ANNUAL REVIEW OF PSYCHOLOGY

ANNUAL REVIEW OF PSYCHOLOGY

VOLUME 53, 2002

SUSAN T. FISKE, *Editor*
Princeton University

DANIEL L. SCHACTER, *Associate Editor*
Harvard University

CAROLYN ZAHN-WAXLER, *Associate Editor*
National Institute of Mental Health

www.annualreviews.org   science@annualreviews.org   650-493-4400

ANNUAL REVIEWS
4139 El Camino Way • P.O. BOX 10139 • Palo Alto, California 94303-0139

ANNUAL REVIEWS
Palo Alto, California, USA

International Standard Serial Number: 0066-4308
International Standard Book Number: 0-8243-0253-2
Library of Congress Catalog Card Number: 50-13143

Annual Review and publication titles are registered trademarks of Annual Reviews.
⊗ The paper used in this publication meets the minimum requirements of American National Standards for Information Sciences—Permanence of Paper for Printed Library Materials, ANSI Z39.48-1992.

Annual Reviews and the Editors of its publications assume no responsibility for the statements expressed by the contributors to this *Annual Review*.

TYPESET BY TECHBOOKS, FAIRFAX, VA
PRINTED AND BOUND IN THE UNITED STATES OF AMERICA

PREFACE

September 11, 2001. December 7, 1941. November 22, 1963. July 4, 1776. Significant dates define the intersection of the global and the personal, the historical-political and the psychological. Although various dates represent defining moments for different generations, the interplay of the person and the world has always motivated much of the psychological enterprise, either directly or indirectly. Psychologists, like other people, wonder about their niche in the intersection of the global and the individual. After individual decisions to donate blood, conserve gas, enlist in the military, promote peace, or manufacture saltpeter, what is the role of psychology in times of national crisis? What is the role of a publication such as the *Annual Review of Psychology*?

Some chapter topics in this volume clearly speak to some origins of current events in individual human actions: aggression, relations between groups, self and social identity, cultural influences on personality, and even the nature of rationality. Others speak directly to the effects of current events on individuals: insomnia and depression, as well as emotions, morbidity, and mortality. Perhaps long-term effects are relevant to chapters on eating disorders, SES and child development, and psychological or psychosocial factors in organic disease. Still other chapters speak to recovery and repair: clinical assessment and the affective dimensions of organizational behavior, as well as motivational beliefs, values, and goals.

None of the chapters' authors write about the events of September 11; indeed, their chapters were already in production by then. And some of these authors may feel that linking their reviews to those events is tenuous at best. Certainly chapters reviewing perception, cognition, and neuroscience relate to these events no more or less than to any ordinary human process and activity, though the practical applications range from people detecting change in satellite photos to people remembering the events they witnessed. Nevertheless, by their very goal of gathering and evaluating psychological science, for presentation to others who research, teach, learn, and treat, they affirm the continuity and value of studying human beings, even in complex, difficult times.

Psychological research, education, and treatment by their nature aim to advance freedom and improve the human condition. Reviews of psychology's progress demonstrate the better side of human nature: freedom of inquiry, pursuit of knowledge, creation of insight, sharing of discovery. Though we are studying neither satellites nor saltpeter, psychologists are studying the people who use them, for better or worse. And that makes a difference.

Susan T. Fiske, Princeton
Daniel L. Schacter, Cambridge
Carolyn Zahn-Waxler, Bethesda

 *Annual Review of Psychology*
Volume 53, 2002

CONTENTS

ANALYSIS OF LATENT VARIABLES

INDEXES

ERRATA

Online log of corrections to the Annual Review of Psychology corrections:
Steven Regeser López and Peter J. Guarnaccia
**Cultural Psychopathology: Uncovering the Social World
of Mental Illness**
Annu. Rev. Psychol. 2000, Vol. 51: 571–598.
http://psych.annualreviews.org/errata.shtml

RELATED ARTICLES

Annu. Rev. Psychol. 2002. 53:1–25

EPISODIC MEMORY: From Mind to Brain

Endel Tulving

Rotman Research Institute of Baycrest Centre, Toronto, Canada, M6A 2E1;
e-mail: tulving@psych.utoronto.ca

Key Words semantic memory, memory systems, amnesia, history of memory, functional neuroimaging, patient K.C.

■ **Abstract** Episodic memory is a neurocognitive (brain/mind) system, uniquely different from other memory systems, that enables human beings to remember past experiences. The notion of episodic memory was first proposed some 30 years ago. At that time it was defined in terms of materials and tasks. It was subsequently refined and elaborated in terms of ideas such as self, subjective time, and autonoetic consciousness. This chapter provides a brief history of the concept of episodic memory, describes how it has changed (indeed greatly changed) since its inception, considers criticisms of it, and then discusses supporting evidence provided by (*a*) neuropsychological studies of patterns of memory impairment caused by brain damage, and (*b*) functional neuroimaging studies of patterns of brain activity of normal subjects engaged in various memory tasks. I also suggest that episodic memory is a true, even if as yet generally unappreciated, marvel of nature.

CONTENTS

INTRODUCTION

With one singular exception, time's arrow is straight. Unidirectionality of time is one of nature's most fundamental laws. It has relentlessly governed all happenings in the universe—cosmic, geological, physical, biological, psychological—as long as the universe has existed. Galaxies and stars are born and they die, living creatures are young before they grow old, causes always precede effects, there is no return to yesterday, and so on and on. Time's flow is irreversible.

0084-6570/02/0201-0001$14.00

The singular exception is provided by the human ability to remember past happenings. When one thinks today about what one did yesterday, time's arrow is bent into a loop. The rememberer has mentally traveled back into her past and thus violated the law of the irreversibility of the flow of time. She has not accomplished the feat in physical reality, of course, but rather in the reality of the mind, which, as everyone knows, is at least as important for human beings as is the physical reality. When Mother Nature watches her favorite creatures turning one of her immutable laws on its head, she must be pleased with her own creativity.

How did Mother Nature do it? We do not yet know, not only because the question has seldom been raised by those who study Mother Nature's ways but also because the brain/mind science that could throw some light on the question is still in its early formative years and many important issues to be explored have not yet been discovered. It will be all a bit clearer a hundred years from now, or a thousand. But there are some clues available even now, and we can make use of them.

The first clue is offered by a perceived absence. There is no evidence that any nonhuman animals—including what we might call higher animals—ever think about what we could call subjective time. Animals are as capable as humans have been at the game of producing more of their kind. They have minds, they are conscious of their world, and they rely as much on learning and memory in acquiring the skills needed for survival as we do (Weiskrantz 1985), but they do not seem to have the same kind of ability humans do to travel back in time in their own minds, probably because they do not need to. The clue suggests that one's sense of subjective time is not a biological necessity. If humans have it, it is an evolutionary frill, necessary for mental time travel. No sense of subjective time, no mental time travel.

A second clue is provided by the realization that, when we do travel back in time, our conscious awareness of our experience is different from our ordinary "on-line" awareness of our environment. We seldom confuse the feeling that we are remembering a past event with the feeling that we are looking at the world, that we are imagining what is on the other side of the mountain, or that we are dreaming. These and other mental activities are conscious, too, but the consciousness is plainly and recognizably different. The term autonoetic has been used to refer to this special kind of consciousness that allows us to be aware of subjective time in which events happened. Autonoetic awareness (or autonoesis) is required for remembering. No autonoesis, no mental time travel.

A third clue is that mental time travel requires a traveler. No traveler, no traveling. The traveler in this case is what is referred to as "self." But an ordinary self will not do. By some criteria at least—the well known Gallup mirror test, for example—some nonhuman primates (chimpanzees and gorillas) also have minds in which their own selves exist as entities different from the rest of the world, but if one assumes that they are not quite capable of the human-type time travel, their selves exist only in the present, whereas ours exist in subjective time.

The three clues—sense of subjective time, autonoetic awareness, and self—point to three central components of a neurocognitive (mind/brain) system that makes mental time travel possible. This (hypothetical) system is called episodic memory, and in this essay I tell its story. Like psychology, episodic memory has a long past but a short history. The concept was first proposed some 30 years ago (Tulving 1972), but it has changed drastically since then and has now reached a stage at which one can, as I am doing now, muse about it as a true marvel of nature.

In this essay I first say a few words about the history of the concept of episodic memory, then describe its current status as not just a psychological but rather a neurocognitive (brain/mind) entity, review criticisms, and end by discussing some evidence. The emphasis in this discussion is squarely on the brain side of the mind/brain equation. The early problems with the concept of episodic memory were largely rooted in the lack of relevant evidence. Moreover, as is almost always the case with purely behavioral data, it was frequently possible to account for relevant findings without invoking the distinction between episodic and semantic memory. Evidence for the separate status of episodic memory at the level of brain activity, however, is more difficult to dismiss or discount. In recent years this kind of evidence (summarized below) has become available.

EARLY HISTORY

The early formulation of the distinction between episodic and semantic memory (Tulving 1972) centered on different kinds and sources of to-be-remembered information (personally experienced events versus general facts). The distinction was readily accepted by the psychological world and regarded by many as a useful heuristic distinction. The initial difficulties consisted of the constraints imposed by the then-prevailing verbal learning tradition as well as the total absence of any relevant data.

By the time I wrote *Elements of Episodic Memory* (Tulving 1983), it had become possible to entertain the thought that the heuristic distinction was useful for the simple reason that it corresponded to biological reality. I proposed, therefore, that episodic and semantic memory represented two functionally separable memory systems. In *Elements* I also made a confession: I had been wrong in 1972 when I had assumed that the traditional, Ebbinghaus-inspired, study/test laboratory experiments of verbal learning and memory had dealt with episodic memory. They had not. Two important features of episodic memory were missing.

One had to do with the contents of what the subjects in the experiments had to learn. Episodic memory is about happenings in particular places at particular times, or about "what," "where," and "when" (Clayton & Dickinson 1998, Nyberg et al. 1996). Traditional laboratory experiments, however, were almost invariably concerned with "what." Subjects are asked, "What do you remember of the presented material?" They report their knowledge in tests such as free recall, cued recall, or recognition. Subjects' memory for "where" and "when" was hardly ever examined. Just about the only exception was provided by studies of "memory judgments," (Hintzman 2000) which, however, were largely ignored by most students of memory, presumably because they did not fit readily into any appropriate theoretical framework. Subsequent history corrected this oversight. There are now on record literally hundreds of studies that are concerned with "what," "where," and "when."

The other missing feature was what I referred to in *Elements* as "recollective experience," or conscious awareness of what had happened in the past. In traditional experiments the experimenter assumes that the overt behavioral response reflects the subject's mental state; that is, that behavior is a faithful index of cognition. The reasoning goes something like this: Surely, if the subject recognizes an item in a recognition test, it means that he remembers it from the list, that is, that he has a conscious recollection of the item's occurrence in the study list. How could it possibly be otherwise?

As subsequent history showed, it could be otherwise. Research on implicit memory (Roediger & McDermott 1993, Schacter 1987a), or so-called nonconscious memory (Jacoby 1991, Toth 2000), has overwhelmingly proved that one and the same behavioral response in a study/test experiment could represent conscious awareness of the retrieved item's experimental history as readily as it could represent total lack of such awareness. In a further development it turned out that when subjects were consciously aware of an item's earlier occurrence in the study list, the awareness could be one of two different kinds. One was referred to as "autonoetic," the other as "noetic." The former, as already mentioned, was used to describe the experiential "flavor" of remembering, or recollection; the latter was used to describe the conscious state that accompanies thinking about (knowing) the world. Thus, even in such sterile situations as list-learning experiments, subjects could either remember the event of an item's appearing in the study list, or know that it occurred, without remembering, and make appropriate experiential judgments (Gardiner 1988, Gardiner & Richardson-Klavehn 2000, Knowlton & Squire 1995, Rajaram 1993, Tulving 1985b). The news here was a further extension of the lessons learned from the studies of implicit memory: One and the same behavioral response (correctly recalled item, or old response in the recognition test) could reflect either of two different states of conscious awareness about the past. The general point made by all these studies, which barely existed at the time of *Elements*, is that there is no necessary correlation between behavior and conscious experience (Tulving 1989) and that in that sense the traditional research was not concerned with episodic memory.

This essay is partly about how the concept of episodic memory came to be what it is today, partly about what it is today, and mainly about how we know or think we know what it is today. The scope of a short essay allows us to discuss only the highlights of what, for want of a better expression, I call the theory of episodic memory, or simply episodic theory, although we are here dealing mostly with conceptual rather than theoretical issues. The theory represents an attempt to formulate a set of interrelated ideas about memory that are internally consistent and reasonably closely tied to the basic empirical facts about memory. A fuller account of the theory of episodic memory is found in Wheeler et al.

(1997); a reasonably up-to-date tabulation of episodic memory's similarities to and differences from semantic memory is found in Tulving & Markowitsch (1998), as well as in Griffiths et al. (1999); one possible extension of the theory, into the relation between the domain of subjective time and evolution of human culture, has been offered elsewhere (Tulving 2001b).

EPISODIC MEMORY TODAY

Today we think of episodic memory as one of the major neurocognitive memory systems (Schacter & Tulving 1994) that are defined in terms of their special functions (what the system does or produces) and properties (how they do it). It shares many features with semantic memory, out of which it grew (Tulving 1984), but it also possesses features that semantic memory does not (Tulving & Markowitsch 1998).

Episodic memory is a recently evolved, late-developing, and early-deteriorating past-oriented memory system, more vulnerable than other memory systems to neuronal dysfunction, and probably unique to humans. It makes possible mental time travel through subjective time, from the present to the past, thus allowing one to re-experience, through autonoetic awareness, one's own previous experiences. Its operations require, but go beyond, the semantic memory system. Retrieving information from episodic memory (remembering or conscious recollection) is contingent on the establishment of a special mental set, dubbed episodic "retrieval mode." Episodic memory is subserved by a widely distributed network of cortical and subcortical brain regions that overlaps with but also extends beyond the networks subserving other memory systems. The essence of episodic memory lies in the conjunction of three concepts—self, autonoetic awareness, and subjectively sensed time.

Let us briefly expand on some of the constituent ideas in this definition of episodic memory.

First, episodic memory is a hypothetical memory system. It is not a particular kind of memory task or test. According to episodic theory, there exist few if any memory tasks used in the laboratory or the clinic that involve a single memory system. In terms of memory systems, all tasks are "multiply determined" (Tulving 1991). The systems' ideas may be assessed in terms of outcomes of tasks, but the logic is a bit more subtle than that inherent in the assumption of the one-to-one mapping of tasks to systems (see Tulving 1983, pp. 55, 77–78). Episodic memory is not just a particular type of retained and retrieved information, and it is not just a particular kind of mental experience, although it is systematically related to both of these. These distinctions may be subtle, but they are important. For instance, if one accepts them, one would not ask a question such as, ". . . how does a systems theorist unambiguously identify a particular memory as being in one system or another. . .?" (Toth & Hunt 1999, p. 233). The answer is that a systems theorist would not, because such questions are uninteresting and lead nowhere.

The concept of memory system, like any other live concept in a developing branch of science, is fluid, and its specific features change over time. But some early ideas are still quite relevant. Because one of my criticisms of the criticisms of multiple systems in general, and episodic memory in particular, is that the critics have misconstrued what they criticize, it is useful here to repeat what I said on the topic when the concept of multiple systems was introduced. In an article entitled, "How many memory systems are there?" I said the following about what memory systems are:

> Memory systems are organized structures of more elementary operating components. An operating component of a system consists of a neural substrate and its behavioral or cognitive correlates. Some components are shared by all systems, others are shared only by some, and still others are unique to individual systems. Different learning and memory situations involve different concatenations of components from one or more systems . . . . Although there is no one-to-one correspondence between tasks and systems . . . they are nonetheless systematically related: A given memory system makes it possible for organisms to perform memory tasks that entail operating components unique to that system. This means, among other things, that intervention with the operation of a system—even if it occurs through a single component of the system—affects all those learning and memory performances that depend on that system . . . . Different systems have emerged at different stages in the evolution of the species, and they emerge at different stages in the development of individual organisms. Thus, they can be ordered from 'lower' to 'higher' systems (or from less to more advanced), provided that it is clearly understood that such attributions are meaningful only with respect to comparisons between combinations of systems, on the one hand, and individual systems alone, on the other . . . . When a new memory system with specialized novel capabilities evolves or develops, it enables the organism to increase the number, and the sophistication, of its memory functions." (Tulving 1985a, pp. 386–87).

More recent and more detailed formulations of systems are available elsewhere (Sherry & Schacter 1987, Schacter & Tulving 1994; see also Schacter et al. 2000).

Episodic memory is oriented to the past in a way in which no other kind of memory, or memory system, is. It is the only memory system that allows people to consciously re-experience past experiences. Its special, and unique, relationship to time, surprisingly, is not widely known. Nor is it, I think, adequately appreciated. Most people naturally associate all memory with the past and are astonished to learn that this is not so.

The theory holds that episodic memory evolved out of semantic memory: Semantic memory appeared long before episodic memory. Many nonhuman animals, especially mammals and birds, possess well-developed knowledge-of-the-world (declarative, or semantic, memory) systems and are capable of acquiring vast amounts of flexibly expressible information. Early humans were like these animals, but at some point in human evolution, possibly rather recently, episodic memory emerged as an "embellishment" of the semantic memory system. The details of this emergence are unknown, and one can only speculate about them (Tulving 2001b). It is not even certain that the evolution of episodic memory was a part of (neo)Darwinian evolution. Episodic memory may represent an instance of the so-called Baldwin effect (Baldwin 1902, Richards 1987).

For nature, the famous tinkerer, to have produced neurocognitive machinery that brings the past into the present is clearly a much greater achievement than evolving the (marvelous) visual system. Many animals have eyes and visual systems, and some of them have been "invented" independently several times in the course of evolution. A system that turns time's arrow into a loop has evolved only once, in only one species, although other species would presumably benefit from it as much as do humans. The singular rarity of the existence of episodic memory in nature presumably reflects the complexity and biological cost of such a system, in terms of both structural components and their operations.

The hypothesis that episodic memory was built on top of the earlier systems, including semantic memory, is in agreement with other ideas and facts about memory. One such is the SPI (serial, parallel, independent) model that postulates process-specific relations among the memory systems (Tulving 1995). Another is the now well-known fact that people can have mental access to their personal past not only in terms of autonoetic remembering but also in terms of nonautonoetic knowing. This state of affairs is reflected in the title of an article by Suparna Rajaram (1993): "Remembering and knowing: two means of access to the personal past."

The notion here is that even before episodic memory emerged in human evolution, humans were capable of acquiring and making use of knowledge about their personal experiences, in the absence of autonoesis, and possibly without a precise temporal "tag." The same scenario holds for nonhuman animals. They too are capable of learning about and from experiences of the past, but without autonoetic awareness that they are doing so (Suddendorf & Corballis 1997). An especially interesting example of the operations of this type of episodic-like memory by food-caching scrub jays has recently been described by Clayton & Dickinson (1998), thereby helping to fill the evolutionary gap between humans, happy possessors of the sophisticated system of episodic memory, and many other animals, capable learners of impersonal and timeless facts of their worlds.

The late (ontogenetic) development of the episodic system is meant to be true in a relative sense. Everyone knows that young children are amazingly efficient learning machines from birth on, and perhaps even earlier, not only with respect to language but many other skills and knowledge as well. According to theory, such learning occurs in the absence of autonoesis and does not require any sense of self in subjective time (cf. McCormack & Hoerl 1999). The late development of episodic memory provides another hint at the complexity of the system. Although it is difficult to put a specific figure on the age when children acquire a more-or-less fully functioning episodic memory system, a rough rule of thumb is that children younger than 4 years of age do not yet have such a system (Perner & Ruffman

1995, Nelson 1993). Wheeler et al. (1997) discuss the issue of development of episodic memory from the perspective of episodic theory at greater length.

CRITICISMS OF EPISODIC MEMORY

As mentioned, most psychologists were happy to use the term episodic memory in a purely descriptive sense, referring to the kinds of experiments that psychologists had been doing since Ebbinghaus: Subjects study some material, and the experimenter tests them for their retention of the material. The suggestion made in *Elements* (Tulving 1983) that episodic and semantic memory are two "functionally different memory systems," however, quickly became controversial, as the saying goes. A controversial idea in science, as everyone knows, means that some people love it, some could not care less, and some are highly opposed to it. Whereas some students of memory were quite willing to begin exploring the hypothesis that there exist real differences between episodic and semantic memory, many others, including those who had had no problem with the heuristic distinction, rejected the hypothesis out of hand.

Critics did not like the thought that there was anything special about episodic memory. The idea was vague, they claimed, it did not follow the established procedure, and it violated the law of parsimony. There was no need to make up imaginary memory systems in order to get on with the task of making theoretical sense of memory facts and phenomena, the critics said. Some did not like the "metaphysics of identifying hidden systems" and the burden of having to try to figure out "in what complex arrangements they may be ordered" (Roediger et al. 1989, p. 36). Some complained that post-hoc dissociations, used to argue for differences between systems, are meaningless because they are not "predicted by a theory" (Hintzman 1984, p. 241). Some did not see any reason to draw any kind of sharp distinction between two kinds of facts: facts about the world and facts about the self (Kihlstrom 1984, p. 244). Some were alarmed at the possibility that many other kinds of memory might be proposed in addition to episodic, and thought it essential to nip the threat of "proliferation of memories" in the bud, lest we end up with the kind of an intellectual disaster that evolved out of the story of instincts (Roediger & Blaxton 1987, pp. 370–71).

Along similar lines, some questioned the wisdom of the misguided believers in separate memory systems, suggesting that our field should show "the maturity to attempt to incorporate a new finding into its abiding viewpoint before offering a proliferation of additional memory stores to account for a few new data points" (Gorfein 1987, p. 383). Some were suspicious of classification of memories because it might be "detrimental to theory" (Ratcliff & McKoon 1986, pp. 312–13). Some believed in multiple memory systems but had doubts about episodic memory: ". . . although a dissociation between autobiographical and nonautobiographical memory is intuitively sensible, the critical question is whether such a dissociation is of a natural kind. One could just as easily split the memory system into . . . memories for all things with sharp boundaries versus all things with fuzzy boundaries . . ." (Cohen 1984, p. 99). Others reviewed the evidence for discrete neurobiological mechanisms that might underlie episodic and semantic memory and concluded that the evidence "does not indicate that episodic and semantic memory arc mediated by discrete neural subsystems" (Horner 1990, p. 281).

Skepticism was expressed about the neuropsychological and the then-barely-existing brain-imaging methods I had suggested would be necessary to get beyond futile psychological arguments (Tulving 1986). These methods were thought to be no more useful for exploring memory than would be the attempts to understand the workings of a computer by smashing it with a sledgehammer to create "lesions" (Ratcliff & McKoon 1986, pp. 312–13). Finally, some critics did not want to give the newborn even a chance at life. Only a year after the proposal of a separate episodic memory system had appeared in print, critics told the world that episodic memory's time had "come and gone" (Hintzman 1984).

These critical comments date from the earlier days of the efforts to work out an acceptable set of ideas about episodic memory. Many of them were pertinent and justifiable, because the evidence at the time was scanty at best, and I said so (Tulving 1986). Other comments were perfectly understandable in light of tradition and well-established practices in the field. Traditions always die hard, and the traditional, unquestioned, and unanalyzed view of memory was unitary.

In terms of practice, as already mentioned, memory research was extremely restricted: lists, verbal materials, measurement of the amount recalled or recognized, and the single-minded focus on the contents of lessons, the "what" component of the information. In this kind of an environment there clearly is little need for any kind of a classification of memory, because memory is highly uniform. Given the emphasis on "what," rather than "where" and "when," given the emphasis on behavior and the irrelevance of experience, given the strangeness of the central concepts of episodic memory, and especially the strangeness of some of the terms (such as autonoetic and noetic), it is not surprising that an intelligent practitioner in traditional memory research would not find anything of interest in the concept of episodic memory. Rejection of the idea as an unparsimonious and unnecessary complication made perfect sense—as long as one kept close to the tradition.

It is more puzzling that even today there are many who have no use for the idea of different memory systems in general and the episodic/semantic distinction in particular. For example, Howe, in a monograph on memory development in young children, dismissed the whole idea of multiple memory systems and advocated the status quo of unitary memory: "Because there is little evidence to support the idea (a) that there are separate memory systems or, (b) that they come on line at different developmental junctures . . . it is perhaps still more parsimonious to view memory as a unitary system that supports a variety of modes of remembering" (Howe 2000, p. 87). Others express similar views: "I am explicitly equating episodic and semantic memory in the sense that there are no separate episodic and semantic memory systems, hierarchically arranged . . . or otherwise" (Glenberg 1997, p. 8). Glenberg thinks that what is (mistakenly) attributed to two separate systems reflects differential use of different memories, methods used to assess them, and different information. Craik (2001) too thinks there is no division between episodic and semantic memory. Like Glenberg, he believes semantic information is usually more accessible than episodic because, by being more general, it receives "more practice." Others in a long list who deny or doubt the reality of multiple systems include McClelland et al. (1995), Toth & Hunt (1999), and Weldon (1999).

What does one do about such criticism? The rules of the game here are the same in episodic memory as they are in the rest of science. If a weakness or flaw of the theory pointed out by a critic is justified, one takes it into account, one way or another, and is grateful to the critic for his or her contribution to the refinement and improvement of the theory. The theory of episodic memory has benefited greatly from such constructive criticism. The situation is different when a criticism essentially reduces to an expression of lack of interest in, no perceived need for, or simple temperamental antagonism to structural as opposed to functional concepts. In such cases one simply agrees to disagree with the critic and proceeds with business on hand. The same solution is usually adopted when the critic complains that all the problems inherent in the new approach have not yet been solved, or even tackled. These kinds of criticism are comparable to complaints about young children not being as strong and smart as adults. In a rational world, there is nothing much one can do about them, other than remember what Benjamin Franklin said about electricity, when asked what use it was, and wait.

I do not attempt to deal with the critics in this article, because there is not enough room. However, I briefly touch on one category of criticism because it is prevalent, because it is a waste of time, and because it can be avoided. These are criticisms based on misconceptions of the subject of the criticism, as mentioned earlier. This kind of criticism takes several forms. I consider only one of these. (I must mention parenthetically that in this matter, as in everything else covered in this essay, I can only speak for myself, and for my own understanding of the issues. There are many other students of memory who believe in multiple memory systems whose ideas need not be the same as mine.)

In an article I know has not been totally ignored, I discussed two kinds of primary concepts of memory, having to do with processes and systems. To minimize the probability of misunderstanding, I said that "the classification approach *complements* the process-oriented approach to memory; it is not an alternative to it" (Tulving 1991; emphasis in original). I have not had any reason to change this understanding of the relation between processes and systems. A recent book chapter dealing with the topic was entitled "Study of Memory: Processes and Systems" (Tulving 1999). Nevertheless, a surprisingly large number of people who wish systems would go away think they were introduced to provide rival, alternative ways of explaining experimental and other empirical findings, especially task dissociations (e.g., Roediger et al. 1989, Toth & Hunt 1999, Craik 2001). In a recent collection of papers, entitled *Memory: Systems, Process, or Function?* (Foster & Jelicic 1999), the central question discussed was whether long-term memory is "best regarded as comprising multiple independent systems . . . , as a processing framework . . . , or as a complex function which can be used in a flexible and task-appropriate manner?" (p. 1). In both the title and the guiding question the operative word is "or." The possibility that the correct answer to the question is, "at the very least all of the above," is ignored, for reasons unknown.

BIOLOGICAL REALITY OF EPISODIC MEMORY

By the standards of mature sciences, the amount of relevant evidence in support of episodic memory is still small. In this respect, much remains to be done. However, by the standards of psychology, or cognitive neuroscience, the amount of evidence is respectable. In this respect, the situation has changed greatly from the early days of episodic memory. Most satisfying is the trend one can discern in the accumulation of pertinent data; not only the quantity but, more importantly, the quality of the data is clearly on the upswing.

In the remainder of this essay I discuss evidence related to the issue of biological reality of episodic memory. Is episodic memory just a category in an abstract organizational scheme applied to memory, that is, a figment of a classifier's imagination, or does something like it actually exist as a separate structure/function in the brain?

The question, of course, does not, and cannot at this time, have a complete answer. The issue is far too complex to have been solved in a few years. Therefore, what follows are examples of a progress report. None of the evidence I discuss below, like the evidence I mentioned above, was available in 1983 when I wrote *Elements of Episodic Memory*, and there is a good deal more recent evidence in the literature.

A number of approaches can be, and have been, taken to this issue. I discuss two. One lies in the neuropsychological study of consequences of the kind of brain damage that selectively involve memory processes. The other has to do with functional neuroimaging of healthy young people.

Case studies of neurological patients who, as a result of brain damage caused by accident or disease, suffer from memory impairment frequently provide information useful to the issue of the biological reality of episodic memory. The history of the relevant research neatly illustrates the dictum, "It is difficult for an explorer to find something that he does not know exists." Even serendipity fails in a situation in which a scientist looks at a pattern but does not see it. Even when one scientist sees it and informs others of it, others may not hear the message.

In 1958, in summarizing his extensive clinical neurological investigations of memory and amnesia, Nielsen, a neurologist at UCLA, reported that

> A study of pathways of memory formation has revealed a basic fact not suspected when this study began—there are two separate pathways for two kinds of memories. The one is memories of life experiences centering around the person himself and basically involving the element of time. The other is memories of intellectually acquired knowledge not experienced but learned by study and not personal. (Nielsen 1958, p. 25)

Corresponding to these two kinds of memories, Nielsen said, are two types of amnesia: "Amnesia is of two types: (1) loss of memory for personal experiences (temporal amnesia), and (2) loss of memory for acquired facts (categorical amnesia). Either may be lost without the other." (Nielsen 1958, p. 15). This was one year after the appearance of a report of bilateral resection of large chunks of the medial temporal lobe tissue from the brain of a young man with epileptic seizures, H.M., who became the world's most famous amnesic (Scoville & Milner 1957).

Thus, Nielsen, looking at many patients, saw the separation between what we now call episodic and semantic memory, told the world about it, and essentially nobody heard him. Milner, and later many others, looking initially at a single patient, did not, and, because H.M.'s amnesia was different, possibly could not, see the separation, and so they lumped episodic and semantic memory together. It was only very recently that a distinction between "episodic amnesia for personally experienced events and semantic retrograde amnesia for components of knowledge" (Kapur 1999, p. 800) was again taken under serious scrutiny.

In the meantime, the case of H.M., suffering from the impairment of declarative (now also called explicit) memory, i.e., memory for personal events and memory for general facts (Squire 1992), has dominated the minds of researchers of amnesia, although the possibility is now being considered that the episodic memory impairment in medial temporal lobe amnesic patients is associated with hippocampal damage, whereas semantic memory problems reflect the damage of cortical tissue (Aggleton & Brown 1999, Mishkin et al. 1997).

If episodic memory is a separate entity—anatomical, hodological, physiological, or in some as yet unknown fashion—in the normal brain, it is possible for damage to the brain to occur in such a way that it is deleteriously affected while other kinds of memory are not, or are less affected. Because there are good reasons to believe that the operations of all memory systems are supported by widely distributed and intricately interconnected regions of the brain (Mesulam 1990, Nyberg et al. 2000), the probability of the kind of brain damage that neatly cleaves the brain function along the lines of such complex systems is small. Most of the time the damage affects the components of a number of systems, resulting in the typical, diffuse impairment of memory for facts and memory for events (Squire 1992). But every now and then the low-probability event materializes. The important point is that it is difficult to imagine how, for instance, brain pathology could occur in which the patient loses all episodic memory functions while retaining those that rely on other systems unless there exists the potentiality for such a division in the healthy brain. But such cases, although rare, do occur.

THE CASE OF K.C.

At University of Toronto we have studied one such individual, K.C., over a number of years (Figure 1). His episodic memory is totally dysfunctional and he has no autonoetic consciousness. Otherwise, all his intellectual functions are close to those of an ordinary, normal, healthy person.

Figure 1   K.C., a man who lost his episodic memory as a result of traumatic brain injury in 1981, photographed in 1986 when he was 35 years of age.

K.C. was born in 1951. At the age of 30 he suffered serious closed head injury in a motorcycle accident, with extensive brain lesions in multiple cortical and subcortical brain regions, including medial temporal lobes (Rosenbaum et al. 2000), and consequent severe amnesia (Tulving et al. 1988, Tulving 2001a). As is the case, by definition, with all amnesics, most of K.C.'s cognitive capabilities are intact and indistinguishable from those of many healthy adults. His intelligence and language are normal; he has no problems with reading or writing; his ability to concentrate and to maintain focused attention are normal; his thought processes are clear; he can play the organ, chess, and various card games; his ability to visually imagine things is intact; and his performance on primary (short-term) memory tasks is normal. He knows many objective facts concerning his own life, such as his date of birth, the address of his home for the first 9 years of his life, the names of the some of the schools he attended, the make and color of the car he once owned, and the fact that his parents owned and still own a summer cottage. He knows the location of the cottage and can easily find it on a map of Ontario. He knows its distance from his home in Toronto and how long it takes to drive there in weekend traffic. He also knows that he has spent a lot of time there.

Like many other typical amnesic patients, K.C. is impaired in his ability to pick up novel generic information from his everyday world and in his ability to remember ongoing experiences: He has deep anterograde amnesia for both personal experiences and semantic information. However, his retrograde amnesia is highly asymmetrical: He cannot recollect any personally experienced events, whether one-time or repeated happenings, whereas his semantic knowledge acquired before the critical accident is still reasonably intact. His knowledge of mathematics, history, geography, and other "school subjects," as well as his general knowledge of the world is not greatly different from others' at his educational level.

The outstanding fact about K.C.'s mental make-up is his utter inability to remember any events, circumstances, or situations from his own life. His episodic amnesia covers his whole life, from birth to the present. The only exception is the experiences that, at any time, he has had in the last minute or two. It does not matter how much and how specific information is given to him about any particular event from further back in the past, how memorable the event is by ordinary standards, how long its duration, or how many times he has been asked about it before. He always denies any recollection and does not even acknowledge any sense of familiarity with the event (Tulving et al. 1988).

K.C. has no particular difficulty apprehending and discussing either himself or physical time. He knows many true facts about himself; he also knows what most other people know about physical time: its units, its structure, and its measurement by clocks and calendars. It is his apprehension of subjectively experienced time, the autonoetic (self-knowing) consciousness, that is grossly impaired. The impairment does not encompass only the past; it also extends to the future. Thus, when asked, he cannot tell the questioner what he is going to do later on that day, or the day after, or at any time in the rest of his life. He cannot imagine his future any more than he can remember his past. This aspect of the syndrome he presents suggests that the sense of time with which autonoetic consciousness works covers not only the past but also the future (Tulving 1985b).

The profile of K.C.'s cognitive capabilities suggests that his brain damage greatly impaired his episodic memory and autonoetic consciousness while leaving his semantic memory and noetic consciousness largely intact. There are problems with this interpretation, of course. An obvious one is that his apparently greater ability to retrieve premorbidly acquired semantic compared to episodic information reflects the differential effects of overlearning or rehearsal of the two kinds of information, rather than the operations of different memory systems. Against this possibility are instances in which he can recall factual information that he is unlikely to have rehearsed repeatedly, such as his knowledge of the difference between stalactites and stalagmites, but he cannot bring back to mind memorable happenings lasting for many days, such as his having been evacuated from his home, along with tens of thousands of others following the nearby derailment of a train carrying deadly chemicals. Nevertheless, the hypothesis of more often repeated versus less often repeated experiences, rather than impersonal and personal ones, popular with critics (e.g., Craik 2001), is logically possible.

We did two extensive case experiments with K.C. to compare his episodic and semantic abilities under better controlled conditions. The question was whether he could learn new factual information presented a number of times, for a few seconds each time, despite his inability to bring back to mind the hours-long occasions on which such learning took place. In one experiment (Tulving et al. 1991) we taught him 64 3-word sentences (such as "reporter sent review," and "student withdrew innuendo") over a number of widely distributed learning trials and then tested him with sentence frames (e.g., "reporter sent—") for the missing word. In the second experiment (Hayman et al. 1993) we taught him 96 amusing definitions (such as "mates live in, employees outside: prison" and "performs a daily massage: toothbrush") and tested him with definitions (e.g., "a servant in name only") for the target word (e.g., bridesmaid). Both experiments showed that he was able to learn, slowly but surely, substantial portions of the material and retain the information normally over weeks and months, while not being able to recollect any visits to the laboratory where the learning took place.

Thus, we know that K.C. can learn new factual information in the total absence of any episodic remembering, under conditions in which there is no confounding between the kind of retrieval (episodic versus semantic) and the amount of learning or rehearsal. Other cases have been described in which new semantic learning by densely amnesic patients has been demonstrated (Hamann & Squire 1995, Schacter et al. 1984, Shimamura & Squire 1987). Note again, however, that, as one might expect, there is a good deal of variability in such learning in amnesic patients (Hamann & Squire 1995, Rajaram & Coslett 2000).

The overall pattern of memory impairment shown by K.C.—much more severe for personal, autobiographical experiences than generic, factual knowledge—has been described by others. A case strikingly similar with respect to the clinical picture of K.C., although of different etiology (herpes simplex encephalitis) and different brain pathology, was described in considerable detail by Kitchener et al. (1998). Their patient, R.S., did not reveal any signs of functioning episodic memory, lost as a result of a bout of herpes simplex encephalitis, but he had nevertheless been able to postmorbidly acquire considerable amounts of factual information about people and news events.

Especially interesting in this context are the cases of three young people, described by Vargha-Khadem and her collaborators (1997), who became amnesic at very early ages as a result of anoxic accidents that produced severe bilateral hippocampal atrophy. They too show striking differences between the impaired episodic memory and relative preservation of semantic memory. None of them can reliably remember ongoing experiences and recollect past personal happenings. They also perform in the amnesic range on most standard psychometric memory tests. Remarkably, however, all three have made and are making normal or near-normal progress in school, and all three have acquired normal or near-normal semantic knowledge about the world.

There have been other cases of impaired episodic and largely spared semantic memory. Most of these are less striking than K.C.'s, but the asymmetry has always been easy to detect (Calabrese et al. 1996, Cermak & O'Connor 1983, DellaSala et al. 1993, Kopelman et al. 1999, Levine et al. 1998, Markowitsch et al. 1993, Rousseaux et al. 1997, Viskontas et al. 2000). Summaries of these and other relevant cases, together with discussion, are available in Kapur (1999) and Wheeler & McMillan (2001).

Although all these cases can be understood in terms of the distinction between episodic and other kinds of memory, there have been, of course, as there always are, different interpretations of them. For example, Squire & Zola (1998) think the slow and laborious learning of new factual information by amnesic patients with impaired hippocampally dependent declarative memory, including Vargha-Khadem's young people who learn at school, is made possible by a small, difficult-to-detect degree of preserved episodic memory.

Clinical cases of the kinds summarized here can be quite convincing, especially to those who have met the patients and studied them extensively. But there are problems, too. A major one is that those who have not met such patients and have not worked with them, usually find the reports difficult to believe and tend to simply dismiss the evidence contained in them. At a distance it is easy to imagine all sorts of reasons why any given case might not quite be what it is claimed to be, all the way from malingering on the part of the patient to sloppy methods on the part of the investigator. Another problem has to do with the fact that studies of specially selected patients are deficient in one of the main conditions of science—independent verification. Most researchers do not have access to the kinds of patients they can read about in specialty journals, and even if they did, their patients might behave differently. The rarity of interesting and truly informative cases allows a sceptic to ignore them. Finally, there is Hughling Jackson's famous dictum about what one can and cannot learn about the normal brain from observing the effects of its damage. Under the circumstances, lessons about memory taught by neuropsychology seep into the awareness of outsiders slowly.

FUNCTIONAL NEUROIMAGING OF MEMORY

Functional neuroimaging techniques [such as positron emission tomography (PET) and functional magnetic resonance imaging (FMRI)] as well as electrophysiological recording, from both the scalp and implanted electrodes, make it possible to examine brain activity associated with mental activity. These techniques have many problems, but they represent an immense advance over the situation that prevailed before their development.

The general logic of functional neuroimaging studies is straightforward, although the interpretation of the data yielded by them is not. Different mental activities are supported by the activities in different brain regions. When the subject engages in a given cognitive task, PET or FMRI provide information about the level of cerebral blood flow (PET) or blood oxygenation level (FMRI) in different brain regions. Because changes in blood flow or oxygenation level are known to be correlated with changes in neuronal activity, their patterns (brain maps) provide information about neuronal activity in different brain sites that reflect these processes (Raichle 1994).

In the most popular method used in "imaging cognition," the subtraction method, the brain maps associated with performance on two cognitive tasks are compared. The differences between the two brain maps are assumed to reflect the differences between the two cognitive tasks. The value of such knowledge clearly depends on what is known, or can be reasonably assumed, about the differences between two tasks. As every cognitive task involves a large number of (frequently interacting) processes, the interpretation of the brain maps yielded by the subtraction method is constrained by the goodness of one's knowledge of the cognitive "ingredients" of the compared tasks. (For a more detailed analysis on the method and limitations of neuroimaging studies, see Buckner & Tulving 1995, Cabeza & Nyberg 2000, Raichle 1994)

The vagaries of the functional neuroimaging techniques and the problems inherent in the interpretation of the obtained results can be mitigated by relying on the traditional scientific standbys of converging results from many studies and guidance by theory. Any given individual study can always be interpreted in many ways. Interpretation of empirical regularities that emerge from a larger number of studies is necessarily more constrained.

One such empirical regularity that has been yielded by PET and FMRI studies of episodic memory is referred to as the HERA (hemispheric encoding/retrieval asymmetry) model: Left prefrontal cortex is differentially more involved than right in encoding information into episodic memory, whereas right prefrontal cortex is differentially more involved than left in episodic memory retrieval. Because episodic encoding processes usually involve semantic memory retrieval, the HERA model assigns semantic-memory retrieval also to the left frontal lobe. The empirical regularity is called a model, because it is described in terms of cognitive-memory concepts of encoding and retrieval, as well as the concepts of episodic and semantic memory. Without these concepts, it would be awkward to describe the regularity.

HERA emerged from initial PET studies investigating encoding and retrieval processes in episodic memory, done in Toronto (Kapur et al. 1994; Moscovitch et al. 1995; Tulving et al. 1994a,b), the Hammersmith Hospital in London (Shallice et al. 1994, Fletcher et al. 1995), and Washington University (Squire et al. 1992, Buckner et al. 1995). A large number of subsequent studies have confirmed the initial findings. The HERA pattern holds not only for verbal materials but also for nonverbal ones (Buckner et al. 1996, Haxby et al. 1996, Köhler et al. 1998, Moscovitch et al. 1995, Nyberg et al. 1996a, Owen et al. 1996; see also Andreasen et al. 1996). This is despite the fact that, orthogonally to the HERA pattern, there are other data showing hemispheric asymmetry for cognitive processing of different kinds of information: Words are processed predominantly in the left hemisphere, whereas unfamiliar faces are processed in the right hemisphere (Kelley et al. 1998, Wagner et al. 1998b).

The HERA model implies that frontal lobes are heavily involved in episodic memory processes, thus confirming earlier suggestions that this might be the case (Schacter 1987, Squire 1987). The relations among episodic memory, autonoetic consciousness, and the frontal lobes have been discussed at some length by Wheeler et al. (1997). At any rate, in addition to telling us something about what brain regions are involved in memory processes such as encoding and retrieval, HERA also provides support to the biological reality of the distinction between episodic and semantic memory. The fact that semantic retrieval seems to be localized largely to the left, whereas episodic retrieval involves additional processes subserved by regions in the right hemisphere (Buckner 1996) points to basic differences in the neuroanatomy of the two memory systems (Desgranges et al. 1998; Fletcher et al. 1995, 1997).

The right frontal activation associated with episodic retrieval stands in striking contrast to semantic-memory retrieval, which is seldom observed in the right hemisphere (Cabeza & Nyberg 2000, Nyberg 1998). In studies designed to further specify the meaning of such a contrast, it was found that the frontal activation, especially on the right, is associated not necessarily with successful remembering of previously studied material but rather, or additionally, with the episodic memory retrieval mode, mentioned above. The data from these studies (Buckner et al. 1998, Kapur et al. 1995, Nyberg et al. 1995, Rugg et al. 1997, Schacter et al. 1996, Wagner et al. 1998a) showed frontal activation not only when subjects successfully recognized previously studied items but also when they tried to do so but failed, because the test items had not been encountered before.

This pattern of data points to the possibility that the right frontal activation reflects retrieval attempt or episodic retrieval mode (Tulving 1983) rather than, or perhaps in addition to, retrieval success.

Retrieval mode represents a mental (neurocognitive) state, a "set," required for remembering earlier experiences as well as for remembering that something did not happen. In a recent analysis of PET data pooled over several different studies in which subjects had been given episodic recognition tests, involving a total of 53 subjects (Lepage et al. 2000), we succeeded in identifying 6 different "retrieval mode sites" in the brain. A retrieval mode site was defined as any brain region that is significantly more active during episodic retrieval than during episodic encoding (or semantic retrieval), and that is equally active when recovery succeeds and when it fails. These sites were all in the frontal lobes: five in prefrontal cortex, three strong ones in the right and two weaker ones in the left hemisphere, and one in the medial anterior cingulate. No similar sites were seen in any other part of the brain.

Episodic retrieval mode involves a number of different processes (Lepage et al. 2000), but because of the limitations of the study we do not know which, or which combination, of these was associated with activation observed at which retrieval mode site. In keeping with the episodic theory, it is possible to imagine that at least some of these frontal activations reflect the mental time travel component of the recognition test. In order for the subject to actually remember that he saw, or did not see, a test item in the study list he must "travel back" to the study episode. Future work no doubt will clarify the matter. However, it is encouraging to see the data point to the likelihood that the frontal lobes, recent appearances on the evolutionary scene, are centrally involved, presumably in close interaction with other regions (McIntosh 1999), in the execution of episodic memory's most distinguishing feature, mental time travel.

CONCLUSION

Is the issue of the special status of episodic memory settled now? In at least one way it is, and in some others it will probably never be settled. In my 1983 monograph, when I posed a similar question, I wrote,

> An issue as complex as the one with which we are concerned is unlikely to be resolved on the basis of a handful of experiments and clinical observations. The debate will undoubtedly continue, and more evidence will be generated that bears on the issue. The consensus that eventually will emerge is going to be shaped by the outcome of a large number of systematic studies, empirical observations, evaluation of the evidence, and rational thought. In the process, the original question, too, is likely to be changed; it is not just the relation between episodic and semantic systems that is going to be studied but also the relation of these two systems on the one hand to other memory systems on the other." (Tulving 1983, p. 99)

At that time we were indeed talking about a handful of half-relevant experiments and a few pertinent clinical observations. Now we have available what by comparison could be thought of as masses of data but that in the bigger reality of living and developing science is still a mere pittance. This is why the debate will continue, and it is in this sense that the matter is not yet settled.

However, it is settled in the sense that the concept of episodic memory is here to stay. It is now a permanent fixture in the thinking about memory in the minds of many memory researchers all over the world, in a way in which memory for things with firm versus fuzzy boundaries or other comparable notions is not. No more is it just an idea about how memory is organized; it now has become a concept that has a home, even if still a hidden one, in the brain. It is thereby a part of the objective reality.

Finally, what about time's arrow that is bent into a loop by episodic memory? Does episodic memory, or the fact that healthy humans can think about their own past, violate the law of unidirectionality of time? Is it really a marvel of nature? Surely this story line is too dramatic, even absurd. An event happens, a person experiences it, memory traces are laid down representing the event, the past vanishes and is replaced by the present. The memory traces of the event continue to exist in the present, they are retrieved, and the person remembers the event. This, in a nutshell, has been the understanding of how memory works. It is simple and straightforward; there is no need or room for magic, or marvel. There is certainly no violation of any law of time.

The common sense reflected in this theory is seduced by the word 'remember' which, in everyday usage, does not distinguish between re-experiencing the past on one hand and all other, temporally neutral, consequences of acts of learning on the other. Moreover, every person's possession of the capability of mental time travel works against the appreciation of the rarity of this capability. A barn owl, were it to reflect on its mental powers, probably would not think much of anyone's ability to catch mice in the dark, just as people in some erewhon where all children, in the course of growing up, learn to walk on water would not give the matter a second thought. Because everyone does it, there is nothing marvelous about it.

If there is hope for a more appropriate assessment of the uniqueness of episodic memory and autonoetic consciousness, it may come through the realization that mental time travel involves awareness not only of what has been but also of what may come. This awareness allows autonoetic creatures to reflect on, worry about, and make plans for their own and their progeny's future in a way that those without this capability possibly could not. *Homo sapiens*, taking full advantage of its awareness of its continued existence in time, has transformed the natural world into one of culture and civilization that our distant ancestors, let alone members of other species, possibly could not imagine.

It took biological evolution a long time to build a time machine in the brain, and it has managed to do it only once, but the consequences have been enormous: By virtue of their mental control over time, human beings now wield powers on earth that in many ways rival or even exceed those of nature itself. It is difficult to imagine a marvel of nature greater than that.

Visit the Annual Reviews home page at www.AnnualReviews.org

LITERATURE CITED

Aggleton JP, Brown MW. 1999. Episodic memory, amnesia and the hippocampal-anterior thalamic axis. *Behav. Brain Sci.* 22:425–44

Andreasen NC, O'Leary DS, Arndt S, Cizadlo T, Hurtig R, et al. 1996. Neural substrates of facial recognition. *J. Neuropsychiatry Clin. Neurosci.* 8:139–49

Baldwin JM. 1902. *Development and Evolution.* New York: Macmillan

Buckner RL. 1996. Beyond HERA: contributions of specific prefrontal brain areas to long-term memory. *Psychonom. Bull. Rev.* 3:149–58

Buckner RL, Koutstaal W, Schacter DL, Dale AM, Rotte M, Rosen BR. 1998. Functional-anatomic study of episodic memory retrieval II. Selective averaging of event-related FMRI trials to test the retrieval success hypothesis. *NeuroImage* 7:163–75

Buckner RL, Petersen SE, Ojemann JG, Miezin FM, Squire LR, Raichle ME. 1995. Functional anatomical studies of explicit and implicit memory retrieval tasks. *J. Neurosci.* 15:12–29

Buckner RL, Raichle ME, Miezin FM, Petersen SE. 1996. Functional anatomical studies of memory retrieval for auditory words and visual pictures. *J. Neurosci.* 16:6219–35

Buckner RL, Tulving E. 1995. Neuroimaging studies of memory: theory and recent PET results. In *Handbook of Neuropsychology*, ed. F Boller, J Grafman, 10:439–66. Amsterdam: Elsevier

Cabeza R, Nyberg L. 2000. Imaging cognition. II. An empirical review of 275 PET and FMRI studies. *J. Cogn. Neurosci.* 12:1–47

Calabrese P, Markowitsch HJ, Durwen HF, Widlitzek H, Haupts M, et al. 1996. Right temporofrontal cortex as critical locus for the ecphory of old episodic memories. *J. Neurol. Neurosurg. Psychiatry* 61 (3):304–10

Cermak LS, O'Connor M. 1983. The antero-grade and retrograde retrieval ability of a patient with amnesia due to encephalitis. *Neuropsychologia* 21:213–34

Clayton NS, Dickinson A. 1998. Episodic-like memory during cache recovery by scrub jays. *Nature* 395:272–74

Cohen NJ. 1984. Preserved learning capacity in amnesia: evidence for multiple memory systems. In *Neuropsychology of Memory*, ed. LR Squire, N Butters, pp. 83–103. New York: Guilford

Craik FIM. 2001. Human memory and age-ing. *Proceedings of the 27th International Congress of Psychology, Stockholm, August 2000.* In press

DellaSala S, Laiacona M, Spinnler H, Trivelli C. 1993. Autobiographical recollection and frontal damage. *Neuropsychologia* 31 (8):823–39

Desgranges B, Baron JC, Eustache F. 1998. The functional neuroanatomy of episodic memory: the role of the frontal lobes, the hippocampal formation, and other areas. *NeuroImage* 8:198–213

Fletcher PC, Dolan RJ, Frith CD. 1995. The functional anatomy of memory. *Experientia* 51:1197–207

Fletcher PC, Frith CD, Rugg MD. 1997. The functional neuroanatomy of episodic memory. *Trends Neurosci.* 20:213–18

Foster JK, Jelicic M, eds. 1999. *Memory: Systems, Process, or Function?* Oxford: Oxford Univ. Press

Gardiner JM. 1988. Functional aspects of recollective experience. *Mem. Cogn.* 16:309–13

Gardiner JM, Richardson-Klavehn A. 2000. Remembering and knowing. See Tulving & Craik 2000, pp. 229–44

Glenberg AM. 1997. What memory is for. *Behav. Brain Sci.* 20:1–55

Gorfein DS. 1987. Functional dissociation: comments on the chapter by Roediger and Blaxton. See Gorfein & Hoffman 1987, pp. 381–83

Gorfein DS, Hoffman RR, eds. 1987. *Memory*

and Learning: The Ebbinghaus Centennial Conference. Hillsdale, NJ: Erlbaum

Griffiths DP, Dickinson A, Clayton NS. 1999. Declarative and episodic memory. What can animals remember about their past? *Trends Cogn. Sci.* 3(2):74–80

Hamann SB, Squire LR. 1995. On the acquisition of new declarative knowledge in amnesia. *Behav. Neurosci.* 109:1027–44

Haxby JV, Ungerleider LG, Horwitz B, Maisog JM, Rapoport SL, Grady CL. 1996. Face encoding and recognition in the human brain. *Proc. Natl. Acad. Sci. USA* 93:922–27

Hayman CAG, Macdonald CA, Tulving E. 1993. The role of repetition and associative interference in new semantic learning in amnesia. *J. Cogn. Neurosci.* 5:375–89

Hintzman DL. 1984. Episodic versus semantic memory: a distinction whose time has come—and gone? *Behav. Brain Sci.* 7:240–41

Hintzman DL. 2000. Memory judgements. See Tulving & Craik 2000, pp. 165–77

Horner MD. 1990. Psychobiological evidence for the distinction between episodic and semantic memory. *Neuropsychol. Rev.* 1:281–321

Howe ML. 2000. *The Fate of Early Memories.* Washington, DC: Am. Psychol. Assoc.

Jacoby LL. 1991. A process dissociation framework: separating automatic from intentional uses of memory. *J. Mem. Lang.* 30:513–41

Kapur N. 1999. Syndromes of retrograde amnesia: a conceptual and empirical analysis. *Psychol. Bull.* 125:800–25

Kapur S, Craik FIM, Jones C, Brown GM, Houle S, Tulving E. 1995. Functional role of the prefrontal cortex in retrieval of memories: a PET study. *NeuroReport* 6:1880–84

Kapur S, Craik FIM, Tulving E, Wilson AA, Houle S, Brown GM. 1994. Neuroanatomical correlates of encoding in episodic memory: levels of processing effect. *Proc. Natl. Acad. Sci. USA* 91:2008–11

Kelley WM, Miezin FM, McDermott KB,

Buckner RL, Raichle ME, et al. 1998. Hemispheric specialization in human dorsal frontal cortex and medial temporal lobe for verbal and nonverbal memory encoding. *Neuron* 20:927–36

Kihlstrom JF. 1984. A fact is a fact is a fact. *Behav. Brain Sci.* 7:243–44

Kitchener EG, Hodges JR, McCarthy R. 1998. Acquisition of post-morbid vocabulary and semantic facts in the absence of episodic memory. *Brain* 121:1313–27

Knowlton BJ, Squire LR. 1995. Remembering and knowing: two different expressions of declarative memory. *J. Exp. Psychol.: Learn. Mem. Cogn.* 21:699–710

Köhler S, Moscovitch M, Winocur G, Houle S, McIntosh AR. 1998. Networks of domain-specific and general regions involved in episodic memory for spatial location and object identity. *Neuropsychologia* 36:129–42

Kopelman MD, Stanhope N, Kingsley D. 1999. Retrograde amnesia in patients with diencephalic, temporal lobe, or frontal lesions. *Neuropsychologia* 37:939–58

Lepage M, Ghaffar O, Nyberg L, Tulving E. 2000. Prefrontal cortex and episodic memory retrieval mode. *Proc. Natl. Acad. Sci. USA* 97:506–11

Levine B, Black SE, Cabeza R, Sinden M, McIntosh AR, et al. 1998. Episodic memory and the self in a case of isolated retrograde amnesia. *Brain* 121:1951–73

Markowitsch HJ, Calabrese P, Liess J, Haupts M, Durwen HF, Gehlen W. 1993. Retrograde amnesia after traumatic injury of the frontotemporal cortex. *J. Neurol. Neurosurg. Psychiatry* 56 (9):988–92

McClelland JL, McNaughton BL, O'Reilly RC. 1995. Why there are complementary learning systems in the hippocampus and neocortex: insights from the successes and failures of connectionist models of learning and memory. *Psychol. Rev.* 102:419–57

McCormack T, Hoerl C. 1999. Memory and temporal perspective: the role of temporal frameworks in memory development. *Dev. Rev.* 19:154–82

McIntosh AR. 1999. Mapping cognition to the brain through neural interaction. *Memory* 7:523–48

Mesulam MM. 1990. Large-scale neurocognitive networks and distributed processing for attention, language, and memory. *Ann. Neurol.* 28:597–613

Mishkin M, Suzuki WA, Gadian DG, Vargha-Khadem F. 1997. Hierarchical organization of cognitive memory. *Philos. Trans. R. Soc. London B* 352:1461–67

Moscovitch M, Kapur S, Köhler S, Houle S. 1995. Distinct neural correlates of visual long-term memory for spatial location and object identity: a positron emission tomography (PET) study in humans. *Proc. Natl. Acad. Sci. USA* 92:3721–25

Nelson K. 1993. The psychological and social origins of autobiographical memory. *Psychol. Sci.* 4:7–14

Nielsen JM. 1958. *Memory and Amnesia.* Los Angeles: San Lucas

Nyberg L. 1998. Mapping episodic memory. *Behav. Brain Res.* 90:107–14

Nyberg L, Cabeza R, Tulving E. 1996a. PET studies of encoding and retrieval: the HERA model. *Psychonom. Bull. Rev.* 3:135–48

Nyberg L, Habib R, Tulving E, Cabeza R, Houle S, et al. 2000. Large scale neurocognitive networks underlying episodic memory. *J. Cogn. Neurosci.* 12:163–73

Nyberg L, McIntosh AR, Cabeza R, Habib R, Tulving E. (1996b). General and specific brain regions involved in encoding and retrieval of events: what, where, and when. *Proc. Natl. Acad. Sci. USA* 93:11280–11285

Nyberg L, Tulving E, Habib R, Nilsson L-G, Kapur S, et al. 1995. Functional brain maps of retrieval mode and recovery of episodic information. *NeuroReport* 7:249–52

Perner J, Ruffman T. 1995. Episodic memory and autonoetic consciousness: developmental evidence and a theory of childhood amnesia. *J. Exp. Child Psychol.* 59:516–48

Raichle ME. 1994. Images of the mind: studies

with modern imaging techniques. *Annu. Rev. Psychol.* 45:333–56

Rajaram S. 1993. Remembering and knowing: two means of access to the personal past. *Mem. Cogn.* 21:89–102

Rajaram S, Coslett HB. 2000. New conceptual associative learning in amnesia. *Mem. Lang.* 43:291–315

Ratcliff R, McKoon G. 1986. More on the distinction between episodic and semantic memories. *J. Exp. Psychol.: Learn. Mem. Cogn.* 12:312–13

Richards RJ. 1987. *Darwin and the Emergence of Evolutionary Theories of Mind and Behavior.* Chicago: Univ. Chicago Press

Roediger HL III, Blaxton TA. 1987. Retrieval modes produce dissociations in memory for surface information. See Gorfein & Hoffman 1987, pp. 349–79

Roediger HL III, McDermott KB. 1993. Implicit memory in normal human subjects. In *Handbook of Neuropsychology*, ed. H Spinnler, F Boller, pp. 63–131. Amsterdam: Elsevier

Roediger HL III, Weldon MS, Challis BH. 1989. Explaining dissociations between implicit and explicit measures of retention: a processing account. In *Varieties of Memory and Consciousness: Essays in Honour of Endel Tulving*, ed. HL Roediger III, FIM Craik, pp. 3–42. Hillsdale, NJ: Erlbaum

Rosenbaum RS, Priselac S, Köhler S, Black S, Gao F, et al. 2000. Remote spatial memory in an amnesic person with extensive hippocampal lesions. *Nat. Neurosci.* 3:1044–48

Rousseaux M, Godfrey O, Cabaret M, Bernati T, Pruvo JP. 1997. Retrograde memory after rupture of aneurysms of the anterior communicating artery. *Rev. Neurolog.* 153 (11):659–68

Rugg MD, Fletcher PC, Frith CD, Frackowiak RS, Dolan RJ. 1997. Brain regions supporting intentional and incidental memory: a PET study. *NeuroReport* 8:1283–87

Schacter DL. 1987a. Implicit memory: history and current status. *J. Exp. Psychol.: Learn. Mem. Cogn.* 13:501–18

Schacter DL. 1987b. Memory, amnesia, and frontal lobe dysfunction. *Psychobiology* 15:21–36

Schacter DL, Alpert NM, Savage CR, Rauch SL. 1996. Conscious recollection and the human hippocampal formation: evidence from positron emission tomography. *Proc. Natl. Acad. Sci. USA* 93:321–25

Schacter DL, Harbluk J, McLachlan D. 1984. Retrieval without recollection: an experimental analysis of source amnesia. *J. Verb. Learn. Verb. Behav.* 23:593–611

Schacter DL, Tulving E. 1994. What are the memory systems of 1994? In *Memory Systems*, ed. DL Schacter, E Tulving, pp. 1–38. Cambridge, MA: MIT Press

Schacter DL, Wagner AD, Buckner R. 2000. Memory systems of 1999. See Tulving & Craik 2000, pp. 627–43

Scoville WB, Milner B. 1957. Loss of recent memory after bilateral hippocampal lesions. *J. Neurol. Neurosurg. Psychiatry* 20:11–21

Shallice T, Fletcher P, Frith CD, Grasby P, Frackowiak RSJ, Dolan RJ. 1994. Brain regions associated with acquisition and retrieval of verbal episodic memory. *Nature* 368:633–35

Sherry DF, Schacter DL. 1987. The evolution of multiple memory systems. *Psychol. Rev.* 94:439–54

Shimamura AP, Squire LR. 1987. A neuropsychological study of fact memory and source amnesia. *J. Exp. Psychol.: Learn. Mem. Cogn.* 13:464–73

Squire LR. 1987. *Memory and Brain.* New York: Oxford Univ. Press

Squire LR. 1992. Memory and the hippocampus: a synthesis from findings with rats, monkeys, and humans. *Psychol. Rev.* 99:195–231

Squire LR, Ojemann JG, Miezin FM, Petersen SE, Videen TO, Raichle ME. 1992. Activation of the hippocampus in normal humans: a functional anatomical study of memory. *Proc. Nat. Sci. USA* 89:1837–41

Squire LR, Zola S. 1998. Episodic memory, semantic memory, and amnesia. *Hippocampus* 8:205–11

Suddendorf T, Corballis MC. 1997. Mental time travel and the evolution of the human mind. *Genet. Soc. Gen. Psychol. Monogr.* 123:133–67

Toth JP. 2000. Nonconscious forms of memory. See Tulving & Craik 2000, pp. 245–61

Toth JP, Hunt RR. 1999. Not one versus many, but zero versus any: structure and function in the context of the multiple memory systems debate. See Foster & Jelicic 1999, pp. 232–72

Tulving E. 1972. Episodic and semantic memory. In *Organization of Memory*, ed. E Tulving, W Donaldson, pp. 381–403. New York: Academic

Tulving E. 1983. *Elements of Episodic Memory.* Oxford: Clarendon

Tulving E. 1984. Relations among components and processes of memory. *Behav. Brain Sci.* 7:257–68

Tulving E. 1985a. How many memory systems are there? *Am. Psychol.* 40:385–98

Tulving E. 1985b. Memory and consciousness. *Can. Psychol.* 26:1–12

Tulving E. 1986. What kind of a hypothesis is the distinction between episodic and semantic memory? *J. Exp. Psychol. Learn. Mem. Cogn.* 12:307–11

Tulving E. 1989. Memory: performance, knowledge, and experience. *Eur. J. Cogn. Psychol.* 1:3–26

Tulving E. 1991. Concepts of human memory. In *Memory: Organization and Locus of Change*, ed. L Squire, G Lynch, NM Weinberger, JL McGaugh, pp. 3–32. New York: Oxford Univ. Press

Tulving E. 1995. Organization of memory: Quo vadis? In *The Cognitive Neurosciences*, ed. MS Gazzaniga, pp. 839–47. Cambridge, MA: MIT Press

Tulving E. 1999. On the uniqueness of episodic memory. In *Cognitive Neuroscience of Memory*, ed. L-G Nilsson, HJ Markowitsch, pp. 11–42. Göttingen: Hogrefe & Huber

Tulving E. 2001a. The origin of autonoesis in episodic memory. In *The Nature of Remembering: Essays in Honor of Robert G. Crowder*, ed. HL Roediger, JS Nairne, I Neath, AM Suprenant, pp. 17–34. Washington, DC: Am. Psychol. Assoc.

Tulving E. 2001b. Chronesthesia: awareness of subjective time. In *The Age of the Frontal Lobes*, ed. DT Stuss, RC Knight. In press

Tulving E, Craik FIM, eds. 2000. *The Oxford Handbook of Memory.* New York: Oxford Univ. Press

Tulving E, Hayman CAG, Macdonald CA. 1991. Long-lasting perceptual priming and semantic learning in amnesia: a case experiment. *J. Exp. Psychol.: Learn. Mem. Cogn.* 17:595–617

Tulving E, Kapur S, Craik FIM, Moscovitch M, Houle S. 1994a. Hemispheric encoding/retrieval asymmetry in episodic memory: positron emission tomography findings. *Proc. Natl. Acad. Sci. USA* 91:2016–20

Tulving E, Kapur S, Markowitsch HJ, Craik FIM, Habib R, Houle S. 1994b. Neuroanatomical correlates of retrieval in episodic memory: auditory sentence recognition. *Proc. Natl. Acad. Sci. USA* 91:2012–15

Tulving E, Markowitsch HJ. 1998. Episodic and declarative memory: role of the hippocampus. *Hippocampus* 8:198–204

Tulving E, Schacter DL, McLachlan DR, Moscovitch M. 1988. Priming of semantic autobiographical knowledge: a case study of retrograde amnesia. *Brain Cogn.* 8:3–20

Vargha-Khadem F, Gadian DG, Watkins KE, Connelly A, Van Paesschen W, Mishkin M. 1997. Differential effects of early hippocampal pathology on episodic and semantic memory. *Science* 277:376–80

Viskontas IV, McAndrews MP, Moscovitch M. 2000. Remote episodic memory deficits in patients with unilateral temporal lobe epilepsy and excisions. *J. Neurosci.* 20:5853–57

Wagner AD, Desmond JE, Glover G, Gabrieli JDE. 1998a. Prefrontal cortex and recognition memory: FMRI evidence for context-dependent retrieval processes. *Brain* 121:1985–2002

Wagner AD, Poldrack RA, Eldridge LL, Desmond JE, Glover G, Gabrieli JDE. 1998b. Material-specific lateralization of prefrontal activation during episodic encoding and retrieval. *NeuroReport* 9:3711–17

Weiskrantz L, ed. 1985. Animal intelligence. *Proceedings of a Royal Society Discussion Meeting.* Oxford, UK: Clarendon

Weldon MS, 1999. The memory chop shop: issues in the search for memory systems. See Foster & Jelicic 1999, pp. 162–204

Wheeler MA, Stuss DT, Tulving E. 1997. Toward a theory of episodic memory: the frontal lobes and autonoetic consciousness. *Psychol. Bull.* 121:331–54

Wheeler MA, McMillan CT. 2001. Focal retrograde amnesia and the episodic-semantic distinction. *Cogn. Affect. Behav. Neurosci.* 1:22–37

Annu. Rev. Psychol. 2002. 53:27–51

HUMAN AGGRESSION

Craig A. Anderson and Brad J. Bushman

Department of Psychology, Iowa State University, Ames, Iowa 50011-3180;
e-mail: caa@iastate.edu, bushman@iastate.edu

Key Words violence, harm, theory, general aggression model

■ **Abstract** Research on human aggression has progressed to a point at which a unifying framework is needed. Major domain-limited theories of aggression include cognitive neoassociation, social learning, social interaction, script, and excitation transfer theories. Using the general aggression model (GAM), this review posits cognition, affect, and arousal to mediate the effects of situational and personological variables on aggression. The review also organizes recent theories of the development and persistence of aggressive personality. Personality is conceptualized as a set of stable knowledge structures that individuals use to interpret events in their social world and to guide their behavior. In addition to organizing what is already known about human aggression, this review, using the GAM framework, also serves the heuristic function of suggesting what research is needed to fill in theoretical gaps and can be used to create and test interventions for reducing aggression.

CONTENTS

0084-6570/02/0201-0027$14.00

INTRODUCTION

In its most extreme forms, aggression is human tragedy unsurpassed. Hopes that the horrors of World War II and the Holocaust would produce a worldwide revulsion against killing have been dashed. Since World War II, homicide rates have actually increased rather than decreased in a number of industrialized countries, most notably the United States. Thus, in recent years there has been renewed interest in learning why humans sometimes behave aggressively.

Some of the causes of increased violence have been identified. For example, the accessibility of guns (O'Donnell 1995), global warming (Anderson et al. 1997), violence against children in schools and homes (Hyman 1995, Straus 2000), and the widespread exposure to violent entertainment media (Bushman & Huesmann 2001) all contribute to the high level of violence and aggression in modern societies. Recent psychological research has yielded promising new treatments (e.g., Borduin 1999), new empirical discoveries (e.g., Baumeister et al. 1996, Bushman 1995), and new theoretical analyses (e.g., Eron et al. 1994, Geen & Donnerstein 1998, Huesmann et al. 1996).

We begin by offering some basic definitions. Next we describe several domain-specific theories of aggression. Finally we describe the general aggression model, an integrative framework that will bring more order and structure to the field of aggression. Subsequent sections address inputs, routes, and outcomes of aggression, illustrating recent advances in aggression research.

BASIC DEFINITIONS

Aggression

Human aggression is any behavior directed toward another individual that is carried out with the *proximate* (immediate) intent to cause harm. In addition, the perpetrator must believe that the behavior will harm the target, and that the target is motivated to avoid the behavior (Bushman & Anderson 2001, Baron & Richardson 1994, Berkowitz 1993, Geen 2001).

Accidental harm is not aggressive because it is not intended. Harm that is an incidental by-product of helpful actions is also not aggressive, because the harm-doer believes that the target is not motivated to avoid the action (e.g., pain experienced during a dental procedure). Similarly, the pain administered in sexual masochism is not aggressive because the victim is not motivated to avoid it—indeed, the pain is actively solicited in service of a higher goal (Baumeister 1989).

Violence

Violence is aggression that has extreme harm as its goal (e.g., death). All violence is aggression, but many instances of aggression are not violent. For example, one child pushing another off a tricycle is an act of aggression but is not an act of violence.

Hostile vs. Instrumental Aggression

Hostile aggression has historically been conceived as being impulsive, thoughtless (i.e., unplanned), driven by anger, having the ultimate motive of harming the target, and occurring as a reaction to some perceived provocation. It is sometimes called affective, impulsive, or reactive aggression. *Instrumental aggression* is conceived as a premeditated means of obtaining some goal other than harming the victim, and being proactive rather than reactive (Berkowitz 1993, Geen 2001). Our recent analysis (Bushman & Anderson 2001) modifies these definitions in two ways. First, we distinguish between proximate and ultimate goals. We view intention to harm as a necessary feature of all aggression (as in purely hostile aggression models), but it is necessary only as a proximate goal. Second, we distinguish between different types of aggression at the level of ultimate goal. Thus, both robbery and physical assault are acts of aggression because both include intention to harm the victim at a proximate level. However, they typically differ in ultimate goals, with robbery serving primarily profit-based goals and assault serving primarily harm-based goals. In short, our definition allows us to discuss the commonalities in and distinctions between affective and instrumental aggression, while including aggression that has mixed motives.

DOMAIN SPECIFIC THEORIES OF AGGRESSION

Five main theories of aggression guide most current research. The theories themselves overlap considerably, which is what instigated early attempts to integrate them into a broader framework (Anderson et al. 1995, 1996a).

Cognitive Neoassociation Theory

Berkowitz (1989, 1990, 1993) has proposed that aversive events such as frustrations, provocations, loud noises, uncomfortable temperatures, and unpleasant odors produce negative affect. Negative affect produced by unpleasant experiences automatically stimulates various thoughts, memories, expressive motor reactions, and physiological responses associated with both fight and flight tendencies. The fight associations give rise to rudimentary feelings of anger, whereas the flight associations give rise to rudimentary feelings of fear. Furthermore, cognitive neoassociation theory assumes that cues present during an aversive event become associated with the event and with the cognitive and emotional responses triggered by the event.

In cognitive neoassociation theory, aggressive thoughts, emotions, and behavioral tendencies are linked together in memory (Collins & Loftus 1975). Figure 1 contains a simplified schematic of an associative memory structure in which the concept of "gun" is linked to a number of aggression-related concepts (CA Anderson et al. 1998). Concepts with similar meanings (e.g., hurt, harm) and concepts that frequently are activated simultaneously (e.g., shoot, gun) develop strong associations. In Figure 1 associations are illustrated by lines between the concepts, with thicker lines representing stronger associations and shorter distances representing greater similarity of meaning. When a concept is primed or activated, this activation spreads to related concepts and increases their activation as well.

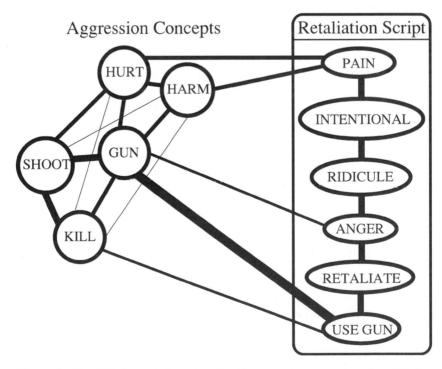

Figure 1   Simplified associative network with aggression concepts and a retaliation script (from CA Anderson et al. 1998).

Cognitive neoassociation theory also includes higher-order cognitive processes, such as appraisals and attributions. If people are motivated to do so, they might think about how they feel, make causal attributions for what led them to feel this way, and consider the consequences of acting on their feelings. Such deliberate thought produces more clearly differentiated feelings of anger, fear, or both. It can also suppress or enhance the action tendencies associated with these feelings.

Cognitive neoassociation theory not only subsumes the earlier frustration-aggression hypothesis (Dollard et al. 1939), but it also provides a causal mechanism for explaining why aversive events increase aggressive inclinations, i.e., via negative affect (Berkowitz 1989). This model is particularly suited to explain hostile aggression, but the same priming and spreading activation processes are also relevant to other types of aggression.

Social Learning Theory

According to social learning theories (Bandura 1983, 2001; Mischel 1973, 1999; Mischel & Shoda 1995), people acquire aggressive responses the same way they acquire other complex forms of social behavior—either by direct experience or by observing others. Social learning theory explains the acquisition of aggressive behaviors, via observational learning processes, and provides a useful set of concepts for understanding and describing the beliefs and expectations that guide social behavior. Social learning theory—especially key concepts regarding the development and change of expectations and how one construes the social world—is particularly useful in understanding the acquisition of aggressive behaviors and in explaining instrumental aggression. For example, Patterson's work on family interactions and the development of antisocial behavior patterns relies heavily on this approach (Patterson et al. 1989, 1992).

Script Theory

Huesmann (1986, 1998) proposed that when children observe violence in the mass media, they learn aggressive scripts. Scripts define situations and guide behavior: The person first selects a script to represent the situation and then assumes a role in the script. Once a script has been learned, it may be retrieved at some later time and used as a guide for behavior. This approach can be seen as a more specific and detailed account of social learning processes.

Scripts are sets of particularly well-rehearsed, highly associated concepts in memory, often involving causal links, goals, and action plans (Abelson 1981, Schank & Abelson 1977). When items are so strongly linked that they form a script, they become a unitary concept in semantic memory. Furthermore, even a few script rehearsals can change a person's expectations and intentions involving important social behaviors (Anderson 1983, Anderson & Godfrey 1987, Marsh et al. 1998). A frequently rehearsed script gains accessibility strength in two ways. Multiple rehearsals create additional links to other concepts in memory, thus increasing the number of paths by which it can be activated. Multiple rehearsals also increase the strength of the links themselves. Thus, a child who has witnessed several thousand instances of using a gun to settle a dispute on television is likely to have a very accessible script that has generalized across many situations. In other words, the script becomes chronically accessible. This theory is particularly useful in accounting for the generalization of social learning processes and the automatization (and simplification) of complex perception-judgment-decision-behavioral processes. Figure 1 includes an example of one simple aggression script involving retaliation.

Excitation Transfer Theory

Excitation transfer theory (Zillmann 1983) notes that physiological arousal dissipates slowly. If two arousing events are separated by a short amount of time, arousal from the first event may be misattributed to the second event. If the second event is related to anger, then the additional arousal should make the person even angrier. The notion of excitation transfer also suggests that anger may be extended over long periods of time if a person has consciously attributed his or her heightened arousal to anger. Thus, even after the arousal has dissipated the person remains ready to aggress for as long as the self-generated label of anger persists.

Social Interaction Theory

Social interaction theory (Tedeschi & Felson 1994) interprets aggressive behavior (or coercive actions) as social influence behavior, i.e., an actor uses coercive actions to produce some change in the target's behavior. Coercive actions can be used by an actor to obtain something of value (e.g., information, money, goods, sex, services, safety), to exact retributive justice for perceived wrongs, or to bring about desired social and self identities (e.g., toughness, competence). According to this theory, the actor is a decision-maker whose choices are directed by the expected rewards, costs, and probabilities of obtaining different outcomes.

Social interaction theory provides an explanation of aggressive acts motivated by higher level (or ultimate) goals. Even hostile aggression might have some rational goal behind it, such as punishing the provocateur in order to reduce the likelihood of future provocations. This theory provides an excellent way to understand recent findings that aggression is often the result of threats to high self-esteem, especially to unwarranted high self-esteem (i.e., narcissism) (Baumeister et al. 1996, Bushman & Baumeister 1998).

THE GENERAL AGGRESSION MODEL

A Heap of Stones is Not a House

"Science is built up with fact, as a house is with stone.
But a collection of fact is no more a science than a heap of stones is a house."
Jules Henri Poincaré

Poincaré's analogy fits the scientific study of aggression. The several current domain-specific theories are the important stones awaiting blueprints, mortar, and a construction crew to build the much more useful house, a general theory of human aggression.

This chapter presents the most recent version of our integrative framework, called the general aggression model (GAM). This theoretical framework was designed to integrate existing mini-theories of aggression into a unified whole. We have fruitfully used various forms of this model for several years (e.g., Anderson 1997; K.B. Anderson et al. 1998; Anderson et al. 1995, 1996a; Anderson & Dill 2000; Bushman & Anderson 2001; Lindsay & Anderson 2000). This general model has at least four advantages over smaller domain theories. First, it is more parsimonious than the set of existing mini-theories. Second, it better explains aggressive acts that are based on multiple motives, e.g., both instrumental and affect-based aggression (Bushman & Anderson 2001). Third, it will aid in the development of more comprehensive interventions designed to treat individuals who are chronically aggressive; many current treatment attempts fail because they focus on only one specific type of aggression or use only one mini-theoretical approach to treatment (Tate et al. 1995). Fourth, it provides broader insights about child rearing and development issues, thus enabling parents, teachers, and public policy makers to make better decisions about child-rearing practices (Zigler et al. 1992).

We believe that GAM provides a useful integrative framework for domain-specific theories of aggression, transforming a heap of stones into a house. For this chapter we have expanded earlier versions of the model (e.g., Anderson 1997; Anderson et al. 1995, 1996a; Anderson & Dill 2000; K.B. Anderson et al. 1998). Specifically, we have dropped the "affective" part of the earlier general affective aggression model, based on the new and broadening definitions of the proximate and ultimate goals of aggression elucidated in Bushman & Anderson (2001). GAM draws heavily on recent work on the development and use of knowledge structures for perception, interpretation, decision making, and action (e.g., Bargh 1996, Collins & Loftus 1975, Fiske & Taylor 1991, Higgins 1996, Wegner & Bargh 1998). Key features include the ideas that knowledge structures (*a*) develop out of experience; (*b*) influence perception at multiple levels, from basic visual patterns to complex behavioral sequences; (*c*) can become automatized with use; (*d*) can contain (or are linked to) affective states, behavioral programs, and beliefs; and (*e*) are used to guide people's interpretations and behavioral responses to their social (and physical) environment. Three particularly relevant subtypes of knowledge structures are (*a*) *perceptual schemata*, which are used to identify phenomena as simple as everyday physical objects (chair, person) or as complex as social events (personal insult); (*b*) *person schemata*, which include beliefs about a particular person or groups of people; and (*c*) *behavioral scripts*, which contain information about how people behave under varying circumstances.

Knowledge structures include affect in three different ways. First, they contain links to experiential affect "nodes" or concepts. When a knowledge structure containing anger is activated, anger is experienced. Second, they include knowledge about affect, such as when a particular emotion should be experienced, how

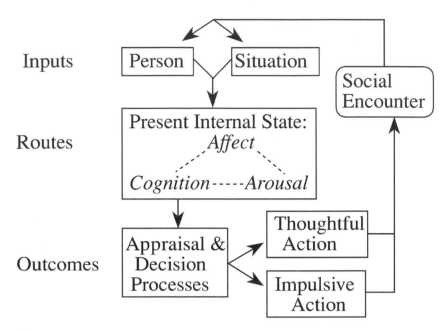

Figure 2   The general aggression model episodic processes.

emotions influence people's judgments and behavior, and so on. Third, a script may include affect as an action rule (Abelson 1981). For example, a personal insult script may prescribe aggressive retaliation but only if anger is at a high level or fear is at a low level.[1]

GAM focuses on the "person in the situation," called an *episode*, consisting of one cycle of an ongoing social interaction. Figure 2 presents a simplified version of the main foci of the model. The three main foci concern (*a*) person and situation inputs; (*b*) cognitive, affective, and arousal routes through which these input variables have their impact; and (*c*) outcomes of the underlying appraisal and decision processes.

INPUTS

Aggression research focuses on discovering what biological, environmental, psychological, and social factors influence aggressive behavior, and on how to use these discoveries to reduce unwarranted aggression. These factors can be

---

[1]See Anderson & Dill 2000, Anderson et al. 2000, Bushman & Anderson 2001 for additional details about types of knowledge structures key to understanding human aggression and the advantages of this approach.

categorized as features of the situation or as features of the person in the situation. The following list of personological and situational input variables is illustrative of key causal factors. Though this list is somewhat biased towards recent research and is not comprehensive, discussing it in a GAM framework leads to a simpler and more comprehensive understanding of human aggression than is possible using the mini-theory approach so commonly used throughout contemporary psychology. Specifically, GAM indicates the types of underlying processes to examine to see how various inputs lead to aggressive (or nonaggressive) behavior.[2]

Person Factors

Person factors include all the characteristics a person brings to the situation, such as personality traits, attitudes, and genetic predispositions. Stable person factors are those that display consistency across time, across situations, or across both. This consistency is largely the result of the person's consistent use of schemata, scripts, and other knowledge structures (Mischel 1999, Mischel & Shoda 1995). In a very real sense, personality is the sum of a person's knowledge structures. Knowledge structures also influence what situations a person will selectively seek out and what situations will be avoided, further contributing to trait-like consistency. Together, person factors comprise an individual's preparedness to aggress.

TRAITS   Certain traits predispose individuals to high levels of aggression. One recent breakthrough, for example, was the discovery that certain types of people who frequently aggress against others do so in large part because of a suscepti-bility towards hostile attribution, perception, and expectation biases (e.g., Crick & Dodge 1994, Dill et al. 1997). Another recent breakthrough contradicts long-standing beliefs of many theoreticians and the lay public alike: A type of high self-esteem (and not low self-esteem) produces high aggression. Specifically, in-dividuals with inflated or unstable self-esteem (narcissists) are prone to anger and are highly aggressive when their high self-image is threatened (Baumeister et al. 1996, Bushman & Baumeister 1998, Kernis et al. 1989). Both discoveries fit the GAM knowledge structure approach quite well.

SEX   Males and females differ in aggressive tendencies, especially in the most violent behaviors of homicide and aggravated assault. The ratio of male to fe-male murderers in the United States is about 10:1 (FBI 1951–1999). Laboratory studies often show the same type of sex effect, but provocation dramatically re-duces sex differences in physical aggression, and specific types of provocation differentially affect male and female aggression (Bettencourt & Miller 1996). The preferred types of aggression also differ for males and females. Males prefer di-rect aggression, whereas females prefer indirect aggression (e.g., Oesterman et al.

---

[2]Space limitations preclude detailed discussion of how biological factors operate within GAM. Briefly, we believe that genetic and other biological factors operate via influences on learning, decision-making, arousal, and affective processes (see Scarpa & Raine 2000).

1998). Developmental research suggests that many of these differences result from different socialization experiences (White 2001). However, evolutionary explanations of some key gender differences also have received empirical support (Buss & Shackelford 1997, Campbell 1999, Geary 1998). For example, males are more upset by sexual infidelity of their mates than by emotional infidelity, whereas the opposite pattern occurs for females (Geary et al. 1995). In all of these examples, our understanding of sex differences in aggression is greatly enhanced by the discovery of differential affective reactions.

BELIEFS   Many types of beliefs play a role in preparedness to aggress. Efficacy-related beliefs are particularly important (e.g., Bandura 1977). Those who believe that they can successfully carry out specific aggressive acts (*self-efficacy*) and that these acts will produce the desired outcomes (*outcome efficacy*) are much more likely to select aggressive behaviors than those who are not so confident of the efficacy of aggressive acts. Aggression-related beliefs significantly predict future levels of aggressive behavior (Huesmann & Guerra 1997). The source of such beliefs in children is often the family (Patterson et al. 1989, 1992).

ATTITUDES   Attitudes are general evaluations people hold about themselves, other people, objects, and issues (Petty & Cacioppo 1986, p. 4). Positive attitudes towards violence in general also prepare certain individuals for aggression. More specific positive attitudes about violence against specific groups of people also increase aggression against those people. For example, attitudes about violence against women are positively related to sexual aggressiveness against women (e.g., Malamuth et al. 1995). Males prone to aggress against women are not generally aggressive against all people in all situations; rather, they specifically target women (but not men) who have provoked them (Anderson 1996).

VALUES   Values—beliefs about what one should or ought to do—also play a role in aggression preparedness. For many people, violence is a perfectly acceptable method of dealing with interpersonal conflict, perhaps even a preferred method. For example, the value system in parts of the southern and western regions of the United States dictates that affronts to personal honor must be answered, preferably with violence (Nisbett & Cohen 1996). There is evidence that some youth gang violence results from similar codes of honor and personal respect (Baumeister & Boden 1998).[3]

LONG-TERM GOALS   Long-term, abstract goals also influence the preparedness of the individual for aggression. For example, the overriding goal of some gang members is to be respected and feared (Horowitz & Schwartz 1974, Klein & Maxson

---

[3]Though Nisbett & Cohen present evidence that a culture of honor is positively related to violence, their claim that this "explains away" apparent hot temperature effects on violent crime is not supported by recent empirical and theoretical analyses (Anderson et al. 2000, Berkowitz 2001).

1989). Such a goal obviously colors one's perceptions of episodes, values, and beliefs about the appropriateness of various courses of action. Similarly, a personal life goal of obtaining wealth can increase one's preparedness for instrumental aggression.

SCRIPTS   The interpretational and behavioral scripts a person brings to social situations influences that person's preparedness for aggression (Huesmann 1988, 1998). Scripts are composed of many of the preceding elements.

Situational Factors

Situational factors include any important features of the situation, such as presence of a provocation or an aggressive cue. Like the person factors, situational factors influence aggression by influencing cognition, affect, and arousal.

AGGRESSIVE CUES   Aggressive cues are objects that prime aggression-related concepts in memory. For instance, Berkowitz & LePage (1967) found that the mere presence of guns (versus badminton racquets and shuttlecocks) increased the aggressive behavior of angered research participants (see Carlson et al. 1990 for a meta-analytic confirmation of this phenomenon). More recently, our understanding of the weapons effect has been enhanced by the discovery that weapon pictures and words automatically prime aggressive thoughts (CA Anderson et al. 1998). Other situational variables that increase aggression, such as exposure to violent television, movies, or video games, also appear to do so via cognitive cueing effects (Anderson & Dill 2000, Bushman 1998).

PROVOCATION   Perhaps the most important single cause of human aggression is interpersonal provocation (Berkowitz 1993, Geen 2001). Provocations include insults, slights, other forms of verbal aggression, physical aggression, interference with one's attempts to attain an important goal, and so on. One emerging line of research concerns workplace violence, aggression, and bullying (Cowie et al. 2001, Folger & Baron 1996). One study (Baron 1999) found that perceived injustice was positively related to workplace aggression.

FRUSTRATION   Frustration can be defined as the blockage of goal attainment. Most provocations can be seen as a type of frustration in which a person has been identified as the agent responsible for the failure to attain the goal. Even frustrations that are fully justified have been shown to increase aggression against the frustrating agent (e.g., Dill & Anderson 1995) and against a person who was not responsible for the failure to attain the goal (e.g., Geen 1968). More recent work has shown that displaced aggression, wherein the target of aggression is not the person who caused the initial frustration, is a robust phenomenon (Marcus-Newhall et al. 2000, Pedersen et al. 2000). Whether such frustration effects operate primarily by influencing cognitions, affect, or arousal is unclear.

PAIN AND DISCOMFORT   Other research has shown that even nonsocial aversive conditions (e.g., hot temperatures, loud noises, unpleasant odors) increase aggression (Berkowitz 1993). Acute aversive conditions, such as pain produced by immersing a hand in a bucket of ice water, increase aggression (e.g., Berkowitz et al. 1981). General discomfort, such as that produced by sitting in a hot room, can also increase aggression; this effect appears to be mediated primarily by increasing negative affect, though there may be cognitive and arousal processes at work too (Anderson et al. 2000).

DRUGS   Various drugs such as alcohol and caffeine can also increase aggression (Bushman 1993). These effects appear to be indirect rather than direct; Bushman (1997) found that aggression-facilitating factors (e.g., provocation, frustration, aggressive cues) have a much stronger effect on people who are under the influence of drugs than on people who are not.

INCENTIVES   The types of incentives that can increase aggression are as numerous as the number of objects that people want or desire. Indeed, the whole advertisement industry rests on the goal of making people want more things (e.g., Kilbourne 1999). By increasing the value of an object, one changes the implicit or explicit perceived cost/benefit ratios, thereby increasing premeditated, instrumental aggression. Momentary appearance of an incentive, such as money left on a table, can also influence aggression in a less premeditated way.

ROUTES

Input variables influence the final outcome behavior through the *present internal state* that they create. For instance, trait hostility and exposure to violent movie scenes interactively influence accessibility of aggressive thoughts (Anderson 1997), aggressive affect (Bushman 1995), and aggressive behavior (Bushman 1995). The internal states of most interest concern cognition, affect, and arousal.

Cognition

HOSTILE THOUGHTS   Some input variables influence aggressive behavior by increasing the relative accessibility of aggressive concepts in memory. Frequent activation of a concept results in its becoming chronically accessible, whereas an immediate situational activation results in making the concept accessible for a short time (e.g., Bargh et al. 1988; Sedikides & Skowronski 1990). The temporary increase in the accessibility is often called priming. A host of factors, such as media violence, can prime aggressive thoughts (e.g., Anderson & Dill 2000, Bushman 1998).

SCRIPTS   Huesmann (1998) has described in detail the basic processes underlying the development of highly accessible aggressive scripts. Similarly, the hostile attribution biases characteristic of aggressive children can be seen as instances of hostility-related scripts (Crick & Dodge 1994, Dodge & Coie 1987).

Affect

MOOD AND EMOTION   Input variables can also directly influence affect, setting the stage for later effects on aggressive behavior. For example, pain increases state hostility or anger (Berkowitz 1993, K.B. Anderson et al. 1998). Uncomfortable temperatures produce a small increase in general negative affect and a larger increase in aggressive affect (Anderson et al. 1996a). Exposure to violent movie clips also increases hostile feelings (Anderson 1997, Bushman 1995, Bushman & Geen 1990, Hansen & Hansen 1990).

Many personality variables are related to hostility-related affect. For example, trait hostility as measured by self-report scales is positively related to state hostility (Anderson 1997, K.B. Anderson et al. 1998, Bushman 1995).

EXPRESSIVE MOTOR RESPONSES   Expressive motor responses are the automatic reactions that occur in conjunction with specific emotions, largely in the face. Even in early infancy, unexpected pain (e.g., immunization inoculations) quickly produces "a clear cut, full-faced anger expression" (Izard 1991, p. 245). Berkowitz (1993) postulated that aversive experiences directly activate aggression-related motor programs that go beyond mere facial expression. This notion fits well with our knowledge structure approach in that many knowledge structures (such as scripts) include action tendencies that are activated whenever the knowledge structure itself reaches threshold.

Arousal

Arousal can influence aggression in three ways. First, arousal from an irrelevant source can energize or strengthen the dominant action tendency, including aggressive tendencies. If a person is provoked or otherwise instigated to aggress at the time that increased arousal occurs, heightened aggression can result (Geen & O'Neal 1969). Second, arousal elicited by irrelevant sources (e.g., exercise) can be mislabeled as anger in situations involving provocation, thus producing anger-motivated aggressive behavior. This mislabeling process has been demonstrated in several studies by Zillmann (1983, 1988), who has named it excitation transfer. Excitation transfer theory suggests that this type of arousal effect may persist over a long period. Even after the arousal has dissipated, the individual may remain potentially aggressive for as long as the self-generated label of "angry" persists. A third, and as yet untested, possibility is that unusually high and low levels of arousal may be aversive states, and may therefore stimulate aggression in the same way as other aversive or painful stimuli.

A large number of situational variables influence both physiological and psychological arousal. Exercise increases both, whereas alcohol decreases both. Interestingly, changes in physiological and psychological arousal do not always coincide. Hot temperatures increase heart rate while simultaneously decreasing perceived arousal. This suggests that heat might increase aggression through the arousal route (Anderson et al. 2000).

Interconnections

As shown in Figure 2, the contents of these three routes are highly interconnected. That cognitions and arousal influence affect is an idea that goes back several generations, through Schachter & Singer (1962) and William James (1890). Affect also influences cognition and arousal (Bower 1981). Research has shown that people often use their affective state to guide inference and judgment processes (Forgas 1992, Schwarz & Clore 1996). At a theoretical level, one can view affect as a part of semantic memory that can be primed via spreading activation processes. Thus, hostile cognitions might make hostile feelings more accessible, and vice versa.

OUTCOMES

The third focus, on outcomes, includes several complex information processes, ranging from the relatively automatic to the heavily controlled (e.g., Robinson 1998, Smith & Lazarus 1993). As shown in Figure 2, results from the inputs enter into the appraisal and decision processes through their effects on cognition, affect, and arousal. In Figure 3 the more automatic processes are labeled "immediate appraisal," whereas the more controlled processes are labeled "reappraisal." The outcomes of these decision processes themselves determine the final action of the episode. The final outcomes then cycle through the social encounter to become part of the inputs for the next episode, as depicted in Figure 2.

The appraisal and decision processes depicted in Figure 3 are taken from research on spontaneous inferences (Krull 1993, Krull & Dill 1996, Uleman 1987)

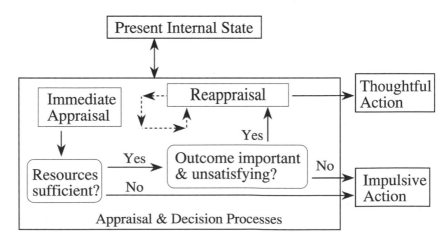

Figure 3 The general aggression model: expanded appraisal and decision processes.

and on explanation and attribution processes (Anderson et al. 1996). To conserve space, we present only a brief tour here.

Immediate appraisal is automatic, i.e., relatively effortless, spontaneous, and occurring without awareness. Depending on the circumstances, immediate appraisal may produce either an automatic trait or situational inference. For example, if a person (target) has been thinking aggressive thoughts and is bumped by another person (actor), the target is likely to perceive the bump as an aggressive act by the actor. However, if the target has been thinking about how crowded the room is, the same bump is likely to be immediately perceived as an accidental consequence of the crowded situation. The present internal state determines, to a great extent, which type of automatic inference is generated. And of course, both person and situation factors determine the present internal state. Thus, Crick & Dodge's (1994) hostile-attribution-bias children bring to the situation a readiness to see intentional affronts where none exists.

Immediate appraisals include affective, goal, and intention information. An aggressive appraisal may include anger-related affect, a retaliation goal, and a specific intention to carry out that goal. However, the exact response will differ considerably from person to person, depending on the person's social learning history (i.e., their personality) and present state of mind (i.e., which knowledge structures are currently most accessible).

What happens after immediate appraisal depends on other resources. If the person has sufficient resources (time, cognitive capacity) and if the immediate appraisal outcome is both important and unsatisfying, then the person will engage a more effortful set of reappraisals. Otherwise, impulsive action results, action that may be aggressive or nonaggressive depending on the content of the immediate appraisal.

Reappraisal involves searching for an alternative view of the situation. It can include a search for relevant information about the cause of the event, a search for relevant memories, and a search for features of the present situation. Reappraisal may include numerous cycles as alternatives are considered and discarded. At some point the recycling process ceases and a thoughtful course of action occurs. If reappraisal leads the person to believe that the bump was an intentionally harmful act, the person may well respond with a thoughtful aggressive action, which may be coldly calculating or may still have hot affective characteristics. Indeed, the reappraisal can increase the level of anger as past wrongs are dredged up from memory or as the damage to one's social image becomes more apparent. Note that the "present internal state" is affected by both types of appraisal, indicated by the double-headed arrow in Figure 3.

PERSONALITY PROCESSES

Just because GAM focuses on the episode and the present internal state does not mean that either the past or the future are irrelevant. The past is represented by what people bring with them to the present episode. Similarly, the future is represented by the person's plans, expectations, goals, and other similar knowledge structures.

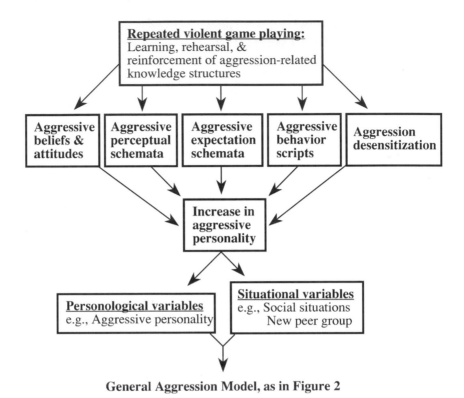

General Aggression Model, as in Figure 2

Figure 4   The general aggression model personality processes.

Repeatedly exposing children to certain factors (e.g., media violence, poor parenting) produces aggressive adults (Huesmann & Miller 1994, Patterson et al. 1992). Such long-term effects result from the development, automatization, and reinforcement of aggression-related knowledge structures. Figure 4 identifies five types of such knowledge structures. In essence, the creation and automatization of these aggression-related knowledge structures and the desensitization effects change the individual's personality. Long-term consumers of violent media, for example, can become more aggressive in outlook, perceptual biases, attitudes, beliefs, and behavior than they were before the repeated exposure, or would have become without such exposure.

Theoretically, these long-term changes in aggressive personality operate in the immediate situation through both types of episodic process input variables depicted in Figure 2: person and situation variables. The link to person variables is obvious—the person is now more aggressive in outlook and propensity. Less obvious is how long-term effects of repeated exposure to maladaptive situations can systematically change other situational variables.

Huesmann & Miller (1994) proposed a model of the long-term social and academic effects of repeated exposure to television violence. A generalized version of this model accounts for other long-term effects, too. As a child becomes more aggressive, the social environment responds. The types of people who are willing to interact with the child, the types of interactions that are held, as well as the types of situations made available, all change. Interactions with teachers, parents, and nonaggressive peers are likely to degenerate, whereas interactions with other "deviant" peers may well increase. Repeated exposure to other situational factors that produce short-term increases in aggression, described earlier, are believed to produce long-term increases in a similar manner.

RELATED PHENOMENA

Opportunity

There are several other features of human aggression that must be successfully explained by any "general" model. For instance, one powerful predictor of aggression is opportunity, or the social situation (Goldstein 1994). Some situations restrict opportunities to aggress; others provide good opportunities. Church services contain many impediments to aggression—witnesses, strong social norms against aggression, and specific nonaggressive behavioral roles for everyone in attendance. Country/Western bars on Saturday nights present better opportunities for aggression. Many aggression facilitators are present: alcohol, aggressive cues, aggression-prone individuals, males competing for the attention of females, and relative anonymity. This phenomenon fits well with GAM and its underlying knowledge structure approach.

Overriding Inhibitions

Another phenomenon of interest has garnered increased attention in recent years—the aggression inhibitions that normally operate in most people. Several research groups have independently identified and discussed how these inhibitions are sometimes overridden (Bandura 2001; Bandura et al. 1996; Keltner & Robinson 1996; Staub 1989, 1998). Most people do not commit extreme acts of violence even if they could do so with little chance of discovery or punishment. Such self-regulation is due, in large part, to the fact that people cannot easily escape the moral standards that they apply to themselves. Self-image, self-standards, and sense of self-worth are used in normal self-regulation of behavior. However, people with apparently normal moral standards sometimes behave reprehensibly towards others, by committing such actions as murder, torture, and even genocide. Two particularly important mechanisms that allow people to disengage their normal moral standards involve moral justification and victim dehumanization. Common justifications for extreme and mass violence include "it is for the person's own good," or the good of the society, or that personal honor demands the violent action. These justifications can be applied at multiple levels, from a parent's abuse of a child to a genocidal war. Dehumanizing the victim operates by making sure that one's moral standards are simply not applicable. War propaganda obviously fits this mechanism, but people also use it at an individual level. Potential victims are placed in the ultimate outgroup—one that has no human qualities. In essence, new knowledge structures are created that explicitly move the target group into a category for which aggression is not only acceptable, but a part of the script.

Several of the more "acute" factors influencing aggression may also operate by reducing inhibitions. For instance, some drugs reduce aggression inhibitions, though the exact mechanism is unknown (e.g., Bushman 1997). Similarly, extreme anger or agitation may increase aggression by reducing inhibitions.

Shared Motivations

People require more than food and shelter to survive. From an evolutionary standpoint, the species also requires an ability and propensity to work cooperatively in social groups. Several common social needs appear repeatedly in the writings of scholars across many areas of psychology (e.g., Baumeister & Leary 1995, Hogan 1998). One such list might include the needs to (a) view oneself positively (self-esteem); (b) believe that others view the self positively (social esteem); (c) believe the world as a just place, if not here then in the hereafter; (d) belong to a social group; (e) view one's group positively (group esteem).

Threats to these needs are often the source of aggressive behavior. Of course, an individual's learning history determines to a great extent what kinds of behaviors will be linked to various threats. Nonetheless, it is striking how often aggression is the dominant response to such threats. We suggest two sources for this commonality. First, aggression frequently works in the short run, especially for big people who wish to control the behavior of small people (e.g., parents punishing children, male-on-female aggression). Second, there seems to be a "preparedness" (Berkowitz 1993, Seligman 1970) to emit aggressive behaviors when faced with pain, physical or psychological. Perhaps the anger-aggression linkage is one that humans are evolutionarily prepared to learn.

Role of Anger

In recent years, aggression scholars have questioned the traditional assumption that anger causes aggression (e.g., Berkowitz 1993, Geen 2001). We believe anger plays several causal roles in aggression (see Berkowitz 2001). First, anger reduces inhibitions against aggressing in at least two ways. Anger sometimes provides a justification for aggressive retaliation—it is part of the decision rule in the aggression script. Anger may sometimes interfere with higher-level cognitive processes, including those normally used in moral reasoning and judgment, which are part of the reappraisal process.

Second, anger allows a person to maintain an aggressive intention over time. Anger increases attention to the provoking events, increases the depth of processing of those events, and therefore improves recall of those events. Thus, anger allows one to reinstate the state that was present in the originally provoking situation.

Third, anger (like other emotions) is used as an information cue. It informs people about causes, culpability, and possible ways of responding (e.g., retaliation). If anger is triggered in an ambiguous social situation, the anger experience itself helps resolve the ambiguities, and does so in the direction of hostile interpretations.

Fourth, anger primes aggressive thoughts, scripts, and associated expressive-motor behaviors. Such anger-related knowledge structures are used to interpret the situation and to provide aggressive responses to the situation. One related consequence of the many links between anger and various knowledge structures is that people frequently pay more attention to anger-related stimuli than to similar neutral stimuli (Cohen et al. 1998).

Fifth, anger energizes behavior by increasing arousal levels. Given that aggression-related knowledge structures are also primed by anger, aggressive behavior is one likely form of behavior that is energized by anger.

Interventions

GAM fully accounts for the fact that attempts to change overly aggressive individuals become increasingly less successful as these individuals become older. With increasing life experiences, one's typical construal of the social world is largely based on well-rehearsed and accessible knowledge structures, which are inherently difficult to change.

Similarly, the model accounts for the fact that narrowly based prevention or treatment programs tend not to work, probably because there are so many ways that maladaptive knowledge structures can be learned. The most successful interventions appear to be those that address multiple sources of potentially maladaptive learning environments, and do so at a relatively young age (e.g., Zigler et al. 1992).

Attempts at treatment or "rehabilitation" of violent adults, usually done in the context of prison programs, have led to a general consensus of failure. Many treatments have been tried with violent juvenile offenders, including such things as "boot camps," individual therapy, "scared straight" programs, and group therapy. Unfortunately, there is little evidence of sustained success for any of these approaches. One problem is that these approaches do not address the wide range of factors that contribute to the development and maintenance of violent behavior. However, there is evidence that treatment can have a significant beneficial impact on violent juvenile offenders (e.g., Simon 1998).

One approach that appears promising is multisystemic therapy (Borduin 1999, Henggeler et al. 1998). Multisystemic therapy is a family-based approach that first identifies the major factors contributing to the delinquent and violent behaviors of the individual undergoing treatment. Biological, school, work, peer-group, family, and neighborhood factors are examined. Intervention is then tailored to fit the individual constellation of contributing factors. Opportunities to observe and commit further violent and criminal offenses are severely restricted, whereas prosocial behavior opportunities are greatly enhanced and rewarded. Both the long-term success rate and the cost/benefit ratio of this approach have greatly exceeded other attempts at treating violent individuals.

In sum, GAM provides a useful framework for understanding and integrating what is already known about human aggression. It provides the mortar and structure to hold together the current domain-specific aggression theories so they form a house rather than a heap of stones. It incorporates smaller domain-specific aggression theories. It organizes recent theories of the development and persistence of the aggressive personality. It serves the heuristic function of suggesting important directions for future research designed to fill in theoretical gaps. Finally, it provides direction for creating and testing interventions designed to reduce unnecessary human aggression. As Immanuel Kant once remarked, research without theory is blind. We believe that theory-based aggression research can reduce the level of violence in society by increasing our understanding of the causes of aggression and violence.

ACKNOWLEDGMENTS

This work was supported in part by a Big XII Faculty Fellowship to the second author. We thank Dave Geary, Al Bandura, Bruce Bartholow, Jeff Valentine, and Anne Powers for helpful comments. We also thank all those individuals who responded to our request for suggested topics to be included in this chapter, and apologize to those whose excellent suggestions could not be accommodated owing to space limitations.

Visit the Annual Reviews home page at www.AnnualReviews.org

LITERATURE CITED

Abelson RP. 1981. Psychological status of the script concept. *Am. Psychol.* 36:715–29

Anderson CA. 1983. Imagination and expectation: the effect of imagining behavioral scripts on personal intentions. *J. Pers. Soc. Psychol.* 45:293–305

Anderson CA. 1997. Effects of violent movies and trait irritability on hostile feelings and aggressive thoughts. *Aggress. Behav.* 23:161–78

Anderson CA, Anderson KB, Deuser WE. 1996a. Examining an affective aggression framework: weapon and temperature effects on aggressive thoughts, affect, and attitudes. *Pers. Soc. Psychol. B* 22:366–76

Anderson CA, Anderson KB, Dorr N, DeNeve KM, Flanagan M. 2000. Temperature and aggression. In *Advances in Experimental Social Psychology*, ed. M Zanna, 32:63–133. New York: Academic

Anderson CA, Benjamin AJ, Bartholow BD. 1998. Does the gun pull the trigger? Automatic priming effects of weapon pictures and weapon names. *Psychol. Sci.* 9:308–14

Anderson CA, Bushman BJ, Groom RW. 1997. Hot years and serious and deadly assault:

empirical tests of the heat hypothesis. *J. Pers. Soc. Psychol.* 16:1213–23

Anderson CA, Deuser WE, DeNeve K. 1995. Hot temperatures, hostile affect, hostile cognition, and arousal: tests of a general model of affective aggression. *Pers. Soc. Psychol. B* 21:434–48

Anderson CA, Dill KE. 2000. Video games and aggressive thoughts, feelings, and behavior in the laboratory and in life. *J. Pers. Soc. Psychol.* 78:772–90

Anderson CA, Godfrey S. 1987. Thoughts about actions: the effects of specificity and availability of imagined behavioral scripts on expectations about oneself and others. *Soc. Cogn.* 5:238–58

Anderson CA, Krull DS, Weiner B. 1996. Explanations: processes and consequences. See Higgins & Kruglanski 1996, pp. 271–96

Anderson KB. 1996. *Cognitive and personality predictors of male-on-female aggression: an integration of theoretical perspectives.* Unpublished PhD dissertation thesis. Univ. Missouri

Anderson KB, Anderson CA, Dill KE, Deuser WE. 1998. The interactive relations between trait hostility, pain, and aggressive thoughts. *Aggress. Behav.* 24:161–71

Bandura A. 1977. *Social Learning Theory.* New York: Prentice Hall

Bandura A. 1983. Psychological mechanisms of aggression. See Geen & Donnerstein 1983, pp. 11–40

Bandura A. 2001. Social cognitive theory: an agentic perspective. *Annu. Rev. Psychol.* 52:1–26

Bandura A, Barbaranelli C, Caprara GV, Pastorelli C. 1996. Mechanisms of moral disengagement in the exercise of moral agency. *J. Pers. Soc. Psychol.* 71:364–74

Bargh JA. 1996. Automaticity in social psychology. See Higgins & Kruglanski 1996, pp. 169–83

Bargh JA, Lombardi WJ, Higgins ET. 1988. Automaticity of chronically accessible constructs in person X situation effects on person perception: It's just a matter of time. *J. Pers. Soc. Psychol.* 55:599–605

Baron RA. 1999. Social and personal determinants of workplace aggression: evidence for the impact of perceived injustice and the Type A behavior pattern. *Aggress. Behav.* 25:281–96

Baron RA, Richardson DR. 1994. *Human Aggression.* New York: Plenum. 2nd ed.

Baumeister RF. 1989. *Masochism and the Self.* Hillsdale, NJ. Erlbaum

Baumeister RF, Boden JM. 1998. Aggression and the self: high self-esteem, low self-control, and ego threat. See Geen & Donnerstein 1998, pp. 111–37

Baumeister RF, Leary MR. 1995. The need to belong: desire for interpersonal attachments as a fundamental human motivation. *Psychol. Bull.* 117:497–529

Baumeister RF, Smart L, Boden JM. 1996. Relation of threatened egotism to violence and aggression: the dark side of high self-esteem. *Psychol. Rev.* 103:5–33

Berkowitz L. 1989. Frustration-aggression hypothesis: examination and reformulation. *Psychol. Bull.* 106:59–73

Berkowitz L. 1990. On the formation and regulation of anger and aggression: a cognitive-neoassociationistic analysis. *Am. Psychol.* 45:494–503

Berkowitz L. 1993. Pain and aggression: some findings and implications. *Motiv. Emot.* 17:277–93

Berkowitz L. 2001. Affect, aggression and antisocial behavior. In *Handbook of Affective Sciences,* ed. RJ Davidson, K Scherer, HH Goldsmith. New York/Oxford UK: Oxford Univ. Press. In press

Berkowitz L, Cochran ST, Embree MC. 1981. Physical pain and the goal of aversively stimulated aggression. *J. Pers. Soc. Psychol.* 40:687–700

Berkowitz L, LePage A. 1967. Weapons as aggression-eliciting stimuli. *J. Pers. Soc. Psychol.* 7:202–7

Bettencourt BA, Miller N. 1996. Gender differences in aggression as a function of provocation: a meta-analysis. *Psychol. Bull.* 119:422–47

Borduin CM. 1999. Multisystemic treatment

of criminality and violence in adolescents. *J Am. Acad. Child Adolesc. Psychiatry* 38:242–49

Bower G. 1981. Mood and memory. *Am. Psychol.* 36:129–48

Bushman BJ. 1993. Human aggression while under the influence of alcohol and other drugs: an integrative research review. *Curr. Dir. Psychol. Sci.* 2:148–52

Bushman BJ. 1995. Moderating role of trait aggressiveness in the effects of violent media on aggression. *J. Pers. Soc. Psychol.* 69:950–60

Bushman BJ. 1997. Effects of alcohol on human aggression: validity of proposed explanations. In *Recent Developments in Alcoholism: Alcohol and Violence*, ed. D Fuller, R Dietrich, E Gottheil, 13:227–43. New York: Plenum

Bushman BJ. 1998. Priming effects of violent media on the accessibility of aggressive constructs in memory. *Pers. Soc. Psychol. Bull.* 24:537–45

Bushman BJ, Anderson CA. 2001. Is it time to pull the plug on the hostile versus instrumental aggression dichotomy? *Psychol. Rev.* 108:273–79

Bushman BJ, Baumeister RF. 1998. Threatened egotism, narcissism, self-esteem, and direct and displaced aggression: Does self-love or self-hate lead to violence? *J. Pers. Soc. Psychol.* 75:219–29

Bushman BJ, Geen RG. 1990. Role of cognitive-emotional mediators and individual differences in the effects of media violence on aggression. *J. Pers. Soc. Psychol.* 58:156–63

Bushman BJ, Huesmann LR. 2001. Effects of televised violence on aggression. In *Handbook of Children and the Media*, ed. D Singer, J Singer, pp. 223–54. Thousand Oaks, CA: Sage

Buss DM, Shackelford TK. 1997. From vigilance to violence: mate retention tactics in married couples. *J. Pers. Soc. Psychol.* 72:346–61

Campbell A. 1999. Staying alive: evolution, culture, and women's intrasexual aggression. *Behav. Brain Sci.* 22:203–52

Carlson M, Marcus-Newhall A, Miller N. 1990. Effects of situational aggression cues: a quantitative review. *J. Pers. Soc. Psychol.* 58:622–33

Cohen DJ, Eckhardt CI, Schagat KD. 1998. Attention allocation and habituation to anger-related stimuli during a visual search task. *Aggress. Behav.* 24:399–409

Collins AM, Loftus EF. 1975. A spreading activation theory of semantic processing. *Psychol. Rev.* 82:407–28

Cowie H, Naylor P, Rivers I, Smith PK, Pereira B. 2001. Measuring workplace bullying. *Aggress. Violent Behav.* In press

Crick NR, Dodge KA. 1994. A review and reformulation of social information processing mechanisms in children's adjustment. *Psychol. Bull.* 115:74–101

Dill J, Anderson CA. 1995. Effects of justified and unjustified frustration on aggression. *Aggress. Behav.* 21:359–69

Dill KE, Anderson CA, Anderson KB, Deuser WE. 1997. Effects of aggressive personality on social expectations and social perceptions. *J. Res. Pers.* 31:272–92

Dodge KA, Coie JD. 1987. Social information-processing factors in reactive and proactive aggression in children's peer groups. *J. Pers. Soc. Psychol.* 53:1146–58

Dollard J, Doob L, Miller N, Mowrer O, Sears R. 1939. *Frustration and Aggression*. New Haven, CT: Yale Univ. Press

Eron LD, Gentry JH, Schlegel P. 1994. *Reason to Hope: A Psychosocial Perspective on Violence and Youth*. Washington, DC: Am. Psychol. Assoc.

FBI. 1951–1999. *Uniform Crime Reports for the United States*. Fed. Bur. Invest., Dep. Justice, Washington, DC: US GPO

Fiske ST, Taylor SE. 1991. *Social Cognition*. New York: McGraw-Hill. 2nd ed.

Folger R, Baron RA. 1996. Violence and hostility at work: a model of reactions to perceived injustice. In *Violence on the Job: Identifying Risks and Developing Solutions*. ed. G VandenBos, E Bulatao, pp. 51–85. Washington, DC: Am. Psychol. Assoc.

Forgas JP. 1992. Affect in social judgments and

decisions: a multiprocess model. *Adv. Exp. Soc. Psychol.* 25:227–75

Geary DC. 1998. Male, female: the evolution of human sex differences. Washington, DC: Am. Psychol. Assoc.

Geary DC, Rumsey M, Bow-Thomas CC, Hoard MK. 1995. Sexual jealousy as a facultative trait: evidence from the pattern of sex differences in adults from China and the United States. *Ethol. Sociobiol.* 16:355–83

Geen RG. 1968. Effects of frustration, attack, and prior training in aggressiveness upon aggressive behavior. *J. Pers. Soc. Psychol.* 9:316–21

Geen RG. 2001. *Human Aggression.* Taylor & Francis. 2nd ed.

Geen RG, Donnerstein E, eds. 1983. *Aggression: Theoretical and Empirical Reviews,* Vol. 1. New York: Academic

Geen RG, Donnerstein E, eds. 1998. *Human Aggression: Theories, Research and Implications for Policy.* New York: Academic

Geen RG, O'Neal EC. 1969. Activation of cue-elicited aggression by general arousal. *J. Pers. Soc. Psychol.* 11:289–92

Goldstein AP. 1994. *The Ecology of Aggression.* New York: Plenum

Hansen CH, Hansen RD. 1990. The influence of sex and violence on the appeal of rock music videos. *Commun. Res.* 17:212–34

Henggeler SW, Schoenwald SK, Borduin CM, Rowland MD, Cunningham PB. 1998. *Multisystemic Treatment of Antisocial Behavior in Children and Adolescents.* New York: Guilford

Higgins E, Kruglanski A, eds. 1996. *Social Psychology: Handbook of Basic Principles.* New York: Guilford

Higgins ET. 1996. Knowledge activation: accessibility, applicability, and salience. See Higgins & Kruglanski 1996, pp. 133–68

Hogan R. 1998. Reinventing personality. *J. Soc. Clin. Psychol.* 17:1–10

Horowitz R, Schwartz G. 1974. Honor, normative ambiguity, and gang violence. *Am. Sociol. Rev.* 39:238–51

Huesmann LR. 1986. Psychological processes promoting the relation between exposure to media violence and aggressive behavior by the viewer. *J. Soc. Issues* 42:125–40

Huesmann LR. 1988. An information-processing model for the development of aggression. *Aggress. Behav.* 14:13–24

Huesmann LR. 1998. The role of social information processing and cognitive schema in the acquisition and maintenance of habitual aggressive behavior. See Geen & Donnerstein 1998, pp. 73–109

Huesmann LR, Becker JV, Dutton MA, Coie J, Gladue BA, et al, eds. 1996. *Reducing Violence: A Research Agenda—A Human Capital Initiative Report.* Washington, DC: Am. Psychol. Assoc.

Huesmann LR, Guerra NG. 1997. Children's normative beliefs about aggression and aggressive behavior. *J. Pers. Soc. Psychol.* 72:408–19

Huesmann LR, Miller LS. 1994. Long-term effects of repeated exposure to media violence in childhood. In *Aggressive Behavior: Current Perspectives*, ed. LR Huesmann, pp. 153–86. New York: Plenum

Hyman IA. 1995. Corporal punishment, psychological maltreatment, violence, and punitiveness in America: research, advocacy, and public policy. *Appl. Prev. Psychol.* 4:113–30

Izard CE. 1991. *The Psychology of Emotion.* New York: Plenum

James W. 1890. *Principles of Psychology.* New York: Holt

Keltner D, Robinson RJ. 1996. Extremism, power, and the imagined basis of social conflict. *Curr. Dir. Psychol. Sci.* 5:101–5

Kernis MH, Grannemann BD, Barclay LC. 1989. Stability and level of self-esteem as predictors of anger arousal and hostility. *J. Pers. Soc. Psychol.* 56:1013–22

Kilbourne J. 1999. *Can't Buy My Love: How Advertising Changes the Way We Think and Feel.* New York: Simon & Schuster

Klein MW, Maxson CK. 1989. Street gang violence. In *Violent Crime, Violent Criminals*, ed. N Weiner, M Wolfgang, pp. 198–234. Newbury Park, CA: Sage

Krull DS. 1993. Does the grist change the mill?:

the effect of perceiver's goal on the process of social inference. *Pers. Soc. Psychol. B* 19:340–48

Krull DS, Dill JC. 1996. On thinking first and responding fast: flexibility in social inference processes. *Pers. Soc. Psychol. B* 22:949–59

Lindsay JJ, Anderson CA. 2000. From antecedent conditions to violent actions: a general affective aggression model. *Pers. Soc. Psychol. B* 26:533–47

Malamuth NM, Linz D, Heavey CL, Barnes G, Acker M. 1995. Using the confluence model of sexual aggression to predict men's conflict with women: a 10-year follow-up study. *J. Pers. Soc. Psychol.* 69:353–69

Marcus-Newhall A, Pedersen WC, Carlson M, Miller N. 2000. Displaced aggression is alive and well: a meta-analytic review. *J. Pers. Soc. Psychol.* 78:670–89

Marsh RL, Hicks JL, Bink ML. 1998. Activation of completed, uncompleted, and partially completed intentions. *J. Exp. Psychol. Learn.* 24:350–61

Mischel W. 1973. Toward a cognitive social learning reconceptualization of personality. *Psychol. Rev.* 80:252–83

Mischel W. 1999. Personality coherence and dispositions in a cognitive-affective personality (CAPS) approach. In *The Coherence of Personality: Social-Cognitive Bases of Consistency, Variability, and Organization*, ed. D Cervone, Y Shoda, pp. 37–60. New York: Guilford

Mischel W, Shoda Y. 1995. A cognitive-affective system theory of personality: reconceptualizing situations, dispositions, dynamics, and invariance in personality structure. *Psychol. Rev.* 102:246–68

Nisbett RE, Cohen D. 1996. *Culture of Honor: The Psychology of Violence in the South.* Boulder, CO: Westview

O'Donnell CR. 1995. Firearm deaths among children and youth. *Am. Psychol.* 50:771–76

Oesterman K, Bjoerkqvist K, Lagerspetz KMJ, Kaukiainen A, Landau SF, et al. 1998. Cross-cultural evidence of female indirect aggression. *Aggress. Behav.* 24:1–8

Patterson GR, DeBaryshe BD, Ramsey E. 1989. A developmental perspective on antisocial behavior. *Am. Psychol.* 44:329–35

Patterson GR, Reid JB, Dishion TJ. 1992. *Antisocial Boys.* Eugene, OR: Castalia

Pedersen WC, Gonzales C, Miller N. 2000. The moderating effect of trivial triggering provocation on displaced aggression. *J. Pers. Soc. Psychol.* 78:913–27

Petty RE, Cacioppo JT. 1986. *Communication and Persuasion: Central and Peripheral Routes to Attitude Change.* New York: Springer-Verlag

Robinson MD. 1998. Running from William James' bear: a review of preattentive mechanisms and their contributions to emotional experience. *Cogn. Emot.* 12:667–96

Scarpa A, Raine A. 2000. Violence associated with anger and impulsivity. In *The Neuropsychology of Emotion*, ed. J Borod, pp. 320–39. New York: Oxford Univ. Press

Schachter S, Singer J. 1962. Cognitive, social, and physiological determinants of emotional state. *Psychol. Rev.* 69:379–99

Schank RC, Abelson RP. 1977. *Scripts, Plans, Goals and Understanding: An Inquiry into Human Knowledge Structures.* Hillsdale, NJ: Erlbaum

Schwarz N, Clore GL. 1996. Feelings and phenomenal experiences. See Higgins & Kruglanski 1996, pp. 433–65

Sedikides C, Skowronski JJ. 1990. Towards reconciling personality and social psychology: a construct accessibility approach. *J. Soc. Behav. Pers.* 5:531–46

Seligman MEP. 1970. On the generality of the law of learning. *Psychol. Rev.* 77:406–18

Simon, LMJ. 1998. Does criminal offender treatment work? *Appl. Prev. Psychol.* 7:137–59

Smith CA, Lazarus RS. 1993. Appraisal components, core relational themes, and the emotions. *Cogn. Emot.* 7:233–69

Staub E. 1989. *The Roots of Evil: The Origins of Genocide and Other Group Violence.* New York: Cambridge Univ. Press

Staub E. 1998. Breaking the cycle of genocidal

violence: healing and reconciliation. In *Perspectives on Loss: A Sourcebook*, ed. J Harvey. Philadelphia: Taylor & Francis

Straus MA. 2000. *Beating the Devil out of Them: Corporal Punishment by American Families and its Effects on Children*. Somerset, NJ: Transaction. 2nd ed.

Tate DC, Reppucci ND, Mulvey EP. 1995. Violent juvenile delinquents: treatment effectiveness and implications for future action. *Am. Psychol.* 50:777–81

Tedeschi JT, Felson RB. 1994. *Violence, Aggression, & Coercive Actions*. Washington, DC: Am. Psychol. Assoc.

Uleman JS. 1987. Consciousness and control: the case of spontaneous trait inferences. *Pers. Soc. Psychol. B* 13:337–54

Wegner DM, Bargh JA. 1998. Control and automaticity in social life. In *The Handbook of Social Psychology*, ed. D Gilbert, S Fiske, G Lindzey, pp. 446–96. New York: McGraw-Hill

White JW. 2001. Gendered aggression across the lifespan. In *Encyclopedia of Gender*. In press

Zigler E, Taussig C, Black K. 1992. Early childhood intervention: a promising preventative for juvenile delinquency. *Am. Psychol.* 47:997–1006

Zillmann D. 1983. Arousal and aggression. See Geen & Donnerstein 1983 pp. 75–102

Zillmann D. 1988. Cognition-excitation interdependencies in aggressive behavior. *Aggress. Behav.* 14:51–64

Annu. Rev. Psychol. 2002. 53:53–81

REMEMBERING OVER THE SHORT-TERM:
The Case Against the Standard Model

James S. Nairne

*Purdue University, Department of Psychological Sciences, Purdue University,
West Lafayette, Indiana 47907-1364;
e-mail: nairne@psych.purdue.edu*

Key Words short-term memory, rehearsal, decay, activation, working memory

■ **Abstract** Psychologists often assume that short-term storage is synonymous with *activation*, a mnemonic property that keeps information in an immediately accessible form. Permanent knowledge is activated, as a result of on-line cognitive processing, and an activity trace is established "in" short-term (or working) memory. Activation is assumed to decay spontaneously with the passage of time, so a refreshing process—rehearsal—is needed to maintain availability. Most of the phenomena of immediate retention, such as capacity limitations and word length effects, are assumed to arise from trade-offs between rehearsal and decay. This "standard model" of how we remember over the short-term still enjoys considerable popularity, although recent research questions most of its main assumptions. In this chapter I review the recent research and identify the empirical and conceptual problems that plague traditional conceptions of short-term memory. Increasingly, researchers are recognizing that short-term retention is cue driven, much like long-term memory, and that neither rehearsal nor decay is likely to explain the particulars of short-term forgetting.

CONTENTS

0084-6570/02/0201-0053$14.00

INTRODUCTION

How do we remember over the short term? It is clearly adaptive to keep recent information available in some kind of accessible form. It would be difficult to comprehend spoken language, which occurs sequentially, or read any kind of text without remembering the early part of an utterance or the themes relevant to a passage. Virtually all complex cognitive activities—reading, reasoning, problem-solving—require access to intermediate steps (as in adding or multiplying two-digit numbers in the head) or other situation-specific information (Baddeley 1992, Kintsch & VanDijk 1978). What then are the psychological mechanisms, or systems, that drive and control such short-term maintenance?

For many years psychologists have essentially agreed about the main mechanism controlling the temporary storage of information. The generally accepted view—referred to here as the standard model—is that short-term storage arises from *activation*, a mnemonic property that keeps information in an immediately accessible form. Permanent knowledge is activated, as a byproduct of on-line cognitive processing, and comes to reside "in" short-term (or working) memory. Short-term memory, as a whole, is simply defined as the collective set of this activated information in memory (e.g., Cowan 1995, Shiffrin 1999). Activation is assumed to be fragile, however, and it can be quickly lost—through the operation of *decay*—in the absence of rehearsal. The decay process has adaptive value because it enables us to update our memories continuously, removing recently activated information that is no longer needed (e.g., Bjork 1975). When necessary, rehearsal can counteract decay, refreshing activation, much like a juggler can temporarily defy the force of gravity by repeatedly tossing plates back up into the air.

The simplicity of the standard model is clearly a virtue, but is it empirically justified? On the surface, the standard model violates a number of well-known tenets of memory theory. For example, decay has been roundly rejected as a vehicle for long-term forgetting for decades, certainly since the seminal arguments of John McGeoch in the 1930s (McGeoch 1932). More importantly, remembering in the standard model is tied directly to activation, an inherent property of a trace; items are more recallable, or closer to the recall threshold, because they are in an "active" state (e.g., Engle et al. 1999, Lovett et al. 1999). Yet, one of the lessons of modern memory theory is that items do not have "strength," or special mnemonic properties, outside of particular retrieval environments. Remembering is always a joint function of trace properties and retrieval cues (e.g., Tulving 1983), so how can a single trace property—activation—be synonymous with remembering?

It is possible that remembering over the short term is a special case, requiring theoretical proposals that do not apply in more general arenas, but the empirical case should be strong. As I review in the next section, the empirical case for the standard model did, in fact, once seem very strong (see also Baddeley 1990). A number of empirical phenomena strongly support a time-based rehearsal plus decay model. However, as this chapter demonstrates, the case for the standard model has lost much of its secure footing over the past decade. The theoretical viability of its main assumptions, particularly those centering on rehearsal and decay, is now in question. In the last section of the chapter I consider alternative ways of conceptualizing how we remember over the short term. Increasingly, researchers are recognizing that short-term retention is cue driven, much like long-term retention, and that simple appeals to either rehearsal or decay are unlikely to explain the particulars of short-term forgetting (e.g., Brown et al. 2000; Lewandowsky 1999; Nairne 1996, 2001; Tehan & Fallon 1999).

THE STANDARD MODEL: REHEARSAL PLUS DECAY

As noted above, activation is the vehicle for temporary storage in the standard model. Items, once activated, are assumed to exist in a state of immediate accessibility (McElree 1998); the amount of activation, in turn, accrues from a continual trade-off between rehearsal and decay. This account has intuitive appeal—it maps well onto phenomenological experience—and it is easily expressed with concrete metaphors. For instance, think about a juggler trying to maintain a set of four plates. Tossing a plate can be seen as a kind of activation; the height of the toss corresponds roughly to the amount of activation achieved. The juggler is able to maintain a set of activated items (plates) to the extent that each can be caught and re-tossed before gravity reduces it to an irretrievable state.

The juggling metaphor is apt because it can be naturally extended to most of the well-known phenomena of immediate memory (see Nairne 1996). For example, there is a content capacity associated with juggling—the number of plates that can be held aloft—that depends on a trade-off between the juggler's skill and the constant force of gravity. If the hand movements of the juggler are particularly skillful, content capacity increases just as the content capacity of immediate memory (memory span) appears to increase directly with the speed or effectiveness of rehearsal. Moreover, the content capacity of a juggler is not a fixed property of a limited-capacity space—air—but rather depends directly on the effectiveness of the reactivation process. A juggler can easily double his or her net content capacity by binding plates together, just as the capacity of immediate memory can be dramatically increased through semantic binding into chunks (Miller 1956).

The main assumptions of the standard model—activation, rehearsal, and decay—are prominent in a host of current theoretical accounts of short-term retention. Probably the best-known example of a "juggler" model is the working memory model of Baddeley & Hitch (1974; see also Baddeley 1992), particularly the component known as the phonological loop. The phonological loop is the subsystem of working memory that controls short-term retention of verbal material. The loop is divided into two parts: a phonological store, which is the storage location for activated information, and a rehearsal/recoding device called the articulatory control process. Information in the phonological store is assumed to decay in roughly 2 s (which is analogous to a constant force of gravity) and can be refreshed, via rehearsal, by the articulatory control process (tossing plates into the air). Capacity limitations in immediate retention—e.g., the magic number seven—are assumed to arise from trade-offs between decay and loop-based rehearsal.

There are many variants of the working memory model in the current literature (see Miyake & Shah 1999) and there are even updated versions of the Baddeley model itself. For example, Baddeley (2000) has recently added another temporary storage system to his model—the episodic buffer—to explain, in part, how verbal material can be maintained when the phonological loop is unavailable. A number of formal simulation models also mimic the standard model and Baddeley's model in particular (e.g., Burgess & Hitch 1999, Henson 1998, Page & Norris 1998). Each relies on rehearsal plus decay to explain the particulars of short-term retention, although most of the simulation models do contain additional machinery to handle cue-driven retrieval effects. I review a selection of these simulation models in more detail in the final major section of this chapter.

Finally, Cowan's (1988, 1995) conception of short-term memory also shares many, but not all, of the features of the standard model. Cowan assumes that short-term memory represents a nested subset of long-term memory; specifically, it comprises those portions of long-term memory that are currently active. Cowan further distinguishes among activation levels—e.g., some items are especially active because they sit in the focus of attention—but it is important to note that (a) short-term retention is generally tied to an item's activation level and (b) activation is assumed to be lost, normally through decay, as a direct function of time. Cowan acknowledges that factors other than rehearsal and/or decay can influence activation levels and retention, but the basic components of the "juggler" model are well represented in the Cowan model.

Articulation Rate and Span

Empirically, the assumptions of the standard model receive their most convincing support from studies showing a systematic relationship between overt articulation rate and memory span. Articulation rate is assumed to correlate with the speed of internal rehearsal (Landauer 1962), and it turns out to be related in a roughly linear fashion to remembering over the short-term (Baddeley et al. 1975, Schweickert & Boruff 1986). The faster the overt articulation rate, the higher the recorded memory span. One of the best-known examples of this relationship is the word-length effect: Lists of short words (defined in terms of spoken duration) are remembered better than lists of long words, holding constant factors such as letter length and number of syllables (Baddeley et al. 1975).

This relation between articulation rate and memory span is well documented and noncontroversial, although some questions remain about the exact form of the function—e.g., linear or possibly quadratic (Brown & Hulme 1995, Schweickert et al. 1990). The relationship holds at the level of aggregate data as well as for individual subjects. Individual differences in immediate memory performance, for both children and adults, are predicted well by individual articulation rates (Baddeley et al. 1975, Tehan & Lalor 2000). One can even predict differences in digit span cross-culturally by knowing how rapidly digits can be pronounced in a given language. If digit names can be spoken relatively quickly, as in English or Chinese, memory span tends to be higher than if the corresponding digit names take longer to pronounce (e.g., Welsh or Arabic) (Ellis & Hennelly 1980, Naveh-Benjamin & Ayres 1986).

Additional evidence comes from studies measuring retention in the absence of rehearsal. Rehearsal can be prevented, or at least disrupted, by requiring subjects to engage in articulatory suppression during the study and recall of a memory list (saying "the" or "bla" repeatedly aloud); alternatively, one can test young children who lack the ability to rehearse strategically. In the former case—with articulatory suppression—immediate memory performance declines significantly and the word-length effect disappears (Baddeley et al. 1984). In the latter case, young children who fail to rehearse consistently often show little sensitivity to spoken duration in immediate retention, at least when material is presented visually (Gathercole & Hitch 1993). As children age, their mean articulation rate increases and their memory span grows in a roughly proportionate manner (Hitch & Halliday 1983, Hulme et al. 1984, Nicolson 1981).

Collectively, these data seem to offer compelling support for the standard model. Articulation rate, and inferentially the speed of internal rehearsal, varies in a more or less direct way with memory span. In the absence of rehearsal, immediate memory performance declines and no longer shows the clean connection with spoken word duration. However, as we shall see, the empirical case loses much of its vigor on closer inspection. Over the past decade, a number of important exceptions to the data patterns listed above have appeared: For example, it turns out that articulation rate and span are not always closely related, and spoken duration effects sometimes emerge in the absence of rehearsal. Moreover, the theoretical assumptions of the standard model, when examined closely, turn out to contain an unsettling amount of ambiguity. In the sections that follow, I examine the discrepant data—first for rehearsal and then for the process of decay—and discuss the conceptual problems that remain unresolved.

PROBLEMS WITH REHEARSAL

I begin by discussing some of the empirical difficulties associated with the rehearsal arm of the standard model. At the outset, it is worth noting that proponents of the standard model (e.g., Baddeley 1992) rarely, if ever, specify the dynamics of the rehearsal process in any kind of systematic way. As Brown & Hulme (1995) observed, "if rehearsal does exert an important causal influence on memory span, it is clearly necessary to know exactly when such rehearsal is taking place" (Brown & Hulme 1995, p. 599). Yet, the protocol of covert rehearsal is likely to change with a host of variables, such as list length, modality of presentation, presentation rate, lexicality, or interitem similarity. Does rehearsal occur only during stimulus input, or does it also occur during response output? Does it matter whether one rehearses based primarily on sound, or is it necessary to access meaning in order to maintain the activation of permanent knowledge? The idea of the standard "rehearsal + decay" model seems simple enough, but its actual implementation is likely to be quite complex.

Dissociating Rehearsal and Span

In its simplest form, the standard model assumes that most of the variability in immediate retention is attributable to rehearsal. Decay is presumably fixed, like gravity, so effective remembering over the short term hinges on one's ability to maintain activation in the face of decay. Such an account is clearly undermined by the fact that recall differences can emerge when articulation rates are held constant. For example, Schweickert et al. (1990) measured pronunciation rates for lists containing phonologically similar and dissimilar items. Similarity had no significant influence on pronunciation rate (similar = 3.01 items/sec; dissimilar = 2.92 items/sec), but produced substantial memory span differences (similar = 5.62 items; dissimilar = 7.06 items). Comparable results were obtained by Hulme & Tordoff (1989) in a study using children, although small differences in articulation rate favoring the dissimilar items were found in one of their experiments.

Dissociations between articulation rate and span have been reported frequently over the past decade. Hulme et al. (1991) found that words produced significantly higher memory spans than nonwords, even when articulation rates were matched for the item types; in fact, the articulation rates for nonwords were actually slightly higher than for the words, yet the words consistently produced the higher memory spans (Hulme et al. 1999). Similar results have been found recently for high- and low-frequency words (Hulme et al. 1997, Roodenrys et al. 1994) and for concrete versus abstract words (Walker & Hulme 1999). In each case, clear immediate memory differences emerged that were independent of articulation rate.

Other researchers have found that manipulations of item duration sometimes fail to produce concomitant changes in immediate memory performance. Caplan et al. (1992) used lists containing short- and long-duration words matched for number of syllables and phonemes and found no memory advantage for the short-duration words; in fact, the word length effect actually reversed when duration was manipulated by using "lax" vowels of short duration (e.g., carrot) and "tense" vowels of long duration (e.g., spider). Caplan et al. (1992) pointed to the phonological structure of a word, rather than its spoken duration, as the major determinant of the magnitude of the word length effect. Service (1998) reached a similar conclusion in a study using Finnish stimuli, which allow one to vary duration by manipulating combinations of the same acoustic and articulatory features. Lastly, Lovatt et al.

(2000) varied spoken duration in disyllabic words, holding constant a host of potentially confounding factors (e.g., frequency, familiarity, number of phonemes) and failed to find any advantage for short-duration words across several experiments; word duration effects emerged only when the original word pools used by Baddeley et al. (1975) were employed as stimuli.

Ironically, Baddeley et al. (1975) suggested decades ago that certain variables such as meaningfulness, list length, and interpolated delay might affect span without significantly changing reading or articulation rate (Baddeley et al. 1975, p. 583). The data just described confirm this basic intuition, as does the companion finding that items of differing spoken duration need not lead to measurable changes in immediate memory performance. These results are inconsistent with any simple form of the standard model, unless one is willing to assume that decay rates are variable across materials or that additional storage assumptions (e.g., the episodic buffer) can be added to handle the troublesome data. One could explain the findings of Schweickert et al. (1990), for example, by assuming that items decay faster in an environment high in phonological similarity (i.e., Posner & Konick 1966). One might also assume that decay rates are relatively faster for nonwords, low-frequency words, and abstract words, but such assumptions detract from the elegant simplicity of the rehearsal plus decay idea.

Other evidence can be marshaled in support of articulatory processes in immediate retention, although the implications of the data are unclear. For example, Wilson & Emmorey (1998) recently found a duration-based word length effect using word lists generated from American Sign Language. Lists composed of short signs were remembered better than lists of long signs under conditions in which "length" could be attributed uniquely to the duration of the signing process. Of course, one can question the relevance of these data to immediate retention and rehearsal of verbal lists, although Wilson (2001) argues that memory for sign language follows the same general principles as memory for spoken lists. In addition, Cowan et al. (1997b) were able to produce an artificial word length effect by instructing subjects to pronounce words either quickly or slowly at presentation and during recall. Given that the same word set was used in the "short" and "long" condition, these data suggest a role for articulation time (see also Cowan et al. 2000). Again, however, the experimental conditions are unusual and it is difficult to know what effect the instructional manipulation truly had on the subject's retention strategies (see Service 1998).

Eliminating Rehearsal

As noted earlier, the fact that item-duration effects can be eliminated under articulatory suppression is usually seen as strong support for the rehearsal arm of the model. Baddeley et al. (1975) found that the word length effect was eliminated under articulatory suppression when lists were presented visually but not aloud. Later work in the same laboratory found that the word length effect could be eliminated under auditory presentation as long as the subject was required to continue the articulatory suppression throughout the recall period (Baddeley et al. 1984). Why the pattern depends on the modality of presentation has never been adequately explained, although the standard model can handle the finding by assuming that the dynamics of rehearsal depend on presentation modality. For example, Baddeley et al. (1984) suggested that there is a "greater compatibility of an articulatory response to auditory material than to visual," perhaps as a consequence of language learning.

More recent evidence, though, further complicates the picture. LaPointe & Engle (1990) found that articulatory suppression eliminates the word length effect only when list items are drawn from a restricted set. If different words are used on every trial, the word length effect remains under articulatory suppression even for visually presented items. Similarly, Caza & Belleville (1999) tested immediate serial recall of words and nonwords under articulatory suppression (during input and the output period) and still found a large advantage for the words (see also Bourassa & Besner 1994, Tehan & Humphreys 1988). Thus, the presence of active rehearsal is not needed to obtain item-based differences in immediate retention.

Word length effects also occur under conditions of extremely rapid visual presentation. Coltheart & Langdon (1998) presented lists of either short or long words at rates approximating 100 msec/item. Presenting an entire list in well under a second, it was argued, should make normal rehearsal virtually impossible. Yet, a highly reliable word length effect was found; moreover, the word length effect was eliminated, under these same rapid presentation conditions, when subjects engaged in concurrent articulatory suppression. Word length effects are also found in patients suffering from serious articulatory difficulties. Baddeley & Wilson (1985) studied patients with dysarthria—that is, patients who lack the capacity to control their articulatory muscles. These individuals cannot speak overtly, although more central aspects of speech planning may remain intact, yet show significant word length effects in immediate recall (see also Bishop & Robson 1989, Vallar & Cappa 1987).

At face value, these data seem troubling for the standard model. In the absence of rehearsal, word length effects can remain. However, the standard model does not necessarily predict that the word length effect should be eliminated under these conditions: Long words, by definition, are associated with longer presentation durations. This means that one would expect the word length effect to disappear in the absence of rehearsal only when the total presentation time has been equated for short and long lists. Suppose it takes 1 s to present a long word and only 0.5 s to present a short word. For pure lists of any length, then, the retention interval for a given long item in the list, with the exception of the last list item, will be longer than for the comparable item in the short list (e.g., for lists of 6 items, 5 s will elapse before the first long item can be recalled versus only 2.5 s for the first short item). Assuming decay, we would expect a word length effect under these circumstances, even without considering rehearsal as a factor (or by assuming that all words are rehearsed only once). In many experimental studies of the word length effect, item presentation rates are controlled (e.g., 1–2 s per item) so the total passage of time elapsing during presentation is, in principle, controlled. However, as reviewed in the next section, the main locus of the word length effect appears to be at output— during recall, when output timing is rarely controlled experimentally.

Output Effects

There is considerable evidence to suggest that word length effects originate, at least in part, during recall output. First, as discussed above, when list items are presented aloud, articulatory suppression eliminates the word length effect only if it occurs during output. Importantly, Baddeley et al. (1984) controlled for output times in these studies by allowing subjects to write down long words in an abbreviated form (e.g., hippo for hippopotamus). Thus, assuming control over the passage of time, these data are largely consistent with the predictions of the standard model (assuming some rehearsal occurs at output). Second, several investigators have found that the word length effect is reduced or eliminated when retention is tested using a probe task rather than serial recall (Avons et al. 1994, Henry 1991). In a probe task, subjects are required to recall only one item at test from a randomly chosen serial position, thus sharply reducing the potential for output-based memory effects.

Converging evidence comes from studies employing mixed lists of short and long words. Cowan et al. (1992) varied whether short and long words occurred early or late in a presentation sequence—i.e., there were lists that began with short words and ended with long words and vice versa. At the point of test, subjects were cued randomly to recall the items in either a forward or a backward direction. The important finding was that recall level was determined by which kind of word was output first. When short words were recalled first (i.e., forward recall of short-long lists or backward recall of long-short lists), performance was better than when long words were output first. Note that at the point of recall presentation time was equated for all the list types, so the performance differences must have arisen during output.

Of course, pinpointing the locus of word length effects at output does not mean that rehearsal is responsible. Again, the raw passage of time could be critical: Recalling long words first imposes more of an output delay on the remaining words than recalling short words first. In fact, when spoken recall protocols are analyzed in microscopic detail, it turns out that both the duration of the recall response and the pauses that occur between recall responses are importantly related to span. A number of studies have found that interword pause durations correlate significantly with span (e.g., Cowan et al. 1998, Tehan & Lalor 2000), yet these durations are far too short for any useful covert rehearsal (ranging from 100 to 300 msec). Moreover, output pauses are not affected by word length, nor do they correlate significantly with articulation rate (Cowan et al. 1998). Instead, they tend to correlate with retrieval factors such as memory search rate or the ease of cue-driven redintegration (see Hulme et al. 1999). It is difficult to see from these data how covert rehearsal processes could be involved.

Finally, if the durations of the output pauses are too short for rehearsal, then when can rehearsal be occurring during output? There are two remaining possibilities: Rehearsal could be occurring during the actual output responses or during the preparatory interval preceding recall. The former case seems unlikely—in fact, one could argue that rehearsal at any point after output has begun is likely to have a detrimental effect because one would need to coordinate two sets of items, the output set and the rehearsal set (Avons et al. 1994). It is more likely that some rehearsal occurs during the preparatory interval immediately preceding recall. However, these intervals usually show no correlation with either memory span or articulation rate (e.g., Cowan et al. 1998, Hulme et al. 1999, Tehan & Lalor 2000). From this perspective, then, there is little support for the proposal of output-based rehearsal processes.

Summary

The widely held belief that internal rehearsal plays a large role in remembering over the short term, refreshing activation, rests primarily on the well-documented relationship between articulation rate and span. However, as the preceding section indicates, there are many reasons to question whether the correlation between articulation and span is actually caused by rehearsal. Perhaps most telling are the repeated failures to replicate item duration effects when other potentially confounding factors are controlled (e.g., Caplan et al. 1992, Service 1998, Lovatt et al. 2000). Short and long items differ on a number of dimensions other than spoken duration (e.g., familiarity, frequency, phonological complexity) and any of these factors (or their combination) could potentially contribute to memory success. Early reports indicated that there might be a pure effect of time when these other factors are controlled (Baddeley et al. 1975), but more recent research suggests otherwise.

It is also well documented that many item-based differences in immediate retention remain when (a) rehearsal is disrupted or blocked and (b) articulation rates are held constant. In the former case, the passage of time could be held responsible—that is, through differential decay—but there is no simple way for the standard model to explain the large span differences found at matched articulation rates. Thus, the span advantage seen for words over nonwords, high-frequency over low-frequency words, or concrete over abstract words must be attributable to factors other than those contained in the rehearsal plus decay assumptions of the standard model. What then accounts for the overall relationship between measures of articulation and immediate retention? One possibility is that there is some unspecified third factor that is associated with both rapid articulation ability and memory skill. Cowan (1999) recently suggested that "the ability to read or extract information from phonological memory quickly" might be involved; Tehan & Lalor (2000) agree, proposing that lexical access is a more potent predictor of individual differences in span than articulation rate. Others have suggested that the length of a word, and thereby its complexity, affects articulation rate as well as the ease of interpreting or "deblurring" the retrieval cues needed for immediate retention (e.g., Neath & Nairne 1995). I return to interpretations of this type in the section Reconceptualizing Short-Term Memory.

Finally, what is the role of rehearsal in remembering over the short-term? The subjective reality of rehearsal seems clear enough, and there is evidence from neuroimaging work that internal rehearsal is correlated with distinct neural activity (see Awh et al. 1996, Smith & Jonides 1997). It seems likely that rehearsal could serve as a mechanism for re-presentation of the stimulus material—that is, discrete rehearsals might produce copies of an item in memory (as in overt recall) that enhance later memory. Multiple presentations would be expected to increase the variability of contextual encoding and effectively shorten the functional retention interval (see Tan & Ward 2000). Importantly, however, rehearsal produces its benefits in this scenario not because it refreshes a decaying trace, as in the juggler model, but rather because it promotes the success of a cue-driven retrieval process.

PROBLEMS WITH DECAY

The second arm of the standard model is *decay*, defined as the loss of trace information exclusively as a function of time. Activation, the vehicle for short-term storage, is believed to decay spontaneously, much like a plate tossed into the air falls spontaneously from the force of gravity. Of course, the fact that forgetting proceeds with time is self-evident—but is it really the passage of time that causes the forgetting? Time is correlated with forgetting, but it may be the events that happen in time that are actually responsible for the loss. The famous analogy used by McGeoch (1932) was of an iron bar left out to rust in the open air—the accumulation of rust develops over time, but it is oxidation, not time per se, that is actually responsible.

With the exception of short-term memory environments, decay is rarely, if ever, used by memory theorists seeking to explain forgetting. There are both empirical and theoretical reasons to reject the concept. First, long-term retention can stay constant, or even improve, with the passage of time (e.g., spontaneous recovery and reminiscence). Second, the rate and extent of forgetting often depend on the specific activities that occur during the retention interval. For example, the similarity between original and interpolated learning determines how much forgetting one sees for the original material (e.g., Osgood 1953). Neither of these empirical results can be explained through a simple appeal to decay. Importantly, as discussed below, both of these results apply to remembering over the short term.

Theoretically, the concept of decay is equally troubling. To propose that memories are lost spontaneously with time ignores the potential contribution of the retrieval environment (e.g., Tulving 1983). In the standard model remembering is essentially tied to a property of the trace—activation—and no claims are made about the effectiveness of retrieval cues. One could assume that short-term memory is also influenced by the availability of retrieval cues (e.g., Nairne 1990a, 2001), but this undercuts the explanatory power of the decay concept. Trace features might be lost over time, in a process akin to radioactive decay, but the effects on memory will depend on the cues present at the time of test. In principle, losing trace features could produce a trace that is actually more compatible with the cues present at time 2 than at time 1, producing little loss or even improved retention. Such a view is widely accepted in the study of long-term memory, in which the passage of time per se is rejected as a sufficient condition for forgetting, but similar analyses are rarely, if ever, made in the short-term memory literature.

Why does decay remain popular? Part of the reason may be phenomenological: We have all experienced the rapid loss of information from consciousness, although the specific cause of the loss is not consciously apparent. More likely, though, the reason is historical. In the original Brown-Peterson experiments (Brown 1958, Peterson & Peterson 1959) requiring subjects to count backward, or read a list of digits, after presentation produced rapid loss in memory for letters. This result was considered striking for two reasons: First, the length of the to-be-remembered series was well below span (e.g., three consonants); second, the to-be-remembered information (letters) and the distractor activity (counting backward) were highly dissimilar. Similarity was believed to be the major determinant of interference at the time, so it was difficult for researchers to explain the rapid loss. Of course, as I discuss below, subsequent work showed that it is not interference from the distractor task per se that is the major cause of forgetting; instead, it is the interference produced by memories from prior trials (e.g., Keppel & Underwood 1962, Nairne et al. 1997).

Dissociating Time and Forgetting

In fact, it is relatively easy to falsify simple versions of decay theory. If time passes and there is no memory loss, or perhaps an improvement in retention, then factors other than decay must be operating. In the standard model rehearsal counteracts decay through reactivation of the trace. However, a number of studies have found little, or no, forgetting in contexts in which rehearsal is unlikely. For example, Greene (1996) found no evidence for loss in the traditional Brown-Peterson paradigm when distractor length was manipulated between subjects (see also Turvey et al. 1970). In the more traditional application, in which retention interval is manipulated within subjects, Keppel & Underwood (1962) reported essentially no forgetting on the first trial. Comparable results have been found by others (e.g., Gorfein 1987), although Baddeley & Scott (1971; see next section) did report small amounts of loss on the first trial during the first few seconds of the retention interval.

Keppel & Underwood (1962) suggested that interference from prior trials is responsible for forgetting in most short-term memory environments. Researchers commonly use the same set of items across trials, or sample from a small set (e.g., consonants), so one could easily become confused about the exact position occupied by an item on a given trial. Nairne et al. (1999) attempted to minimize interference by using different items on every trial and reconstruction of order as the retention measure; in a reconstruction test the just-presented items are given back in random order and the task is to place the items into their original presentation order. Under these conditions very little evidence of forgetting was found across retention intervals ranging from 2 to 96 s—e.g., reconstruction performance averaged 78% correct after 2 s of distraction and 73% correct after 96 s.

Historically, proponents of the standard model have explained data like these by appealing to long-term memory (e.g., Atkinson & Shiffrin 1968, Cowan 1995). In the absence of interference, such as on the first trial of an experimental session, subjects can recover information from long-term memory, which essentially masks the contribution of decay in short-term memory. Thus, little short-term forgetting is expected under these circumstances, even though the short-term memory trace presumably continues to decay. This kind of account can easily handle the recent findings of Nairne et al. (1997), showing that the word length effect, like distractor effects, emerges only after several trials in an experimental session. Again, on early trials both item types can be recovered from long-term memory, where decay and activities designed to prevent decay (rehearsal), play less of a role. As long-term memory becomes cluttered from prior trials, however, the subject shifts strategically to short-term memory, for which time-based factors are important.

On reflection, it is difficult to see why this account has such wide appeal. First, there is no direct evidence confirming that subjects actually do shift from long- to short-term retrieval within an experimental session. Moreover, Nairne & Kelley (1999) found that the phonological similarity effect remains robust when interference from prior trials is minimized. If subjects tend to rely on recovery from long-term memory in an "uncluttered" environment, then phonological similarity should play a reduced role (i.e., because long-term retrieval tends to be influenced more by semantic factors). Second, and more troubling, short-term memory is assigned a kind of "back-up" status in this account—that is, something to be used only when recovery from long-term memory is problematic. It suggests that a subject's first line of defense is to recover information from long-term memory; recovery from short-term memory occurs only when long-term traces are difficult to access. Yet, of course, in most natural environments people have not been exposed to multiple "lists" of to-be-remembered information. Thus, in the prototypical case—remembering a telephone number—it is not clear why short-term memory would even be needed.

A better explanation is given by general distinctiveness accounts, which assume that forgetting is caused by a failure to discriminate current trial information from information presented on previous trials (e.g., Baddeley 1976, Brown et al. 2001). There is limited forgetting on the first trial in a Brown-Peterson task because there are no prior trials to produce interference; also, when interference is reduced by using different items on every trial, the amount of forgetting should be sharply reduced (Nairne et al. 1999). The crucial role played by prior trials is illustrated nicely in a study by Turvey et al. (1970) that uses a version of the Brown-Peterson task. Different groups of subjects were asked to count backward as a distractor activity for group-specific intervals (e.g., one group counted for 10 s, another for 15 s, and another for 20 s). Foreshadowing Greene (1996), equivalent amounts of forgetting were found across groups in this between-subject design (0.33, 0.30, and 0.30, respectively). On the critical trial, however, all groups were switched to the same 15 s distractor period. Retention performance dropped in the 10-s group (from 0.33 to 0.20), stayed roughly constant in the 15-s group (0.30 to 0.28) and improved in the 20-s group (0.30 to 0.38). Note that the passage of time—and therefore the opportunity for decay—was equated across the groups on the critical 15-s trial, yet performance depended on the timing of prior trials.

One can parsimoniously explain these data by assuming that the relative, rather than absolute, durations of distractor activity affect the discriminability of target information at test (Baddeley 1976). Memory improves whenever target items can be easily discriminated from the memories created by prior trials. According to distinctiveness accounts, it is the ratio of the interpresentation interval to the length of the current retention interval that matters. In the Turvey et al. (1970) case, the interpresentation interval corresponds to the period separating the presentation of the to-be-remembered information on trial N-1 from the presentation on trial N. Note that on the critical trial containing 15 s of distraction, prior trial information is relatively "closer" in time for the 10-s group ($10/15 = 0.67$) than for the 15-s group ($15/15 = 1.0$) or the 20-s group ($20/15 = 1.33$). The actual data are predicted well by these ratios. The Turvey et al. (1970) data are particularly important in the present context because they show that short-term memory performance can decrease, stay the same, or even increase depending on timing variables. Comparable results have been found in other contexts: Neath & Knoedler (1994), for example, showed that memory for early items in a list sometimes improves as the length of the retention interval increases (see also Bjork 2001, Wright et al. 1985). Once again, such a finding is inconsistent with the notion of decay, although it can be handled relatively easily by simple distinctiveness accounts (Neath 1998).

The Role of Intervening Activity

The preceding studies establish quite clearly that the passage of time is not necessarily a predictor of memory loss. Time is often correlated with forgetting, but the correlation is far from perfect. The exceptions are important, though, because they help to falsify simpleminded notions of decay. Decay theories also have trouble explaining why forgetting can depend on the specific activities that occur during the retention interval. In his original work on the distractor paradigm, Brown (1958) found that the similarity between the distractor activity and the to-be-remembered material played only a minor role. However, subsequent researchers have established that the nature of the distractor activity clearly does matter (see Greene 1992).

For example, significantly more forgetting is found in a short-term memory environment when the modalities of presentation and distraction match. More forgetting is found when target items are presented aloud and the distractor activity is also auditory (Elliott & Strawhorn 1976, Proctor & Fagnani 1978). Semantic (Dale & Gregory 1966) and phonological (Wickelgren 1965) similarity between the presented items and the content of distraction also increase the amount of short-term forgetting. Interference from prior study trials may be the major determinant of short-term forgetting (i.e., proactive interference), but it is now generally agreed that similarity-based retroactive interference also plays a role.

Additional support for modality-specific interference comes from the extensive literature on the suffix effect (for reviews see Crowder 1976, Greene 1992). The suffix effect refers to the reduction in recency recall that occurs when auditory lists end with a redundant (nonrecalled) verbal item. The amount of interference obtained tends to vary directly with the acoustic similarity between the suffix and final list item. Silently presented suffixes do not generally lead to recency reduction, nor do suffixes that simply share a meaningful relation to the final list item. Successful models of the suffix effect generally assume that the auditory suffix interferes with, or "overwrites," the sensory features of the last list item, leading to poorer immediate retention (e.g., Nairne 1990a). Importantly, this modality-specific interference operates over very short time windows. If the suffix is delayed for a second or two following the last list item, the suffix effect is sharply reduced. It therefore seems clear that similarity-based interference can occur over intervals encompassed by activation-based accounts of immediate retention.

Several investigators have attempted to reduce the similarity between the target material and the distractor task to such an extent that interference between the two seems unlikely (e.g., Cowan et al. 1997a, Reitman 1974). For example, Cowan et al. (1997a) presented pairs of short tones that differed slightly in frequency and asked the subject to decide whether the second tone was higher or lower in pitch than the first. The delay between the tones ranged up to 12 s, during which the subject performed a silent distracting task (tracking the movement of a visual icon on a computer screen). The tracking task should have produced little or no interference with the tone comparison task, because the two are quite dissimilar, yet correct performance on the tone task declined significantly with delay.

This time-based performance loss seems consistent with decay theory. Note that a comparable result would not be found with verbal material because the subject could presumably rehearse the material during the retention interval. The fact that significant loss occurred, with essentially no interfering material present (and rehearsal possible, in principle), suggests that the forgetting was due uniquely to the passage of time. However, in a subsequent reanalysis of their data, Cowan et al. (2001) discovered that the relative distinctiveness of the tones on the current comparison trial influenced the amount of measured forgetting. Just as in the Turvey et al. (1970) data, performance depended on the ratio of the interpresentation interval to the current retention interval. Cowan et al. (2001) concluded that the relative distinctiveness of the tones predicted memory loss as well or better than the pure passage of time.

Summary

In his famous attack on Thorndike's "law of disuse," McGeoch (1932) used the fact that memory sometimes fails to decline, or even improves, over time as powerful evidence against the idea that information spontaneously decays. He also pointed to the fact that long-term memory for a given set of materials often depends on the specific activities that occur during the retention interval (i.e., retroactive interference). Historically, most memory theorists have accepted these arguments and rejected decay as an explanatory concept for long-term remembering. However, for short-term memory the situation is quite different—decay plays a prominent role in the standard model and is widely accepted as one of the main determinants of short-term forgetting.

As the preceding review indicates, both of the main arguments used by McGeoch (1932) to attack decay in long-term remembering apply to short-term remembering as well. Short-term memory can decrease, stay constant, or even improve over time depending on the situation. The specific activities that occur during the retention interval also matter—e.g., the more similar the distractor material is to the target material, the more forgetting one typically sees. Of course, the fact that short-term retention is influenced by interference does not rule out decay—both interference and decay could be operating in short-term memory environments. In fact, Baddeley (1990) has argued that both factors are important, with decay exerting its main influence in only the first few seconds of the retention interval. As discussed above, Baddeley & Scott (1971) attempted to replicate the findings of Keppel & Underwood (1962)—using longer lists to avoid ceiling effects—and found small amounts of forgetting on the first trial. The loss was virtually complete by 5 s, leading to the conclusion that decay occurs very rapidly and plays only a subsidiary role in the Brown-Peterson task. As Baddeley (1990) put it, ". . . something like trace decay occurs in the Peterson task, but is complete within five seconds, and is certainly not sufficient to explain the substantial forgetting that occurs in the standard paradigm" (Baddeley 1990, p. 48). The idea that decay occurs quickly is important because it fits the assumption of the standard model that activation is lost in a second or two and must be refreshed through rehearsal.

However, it is difficult to see how proponents of decay can explain all the situations in which time exerts no influence. For instance, as reviewed in the previous section, current research indicates that it is complexity, rather than actual duration, that mediates most word length effects in immediate recall. Again, long durations can actually lead to better immediate memory in some situations. Moreover, several researchers have reported that output duration is a better predictor of memory span than presentation duration, and the typical output period far exceeds the 2-s decay window (e.g., Dosher 1999, Hulme et al. 1999). Finally, as I discuss in the next section, it is possible to construct relatively successful models of immediate memory that reject decay and rely entirely on various forms of interference to explain short-term forgetting (e.g., Brown & Hulme 1995, Brown et al. 2000, Nairne 1990a, Neath & Nairne 1995). For example, Brown et al. (2001) have shown how the data of Baddeley & Scott (1971)—limited forgetting over the first few seconds of distraction—can be explained by appealing to intrasequence interference; that is, interference produced among the items in a current to-be-remembered list (see also Melton 1963). As I discuss below, one of the major advantages that models of this type have over the standard model is their assumption that remembering is cue driven.

RECONCEPTUALIZING SHORT-TERM MEMORY

In this section I discuss alternatives to the standard model. As noted throughout, one of the most important conceptual hurdles faced by activation accounts is the proposal that recovery from short-term memory is essentially independent of cueing. Kintsch and colleagues recently noted that questions about retrieval touch on "the essence of working memory because of the common assumption that information 'in' working memory is directly and effortlessly retrievable" (Kintsch et al. 1999). This notion does not fit the commonly accepted mnemonic principle that all remembering is cue dependent. As Endel Tulving put it, "Every phenomenon of episodic memory depends on both storage and retrieval conditions" (Tulving 1983)—every phenomenon, apparently, except activated items in short-term memory.

The proposal that retrieval from activated memory and retrieval from long-term memory "differ in important ways" (Cowan 1999) receives some support from microscopic analyses of reaction time patterns in short- and long-term retrieval environments. For example, several researchers have found that the retrieval dynamics for the last few items in a memory list are different than for earlier items (e.g., McElree & Dosher 1989, McElree 1998, Wickelgren et al. 1980). There are also classic studies showing that the recency effect in free recall, which is believed by many to reflect the dumping of activated information, is sensitive to different variables than the primacy and asymptotic portions of the serial position curve (e.g., Glanzer & Cunitz 1966). However, these studies do not establish how retrieval over the immediate term is actually accomplished. Remembering over the short term may still be cue driven, as in long-term memory, but the cues controlling performance may simply change across retention environments (Brown et al. 2000, Burgess & Hitch 1999). Indeed, many other studies have found that remembering over the short and long term show similarities and can often be fit with the same type of model (e.g., Brown et al. 2000, Nairne 1990b, 1991).

Cue-Driven Immediate Retention

There are many factors that have influenced the movement toward cue-driven accounts of immediate retention. One factor is the sensitivity of immediate recall to item-specific variables such as lexicality, word frequency, and concreteness. As noted above, in the standard model there is no obvious reason why lexicality or concreteness should affect the availability of an item, once activated, yet each produces large and consistent effects on immediate recall. Researchers generally refer to these effects as long-term memory contributions to immediate memory, and they are increasingly assumed to arise from a redintegration process wherein the decayed or degraded immediate memory trace is used as a cue to sample an appropriate candidate from long-term memory (e.g., Hulme et al. 1999, Nairne 1990a, Schweickert 1993).

More direct evidence for cueing effects comes from work on "release" from proactive interference (Wickens 1970). In the prototypical paradigm, subjects receive immediate memory trials in which successive lists are drawn from the same conceptual class (e.g., pieces of furniture, animals, or rhyme categories). Performance typically declines over trials, presumably because it becomes increasingly difficult to discriminate items on the current trial from conceptually similar items that occurred on previous trials. On trial N + 1 list items are drawn from a new conceptual class (e.g., moving from furniture to animals) and performance dramatically improves, a finding known as release from proactive interference. A standard interpretation of this effect is that people use the conceptual class as a "cue" to guide short-term recall; the effectiveness of the cue, in turn, is determined by the degree of cue overload (Watkins & Watkins 1975). On build-up trials, the cue becomes overloaded—that is, it predicts many items—and performance suffers; on release trials, the conceptual cue uniquely specifies the items on the current trial and performance gains are recorded.

Strong support for the cueing interpretation of proactive interference comes from studies manipulating the nature of the cues at test. For example, one can obtain release from proactive interference at the point of test, after the list has been presented, if discriminating cues are provided (Dillon & Bittner 1975, Gardiner et al. 1972). Recently, Tehan & Humphreys (1996, 1998) demonstrated the power of a distinctive cue in a paradigm requiring subjects to remember the second of two four-item trial blocks (on some trials people are asked to recall after the first block to guarantee attention to the first block). The critical manipulation varied whether items in the first block shared conceptual properties with items in the second, to-be-recalled, block—e.g., the first block might contain the items "jail-silk-orange-peach," whereas the second block contains "page-leap-carrot-witch." Note that orange and carrot share certain conceptual properties (color, edible, etc.). Tehan & Humphreys (1996) found that if subjects were asked to recall the "vegetable" from the second block, no interference was found (orange is not a vegetable). However, if the cue was "type of juice," recall of carrot was impaired if orange occurred in the first block. Thus, susceptibility to proactive interference depended entirely on the type of cue presented at test.

Evidence for cue-driven immediate retention also comes from the analysis of errors in immediate recall. Errors are usually not random, but rather follow certain rules, suggesting that position of occurrence may be an important retrieval cue. For example, when an item is recalled in the wrong serial position in immediate recall, it tends to be placed in a nearby position. One typically finds regular error gradients that drop off with distance from the original position of occurrence (e.g., Healy 1974). If lists are grouped and subjects misplace an item from one group into another group, the item tends to be placed in an identical relative serial position (e.g., Henson 1999). Finally, when people intrude an item from a previous list, it is likely to have occurred at the same serial position in the previous list (Estes 1991). These data suggest that people are not simply outputting activated items directly from short-term memory, but rather are using position of occurrence as a retrieval cue to decide what happened moments before.

Although there may be disagreements about which cues predominate, collectively these data have led many short-term memory theorists to conclude that remembering over the short term is definitely cue driven. As I discuss below, recent formal models of immediate retention tend to be cue driven, although some are hybrid models that assume that some form of "direct retrieval" from short-term memory is possible. Even accounts that closely mimic the assumptions of the standard model, such as Baddeley's working memory model (Baddeley 1986), recognize that direct retrieval cannot explain all the particulars of immediate retention. For example, it is difficult to derive the phonological similarity effect—poorer memory for lists composed of similar sounding items—from the assumptions of the standard model. Working memory proponents generally assume that memory is impaired because recall requires "... discrimination among the memory traces ... similar traces will be harder to discriminate, leading to a lower level of recall" (Baddeley 1990). The discrimination process is left unspecified, but it is in all likelihood cue driven.

Hybrid Models

The term hybrid model refers to a class of current models that retain important elements of the standard model—e.g., activation-based remembering, rehearsal, and/or decay—but assume that retrieval cues play an important role in short-term remembering as well. A detailed review of these models is beyond the scope of this article, so I provide only a few brief descriptions here. Schweickert (1993) has proposed a multinomial processing tree model that closely mimics the standard model except for the proposal of an additional redintegration stage. List presentation leads to the formation of active traces in short-term memory, which over time become degraded. Schweickert is noncommittal about the actual process controlling degradation, assuming that either decay or interference may contribute. During recall, the subject's first line of attack is a "direct readout" of the active trace, as in the standard model, which occurs successfully with probability I. If direct readout fails (with probability 1-I), an attempt is made to interpret the degraded trace through redintegration.

This second stage of Schweickert's model—the interpretation or redintegration stage—provides a vehicle for explaining many of the findings discussed above that have proven troubling for the standard model. The degraded trace becomes a cue of sorts that is interpreted by accessing long-term knowledge, particularly about language processing (see also Hulme et al. 1997). It is in the redintegration stage that the effects of lexicality, word frequency, and concreteness are presumed to occur. For example, the degraded traces for words are presumably easier to interpret than those for nonwords, leading to the lexicality effect in immediate recall. By placing the locus in the redintegration stage, the model is able to dissociate so-called long-term memory influences, such as lexicality and frequency, from the effects of articulation rate, which are presumed to primarily affect the direct readout stage.

One of the advantages of the multinomial tree model is its clear predictions about how different variables should interact. Word length and lexicality are assumed to selectively influence different stages of the recall process: Word length affects the probability of trace degradation (for the same reasons described by the standard model), and lexicality affects the probability of trace interpretation. As a result, these factors, when combined factorially, are expected to produce an underadditive interaction in correct recall. Just this pattern has been obtained in relevant studies— i.e., the size of the word length effect is smaller for words than nonwords (Besner & Davelaar 1982). Thus, by adding the cue-drive, redintegration stage, the model can handle findings that seem to falsify the standard model. At the same time, Schweickert's model is silent about the mechanisms or processes that actually underlie the act of recall. For example, how is "direct readout" accomplished? Is it cue driven, or is the information available by virtue of its activation alone? It may turn out that the model's assumptions about the need for separate and independent routes to recall are well justified, but that its implied assumptions about decay and direct readout are not.

The "start-end" model proposed recently by Henson (1998) is another example of a hybrid model. Henson (1998) assumes that items are coded relative to the beginning and end of a sequence. Essentially, items are associated with position codes, and these position codes are then used as cues to drive recall. In this sense, the deep structure of the model differs significantly from the standard model— items are not activated and immediately accessible, but rather are selected for recall on the basis of a cued-driven response competition process. Through simulations, Henson (1998) has shown how this machinery can be used to explain much of the phenomena of immediate and delayed retention of serial order, such as serial position curves, error distributions, grouping effects, and modality effects. However, the model is unable to explain word length effects and phonological similarity effects without additional assumptions.

To handle time- and item-based effects, Henson (1998) appeals to the main assumptions of the standard model. In particular, he assumes that "each presentation and rehearsal of an item activates its phonological representation to a fixed amount that subsequently undergoes exponential decay" (Henson 1998, p. 106). The activation process increases the probability of recall directly, by bringing an item closer to its recall threshold, although it can increase the chances of phonological confusions as well (thus explaining the phonological similarity effect). Word length effects are explained by appealing to the dynamics of rehearsal: Long words tend to receive less activation, because they cannot be rehearsed as efficiently, and recall suffers as a result. Thus, as in the standard model, activation plays a role as a mnemonic property that is independent of any cueing mechanism. For the reasons described throughout this article, these assumptions of the start-end model are not well supported by the data.

Unitary Models

The two models just described are examples of current hybrid models. There have been other efforts to combine elements of the standard model with some kind of cue-based mechanism (e.g., Burgess & Hitch 1999), but I turn my attention now to models that contain virtually no assumptions in common with the standard model. These models assume no direct connection between activation level and memory success, propose little or no role for rehearsal, and reject the concept of decay in favor of item-based interference. I refer to these models as unitary models because they also assume similar processes for short- and long-term remembering (what differs is the retrieval cues in effect). Although not reviewed here, there is considerable evidence suggesting that short- and long-term memory often follow similar rules (e.g., Brown et al. 2000, Melton 1963, Nairne 1991, Crowder & Neath 1991).

The feature model (Nairne 1988, 1990a) is an example of a unitary model. All remembering over the short term is cue driven in this model, based on an analysis of residual processing records. What sits in short-term memory is not an activated "item" that can be directly retrieved, but rather a constellation of activated cues that the subject uses to reconstruct what happened moments before. In most cases, these "cues" consist of remnants of prior processing records—e.g., records of just-presented list items that have become degraded through interference. A recall candidate is selected from long-term memory, based on a similarity-driven sampling rule (a choice rule), in a manner resembling that employed by context models of categorization (e.g., Nosofsky 1986). Importantly, it is not the match between the to-be-interpreted cues and long-term memory candidates that turns out to be important; instead, what determines performance is how well cues uniquely specify one or more of the target items (see Nairne 2001).

Short-term forgetting in this model occurs because the available cues become poor predictors of the target items. Processing records are overwritten by subsequently occurring material (as a function of similarity), making it more difficult to interpret the records correctly. Basing interference on similarity enables the model to explain why performance can depend on the specific activities that occur during the retention interval, and it helps explain benchmark phenomena such as the phonological similarity effect as well. Overall, increasing the similarity among list items tends to reduce the predictive value of common features; any given residual cue tends to be predictive of several target items (it becomes overloaded), which lowers the chances of remembering a given target item in its correct position. Performance declines with increasing list length for a very similar reason. Cues in short-term memory are effective only to the extent that they are distinctive—that is, they uniquely predict target items.

Simulations of the feature model have been applied to most of the phenomena of immediate memory with success (see Nairnc 1990a; Neath & Nairne 1995; Neath 1998, 1999). For example, Neath & Nairne (1995) demonstrated how the feature model can handle the nearly linear relation between articulation rate and span, as well as the interactions found between word length, modality of presentation, and articulatory suppression. Neath (2000) has recently shown how the model can account for the rather complex effects of irrelevant speech on short-term memory performance (see also Surprenant et al. 2000). For the present purposes, the important point is that these effects are simulated without any recourse to either rehearsal or decay. No special mnemonic properties are assigned to the activated contents of short-term memory—they merely act as retrieval cues that may or may not lead to correct retrieval. People forget with an increasing delay because retrieval cues change with time, not because of spontaneous decay. Such a cue-based model can easily handle the fact that memory may remain constant, or even improve, as time passes. Provided that distinctive cues are not interfered with by subsequent material, or are reinstated in some way, immediate memory should remain at high levels.

Cue-dependent forgetting is also central to the OSCAR model proposed recently by Brown et al. (2000) and to the phonological loop model of Burgess & Hitch (1999). Both models assume that associations are formed between items, represented as feature vectors, and dynamic context signals. Context signals are represented as sets of oscillators that change systematically, at idiosyncratic rates, over time. At recall, the context signal is reset—the oscillators are "rewound"— and each successive state is used as a cue to recall associated items. The details of the storage assumptions are beyond the scope of this article, but the product of the cueing process tends to be a blurry record, requiring a cleanup or redintegration stage. It is during the redintegration stage, which in OSCAR is driven by a similarity-based comparison process, that many important recall phenomena, such as the phonological similarity effect, primarily arise (see also Lewandowsky 1999).

The major difference between OSCAR and the loop model (Burgess & Hitch 1999) is the failure of OSCAR to incorporate the assumptions of the standard model. The phonological loop model is actually a hybrid model—recall is cue driven, but rehearsal and decay are used to account for a number of recall effects. OSCAR essentially rejects the concept of decay and assumes that the same principles apply over a wide range of time scales. As a result, OSCAR has some trouble accounting for rehearsal-based effects, such as the word length effect, which can be easily handled by the loop account. However, as we have seen above, the evidence for rehearsal and decay is mixed at best, and it is possible to explain time-based effects in alternative ways (e.g., through interference; see Neath & Nairne 1995, Brown et al. 2000). Moreover, unitary models such as OSCAR are potentially capable of explaining a wider range of data, over both short- and long-term time scales, because they do not rely on the mnemonic properties of activation. Because retrieval in the standard model is cue independent, relying solely on activation, it must differ in a fundamental way from the retrieval processes governing long-term retention.

SUMMARY AND CONCLUSIONS

The preceding two sections provide a brief and selective review of some recent formal models covering immediate retention. In each of these models remembering over the short term is assumed to be primarily cue driven, although rehearsal and decay—the two main assumptions of the standard model—contribute to performance in some cases. Focusing on cue-driven processes, as opposed to the direct retrieval of activated "items," offers a number of advantages. First, and perhaps most importantly, it lays the groundwork for a truly unified account of remembering. Virtually all researchers recognize that long-term remembering is cue driven; acknowledging that short-term remembering is cue driven as well helps explain why short- and long-term retention often show similarities, and it releases the theorist from the unreasonable assumption that activated traces have special properties outside of particular retrieval environments.

More concretely, cue-driven accounts easily handle the item-specific long-term memory influences that characterize remembering over the short term. As we have seen, immediate retention is influenced by a number of variables, such as lexicality, word frequency, and concreteness, that are likely to affect one's ability to sample an appropriate recall candidate from long-term memory. In addition, it is easy to see how memory performance could decrease, stay constant, or even improve over time depending on the available constellation of retrieval cues. In unitary models, such as the feature model, short-term memory is simply conceived as a repository for cues that are used for reconstructing the immediate past. No items are stored—only feature-based cues that are, by themselves, not recallable. Such a conceptualization is vastly different from intuitive notions about activated items "sitting" in short-term memory awaiting direct recall.

This kind of view also has no trouble handling the possibility that inhibitory effects will occur in immediate retention. It is almost certainly the case that item accessibility can be lowered over the short term—that is, you become less likely to remember an item—and there is no easy way to represent inhibition in the standard model. Rather than assuming an item is in some special state of inaccessibility, one can assume that there are simply cue constellations that reduce the likelihood of recovering an item as a possible response (response suppression mechanisms may also be at work in some instances). Note that inhibition conceived in this way is not a special state of the item; it is simply a byproduct of the particular cue constellation that happens to be driving memory.

What role then should the standard model play in our efforts to understand how we remember over the short term? The juggler metaphor certainly has heuristic value, and it provides a nice organizational rubric for a variety of immediate memory phenomena. However, even as a heuristic, the standard model is misleading. It leads one to the conclusion that forgetting rates are fixed, like gravity, rather than variable, as much of the data suggest. It also suggests that the main vehicle for short-term storage is rehearsal when, in fact, much of the variability in immediate retention turns out to be independent of rehearsal. Finally, it leads one to the conclusion that remembering is a direct byproduct of activation. Whereas it may be reasonable to propose activation in the brain, it is not activation per se that predicts performance. It is the interpretation of that activation, through a cue-driven retrieval process, that explains how we remember over the short term.

ACKNOWLEDGMENTS

I thank Gordon Brown, Ian Neath, and Gerry Tehan for many thoughtful discussions about the ideas presented in this review. Thanks are also due to Nelson Cowan and Margaret Wilson for commenting on an earlier version of the manuscript.

Visit the Annual Reviews home page at www.AnnualReviews.org

LITERATURE CITED

Atkinson RC, Shiffrin RM. 1968. Human memory: a proposed system and its control processes. In *The Psychology of Learning and Motivation*, ed. KW Spence, JT Spence, 2:89–105. New York: Academic

Avons SE, Wright KL, Pammer K. 1994. The word-length effect in probed and serial recall. *Q. J. Exp. Psychol.* 20:249–64

Awh E, Jonides J, Smith EE, Schumacher EH, Koeppe RA, Katz S. 1996. Dissociation of storage and rehearsal in verbal working memory: evidence from positron emission tomography. *Psychol. Sci.* 7:25–31

Baddeley AD. 1976. *The Psychology of Memory*. New York: Basic Books

Baddeley AD. 1986. *Working Memory*. Oxford: Oxford Univ. Press

Baddeley AD. 1990. *Human Memory: Theory and Practice*. Oxford: Oxford Univ. Press

Baddeley AD. 1992. Working memory. *Science* 255:556–59

Baddeley AD. 2000. The episodic buffer: a new component of working memory? *Trends Cogn. Sci.* 4:417–23

Baddeley AD, Hitch G. 1974. Working memory. In *The Psychology of Learning and Moti-*

vation, ed. GH Bower, 8:647–67. New York: Academic

Baddeley AD, Lewis VJ, Vallar G. 1984. Exploring the articulatory loop. *Q. J. Exp. Psychol.* 36:233–52

Baddeley AD, Scott D. 1971. Short term forgetting in the absence of proactive interference *Q. J. Exp. Psychol.* 23:275–83

Baddeley AD, Thomson N, Buchanan M. 1975. Word length and the structure of short-term memory. *J. Verbal Learn. Verbal Behav.* 14:575–89

Baddeley AD, Wilson B. 1985. Phonological coding and short-term memory in patients without speech. *J. Mem. Lang.* 24:490–502

Besner D, Davelaar E. 1982. Basic processes in reading: two phonological codes. *Can. J. Psychol.* 36:701–11

Bishop DVM, Robson J. 1989. Unimpaired short-term memory and rhyme judgment in congenitally speechless individuals: implications for the notion of 'articulatory coding'. *Q. J. Exp. Psychol.* 41A:123–41

Bjork RA. 1975. Short-term storage: the output of a central processor. In *Cognitive Theory*, ed. F Restle, RM Shiffrin, NJ Castellan,

HR Lindman, DB Pisoni, 1:151–72. Hillsdale, NJ: Erlbaum

Bjork RA. 2001. Recency and recovery in human memory. See Roediger et al. 2001, pp. 211–32

Bourassa D, Besner D. 1994. Beyond the articulatory loop: a semantic contribution to serial order recall of subspan lists. *Psychol. Bull. Rev.* 1:122–25

Brown GDA, Hulme C. 1995. Modeling item length effects in memory span: no rehearsal needed? *J. Mem. Lang.* 34:594–21

Brown GDA, Neath I, Chater N. 2001. SIMPLE: a local distinctiveness model of scale—invariant memory and perceptual identification. Unpublished manuscript

Brown GDA, Preece T, Hulme C. 2000. Oscillator-based memory for serial order. *Psychol. Rev.* 107:127–81

Brown J. 1958. Some tests of the decay theory of immediate memory. *Q. J. Exp. Psychol.* 10:12–21

Burgess N, Hitch GJ. 1999. Memory for serial order: a network model of the phonological loop and its timing. *Psychol. Rev.* 106:551–81

Caplan D, Rochon E, Waters GS. 1992. Articulatory and phonological determinants of word-length effects in span tasks. *Q. J. Exp. Psychol.* 45A:177–92

Caza N, Belleville S. 1999. Semantic contribution to immediate serial recall using an unlimited set of items: evidence for a multilevel capacity view of short-term memory. *Int. J. Psychol.* 34:334–38

Coltheart V, Langdon R. 1998. Recall of short word lists presented visually at fast rates: effects of phonological similarity and word length. *Mem. Cogn.* 26:330–42

Cowan N. 1988. Evolving conceptions of memory storage, selective attention, and their mutual constraints within the human information processing system. *Psychol. Bull.* 104:163–91

Cowan N. 1995. *Attention and Memory: An Integrated Framework.* New York: Oxford Univ. Press

Cowan N. 1999. The differential maturation of two processing rates related to digit span. *J. Exp. Child Psychol.* 72:193–209

Cowan N, Day L, Saults JS, Keller TA, Johnson Y, Flores L. 1992. The role of verbal output time in the effects of word length on immediate memory. *J. Mem. Lang.* 31:1–17

Cowan N, Nugent LD, Elliot EM, Geer T. 2000. Is there a temporal basis of the word length effect? A response to Service (1998). *Q. J. Exp. Psychol.* 53A:647–60

Cowan N, Saults JS, Nugent LD. 1997a. The role of absolute and relative amounts of time in forgetting within immediate memory: the case of tone pitch comparisons. *Psychol. Bull. Rev.* 4:393–97

Cowan N, Saults JS, Nugent LD. 2001. The ravages of absolute and relative amounts of time on memory. See Roediger et al. 2001, pp. 315–30

Cowan N, Wood NL, Nugent LD, Treisman M. 1997b. There are two word length effects in verbal short-term memory: opposed effects of duration and complexity. *Psychol. Sci.* 8:290–95

Cowan N, Wood NL, Wood PK, Keller TA, Nugent LD, Keller CV. 1998. Two separate verbal processing rates contributing to short-term memory span. *J. Exp. Psychol.: Gen.* 127:141–60

Crowder RG. 1976. *Principles of Learning and Memory.* Hillsdale, NJ: Erlbaum

Crowder RG, Neath I. 1991. The microscope metaphor in human memory. See Hockley & Lewandowsky 1991, pp. 111–25

Dale HC, Gregory M. 1966. Evidence of semantic coding in short-term memory. *Psychol. Sci.* 5:153–54

Dillon RF, Bittner LA. 1975. Analysis of retrieval cues and release from proactive inhibition. *J. Verbal Learn. Verbal Behav.* 14:616–22

Dosher BA. 1999. Item interference and time delays in working memory: immediate serial recall. *Int. J. Psychol.* 34:276–84

Elliott LA, Strawhorn RJ. 1976. Interference in short-term memory from vocalization: aural versus visual modality differences. *J. Exp. Psychol.: Hum. Learn. Mem.* 2:705–11

Ellis NC, Hennelly RA. 1980. A bilingual word-length effect: implications for intelligence testing and the relative ease of mental calculation in Welsh and English. *Br. J. Psychol.* 71:43–52

Engle RW, Kane MJ, Tuholski SW. 1999. Individual differences in working memory capacity and what they tell us about controlled attention, general fluid intelligence, and functions of the prefrontal cortex. See Miyake & Shaw 1999, pp. 102–34

Estes WK. 1991. On types of item coding and source of recall in short-term memory. See Hockley & Lewandowsky 1991, pp. 155–74

Gardiner JM, Craik FIM, Birtwistle J. 1972. Retrieval cues and release from proactive inhibition. *J. Verbal Learn. Verbal Behav.* 11:778–83

Gathercole SE, Hitch GJ. 1993. Developmental changes in short-term memory: a revised working memory perspective. In *Theories of Memory*, ed. AF Collins, SE Gathercole, MA Conway, PE Morris, pp. 189–210. Hove, UK: Erlbaum

Glanzer M, Cunitz AR. 1966. Two storage mechanisms in free recall. *J. Verbal Learn. Verbal Behav.* 5:351–60

Gorfein DS. 1987. Explaining context effects on short-term memory. In *Memory and Learning: The Ebbinghaus Centennial Conference*, ed. DS Gorfein, RR Hoffman. Hillsdale, NJ: Erlbaum

Greene RL. 1992. *Human Memory: Paradigms and Paradoxes*. Hillsdale, NJ: Erlbaum

Greene RL. 1996. The influence of experimental design: the example of the Brown-Peterson paradigm. *Can. J. Exp. Psychol.* 50:240–42

Healy AF. 1974. Separating item from order information in short-term memory. *J. Verbal Learn. Verbal Behav.* 13:644–55

Henry LA. 1991. Development of auditory memory span: the role of rehearsal. *Br. J. Dev. Psychol.* 9:493–511

Henson RNA. 1998. Short-term memory for serial order: the Start-End Model. *Cogn. Psychol.* 36:73–37

Henson RNA. 1999. Positional information in short-term memory: relative or absolute? *Mem. Cogn.* 27:915–27

Hitch GJ, Halliday MS. 1983. Working memory in children. *Philos. Trans. R. Soc. London Ser. B* 302:324–40

Hockley WE, Lewandowsky S, eds. 1991. *Relating Theory and Data: Essays on Human Memory in Honor of Bennet B. Murdock.* Hillsdale, NJ: Erlbaum

Hulme C, Maughan S, Brown GDA. 1991. Memory for familiar and unfamiliar words: evidence for a long-term memory contribution to short-term memory span. *J. Mem. Lang.* 30:685–701

Hulme C, Newton P, Cowan N, Stuart G, Brown G. 1999. Think before you speak: pauses, memory search, and trace redintegration processes in verbal memory span. *J. Exp. Psychol.: Learn. Mem. Cogn.* 25:447–63

Hulme C, Roodenrys S, Schweickert R, Brown GDA, Martin S, Stuart G. 1997. Word frequency effects on short-term memory tasks: evidence for a multinomial processing tree model of immediate serial recall. *J. Exp. Psychol.: Learn. Mem. Cogn.* 23:1217–32

Hulme C, Thomson N, Muir C, Lawrence A. 1984. Speech rate and the development of short-term memory span. *J. Exp. Child Psychol.* 38:241–53

Hulme C, Tordoff V. 1989. Working memory development: the effects of speech rate word length and acoustic similarity on serial recall. *J. Exp. Child Psychol.* 47:72–87

Keppel G, Underwood BJ. 1962. Proactive inhibition in short-term retention of single items. *J. Verbal Learn. Verbal Behav.* 1:153–61

Kintsch W, Healy AF, Hegarty M, Pennington BF, Salthouse TA. 1999. Models of working memory: eight questions and some general answers. See Miyake & Shah 1999, pp. 412–41

Kintsch W, VanDijk TA. 1978. Toward a model of text comprehension and production. *Psychol. Rev.* 85:363–94

Landauer TK. 1962. Rate of implicit speech. *Percept. Mot. Skills* 15:646

LaPointe LB, Engle RW. 1990. Simple and

complex spans as measures of working memory capacity. *J. Exp. Psychol.: Learn. Mem. Cogn.* 16:1118–33

Lewandowsky S. 1999. Redintegration and response suppression in serial recall: a dynamic network model. *Int. J. Psychol.* 34:434–46

Lovatt P, Avons SE, Masterson J. 2000. The word-length effect and disyllabic words. *Q. J. Exp. Psychol.* 53A:1–22

Lovett MC, Reder LM, Lebiere C. 1999. Modeling working memory in a unified architecture. See Miyake & Shah 1999, pp. 135–82

McElree B. 1998. Attended and non-attended states in working memory: accessing categorized structures. *J. Mem. Lang.* 38:225–52

McElree B, Dosher BA. 1989. Serial position and set size in short-term memory: the time course of recognition. *J. Exp. Psychol.: Gen.* 118:346–73

McGeoch JA. 1932. Forgetting and the law of disuse. *Psychol. Rev.* 39:352–70

Melton AW. 1963. Implications of short-term memory for a general theory of memory. *J. Verbal Learn. Verbal Behav.* 2:1–21

Miller GA. 1956. The magical number seven plus or minus two: some limits on our capacity for processing information. *Psychol. Rev.* 63:81–97

Miyake A, Shah P. 1999. *Models of Working Memory.* Cambridge: Cambridge Univ. Press

Nairne JS. 1988. A framework for interpreting recency effects in immediate serial recall. *Mem. Cogn.* 16:343–52

Nairne JS. 1990a. A feature model of immediate memory. *Mem. Cogn.* 18:251–69

Nairne JS. 1990b. Similarity and long-term memory for order. *J. Mem. Lang.* 29:733–46

Nairne JS. 1991. Positional uncertainty in long-term memory. *Mem. Cogn.* 19:332–40

Nairne JS. 1996. Short-term/working memory. In *Memory*, ed. EL Bjork, RA Bjork, pp. 101–26. New York: Academic

Nairne JS. 2001. A functional analysis of primary memory. See Roediger et al. 2001, pp. 283–96

Nairne JS, Kelley MR. 1999. Reversing the phonological similarity effect. *Mem. Cogn.* 27:45–53

Nairne JS, Neath I, Serra M. 1997. Proactive interference plays a role in the word-length effect. *Psychol. Bull. Rev.* 4:541–45

Nairne JS, Whiteman HL, Kelley MR. 1999. Short-term forgetting of order under conditions of reduced interference. *Q. J. Exp. Psychol.* 52A:241–51

Naveh-Benjamin M, Ayres TJ. 1986. Digit span, reading rate, and linguistic relativity. *Q. J. Exp. Psychol.* 38A:739–51

Neath I. 1998. *Human Memory: An Introduction to Research Data and Theory.* Pacific Grove, CA: Brooks/Cole

Neath I. 1999. Modelling the disruptive effects of irrelevant speech on order information. *Int. J. Psychol.* 34:416–24

Neath I. 2000. Modeling the effects of irrelevant speech on memory. *Psychol. Bull. Rev.* 7:403–23

Neath I, Knoedler AJ. 1994. Distinctiveness and serial position effects in recognition and sentence processing. *J. Mem. Lang.* 33:776–95

Neath I, Nairne JS. 1995. Word-length effects in immediate memory: overwriting trace-decay theory. *Psychol. Bull. Rev.* 2:429–41

Nicolson R. 1981. The relationship between memory span and processing speed. In *Intelligence and Learning*, ed. M Friedman, JP Das, N O'Conner. New York: Plenum

Nosofsky RM. 1986. Attention, similarity, and the identification-categorization relationship. *J. Exp. Psychol.: Gen.* 115:39–57

Osgood CE. 1953. *Method and Theory in Experimental Psychology.* New York: Oxford Univ. Press

Page MPA, Norris D. 1998. The primacy model: a new model of immediate serial recall. *Psychol. Rev.* 105:761–81

Peterson LR, Peterson MJ. 1959. Short-term retention of individual verbal items. *J. Exp. Psychol.* 58:193–98

Posner MI, Konick AW. 1966. On the role of interference in short-term retention. *J. Exp. Psychol.* 72:221–31

Proctor RW, Fagnani CA. 1978. Effects of

distractor-stimulus modality in the Brown-Peterson distractor task. *J. Exp. Psychol.: Hum. Learn. Mem.* 4:676–84

Reitman JS. 1974. Without surreptitious rehearsal information in short-term memory decays. *J. Verbal Learn. Verbal Behav.* 13:365–77

Roediger HL III, Nairne JS, Neath I, Suprenant AM, eds. 2001. *The Nature of Remembering: Essays in Honor of Robert G. Crowder.* Washington, DC: Am. Psychol. Assoc.

Roodenrys S, Hulme C, Alban J, Ellis AW, Brown GD. 1994. Effects of word frequency and age of acquisition on short-term memory span. *Mem. Cogn.* 22:695–701

Schweickert R. 1993. A multinomial processing tree model for degradation and redintegration in immediate recall. *Mem. Cogn.* 21:167–75

Schweickert R, Boruff B. 1986. Short-term memory capacity: magic number or magic spell? *J. Exp. Psychol.: Learn. Mem. Cogn.* 12:419–25

Schweickert R, Guentert L, Hersberger L. 1990. Phonological similarity, pronunciation rate, and memory span. *Psychol. Sci.* 1:74–77

Service E. 1998. The effect of word length on immediate serial recall depends on phonological complexity not articulatory duration. *Q. J. Exp. Psychol.* 51A:283–304

Shiffrin RM. 1999. 30 years of memory. In *On Human Memory: Evolution Progress and Reflections of the 30th Anniversary of the Atkinson-Shiffrin Model*, ed. C Izawa, pp. 17–33. Mahwah, NJ: Erlbaum

Smith EE, Jonides J. 1997. Working memory: a view from neuroimaging. *Cogn. Psychol.* 33:5–42

Surprenant AM, LeCompte DC, Neath I. 2000. Manipulations of irrelevant information: suffix effects with articulatory suppression and irrelevant speech. *Q. J. Exp. Psychol.* 53A:325–48

Tan L, Ward G. 2000. A recency-based account of the primacy effect in free recall. *J. Exp. Psychol.: Learn. Mem. Cogn.* 26:1589–625

Tehan G, Fallon AB. 1999. A connectionist model of short-term cued recall. In *Prospec-

tives in Cognitive Science*, ed. J Wiles, T Dartnell, pp. 221–37. Stamford, CT: Ablex

Tehan G, Humphreys MS. 1988. Articulatory loop explanations of memory span and pronunciation rate correspondence: A cautionary note. *Bull. Psychon. Soc.* 26:293–96

Tehan G, Humphreys MS. 1996. Cuing effects in short-term recall. *Mem. Cogn.* 24:719–32

Tehan G, Humphreys MS. 1998. Creating proactive interference in immediate recall: building a dog from a dart, a mop and a fig. *Mem. Cogn.* 26:477–89

Tehan G, Lalor DM. 2000. Individual differences in memory span: the contribution of rehearsal access to lexical memory and output speed. *Q. J. Exp. Psychol.* 53A:1012–38

Tulving E. 1983. *Elements of Episodic Memory.* New York: Oxford Univ. Press

Turvey MT, Brick P, Osborn J. 1970. Proactive interference in short-term memory as a function of prior-item retention interval. *Q. J. Exp. Psychol.* 22:142–47

Vallar G, Cappa SF. 1987. Articulation and verbal short-term memory: evidence from Anarthria. *Cogn. Neurosci.* 4:55–78

Walker I, Hulme C. 1999. Concrete words are easier to recall than abstract: evidence for a semantic contribution to short-term serial recall. *J. Exp. Psychol.: Learn. Mem. Cogn.* 25:1256–71

Watkins OC, Watkins MJ. 1975. Buildup of proactive inhibition as a cue-overload effect. *J. Exp. Psychol.: Human Learn. Mem.* 104:442–52

Wickelgren WA. 1965. Acoustic similarity and retroactive interference in short-term memory. *J. Verbal Learn. Verbal Behav.* 4:53–61

Wickelgren WA, Corbett AT, Dosher BA. 1980. Priming and retrieval from short-term memory: a speed-accuracy tradeoff analysis. *J. Verbal Learn. Verbal Behav.* 19:387–404

Wickens DD. 1970. Encoding categories of words: an empirical approach to meaning. *Psychol. Rev.* 77:771–15

Wilson M. 2001. The case for sensorimotor coding in working memory. *Psychol. Bull. Rev.* 8:44–57

Wilson M, Emmorey K. 1998. A "word length effect" for sign language: further evidence on the role of language in structuring working memory. *Mem. Cogn.* 26:584–90

Wright AA, Santiago HC, Sands SF, Kendrick DF, Cook RG. 1985. Memory processing of serial lists by pigeons, monkeys and people. *Science* 229:287–89

Annu. Rev. Psychol. 2002. 53:83–107

EMOTIONS, MORBIDITY, AND MORTALITY:
New Perspectives from Psychoneuroimmunology

Janice K. Kiecolt-Glaser[1], Lynanne McGuire[2], Theodore F. Robles[3], and Ronald Glaser[4]

[1,2]Department of Psychiatry and [4]Department of Molecular Virology, Immunology, and Medical Genetics, The Ohio State University College of Medicine, 1670 Upham Drive, Columbus, Ohio 43210; e-mail: Kiecolt-Glaser.1@osu.edu
[3]Department of Psychology, The Ohio State University, Columbus, Ohio 43210; e-mail: robles.8@osu.edu

Key Words depression, immune function, social support, interleukin 6

■ **Abstract** Negative emotions can intensify a variety of health threats. We provide a broad framework relating negative emotions to a range of diseases whose onset and course may be influenced by the immune system; inflammation has been linked to a spectrum of conditions associated with aging, including cardiovascular disease, osteoporosis, arthritis, type 2 diabetes, certain cancers, Alzheimer's disease, frailty and functional decline, and periodontal disease. Production of proinflammatory cytokines that influence these and other conditions can be directly stimulated by negative emotions and stressful experiences. Additionally, negative emotions also contribute to prolonged infection and delayed wound healing, processes that fuel sustained proinflammatory cytokine production. Accordingly, we argue that distress-related immune dysregulation may be one core mechanism behind a large and diverse set of health risks associated with negative emotions. Resources such as close personal relationships that diminish negative emotions enhance health in part through their positive impact on immune and endocrine regulation.

CONTENTS

0084-6570/02/0201-0083$14.00

INTRODUCTION

The idea that emotions are linked with morbidity and mortality has existed for over two millennia (Sternberg 1997). Hippocrates (c. 500 B.C.) theorized that health was related to the balance of four bodily humors, which contributed to specific temperaments. Galen (A.D. 131–201) took this idea further, proposing that a balance of the "passions" was essential for physical health. Indeed, severe emotional reactions were considered causes of diseases such as stroke, birth defects, asthma, ulcers, and, ultimately, even death (Sternberg 1997). These beliefs persisted through the medieval period and the early Renaissance; in *The Anatomy of Melancholy*, Robert Burton (1621/1893) wrote, "the mind most effectually works upon the body, producing by his passions and perturbations miraculous alterations . . . cruel diseases and sometimes death itself." Although this idea dominated medical practice for much of early civilization, in the modern era the science of the biological bases of health and disease has far surpassed the science of emotions. In this review we consider new evidence that suggests how negative emotions may contribute to disease and death through immune dysregulation.

We first address the evidence that negative emotions are related to morbidity and mortality. We highlight the consequences of depression, anxiety, and hostility, three broad emotions that have been linked to verifiable health outcomes; although there are many potential common paths among the negative emotions, there is also evidence that different emotions may make unique contributions to some disease processes (Leventhal et al. 1998). Next we consider key pathways, focusing on a central immunological mechanism that serves as a gateway for a range of age-associated diseases, the dysregulation of proinflammatory cytokine production. In the final section we consider vulnerability and resilience factors, including sociodemographic variables, personality traits and coping, social relationships, and positive emotions.

Although it is clear that negative emotions can intensify a wide variety of health threats, positive emotions have received considerably less attention, perhaps related to the prevailing view of physical and mental health as the absence of disease and negative emotions (Ryff & Singer 1998), as well as the fact that positive emotions are fewer in number and less differentiated than negative emotions (Ellsworth & Smith 1988). Indeed, although a substantial empirical literature exists for "depression" and objective measures of health, almost none exists for "happiness" and health, and thus we concentrate on the former.

This review concentrates on the pathways from negative emotions to illness and death; the effects of disease on emotional distress will not be addressed in any detail, although the relationships are clearly bidirectional. Indeed, cytokines have substantial effects on the central nervous system, including production and enhancement of negative moods, physical symptoms including lethargy and fatigue, and a range of sickness behaviors from shivering to loss of appetite (Leventhal et al. 1998, Watkins & Maier 2000); accordingly, negative emotions may also reflect a prodromal or active disease process (Leventhal et al. 1998). In fact, although we focus on the impact of emotions on immune and endocrine responses and disease, there is plausible evidence that the immune system has a role in the neuroendocrine and behavioral features of both depressive and anxiety disorders (Miller 1998).

NEGATIVE EMOTIONS, MORBIDITY, AND MORTALITY: THE EVIDENCE

Depression

Depression is the most common psychiatric illness, and both major depression and subthreshold depressive symptoms carry substantial health risks. A number of well-controlled prospective studies have linked depressive symptoms with coronary heart disease (CHD), the leading cause of death in the United States. For example, a 13-year prospective study suggested that individuals with major depression had a 4.5 times greater risk of a heart attack compared with those with no history of depression (Pratt et al. 1996). Depressive symptoms also place patients at jeopardy; across a series of studies, healthy individuals who had elevated depression scores at baseline had a 1.5- to 2-fold increased risk for a first heart attack (Glassman & Shapiro 1998). Not surprisingly, patients who had preexisting cardiovascular disease also had poorer outcomes if they were depressed (Glassman & Shapiro 1998); mortality among patients who had suffered a heart attack was four times higher among the depressed than the nondepressed (Frasure-Smith et al. 1993).

One recent well-controlled study found that chronic depressed mood was linked to cancer risk; after adjusting for sociodemograhic variables and risk factors, the hazard ratio across a range of cancers was 1.88 (Penninx et al. 1998b). In contrast to these findings, other researchers have not found evidence for a link between depression and malignant disease (Croyle 1998, Whooley & Browner 1998). However, most prior literature has relied on a single assessment of depressive symptoms; when Penninx et al. (1998b) used a similar strategy with their own data, they did not find the relationship between dysphoria and cancer that emerged when depressive symptoms exceeded cut points at baseline as well as 3 and 6 years before baseline. Thus, some of the inconsistencies among cancer studies may reflect methodological differences. Additionally, it should also be noted that many related cancer studies have assessed a wide range of malignancies with very different etiologies, genetic contributions, behavioral influences (e.g., smoking), etc.; the heterogeneity makes it difficult to assess evidence in this arena. Our mechanistic discussion in the next section suggests that some cancers may show stronger relationships with negative emotions than others (Ershler & Keller 2000).

Depression influences outcomes in a variety of other illnesses. Depressed mood was an independent risk factor for all-cause mortality in medical inpatients (Herrmann et al. 1998). Among 1286 persons who were 71 or older, baseline depressive symptoms predicted greater physical decline over the subsequent 4 years (Penninx et al. 1998a). Depression heightens the risk for osteoporosis; either past or current depression in women was associated with lower bone mineral density (Michelson et al. 1996). Among older men, depressed mood at baseline was associated with an increased risk for declines in muscle strength over a 3-year period; important as an indication of current physical functioning, grip strength is also a powerful predictor of future functional limitations and disability (Rantanen et al. 2000). Depression has also been associated with reduced rehabilitation effectiveness in a spectrum of diseases (e.g., stroke, fractures, and pulmonary disease) (Katz 1996). Similarly, depressed diabetics are less likely to follow recommendations for dietary management and glycemic control (Katon 1998).

Pain, a pervasive medical problem, accounts for substantial levels of disability and contributes greatly to the overall burden of illness (Turk & Melzack 1992). Inextricably linked to depression and other negative moods, pain can increase disease severity and mortality (Staats 1999, Wells et al. 1989). Pain can provoke increases in heart rate and blood pressure, enhance secretion of stress-related hormones including catecholamines and cortisol, and dysregulate a range of immunological activities (Kiecolt-Glaser et al. 1998, Liebeskind 1991). Additionally, pain may disrupt many aspects of physical, mental, and social functioning (Leventhal et al. 1998). Accordingly, depression can amplify morbidity by magnifying pain and disability across a range of acute and chronic health problems.

How large are the effects? For mortality, the increased risk among elderly women in one large study was ". . . similar to that conferred by other cardiovascular risk factors, such as hypertension, cigarette smoking, hyperlipidemia, obesity, and diabetes" (Whooley & Browner 1998, p. 2132). In another study, depression at baseline increased the risk that participants would develop a disability over the next 6 years by 73% (Penninx et al. 1999). Data from 11,242 outpatients in the Medical Outcomes Study showed that patients with either a current depressive disorder or depressive symptoms in the absence of a syndromal disorder had worse physical, social, and role function, worse perceived current health, and greater bodily pain than patients with no chronic conditions (Wells et al. 1989). The poorer functioning that was uniquely associated with depressive symptoms was comparable to—or even worse than—that uniquely associated with eight chronic medical conditions. Thus, the increased morbidity and mortality associated with depression is substantial.

Anxiety

Although depression has been the best-studied negative emotion, anxiety also has adverse effects, particularly in the cardiovascular realm, where it plays a role in the development of CHD and contributes to poorer prognosis after acute coronary events, including death and recurrent ischemic events. Phobic, panic-like anxiety predicted 3 times the risk of fatal CHD at a 7-year follow-up compared with no anxiety (Haines et al. 1987). In data from the Normative Aging Study higher levels of anxiety were associated with almost double the risk of fatal CHD (Kawachi et al. 1994b). Similarly, men in the Health Professionals Follow-up Study who reported the highest levels of anxiety had more than double the risk for fatal CHD and nonfatal myocardial infarction (Kawachi et al. 1994a). Anxiety symptoms were associated with significantly increased risk of myocardial infarction and coronary-related death over a 20-year period in women who were homemakers (Eaker et al. 1992). Anxiety also has negative consequences for recovery from surgery (Kiecolt-Glaser et al. 1998).

Hostility/Anger

Chronic anger and hostility also negatively impact health. One excellent 9-year population-based study found that men high in hostility had more than twice the risk of all-cause and cardiovascular mortality compared with men low in hostility (Everson et al. 1997). Similarly, a large prospective study of employees found that hostility predicted the total number of long-term medically certified absences over a 4-year period among men but not women (Vahtera et al. 1997). Indeed, a rigorous meta-analysis concluded that hostility was a robust risk factor for CHD, as well as for all-cause mortality (Miller et al. 1996).

Although the weight of the evidence clearly implicates negative emotions, particularly depression, in all-cause mortality, the findings have been inconsistent, the discrepancies undoubtedly fueled by notable methodological shortcomings in a number of studies, including small samples, low mortality, brief follow-up periods, incomplete follow-up, and absence of control for relevant health behaviors or premorbid status (Schulz et al. 2000). Successive assessments that provide information on health problems, medications, smoking, and alcohol use are crucial; indeed, the absence of positive findings in some studies may well be related to failure to assess and control for smoking and alcohol use (Wulsin et al. 1999), key health behaviors that impact a spectrum of diseases (Kiecolt-Glaser & Glaser 1988). The effects are clearly bidirectional, and illness can enhance the risk for the development of depression and anxiety symptoms and disorders (Katz 1996). Despite these methodological shortcomings, it is clear that the burdens and stresses that stimulate psychological morbidity also have clear and notable consequences for physical health.

PATHWAYS

Morbidity, Mortality, and Aging: Central Immunological Mechanisms

Emotions can affect health through many pathways; these influences may occur indirectly, through health behaviors or compliance with medical regimens, and directly, through alterations in the functioning of the central nervous system, immune, endocrine, and cardiovascular systems. The primary focus of our mechanistic discussion will be the immune and endocrine pathways to age-related changes in health; our choice is based on recent evidence that implicates dysregulation of proinflammatory cytokines, particularly interleukin 6 (IL-6), as a central component across a range of diseases in older adults. We first provide a brief introduction to cytokines, followed by a review of evidence relating cytokine dysregulation to a spectrum of health problems.

Cytokines are protein substances released by cells that serve as intercellular signals to regulate the immune response to injury and infection. The relevance of cytokines to the biobehavioral sciences is illustrated by the appearance of reviews of cytokine biology in psychiatric and psychological literature (Kronfol & Remick 2000, Maier & Watkins 1998). The signaling properties of cytokines are similar to classic hormones of the endocrine system, and cytokines can be differentiated into two basic classes based on their effects on the immune response, proinflammatory and antiinflammatory. The proinflammatory cytokines include IL-1, IL-6, and tumor necrosis factor (TNF); they promote inflammation, a beneficial reaction in early immune responses to infection and injury (Glaser et al. 1999a). The primary actions of these cytokines are attracting immune cells to the site of infection or injury and causing them to become activated to respond. Secondary actions include changes in physiology that promote inflammation, such as alterations in metabolism and temperature regulation. Antiinflammatory cytokines such as IL-10 and IL-13 dampen the immune response, causing, for instance, decreased cell function and synthesis of other cytokines.

The immune system's inflammatory response can be triggered in a variety of ways, including infection and trauma. The mechanisms associated with inflammation are critical to resolving infections and repairing tissue damage; however, chronic or recurring infections can provoke pathological changes (Hamerman 1999). For example, low levels of persistent inflammation may result when chronic infectious processes such as periodontal disease, urinary tract infections, chronic pulmonary disease, and chronic renal disease persistently stimulate the immune system, with the greatest repercussions among older adults who already show age-related increases in IL-6 production (Cohen 2000).

Indeed, inflammation has recently been linked to a spectrum of conditions associated with aging, including cardiovascular disease, osteoporosis, arthritis, type 2 diabetes, certain lymphoproliferative diseases or cancers (including multiple myeloma, non-Hodgkin's lymphoma, and chronic lymphocytic leukemia), Alzheimer's disease, and periodontal disease (Ershler & Keller 2000). The association between cardiovascular disease and IL-6 is related in part to the central role that this cytokine plays in promoting the production of C-reactive protein (CRP), recently recognized as an important risk factor for myocardial infarction (Papanicolaou et al. 1998). For example, high concentrations of CRP predicted the risk of future cardiovascular disease in apparently healthy men (Ridker et al. 1997). Further studies provided mechanistic links: chronic infections amplified the risk for development of atherosclerosis fourfold in subjects who were free of carotid atherosclerosis at baseline, conferring increased risk even in subjects lacking conventional vascular risk factors (Kiechl et al. 2001). Indeed, the increased risk for artery-clogging plaque was greater than that conferred by elevated blood pressure or cholesterol (Kiechl et al. 2001). Cardiovascular disease is the leading cause of death, and individuals with high levels of both IL-6 and CRP were 2.6 times more likely to die over a 4.6-year period than those who were low on both (Harris et al. 1999).

More globally, chronic inflammation has been suggested as one key biological mechanism that may fuel declines in physical function leading to frailty, disability, and, ultimately, death (Hamerman 1999, Taaffe et al. 2000). For example, elevated serum IL-6 levels predicted future disability in older adults, a finding the authors suggest may reflect the effects of the cytokine on muscle atrophy, and/or to the pathophysiologic role played by the cytokine in particular diseases (Ferrucci et al. 1999). Proinflammatory cytokines including IL-6 may slow muscle repair following injury and accelerate muscle wasting (Cannon 1995); indeed, IL-6 and CRP also play a pathogenic role in a range of diseases associated with disability among the elderly (e.g., osteoporosis, arthritis, and congestive heart failure) (Ferrucci et al. 1999). In this context it is interesting that IL-6 is also associated with self-rated health (Cohen et al. 1997a), a robust predictor of mortality (Leventhal et al. 1998). Thus, the clinical importance of immunological dysregulation for older adults is highlighted by increased risks across diverse conditions and diseases.

Emotions and Immune System Alterations

There is excellent evidence that depression and anxiety enhance the production of proinflammatory cytokines, including IL-6 (Dentino et al. 1999; Lutgendorf et al. 1999; Maes et al. 1995, 1999, 1998). Higher plasma IL-6 levels were associated with greater distress in a sample of community women (Lutgendorf et al. 1999). Women who were caregiving for a relative with Alzheimer's disease had higher levels of plasma IL-6 than either women who were anticipating a housing relocation or community controls (Lutgendorf et al. 1999); the finding was particularly noteworthy because caregivers were 6–9 years younger, on average, than women in the other two groups. Chronic fatigue patients showed increases in IL-6 following a severe life stressor (Hurricane Andrew) (Costello et al. 1998). Following successful pharmacologic treatment, elevated IL-6 levels declined in patients with a major depression diagnosis (Sluzewska et al. 1995).

Both physical and psychological stressors can provoke transient increases in proinflammatory cytokines (DeRijk et al. 1997, Zhou et al. 1993); in animal models both stress and administration of epinephrine elevated plasma IL-6, consistent with evidence that IL-6 production is stimulated through β-adrenergic receptors, among other pathways (Papanicolaou et al. 1998). Thus, production of IL-6 and other proinflammatory cytokines can be directly stimulated by negative emotions and stressful experiences, providing one direct pathway.

Negative emotions also contribute indirectly to the immune dysregulation evidenced by proinflammatory cytokine overproduction. Repeated, chronic, or slow-resolving infections or wounds enhance secretion of proinflammatory cytokines, a process that can serve to further inhibit certain aspects of immune responses (e.g., IL-2, an important defense against infection), and thus may contribute to the immunodepression of aging (Catania et al. 1997). Stress impedes the immune response to infectious challenges, amplifying risks for contagion and prolonged illness episodes (Glaser et al. 1999b, Kiecolt-Glaser et al. 1996a, Sheridan et al. 1991); distress also provokes substantial delays in wound healing (Glaser et al. 1999a, Kiecolt-Glaser et al. 1995, Marucha et al. 1998) and enhances the risk for wound infection after injury (Rojas et al. 2001). Thus, negative emotions such as depression or anxiety can directly affect the cells of the immune system and either up- or down-regulate the secretion of proinflammatory cytokines; in addition, negative emotions may also contribute to prolonged or chronic infections or delayed wound healing, processes that indirectly fuel proinflammatory cytokine production. These changes are likely to be greatest, and to carry the highest health risks, among the elderly.

Although our focus thus far has been on the health consequences associated with secretion of proinflammatory cytokines, negative emotions can also have direct adverse effects on a variety of other immunological mechanisms; both animal and human studies have provided convincing evidence that these immune alterations are consequential for health. For example, to help demonstrate causal relationships between psychosocial stressors and the development of infectious illness, investigators have inoculated subjects with a variety of vaccines (Glaser et al. 1992, 2000, Kiecolt-Glaser et al. 1996a, Morag et al. 1999, Vedhara et al. 1999). Vaccine responses demonstrate clinically relevant alterations in immunological responses to challenge under well-controlled conditions; accordingly, they serve as a proxy for response to an infectious agent. More distressed and anxious individuals produced immune responses to vaccines that were delayed, substantially weaker, and/or shorter lived; as a consequence, it is reasonable to assume these same individuals would also be slower to develop immune responses to other pathogens; thus, they could be at greater risk for more severe illness. Consistent with this argument, adults who show poorer responses to vaccines also experience higher rates of clinical illness, as well as longer-lasting infectious episodes (Burns & Goodwin 1990, Patriarca 1994). In addition, other researchers have shown that distress can alter susceptibility to cold viruses (Cohen et al. 1998).

Increased susceptibility to pathogens is a serious health problem for older adults. For example, although influenza is rarely fatal among healthy younger adults, together influenza and pneumonia, a common complication of influenza virus infection, constitute the fourth leading cause of death among individuals who are 75 or older (Yoshikawa 1983); distressed older adults demonstrate poorer responses to both influenza and pneumococcal vaccines (Glaser et al. 2000, Kiecolt-Glaser et al. 1996a, Vedhara et al. 1999). Thus, data from human studies now provide solid evidence that negative emotions can increase susceptibility to infectious disease via alterations in the immune response.

Emotions and Neuroendocrine Alterations

The endocrine system serves as one prominent gateway across a spectrum of diseases because emotions provoke the release of pituitary and adrenal hormones that have multiple effects, including alterations in cardiovascular and immune function (Glaser & Kiecolt-Glaser 1994, Rozanski et al. 1999). Both anxious and depressed moods can activate the sympathetic-pituitary-adrenal medullary axis, as well as the hypothalamic-pituitary-adrenocortical (HPA) axis (Miller 1998). Numerous studies have suggested that a variety of emotion-responsive hormones including the catecholamines (norepinephrine and epinephrine), adrenocorticotropin hormone, cortisol, growth hormone, and prolactin can impel quantitative and qualitative changes in immune function, and there is bi-directional feedback between the endocrine and immune systems (Rabin 1999). For example, depression can substantially boost cortisol, and elevations in cortisol can provoke multiple adverse immunological changes including defects in vaccine responses (Vedhara et al. 1999) and wound healing (Padgett et al. 1998). In contrast to the generally negative effects of cortisol, growth hormone can enhance many aspects of immune function (Malarkey et al. 1996); growth hormone is lower in depressed patients (Dinan 1998), and growth hormone gene expression is altered in mononuclear cells of chronically distressed caregivers (Malarkey et al. 1996). Additionally, both anxious and depressive disorders and symptoms can elevate catecholamines; although brief increases in response to acute stressors may be advantageous under many circumstances, longer-term increases are generally associated with immunological down-regulation (Malarkey et al. 1996).

The hypercortisolemia associated with clinical depression is well documented (DeRijk et al. 1997); however, the endocrine system's involvement in the pathogenesis of many stress-related disease processes is also likely mediated in part through frequent small daily excursions in hormonal levels following stressful events, and/or through disturbance of diurnal rhythms (Dhabhar & McEwen 1997). The ability to "unwind" after stressful encounters, i.e., quicker return to one's neuroendocrine baseline, influences the total burden that stressors place on an individual (Frankenhaeuser 1986). Stressors that are resistant to behavioral coping, particularly stressors perceived as unpredictable and uncontrollable, may continue to be associated with elevated stress hormones even after repeated exposure (Baum et al. 1993).

Our prior discussion focused on age-related immune dysregulation; thus, it is important to note that cytokines such as IL-6 also influence the functioning of the endocrine system, one of the many bi-directional relationships between the two systems. IL-6 is a potent stimulator of corticotropin-releasing hormone production, a mechanism that leads to heightened HPA activity, including elevated levels of plasma adrenocorticotropin hormone, followed by increased cortisol levels

(Dentino et al. 1999). Thus, negative emotions that dysregulate IL-6 secretion may also promote neuroendocrine alterations that have immune consequences.

The complexity of these potential interactions is further underscored by one line of research that suggests that once cortisol levels rise, they can initiate, perpetuate, or aggravate syndromal depression, depression-like behaviors, and depressive symptoms such as anxiety, insomnia, and poor memory (Wolkowitz & Reus 1999). Such data are consistent with the conceptualization of major depression as a dysfunction in the stress response (Sternberg et al. 1992), as well as evidence that both emotional distress and disease may be prompted by common genetic and constitutional variables (Leventhal et al. 1998). For example, first-degree relatives of depressed patients who have never been clinically depressed have HPA axis responses similar to their affected relatives and different from controls (Holsboer et al. 1995). Similarly, a 10-year follow-up of adolescents who had served as part of a normal control group showed that the baseline pattern of sleep-related growth hormone secretion was predictive of subsequent depressive episodes (Coplan et al. 2000). Accordingly, the health hazards associated with negative emotions'are likely to reflect multiple interacting risk factors, including important genetic influences.

Although there are common genetic influences for depression and neuroendocrine dysregulation, sufficiently stressful circumstances can also produce clinically significant immune and endocrine dysregulation in individuals who are not at risk. For example, the chronic strains of dementia spousal caregiving were related to the onset of syndromal depressive disorders in older adults who had no prior evidence of vulnerability through either personal or family history (Dura et al. 1990). Moreover, although only a minority of caregivers develop syndromal disorders, men and women who provide long-term care for a spouse or parent with Alzheimer's disease typically report high levels of distress as they attempt to cope with the family member's problematic behaviors; this stressor has been associated with prolonged endocrine and immune dysregulation, as well as health changes, including alterations in vaccine response and wound healing (Castle et al. 1995; Esterling et al. 1994, 1996; Glaser et al. 1998; Irwin et al. 1991; Kiecolt-Glaser et al. 1996a; Malarkey et al. 1996; Mills et al. 1999; Vedhara et al. 1999; Wu et al. 1999).

Health Behaviors

In addition to the direct influences of psychological states on physiological function, distressed individuals are more likely to have health habits that put them at greater risk, including poorer sleep, a greater propensity for alcohol and drug abuse, poorer nutrition, and less exercise, and these health behaviors have cardiovascular, immunological, and endocrinological consequences (Kiecolt-Glaser & Glaser 1988). Psychosocial stressors that increase adverse health behaviors also provoke maladaptive physiological changes. For example, deep sleep provides the normal stimulus for much of the release of growth hormone, which enhances multiple aspects of immune function; thus, stressors that modify the architecture of sleep also lessen secretion of growth hormone (Veldhuis & Iranmanesch 1996). Moreover, even partial sleep loss one night results in elevated cortisol levels the next evening (Leproult et al. 1997). Adverse health behaviors can interact with one another; for example, heavy alcohol use is linked to poorer sleep and nutrition. Smoking makes substantial contributions to morbidity and mortality; depressed patients are more likely to smoke and less likely to quit than nondepressed individuals (Wulsin et al. 1999). Depressed patients may be less likely to seek medical care and take prescribed medications than those who are not depressed (Penninx et al. 1999, Whooley & Browner 1998).

Higher plasma IL-6 and CRP levels are associated with adverse health habits: Values for both are higher in smokers than nonsmokers, in individuals who report less physical activity, and in those with a higher body mass index (Ferrucci et al. 1999, Taaffe et al. 2000). However, health habits including smoking, physical activity, and alcohol use have typically explained only a small part of the excess mortality associated with depression among older adults, e.g., Penninx et al. (1999). Similarly, IL-6 has robust relationships with morbidity and mortality, even after controlling for health behaviors (Ferrucci et al. 1999, Taaffe et al. 2000); more broadly, behavioral studies have demonstrated reliable psychological influences on immune function in populations selected in part on the basis of health habits (Kiecolt-Glaser et al. 1993). Thus, health behaviors, although obviously important, are not sufficient to explain the relationship between emotions and disease.

We have focused on the immune and endocrine systems, but there are obviously many other physiological pathways through which emotions can influence health, including cardiovascular and neurobiological circuitry (Davidson et al. 2001, Krantz & McCeney 2001, Leventhal et al. 1998). However, many lines of evidence now indicate that IL-6 may function as a "... global marker of impending deterioration in health status in older adults" (Ferrucci et al. 1999, p. 645). We have argued that negative emotions directly prompt immune dysregulation, and these processes may lead to subsequent maladaptive immune and endocrine changes. Thus, research that addresses the dysregulation of the immune and endocrine systems associated with negative emotions could substantially enhance our understanding of psychological influences on health, particularly among the elderly.

Allostatic Load: Conceptual Similarities and Differences

The immune dysregulation we are discussing is consistent with the broad allostatic load formulation, the "... long-term effect of the physiologic response to stress" (McEwen 1998, p. 171); however, the breadth of disease outcomes addressed and the operationalization of the concepts and pathways are somewhat different. Investigators have used a broad battery of measures to gauge allostatic load, including blood pressure, overnight urinary cortisol and catecholamine excretion, waist to hip ratio, glycosylated hemoglobin, the ratio of serum high-density lipoprotein in the total serum cholesterol concentration, and dehydroepiandrosterone (DHEA) sulfate; individuals with higher scores on this broad battery were more likely to have incident cardiovascular disease as well as declines in cognitive and physical function when assessed at a 3-year follow-up (Seeman et al. 1997).

In concert with the underlying tenets of the allostatic load formulation (McEwen 1998), emotional influences on the HPA and sympathetic-pituitary-adrenal medullary axes—and potential long-term changes in each—are a central focus of our mechanistic discussion. Within both frameworks chronic stress is highlighted, with its capacity for inducing long-term decline via overexposure to stress hormones. However, our mechanistic path focuses more narrowly on the implications of adverse neuroendocrine changes for immune modulation, as well as the bidirectional feedback from the immune system to the endocrine system—the stimulation of corticotropin-releasing hormone by IL-6—on the spectrum of inflammation-related health outcomes discussed earlier. Clearly, the battery of health indices described above (Seeman et al. 1997) have important prognostic value; however, even after the point at which risk factors such as cholesterol, hypertension, and obesity predict health deterioration less successfully among the very old, chronic inflammation continues to be an important marker (Ferrucci et al. 1999). Finally, we place a greater emphasis on the toll that daily stress plays via immune dysregulation—the extent to which negative emotions contribute to prolonged infection and delayed wound healing, processes that fuel sustained proinflammatory cytokine production. Thus, in the final section we address the enormous variability in stress responsiveness by reviewing literature related to resilience and vulnerability factors identified in psychoneuroimmunology research to date.

VULNERABILITY AND RESILIENCE FACTORS

Sociodemographic Variables

AGE   Biologically, the largest deleterious or enhancing consequences of negative and positive emotions are likely to occur when biological vulnerability is greatest: early and late in life. Although our primary focus has been on aging, intense emotional experiences have the capacity to permanently alter neuroendocrine and autonomic responses, and these may be most consequential when they occur early in life. For example, women with a history of childhood abuse are at substantially greater risk for depressive and anxiety disorders; they also show larger pituitary-adrenal and autonomic responses to laboratory stressors than controls (Heim et al. 2000, Lemieux & Coe 1995) and possibly experience long-term immunological alterations (De Bellis et al. 1996). Data on maternal separation in nonhuman primates provides strong supportive evidence from a well-characterized animal model (Coe 1993).

Changes in immune function associated with aging have already been addressed. In addition, however, older adults appear to show greater immunological impairments associated with distress or depression than younger adults (Herbert &

Cohen 1993, Kiecolt-Glaser et al. 1996a, Schleifer et al. 1989). Further, older adults may be more vulnerable to negative emotions due to smaller social support networks (Carstensen 1992). In contrast, however, the intensity of emotional reactions may also decline with aging, providing some protection (Leventhal et al. 1998).

Finally, the impact of age may vary through its association with other individual differences, related to changes in social, psychological, and biological resources (Leventhal et al. 1998). For example, age of onset of depression interacted with gender such that onset after age 70 in women most strongly predicted increased morbidity and mortality among adults seeking treatment for depression (Philibert et al. 1997). Thus, aging can interact with distress and depression to enhance risks for morbidity and mortality among older adults.

GENDER   There are established gender differences in well-being, including differences in major psychopathology (e.g., depression is more common in women) and negative and positive moods, that may derive from biological, personality, and sociocultural influences (Nolen-Hoeksema & Rusting 1999). Surprisingly, there has been inconsistent attention paid to possible gender differences in emotion and health relationships, making it difficult to draw conclusions at this time. Some studies have used only males or females, and others have not systematically examined gender effects. For example, a meta-analysis of hostility and health concluded that too few studies have reported results by sex to draw conclusions at this time (Miller et al. 1996).

Estrogen and androgens can repress IL-6 expression, and thus age-related increases in IL-6 gene expression and serum levels are thought to be related in part to the aging of the endocrine system (Ershler & Keller 2000). These linkages suggest that longitudinal comparisons of postmenopausal women who are taking hormone replacement therapy with those who are not would be one potentially profitable avenue for exploration.

More broadly, gender effects have been demonstrated both in emotional experiences (e.g., cognitive, physiological responses), and in health outcomes (Frankenhaeuser 1991, Stoney et al. 1987, Verbrugge 1982). Differential rates of depression, anxiety, and hostility in men and women may lead to different overall associations between gender and health outcomes. Furthermore, men and women may experience similar emotions differently, perhaps in part due to different constellations of additional vulnerability and resilience factors (e.g., age, social support), resulting in different associations with health outcomes (Kiecolt-Glaser & Newton 2001, Taylor et al. 2000b). For example, an interaction between depression severity, age, and gender was recently found such that among the elderly, severe depression was associated with increased mortality in men and women, whereas mild depression predicted increased mortality solely in men (Schoevers et al. 2000). In another example, among community dwelling adults, chronic strain, low sense of mastery, and rumination were more common in women than in men and mediated the greater prevalence of depression in women (Nolen-Hoeksema et al. 1999). It is possible that differences in the qualitative experience of emotions may be associated with different health behavior and physiological reactivity patterns, leading to different health outcomes. An important focus for future research is the manner in which gender may act as a vulnerability or resilience factor in its interaction with emotion and health outcomes, and the contribution of additional contextual variables such as age and social support in these relationships.

SOCIOECONOMIC STATUS   Socioeconomic status (SES), typically measured by education, income, and occupation, has inverse relationships with major depression, depressive symptoms, and hostility (Adler et al. 1994). SES also shows strong inverse relationships with most major causes of morbidity and mortality across populations (Taylor et al. 1997). The relationships are so strong that although lower SES groups have higher rates of morbidity and mortality, differences in social position relate to risk even at the upper levels of the hierarchy (Adler et al. 1994). The longer-term stressors associated with immune alterations include "burnout" at work (Lerman et al. 1999), job strain (Kawakami et al. 1997), and unemployment (Arnetz et al. 1991). Taylor and colleagues (1997) suggest that social class and race provide a context for understanding the impact of unhealthy environments, with one initial route to increased risk via obvious differential exposures to chronic stress.

RACE   Racial and ethnic disparities in morbidity and mortality exist in a number of health-related conditions, including cancer, cardiovascular disease, diabetes, HIV/AIDS, and preventable infectious illness (Williams 1997), all of which involve the immune system. These differences are due in part to dispositional risk factors, health behavioral risk factors (Myers et al. 1995), and SES, which are not exclusive to particular ethnic groups. For example, a higher prevalence of AIDS indicator conditions (e.g., tuberculosis, pneumonia) has been found in HIV-positive racial and ethnic minorities compared with HIV-positive whites, and is probably influenced by differential exposure to etiologic agents, diagnosis and reporting, and access to treatment (Hu et al. 1995). Racial and ethnic differences in health-related outcomes may be associated with mental health disparities, such as rates of depression, that may be driven by SES and ethnic differences in seeking treatment (US Dep. of Health and Human Services 1999). At the same time, there appear to be direct relationships between ethnicity and health, such as poorer health outcomes among African Americans across the socioeconomic strata (Williams & Collins 1995).

The immunological and genetics literatures generally suggest a genetic contribution to disease risk stratified by race/ethnicity, particularly for autoimmune disorders (Hess & Farhey 1994, Kalman & Lublin 1999), and these differences may be due to genetic factors such as cytokine polymorphisms. Despite these genetic stratifications, the concept of "race" is not a true biological characteristic, and the construct of "ethnicity" is atheoretical; both can lead to simplistic interpretations of intergroup differences (Meyerowitz et al. 1998, Williams 1997). Moreover, given that genetic factors generally determine susceptibility, but not development of disease, racial and ethnic influences on emotions, immunity, and health may be best understood along multiple dimensions, including culture, ethnic identity, and minority status (Phinney 1996).

Personality Traits and Coping

Personality and coping styles reflect individual differences in appraisal and response to stressful situations, and both have been associated with the onset and course of chronic and progressive health problems (Scheier & Bridges 1995). In fact, in longitudinal studies, personality and coping characteristics have predicted physical illness and mortality in initially healthy adults (Maruta et al. 2000, Peterson et al. 1988), as well as in HIV-seropositive gay men (Cole et al. 1997, 1996; Reed et al. 1999) and adults undergoing bone marrow transplant (Molassiotis et al. 1997). There is evidence that personality, coping, and emotions may interact to increase or decrease individuals' risk of negative health outcomes. For example, the co-existence of the type "D" distressed personality style, including depressive and anxiety symptoms, and social inhibition, predicted cardiac morbidity and mortality over a 10-year period (Denollet & Brutsaert 1998, Denollet et al. 1996), whereas greater optimism, indicative of a positive emotion personality style, predicted better health outcomes among cardiac patients (Scheier et al. 1999).

A potent resilience factor for health outcomes may be the induction and maintenance of positive emotion through personality and coping styles. The broaden-and-build model of positive emotions (Fredrickson 1998) posits a broadening of the individual's scope of attention, cognition, and action, and building of physical, intellectual, and social resources. Positive emotion may include, but is not limited to, positive reappraisal of stressful life events (Folkman & Moskowitz 2000), finding meaning (Taylor 1983), developing positive illusions (Taylor et al. 2000a), and situational or dispositional optimism (Scheier & Carver 1992, Taylor 1989). Furthermore, positive emotions might "undo" the aftereffects of negative emotions, particularly in physiological recovery (Fredrickson 1998). Positive emotion has been associated with better health outcomes, for example among male heart attack survivors (Affleck et al. 1987) and HIV-seropositive men experiencing bereavement (Bower et al. 1998). The pathways through which positive emotions impact health outcomes are not well known at this point, but likely occur through endocrine and immune mechanisms, as well as indirectly through health behaviors (Aspinwall & Brunhart 1996, Shepperd et al. 1996).

Personality and coping styles may predispose individuals toward greater relative negative or positive emotions, thereby maintaining physiological alterations associated with emotions. For example, personality and coping styles, such as repression, rejection sensitivity, attributional style, and sociability, have been associated with altered immune cell counts in peripheral blood and dysregulated cellular immune function (Segerstrom 2000). Notably, given our earlier discussion, one positive coping strategy, attendance at religious services, has been associated with lower levels of IL-6 in a large community sample of older adults (Koenig et al. 1997). Thus, the relationships among personality and coping styles and health outcomes may be mediated by their influences on negative and positive emotions and immune function, and these relationships are likely to be strongest in the context of relevant stressful events.

Social Relationships

Data from large, well-controlled epidemiological studies suggest that social isolation constitutes a major risk factor for morbidity and mortality, with statistical effect sizes comparable to those of such well-established health risk factors as smoking, blood pressure, blood lipids, obesity, and physical activity (House et al. 1988). Immunological alterations provide one possible physiological pathway: the link between personal relationships and immune function is one of the most robust findings in psychoneuroimmunology (Uchino et al. 1996). For example, better responses on two immunological assays were associated with higher social support in women whose husbands were being treated for urologic cancer (Baron et al. 1990). Medical students who reported better social support mounted a stronger immune response to a hepatitis B vaccine than those with less support (Glaser et al. 1992). Individuals with fewer social ties were more susceptible to respiratory viruses (Cohen et al. 1997b). Spousal caregivers of dementia sufferers who reported lower levels of social support on entry into a longitudinal study and who were most distressed by dementia-related behaviors showed the greatest and most uniformly negative changes in immune function one year later (Kiecolt-Glaser et al. 1991). Several researchers reported immunological differences between subjects who disclosed traumatic or upsetting events, compared with those in a nondisclosure condition (Christensen et al. 1996, Esterling et al. 1990, Pennebaker et al. 1988, Petrie et al. 1995). Loss of a spouse or partner through bereavement or divorce is associated with poorer immune function for a period of time (Irwin et al. 1987; Kemeny et al. 1995; Kiecolt-Glaser et al. 1987, 1988; Schleifer et al. 1983).

Marriage is obviously an important relationship, and marital quality has been associated with immune and endocrine function (Kiecolt-Glaser & Newton 2001). For example, women with rheumatoid arthritis were followed for 12 weeks (Zautra et al. 1998); although both immune function and clinician's ratings changed during a week of increased interpersonal stress, women who reported more positive spousal interaction patterns and less spousal criticism or negativity did not show as large an increase in clinical symptoms.

However, when close relationships are discordant, they can also be associated with depression and immune dysregulation. Both syndromal depression and depressive symptoms were strongly associated with marital discord (Beach et al. 1998, Fincham & Beach 1999). In addition, pervasive differences in endocrine and immune function were reliably associated with hostile behaviors during marital conflict among diverse samples that included newlyweds selected on the basis of stringent mental and physical health criteria, as well as couples married an average of 42 years (Kiecolt-Glaser et al. 1997, 1993, 1996b; Malarkey et al. 1994). Thus, although supportive personal relationships are associated with better immune function (Kiecolt-Glaser & Newton 2001, Uchino et al. 1996), close personal relationships that are chronically abrasive or stressful may provoke depression and other negative emotions as well as persistent immune and endocrine dysregulation.

CONCLUSIONS

We suggest that researchers interested in psychological influences on health should expand their consideration of the range of diseases whose onset and course may be influenced by the immune system; inflammation has recently been linked to a spectrum of conditions associated with aging, including cardiovascular disease, osteoporosis, arthritis, type 2 diabetes, certain lymphoproliferative diseases or cancers, Alzheimer's disease, frailty and functional decline, and periodontal disease (Ershler & Keller 2000). Production of IL-6 and other proinflammatory cytokines that influence these and other conditions can be directly stimulated by negative emotions and stressful experiences, providing one direct pathway from emotions to health. In addition, negative emotions may also contribute to prolonged infection or delayed wound healing, processes that fuel sustained proinflammatory cytokine production. Accordingly, we argue that distress-related immune dysregulation may be one core mechanism behind the health risks associated with negative emotions. These direct and indirect processes pose the greatest health risks for older adults who already show age-related increases in proinflammatory cytokine production. Thus, aging interacts with negative emotions to enhance risks for morbidity and mortality among older adults. Finally, the psychoneuroimmunology literature provides evidence that resources such as close personal relationships or personality and coping styles that diminish negative emotions may enhance health in part through their positive impact on immune and endocrine regulation.

ACKNOWLEDGMENTS

Work on this article was supported by NIH grants K02 MH01467, R37 MH42096, K02 MH01467, PO1 AG16321, P50 DE17811, and T32 MH18831.

Visit the Annual Reviews home page at www.AnnualReviews.org

LITERATURE CITED

Adler N, Boyce T, Chesney M, Cohen S, Folkman S, et al. 1994. Socioeconomic status and health. *Am. Psychol.* 49:15–24

Affleck G, Tennen H, Croog S, Levine S. 1987. Causal attribution, perceived benefits, and morbidity after a heart attack: an 8-year study. *J. Consult. Clin. Psychol.* 55:29–35

Arnetz BB, Brenner SO, Levi L, Hjelm R, Petterson IL, et al. 1991. Neuroendocrine and immunologic effects of unemployment and job insecurity. *Psychother. Psychosom.* 55:76–80

Aspinwall LG, Brunhart SM. 1996. Distinguishing optimism from denial: optimistic beliefs predict attention to health threats. *Pers. Soc. Psychol. Bull.* 22:993–1003

Baron RS, Cutrona CE, Hicklin D, Russell DW, Lubaroff DM. 1990. Social support and immune function among spouses of cancer patients. *J. Pers. Soc. Psychol.* 59:344–52

Baum A, Cohen L, Hall M. 1993. Control and intrusive memories as possible determinants of chronic stress. *Psychosom. Med.* 55:274–86

Beach SRH, Fincham FD, Katz J. 1998. Marital therapy in the treatment of depression: toward a third generation of therapy and research. *Clin. Psychol. Rev.* 18:635–61

Bower JE, Kemeny ME, Taylor SE, Fahey JL. 1998. Cognitive processing, discovery of meaning, CD4 decline, and AIDS-related mortality among bereaved HIV-seropositive men. *J. Consult. Clin. Psychol.* 66:979–86

Burns EA, Goodwin JS. 1990. Immunology and infectious disease. In *Geriatric Medicine*, ed. CK Cassel, DE Risenberg, LB Sorensen, JR Walsh, pp. 312–29. New York: Springer-Verlag

Burton R. 1893. (1621) *The Anatomy of Melancholy*, Vol. I, ed. AR Shilleto. London: Bell & Sons

Cannon J. 1995. Cytokines in aging and muscle homeostasis. *J. Gerontol. A Biol. Sci. Med. Sci.* 50:120–23

Carstensen LL. 1992. Social and emotional patterns in adulthood: support for socioemotional selectivity theory. *Psychol. Aging* 10:331–38

Castle S, Wilkins S, Heck E, Tanzy K, Fahey J. 1995. Depression in caregivers of demented patients is associated with altered immunity: impaired proliferative capacity, increased CD8+, and a decline in lymphocytes with surface signal transduction molecules (CD38) and a cytotoxicity marker (CD56+CD8+). *Clin. Exp. Immunol.* 101:487–93

Catania A, Airaghi L, Motta P, Manfredi MG, Annoni G, et al. 1997. Cytokine antagonists in aged subjects and their relation with cellular immunity. *J. Gerontol. A Biol. Sci.* 52A:B93–97

Christensen AJ, Edwards DL, Wiebe JS, Benotsch EG, McKelvey L, et al. 1996. Effect of verbal self-disclosure on natural killer cell activity: moderating influence of cynical hostility. *Psychosom. Med.* 58:150–55

Coe C. 1993. Psychosocial factors and immunity in nonhuman primates: a review. *Psychosom. Med.* 55:298–308

Cohen HJ, Pieper CF, Harris T, Rao K, Currie MMK. 1997a. The association of plasma IL-6 levels with functional disability in community-dwelling elderly. *J. Gerontol. A Biol. Sci. Med. Sci.* 52:M201–8

Cohen HJ. 2000. Editorial: in search of the underlying mechanisms of frailty. *J. Gerontol. A. Biol. Sci. Med. Sci.* 55:M706–8

Cohen S, Doyle WJ, Skoner DP, Rabin BS, Gwaltney JM. 1997b. Social ties and susceptibility to the common cold. *JAMA* 277:1940–44

Cohen S, Frank E, Doyle WJ, Skoner DP, Rabin BS, Gwaltney JM. 1998. Types of stressors that increase susceptibility to the common cold in healthy adults. *Health Psychol.* 17:214–23

Cole SW, Kemeny ME, Taylor SE. 1997. Social identity and physical health: accelerated HIV progression in rejection-sensitive gay men. *J. Pers. Soc. Psychol.* 72:320–35

Cole SW, Kemeny ME, Taylor SE, Visscher BR, Fahey JL. 1996. Accelerated course of human immunodeficiency virus infection in gay men who conceal their homosexual identity. *Psychosom. Med.* 58:1–13

Coplan JD, Wolk SI, Goetz RR, Ryan ND, Dahl RE, et al. 2000. Nocturnal growth hormone secretion studies in adolescents with or without major depression re-examined: integration of adult follow-up data. *Biol. Psychiatry* 47:594–604

Costello N, Antoni M, Baldewicz T, Lutgendorf S, Klimas N, Schneiderman N. 1998. Coping and emotional expression effects upon distress, illness burden, and cytokines in CFS patients after Hurricane Andrew. *Psychosom. Med.* 60:121–22

Croyle RT. 1998. Depression as a risk factor for cancer: renewing a debate on the psychobiology of disease. *J. Natl. Cancer Inst.* 90:1856–57

Davidson RJ, Pizzagalli D, Nitschke JB, Putnam K. 2001. Depression: perspectives from affective neuroscience. *Annu. Rev. Psychol.* 53:545–74

De Bellis MD, Burke L, Trickett PK, Putnam FW. 1996. Antinuclear antibodies and thyroid function in sexually abused girls. *J. Trauma. Stress* 9:369–78

Denollet J, Brutsaert DL. 1998. Personality, disease severity, and the risk of long-term cardiac events in patients with a decreased ejection fraction after myocardial infarction. *Circulation* 97:167–73

Denollet J, Sys SU, Stroobant N, Rombouts H, Gillebert TC, Brutsaert DL. 1996. Personality as independent predictor of long-term mortality in patients with coronary heart disease. *Lancet* 347:417–21

Dentino AN, Pieper CF, Rao KMK, Currie MS, Harris T, et al. 1999. Association of interleukin-6 and other biologic variables with depression in older people living in the community. *J. Am. Geriatr. Soc.* 47:6–11

DeRijk R, Michelson D, Karp B, Petrides J, Galliven E, et al. 1997. Exercise and circadian rhythm-induced variations in plasma cortisol differentially regulate interleukin-1β (IL-1β), IL-6, and tumor necrosis factor-α (TNF-α) production in humans: high sensitivity of TNF-α and resistance of IL-6. *J. Clin. Endocrinol. Metab.* 82:2182–92

Dhabhar FS, McEwen BS. 1997. Acute stress enhances while chronic stress suppresses cell-mediated immunity *in vivo*: a potential role for leukocyte trafficking. *Brain Behav. Immun.* 11:286–306

Dinan TG. 1998. Psychoneuroendocrinology of depression. *Psychiatr. Clin. North Am.* 21:325–39

Dura J, Stukenberg K, Kiecolt-Glaser JK. 1990. Chronic stress and depressive disorders in older adults. *J. Abnorm. Psychol.* 99:284–90

Eaker ED, Pinsky J, Castelli WP. 1992. Myocardial infarction and coronary death among women: psychosocial predictors from a 20-year follow-up of women in the Framingham Study. *Am. J. Epidemiol.* 135:854–64

Ellsworth PC, Smith C. 1988. Shades of joy: patterns of appraisal differentiating pleasant emotions. *Cogn. Emot.* 2:301–31

Ershler W, Keller E. 2000. Age-associated increased interleukin-6 gene expression, late-life diseases, and frailty. *Annu. Rev. Med.* 51:245–70

Esterling BA, Antoni M, Kumar M, Schneiderman N. 1990. Emotional repression, stress disclosure responses, and Epstein-Barr viral capsid antigen titers. *Psychosom. Med.* 52:397–410

Esterling BA, Kiecolt-Glaser JK, Bodnar J, Glaser R. 1994. Chronic stress, social support, and persistent alterations in the natural killer cell response to cytokines in older adults. *Health Psychol.* 13:291–99

Esterling BA, Kiecolt-Glaser JK, Glaser R. 1996. Psychosocial modulation of cytokine-induced natural killer cell activity in older adults. *Psychosom. Med.* 58:264–72

Everson SA, Kauhanen J, Kaplan GA, Goldberg DE, Julkunen J, et al. 1997. Hostility and increased risk of mortality and acute myocardial infarction: the mediating role of behavioral risk factors. *Am. J. Epidemiol.* 146:142–52

Ferrucci L, Harris T, Guralnik J, Tracy R, Corti M, et al. 1999. Serum IL-6 level and the development of disability in older persons. *J. Am. Geriatr. Soc.* 47:639–46

Fincham FD, Beach SR. 1999. Conflict in marriage: implications for working with couples. *Annu. Rev. Psychol.* 50:47–77

Folkman S, Moskowitz JT. 2000. Positive affect and the other side of coping. *Am. Psychol.* 55:647–54

Frankenhaeuser M. 1986. A psychobiological framework for research on human stress and coping. In *Dynamics of Stress: Physiological, Psychological, and Social Perspectives,* ed. MH Appley, R Trumbull, pp. 101–16. New York: Plenum

Frankenhaeuser M. 1991. The psychophysiology of sex differences as related to occupational status. In *Women, Work, and Health and Opportunities*, ed. M Frankenhaeuser, U Lundberg, M Chesney, pp. 39–61. New York: Plenum

Frasure-Smith N, Lesperance F, Talajic M. 1993. Depression following myocardial infarction: impact on 6-month survival. *JAMA* 270:1819–25

Fredrickson BL. 1998. What good are positive emotions? *Rev. Gen. Psychol.* 2:271–99

Glaser R, Kiecolt-Glaser JK, eds. 1994. *Handbook of Human Stress and Immunity*. San Diego: Academic

Glaser R, Kiecolt-Glaser JK, Bonneau RH, Malarkey W, Kennedy S, Hughes J. 1992. Stress-induced modulation of the immune response to recombinant hepatitis B vaccine. *Psychosom. Med.* 54:22–29

Glaser R, Kiecolt-Glaser JK, Malarkey WB, Sheridan JF. 1998. The influence of psychological stress on the immune response to vaccines. *Ann. NY Acad. Sci.* 840:656–63

Glaser R, Kiecolt-Glaser JK, Marucha PT, MacCallum RC, Laskowski BF, Malarkey WB. 1999a. Stress-related changes in proinflammatory cytokine production in wounds. *Arch. Gen. Psychiatry* 56:450–56

Glaser R, Rabin B, Chesney M, Cohen S, Natelson B. 1999b. Stress-induced immunomodulation—implications for infectious diseases? *JAMA* 281:2268–70

Glaser R, Sheridan JF, Malarkey WB, MacCallum RC, Kiecolt-Glaser JK. 2000. Chronic stress modulates the immune response to a pneumococcal vaccine. *Psychosom. Med.* 62:804–7

Glassman AH, Shapiro PA. 1998. Depression and the course of coronary artery disease. *Am. J. Psychiatry* 155:4–11

Haines AP, Imeson JD, Meade TW. 1987. Phobic anxiety and ischemic heart disease. *Br. Med. J. Clin. Res. Educ.* 295:297–99

Hamerman D. 1999. Toward an understanding of frailty. *Ann. Intern. Med.* 130:945–50

Harris T, Ferrucci L, Tracy R, Corti M, Wacholder S, et al. 1999. Associations of elevated interleukin-6 and C-reactive protein levels with mortality in the elderly. *Am. J. Med.* 106:506–12

Heim C, Ehlert U, Hellhammer D. 2000. The potential role of hypocortisolism in the pathophysiology of stress-related bodily disorders. *Psychoneuroendocrinology* 25:1–35

Herbert TB, Cohen S. 1993. Depression and immunity: a meta-analytic review. *Psychol. Bull.* 113:472–86

Herrmann C, Brand-Driehorst S, Kaminsky B, Leibing E, Staats H, Ruger U. 1998. Diagnostic groups and depressed mood as predictors of 22-month mortality in medical inpatients. *Psychosom. Med.* 60:570–77

Hess EV, Farhey Y. 1994. Epidemiology, genetics, etiology, and environment relationships of systemic lupus erythematosus. *Curr. Opin. Rheumatol.* 6:474–80

Holsboer F, Lauer C, Schreiber W, Krieg J. 1995. Altered hypothalamic-pituitary-adrenocortical regulation in healthy subjects at high familial risk for affective disorders. *Neuroendocrinology* 62:340–47

House JS, Landis KR, Umberson D. 1988. Social relationships and health. *Science* 241:540–45

Hu DJ, Fleming PL, Castro KG, Jones JL, Bush TJ, et al. 1995. How important is race/ethnicity as an indicator of risk for specific AIDS-defining conditions? *J. AIDS Hum. Retrovirol.* 10:374–80

Irwin M, Brown M, Patterson T, Hauger R, Mascovich A, Grant I. 1991. Neuropeptide Y and natural killer cell activity: findings in depression and Alzheimer caregiver stress. *FASEB J.* 5:3100–7

Irwin M, Daniels M, Weiner H. 1987. Immune and neuroendocrine changes during bereavement. *Psychiatr. Clin. North Am.* 10:449–65

Kalman B, Lublin FD. 1999. The genetics of multiple sclerosis: a review. *Biomed. Pharmacother.* 53:358–70

Katon W. 1998. The effect of major depression on chronic medical illness. *Semin. Clin. Neuropsychiatry* 3:82–86

Katz IR. 1996. On the inseparability of mental and physical health in aged persons: lessons from depression and medical comorbidity. *Am. J. Geriatr. Psychiatry* 4:1–16

Kawachi I, Colditz GA, Ascherio A, Rimm EB, Giovannucci E, et al. 1994a. Prospective study of phobic anxiety and risk of coronary heart disease in men. *Circulation* 89:1992–97

Kawachi I, Sparrow D, Vokonas PS, Weiss ST. 1994b. Symptoms of anxiety and risk of coronary heart disease. The Normative Aging Study. *Circulation* 90:2225–29

Kawakami N, Tanigawa T, Araki S, Nakata A, Sakurai S, et al. 1997. Effects of job strain on helper-inducer (CD4+CD29) and suppressor-inducer (CD4+CD45RA) T cells in Japanese blue-collar workers. *Psychother. Psychosom.* 66:192–98

Kemeny ME, Weiner H, Duran R, Taylor SE, Visscher B, Fahey JL. 1995. Immune system changes after the death of a partner in HIV-positive gay men. *Psychosom. Med.* 57:547–54

Kiechl S, Egger G, Mayr M, Wiedermann CJ, Bonora E, et al. 2001. Chronic infections and the risk of carotid atherosclerosis: prospective results from a large population study. *Circulation* 103:1064–70

Kiecolt-Glaser JK, Dura JR, Speicher CE, Trask OJ, Glaser R. 1991. Spousal caregivers of dementia victims: longitudinal changes in immunity and health. *Psychosom. Med.* 53:345–62

Kiecolt-Glaser JK, Fisher LD, Ogrocki P, Stout JC, Speicher CE, Glaser R. 1987. Marital quality, marital disruption, and immune function. *Psychosom. Med.* 49:31–34

Kiecolt-Glaser JK, Glaser R. 1988. Methodological issues in behavioral immunology research with humans. *Brain Behav. Immun.* 2:67–78

Kiecolt-Glaser JK, Glaser R, Caciopp JT, MacCallum RC, Snydersmith M, et al. 1997. Marital conflict in older adults: endocrinological and immunological correlates. *Psychosom. Med.* 59:339–49

Kiecolt-Glaser JK, Glaser R, Gravenstein S,

Malarkey WB, Sheridan J. 1996a. Chronic stress alters the immune response to influenza virus vaccine in older adults. *Proc. Natl Acad. Sci. USA* 93:3043–47

Kiecolt-Glaser JK, Kennedy S, Malkoff S, Fisher L, Speicher CE, Glaser R. 1988. Marital discord and immunity in males. *Psychosom. Med.* 50:213–29

Kiecolt-Glaser JK, Malarkey WB, Chee M, Newton T, Cacioppo JT, et al. 1993. Negative behavior during marital conflict is associated with immunological down-regulation. *Psychosom. Med.* 55:395–409

Kiecolt-Glaser JK, Marucha PT, Malarkey WB, Mercado AM, Glaser R. 1995. Slowing of wound healing by psychological stress. *Lancet* 346:1194–96

Kiecolt-Glaser JK, Newton T. 2001. Marriage and health: his and hers. *Psychol. Bull.* In press

Kiecolt-Glaser JK, Newton T, Cacioppo JT, MacCallum RC, Glaser R, Malarkey WB. 1996b. Marital conflict and endocrine function: Are men really more physiologically affected than women? *J. Consult. Clin. Psychol.* 64:324–32

Kiecolt-Glaser JK, Page GG, Marucha PT, MacCallum RC, Glaser R. 1998. Psychological influences on surgical recovery: perspectives from psychoneuroimmunology. *Am. Psychol.* 53:1209–18

Koenig H, Cohen H, George L, Hays J, Larson D, Blazer D. 1997. Attendance at religious services, interleukin-6, and other biological parameters of immune function in older adults. *Int. J. Psychiatry Med.* 27:233–50

Krantz DS, McCeney MK. 2001. Effects of psychological and social factors on organic disease: a critical assessment of research on coronary heart disease. *Annu. Rev. Psychol.:* 53:341–69

Kronfol Z, Remick DG. 2000. Cytokines and the brain: implications for clinical psychiatry. *Am. J. Psychiatry* 157:683–94

Lemieux A, Coe C. 1995. Abuse-related post-traumatic stress disorder: evidence for chronic neuroendocrine activation in women. *Psychosom. Med.* 57:105–15

Leproult R, Copinschi G, Buxton O, Cauter EV. 1997. Sleep loss results in an elevation of cortisol levels the next evening. *Sleep* 20:865–70

Lerman Y, Melamed S, Shragin Y, Kushnir T, Rotgoltz Y, et al. 1999. Association between burnout at work and leukocyte adhesiveness/aggression. *Psychosom. Med.* 61:828–33

Leventhal H, Patrick-Miller L, Leventhal EA, Burns EA. 1998. Does stress-emotion cause illness in elderly people? In *Annual Review of Gerontology and Geriatrics*, Vol. 17. *Focus on Emotion and Adult Development*, ed. KW Schaie, MP Lawton, pp. 138–84. New York: Springer

Liebeskind JC. 1991. Pain can kill. *Pain* 44:3–4

Lutgendorf SK, Garand L, Buckwalter KC, Reimer TT, Hong S, Lubaroff DM. 1999. Life stress, mood disturbance, and elevated interleukin-6 in healthy older women. *J. Gerontol. A Biol. Sci. Med. Sci.* 54A:M434–39

Maes M, Bosmans E, De Jongh R, Kenis G, Vandoolaeghe E, Neels H. 1995. Increased serum IL-6 and IL-1 receptor antagonist concentrations in major depression and treatment resistant depression. *Cytokine* 9:853–58

Maes M, Lin A, Delmeire L, Van Gastel A, Kenis G, et al. 1999. Elevated serum interleukin-6 (IL-6) and IL-6 receptor concentrations in posttraumatic stress disorder following accidental man-made traumatic events. *Biol. Psychiatry* 45:833–39

Maes M, Song C, Lin A, De JR, Van GA, et al. 1998. The effects of psychological stress on humans: increased production of proinflammatory cytokines and a Th1-like response in stress-induced anxiety. *Cytokine* 10:313–18

Maier SF, Watkins LR. 1998. Cytokines for psychologists: implications of bidirectional immune-to-brain communication for understanding behavior, mood, and cognition. *Psychol. Rev.* 105:83–107

Malarkey W, Kiecolt-Glaser JK, Pearl D, Glaser R. 1994. Hostile behavior during marital conflict alters pituitary and adrenal hormones. *Psychosom. Med.* 56:41–51

Malarkey WB, Wu H, Cacioppo JT, Malarkey KL, Poehlmann KM, et al. 1996. Chronic stress down regulates growth hormone gene expression in peripheral blood mononuclear cells of older adults. *Endocrine* 5:33–39

Marucha PT, Kiecolt-Glaser JK, Favagehi M. 1998. Mucosal wound healing is impaired by examination stress. *Psychosom. Med.* 60:362–65

Maruta T, Colligan RC, Malinchoc M, Offord KP. 2000. Optimists vs pessimists: survival rate among medical patients over a 30-year period. *Mayo Clin. Proc.* 75:140–43

McEwen BS. 1998. Protective and damaging effects of stress mediators. *N. Engl. J. Med.* 338:171–79

Meyerowitz BE, Richardson J, Hudson S, Leedham B. 1998. Ethnicity and cancer outcomes: behavioral and psychosocial considerations. *Psychol. Bull.* 123:47–70

Michelson D, Stratakis C, Hill L, Reynolds J, Galliven E, et al. 1996. Bone mineral density in women with depression. *N. Engl. J. Med.* 335:1176–81

Miller AH. 1998. Neuroendocrine and immune system interactions in stress and depression. *Psychiatr. Clin. North Am.* 21:443–63

Miller TQ, Smith TW, Turner CW, Guijarro ML, Hallet AJ. 1996. A meta-analytic review of research on hostility and physical health. *Psychol. Bull.* 119:322–48

Mills PJ, Yu H, Ziegler MG, Patterson TL, Grant I. 1999. Vulnerable caregivers of patients with Alzheimer's disease have a deficit in circulating CD62L-T lymphocytes. *Psychosom. Med.* 61:168–74

Molassiotis A, Van Den Akker OB, Milligan DW, Goldman JM. 1997. Symptom distress, coping style and biological variables as predictors of survival after bone marrow transplantation. *J. Psychosom. Res.* 42:275–85

Morag M, Morag A, Reichenberg A, Lerer B, Yirmiya R. 1999. Psychological variables as predictors of rubella antibody titers and fatigue—a prospective, double blind study. *J. Psychiatr. Res.* 33:389–95

Myers HF, Kagawa-Singer M, Kumanyika SK, Lex BW, Markides KS. 1995. Panel III. Behavioral risk factors related to chronic diseases in ethnic minorities. *Health Psychol,* 14:613 21

Nolen-Hoeksema S, Larson J, Grayson C. 1999. Explaining the gender difference in depressive symptoms. *J. Pers. Soc. Psychol.* 77:1061–72

Nolen-Hoeksema S, Rusting CL. 1999. Gender differences in well-being. In *Well-being: The Foundations of Hedonic Psychology*, ed. D Kahneman, E Diener, pp. 330–50. New York: Russell Sage Found.

Padgett DA, Marucha PT, Sheridan JF. 1998. Restraint stress slows cutaneous wound healing in mice. *Brain Behav. Immun.* 12:64–73

Papanicolaou DA, Wilder RL, Manolagas SC, Chrousos GP. 1998. The pathophysiologic roles of interleukin-6 in human disease. *Ann. Int. Med.* 128:127–37

Patriarca PA. 1994. A randomized controlled trial of influenza vaccine in the elderly. *JAMA* 272:1700–1

Pennebaker JW, Kiecolt-Glaser JK, Glaser R. 1988. Disclosure of trauma and immune function: health implications for psychotherapy. *J. Consult. Clin. Psychol.* 56:239–45

Penninx BWJH, Guralnik JM, Ferrucci L, Simonsick EM, Deeg DJH, Wallace RB. 1998a. Depressive symptoms and physical decline in community-dwelling older persons. *JAMA* 279:1720–26

Penninx BWJH, Guralnik JM, Pahor M, Ferrucci L, Cerhan JR, et al. 1998b. Chronically depressed mood and cancer risk in older persons. *J. Natl. Cancer Inst.* 90:1888–93

Penninx BWJH, Leveille S, Ferrucci L, van Eijk JTM, Guralnik JM. 1999. Exploring the effect of depression on physical disability: longitudinal evidence from the established populations for epidemiologic studies of the elderly. *Am. J. Public Health* 89:1346–52

Peterson C, Seligman MEP, Vaillant GE. 1988. Pessimistic explanatory style is a risk factor for physical illness: a thirty-five-year longitudinal study. *J. Pers. Soc. Psychol.* 55:23–27

Petrie KJ, Booth RJ, Pennebaker JW, Davison KP, Thomas MG. 1995. Disclosure of trauma and immune response to a hepatitis B vaccination program. *J. Consult. Clin. Psychol.* 63:787–92

Philibert RA, Richards L, Lynch CF, Winokur G. 1997. The effect of gender and age at onset of depression on mortality. *J. Clin. Psychiatry* 58:355–60

Phinney JS. 1996. When we talk about American ethnic groups, what do we mean? *Am. Psychol.* 51:918–27

Pratt LA, Ford DE, Crum RM, Armenian HK, Gallo JJ, Eaton WW. 1996. Depression, psychotropic medication, and risk of myocardial infarction. *Circulation* 94:3123–29

Rabin BS. 1999. *Stress, Immune Function, and Health: The Connection.* New York: Wiley-Liss

Rantanen T, Penninx BWJH, Masaki K, Lintunen T, Foley D, Guralnik JM. 2000. Depressed mood and body mass index as predictors of muscle strength decline in old men. *J. Am. Geriatr. Soc.* 48:613–17

Reed GM, Kemeny ME, Taylor SE, Visscher BR. 1999. Negative HIV-specific expectancies and AIDS-related bereavement as predictors of symptom onset in asymptomatic HIV-positive gay men. *Health Psychol.* 18:354–63

Ridker PM, Cushman M, Stampfer MJ, Tracy RP, Hennekens CH. 1997. Inflammation, aspirin, and the risk of cardiovascular disease in apparently healthy men. *N. Engl. J. Med.* 336:973–79

Rojas I, Padgett DA, Sheridan JF, Marucha PT. 2001. Stress-induced susceptibility to bacterial infection during cutaneous wound healing. *Brain Behav. Immun.* In press

Rozanski A, Blumenthal JA, Kaplan J. 1999. Impact of psychological factors on the pathogenesis of cardiovascular diseases. *Circulation* 99:2192–217

Ryff CD, Singer BS. 1998. The contours of positive human health. *Psychol. Inq.* 9:1–28

Scheier MF, Bridges MW. 1995. Person variables and health: personality predispositions and acute psychological states as shared determinants for disease. *Psychosom. Med.* 57:255–68

Scheier MF, Carver CS. 1992. Effects of optimism on psychological and physical well-being: theoretical overview and empirical update. *Cogn. Ther. Res.* 16:201–28

Scheier MF, Matthews KA, Owens JF, Schulz R, Bridges MW, et al. 1999. Optimism and rehospitalization after coronary artery bypass graft surgery. *Arch. Intern. Med.* 159:829–35

Schleifer SJ, Keller SE, Bond RN, Cohen J, Stein M. 1989. Major depressive disorder and immunity. *Arch. Gen. Psychiatry* 46:81–87

Schleifer SJ, Keller SE, Camerino M, Thorton JC, Stein M. 1983. Suppression of lymphocyte stimulation following bereavement. *JAMA* 250:374–77

Schoevers RA, Geerlings MI, Beekman AT, Penninx BWJH, Deeg DJH, et al. 2000. Association of depression and gender with mortality in old age: results from the Amsterdam Study of the Elderly (AMSTEL). *Br. J. Psychiatry* 177:336–42

Schulz R, Beach SR, Ives DG, Martire LM, Ariyo AA, Kop WJ. 2000. Association between depression and mortality in older adults. *Arch. Intern. Med.* 160:1761–68

Seeman TE, Singer BH, Rowe JW, Horwitz RI, McEwen BS. 1997. Price of adaptation—allostatic load and its health consequences: MacArthur Studies of Successful Aging. *Arch. Intern. Med.* 157:2259–68

Segerstrom SC. 2000. Personality and the immune system: models, methods, and mechanisms. *Ann. Behav. Med.* 22:180–90

Shepperd JA, Maroto JJ, Pbert LA. 1996. Dispositional optimism as a predictor of health changes among cardiac patients. *J. Res. Pers.* 30:517–34

Sheridan JF, Feng N, Bonneau RH, Allen CM, Huneycutt BS, Glaser R. 1991. Restraint-induced stress differentially affects anti-viral cellular and humoral immune responses. *J. Neuroimmunol.* 31:245–55

Sluzewska A, Rybakowski JK, Laciak M, Mackiewicz A, Sobieska M, Wiktorowicz K. 1995. Interleukin-6 serum levels in de-

pressed patients before and after treatment with fluoxetine. *Ann. NY Acad. Sci.* 762:474–76

Staats PS. 1999. Pain, depression and survival. *Am. Fam. Physician* 60:42–43

Sternberg EM. 1997. Emotions and disease: from balance of humors to balance of molecules. *Nat. Med.* 3:264–67

Sternberg EM, Chrousos GP, Wilder RL, Gold PW. 1992. The stress response and the regulation of inflammatory disease. *Ann. Intern. Med.* 117:854–66

Stoney CM, Davis MC, Matthews KA. 1987. Sex differences in physiological responses to stress and in coronary heart disease: a causal link? *Psychophysiology* 24:127–31

Taaffe DR, Harris TB, Ferrucci L, Rowe J, Seeman TE. 2000. Cross-sectional and prospective relationships of interleukin-6 and C-reactive protein with physical performance in elderly persons: MacArthur Studies of Successful Aging. *J. Gerontol. A. Biol. Sci. Med. Sci.* 55:M709–15

Taylor SE. 1983. Adjustment to threatening events: a theory of cognitive adaptation. *Am. Psychol.* 38:1161–73

Taylor SE. 1989. *Positive Illusions: Creative Self-Deception and the Healthy Mind.* New York: Basic Books

Taylor SE, Kemeny ME, Reed GM, Bower JE, Gruenewald TL. 2000a. Psychological resources, positive illusions, and health. *Am. Psychol.* 55:99–109

Taylor SE, Klein LC, Lewis BP, Gruenewald TL, Gurung RAR, Updegraff JA. 2000b. Biobehavioral responses to stress in females: tend-and-befriend, not fight-or-flight. *Psychol. Rev.* 107:411–29

Taylor SE, Repetti RL, Seeman T. 1997. Health psychology: What is an unhealthy environment and how does it get under the skin? *Annu. Rev. Psychol.* 48:411–47

Turk DC, Melzack R. 1992. The measurement of pain and the assessment of people experiencing pain. In *Handbook of Pain Assessment*, ed. DC Turk, R Melzack, pp. 3–12. New York: Guilford

US Dep. Health and Human Services. 1999.

Mental Health: A Report of the Surgeon General. US Dep. Health Hum. Serv., Substance Abuse Mental Health Serv. Admin., Cent. Mental Health Serv., Natl. Inst, Health, Natl. Inst. Mental Health, Rockville, MD

Uchino BN, Cacioppo JT, Kiecolt-Glaser JK. 1996. The relationship between social support and physiological processes: a review with emphasis on underlying mechanisms. *Psychol. Bull.* 119:488–531

Vahtera J, Kivimaki M, Koskenvuo M, Pentti J. 1997. Hostility and registered sickness absences: a prospective study of municipal employees. *Psychol. Med.* 27:693–701

Vedhara K, Cox NKM, Wilcock GK, Perks P, Hunt M, et al. 1999. Chronic stress in elderly carers of dementia patients and antibody response to influenza vaccination. *Lancet* 353:627–31

Veldhuis JD, Iranmanesch A. 1996. Physiological regulation of the human growth hormone (GH)-insulin-like growth factor type I (IGF-I) axis: predominant impact of age, obesity, gonadal function, and sleep. *Sleep* 19:S221–24

Verbrugge LM. 1982. Sex differentials in health. *Public Health Rep.* 97:417–37

Watkins LR, Maier SF. 2000. The pain of being sick: implications of immune-to-brain communication for understanding pain. *Annu. Rev. Psychol.* 51:29–57

Wells KB, Stewart A, Hays RD, Burnam A, Rogers W, et al. 1989. The functioning and well-being of depressed patients. *JAMA* 262: 914–19

Whooley MA, Browner WS. 1998. Association between depressive symptoms and mortality in older women. *Arch. Intern. Med.* 158: 2129–35

Williams DR. 1997. Race and health: basic questions, emerging directions. *Ann. Epidemiol.* 7:322–33

Williams DR, Collins C. 1995. U.S. socioeconomic and racial differences in health: Patterns and Explanations. *Annu. Rev. Sociol.* 21:349–86

Wolkowitz OM, Reus VI. 1999. Treatment of depression with antiglucocorticoid drugs. *Psychosom. Med.* 61:698–711

Wu H, Wang J, Cacioppo JT, Glaser R, Kiecolt-Glaser JK, Malarkey WB. 1999. Chronic stress associated with spousal caregiving of patients with Alzheimer's dementia is associated with down-regulation of B-lymphocyte GH mRNA. *J. Gerontol. A Med. Sci.* 54:M212–15

Wulsin LR, Vaillant GE, Wells VE. 1999. A systematic review of the mortality of depression. *Psychosom. Med.* 61:6–17

Yoshikawa TT. 1983. Geriatric infectious diseases: an emerging problem. *J. Am. Geriatr. Soc.* 31:34–39

Zautra AJ, Hoffman JM, Matt KS, Yocum D, Potter PT, et al. 1998. An examination of individual differences in the relationship between interpersonal stress and disease activity among women with rheumatoid arthritis. *Arthritis Care Res.* 11:271–79

Zhou D, Kusnecov AW, Shurin MR, DePaoli M, Rabin BS. 1993. Exposure to physical and psychological stressors elevates plasma interleukin 6: relationship to the activation of hypothalamic-pituitary-adrenal axis. *Endocrinology* 133:2523–30

Annu. Rev. Psychol. 2002. 53:109–32

MOTIVATIONAL BELIEFS, VALUES, AND GOALS

Jacquelynne S. Eccles and Allan Wigfield

Institute for Social Research, University of Michigan, Ann Arbor, Michigan 48106;
e-mail: jeccles@isr.umich.edu

Key Words   expectancies, task value, goal theory, efficacy, volition, self-regulation

■ **Abstract**   This chapter reviews the recent research on motivation, beliefs, values, and goals, focusing on developmental and educational psychology. The authors divide the chapter into four major sections: theories focused on expectancies for success (self-efficacy theory and control theory), theories focused on task value (theories focused on intrinsic motivation, self-determination, flow, interest, and goals), theories that integrate expectancies and values (attribution theory, the expectancy-value models of Eccles et al., Feather, and Heckhausen, and self-worth theory), and theories integrating motivation and cognition (social cognitive theories of self-regulation and motivation, the work by Winne & Marx, Borkowski et al., Pintrich et al., and theories of motivation and volition). The authors end the chapter with a discussion of how to integrate theories of self-regulation and expectancy-value models of motivation and suggest new directions for future research.

CONTENTS

0084-6570/02/0201-0109$14.00

OVERVIEW

The Latin root of the word "motivation" means "to move"; hence, in this basic sense the study of motivation is the study of action. Modern theories of motivation focus more specifically on the relation of beliefs, values, and goals with action. In this chapter we review the work growing out of these theories of achievement motivation with a particular emphasis on developmental and educational psychology. Furthermore, although motivation theories have emerged from different intellectual traditions (Weiner 1992), we focus on those that are most closely linked to expectancy-value models of behavior. Expectancies refer to beliefs about how one will do on different tasks or activities, and values have to do with incentives or reasons for doing the activity. We use this perspective to organize our presentation, by grouping motivational theories into four broad categories. The first focuses on beliefs about competence and expectancy for success. The second focuses on the reasons why individuals engage in different activities; these theories include constructs such as achievement values, intrinsic and extrinsic motivation, interests, and goals. The third integrates expectancy and value constructs. The fourth draws links between motivational and cognitive processes. We consider each perspective in turn.

THEORIES FOCUSED ON EXPECTANCY

Several theories focus on individuals' beliefs about their competence and efficacy, expectancies for success or failure, and sense of control over outcomes; these beliefs are directly related to the question, "Can I do this task?". In general, when people answer this question affirmatively they perform better and are motivated to select more challenging tasks.

Self-Efficacy Theory

Bandura (1997) proposed a social cognitive model of motivation focused on the role of perceptions of efficacy and human agency. Bandura defined self-efficacy as individuals' confidence in their ability to organize and execute a given course of action to solve a problem or accomplish a task; he characterized it as a multidimensional construct that varies in strength, generality, and level (or difficulty). Thus, some people have a strong sense of self-efficacy and others do not; some have efficacy beliefs that encompass many situations, whereas others have narrow efficacy beliefs; and some believe they are efficacious even on the most difficult tasks, whereas others belief they are efficacious only on easier tasks.

As in expectancy-value theory and attribution theory, Bandura's self-efficacy theory focuses on expectancies for success. However, Bandura distinguished between two kinds of expectancy beliefs: outcome expectations—beliefs that certain behaviors will lead to certain outcomes (e.g., the belief that practicing will improve one's performance)—and efficacy expectations—beliefs about whether one can effectively perform the behaviors necessary to produce the outcome (e.g., "I can practice sufficiently hard to win the next tennis match"). These two kinds of expectancy beliefs are different because individuals can believe that a certain behavior will produce a certain outcome (outcome expectation), but may not believe they can perform that behavior (efficacy expectation). Indeed, Bandura proposed that individuals' efficacy expectations are the major determinant of goal setting, activity choice, willingness to expend effort, and persistence.

The self-efficacy construct has been applied to behavior in many domains including school, health, sports, therapy, and even snake phobia (see Bandura 1997). By and large, the evidence is very supportive of the theoretical predictions. For example, high personal academic expectations predict subsequent performance, course enrollment, and occupational aspirations choice (see Bandura 1997, Bandura et al. 2001).

Control Theories

Locus of control theories are another type of expectancy-based theory (Crandall et al. 1965, Rotter 1966). According to these theories, one should expect to succeed to the extent that one feels in control of one's successes and failures (i.e., one has an internal locus of control). Evidence supports this prediction (see Findley & Cooper 1983, Weisz 1984). Recent locus of control theorists have elaborated broader conceptual models of control. Connell (1985), for example, added *unknown control* as a third control belief category and argued that younger children are particularly likely to use this category. He also demonstrated that not knowing the cause of one's successes and failures undermines one's motivation to work on the associated tasks.

Connell & Wellborn (1991) also integrated control beliefs into a broader theoretical framework in which they proposed three basic psychological needs: competence, autonomy, and relatedness. They linked control beliefs to competence needs: Children who believe they control their achievement outcomes should feel more competent. They hypothesized that the extent to which these needs are fulfilled is influenced by following characteristics of their family, peer, and school contexts: the amount of structure, the degree of autonomy provided, and the level of involvement in the children's activities. Finally, they proposed that the ways in which these needs are fulfilled determine engagement in different activities. When the needs are fulfilled, children will be fully engaged. When one or more of the needs is not fulfilled, children will become disaffected and unmotivated (see Connell et al. 1994, Skinner & Belmont 1993 for supportive evidence).

Ellen Skinner and her colleagues (e.g., Skinner 1995, Skinner et al. 1998) proposed a more elaborate model of perceived control. Focusing on understanding goal-directed activity, Skinner described three critical beliefs: means-ends beliefs, control beliefs, and agency beliefs. Means-ends beliefs concern the expectation that particular causes can produce certain outcomes; these causes include causal attributions (Weiner 1985) and unknown control. Agency beliefs are the expectations that one has access to the means needed to produce various outcomes. Control beliefs are the expectations individuals have that they can produce desired events. All three sets of beliefs influence performance on achievement tasks. Skinner et al. (1998) charted the development of these beliefs over the school years and looked at relations of children's perceived control to the ways children perceived that teachers treated them. Children who believed teachers were warm and supportive developed a more positive sense of their control over outcomes.

THEORIES FOCUSED ON THE REASONS FOR ENGAGEMENT

Although theories dealing with competence, expectancy, and control beliefs provide powerful explanations of individuals' performance on different kinds of achievement tasks, these theories do not systematically deal with the reasons individuals have for engaging in different achievement tasks. Even if people are certain they can do a task, they may have no compelling reason to do it. The theories presented in this section focus on the question of why.

Intrinsic Motivation Theories

Several theories focus on the distinction between intrinsic and extrinsic motivation (see Sansone & Harackiewicz 2000). When individuals are intrinsically motivated, they engage in an activity because they are interested in and enjoy the activity. When extrinsically motivated, individuals engage in activities for instrumental or other reasons, such as receiving a reward.

SELF-DETERMINATION THEORY   Given the growing evidence that extrinsic incentives and pressures can undermine motivation to perform even inherently interesting activities, Deci & Ryan (1985) proposed self-determination theory in which they integrated two perspectives on human motivation: (*a*) Humans are motivated to maintain an optimal level of stimulation (Hebb 1955), and (*b*) humans have basic needs for competence (White 1959) and personal causation or self-determination (deCharms 1968). They argued that people seek out optimal stimulation and challenging activities and find these activities intrinsically motivating because they have a basic need for competence. In addition, they argued that intrinsic motivation is maintained only when actors feel competent and self-determined. Evidence that intrinsic motivation is reduced by exerting external control and by giving negative competence feedback supports this hypothesis (see Cameron & Pierce 1994, Deci & Ryan 1985, Deci et al. 1999).

Deci & Ryan (1985) also argued that the basic needs for competence and self-determination play a role in more extrinsically motivated behavior. Consider, for example, a student who consciously and without any external pressure selects a specific major because it will help him earn a lot of money. This student is guided by his basic needs for competence and self-determination, but his choice of major is based on reasons totally extrinsic to the major itself. Finally, Deci & Ryan (1985) postulated that a basic need for interpersonal relatedness explains why people turn external goals into internal goals through internalization.

Deci, Ryan, and their colleagues (see Ryan & Deci 2000) have extended the extrinsic-intrinsic motivation dichotomy in their discussion of internalization—the process of transferring the regulation of behavior from outside to inside the individual. When individuals are self-determined, their reasons for engaging in behavior are fully internalized (see Grolnick et al. 2000 for discussion of the development of self-regulation). Deci and colleagues defined several levels in the process of going from external to internalized regulation. These are *external* (regulation coming from outside the individual); *introjected* (internal regulation based on feelings that one has to do the behavior); *identified* [internal regulation based on the utility of that behavior (e.g., studying hard to get grades to get into college)]; and *integrated* (regulation based on what the individual thinks is valuable and important to the self). Even this last level, however, is not fully internalized and self-determined.

FLOW THEORY   Csikszentmihalyi (1988) defined intrinsically motivated behavior in terms of the immediate subjective experience that occurs when people are engaged in an activity. Expert climbers, dancers, chess players, basketball players, and composers describe their experiences when fully engaged in terms of an emotional state Csikszentmihalyi labeled "flow," characterized by (*a*) a holistic feeling of being immersed in, and carried by, an activity; (*b*) a merging of action and awareness; (*c*) focus of attention on a limited stimulus field; (*d*) lack of self-consciousness; and (*e*) feeling in control of one's actions and the environment. Flow is only possible when a person feels that the opportunities for action in a given situation match his or her ability to master the challenges. The challenge of an activity may be concrete or physical like the peak of a mountain to be scaled or abstract and symbolic like a set of musical notes to be performed, a story to be written, or a puzzle to be solved. Recent research has shown that both the challenges and skills must be relatively high before a flow experience becomes possible (Massimini & Carli 1988).

At first sight, the theories of Deci & Ryan and Csikszentmihalyi seem to be very different. Deci & Ryan (1985) conceptualize intrinsic motivation in terms of innate, basic needs, whereas Csikszentmihalyi stresses subjective experience. We suggest, however, that this difference reflects two sides of the same coin. As Schneider (2001) has argued, one has to distinguish between immediate reasons (e.g., enjoyment) and ultimate reasons of behavior (e.g., survival). Intrinsically motivated behavior can be conducive to ultimate goals even though the actor is only motivated by immediate incentives. A typical case is exploratory or play behavior. Both types of behavior help to increase an individual's competence, but they are usually performed because they are exciting, pleasurable, or enjoyable. This distinction between immediate and ultimate causes of behavior makes it possible to reconcile the positions of Deci & Ryan and Csikszentmihalyi. Deci & Ryan (1985) focus on ultimate reasons of behavior, whereas Csikszentmihalyi (1988) focuses mainly on immediate reasons. Csikszentmihalyi & Massimini (1985) have suggested that the experience of flow is a reward that ensures that individuals will seek to increase their competence. According to Csikszentmihalyi, the repeated experience of flow is only possible when individuals seek out increasingly challenging tasks and expand their competencies to meet these challenges. Thus, the experience of flow should reinforce behaviors underlying development.

INDIVIDUAL DIFFERENCE THEORIES OF INTRINSIC MOTIVATION   Until recently, intrinsic motivation researchers have focused primarily on conditions, components, and consequences of intrinsic motivation without making a distinction between intrinsic motivation as a state versus intrinsic motivation as a traitlike characteristic. However, interest in traitlike individual differences in intrinsic motivation is increasing, particularly among educational and sport psychologists (see Amabile et al. 1994; Gottfried 1990; Nicholls 1984, Nicholls et al. 1990). These researchers define this enduring intrinsic motivational orientation in terms of (*a*) preference for hard or challenging tasks, (*b*) learning that is driven by curiosity or interest, and (*c*) striving for competence and mastery. The second component is most central to the idea of intrinsic motivation. Both preference for hard tasks and striving for competence can be linked to either extrinsic or more general need-achievement motivation. Nonetheless, empirical findings suggest that the three components are highly correlated. In addition, evidence suggests that high levels of traitlike intrinsic motivation facilitate positive emotional experience (Matsumoto & Sanders 1988), mastery-oriented coping with failure, high academic achievement (Benware & Deci 1984), and use of appropriate learning strategies (Pintrich & Schrauben 1992).

Interest Theories

There has been a recent upsurge in work on the concept of "interest" (e.g., Alexander et al. 1994, Hidi & Harackiewicz 2001, Schiefele 1999). These researchers differentiate between individual and situational interest. Individual interest is a relatively stable evaluative orientation towards certain domains; situational interest is an emotional state aroused by specific features of an activity or a task. Two aspects or components of individual interest are distinguishable (Schiefele 1999): feeling-related and value-related valences. Feeling-related valences refer to the feelings that are associated with an object or an activity—feelings such as involvement, stimulation, or flow. Value-related valences refer to the attribution of personal significance or importance to an object or activity. In addition, both feeling-related and value-related valences are directly related to the object or activity rather than to the relation of this object or activity to other objects or events. For example, if students associate mathematics with high personal significance because mathematics can help them get prestigious jobs, then we would not speak of interest. Although feeling-related and value-related valences are highly correlated (Schiefele 1999), it is useful to differentiate between them because some individual interests are likely based primarily on feelings, whereas other interests are more likely to be based on personal significance (see Eccles et al. 1998b, Wigfield & Eccles 1992).

Much research on individual interest has focused on its relation to the quality of learning (see Alexander et al. 1994, Renninger et al. 1992, Schiefele 1999). In general, there are significant but moderate relations between interest and text learning. More importantly, interest is more strongly related to indicators of deep-level learning (e.g., recall of main ideas, coherence of recall, responding to deeper comprehension questions, representation of meaning) than to surface-level learning (e.g., responding to simple questions, verbatim representation of text) (Schiefele 1999).

Most of the research on situational interest has focused on the characteristics of academic tasks that create interest (e.g., Hidi & Baird 1986). The following text features have been found to arouse situational interest and promote text comprehension and recall: personal relevance, novelty, activity level, and comprehensibility (Hidi & Baird 1986; see Schiefele 1999).

Goal Theories

Motivation researchers have become very interested in children's achievement goals and their relation to achievement behavior (see Ames 1992, Anderman et al. 2001, Covington 2000, Dweck 1999, Pintrich 2000b). Several different approaches have emerged. For instance, Bandura (1997) and Schunk (1990) have shown that specific, proximal, and somewhat challenging goals promote both self-efficacy and improved performance. Other researchers have defined and investigated broader goal orientations (e.g., Ames 1992, Blumenfeld 1992, Butler 1993, Dweck 1999, Nicholls 1984). For example, Nicholls and his colleagues (e.g., Nicholls et al. 1990) defined two major kinds of motivationally relevant goal patterns or orientations: ego-involved goals and task-involved goals. Individuals with ego-involved goals seek to maximize favorable evaluations of their competence and minimize negative evaluations of competence. Questions like "Will I look smart?" and "Can I outperform others?" reflect ego-involved goals. In contrast, with task-involved goals, individuals focus on mastering tasks and increasing their competence. Questions such as "How can I do this task?" and "What will I learn?" reflect task-involved goals. Dweck and her colleagues provided a complementary analysis (see Dweck 1999) distinguishing between performance goals (like ego-involved goals) and learning goals (like task-involved goals). Similarly, Ames (1992) distinguished between the association of performance goals (like ego-involved goals) and mastery goals (like task-focused goals) with both performance and task choice. With ego-involved (or performance) goals, children try to outperform others, and are more likely to perform tasks they know they can do. Task-involved (or mastery-oriented) children choose challenging tasks and are more concerned with their own progress than with outperforming others.

An important advance in this area is the distinction between performance-approach and performance-avoid goals (Elliott & Church 1997, Midgley et al. 1998, Skaalvik 1997). This distinction arose in part because of some inconsistent evidence about the effects of performance goals on various outcomes. As the name implies, performance-approach goals imply engagement in achievement tasks for performance reasons, whereas performance-avoid goals concern disengagement in order not to appear stupid. Generally, performance-approach goals appear to have more positive consequences on motivation and achievement than do performance-avoid goals (see Anderman et al. 2001 for review). However, there is some disagreement among goal theories about the positive consequences of performance-approach goals (see Midgley et al. 2001). This distinction is quite similar to the distinction originally made by Atkinson (1964) between the approach and avoidance components of need-achievement motivation.

Other researchers (e.g., Ford 1992, Wentzel 1991) have adopted a more complex perspective on goals and motivation, arguing that there are many different kinds of goals individuals can have in achievement settings. For example, Ford proposed a complex theory based on the assumption that humans are goal directed and self-organized (e.g., Ford 1992, Ford & Nichols 1987). He defined goals as desired end states people try to attain through the cognitive, affective, and biochemical regulation of their behavior. Furthermore, Ford viewed goals as only one part of motivation; in his model motivation is defined as the product of goals, emotions, and personal agency beliefs.

Although Ford and Nichols (Ford 1992, Ford & Nichols 1987) outlined an extensive taxonomy of goals, they distinguished most broadly between within-person goals (desired within-person consequences) and person-environment goals (desired relationship between the person and their environment). Similar to Rokeach's (1979) human values and Eccles' (1987) attainment value, the within-person goals include affective goals (e.g., happiness, physical well-being), cognitive goals (e.g., exploration, intellectual creativity), and subjective organization goals (e.g., unity, transcendence). The person-environment goals include self-assertive goals such as self-determination and individuality, integrative social relationship goals such as belonging and social responsibility, and task goals such as mastery, material gain, and safety. Although Ford & Nichols (1987) developed measures to assess all 24 goals specified in Ford's model, their evidence suggests that people typically rely on a much smaller cluster of core goals in regulating their behavior. Ford (1992) also developed an important set of principles for optimizing motivation, based on the tenets of his theory.

Wentzel (e.g., 1991, 1993) has examined the multiple goals of adolescents in achievement settings. Wentzel's view on goals differs from the views of theorists like Dweck and Nichols in that she focuses on the content of children's goals, rather than on mastery versus performance criteria of success. Wentzel has demonstrated that both social and academic goals relate to adolescents' school performance and behavior (see Juvonen & Wentzel 1996 for social goals and social motivation). For instance, Wentzel (1991) has found that the goals related to school achievement include seeing oneself as successful, dependable, wanting to learn new things, and wanting to get things done. Higher-achieving students have higher levels of both social responsibility and achievement goals than lower-achieving students (Wentzel 1993, 1994). Similarly, Wentzel (1994) documented the association among middle school children's prosocial goals of helping others, academic prosocial goals such as sharing learning with classmates, peer social responsibility goals such as following through on promises made to peers, and academic social responsibility goals such as following the teacher's instructions. Prosocial goals (particularly academic prosocial goals) related positively to peer acceptance. Interestingly, academic responsibility goals related negatively to peer acceptance but positively to acceptance by teachers. Further, positive prosocial and academic goals related positively to prosocial behaviors (as rated by teachers) and negatively to irresponsible behaviors. Finally, the pursuit of positive social goals was facilitated by perceived support from teachers and peers.

THEORIES INTEGRATING EXPECTANCY
AND VALUE CONSTRUCTS

Attribution Theory

Weiner's attribution theory has been a major theory of motivation for the past 30 years (see Graham 1991, Weiner 1985). We place this theory in this section for two reasons: First, Weiner was a student of Atkinson, who developed the expectancy-value model of achievement motivation. Weiner always has acknowledged his connection to Atkinson's framework, although his attribution model departs from Atkinson's model in many ways. Second, attribution models include beliefs about ability and expectancies for success, along with incentives for engaging in different activities, including valuing of achievement (see Graham & Taylor 2001).

Fundamentally, attribution theorists emphasize that individuals' interpretations of their achievement outcomes, rather than motivational dispositions or actual outcomes, determine subsequent achievement strivings. Weiner argued that the individual's causal attributions (or explanations) for achievement outcomes determine subsequent achievement strivings and, thus, are key motivational beliefs.

Weiner and his colleagues (see Weiner 1992) identified ability, effort, task difficulty, and luck as the most important achievement attributions. They classified these attributions into three causal dimensions: locus of control, stability, and controllability. The locus of control dimension has two poles: internal versus external locus of control. The stability dimension captures whether causes change over time or not. For instance, ability was classified as a stable, internal cause, and effort was classified as unstable and internal. Controllability contrasts causes one can control, such as skill/efficacy, from causes one cannot control, such as aptitude, mood, others' actions, and luck.

Weiner and his colleagues (see Weiner 1985, 1992) demonstrated that each of these causal dimensions has unique influences on various aspects of achievement behavior. The stability dimension influences individuals' expectancies for success: Attributing an outcome to a stable cause such as ability or skill has a stronger influence on expectancies for future success than attributing an outcome to an unstable cause such as effort. The locus of control dimension is linked most strongly to affective reactions. For instance, attributing success to an internal cause enhances one's pride or self-esteem, but attributing that success to an external cause enhances one's gratitude; attributing failure to internal causes is linked to shame, but attributing it to external causes is linked to anger. Weiner also argued that each dimension has important affective consequences.

Modern Expectancy-Value Theory

Modern expectancy-value theories (e.g., Eccles 1987; Eccles et al. 1983; Wigfield & Eccles 1992, 2001, Feather 1988) are based in Atkinson's (1964) expectancy-value model in that they link achievement performance, persistence, and choice most directly to individuals' expectancy-related and task-value beliefs. However, they differ from Atkinson's expectancy-value theory in several ways. First, both the expectancy and value components are more elaborate and are linked to a broader array of psychological and social/cultural determinants. Second, expectancies and values are assumed to be positively related to each other, rather than inversely related, as proposed by Atkinson.

THE ECCLES ET AL. EXPECTANCY-VALUE MODEL   Eccles and her colleagues have elaborated and tested an expectancy-value model of achievement-related choices (e.g., Eccles et al. 1983, 1984; Meece et al. 1990). In this model choices are assumed to be influenced by both negative and positive task characteristics, and all choices are assumed to have costs associated with them precisely because one choice often eliminates other options. Consequently, the relative value and probability of success of various options are key determinants of choice.

The most recent version of this model is depicted in Figure 1. Expectancies and values are assumed to directly influence performance, persistence, and task choice. Expectancies and values are assumed to be influenced by task-specific beliefs such as perceptions of competence, perceptions of the difficulty of different tasks, and individuals' goals and self-schema. These social cognitive variables, in turn, are influenced by individuals' perceptions of other peoples' attitudes and expectations for them, by their affective memories, and by their own interpretations of their previous achievement outcomes. Individuals' task perceptions and interpretations

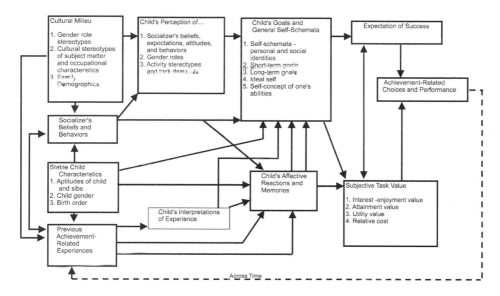

Figure 1   The Eccles et al. expectancy-value model of achievement.

of their past outcomes are assumed to be influenced by socializer's behavior and beliefs and by cultural milieu and unique historical events.

Eccles and colleagues defined expectancies for success as individuals' beliefs about how well they will do on upcoming tasks, either in the immediate or longer-term future. These expectancy beliefs are measured in a manner analogous to measures of Bandura's (1997) personal efficacy expectations. Thus, in contrast to Bandura's claim that expectancy-value theories focus on outcome expectations, the focus in this model is on personal or efficacy expectations.

Eccles et al. (1983) defined beliefs about ability as individuals' evaluations of their competence in different areas. In the expectancy-value model ability beliefs are conceived as broad beliefs about competence in a given domain, in contrast to one's expectancies for success on a specific upcoming task. However, their empirical work has shown that children and adolescents do not distinguish between these two different levels of beliefs. Apparently, even though these constructs can be theoretically distinguished from each other, in real-world achievement situations they are highly related and empirically indistinguishable.

Eccles et al. (1983) outlined four components of task-value: attainment value, intrinsic value, utility value, and cost. Like Battle (1966), they defined attainment value as the personal importance of doing well on the task. Drawing on self-schema and identity theories (e.g., Markus & Wurf 1987), they also linked attainment value to the relevance of engaging in a task for confirming or disconfirming salient aspects of one's self-schema (i.e., because tasks provide the opportunity to demonstrate aspects of one's actual or ideal self-schema, such as masculinity, femininity, and/or competence in various domains, tasks will have higher attainment value to the extent that they allow the individual to confirm salient aspects of these self-schemata). This component of value relates most directly to the perspective on values espoused by Feather (1988) and Rokeach (1979).

Intrinsic value is the enjoyment the individual gets from performing the activity or the subjective interest the individual has in the subject. This component of value is similar to the construct of intrinsic motivation as defined by Harter (1981), and by Deci and his colleagues (e.g., Deci & Ryan 1985), and to the constructs of interest and flow as defined by Csikszentmihalyi (1988), Renninger (Renninger et al. 1992), and Schiefele (1999).

Utility value is determined by how well a task relates to current and future goals, such as career goals. A task can have positive value to a person because it facilitates important future goals, even if he or she is not interested in the task for its own sake. For instance, students often take classes they do not particularly enjoy but that they need to take to pursue other interests, to please their parents, or to be with their friends. In one sense then this component captures the more "extrinsic" reasons for engaging in a task (see Deci & Ryan 1985, Harter 1981). However, it also relates directly to an individual's internalized short- and long-term goals.

Finally, Eccles and her colleagues identified cost as a critical component of value (Eccles et al. 1983, Eccles 1987). Cost is conceptualized in terms of the negative aspects of engaging in the task, such as performance anxiety and fear of both failure and success, as well as the amount of effort needed to succeed and the lost opportunities that result from making one choice rather than another.

Eccles and her colleagues have shown that ability self-concepts and performance expectancies predict performance in mathematics and English, whereas task values predict course plans and enrollment decisions in mathematics, physics, and English and involvement in sport activities even after controlling for prior performance levels (Eccles 1987, Eccles et al. 1983, Eccles et al. 1984, Meece et al. 1990). They have also shown that both expectancies and values predict career choices (see Eccles et al. 1998a). These findings suggest a possible modification to the model in Figure 1, in which direct paths are drawn from both expectancies and values to performance, persistence, and choice. These results suggest reconsidering the paths from expectancies to choice once prior achievement level is controlled, and from values to performance (see Wigfield & Eccles 1992).

An important question is how people's competence beliefs relate to their subjective task values. According to both the Eccles et al. model and Bandura's (1997) self-efficacy theory, ability self-concepts should influence the development of task values. In support, Mac Iver et al. (1991) found that changes in junior high school students' competence beliefs over a semester predicted change in children's interest much more strongly than vice versa. Does the same causal ordering occur in younger children? Bandura (1997) argued that interests emerge out of one's sense of self-efficacy and that children should be more interested in challenging than in easy tasks. Taking a more developmental perspective, Wigfield (1994) proposed that initially, young children's competence and task-value beliefs are likely to be relatively independent of each other. Over time, particularly in the achievement domain, children may begin to attach more value to activities in which they do well, for two reasons: First, through processes associated with classical conditioning, the positive effect one experiences when one does well should become attached to the successful activities (see Eccles et al. 1983). Second, lowering the value one attaches to difficult activities is likely to be an effective way to maintain a positive global sense of efficacy and self-esteem (see Eccles et al. 1998b, Harter 1990). Thus, at some point competence-related beliefs and values should become positively related to one another; Wigfield et al. (1997) demonstrated this empirically.

FEATHER'S WORK ON VALUES   Feather (e.g., 1988, 1992) extended Atkinson's original expectancy-value model in important ways by broadening the conceptualization of value. Drawing on Rokeach's (1979) work, he defined values as a set of stable, general beliefs about what is desirable and postulated that these beliefs emerge from both society's norms and the individual's core psychological needs and sense of self. He integrated Rokeach's approach to values into the expectancy-value approach to need-achievement by arguing that values are one class of motives that lead individuals to perform acts they think should be done. Individuals' values influence the attractiveness of different goal objects and, consequently, the motivation to attain these goals. Feather (1988, 1992) has confirmed these ideas for several types of behavior including joining political action groups and selecting academic majors. In addition, he found that values and ability perceptions are positively rather than inversely related, suggesting that values are determined by influences other than just the difficulty of the task—influences such as the features of the goal object itself, the valence of success and failure to the individual, and the probability of succeeding on the task. He also concluded that we know little about the origins of these task values.

HECKHAUSEN'S EXPECTANCY-VALUE MODEL   In his general expectancy-value model, Heckhausen (see 1991) attempted to integrate a number of different approaches to motivation. The resulting model distinguished between four different types of expectancies: situation-outcome (subjective probability of attaining an outcome in a specific situation without acting), action-outcome (subjective probability of attaining an outcome by one's actions), action-by-situation-outcome (subjective probability that situational factors facilitate or impede one's action-outcome expectancy), and outcome-consequence (subjective probability of an outcome to be associated with a specific consequence). It is important to note that in Heckhausen's model outcomes are the immediate results of one's actions. These immediate results are or are not followed by various consequences (e.g., self-evaluation, external evaluation). They do not have any incentive value on their own. Incentive value is only attributed to the consequences of one's actions. Therefore, the motivation to act depends mainly on the value attached to the consequences of one's behavior.

In sum, expectancy-value models continue to be prominent. The most important contributions of the contemporary models are the elaboration of the values construct and the discussion of whether expectancies and values relate differentially to performance and choice. More work is needed on how the links of expectancies and values to performance and choice change across ages (see Eccles et al. 1993, Wigfield 1994) and on the links between expectancies and values.

Like attribution theory, goal theory, and self-efficacy theory, modern expectancy-value theory can be criticized for emphasizing the rational cognitive processes leading to motivation and behavior. For example, Fischoff et al. (1982) argued that the logical, rational decision-making processes of determining expectancies and valences are often not used because people prefer simpler, but more fallible and optimistic, decision-making strategies. They also argued that task values shift fairly rapidly, particularly for unfamiliar tasks. These criticisms are likely to be particularly à propos when these models are considered from a developmental perspective (see Wigfield 1994). However, the impressive body of research showing the relations of expectancy and values to different kinds of performance and choice supports the continuing viability of these models. Furthermore, as conceptualized by Eccles and her colleagues, values are linked to more stable self-schema and identity constructs and choice is not necessarily the result of conscious rational decision-making processes (see Eccles 1987, Eccles & Harold 1992). By including affective memories, culturally based stereotypes, and identity-related constructs and processes as part of the theoretical system, Eccles and her colleagues have included less rational processes in motivated behavioral choices.

Self-Worth Theory

Before leaving the straight motivation theories, we want to add one more that is not easily classifiable in terms of expectancies and values. We include it in this section because it does link ability-related and value-related constructs to motivated behavior in academic settings. In addition, however, it focuses on mental health as a key determinant of the relation of expectancies and values to achievement behaviors.

In his self-worth theory, Covington (see 1992, 1998) defined the motive for self-worth as the tendency to establish and maintain a positive self-image, or sense of self-worth. Because children spend so much time in classrooms and are evaluated so frequently there, Covington argued that a key way to maintain a sense of self-worth is to protect one's sense of academic competence. That is, children need to believe they are academically competent in order to think they have worth as a person in the school context. Therefore, children will try to maximize, or at least protect, their sense of academic competence in order to maintain their self-worth. One way to accomplish this is by making causal attributions that enhance one's sense of academic competence and control. Covington & Omelich (1979) demonstrated that both college students' and younger individuals' most-preferred attributions for success are ability and effort; the most-preferred attribution for failure was not trying. Attributing failure to lack of ability was a particularly problematic attribution that students preferred to avoid.

However, school evaluation, competition, and social comparison make it difficult for many children to maintain the belief that they are competent academically. Covington (1992) discussed the strategies many children develop to avoid appearing to lack ability. These include procrastination, making excuses, avoiding challenging tasks, and perhaps most important, not trying. Covington & Omelich (1979) referred to effort as a "double-edged sword," because although trying is important for success (and is encouraged by both teachers and parents), if children try and fail, it is difficult to escape the conclusion that they lack ability. Therefore, if failure seems likely, some children will not try, precisely because trying and failing threatens their ability self-concepts. Covington called such strategies "failure avoiding strategies." Furthermore, Covington discussed how even high-achieving students can be failure avoidant. Rather than responding to a challenging task with greater effort, these students may try to avoid the task in order to maintain both their own sense of competence, and others' conclusions regarding their competence. Covington (1992) suggested that reducing the frequency and salience of competitive, social comparative, and evaluative practices, and focusing instead on effort, mastery, and improvement, would allow more children to maintain their self-worth without having to resort to these failure-avoiding strategies (see Covington 1998 for further suggestions on how to enhance students' motivation). Recent school reform efforts support these suggestions (e.g., Ames 1992, Maehr & Midgley 1996).

Some work in the self-concept area, however, raises questions about Covington's contention that academic competence beliefs are the strongest determinant of self-worth. For example, Harter (1990) has shown that self-concepts regarding physical appearance and social competence more strongly predict self-worth than academic self-concepts (see Harter 1998). Perhaps academic self-competence is not as strong a predictor of self-worth as Covington claims for all individuals. In fact, several investigations suggest that the power of any particular self-concept to influence one's self-worth is dependent on the value one attaches to this competence domain and that people may reduce the value they attach to those tasks at which they expect to fail in order to maintain their sense of self-worth (e.g., Eccles 1993, Harter 1998).

THEORIES INTEGRATING MOTIVATION AND COGNITION

Motivation theorists increasingly are interested in the ways in which motivation and cognition work together. One large body of this work concerns how individuals regulate their behavior to meet their learning goals (see Boekaerts et al. 2000, Schunk & Zimmerman 1994). Other theorists have studied the links between motivation and the use of various cognitive strategies (e.g., Alexander et al. 1994,

Pintrich et al. 1993). Furthermore, theorists such as Kuhl (1987) and Corno (1993) have argued for the distinction between motivation and volition, with motivation guiding decisions about engaging in particular activities, and volition guiding the behaviors used to attain the goal. Broadly, these theorists focus on two issues: how motivation gets translated into regulated behavior, and how motivation and cognition are linked.

Social Cognitive Theories of Self-Regulation and Motivation

Reviewing the extensive literature on the self-regulation of behavior is beyond the scope of this chapter (see Boekaerts et al. 2000). We focus on the work of Zimmerman, Schunk, and their colleagues, because they directly link motivation to self-regulation. Zimmerman (1989) described self-regulated students as being metacognitively, motivationally, and behaviorally active in their own learning processes and in achieving their own goals. Zimmerman posited reciprocally related personal, environmental, and behavioral determinants of self-regulated learning that allow individuals to control the extent to which they are self-regulated through personal and behavioral actions and choices. He also acknowledged that context is important in that some environments do not allow much latitude in choice of activities or approaches, making self-regulation more difficult.

According to Zimmerman (2000), self-regulated learners have three important characteristics: They use a variety of self-regulated strategies (active learning processes that involve agency and purpose); they believe they can perform efficaciously; and they set numerous and varied goals for themselves. Furthermore, self-regulated learners engage in three important processes: self-observation (monitoring of one's activities); self-judgment (evaluation of how well one's own performance compares to a standard or to the performance of others); and self-reactions (reactions to performance outcomes). When these reactions are favorable, particularly in response to failure, students are more likely to continue. The favorableness of one's reaction to failure is determined by how individuals interpret their difficulties and failures.

In his discussions of self-efficacy and self-regulation, Schunk (e.g., 1990, Schunk & Zimmerman 1994, Schunk & Ertmer 2000) emphasized the reciprocal roles of goal setting, self-evaluation, and self-efficacy. He discussed goals in two ways: Initially, he demonstrated that when goals are proximal, specific, and challenging they are most effective in motivating children's behavior and increasing their sense of self-efficacy (see Schunk 1990). More recently, Schunk & Zimmerman (1994) discussed how self-efficacy might be influenced by the learning and performance goal types discussed earlier, suggesting that self-efficacy should be higher under learning than under performance goals; some research supports this claim (e.g., Elliott & Dweck 1988, Meece et al. 1988).

In sum, the social cognitive view of self-regulation emphasizes the importance of self-efficacy beliefs, causal attributions, and goal setting in regulating behavior directed at accomplishing a task or activity. Once children engage in a task, then they must monitor their behavior, judge its outcomes, and react to those outcomes in order to regulate what they do. Schunk & Zimmerman (1994) concluded that assessing the interactions of self-efficacy, goals, and attributions is one of the most important tasks for future research in this area.

Theories Linking Motivation and Cognition

Some motivation researchers are interested in how motivation and cognition interact to influence self-regulated learning (e.g., Borkowski & Muthukrishna 1995, Winne & Marx 1989). Winne & Marx (1989) posited that motivation should be conceived in cognitive processing terms, and that motivational thoughts and beliefs are governed by the basic principles of cognitive psychology, differing from other thoughts and beliefs only in their content. Winne & Marx further discussed the conditions under which tasks are performed, the operations needed to complete the task, the product the student produces when the task is completed, and the evaluation of the task and how motivation can influence each aspect.

Borkowski and his colleagues (Borkowski et al. 1990, Borkowski & Muthukrishna 1995) developed a model highlighting the interaction of the following cognitive, motivational, and self-processes: knowledge of oneself (including one's goals, possible selves, and sense of self-worth), domain-specific knowledge, strategy knowledge, and personal-motivational states (including attributional beliefs, self-efficacy, and intrinsic motivation). Together these components are assumed to influence performance.

Pintrich and his colleagues outlined a model of the relations between motivation and cognition (Pintrich 2000a,b). This model incorporates several components including student entry characteristics (such as prior achievement levels); the social aspects of the learning setting (e.g., the social characteristics of the tasks and the interactions between students and teachers during instruction); several motivational constructs derived from expectancy-value and goal theories (expectancies, values, and affect); and various cognitive constructs (e.g., background knowledge, learning strategies, and self-regulatory and metacognitive strategies). Pintrich and colleagues postulated that the cognitive and motivational constructs influence each other as well as being influenced by the social context. In turn, both the cognitive and motivational constructs are assumed to influence students' involvement with their learning and, consequently, achievement outcomes. In support, Pintrich & De Groot (1990) found that students' achievement values determined initial engagement decisions and that their self-efficacy facilitated both engagement and performance in conjunction with cognitive and self-regulation strategies.

Both the Borkowski & Muhukrishna and Pintrich models are important because they specify possible links between motivation and cognition, which each research group has begun to test. Many of the possible links remain unexamined, however. Pintrich et al. (1993) presented a more fully articulated discussion of links of motivation and cognition, with specific reference to conceptual change. They discussed how traditional "cold" cognitive psychological models of conceptual change do not consider the motivational and contextual factors that likely influence conceptual development. They described and provided preliminary evidence of how various classroom and motivational factors such as goals, achievement values, efficacy beliefs, and control beliefs can influence whether students change their mental concepts. They also stressed the relative paucity of research on these relations.

Theories of Motivation and Volition

The term "volition" refers to both the strength of will needed to complete a task, and the diligence of pursuit (Corno 1993). Kuhl (e.g., 1987) argued that many motivational theorists have ignored volitional processes by assuming that motivation leads directly to outcomes. He argued instead that motivational processes only lead to the decision to act. Once the individual engages in action, volitional processes take over and determine whether or not the intention is fulfilled (see also Zimmerman 1989). A variety of distracters and other opportunities can waylay even the strongest intentions to complete a task or activity. Kuhl (1987) proposed several specific volitional strategies to explain persistence in the face of distractions and other opportunities: cognitive control strategies that help individuals stay focused on the relevant information, avoid distracting information, and optimize decision-making including selective attention, encoding control, and parsimony of information processing. Emotional control strategies involve keeping inhibiting emotional states like anxiety and depression in check. Motivational control strategies involve strengthening the current behavior's motivational base, particularly when the intention is weak relative to other possible competing intentions. Environmental control means constraining (or enhancing) one's environment to facilitate the motivated behavior, e.g., turning off the TV while studying. Finally, Kuhl proposed that some individuals (those with an "action orientation") are more likely to engage in these volitional strategies than "state-oriented" individuals.

Corno (1993) provided several examples of the volitional challenges students face (e.g., coordinating multiple demands and desires such as doing homework, watching TV, or calling a friend; dealing with the many distractions in any particular context, such as a classroom; and clarifying often vaguely specified goals and assignments). She focused on Kuhl's (1987) motivation and emotion control strategies because strengthening one's motivation to complete a task and managing one's negative emotional states are often crucial to successful academic performance. Corno also argued that volition is a broader concept than self-regulation because volition includes personality characteristics, aptitudes, and other cognitive processes, whereas most models of self-regulation focus more narrowly on self-monitoring and self-evaluation (see also Corno & Kanfer 1993).

Integrating Theories of Self-Regulation and Expectancy-Value Models of Motivation

Wigfield & Eccles (2001) discussed possible integrations of self-regulatory and expectancy-value models. They noted that a variety of models of self-regulation include competence or efficacy beliefs as crucial influences on self-regulation.

Some models of self-regulation include a consideration of achievement values (e.g., Rheinberg et al. 2000, Schunk & Ertmer 2000). Rheinberg et al. specified different questions individuals pose to themselves concerning potential links of their actions to desired outcomes. One of the questions is a "values" question: Are the consequences of the action important enough to me? If the answer is yes, the individual more likely will undertake the action. If no, then engagement is less likely.

Generally, however, those posing models of self-regulation emphasize goals rather than values; goals are given a prominent role in leading people to action (e.g., Boekaerts & Niemivirta 2000; Carver & Scheier 2000; Pintrich 2000a,b; Schunk & Ertmer 2000; Zimmerman 2000). Furthermore, Carver & Scheier (2000) and Shah & Kruglanski (2000) posit that some goals are organized in hierarchies. For Carver & Scheier the importance of the goal is a basis for the goal hierarchy; goals at higher levels of the hierarchy are thought to be more important to the individual. From the perspective of expectancy-value theory, goal hierarchies also could be organized around the other aspects of task value. Different goals may be more or less useful to the individual or more or less interesting. We have predicted that the relative value attached to the goal should influence its placement in a goal hierarchy, as well as the likelihood that the individual will try to attain the goal (see Eccles 1987, Wigfield & Eccles 2001, for further discussion). The further integration of work on cognition, motivation, and self-regulation will remain an important topic for motivation researchers during the next decade.

CONCLUSION

By focusing on individuals' beliefs, values, and goals, motivation researchers have learned much about the reasons why individuals choose to engage or disengage in different activities, and how individuals' beliefs, values, and goals relate to their achievement behaviors. Various theoretical perspectives on these issues are flourishing, and motivation research remains very active.

We close by noting three important issues that need further study. First, although various theoretical models are flourishing, there is a need for theoretical integration in the field, particularly with respect to models that incorporate competence and expectancy belief constructs. Although there are some differences across these constructs, the similarities likely outweigh the differences. The proliferation of different terms (and measures) for similar constructs makes theoretical integration more difficult.

Second, the focus on belief, values, and goal constructs has led to important advances in the field of motivation. Yet as noted earlier, this focus may overemphasize rational, cognitive processes in motivation, at the expense of affective and other processes. Those writing about cognitive-motivational links also have discussed how "cold" cognitive models cannot adequately capture conceptual change; there is a need to consider affect as well (Pintrich et al. 1993). Within the motivation field, affective processes have not received systematic attention, except in the case of attribution theory. It is time for motivation researchers to investigate such processes more fully (see Roeser 1997).

Finally, as in many areas of psychology, the role of context has become increasingly important to motivation theorists (e.g., Eccles & Midgley 1989, Turner & Meyer 1999, Urdan 1999). Space does not allow for a consideration of contextual influences in this chapter, but it is clear from recent work that the kinds of classroom and school contexts children are in greatly influence their motivation and achievement in complex ways (see Eccles et al. 1998b, Stipek 1998, Stipek & Seal 2001). It is difficult if not impossible to understand students' motivation without understanding the contexts they are experiencing. The complex interactions of context and the individual need further explication.

Visit the Annual Reviews home page at www.AnnualReviews.org

LITERATURE CITED

Alexander PA, Kulikowich JM, Jetton TL. 1994. The role of subject-matter knowledge and interest in the processing of linear and nonlinear texts. *Rev. Educ. Res.* 64:201–52

Amabile TM, Hill KG, Hennessey BA, Tighe EM. 1994. The Work Preference Inventory: assessing intrinsic and extrinsic motivational orientations. *J. Pers. Soc. Psychol.* 66:950–67

Ames C. 1992. Classrooms: goals, structures, and student motivation. *J. Educ. Psychol.* 84:261–71

Ames R, Ames C, eds. 1989. *Research on Motivation in Education*, Vol. 3. New York: Academic

Anderman EM, Austin AC, Johnson DM. 2001. The development of goal orientation. See Wigfield & Eccles 2001. In press

Atkinson JW. 1964. *An Introduction to Motivation*. Princeton, NJ: Van Nostrand

Bandura A. 1997. *Self-Efficacy: The Exercise of Control*. New York: Freeman

Bandura A, Barbaranelli C, Caprara GV, Pastorelli C. 2001. Self-efficacy beliefs as shapers of children's aspirations and career trajectories. *Child Dev.* 72:187–206

Battle E. 1966. Motivational determinants of academic competence. *J. Pers. Soc. Psychol.* 4:534–642

Benware CA, Deci EL. 1984. Quality of learning with an active versus passive motivational set. *Am. Educ. Res. J.* 21:755–65

Blumenfeld PC. 1992. Classroom learning and motivation: clarifying and expanding goal theory. *J. Educ. Psychol.* 84:272–81

Boekaerts M, Niemivirta M. 2000. Self-regulated learning: finding a balance between learning goals and ego protective goals. See Boekaerts et al. 2000, pp. 417–50

Boekaerts M, Pintrich PR, Zeidner MH, eds. 2000. *Handbook of Self-Regulation*. San Diego, CA: Academic

Borkowski JG, Carr M, Relliger E, Pressley M. 1990. Self-regulated cognition: interdependence of metacognition, attributions, and self-esteem. In *Dimensions of Thinking and Cognitive Instruction*, Vol. 1, ed. B Jones, L Idol. Hillsdale, NJ: Erlbaum

Borkowski JG, Muthukrisna N. 1995. Learning environments and skill generalization: how contexts facilitate regulatory processes and efficacy beliefs. In *Recent Perspectives on Memory Development*, ed. F Weinert, W Schneider. Hillsdale, NJ: Erlbaum

Butler R. 1993. Effects of task- and ego-achievement goals on information seeking during task engagement. *J. Pers. Soc. Psychol.* 65:18–31

Cameron J, Pierce WD. 1994. Reinforcement, reward, and intrinsic motivation: a meta-analysis. *Rev. Educ. Res.* 64:363–423

Carver CS, Scheier MF. 2000. On the structure of behavioral self-regulation. See Boekaerts et al. 2000, pp. 41–84

Connell JP. 1985. A new multidimensional

measure of children's perception of control. *Child Dev.* 56:1018–41

Connell JP, Spencer MB, Aber JL. 1994. Educational risk and resilience in African American youth: context, self, and action outcomes in school. *Child Dev.* 65:493–506

Connell JP, Wellborn JG. 1991. Competence, autonomy, and relatedness: a motivational analysis of self-system processes. In *Minnesota Symposia on Child Psychology*, ed. M 'Gunnar, LA Sroufe, 23:43–77. Hillsdale, NJ: Erlbaum

Corno L. 1993. The best-laid plans: modern conceptions of volition and educational research. *Educ. Res.* 22:14–22

Corno L, Kanfer R. 1993. The role of volition in learning and performance. In *Review of Research in Education*, Vol. 29, ed. L Darling-Hammond. Washington, DC: Am. Educ. Res. Assoc.

Covington MV. 1992. *Making the Grade: A Self-Worth Perspective on Motivation and School Reform*. New York: Cambridge Univ. Press

Covington MV. 1998. *The Will to Learn: A Guide for Motivating Young People*. New York: Cambridge Univ. Press

Covington MV. 2000. Goal theory, motivation, and school achievement: an integrative review. *Annu. Rev. Psychol.* 51:171–200

Covington MV, Omelich CL. 1979. Effort: the double-edged sword in school achievement. *J. Educ. Psychol.* 71:169–82

Crandall VC, Katkovsky W, Crandall VJ. 1965. Children's beliefs in their own control of reinforcements in intellectual-academic achievement situations. *Child Dev.* 36:91–109

Csikszentmihalyi M. 1988. The flow experience and its significance for human psychology. See Csikszentmihalyi & Csikszentmihalyi 1988, pp. 15–35

Csikszentmihalyi M, Csikszentmihalyi IS, eds. 1988. *Optimal Experience: Psychological Studies of Flow in Consciousness*. Cambridge, MA: Cambridge Univ. Press

Csikszentmihalyi M, Massimini F. 1985. On the psychological selection of bio-cultural

information. *New Ideas Psychol.* 3:15–138

deCharms R. 1968. *Personal Causation: The Internal Affective Determinants of Behavior*. New York: Academic

Deci EL, Koestner R, Ryan RM. 1999. A meta-analytic review of experiments examining the effects of extrinsic rewards on intrinsic motivation. *Psychol. Bull.* 125:627–68

Deci EL, Ryan RM. 1985. *Intrinsic Motivation and Self-Determination in Human Behavior*. New York: Plenum

Dweck C. 1999. *Self-Theories: Their Role in Motivation, Personality, and Development*. Philadelphia: Psychol. Press

Eccles JS. 1987. Gender roles and women's achievement-related decisions. *Psychol. Women Q.* 11:135–72

Eccles JS. 1993. School and family effects on the ontogeny of children's interests, self-perceptions, and activity choice. In *Nebraska Symposium on Motivation, 1992: Developmental Perspectives on Motivation*, ed. J Jacobs, pp. 145–208. Lincoln: Univ. Nebr. Press

Eccles JS, Adler TF, Meece JL. 1984. Sex differences in achievement: a test of alternate theories. *J. Pers. Soc. Psychol.* 46:26–43

Eccles JS, Barber B, Jozefowicz D. 1998a. Linking gender to educational, occupational, and recreational choices: applying the Eccles et al. model of achievement-related choices. In *Sexism and Stereotypes in Modern Society: The Gender Science of Janet Taylor Spence*, ed. WB Swann, JH Langlois, LA Gilbert, pp. 153–92. Washington, DC: Am. Psychol. Assoc.

Eccles JS, Harold RD. 1992. Gender differences in educational and occupational patterns among the gifted. In *Talent Development: Proceedings from the 1991 Henry B. and Jocelyn Wallace National Research Symposium on Talent Development*, ed. N Colangelo, SG Assouline, DL Ambroson, pp. 3–29. Unionville, NY: Trillium

Eccles JS, Midgley C. 1989. Stage/environment fit: developmentally appropriate classrooms for early adolescents. See Ames & Ames 1989, pp. 139–81

Eccles JS, Wigfield A, Schiefele U. 1998b. Motivation. See Eisenberg 1998, pp. 1017–95

Eccles (Parsons) J, Adler TF, Futterman R, Goff SB, Kaczala CM, et al. 1983. Expectancies, values, and academic behaviors. In *Achievement and Achievement Motivation*, ed. JT Spence, pp. 75–146. San Francisco: Freeman

Eisenberg N, ed. 1998. *Handbook of Child Psychology*, Vol. 3. New York: Wiley. 5th ed.

Elliott A, Church M. 1997. A hierarchical model of approach and avoidance achievement motivation. *J. Pers. Soc. Psychol.* 72: 218–32

Elliott ES, Dweck CS. 1988. Goals: an approach to motivation and achievement. *J. Pers. Soc. Psychol.* 54:5–12

Feather NT. 1988. Values, valences, and course enrollment: testing the role of personal values within an expectancy-value framework. *J. Educ. Psychol.* 80:381–91

Feather NT. 1992. Values, valences, expectations, and actions. *J. Soc. Issues* 48:109–24

Findley MJ, Cooper HM. 1983. Locus of control and academic achievement: a literature review. *J. Pers. Soc. Psychol.* 44:419–27

Fischhoff B, Goitein B, Shapira Z. 1982. The experienced utility of expected utility approaches. In *Expectations and Actions: Expectancy-Value Models in Psychology*, ed. NT Feather, pp. 315–39. Hillsdale, NJ: Erlbaum

Ford ME. 1992. *Human Motivation: Goals, Emotions, and Personal Agency Beliefs*. Newbury Park, CA: Sage

Ford ME, Nichols CW. 1987. A taxonomy of human goals and some possible application. In *Humans as Self-Constructing Living Systems: Putting the Framework to Work*, ed. ME Ford, DH Ford, pp. 289–311. Hillsdale, NJ: Erlbaum

Gottfried AE. 1990. Academic intrinsic motivation in young elementary school children. *J. Educ. Psychol.* 82:525–38

Graham S. 1991. A review of attribution theory in achievement contexts. *Educ. Psychol. Rev.* 3:5–39

Graham S, Taylor AZ. 2001. Ethnicity, gender, and the development of achievement values. See Wigfield & Eccles 2001. In press

Grolnick WS, Gurland ST, Jacob KF, Decourcey W. 2000. The development of self-determination in middle childhood and adolescence. Motivating the academically unmotivated: a critical issue for the 21st century. *Rev. Educ. Res.* 70:151–80

Harter S. 1981. A new self-report scale of intrinsic versus extrinsic orientation in the classroom: motivational and informational components. *Dev. Psychol.* 17:300–12

Harter S. 1990. Causes, correlates and the functional role of global self-worth: a life-span perspective. In *Perceptions of Competence and Incompetence Across the Life-Span*, ed. J Kolligian, R Sternberg, pp. 67–98. New Haven, CT: Yale Univ. Press

Harter S. 1998. Developmental perspectives on the self-system. See Eisenberg 1998, pp. 553–618

Hebb DO. 1955. Drives and the C.N.S. (conceptual nervous system). *Psychol. Rev.* 62:243–54

Heckhausen H. 1991. *Motivation and Action*. Berlin: Springer-Verlag

Hidi S, Baird W. 1986. Interestingness—a neglected variable in discourse processing. *Cogn. Sci.* 10:179–94

Hidi S, Harackiewicz JM. 2001. Motivating the academically unmotivated: a critical issue for the 21st century. *Rev. Educ. Res.* 70:151–80

Juvonen J, Wentzel KR. 1996. *Social Motivation: Understanding Children's School Adjustment*. New York: Cambridge Univ. Press

Kuhl J. 1987. Action control: the maintenance of motivational states. In *Motivation, Intention, and Volition*, ed. F Halisch, J Kuhl, pp. 279–307. Berlin: Springer-Verlag

Mac Iver DJ, Stipek DJ, Daniels DH. 1991. Explaining within-semester changes in student effort in junior high school and senior high school courses. *J. Educ. Psychol.* 83:201–11

Maehr ML, Midgley C. 1996. *Transforming School Cultures*. Boulder, CO: Westview

Markus H, Wurf E. 1987. The dynamic self-concept: a social psychological perspective. *Annu. Rev. Psychol.* 38:299–337

Massimini F, Carli M. 1988. The systematic assessment of flow in daily experience. See Csikszentmihalyi & Csikszentmihalyi 1988, pp. 266–87

Matsumoto D, Sanders M. 1988. Emotional experiences during engagement in intrinsically and extrinsically motivated tasks. *Motiv. Emot.* 12:353–69

Meece JL, Blumenfeld PC, Hoyle RH. 1988. Students' goal orientations and cognitive engagement in classroom activities. *J. Educ. Psychol.* 80:514–23

Meece JL, Wigfield A, Eccles JS. 1990. Predictors of math anxiety and its consequences for young adolescents' course enrollment intentions and performances in mathematics. *J. Educ. Psychol.* 82:60–70

Midgley C, Kaplan A, Middleton M. 2001. Performance-approach goals: good for what, for whom, under what circumstances, and at what cost? *J. Educ. Psychol.* 93:77–86

Midgley C, Kaplan A, Middleton M, Maehr ML, Urdan T, et al. 1998. The development and validation of scales assessing students' goal orientations. *Contemp. Educ. Psychol.* 23:113–31

Nicholls JG. 1984. Achievement motivation: conceptions of ability, subjective experience, task choice, and performance. *Psychol. Rev.* 91:328–46

Nicholls JG, Cobb P, Yackel E, Wood T, Wheatley G. 1990. Students' theories of mathematics and their mathematical knowledge: multiple dimensions of assessment. In *Assessing Higher Order Thinking in Mathematics*, ed. G Kulm, pp. 137–54. Washington, DC: Am. Assoc. Adv. Sci.

Pintrich PR. 2000a. An achievement goal perspective on issues in motivation terminology, theory, and research. *Contemp. Educ. Psychol.* 25:92–104

Pintrich PR. 2000b. The role of goal orientation in self-regulated learning. See Boekaerts et al. 2000, pp. 452–502

Pintrich PR, De Groot EV. 1990. Motivational and self-regulated learning components of classroom academic performance. *J. Educ. Psychol.* 82:33–40

Pintrich PR, Marx RW, Boyle RA. 1993. Beyond cold conceptual change: the role of motivational beliefs and classroom contextual factors in the process of conceptual change. *Rev. Educ. Res.* 63:167–99

Pintrich PR, Schrauben B. 1992. Students' motivational beliefs and their cognitive engagement in classroom academic tasks. In *Student Perceptions in the Classroom*, ed. DH Schunk, JL Meece, pp. 149–83. Hillsdale, NJ: Erlbaum

Renninger KA, Hidi S, Krapp A, eds. 1992. *The Role of Interest in Learning and Development*. Hillsdale, NJ: Erlbaum

Rheinberg F, Vollmeyer R, Rollett W. 2000. Motivation and action in self-regulated learning. See Boekaerts et al. 2000, pp. 503–29

Roeser RW. 1997. On schooling and mental health: introduction to the special issue. *Educ. Psychol.* 33:129–34

Rokeach M. 1979. From individual to institutional values with special reference to the values of science. In *Understanding Human Values*, ed. M Rokeach, pp. 47–70. New York: Free Press

Rotter JB. 1966. Generalized expectancies for internal versus external control of reinforcement. *Psychol. Monogr.* 80:1–28

Ryan RM, Deci E. 2000. Intrinsic and extrinsic motivations: classic definitions and new directions. *Contemp. Educ. Psychol.* 25:54–67

Sansone C, Harackiewicz JM. 2000. *Intrinsic and Extrinsic Motivation: The Search for Optimal Motivation and Performance*. New York: Academic

Schiefele U. 1999. Interest and learning from text. *Sci. Stud. Read.* 3:257–80

Schneider K. 2001. Intrinsisch (autotelisch) motiviertes Verhalten dargestellt an den Beispielen des Neugierverhaltens sowie verwandter Verhaltenssysteme (Spielen und leistungsmotiviertes Handeln). In *Motivation, Volition, Handlung (Enzykl. Psychol. C, Ser. Motiv. Emot., Bd. 4)*, ed. H Heckhausen, J Kuhl. Gottingen: Hogrefe. In press

Schunk DH. 1990. Goal setting and self-efficacy during self-regulated learning. *Educ. Psychol.* 25:71–86

Schunk DH, Ertmer PA. 2000. Self-regulatory and academic learning self-efficacy enhancing interventions. See Boekaerts et al. 2000, pp. 631–49

Schunk DH, Zimmerman BJ, eds. 1994. *Self-Regulation of Learning and Performance.* Hillsdale, NJ: Erlbaum

Shah JY, Kruglanski AW. 2000. Aspects of goal networks: implications for self-regulation. See Boekaerts et al. 2000, pp. 86–110

Skaalvik E. 1997. Self-enhancing and self-defeating ego orientation: relations with task and avoidance orientation, achievement, self-perception, and anxiety. *J. Educ. Psychol.* 89:71–81

Skinner EA. 1995. *Perceived Control, Motivation, and Coping.* Thousand Oaks, CA: Sage

Skinner EA, Belmont MJ. 1993. Motivation in the classroom: reciprocal effects of teacher behavior and student engagement across the school year. *J. Educ. Psychol.* 85:571–81

Skinner EA, Zimmer-Gembeck MJ, Connell JP. 1998. Individual differences and the development of perceived control. *Monogr. Soc. Res. Child Dev.* 63(Ser. No. 254, No. 2–3)

Stipek DJ. 1998. *Motivation to Learn: From Theory to Practice.* Boston: Allyn & Bacon

Stipek DJ, Seal K. 2001. *Motivated Minds: Raising Children to Love Learning.* New York: Holt & Co

Turner JC, Meyer DK. 1999. Integrating classroom context into motivation theory and research: rationale, methods, and implications. See Urdan 1999, pp. 87–122

Urdan T, ed. 1999. *The Role of Context: Advances in Motivation and Achievement,* Vol. 11. Stamford, CT: JAI Press

Weiner B. 1985. An attributional theory of achievement motivation and emotion. *Psychol. Rev.* 92:548–73

Weiner B. 1992. *Human Motivation: Metaphors, Theories, and Research.* Newbury Park, CA: Sage

Weisz JP. 1984. Contingency judgments and achievement behavior: deciding what is controllable and when to try. In *The Development of Achievement Motivation,* ed. JG Nicholls, pp. 107–36. Greenwich, CT: JAI Press

Wentzel KR. 1991. Relations between social competence and academic achievement in early adolescence. *Child Dev.* 62:1066–78

Wentzel KR. 1993. Does being good make the grade? Social behavior and academic competence in middle school. *J. Educ. Psychol.* 85:357–64

Wentzel KR. 1994. Relations of social goal pursuit to social acceptance, and perceived social support. *J. Educ. Psychol.* 86:173–82

White RH. 1959. Motivation reconsidered: the concept of competence. *Psychol. Rev.* 66:297–333

Wigfield A. 1994. Expectancy-value theory of achievement motivation: a developmental perspective. *Educ. Psychol. Rev.* 6:49–78

Wigfield A, Eccles J. 1992. The development of achievement task values: a theoretical analysis. *Dev. Rev.* 12:265–310

Wigfield A, Eccles JS, eds. 2001. *The Development of Achievement Motivation.* San Diego, CA: Academic. In press

Wigfield A, Eccles JS. 2001. The development of competence-related beliefs and achievement task values from childhood to adolescence. See Wigfield & Eccles 2001. In press

Wigfield A, Eccles JS, Yoon KS, Harold RD, Arbreton A, et al. 1997. Changes in children's competence beliefs and subjective task values across the elementary school years: a three-year study. *J. Educ. Psychol.* 89:451–69

Winne PH, Marx RW. 1989. A cognitive-processing analysis of motivation with classroom tasks. See Ames & Ames 1989, pp. 223–37

Zimmerman BJ. 1989. A social cognitive view of self-regulated learning. *J. Educ. Psychol.* 81:329–39

Zimmerman BJ. 2000. Attaining self-regulation: a social-cognitive perspective. See Boekaerts et al. 2000, pp. 13–39

Annu. Rev. Psychol. 2002. 53:133–60

CULTURAL INFLUENCES ON PERSONALITY

Harry C. Triandis[1] and Eunkook M. Suh[2]

[1]Department of Psychology, University of Illinois, Champaign-Urbana, Champaign, Illinois; e-mail: Triandis@uiuc.edu
[2]Department of Psychology and Social Behavior, University of California, Irvine, California; e-mail: Esuh@uci.edu

Key Words individualism, collectivism, Big Five, indigenous psychologies, universals

■ **Abstract** Ecologies shape cultures; cultures influence the development of personalities. There are both universal and culture-specific aspects of variation in personality. Some culture-specific aspects correspond to cultural syndromes such as complexity, tightness, individualism, and collectivism. A large body of literature suggests that the Big Five personality factors emerge in various cultures. However, caution is required in arguing for such universality, because most studies have not included emic (culture-specific) traits and have not studied samples that are extremely different in culture from Western samples.

CONTENTS

0084-6570/02/0201-0133$14.00

INTRODUCTION

Recent *Annual Reviews of Psychology* have had chapters dealing with personality (Wiggins & Pincus 1992, Magnusson & Töerestad 1993, Revelle 1995) and with culture (Shweder & Sullivan 1993, Bond & Smith 1996a, Cooper & Denner 1998), but not with both culture and personality. The culture and personality topic is controversial. Bruner (1974) assessed the field as a "magnificent failure." Shweder (1991) saw little that can be considered positive in this field. For instance, Shweder argued that (*a*) individual differences in conduct are narrowly context dependent and do not generalize across contexts. Thus, global traits do not exist. Shweder further argued that (*b*) early childcare practices per se do not have predictable consequences for adult character, (*c*) the greater the cultural variation, the smaller is the situational comparability, and that (*d*) "objective" conditions, such as reinforcers and other "external" stimulus events, do not predict the accommodation of an organism to its environment.

More positive evaluations have emerged recently (e.g., Lee et al. 1999a). Lee et al. (1999b) edited a book that vigorously defended the utility of culture and personality studies, summarized the history of this topic, and provided chapters about Mexican, Chinese, African, German, Indian, and Japanese personality, as well as studies for the improvement of interaction across cultures. Piker (1998) thought that Shweder's objections to previous work employed "straw dummy tactics" (p. 21).

McCrae and his colleagues (McCrae 2000, McCrae et al. 2000) also presented a view diametrically opposite to Shweder (1991). According to McCrae et al., global traits do exist. They claim that "studies of heritability, limited parental influence, structural invariance across cultures and species, and temporal stability all point to the notion that personality traits are more expressions of human biology than products of life experience" (p. 177). This view places too much emphasis on biology, and more balanced assessments of the influence of genes and environment (e.g., Maccoby 2000) suggest that personality corresponds to the area of a quadrangle, one side of which is genes and the other, environment. In short, personality emerges under the influence of both genes and environment. Furthermore, behavior is likely to be a function of not only culture and personality but also the interaction between personality and the situation. We review studies where most of the variance in behavior is a function of such interactions.

In any case, McCrae et al. (2000) argued that there are basic tendencies (neuroticism, extraversion, openness, agreeableness, and conscientiousness) that are independent of culture. For example, animal psychologists (e.g., Gosling & John 1999) have identified personality traits (such as extroversion and dominance) in some higher animals, so at a basic level, contrary to Shweder's view, such traits are likely to exist (see also Munroe 1999). Many of Shweder's other points can be criticized in similar ways, leading us to agree with Piker's (1998) comments.

Shweder (1991) proposed that cultural psychology would provide the way to think about culture and personality. He recommended "thick description" of the cultural practices without attempts at generalizations. However, the facts of phylogenetic continuity make generalizations possible. We can examine universals across cultures while admitting that the meaning that individuals give to a particular event may differ from culture to culture and must be incorporated in our understanding of the way culture is related to individual differences in behavior. Thus, in this chapter we take a position that is intermediate between Shweder (1991) and McCrae et al. (2000). We look for universal generalizations, while at the same time admitting emic (culture-specific) information.

Personality is shaped by both genetic and environmental influences. Among the most important of the latter are cultural influences. Culture is transmitted through language and the modeling of behavior when conditions permit humans to communicate through shared language, by living in the same historic period, and when they are sufficiently proximal to influence each other. The overarching model of cultural influences on personality that we have adopted in this chapter is that though biological factors have an important role in shaping personality, they do not account for most of the variance. Ecology, among other factors, shapes the culture, which in turn shapes the socialization patterns, which shape some of the variance of personality (Maccoby 2000). For example, Rohner (1986, 1999) has shown reliable links between socialization practices and personality. Both within and between cultures when parents accept their children (there is much hugging, comforting), the children become sociable, emotionally stable, have high self-esteem, feel self-adequate, and have a positive world view. When parents are rejecting (hitting, using sarcastic language, humiliating, neglecting), their children become adults who are hostile, unresponsive, unstable, immaturely dependent, and have impaired self-esteem and a negative world view.

Of course, historical factors and cultural diffusion also shape cultures, but limitations of space preclude their discussion. Broad empirical support for such a model does exist (e.g., Singelis & Brown 1995). In addition to these factors, we consider other constructs that are needed for a better understanding of the way culture influences personality.

SOME DEFINITIONS

Culture

The conceptualization of culture is by no means a simple matter. One possible way to think about culture is that "culture is to society what memory is to individuals" (Kluckhohn 1954). It includes what has worked in the experience of a society, so that it was worth transmitting to future generations. Sperber (1996) used the analogy of an epidemic. A useful idea (e.g., how to make a tool) is adopted by more and more people and becomes an element of culture (Campbell 1965). Barkow et al. (1992) distinguished three kinds of culture: metaculture, evoked culture, and epidemiological culture. They argue that "psychology underlies culture and society, and biological evolution underlies psychology" (p. 635). The biology that has been common to all humans as a species distinguishable from other species, results in a "metaculture" that corresponds to panhuman mental contents and organization. Biology in different ecologies results in "evoked culture" (e.g., hot climate leads to light clothing), which reflects domain-specific mechanisms that are triggered by local circumstances, and leads to within-group similarities and between-groups differences. What Sperber describes, Barkow et al. call "epidemiological culture."

Elements of culture are shared standard operating procedures, unstated assumptions, tools, norms, values, habits about sampling the environment, and the like. Because perception and cognition depend on the information that is sampled from the environment and are fundamental psychological processes, this culturally influenced sampling of information is of particular interest to psychologists. Cultures develop conventions for sampling information and determine how much to weigh the sampled elements from the environment (Triandis 1989). For example, people in hierarchical cultures are more likely to sample clues about hierarchy than clues about aesthetics. Triandis (1989) argued that people in individualist cultures, such as those of North and Western Europe and North America, sample with high probability elements of the personal self (e.g., "I am busy, I am kind"). People from collectivist cultures, such as those of Asia, Africa, and South America, tend to sample mostly elements of the collective self (e.g., "my family thinks I am too busy, my co-workers think I am kind") (Triandis et al. 1990, Trafimow et al. 1991).

Personality

Funder (1997) defined personality as "an individual's characteristic pattern of thought, emotion, and behavior, together with the psychological mechanisms—hidden or not—behind those patterns" (pp. 1–2). Characteristic sampling of the information in the environment, which corresponds to the sampling that occurs in different cultures, can be one of the bases of individual differences in personality.

Personality may also be conceptualized as a configuration of cognitions, emotions, and habits activated when situations stimulate their expression. Generally, they determine the individual's unique adjustment to the world. This view is supported by data that indicate the importance of the situation. For example, the authoritarian personality is characterized by submission to authorities, aggression toward people who are different, and conventionalism (Pettigrew 1999). Interestingly, Russians who are high on this trait reject laissez-faire individualism, whereas Americans who are high on this trait support this type of individualism (McFarland et al. 1992). Rejection of individualism is consistent with Russian conventionalism, whereas support for individualism is consistent with American conventionalism.

Level of Analysis

Studies that use culture as the N can provide different results than studies that use individuals as the N. Thus, below we attempt to make explicit the level of analysis that was used in a particular study.

Indigenous, Cultural, and Cross-Cultural Psychologies

Many theoretical perspectives are used when studying the relationship between culture and psychology (Cooper & Denner 1998). The most important are the indigenous, cultural, and cross-cultural perspectives. The differences in perspectives have implications for the methodology that is likely to be used in studying personality. For example, personality tests developed in one culture and translated for use in other cultures are likely to be insensitive to cultural differences and to produce distorted results (Greenfield 1997). Cultural and indigenous psychologists do not use such tests; they use mostly ethnographic methods. Cross-cultural psychologists attempt to measure the same construct equivalently in each culture with culturally sensitive methods.

Triandis (2000b) outlined several differences among these approaches and argued that all three are needed. Converging findings using these approaches are most likely to be reliable and valid. This is also the view of Marsella et al. (2000) who, after an excellent review of the history of culture and personality studies, emphasized the use of qualitative (ethnosemantic) methods in conjunction with quantitative methods. The ethnosemantic methods include (*a*) the elicitation of all personality terms in the particular language, (*b*) the organization by research participants of the terms into naturally occurring structures, (*c*) the derivation of the meanings (e.g., spontaneous associations) of these structures, and (*d*) the linking of the terms to actual behaviors. For example, researchers might use the antecedent-consequent method (Triandis 1972) ("If one is Y then one 'would' or 'would not' do X") to determine the link between personality terms and behaviors in different cultures. It is very likely that the emic structures obtained with these methods will have some resemblance to the etic structures obtained by Western methods. Finding such convergence allows us to compare personalities across cultures (using the etic dimensions) and also describe personalities with culturally sensitive elements (using the emic dimensions).

Church & Lonner (1998) edited a special issue of the *Journal of Cross-Cultural Psychology*, which utilized this convergent point of view. They included papers that linked personality and culture from the perspective of cultural (Markus & Kitayama 1998), indigenous (Ho 1998), and evolutionary psychology (MacDonald 1998). Church (2000) has provided an impressive model of culture and personality that integrated many of these approaches, especially the trait and cultural psychological approaches. According to the model, traits exist in all cultures, but account for behavior less in collectivist than in individualist cultures. Situational determinants of behavior are important universally, but more so in collectivist than in individualist cultures. Cognitive consistency among psychological processes and between psychological processes and behavior occurs universally, but is less important in collectivist than in individualist cultures.

Ecology to Culture Links

Ecology (terrain, climate, flora and fauna, natural resources) is linked to the maintenance system (subsistence and settlement patterns, social structures, means of production) and to subjective culture. For example, large mountains and wide seas reduce the probability of cultural diffusion. Thus, the homogeneity of relatively isolated cultures (e.g., Japan in contrast to China) is likely to be high. Homogeneity makes a culture "tight," that is, its members have many rules and norms about behavior and punish those who deviate, even in minor ways, from norms. In tight cultures, such as Singapore, adolescents conform to the societal norms and do not engage in risk behaviors, such as experimenting with alcohol, tobacco, physical violence, or sexual intercourse (Ball & Moselle 1995). In "loose" cultures people are more likely to react to deviations from normative behaviors by saying "It does not matter."

An interesting ecological variable is whether the resources that a population needs for survival have high (e.g., cattle) or low (e.g., trees) mobility. Cultures where wealth is easily moveable develop a "culture of honor" in which people are socialized to be fierce and to react aggressively to insults, so that strangers will be discouraged from stealing their moveable goods. Nisbett & Cohen (1996) showed that a culture of honor is more common in the South than in the northern regions of the United States. Cohen et al. (1996) showed that, compared with students from the North, students from the South were more easily provoked and became more aggressive when verbally insulted.

Climate can also influence culture. For example, Van de Vliert et al. (1999) argued that temperature is related to violence. Data from 136 countries show a curvilinear pattern, with violence very low in cold climates (e.g., Finland), very high in warm climates (e.g., Pakistan), and moderately high in extremely hot climates (e.g., Malaysia). In warm climates the survival of offspring is possible even without the significant investment of fathers. This frees men to sire children with multiple mates and leads to greater competition among the men, and ultimately to "masculine" cultures where men are more dominant, assertive, and tough.

The cultures that emerge in different parts of the world often reflect the availability of flora, fauna, and other resources, as well as historical factors, such as migrations, wars, revolutions, and inventions. There is little inequality in hunting and gathering cultures, because food (resources) cannot be preserved for a long time, so it is not possible for one group to accumulate resources (O'Kelly & Carney 1986). The greatest inequality is in societies where inventors are financially successful and become differentiated from their peers.

The maintenance system (food gathering, agriculture, manufacturing, services) is linked to cultural syndromes (i.e., shared elements of subjective culture, such as attitudes, norms, and values that are organized around a theme) (Triandis 1996). For example, among hunters individual action is often more valuable than collective action, whereas among agricultural people collective action (e.g., building an irrigation system) is often extremely valued. The result is that hunting cultures are more individualist than farming cultures (Berry 1976) and the latter are more conforming than the former, an attribute that is associated with collectivism (Bond & Smith 1996b).

Both the genetic system (e.g., levels of arousal, activity, universals of emotions) and the cultural system are shaped by evolution (Tooby & Cosmides 1992). Culture includes socialization patterns, which shape personality (Maccoby 2000). In the sections that follow we review studies showing the specifics of some of the links we have just discussed.

DIMENSIONS OF CULTURE

Complexity

Cultures differ in complexity (Chick 1997). The most contrast is found between hunters/gatherers and information societies. Gross national product per capita, although not sufficient, is one index of cultural complexity. Other indices include the percent of the population that is urban, the size of cities, personal computers per capita, etc.

Tightness

In tight cultures norms are imposed tightly (see above). In loose cultures deviation from norms is tolerated. Such tolerance is found in relatively heterogeneous societies (where several normative systems are present), where people do not depend on each other much, and where population density (e.g., opportunity for surveillance) is low. An open frontier is related to looseness (Triandis 1994, 1995).

Collectivism

Triandis (1994, 1995) proposed the hypothesis that collectivism is high in cultures that are simple and tight. Carpenter (2000) obtained empirical support for the correlation of collectivism and tightness. In collectivist cultures people are interdependent with their in-groups (family, tribe, nation, etc.), give priority to the goals of their in-groups, shape their behavior primarily on the basis of in-group norms, and behave in a communal way (Mills & Clark 1982).

There are many kinds of collectivist cultures. One important distinction is between vertical (e.g., India) and horizontal (e.g., the Israeli kibbutz) collectivist cultures. Vertical cultures are traditionalist and emphasize in-group cohesion, respect for in-group norms, and the directives of authorities (Bond & Smith 1996b). For instance, vertical collectivism is correlated with right wing authoritarianism (Altemeyer 1996), the tendency to be submissive to authority and to endorse conventionalism. Both vertical collectivism and right wing authoritarianism correlate positively with age and religiosity, and negatively with education and exposure to diverse persons (Pettigrew 1999, Triandis 1995). Horizontal collectivist cultures emphasize empathy, sociability, and cooperation (Triandis & Gelfand 1998). Gabriel & Gardner (1999) recently found another variation of collectivism between genders. According to their research, male collectivism is derived from group memberships (e.g., "I am an American"); female collectivism is derived from specific relationships (e.g., "I am Amanda's best friend").

A defining character of people in collectivist cultures is their notable concern with relationships. For example, Ohbuchi et al. (1999) showed that collectivists in conflict situations are primarily concerned with maintaining relationships with others, whereas individualists are primarily concerned with achieving justice. Thus, collectivists prefer methods of conflict resolution that do not destroy relationships (e.g., mediation), whereas individualists are willing to go to court to settle disputes (Leung 1997).

Individualism

At the cultural level of analysis (in which the number of cultures is the N of the analyses), individualism is the other pole of collectivism. In vertical individualist cultures (e.g., US corporate cultures) competitiveness is high, and one must be "the best" in order to climb the hierarchy. In horizontal individualist cultures (e.g., Australia, Sweden) hierarchical differentiation is de-emphasized, and the emphasis is on self-reliance, independence from others, and uniqueness (Triandis & Gelfand 1998). This is only a partial list of dimensions of cultural variation. Many more (e.g., Hofstede et al. 1998) have been proposed, but limitations of space do not allow their presentation here.

Recent Findings on Individualism and Collectivism

Greenfield (1999) suggested that the individualism-collectivism contrast corresponds to the "deep structure" of cultural differences. We concur and thus feel that it deserves special attention and emphasis in this review. In recent years there were almost 100 studies published annually examining some phenomenon from the point of view of these cultural patterns. For example, Marc Bornstein (e.g., Bornstein et al. 1999) has published numerous studies concerning mother-child interactions in several cultures and has found that the contrast between collectivism and individualism provides a helpful framework for the findings. Although a complete review of this literature is beyond the scope of this chapter, a number of key recent findings are summarized in this review.

The terms individualism and collectivism are used at the cultural level of analysis, where the number of observations is the number of cultures (e.g., Hofstede 1980). In such data individualism is the polar opposite of collectivism. As mentioned above, results at the cultural level may differ from results at the individual level of analysis. Thus, different terms are used to indicate the level of analysis. Individualism and collectivism are used at the cultural level, whereas at the individual level of analysis (i.e., within-culture analyses), the corresponding terms are *idiocentrism* and *allocentrism* (Triandis et al. 1985). Idiocentrism and allocentrism are personality attributes that are often orthogonal to each other. Idiocentrics emphasize self-reliance, competition, uniqueness, hedonism, and emotional distance from in-groups. Allocentrics emphasize interdependence, sociability, and family integrity; they take into account the needs and wishes of in-group members, feel close in their relationships to their in-group, and appear to others as responsive to their needs and concerns (Cross et al. 2000). It is possible for individuals to be high or low on both allocentrism and idiocentrism, though this may depend on culture. For instance, Verkuyten & Masson (1996) found that allocentrism and idiocentrism were unrelated in a collectivist sample but negatively correlated in an individualist sample.

In all cultures there are both idiocentrics and allocentrics, in different proportions (Triandis et al. 2001). Generally speaking, in collectivist cultures there are about 60% allocentrics and in individualist cultures about 60% idiocentrics. The allocentrics in individualist cultures are more likely than the idiocentrics to join groups—gangs, communes, unions, etc. The idiocentrics in collectivist cultures are more likely than the allocentrics to feel oppressed by their culture and to seek to leave it.

At the Cultural Level of Analysis

The collectivism-individualism cultural syndrome has been studied intensively (for review, see Kagitcibasi 1997; Markus & Kitayama 1991; Triandis 1989, 1995). Collectivism-individualism are broader terms than interdependence-independence as used by Markus & Kitayama. The latter refer to self-construal which is only an aspect of the cultural syndrome of collectivism-individualism. An important goal of collectivists is to fulfill their duties and obligations. Triandis (1995) pointed out that collectivists usually have few in-groups, whereas individualists have many. Thus, the social obligations of collectivists are quite focused, whereas those of individualists are fluid and may be converted to obligations to the larger society rather than to specific in-groups. Consistent with this observation, Oyserman et al. (1998) found that collectivism increased obligation to the in-group when in-group membership was made salient.

COGNITION   People in collectivist cultures see the environment as more or less fixed (stable norms, obligations, duties) and themselves as changeable, ready to "fit in." People in individualist cultures see themselves as more or less stable (stable attitudes, personality, rights) and the environment as changeable (e.g., if they do not like the job they change jobs) (Chiu et al. 1997, Chiu & Hong 1999, Hong et al. 2001, Su et al. 1999).

Norenzayan et al. (1999) claim, for instance, that East Asians making dispositional attributions see traits as quite malleable, whereas Western individualist samples see them as fixed. They reviewed a wide range of information, from laboratory studies to ethnographies, and concluded that probably all cultures make dispositional attributions. Cultural differences occur because samples from East Asia make situational attributions much more frequently and to a greater extent than samples from the West (see also Krull et al. 1999). Furthermore, Choi & Nisbett (2000) found that East Asians have a higher tolerance for contradictions than do Americans and thus are less surprised than Americans when they are presented with inconsistencies, such as a plausible hypothesis that was not supported. Choi & Nisbett (2000) suggest that the logical thinking of Western samples has advantages in the development of science, whereas the more holistic thinking of Eastern samples has advantages for the maintenance of interpersonal order and harmony within the in-group (sensitivity in interpersonal relations, saving face, and the like).

MOTIVATION   The greater the complexity, and therefore individualism, the more people desire to have many choices and to be unique. Kim & Markus (1999) used several methods to show that in some cultures people are highly motivated to be unique, whereas in others people prefer to be like everyone else. Iyengar & Lepper (1999) found that children of European-American backgrounds were more motivated when they had a choice and showed less motivation when authorities or peers made the choice for them. Conversely, Asian-American children were less motivated when given a personal choice, whereas having choices made for them by trusted authority figures and peers actually produced the highest levels of intrinsic motivation and performance.

Motivation in individualist cultures increases following success. In collectivist cultures it increases following failure, because the individual focuses on how to change the self and improve the fit between self and the demands of the social environment (Heine et al. 2000). Munro et al. (1997) recently edited a volume devoted to the relationships between culture and various types of motivation (e.g., work, religious, social, sexual).

EMOTION   The prototypical emotions experienced by collectivist and individualist cultural members appear to be different. In a study by Kitayama et al. (2000) Americans reported more positive disengaged emotions (superior, proud, top of the world), whereas Japanese reported more interpersonally engaged emotions (friendly feelings, feel close, respect). Also, compared with the Japanese, Americans reported more positive than negative emotions. Mesquita (2001) reported that emotions in collectivist cultures tend to be embedded in relationships and are perceived to reflect the status of those relationships. Similar emotions may be instantiated in self-focused or other-focused ways in individualist and collectivist cultures, respectively.

In addition to the difference in the content of emotions, the weights that collectivists and individualists assign to their emotional experience as a whole seem to differ. For instance, Suh et al. (1998) found that emotions are strong predictors of life satisfaction in individualist cultures, whereas social norms (approval by others) strongly predict the satisfaction of collectivists. Levine et al. (1995) also found that emotional factors (i.e., love) play a more decisive role in major personal decisions such as marriage in individualist than in collectivist cultures.

SELF-DESCRIBED PERSONALITY TRAITS   Grimm et al. (1999) examined the self-described personality traits, values, and moods of students in an individualist (United States) and a collectivist (Philippines) culture. They predicted that the Filipino sample would rate themselves lower than the US sample on individualist traits (e.g., independence, pleasure seeking, assertiveness) and higher on collectivist traits (e.g., attentiveness, respectfulness, humility, cooperativeness). The data were generally supportive of the differences on the individualist traits, but there were no cultural differences on the collectivist traits.

WELL-BEING   People in individualist cultures have more positive self-esteem (Heine et al. 1999) and are more optimistic (Lee & Seligman 1997) than people in collectivist cultures, and those factors are associated with high subjective well-being (for a review, see Suh 2000). Triandis (2000a) has proposed a wide range of factors that might contribute to cultural differences in subjective well-being. The more important ones are a good fit between personality and culture, openness to new experiences, extroversion, environmental mastery, personal growth, purpose in life, and self-acceptance (for further discussions on culture and well-being, see Diener & Suh 2000).

SOCIAL BEHAVIOR   People in collectivist cultures belong to groups as a matter of right, by birth or marriage, whereas those in individualist cultures often have to earn their membership in a group. Thus, the former rarely develop excellent skills for entering new groups, whereas the latter are more likely to acquire such skills (Cohen 1991). People in collectivist cultures usually establish intimate and long-term relationships (Verma 1992). People in individualist cultures usually establish nonintimate and short-term relationships.

Collectivist cultural members are strongly influenced by the behaviors and thoughts of other people. For instance, Cialdini et al. (1999) examined how people responded to a request to participate in a market survey. They found that people from collectivist cultures were influenced by social proof arguments (e.g., your peers have complied with this request). People from individualist cultures, however, were influenced more by commitment/consistency arguments (e.g., you have complied to a similar request in the past).

In recreational settings the typical group in collectivist cultures (a) has stable membership, (b) is relatively large (more than three people), and (c) meets frequently. Choi (1996) found that during recreation individuals in collectivist cultures are more likely to engage in joint activities with family members and friends, whereas individuals in individualistic cultures are more likely to engage in activities alone (see also Brandt 1974). The typical recreation group in individualist cultures (a) has variable membership, (b) is often small (two or three people) or very large, and (c) meets infrequently. The cocktail party, after all, was invented by individualists!

COMMUNICATION   People in collectivist cultures use indirect and face-saving communication more than people in individualist cultures (Holtgraves 1997). Lin (1997) points out that ambiguity in communication can be very helpful in a vertical collectivist culture such as China, where clarity may result in sanctions. One cannot point out to an official that he is not correct. The Chinese, he indicates, admire people who are frank, such as Judge Bao (p. 369), but do not emulate him.

During communication people in collectivist cultures frequently use "we"; individualists use "I." In vertical cultures the very use of words is different depending on whether a lower status person is talking to a higher status person or vice versa. Such differences in word use are not so frequent in horizontal cultures. In fact, the languages used by people in collectivist cultures often do not require the use of "I" and "you," whereas the languages used by individualists do (Kashima & Kashima 1998). In Japan, as well as among many Native Americans, silence is acceptable. In fact, some Japanese women think that a silent male is going to be economically successful and will be a good provider and husband (Ishikawa 1970, written in Japanese, reported in Hasegawa 1996). Silence is embarrassing to people in individualist cultures, whereas it is a sign of strength for some people in collectivist cultures (Iwao 1993).

ETHICS   There are three moral codes: community, autonomy, and divinity (Rozin et al. 1999). Community codes are especially important to people in collectivist cultures, whereas autonomy codes are important in individualist cultures. They evoke different emotions. Violation of communal codes, including hierarchy, evokes contempt; violation of the autonomy code (e.g., individual rights) evokes anger. Violation of the divinity code (purity, sanctity) evokes disgust. Data from Japan and the United States support the theory (Rozin et al. 1999).

Indians see helping an in-group member as duty-based, whereas Americans see it more as a matter of personal choice (Miller 1997). In fact, Americans are less likely to feel responsible than are Indians for helping siblings or colleagues whom they personally do not like. The judgments of Indians were not affected by liking (Miller & Bersoff 1998). Morality among people in collectivist cultures is more contextual, and the supreme value is the welfare of the collective. Ma (1988) has provided a Chinese perspective on moral judgment that differs from the individualistic perspective of Kohlberg (1981).

Lying is a more acceptable behavior in collectivist than in individualist cultures, if it saves face or helps the in-group. There are traditional ways of lying that are understood as "correct behavior." Trilling (1972) argues that when people have a strong sense that they themselves determine who they are, as is characteristic of people in individualist cultures, they are more likely to seek sincerity and authenticity. By contrast, when they feel swept by traditions and obligations, as is more likely among people in collectivist cultures, they de-emphasize authenticity. Triandis et al. (2001) found evidence of greater tendencies toward deception among collectivist samples.

Many observers have emphasized the importance of saving face in collectivist cultures (Hu 1944, Ho 1976). Moral persons behave as their roles, in-group members, and society stipulate. If the individual deviates from such ideal behavior, there is loss of face, not only for the individual, but also for the whole in-group. In many collectivist cultures morality consists of doing what the in-group expects. When interacting with the out-group, it is sometimes considered "moral" to exploit and deceive. In other words, morality is applicable to only some members of one's social environment.

Leung (1997) reviewed several empirical studies concerned with the way resources are distributed. He concluded that in general, in equal status situations, equality is preferred in collectivist and equity in individualist cultures. Equal distribution is associated with solidarity, harmony, and cohesion, so it fits with the values of people in collectivist cultures. Equity is compatible with productivity, competition, and self-gain, so it fits with the values of people in individualist cultures. Some people in collectivist cultures even show a generosity rule when exchanging with in-group members. That is, they use equality even when their contribution is clearly higher than that of other members (Hui et al. 1991).

Church (2000) has summarized the major differences between individualist and collectivist cultures. The following are especially important in comparisons of collectivist and individualist cultures: (*a*) People in collectivist cultures focus on contexts more than on internal processes in predicting the behavior of others; (*b*) individual behaviors are less consistent in collectivist cultures across situations; and (*c*) in collectivist cultures behavior is more predictable from norms and roles than from attitudes.

At the Individual Level of Analysis

All humans have access to both individualist and collectivist cognitive structures, but the accessibility to these structures differs. In individualist cultures people have more access to the individualist cognitive structures and are idiocentric, whereas in collectivist cultures people have more access to the collectivist cognitive structures and are allocentric. A simple prime, such as asking people to think for two minutes about what they have in common with their family and friends, shifts people toward allocentrism, whereas thinking of what makes one different from family and friends shifts one to idiocentrism (Trafimow et al. 1991). "Frame switching" among bicultural individuals is common. For instance, priming with the US Capitol or a Chinese building results in tendencies toward idiocentrism or allocentrism, respectively (Hong et al. 2000). That is, they see the self as either stable or malleable, behavior as determined by dispositional or situational factors, and the like, as discussed above.

Allocentrics tend to define themselves with reference to social entities to a greater extent than do idiocentrics (Triandis et al. 1990). Traditional samples that have acculturated to individualist cultures show this tendency less, especially when they are highly educated. For example, Altrocchi & Altrocchi (1995) found that the least acculturated Cook Islanders used about 57% social content in describing themselves, whereas Cook Islanders born in New Zealand used 20%, and New Zealanders used 17% social content. Similarly, Ma & Schoeneman (1997) reported 84% social content for Sumbaru Kenyans, 80% for Maasai Kenyans, but only 12% for American students, and 17% for Kenyan students. Idiocentrics tend to use traits in describing other people (Duff & Newman 1997) and focus on internal dispositions in making attributions (Menon et al. 1999). Compared with idiocentrics, allocentrics use the context, the situation, and the group's perspective more in making attributions (Choi et al. 1999, Menon et al. 1999) and evaluating their lives (Suh & Diener 2001) and tend to be more field-dependent and think in more holistic terms (Ji et al. 2000).

Allocentrics are also more ethnocentric than idiocentrics; they have very positive attitudes about their in-groups and quite negative attitudes about their out-groups (Lee & Ward 1998). Allocentrics see a large distance between self and enemies and a relatively small distance between self and friend. Idiocentrics see a relatively large distance between self and all others. In short, large differentiation occurs between self and others among idiocentrics; between in-group and out-groups among allocentrics (Iyengar et al. 1999).

Several important personality characteristics distinguish idiocentrics and allocentrics. For instance, idiocentrics tend toward dominance, while allocentrics tend to be agreeable (Moskowitz et al. 1994). Realo et al. (1997) developed a measure of allocentrism in Estonia and tested its convergence with the Big Five. They found a negative correlation between openness and allocentrism and positive correlations between agreeableness and conscientiousness and allocentrism. Watson et al. (1998) found that allocentrism was correlated with social responsibility and negatively correlated with normlessness; idiocentrism was correlated with high self-esteem and normlessness. Other studies show that compared with idiocentrics, allocentrics have low self-esteem, are easily embarrassed (Singelis et al. 1999), show greater tendencies toward affiliation, are more sensitive to rejection, and have a lower need for uniqueness (Yamaguchi et al. 1995). Matsumoto et al. (1997) developed and validated an inventory that measures allocentric and idiocentric tendencies.

In studies by Dion & Dion (1996) idiocentrism was related to less intimacy and poorer adjustment in romantic love relationships. Self-actualization, a prototypical individualist construct, was related to more gratification with love, yet less love for the partner and less caring for the needs of the partner, suggesting that idiocentrism may be a factor in the high divorce rate of individualist countries (Dion & Dion 1996).

The motive structure of allocentrics reflects receptivity to others, adjustment to the needs of others, and restraint of own needs and desires. The basic motives emphasized by idiocentrics reflect internal needs, such as rights and capacities, including the ability to withstand social pressures (Markus & Kitayama 1991, Bond & Smith 1996b). Achievement motivation is socially oriented among allocentrics, and individually oriented among idiocentrics. Yu & Yang (1994) developed separate scales for these two kinds of motivation and showed that these scales are uncorrelated among allocentrics. Gabrenya & Hwang (1996) provide an excellent description of social interaction in China that illustrates most of the points presented above.

Social behavior depends on the interaction of personality and situation. When idiocentrics and allocentrics were randomly assigned to individualist and collectivist situations, the most cooperation occurred among allocentrics in collectivist situations (Chatman & Barsade 1995). In Chatman & Barsade's study, the situation was a powerful factor in determining the level of cooperation, but the interaction of personality and situation was equally important. Situations may also have implications for the kinds of behaviors that will emerge. For instance,

Kitayama et al. (1997) showed that situations freely generated by Americans are conducive to self-enhancement, and Americans are likely to be high in self-enhancement. Japanese-generated situations tend to be conducive to self-criticism, and the Japanese are likely to engage in self-criticism. Kitayama & Markus (1999) showed that the Japanese self, while internally consistent, allows the coexistence of contrasting elements, making it possible for the Japanese to be both explicitly self-critical and implicitly to evaluate themselves in a positive way. Perhaps because of this coexistence of contrasting elements of the self, on average, collectivists view themselves as more flexible across social situations than individualists do (Suh 2001).

What is the ideal relation between culture (e.g., individualism) and personality (e.g., idiocentrism)? There is some empirical support for the "culture fit" hypothesis, which states that allocentrics are better adjusted in a collectivist culture and idiocentrics are better adjusted in an individualist culture (Schmitz 1994, Ward & Chang 1997). However, there is also evidence that individuals who are high on both allocentrism and idiocentrism are especially well-adjusted to their environment (Imamoglou 1998). Also, those who were raised in a collectivist culture and become acculturated to an individualist culture are high in both allocentrism and idiocentrism (Yamada & Singelis 1999). More needs to be explored about how individual tendencies (e.g., allocentrism) unfold and change in the context of both congruent (collectivistic) and incongruent (individualistic) cultural situations.

DIMENSIONS OF PERSONALITY

The Big Five, Seven, and Other Arguments

Given that all humans are one species and that personality has genetic roots (Rieman et al. 1997), the similarities among cultural groups are likely to be greater than the differences. Not surprisingly, most personality researchers emphasize the similarities in personality structure across cultures. Goldberg (1981) makes the case that the Big Five may be universal, because they each have important survival qualities in all cultures. De Raad et al. (1998) offer a review of the cross-cultural findings on the Big Five personality factors.

The research program of McCrae and Costa suggests that the basic personality traits are transcultural. They argue that (a) the same personality structure has emerged in a wide variety of cultures (Digman & Shmelyov 1996, McCrae & Costa 1997, Pulver et al. 1995, Yang et al. 1999), (b) traits show the same pattern of developmental change in adulthood (McCrae et al. 1999, 2000), (c) traits are biologically based (Jang et al. 1998), and (d) acculturation effects are as predicted (McCrae et al. 1998b). For example, exposing Chinese to Canadian culture increases their openness, cheerfulness, and indiscriminate pro-social behavior and attitudes.

McCrae et al. (1998a) show very similar structures in different cultures, though they admit that the French varimax factors are about 15 degrees off from the American position, and the Japanese factors are 35 degrees away from the American position. Butcher et al. (1998) make the same claim for the MMPI-2, as a measure of abnormal personality. Somer & Goldberg (1999) reported that four of the five factors were clearly detectable in the structure of Turkish trait descriptive adjectives.

Instead of using the traditional lexical approach, several studies have examined the Big Five structures through other methods. Paunonen et al. (2000) constructed a nonverbal test of personality, consisting of a target person engaging in various trait-related behaviors, and found the five factors in data from Canada, England, the Netherlands, Norway, and Israel. Working with parental descriptions of child personality, Kohnstamm et al. (1998) found that in the seven countries they examined, the Big Five provided the most important categories for the classification of these descriptions.

Williams et al. (1998) linked the Big Five with individualism and collectivism. They obtained a cluster of countries that was individualist and low in power distance and a cluster that was collectivist and less economically developed. Interestingly, however, Japan and Singapore belonged to the first cluster. In the individualist cultures the more important traits were internal (e.g., dominant, distrustful, unscrupulous), whereas in the collectivist countries they were external (handsome, polished, healthy). Again, we see the emphasis on internal factors among individualists and external factors among collectivists.

Although the overall evidence in support of the Big Five structure is impressive, cross-cultural generalizations still require caution. The special issue edited by McCrae (2000) does a commendable job of including papers by critics. Bock (2000), for instance, argues that there is much within-culture variability, and any characterization of a culture on the basis of the location of the sample on the five factors will be an oversimplification. In another paper, Bond (2000) finds a *Chinese tradition* factor that was derived from emic personality studies and shows that when this factor is included in a study, it increases the predictability of behavior. One important comment made by Church & Katigbak (2000) is that traits do not predict behavior as well in collectivist as in individualist cultures.

Our own reaction to this research program is also critical. First, most of the data were collected from college students or students of secondary and technical schools (Draguns et al. 2000). In the earlier section we pointed out that education is linked with idiocentrism. We do not know what the structures would be with very allocentric research participants or with those who did not have the benefit of extensive schooling, e.g., illiterates. Schooling is a major factor in the way people are able to reason (Luria 1976) and respond to personality instruments.

Related to that criticism is the observation that the cultural distance between the American samples and the samples from the other cultures that have been investigated thus far was not especially large. Cultural distance reflects differences in language families, socio-economic level, family structure, religion, and values

(Triandis 1994). Values differ substantially among cultures (Schwartz 1992, 1994). Todd (1983) has identified eight types of family structure. A simple term like "aunt" may convey different meanings in different family structures. Noneducated samples from nonliterate cultures that have very different religions, standards of living, and values, for instance, have not been studied much so far. Because most cross-cultural studies of the Big Five used samples that are not very distant in culture, we cannot be sure as yet that the same factor structures will occur universally.

Second, cultural differences in the way people sample the environment may change the factor structure. The Big Five are etic dimensions of personality. It is possible to use indigenous markers of these five factors, which results in a quasi-indigenous personality inventory, as was done for Castilian Spanish by Benet-Martinez & John (2000). However, one step further is to use both etic and emic items (Diaz-Loving 1998, 1999). In the few cases in which the etic plus emic strategy was used, the Big Five structure survived some of the time, but not always. Such strategies resulted in new factors that apparently are more adequate for the description of personality in one culture than in another. For instance, Di Blas & Forzi (1999) found that the Big Five structure was replicated in Italian when they imposed an etic definition of the personality dimensions. However, when they incorporated an emic perspective, a three-factor structure emerged as the most satisfactory solution. Di Blas et al. (2000) found that when the evaluative and descriptive aspects of the Italian personality inventory were distinguished, three factors were obtained: evaluation, tightness (e.g., self-controlled) versus looseness (e.g., impulsive), and assertive versus unassertive. Katigbak et al. (1996) developed an indigenous Filipino personality inventory that had six factors. They found that it could be matched to the Big Five or the Big Seven, but only after significant adjustment. Benet-Martinez (1999) found that seven factors were best in describing personality in a Spanish sample.

Third, the original set of traits that was used in the development of the Big Five excluded a number of potential descriptors. According to Almagor et al. (1995), the original Allport-Odbert and Norman lists of personality traits excluded evaluative terms and terms describing temporary states (e.g., mood states). This resulted in the elimination of some factors, so that seven instead of five factors emerged when a more complete list of traits (in Hebrew) was used. Benet-Martinez & Waller (1997) started with traits listed in the unabridged Spanish dictionary and also obtained seven factors.

China is culturally more distant from the United States than Israel or Spain. When an etic plus emic personality inventory was administered in China, the results were even more discrepant (Cheung et al. 1996). The Chinese Personality Assessment Inventory (CPAI) used scales that were specific to Chinese culture (such as the Ah-Q mentality, found in a well-known fictional character in Chinese literature of the early twentieth century). It also used traits found in the Big Five. It obtained four factors that accounted for only 59% of the total variance and had no obvious relationship to the Big Five. When Cheung & Leung (1998) administered the CPAI in Hong Kong and the People's Republic of China, they obtained four factors in both places that did not match the Big Five. Furthermore, when they administered the Big Five items jointly with the Chinese personality inventory, they were able to identify the neuroticism, extraversion, agreeableness, and conscientiousness factors, but not the openness factor. There was also a Chinese tradition factor that had no relationship to the Big Five. It appears that the openness factor is problematic in several studies. One possibility is that because collectivism is negatively correlated with openness (Realo et al. 1997), openness emerges more readily in individualist cultures, particularly among student samples that tend to be idiocentric, than in collectivist cultures.

The utility of the etic plus emic approach can be seen when the addition of the emic factors increases predictability on some criterion. For example, Zhang & Bond (1998) found that adding an indigenous personality factor to the Big Five increased the predictability of "filial piety" in two Chinese societies.

Cultural psychologists have gone even further and developed inventories that were entirely emic. For example, La Rosa & Diaz-Loving (1991) developed a list of 700 traits by discussing the topic with 118 Mexican high school and university students. After a series of factor analyses they found 9 factors that had little resemblance to the Big Five. Diaz-Guerrero & Diaz-Loving (1994) went even further and proposed that psychologists should use different inventories depending on whether they are interested in studying clinical, educational, industrial, criminal, or social samples.

Guanzon-Lapena et al. (1998) developed four indigenous Philippine personality measures (with different samples). They were able to conceptually match their factors with the Big Five. However, they stressed that they do not claim that their factors "really" corresponded to the Big Five (p. 265). They concluded that "(a) Each of the Big Five domains is represented by one or more dimensions from each of the indigenous instruments; and (b) None of the indigenous dimensions is so culturally unique that it is unrecognizable to non-Filipinos ..." (p. 265). They further pointed out that some dimensions such as social curiosity, excessive conformity, respectfulness, low tolerance for teasing, and thriftiness are especially relevant to a collectivist culture, such as the Philippines. Church et al. (1997) had Filipinos rate the self on 861 Tagalog trait adjectives and another Filipino sample rate it on 280 marker variables. In both cases, they obtained seven factors.

The assessment of personality across cultures is difficult because there are many ways in which nonequivalence of factors may emerge. Paunonen & Ashton (1998) pointed out that nonequivalence of the Big Five factor structure could be due to such factors as poor item translation, lack of item relevance, trait-level differences, trait-structure differences, differential causal links, response style differences, test-format problems, and differential analytic methods. They concluded that if the Big Five structure is obtained in other cultures it means that these factors are applicable in the other cultures. On the other hand, if the Big Five factor structure does not emerge, that does not necessarily mean that the factors are not applicable, because any one of the 10 methodological factors that can create nonequivalence might be operating. The inability to falsify the hypothesis that the Big Five are universal is a glaring weakness of this hypothesis.

Saucier et al. (2000) identified 18 methodological factors that may give the impression of nonequivalence of factor structures. They asked, When is a difference in factor structures a "real" difference? The two-factor solution, they think, is undoubtedly universal and may correspond to individualism and collectivism. The two-factor solution includes dynamism and individual ascendance as one factor and social propriety and community as the other factor. They also explored if the three- or four-factor solutions may be universal. They concluded by pointing out that "a model of descriptions does not provide a model of causes, and the study of personality lexicons should not be equated with the study of personality" (p. 43).

De Raad et al. (1998) culled trait terms from various lexicons and constructed a representative sample of trait terms and then obtained factor structures in eight Western cultures. They computed Tucker (1951) congruence coefficients between the factor structures of these cultures and the American English solution. They concluded that three or four of the Big Five factors can be identified in all cultures. The openness factor of the Big Five was again problematic. However, whether the coefficients of congruence were high enough to permit calling the factors "equivalent" is a matter of opinion. According to Tucker (personal communication, 1975), the level of his coefficient needs to reach 0.90 in order to call a factor "the same." None of the coefficients reported by de Raad et al. reached that level (they ranged from 0.23 to 0.85). It is up to the reader to decide if the factors are really equivalent.

In sum, although the Big Five seem well-established in individualist cultures, only four of these factors appear consistently in all cultures, and depending on the list of traits that one starts with, one may obtain indigenous factors or more than five factors. Also, it is worth noting that even if the taxonomies of personality are universal, it does not guarantee their identical usage (Atran 1993, Choi et al. 1997).

FUTURE DIRECTIONS

Spiro (1993) provided an extensive critique of the work of Markus & Kitayama (1991) and others who contrasted individualist and collectivist cultures. He thought that this characterization of such cultures is "wildly overdrawn." He emphasized that culturally normative conceptions are not necessarily manifested in the behavior of individuals. This suggests the need for research that will examine how the constructs are to be conceived. Triandis (1989) presented a probabilistic conception that emphasizes that in individualist cultures people sample mostly internal attributes of individuals and aspects of the personal self, whereas in collectivist cultures people sample mostly the collective aspects of the self. Is this conception useful in predicting behaviors? How is that conception related to differences in the ecology? In turn, how are differences in ecology related to differences in socialization practices?

The study of cultural syndromes also requires the examination of hypotheses about the relationships among the syndromes. For example, is it in fact the case that collectivism is correlated with tightness and also with cultural simplicity? Carpenter's (2000) data suggest that they are correlated, but more work is needed. Is it in fact the case that individualism is correlated with cultural complexity and also with looseness? How are these attributes related to personality? Is cultural complexity related to cognitive complexity? Is tightness related to conscientiousness?

The emic plus etic description of personality will require data from many cultures, especially nonliterate ones, and the integration of the information obtained from these studies with the study of cultural syndromes. In addition, researchers need to probe each of the Big Five traits more deeply. A recent study by Lucas et al. (2000), for instance, suggests that sensitivity to positive reward is a universally significant feature of extraversion. Many more questions need to be addressed concerning the precise meaning and importance of the Big Five traits across cultures. For instance, are traits especially relevant to successful functioning in one culture different from those of another? We speculate that agreeableness may be particularly important in cultures that emphasize interpersonal harmony, whereas surgency may be more important in individualist cultures.

Finally, an important direction would be the study of culture change and its impact on personality. For instance, as globalization increasingly pushes different cultures to interact with each other, what kinds of "culturally hybrid" personalities will emerge?

SUMMARY AND CONCLUSION

We reviewed links between ecology and culture, and cultural syndromes and personality. In addition, we identified dimensions of socialization that are related to cultural syndromes, such as the emphasis on child independence found in individualist cultures and the emphasis on dependence found in collectivist cultures. In addition to the significant findings that continue to emerge at the cultural level of individualism and collectivism, sophisticated theories and methodologies are being developed to understand the personal characteristics of idiocentric and allocentric individuals within a culture.

A large volume of cross-cultural evidence has been accumulated in recent years in support of the structural stability of the Big Five model. Although the sheer amount of evidence in support of the Big Five model is impressive, we have highlighted several limitations in the current research that are worth considering before making sweeping generalizations about the Big Five. A challenging but highly promising future direction for the study of culture and personality is to find ways to successfully incorporate emic as well as etic elements of culture into the field's research methods and theories.

ACKNOWLEDGMENTS

We thank Karen Feasel, Susan Fiske, and Fred Kanfer for helpful comments on earlier versions of this chapter.

Visit the Annual Reviews home page at www.AnnualReviews.org

LITERATURE CITED

Almagor M, Tellegen A, Waller NG. 1995. The Big Seven: a cross-cultural replication and further exploration of the basic dimensions of natural language trait descriptors. *J. Pers. Soc. Psychol.* 69:300–7

Altemeyer R. 1996. *The Authoritarian Specter.* Cambridge, MA: Harvard Univ. Press

Altrocchi J, Altrocchi L. 1995. Polyfaceted psychological acculturation in Cook Islanders. *J. Cross-Cult. Psychol.* 26:426–40

Atran S. 1993. Core domains versus scientific theories: evidence from systematics and Itza-Maya folkbiology. In *Domain Specificity in Cognition and Culture,* ed. L Hirschfeld, S Gelman, pp. 316–40. New York: Cambridge Univ. Press

Ball J, Moselle K. 1995. Health risk behaviors of adolescents in Singapore. *Asian J. Psychol.* 1:54–62

Barkow G, Cosmides L, Tooby J, eds. 1992. *The Adapted Mind: Evolutionary Psychology and the Generation of Culture.* New York: Oxford Univ. Press

Benet-Martinez V. 1999. Exploring indigenous Spanish personality constructs with a combined emic-etic approach. In *Latest Contributions to Cross-Cultural Psychology,* ed. JC Lasry, JG Adair, KL Dion, pp. 151–75. Lisse, The Netherlands: Swets & Zeitliner

Benet-Martinez V, John OP. 2000. Towards the development of quasi-indigenous personality constructs: measuring Los Cinco Grandes in Spain with indigenous Castilian markers. *Am. Behav. Sci.* 44:141–57

Benet-Martinez V, Waller NG. 1997. Further evidence for the cross-cultural generality of the big seven factor model: indigenous and imported Spanish personality constructs. *J. Pers.* 65:567–98

Berry JW. 1976. *Human Ecology and Cognitive Style.* Beverly Hills, CA: Sage

Bock PK. 2000. Culture and personality revisited. *Am. Behav. Sci.* 44:32–40

Bond MH. 2000. Localizing the imperial outreach: the Big Five and more in Chinese culture. *Am. Behav. Sci.* 44:63–72

Bond MH, Smith PB. 1996a. Cross-cultural social and organizational psychology. *Annu. Rev. Psychol.* 47:205–35

Bond R, Smith PB. 1996b. Culture and conformity: a meta-analysis of studies using Asch's (1952b, 1956) line judgment task. *Psychol. Bull.* 119:111–37

Bornstein MH, Haynes OM, Pascual L, Painter KM, Galperin C. 1999. Play in two societies: pervasiveness of process, specificity of structure. *Child Dev.* 70:317–31

Brandt VS. 1974. Skiing cross-culturally. *Curr. Anthropol.* 15:64–66

Bruner J. 1974. Concluding comments and summary of conference. In *Readings in Cross-Cultural Psychology,* ed. JLM Dawson, WJ Lonner, pp. 381–91. Hong Kong: Univ. Hong Kong Press

Butcher JN, Lim J, Nezami E. 1998. Objective study of abnormal personality in cross-cultural settings: the Minnesota Multiphasic Personality Inventory (MMPI–2). *J. Cross-Cult. Psychol.* 29:189–211

Campbell DT. 1965. Variation and selective retention in socio-cultural evolution. In *Social Change in Developing Areas,* ed. HR Barringer, G Blanksten, R Mack, pp. 19–49. Cambridge, MA: Schenkman

Carpenter S. 2000. Effects of cultural tightness and collectivism on self-concept and causal attributions. *Cross-Cult. Res.* 34:38–56

Chatman JA, Barsade SG. 1995. Personality,

organizational culture, and cooperation: evidence from a business simulation. *Adm. Sci. Q.* 40:423–43

Cheung FM, Leung K. 1998. Indigenous personality measures: Chinese examples. *J. Cross-Cult. Psychol.* 29:233–48

Cheung FM, Leung K, Fan RM, Song W-Z, Zhang J-X, Zhang J-P. 1996. Development of the Chinese Personality Assessment Inventory. *J. Cross-Cult. Psychol.* 27:181–99

Chick G. 1997. Cultural complexity: the concept and its measurement. *Cross-Cult. Res.* 31:275–307

Chiu C, Dweck CS, Tong JY, Fu JH. 1997. Implicit theories and concepts of morality. *J. Pers. Soc. Psychol.* 73:923–40

Chiu C, Hong Y. 1999. Social identification in a political transition: the role of implicit beliefs. *Intern. J. Intercult. Relat.* 23:297–318

Choi I, Nisbett RE. 2000. Cultural psychology of surprise: holistic theories and recognition of contradiction. *J. Pers. Soc. Psychol.* 79:890–905

Choi I, Nisbett RE, Norenzayan A. 1999. Causal attribution across cultures: variation and universality. *Psychol. Bull.* 125:47–63

Choi I, Nisbett RE, Smith EE. 1997. Culture, category salience, and inductive reasoning. *Cognition* 65:15–32

Choi Y-E. 1996. *The Self in Different Contexts: Behavioral Analysis.* Montreal: Int. Congr. Psychol.

Church AT. 2000. Culture and personality: toward an integrated cultural trait psychology. *J. Pers.* 69:651–703

Church AT, Katigbak MS. 2000. Trait psychology in the Philippines. *Am. Behav. Sci.* 44:73–94

Church AT, Lonner WJ. 1998. The cross-cultural perspective in the study of personality: rationale and current research. *J. Cross-Cult. Psychol.* 29:32–62

Church AT, Reyes JA, Katigbak MS, Grimm SD. 1997. Filipino personality structure and the big five model. *J. Pers.* 65:477–528

Cialdini RB, Wosinska W, Barrett DW, Butner J, Gornik-Durose M. 1999. Compliance with a request in two cultures: the differential influence of social proof and commitment/consistency on collectivists and individualists. *Pers. Soc. Psychol. Bull.* 25:1242–53

Cohen D, Nisbett RE, Bowdle BF, Schwarz N. 1996. Insult, aggression, and the Southern culture of honor: an "experimental ethnography." *J. Pers. Soc. Psychol.* 70:945–60

Cohen R. 1991. *Negotiating Across Cultures.* Washington, DC: US Inst. Peace Press

Cooper CR, Denner J. 1998. Theories linking culture and psychology: universal and community-specific processes. *Annu. Rev. Psychol.* 49:559–84

Cross SE, Bacon P, Morris M. 2000. The relational-interdependent self-construal and relationships. *J. Pers. Soc. Psychol.* 78:791–98

De Raad B, Perugini M, Hrebickova M, Szarota P. 1998. Lingua franca of personality: taxonomies and structures based on the psycholexical approach. *J. Cross-Cult. Psychol.* 29:212–32

Diaz-Guerrero R, Diaz-Loving R. 1994. Personality across cultures. In *Cross-Cultural Topics in Psychology*, ed. LL Adler, UP Gielen, pp. 125–38. Westport, CT: Praeger

Diaz-Loving R. 1998. Contributions of Mexican ethnopsychology to the resolution of the etic-emic dilemma in personality. *J. Cross-Cult. Psychol.* 29:104–18

Diaz-Loving R. 1999. The indiginisation of psychology. Birth of a new science or rekindling of an old one? *Appl. Psychol.: Intern. Rev.* 48:433–50

Di Blas L, Forzi M. 1999. Refining a descriptive structure of personality attributes in the Italian language: the abridged Big Three circumplex structure. *J. Pers. Soc. Psychol.* 76:451–81

Di Blas L, Forzi M, Peabody D. 2000. Evaluative and descriptive dimensions from Italian personality factors. *Eur. J. Personal.* 14:279–90

Diener E, Suh EM, eds. 2000. *Subjective Well-Being Across Cultures.* Cambridge, MA: MIT Press

Digman JM, Shmelyov AG. 1996. The structure of temperament and personality in Russian children. *J. Pers. Soc. Psychol.* 71:341–51

Dion KK, Dion KL. 1996. Cultural perspectives on romantic love. *Pers. Relat.* 3:5–17

Draguns J, Krylova AV, Oryol VE, Rukavishnikov AA, Martin TA. 2000. Personality characteristics of the Netsy in the Russian Arctic. *Am. Behav. Sci.* 44:126–40

Duff KJ, Newman LS. 1997. Individual differences in the spontaneous construal of behavior: idiocentrism and the automatization of the trait inference process. *Soc. Cogn.* 15:217–41

Earley PC, Erez M, eds. 1997. *New Perspectives on International Industrial and Organizational Psychology.* San Francisco: Lexington

Funder D. 1997. *The Personality Puzzle.* New York: Norton

Gabrenya WK, Hwang K-K. 1996. Chinese social interaction: harmony and hierarchy on the good earth. In *The Handbook of Chinese Psychology*, ed. MH Bond, pp. 309–21. Hong Kong: Oxford Univ. Press

Gabriel S, Gardner WL. 1999. Are there "his" and "hers" types of interdependence? The implications of gender differences in collective versus relational interdependence for affect, behavior, and cognition. *J. Pers. Soc. Psychol.* 77:642–55

Goldberg L. 1981. Language and individual differences: the search for universals in personality lexicons. In *Review of Personality and Social Psychology*, ed. L Wheeler, pp. 141–61. Beverly Hills, CA: Sage

Gosling SD, John OP. 1999. Personality dimensions in non-human animals: a cross-species review. *Curr. Dir. Psychol. Sci.* 8:69–73

Greenfield P. 1997. You can't take it with you. Why ability assessments don't cross cultures. *Am. Psychol.* 52:1115–24

Greenfield P. 1999. *Three approaches to the psychology of culture: Where do they come from? Where can they go?* Presented at 3rd Conf. Asian Assoc. Soc. Psychol., Taiwan

Grimm SD, Church AT, Katigbak MS, Reyes

JA. 1999. Self-described traits, values, and moods associated with individualism and collectivism: testing I-C theory in an individualistic (U.S.) and a collectivistic (Philippine) culture. *J. Cross-Cult. Psychol.* 30:466–500

Guanzon-Lapena MA, Church AT, Carlota AJ, Katigbak MS. 1998. Indigenous personality measures: Philippine examples. *J. Cross-Cult. Psychol.* 29:249–70

Hasegawa T. 1996. *Silence in Japan and the United States.* MS thesis. Calif. State Univ. Fullerton

Heine SJ, Kitayama S, Lehman DR, Takata T, Ide E, et al. 2000. *Divergent Consequences of Success and Failure in Japan and North America: An Investigation of Self-Improving Motivations and Malleable Selves.* Univ. B.C., Vancouver, Can.

Heine SJ, Lehman DR, Markus HR, Kitayama S. 1999. Is there a universal need for positive self-regard? *Psychol. Rev.* 106:766–94

Ho D Y-F. 1998. Indigenous psychologies: Asian perspectives. *J. Cross-Cult. Psychol.* 29:88–103

Ho D Y-F. 1976. On the concept of face. *Am. J. Sociol.* 81:867–90

Hofstede G. 1980. *Culture's Consequences.* Beverly Hills, CA: Sage

Hofstede G, Arrindell WA, Best DL, De Mooij M, Hoppe MH, et al. 1998. *Masculinity and Femininity: The Taboo Dimension of National Cultures.* Thousand Oaks, CA: Sage

Holtgraves T. 1997. Styles of language use: individual and cultural variability in conversational indirectness. *J. Pers. Soc. Psychol.* 73:624–37

Hong Y, Ip G, Chiu C, Morris MW, Menon T. 2001. Cultural identity and dynamic construction of the self: collective duties and individual rights in Chinese and American cultures. *Soc. Cogn.* In press

Hong Y, Morris MW, Chiu C, Benet-Martinez V. 2000. Multiple minds: a dynamic constructivist approach to culture and cognition. *Am. Psychol.* 55:709–20

Hu HC. 1944. The Chinese concepts of face. *Am. Anthropol.* 46:45–64

Hui CH, Triandis HC, Yee C. 1991. Cultural differences in reward allocation: Is collectivism the explanation? *Br. J. Soc. Psychol.* 30:145–57

Imamoglou EO. 1998. Individualism and collectivism in a model and scale of balanced differentiation and integration. *J. Psychol.* 132:95–105

Iwao S. 1993. *The Japanese Woman: Traditional Image and Changing Reality.* New York: Free Press

Iyengar SS, Lepper MR. 1999. Rethinking the value of choice: a cultural perspective on intrinsic motivation. *J. Pers. Soc. Psychol.* 76:349–66

Iyengar SS, Lepper MR, Ross L. 1999. Independence from whom? Interdependence from whom? Cultural perspectives on ingroups versus outgroups. See Prentice & Miller 1999, pp. 273–301

Jang KL, McCrae RR, Angleitner A, Rieman R, Livesley WJ. 1998. Heritability of facet-level traits in a cross-cultural twin sample: support for a hierarchical model of personality. *J. Pers. Soc. Psychol.* 74:1556–65

Ji L-J, Peng K, Nisbett RE. 2000. Culture, control and perception of relationships in the environment. *J. Pers. Soc. Psychol.* 78:943–55

Kagitcibasi C. 1997. Individualism and collectivism. In *Handbook of Cross-Cultural Psychology*, ed. JW Berry, MH Segall, C Kagitcibasi, pp. 1–50. Boston: Allyn & Bacon. 2nd ed.

Kashima ES, Kashima Y. 1998. Culture and language: the case of cultural dimensions and personal pronoun use. *J. Cross-Cult. Psychol.* 29:461–86

Katigbak MS, Church AT, Akamine TX. 1996. Cross-cultural generality of personality dimensions: relating indigenous and imported dimensions in two cultures. *J. Pers. Soc. Psychol.* 70:99–114

Kim H, Markus HR. 1999. Deviance or uniqueness, harmony or conformity? A cultural analysis. *J. Pers. Soc. Psychol.* 77:785–800

Kim U, Triandis HC, Kagitcibasi C, Choi S-C, Yoon G, eds. 1994. *Individualism and Collectivism: Theory, Method, and Applications.* Newbury Park, CA: Sage

Kitayama S, Markus HR. 1999. Yin and Yang of the Japanese self: the cultural psychology of personality coherence. In *The Coherence of Personality: Social-Cognitive Bases of Consistency, Variability and Organization*, ed. D Cervone, Y Shoda, pp. 242–301. New York: Guilford

Kitayama S, Markus HR, Kurokawa M. 2000. Culture, emotion, and well-being: good feelings in Japan and the United States. *Cogn. Emot.* 14:93–124

Kitayama S, Markus HR, Matsumoto H, Norasakkunkit V. 1997. Individual and collective processes in the construction of the self: self-enhancement in the United States and self-criticism in Japan. *J. Pers. Soc. Psychol.* 72:1245–67

Kluckhohn C. 1954. Culture and behavior. In *Handbook of Social Psychology*, ed. G Lindzey, 2:921–76. Cambridge, MA: Addison-Wesley

Kohlberg L. 1981. *Essays on Moral Development.* New York: Harper & Row

Kohnstamm GA, Halverson CF Jr, Mervielde I, Havill VL. 1998. *Parental Descriptions of Child Personality: Developmental Antecedents of the Big Five?* Mahwah, NJ: Erlbaum

Krull DS, Loy MH-M, Lin J, Wang C-F, Chen S, Zhao X. 1999. The fundamental attribution error: correspondence bias in individualist and collectivist cultures. *Pers. Soc. Psychol. Bull.* 25:1208–19

La Rosa J, Diaz-Loving R. 1991. Evaluacion de autoconcepto: una escala multidimensional. *Rev. Latinoam. Psicol.* 23:15–33

Lee L, Ward C. 1998. Ethnicity, idiocentrism-allocentrism, and intergroup attitudes. *J. Appl. Soc. Psychol.* 28:109–23

Lee Y-T, McCauley CR, Draguns JG, eds. 1999a. *Personality and Person Perceptions Across Cultures.* Mahwah, NJ: Erlbaum

Lee Y-T, McCauley CR, Draguns JG. 1999b. Why study personality in culture? See Lee et al. 1999a, pp. 3–22

Lee Y-T, Seligman MEP. 1997. Are Americans

more optimistic than the Chinese? *Pers. Soc. Psychol. Bull.* 23:32–40

Leung K. 1997. Negotiation and reward allocations across cultures. See Earley & Erez 1997, pp. 640–75

Levine R, Sato S, Hashimoto T, Verma J. 1995. Love and marriage in eleven cultures. *J. Cross-Cult. Psychol.* 26:554–71

Lin Z. 1997. Ambiguity with a purpose. The shadow of power in communication. See Earley & Erez 1997, pp. 363–76

Lucas RE, Diener E, Grob A, Suh EM, Shao L. 2000. Cross-cultural evidence for the fundamental features of extraversion. *J. Pers. Soc. Psychol.* 79:452–68

Luria AR. 1976. *Cognitive Development: Its Cultural and Social Foundations.* Cambridge, MA: Harvard Univ. Press

Ma HK. 1988. The Chinese perspective on moral judgment and development. *Int. J. Psychol.* 23:201–27

Ma V, Schoeneman TJ. 1997. Individualism versus collectivism: a comparison of Kenyan and American self-concepts. *Basic Appl. Soc. Psychol.* 19:261–73

Maccoby EE. 2000. Parenting and its effects on children: on reading and misreading behavior genetics. *Annu. Rev. Psychol.* 51:1–27

MacDonald K. 1998. Evolution, culture, and the five-factor model. *J. Cross-Cult. Psychol.* 29:119–49

Magnusson D, Törestad B. 1993. A holistic view of personality: a model revisited. *Annu. Rev. Psychol.* 44:427–52

Markus H, Kitayama S. 1991. Culture and self: implications for cognition, emotion, and motivation. *Psychol. Rev.* 98:224–53

Markus H, Kitayama S. 1998. The cultural psychology of personality. *J. Cross-Cult. Psychol.* 29:63–87

Marsella AJ, Dubanoski J, Hamada WC, Morse H. 2000. The measurement of personality across cultures: historical, conceptual, and methodological considerations. *Am. Behav. Sci.* 44:41–62

Matsumoto D, Weissman MD, Preston K, Brown BR, Kupperbusch C. 1997. Context-specific measurement of individualism-collectivism on the individual level: the Individualism-Collectivism Interpersonal Assessment Inventory. *J. Cross-Cult. Psychol.* 28:743–67

McCrae RR. 2000. Trait psychology and the revival of personality-and-culture studies. *Am. Behav. Sci.* 44:10–31

McCrae RR, Costa PT Jr. 1997. Personality trait structure as a human universal. *Am. Psychol.* 52:509–16

McCrae RR, Costa PT Jr, Pedroso de Lima M, Simoes A, Ostendorf F, et al. 1999. Age differences in personality across the adult life span: parallels in five cultures. *Dev. Psychol.* 35:466–77

McCrae RR, Costa PT Jr, del Pilar GH, Rolland J-P, Parker WD. 1998a. Cross-cultural assessment of the five factor model: the revised NEO personality inventory. *J. Cross-Cult. Psychol.* 29:171–88

McCrae RR, Costa PT Jr, Ostendorf F, Angleitner A, Hrebickova M, et al. 2000. Nature over nurture: temperament, personality, and lifespan development. *J. Pers. Soc. Psychol.* 78:173–86

McCrae RR, Yik MSM, Trapnell PD, Bond MH, Paulhus DL. 1998b. Interpreting personality profiles across cultures: bilingual, acculturation, and peer rating studies of Chinese undergraduates. *J. Pers. Soc. Psychol.* 74:1041–55

McFarland S, Ageyev V, Abalakina-Paap M. 1992. Authoritarianism in the former Soviet Union. *J. Pers. Soc. Psychol.* 63:1004–10

Menon T, Morris MW, Chiu C-Y, Hong Y-Y. 1999. Culture and the construal of agency: attribution to individual versus group dispositions. *J. Pers. Soc. Psychol.* 76:701–17

Mesquita B. 2001. Emotions in collectivist and individualist contexts. *J. Pers. Soc. Psychol.* 80:68–74

Miller JG. 1997. Cultural conceptions of duty. See Munro et al. 1997, pp. 178–92

Miller JG, Bersoff DM. 1998. The role of liking in perceptions of the moral responsibility to help: a cultural perspective. *J. Exp. Soc. Psychol.* 34:443–69

Mills J, Clark MS. 1982. Exchange and communal relationships. In *Review of Personality and Social Psychology*, ed. L Wheeler, 3:121–44. Beverly Hills, CA: Sage

Moskowitz DS, Suh EJ, Desaulniers J. 1994. Situational influences on gender differences in agency and communion. *J. Pers. Soc. Psychol.* 66:753–61

Munro D, Schumaker JF, Carr SC, eds. 1997. *Motivation and Culture*. New York: Routledge

Munroe RL. 1999. A behavioral orientation. *Ethos* 27:104–14

Nisbett RE, Cohen D. 1996. *Culture of Honor: The Psychology of Violence in the South*. Boulder, CO: Westview

Norenzayan A, Choi I, Nisbett RE. 1999. Eastern and Western perceptions of causality for social behavior: lay theories about personalities and situations. See Prentice & Miller 1999, pp. 239–72

Ohbuchi K-I, Fukushima O, Tedeschi JT. 1999. Cultural values in conflict management: goal orientation, goal attainment, and tactical decision. *J. Cross-Cult. Psychol.* 30:51–71

O'Kelly CG, Carney LS. 1986. *Women and Men in Society*. Belmont, CA: Wadsworth. 2nd ed.

Oyserman D, Sakamoto I, Lauffer A. 1998. Cultural accommodation: hybridity and the framing of social obligation. *J. Pers. Soc. Psychol.* 74:1606–18

Paunonen SV, Ashton MC. 1998. The structural assessment of personality across cultures. *J. Cross-Cult. Psychol.* 29:150–70

Paunonen SV, Zeidner M, Engvik HA, Oosterveld P, Maliphant R. 2000. The nonverbal assessment of personality in five cultures. *J. Cross-Cult. Psychol.* 31:220–39

Pettigrew TF. 1999. Placing authoritarianism in social context. *Polit. Groups Individ.* 8:5–20

Piker S. 1998. Contributions of psychological anthropology. *J. Cross-Cult. Psychol.* 29:9–31

Prentice DA, Miller DT, eds. 1999. *Cultural Divides: Understanding and Overcoming Group Conflict*. New York: Russell Sage Found.

Pulver A, Allik J, Pulkkinen L, Haemaelaeinen M. 1995. A Big Five personality inventory in two non-Indo-European languages. *Eur. J. Pers.* 9:109–24

Realo A, Allik J, Vadi M. 1997. The hierarchical structure of collectivism. *J. Res. Pers.* 31:93–116

Revelle W. 1995. Personality processes. *Annu. Rev. Psychol.* 46:295–328

Rieman R, Angleitner A, Strelau J. 1997. Genetic and environmental influences on personality: a study of twins reared together using self- and peer-report NEO-FFI scales. *J. Pers.* 65:449–75

Rohner RP. 1986. *The Warmth Dimension: Foundations of Parental Acceptance-Rejection Theory*. Newbury Park, CA: Sage

Rohner RP. 1999. Acceptance and rejection. In *Encyclopedia of Human Emotions*, ed. D Levinson, J Ponzetti, P Jorgensen, 1:6–14. New York: Macmillan

Rozin P, Lowery L, Imada S, Haidt J. 1999. The CAD triad hypothesis: a mapping between three moral emotions (contempt, anger, disgust) and three moral codes (community, autonomy, divinity). *J. Pers. Soc. Psychol.* 76:574–86

Saucier G, Hampson SE, Goldberg LR. 2000. Cross-language studies of lexical personality factors. In *Advances In Personality Psychology*, ed. SE Hampson, 1:1–36. Hove, UK: Psychology Press

Schmitz PG. 1994. Acculturation and adaptation processes among immigrants in Germany. In *Journeys into Cross-Cultural Psychology*, ed. A-M Bouvy, FJR van de Vijver, P Boski, PG Schmitz, pp. 142–57. Lisse, The Netherlands: Swets & Zeitlinger

Schwartz SH. 1992. Universals in the content and structure of values: theoretical advances and empirical tests in 20 countries. In *Advances in Experimental Social Psychology*, ed. M Zanna, 25:1–66. New York: Academic

Schwartz SH. 1994. Beyond individualism and collectivism: new cultural dimensions of values. See Kim et al. 1994, pp. 85–122

Shweder RA. 1991. Rethinking culture and personality theory. *Thinking Through Cultures: Expeditions in Cultural Psychology*, ed. RA Schweder, pp. 269–312. Cambridge, MA. Harvard Univ. Press

Shweder RA, Sullivan MA. 1993. Cultural psychology: Who needs it? *Annu. Rev. Psychol.* 44:497–23

Singelis TM, Bond MH, Sharkey WF, Lai CS-Y. 1999. Unpackaging culture's influence on self-esteem and embarrassability. *J. Cross-Cult. Psychol.* 30:315–41

Singelis TM, Brown WJ. 1995. Culture, self, and collectivist communication: linking culture to individual behavior. *Hum. Commun. Res.* 21:354–89

Somer O, Goldberg LR. 1999. The structure of Turkish trait descriptive adjectives. *J. Pers. Soc. Psychol.* 76:431–50

Sperber D. 1996. *Explaining Culture: A Naturalistic Approach*. Oxford: Blackwell

Spiro ME. 1993. Is the Western conception of the self "peculiar" within the context of world cultures? *Ethos* 21:107–53

Su SK, Chiu C, Hong Y, Leung K, Peng K, Morris MW. 1999. Self-organization and social organization: U. S. and Chinese constructions. In *The Psychology of the Social Self*, ed. TR Tyler, RM Kramer, OP John, pp. 193–222. Mahwah, NJ: Erlbaum

Suh E, Diener E, Oishi S, Triandis HC. 1998. The shifting basis of life satisfaction judgments across cultures: emotions versus norms. *J. Pers. Soc. Psychol.* 74:482–93

Suh EM. 2001. *Culture, Identity Consistency, and Subjective Well-Being*. Univ. Calif., Irvine. Submitted

Suh EM. 2000. Self, the hyphen between culture and subjective well-being. In *Culture and Subjective Well-Being*, ed. E Diener, EM Suh, pp. 63–87. Cambridge, MA: MIT Press

Suh EM, Diener E. 2001. *The Role of the Self in Life Satisfaction Judgments: Weighing Emotion and Social Information Differently*. Univ. Calif., Irvine. Submitted

Todd E. 1983. *La Troisieme Planete*. Paris: Editions Seuil

Tooby J, Cosmides L. 1992. The psychological foundations of culture. See Barkow et al. 1992, pp. 3–136

Trafimow D, Triandis HC, Goto S. 1991. Some tests of the distinction between private self and collective self. *J. Pers. Soc. Psychol.* 60:640–55

Triandis HC. 1972. *The Analysis of Subjective Culture*. New York: Wiley

Triandis HC. 1989. The self and social behavior in different cultural contexts. *Psychol. Rev.* 96:269–89

Triandis HC. 1994. *Culture and Social Behavior*. New York: McGraw-Hill

Triandis HC. 1995. *Individualism and Collectivism*. Boulder, CO: Westview

Triandis HC. 1996. The psychological measurement of cultural syndromes. *Am. Psychol.* 51:407–15

Triandis HC. 2000a. Cultural syndromes & subjective well-being. See Diener & Suh 2000, pp. 13–37

Triandis HC. 2000b. Dialectics between cultural and cross-cultural psychology. *Asian J. Soc. Psychol.* 3:185–95

Triandis HC, Carnevale P, Gelfand M, Robert C, Wasti A, et al. 2001. Culture, personality and deception. *Int. J. Cross-Cult. Manage.* 1:73–90

Triandis HC, Gelfand M. 1998. Converging measurements of horizontal and vertical individualism and collectivism. *J. Pers. Soc. Psychol.* 74:118–28

Triandis HC, Leung K, Villareal M, Clack FL. 1985. Allocentric versus idiocentric tendencies: convergent and discriminant validation. *J. Res. Pers.* 19:395–415

Triandis HC, McCusker C, Hui CH. 1990. Multimethod probes of individualism and collectivism. *J. Pers. Soc. Psychol.* 59:1006–20

Trilling L. 1972. *Sincerity and Authenticity*. London: Oxford Univ. Press

Tucker LJ. 1951. *A method for synthesis of factor analysis studies. Personnel Res. Rep. No. 984*, Dep. Army. Washington, DC

Van de Vliert E, Schwartz SH, Huismans SE, Hofstede G, Daan S. 1999. Temperature, cultural masculinity, and domestic political violence: a cross-national study. *J. Cross-Cult. Psychol.* 30:291–314

Verkuyten M, Masson K. 1996. Culture and gender differences in the perception of friendship by adolescents. *Int. J. Psychol.* 31:207–17

Verma J. 1992. Allocentrism and relational orientation. In *Innovations in Cross-Cultural Psychology*, ed. S Iwawaki, Y Kashima, K Leung, pp. 152–63. Lisse, The Netherlands: Swets & Zeitlinger

Ward C, Chang WC. 1997. "Cultural fit:" a new perspective on personality and sojourner adjustment. *Int. J. Intercult. Relat.* 21:525–33

Watson PJ, Sherbak J, Morris RJ. 1998. Irrational beliefs, individualism-collectivism, and adjustment. *Pers. Individ. Differ.* 24:173–79

Wiggins JS, Pincus AL. 1992. Personality: structure and assessment. *Annu. Rev. Psychol.* 43:473–504

Williams JE, Satterwhite RC, Saiz JL. 1998.

The Importance of Psychological Traits: A Cross-Cultural Study. New York: Plenum

Yamada A, Singelis T. 1999. Biculturalism and self-construal. *Int. J. Intercult. Relat.* 23:697–709

Yamaguchi S, Kuhlman DM, Sugimori S. 1995. Personality correlates of allocentric tendencies in individualist and collectivist cultures. *J. Cross-Cult. Psychol.* 26:658–72

Yang J, McCrae RR, Costa PT, Dai X, Yao S, et al. 1999. Cross-cultural personality assessment in psychiatric populations: the NEO-PI-R in the People's Republic of China. *Psychol. Assess.* 11:359–68

Yu A-B, Yang K-S. 1994. The nature of achievement motivation in collectivist societies. See Kim et al. 1994, pp. 239–50

Zhang J, Bond MH. 1998. Personality and filial piety among college students in two Chinese societies: the added value of indigenous constructs. *J. Cross-Cult. Psychol.* 29:402–17

Annu. Rev. Psychol. 2002. 53:161–86

SELF AND SOCIAL IDENTITY*

Naomi Ellemers,[1] Russell Spears,[2] and Bertjan Doosje[2]

[1]*Department of Social and Organizational Psychology, Leiden University, P.O. Box 9555, 2300 RB Leiden, The Netherlands; e-mail: Ellemers@fsw.leidenuniv.nl*
[2]*Department of Social Psychology, University of Amsterdam, Roetersstraat 15, 1018 WB Amsterdam, The Netherlands; e-mail: SP_Spears@macmail.psy.uva.nl, SP_Doosje@macmail.psy.uva.nl*

Key Words identity threat, group commitment, social context, identity functions, group distinctiveness

■ **Abstract** In this chapter, we examine the self and identity by considering the different conditions under which these are affected by the groups to which people belong. From a social identity perspective we argue that group commitment, on the one hand, and features of the social context, on the other hand, are crucial determinants of central identity concerns. We develop a taxonomy of situations to reflect the different concerns and motives that come into play as a result of threats to personal and group identity and degree of commitment to the group. We specify for each cell in this taxonomy how these issues of self and social identity impinge upon a broad variety of responses at the perceptual, affective, and behavioral level.

CONTENTS

---

*Author's note: The order in which the authors' names are listed does not reflect their relative input into this product. It has been a truly collective enterprise.

INTRODUCTION

Issues of self and identity are usually conceptualized at the level of the personal self. Although this tradition emphasizes the importance of social roles and social interactions for the awareness of who one is (see Banaji & Prentice 1994, Baumeister 1998), these are mainly considered as interindividual processes, in terms of how reflected appraisals from others contribute to the definition of self (see Swann et al. 2000) or may help fulfill a generic need to belong (see Baumeister & Leary 1995, Leary & Baumeister 2000). In this chapter, using social identity theory (Tajfel 1978, Tajfel & Turner 1979) and self-categorization theory (Turner 1987, 1999), we focus on the different conditions under which issues of selfhood and identity are affected by the groups to which people belong. For this purpose we develop a taxonomy of situations in which different identity concerns play a role, and accordingly, where the social self serves different functions and motives. We then proceed by specifying for each cell in this taxonomy how these issues of self and identity impinge upon a broad variety of perceptual, affective, and behavioral responses.

BASIC PRINCIPLES

Personal versus Collective Self

Concern with the personal self and issues of personal identity as an explanatory frame for understanding social behavior dominates theoretical accounts and empirical work even when group processes and intergroup relations are the object of investigation. For instance, group cohesion is often conceptualized as stemming from interpersonal ties between individual group members (see also Hogg 1992, Prentice et al. 1994), effects of the group on people's self-definitions are examined by assessing expectations of individual ingroup members about each other (Swann et al. 2000), or the tendency to either associate with or distance the self from particular groups is explained by considering how membership in the group can be beneficial for the individual in question (e.g., Luhtanen & Crocker 1991).

Western societies, in which most of this theorizing and research has been carried out, can be characterized as cultural contexts with a strong emphasis on personal identities and individual achievements (Hofstede 1980, Triandis 1989). As a result, the primary emphasis in social psychological theory and research is on the analysis of individual processes and interpersonal interaction. This concern with the individual self also permeates commonly used research paradigms, in which manipulations and measures expressly or inadvertently focus on the individual self or on interpersonal comparisons with other ingroup members. Furthermore, in laboratory experimentation with the "minimal group paradigm," categorizations are often arbitrary and temporary, resulting in groups with no history and no future (Doosje et al. 2001). This implies that overall levels of group commitment tend to remain relatively low in these studies, which is likely to diminish concerns with group-level outcomes. It is perhaps no wonder that the observed effects seem to confirm the notion that even in social situations personal identities tend to be primary (Gaertner et al. 1999, Simon 1997).

Nevertheless, there is a substantial body of research reporting on phenomena that illustrate the powerful impact of people's social identities on their perceptions, emotions, and behavior. Examples include sports team members who personally take the blame for a team loss (Taylor & Doria 1981), research participants who stick together with an unsuccessful group, even when they have the opportunity to leave (Ellemers et al. 1997), or activists who may jeopardize their personal well-being for causes or principles that are unlikely to affect their own immediate outcomes (e.g., animal rights and environmental activists; e.g., Drury & Reicher 2000). The lengths that people sometimes go to in order to protect their group, and the collective self, also belie the notion that the collective self is necessarily subservient to the individual self (Gaertner et al. 1999). Perhaps the most extreme form of individual self-sacrifice in the collective cause is the case of kamikaze pilots and suicide bombers. Thus, there are numerous examples of impactful social behavior that cannot always easily be explained by referring to the personal self or individual identity maintenance concerns. Instead, such observations are more compatible with the notion that there are situations in which people's collective selves and social identities may guide their perceptual, affective, and behavioral responses in important ways.

Rather than trying to decide whether the individual self or the collective self is more important, we think a more fruitful approach is to specify the conditions under which one is likely to take precedence over the other, and with what effect. An important contribution to our understanding of these issues is provided by the social identity approach, subsuming both social identity theory (Tajfel 1978, Tajfel & Turner 1979) and self-categorization theory (Turner 1987). This theoretical framework emphasizes the interaction between social identity as a perceiver factor implicating different aspects of the self (or different social selves), and social contextual factors that either enhance or diminish the meaningfulness of personal as well as social identities. We consider each of these factors in turn.

Social Identity and Group Commitment

At first sight, it would seem that processes associated with the collective self are often similar to those that occur for the individual self, except that they occur at the group level instead of at an individual level (e.g., a concern with positive esteem). However, the inclusion of group-based aspects of self and identity also implies that additional issues and processes come into play, so that theoretical and empirical insights on topics such as self-perception, self-esteem, or self-presentation cannot simply be transferred from the individual level to the group level (e.g., Schmitt et al. 2000, Schopler & Insko 1992). Moreover, the interaction and competition between the personal and collective levels of self add a further level of complexity (Spears 2001).

Whereas the personal self is defined as a unitary and continuous awareness of who one is (Baumeister 1998), it is less clear how we should conceive of the social self, which can be as varied as the groups to which we belong. Each of us has a range of different, cross-cutting, social identities, including those derived from highly meaningful and clearly delineated groups (e.g., psychology professors) as well as those referring to more abstract and perhaps ambiguous social categories (e.g., fellow Europeans). An important consequence is that differential perceptions of self and others may emerge, depending on which identity is most salient (Crisp & Hewstone 2001, Haslam & Turner 1992, Mussweiler et al. 2000, Spears 2001, Van Rijswijk & Ellemers 2001). Thus, the extent to which group characteristics and group processes affect the social self may differ from one group member to the next, depending on the extent to which they consider themselves in terms of that particular group membership (Ellemers et al. 1999c).

One source of confusion in the literature is that the term "social identification" has been used to refer to the content of the identity itself, as well as to indicate the strength of the association with a particular social category. These are essentially different components of the social identity, which although related, may operate relatively independently of each other (Ellemers et al. 1999b; see also Jackson, 2001, Smith Murphy & Coats 1999). To avoid confusion here, we reserve the term "social identity" to refer to the nature or content of a particular identity, whereas we use the term "commitment" to indicate the strength of people's ties with that particular group.

This conceptual distinction makes it easier to understand that people may feel strongly committed to groups that confer a negative identity upon them. For example, the employees of Baan, an IT company in the Netherlands, were strongly tied together by the fact that they all came from a small, highly religious community. As a result, when profits plummeted, instead of leaving for a more financially sound company, employees started daily prayers in the hope that the firm might yet be saved from bankruptcy (Baltesen 2000). The strength of their commitment did not waver, even though the object of their identification was no longer attractive from an outsider's perspective. We argue that when collective identities are concerned, the level of commitment to a particular group or category determines how group characteristics, norms, or outcomes will influence the perceptual, affective, and behavioral responses of individuals belonging to that group.

The Importance of Social Context

A central point of departure in the social identity approach is that the impact of social groups on the way people see themselves and others around them cannot be understood without taking into consideration the broader social context in which they function. Early formulations of this theoretical position (Tajfel 1978, Tajfel & Turner 1979) focused on the proposition that social structures can be characterized by a number of key features (namely the permeability of group boundaries, the stability of group statuses, and the legitimacy of current status relations) that are also important determinants of the likelihood that people self-define either at the individual level or at the group level. Empirical work confirmed that people were more inclined to identify as group members when group status was unstable (promoting intergroup competition and social change), whereas the individual level of self-definition was more salient when group boundaries were permeable or inclusion in the group seemed illegitimate (see Ellemers 1993 for an overview).

Further developments in the self-categorization tradition have elaborated on more immediate social contextual factors that may influence self-definitions and identity concerns (Turner 1987). The basic assumption here is that the relevant social context determines which categorization seems most suitable to provide a meaningful organization of social stimuli, and hence which identity aspects become salient as guidelines for the perceptions and behavior of those who operate within that context (e.g., Oakes 1987; see also Deaux & Major 1987). Accordingly, research has demonstrated that people perceive their own and other groups in terms of different characteristics, depending on which comparison group or comparative domain provides the frame for their judgments (e.g., Doosje et al. 1998, Haslam & Turner 1992, Van Rijswijk & Ellemers 2001).

Taking this reasoning one step further, it has been argued that we should not conceive of certain social identities as inherently attractive or unattractive. Instead, the same group membership may be seen either as identity enhancing or as jeopardizing a positive sense of self, depending on whether it compares favorably or unfavorably to other groups that are relevant in that context. For instance, whereas psychology students could establish a positive identity when comparing their intelligence with arts students, or their creativity with physics students, they felt inferior when comparing themselves with physics students in terms of intelligence, or with arts students in terms of creativity (Spears et al. 1997a). Thus, it is the social context, rather than specific group features, that determines the evaluative flavor of any given group membership. An intriguing consequence is that the motivational implications of a particular social identity are shaped by these contextual features, which may include the nature of characteristics associated with other groups.

These more socio-structural and social comparative treatments of context in social identity and self-categorization theories point to two related but distinct features of context relevant to our analysis. First, the context provides feedback about one's social position (of the person in the group, of the group in relation to other groups) that can provide a sense of security (even superiority) or engender a source of threat to self (Ouwerkerk & Ellemers 2001). At the group level, social status and group distinctiveness are the main contextual factors that produce this threat. Second, the context also constitutes the social reality that facilitates or restricts attempts to cope with these potential threats. Stability, permeability, legitimacy and the validity of comparison information are all examples of contextual factors that can be used to develop and choose feasible strategies designed to address self-relevant concerns such as identity threat (Doosje et al. 1999b, Ellemers & Van Rijswijk 1997).

To summarize, the social context is both a source of threat and source of potential resources to deal with threats. Commitment to the group is a crucial moderating factor that determines the responses to these circumstances and the use of the resources available. We now develop a theoretical taxonomy that further specifies the responses to combinations of identity threats and group commitment and elaborates the role of the personal and collective identities therein.

Identity Concerns and Self Motives: Towards a Taxonomy

In the previous section, we argued that different social situations may have specific implications for issues of self and identity. Of course, some group-based identities may be so central to the person that they become chronically salient. In a similar vein, some intergroup comparisons may be so pervasive that they dominate a variety of social contexts and overpower other social identities. More generally, commitment to identity and social contextual features interact, combining to form into a limited number of meaningful social situations (Spears et al. 1999, Turner 1999). To examine this more systematically, we have crossed commitment and context dimensions to form a taxonomy of situations in which different identity concerns arise, and hence, different perceptual, affective, and behavioral responses may be anticipated.

A central feature of this taxonomy is that it specifies particular identity concerns as well as the conditions under which they are most likely to play a role. Although the differences between the cells should be seen in gradual rather than absolute terms, the proposed organization of situations structures our discussion of which identity concerns are expected to emerge and the functional implications of self-related responses in the different classes of situations. An important property of social contexts for the self is their propensity to induce some form of threat to individuals or to the group, which calls for some (coping) response (see also Branscombe et al. 1999a). We propose that the consequences of such threat (or its absence) for the self, and hence the resulting responses, may be fundamentally different depending on the level of commitment to the group in question.

Our treatment is somewhat asymmetrical, reflecting the dominant concerns in the literature. We concentrate primarily on conditions of threat because these most often require and invoke responses, which also tend to vary according to level of self and group commitment. We therefore neglect situations in which the personal or group self actually benefits in some way. Although psychologically interesting, these contexts are beyond the scope of this chapter. However, it is important to observe that conditions of group advantage are receiving increasing attention, and the role of this factor in intergroup processes is increasingly being acknowledged and researched (see e.g., Branscombe 1998, Leach et al. 2001).

TABLE 1   Primary concerns and motives of the social self: a taxonomy

	Group Commitment	
	Low	High
No threat	**1.**	**2.**
Concern:	Accuracy/efficiency	Social meaning
Motive:	Noninvolvement	Identity expression
Individual-directed threat	**3.**	**4.**
Concern:	Categorization	Exclusion
Motive:	Self-affirmation	Acceptance
Group-directed threat	**5.**	**6.**
Concern:	Value	Distinctiveness, value
Motive:	Individual mobility	Group-affirmation

We first consider no-threat situations in which people are mainly concerned with forming accurate impressions efficiently or trying to make sense of their own group identity under different conditions of group commitment. We then move into situations in which a threat to the individual self may stem from the relationship between the individual and the group. For those with low commitment, inclusion in the group may be threatening, whereas the possibility of exclusion from the group or category can be a source of threat when commitment is high. Finally, we address contexts in which group identity is threatened, the terrain of much work in the social identity tradition. How people respond when either the value or the distinctiveness of their group is called into question is again crucially affected by commitment to the group. Along with the different identity concerns that may arise, we aim to specify the functions of self associated with each situation and specific concerns and resulting motives that arise (Table 1). We now address the six cells in turn and examine in greater detail the responses and strategies that are likely to emerge corresponding to the different identity concerns.

RESPONSES AND STRATEGIES

Cell 1: No Threat, Low Group Commitment: Noninvolvement

The first cell of our taxonomy does not implicate the self, at least in terms of commitment to a group self or through contextual threats to self. The predominant response to surrounding social stimuli is therefore one of noninvolvement. The characteristic response profile for this cell is that it will primarily have implications for perception, but less (if at all) for affect and behavior. The concern for social perception under these conditions is accuracy or sense-making on the one hand and efficiency on the other (often with a trade-off between these two).

There have been different theoretical approaches addressing this issue. Within social cognition, as a result of the information processor metaphor in the heuristics and biases tradition, categorization and stereotyping have come to be regarded as ways of managing the surfeit of social information efficiently, especially under conditions of limited personal involvement (e.g., Fiske et al. 1999). Because the group self is largely uninvolved, it will not bias perception, at least not in group-serving ways, although efficiency concerns may lead to other kinds of information processing biases associated with simplification (Fiske et al. 1999, Macrae & Bodenhausen 2000). These approaches often make a distinction between categorization and stereotype activation (which occur relatively automatically or effortlessly) on the one hand, and more effortful individuation on the other, and they therefore have a dual-process character (Brewer & Harasty Feinstein 1999, Fiske et al. 1999). However, other models have argued that knowledge activation and application processes underlying social perception can be understood without making such a clear division in processing terms (e.g., Kunda & Thagard 1996, McGarty 1999), suggesting that it may be less clear whether the function of categorization and stereotyping is to simplify or save energy, rather than to reflect learned associations of the social world in general.

Research in the tradition of self-categorization theory has focused on the contextual determinants of social perception, showing how stereotyping (and other related processes) shifts with the judgmental context (Haslam et al. 1992, Oakes et al. 1994). According to this approach, social perception is essentially context sensitive and comparative, and the emphasis is more on contextual relevance and sense making than on accuracy or efficiency concerns per se.

The self (individual or collective) might be implicated in cell 1 not through a threat to identity, but through more instrumental motives relating to relevant goals, outcomes, and relevant audiences. Under these conditions the noninvolved character clearly changes and the role of motivation and affect become more apparent. This issue has been approached from the perspective of the different traditions already described. For example, research by Fiske and her colleagues on the effects of interdependence and anticipated interaction shows that when people have a self-interested relation to others, attention becomes focused to better predict their behavior: The cognitive miser becomes the motivated tactician (Fiske et al. 1999). Within the self-categorization tradition, research has also shown how behavior can reflect strategic self-presentational concerns under conditions of accountability to others (e.g., Ellemers et al. 1999a, Reicher et al. 1995).

To summarize, in cell 1 of our taxonomy, relevant theories focus on social perception, rather than affective and behavioral responses, and generally they reflect noninvolvement unless the self is directly implicated. Approaches differ as to whether social perception for the uninvolved perceiver should be seen as biased by lack of motivation or processing resources (as the limited information processing metaphor implies), or not necessarily, as self-categorization theorists have argued. This may depend on whether perception in terms of individuals and individual characteristics is seen as more valid than perception in terms of group identities and attributes, which is itself arguably a question of level of self-definition and social context (Reynolds & Oakes 2000, Spears et al. 1997b).

Cell 2: No Threat, High Commitment: Identity Expression

In this cell of our taxonomy, commitment to the group identity is increased. The main implication is that social perception now acquires a self-relevant and self-relative character at the group level. As a consequence, responses are no longer restricted to the perceptual realm but also involve affect and behavior. However, behavior in this cell still lacks the urgency that it can be given by threats to identity. The importance of group identity means the primary concern here will be to express and affirm this identity. We now consider ways in which this identity-expressive function manifests itself in the domains of perception, affective response, and behavior.

When group identity is not yet clear, but there is a commitment to the incipient identity, there is likely to be an attempt to create a distinctive identity by distinguishing and differentiating the group from outgroups in the comparative context. This process is similar to the sense-making process described in the previous section, but here the aim is not simply to make sense of the external world, but to define the group-self as distinct from other groups. Spears et al. (2001b) have referred to this process of gaining a distinctive self as "creative distinctiveness," and evidence indicates that indistinct groups such as minimal groups can be more likely to differentiate themselves than more meaningful groups as a way of creating a distinctive group identity. Along similar lines, Hogg and colleagues have pointed to the experience of uncertainty in relation to group membership (e.g., Mullin & Hogg 1998), arguing that this may motivate people to define the situation and their relation in it, by displaying group-affirming responses.

If group identity is already formed and clear-cut, social perception and attempts at intergroup differentiation are predicted to follow principles set out in social identity theory (Tajfel & Turner 1979) and self-categorization theory (Turner 1987). Following the meta-contrast principle, groups tend to endorse group norms and conform to the prototypical ingroup position (maximizing intergroup differences and intragroup similarities) while also perceiving the outgroup in stereotypic terms (Turner 1987). A key difference from the influence of social context on perception described in the previous cell is that commitment to the group introduces the motivation to differentiate the ingroup (a distinctiveness motive) in positive ways (an enhancement motive) (Tajfel & Turner 1979). Because the group is not threatened in this context, satisfaction of group distinctiveness may often be sufficient, however (Spears et al. 2001b). For example, research shows that for groups that are compared on different dimensions, it may be possible to concede superiority to the outgroup on their dimension as a way of maintaining distinctiveness, as long as there are alternative dimensions available to derive some positive character for the ingroup (Doosje et al. 1998, Ellemers et al. 1999a, Mummendey & Schreiber 1983, Van Knippenberg 1984).

Turning to the affective processes, there is empirical support for the theoretical position that positive differentiation can enhance group esteem, although the evidence is mixed (see Hogg & Abrams 1988, Long & Spears 1997, Rubin & Hewstone 1998 for reviews). However, one of the problems with the so-called self-esteem hypothesis is that when group identity is not threatened, it is not clear that differentiation should function to enhance self-esteem, especially if group distinctiveness is satisfied. The interpretation of research findings is further obscured by conceptualization and measurement issues, with early tests focusing on personal rather than collective measures of esteem, and measures defined in trait rather than state terms (e.g., Luhtanen & Crocker 1991; see Long & Spears 1997, Rubin & Hewstone 1998).

At the behavioral level, group commitment is usually associated with prosocial behavior, such as volunteering to support group members who suffer from illness (e.g., Simon et al. 2000) or helping colleagues at work (Ellemers et al. 1998). However, the motive here is to differentiate between the ingroup and outgroup, which implies that commitment may also have negative effects, such as outgroup derogation (see Hinkle & Brown 1988). Thus, the general pattern is that commitment will enhance conformity to group norms (e.g., Doosje et al. 1999a, Terry & Hogg 1996), which may just as easily result in behavior that may be considered antisocial or deviant from the outside (e.g., Postmes & Spears 1998, Reicher et al. 1995) as prescribe fair behavior towards outgroup members (Jetten et al. 1999). One paradoxical consequence of such self-categorization effects is that strong commitment can also result in individual behavior where this is normative for the group (Ellemers et al. 1999a, Jetten et al. 2001c). Thus, group commitment is crucial in distinguishing group behavior from truly individual behavior (Spears 2001).

To summarize, the characteristic concern in cell 2 is the presence of a clear meaningful group identity coupled to commitment to this identity. The main function is therefore to create a distinctive identity when it is not yet established, or to express it on meaningful dimensions of differentiation when it is. In addition to shifting social perception to group attributes, group commitment is likely to implicate collective esteem and motivate behavioral differentiation.

Cell 3: Self-Directed Threat, Low Commitment: Self-Affirmation

"I don't want to belong to any club that will accept me as a member."
Groucho Marx

For someone with a low degree of commitment to the group to be categorized as a member of this group may threaten the individual self. Even those who can technically be considered as category members may experience the particular group as a (psychological) outgroup. Such resistance to categorization may stem from a variety of motives, including (*a*) the desire to establish individual uniqueness, (*b*) a conviction that the categorization is not relevant to the situation at hand, (*c*) the view that other additional categorizations should also be taken into account, or (*d*) resentment of losing personal control when a particular categorization is imposed by others. These responses have implications for self-perception, as well as affect and behavior.

In optimal distinctiveness theory, Brewer (1991, Pickett & Brewer 2001) argues that people find it aversive to be assimilated into large groups and should therefore prefer inclusion in relatively smaller groups (see also Frable 1993, Snyder & Fromkin 1980). Here we propose that especially under conditions of low group commitment (which may also occur in minority groups) people prefer to be seen as separate individuals rather than being lumped together as a group. A consequence at the perceptual level is that those who think they are inappropriately categorized should tend to emphasize intragroup differences. Spears et al. (1999) report evidence that under conditions of category salience, less committed group members try to individuate the ingroup. In a similar vein, when the categorization seems inappropriate to the situation at hand, group members are likely to perceive themselves in terms of individually distinctive attributes, which may be nonprototypical for their group. For instance, there is evidence that high ranking women in organizations make a point of emphasizing self-descriptive traits that are relevant to their position at work (e.g., competitive, ambitious) but set them apart from their gender category (see Ellemers 2001 for an overview).

Whereas they may not be able to deny belonging to a particular group, people may often resist being viewed in terms of that category exclusively. Attempts to convey some personal uniqueness may take the form of creating a richer picture of the self, by emphasizing additional identities. For instance, a study of Portuguese immigrants in the Netherlands revealed that when it was likely that they would be categorized as minority group members (given that they were judged by the Dutch host group) they emphasized their dual identity, by decreasing identification with the native (Portuguese) group while emphasizing their identity as members of the host society (Ellemers et al. 1999a).

In terms of affective reactions, Lemyre & Smith (1985) have argued that in minimal groups, the very act of being categorized can be threatening. This is probably because of the low group commitment that is generally associated with such minimal contexts. Indeed, there is empirical evidence that people are generally less willing to be considered in terms of categorizations that are ascribed to them or imposed upon them by others than to being included in groups whose membership they have earned or chosen (Ellemers et al. 1999b). Barreto & Ellemers (2001) showed that resistance against an imposed categorization occurs when people's preferred self-categorizations are neglected (see also Hornsey & Hogg 2000). There is also evidence that categorization can be physiologically arousing for low group identifiers, regardless of the value associated with the ingroup (Branscombe et al. 1999a). Such aversion to categorization does not have to be general but may be context specific, as when gender or ethnic group membership is applied in a work setting where it should be irrelevant.

Although the general aim in this cell may be to counter the effects of categorization, sometimes the behavioral consequences of unsolicited categorization are beyond one's control, as in the case of stereotype threat (Steele & Aronson 1995, Crocker et al. 1998, Steele 1997). This refers to the phenomenon that members of stigmatized groups typically underperform on dimensions on which their group stereotypically under-achieves (e.g., African Americans in intellectual domains, women in mathematics). Recent empirical evidence indicates that similar under-mining effects of stereotypic expectations for the performance of individual group members can been observed for nonstigmatized groups (e.g., Leyens et al. 2000, Marx et al. 1999, Stone et al. 1999). Indeed, even an awareness of positive stereo-typic expectations (i.e., with respect to the mathematical skills of Asian-American women) impaired participants' math performance (Cheryan & Bodenhausen 2000; Shih, Pittinsky, & Ambadi 1999).

It seems that these are all instances of the general phenomenon that people tend to underperform when they are subjected to category-based expectations in situations in which they might prefer to be judged in terms of individual merit (or not at all). There is some evidence that concern with an unwanted categorization takes up cognitive resources (Smart & Wegner 1999) and diminishes concentration on the task at hand (Cheryan & Bodenhausen 2000). Indeed, a study in which ethnicity salience was manipulated in a more subtle way resulted in enhanced performance, indicating behavioral affirmation of the category stereotype (Cheryan & Bodenhausen 2000), in line with cell 2 of our taxonomy.

A somewhat paradoxical behavioral result of category threat can be to display ingroup bias. Although those who possess attractive individual characteristics (e.g., high individual ability) are more likely than others to resist categorization, as ev-idenced by decreased group identification (Ellemers 1993), when such unwanted categorization seems inevitable, uncommitted group members may resort to in-group bias to salvage their personal identity. Similarly, Long & Spears (1997) found that, in a group context, people high in personal self-esteem tended to show more ingroup bias than those low in personal self-esteem. Thus, what is charac-teristically seen as group-serving behavior can also come about as an attempt to compensate for more individual concerns when categorization seems inevitable.

To summarize, there is some evidence that threat to the individual self resulting from category inclusion can prompt perceptual, affective, and behavioral responses designed to affirm individual identity or alternative identities and/or to use other compensation strategies. An unwillingness to be categorized in one particular category does not necessarily mean an aversion to being categorized in general. Groucho Marx was happy enough to be a Marx brother—he just did not want to be a member of a "club."

Cell 4: Self-Directed Threat, High Commitment: Acceptance

When the person is committed to the group, the individual self is not threatened by categorization, but rather by lack of acceptance in the valued group or even exclusion. Accordingly, responses in this cell are in many respects opposite to those considered in the previous section. Perceived exclusion or rejection by the valued group will result in negative affect and attempts to gain acceptance. Even if the threat to self does not derive from potential exclusion, highly committed group members may seek refuge in the group as a way of compensating for their individual shortcomings. Baumcistei & Leary (1995) refer to similar considerations, although they propose a generic need to belong, whereas we propose that this need only emerges in particular contexts and in relation to groups to which one feels highly committed.

Whereas one perceptual consequence of such threat from the perspective of the self would be to recognize one's peripheral status, paradoxically, the concern with acceptance may repress acknowledgment of possible rejection from the group. For instance, a study by Jetten et al. (2001b) revealed that under the threat of future rejection, highly committed group members perceived greater ingroup homogeneity, which could be seen as an attempt to feel more included (see also Pickett & Brewer 2001). In this case perception may reflect a motivated defensive response. The primary observable responses to this form of threat are therefore likely to be affective and behavioral, reflecting and designed to cope with this threat.

In terms of the affective reactions, evidence shows that new members of groups tend to be more anxious and lack confidence reflecting acceptance concerns (e.g., Moreland 1985). Jetten et al. (2001b) showed that highly committed peripheral group members who anticipated future acceptance showed more positive and fewer negative emotions than those who were less committed. Jetten et al. (2001a) investigated the affective consequences of having an insecure peripheral position in the group (versus secure and prototypical) and examined how shifts in position over time affected personal and collective self-esteem. Shifts to more prototypical positions enhanced collective self-esteem, whereas shifts to more peripheral positions enhanced personal self-esteem—presumably reflecting reduced commitment to the group.

A further affective consequence of marginal status is that people will likely value prototypical group members more but may be especially critical of others also perceived to be marginal. Ironically, black sheep (Marques & Paez 1995), at least those who are committed to the group, may be the severest critics of fellow black sheep. Schmitt & Branscombe (2001) showed that highly identified males who received feedback that they were atypical of their gender (unmasculine) tended to value prototypical males even more, but liked peripheral males (like themselves) even less, than when not so threatened (see also Jetten et al. 2001b). In sum, acceptance motives and identity concerns can even outweigh similarity-attraction principles.

A marginal status within the group, and the motivation to improve this, is also reflected in behavioral strategies. One such strategy is to display group prototypical behavior, particularly when visible to ingroup members. Although ingroup helping clearly qualifies as behavior that may earn approval of other ingroup members, displays of allegiance to the group may also result in individualistic (Barreto & Ellemers 2000) or even antisocial behavior, depending on the relevant group norms.

For example, Noel et al. (1995) showed that peripheral group members were more likely than core members to derogate outgroups, especially when identifiable to the ingroup.

To summarize, those who are committed to the group but threatened by exclusion may try to emphasize their inclusion in perceptual ways (e.g., homogeneity). They are likely to experience negative affect at the prospect of exclusion and respond by behavioral conformity to the group, of which ingroup bias is just one form.

Cell 5: Group-Directed Threat, Low Commitment: Individual Mobility

In this cell we consider how people respond to a threat to their group's value when they are not particularly committed to the group. Here the dominant motive is to avoid the negative group identity that has been imposed and possibly align with preferable ones, such as those instrumental to the individual self. First, however, we should resolve the seeming contradiction that a negative evaluation of one's group should be perceived as threatening to the individual self for those low in group commitment. To the extent that a nonvalued identity is called into question, it would seem that this need not necessarily be perceived as threatening to the self. Indeed, some have proposed that self-affirmation strategies may not be necessary if the individual self is primary or stronger than the group self (Gaertner et al. 1999), which may be particularly true for those with low commitment to the group.

Others have argued that explaining negative reactions of others to the self by referring to the category (as in attributions to prejudice) may actually form a way of protecting the individual self (Crocker et al. 1998). However, the generality of this strategy has been disputed (e.g., Schmitt & Branscombe 2001); unless they can hide their group membership, members of stigmatized groups are likely to be chronically treated in terms of their devalued group membership, regardless of their group commitment. Thus, it would be misleading to assume that low group commitment is always sufficient to protect the individual self from negative group identities.

An example of a perceptual coping response is provided by evidence that group members who learn their group has a negative value tend to emphasize the heterogeneity within the group (especially when the social reality allows for this), which may help convey that unfavorable group features do not necessarily apply to the individual self (see Doosje et al. 1999b). Although emphasizing heterogeneity within groups could also be interpreted as a group level way of undermining the implications of overall differences between groups, further research confirmed that only people with low commitment to the group used this variability strategy (Doosje et al. 1995). Accordingly, in addition to these instrumental perceptions of the group, in the face of group-value threat uncommitted members reported relatively low levels of self-stereotyping (Ellemers 2001, Spears et al. 1997a). Similarly, Mussweiler et al. (2000) found that when their group is depicted negatively, people shift their self-definition to another identity, provided that they have high self-esteem (see Tajfel and Turner 1979 for further "social creativity" strategies).

Turning to the affective realm, there is considerable empirical support for the view that receiving negative feedback about one's group can lead to negative mood (e.g., McFarland & Buehler 1995) and reduced personal self-esteem (see Ellemers & Barreto 2000 for an overview). Furthermore, under minimal group conditions (when group commitment is typically low), a threat to the value of the group often results in reduced ingroup identification (Ellemers 1993). Once this has happened, identification is likely to stay low even while the group develops over time, as long as the group-level feedback remains negative. Indeed, under these circumstances, people are only prepared to build affective ties with their group when it is certain that their status will improve in the near future. This reflects an individually instrumental attitude, where the less committed try to distance themselves from the group affiliation in a threatened situation (Doosje et al. 2001).

Perhaps the most straightforward behavioral response to group-value threat for those with low commitment is to try to leave the group and gain access to another, more attractive group. This behavioral strategy has been denoted with different terms in different theoretical and research traditions, including exit, passing, or individual mobility (Tajfel 1978, Tajfel & Turner 1979). The process of mobility can involve dissatisfaction with membership of the threatened group (Ellemers 1993) and resistance of the identification of self as an ingroup member (Cialdini et al. 1976). As a result, individually mobile group members decline opportunities to improve the standing of their group (Wright et al. 1990) or to help other group members (Ellemers 2001) while showing anticipatory identification with a more attractive group (Ellemers 1993, Ellemers et al. 1997). However, when group boundaries are impermeable, this cuts off the mobility route, leading to other social creativity strategies (associated with the perceptual realm), or in more chronic and extreme circumstances leading to internalization of inferiority (e.g., Jost & Banaji 1994).

Threat comes not just from the relative status or performance of the group, but also reflects the moral value associated with its treatment of others (Branscombe et al. 1999a), and this can have distinctive affective consequences. When a group's moral integrity is threatened, for example when a national history of exploiting another nation is made salient, those who are less committed tend to suffer most from negative affective reactions such as guilt (e.g., Doosje et al. 1998). Such collective guilt in turn can have distinctive behavioral reactions resulting in some sort of restitution on behalf of the victimized group (Branscombe et al. 2001, Swim & Miller 1999). Thus, members who care least for their group are most likely to experience negative affective reactions as a result of their group membership. As a result, the least committed group members are most inclined to show prosocial behavior, in this case towards the harmed group, again underlining that there is no simple relation between group commitment and behavior.

To summarize, group-level threat combined with low group commitment can have a number of perceptual, affective, and behavioral consequences designed to protect the individual self or seek out a preferred social identity, although low commitment can also increase the chances of prosocial responses, as in the case of the morality threat implied by collective guilt.

Cell 6: Group-Directed Threat, High Commitment: Group Affirmation

In this last cell of our taxonomy, we focus on the situation in which the threat is directed at the group level and members feel highly committed to their group. Two important sources of group threat can be distinguished in this context: threat in terms of value (in terms of status or morality) and threats to group distinctiveness.

In terms of threat to group value qua status, social identity theory proposes that perceptual, affective, and behavioral responses are instrumentally aimed at differentiation and group affirmation. Thus, at the perceptual level, highly committed group members may stress the homogeneity of the ingroup (Doosje et al. 1995), differentiate between groups (Spears et al. 1999), display relatively high levels of self-stereotyping (Spears et al. 1997a), or affirm the collective self in other ways (see also Steele 1987). These variables can be interpreted as indicators of a state of mind that is conducive to collective group behavior aimed at challenging the source of threat and changing the present status configuration insofar as it is unfavorable for the ingroup (Doosje et al. 1999a), although these need to take into account the social reality constraints of intergroup differences (Ellemers et al. 1999a).

In terms of affective responses, although threats to value are likely to impact negatively on esteem (as for those with low commitment), a more collective coping response among those who are committed to the group will lead them to display even stronger group affiliation, expressing their loyalty to the devalued group. Indeed, it has been observed that people have a tendency to emphasize group cohesiveness when the value of the group is threatened (Branscombe et al. 1999b, Turner et al. 1984). Subsequent research has shown that these affective reactions in terms of expressing one's loyalty to the group are most prominent for those who were already committed to the group. Thus, highly committed members are most likely to stick together with their group in terms of identification, even when there is no realistic chance of improving its status position (Doosje et al. 2001).

Threats to group value may take different forms depending on contextual factors (social structure and comparison groups) and will result in different affective reactions. For example, when their group's values are threatened, members of powerful groups are more likely to express anger and contempt towards an outgroup than members of weak or submissive groups. In addition, the inclination to move against the outgroup, which is stronger among powerful groups than among weak groups, is mediated by anger but not by contempt (Dijker 1987, Fiske et al. 2001, Mackie et al. 2000, Smith 1993).

At the behavioral level, high commitment in combination with group threat is likely to give rise to intergroup differentiation tendencies aimed at improving the ingroup's status position. This suggestion is in line with social identity theory, which predicts competitive behavior among highly committed members when the group's status is threatened by comparison with a higher status outgroup (Tajfel & Turner 1979). Such competitiveness might be expressed in a number of different ways. For example, people may derogate outgroup members when the value of the ingroup is threatened (e.g., Branscombe & Wann 1994). Alternatively, when highly committed group members are faced with low group status, they are likely to engage in attempts to redress the situation by means of collective action (Kelly & Breinlinger 1996), as has been observed for a variety of social groups, ranging from workers (e.g., Veenstra & Haslam 2000) to gay people (Simon et al. 1998).

When the moral value of a group is threatened, in contrast to less committed group members those who feel highly committed to their group are unlikely to express high levels of guilt (Doosje et al. 1998). Instead, they are more inclined to display defensive reactions when their group's moral value is challenged (e.g., by downplaying the credibility of the presented negative image of their group). In behavioral terms, it accordingly seems that highly committed members are generally not in favor of acknowledging their group's culpability by official apologies to the harmed group, but prefer to deal with the situation by offering financial reparation (Branscombe et al. 2001).

Another fundamental source of threat is when the distinctiveness of the group is undermined by comparison to similar outgroups. A central principle within social identity theory is the motivation to seek or maintain group distinctiveness (Tajfel 1978, Tajfel & Turner 1979; see also Brewer 1991, Spears et al. 2001b). This speaks to the very existence and raison d'être of the group as an entity and thus addresses the identity expression function. Distinctiveness threat is less of an issue for those with low group commitment because it further undermines the sense of group identity and promotes recategorization at the superordinate level (Jetten et al. 1999). Those who are highly committed, however, are clear about their group identity and motivated to preserve its distinctiveness.

In terms of perceptions, threats to group distinctiveness combined with a high level of commitment are likely to result in a high degree of self-stereotyping (Spears et al. 1997a) and greater differentiation on stereotypic dimensions (Jetten et al. 2001d). In terms of affective reactions, for highly committed group members a threat to group distinctiveness is expected to give rise to reactions that induce conflict between the ingroup and the outgroup and the motivation to restore distinctiveness (Spears et al. 2001b). In the behavioral realm, distinctiveness threat elicits the desire to clearly differentiate the ingroup from other groups, which may take the form of overt discrimination (Jetten et al. 1999), especially for those central or most committed to the group (Jetten et al. 2001d). Group distinctiveness threat combined with high commitment may even lead to displays of hatred and disgust towards the outgroup as a result of the motivation to sharpen group boundaries

(Keltner & Haidt 1999). Moreover, intergroup similarity only provides a basis for contact so long as differentiation is possible (Roccas & Schwartz 1993). However, similarities perceived as aversive in one intergroup context may form the basis for common categorization if distinctiveness concerns are addressed (Hornsey & Hogg 2000).

Although generally speaking, group members prefer their group to be positively distinct from other groups (Mummendey & Schreiber 1983), for committed group members it may be of paramount importance to establish a distinctive group identity per se (Spears et al. 2001b). In such situations the distinctiveness motive takes precedence over a desire for ingroup superiority, so that highly committed group members may settle for a negative identity rather than being regarded positively at the expense of group distinctiveness. For example, Polish students who were strongly committed to their national identity claimed to have an array of clearly negative but group-defining characteristics (Mlicki & Ellemers 1996).

To summarize, group-level threat combined with high group commitment is associated with perceptual, affective, and behavioral reactions aimed at the group reasserting itself in terms of either value or distinctiveness. This may lead to a high degree of self-stereotyping, expressions of strong ingroup loyalty, and a readiness for collective action. The quest for clear intergroup differentiation may paradoxically lead highly committed group members to cultivate negative traits and/or behaviors, insofar as they seem to underline the group's distinct identity.

CONCLUSIONS AND DIRECTIONS FOR FUTURE RESEARCH

With this chapter we have integrated theoretical insights and empirical research in the area of self and social identity in terms of a taxonomy of situations defined by the level of group commitment and social contextual characteristics. We reviewed representative research relevant for each of the cells in the resulting matrix. We have shown that whereas strength of commitment to the group indicates the likelihood that a particular (social) identity will be relevant to the individual in question, the nature of the resulting perceptual, affective, or behavioral responses depends on interaction with the relevant social context and which aspects of the self are secure or threatened. We now try to derive some more general conclusions from our review in terms of this analytical framework.

First, from the literature it is evident that the bulk of research is most relevant to two of the situations that we distinguish. Most social-cognitive work on self and social identity has examined situations in which the self remains uninvolved, as group commitment is low, and no threat is present (cell 1 of our taxonomy). Conversely, research in the social identity tradition has primarily tried to uncover how highly committed group members respond to group level threats (as in cell 6 of our taxonomy). As a result, it should be clear that some cells of our taxonomy deserve further research attention. In a similar vein, whereas we have examined research on perceptual, affective, and behavioral responses, some modes are overrepresented in some cells and underrepresented in others (e.g., perceptual responses mainly occur in cell 1, whereas research in cell 6 focuses more on behavioral responses), and other forms of response (e.g., affective responses) are less researched. As well as reflecting the focus in the literature, this informs us of the relevance of affect and action under conditions in which the self is threatened.

Another consequence of this exercise is that this has forced us to indicate the differences between conditions that at first sight may seem quite similar and have previously been confounded. For example, instances of self-affirmation (as in cell 3) are often considered in conjunction with attempts at individual mobility (in cell 5). At first sight these may indeed seem to represent similar motives, but our analysis proposes that there is a fundamental difference between them. Responses to categorization threat (cell 3) involve resisting the very idea that individuals are treated as category members (even though such resistance may not be generic but can be highly context-specific). By contrast, threat to the value of the group (cell 5) may elicit individual mobility attempts, which imply that the category system may be accepted, and only one's position within that system is disputed. To complicate matters further, the psychological and strategic processes that take place when group members aim at individual mobility (in cell 5) may involve temporary distancing of self from group, resembling the processes that occur when people reject categorization altogether (as in cell 3), as a step toward achieving inclusion in another more attractive group. As such, perceptions (e.g., distancing oneself from the group) and affective reactions (e.g., decreased level of ingroup identification) may be a first step necessary to prepare for other behavior (e.g., leaving the group).

By organizing our review according to a limited number of cells, we have tried to show that a range of observable responses may stem from a distinct pattern of underlying motives and regulatory mechanisms, due to credibility considerations relating to social reality constraints (Ellemers et al. 1999a, Spears et al. 2001a) and the feasibility of different response strategies derived from socio-structural conditions (Ouwerkerk et al. 1999). Thus, identical forms of behavior (i.e., ingroup favoritism) may either constitute an attempt to improve the standing of the group (as when highly committed group members are confronted by group-value threat, cell 6), or result from the desire to salvage one's individual identity when it is inevitably submerged in the group (i.e., under low commitment and categorization threat, cell 3).

One important conclusion of this is that responses should not be considered in isolation or taken at face value as necessarily reflecting privately held views. Responses may often be strategic, addressing identity-expressive concerns and instrumental concerns directed by goals attuned to the dominant level of self, which take into account the constraints and possibilities present in context (Ellemers & Barreto 2000, Ellemers et al. 1999a, Spears et al. 2001a). Consideration of the different underlying goals and motives associated with combinations of self and contextual conditions is essential to explain why superficially similar as well as different response patterns emerge. The joint examination of perceptual, affective, and behavioral consequences and the moderating role of group commitment provides insight into these patterns, as it helps to predict where essential differences are likely to occur.

Another theoretical point that can be derived from the discussion of our taxonomy is that identical conditions may have positive as well as negative consequences, both for the individual and from the perspective of the social system as a whole. For instance, whereas it has been argued that inclusion in a group may serve important self-protective functions (e.g., Leary & Baumeister 2000), we have seen that people may suffer from being categorized against their will, for instance by showing performance impairment due to stereotype threat. In our view, whether or not people feel committed to the group in question is an important determinant of how they respond to the relevant social context and its implications.

Similar interactive effects also imply that the role of group commitment can differ substantially as a function of group context as well as identity content. It is often assumed that high commitment leads to prosocial behavior, and that this is beneficial from a societal perspective. However, this is not necessarily the case. Group commitment only predicts prosocial behavior towards the ingroup, but can also cause outgroup derogation. Indeed, compliance with group norms may just as easily elicit individualistic, antisocial, or "deviant" behavior. Thus, even when focusing on a particular cell of our taxonomy, it is important to distinguish between different sorts of group contexts, and to specify the content of identity and norms prescribing behavior.

One important issue we have touched on only incidentally in this review is how precisely to explain the emergence of group commitment, or commitment to any level of self for that matter. This question has not been a high priority in social psychological research in which commitment is often been treated as an independent variable. Commitment to particular identities is likely to emerge over time according to the same process of interaction between identity and context that we have used to guide our analysis (Spears et al. 1999, Turner 1999). For example, chronic threats to group identity, especially where the social identity is difficult to escape, may turn the disinterested into the committed over time (Condor 1996, Doosje et al. 2001). Indeed, the strategic functions of the responses we have been discussing only make sense in a temporal context in which there is hope and scope to change an unfavorable status quo (Ellemers 1993, Spears et al. 2001a, Tajfel & Turner 1979).

To conclude, we have focused on social identity in different group contexts and have analyzed how both the individual and the collective self are implicated in a range of different group situations. In order to specify the different concerns and motivations that may play a role, we developed a taxonomy with which to analyze the perceptual, affective, and behavioral consequences of the different combinations of group commitment and identity threat. We think this provides a useful analytic tool with which to interpret the current literature on the social self (both collective and personal) in group contexts, as well as serving as a framework for understanding future research in this area.

Visit the Annual Reviews home page at www.AnnualReviews.org

LITERATURE CITED

Abrams DA, Hogg MA, eds. 1988. *Social Identity Theory: Constructive and Critical Advances.* Hemel Hempstead, UK: Harvester Wheatsheaf

Baltesen R. 2000. Maar het Baan-gevoel blijft. *FEM/DeWeek.* 21:22–24

Banaji MR, Prentice DA. 1994. The self in social contexts. *Annu. Rev. Psychol.* 45:297–332

Barreto M, Ellemers N. 2000. You can't always do what you want: social identity and self-presentational determinants of the choice to work for a low status group. *Pers. Soc. Psychol. Bull.* 26:891–906

Barreto M, Ellemers N. 2001. The Impact of respect vs. neglect of self-identities on identification and group loyalty. *Pers. Soc. Psychol. Bull.* In press

Baumeister RF. 1998. The self. See Gilbert et al. 1998, pp. 680–740

Baumeister RF, Leary MR. 1995. The need to belong: desire for interpersonal attachments as a fundamental human motivation. *Psychol. Bull.* 117:497–529

Branscombe NR. 1998. Thinking about one's gender group's privileges or disadvantages: consequences for well being in women and men. *Br. J. Soc. Psychol.* 37:167–84

Branscombe NR, Doosje B, McGarty C. 2001. The antecedents, experience, and consequences of collective guilt. See Mackie & Smith 2001. In press

Branscombe NR, Ellemers N, Spears R, Doosje B. 1999a. See Ellemers et al. 1999c, pp. 35–58

Branscombe NR, Schmitt MT, Harvey RD. 1999b. Perceiving pervasive discrimination among African Americans: implications for group identification and well-being. *J. Pers. Soc. Psychol.* 77:135–49

Branscombe NR, Wann DL. 1994. Collective self-esteem consequences of outgroup derogation when a valued social identity is on trial. *Eur. J. Soc. Psychol.* 24:641–57

Brewer MB. 1991. The social self: on being the same and different at the same time. *Pers. Soc. Psychol. Bull.* 17:4750–82

Brewer MB, Harasty Feinstein AS. 1999. Dual processes in the cognitive representation of persons and social categories. See Chaiken & Trope 1999, pp. 253–70

Chaiken S, Trope Y. 1999. *Dual Process Theories in Social Psychology.* New York: Guilford

Cheryan S, Bodenhausen GV. 2000. When positive stereotypes threaten intellectual performance: the psychological hazards of "model minority status." *Psychol. Sci.* 11:399–402

Cialdini RB, Borden RJ, Thorne A, Walker MR, Freeman S, Sloan LR. 1976. Basking in reflected glory: three (football) field studies. *J. Pers. Soc. Psychol.* 34:366–75

Condor S. 1996. Social identity and time. In *Social Groups and Identities: Developing the Legacy of Henri Tajfel,* ed. P Robinson, pp. 285–315. Oxford: Butterworth Heinemann

Crisp RJ, Hewstone M. 2001. Multiple categorization and implicit intergroup bias: differential category dominance and the positive-negative asymmetry effect. *Eur. J. Soc. Psychol.* 31:45–62

Crocker J, Major B, Steele C. 1998. Social stigma. See Gilbert et al. 1998, pp. 504–53

Deaux K, Major B. 1987. Putting gender into context: an interactive model of gender-related behavior. *Psychol. Rev.* 94:369–89

Dijker AJM. 1987. Emotional reactions to ethnic minorities. *Eur. J. Soc. Psychol.* 17:305–25

Doosje B, Branscombe NR, Spears R, Manstead ASR. 1998. Guilty by association: when one's group has a negative history. *J. Pers. Soc. Psychol.* 75:872–86

Doosje B, Ellemers N, Spears R. 1995. Perceived intragroup variability as a function of group status and identification. *J. Exp. Soc. Psychol.* 31:410–36

Doosje B, Ellemers N, Spears R. 1999a. Commitment and intergroup behaviour. See Ellemers et al. 1999c, pp. 84–106

Doosje B, Haslam SA, Spears R, Oakes PJ, Koomen W. 1998. The effect of comparative context on central tendency and variability judgments and the evaluation of group characteristics. *Eur. J. Soc. Psychol.* 28:173–84

Doosje B, Spears R, Ellemers N. 2001. The dynamic and determining role of ingroup identification: responses to anticipated and actual changes in the intergroup status hierarchy. *Br. J. Soc. Psychol.* In press

Doosje B, Spears R, Ellemers N, Koomen W. 1999b. Perceived group variability in intergroup relations: the distinctive role of social identity. *Eur. Rev. Soc. Psychol.* 10:41–74

Drury J, Reicher S. 2000. Collective action and psychological change: the emergence of new social identities. *Br. J. Soc. Psychol.* 39:579–604

Ellemers N. 1993. Influence of socio-structural variables on identity enhancement strategies. *Eur. Rev. Soc. Psychol.* 4:27–57

Ellemers N. 2001. Individual upward mobility and the perceived legitimacy of intergroup relations. See Jost & Major 2001

Ellemers N, Barreto M. 2000. The impact of relative group status: affective, perceptual and behavioural consequences. In *The Blackwell Handbook of Social Psychology*, Vol. 4. *Intergroup Processes*, ed. R Brown, S Gaertner, pp. 324–43. Oxford: Blackwell

Ellemers N, Barreto M, Spears R. 1999a. Commitment and strategic responses to social context. See Ellemers et al. 1999c, pp. 127–46

Ellemers N, De Gilder D, Van den Heuvel H. 1998. Career-oriented versus team-oriented commitment and behavior at work. *J. Appl. Psychol.* 83:717–30

Ellemers N, Kortekaas P, Ouwerkerk J. 1999b. Self-categorization, commitment to the group and social self-esteem as related but distinct aspects of social identity. *Eur. J. Soc. Psychol.* 28:371–98

Ellemers N, Spears R, Doosje B. 1997. Sticking together or falling apart: ingroup identification as a psychological determinant of group commitment versus individual mobility. *J. Pers. Soc. Psychol.* 72:617–26

Ellemers N, Spears R, Doosje B, eds. 1999c. *Social Identity: Context, Commitment, Content*. Oxford: Blackwell

Ellemers N, Van Rijswijk W. 1997. Identity needs versus social opportunities: the use of group-level and individual level identity management strategies. *Soc. Psychol. Q.* 60:52–65

Fiske ST, Cuddy AJC, Glick P. 2001. Emotions up and down: intergroup emotions result from perceived status and competition. See Mackie & Smith 2001. In press

Fiske ST, Lin MH, Neuberg SL. 1999. The continuum model: ten years later. See Chaiken & Trope 1999, pp. 231–54

Frable DES. 1993. Being and feeling unique: statistical deviance and psychological marginality. *J. Pers.* 61:85–110

Gaertner L, Sedikides C, Graetz K. 1999. In search of self-definition: motivational primacy of the collective self, or contextual primacy? *J. Pers. Soc. Psychol.* 76:5–18

Gilbert DT, Fiske SR, Lindzey G, eds. 1998. *The Handbook of Social Psychology*. New York: McGraw-Hill

Haslam SA, Turner JC. 1992. Context-dependent variation in social stereotyping. 2. The relationship between frame of reference, self-categorization and accentuation. *Eur. J. Soc. Psychol.* 22:251–77

Haslam SA, Turner JC, Oakes PJ, McGarty C, Hayes BK. 1992. Context-dependent variation in social stereotyping. 1. The effects of intergroup relations as mediated by social change and frame of reference. *Eur. J. Soc. Psychol.* 22:3–20

Hinkle S, Brown R. 1988. Intergroup comparison and social identity: some links and lacunae. See Abrams & Hogg 1988, pp. 48–70

Hofstede G. 1980. *Culture's Consequences: International Differences in Work-Related Values*. Beverly Hills, CA: Sage

Hogg MA. 1992. *The Psychology of Group Cohesiveness: From Attraction to Social Identity*. New York: Harvester Wheatsheaf

Hogg MA, Abrams DA. 1988. Social motivation, self-esteem and social identity. See Abrams & Hogg 1988, pp. 28–47

Hornsey MJ, Hogg MA. 2000. Subgroup relations: a comparison of the mutual intergroup differentiation and common ingroup identity models of prejudice reduction. *Pers. Soc. Psychol. Bull.* 26:242–56

Jackson JW. 2001. Ingroup attitudes as a function of different dimensions of group identification and perceived intergroup conflict. *Self Identity*. In press

Jetten J, Branscombe NR, Spears R. 2001a. On being peripheral: effects of identity security on personal and collective self-esteem. *Eur. J. Soc. Psychol.* In press

Jetten J, Branscombe NR, Spears R, McKimmie B. 2001b. Predicting the paths of peripherals: the interaction of identification and future possibilities. Submitted

Jetten J, Postmes T, McAuliffe B. 2001c. We're all individuals: group norms of individualism and collectivism, levels of identification, and identity threat. *Eur. J. Soc. Psychol.* In press

Jetten J, Spears R, Manstead ASR. 1999. Group distinctiveness and intergroup discrimination. See Ellemers et al. 1999c, pp. 107–26

Jetten J, Spears R, Manstead ASR. 2001d. Similarity as a source of discrimination: The role of group identification. *Eur. J. Soc. Psychol.* In press

Jost JT, Major B, eds. 2001. *The Psychology of Legitimacy: Emerging Perspectives on Ideology, Justice, and Intergroup Relations*. New York: Cambridge Univ. Press

Jost JT, Banaji MR. 1994. The role of stereotyping in system-justification and the production

of false consciousness. *Br. J. Soc. Psychol.* 33:1–27

Kelly C, Breinlinger S. 1996. *The Social Psychology of Collective Action: Identity, Injustice, and Gender*. London: Taylor & Francis

Keltner D, Haidt J. 1999. Social functions of emotions at four levels of analysis. *Cogn. Emot.* 13:505–21

Kunda Z, Thagard P. 1996. Forming impressions from stereotypes, traits, and behaviors: a parallel-constraint-satisfaction theory. *Psychol. Rev.* 103:284–308

Leach CW, Snider SL, Iyer A. 2001. "Poisoning the consciences of the fortunate": The experience of relative advantage and support for social equality. In *Relative Deprivation: Specification, Development, and Integration*, ed. I Walker, HJ Smith. New York: Cambridge Univ. Press. In press

Leary MR, Baumeister RF. 2000. The nature and function of self-esteem: sociometer theory. *Adv. Exp. Soc. Psychol.* 32:1–62

Lemyre L, Smith PM. 1985. Intergroup discrimination and self-esteem in the minimal group paradigm. *J. Pers. Soc. Psychol.* 49:660–70

Leyens JP, Désert M, Croizet JC, Darcis C. 2000. Stereotype threat: Are lower status and history of stigmatization preconditions of stereotype threat? *Pers. Soc. Psychol.* 26:1189–99

Long K, Spears R. 1997. The self-esteem hypothesis revisited: differentiation and the disaffected. See Spears et al. 1997c, pp. 296–317

Luhtanen R, Crocker J. 1991. Self-esteem and intergroup comparisons: toward a theory of collective self-esteem. In *Social Comparison: Contemporary Theory and Research*, ed. J Suls, TA Wills, pp. 211–36. Hillsdale, NJ: Erlbaum

Mackie DM, Devos T, Smith ER. 2000. Intergroup emotions: explaining offensive action tendencies in an intergroup context. *J. Pers. Soc. Psychol.* 79:602–16

Mackie DM, Smith E, eds. 2001. *From Prejudice to Intergroup Emotions: Differentiated Reactions to Social Groups*. Philadelphia: Psychology Press. In press

Macrae CN, Bodenhausen GV. 2000. Social cognition: thinking categorically about others. *Annu. Rev. Psychol.* 51:93–120

Marques JM, Paez D. 1995. The "Black Sheep effect": social categorization, rejection of ingroup deviates, and perception of group variability. *Eur. Rev. Soc. Psychol.* 5:37–68

Marx DM, Brown JL, Steele CH. 1999. Allport's legacy and the situational press of stereotypes. *J. Soc. Issues* 55:491–502

McFarland C, Buehler R. 1995. Collective self-esteem as a moderator of the frog-pond effect in reactions to performance feedback. *J. Pers. Soc. Psychol.* 68:1055–70

McGarty C. 1999. *Categorization in Social Psychology*. London: Sage

Mlicki P, Ellemers N. 1996. Being different or being better? National stereotypes and identifications of Polish and Dutch students. *Eur. J. Soc. Psychol.* 26:97–114

Moreland RL. 1985. Social categorization and the assimilation of "new" group members. *J. Pers. Soc. Psychol.* 48:1173–90

Mullin B, Hogg MA. 1998. Dimensions of subjective uncertainty in social identification and minimal group discrimination. *Br. J. Soc. Psychol.* 37:345–65

Mummendey A, Schreiber HJ. 1983. Better or different? Positive social identity by discrimination against or differentiation from outgroups. *Eur. J. Soc. Psychol.* 13:389–97

Mussweiler R, Gabriel S, Bodenhausen GV. 2000. Shifting social identities as a strategy for deflecting threatening social comparisons. *J. Pers. Soc. Psychol.* 79:398–409

Noel JG, Wann DL, Branscombe NR. 1995. Peripherical ingroup membership status and public negativity towards outgroups. *J. Pers. Soc. Psychol.* 68:127–37

Oakes PJ. 1987. The salience of social categories. See Turner et al. 1987, pp. 42–67

Oakes PJ, Haslam SA, Turner JC. 1994. *Stereotyping and Social Reality*. Oxford: Blackwell

Ouwerkerk JW, Ellemers N. 2001. The benefits of being disadvantaged: performance-related circumstances and consequences of intergroup comparisons. *Eur. J. Soc. Psychol.* In press

Ouwerkerk JW, Ellemers N, De Gilder D. 1999. Group commitment and individual effort in experimental and organizational contexts. See Ellemers et al. 1999c, pp. 184–204

Pickett CL, Brewer MB. 2001. Assimilation and differentiation needs as motivational determinants of perceived ingroup and outgroup homogeneity. *J. Exp. Soc. Psychol.* In press

Postmes T, Spears R. 1998. Deindividuation and anti-normative behavior: a meta-analysis. *Psychol. Bull.* 123:238–59

Prentice DA, Miller DT, Lightdale JR. 1994. Asymmetries in attachments to groups and to their members—distinguishing between common-identity and common-bond groups. *Pers. Soc. Psychol. Bull.* 20:484–93

Reicher SD, Spears R, Postmes T. 1995. A social identity model of deindividuation phenomena. *Eur. Rev. Soc. Psychol.* 6:161–89

Reynolds KJ, Oakes PJ. 2000. Variability in impression formation: investigating the role of motivation, capacity, and the categorization process. *Pers. Soc. Psychol. Bull.* 26:355–73

Roccas S, Schwartz SH. 1993. Effects of intergroup similarity on intergroup relations. *Eur. J. Soc. Psychol.* 23:581–95

Rubin M, Hewstone M. 1998. Social identity theory's self-esteem hypothesis: a review and some suggestions for clarification. *Pers. Soc. Psychol. Rev.* 2:40–62

Schmitt MT, Branscombe NR. 2001. The good, the bad, and the manly: effects of threats to one's prototypicality on evaluations of fellow ingroup members. *J. Exp. Soc. Psychol.* In press

Schmitt MT, Silvia PJ, Branscombe NR. 2000. The intersection of self-evaluation maintenance and social identity theories: intragroup judgment in interpersonal and intergroup contexts. *Pers. Soc. Psychol. Bull.* 26:1598–606

Schopler J, Insko CA. 1992. The discontinuity effect in interpersonal and intergroup relations: generality and mediation. *Eur. Rev. Soc. Psychol.* 3:121–51

Shih M, Pittinsky TL, Ambadi N. 1999.

Stereotype susceptibility: identity salience and shifts in quantitative performance. *Psychol. Sci.* 10:80–83

Simon B, Loewy M, Stürmer S, Weber U, Freytag P, et al. 1998. Collective identification and social movement participation. *J. Pers. Soc. Psychol.* 74:646–58

Simon B, Stürmer S, Steffens K. 2000. Helping individuals or group members? The role of individual and collective identification in AIDS-volunteerism. *Pers. Soc. Psychol. Bull.* 26:497–506

Simon B. 1997. Self and group in modern society: ten theses on the individual self and the collective self. See Spears et al. 1997c, pp. 318–35

Smart L, Wegner DM. 1999. Covering up what can't be seen: concealable stigma and mental control. *J. Pers. Soc. Psychol.* 77:474–86

Smith ER. 1993. Social identity and social emotions: toward new conceptualizations of prejudice. In *Affect, Cognition and Stereotyping: Interactive Processes in Group Perception*, ed. DM Mackie, DL Hamilton, pp. 297–315. San Diego, CA: Academic

Smith ER, Murphy J, Coats S. 1999. Attachment to groups: theory and measurement. *J. Pers. Soc. Psychol.* 77:94–110

Snyder CR, Fromkin HL. 1980. *Uniqueness: The Human Pursuit of Difference*. New York: Plenum

Spears R. 2001. The interaction between the individual and the collective self: self-categorization in context. In *Individual Self, Relational Self, and Collective Self: Partners, Opponents or Strangers?*, ed. C Sedikides, MB Brewer. Philadelphia, PA: Psychology Press. In press

Spears R, Doosje B, Ellemers N. 1997a. Self-stereotyping in the face of threats to group status and distinctiveness: the role of group identification. *Pers. Soc. Psychol. Bull.* 23:538–53

Spears R, Doosje B, Ellemers N. 1999. Commitment and the context of social perception. See Ellemers et al. 1999c, pp. 59–83

Spears R, Jetten J, Doosje B. 2001a. The (il)legitimacy of ingroup bias: from social re-

ality to social resistance. See Jost & Major 2001. In press

Spears R, Jetten J, Scheepers D, 2001b. Distinctiveness and the definition of collective self: a tripartite model. In *Psychological Perspectives on Self and Identity*, ed. A Tesser, JV Wood, DA Stapel, Vol. 2. Lexington, VA: Am. Psychol. Assoc. In press

Spears R, Oakes PJ, Ellemers N, Haslam SA. 1997b. The social psychology of stereotyping and group life. See Spears et al. 1997c, pp. 1–19

Spears R, Oakes PJ, Ellemers N, Haslam SA. 1997c. *Introduction: the Social Psychology of Stereotyping and Group Life*. Oxford: Blackwell

Steele CM. 1987. The psychology of self-affirmation: sustaining the integrity of the self. In *Advances in Experimental Social Psychology*, ed. L Berkowitz, 21:261–302. New York: Academic

Steele CM. 1997. A threat in the air: how stereotypes shape intellectual identity and performance. *Am. Psychol.* 52:613–29

Steele CM, Aronson J. 1995. Stereotype threat and the intellectual test performance of African Americans. *J. Pers. Soc. Psychol.* 69:797–811

Stone J, Lynch CI, Sjomeling M, Darley JM. 1999. Stereotype threat effects on black and white athletic performance. *J. Pers. Soc. Psychol.* 77:1213–27

Swann WB, Milton LP, Polzer JT. 2000. Should we create a niche or fall in line? Identity negotiation and small group effectiveness. *J. Pers. Soc. Psychol.* 79:238–50

Swim JK, Miller DL. 1999. White guilt: its antecedents and consequences for attitudes toward affirmative action. *Pers. Soc. Psychol. Bull.* 25:500–14

Tajfel H. 1978. *Differentiation Between Social Groups: Studies in the Social Psychology of Intergroup Relations*. New York: Academic

Tajfel H, Turner J. 1979. An integrative theory of intergroup conflict. In *The Social Psychology of Intergroup Relations*, ed. WG Austin, S Worchel, pp. 33–48. Monterey, CA: Brooks-Cole

Taylor DM, Doria JR. 1981. Self-serving and group-serving bias in attribution. *J. Soc. Psychol.* 113:201–11

Terry DJ, Hogg MA. 1996. Group norms and the attitude-behavior relationship: a role for group identification. *Pers. Soc. Psychol. Bull.* 22:776–93

Triandis HC. 1989. The self and social behavior in differing cultural contexts. *Psychol. Rev.* 96:506–20

Turner JC. 1987. A self-categorization theory. See Turner et al. 1987, pp. 42–67

Turner JC. 1999. Some current issues in research on social identity and self-categorization theories. See Ellemers et al. 1999c, pp. 6–34

Turner JC, Hogg MA, Oakes PJ, Reicher SD, Wetherell MS, eds. 1987. A self-categorization theory. In *Rediscovering the Social Group: A Self-Categorization Theory.* Oxford: Basil Blackwell

Turner JC, Hogg MA, Oakes PJ, Smith PM.

1984. Failure and defeat as determinants of group cohesiveness. *Br. J. Soc. Psychol.* 23:97–111

Van Knippenberg A. 1984. Intergroup differences in group perceptions. In *The Social Dimension: European Developments in Social Psychology*, ed. H Tajfel, pp. 560–78. Cambridge: Cambridge Univ. Press

Van Rijswijk W, Ellemers N. 2002. Context effects on the application of stereotype content to multiple categorizable targets. *Pers. Soc. Psychol. Bull.* 28:In press

Veenstra K, Haslam SA. 2000. Willingness to participate in industrial protest: exploring social identification in context. *Br. J. Soc. Psychol.* 39:153–72

Wright SC, Taylor DM, Moghaddam FM. 1990. Responding to membership in a disadvantaged group: from acceptance to collective protest. *J. Pers. Soc. Psychol.* 58:994–1003

Annu. Rev. Psychol. 2002. 53:187–213

CAUSES OF EATING DISORDERS

Janet Polivy[1] and C. Peter Herman[2]

[1]*Department of Psychology, University of Toronto, Erindale Campus, Mississauga, Ontario, Canada L5L 1C6; e-mail: polivy@psych.utoronto.ca*
[2]*Department of Psychology, University of Toronto, Toronto, Ontario, Canada M5S 1A1; e-mail: herman@psych.utoronto.ca*

Key Words anorexia nervosa, bulimia nervosa, contributory factors, identity, control

■ **Abstract** Anorexia nervosa and bulimia nervosa have emerged as the predominant eating disorders. We review the recent research evidence pertaining to the development of these disorders, including sociocultural factors (e.g., media and peer influences), family factors (e.g., enmeshment and criticism), negative affect, low self-esteem, and body dissatisfaction. Also reviewed are cognitive and biological aspects of eating disorders. Some contributory factors appear to be necessary for the appearance of eating disorders, but none is sufficient. Eating disorders may represent a way of coping with problems of identity and personal control.

CONTENTS

INTRODUCTION

In the late 1960s, the previously obscure and extremely rare disorder anorexia nervosa (AN) became much more prevalent in Western societies. Young females from middle- and upper-class families were starving themselves, sometimes to death. The next decade saw the emergence of a new eating disorder, bulimia nervosa (BN), wherein young women alternated self-starvation with bingeing, usually followed by purging (i.e., active attempts to rid the body of calories). Clinicians and

0084-6570/02/0201-0187$14.00

187

the media focused intensively on these new disorders, which supplanted obesity as the primary eating disorder; indeed, obesity was removed from the Diagnostic and Statistical Manual (DSM) of Mental Disorders in the 1980s. Research on these new disorders grew at about the same rate as the disorders themselves. Some interesting historical research (Bemporad 1997) uncovered evidence of both AN and BN having existed since ancient times, but certainly not to the same extent—and possibly not in the same way—as at present. By the turn of the millennium, AN and BN were well-established—as was the research enterprise—but a clear understanding of the source of the disorders or how to prevent or treat them remained elusive.

In this chapter, we first describe the disorders; the bulk of the chapter is devoted to a review of research (and speculation) on the causes of eating disorders, emphasizing the discriminant validity of causal factors (i.e., why one person develops an eating disorder, whereas another seemingly similar person in a seemingly similar situation does not). One major area we do not review is treatment research; this decision is dictated mainly by space limitations, but also by the fact that studies on treatment are only loosely related to research on eating disorder's (ED) causes. Another arguable decision is to ignore binge eating disorder and eating disorder not otherwise specified, recently identified EDs; again, space limitations require strict focus on the major EDs.

DIAGNOSTIC CRITERIA AND CORE PATHOLOGICAL FEATURES

In this chapter we follow the convention of the research literature and consider AN and BN as separate disorders. How—or even whether—to separate the eating disorders, however, has been debated vigorously. The core symptoms (e.g., body dissatisfaction; preoccupation with food, weight, and shape; certain ego deficits) do not necessarily distinguish AN from BN patients, even if the diagnostic criteria for the two EDs differ. The spectrum hypothesis (VanderHam et al. 1997) considers the EDs as one syndrome with different manifestations.

According to the DSM-IV [American Psychiatric Association (APA) 1994], the diagnostic criteria for AN are maintaining a body weight at a level less than 85% of normal weight for age and height, an intense fear of fatness, disturbed experience of one's body weight or shape, and amenorrhea for at least three consecutive menstrual cycles. Although many AN patients engage in compulsive exercising, restrictor-type AN patients are distinguished by their resolute refusal to eat (much), whereas bulimic-type AN patients regularly engage in binge eating and purging. Some have questioned the wisdom of retaining amenorrhea as a diagnostic criterion (Cachelin & Maher 1998, Garfinkel et al. 1996); we could extend the argument to the 85% weight criterion.

The DSM-IV criteria for BN include recurrent episodes of both binge eating (i.e., eating a larger amount of food than most people would eat in a similar time and circumstances, and a feeling of lack of control of one's eating during the episode) and compensatory behaviors (such as purging, exercising, or fasting) to prevent weight gain from the overeating. These behaviors must occur at least twice a week for a minimum of 3 months. In addition, self-evaluation is overly dependent on body weight and shape. Note that bingeing and purging are characteristics of one major type of AN, which leads to understandable confusion between AN and BN[1]; BN may differ from bulimic-type AN only in that BN patients are unable to suppress their weight below the 85% cut-off and thus fail to display amenorrhea. AN is an exclusionary criterion for BN, which otherwise might be confused with bulimic-type AN. A further subdivision of BN into purging-type (i.e., use of self-induced vomiting or laxative, diuretic, or enema abuse) and nonpurging type (i.e., fasting, exercising, or other nonpurging means of compensating for binge eating) would seem to differ only in the preferred tactic for eliminating calories and probably has little conceptual significance (APA 1994).

Although bingeing is a diagnostic feature of BN and bulimic-type AN, we have little guidance as to how to identify a binge (Herman & Polivy 1996). Exactly how much food is a larger-than-normal amount of food? How are we to assess the loss of control that allegedly characterizes binges (Johnson et al. 2000)? If an eating episode displayed only one aspect—a huge amount of food or loss of control but not both—would it still be a binge?

One correlative feature that distinguishes BN from AN is impulsivity. Sexual promiscuity, suicide attempts, drug abuse, and stealing or shoplifting are frequently noted in BN patients (e.g., Matsunaga et al. 2000; Wiederman & Pryor 1996). Indeed, impulsiveness may be what makes an aspiring anorexic into a bulimic; if an individual intent on restricting her intake cannot resist food under certain circumstances, she may capitulate to temptation, binge, and then feel obliged to compensate afterward. This pattern would seem to characterize both BN and bulimic-type AN patients, the only difference being the weight level around which they fluctuate.

Incidence and Prevalence

The incidence of AN and BN has increased markedly during the past 50 years, although there is some reason to believe that at least some of the increase is due to greater awareness and reporting of these disorders (Wakeling 1996). Precise estimates of incidence and prevalence vary wildly, perhaps because those who suffer from these disorders are often reluctant to reveal their condition. Prevalence estimates tend to range from about 3% to 10% of at-risk females (those between 15 and 29 years of age), with BN patients outnumbering AN patients by at least 2 to 1. Those with AN frequently deny any illness and are often seen for treatment only because of the concern of those close to them that their lives may be in

---

[1]Indeed, Gleaves et al. (2000) found that restrictor-type AN is more distinct from bulimic-type AN than bulimic-type AN is from BN. It has been argued that bulimic-type AN should simply be considered BN.

imminent danger. Those with BN, because their appearance is usually normal and their bingeing and purging occur in private, are usually more difficult to detect, although BN patients are more likely to present themselves for treatment, because the binge-purge cycle is often profoundly disturbing to them. (AN patients frequently appear to be indifferent to their disorder.) The prevalence of partial EDs is at least twice that of full-syndrome EDs. Longitudinal studies suggest a progression from less to more severe disturbances, with normal dieters occasionally becoming pathological dieters, who in turn occasionally progress to partial- or full-syndrome EDs (Shisslak et al. 1995). It must be remembered, though, that whereas normal dieting is a frequent precursor of EDs, most normal dieters do not progress to the point of pathology. One of the most significant questions facing us is why some dieters progress to EDs whereas most do not.

Prognosis

There is no easy treatment for EDs. About a third of patients continue to meet diagnostic criteria 5 years and longer after initial treatment (Fairburn et al. 2000, Keel et al. 1999). Estimates of mortality (including suicide) rates range from just over 5% to just over 8% (Herzog et al. 2000, Steinhausen et al. 2000). Still, more than 50% of patients show significant improvement more than 5 years after beginning treatment (Casper & Jabine 1996, Herpertzdahlmann et al. 1996, Steinhausen et al. 2000). Some research (e.g., Keel et al. 1999) has explored predictors of success in treatment, but there has been little investigation into natural recovery, self-cure, or remission of EDs without treatment. Perhaps only the most intractable cases find their way into treatment.

CAUSES OF EATING DISORDERS

The main purpose of this chapter is to survey the various attempts to explain why some people develop eating disorders. The literature displays an uneasy balance between studies exploring the role of particular putative causal factors and theories that attempt to combine such factors into a comprehensive whole. The main obstacles facing these attempts are, first and foremost, the virtual impossibility of conducting true experimental research in which a putative causal factor is manipulated, and secondly, the difficulty of combining all such factors into a model that is not unwieldy. A large proportion of studies examine AN and/or BN patients (and sometimes a healthy or psychiatrically impaired control group) with an eye to isolating correlates of the disorder, often in the vague hope that correlates can be persuasively argued into causes. The difficulty of finding suitable samples of ED patients to test has led to a proliferation of studies examining correlates of ED symptomatology as it exists in more-or-less normal populations. Any sample of high school or college females (and even males) will manifest a distribution of self-reported symptoms (albeit far short of true pathology), which may be leveraged by extrapolation and the confusion of correlation and causation (especially in cross-sectional data) into examinations of the causes of EDs. The difficulty of doing proper research, along with the relative infancy of this field of research, should make us tolerant of these shortcomings. Still, the explanatory achievements to date are modest. Some theorists, such as Bruch (1973), have provided elegant theories; however, empirical data to confirm this and other theories are incomplete and inconclusive at this point.

Literally thousands of studies, plus numerous books and chapters, have attempted to specify exactly what causes EDs. The consensual approach to integrating the various factors that contribute to EDs is the "biopsychosocial" model. This model has the advantage of taking into account all sorts of factors—ranging from the broadly cultural to the narrowly biological, with stops along the way for familial, social, cognitive, learning, personality, and other factors—that have been alleged to make a difference (Leung et al. 1996). The model lacks specificity, however; moreover, each version of the biopsychosocial model differs from the next. Space limitations preclude an exhaustive review here, but we attempt to provide an overview of the most salient findings and issues. We begin at the broadest level with culture, proceed to familial and social factors, and then examine individual factors such as personality, cognition, and physiology.

Sociocultural Contributors to Eating Disorders

Eating disorders do not occur uniformly in all cultures at all times. An obsession with slimness—a core feature of EDs—is concentrated in cultures in which food is abundant. In cultures of scarcity, the ideal body shape is much more likely to be rotund, suggesting that ideals tend toward what is difficult to achieve. In this sense, then, a culture of caloric abundance may be considered a cause of EDs. It is important to note from the outset, however, that this cause is not specific; growing up in a culture of abundance, while perhaps increasing the chances of your developing an ED, does not make it likely that you will develop an ED; after all, most people in even the most affluent of cultures do *not* develop EDs. A culture of abundance should be regarded as at most a background cause. Such a culture may value slimness, but whether a particular individual takes this valuation to a pathological extreme depends on additional factors. For instance, there is variation in the extent to which people internalize our culture's valuation of slimness, and the extent of such internalization predicts body dissatisfaction, drive for thinness, and certain bulimic characteristics (Stormer & Thompson 1996, Stice 2001). What factors, though, determine the extent to which the value of thinness is internalized? We must refer to more individual factors (see below).

Initially, it was believed (see e.g., Garfinkel & Garner 1982) that the idealization of slimness, and the consequent tendency toward EDs, was concentrated in the upper-SES strata of the culture of abundance, where after all, abundance is even greater. As our culture becomes increasingly homogenized, with media images of a thin ideal physique now permeating every corner of society, EDs have become correspondingly more democratic (Gard & Freeman 1996, Striegel-Moore 1997).

Not surprisingly, the media are often blamed for the (increasing) incidence of EDs, on the grounds that media images of idealized (slim) physiques motivate or even force people to attempt to achieve slimness themselves. The media are accused of distorting reality, in that the models and celebrities portrayed in the media are either naturally thin (i.e., at the tail of the normal distribution of body weight) and thus unrepresentative of normality, or unnaturally thin (i.e., the products of exceptional exertions to achieve and maintain a slim physique). As with the culture of abundance, idealized media images are at best a background cause of EDs. Exposure to the media is so widespread that if such exposure were *the* cause of EDs, then it would be difficult to explain why anyone would *not* be eating-disordered. Furthermore, as Tiggemann & Pickering (1996, p. 202) noted upon discovering that among girls, body dissatisfaction and drive for thinness were associated with increased exposure to certain types of TV shows, "although it is tempting to conclude that watching a large dose of thin idealized images on television leads to dissatisfaction with one's body, a correlation cannot determine causality. An alternative scenario, for example, might be that those most dissatisfied with their bodies or wishing to be thinner, seek out or are more interested in particular types of television."

The idealization of slimness and derogation of fatness in cultures of abundance is more intense for females than for males (Striegel-Moore 1993, 1997). This sex-linked valuation of thinness is usually invoked to account for the fact that EDs are more than 10 times more prevalent in females than in males (Striegel-Moore 1997). As a result of the societal disparagement of overweight and glorification of underweight, many—perhaps most—young women express dissatisfaction with their weight and shape. This dissatisfaction often has emotional overtones of self-disgust. Body dissatisfaction, in fact, may be regarded as an essential precursor (and continuing accompaniment) of EDs. The more intense this dissatisfaction, the more likely that one will undertake attempts to lose weight. When combined with other pathogens (see below), these attempts may well eventuate in AN (if the individual has particularly strong restraints on eating) or BN (if she does not).

Like the media, peer influence is often cited as a contributor to EDs (e.g., Levine et al. 1994, Shisslak et al. 1998, Stice 1998, Wertheim et al. 1997). Adolescent girls learn certain attitudes (i.e., the importance of slimness) and behaviors (i.e., dieting, purging) from their peers (Levine et al. 1994), both by example and encouragement and by way of teasing for failure to adhere to peer norms. Adolescent female friendship cliques tend to be homogenous with respect to body-image concerns (Paxton et al. 1999), suggesting direct peer influence; however, the possibility remains that cliques do not influence their members so much as "recruit" them on the basis of shared concerns (Ennett & Bauman 1994). It is difficult to weigh the relative importance of peer influence, as opposed, say, to the influence of the media or the family, which teach the same lessons; some evidence suggests that peers and family are more potent influences than the media (Stice 1998), whereas other studies find the reverse (Wertheim et al. 1997). Moreover, peer influence, like these other influences, is so broad and pervasive that it ought to cause more pathology than actually occurs. Paxton et al.'s (1999) analysis reminds us that not all peers are equally concerned about attaining a slim physique, so blanket condemnation of peer influence or pressure is unwarranted.

Media and peer pressure no doubt impinge more powerfully on females than on males, but we should not be too complacent about explaining the huge disproportion of females among ED patients solely in terms of these influences. At the very least, we must consider the possibility that it is not simply that our culture exhorts females (more than males) to be thin; it may be the case that females are more attentive than are males to such exhortations, for various reasons that are examined below.

Among American women, blacks were thought to be "protected" from EDs owing to the reduced pressure on them to be thin. Black men prefer heavier women than do white men (see e.g., Greenberg & Laporte 1996), and black women (e.g., Powell & Kahn 1995) and children (Thompson et al. 1997) have larger ideal physiques. Thus, when black women develop an ED, it is more likely to be binge eating disorder, an ED that does not prominently feature a drive toward thinness (Striegel-Moore & Smolak 1996). Still, recent case reports (Striegel-Moore 1997; Striegel-Moore & Smolak 1996) suggest that the diffusion of the thin ideal has reached the black subculture as well. The widespread adoption of the dominant American cultural ideals (in American ethnic subcultures and indeed around the world) has meant that "ethnicity" no longer protects individuals from AN and BN (e.g., Chamorro & Flores-Ortiz 2000, Mumford & Choudry 2000, Polivy et al. 2001). Evidence that high-income black women are just as dissatisfied as are high-income white women suggests that whatever black-white differences may exist in population samples may be more a function of SES than of race (Caldwell et al. 1997).

The influence of sociocultural factors in the context of EDs can be summarized succinctly as the idealization of thinness, which is sometimes regarded as a principal cause of EDs on its own. More plausibly, it may channel women's dissatisfactions and distress toward a focus on body shape and size, providing an outlet for individual pathology; thinness is thus relentlessly pursued by those who see no better way to solve their problems. As we narrow our focus toward individual pathology, we now move to family influences.

Familial Influences on Eating Disorders

In what ways might families contribute to EDs? The most obvious way is by encouraging EDs. Families (and friends) often praise AN patients' slenderness, and envy the self-control and discipline required to achieve it (Branch & Eurman 1980); this reinforcement frequently persists even when the anorexic becomes severely emaciated. Of course, this reinforcement does not cause the disorder so much as help to perpetuate it. Certainly, people with AN do not require family approval in order to starve themselves. In fact, those with AN as often as not use their families' increasing concerns about their inordinate slimness as a manipulative tool (Branch & Eurman 1980, Minuchin et al. 1978).

Family dynamics have been implicated not only in the perpetuation of EDs but also in their development (e.g., Minuchin et al. 1978). Case reports and studies of family interaction show eating-disordered families to be enmeshed, intrusive, hostile, and negating of the patient's emotional needs (Minuchin et al. 1978) or overly concerned with parenting (Shoebridge & Gowers 2000); some, such as Minuchin, have argued that the entire family unit must be treated if therapy is to be effective. Within the past few years, several studies have found that attachment processes are abnormal in eating-disordered populations; insecure attachment is common in this group (Ward et al. 2000a,b). Ward and colleagues (Ward et al. 2000b, p. 279), however, conclude that "many of these (family dysfunction) characteristics are regarded as secondary to the presence of an ill family member, rather than causative."

ED patients generally describe a critical family environment, featuring coercive parental control (Haworth-Hoeppner 2000). Adolescents who perceive family communication, parental caring, and parental expectations as low and those who report sexual or physical abuse are at increased risk for developing EDs (Haudek et al. 1999, Neumark-Sztainer et al. 2000). BN patients also report greater parental intrusiveness, specifically maternal invasion of privacy, jealousy, and competition, as well as paternal seductiveness (Rorty et al. 2000). In contrast, perceived parental encouragement of autonomy is associated with less dieting behavior (Strong & Huon 1998), possibly serving a protective function against EDs.

Mothers of girls with EDs may well have an influence on their daughters' pathology. They think that their daughters should lose more weight and describe them as less attractive than do comparison mothers or the girls themselves (Hill & Franklin 1998, Pike & Rodin 1991). Mothers of ED patients are more dissatisfied with the general functioning of the family system and are themselves more eating-disordered than are mothers of girls who do not have EDs (Hill & Franklin 1998, Pike & Rodin 1991). Direct maternal comments appear to be more powerful influences than is simple modeling of weight and shape concerns (Ogden & Steward 2000, Smolak et al. 1999), although even modeling does appear to affect elementary schoolchildren's weight and shape-related attitudes and behaviors (Smolak et al. 1999). Mothers' critical comments prospectively predicted ED outcome for their daughters (Vanfurth et al. 1996).

Mothers who themselves have an ED tend to have a negative influence on their children's attitudes and behaviors, feeding them irregularly, using food for nonnutritive purposes, and expressing concern about their daughters' weight as early as the age of 2. By 5 years of age, these children exhibit greater negative affect than do the offspring of mothers without EDs and are at serious risk for the later development of an ED (Agras et al. 1999). In fact, maternal EDs produce childhood feeding problems in offspring (Whelan & Cooper 2000), and 50% of children of mothers with EDs have psychiatric disorders (Hodes et al. 1997).

Most studies of family functioning are, predictably, correlational, making it difficult to determine whether family dysfunction contributes to EDs, EDs contribute to family dysfunction, or some common factor contributes to both. Moreover, the role of the family is often ascertained by retrospective questioning, further undermining our certainty about what caused what. Finally, case studies of dysfunctional/eating-disordered families, in the absence of control families, preclude any certainty about whether these family problems are unique to families with a member who suffers from an ED.[2]

If we were to conclude that negative family influences were in fact responsible for the development of EDs, we would still need to ask exactly how a dysfunctional family induces EDs. Below, we consider the possibility that problems of identity and/or control are central to EDs, with the individual attempting to resolve these problems by investing emotionally and behaviorally in the pursuit of slimness. The family, of course, may contribute directly to problems of identity or control and may also suggest the solution, by emphasizing slimness as a panacea. Steiger et al. (1996) conclude that families (including so-called normal families as well) may transmit eating concerns, but such transmission may not be sufficient for the emergence of an ED, which requires "some additional vulnerability factor" (p. 156), either biological or experiential. This brings us to the consideration of individual factors that conduce to the development of EDs.

Individual Risk Factors

There are many factors specific to the individual that have been proposed as contributors to the development of EDs. Some of these factors (e.g., personality traits, self-esteem deficits) are seen as resident in the individual, whereas others involve personal experiences and seem to fall somewhere between the environment and the individual. The latter accordingly is examined first.

EXPERIENCES CONTRIBUTING TO EATING DISORDER DEVELOPMENT   Interpersonal experiences that have been most frequently linked to the development of EDs include abuse, trauma, and teasing. Self-reports of having been teased about one's appearance or body shape are associated with increased ED symptomatology

---

[2]A dramatically different approach to assessing familial influences on EDs is behavior genetic analysis, which includes common (familial) environment as a potential explanation of twin concordance. The Virginia group found a substantial familial influence on BN (Kendler et al. 1995) but later reversed itself, deciding that "the tendency to focus on common or familial environment as playing a primary causal role in the development of disordered eating is overemphasized" (Bulik et al. 1998, p. 1216). The often implausibly huge heritability coefficients for EDs (see below) leaves the skeptical reviewer disinclined to draw conclusions about family influence on the basis of genetics-vs.-environment models. Moreover, as Spelt & Meyer (1995) point out, the absence of common family environment effects in twin studies may simply mean that children react differently to family environment influences, not that such influences do not exist.

(Lunner et al. 2000). Similarly, ED patients report more premorbid life stresses and difficulties than do controls (e.g., Raffi et al. 2000, Schmidt et al. 1997, Welch et al. 1997). The joint occurrence (and possible mutual influence) of stressful life events and affective deficiencies such as low self-esteem, depressed mood, anhedonia, generalized anxiety, and irritability may be particularly pathogenic for BN (Raffi et al. 2000).

The influence of childhood abuse is somewhat more complex. There does appear to be a connection between childhood sexual abuse (CSA) and bulimic symptomatology (Everill & Waller 1995), although CSA is also associated with depression and other psychological disturbances. Not surprisingly, all of these problems are more likely to be associated with CSA in conjunction with other physical and emotional abuse and when the family does not provide support (deGroot & Rodin 1999). Some, however, maintain that BN patients do not have an elevated incidence of CSA, although the severity of the abuse may be greater (Groth-Marnat & Michel 2000). Casper & Lyubomirsky (1997) argue that sexual abuse causes BN only indirectly, by conducing to individual psychopathology. Kent & Waller (2000) maintain that childhood emotional abuse (CEA)—possibly through its profound influence on self-esteem and anxiety—is the only type of childhood trauma that predicts eating pathology in adults.

How might abuse lead to EDs? It has been argued abuse induces intolerable emotions and undermines identity. EDs serve as desperate attempts to regulate overwhelming negative affect and to construct a coherent sense of self when internal structures are lacking (Rorty & Yager 1996). Similarly, EDs have been seen as coping mechanisms favored by women who do not have more constructive ways of dealing with personal crises (Troop 1998).

How do EDs serve to deal with continuing emotional or identity problems? By refocusing one's attention onto weight, shape, and eating, one enters a domain in which one can gain some emotional control. The AN patient achieves at least partial emotional gratification by avoiding food and achieving slimness (albeit never enough). The BN patient gains emotional relief by bingeing (and then by purging). For both, obsessive focus on weight loss and its associated tactics provide a narrow, apparently viable way to channel identity concerns (and to avoid dealing with broader issues). More recent theorists concur that an extreme need to control both eating and other aspects of behavior is a central feature of EDs (Fairburn et al. 1999). Gaining a sense of control and pride in one's ability to control one's eating combats the feeling of being taken over by thoughts of food or of lacking control of one's thoughts, eating, and weight (Serpell et al. 1999). An experimental induction of loss of perceived control led ED patients to report feeling fatter and more pessimistic (Waller & Hodgson 1996).

AFFECTIVE INFLUENCES   Although a temperamental characteristic such as negative emotionality is unlikely to lead to EDs in and of itself, stress and negative mood are commonly reported antecedents for EDs (e.g., Ball & Lee 2000, Leon et al. 1997). For example, BN patients have elevated self-directed hostility scores, even controlling for other factors such as mood and family hostility level

(Friedman et al. 1997), and women with EDs score higher than controls in guilt, covert hostility (BN) (Allen et al. 1998), and suppressed anger (AN) (Geller et al. 2000). Furthermore, negative affect has been shown to mediate the relation between dieting and binge eating, although dieting and negative affect remain independent risk factors for binge eating (Stice et al. 2000a). It may be, though, that negative affectivity increases vulnerability for overall psychopathology rather than EDs per se (Leon et al. 1997). Longitudinal studies often find that although initial depressed mood and self-perceptions predict later ED symptomatology, none of these predictors remain significant if initial disordered eating is ruled out. Thus, affective factors may not be etiologically important for EDs, although they may be associated with subclinical eating problems (Wichstrom 2000).

A functional relation between negative affect and ED symptoms has been proposed (e.g., Steinberg et al. 1989). According to Johnson & Larson (1982), people with BN attempt to elevate their mood by eating; purging allows them to avoid gaining weight. Unfortunately, the bulimic eventually realizes that the binges are out of control, and begins to feel guilty and dread eating. Eating no longer provides relief, but rather induces negative emotions such as guilt. Purging may then relieve the guilt, as well as discharging anger. It is thus possible that purging eventually replaces bingeing as a means of tension reduction (Johnson & Larson 1982). In fact, BN patients report reduced anxiety and depression following a binge/purge episode (Sanftner & Crowther 1998, Steinberg et al. 1989). After bingeing in the laboratory, bulimics reported reduced anxiety, tension, and guilt, although depression was unchanged (Kaye et al. 1986). Bulimic behaviors also reduce anger, particularly when the individual has a strong tendency to avoid expressing that emotion (Milligan & Waller 2000).

The co-occurrence of ED and mood disorders (particularly depression) has been frequently noted and may reflect primary mood disturbance in EDs, mood disorders secondary to EDs, or common third variables (biological or psychosocial) leading to both, such as genetic or familial transmission. The lack of a well-organized body- and self-image is unique to EDs, however (Steiger et al. 1992). Some evidence supports the primacy of the ED; ED symptoms and dietary restraint predicted subsequent depression in initially nondepressed individuals (Stice et al. 2000b). Some studies find that ED onset follows that of mood disorder (Godart et al. 2000, Gruber & Dilsaver 1996), whereas still others suggest that depression and anxiety are more state-dependent features that resolve when ED symptoms remit (Lehoux et al. 2000). Actually inducing negative affect increases body dissatisfaction and body-size perception in BN patients (Carter et al. 1996; Kulbartz-Klatt et al. 1999), suggesting that whichever is primary, negative affect can contribute to ED symptoms.

SELF-ESTEEM   Low self-esteem may conduce to a variety of disorders, including EDs (e.g., Fairburn et al. 1997, Leary et al. 1995, Striegel-Moore 1997). Self-esteem reflects how others react to the individual; thus, (perceived) rejection may cause lower self-esteem and maladaptive behaviors, including EDs. Furthermore, dieting, which is highly prone to disruptions that result in overeating, often produces a downward spiraling of self-esteem that contributes more specifically to EDs (as opposed to, say, depression) (Heatherton & Polivy 1992). Shape- and weight-based self-esteem is reduced in ED patients (Geller ct al. 1998), and prospective research confirms that girls with low self-esteem are more likely to develop disordered eating in the next few years (Button et al. 1996).

Empirically, self-esteem has been found to moderate perfectionism and feeling overweight in predicting bulimic symptoms (Bardone et al. 2000, Vohs et al. 1999). Women high in perfectionism, who consider themselves overweight exhibit bulimic symptoms only if they have low self-esteem (i.e., if they doubt they can attain their high body standards); women with high self-esteem and the same diathesis-stress conditions are less likely to exhibit bulimic symptoms. Similarly, low self-esteem and negative affect predicted ED symptomatology 4 years later (Leon et al. 1997). Moreover, a program aimed at improving self-esteem in 11- to 14-year-olds resulted in lowered incidence of weight loss and ED symptomatology 1 year later in participants considered at risk when the program began (O'Dea & Abraham 2000). Finally, lower self-esteem in ED patients predicts worse outcome (Hesse-Biber et al. 1999, VanderHam et al. 1998). Alternatively, women who recover from BN report an increase in their self-esteem (Troop et al. 2000).

BODY DISSATISFACTION   Negative affect and negative feelings about the self are channeled in ED more specifically into negative feelings about the body or body dissatisfaction (BD).[3] BD is sometimes operationalized as the gap between one's actual and ideal weight/shape; however, this is inappropriate, because one may see one's body as far from ideal and yet still be reasonably satisfied with it. More direct assessment of BD involves asking people specifically how (dis)satisfied they are with their bodies or parts thereof.

Virtually all conceptualizations of EDs—including the DSM criteria—make reference to BD. Most models of EDs involving multiple factors (e.g., Stice 2001) assign BD a prominent causal role. BD (sometimes referred to as weight concern) is often associated with dieting behavior; indeed, BN and AN are sometimes referred to as the dieting disorders. Dieting has been posited to precipitate, if not cause, bingeing (Polivy & Herman 1985) and EDs in general (Polivy & Herman 1987; Stice 2000a, 2001), and it is BD that presumably causes dieting. Weight concern and dieting help to predict the emergence of an ED (e.g., Joiner et al. 1997, Steiger et al. 1996, Stice et al. 1998), and bulimic women seek out the

---

[3]The broader construct of "negative body image" comprises both body dissatisfaction and body misperception—typically, overestimation of one's actual body size. Although both types of body image problems can in principle drive weight loss attempts, and although they may well overlap empirically, it is possible to experience one and not the other (Stormer & Thompson 1996). For a time, misperception was considered a critical aspect of EDs and research on it flourished, but its importance has faded in recent years. ED-control differences in misperception are much weaker than are comparable differences in dissatisfaction (Cash & Deagle 1997).

very appearance feedback that is likely to aggravate these concerns (Joiner 1999). Moreover, such interest in negative appearance feedback predicts the development of later symptoms, via the mediating effects of increased body dissatisfaction Conversely, satisfaction with one's weight acts as a "protective" factor in adolescent girls who are otherwise at high risk for developing EDs (Chandy et al. 1995).

Most of the alleged causes of EDs that we have reviewed operate through BD. Thus, media influence is thought to precipitate EDs by making women feel dissatisfied with their appearance. Family and peer pressure, teasing, and more individual psychological influences such as general anxiety converge on the "final common pathway" of BD (Paxton et al. 1999).

In our view, while BD is probably a necessary factor in the emergence of EDs, it is not sufficient. After all, it is possible to be dissatisfied with one's body and yet not do anything about it. Why is it that of two dissatisfied people, one throws herself into (usually futile) attempts to achieve a satisfactory body, whereas the other remains dissatisfied but does not diet/starve, binge, or purge? The determining factor, we suggest, is whether or not the individual seizes upon weight and shape as the answer to the problems of identity and control. Some young women become invested in achieving a "perfect" body as an existential project (i.e., as a way of giving their lives meaning, coherence, and emotional fulfillment that are otherwise lacking). Some become invested in achieving complete control over their eating, weight, and shape, believing that control in these domains is possible even though such control is not possible elsewhere in their lives. For many with EDs, these two goals overlap. In the final analysis, BD may contribute to EDs primarily by conferring purpose: The narrow ambitions of the ED patient—in particular, the exclusive focus on weight—may make her life simpler, more certain, and more efficacious. "She finds a maladaptive solution to her suffering, confusion, and sense of inadequacy by identifying herself with her weight" (Vitousek & Hollon 1990, p. 197).

COGNITIVE FACTORS   EDs feature several cognitive aberrations, including obsessive thoughts, inaccurate judgments, and rigid thinking patterns. The prominence of these has suggested that cognitive pathology may contribute to EDs. Schematicity for weight, and using one's weight as a basis for self-evaluation, are central features of both AN and BN and contribute to the persistence of EDs (Vitousek & Hollon 1990). An obsession with becoming thin may be seen as driving AN (and is present in BN as well). Judging one's own body to be larger than it really is may justify a relentless pursuit of thinness. Examination of cognitions in EDs has been stimulated by two developments: (*a*) the ascendancy of cognitive-behavior therapy for EDs, which is premised on the notion that normalizing cognitions may prove effective against EDs and (*b*) the importation of well-developed experimental paradigms for studying cognition.

Obsessive thoughts   Individuals with EDs tend to spend an inordinate amount of time obsessing about food/eating, weight/shape, and related matters (Gleaves et al. 2000). One survey (Sunday et al. 1995) found that 74% of ED patients spent more than 3 hours/day on obsessional thoughts; 42% spent more than 8 hours/day! Sixty-two percent had fewer than 3 hours/day entirely free of such obsessive thoughts, and 37% had no free hours at all. Most (72%) patients tried to suppress these obsessive thoughts, but "50% were not successful and felt that they had little or no control over the preoccupations" (Sunday et al. 1995, p. 241). About 20% of the patients—especially restricting anorexics—found the obsessive thoughts comforting and did not wish to be rid of them; more than half the patients considered the obsessions to be ego-syntonic.

Perfectionism   Related to obsession is perfectionism, the belief that one must (strive to) be perfect. Perfectionism can easily be applied to eating, weight, and shape. Perfectionism is not a defining characteristic of eating disorders but it has long been thought to be involved in AN and, to a lesser extent, BN (Garner et al. 1983, 1984). Hewitt et al. (1995) argue that perfectionism can contribute to eating disorders by making normal shortcomings more traumatic or by making a normal body a sign of imperfection. The eating disorder inventory (EDI) (Garner et al. 1983) includes a perfectionism subscale.

AN patients display elevated scores on paper-and-pencil measures of perfectionism (Bastiani et al. 1995). The fact that some indices of perfectionism remain high even after weight restoration suggests that perfectionism may be a precursor of AN; this view accords with Strober's (1991) theory in which self-doubting perfectionism is one of a small number of characteristics that predispose one to AN. Bruch (1973) and Casper (1983) also accord perfectionism a causal role in AN. Recent debates contrasting self-imposed perfectionism and other-imposed perfectionism add further complexities to the analysis of EDs (Hewitt et al. 1995); whom are ANs trying to please, themselves or others?

Dissociation   One of the more profound psychological tactics used to escape unpleasant realities is to adopt the dynamic defense of dissociation, in which traumatic elements are split off from focal consciousness, which turns instead to something more tractable. In BN "immersion" in the binge may protect the individual from emotional distress (Heatherton & Baumeister 1991, Lacey 1986). Evidence for dissociative tendencies in EDs—as measured using the self-report Dissociative Experiences Scale (Bernstein & Putnam 1986)—is not very impressive, however. In their review Everill & Waller (1995) claim that "high levels of dissociative tendencies have been reported in eating-disordered women" (p. 4), but these same authors found that bulimic women display only a weak elevation of Dissociative Experiences Scale scores (Everill et al. 1995). Valdiserri & Kihlstrom conclude that "within the population of normal college-age women . . . there appears to be no particular relationship between abnormal eating and dissociative experiences" (1995, p. 149).

Cognitive style   ED patients display evidence of abnormal cognitive style or information processing. For instance, BNs are much quicker than are restricting ANs on the Matching Familiar Figures Test, reflecting their greater impulsiveness (Kaye et al. 1995). Such aberrations might contribute to their disorder; Bruch (1973) argued that ANs engaged in unwarranted all-or-none thinking, which might lead them to regard themselves as failures after even minor infractions.

Cognitive bias   ED patients display aberrations in information processing and memory, especially for material related to weight, shape, and food. Although there are many controversies pertaining to technical issues, the consensus from studies assessing cognitive bias such as those using the modified Stroop (color-naming) (e.g., Green et al. 1999) and dot/visual probe (e.g., Rieger et al. 1998) paradigms is clear: BNs tend to show bias for weight/shape words (compared with control words), whereas ANs are more likely to show bias for food words. What is less clear is the value of this discovery. We already knew that ED patients have an emotional concern with weight and shape; this is a defining feature of the disorders. That normal dieters and possibly hungry people in general (Mogg et al. 1998) also show attentional bias to shape and food stimuli renders the findings in ED patients even less important.

Studies of memory bias make the same point, with ED patients showing differential memory for disorder-related material (e.g., Hermans et al. 1998, Sebastian et al. 1996). Even if it were established conclusively that ED patients are schematic for weight, shape, and food information, "it is, however, still unclear what role (if any) these schemata play in the etiology of anorexia nervosa" (Hermans et al. 1998, p. 199) or in BN. It seems just as likely that a preoccupation with food is a result as it is a cause of weight loss (see Herman & Polivy 1993).

BIOLOGICAL INFLUENCES   Because EDs so prominently involve appetite— apparent lack of appetite in the case of AN and apparently uncontrollable appetite in the case of BN—there is an understandable temptation to look for biological causes of these disorders. There are all sorts of biological abnormalities associated with EDs, some of which we review. Researchers in this area have for the most part shown commendable reluctance to promote biological correlates of EDs into candidate causes, probably because of repeated warnings that AN and BN both have the potential to disrupt appetitive and broader neuroendocrine systems, so that biological anomalies may be just as likely to be effects as causes. Indeed, many of the anomalies are well-known effects of starvation or stress, undermining their causal candidacies. The preferred approach to identifying biological (or any other class of potential) causes is to conduct prospective research in which a normal (pre-symptomatic) sample is assessed, permitting the identification of differential predictors of eventual ED, and avoiding the contaminating influence of the ED on the predictor. As Leon et al. (1997, p. 407) note, however, "the assessment of many types of biological risk factors is often too costly and invasive to be done in prospective studies with large nonclinical samples." (The same can be said for many nonbiological risk factors as well.)

Genetics   Twin and family studies provide evidence for the genetic transmission of EDs, although such evidence is not conclusive. For one thing, behavior genetics currently emphasizes environmental factors as much as genetic factors. (The double irony of modern behavior genetics is that not only does it not necessarily focus on genetics, but it also rarely focuses on behavior. In the case of EDs, the criterion is usually either clinical diagnosis or questionnaire responses, both of which are only remotely related to actual behavior.) Family studies (see Spelt & Meyer 1995 for a review) indicate that EDs aggregate in families, but such studies cannot easily disentangle genetic from environmental transmission. Very high heritability coefficients—reflecting the relative importance of strictly genetic factors—have been claimed for both AN and BN. Klump et al.'s (2000) reading of the literature leads them to conclude that 50–83% of the variance in AN and BN is genetic. These estimates are based on twin studies, which may yield artifactually high heritability estimates, owing to contrast and assimilation effects and the skewing effect of nonadditive genetic variance (Plomin et al. 1990). More troubling, in our view, is the common finding that not only the disorder itself but also the associated attitudes (concerns, fears, and preoccupations) are highly heritable (Klump et al. 2000). We are prepared to concede a role for genetics in the regulation of physiological parameters that might in principle contribute to an ED; however, statistics notwithstanding, it is difficult to understand how genes influence these attitudes, which in turn influence the development of the disorder. We are confronted with analyses that purport to show *that* genes have a major influence on EDs, but that do not indicate *how*. A persuasive case for genetic influence awaits a clearer indication of the pathways from genes to (pathological) behavior, affect, and cognition (Allison 1997). As Hewitt (1997, p. 355) concludes, "although there is consistent evidence of genetic factors influencing vulnerability to eating disorders, the details are far from clear."

Neuroendocrine factors   Just as the former ED, obesity, was often explained as "glandular" in origin, so current EDs are often seen as explicable in terms of neuroendocrine dysfunction, which might or might not itself be genetic in origin. Such dysfunction might be primary (i.e., a hormonal aberration triggers the disorder) or mediational (i.e., stress or some other environmental factor disrupts hormonal functioning, which in turn affects eating). Because appetite is commonly regarded as responsive to hormonal controls, a neuroendocrine explanation for EDs is attractive. The major problem with such an explanation is that EDs are not simply disorders of appetite. Almost everyone sees AN as principally attributable to the relentless pursuit of thinness (RPT) that dictates restrictive food intake, which leads directly to AN. What causes RPT is debatable, but it is difficult to see how appetite suppression could precede RPT (unless you wanted to construct a convoluted scenario in which RPT develops as an ex post facto attitudinal justification for not eating). In the most prevalent view of BN, RPT and restrictive intake precedes bingeing, and bingeing is simply a breakdown of restraint (e.g., Polivy & Herman 1985, Stice et al. 1998). An alternative view of BN regards bingeing as primary and restrictive intake as secondary and compensatory (e.g., Bulik et al. 1997, Mussell et al. 1997); this minority view might possibly be compatible with a primary neuroendocrine disorder, but it does not easily accommodate the centrality of RPT in BN.

One notable feature of neuroendocrine accounts of EDs is that AN and BN are seen as virtual opposites, whereas most other theories regard them as more alike than different. The neuroendocrine approach emphasizes starving (AN) versus bingeing (BN). What factors might go awry to produce the extremes of normal appetite?

One possibility would be primary dysfunction of the hypothalamus, the "seat" of appetite. The evidence that AN is due to a disturbance of the hypothalamus, either structural or functional, is weak. "Although structural lesions involving the hypothalamus can lead to cachectic states, . . . a syndrome that fulfills strict criteria for AN is excessively rare. . . . there is no good evidence for a primary hypothalamic disorder in AN in general, although this possibility is not excluded" (Study Group on Anorexia Nervosa [SGAN] 1995, p. 239). The SGAN indicates (p. 237) that "a combination of elevated CRH (corticotropin-releasing hormone) and elevated AVP (arginine vasopressin) may have a key role in sustaining the reduced food intake that is characteristic of the disorder," but note the careful wording: the hormonal abnormality is characterized as "sustaining" the reduced intake, not causing it.

Although tests of hormonal functioning and evidence of hormonal aberrations in AN are both prevalent, the balance of opinion is that these aberrations are not what cause the disorder (Leung et al. 1996). "In fact, refeeding alone, leading to consistent weight gain and balanced nutrition, reverses the endocrine changes observed in AN" (SGAN 1995, p. 238).

One popular neurochemical candidate cause for EDs is serotonin (Brewerton 1995). Might ANs suffer from increased 5-Hydroxytryptamine (HT) activity, which would be consistent with their generally obsessive-compulsive approach to life, even after recovery from AN (SGAN 1995)? Both AN and obsessive-compulsive disorder (OCD) are responsive to fluoxetine, leading some to speculate that AN might simply be a variant of OCD (Pryor et al. 1995). By contrast, BN has been interpreted in terms of a 5-HT deficit (and a possible connection to both impulsivity and seasonal affective disorder). Recovered BNs show persistent abnormalities related to serotonin function, suggesting that such abnormalities may underlie the development of BN (Kaye et al. 1998). Serotonin imbalance has more surface appeal than most other biological hypotheses of ED, but the case is not yet strong. Recovered ANs do not show persistent 5-HT anomalies (O'Dwyer et al. 1996), leading Ward et al. (2000c) to conclude that "an abnormality of serotonin regulation is unlikely to be a major vulnerability factor in AN" (p. 283). Moreover, the excess/AN vs. deficit/BN explanation would seem to have difficulty accounting for alternating restriction and bingeing, which occurs to some extent in BN and more dramatically in bulimic-type AN.

Other biologically based factors   One interesting theme in much of the research is that biological factors can act to perpetuate a disorder that might not initially have been biological in origin. For instance, very-low-weight AN patients show olfactory impairment; such impairment is in all probability a consequence of starvation, but may act to diminish the appeal of food (Fedoroff et al. 1995). Similarly, food may not appeal to ANs because it loses its "incentive-value"; this decline in incentive value may be a consequence of ironic aversive taste conditioning in food-deprived individuals (Pinel et al. 2000). Gastric distress and bloating, commonly reported in EDs, may also make eating aversive (e.g., Krahn et al. 1996).

Addiction models of EDs have been proposed (Wilson 1991). In the case of BN, the emphasis is on craving. Just as an addict craves a drug, BNs are postulated to experience intense food cravings, which may be due to exaggerated cephalic phase responses to food cues and/or distress, which has been associated with overeating in the past (e.g., Wilson 1991, Woods & Brief 1988). ANs may be "addicted" to the body's endogenous opioids, which are released in self-starvation accompanied by excessive exercise (Davis & Claridge 1998). Wilson dismisses the addiction model because of the lack of evidence for an addictive personality; the model does not address the core clinical characteristics of EDs (such as RPT) or the identified underlying psychopathology (such as low self-esteem, interpersonal distrust, and feelings of ineffectiveness), and it fails to account for psychobiological connections between dieting and EDs. Like Wilson, we are reluctant to apply the addiction metaphor to EDs.

Lack of internal awareness   Lack of interoceptive awareness (LIA) refers to an inability to accurately identify internal states or feelings, including physiological states (such as hunger and satiety) and emotional states (Garner et al. 1983). (Note that the problem is not an inability to detect internal states, but rather an inability to identify them.) It has long been argued (since at least Bruch 1969) that defective interoceptive awareness may produce confusion, so that the individual misinterprets her emotions as hunger, with the result that emotional arousal may trigger eating or even bingeing. By the same token, it seems possible that genuine hunger may not be perceived even when it is there (AN?), just as it may be perceived when it is not there (BN?).

There is little question that ED patients suffer from LIA (as reflected in its incorporation into the EDI). Questions remain, though, as to whether LIA is a cause or a consequence of EDs, and whether it should be regarded as a biological, perceptual, or cognitive problem. Bruch (1973) regarded LIA as a consequence of faulty learning beginning in infancy, when caretakers do not provide food merely to assuage hunger, but in response to all expressions of distress. Bruch further theorized that such faulty learning undermines trust in one's body and increases the need to control both the body and the self, which are seen as intertwined.

CONCLUSIONS

Reviewing the literature on EDs leaves us with many questions about how these disorders develop. To some extent, this may be unavoidable; research on clinical syndromes is of necessity mostly nonexperimental, and nonexperimental data preclude causal inferences. Unfortunately, many researchers lose sight of this limitation in their efforts to explain these syndromes. Moreover, the interaction of etiological factors in a complex behavioral syndrome such as EDs is difficult if not impossible to capture. There are so many possible influences that their particular combination in any given individual becomes almost unique, and thus impractical to generalize to others. Finally, much of the literature consists of atheoretical attempts to measure and correlate particular researchers' favorite variables, rather than attempting to test etiological hypotheses about EDs. This is not to say that there are not theoreticians doing systematic studies testing conceptual views of the disorder, but such research is often overshadowed by the myriad studies in this area that do not rely on theoretical underpinnings. The noise-to-signal ratio in the literature is thus higher than one would like.

Eating disorders did not emerge as a serious problem until the late 1970s, so perhaps it is not surprising that a mere 25 years later we still seem to be so far from understanding their etiology. In fact, how much do we really know about the causes of other, longer-studied disorders such as depression? As with the EDs, we know that there is a biological/genetic contribution in at least some, though not all, depressives, and that life stresses along with psychological factors such as low self-esteem also make a contribution. We are still incapable, though, of predicting who will develop depression, when, and why other at-risk individuals will be spared. The literature suggests that EDs result similarly from the convergence of several facilitating factors, but the causal mechanisms are not yet identified. No single agent seems to be sufficient, but we may perhaps distinguish among stronger and weaker contributory factors.

What factors appear to be most necessary for the development of EDs? It is difficult to imagine developing an ED without the presence of body dissatisfaction, although the majority of individuals who are dissatisfied with their bodies will never go on to develop an ED. Similarly, negative emotion (such as depression or anxiety) and markedly low self-esteem are prominent features of EDs, and seem to be virtually invariant precursors of their development. Other elements that appear to be strongly implicated in the development of EDs include environmental stressors (usually the triggering factor) and cognitive distortions such as obsessive thoughts (e.g., that one is too fat). Finally, personality features such as a need for control (over oneself or one's body) and inadequate identity formation have been plausibly suggested as being necessary for the development of an ED.

What about the other risk factors that have received so much research attention? Sociocultural pressure to be thin, family influences such as criticism or enmeshment, dieting, biological contributors, genetic predisposition, personality variables such as perfectionism, dissociation, maturity fears, and interpersonal distrust all appear to contribute to the development of EDs, and the more of them impinging on an individual, the greater the risk. Some or all of these may contribute to the features delineated in the preceding paragraph, or they may contribute in their own right. Although it may turn out that one or more of these factors will be shown to be a prime cause of EDs, for the moment their connection seems less central, although clearly this is a judgment call.

Establishing which factors are more tightly linked to EDs does not bring us closer to understanding the mechanism underlying EDs. On the one hand, we are left with the question of what produces these causal factors (e.g., body dissatisfaction, identity deficits) in the first place; on the other, establishing the connection does not explain the process of going from the cause (body dissatisfaction, identity deficits) to the effects (EDs). Arguably, effective treatment does not require a full understanding of mechanisms. (We can treat headaches with aspirin without understanding either where the headache came from or how aspirin works.) Still, as scientists, our first obligation must be understanding. Our review indicates that we are a long way from understanding EDs. Constraints on research in this field will not make it easy to achieve empirical or conceptual progress. As with other psychological problems, we may have to be satisfied with recognizing contributory risk factors and devising therapies to help alleviate the discomfort, without conclusive proof of exactly what causes the disorder in any individual.

Visit the Annual Reviews home page at www.AnnualReviews.org

LITERATURE CITED

Agras S, Hammer L, McNicholas F. 1999. A prospective study of the influence of eating–disordered mothers on their children. *Int. J. Eat. Disord.* 25:253–62

Allen FCL, Scannell ED, Turner HR. 1998. Guilt and hostility as coexisting characteristics of bulimia nervosa. *Aust. Psychol.* 33:143–47

Allison D. 1997. Issues in mapping genes for eating disorders. *Psychopharmacol. Bull.* 33:359–68

Am. Psychiatr. Assoc. 1994. *Diagnostic and Statistical Manual of Mental Disorders.* Washington, DC: Am. Psychiatr. Assoc. 4th ed.

Ball K, Lee C. 2000. Relationships between psychological stress, coping and disordered eating: a review. *Psychol. Health* 14:1007–1035

Bardone AM, Vohs KD, Abramson LY, Heatherton TF, Joiner TE. 2000. The confluence of perfectionism, body dissatisfaction, and low self-esteem predicts bulimic symptoms: clinical implications. *Behav. Ther.* 31:265–80

Bastiani AM, Rao R, Weltzin T, Kaye WH.

1995. Perfectionism in anorexia nervosa. *Int. J. Eat. Disord.* 17:147–52

Bemporad JR. 1997. Cultural and historical aspects of eating disorders. *Theor. Med.* 18:401–20

Bernstein EM, Putnam FW. 1986. Development, reliability, and validity of a dissociation scale. *J. Nerv. Ment. Dis.* 174:727–34

Branch CHH, Eurman LJ. 1980. Social attitudes toward patients with anorexia nervosa. *Am. J. Psychiatry* 137:631–32

Brewerton TD. 1995. Review: toward a unified theory of serotonin dysregulation in eating and related disorders. *Psychoneuroendocrinology* 20:561–90

Bruch H. 1969. Hunger and instinct. *J. Nerv. Ment. Dis.* 149:91–114

Bruch H. 1973. *Eating Disorders: Obesity, Anorexia Nervosa and the Person Within.* New York: Basic Books

Bulik CM, Sullivan PF, Carter FA, Joyce PR. 1997. Initial manifestations of disordered eating behavior: dieting versus bingeing. *Int. J. Eat. Disord.* 22:195–201

Bulik CM, Sullivan PF, Kendler KS. 1998. Heritability of binge-eating and broadly defined bulimia nervosa. *Biol. Psychiatry* 44:1210–18

Button EJ, Sonugabarke EJS, Davies J, Thompson M. 1996. A prospective study of self-esteem in the prediction of eating problems in adolescent schoolgirls: questionnaire findings. *Br. J. Clin. Psychol.* 35:193–203

Cachelin FM, Maher BA. 1998. Is amenorrhea a critical criterion for anorexia nervosa? *J. Psychosom. Res.* 44:435–40

Caldwell MB, Brownell KD, Wilfley DE. 1997. Relationship of weight, body dissatisfaction, and self-esteem in African American and white female dieters. *Int. J. Eat. Disord.* 22:127–30

Carter FA, Bulik CM, Lawson RH, Sullivan PF, Wilson JS. 1996. Effect of mood and food cues on body image in women with bulimia and controls. *Int. J. Eat. Disord.* 20:65–76

Cash TF, Deagle EA. 1997. The nature and extent of body-image disturbances in anorexia nervosa and bulimia nervosa: a meta-analysis. *Int. J. Eat. Disord.* 22:107–25

Casper RC. 1983. Some provisional ideas concerning the psychologic structure in anorexia nervosa and bulimia. In *Anorexia Nervosa: Recent Developments in Research*, ed. PL Darby, PE Garfinkel, DM Garner, DV Coscina, pp. 387–92. New York: Liss

Casper RC, Jabine LN. 1996. An eight-year follow-up: outcome from adolescent compared to adult onset anorexia nervosa. *J. Youth Adolesc.* 25:499–517

Casper RC, Lyubomirsky S. 1997. Individual psychopathology relative to reports of unwanted sexual experiences as predictor of a bulimic eating pattern. *Int. J. Eat. Disord.* 21:229–36

Chamorro R, Flores-Ortiz Y. 2000. Acculturation and disordered eating patterns among Mexican American women. *Int. J. Eat. Disord.* 28:125–29

Chandy JM, Harris L, Blum RW, Resnick MD. 1995. Female adolescents of alcohol misusers: disordered eating features. *Int. J. Eat. Disord.* 17:283–89

Davis C, Claridge G. 1998. The eating disorders as addiction: a psychobiological perspective. *Addict. Behav.* 23:463–75

deGroot J, Rodin G. 1999. The relationship between eating disorders and childhood trauma. *Psychiatr. Ann.* 29:225–29

Ennett ST, Bauman KE. 1994. The contribution of influence and selection to adolescent peer group homogeneity: the case of adolescent cigarette smoking. *J. Pers. Soc. Psychol.* 67:653–63

Everill JT, Waller G. 1995. Reported sexual abuse and eating psychopathology: a review of the evidence for a causal link. *Int. J. Eat. Disord.* 18:1–11

Everill JT, Waller G, Macdonald W. 1995. Dissociation in bulimic and non-eating-disordered women. *Int. J. Eat. Disord.* 17:127–34

Fairburn CG, Cooper Z, Doll HA, Norman P, O'Connor M. 2000. The natural course of bulimia nervosa and binge eating disorder in young women. *Arch. Gen. Psychiatry* 57:659–65

Fairburn CG, Shafran R, Cooper Z. 1999. Invited essay: a cognitive behavioural theory of anorexia nervosa. *Behav. Res. Ther.* 37:1–13

Fairburn CG, Welch SL, Doll HA, Davies BA, O'Connor ME. 1997. Risk factors for bulimia nervosa—a community-based case-control study. *Arch. Gen. Psychiatry* 54:509–17

Fedoroff IC, Stoner SA, Andersen AE, Doty RL, Rolls BJ. 1995. Olfactory dysfunction in anorexia nervosa. *Int. J. Eat. Disord.* 18:71–77

Friedman MA, Wilfley DE, Welch RR, Kunce JT. 1997. Self-directed hostility and family functioning in normal-weight bulimics and overweight binge eaters. *Addict. Behav.* 22:367–75

Gard MCE, Freeman CP. 1996. The dismantling of a myth: a review of eating disorders and socioeconomic status. *Int. J. Eat. Disord.* 20:1–12

Garfinkel PE, Garner DM. 1982. *Anorexia Nervosa: A Multidimensional Perspective.* New York: Brunner/Mazel

Garfinkel PE, Lin E, Goering P, Spegg C,

Goldbloom D, et al. 1996. Should amenorrhoea be necessary for the diagnosis of anorexia nervosa? Evidence from a Canadian community sample. *Br. J. Psychiatry* 168:500–6

Garner DM, Olmsted MP, Polivy J. 1983. Development and validation of a multidimensional eating disorder inventory for anorexia nervosa and bulimia. *Int. J. Eat. Disord.* 2:15–34

Garner DM, Olmsted MP, Polivy J, Garfinkel PE. 1984. Comparison between weight preoccupied women and anorexia nervosa. *Psychosom. Med.* 46:255–66

Geller J, Cockell SJ, Goldner EM. 2000. Inhibited expression of negative emotions and interpersonal orientation in anorexia nervosa. *Int. J. Eat. Disord.* 28:8–19

Geller J, Johnston C, Madsen K, Goldner EM, Remick RA, Birmingham CL. 1998. Shape- and weight-based self-esteem and the eating disorders. *Int. J. Eat. Disord.* 24:285–98

Gleaves DH, Lowe MR, Snow AC, Green BA, Murphy-Eberenz KP. 2000. Continuity and discontinuity models of bulimia nervosa: a taxometric investigation. *J. Abnorm. Psychol.* 109:56–68

Godart NT, Flament MF, Lecrubier Y, Jeammet P. 2000. Anxiety disorders in anorexia nervosa and bulimia nervosa: co-morbidity and chronology of appearance. *Eur. Psychiatry* 15:38–45

Green M, Corr P, DeSilva L. 1999. Impaired color naming of body shape-related words in anorexia nervosa: affective valence or associative priming? *Cogn. Ther. Res.* 23:413–22

Greenberg DR, Laporte DJ. 1996. Racial differences in body type preferences of men for women. *Int. J. Eat. Disord.* 19:275–78

Groth-Marnat G, Michel N. 2000. Dissociation, comorbidity of dissociative disorders, and childhood abuse in a community sample of women with current and past bulimia. *Soc. Behav. Pers.* 28:279–92

Gruber NP, Dilsaver SC. 1996. Bulimia and anorexia nervosa in winter depression: lifetime rates in a clinical sample. *J. Psychiatry Neurosci.* 21:9–12

Haudek C, Rorty M, Henker B. 1999. The role of ethnicity and parental bonding in the eating and weight concerns of Asian-American and Caucasian college women. *Int. J. Eat. Disord.* 25:425–33

Haworth-Hoeppner S. 2000. The critical shapes of body image: the role of culture and family in the production of eating disorders. *J. Marriage Fam.* 62:212–27

Heatherton TF, Baumeister RF. 1991. Binge-eating as escape from self-awareness. *Psychol. Bull.* 110:86–108

Heatherton TF, Polivy J. 1992. Chronic dieting and eating disorders: a spiral model. In *The Etiology of Bulimia: The Individual and Familial Context*, ed. J Crowther, SE Hobfall, MAP Stephens, DL Tennenbaum, pp. 133–55. Washington, DC: Hemisphere

Herman CP, Polivy J. 1993. Mental control of eating: excitatory and inhibitory food thoughts. In *Handbook of Mental Control*, ed. DM Wegner, JW Pennebaker, pp. 491–505. Englewood Cliffs, NJ: Prentice-Hall

Herman CP, Polivy J. 1996. What does abnormal eating tell us about normal eating? In *Food Choice, Acceptance, and Consumption*, ed. H Meiselman, H MacFie, pp. 207–38. London: Blackie Acad. Prof.

Hermans DG, Pieters G, Eelen P. 1998. Implicit and explicit memory for shape, body weight, and food-related words in patients with anorexia nervosa and nondieting controls. *J. Abnorm. Psychol.* 107:193–202

Herpertzdahlmann B, Wewetzer C, Hennighausen K, Remschmidt H. 1996. Outcome, psychosocial functioning, and prognostic factors in adolescent anorexia nervosa as determined by prospective follow-up assessment. *J. Youth Adolesc.* 25:455–71

Herzog DB, Greenwood DN, Dorer DJ, Flores AT, Ekeblad ER, et al. 2000. Mortality in eating disorders: a descriptive study. *Int. J. Eat. Disord.* 28:20–26

Hesse-Biber S, Marino M, Watts-Roy D. 1999. A longitudinal study of eating disorders among college women—factors that influence recovery. *Gender Soc.* 13:385–408

Hewitt JK. 1997. Behavior genetics and eating

disorders. *Psychopharmacol. Bull.* 33:355–58

Hewitt PL, Flett GL, Ediger E. 1995. Perfectionism traits and perfectionistic self-presentation in eating disorder attitudes, characteristics, and symptoms. *Int. J. Eat. Disord.* 18:317–26

Hill AJ, Franklin JA. 1998. Mothers, daughters and dieting: investigating the transmission of weight control. *Br. J. Clin. Psychol.* 37:3–13

Hodes M, Timimi S, Robinson P. 1997. Children of mothers with eating disorders: a preliminary study. *Eur. Eat. Disord. Rev.* 5:11–24

Johnson C, Larson R. 1982. Bulimia: an analysis of moods and behavior. *Psychosom. Med.* 44:341–51

Johnson WG, Boutelle KN, Torgrud L, Davig JP, Turner S. 2000. What is a binge? The influence of amount, duration, and loss of control criteria on judgments of binge eating. *Int. J. Eat. Disord.* 27:471–79

Joiner TE. 1999. Self-verification and bulimic symptoms: Do bulimic women play a role in perpetuating their own dissatisfaction and symptoms? *Int. J. Eat. Disord.* 26:145–51

Joiner TE, Heatherton TF, Rudd MD, Schmidt NB. 1997. Perfectionism, perceived weight status, and bulimic symptoms: two studies testing a diathesis-stress model. *J. Abnorm. Psychol.* 106:145–53

Kaye WH, Bastiani AM, Moss H. 1995. Cognitive style of patients with anorexia nervosa and bulimia nervosa. *Int. J. Eat. Disord.* 18:287–90

Kaye WH, Greeno CG, Moss H, Fernstrom J, Fernstrom M. 1998. Alterations in serotonin activity and psychiatric symptoms after recovery from bulimia nervosa. *Arch. Gen. Psychiatry* 55:927–35

Kaye WH, Gwirtzman HE, George DT, Weiss SR, Jimerson DC. 1986. Relationship of mood alterations to bingeing behavior in bulimia. *Br. J. Psychiatry* 149:479–85

Keel PK, Mitchell JE, Miller KB, Davis TL, Crow SJ. 1999. Long-term outcome of bulimia nervosa. *Arch. Gen. Psychiatry* 56:63–69

Kendler KS, Walters EE, Neale MC, Kessler RC, Heath AC, Eaaves LJ. 1995. The structure of the genetic and environmental risk factors for six major psychiatric disorders in women. *Arch. Gen. Psychiatry* 52:374–83

Kent A, Waller G. 2000. Childhood emotional abuse and eating psychopathology. *Clin. Psychol. Rev.* 20:887–903

Klump K, McGue M, Iacono WG. 2000. Age differences in genetic and environmental influences on eating attitudes and behaviors in preadolescent and adolescent female twins. *J. Abnorm. Psychol.* 109:239–51

Krahn D, Kurth C, Nairn K, Redmond L, Drewnowski A, Gomberg E. 1996. Dieting severity and gastrointestinal symptoms in college women. *J. Am. Coll. Health* 45:67–71

Kulbartz-Klatt YJ, Florin I, Pook M. 1999. Bulimia nervosa: mood changes do have an impact on body width estimation. *Br. J. Clin. Psychol.* 38:279–87

Lacey JH. 1986. Pathogenesis. In *Current Approaches: Bulimia Nervosa*, ed. LJ Downey, JC Malkin, pp. 17–26. Birmingham, Engl.: Dupar Med.

Leary MR, Schreindorfer LS, Haupt AL. 1995. The role of low self-esteem in emotional and behavioral problems: Why is low self-esteem dysfunctional? *J. Soc. Clin. Psychol.* 14:297–314

Lehoux PM, Steiger H, Jabalpurlawa S. 2000. State/trait distinctions in bulimic syndromes. *Int. J. Eat. Disord.* 27:36–42

Leon GR, Keel PK, Klump KL, Fulkerson JA. 1997. The future of risk factor research in understanding the etiology of eating disorders. *Psychopharmacol. Bull.* 33:405–11

Leung F, Geller J, Katzman M. 1996. Issues and concerns associated with different risk models for eating disorders. *Int. J. Eat. Disord.* 19:249–56

Levine MP, Smolak L, Moodey AF, Shuman MD, Hessen LD. 1994. Normative developmental challenges and dieting and eating disturbances in middle school girls. *Int. J. Eat. Disord.* 15:11–20

Lunner K, Werthem EH, Thompson JK, Paxton SJ, McDonald F, Halvaarson KS. 2000.

A cross-cultural examination of weight-related teasing, body image, and eating disturbance in Swedish and Australian samples. *Int. J. Eat. Disord.* 28:430–35

Matsunaga H, Kiriike N, Iwasaki Y, Miyata A, Matsui T. 2000. Multi-impulsivity among bulimic patients in Japan. *Int. J. Eat. Disord.* 27:348–52

Milligan RJ, Waller G. 2000. Anger and bulimic psychopathology among nonclinical women. *Int. J. Eat. Disord.* 28:446–50

Minuchin S, Rosman BL, Baker L. 1978. *Psychosomatic Families: Anorexia Nervosa in Context.* Cambrige, MA: Harvard Univ. Press

Mogg K, Bradley BP, Hyare H, Lee S. 1998. Selective attention to food-related stimuli in hunger: Are attentional biases specific to emotional and psychopathological states, or are they also found in normal drives states? *Behav. Res. Ther.* 36:227–37

Mumford DB, Choudry IY. 2000. Body dissatisfaction and eating attitudes in slimming and fitness gyms in London and Lahore: a cross-cultural study. *Eur. Eat. Disord. Rev.* 8:217–24

Mussell MP, Mitchell JE, Fenna CJ, Crosby RD, Miller JP, Hoberman HM. 1997. A comparison of onset of binge eating versus dieting in the development of bulimia nervosa. *Int. J. Eat. Disord.* 21:353–60

Neumark-Sztainer D, Story M, Hannan PJ, Beuhring T, Resnick MD. 2000. Disordered eating among adolescents: associations with sexual/physical abuse and other familial/psychosocial factors. *Int. J. Eat. Disord.* 28:249–58

O'Dea JA, Abraham S. 2000. Improving the body image, eating attitudes, and behaviors of young male and female adolescents: a new educational approach that focuses on self-esteem. *Int. J. Eat. Disord.* 28:43–57

O'Dwyer AM, Lucey JV, Russell GF. 1996. Serotonin activity in anorexia nervosa after long-term weight restoration: response to D-fenfluramine challenge. *Psychol. Med.* 26:353–59

Ogden J, Steward J. 2000. The role of the mother-daughter relationship in explaining weight concern. *Int. J. Eat. Disord.* 28:78–83

Paxton SJ, Schutz HK, Wertheim ES, Muir SL. 1999. Friendship clique and peer influences on body image concerns, dietary restraint, extreme weight-loss behaviors, and binge eating in adolescent girls. *J. Abnorm. Psychol.* 108:255–66

Pike KM, Rodin J. 1991. Mothers, daughters, and disordered eating. *J. Abnorm. Psychol.* 100:198–204

Pinel JPJ, Assanand S, Lehman DR. 2000. Hunger, eating, and ill health. *Am. Psychol.* 55:1105–16

Plomin R, Chipuer HM, Loehlin JC. 1990. Behavioral genetics and personality. In *Handbook of Personality Theory and Research*, ed. LA Pervin, pp. 225–43. New York: Guilford

Polivy J, Herman CP. 1985. Dieting and binging: a causal analysis. *Am. Psychol.* 40:193–201

Polivy J, Herman CP. 1987. The diagnosis and treatment of normal eating. *J. Consult. Clin. Psychol.* 55:635–44

Polivy J, Herman CP, Mills J, Wheeler HB. 2001. Eating disorders in adolescence. In *The Blackwell Handbook of Adolescence*, ed. G Adams, M Berzonsky. Oxford: Blackwell. In press

Powell AD, Kahn AS. 1995. Racial differences in women's desires to be thin. *Int. J. Eat. Disord.* 17:191–95

Pryor TL, Martin RL, Roach N. 1995. Obsessive-compulsive disorder, trichotollimania, and anorexia nervosa: a case report. *Int. J. Eat. Disord.* 18:375–79

Raffi AR, Rondini M, Grandi S, Fava GA. 2000. Life events and prodromal symptoms in bulimia nervosa. *Psychol. Med.* 30:727–31

Rieger E, Schotte DE, Touyz SW, Beumont PJV, Griffiths R, Russell J. 1998. Attentional biases in eating disorders: a visual probe detection procedure. *Int. J. Eat. Disord.* 23:199–205

Rorty M, Yager J. 1996. Histories of childhood trauma and complex posttraumatic sequelae in women with eating disorders. *Psychiatr. Clin. N. Am.* 19:773–87

Rorty M, Yager J, Rossotto E, Buckwalter G. 2000. Parental intrusiveness in adolescence recalled by women with a history of bulimia nervosa and comparison women. *Int. J. Eat. Disord.* 28:202–8

Sanftner JL, Crowther JH. 1998. Variability in self-esteem, moods, shame and guilt in women who binge. *Int. J. Eat. Disord.* 23: 391–97

Schmidt U, Tiller J, Blanchard M, Andrews B, Treasure J. 1997. Is there a specific trauma precipitating anorexia nervosa? *Psychol. Med.* 27:523–30

Sebastian SB, Williamson DA, Blouin DC. 1996. Memory bias for fatness stimuli in the eating disorder. *Cogn. Ther. Res.* 20:275–86

Serpell L, Treasure J, Teasdale J, Sullivan V. 1999. Anorexia nervosa: friend or foe? *Int. J. Eat. Disord.* 25:177–86

Shisslak CM, Crago M, Estes LS. 1995. The spectrum of eating disturbances. *Int. J. Eat. Disord.* 18:209–19

Shisslak CM, Crago M, McKnight KM, Estes LS, Gray N, Parnaby OG. 1998. Potential risk factors associated with weight control behaviors in elementary and middle school girls. *J. Psychosom. Res.* 44:301–13

Shoebridge P, Gowers SG. 2000. Parental high concern and adolescent-onset anorexia nervosa—a case-control study to investigate direction of causality. *Br. J. Psychiatry* 176:132–37

Smolak L, Levine MP, Schermer F. 1999. Parental input and weight concerns among elementary school children. *Int. J. Eat. Disord.* 25:263–71

Spelt J, Meyer JM. 1995. Genetics and eating disorders. In *Behavior Genetic Approaches in Behavioral Medicine*, ed. JR Turner, LR Cardon, JK Hewitt, pp. 167–85. New York: Plenum

Steiger H, Leung FYK, Puentes-Neuman G, Gottheil N. 1992. Psychological profiles of adolescent girls with varying degrees of eating and mood disturbances. *Int. J. Eat. Disord.* 11:121–31

Steiger H, Stotland S, Trottier J, Ghadirian AM. 1996. Familial eating concerns and psychopathological traits: causal implications of transgenerational effects. *Int. J. Eat. Disord.* 19:147–57

Steinberg S, Tobin D, Johnson C. 1989. The role of bulimic behaviors in affect regulation: different functions for different patient subgroups? *Int. J. Eat. Disord.* 9:51–55

Steinhausen HC, Seidel R, Metzke CW. 2000. Evaluation of treatment and intermediate and long-term outcome of adolescent eating disorders. *Psychol. Med.* 30:1089–98

Stice E. 1998. Modeling of eating pathology and social reinforcement of the thin-ideal predict onset of bulimic symptoms. *Behav. Res. Ther.* 36:931–44

Stice E. 2001. A prospective test of the dual-pathway model of bulimic pathology: mediating effects of dieting and negative affect. *J. Abnorm. Psychol.* 110:1–12

Stice E, Akutagawa D, Gaggar A, Agras WS. 2000a. Negative affect moderates the relation between dieting and binge eating. *Int. J. Eat. Disord.* 27:218–29

Stice E, Hayward C, Cameron RP, Killen JD, Taylor CB. 2000b. Body-image and eating disturbances predict onset of depression among female adolescents: a longitudinal study. *J. Abnorm. Psychol.* 109:438–44

Stice E, Shaw H, Nemeroff C. 1998. Dual pathway model of bulimia nervosa: longitudinal support for dietary restraint and affect-regulation mechanisms. *J. Soc. Clin. Psychol.* 17:129–49

Stormer SM, Thompson JK. 1996. Explanations of body image disturbance: a test of maturational status, negative verbal commentary, social comparison, and sociocultural hypotheses. *Int. J. Eat. Disord.* 19:193–202

Striegel-Moore R. 1993. Etiology of binge eating: a developmental perspective. In *Binge Eating: Nature, Assessment and Treatment*, ed. CG Fairburn, GT Wilson, pp. 144–72. New York: Guilford

Striegel-Moore R. 1997. Risk factors for eating disorders. *Ann. NY Acad. Sci.* 817:98–109

Striegel-Moore R, Smolak L. 1996. The role of race in the development of eating disorders. In *The Developmental Psychopathology of Eating Disorders: Implications for Research, Prevention, and Treatment*, ed. MP Levine, LL Smolak, R Striegel-Moore, pp. 259–84. Hillsdale, NJ: Erlbaum

Strober M. 1991. Disorders of the self in anorexia nervosa: an organismic-developmental paradigm. In *Psychodynamic Treatment of Anorexia Nervosa and Bulimia*, ed. CL Johnson, pp. 354–73. New York: Guilford

Strong KG, Huon GF. 1998. An evaluation of a structural model for studies of the initiation of dieting among adolescent girls. *J. Psychosom. Res.* 44:315–26

Study Group Anorexia Nervosa. 1995. Anorexia nervosa: directions for future research. *Int. J. Eat. Disord.* 17:235–41

Sunday SR, Halmi KA, Einhorn A. 1995. The Yale-Brown-Cornell eating disorder scale: a new scale to assess eating disorder symptomatology. *Int. J. Eat. Disord.* 18:237–45

Thompson SH, Corwin SJ, Sargent RG. 1997. Ideal body size beliefs and weight concerns of fourth-grade children. *Int. J. Eat. Disord.* 21:279–84

Tiggemann M, Pickering AS. 1996. Role of television in adolescent women's body dissatisfaction and drive for thinness. *Int. J. Eat. Disord.* 20:199–203

Troop NA. 1998. Eating disorders as coping strategies: a critique. *Eur. Eat. Disord. Rev.* 6:229–37

Troop NA, Schmidt VA, Turnbull SJ, Treasure JL. 2000. Self-esteem and responsibility for change in recovery from bulimia nervosa. *Eur. Eat. Disord. Rev.* 8:384–93

Valdiserri S, Kihlstrom J. 1995. Abnormal eating and dissociative experiences: a further study of college women. *Int. J. Eat. Disord.* 18:145–50

VanderHam T, Meulman JJ, VanStrien DC, vanEngeland H. 1997. Empirically based subgrouping of eating disorders in adolescents: a longitudinal perspective. *Br. J. Psychiatry* 170:363–68

VanderHam T, VanStrien DC, vanEngeland H. 1998. Personality characteristics predict outcome of eating disorders in adolescents: a 4-year prospective study. *Eur. Child Adolesc. Psychiatry* 7:79–84

Vanfurth EF, Vanstrien DC, Martina LML, Vanson MJM, Hendrickx JJP, vanEngeland H. 1996. Expressed emotion and the prediction of outcome in adolescent eating disorders. *Int. J. Eat. Disord.* 20:19–31

Vitousek KB, Hollon SD. 1990. The investigation of schematic content and processing in eating disorders. *Cogn. Ther. Res.* 14:191–214

Vohs KD, Bardone AM, Joiner TE, Abramson LY, Heatherton TF. 1999. Perfectionism, perceived weight status, and self-esteem interact to predict bulimic symptoms: a model of bulimic symptom development. *J. Abnorm. Psychol.* 108:695–700

Wakeling A. 1996. Epidemiology of anorexia nervosa. *Psychiatry Res.* 62:3–9

Waller G, Hodgson S. 1996. Body image distortion in anorexia and bulimia nervosa—the role of perceived and actual control. *J. Nerv. Ment. Dis.* 184:213–19

Ward A, Ramsay R, Treasure JL. 2000a. Attachment research in eating disorders. *Br. J. Med. Psychol.* 73:35–51

Ward A, Ramsay R, Turnbull S, Benedettini M, Treasure J. 2000b. Attachment patterns in eating disorders: past in the present. *Int. J. Eat. Disord.* 28:370–76

Ward A, Tiller J, Treasure J, Russell G. 2000c. Eating disorders: psyche or soma? *Int. J. Eat. Disord.* 27:279–87

Welch SL, Doll HA, Fairburn CG. 1997. Life events and the onset of bulimia nervosa: a controlled study. *Psychol. Med.* 27:515–22

Wertheim EH, Paxton SJ, Schutz HK, Muir SL. 1997. Why do adolescent girls watch their weight? An interview study examining sociocultural pressures to be thin. *J. Psychosom. Res.* 42:345–55

Whelan E, Cooper PJ. 2000. The association

between childhood feeding problems and maternal eating disorder: a community study. *Psychol. Med.* 30:69–77

Wichstrom L. 2000. Psychological and behavioral factors unpredictive of disordered eating: a prospective study of the general adolescent population in Norway. *Int. J. Eat. Disord.* 28:33–42

Wiederman MW, Pryor T. 1996. Multi-impulsi-

vity among women with bulimia nervosa. *Int. J. Eat. Disord.* 20:359–65

Wilson GT. 1991. The addiction model of eating disorders: a critical analysis. *Adv. Behav. Res. Ther.* 13:27–72

Woods SC, Brief DJ. 1988. Physiological factors. In *Assessment of Addictive Behaviors*, ed. DM Donovan, GA Marlatt, pp. 296–322. New York: Guilford

Annu. Rev. Psychol. 2002. 53:215–43

INSOMNIA: Conceptual Issues in the Development, Persistence, and Treatment of Sleep Disorder in Adults

Colin A. Espie

Department of Psychological Medicine, University of Glasgow, Academic Centre, Gartnavel Royal Hospital, 1055 Great Western Road, Glasgow, G12 0XH, Scotland; e-mail: c.espie@clinmed.gla.ac.uk

Key Words   cognitive-behavior therapy, circadian rhythm, sleep homeostasis

■ **Abstract**   This paper critically reviews the evidence base for previously reported conceptual models of the development and persistence of insomnia. Although a number of perspectives have some empirical support, no one approach emerges as preeminent. Importantly, the efficacy of any particular psychological intervention cannot be taken as confirmation of presumed, underlying mechanisms. An integrated psychobiological inhibition model of insomnia is developed that accounts for the research data. The model views insomnia as arising from inhibition of de-arousal processes associated with normal sleep. It is proposed that sleep homeostatic and circadian factors are compromised by impairment of the automaticity and plasticity associated with good sleep, and that cognitive/affective processes activate the clinical complaint of insomnia. Common pathways for the action of cognitive-behavioral interventions are identified, and a research agenda is set for further conceptual and clinical study.

CONTENTS

0084-6570/02/0201-0215$14.00

AN INTRODUCTION TO INSOMNIA

The *Diagnostic and Statistical Manual of Mental Disorders* (DSM-IV) defines primary insomnia as a complaint lasting for at least 1 month of difficulty initiating and/or maintaining sleep or of nonrestorative sleep (Am. Psychiatr. Assoc. 1994). The International Classification of Sleep Disorders-Revised (ICSD-R) uses the term "psychophysiologic insomnia" for such a complaint and associated decreased functioning during wakefulness. (Am. Sleep Disorders Assoc. 1997). ICSD-R regards insomnia of 6-month duration as chronic. Both systems differentiate insomnia from circadian rhythm disorders, in which timing of the major sleep period is out of alignment with the local clock; from parasomnias, in which behavioral events occur in association with sleep (e.g., sleepwalking, night terrors); and from secondary insomnias, in which psychiatric, neurologic, or medical problems present. Disorders such as sleep apnea, with associated respiratory impairment, and disorders of excessive sleepiness (e.g., narcolepsy) are also classified separately.

Conservative estimates for chronic insomnia range from 9–12% in adulthood and up to 20% in later life, and women present about two times more than men (Bixler et al. 1979, Mellinger et al. 1985, Ford & Kamerow 1989, Gallup Organisation 1991, Foley et al. 1995, Hoch et al. 1997). Sleep disturbance is a common complaint in general practice (Shocat et al. 1999) and once established may persist over many years (Mendelson 1995). Insomnia therefore constitutes a considerable public health problem. The direct costs of assessing and treating insomnia were approximated as $14 billion in the United States and FF10 billion in France in 1995 (Walsh & Engelhardt 1999, Leger et al. 1999).

Polysomnographic assessment (PSG) comprises monitoring of the electroencephalogram (EEG) along with muscle activity, eye movement, respiration, and blood oxygen saturation levels. However, PSG is not required unless clinical presentation raises the possibility of disorders such as sleep apnea (Gillin & Byerley 1990, Douglas et al. 1992, Reite et al. 1995, Am. Sleep Disorders Assoc. 1995a). Actigraphic assessment is helpful to identify disorders of circadian function. The wrist actigraph provides data on body movement over extended periods (typically 1 minute epochs for several weeks) and is a reliable index of sleep parameters (Sadeh et al. 1995, Am. Sleep Disorders Assoc. 1995b).

In practice, structured interview is recommended (Buysse et al. 1989, Morin 1993, Spielman & Anderson 1999, Espie 2000), supplemented by a sleep diary completed upon waking, comprising information on sleep-onset latency (SOL), wake time after sleep-onset, and total sleep time (Espie 1991). Time in bed (TIB) is calculated by subtracting rising time from bedtime, and the sleep efficiency index is computed as the ratio of total sleep time to TIB expressed as a percentage. A sleep efficiency index of 85% is the upper limit for poor sleep (Frankel et al. 1976, Coates et al. 1982), and a minimum SOL or wake time after sleep-onset of 30 minutes per night is a threshold for clinical significance (Espie et al. 1989a, 2001a). Baseline values in outcome studies, however, are typically twice this level (Morin et al. 1999b). With medication, alcohol, and ratings of sleep quality commonly included, the sleep diary quantifies sleep experience and permits study of night-to-night variability, which is important because unpredictability of sleep is a feature of insomnia (Coates et al. 1982, Roth et al. 1976).

The American Academy of Sleep Medicine (AASM) has published practice parameters for the assessment (Chesson et al. 2000) and nonpharmacological treatment of insomnia (Chesson et al. 1999). The latter were derived from systematic review (Morin et al. 1999b) following meta-analyses demonstrating the efficacy of cognitive-behavioral treatment (CBT) for adults (Morin et al. 1994, Murtagh & Greenwood 1995). Another review came to similar conclusions (Edinger & Wohlgemuth 1999). Furthermore, clinical effectiveness studies have produced comparable results (Espie et al. 2001a,b), and CBT with or without pharmacotherapy compares favorably with pharmacotherapy alone for older adults (Morin et al. 1999a). CBT, therefore, may be the treatment of first choice for chronic insomnia (Espie 1999). The role of hypnotic medication has been debated (Kripke 2000, Kramer 2000, Buysse 2000), there being little evidence of long-term efficacy for any drug. Recent textbooks also provide useful discussion: Lichstein & Morin (2000) focus on late-life insomnia, and Pressman & Orr (1997) provide an overview of insomnia in medical patients. Finally, an AASM working group on research diagnostic criteria will report in 2002 (Edinger et al. 2002). Thus, there is a sizeable, systematic, and practitioner-oriented literature on insomnia. The conceptual foundations of insomnia, however, have been more neglected, and it seems timely to review models of the development, persistence, and treatment of insomnia, to evaluate explanatory mechanisms, and to propose an evidence-based integrated model.

THE CONCEPTUAL BASIS FOR THE DEVELOPMENT AND MAINTENANCE OF INSOMNIA

A wide range of factors may play some part in insomnia. It may be helpful to consider each of these before presenting a proposed integrated model.

Normal Sleep in Human Development

Wakefulness is not pathological. On the contrary, it might be considered the preferred state because a primary function of sleep is to ensure wakeful cortical function (Horne 1988). Prolonged wakefulness reliably induces sleep, and failure to obtain at least a core amount (sleep deprivation) leads to impaired function. Two processes interact in normal sleep (Borbely 1994). The sleep homeostat "drives" the sleep-wake schedule toward a balanced requirement because prolonged wakefulness accrues "sleep debt" (Carskadon & Dement 1981) and sleep pays off the debt; the circadian timer regulates the biological clock in approximation to the 24-hour clock (Borbely 1994, Moore-Ede et al. 1982). These processes also regulate type of sleep (Dement 1960). Thus, young children have longer sleep periods than adults and have higher proportions of rapid eye movement (REM) and "deep sleep" (non-REM stages 3 and 4). Similarly, insufficient sleep induces recovery sleep comprising proportionately more REM and deep sleep. The sleep of older adults is more fragmented and lighter (Bliwise 1993, Carskadon et al. 1982), and homeostatic drive declines with age (Buysse et al. 1993), when disturbances of the sleep-wake schedule are less well tolerated (Webb 1981, Monk et al. 1992). Thus, increasing age represents a vulnerability factor to sleep disturbance.

Quality of Sleep

Investigations of PSG and self-report generally reveal modest positive correlation. Poor sleepers overestimate sleep disturbance relative to objective criteria (see Espie 1991, pp. 17–18). However, insomniacs have reported being awake when roused from light sleep (Borkovec et al. 1981), and modified EEG criteria are associated with greater accuracy (Coates et al. 1982). There is debate over whether insomniacs are sleepy in the daytime (Seidel et al. 1984, Mendelson et al. 1984, Chambers & Keller 1993, Lichstein et al. 1994). However, sleep should not be considered only in terms of chronobiological "fitness for purpose." The quality of the sleep experience is important. Indeed, ratings of sleep quality do not necessarily correlate highly even with subjective reports of sleep pattern. Unpublished analyses from our recent clinical cohort (Espie et al. 2001b; n = 139) reveal modest inverse association of SOL and wake time after sleep-onset with ratings of "sleep enjoyment" (r = −0.30 and −0.31) and "restedness after sleep" (−0.22 and −0.19).

Predisposing, Precipitating, and Perpetuating Factors

How then might insomnia develop? A useful conceptualization comprises predisposing, precipitating, and perpetuating components (Spielman & Glovinsky 1991). Both DSM-IV and ICSD-R report familial association with light, disrupted sleep, and ICSD-R reports anxious over-concern with health as predisposing. Indeed, insomniacs appear prone to introspection and worry (e.g., Kales et al. 1984, Edinger et al. 1988, Lundh et al. 1995, Schramm et al. 1995). Research suggesting elevated autonomic and metabolic rates also implies a vulnerability factor (Bonnet & Arand 1995, 1997a). However, predisposing factors alone are unlikely to create imbalance in sleep homeostasis or circadian timing, although they might impair sleep quality and, potentially, lead to sleep state misperception (see also Bonnet &

Arand 1997b). Reduced "plasticity" (see below) might also be a predispositional factor.

Transient sleep disorder is a likely context in which to identify precipitating factors. ICSD-R defines adjustment sleep disorder associated temporally with acute stress, conflict, or environmental change, and shiftwork schedule disorder as a transient phenomenon relating to work schedules. Because the homeostat and timer regulate natural variation, it can be hypothesized that there is generally sufficient plasticity to absorb the impact of such events, and to survive more prolonged change. The severity and impact of events may need to be greater to precipitate sleep disturbance in the absence of predisposing factors. Nevertheless, studies investigating the onset of chronic insomnia have commonly found that stress or life change was a factor at the time (Healey et al. 1981, Kales & Vgontzas 1992, Morgan & Clarke 1997). Presumably, some other mechanism accounts for the persistence of a sleep problem. Why only some disturbances develop into chronic insomnia when others spontaneously remit, and why good sleep can persist during chronic stress are important questions requiring further study.

To summarize, predisposition may interact with precipitating factors to create temporary sleep disruption, but in the absence of perpetuating factors, the plasticity of the sleep-wake schedule would drive toward homeostasis and reestablish good sleep. The literature has focused primarily on presumed factors maintaining insomnia.

Mental Disorder

A common misconception is that insomnia is a symptom not meriting treatment in its own right. However, insomnia can be either a symptom (e.g., a complaint of difficulty falling asleep) or a disorder (i.e., complaint plus significant distress and functional impairment) (Harvey 2001a, Lichstein 2000). The misconception is particularly evident in the mental health field but is unsupported by the literature.

Ford & Kamerow (1989) reported on 8000 respondents, revealing that the risk of developing depression was much higher in those with preexisting insomnia. Similarly, Eaton et al. (1995) reported that having a sleep problem was the highest precursor in terms of attributable risk, identifying 47% of new cases of depression the following year. Other longitudinal studies have confirmed such findings. One report on 262 older adults suggested that frequency of depressed affect related to poor sleep, even when age, sex, and health status were accounted for (Rodin et al. 1988). Breslau et al.'s (1996) work on 1007 21–30-year-olds found that gender-adjusted relative risk for major depression in people with a history of insomnia was 4.0 (95% CI 2.2–7.0). Weissman et al.'s (1997) epidemiological survey reported an odds ratio of 5.4 (95% CI 2.6–11.1) for first-onset depression in 414 people with insomnia and no psychiatric history. Insomnia was also an independent risk factor for panic disorder and obsessive compulsive disorder. Finally, the Johns Hopkins Precursors Study found that insomnia in young men was indicative of greater risk for depression and psychiatric distress that persists for 30 years (Chang et al. 1997).

Thus, insomnia cannot be accounted for simply as presumed mental disorder. Furthermore, sleep disturbance often fails to resolve upon recovery from depression. However, the possibility that insomnia shares some psychobiological diathesis with anxiety and mood disorder is worthy of further investigation.

Faulty Conditioning

Since first proposed by Bootzin (1972), an understanding of insomnia as the product of maladaptive sleep habits has had considerable appeal. Good sleep is seen as coming under the stimulus control of the bedroom environment, which acts as a discriminative stimulus for sleep (Bootzin et al. 1991). Difficulty falling asleep may result either from failure to establish discriminative stimuli for sleep or the presence of stimuli incompatible with sleep. Poor stimulus control, therefore, might compete with sleep drive by strengthening conditioned arousal, and with circadian timing by doing so at normal bedtime. The insomniac may also nap in an armchair and so strengthen associations between sleep and nonsleeping environments. Stimulus control treatment instructions comprise lying down to sleep only when sleepy, avoiding using the bed for activities other than sleep (sexual activity excepted), getting up if unable to sleep quickly (within 15–20 minutes), repeating rising from bed as necessary throughout the night, getting up the same time every day, and avoiding napping (Bootzin 1972, Bootzin & Epstein 2000).

Only a few studies have investigated conditioning in insomnia. Haynes et al. (1982) compared student insomniacs and noninsomniacs on 12 sleep-incompatible behaviors, but found only one that differentiated the groups. Furthermore, duration of engagement in sleep-incompatible activity was unrelated to SOL. They had previously reported that the number of sleep-incompatible behaviors was not related to sleep difficulty (Haynes et al. 1974). Although over half the chronic insomniacs in Espie et al.'s (1989a) outcome study reported reading or watching TV in bed, there was no comparison group of good sleepers. Tokarz & Lawrence (1974) separated situational (reestablishing bedroom cues for sleep) from temporal components (regularizing sleep routines) and found both reduced SOL in their student sample. Zwart & Lisman (1979) conducted a study of 47 undergraduates assigned to stimulus control (all instructions), temporal control (lie down only when sleepy, rise at same time each day, do not nap), noncontingent control (a fixed number of risings within 20 minutes of retiring), countercontrol (sit up in bed and read, watch TV etc. if unable to sleep), or no treatment. They found countercontrol as effective as stimulus control, suggesting that it may ensure contingent disruption of bed and bedtime as cues for mental arousal. Davies et al. (1986) used countercontrol with older adults and found it moderately effective, although their 30% reduction in wake time after sleep-onset is less than typically reported in this population (Morin et al. 1999c).

In spite of equivocal evidence for the mechanism of effect (i.e., is it a stimulus control paradigm?), there has been little recent work on the conceptual basis of stimulus control. Harvey (2000a) reported that primary insomniacs did not differ from good sleepers on daytime napping, variable sleep scheduling, whether they stayed in bed or got up when unable to sleep, or on engagement in sleep-incompatible activities. Nevertheless, significantly lower sleep efficiency is typical of insomniacs, and this may evidence the need for improved stimulus control. Interestingly, Bootzin has reported that stimulus control reduces sleep anticipatory anxiety as well as improving sleep (Bootzin et al. 1999). More research is required because stimulus control interventions have consistently been found to be efficacious in meta-analyses (Morin et al. 1994, 1999b; Murtagh & Greenwood 1995). Indeed, they are the only procedures recommended by AASM as comprising "standard" nonpharmacological treatment for insomnia (Chesson et al. 1999).

Poor Chronobiological Timing

In sleep phase disorders people sleep relatively normally, but during the "wrong" hours. In Delayed Sleep Phase Syndrome (DSPS), for example, in which the sleep period is phase delayed, subjects experience sleep-onset insomnia if they attempt to sleep before they are ready to sleep, and in advanced sleep phase syndrome sleep-onset is early and the phase advance results in early waking. In primary insomnia there may be an element of chronobiological dysfunction. For example, some insomniacs go to bed early and spend excessive time in bed either habitually as in the case of older adults, or as a response to having slept poorly on previous nights (Morgan 2000, Morin 1993). This contributes to poor sleep efficiency, which is affected both by TIB and total sleep time (see above), and can be improved by spending less time in bed, sleeping longer, or by a combination of the two. Similarly, napping reduces nighttime sleep drive in adults. The literature may have failed to discriminate adequately between circadian disorders and primary insomnia (Morris et al. 1990, Lack & Wright 1993). In particular, DSPS may not have been identified in studies involving younger populations. Research diagnostic criteria require clarification (Edinger et al. 2002).

It is suggested that, in the absence of competing factors, good sleep is associated with optimal, stable, and accurate circadian timing. Stimulus control instructions contain elements of temporal adjustment (see Lacks 1987, pp. 51–53; Espie 1991, pp. 51–55) and may provide *zeitgebers* (Aschoff 1951) for healthy sleep. Sleep restriction is another technique that may act both as a circadian harmonic and a reinforcer of homeostatic drive. Patients are encouraged to reduce bedtime hours (by staying up late and/or rising earlier) to approximate TIB closer to actual sleep duration (Spielman et al. 1987). Sleep restriction compresses sleep toward greater continuity, reduces wakefulness in bed, and increases sleep efficiency. Once the sleep pattern is improved, TIB may be extended, at a rate of 15 minutes per night per week, until the patient no longer gains further sleep or sleep efficiency is at risk of being reduced. Wohlegemuth & Edinger (2000) reviewed empirical findings on the efficacy of sleep restriction, and the AASM support sleep restriction as a "guideline" intervention for insomnia (Chesson et al. 1999). The synergy between stimulus control and sleep restriction is evident, and they are often presented together. We use the term "sleep scheduling" for the combination (Espie et al. 1998, 2001b).

Recent interest in using appropriately timed bright light exposure to entrain circadian timing also focuses attention on possible chronobiological explanations of sleep disorder. Early evening bright light shifts the circadian rhythm of core body temperature and improves PSG-defined sleep in sleep-maintenance insomnia (Campbell et al. 1993), and morning light reduces SOL (Lack et al. 1995). Light exposure may also have a role in managing sleep disturbance in dementia (e.g., Satlin et al. 1992).

Physiological Hyper-Arousal

In 1967 Monroe conducted an influential study comparing 16 good sleepers with 16 poor sleepers, suggesting that poor sleepers exhibit heightened autonomic arousal (higher rectal temperature, vasoconstrictions per minute, perspiration rate, skin conductunce, body movements per hour) both prior to and during sleep. This work has been partly replicated (Stepanski et al. 1989), but other studies have failed to demonstrate arousal differentials. Higher levels of hormones indicative of adreno-cortical activity have been both supported (Johns et al. 1971, Adam et al. 1986) and denied (Frankel et al. 1973). Other early work reported less rapid decline in heart rate associated with sleep in insomniacs, but others found no significant relationship between sleep-onset and heart rate or frontalis electromyography (EMG) (Haynes et al. 1974, Good 1975, Browman & Tepas 1976). Now that heart rate variability in the progression through sleep is better understood in normal subjects (e.g., Baharav et al. 1995, Bonnet & Arand 1997a), further comparative study seems warranted. Freedman & Sattler (1982) found that, prior to sleep-onset, insomniacs had higher frontalis and chin EMG than good sleepers, and the literature on relaxation and/or biofeedback treatments (e.g., Borkovec & Weerts 1976, Borkovec & Sides 1979, Freedman & Papsdorf 1976) might appear to support muscle tension as a problem in insomnia. However, there is limited evidence of tension reduction as the active mechanism, and posttreatment changes in EMG, heart rate, or respiration have proven elusive (see Espie 1991, pp. 43–45; Bootzin & Rider 1997, pp. 322–26 for review).

Interest in physiological arousal has been rekindled by evidence that insomniacs display measurable neurobiological differences from normal sleepers. Bonnet & Arand (1995) compared 10 objectively defined insomniacs with age-, sex-, and weight-matched controls and found they had significantly increased oxygen use both day and night. They suggested that increased 24-hour metabolic rate could be magnified by stress or viewed as a "higher arousal set point." In a complementary controlled study, 9 subjects with sleep state misperception (SSM) were also found to have increased metabolic rate, but less so than the primary insomniacs (Bonnet & Arand 1997b), raising the possibility that SSM is a mild version of, or precursor to, psychophysiological insomnia. Hyper-arousal has also been investigated in PSG studies. Early reports suggested insomniacs had more beta and fewer alpha frequencies in their EEG (Freedman 1987, Freedman & Sattler 1982). Recently, Merica et al. (1998) compared spectral characteristics of 20 insomniacs and 19 controls. For all frequencies below beta, insomniacs had slower rise rates and reached lower levels, whereas beta power was increased. In REM, insomniacs showed lower levels in delta and theta bands, whereas power in faster bands was increased. These findings are consistent with slow wave deficiency in insomnia accompanied by hyper-arousal of the CNS, suggesting that insomnia may result from increased cortical activation. They noted, however, that homeostatic control of slow wave activity appeared to be intact in the patient population. A study by Loewy & Bootzin (1998) also investigated hyper-arousal and found that event-related EEG activity, as measured by auditory evoked potentials, provided evidence of information processing during sleep.

Importantly, however, not all objective poor sleepers complain of insomnia, and not all subjective insomniacs have poor sleep (Edinger et al. 2000), suggesting that physiological arousal alone is an insufficient explanation.

Cognitive Hyper-Arousal

It was first reported 25 years ago that poor sleepers complain of mental alertness more than physiological arousal (Evans 1977). Other studies have consistently associated cognitive arousal more strongly with sleep disruption, and "having an overactive mind" has been the attribution rated most highly, both by insomniacs and noninsomniacs (Lichstein & Rosenthal 1980, Nicassio et al. 1985, Broman & Hetta 1994). Espie et al. (1989a) reported that the cognitive items of the Sleep Disturbance Questionnaire (e.g., "my mind keeps turning things over," "I am unable to empty my mind") were the most highly rated; Harvey (2000b) recently replicated these findings. The Sleep Disturbance Questionnaire has been found to have modest internal consistency ($\alpha = 0.67$) (Espie et al. 2000). Although there is no gold standard measure of cognitive activity, the Pre-Sleep Arousal Scale (Nicassio et al. 1985) is widely used and has satisfactory internal consistency for its somatic and cognitive subscales ($\alpha = 0.81$ and $\alpha = 0.76$, respectively). These constructs have some degree of independence (74% unshared variance). The cognitive subscale of the Pre-Sleep Arousal Scale has also demonstrated modest ($r = 0.35$) validity compared with voice-activated recordings of presleep thoughts as a criterion measure (Wicklow & Espie 2000).

Population survey confirms that people dissatisfied with sleep report mental activity near bedtime (Ohayon et al. 1997). However, there are conflicting conclusions from studies of the relationship between cognitive activity and sleep latency. Van Egeren et al. (1983) found that audiotape-recorded cognitions were significantly correlated with subjective sleep latency, but not with polysomnographic (PSG) assessment sleep, whereas Borkovec et al. (1979) and Kuisk et al. (1989) reported more frequent cognitive activity in insomnia confirmed by PSG. Sanavio (1988) reported a low correlation ($r = 0.09$) between presleep intrusion and self-reported sleep latency, and furthermore, found no advantage of a tailored cognitively focused program in the treatment of sleep-onset insomnia. The possibility, therefore, remains that cognitive arousal is an epiphenomenon of nighttime wakefulness (Freedman & Sattler 1982, Morin 1993).

Support for a cognitive model has also come from studies involving experimental manipulation of presleep cognitive intrusions (e.g., Gross & Borkovec 1982, Hall et al. 1996). However, Haynes et al. (1981) exposed insomniacs and noninsomniacs to brief stressors and found a decrease in subjective and objective SOL among insomniacs on stress nights. They concluded that a mental processing task that disrupts sleep-related cognitive events may decrease SOL, implying that the nature of the intrusions may be critical to the effect upon sleep. Therefore, failure to differentiate thought content could result in limited comparability between studies.

Dysfunctional Thinking

The importance of emotional arousal has been stressed, because affect-laden cognitions are more likely to interfere with sleep (Espie 1991, Morin 1993, Haynes et al. 1981, Coyle & Watts 1991). Beliefs about the negative experiences and consequences of insomnia may foster the clinical complaint. This parallels research on "worry," posited as a generic trait (Barlow 1988, Meyer et al. 1990), and studies on unwanted intrusive thoughts (Rachman & De Silva 1978, Reynolds & Salkovskis 1992). Negative and distressing cognitions are likely to contribute to the development of obsessions; however, it is not the thoughts per se that are untypical or pathological, but the meaning and concern attributed to them (Clark & Purdon 1993, 1995). The conceptual relatedness of nighttime and daytime intrusions, therefore, appears considerable.

Insomniacs have more negative thoughts than good sleepers at bedtime (Nicassio et al. 1985, Van Egeren et al. 1983, Kuisk et al. 1989), and such thinking is reported even when wakened from light sleep (Borkovec et al. 1981). The thoughts of insomniacs may be dependent on emotional state. Investigating the relationship between worry and insomnia, Watts et al. (1994) found that much of the presleep mental activity of "worried insomniacs" revolved around work and general mental activity. In contrast, thoughts of "nonworried insomniacs" focused on the sleep process itself. Insomniacs may also feel less in control of their thinking (Watts et al. 1995). Gendron et al. (1998) reported that insomniacs with comorbid generalized anxiety disorder had greater cognitive activity at bedtime than insomniacs without generalized anxiety disorder, evaluated their thoughts as more intrusive and worrisome, and attempted cognitive avoidance strategies more frequently.

Morin (1993) has argued that beliefs and attitudes play a critical role. He devised a 30-item questionnaire to identify irrational, affect-laden thoughts that intrude prior to sleep-onset (dysfunctional beliefs and attitudes about sleep scale) (Morin 1993, Morin et al. 1993). This scale comprises misconceptions about the causes of insomnia, misattributions or amplifications of the consequences of insomnia, unrealistic sleep expectations, diminished perceptions of control, and faulty beliefs about sleep-promoting practices. It has satisfactory psychometric properties and sensitivity to change after cognitive-behavioral treatment (CBT) (Espie et al. 2000, Morin et al. 2001), and may help identify subgroups of the insomniac population (Edinger et al. 1998). Furthermore, those with subjective insomnia report more dysfunctional sleep-related cognitions than do those with objective insomnia (Edinger et al. 2000), consistent with the view that cognition/affect may influence sleep report and perhaps mediate insomniac complaint.

Formal analysis of sleep-interfering cognitions has been reported in several studies. Coyle & Watts (1991) used an extended version of the Sleep Disturbance Questionnaire (Espie et al. 1989a) and reported two distinct factors: "sleep attitudes," reflecting anxiety about the sleep process, and "mental activity," reflecting nonspecific cognitive activity. Six factors of nighttime intrusive thoughts, i.e., trivial topics, thoughts about sleep, family and long-term concerns, positive plans and concerns, somatic preoccupations, and work and recent concerns, were identified in a study of young adults (Watts et al. 1994). Extending these findings by using a good-sleeper comparison group, Harvey (2000b) reported that presleep cognitive activity of insomniacs could be distinguished by being more focused upon worry about not getting to sleep, general worries, solving problems, the time, and noises in the house, and less focused upon "nothing in particular."

A study by Fichten et al. (1998) of the thoughts of older adults during wakeful periods yielded a 3-factor solution of generalized positive thinking, generalized negative thinking, and thoughts related to sleep. They suggested that insomniacs use positive thinking as a buffer to combat negative intrusions. Also recently, Wicklow & Espie (2000) obtained voice-activated audiotape recordings of spontaneous thoughts and sleep actigraphic data from 21 poor sleepers over 3 consecutive nights. Content analysis yielded 8 categories of presleep intrusion, and a regression model indicated that thinking about sleep and the anticipated consequences of poor sleep, along with general problem-solving were the strongest predictors of objective SOL. Intrusions were subsumed under one of 3 factors: active problem-solving (e.g., rehearsing/planning events), present state monitoring (e.g., thinking about sleep/not sleeping) and environmental reactivity (e.g., attending to external noises).

Paradox and Ironic Control

This model of insomnia proposes that anxiety responses may be conditioned not only to external, situational cues but also to the individual's behavior (Ascher & Turner 1979, Espie & Lindsay 1985, Espie 1991). Fear of performance failure (insomnia) and of anticipated negative consequences of that failure is described as performance anxiety. In paradoxical treatment counterproductive attempts to fall asleep are replaced by the intention of remaining passively awake or by giving up any direct effort to fall asleep (Ascher & Turner 1980, Fogle & Dyal 1983). This rationale is supportable in that good sleepers do not use any strategies to fall asleep. Paradoxical intention has demonstrated efficacy in controlled trials (Turner & Ascher 1979, Espie et al. 1989b) and is an intervention that reflects a "moderate degree of clinical certainty" according to the AASM (Chesson et al. 1999). Paradox continues to be used within multicomponent CBT (e.g., Espie et al. 2001b) and may be particularly useful with patients who are resistant and reactive to therapeutic suggestions (Shoham et al. 1995).

Further evidence for this type of mechanism was provided by Ansfield et al. (1996), who explored the effects of different sleep-onset instructions in good sleepers under high or low mental load. Paradoxical wakefulness was found amongst those attempting to sleep while listening to marching music. This was interpreted in terms of Wegner's (1994) theory of a self-loading system that suggests that under certain conditions the thwarted attempt to control a particular mental state can yield the opposite of what is desired. They hypothesized that failure to fall asleep on a few occasions could occur when sleep is attempted under transitory mental loads, such as at times of stress. Eventually, a person's thoughts about being unable to sleep could constitute a debilitating mental load, which when combined with the continuing frustrated desire to fall asleep, could lead to chronic insomnia.

Harvey (2001b) has explored the effects of suppressing presleep cognitive activity on sleep-onset latency. A cohort of insomniacs and good sleepers were allocated to either a suppression condition ("suppress the thought most likely to dominate your thinking as you get into bed") or nonsuppression condition ("think about anything as you get into bed, including the thought you would most likely think about as you go to sleep"). Suppress participants reported longer sleep latencies and poorer sleep quality, regardless of whether they were insomniac or not. Harvey concluded that thought suppression appeared to have the opposite effect in that it prevented sleep-onset, in a manner consistent with Wegner's theory of ironic mental control.

There are parallels between Wegner's theory and the performance anxiety model that gave rise to the adaptation of paradoxical intention from the work of Frankl (1960). Indeed, Ansfield et al. (1996) propose that their results are consistent with theories of cyclic escalation of anxiety disorders (Ascher 1981) and worry about sleep (Borkovec 1982).

AN INTEGRATED PSYCHOBIOLOGICAL MODEL
OF NORMAL SLEEP

There are, thus, differing explanations of insomnia, each having some empirical support. The rest of this paper attempts to integrate this evidence into a conceptual framework. A model of the normal sleep process is presented first, because a perspective on the pathway to sleeping well is likely to inform understanding of the development, maintenance, and treatment of insomnia.

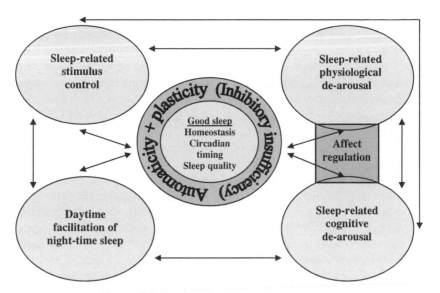

Figure 1   A psychobiological model of good sleep. Insomnia is proposed as resulting from chronic inhibition of one or more of the component processes.

Figure 1 summarizes hypothesized processes and interactions in normal sleep. The model proposes good sleep as the natural state of the human organism—its default state. That is, homeostatic and circadian processes, under normal circumstances, default to good sleep, not to insomnia. The core of the model is involuntary, harmonious interaction between homeostat and timer, which is associated with the self-perception of good quality sleep. Like all neurobehavioral systems, good sleep is assumed to have both functional plasticity and automaticity. These are presented as protective properties, "defending" the core.

Plasticity refers to the "absorb and readjust" capability of the sleep-wake system to accommodate living in the real world where situational and personal factors provoke variance and challenge normal, stable functioning. Night-to-night variability is tolerated but minimized by the good sleeper, for whom the sleep homeostat drives sleep-related behaviors effectively. In acute insomnia the norm would be recovery of sleep pattern, again reflecting the system's plasticity in function and default regression towards good sleep. Automaticity refers to the involuntary nature of the well-adjusted schedule, to the habitual, conditioned associations that are part of its stimulus control paradigm, and to the implicit expectations and assumptions the good sleeper has about sleep continuity and sleep quality. It is tempting to think of the model as the good sleeper's list of ingredients for good sleep, but that would be misleading. The good sleeper is not thought of as following a recipe to produce the perfect sleep. Rather, the good sleeper is regarded as essentially passive because internal and external cues act as automated setting conditions for sleep. Endogenous cues to sleep such as physical and mental fatigue interact reciprocally with exogenous cues in the home environment. The good sleeper sleeps just as he walks, or talks—without thinking about it. This, presumably, is the insomniac's ambition.

The defensive properties of the good sleep paradigm, therefore, are seen as maintained by four interacting subsystems: sleep-stimulus control, physiological de-arousal, cognitive de-arousal, and daytime facilitation. In a reciprocal way, sleep homeostasis, circadian timing, and sleep quality serve to reinforce and maintain these behavioral, cognitive, and biological processes. That is, good sleep begets good psychobiological preparation for sleep, which begets good sleep.

The model predicts that the good sleeper accurately interprets physiological and mental signs of sleep readiness and, once in the bedroom, the stimulus environment there further reinforces de-arousal. Regular sleep habits for retiring and rising constitute a good predictive framework that exhibits both sensitivity and specificity. In terms of the former, a high percentage of nights that follow this pattern is associated with efficient sleep. In terms of the latter, sleep is highly specific to the bedroom and wakefulness to other environments; i.e., the good sleeper is less likely to lie awake in bed or need to sleep in the day or evening. Effective stimulus control reinforces not only circadian timing and sleep homeostasis but also contributes to cognitive de-arousal because high sleep efficiency precludes cognitive intrusion in bed. Both physiological and cognitive de-arousal are presumed to occur in parallel. Active information-processing recedes as the wake system disengages and the sleep system engages. The good sleeper is less likely to use time in bed for problem-solving or anxious thinking, nor have time to do so because sleep-onset is rapid, and nervous system adaptations proceed unhindered because the good sleeper has few inaccurate expectations or worries about sleep or wakefulness.

Crucially, the good sleeper experiences little affect associated with sleep. Affect regulation, which represents an interaction between cognitive and physiological processes, is proposed as functional when affect is essentially neutral. Dysregulation would occur with strong (negative or positive) emotions, both of which are arousing. Similarly, the good sleeper is seen as having few conscious expectations of sleep and puts no direct effort into the sleep process. Daytime attitudes and behaviors may also facilitate sleep. The good sleeper may make fewer attributions of daytime mood and performance to the preceding night's sleep. For example, when irritable or fatigued, he may be more likely to associate these with proximal events (e.g., pressure of work) than view them as contingencies of sleep pattern or sleep quality. Also, the good sleeper may be more effective at managing state/trait symptoms and/or may put less pressure on sleep to compensate for any excessive daytime routines.

Thus, the common pathway in the maintenance of sleep homeostasis, circadian timing, and sleep quality is proposed as an involuntary process of psychobiological de-arousal within which there is insufficient mental, behavioral, or physiological inhibition to impair the automaticity and plasticity of sleep. Implicit in the model is the expectation of regression towards normal sleep because of its fundamental importance both developmentally and functionally.

UNDERSTANDING INSOMNIA WITHIN THE PSYCHOBIOLOGICAL INHIBITION MODEL

At the simplest level, insomnia may be seen as a failure of automated sleep activation and maintenance. More specifically, insomnia may arise from acute inhibition of one or more of the processes normally contributing to good sleep (precipitating stage), perhaps in predisposed individuals, which may become persistent when chronic inhibition develops, preventing the natural recovery of good sleep (perpetuating stage). This conceptualization seems consistent with the lack of pathology or fundamental disorder of sleep-wake function in primary insomnia. Insomnia is proposed, therefore, as persistent loss of expression of normal sleep. The conceptualization is also consistent with evidence that chronic insomnia is amenable to cognitive-behavioral intervention (Morin et al. 1994, 1999b; Murtagh & Greenwood 1995). CBT may act to overcome inhibitory mechanisms and reestablish adaptive mental and situational "setting conditions" for the restoration of normal sleep.

Automaticity and plasticity would be weakened by inhibitory feedback from one or more of the attendant psychobiological processes (Figure 1 and Table 1). For example, poor stimulus control represented by sleep-incompatible behavior, diminished sleep-wake sensitivity and specificity, and irregular sleep habits could inhibit sleep and maintain insomnia. Similarly, affect-laden thinking would undermine cognitive de-arousal. The notion of "inhibitory sufficiency" is introduced because good sleepers do not necessarily observe all the rules of sleep preparation; e.g., good sleepers may read, drink caffeinated beverages, spend time anxiously reflecting on the day while in bed, be poor daytime copers, etc., without ever becoming insomniac. It helps to account for those individuals who are under chronic stress but who apparently still sleep well. Inhibitory sufficiency, therefore, represents the critical mass of inhibition required to outweigh the stability of an individual's default sleep pattern. Theoretically, it would need to be higher where there is strong sleep homeostasis and/or circadian timing, and less where there is predisposition to insomnia, strong precipitating factors or limited protection afforded by plasticity and automaticity.

Table 1 presents detail of the elements of the model and how they may become inhibited. Poor sleep-related stimulus control would be observed where the bedroom becomes a conditioned focus for waking activity and where the sensitivity/specificity of the sleep-wake schedule is compromised, primarily by remaining awake in bed, but also by sleeping in the daytime. Attempting to sleep longer on recovery nights and spending too long in bed could also inhibit the continuity and automaticity of sleep by reducing sleep efficiency. Stimulus control and sleep restriction treatments may be effective because they counteract the process of inhibition (stay up until sleepy, compress time in bed, etc.) and reinstate default sleep. The instruction to get up if not asleep within 15 minutes may also attenuate the inhibition associated with effort to sleep, as it can be likened to a "give up trying" instruction.

TABLE 1 Insomnia within the psychobiological inhibition model.

Factors contributing to good sleep	Insomnia: factors inhibitory to sleep homeostasis and circadian timing, and to the protection of good sleep afforded by automaticity and plasticity
Sleep stimulus control	
Sleep-compatible conditioning	Conditioned association of sleep-incompatible, waking activities (e.g., reading, watching TV, eating, talking, problem-solving) with bed and bedroom environment; keeping the light on
Sleep-wake sensitivity/specificity	Environmental latitude in sleep and wake behaviors: lying awake in bed either presleep or upon wakening, sleeping in the day, sleeping elsewhere than in bed
Regular sleep habits	Variable and/or reactive patterns: changing times for retiring and rising, extending time in bed to catch up on sleep, sleeping in at weekends, spending longer in bed than current sleep requirement—reduced sleep efficiency
Physiological de-arousal	
Sleep system engagement	Not feeling tired at bedtime, in bed too early, keeping the light on, sleep-incompatible activities, anxiety, trying too hard to sleep, tension, heart rate variability
Wake system disengagement	As above; active thinking and problem-solving, self-monitoring of internal (bodily and mental) cues, hypervigilance, poor sleep hygiene
Good sleep hygiene	Stimulants (e.g., caffeine, nicotine) in excess/near bedtime; alcohol withdrawal symptoms during the night; active exercise late evening; bedroom stuffy, hot, or cold; bed uncomfortable
Cognitive de-arousal	
Minimal cognitive drive	Rehearsing/planning/problem-solving thoughts in bed, thinking about events the previous or next day, preoccupation with sleep/sleeplessness, "stimulus hungry" mind, mind racing, unable to "switch off"
Accurate sleep-wake attribution	Dysfunctional beliefs and attitudes about sleep and consequences of not sleeping, not expecting to sleep, catastrophic thoughts, concern about next day well-being and coping
Affect regulation	
Minimal affect	Worry, anxiety, frustration, negativity or excitement, intensity in emotional tone associated with above cognitive or physiological processes
Minimal effort to sleep	Sleeplessness preoccupying: trying to control sleep/overcome insomnia, attempts to suppress thoughts/suppress affect, self-monitoring of alert/sleepiness state, performance effort to fall asleep, performance anxiety
Daytime facilitation of night sleep	
Accurate wake-sleep attribution	Attribution of impaired daytime mood, attention, performance to quality of sleep; expectation that sleep should compensate; blaming problems on insomnia; fatigue seen as pathognomic of insomnia; perception of self as insomniac
Effective coping skills	Experiencing time pressure; problems relaxing; worry, frustration, low mood; active late into evening; poor wind down

Some insomniacs report not being tired at bedtime, which undermines physiological de-arousal, and evidence of wakefulness when aroused from light sleep suggests slower engagement of the sleep system. Studies revealing elevated autonomic symptoms in poor sleepers suggest that inhibition of normal arousal is problematic. Sleep hygiene is traditionally regarded as a behavioral strategy. However, its components are primarily physiological in terms of the model of sleep inhibition. Excessive use of caffeine and strenuous exercise delay sleep onset, presumably through heightened arousal. Indeed, in one experimental study 400 mg of caffeine three times per day for one week produced increased arousal on metabolic measures and reports typical of insomniac complaint (Bonnet & Arand 1992). Similarly, environmental factors (temperature, humidity, light) could inhibit sleep physiologically. Use of alcohol may lead to dehydration or provoked awakenings because of ethanol metabolism. Observing good sleep hygiene, therefore, would remove some potential inhibitors of sleep. Similarly, relaxation-based treatments may either reciprocally inhibit autonomic activity (Wolpe 1958) and thus counteract the maintenance of physiological arousal or, perhaps more likely, facilitate mental (and physiological) de-arousal.

Problems with cognitive de-arousal appear central to insomnia. Insomniacs report intrusive thinking; some of this is reflective, but much is also worrisome. The active mind is likely to inhibit de-arousal, particularly where accompanied by negatively toned affect. The insomniac typically becomes concerned about sleeplessness and its immediate and longer-term negative consequences. This gives rise to emotional upset, ironic urgency, and performance anxiety associated with failed efforts to regain perceived loss of control over sleep. Indeed, the development of attentional bias for sleep- or insomnia-related thoughts may help to explain the maintenance of sleep disorders even after proximal sources of transient sleeplessness (e.g., stress) have passed. The fact that attempts to suppress thinking produce sleep disturbance even in normal sleepers is further evidence of insomnia arising from cognitively mediated sleep inhibition. Insomniacs often try too hard, thereby obviating passive acceptance of sleep, which is a hallmark of the good sleeper. The success of cognitive strategies for insomnia may depend, therefore, upon the extent to which they disable sleep-interfering mentation and affect. The central paradox is that deliberate efforts to do so fail to emulate the automatic nature of sleep-onset in good sleepers and may exacerbate preexisting sleep inhibition. The less direct mechanisms of behavioral interventions such as stimulus control upon cognitive processes therefore merit further attention, as do techniques using paradoxical instructions.

It is specious, of course, to set up physiological and cognitive arousal in direct competition. The psychobiological inhibition model presumes interaction between physiological, cognitive, affective, and behavioral subsystems, and indeed between daytime and nighttime variables. These relationships are represented by arrows in Figure 1. Their interaction contributes positively to the maintenance of good sleep. The corollary, however, is that interaction would also compound inhibitory effects. Indeed, Born et al. (1999) have demonstrated that normal sleepers, told that they would be woken at 6 A.M., had significant increases in adrenocorticotropin during the hour preceding waking. This suggests that some form of cognitive priming may be linked to sleep-related biological responses.

Less attention has been paid to how daytime factors could contribute to insomnia. Good sleep may be inhibited by daytime preoccupation with impairments perceived to result from poor sleep. Just as attributional (sleep-wake) error can contribute to sleeplessness during the night, so it may form dysfunctional sleep-related schema during the day (wake-sleep). Self-perception of being insomniac may influence interpretation of everyday experiences, such as feeling fatigued or irritable, in a manner comparable to obsessional disorders in which special meaning is attributed to common thoughts and behaviors. Just as some people differ from controls only in respect of their interpretation of events, some insomniacs have normal or close-to-normal sleep, but perceive it to be abnormal. Insomniacs have been characterized as prone to worry and internalizing of anxiety. Such traits may be reinforced in the day, not only during the night. Furthermore, failure to manage daytime concerns effectively may put pressure on sleep when, in the absence of other stimulation or distraction, the insomniac spends time thinking, rehearsing, planning, and worrying. The model, therefore, includes poor coping skills and disturbed daytime affect as factors that may undermine preparation for sleep and may contribute to behavioral and cognitive sleep inhibition.

It may seem counterintuitive or even arbitrary to talk in terms of inhibition of de-arousal rather than excitation (hyper-arousal). However, the definition of insomnia as failure of expression of an essentially normal underlying sleep process is defensible. To remain awake the insomniac does not need to be hyper-aroused any more than one needs to be hyper-aroused at any other time to remain awake. Hyper-arousal is a sufficient but not necessary precondition to wakefulness. Furthermore, even if hyper-arousal were to occur initially to delay sleep it would not follow that remaining hyper-aroused would be necessary to stay awake thereafter. By comparison, if an individual is becoming sleepy (de-aroused) but subsequently becomes wakeful, it only seems necessary to infer that there has been attenuation of the de-arousal, and that explanation also seems sufficient. It is not being argued that hyper-arousal never occurs, but rather that inhibition of de-arousal does always occur. Inhibition is the lowest common denominator that can be reliably deduced. It is suggested that insomnia as a disorder of initiating or maintaining sleep is at its core a disorder of sleep engagement, not a disorder of excessive arousal.

Nevertheless, the model does account for hyper-arousal in insomnia. Hyper-arousal clearly would inhibit sleep, but it is hypothesized that there is within-group variability in insomnia (i.e., not all insomniacs are hyper-aroused). Variability between populations of insomniacs studied might explain apparently discrepant results reporting both physiological and mental measurement. Physiological hyper-arousal may be a distinct subtype of insomnia. De-arousal, however, is suggested as the reliable correlate of good quality sleep; anything else at or above a level sufficient to inhibit sleep may be associated with insomnia.

Why then has cognitive arousal been more strongly associated with insomnia than physiological arousal? It is suggested that cognition is invariably symptomatic of insomniacs' subjective nighttime experience, whereas physiological arousal is less invariably so. Accordingly, when asked to rate or attribute sleeplessness, insomniacs are likely to stress mentation and/or affect rather than physiological symptoms. There may be interpretation bias, and the possibility that cognitive activity is simply an epiphenomenon of sustained wakefulness or a by-product of the measurement process cannot yet be excluded. However, the cognitive/affective component of primary insomnia does seem to be a sine qua non in clinical practice. Like physiological arousal, cognitive arousal may represent a continuous dimension from de-arousal to hyper-arousal, exhibiting individual variability, but once again, de-arousal appears to be the correlate of good sleep. This helps to explain the common finding that insomniacs consistently appear hyper-aroused, relative to good sleepers, on measures such as the cognitive subscale of the Pre-Sleep Arousal Scale. It cannot be stated with conviction that they are hyper-aroused in any absolute sense, but it may be reasonably inferred that they are not de-arousing.

It should be noted that the model can also be applied to sleep-maintenance insomnia. This subtype is more commonly associated with mid- to late-life, when a propensity to lighter, more broken sleep develops and automaticity and plasticity may be compromised. It is suggested that in sleep-maintenance insomnia there is inhibition of the rapid, automated de-arousal response to the brief wakeful experiences typically found in older good sleepers. This results in more conscious processing of arousals, more frequent arousals, and times of extended wakefulness with difficulty returning to sleep. One way in which inhibition might occur would be through attentional bias for arousal and threat-related cues. The insomniac may selectively attend to brief arousals in the night and interpret these by means of established schema as evidence of inability to sleep. This could then set up the pernicious cycle of inaccurate attribution, affect, effort to sleep, physiological arousal and engagement of the wake system.

It is proposed, therefore, that the common pathway in insomnia is inhibition of the expression of normal sleep. It is further suggested that, whereas any of the subsystems may contribute to inhibition, it is cognitive/affective factors that serve as the "activating agent" for the phenomenology of insomnia and presentation of clinical complaint. This is evidenced by the consistent association of intrusive, affect-laden cognitions with primary insomnia and by the fact that some self-reported good sleepers sleep as poorly as insomniacs, but without experiencing concerns about sleep (Edinger et al. 2000). In the psychobiological inhibition model such cognitions are presumed to pervade nighttime and/or daytime thinking. A corollary to the suggestion of activation is that, if CBT intervention is to be effective, it must somehow close this cognitive/affective gate. This again is consistent with the proposition that stimulus control may achieve its effects by fostering cognitive de-arousal. Similarly, sleep restriction might be regarded as a paradigm involving behavioral experiments to evaluate assumptions about sleep requirements and their consequences. The circadian readjustments that form part of both stimulus control and sleep restriction may, of course, take place without synchronous cognitive conceptual shift, but if that is the case it is suggested that insomnia complaint is likely to persist.

Relationship of the Psychobiological Inhibition Model to Other Models of Insomnia

Espie (1991, pp. 39–56) proposed a framework in which insomnia was conceptualized as mediating from activation of nervous system (central, autonomic), psychological (cognitive, emotional), or environmental (situational, temporal) arousal. These elements can all be accommodated in the current model, although the emphasis is now upon inhibition, impairing the automaticity of normal sleep. Daytime factors are also factored into the new model, and further detail of the cognitive dimension (from Espie 1992, Espie & Wicklow 2001) is presented in the cognitive de-arousal component.

Morin (1993, pp. 46–60) also presented an integrative conceptualization of insomnia. He suggested that hyper-arousal (emotional, cognitive, physiologic) is the central mediating feature of insomnia, which interacts with dysfunctional cognitions, maladaptive habits, and perceived consequences of insomnia. Although the psychobiological inhibition model makes no requirement of hyper-arousal, Morin's emphasis on cognitive factors parallels the cognitive/affective activation agent presented here. The role of dysfunctional thoughts and beliefs in the psychobiological inhibition model is consistent with Edinger et al.'s (2000) interpretation that these influence self-perception of insomnia and insomniac report. Morin also stressed the bi-directional influence of the components, such that consequences often become causes and vice versa, similar to the proposed reciprocal interaction of the elements of the psychobiological inhibition model.

Perlis et al. (1997) discussed discrepancies between PSG and subjective appraisal of sleep. They suggested that inconsistencies may be explained by the presence of high frequency EEG activity in insomnia around sleep-onset, which interferes with the development of mesograde amnesia, and results in insomniacs having blurred phenomenological distinction between sleep and wakefulness. The psychobiological inhibition model can accommodate such an association but would suggest that cortical arousal represents a failure to de-arouse, with hyper-arousal presenting only in some insomniacs. The reciprocal interaction between maintained physiological and psychological processes would inhibit both the transition to slower EEG activity and the experience of sleep-onset, but the model would suggest that it is cognitive/affective inhibition that is the more likely activating factor.

It is also noteworthy that the psychobiological inhibition model is consistent with Spielman's (1991) model of insomnia acquisition (presented above) and with Edgar's (1996) "opponent process" model. The latter proposes that circadian timing promotes wakefulness and opposes sleep drive, and that prolonged wakefulness leads to compensatory sleep responses. The psychobiological inhibition model assumes such an interaction between homeostat and timer, but also describes how such an automated interaction may be inhibited by thoughts, emotions, and behavioral changes.

Some Implications of the Cognitively Activated Psychobiological Inhibition Model

This model raises testable hypotheses and suggests mechanisms for treatment effects. It is only possible to touch upon some of these. The central premise is that in insomnia the expression of normal sleep is chronically inhibited. Therefore, further study of sleep-related de-arousal in good sleepers is required. The model predicts phenomenology comprising attitudinal passivity towards sleep, with neutral expectations, compared with the negativity and worry of the insomniac. In terms of automaticity, it is suggested that the good sleeper is like the experienced car driver who executes a complex series of operations with minimal attentional load. In comparison, the insomniac is like the anxious learner driver: vigilant, deliberate, and errorful. The concept of automaticity in human learning has long been discussed as part of information-processing theory (Shiffrin & Schneider 1977). Its application to sleep and insomnia could be fruitful. The ability to automate is, presumably hard-wired in order to overcome problems associated with an otherwise limited-capacity information-processing system. Theories of paradox and ironic mental control are interesting because they emphasize allowing events to take their natural course, and de-emphasize the need for control and success. Effort to sleep and suppression of wakefulness, and its associated mental activity, may disengage automaticity.

Study of within-subject as well as within-group variability may lead to greater appreciation of how similarly or differently good sleepers and insomniacs respond to good and bad nights, in terms of their expectations, affect, and behavior. Furthermore, because cognitive/affective activation is seen as central, insomniacs may be differentiated not only from good sleepers, but also from noncomplaining poor sleepers. It seems important to identify this latter group for formal study and to consider degree/severity of complaint as a correlate of mental arousal/concern. The latter may be an inverse correlate of automaticity. Good sleepers and noncomplaining poor sleepers may make more benign attributions after a bad night, leaving automaticity intact. It is further suggested that sleep state misperception (SSM) may represent cognitive activation and perceived severity equivalent to that found in primary insomnia, thus differentiating SSM from good sleepers and noncomplaining poor sleepers, but not from insomniacs. Longitudinal study of SSM is required to investigate whether or not objective sleep disturbance develops over time. There is a need, however, to develop better measures of sleep quality, with sound psychometric properties, and to investigate the interrelationships between sleep quality, cognitive arousal, dysfunctional beliefs, attributional error, attentional bias, and affect, both in SSM and insomnia.

Comparison of the relapse patterns of various subgroups after bad nights or periods of poorer sleep would be interesting from another perspective. The interaction of sleep homeostasis and circadian timing is thought to demonstrate impaired plasticity in insomniacs, who present sleep pattern variability. Their sleep-wake rhythm may be more brittle, and the repayment of sleep debt may not function as efficiently. Unfortunately, research data are usually analyzed as weekly mean values, thus concealing within-subject and within-group variability in sleep. Individual raw score variance has been reported only occasionally in insomnia, but further work using such data would be valuable. Theoretically, stability in sleep pattern would be displayed by small raw score standard deviations, and plasticity would be demonstrated by regression from higher values (e.g., at times of acute insomnia) to lower values. The time taken to accommodate and adjust from above to below some threshold value might be a useful measure of plasticity.

The "setting conditions" for insomnia are potentially wide-ranging, and further study employing experimental manipulation of situational, autonomic, mental, and affective variables would be valuable. The model would predict that only manipulations with a cognitive/affective activating component would lead to subjective sleep concern, which can vary independently of sleep disruption. The concept of inhibitory sufficiency requires investigation, and methods need to be developed to titrate experimental "doses" so that outcomes can be related to inputs. For example, if an experiment was conducted on the countercontrol procedure, it would be helpful to use standard stimuli (e.g., text to read, TV program to watch) validated for emotional valence, intrusiveness, imagery potential, etc. It should be borne in mind, of course, that disturbance of a single night is not insomnia, but only a bad night. Care must be taken, therefore, also to consider inhibitory sufficiency from the clinical perspective of generalized and enduring sleep disturbance where, presumably, retrospective experience influences response to prospective experimental factors.

The proposed model suggests that maintained arousal is the necessary and sufficient precondition for insomnia. Clearly, this hypothesis requires validation, and a between-group repeated-measures model utilizing daytime, pre-bedtime, presleep, and early-sleep measures of physiological and cognitive arousal in insomniacs and good sleepers would seem appropriate. This would also identify cases of hyper-arousal, proposed as a subpopulation of insomnia. In terms of intervention, the model suggests that cognitive behavioral strategies may act via the common pathway of disengaging mechanisms inhibitory to de-arousal, and facilitating reestablishment of automated normal sleep. Given the proposed importance of cognitive/affective de-activation, it would be particularly useful to investigate stimulus control and sleep restriction as de-activating in this context e.g., attitudinal shift, relinquishing control, precluding worry from bed. Their contribution to circadian timing and homeostatic drive, along with such de-activation, may explain the positive clinical outcomes achieved using these procedures. Specific cognitive interventions need to be explored in terms of direct versus indirect action upon sleep-related variables. Automaticity would predict that indirect (e.g., paradoxical) methods would be more efficacious than those that focus attention and intervention directly upon sleep or upon sleep-related thoughts.

CONCLUSION

Although there are a number of perspectives on the etiology and maintenance of insomnia, each of which has some empirical support, the conceptual basis lags some way behind treatment methodology and the evaluation of efficacy and effectiveness. An integrated psychobiological model has been proposed that differentiates insomnia from normal sleep in terms of inhibitory mechanisms and processes. It is hoped that the hypotheses raised here will stimulate interest in further experimental and clinical study, and that the resultant research process will improve both understanding and management of this common condition.

ACKNOWLEDGMENTS

The author was supported by research grants from Chief Scientist Office, Scottish Executive Health Department: Novel Health Research Initiative and CZH/4/2. Thanks to Dr. Charles M. Morin, Université Laval, Québec City; Dr. Daniel J. Buysse, Western Psychiatric Institute and Clinics, Pittsburgh, PA; and Dr. Allison G. Harvey, University of Oxford, UK for their helpful comments on an earlier version of this manuscript.

Visit the Annual Reviews home page at www.AnnualReviews.org

LITERATURE CITED

Adam K, Tomeny M, Oswald I. 1986. Physiological and psychological differences between good and poor sleepers. *J. Psychiatr. Res.* 20:301–16

Am. Psychiatr. Assoc. 1994. *Diagnostic and Statistical Manual of Mental Disorders (DSM–IV)*. Washington, DC: APA. 4th ed.

Am. Sleep Disorders Assoc. 1995a. Practice parameters for the use of polysomnography in the evaluation of insomnia. *Sleep* 18:55–57

Am. Sleep Disorders Assoc. 1995b. Practice parameters for the use of actigraphy in the clinical assessment of sleep disorders. *Sleep* 18:285–87

Am. Sleep Disorders Assoc. 1997. *International Classification of Sleep Disorders: Diagnostic and Coding Manual*. Rochester, MA: ASDA. Revised ed.

Ansfield ME, Wegner DM, Bowser R. 1996. Ironic effects of sleep urgency. *Behav. Res. Ther.* 34:523–31

Ascher LM. 1981. Employing paradoxical intention in the treatment of agoraphobia. *Behav. Res. Ther.* 19:533–42

Ascher LM, Turner RM. 1979. Paradoxical intention and insomnia: an experimental investigation. *Behav. Res. Ther.* 17:408–11

Ascher LM, Turner RM. 1980. A comparison of two methods for the administration of paradoxical intention. *Behav. Res. Ther.* 18:121–26

Aschoff J. 1951. Die 24 stunden Periodik der Maus unter konstanten umge-bungs bedingungen. ("The 24-hour period of the mouse under constant environmental conditions.") *Naturwissenschaften* 38:506–7

Baharav A, Kotagal S, Gibbons V, Rubin BK, Pratt G, et al. 1995. Fluctuations in autonomic nervous activity during sleep displayed by power spectrum analysis of heart rate variability. *Neurology* 45:1183–87

Barlow DH. 1988. *Anxiety and its Disorders*. New York: Guilford

Bixler EO, Kales A, Soldatos CR, Kales JD,

Healy B. 1979. Prevalence of sleep disorders in the Los Angeles metropolitan area. *Am. J. Psychiatry* 136:1257–62

Bliwise DL. 1993. Sleep in normal aging and dementia. *Sleep* 16:40–81

Bonnet MH, Arand DL. 1992. Caffeine use as a model of acute and chronic insomnia. *Sleep* 15:526–36

Bonnet MH, Arand DL. 1995. 24 hour metabolic rate in insomniacs and matched normal sleepers. *Sleep* 18:581–88

Bonnet MH, Arand DL. 1997a. Heart rate variability: sleep stage, time of night, and arousal influences. *Electroencephalogr. Clin. Neurophysiol.* 102:390–96

Bonnet MH, Arand DL. 1997b. Physiological activation in patients with sleep state misperception. *Psychosom. Med.* 59:533–40

Bootzin RR. 1972. A stimulus control treatment for insomnia. *Proc. Am. Psychol. Assoc.*, pp. 395–96

Bootzin RR, Epstein DR. 2000. Stimulus control. See Lichstein & Morin 2000, pp. 167–84

Bootzin RR, Epstein D, Wood JM. 1991. Stimulus control instructions. See Hauri 1991, pp. 19–28

Bootzin RR, Lack L, Wright H. 1999. Efficacy of bright light and stimulus control instructions for sleep onset insomnia. *Sleep* 22(Suppl. 1):53–54

Bootzin RR, Rider SP. 1997. Behavioural techniques and biofeedback for insomnia. See Pressman & Orr 1997, pp. 315–28

Borbely AA. 1994. Sleep homeostasis and models of sleep regulation. In *Principles and Practice of Sleep Medicine*, ed. MH Kryger, T Roth, WC Dement, pp. 309–20. Philadelphia, PA: Saunders. 1067 pp. 2nd ed.

Borkovec TD. 1982. Insomnia. *J. Consult. Clin. Psychol.* 50:880–95

Borkovec TD, Grayson JB, O'Brien GT, Weerts TC. 1979. Relaxation treatment of pseudoinsomnia and idiopathic insomnia; an electroencephalographic evaluation. *J. Appl. Behav. Anal.* 12:37–54

Borkovec TD, Lane TW, Van Oot PA. 1981. Phenomenology of sleep among insomniacs and good sleepers: wakefulness experience

when cortically asleep. *J. Abnorm. Psychol.* 90:607–9

Borkovec TD, Sides JK. 1979. Critical procedural variables related to the physiological effects of progressive relaxation: a review. *Behav. Res. Ther.* 17:119–25

Borkovec TD, Weerts TC. 1976. Effects of progressive relaxation on sleep disturbance: an electroencephalographic evaluation. *Psychosom. Med.* 38:173–80

Born J, Hansen K, Marshall L, Molle M, Fehm HL. 1999. Timing the end of nocturnal sleep. *Nature* 397:29–30

Breslau N, Roth T, Rosenthal L, Andreski P. 1996. Sleep disturbance and psychiatric disorders: a longitudinal epidemiological study of young adults. *Biol. Psychiatry* 39:411–18

Broman JE, Hetta J. 1994. Perceived pre-sleep arousal in patients with persistent psychophysiologic and psychiatric insomnia. *Nord. J. Psychiatry* 48:203–7

Browman C, Tepas D. 1976. The effects of pre-sleep activity on all-night sleep. *Psychophysiology* 13:536–40

Buysse DJ. 2000. Rational pharmacotherapy for insomnia: time for a new paradigm. *Sleep Med. Rev.* 4:521–27

Buysse DJ, Monk TH, Reynolds CF, Mesiano D, Houck PR, et al. 1993. Patterns of sleep episodes in young and elderly adults during a 36-hour constant routine. *Sleep* 16:632–37

Buysse DJ, Reynolds CF, Monk TH, Berman SR, Kupfer DJ. 1989. The Pittsburgh Sleep Quality Index: a new instrument for psychiatric practice and research. *Psychiatry Res.* 28:193–213

Campbell SS, Dawson D, Anderson MW. 1993. Alleviation of sleep maintenance insomnia with timed exposure to bright light. *J. Am. Geriatr. Soc.* 41:829–36

Carskadon MA, Brown ED, Dement WC. 1982. Sleep fragmentation in the elderly: relationship to daytime sleep tendency. *Neurobiol. Aging* 3:321–27

Carskadon MA, Dement WC. 1981. Cumulative effects of sleep restriction on daytime sleepiness. *Psychophysiology* 18:107–13

Chambers MJ, Keller B. 1993. Alert insomniacs: Are they really sleep deprived? *Clin. Psychol. Rev.* 13:649–66

Chang PP, Ford DE, Mead LA, Patrick-Cooper L, Klag MJ. 1997. Insomnia in young men and subsequent depression. The Johns Hopkins Precursors Study. *Am. J. Epidemiol.* 146:105–14

Chesson AL, Anderson WM, Littner M, Davila D, Hartse K, et al. 1999. Practice parameters for the nonpharmacologic treatment of chronic insomnia. *Sleep* 22:1128–33

Chesson AL, Hartse K, Anderson WM, Davila D, Johnson S, et al. 2000. Practice parameters for the evaluation of chronic insomnia. *Sleep* 23:237–41

Clark DA, Purdon CL. 1993. New perspectives for a cognitive theory of obsessions. *Aust. Psychol.* 28:161–67

Clark DA, Purdon CL. 1995. The assessment of unwanted intrusive thoughts: a review and critique of the literature. *Behav. Res. Ther.* 33:967–76

Coates TJ, Killen JD, George J, Marchini E, Silverman S, et al. 1982. Estimating sleep parameters: a multitrait-multimethod analysis. *J. Consult. Clin. Psychol.* 50:345–52

Coyle K, Watts FN. 1991. The factorial structure of sleep dissatisfaction. *Behav. Res. Ther.* 29:513–20

Davies R, Lacks P, Storandt M, Bertelson AD. 1986. Countercontrol treatment of sleep-maintenance insomnia in relation to age. *Psychol. Aging* 1:233–38

Dement W. 1960. The effect of dream deprivation. *Science* 131:1705–7

Douglas NJ, Thomas S, Tan MA. 1992. The clinical value of polysomnography. *Lancet* 339:347–50

Eaton WW, Badawi MD, Melton B. 1995. Prodromes and precursors: epidemiologic data for primary prevention of disorders with slow onset. *Am. J. Psychiatry* 152:967–72

Edgar DM. 1996. Circadian control of sleep/wakefulness: implications in shiftwork and therapeutic strategies. In *Physiological Basis of Occupational Health: Stressful Environ-*

ments, ed. K Shiraki, S Sagawa, MK Yousef, pp. 253–65. Amsterdam: Academic

Edinger JD, Glenn DM, Bastian LA, Fins AI. 1998. The roles of dysfunctional cognitions and other person factors in mediating insomnia complaints. *Sleep* 21(Suppl.):144

Edinger JD, Stout AL, Hoelscher TJ. 1988. Cluster analysis of insomniacs' MMPI profiles: relation of subtypes to sleep history and treatment outcome. *Psychosom. Med.* 50:77–87

Edinger JD, Sullivan RJ, Bastian LA, Hope TV, Young M, et al. 2000. Insomnia and the eye of the beholder: Are there clinical markers of objective sleep disturbances among adults with and without insomnia complaints? *J. Consult. Clin. Psychol.* 68:586–93

Edinger JD, Wohlgemuth W. 1999. The significance and management of persistent primary insomnia: the past, present and future of behavioral insomnia therapies. *Sleep Med. Rev.* 3:101–18

Edinger JD, et al. 2002. AASM:RDC paper. In preparation

Espie CA. 1991. *The Psychological Treatment of Insomnia.* Chichester, UK: Wiley. 260 pp.

Espie CA. 1992. *Getting ready for bed: cognitive tasks and outcomes which promote good sleep.* Presented at World Congr. Cogn. Ther., Toronto

Espie CA. 1999. Cognitive behaviour therapy as the treatment of choice for primary insomnia. *Sleep Med. Rev.* 3:97–99

Espie CA. 2000. Assessment and differential diagnosis of insomnia. See Lichstein & Morin 2000, pp. 81–108

Espie CA, Brindle SJ, Tessier S, Dawson S, Hepburn T, et al. 1998. Supervised cognitive-behavior therapy for insomnia in general medical practice—preliminary results from the West of Scotland program. In *Behavior and Cognitive Therapy Today: Essays in Honour of Hans J. Eysenck,* ed. E Sanavio, pp. 67–75. Amsterdam: Elsevier. 339 pp.

Espie CA, Brooks DN, Lindsay WR. 1989a. An evaluation of tailored psychological treatment for insomnia in terms of statistical and clinical measures of outcome. *J. Behav. Ther. Exp. Psychiatry* 20:143–53

Espie CA, Inglis SJ, Harvey L. 2001a. Predicting clinically significant response to cognitive behavior therapy (CBT) for chronic insomnia in general practice: analyses of outcome data at 12 months post-treatment. *J. Consult. Clin. Psychol.* 69:58–66

Espie CA, Inglis SJ, Harvey L, Tessier S. 2000. Insomniacs' attributions: psychometric properties of the Dysfunctional Beliefs and Attitudes about Sleep Scale and the Sleep Disturbance Questionnaire. *J. Psychosom. Res.* 48:141–48

Espie CA, Inglis SJ, Tessier S, Harvey L. 2001b. The clinical effectiveness of cognitive behaviour therapy for chronic insomnia: implementation and evaluation of a sleep clinic in general medical practice. *Behav. Res. Ther.* 39:45–60

Espie CA, Lindsay WR. 1985. Paradoxical intention in the treatment of chronic insomnia: six cases illustrating variability in therapeutic response. *Behav. Res. Ther.* 23:703–9

Espie CA, Lindsay WR, Brooks DN, Hood EH, Turvey T. 1989b. A controlled comparative investigation of psychological treatments for chronic insomnia. *Behav. Res. Ther.* 27:51–56

Espie CA, Wicklow A. 2001c. Cognitive therapy for insomnia. In *Sleep and Psychiatry*, ed. C Shapiro, EP Sloan. Cambridge: Cambridge Univ. Press. In press

Evans FJ. 1977. Subjective characteristics of sleep efficiency. *J. Abnorm. Psychol.* 86:561–64

Fichten CS, Libman E, Creit L, Amsel R, Tagalakis V, et al. 1998. Thoughts during awake times in older good and poor sleepers—the self-statement test: 60+. *Cogn. Res. Ther.* 22:1–20

Fogle DO, Dyal JA. 1983. Paradoxical giving up and the reduction of sleep performance anxiety in chronic insomniacs. *Psychoth.: Theory, Res. Practice* 20:21–30

Foley DJ, Monjan AA, Brown SL, Simonsick EM, Wallace RB, et al. 1995. Sleep complaints among elderly persons: an epidemiologic study of three communities. *Sleep* 18:425–33

Ford DE, Kamerow DB. 1989. Epidemiologic study of sleep disturbances and psychiatric disorders. *JAMA* 262:1479–84

Frankel BL, Buchbinder R, Coursey RD, Snyder F. 1973. Sleep patterns and psychological test characteristics of chronic primary insomniacs. *Sleep Res.* 2:149

Frankel BL, Buchbinder R, Coursey RD, Snyder F. 1976. Recorded and reported sleep in primary chronic insomnia. *Arch. Gen. Psychiatry* 33:615–23

Frankl VE. 1960. Paradoxical intention: a logotherapeutic technique. *Am. J. Psychoth.* 14:520–35

Freedman R. 1987. Chronic insomniacs: replication of Monroe's findings. *Psychophysiology* 24:721–22

Freedman R, Papsdorf J. 1976. Biofeedback and progressive relaxation treatment of sleep-onset insomnia: a controlled all-night investigation. *Biofeedback Self-Regul.* 1:253–71

Freedman R, Sattler HI. 1982. Physiological and psychological factors in sleep-onset insomnia. *J. Abnorm. Psychol.* 91:380–89

Gallup Org. 1991. *Sleep in America*. Princeton, NJ: Gallup

Gendron L, Blais FC, Morin CM. 1998. Cognitive activity among insomniac patients. *Sleep* 21:130

Gillin JC, Byerley WF. 1990. The diagnosis and management of insomnia. *N. Engl. J. Med.* 322:239–48

Good R. 1975. Frontalis muscle tension and sleep latency. *Psychophysiology* 12:465–67

Gross RT, Borkovec TD. 1982. Effects of a cognitive intrusion manipulation on the sleep-onset latency of good sleepers. *Behav. Ther.* 13:117–24

Hall M, Buysse DJ, Reynolds CF, Kupfer DJ, Baum A. 1996. Stress related intrusive thoughts disrupt sleep onset and continuity. *Sleep Res.* 25:163

Harvey AG. 2000a. Sleep hygiene and sleep-onset insomnia. *J. Nerv. Mental Dis.* 188:53–55

Harvey AG. 2000b. Pre-sleep cognitive activity in insomnia: a comparison of sleep-onset insomniacs and good sleepers. *Br. J. Clin. Psychol.* 39:275–06

Harvey AG. 2001a. Insomnia: symptom or diagnosis. *Clin. Psychol. Rev.* In press

Harvey AG. 2001b. Attempted suppression of pre-sleep cognitive activity in insomnia. *Cogn. Res. Ther.* In press

Hauri P, ed. 1991. *Case Studies in Insomnia.* New York: Plenum

Haynes SN, Adams AE, Franzen M. 1981. The effects of presleep stress on sleep-onset insomnia. *J. Abnorm. Psychol.* 90:601–6

Haynes SN, Adams AE, West S, Kamens L, Safranek R. 1982. The stimulus control paradigm in sleep-onset insomnia: a multimethod assessment. *J. Psychosom. Res.* 26: 333–39

Haynes SN, Follingstad DR, McGowan WT. 1974. Insomnia: sleep patterns and anxiety levels. *J. Psychosom. Res.* 18:69–74

Healey ES, Kales A, Monroe LJ, Bixler EO, Chamberlin K, et al. 1981. Onset of insomnia: role of life-stress events. *Psychosom. Med.* 43:439–51

Hoch CC, Dew MA, Reynolds CF, Buysse DJ, Nowell PD, et al. 1997. Longitudinal changes in diary- and laboratory-based sleep measures in healthy "old old" and "young old" subjects: a three-year follow-up. *Sleep* 20:192–202

Horne J. 1988. *Why We Sleep.* Oxford: Oxford Univ. Press. 319 pp.

Johns MW, Gay MP, Masterton JP, Bruce DW. 1971. Relationship between sleep habits, adrenocortical activity and personality. *Psychosom. Med.* 3:499–508

Kales A, Bixler EO, Vela-Bueno A, Cadieux RJ, Soldatos CR, et al. 1984. Biopsychobehavioural correlates of insomnia. III. Polygraphic findings of sleep difficulty and their relationship to psychopathology. *Intern. J. Neurosci.* 23:43–56

Kales A, Vgontzas AN. 1992. Predisposition to and development and persistence of chronic insomnia: importance of psychobehavioural factors. *Arch. Intern. Med.* 152:1570–72

Kramer M. 2000. Hypnotic medication in the treatment of chronic insomnia: non nocere! Doesn't anyone care? *Sleep Med. Rev* 4:529–41

Kripke D. 2000. Hypnotic drugs: deadly risks, doubtful benefits. *Sleep Med. Rev.* 4:5–20

Kuisk KA, Bertelson AD, Walsh JK. 1989. Presleep cognitive hyperarousal and affect as factors in objective and subjective insomnia. *Percept. Mot. Skills* 69:1219–25

Lack L, Wright H. 1993. The effect of evening bright light in delaying the circadian rhythms and lengthening the sleep of early morning awakening insomniacs. *Sleep* 16:436–43

Lack L, Wright H, Paynter D. 1995. The treatment of sleep onset insomnia with morning bright light. *Sleep Res.* 24A:338

Lacks P. 1987. *Behavioral Treatment for Persistent Insomnia.* New York: Pergamon. 164 pp.

Leger D, Levy E, Paillard M. 1999. The direct economic costs of insomnia in France. *Sleep* 22(Suppl. 2):394–401

Lichstein KL. 2000. Secondary insomnia. See Lichstein & Morin 2000, pp. 297–320

Lichstein KL, Morin CM. 2000. *Treatment of Late Life Insomnia.* Thousand Oaks, CA: Sage. 354 pp.

Lichstein KL, Rosenthal TL. 1980. Insomniacs' perceptions of cognitive versus somatic determinants of sleep disturbance. *J. Abnorm. Psychol.* 89:105–7

Lichstein KL, Wilson NM, Noe SL, Aguillard RN, Bellur SN. 1994. Daytime sleepiness in insomnia: behavioral, biological and subjective indices. *Sleep* 17:693–702

Loewy DH, Bootzin RR. 1998. Event-related potential measures of information processing in insomniacs at bedtime and during sleep. *Sleep* 21(Suppl.):98

Lundh LG, Broman JE, Hetta J. 1995. Personality traits in patients with persistent insomnia. *Pers. Individ. Differ.* 18:393–403

Mellinger GD, Balter MB, Uhlenhuth EH. 1985. Insomnia and its treatment: prevalence and correlates. *Arch. Gen. Psychiatry* 42:225–32

Mendelson WB. 1995. Long-term follow-up of chronic insomnia. *Sleep* 18:698–701

Mendelson WB, Garnett D, Linnoila M. 1984. Do insomniacs have impaired daytime functioning? *Biol. Psychiatry* 19:1261–64

Merica H, Blois R, Gaillard JM. 1998. Spectral characteristics of sleep EEG in chronic insomnia. *Eur. J. Neurosci.* 10:1826–34

Meyer TJ, Miller ML, Metzger RL, Borkovec TD. 1990. Development and validation of the Penn State Worry Questionnaire. *Behav. Res. Ther.* 28:487–95

Monk TH, Reynolds CF, Machen MA, Kupfer DJ. 1992. Daily social rhythms in the elderly and their relationship to objectively recorded sleep. *Sleep* 15:322–29

Moore-Ede MC, Sulzman FM, Fuller CF. 1982. *The Clocks that Time Us.* Cambridge, MA: Harvard Univ. Press

Morgan K. 2000. Sleep and aging. See Lichstein & Morin 2000, pp. 3–36

Morgan K, Clarke D. 1997. Risk factors for late-life insomnia in a representative general practice sample. *Br. J. Gen. Pract.* 47:166–69

Morin CM. 1993. *Insomnia: Psychological Assessment and Management.* New York: Guilford. 238 pp.

Morin CM, Blais F, Savard J. 2001. Are changes in beliefs and attitudes about sleep related to sleep improvements in the treatment of insomnia? *Behav. Res. Ther.* In press

Morin CM, Colecchi C, Stone J, Sood R, Brink D. 1999a. Behavioral and pharmacological therapies for late-life insomnia: a randomised controlled trial. *JAMA* 281:991–99

Morin CM, Culbert JP, Schwartz MS. 1994. Non-pharmacological interventions for insomnia: a meta-analysis of treatment efficacy. *Am. J. Psychiatry* 151:1172–80

Morin CM, Hauri PJ, Espie CA, Spielman A, Buysse DJ, et al. 1999b. Nonpharmacologic treatment of insomnia: an American Academy of Sleep Medicine Review. *Sleep* 22:1134–56

Morin CM, Mimeault V, Gagne A. 1999c. Non-pharmacological treatment of late-life insomnia. *J. Psychosom. Res.* 46:103–16

Morin CM, Stone J, Trinkle D, Mercer J,

Remsberg S. 1993. Dysfunctional beliefs and attitudes about sleep among older adults with and without insomnia complaints. *Psychol. Aging* 8:463–67

Morris M, Lack L, Dawson D. 1990. Sleep-onset insomniacs have delayed temperature rhythms. *Sleep* 13:1–14

Murtagh DR, Greenwood KM. 1995. Identifying effective psychological treatments for insomnia: a meta-analysis. *J. Consult. Clin. Psychol.* 63:79–89

Nicassio PM, Mendlowitz DR, Fussell JJ, Petras L. 1985. The phenomenology of the pre-sleep state: the development of the pre-sleep arousal scale. *Behav. Res. Ther.* 23:263–71

Ohayon MM, Caulet M, Guilleminault C. 1997. How a general population perceives its sleep and how this relates to the complaint of insomnia. *Sleep* 20:715–23

Perlis ML, Giles DE, Mendelson WB, Bootzin RR, Wyatt JK. 1997. Psychophysiological insomnia: the behavioural model and a neurocognitive perspective. *J. Sleep Res.* 6:179–88

Pressman MR, Orr WC. 1997. *Understanding Sleep. The Evaluation and Treatment of Sleep Disorders.* Washington, DC: Am. Psychol. Assoc. 566 pp.

Rachman S, De Silva P. 1978. Abnormal and normal obsessions. *Behav. Res. Ther.* 16: 233–48

Reite M, Buysse D, Reynolds C, Mendelson W. 1995. The use of polysomnography in the evaluation of insomnia. *Sleep* 18:58–70

Reynolds M, Salkovskis PM. 1992. Comparison of positive and negative intrusive thoughts and experimental investigation of the differential effects of mood. *Behav. Res. Ther.* 30:273–81

Rodin J, McAvay G, Timko C. 1988. A longitudinal study of depressed mood and sleep disturbances in elderly adults. *J. Gerontol.* 43:45–53

Roth T, Kramer M, Lutz T. 1976. The nature of insomnia: a descriptive summary of a sleep clinic population. *Compr. Psychiatry* 17:217–20

Sadeh A, Hauri PJ, Kripke DF, Lavie P. 1995.

The role of actigraphy in the evaluation of sleep disorders. *Sleep* 18:288–302

Sanavio E. 1988. Pre-sleep cognitive intrusions and treatment of onset-insomnia, *Behav. Res. Ther.* 26.431–39

Satlin A, Volicer L, Ross V, Herz L, Campbell S. 1992. Bright light treatment of behavioral and sleep disturbances in patients with Alzheimer's disease. *Am. J. Psychiatry* 149:1028–32

Schramm E, Hohagen F, Kappler C, Grasshoff E, Berger M. 1995. Mental comorbidity of chronic insomnia in general practice attenders using DSM-III-R. *Acta Psychiatr. Scand.* 91:10–17

Seidel WF, Ball S, Cohen S, Patterson N, Yost D, et al. 1984. Daytime alertness in relation to mood, performance, and nocturnal sleep in chronic insomniacs and noncomplaining sleepers. *Sleep* 7:230–38

Shiffrin RM, Schneider W. 1977. Controlled and automatic human information processing. II. Perceptual learning, automatic attending, and a general theory. *Psychol. Rev.* 84:127–90

Shocat T, Umphress J, Israel AG, Ancoli-Israel S. 1999. Insomnia in primary care patients. *Sleep* 22(Suppl. 2):S359–65

Shoham V, Bootzin RR, Rohrbaugh M, Urry H. 1995. Paradoxical versus relaxation treatment for insomnia: the moderating role of reactance. *Sleep Res.* 24A:365

Spielman AJ, Anderson MW. 1999. The clinical interview and treatment planning as a guide to understanding the nature of insomnia: the CCNY Interview for Insomnia. In *Sleep Disorders Medicine: Basic Science, Technical Considerations and Clinical Aspects*, ed. S Chokroverty, pp. 385–426. Boston: Butterworth-Heinemann. 2nd ed.

Spielman AJ, Glovinsky PB. 1991. The varied nature of insomnia. See Hauri 1991, pp. 1–15

Spielman AJ, Saskin P, Thorpy MJ. 1987. Treatment of chronic insomnia by restriction of time in bed. *Sleep* 10:45–56

Stepanski EJ, Glinn M, Fortier J, Sicklesteel J, Zorick FJ, et al. 1989. Physiological re-

activity in chronic insomnia. *Sleep Res.* 18: 306

Tokarz T, Lawrence P. 1974. *An analysis of temporal and stimulus control factors in the treatment of insomnia*. Presented at Assoc. Adv. Behav. Ther., Chicago

Turner RM, Ascher LM. 1979. A controlled comparison of progressive relaxation, stimulus control and paradoxical intention therapies for insomnia. *J. Consult. Clin. Psychol.* 47:500–8

Van Egeren L, Haynes SN, Franzen M, Hamilton J. 1983. Presleep cognitions and attributions in sleep-onset insomnia. *J. Behav. Med.* 6:217–32

Walsh JK, Engelhardt CL. 1999. The direct economic costs of insomnia in the US for 1995. *Sleep* 22(Suppl. 2):386–93

Watts FN, Coyle K, East MP. 1994. The contribution of worry to insomnia. *Br. J. Clin. Psychol.* 33:211–20

Watts FN, East MP, Coyle K. 1995. Insomniacs' perceived lack of control over sleep. *Psychol. Health* 10:81–95

Webb WB. 1981. Sleep stage responses of older and younger subjects after sleep deprivation. *Electroencephalogr. Clin. Neurophysiol.* 52:368–71

Wegner DM. 1994. Ironic processes of mental control. *Psychol. Rev.* 101:34–52

Weissman MM, Greenwald MA, Nino-Murica G, Dement WC. 1997. The morbidity of insomnia uncomplicated by psychiatric disorders. *Gen. Hosp. Psychiatry* 19:245–50

Wicklow A, Espie CA. 2000. Intrusive thoughts and their relationship to actigraphic measurement of sleep: towards a cognitive model of insomnia. *Behav. Res. Ther.* 38:679–93

Wohlegemuth WK, Edinger JD. 2000. Sleep restriction therapy. See Lichstein & Morin 2000, pp. 147–66

Wolpe J. 1958. *Psychotherapy by Reciprocal Inhibition*. Stanford, CA: Stanford Univ. Press

Zwart CA, Lisman SA. 1979. Analysis of stimulus control treatment of sleep-onset insomnia. *J. Consult. Clin. Psychol.* 47:113–19

Annu. Rev. Psychol. 2002. 53:245–77

CHANGE DETECTION

Ronald A. Rensink

Departments of Psychology and Computer Science, University of British Columbia, Vancouver, British Columbia, V6T 1Z4 Canada; e-mail: rensink@psych.ubc.ca

Key Words   change blindness, visual attention, scene perception, eye movements, visual memory

■ **Abstract**   Five aspects of visual change detection are reviewed. The first concerns the concept of *change* itself, in particular the ways it differs from the related notions of *motion* and *difference*. The second involves the various methodological approaches that have been developed to study change detection; it is shown that under a variety of conditions observers are often unable to see large changes directly in their field of view. Next, it is argued that this "change blindness" indicates that focused attention is needed to detect change, and that this can help map out the nature of visual attention. The fourth aspect concerns how these results affect our understanding of visual perception—for example, the implication that a sparse, dynamic representation underlies much of our visual experience. Finally, a brief discussion is presented concerning the limits to our current understanding of change detection.

CONTENTS

0084-6570/02/0201-0245$14.00

INTRODUCTION

Change detection is the apprehension of change in the world around us. The ability to detect change is important in much of our everyday life—for example, noticing a person entering the room, coping with traffic, or watching a kitten as it runs under a table. However, in spite of the pervasiveness of change detection in our lives, it has proven surprisingly difficult to study. Only recently have various approaches begun to converge in terms of what it is and how it is carried out.

As used here, the term change detection pertains primarily to the visual processes involved in first noticing a change. It denotes not only detection proper (i.e., the observer reporting on the existence of the change), but also identification (reporting what the change is) and localization (reporting where it is). The perception of dynamic patterns per se (e.g., the perception of movement) is not discussed in detail here, since this involves a formidable set of issues in its own right (see e.g., Jacobs et al. 1988). Likewise, the focus is on behavioral measures and their interpretation rather than investigations into underlying neural systems.

Restricted in this way, change detection might appear to be a fairly straightforward process. However, empirical studies have repeatedly proven otherwise. For example, we as observers tend to believe we could immediately detect any change in front of us if it were sufficiently large (Levin et al. 2000). However, this is not so: Under a wide variety of conditions we can be amazingly blind to changes, failing to see them even when they are large, repeatedly made, and anticipated (for reviews, see Rensink 2000a, Simons & Levin 1997). This "change blindness" (Rensink et al. 1997) is a striking phenomenon, one that has often served as the flip side of change detection: Just as our ability to detect change has cast light on some perceptual mechanisms, so has our inability to detect it cast light on others.

The study of change detection can be loosely divided into three phases. The first, occurring roughly between the mid-1950s and mid-1960s, included the work of French (1953) on changes in position in dot arrays and Hochberg (1968) on changes to faces; here, change usually occurred during a temporal gap of several seconds. Meanwhile, studies such as Ditchburn's (1955) and Wallach & Lewis's (1966) investigated displacements made during an eye movement (or *saccade*). All studies showed observers to be surprisingly poor at detecting changes made contingent on a temporal gap or a saccade. However, no attempt was made to incorporate the entire set of findings into a systematic framework.[1]

The second phase took place during the 1970s, with some work continuing into the 1980s. Examples here include Pollack (1972), Phillips & Singer (1974), and Pashler (1988), who systematically investigated the limits of the detection of gap-contingent changes in arrays of simple figures. This work—along with that on visual integration—formed the basis for the proposal of a limited-capacity visual short-term memory (vSTM). Concurrent with these developments, studies such as those by Mack (1970), Bridgeman et al. (1975), and McConkie & Zola (1979) showed that observers were poor at detecting saccade-contingent change under a variety of conditions. Although a considerable body of knowledge about this phenomenon was eventually gathered (see e.g., Bridgeman et al. 1994), no integration with the work on gap-contingent changes was achieved.

The third phase began in the early 1990s and has continued to the present. Examples are Simons (1996), Rensink et al. (1997), and Henderson & Hollingworth (1999a). Work here can be distinguished from previous approaches in at least one of three ways: (*a*) Stimuli are more realistic—e.g., images of real-world scenes or dynamic events; (*b*) repeated rather than single changes are used, allowing the use of time as a measure of performance; and (*c*) an emphasis on integrating results obtained via different kinds of manipulations—e.g., the identification of transsaccadic memory with vSTM (Irwin 1991), which connected saccade-contingent and gap-contingent change blindness. These studies emphasize the idea that change detection is not a marginal process, but involves mechanisms central to the way we perceive our world.

DISTINCTIONS AND DEFINITIONS

As with many ideas in psychology, the concept of change initially appears unproblematic, but upon closer examination contains subtleties that may cause great confusion unless carefully handled. Indeed, the concept of change has had a particularly long and tortuous history, extending back at least to the time of the pre-Socratic philosophers, when it formed the basis for a host of problems. Some

---

[1]The work on saccade-contingent change was intended to address the question of how visual experience could remain stable in the face of constant eye movements. These and later studies did help develop a framework for this problem (see e.g., Bridgeman et al. 1994). However, there does not appear to have been a serious attempt to relate the work on saccade-contingent change to the work on gap-contingent change, or to the issue of visual memory in general.

of these problems—such as the paradoxes of Zeno of Elea—were highly intricate, taking centuries to resolve[2] (see e.g., Kirk & Raven 1957); indeed, several persist to this day.

Consequently, this section focuses on some of the basic issues pertaining to the concept of change. In particular, it attempts to clarify the distinctions (and relations) between change, motion, and difference. These distinctions are examined from the perspectives of both physical description and perceptual mechanism.

Change vs. Motion

The word *change* generally refers to a transformation or modification of something over time. As such, this notion presumes a nonchanging substrate on which changes are imposed. More precisely, change is defined here as the transformation over time of a well-defined, enduring structure. The complexity of the structure does not matter—it can range from an undifferentiated particle to a highly articulated object. All that is required is that the structure continues to exist over the course of its transformation. Although such continuity can be defined in a variety of ways, the most appropriate appears to be spatiotemporal continuity (see e.g., Smith 1998).

Stated this way, an important distinction can be drawn between change and *motion*. Motion is often taken to refer to change of position over time. However, consider a situation such as a flowing stream. Here, the critical property is the velocity at each point in space; the complete array of these velocities forms a motion field. Referencing temporal variation to space in this way allows motion to be treated much like color or brightness, so that constructs such as borders can be defined on the basis of the motion pattern. More generally, motion can refer to the temporal variation at a point in space of any measurable quantity (see e.g., Adelson & Bergen 1991).

Thus, motion is most usefully defined as variation referenced to location, whereas change is referenced to structure.[3] This distinction has important consequences for the perceptual processes involved. For example, motion can generally

---

[2]Perhaps the most famous of these is the paradox of Achilles and the tortoise, which involves change in position (i.e., movement). A tortoise is given a head start in a race with Achilles. It is then argued that Achilles can never overtake the tortoise, for by the time he arrives at the previous location of the tortoise, the tortoise will have moved yet further ahead. Based on apparent paradoxes such as this, some early thinkers (e.g., Parmenides of Elea) argued that change was impossible, and that the perception of change was therefore illusory (see e.g., Kirk & Raven 1957).

[3]This distinction can always be maintained, even when the variations are smooth and pertain to position. For the simple case of smoothly moving particles, for example, there exist two distinct ways of describing the situation (Batchelor 1967, pp. 71–73). The first is an Eulerian specification, in which derivatives are defined with respect to a fixed point in space. The second is a Lagrangian specification, in which derivatives are defined with respect to the path of a particular (arbitrarily small) element. The two forms are generally different, and describe different quantities: motion and (position) change, respectively.

be described in terms of local derivatives—no other structure is needed.[4] Motion detectors can therefore be located at the initial stages of visual processing, where spatial representations have minimal complexity (see e.g., Hildreth & Koch 1987, Nakayama 1985). In contrast, change is referenced to a particular structure that must maintain spatiotemporal continuity, and so more sophisticated processes are needed.

In this view, then, the transformation of any external entity is picked up by two concurrent perceptual systems: one describing motion (variation referenced to location), and the other change (variation referenced to a structure).[5] Although the outputs of these systems are often correlated, they can sometimes be decoupled, e.g., by their differential response to different stimuli (Seiffert & Cavanagh 1998), or by using transformations that occur beyond the temporal window of most motion detectors, a window of approximately 50–80 ms (e.g., Woodhouse & Barlow 1982, van der Grind et al. 1986).

Dynamic vs. Completed Change

Another important distinction is that between the detection of *dynamic* change (i.e., seeing a change in progress) and the detection of *completed* change (i.e., seeing that something has changed). Loosely speaking, this distinction reflects the difference between present progressive and past perfect tense.

More precisely, the detection of dynamic change refers to the perception of the transformation itself: The change is perceived as a dynamic visual event. This suggests that the spatiotemporal continuity of the external entity may be reflected in the spatiotemporal continuity of the internal representation. Note that the entity need not be continually present, however. Mechanisms at early levels may allow its representation to be sustained over brief intervals.

In contrast, the detection of completed change refers to the perception that the structure changed at some point, such as might happen if the change took place

---

[4]In general, simple continuity is not enough: Additional conditions are generally required to ensure that the derivatives of that particular order and type can exist (see e.g., Gelfand & Fomin 1963). However, the initial stages of visual processing usually involve only simple first- and second-order derivatives, which are calculated after smoothing by low-pass filters. As such, these quantities exist for virtually all conditions encountered when viewing the world (see e.g., Hildreth & Koch 1987, Marr 1982).

[5]Note that a change in the use of terms is advocated here. For example, "first-order motion" and "second-order motion" pertain to variation referenced to retinotopic space, and so describe types of motion; "third-order motion," however, refers to the tracking of a moving structure and is therefore a misnomer, describing instead a type of movement. This distinction is not just nominal: The mechanisms underlying the perception of motion differ fundamentally from those underlying the perception of movement (e.g., Seiffert & Cavanagh 1998, Sperling & Hoff 2000). More generally, the displacement of an object gives rise to the perception of *motion* (temporal variation of intensity, color, etc.) at various points in the field of view, whereas the object itself is perceived as *moving*.

while the entity was briefly occluded. Phenomenologically, there is no sense of a dynamic transformation; the change is simply noted to have taken place some time in the past. The mechanisms involved here would likely compare a property of a representation in memory against a representation of a currently visible structure, with the continuity of the referents established by means other than the continuity of the visual representation itself.[6]

Change vs. Difference

Finally, it is also important to distinguish between change and difference. As discussed above, *change* refers to the transformation over time of a single structure. In contrast, *difference* refers to a lack of similarity in the properties of two structures. The issue then is to clarify how these two notions differ. To the degree that they are not the same, trying to "spot the difference" between two side-by-side images will be a rather different activity than trying to detect the change in a pair of sequentially presented images (see Gur & Hilgard 1975, Brunel & Ninio 1997, Scott-Brown et al. 2000, Shore & Klein 2000).

It is important to note that the concepts of change and difference do have several elements in common. Both are referenced to structure, with the nature of the structures being unimportant. And both rely on the idea of similarity as applied to one or more of their properties.

However, the two concepts are not the same. To begin with, change refers to a single structure, difference to two. Furthermore, change involves temporal transformation, the measures of similarity pertaining to the same structure at different points in time; this is especially pronounced in dynamic change. In contrast, difference involves no notion of transformation, with similarity defined instead via the atemporal comparison of structures that may or may not exist simultaneously. There consequently appears to be an ordering of sorts: (*a*) dynamic change, with dynamic transformation and spatiotemporal continuity; (*b*) completed change, with inferred transformation and possibly a more abstract kind of continuity; and (*c*) difference, with no transformation (only comparison) and no continuity.

As in the case of motion, these distinctions have implications for the perceptual mechanisms involved. The detection of dynamic change involves spatiotemporal continuity, not only of the external entity, but likely of the internal representations as well. As such, a memory of a fairly sophisticated sort is required, one that not

---

[6]In some sense, these two types of perception are analogous to *modal completion* (i.e., the perception of visible properties not actually in the image to account for gaps between aligned fragments; see e.g., Kanizsa 1979) and *amodal completion* (i.e., the perception that aligned fragments in contact with a visible occluder are parts of the same structure; see e.g., Kanizsa & Gerbino 1982). Detection of dynamic change involves seeing a dynamic visual event that extends over a temporal gap; this is akin to seeing a modally completed surface that extends over a spatial gap. Meanwhile, detecting completed change involves a more abstract linking of items believed to refer to the same spatiotemporal structure; this is like the abstract linking of amodally completed fragments.

only maintains continuity but also supports the perception of a dynamic transformation. In contrast, all that is needed to detect difference is to extract the relevant properties from each entity and compare them at some point; memory need not enable continuity to be determined. Meanwhile, the mechanisms underlying the detection of completed change depend on the kind of continuity involved. If the external entity is somehow tracked, these mechanisms might be largely the same as those used for dynamic change. If the entity is not tracked, the mechanisms could be much the same as those used for detecting difference, along with an additional mechanism to identify the two structures as the same entity at different moments in time.

It is also important to maintain a careful distinction between structures defined as external entities and structures defined as internal representations. For example, a person may be encountered on two different occasions years apart. If the external entity is considered, there exists a set of transformations linking the current manifestation to the previous one; it is therefore the same person, who has simply changed. However, suppose the observer previously knew the person, but does not now recognize him or her. In terms of internal representations, the old and the new manifestations will be seen as different people.

These distinctions not only affect the way that words are used: They also affect the types of experiments considered relevant to a discussion of change detection. For instance, "match-to-sample" experiments (e.g., Biederman & Gerhardstein 1993) do not pertain to change detection, because the test and sample items are not necessarily perceived as corresponding to the same entity. Meanwhile, some "same vs. different" studies (e.g., Carlson-Radvansky & Irwin 1999) do pertain to change detection, because successive stimuli are perceived as the same entity.

EMPIRICAL APPROACHES

As mentioned earlier, the study of change detection has evolved over many years, proceeding through phases that have emphasized different types of stimuli and different types of tasks. All studies, however, rely on the same basic design: An observer is initially shown a stimulus (e.g., a picture or array), a change of some kind is made to this stimulus (e.g., removal or alteration of an element), and the response of the observer is then measured. The wide variety of approaches that have been developed around this design can be categorized via a relatively small number of dimensions.

Contingency of Change

The design of any change-detection experiment must ensure that the results are not due to the detection of motion. Note that the goal is not to eliminate motion detection outright, for a changing stimulus is always accompanied by temporal variations in the incoming light. Rather, the goal is to decouple the outputs of the change- and motion-detection systems. A few studies (e.g., Brawn & Snowden 1999, Castiello & Jeannerod 1991) attempt this via the temporal pattern of responses to a sudden change. Others (e.g., Seiffert & Cavanagh 1998) look at how performance is affected by different types of stimuli. However, for the most part, change and motion have been decoupled by making the change contingent on some event.

Gap-contingent techniques, for example, make the change during a temporal gap (or *interstimulus interval*) between the original and altered stimulus. A patterned mask is sometimes displayed during this gap, although often a simple blank field is used. Examples of this include work by Hochberg (1968), Phillips (1974), Pashler (1988), Simons (1996), and Rensink et al. (1997). Observers are generally poor at detecting change if more than a few items are present.

Saccade-contingent approaches make the change during a saccade of the eyes (see e.g., Sperling & Speelman 1965, Bridgeman et al. 1979, McConkie & Zola 1979, Carlson-Radvansky & Irwin 1995, Grimes 1996, and Henderson & Hollingworth 1999a). In all cases, observers are generally poor at detecting change. Indeed, this is true for position change if even only one item is present, provided it has no global frame of reference.

Shift-contingent techniques make the change during a sudden shift of the entire display; this is like the saccade-contingent technique, but with a simulated saccade [see e.g., Sperling & Speelman (1968) in Sperling (1990), Blackmore et al. 1995]. A considerable amount of change blindness is found both when the eye does and does not move in response to the shift.

Blink-contingent procedures make a change during an eyeblink. An example of this is the work of O'Regan et al. (2000). Again, observers are generally poor at detecting such changes. [This effect was known to movie editors long ago, who would use a sharp noise to induce the blink (see Dmytryk 1984, p. 31)]. Interestingly, change blindness can occur even if the observer is fixating the item being changed.

Splat-contingent techniques make the change simultaneous with the appearance of brief distractors, or *splats* (e.g., Rensink et al. 2000b). The change blindness induced by this technique is less severe than that of others; nevertheless, it still occurs (O'Regan et al. 1999, Rensink et al. 2000b). This shows that change blindness can be induced even when the change itself is completely undisturbed.

Occlusion-contingent change occurs while the changing item is briefly occluded. Examples can be found in the work of Simons & Levin (1998), Vaughan & Yantis (1999), Scholl et al. (1999), and Rich & Gillam (2000). In all cases, changes are much more difficult to detect than when the changing item is not occluded.

Cut-contingent methods involve items in movies, the change being made during a cut from one camera position to another (see e.g., Levin & Simons 1997, 2000). Changes made this way are usually difficult to detect. An interesting exception is that location change can be easily detected if the left-right arrangement of the two leading characters is reversed (see e.g., Arijon 1976, p. 29).

Gradual change, meanwhile, has the transition between original and modified display made slowly, i.e., over the course of several seconds (see e.g., Simons et al. 2000). (Note that the transition must still be fast enough that it can be easily seen once noticed.) Observers have great difficulty detecting this kind of change, even though no disruptions of any kind appear in the display.

Repetition of Change

Studies can also be characterized by the number of times the change is made; this is roughly analogous to the duration of a static presentation in a conventional detection experiment. As for visual experiments generally, brief and extended presentations are complementary approaches, with the weaknesses of the one largely compensated for by the strengths of the other.

In the *one-shot* approach the change is made just once during each trial (Figure 1*a*). Performance is primarily measured by accuracy, although response time is sometimes measured as well [(see e.g., Hochberg 1968, Avons & Phillips 1980, Blackmore et al. 1995, Levin & Simons 1997) Wright et al. 2000]. This technique minimizes the involvement of eye movements and long-term memory.

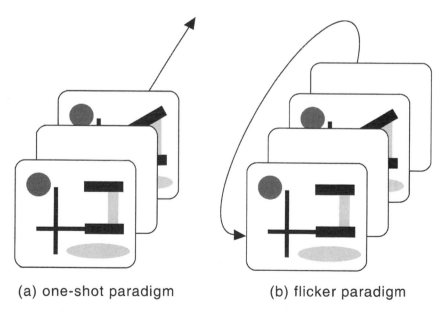

(a) one-shot paradigm   (b) flicker paradigm

Figure 1   Two variants of gap-contingent change. (*a*) One-shot paradigm. The observer views a single alternation of displays and determines if a change occurred. Performance is measured via accuracy of response. (*b*) Flicker paradigm. The observer views a continual cycling of displays and determines if a change is occurring. Performance is measured via response time. Both approaches can also be applied to other kinds of contingent change, such as those made during eye movements or blinks.

It can also distinguish between particular transformations (e.g., blue to yellow, present to absent), which would not be easily separated otherwise.

The *repeated-change* approach, in contrast, has the change made repeatedly until detected, or until the trial ends. Performance is primarily measured via response time, although accuracy is sometimes measured as well (see e.g., Rensink et al. 1997, Hollingworth & Henderson 2000, Aginsky & Tarr 2000, Wallis & Bülthoff 2000). In the case of gap-contingent change, the constantly repeating gaps generate a visible flicker (Figure 1*b*); this technique is therefore known as the *flicker paradigm* (Rensink et al. 1997). Because this technique allows sufficient time to process the input, the finding of change blindness here rules out the possibility that it stems from a failure to consolidate the information in memory (Rensink et al. 2000b).

Content of Display

Another dimension is the content of the displays used. As for visual stimuli generally, this can range from simple static figures on computer monitors to dynamic events in the world itself. The level of realism used reflects a particular choice of trade-offs: Simpler displays afford more control and usually allow results to be more easily analyzed, whereas more realistic displays involve factors more difficult to compensate for, but more applicable to tasks in everyday life.

Simple figures form the simplest type of display; these are typically dots, lines, or letters arranged in circular, linear, or rectangular arrays. If configural effects can be neutralized, such stimuli are well suited for investigating individual mechanisms, because the effects of other processes (e.g., scene organization) are minimal (see e.g., Phillips 1974, Luck & Vogel 1997, Rensink 2000b, Scott-Brown et al. 2000). In all cases, a considerable amount of change blindness occurs whenever more than a few items are present.

Drawings of objects and scenes range from line-based sketches to full-color computer renderings; these are placed into simple arrays or form complete scenes. Such displays are a step towards greater realism, but without the full complexity of real-world stimuli (see e.g., Simons 1996, Henderson & Hollingworth 1999a, Scholl 2000, Williams & Simons 2000). In general, a high degree of change blindness can be induced, although not always as dramatic as that obtained with more realistic stimuli (Hollingworth & Henderson 2000).

Images of objects and scenes provide even more realism. These are photographs of real-world objects, which—as in the case of drawings—are either placed into simple arrays or form complete scenes. Such stimuli have the advantage of avoiding an artificial parsing of objects into parts; in the case of complete scenes, they also avoid an artificial parsing of the scene (see e.g., Blackmore et al. 1995, Grimes 1996, Rensink et al. 1997, Zelinsky 1997, Ro et al. 2001). In all situations, a high degree of change blindness can be induced.

Dynamic displays such as movies also provide a greater degree of realism (e.g., Levin & Simons 1997, Gysen et al. 2000, Wallis & Bülthoff 2000). Again, observers generally have great difficulty detecting change, especially in objects irrelevant to the main events in the presentation. Changes to moving objects appear to be detected more easily than changes to stationary objects (Cyson et al. 2000).

Real-life interactions provide the highest level of realism. An example of this is work by Simons & Levin (1998), in which an experimenter requested directions from an unwitting observer, with an occlusion-contingent switch of experimenters occurring during the interaction. As in the case of other techniques, observers are poor at noticing the change. Wang & Simons (1999) provide another example, with observers detecting changes in the layout of a set of real-world objects. Changes were more difficult to detect if this set was rotated during a temporal gap; interestingly, performance was better if the observer was rotated instead, indicating possible involvement of the vestibular system.

Content of Change

Most studies to date have been careful to ensure that changes made to a display do not introduce a radical change in its overall appearance. For example, a change to a real-world image will be such that both the original and modified images are of the same kind of scene. Care is also taken that no anomalies are caused by the alteration (e.g., an automobile floating in the air), for otherwise, performance could be influenced by the anomaly, and not the change per se.

Even with such constraints, however, changes can be made in many ways. It is difficult to compare different types of changes with each other: Performance depends on the magnitude of the change (Carlson-Radvansky & Irwin 1999, Smilek et al. 2000, Williams & Simons 2000), and there is no simple way to equate the visibility of different kinds of changes. However, a great deal can be learned by examining how change detection is affected by manipulations within each change type.

Of the various types of change, perhaps the simplest is that in the *existence* of an item, i.e., addition or deletion.[7] Examples can be found in Rensink et al. (1997), Henderson & Hollingworth (1999a), Aginsky & Tarr (2000), and Mondy & Coltheart (2000). Provided that the changed item is unique, some deletions appear to be detected more easily than additions. However, this asymmetry may be eliminated—or even reversed—depending on how the initial and modified images are to be used subsequently, suggesting that detection of existence change may be based on a feature-matching process (Agostinelli et al. 1986, Mondy & Coltheart 2000).

---

[7]This simplicity is only in terms of the pattern of light on the retina or the image on a visual display. In terms of entities in the external world, changes in existence are rather special. First, they pertain to the well-defined nature of the entity itself rather than to any particular properties it may have. Second, they are relatively uncommon, being limited to creation and destruction. This latter factor may account for the tendency to interpret a change of existence in a stimulus element as some other kind of change, e.g., a displacement of the corresponding entity to a distant location.

Changes can also be made to various *properties* of an item; these are usually simple features such as orientation, size, shape, or color (e.g., Palmer 1988,
Grimes 1996, Simons 1996, Scott-Brown & Orbach 1998). Three variants are
commonly used: (*a*) change to an item with a property unique in the display,
(*b*) change to an item with a nonunique value, and (*c*) a switch in properties
among two or more items. Detection is best for changes to a unique property, and
worst for switches (Saiki 1999, Rich & Gillam 2000, Wheeler & Treisman 2001).
Performance can differ for different properties (Aginsky & Tarr 2000, Rensink
2000b).

Property changes can also be more complex—e.g., disjunction, where one of
two possible properties can change. This is as easy as detecting a single property
change, indicating that both properties are concurrently encoded (Luck & Vogel
1997, Wheeler & Treisman 2001). Another variant is conjunction, where all items
change one of two properties, with the target changing in both. Such changes are
extremely difficult to detect, as is the absence of change among changing items
(Rensink 1999a, 2001).

Another type of change is that of the semantic *identity* of an item—by rearrang-
ing its parts, for instance, or by substituting an entirely different item altogether.
Examples of this can be found in work by Levin & Simons (1997), Zelinsky (1997),
Archambault et al. (1999), and Williams & Simons (2000). If the change is such
that the overall appearance of the item is maintained (e.g., same overall size or
shape), detection of the change is usually quite poor. Provided that visual similarity
can be taken into account, such an approach may provide a powerful way to map
out the various categories used in visual perception. Related to this is the issue of
how the type of change connects to the item being changed—e.g., detecting the
displacement of a car along its direction of travel (i.e., back and forth), versus a
similar displacement sideways.

Finally, changes can also be made to the spatial arrangement (or *layout*) of
the items in the display. Care must be taken to keep the number of items—and
their properties—constant to avoid confounding factors. (For instance, removing
an item would result in a change in layout, but would also result in a change in
existence.) Examples are French (1953), Pollack (1972), Irwin (1991), Wang &
Simons (1999), and Jiang et al. (2000). Change blindness is generally found for
layout changes involving more than a few items. In some cases, layout change
appears to be easier to detect than feature change (e.g., Simons 1996), whereas in
others it is more difficult (e.g., Mondy & Coltheart 2000). This divergence may
be due to different encoding strategies: In some situations, a group of items might
be seen as a single item, with layout change then corresponding to a change in the
configuration of its parts.

Observer Intention

Another important dimension is the intention of the observer. Intentions affect
the degree to which an observer will expect a change, which in turn can affect

the mechanisms used (see Simons & Mitroff 2001). This is especially important for investigation into the mechanisms involved in everyday vision, which are not usually devoted to the detection of an anticipated change.

At one end of this spectrum is the *intentional* approach. Here, the observer fully expects a change and devotes all available resources to detecting it; as such, this is a good way to examine perceptual capacities. Examples can be found in work by Pollack (1972), Pashler (1988), Jiang et al. (2000), and Wright et al. (2000). Change blindness is generally found under these conditions, even though all resources have been allocated to the task.

A less-extreme variant is the *divided-attention* approach, in which some other task is primary—e.g., memorization of an image for a subsequent memory task (e.g., Grimes 1996, McConkie & Currie 1996). Meanwhile, observers are told that changes may "occasionally" occur, and to report any changes that they notice. Change blindness is again found, although detection still occurs for changes to certain items, such as saccade targets (McConkie & Currie 1996).

At the other end of this spectrum is the *incidental* approach (e.g., Levin & Simons 1997, Rich & Gillam 2000). Here, there is no mention at all of a possible change—observers are typically given some other task as their primary responsibility and are questioned only afterwards about whether they noticed a change. The degree of blindness encountered is generally much higher than that found using intentional approaches. However, some ability to detect change remains.

Type of Task

Tasks can also be classified according to which aspect of the change is involved. As for perception generally, detection is not necessarily identical to localization or identification (see e.g., Henderson 1992, Pashler & Badgio 1987). Comparing performance for different types of task may therefore cast light on the various mechanisms at play.

Detection is perhaps the most widely used type of task; here, the observer simply responds to the presence of a change in the display (e.g., Phillips 1974, Verfaillie et al. 1994, McConkie & Currie 1996, Luck & Vogel 1997, Austen & Enns 2000, Scott-Brown et al. 2000). A high degree of change blindness is generally found.

Localization requires that the observer respond to the location of the change. Examples can be found in the work of Fernandez-Duque & Thornton (2000), Scott-Brown & Orbach (1998), and Smilek et al. (2000). In most cases, observers are relatively poor at determining the location of the change.

Identification is potentially more complex, requiring the observer to respond to the identity of the changing item. Two variants exist: identity of the changing item, and identity of the change itself (i.e., the type of change). Most work to date has been based on identity of the change, although a few studies have also looked at identity of the item (e.g., Palmer 1988, Brawn & Snowden 1999, Wilken et al. 1999, Mondy & Coltheart 2000). Results indicate that identification is more difficult than detection of change.

Type of Response

An important aspect of any psychophysical experiment is the set of mechanisms generating the observer's response. These are determined both by the instructions to the observer (i.e., what aspect of their experience they are told to respond to) and by the choice of system to regard as "responding." Different mechanisms may tap into different perceptual systems; consequently, a great deal may be learned from the various types of response to a change.

Explicit responses are triggered by the conscious visual experience of the observer; these most closely match the intuitive idea of "seeing" a change (e.g., French 1953, Simons 1996, Rensink et al. 1997, Jiang et al. 2000). Two variants exist: "yes/no," in which the observer must answer either "yes" or "no" (or more generally, select from a fixed set of alternatives), and "go/no-go," in which the observer only responds "yes" if the change is seen (or if one particular type or location of change is seen). The go/no-go response has the advantage of guaranteeing that the observer truly did experience the change, although the response bias differs from that of yes/no responses (Wilken et al. 1999). A high degree of change blindness is still found in all cases.

Semi-explicit responses are similar, though triggered by a "feeling" that a change is occurring—no visual experience is involved. This trigger is therefore explicit in some ways (i.e., an awareness that a change is occurring) but not others (i.e., what the change looks like). An example of this can be found in the work of Rensink (1998, 2000a). Although detection of change via this *mindsight* is not immediate, it can precede the visual experience of change by several seconds in approximately one third of observers.

Implicit responses, in contrast, are measured by the extent to which a change not consciously perceived can influence a consciously initiated decision—e.g., how the occurrence of an unseen change affects forced-choice guessing about its possible location. Examples of this can be found in Fernandez-Duque & Thornton (2000), Thornton & Fernandez-Duque (2000), and Williams & Simons (2000). Although implicit detection of change is generally poor, it is above chance levels, suggesting that the underlying mechanisms may provide some information about the location and nature of the item changed.

Visuomotor responses are based on the reaction of a visually guided motor system—usually manual pointing or eye fixation—to a change in the display (e.g., Bridgeman et al. 1979, Goodale et al. 1986, Castiello et al. 1991, Hayhoe et al. 1998). Note that conscious perception of the change must not be able to influence this response. Visuomotor responses are generally faster and more accurate than consciously mediated ones, especially when the display contains only a few items; this is particularly true for location change, although an ability to detect property change also exists (Hayhoe et al. 1998).

ATTENTION AND CHANGE DETECTION

As the previous section shows, a striking blindness to change can be induced under a wide variety of conditions. The sheer range of these conditions—together with the strength and robustness of the effect itself—indicates that the mechanisms involved are central to the way we perceive the world around us. But what might these mechanisms be?

Most results to date can be explained by the thesis that focused attention is needed to see change (Rensink et al. 1997). A change in the world is always accompanied by a motion signal in the input; under normal circumstances, this signal will be unique—or at least larger than the background noise—and thus attract attention to its location (see e.g., Klein et al. 1992). This in turn will enable the change to be seen. However, if this signal is too weak (e.g., is made too slowly or is swamped by transients associated with a saccade, flicker, or splat), it will not draw attention, and change blindness will result.

If this view is correct, the possibility arises of reversing things: Instead of using focused attention to help clarify what change blindness is, change blindness could be used to help clarify what focused attention is. Much has been learned of attention using approaches such as visual search on static displays and priming (see e.g., Pashler 1998). However, the high degree of change blindness found under many conditions might be harnessed to provide results with a high signal-to-noise ratio, which could allow the mechanisms of focused attention to be explored in great detail.

Involvement of Focused Attention

Given the thesis that change detection is mediated by "attention," it is important to specify exactly what is meant by this term, because several different meanings can be ascribed to it (see e.g., Allport 1992). In particular, it is important to determine whether the detection of change is mediated by the focused attention believed to bind together features in the perception of static displays (e.g., Treisman & Gormican 1988).

Evidence is accumulating in favor of this possibility. To begin with, many characteristics of the change-detection process (e.g., speed, capacity, selectivity) are similar to—or at least compatible with—what is known of focused attention (Rensink 2000b). For example, for orientation change, no more than 4–5 items can be monitored simultaneously (Rensink 2000b, Rensink et al. 2000a), a limit similar to that encountered in other types of attentional tasks (e.g., Pashler 1988, Pylyshyn & Storm 1988). In addition, change blindness is reduced for items considered to be "interesting" (Rensink et al. 1997), and by exogenous cues at the location of the change (Scholl 2000). In both types of situations, then, performance is consistent with the drawing of focused attention. Finally, it appears that attentional priming occurs at the location of an item seen to be changing, and that such priming does not occur when there is no visual experience of change (Fernandez-Duque &

Thornton 2000). Again, this supports the view that the relevant quantity is the focused attention involved in the perception of static displays.

Comparison vs. Construction

If attention is needed for change detection, how does it operate? At least two possibilities exist. First, attention could construct a limited number of relatively complex structures (e.g., the object files of Kahneman et al. 1992 or the coherence fields of Rensink 2000c), with these complexes[8] then being the basis for change detection. Alternatively, attention may simply enable a limited amount of comparison on an effectively unlimited amount of information (Scott-Brown et al. 2000).

Several results argue against this latter possibility. First, it cannot explain the failure to combine the detailed contents of successive fixations (Irwin 1991) or why visual search for a changing item should be difficult (Rensink 2000b): If the detailed contents of successive fixations or displays could be accumulated, a distinctive pattern formed from these should be easy to detect. Second, when both the initial and changed displays are presented for increasingly long durations, a limit is reached in the number of items that can be seen to change orientation at any one time (Rensink 2000b). This would not occur if storage were unlimited, because all stored items would eventually be compared, even by a limited-capacity mechanism. Finally, the comparison of items already in (short-term) memory requires about 20 ms/item (Rensink 1999a); if limits on comparison dominated change detection, search for change would also proceed at this rate. However, search typically proceeds at about 100 ms/item (Rensink 2000b), showing that additional operations are involved. Relatively little of change blindness therefore appears to be due to a bottleneck in the comparison process. Rather, detection of change apparently involves the construction of a limited number of structures.

Construction vs. Maintenance

If attention forms complexes capable of supporting change detection, an important issue is then how these are stored in visual short-term memory (vSTM). A commonly held view is that focused attention and vSTM are largely separate, with attention constructing complexes and vSTM maintaining them. However, results on change detection are beginning to alter this picture.

For example, the absence of change is extremely difficult to detect—only one item can be compared at each alternation (Rensink 1999a, 2000a). If several items could be placed into vSTM, this difficulty should not exist, for each item could be examined in turn against the input. Conjunctions of changes are also extremely difficult to detect, also being limited to one per alternation (Rensink 2000a, 2001);

---

[8]The term *complex* is used here to denote the representational structure formed by attention for an item in the stimulus array, without regard to any particular theory. Other terms (such as *object file* or *coherence field*) are associated with particular ideas about the formation and content of complexes, associations that are avoided by use of a more neutral word. The more theory-laden terms are used here only in the context of particular theories of attention.

again, this should not happen if several complexes could be held in vSTM and compared (one at a time, if need be) against the input. Finally, detection of change to a conjunction of features is improved when all items are removed except the test item, again indicating that items are not held in vSTM in bound form (Wheeler & Treisman 2001).

These results show that focused attention and vSTM overlap much more than previously believed, a conclusion also arrived at from other areas of study (see e.g., Cowan 1988). Indeed, the two may simply be different aspects of the same process, with items held in a coherent complex as long as they are attended, but falling apart when attention is withdrawn (Wolfe 1999, Rensink 2000c).

Independence of Attentional Complexes

Several studies (e.g., Luck & Vogel 1997, Rensink 2000b) show that several items can be held by attention at any one time. How are the corresponding complexes related to each other? One possibility is that each is completely independent of the others (Pylyshyn & Storm 1988). Alternatively, a higher-level structure may constrain what can be done with them (Yantis 1992; Rensink 2000a, 2001).

Results from change-detection studies support the latter view. In particular, it appears that although attention can hold on to 4–5 items at a time, there is some pooling of their properties into a single collection point, or *nexus* (Rensink 1999a, 2000c). The number of items attended therefore will depend on the nature of the task. Detecting the presence of change, for example, can be done by attending to several items at a time: All that is needed is a change in the pooled signal. In contrast, determining the absence of a change involves detecting the presence of a nonchanging signal in a signal collected from several changing items; to do this reliably, items must be attended one at a time (see Rensink 2000a, 2001). Note that this constraint would not exist if complexes were independent entities; in such a case, each complex could simply be tested in turn.

Other studies also indicate that complexes are not independent. For example, a high degree of change blindness exists for switches of colors in tracked items (Saiki 1999, Scholl et al. 1999) and for conjunctions of features in stationary items, even when only three items are in the display (Wheeler & Treisman 2001). In both situations, the relevant items are almost certainly attended; if the corresponding complexes were independent, detection should be near perfect. The poor performance actually found indicates a migration of features among the attended items, something much more consistent with a pooled signal. Furthermore, perceiving the identity of a change (e.g., bigger vs. smaller) is more accurate when attention is given to one item than to four, again indicating a pooling of attentional resources (Palmer 1990).

Contents of Attentional Complexes

Another important issue is the content of an attentional complex—the number of features included, the amount of detail for each feature, etc. Previous work (e.g., Kahneman et al. 1992) indicated that this content is relatively sparse, with only a handful of features represented. Results from change-detection studies have reinforced this conclusion. For example, observers in an incidental change-detection task can miss relatively large changes in an item even when it is attended, suggesting that the corresponding complex may be far from a complete representation of the object (Levin & Simons 1997).[9]

Thus, attention may not be concerned with the construction of general-purpose representations, but rather, with the construction of more specialized representations suitable for the task at hand. It appears that at least four properties—e.g., orientation, color, size, and presence of a gap—can be simultaneously represented in a complex (Luck & Vogel 1997), presumably via concurrent systems (Wheeler & Treisman 2001). Furthermore, items can be described not only in terms of their properties, but also their parts and the structural relations between these parts (Carlson-Radvansky & Irwin 1995). Such relations appear to be encoded via a concurrent set of spatial representations, the simplest of these describing the spatial configuration (or layout) of the attended items (Jiang et al. 2000).

Observers are generally good at selecting the properties to be entered into a complex while screening out others. For example, the detection of orientation change is almost entirely unaffected by irrelevant variations in contrast sign (Rensink 2000b). Selection is possible for structural relations as well. For instance, observers can focus on a particular level (local or global) of a compound item, although this appears to be limited to one level at a time (Austen & Enns 2000).

Coherence Theory

The characteristics described above provide a necessary set of constraints on any model of visual attention. One model consistent with all these characteristics is *coherence theory* (Rensink 2000c). This proposal (Figure 2) has three parts:

1. Prior to focused attention is a stage of *early* processing, i.e., processing that is low-level, rapid, and carried out in parallel across the visual field. The resultant structures (*proto-objects*) can be quite sophisticated, describing several aspects of scene structure. However, they have limited spatial coherence. They also have limited temporal coherence: They are volatile, and so are simply replaced by any new stimuli at their location.

2. Focused attention acts as a hand that "grasps" several proto-objects from this constantly regenerating flux. While held, they are part of a *coherence field* representing an individuated object. This field is formed via feedback between low-level proto-objects and a mid-level nexus. The coherence formed

---

[9]Care must be taken in distinguishing between an object defined as a structure in the external world (i.e., a concrete spatiotemporal entity) and as a structure internal to the observer (i.e., an attentional complex). If "object" is taken to be an external structure, then attention to it will encode only some of its properties. As such, attention is necessary but not sufficient to perceive change in an object. If "object" is defined as the contents of the complex, the issue is whether there exists additional selectivity in the comparison process; if not, attention would be both necessary and sufficient to perceive change in this internal structure.

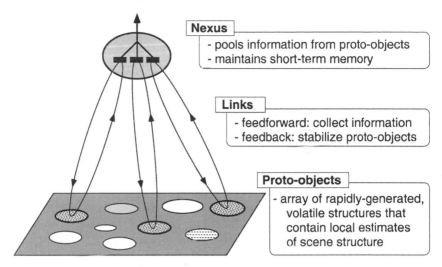

Figure 2   Coherence theory (Rensink 2000c). In the absence of focused attention, low-level structures (proto-objects) are volatile, and thus are simply replaced by the representations of new stimuli at their location. Attention acts by establishing feedback links between a selected set of proto-objects that provides visual properties and a mid-level nexus that stabilizes them; the interacting set of proto-objects, links, and nexus is a coherence field. This interaction allows attended proto-object properties to be held in coherent form, both in time and in space. When the feedback loop is broken, coherence dissolves, with the previously attended proto-objects reverting to a volatile state.

this way allows the object to maintain continuity across brief interruptions; as such, it is perceived as being transformed when new stimuli arrive at its location.

3. To release attention, the feedback loop is broken. The field then loses its coherence, with the object representation dissolving back into its constituent set of volatile proto-objects.

Note that in contrast to previous models of attended complexes (e.g., the object files of Kahneman et al. 1992), coherence theory posits that these structures (the coherence fields) collapse as soon as attention is withdrawn. Furthermore, these complexes are not independent, but are parts of a more integrated structure that loosely corresponds to a concrete instance (or token) of an articulated object.

IMPLICATIONS FOR VISUAL PERCEPTION

According to the arguments put forward in the previous section, attention is needed to see change. But although this thesis—and the developments stemming from it—can explain how observers see (or do not see) change under various conditions, the adoption of this thesis has a number of important implications for various aspects of visual perception. For example, if only a small number of objects have a coherent representation at any one time, why do we experience all the objects in our surroundings as existing simultaneously? If we can implicitly perceive change in the absence of attention, how might this be carried out, and how might it contribute to our visual experience? In general, then, work on change detection is forcing a reconsideration of what it means to see and what might be the mechanisms involved.

Visual Buffer

Among the first casualties of the thesis that attention is needed to see change was the hypothesis of a visual buffer, a spatiotopic memory store believed to accumulate the contents of successive fixations (e.g., Feldman 1985). This was thought to provide a detailed representation of the incoming light that was independent of eye movements; among other things, it was taken as the basis for the richly detailed experience we have of our surroundings. However, the widespread existence of change blindness suggests that no such buffer exists (see Comparison vs. Construction, above), a conclusion consistent with complementary work on the visual integration of information (e.g., Irwin 1996, Henderson 1997). More generally, it appears that the detailed contents of successive presentations—including successive fixations—can never be added, compared, or otherwise combined in their entirety, thereby ruling out any large-scale accumulation of information.

It should be pointed out, however, that there still exists a detailed retinotopic representation of the incoming light at any moment in time. Indeed, it is exactly this that constitutes the output of early vision (see e.g., Rensink 2000c). However, according to coherence theory, this representation does not endure: Unattended proto-objects are quickly replaced whenever the eye (or the visual stimulus) moves and rapidly decay when the eye closes (or the stimulus disappears).

The memory trace of the decaying proto-objects may correspond to the informational persistence (or iconic memory) found using partial-report techniques (e.g., Sperling 1960). Although such memory persists for only about 300 ms, it may nevertheless enable a change in a proto-object to be represented without attention. According to coherence theory, such an unattended change will not be consciously perceived, but it could have other effects. For example, it could be salient, drawing attention to its location sooner than otherwise would have been the case (Rensink et al. 2000a, Smilek et al. 2000). As such, informational persistence may play a larger role in visual perception than previously believed (see Haber 1983). One interesting possibility is that it enables the dynamic transformation that is experienced in dynamic change.

Coherent Structure

Various studies of gap-contingent change (e.g., Pashler 1988, Luck & Vogel 1997, Rensink et al. 2000a) indicate that only about four items can be monitored at a time.

This limit is similar to that obtained from work on saccade-contingent change, and indicates that transsaccadic memory may be largely—if not entirely—identical to vSTM (Irwin 1991). If vSTM and visual attention are also much the same, there may then exist only one system concerned with the formation and maintenance of coherent visual structure. According to coherence theory (Rensink 2000c), this system would be primarily concerned with the perception of objects.

A key issue in determining the viability of this view is the fate of an attentional complex once attention has been withdrawn. Results suggest that the binding of features into coherent complexes does fall apart in the absence of attention (see Construction vs. Maintenance, above), supporting the idea that vSTM and visual attention are largely the same, and thus supporting the proposal of a single system for the formation and maintenance of coherent structure.

Scene Representation

The results of various studies of change detection (and related phenomena such as visual integration) appear to converge on two main points concerning visual representation: (*a*) If it is detailed, it cannot be coherent to any great extent, and (*b*) if it is coherent, it cannot be highly detailed. Thus, no visual representations are both coherent and detailed.

To reconcile this with the coherent, detailed scene we believe we experience, consider what needs to be represented for a task. There is usually little need for a detailed representation of all the objects present; instead, all that is really needed is a representation of only those objects—and those particular properties—involved in the task at hand. If attention can form a coherent representation of any aspect of any object whenever requested, the result will be a *virtual representation* of the scene that will appear to higher levels as if real, i.e., as if all objects simultaneously have detailed, coherent representations (Rensink 2000c).[10] In this view, the notion of a static, all-purpose representation is replaced by that of a dynamic representation highly sensitive to the demands of the task and the expectations of the observer.

It is not yet known whether such a system is actually implemented in the human perceptual system. However, one possibility that is consistent with what is known of human vision is the *triadic architecture* (Rensink 2000c) shown in Figure 3. This is composed of three largely independent systems:

1. *Early processing.* A low-level system that continually generates highly detailed, volatile structures. (This could be, for example, the proto-objects posited by coherence theory.)

---

[10]Note that this applies only to the visual experience of coherent structure—the structure manifested by, e.g., the ability to see change. Nothing is implied about how volatile structure is experienced. It may be, for example, that volatile structures support the visual experience of a dense sea of simple features, although changes per se will still not be seen. If so, the visual impression an observer has of his or her surroundings will be based on just a few coherent structures embedded in this sea.

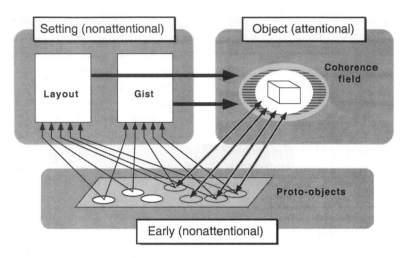

Figure 3   Triadic architecture (Rensink 2000c). Here, visual processing is split into three largely independent systems: (*a*) an *early* system concerned with the rapid formation of sophisticated—but volatile—proto-objects; (*b*) an attentional system concerned with the formation of coherent *objects*; and (*c*) a nonattentional *setting* system that guides attention. According to coherence theory, attention is needed for the visual experience of change, and thus unattended structures do not support such experience. The contribution of unattended structures to the visual experience of static stimuli is indeterminate.

2. *Object system.* A limited-capacity attentional system that stabilizes these and forms them into a coherent object representation. (This could be, for example, the coherence field posited by coherence theory.)

3. *Setting system.* A limited-capacity nonattentional system that helps guide attention. This may be based on the meaning (or *gist*) of the scene and the arrangement (or *layout*) of items in it. These attributes are based on properties obtained via early vision, largely without the involvement of attention.

Here, the constantly regenerating set of proto-objects provides a rapid estimate of the visible properties of the scene. These then form the basis of a rapid determination of scene gist. This—together with possibly longer-lasting layout information—then allows the observer to verify whether the initial impression was correct and to gather additional detail and construct coherent representations whenever required. Note that such a process of sparse construction and verification is believed to underlie much of the conscious perception of scenes (Henderson 1992, Henderson & Hollingworth 1999b).

Dependence on Task

If the formation of coherent structure requires attention, successful perception for everyday tasks must depend on *attentional management*, i.e., deploying attention such that the limited amount of information stabilized is used as effectively as possible. An important part of this is to allocate attention in a way suitable for the task at hand

Evidence of this kind of management appeared in a study that examined search for change in an array of figures (Rensink 1999b). When observers searched for an orientation change, speed was strongly influenced by the shape of the items. However, when the same figures were used in a search for a contrast polarity change, no such influence was found. Apparently, some geometric information did not enter into the representations formed when only nongeometric (i.e., color) information needed to be compared.

Similar effects appeared in a study comparing incidental and intentional detection of changes made during movie cuts (Levin & Simons 1997). Intentional detection was found to be much more accurate than incidental detection, indicating that the only properties put into coherent form (or at least compared) were the minimal ones sufficient for the immediate needs of the observer.

High-Level Knowledge

Another important aspect of attentional management involves the high-level knowledge of the observer. Such knowledge often takes the form of a "chunk," a structure in long-term memory containing a cluster of properties that can be attended and held in vSTM in much the same way as a simple element (e.g., Miller 1956). The contents of a chunk can affect what is attended, and thus what is perceived. Evidence of this was found by Archambault et al. (1999), who had observers learn a set of objects either at a general level of categorization (e.g., "a mug"), or at a specific level (e.g., "the mug owned by Bill"). Detection of change was better for objects learned at a specific level, suggesting that more detailed representations had been formed.

High-level knowledge can also have a more direct influence via the selection of the content of attentional complexes. For example, Simons & Levin (1998) investigated detection of changes to people asking for directions. Observers were more likely to notice the change when the experimenter was considered a member of their social group, suggesting a high-level influence on the amount of information contained in the corresponding complexes.

Another aspect is the control of attention by various objects in a scene. Known objects may be rapidly identified via the setting system, and so preferentially draw (or at least hold) attention. For example, changes to real-world scenes are noticed most quickly for "central interests," i.e., objects or regions mentioned most often in brief verbal descriptions of the scene (Rensink et al. 1997). Although central interests may be preferentially attended in part because of the salience of their features (Shore & Klein 2000), semantic considerations are also involved (Hollingworth & Henderson 2000, Ro et al. 2001).

Finally, if the observer has knowledge of which aspects of a scene are important, this can help guide attention to the appropriate items at the appropriate time. For instance, Werner & Thies (2000) examined the ability of observers to notice changcs in scenes of American football games. Comparing the performance of experts and nonexperts, it was found that experts could spot changes in meaning more quickly and could attentionally scan meaningful scenes more efficiently.

Implicit Perception

The thesis that attention is needed to see change is somewhat ambiguous regarding the implicit detection of change that may occur in the absence of conscious awareness (see Type of Response, above). If "see" denotes any use of light to affect behavior (see Rensink 2000a), this thesis makes the strong claim that no detection of change can occur without attention; if attention is sufficient for conscious experience, this would then rule out the possibility of implicit change detection [a result in accord with some views on implicit perception (e.g., Dulany 1997)]. On the other hand, if "see" is restricted to conscious visual experience, then the thesis says nothing about how the implicit perception of change may be carried out.

Owing to various methodological difficulties, relatively little is known about this type of perception generally (see e.g., Milner & Goodale 1995, Merikle & Reingold 1992). Several studies have examined the response of the visuomotor system to various types of change. Results show that even if the observer does not consciously experience a change, the visuomotor system may still respond to it (e.g., Bridgeman et al. 1975, Goodale et al. 1986, Hayhoe et al. 1998). This has provided much of the support for the proposal that vision is composed of two largely independent streams: an *on-line* stream concerned with immediate visuomotor action and a slower *off-line* stream concerned with object recognition (Milner & Goodale 1995). However, the particular mechanisms underlying visuomotor change detection (including any possible involvement of attention) remain unknown.

Another approach is the forced-choice guessing of unseen changes. For example, observers may be able to guess the location of a change more often than chance, even if they have no awareness that it occurred (Fernandez-Duque & Thornton 2000). Note that the key issue here is not whether detection is "really" implicit, but whether performance accompanied by conscious awareness differs from performance unaccompanied by awareness (Merikle & Reingold 1992). Some evidence (Thornton & Fernandez-Duque 2000) suggests that this is the case, but there is some disagreement on this point (Mitroff & Simons 2000). If implicit detection of change does exist, the neural substrate might be the on-line stream believed to support visuomotor action; alternatively, it might be the setting system of the triadic architecture (Rensink 2000c), a nonattentional system not concerned with conscious perception per se.

It may also be possible to obtain information about these mechanisms via explicit detection of change. For example, Deubel et al. (1996) found that detection of saccade-contingent change improved greatly when the saccade target was blanked and did not reappear until a few hundred milliseconds after the eye had landed. This indicates that some information about position (and perhaps shape) is retained in a latent form not available to conscious perception. An interesting possibility is that this may be the information supporting implicit detection, with the reappearance of the target somehow triggering its transfer to a more explicit system.

OPEN ISSUES

As the previous sections have shown, much has been learned about the nature of change detection, both what it is and what mechanisms may be involved. This in turn has cast considerable light on how the visual system operates. However, many issues concerning the nature of change detection remain open. Some of these involve the properties of the particular mechanisms used—e.g., the capacity of attention/vSTM, the types of units used, etc. (see e.g., Rensink 2000b). However, others are more fundamental and require resolution before change detection itself can be said to be well understood. These latter issues include:

1. *How does identification of change differ from detection of change?* Several studies have shown that identifying a change is more difficult than detecting it (see Type of Task, above). This may be in part because identification is simply a less sensitive process, requiring a higher signal-to-noise ratio. However, different mechanisms appear to be involved (Wilken et al. 1999). If so, it is not clear which ability—if either—should be considered as "basic"; for example, detection may occur via simple comparison, whereas identification may occur via mechanisms underlying the perception of dynamic events. More generally, different mechanisms may be used for various aspects of change perception, including not only detection and identification, but other tasks as well (e.g., localization).

2. *How does implicit detection of change differ from explicit detection of change?* Given the possibility that observers may be able to implicitly detect a change without any awareness of it (see Implicit Perception, above), an important issue is to determine whether this form of perception exists outside of visuomotor responses. If so, a key concern would be the mechanisms involved—not just in the details of their operation, but also how they relate to each other (i.e., whether there exist several separate systems) and how they relate to the mechanisms underlying the explicit detection of change.

3. *Does explicit detection of change involve only a subset of attended information?* Although attention may be needed to explicitly experience change, it is unclear whether such detection is based on all attended information or just a selected subset. Some studies suggest that observers may hold only one property at a time in coherent form (e.g., Ballard et al. 1995, Hayhoe et al. 1998), a result at odds with our impression that we see many properties simultaneously. It could be that our impressions result from a virtual representation that efficiently switches between properties as well as between objects. However, it could also be that our visual experience reflects the many

dimensions being attended, with only a subset of these being compared in any given task.

It is important to resolve this issue, for otherwise characteristics of the comparison mechanism could be ascribed to visual attention, or vice versa. For example, the relatively poor detection of incidental change (e.g., Levin & Simons 1997) cannot be used as conclusive evidence that fewer properties are being attended. It could simply be that fewer properties are being compared. However, careful analysis can often provide information about the attentional structures involved, even if the details of the comparison process are unknown (e.g., Rensink 2000a, 2001).

4. *How might detection of dynamic change differ from detection of completed change?* At a conceptual level, there is a considerable difference between these two types of detection, suggesting that separate mechanisms may be involved (see Dynamic vs. Completed Change, above). However, whether this division really exists in the human visual system remains unknown. Interestingly, a phenomenological dissociation appears to exist in the detection of gap-contingent change, with detection of dynamic change (seeing the dynamic transformation) found for interstimulus intervals of about 300 ms or less, and detection of completed change (seeing that something has changed) for longer intervals (e.g., Phillips 1974, Rensink et al. 2000a; see also Bridgeman et al. 1975). To establish this difference firmly would require behavioral correlates (see Merikle & Reingold 1992). A possible candidate in this regard might be the finding of two separate mechanisms for the detection of displacement: one for intervals less than 200 ms, the other for intervals greater than 500 ms (Palmer 1986).

If the two types of detection are separate, the continued application of attention would likely be needed only for the detection of dynamic change; the detection of completed change might simply then be carried out via a referral to remembered information, with attention perhaps needed only for the comparison operation. This latter possibility may explain the finding that a change can sometimes be explicitly detected when the eye returns to a previously fixated item (Henderson & Hollingworth 1999a); if it can be ascertained that attention is not continually applied to such items, this would indicate that the relevant quantity is indeed remembered information. However, note that such information would not be a complete description of the scene; rather, it would still be a relatively sparse representation, such as the schematic map proposed by Hochberg (1968) for the guidance of eye movements, or the setting system proposed by Rensink (2000c) for the guidance of attention.

5. *How might detection of dynamic change differ from detection of motion?* If there is a separate system for the detection of dynamic change, its maximum temporal range would be approximately 300 ms. This is within the largest temporal range for motion detectors (van der Grind et al. 1986), raising the

possibility that detection of dynamic change is simply a form of motion perception. However, 300 ms is also a duration typical of informational persistence, suggesting that detection of dynamic change may be based on this instead. An interesting possibility in this regard is that changes may be picked up at the level of informational persistence, with these changes becoming explicitly detected only when attention is applied to the relevant structures (see Visual Buffer, above).

One way to settle this issue might be to examine how change detection is affected by a sudden displacement of the stimulus: Performance would decline for a motion-based mechanism, whereas it might remain unaffected for a mechanism referenced to stimulus structure. Evidence for the indifference of dynamic change detection to displacement has been found (Rensink et al. 2000a), providing preliminary support for the existence of separate systems.

6. *How might detection of completed change differ from detection of difference?* If a distinct system exists for the detection of completed change, it might not need to have items continually attended. Instead, a currently visible item would simply be compared with a structure in memory. As such, detection of completed change may differ from perception of difference only in the use of an additional process to establish that the structures being compared refer to the same external entity (see Change vs. Difference, above). However, the detection of completed change can occur after interstimulus intervals of only 300 ms, something difficult to reconcile with the long-term memories that can be involved in the perception of difference. Preliminary work (e.g., Shore & Klein 2000) suggests behavioral differences between the two forms of detection. It may be that several systems are at play, each involving a different time scale, and perhaps different ways of making comparisons.

7. *What are the limits to which change-detection mechanisms can access visual representations?* Although change blindness can arise from a failure to maintain relevant information, it can also arise from a failure to access the relevant representations (see e.g., Simons 2000). For example, the explicit detection of saccade-contingent change is greatly improved when a brief blank follows the landing of the eye (Deubel et al. 1996), showing the existence of preserved information normally inaccessible to the mechanisms underlying the conscious detection of change. Again, such information is unlikely to be a complete and detailed description of the visible scene, being instead a sparser description containing information about particular aspects of it.

More generally, it may be that the group of mechanisms underlying each kind of change detection (e.g., explicit or implicit, dynamic or completed) can access only a subset of the representations used in vision, and that each group accesses a different subset. If so, it becomes important to determine the various types of information that are preserved, the subsets that can be accessed by each group of change-detection mechanisms, and the reasons for these limits.

CLOSING REMARKS

Resolving the many issues centered around change detection will not be easy. However, as the discussion above has indicated, ways exist to investigate the various problems involved. If history is any guide, these investigations will likely lead to effects again at odds with our intuitions. These will then lead to further revisions in our understanding of what change detection is and how it is carried out. And this in turn will improve our ability to explore other aspects of visual perception. Thus, it appears that the concept of change, a concept that caused so many difficulties for so many years, is well on its way to becoming the basis for important new insights into the way we experience the world around us.

ACKNOWLEDGMENTS

I would like to thank Dan Simons and Ian Thornton for their comments on an earlier draft of this paper.

Visit the Annual Reviews home page at www.AnnualReviews.org

LITERATURE CITED

Adelson EH, Bergen JR. 1991. The plenoptic function and the elements of early vision. In *Computational Models of Visual Processing*, ed. M Landy, JA Movshon, pp. 3–20. Cambridge, MA: MIT Press

Aginsky V, Tarr MJ. 2000. How are different properties of a scene encoded in visual memory? *Vis. Cogn.* 7:147–62

Agostinelli G, Sherman SJ, Fazio RH, Hearst ES. 1986. Detecting and identifying change: additions versus deletions. *J. Exp. Psychol.: Hum. Percept. Perform.* 12:445–54

Allport A. 1992. Attention and control: Have we been asking the wrong questions? A critical review of twenty-five years. In *Attention and Performance XIV*, ed. DE Meyer, S Kornblum, pp. 183–218. Cambridge, MA: MIT Press

Archambault A, O'Donnell C, Schyns PG. 1999. Blind to object changes: when learning the same object at different levels of categorization modifies its perception. *Psychol. Sci.* 10:249–55

Arijon D. 1976. *Grammar of the Film Language*. Los Angeles: Silman-James

Austen E, Enns JT. 2000. Change detection: paying attention to detail. *Psyche* 6(11). http://psyche.cs.monash.edu.au/v6/psyche-6-11-austen.html

Avons SE, Phillips WA. 1980. Visualization and memorization as a function of display time and poststimulus processing time. *J. Exp. Psychol.: Hum. Learn. Mem.* 6:407–20

Ballard DH, Hayhoe MM, Pelz JB. 1995. Memory representations in natural tasks. *J. Cogn. Neurosci.* 7:66–80

Batchelor GK. 1967. *An Introduction to Fluid Dynamics*. Cambridge: Cambridge Univ. Press

Biederman I, Gerhardstein PC. 1993. Recognizing depth-rotated objects: evidence and conditions for three-dimensional viewpoint invariance. *J. Exp. Psychol.: Hum. Percept. Perform.* 19:1162–82

Blackmore SJ, Brelstaff G, Nelson K, Troscianko T. 1995. Is the richness of our visual world an illusion? Transsaccadic memory for complex scenes. *Perception* 24:1075–81

Brawn P, Snowden RJ. 1999. Can one pay

attention to a particular color? *Percept. Psychophys.* 61:860–73

Bridgeman B, Hendry D, Stark L. 1975. Failure to detect displacement of the visual world during saccadic eye movements. *Vis. Res.* 15:719–22

Bridgeman B, Lewis S, Heit G, Nagle M. 1979. Relation between cognitive and motor-oriented systems of visual position perception. *J. Exp. Psychol.: Hum. Percept. Perform.* 5:692–700

Bridgeman B, van der Heijden AH, Velichkovsky BM. 1994. A theory of visual stability across saccadic eye movements. *Behav. Brain Sci.* 17:247–92

Brunel N, Ninio J. 1997. Time to detect the difference between two images presented side by side. *Cogn. Brain Res.* 5:273–82

Carlson-Radvansky LA, Irwin DE. 1995. Memory for structural information across eye movements. *J. Exp. Psychol.: Learn. Mem. Cogn.* 21:1441–58

Carlson-Radvansky LA, Irwin DE. 1999. Memory for relational information across cye movements. *Percept. Psychophys.* 61: 919–34

Castiello U, Jeannerod M. 1991. Measuring time to awareness. *NeuroReport* 2:797–800

Castiello U, Paulignan Y, Jeannerod M. 1991. Temporal dissociation of motor responses and subjective awareness. *Brain* 114:2639–55

Cowan N. 1988. Evolving conceptions of memory storage, selective attention, and their mutual constraints with the human information-processing system. *Psychol. Rev.* 104:163–91

Deubel H, Schneider WX, Bridgeman B. 1996. Post-saccadic target blanking prevents saccadic suppression of image displacement. *Vis. Res.* 36:985–96

Ditchburn R. 1955. Eye-movements in relation to retinal action. *Opt. Acta* 1:171–76

Dmytryk E. 1984. *On Film Editing*. Boston: Focal

Dulany DE. 1997. Consciousness in the explicit (deliberative) and implicit (evocative). In *Scientific Approaches to Consciousness*, ed. JD

Cohen, JW Schooler, pp. 179–211. Mahwah, NJ: Erlbaum

Feldman JA, 1985. Four frames suffice: a provisional model of vision and space. *Behav. Brain Sci.* 8:265–89

Fernandez-Duque D, Thornton IM. 2000. Change detection without awareness: Do explicit reports underestimate the representation of change in the visual system? *Vis. Cogn.* 7:323–44

French RS. 1953. The discrimination of dot patterns as a function of number and average separation of dots. *J. Exp. Psychol.* 46:1–9

Gelfand IM, Fomin SV. 1963. *Calculus of Variations*. Transl. RA Silverman. Englewood Cliffs, NJ: Prentice Hall

Goodale MA, Pelisson D, Prablanc C. 1986. Large adjustments in visually guided reaching do not depend on vision of the hand or perception of target displacement. *Nature* 320:748–50

Grimes J. 1996. On the failure to detect changes in scenes across saccades. In *Perception. Vancouver Studies in Cognitive Science*, ed. K Akins, 5:89–109. New York: Oxford Univ. Press

Gur RC, Hilgard ER. 1975. Visual imagery and the discrimination of differences between altered pictures simultaneously and successively presented. *Br. J. Psychol.* 66:341–45

Gysen V, De Graef P, Verfaillie K. 2000. Detection of intrasaccadic changes in stationary and moving objects. *Invest. Ophthalmol. Vis. Sci.* 41:45 (Abstr.)

Haber RN. 1983. The impending demise of the icon: a critique of the concept of iconic storage in visual information processing. *Behav. Brain Sci.* 6:1–54

Hayhoe MM, Bensinger DG, Ballard DH. 1998. Task constraints in visual working memory. *Vis. Res.* 38:125–37

Henderson JM. 1992. Object identification in context: the visual processing of natural scene. *Can. J. Psychol.* 46:319–41

Henderson JM. 1997. Transsaccadic memory and integration during real-world object perception. *Psychol. Sci.* 8:51–55

Henderson JM, Hollingworth A. 1999a. The

role of fixation position in detecting scene changes across saccades. *Psychol. Sci.* 10: 438–43

Henderson JM, Hollingworth A. 1999b. High-level scene perception. *Annu. Rev. Psychol.* 50:243–71

Hildreth EC, Koch C. 1987. The analysis of visual motion: from computational theories to neuronal mechanisms. *Annu. Rev. Neurosci.* 10:477–533

Hochberg J. 1968. In the mind's eye. In *Contemporary Theory and Research in Visual Perception*, ed. RN Haber, pp. 309–31. New York: Holt, Rinehart & Winston

Hollingworth A, Henderson JM. 2000. Semantic informativeness mediates the detection of changes in natural scenes. *Vis. Cogn.* 7:213–35

Irwin DE. 1991. Information integration across saccadic eye movements. *Cogn. Psychol.* 23: 420–56

Irwin DE. 1996. Integrating information across saccadic eye movements. *Curr. Dir. Psychol. Sci.* 5:94–100

Jacobs WJ, Blackburn JR, Buttrick M, Harpur TJ, Kennedy D, et al. 1988. Observations. *Psychobiology* 16:3–19

Jenkin M, Harris LR, eds. 2001. *Vision and Attention.* New York: Springer

Jiang Y, Olson IR, Chun MM. 2000. Organization of visual short-term memory. *J. Exp. Psychol.: Learn. Mem. Cogn.* 26:683–702

Kahneman D, Treisman A, Gibbs B. 1992. The reviewing of object files: object-specific integration of information. *Cogn. Psychol.* 24:175–219

Kanizsa G. 1979. *Organization in Vision.* New York: Praeger

Kanizsa G, Gerbino W. 1982. Amodal completion: seeing or thinking. In *Organization and Representation in Perception*, ed. J Beck, pp. 167–89. Hillsdale, NJ: Erlbaum

Kirk GS, Raven JE. 1957. *The Presocratic Philosophers: A Critical History with a Selection of Texts.* Cambridge: Cambridge Univ. Press

Klein R, Kingstone A, Pontefract A. 1992. Orienting of visual attention. In *Eye Movements and Visual Cognition: Scene Perception and Reading*, ed. K Rayner, pp. 46–65. New York: Springer

Levin DT, Momen N, Drivdahl SB, Simons DJ. 2000. Change blindness blindness: the metacognitive error of overestimating change-detection ability. *Vis. Cogn.* 7:397–412

Levin DT, Simons DJ. 1997. Failure to detect changes to attended objects in motion pictures. *Psychonom. Bull. Rev.* 4:501–6

Levin DT, Simons DJ. 2000. Perceiving stability in a changing world: combining shots and integrating views in motion pictures and the real world. *Media Psychol.* 2:357–80

Luck SJ, Vogel EK. 1997. The capacity of visual working memory for features and conjunctions. *Nature* 390:279–80

Mack A. 1970. An investigation of the relationship between eye and retinal image movement in the perception of movement. *Percept. Psychophys.* 8:291–98

Marr D. 1982. *Vision.* San Francisco: Freeman

McConkie GW, Currie CB. 1996. Visual stability across saccades while viewing complex pictures. *J. Exp. Psychol.: Hum. Percept. Perform.* 22:563–81

McConkie GW, Zola D. 1979. Is visual information integrated across successive fixations in reading? *Percept. Psychophys.* 25:221–24

Merikle PM, Reingold EM. 1992. Measuring unconscious perceptual processes. In *Perception Without Awareness*, ed. RF Bernstein, TS Pittman, pp. 55–80. New York: Guilford

Miller GA. 1956. The magical number seven, plus or minus two: some limits on our capacity for processing information. *Psychol. Rev.* 63:81–97

Milner AD, Goodale MA. 1995. *The Visual Brain in Action.* Oxford: Oxford Univ. Press

Mitroff SR, Simons DJ. 2000. Changes are not localized before they are explicitly detected. *Invest. Ophthalmol. Vis. Sci.* 41:420 (Abstr.)

Mondy S, Coltheart V. 2000. Detection and identification of change in naturalistic scenes. *Vis. Cogn.* 7:281–96

Nakayama K. 1985. Biological motion processing: a review. *Vis. Res.* 25:625–60

O'Regan JK, Deubel H, Clark JJ, Rensink RA. 2000. Picture changes during blinks: looking without seeing and seeing without looking. *Vis. Cogn.* 7:191–211

O'Regan JK, Rensink RA, Clark JJ. 1999. Change blindness as a result of 'mudsplashes.' *Nature* 398:34

Palmer J. 1986. Mechanisms of displacement discrimination with and without perceived movement. *J. Exp. Psychol.: Hum. Percept. Perform.* 12:411–21

Palmer J. 1988. Very short-term visual memory for size and shape. *Percept. Psychophys.* 43:278–86

Palmer J. 1990. Attentional limits on the perception and memory of visual information. *J. Exp. Psychol.: Hum. Percept. Perform.* 16:332–50

Pashler HE. 1988. Familiarity and visual change detection. *Percept. Psychophys.* 44: 369–78

Pashler HE. 1998. *The Psychology of Attention.* Cambridge, MA: MIT Press

Pashler HE, Badgio PC. 1987. Attentional issues in the identification of alphanumeric characters. In *Attention and Performance XII*, ed. M Coltheart, pp. 63–81. Hillsdale, NJ: Erlbaum

Phillips WA. 1974. On the distinction between sensory storage and short-term visual memory. *Percept. Psychophys.* 16:283–90

Phillips WA, Singer W. 1974. Function and interaction of on and off transients in vision. I. *Psychophysics. Exp. Brain Res.* 19:493–506

Pollack I. 1972. Detection of changes in spatial position: III. Dot number or dot density. *Percept. Psychophys.* 12:487–91

Pylyshyn ZW, Storm RW. 1988. Tracking multiple independent targets: evidence for a parallel tracking mechanism. *Spat. Vis.* 3:179–97

Rensink RA. 1998. Mindsight: visual sensing without seeing. *Invest. Ophthalmol. Vis. Sci.* 39:631 (Abstr.)

Rensink RA. 1999a. The magical number one, plus or minus zero. *Invest. Ophthalmol. Vis. Sci.* 40:52 (Abstr.)

Rensink RA. 1999b. Attentional processing of geometric figures. *Perception* 28(Suppl.): 55–56 (Abstr.)

Rensink RA. 2000a. Seeing, sensing, and scrutinizing. *Vis. Res.* 40:1469–87

Rensink RA. 2000b. Visual search for change: a probe into the nature of attentional processing. *Vis. Cogn.* 7:345–76

Rensink RA. 2000c. The dynamic representation of scenes. *Vis. Cogn.* 7:17–42

Rensink RA. 2001. Change blindness: implications for the nature of visual attention. See Jenkin & Harris 2001, pp. 169–88

Rensink RA, Deubel H, Schneider WX. 2000a. The incredible shrinking span: estimates of memory capacity depend on interstimulus interval. *Invest. Ophthalmol. Vis. Sci.* 41:425 (Abstr.)

Rensink RA, O'Regan JK, Clark JJ. 1997. To see or not to see: the need for attention to perceive changes in scenes. *Psychol. Sci.* 8:368–73

Rensink RA, O'Regan JK, Clark JJ. 2000b. On the failure to detect changes in scenes across brief interruptions. *Vis. Cogn.* 7:127–45

Rich A, Gillam B. 2000. Failure to detect changes in color for lines rotating in depth: the effects of grouping and type of color change. *Vis. Res.* 40:1469–87

Ro T, Russell C, Lavie N. 2001. Changing faces: a detection advantage in the flicker paradigm. *Psychol. Sci.* 12:94–99

Saiki J. 1999. Relation blindness: difficulty in detecting a violation of spatial relations in regular rotations of a triangular pattern. *Invest. Ophthalmol. Vis. Sci.* 40:49 (Abstr.)

Scholl BJ. 2000. Attenuated change blindness for exogenously attended items in a flicker paradigm. *Vis. Cogn.* 7:377–96

Scholl BJ, Pylyshyn ZW, Franconeri SL. 1999. When are featural and spatiotemporal properties encoded as a result of attentional allocation? *Invest. Ophthalmol. Vis. Sci.* 40:797 (Abstr.)

Scott-Brown KC, Baker MR, Orbach HS. 2000. Comparison blindness. *Vis. Cogn.* 7: 253–67

Scott-Brown KC, Orbach HS. 1998. Contrast

discrimination, non-uniform patterns, and change blindness. *Proc. R. Soc. London Ser. B* 265:2159–66

Seiffert AE, Cavanagh P. 1998. Position displacement, not velocity, is the cue to motion detection of second-order patterns. *Vis. Res.* 38:3569–82

Shore DI, Klein RM. 2000. The effects of scene inversion on change-blindness. *J. Gen. Psychol.* 127:27–44

Simons DJ. 1996. In sight, out of mind: when object representations fail. *Psychol. Sci.* 7:301–5

Simons DJ. 2000. Current approaches to change blindness. *Vis. Cogn.* 7:1–15

Simons DJ, Franconeri SL, Reimer RL. 2000. Change blindness in the absence of visual disruption. *Perception* 29:1143–54

Simons DJ, Levin DT. 1997. Change blindness. *Trends Cogn. Sci.* 1:261–67

Simons DJ, Levin DT. 1998. Failure to detect changes to people during a real-world interaction. *Psychonom. Bull. Rev.* 5:644–49

Simons DJ, Mitroff SR. 2001. The role of expectations in change detection and attentional capture. See Jenkin & Harris 2001, pp. 189–207

Smilek D, Eastwood JD, Merikle PM. 2000. Does unattended information facilitate change detection? *J. Exp. Psychol.: Hum. Percept. Perform.* 26:480–87

Smith BC. 1998. *On the Origin of Objects.* Cambridge, MA: MIT Press

Sperling G. 1960. The information available in brief visual presentations. *Psychol. Monogr.* 74:1–29

Sperling G. 1990. Comparison of perception in the moving and stationary eye. In *Eye Movements and Their Role in Visual and Cognitive Processes*, ed. E Kowler, pp. 307–51. New York: Elsevier

Sperling G, Hoff CE. 2000. Third-order versus first-order and second-order motion in ambiguous stimuli: competition reveals temporal tuning functions, monocularity/binocularity, and the role of attention. *Perception* 29(Suppl.):83 (Abstr.)

Sperling G, Speelman RG. 1965. Visual spatial

localization during object motion, apparent object motion, and image motion produced by eye movements. *J. Opt. Soc. Am.* 55:1576–77

Thornton IM, Fernandez-Duque D. 2000. An implicit measure of undetected change. *Spat. Vis.* 14:21–44

Treisman A, Gormican S. 1988. Feature analysis in early vision: evidence from search asymmetries. *Psychol. Rev.* 95:15–48

van der Grind WA, Koenderink JJ, van Doorn AJ. 1986. The distribution of human motion detector properties in the monocular visual field. *Vis. Res.* 26:797–810

Vaughan B, Yantis S. 1999. Information preservation during occlusion. *Invest. Ophthalmol. Vis. Sci.* 40:415 (Abstr.)

Verfaillie K, de Troy A, van Rensbergen J. 1994. Transsaccadic integration of biological motion. *J. Exp. Psychol.: Learn. Mem. Cogn.* 20:649–70

Wallach H, Lewis C. 1966. The effect of abnormal displacement on the retinal image during eye movements. *Percept. Psychophys.* 1:25–29

Wallis G, Bülthoff H. 2000. What's scene and not seen: influences of movement and task upon what we see. *Vis. Cogn.* 7:175–90

Wang RF, Simons DJ. 1999. Active and passive scene recognition across views. *Cognition* 70:191–210

Werner S, Thies B. 2000. Is "change blindness" attenuated by domain-specific expertise? An expert-novices comparison of change detection in football images. *Vis. Cogn.* 7:163–73

Wheeler ME, Treisman AM. 2001. Binding in short-term visual memory. *J. Exp. Psychol.: Gen.* In press

Wilken P, Mattingley JB, Korb KB, Webster WR, Conway D. 1999. *Capacity limits for detection versus reportability of change in visual scenes.* Presented at 26th Annu. Austr. Exp. Psychol. Conf., April 9–11, Sydney

Williams P, Simons DJ. 2000. Detecting changes in novel, complex three-dimensional objects. *Vis. Cogn.* 7:297–322

Wolfe JM. 1999. Inattentional amnesia. In *Fleeting Memories*, ed. V Coltheart, pp. 71–94. Cambridge, MA: MIT Press

Woodhouse JM, Barlow HB. 1982. Spatial and temporal resolution and analysis. In *The Senses*, ed. HB Barlow, pp. 152–62. Cambridge: Cambridge Univ. Press

Wright M, Green A, Baker S. 2000. Limitations for change detection in multiple Gabor targets. *Vis. Cogn.* 7:237–52

Yantis S. 1992. Multielement visual tracking: attention and perceptual organization. *Cogn. Psychol.* 24:295–340

Zelinsky G. 1997. Eye movements during change detection search task. *Invest. Ophthalmol. Vis. Sci.* 38:373 (Abstr.)

Annu. Rev. Psychol. 2002. 53.279–307

ORGANIZATIONAL BEHAVIOR:
Affect in the Workplace

Arthur P. Brief[1] and Howard M. Weiss[2]

[1]A. B. Freeman School of Business and Department of Psychology, Tulane University, New Orleans, Louisiana 70118; e-mail: artbrief@tulane.edu
[2]Department of Psychological Sciences, Purdue University, West Lafayette, Indiana 47907; e-mail: weiss@psych.purdue.edu

Key Words moods and emotions, job satisfaction, positive and negative affectivity, work environments, job performance

■ **Abstract** The study of affect in the workplace began and peaked in the 1930s, with the decades that followed up to the 1990s not being particularly fertile. Whereas job satisfaction generally continues to be loosely but not carefully thought of and measured as an affective state, critical work in the 1990s has raised serious questions about the affective status of job satisfaction in terms of its causes as well as its definition and measurement. Recent research has focused on the production of moods and emotions at work, with an emphasis, at least conceptually, on stressful events, leaders, work groups, physical settings, and rewards/punishment. Other recent research has addressed the consequences of workers' feelings, in particular, a variety of performance outcomes (e.g., helping behaviors and creativity). Even though recent interest in affect in the workplace has been intense, many theoretical and methodological opportunities and challenges remain.

CONTENTS

INTRODUCTION

The organizations in which people work affect their thoughts, feelings, and actions in the workplace and away from it. Likewise, people's thoughts, feelings, and actions affect the organizations in which they work. Organizational behavior is an area of inquiry concerned with both sorts of influence: work organizations on people and people on work organizations. The slice of the organizational behavior literature this paper addresses has to do with the feelings of workers, how organizations affect them and how they affect organizations. As should become clear in the following section, we choose to focus on the affective dimensions of organizational behavior because, after a lapse of more than half a century, organizational researchers have begun to demonstrate a serious interest in moods and emotions in the workplace.

The remainder of the paper unfolds as follows. First, the study of workers' feelings is placed in a historical context and, thereby, the boundaries of the chapter are delineated further. Second, the affective status of the job satisfaction construct is assessed very briefly. Third, recent literature pertaining to the production of moods and emotions in the workplace is reviewed, followed by a survey of the effects of moods and emotions experienced in the workplace. Finally, conceptual concerns about workers' feelings not adequately addressed in the organizational literature are raised, and suggestions for how to approach these concerns methodologically are provided. Overall, the intents of the paper are to appraise what is known about affective experiences in organizational settings, to highlight existing gaps in the literature, and to suggest how those gaps might be filled.

THE HISTORICAL CONTEXT

The Rich 1930s and the Leaner Years

The study of affect at work clearly emerged as a scientific research concern in the 1930s, principally in the United States; this likely was made possible by earlier developments that philosophically justified the application of scientific principles to the study of social phenomenon, that supplied the methodological tools necessary to conduct such research, and that created the perceived need for understanding workers' feelings in the minds of those who managed them. Examples of now-classic studies from this period that focused on affect per se or job satisfaction include Fisher & Hanna's (1931) *The Dissatisfied Worker*, Kornhauser & Sharp's (1932) "Employee attitudes; suggestions from a study in a factory," Hersey's (1932) *Workers' Emotions in Shop and Home: A Study of Individual Workers from the Psychological and Physiological Standpoint*, Hoppock's (1935) *Job Satisfaction*, and Roethlisberger & Dickson's (1939) *Management and the Worker*.

The 1930s were exciting times for the study of affect at work, characterized by innovation and discovery as well as a diversity of ideas and methods. For instance, Fisher & Hanna (1931), relying on the findings of a number of case studies, characterized job dissatisfaction as the product of "nonadjustive emotional tendencies" whose associated unrest is misattributed by workers to their job situations. Kornhauser & Sharp (1932) conducted an attitude survey of Kimberly Clark employees, supplemented by interviews, and concluded that "efficiency ratings of employees showed no relationship to their attitudes" (p. 402). Hersey (1932), using a repeated measures design with a small group of skilled workers, observed, among many other things, a clear relationship between daily affect levels and daily performance levels as well as considerable influence of workers' emotional lives at home on their work behaviors. Hoppock (1935), using surveys and interviews of workers in one community (New Hope, Pennsylvania) and in one occupation (teachers), in part found elements of the work environment (e.g., supervision), family expectations, and "emotional maladjustment," all to influence job satisfaction. Roethlisberger & Dickson (1939), based upon a series of studies using a variety of methods in the Hawthorne plant of AT&T's Western Electric division, concluded, for instance, that the workplace's social organization and the individual's interaction with that organization, more than individual differences per se, determined worker adjustment.

The diversity evident in the 1930s soon faded and was replaced by an approach that was conceptually and methodologically narrow. This approach entailed (*a*) construing of affect at work almost exclusively in terms of job satisfaction; (*b*) measuring constructs of interest with structured questionnaires, largely ignoring, for instance, more clinical or qualitative methods; (*c*) focusing on empirical observables to such an extent that adequate attention to theory building too often was excluded; and (*d*) examining the facets of the work environment as causes of job satisfaction while generally neglecting dispositional and extra-work factors such as family and economic circumstances.

Whereas one could speculate on the causes of this narrowing [e.g., the reliance on questionnaires may have been attributable to developments in the measurement of attitudes, and the almost exclusive concern with work environment causes of job satisfaction might have been due to the desire of industrial psychologists to aid management in controlling the workplace (Baritz 1960)], here we address only the results of the narrowing (for more details on the 1930s, see Weiss & Brief 2002). For almost the next half century one workplace event, condition, or outcome after another was correlated with pencil-and-paper measures of job satisfaction, typically not guided by a well-articulated theoretical frame of reference, yielding well in excess of 10,000 studies (Spector 1996)! We will review that literature here; for such reviews see, for example, Locke (1976) and Spector (1997). In the next section, however, we do take a brief look at job satisfaction but only through an affective lens, considering recent approaches that recognize that job satisfaction does not equal affect.

The Hot 1990s

In the mid-1980s and the 1990s, organizational researchers rediscovered affect, expressing interest in both moods and emotions. Here, "moods" are considered to be generalized feeling states that are not typically identified with a particular stimulus and not sufficiently intense to interrupt ongoing thought processes (e.g., Clark & Isen 1982, Thayer 1989); alternatively, "emotions" normally are associated with specific events or occurrences and are intense enough to disrupt thought processes (e.g., Frijda 1993, Simon 1982; for a review of the emotions literature, see Zajonc 1998). Moreover, whereas moods often [but not always (e.g., Russell & Barrett 1999)] are described in terms of their underlying dimensions (e.g., positive and negative) (e.g., Watson 2000), emotions tend to be treated in their discrete forms (e.g., anger, fear, and joy) (e.g., Plutchik 1994). This review focuses on research in organizations on such moods and emotions. Why such research re-emerged as an area of inquiry in organizational behavior is not known, but it likely had a lot to do with the seemingly intense interests moods and emotions were (and are) attracting generally in psychology (e.g., the American Psychological Association launched a new journal, *Emotion*, in 2001). Whatever the cause, there now exists a contemporary literature concerned with affective experiences in organizational settings, to which we now turn.

THE AFFECTIVE STATUS OF JOB SATISFACTION

Definitional Concerns

In 1976, Locke advanced what came to be a highly influential definition of job satisfaction. He defined it as "a pleasurable or positive emotional state resulting from the appraisal of one's job or job experiences" (p. 1300). Thus, job satisfaction came to be considered an affective reaction to one's job. Almost a decade later Organ & Near (1985) recognized that job satisfaction has a cognitive as well as an affective dimension and questioned the extent to which commonly used measures of the construct capture both (also see Pekrun & Frese 1992, Sandelands 1988). Brief & Roberson (1989) empirically explored the affective and cognitive content of three commonly used measures of job satisfaction. They observed that only the Faces scale (Kunin 1955) captured the affective and cognitive components about equally and that the other two highly popular measures investigated mostly tapped the cognitive components. Thus, Brief & Roberson discovered a paradox that remains troublesome today: Job satisfaction generally is construed in affective terms, but typically only its cognitive aspects are measured (also see Porac 1987).

Progress towards a more balanced treatment of job satisfaction, at least conceptually, was made during the 1990s. Motowidlo (1996) defined self-reports of job satisfaction as "*judgments* about the *favorability* of the *work environment*" (p. 176) (also see Pratkanis & Turner 1994). Consistently, but more explicitly, adopting a construal of job satisfaction as an attitude, Weiss (2002) defined it as "a positive (or negative) evaluative judgment one makes about one's job or job situation" (p. 6). Perhaps most closely aligned with the attitude construct is Brief's (1998) definition. Based on Eagly & Chaiken's (1993) assertion that an attitude is "*a psychological tendency that is expressed by evaluating a particular entity with some degree of favor* or *disfavor,*" with "evaluating" referring to "all classes of evaluative responding, whether overt or covert, cognitive, affective, or behavioral" (p. 1), he defined job satisfaction as "*an internal state that is expressed by affectively and/or cognitively evaluating an experienced job with some degree of favor or disfavor*" (p. 86). Brief, like Bagozzi & Burnkrant (1979), as well as others, excluded evaluative responses of the behavioral type because they often are treated as dependent effects of the attitude.

The distinction between job satisfaction as an evaluative judgment and as an attitude with affective as well as cognitive components is not trivial. For example, Weiss (2002, Weiss & Cropanzano 1996) asserted that affective experiences on the job are a cause of job satisfaction (construed as an evaluative judgment); Weiss et al. (1999a) have demonstrated empirically this is so (also see Fisher 2000, Kelloway et al. 1993). It also has been asserted that self-reported affect at work [for example, as gauged by Burke and associates' (1989) Job Affect Scale] is an indicator of the affective component of job satisfaction; Moorman (1993), consistent with the reasoning for instance of Millar & Tesser (1986), has shown that so-called affective- and cognitive-based measures of job satisfaction differentially predict the same criterion. He found a cognitive-based measure to predict "organizational citizenship behaviors" (e.g., Organ 1988) better than an affective-based measure of job satisfaction. Thus, it appears that job satisfaction may be approached productively in at least two ways: (*a*) If job satisfaction is taken as an evaluative judgment, then affect at work can be seen as an antecedent to it, and (*b*) if job satisfaction is taken to have an affective component, then affect at work can be seen to be an indicator of it. Researchers, in the future, should recognize explicitly that these approaches, while distinctive, may not be in conflict (i.e., moods and emotions experienced on the job may be both a cause of job attitudes and an indicator of them) and that each has its own merits.

Regarding the merits of the "affect as a cause approach," for example as advanced in affective events theory (Weiss & Cropanzano 1996), it draws much needed attention to streams of events that can unfold in workplaces and that generate emotional reactions or mood changes. Regarding the merits of the "affect as indicator approach," it, for example, encourages one to consider the components of job satisfaction and how they might be related to consequent behaviors that may be more affectively than cognitively driven or vice versa. Either approach indicates that job satisfaction's affective status was elevated in such a way during the 1990s that it no longer should be acceptable to define job satisfaction one way (affectively) and blindly measure it another (cognitively).

Dispositional Influences

Another way the affective status of job satisfaction has been elevated in recent years is by the recognition that it is influenced by "affective dispositions" (e.g., Judge 1992) or, more precisely, by personality traits that have been labeled temperaments (Watson 2000). These traits are neuroticism [or negative affectivity (NA)] and extraversion [or positive affectivity (PA)], both components of the five-factor model of personality (e.g., Watson & Clark 1992), with individuals high in the former prone to experience a diverse array of negative mood states (e.g., anxiety, depression, hostility, and guilt) and individuals high in the latter prone to describe themselves as cheerful, enthusiastic, confident, active, and energetic. Organizational interest in these traits stems from Staw and associates' (1986) attention-grabbing demonstration that affective disposition gauged when participants were 15 to 18 years of age correlated significantly ($r = 0.35\ p \le 0.01$) with a measure of job satisfaction taken when the participants ranged from about 54 to 62 years of age. Although Staw et al.'s results and dispositional interpretations have not gone uncriticized (e.g., Davis-Blake & Pfeffer 1996, Williams et al. 1996), detected relationships between negative and/or positive affectivity and job satisfaction now are commonplace in the literature (e.g., Agho et al. 1992; Cropanzano et al. 1993; Necowitz & Roznowski 1994; Schaubroeck et al. 1992, 1998; Watson & Slack 1993). Various explanations for these empirical observations have been advanced (Arvey et al. 1991, House et al. 1996, Judge 1992); recent examples of these are presented below.

Following the lead of Schmitt & Bedeian (1982), Watson & Slack (1993), reasoned that job satisfaction and general temperament mutually influence one another. That is, affective dispositions broadly influence the extent to which people are satisfied with and derive pleasure from their jobs (as well as other aspects of their lives), and because job satisfaction is an important life domain, it may lead to more general life satisfaction and better emotional adjustment (i.e., higher trait positive affect and lower trait negative affect). To our knowledge, such a reciprocal relationship remains to be tested.

Drawing on the "instrumental" and "temperamental" views described by McCrae & Costa (1991), Brief et al. (1995) reasoned that high NA individuals (*a*) because of their tendency to dwell on failures and shortcomings of themselves and others, may alienate their co-workers and managers, resulting in more negative interpersonal interactions, thus lowering job satisfaction (also see Burke et al. 1993) and (*b*) because they are more sensitive to negative stimuli, may react with more extreme emotion when experiencing negative job events, thus lowering job satisfaction (also see Parkes 1990). Brief et al. also posited that high NA individuals might respond with diminished pleasure when experiencing positive job events. They attributed such a possibility to high NA individuals (*a*) having a higher threshold for positive stimuli, (*b*) having a lower-magnitude positive mood reaction to positive events, and/or (*c*) experiencing the effects of positive mood–inducing events for shorter periods of time than those low in NA. Brief et al., in a field experiment, did observe an interaction between NA and a positive mood induction such that the induction had less of an effect on job satisfaction among individuals high in NA. This observed interaction, however, could have been attributable to any or all of the three underlying mechanisms they posited.

After Weiss & Cropanzano (1996), Weiss et al. (1999a), as noted earlier, hypothesized that global satisfaction judgments are, in part, a function of "true affective experiences at work or 'the preponderance of pleasant affect' over time" (p. 4); they supported this prediction with daily accounts of mood-at-work data. Moreover, Weiss et al. hypothesized and observed that "dispositional happiness" predicts "average state levels of pleasant-unpleasant mood at work over the course of the mood assessment period" (p. 5). Their results are consistent with a personality–mood at work–job satisfaction causal chain. Brief (1998), in his integrated model of job satisfaction, proposed a somewhat different causal chain: personality–interpretations of job circumstances–job satisfaction, with "interpretations" referring "to how a person construes or apprehends the objective circumstances of his or her job" (p. 96). Whereas one could empirically pit one model against the other, it appears more reasonable to consider that temperaments influence job satisfaction through both mood at work and interpretations of job circumstances, recognizing that moods and interpretations are unlikely to be independent.

Shaw et al. (1999) creatively pursued Larsen & Ketalaar's (1989) assertion that PA and NA represent reward-signal sensitivity and punishment-signal sensitivity, respectively. They argued that not all elements of job satisfaction evolve both sensitivities; in particular, pay evokes reward sensitivity only. Moreover, Shaw et al. hypothesized and, to a considerable degree, empirically demonstrated that NA is unrelated to pay satisfaction and that PA is associated with it; additionally, PA interacted with actual salary level to predict some dimensions of pay satisfaction. The form of the interactions, as predicted, indicated that low PA individuals are much more satisfied with high rather than low pay relative to high PA individuals.

Whereas it is clear that temperaments can influence job satisfaction, the processes by which this happens are not yet well understood. It appears that personality operates through multiple channels to affect job satisfaction, and different elements of job satisfaction may be differentially affected by the same affective trait. Whatever mechanisms may be discovered, the affective status of job satisfaction has been elevated merely by the repeated demonstration that affective dispositional traits such as NA and PA (along with environmental stimuli) are associated with job satisfaction.

Summary

In a knee-jerk fashion, job satisfaction generally continues to be loosely but not carefully thought of as an affective reaction and to be measured in ways that have been assumed, largely uncritically for decades, to tap how workers feel. In the 1990s, however, the construct began to be examined closely in affective terms. Moods and emotions experienced at work have been shown to influence job satisfaction. Can these same moods and emotions also be taken as indicators of job satisfaction? Should job satisfaction be construed as an evaluative judgment or as an attitude with affective and cognitive components? Job satisfaction has been shown to be influenced by temperaments. What are the processes that underlie these relationships? Do these processes vary by the focal job element being evaluated (e.g., pay versus job security)? We have seen the beginnings of a change in the way the relationship between affect and job satisfaction is construed. Whether or not it fully materializes depends on how vigorously answers to the sorts of questions posed here are pursued and, more importantly, the extent to which as yet unasked questions about the affective status of job satisfaction are advanced in ways that capture the interests of researchers.

THE PRODUCTION OF MOODS AND EMOTIONS IN THE WORKPLACE

Exogenous Factors

Obviously, the feelings people experience at work may have been produced elsewhere (e.g., marital problems at home may spill over and affect how one feels at work) (e.g., Hersey 1932). Such carryover states, although important for understanding behaviors in organizations, are not of concern here; rather, this section focuses on factors in the workplace that influence the feelings experienced there. Also exogenous to the workplace and, thus, not the focus of attention are two factors worthy of mention, for they have been considered in the organizational literature: (*a*) diurnal and other recurring cycles in feelings over time and (*b*) dispositional influences on affective states.

Cycles in feelings (i.e., moods) can arise from rhythms related to lifestyle, to sociocultural factors, and to biological factors (e.g., Watson 2000). Weiss et al. (1999a) have conducted perhaps the only modern study designed to examine mood cycles at work. Based upon affective events theory (Weiss & Cropanzano 1996), they expected and observed in a sample of 24 middle managers that mood cycles at work do exist and that individuals differ in their cycles of pleasantness and activation at work. Weiss et al. recognized that "the causes and consequences of these differences remain to be explored," and that more generally, "it is important to emphasize that identifying these cycles is not the same as explaining them" (p. 21).

In the previous sections, we addressed, albeit rather briefly, historical interest in the dispositional basis of affect at work and contemporary concern with dispositional approaches to job satisfaction. Consistent with these observations, we note that, in the 1990s, statistically significant correlations between NA and workplace-experienced depressed mood, anxiety, and other indicators of negative affect were commonplace (e.g., Fortunato et al. 1999, George et al. 1993, Hart et al. 1995, Heinisch & Jex 1997, Schaubroeck et al. 1992, Spector & O'Connell 1994). Typically, these correlations were found in investigations appearing in the job stress literature, in which it is well known that personality plays multiple, influential roles in stress and coping processes whose outcomes often are construed in terms of affect (e.g., George & Brief 2001, Lazarus & Cohen-Charash 2001). George's (1990) demonstration that characteristic levels of the personality traits of PA and NA, within work groups, are positively associated with their corresponding (positive and negative) affective tones. George's (e.g., 1996) work takes affect up to a more aggregate level of analysis with its focus on "group affective tone," which she defines as "consistent or homogenous affective reactions within a group" (p. 78).

Stressful Events/Conditions at Work

Conceptually at least, workplace endogenous factors that produce moods and emotions have been grouped into several not necessarily mutually exclusive categories (e.g., George 1996, George & Brief 1992, Weiss & Cropanzano 1996). Examples of these categories include stressful events (or aversive stimuli), leaders, workgroup characteristics, physical settings, and organizational rewards and punishments. We begin by considering stressful events. The job-related stress literature is massive (with at least one journal, *Work & Stress*, exclusively devoted to the topic), populated by a diversity of theoretical orientations (e.g., Cooper 1998), and too often methodologically muddled (e.g., Hurrell et al. 1998). Because the focus of this chapter is on affect, not job stress per se, we provide examples only of those stress studies that explicitly examined affect. Several studies in the 1990s sought to ascertain if NA is a nuisance in the analysis of job stress because it inflates relationships between self-reports of stressors and strains (e.g., Schaubroeck et al. 1992). These studies, while providing evidence of personality-affect linkages, otherwise have contributed little to understanding the production of moods and emotions at work. The attention focused on NA by job stress researchers may have distracted from efforts aimed at systematically identifying those events/conditions in the workplace associated with negative feelings. It is time to move on.

Signs of the direction of that movement are evident. In an experience sampling study of employed mothers, Williams et al. (1991) observed that self-reported multiple role juggling (i.e., simultaneously attending to demands of different roles) had immediate negative effects on mood; however, habituation to role juggling occurred when mood was examined over time. Moreover, Williams & Alliger (1994), in an experience sampling study of employed parents, found that unpleasant mood spilled over from family to work but pleasant moods had little spillover. (For a conceptual treatment of juggling and emotions, see Wharton & Erickson 1993.) George et al. (1993) observed that the extent of a nurses' exposure to AIDS patients, as part of the nursing role, is positively associated with negative mood at work and that this relationship is moderated by organizational and social support. Hart et al. (1995), among a sample of police officers, found that self-reports of emotion-focused coping with work events was associated with more negative job experiences, which, in turn, were associated with more negative and less positive affect. The most important negative job experiences were shown to be organizationally related (e.g., dealing with administration and supervision) rather than operationally related (e.g., dealing with victims and danger). Zohar (1999), using pooled-time series analysis on daily records of a sample of military parachute trainers, observed that daily occupational hassle severity, measured independently by an expert, predicted end-of-day negative mood. Teuchmann et al. (1999), using an experience sampling methodology with a small sample of accountants, found self-reported time pressure to be associated with negative mood and that perceived control may alleviate this negative effect.

The above six studies exemplify what we believe to be good and bad about what appears to be emerging in the job stress literature pertaining to moods and emotions. On the positive side, the literature seems to be advancing methodologically, with the increased use of experience sampling resulting in less reliance on cross-sectional designs that make inferences about process hazardous. Substantially, on the positive side, with physically threatening conditions of work (e.g., AIDS) being considered, an interest in the social environment at work as a source of distress is being placed in a more proper perspective; that is, threats to physical well-being are beginning to receive the attention they deserve.

On the negative side, several substantive concerns are evident: Discrete emotions tend not to be the focus of study; economic events/conditions have not taken their appropriate place alongside social and physical factors as potential job stressors; and, consistently, the search for potential job stressors is not guided by a widely accepted theoretical frame of reference or even a small set of competitive theories—rather, each empirical investigation seems to be driven by a somewhat unique theoretical orientation. Thus, the job stress literature has yielded relatively little, in a cumulative sense, toward understanding the production of moods and emotions in the workplace, and without theoretical guidance, it is unlikely to do so.

Leaders

Leaders, in various ways, have been theorized to affect how their followers feel (e.g., George 2000). For example, George (1996), following George & Brief

(1992), asserted, "Leaders who feel excited, enthusiastic, and energetic themselves are likely to similarly energize their followers, as are leaders who feel distressed and hostile likely to negatively activate their followers" (p. 84). This idea clearly is evident in the transformational leadership literature, in which the claim is made that these types of leaders use strong emotions to arouse similar feelings in their audiences (e.g., Conger & Kanungo 1998); others have reasoned that managers can foster and shape the arousal of their subordinates through the use of symbols (e.g., Ashforth & Humphrey 1995). Some recent evidence does support the role of leaders in the production of moods and emotions. Fitness (2000), for instance, observed that what angered people depended upon their organizational position. For lower-power workers (e.g., followers), anger was a product of unjust treatment by higher-power workers (e.g., leaders). If the offenses from above involved humiliation, low-power workers experienced moderate to high levels of hate for offenders. Lewis (2000b), in a laboratory study, found that followers observing a leader expressing anger felt more nervous and less relaxed than followers observing a leader expressing sadness or no emotion. In addition, she found that followers observing a leader expressing sadness felt less enthusiasm and more fatigue then followers observing a leader expressing anger or no emotion. Although results like these are interesting, it is clear that the organizational literature is populated with many more ideas about the leader's role in the production of moods and emotions than it is with relevant data.

Work Group Characteristics

Preliminary research suggests that work groups commonly have consistent or homogeneous affective reactions (e.g., George 1990, 1995; conceptually, also see Barsade & Gibson 1998, Sandelands & St. Clair 1993; for counter-evidence, see Barsade et al. 2000); as was noted above, this "group affective tone" is influenced by characteristic levels of personality traits within groups. These characteristic levels of personality have been theorized to be brought about by member similarity resulting from attraction-selection-attrition processes described by Schneider (1987, George 1990). Beyond personality, a number of other factors have been posited to explain why work group members tend to share moods and emotions (e.g., Bartel & Saavedra 2000, George 1996, George & Brief 1992), for example, (*a*) common socialization experiences and common social influences (Hackman 1992); (*b*) similarity of tasks and high task interdependence (see Gallupe et al. 1991, Heath & Jourden 1997 on group task activity per se); (*c*) membership stability; (*d*) mood regulation norms and rules [see, e.g., the literature on emotional labor (e.g., Sutton 1991)]; and (*d*) after Hatfield et al. (1994), emotional contagion (see Pugh 2001 for a study of emotional contagion from employees to customers).

Regarding these work group characteristics, we again observe that ideas far outstrip data. The following examples of recent studies do demonstrate considerable promise, however. Totterdell et al. (1998) showed, in two studies (with community nurses and accountants), that people's moods are influenced by the collective mood of their co-workers over time. Moreover, for the nurses, this result was not dependent on common daily hassles, but was, for instance, on age (with a greater association for older nurses) and commitment to teams (with a greater association for more committed nurses). In a follow-up study of two professional cricket teams, Totterdell (2000) found, with pooled time-series analyses, significant associations between the average of teammates' happy moods and the players' own moods. In addition, these results were independent of hassles and favorable standing in the match and, like Totterdell et al., dependent on player age and commitment to the team. Bartel & Saavedra (2000), based upon a study of 70 work groups, found convergence between observers' reports and self-report indicators of eight distinct mood categories, with the weakest relationships detected for mood categories characterized by low arousal. Convergence in members' mood increased with task and social interdependence, membership stability, and mood regulation norms. We hope the research by Bartel & Saavedra and by Totterdell and his colleagues will help provide the impetus for more research on how work group characteristics affect the production of moods and emotions.

Physical Settings

Very little is known about how physical settings, even broadly construed, affect feelings in the workplace. Oldham et al. (1995) used a quasi-experimental design to observe that music improved the mood states of workers and that this effect was stronger for workers performing relatively simple jobs. Also addressing job complexity were Spector & Jex (1991), who observed that incumbent (but not independent) ratings of job characteristics were associated with anxiety and frustration, leading them to urge caution in the use of incumbent self-reports of job characteristics as indicators of actual work environments. This warning seems not to have been heeded by Saavedra & Kwun (2000), who found, in their sample of managers, that self-reports of job characteristics were related to both independent assessments of activated pleasant and unpleasant affect and went on to treat these results as if they entailed job characteristics, by addressing the implications of them for the actual design of managerial work in their discussion.

A few other studies exemplify what can be considered as falling into the physical setting domain. Rafaeli & Sutton (1990), using structured observations of 194 transactions between cashiers and customers in 5 supermarkets, found store busyness to be related negatively to cashiers' displayed positive emotion, and customer demand (i.e., the extent to which a transaction required a prolonged and complex cashier response) to be related positively to displayed positive emotions. Of course, one must question the degree to which such displayed emotions are congruent with those felt. Locke (1996) provides another example of the study of the "emotional labor" (e.g., Hochschild 1983) process, which concerns the production of displayed feelings. During a year-long study in a pediatric department, she observed the interplay between emotions expressed by patients and their families and those expressed by physicians. Locke found that physicians tended to enact comedic performances in response to families' negative emotions, presumably to display and generate fun, which is incompatible with the anxiety, fear, and despondence patients' families may bring to medical encounters.

As a final example, Wasserman et al. (2000; also see, e.g., Strati 1992, 1996; White 1990), drawing on both qualitative and quantitative data, demonstrated links between the aesthetics of physical cues or symbols in organizations (restaurants and bars) and the emotions felt by potential participants. For instance, research participants reacting to photographs of eclectically designed establishments reported largely pleasant emotions, whereas the reactions to monomorphic designs were considerably more mixed.

In sum, recent organizational research on the relationship between the properties of physical settings and the experience of mood and emotions has been slim and characterized by highly varied theoretical and methodological orientations; little knowledge has accumulated. Obvious properties like temperature, noise, and lighting appear to have been ignored, at least recently, in the organizational literature [for a glimpse of the literature on physical settings outside the organizational arena, see, for example, Sundstrom et al. (1996).]

Organizational Rewards/Punishments

The final category of factors we previously identified as theorized to produce moods and emotions is organizational rewards and punishments. Surprisingly, given their potential import (e.g., Brief & Aldag 1994), we found very few empirical studies in the 1990s and beyond in the organizational literature that addressed linkages between rewards/punishments and workers' feelings. What we did isolate was research that adopted a justice frame of reference (e.g., Folger & Cropanzano 1998, Greenberg 1990). For example, Weiss et al. (1999b) found that happiness was influenced by outcomes, with procedural fairness playing little role; alternatively, guilt, anger, and, to a lesser extent, pride were influenced by specific combinations of outcomes and procedures (also see Bies 2001, Bies & Tripp 2001; see Miller 2001 for a more general treatment of the topic). Whereas these results, because of their provocative nature, suggest that a justice orientation to understanding affective reactions to organizational rewards/punishments is worthwhile, it is most clear that rewards/punishments from an affect standpoint largely have been ignored. This sad state of affairs likely will be best corrected by pursuing multitheoretical avenues, justice being one of them.

Summary

The above treatment of the literature by the categories we identified should not be taken as encompassing all existing approaches to understanding the production of moods and emotions in the workplace. Other, more isolated approaches do exist. For example, we found papers that compared the moods of unemployed and unsatisfactory employed young adults over time (Winefield et al. 1991) and that theorized about the causes of jealousy and envy at work (Vecchio 1995). Even though our review of the recent organizational literature was not comprehensive, several observations appear warranted.

First, personality as a determinant of workplace moods (but not workplace emotions) seems relatively well established; how attributes of the workplace might interact with personality to affect feelings has been approached too narrowly, theoretically, and empirically. Second, in the job stress literature, threats to physical well-being as a source of negative moods and emotions are beginning to draw needed attention; however, as is characteristic of the job stress literature in general, this research has not been conducted with the intent of developing a meta-theory of job stress—a framework to guide the search for those conditions of work likely to produce negative moods and emotions. Third, empirical research on how leaders may affect the feelings of their followers is embryonic; however, it exhibits tremendous promise on theoretical grounds. Fourth, perhaps the most exciting new area of research is that pertaining to group affective tone. Available theory is provocative, and the few empirical results now available generally are supportive of the ideas that have been advanced to explain how work group members come to share their feelings. Fifth, research on affective reactions to the physical work environment is small and eclectic, but interesting. Research that recognizes that customers/clients/patients can be construed as mood and emotion generators and that focuses on the mood and emotional consequences of the workplace aesthetics (including music) seems to be especially intriguing. Sixth, virtually no progress has been made in the past decade toward understanding the effects of organizational rewards and punishments on how workers feel. Finally, the research reviewed here admirably often relied upon longitudinal designs that could allow for the study of process (i.e., how the production of moods and emotions unfolds); however, rarely did studies include objective indicators of those workplace features thought to produce moods and emotions, thereby leaving us too dependent on self-reports, which may not be congruent with more independent measures of the workplace and may, themselves, be influenced by the feelings workers experience (the dependent variables of interest).

In closing, for the past ten years or more, organizational researchers have raised many more questions than they have answered about the production of moods and emotions. We interpret this state of affairs opportunistically, as a beginning or, in light of our earlier historical analysis, as a rebirth. After considering below the consequences of workers' feeling, we turn to gaps in the literature in need of filling; thus, the production of moods and emotions will surface again.

CONSEQUENCES OF MOODS AND EMOTIONS IN THE WORKPLACE

Conceptual Orientations

In the past decade several conceptual discussions of affect appeared that focused either on the organizational consequences of affective states or traits or included discussions of consequences within broader discussions of mood and emotion at work. Stimulated partly by these organizationally focused conceptual pieces and partly by more basic research, empirical work appeared demonstrating the attitudinal or behavioral consequences of affect at work. Among the conceptual pieces published, three stand out. Isen & Baron (1991) presented a wide-ranging discussion of the potential effects of positive affect on a variety of work-relevant attitudes, behaviors, and cognitive processes. Their discussion is notable for its effort to connect organizational issues to basic research on mood, particularly Isen's (1987, 1999, 2000) body of work on positive affect. At the same time, its exclusive focus on positive affect makes it less useful for understanding the effects of negative mood states or discrete emotions. George & Brief (1992) examined the relationship between affective states and what they called "organizational spontaneity," a variant on what has come to be known as extra-role or organizational citizenship behaviors. They argued that mood at work is a proximal cause of spontaneity and that individual mood is, in turn, influenced by individual mood-generating factors both on and off the job as well as group affective tone.

Weiss & Cropanzano (1996) presented a broad discussion of the consequences of affective states and traits at work. Of particular interest is their distinction between affect-driven and judgment-driven behaviors. According to Weiss & Cropanzano, affect-driven behaviors are relatively immediate behavioral and cognitive outcomes of affective states. These effects generally are bounded in time and unmediated by overall evaluative judgments about jobs as a whole or elements of the job experience. Judgment-driven behaviors are outcomes influenced by overall or particular evaluative judgments such as job or facet satisfaction. They further argued that some satisfaction-outcome relationships reported in the literature may be the spurious result of affective states influencing both satisfaction and the particular outcome in question.

Judgments

Most organizational research closely follows findings from the basic research literature on the behavioral and cognitive effects of affective states, particularly moods. That organizational research shows, as we demonstrate, that affective states can influence a variety of performance-relevant outcomes including judgments, attitudinal responses, creativity, helping behavior, and risk taking. We begin by considering judgments.

The effects of affect on judgments have been studied in a number of ways. DeNisi and his associates (Robbins & DeNisi 1994, 1998; Varma et al. 1996) examined the relationship between what they referred to as "interpersonal affect" and performance evaluations. Similar research by Judge & Ferris (1993) examined supervisor liking for a subordinate and supervisor ratings of the subordinate's performance. In aggregate, these kinds of studies showed interpersonal affect and liking to be related to both performance ratings and certain intervening cognitive processes. However, as measured, interpersonal affect and liking seem more assessments of attitudes held toward a subordinate than assessments of any real affective experiences with the subordinate or affective responses to the subordinate. As such, these studies do demonstrate that attitudinal consistency can bias performance judgments, but provide less clarity regarding affective influences on appraisals.

In an interesting twist on the affect-performance evaluation relationship, Fried et al. (1999) examined the relationship between NA and deliberate rating inflation. They argued that raters high on NA would generally produce higher ratings than raters low on NA, through such automatic processes as biased recall. The consequence of these automatic distortions is that high NA raters would have less room or inclination to deliberately inflate their ratings and, therefore, more inflation would be seen among raters low in NA. Whereas Fried et al. did not measure distortion per se, their results did show that NA was positively correlated with self-reports of distortion and that this relationship was moderated by the extent to which supervisors were required to document subordinates' work behaviors and the extent to which appraisals were visible among peers.

Other performance-relevant judgments have been shown to be influenced by affect. Saavedra & Earley (1991) showed that self-efficacy was higher among subjects exposed to a positive affect manipulation than it was among subjects exposed to a negative affect manipulation. Unfortunately, the absence of a neutral affect control group precludes the ability to determine whether positive affect enhances efficacy, negative affect reduces efficacy, or both. Brief et al. (1995) had two groups of employees complete a typical job satisfaction measure. One group was put in a positive mood by the receipt of small gifts. The other group served as a control. Employees in a positive mood reported higher levels of job satisfaction than did employees in the control group. Note that this may be a demonstration of the biasing effects of immediate mood on judgment, rather than of the substantive influence of work-relevant affect on the formation of job attitudes.

Creative Problem Solving

A longstanding laboratory finding is that being in a positive mood can enhance creative problem solving (Isen 1999). This relationship has been tested in the field: Estrada et al. (1997) showed that physicians placed in a positive mood scored better on a test of creativity. Madjar et al. (2001) demonstrated that positive mood, but not negative mood, predicted on the job ratings of creativity and mediated the effects of social support on creativity ratings.

Helping Behaviors

A substantial body of social psychological research has shown that being in a positive mood state generally encourages the display of helping behavior and cooperation and reduces aggression (Isen & Baron 1991). The clear relevance of cooperative, prosocial behaviors to organizations has produced a lot of research examining affect and various forms of helping behavior at work. In a series of studies, George looked at the relationship between positive mood at both individual (George 1991) and group (George 1990, George & Bettenhausen 1990) levels, with prosocial behavior directed at both co-workers and customers. George (1991) found that a self-report of positive mood in the previous week predicted supervisor ratings of altruism on the job and customer service. Moreover, it did so after controlling for beliefs about justice and fairness in the workplace and more dispositional measures of affect. George (1990) found that the negative group affective tone was associated with the level of prosocial behaviors in the group; George & Bettenhausen (1990) found that a leader's positive mood predicted group members' self-reports of customer service behavior.

General Performance

Staw and his colleagues' (Staw & Barsade 1993, Staw et al. 1994, Wright & Staw 1999) research is notable for its thoughtful explication of affect processes that may influence performance. Some of these processes, as the Staw group notes, suggest conflicting predictions about the effects of positive and negative affective states. So, for example, research indicates that positive affective states facilitate creativity and efficacy judgments whereas other research suggests that negative affective states can lead to more thorough canvassing of problem solutions and more accurate judgments. By and large, Staw and his colleagues' research demonstrates a performance facilitation of positive rather than negative affect. For instance, Staw & Barsade (1993) showed facilitative effects of positive affect on decision quality and interpersonal performance, as well as more general indicators of performance.

Negotiations

The negotiation context, with its emphasis on the receipt of favorable or unfavorable outcomes and its opportunity for interpersonal conflict, should be a natural setting for the study of affect. Somewhat surprisingly, few studies of true affect in negotiations context have been conducted (Barry & Oliver 1996, Thompson et al. 1999). Those studies mostly have focused on negotiator tactics and generally find that positive affect enhances cooperation and the search for creative solutions (see, e.g., Baron 1990, Forgas 1998, Pruitt & Carnevale 1993) as well as confidence in being able to achieve positive outcomes (Baron 1990, Kramer et al. 1993). Additionally, Pillutla & Murnighan (1996) have opened up a new line of research focused more on discrete emotions than general affective states. They find that anger reactions can lead negotiators to reject offers that are in their best interests as judged by pure economic standards. Recent conceptual treatments of affect in negotiation processes (e.g., Barry & Oliver 1996, George et al. 1998, Kumar 1997, Thompson, et al. 1999), as well as Pillutla & Murnighan's work on anger, should stimulate more research in this area.

Withdrawal Behaviors

In 1989, George showed that positive, but not negative, moods predicted absenteeism and that positive and negative moods predicted turnover intentions. Research on affect, both state and trait, and withdrawal continued in the 1990s. Cropanzano et al. (1993) argued that commitment was the consequence of affective experiences at work, and because negative affectivity (NA) and positive affectivity (PA) influence emotional reactivity, both traits should predict turnover intentions as mediated by commitment. In two studies they found that NA and PA correlated with turnover intentions, with commitment mediating the effect of PA in both studies and NA in one. George & Jones (1996) examined the interactive effects of values, positive moods, and satisfaction in predicting turnover intentions and found that positive mood predicted turnover intentions both in isolation and interacting with satisfaction and value fulfillment. In a longitudinal field study, Pelled & Xin (1999) showed that both positive and negative mood at work predicted subsequent absenteeism, although positive mood was more influential. In contrast, only negative mood states predicted subsequent turnover. In the aggregate, these studies all point to the importance of examining affective experiences when studying withdrawal behaviors, although the somewhat conflicting findings regarding positive and negative states indicate a need for more research on the processes that explain these effects.

Summary

It seems fair to say that examinations of the performance consequences of affect have been characterized by somewhat more sophisticated discussions of process than have traditional examinations of satisfaction-performance relationships. Much of the affect research has been well grounded in basic research, particularly that pertaining to the behavioral and judgment consequences of mood states. Specific affect studies have been as likely to focus on specific performance–related behaviors or judgments (e.g., creativity, goal persistence, and helping behavior) as on general performance assessments. Overall, thus far, the results appear more positive than what the field has been used to with job satisfaction. That being said, there have been certain limitations to the research on outcomes of affective states, which are addressed below.

OVERALL CONCLUSIONS AND RESEARCH DIRECTIONS

The Narrowness of Organizational Research

The study of affect across psychology is wide-ranging in terms of its research programs: the problems identified, the methods used in seeking solutions to those problems, and the tentative solutions that have been produced. The study of affect in organizations is narrow in its problems and methods. That narrowness could be considered appropriate if it was the consequence of a thoughtful examination of the breadth of basic research followed by a series of judgments about what is and is not relevant to understanding behavior in organizations. Unfortunately, that does not appear to be the reason for the discrepancy. Our goal in this section is not to review basic research on moods and emotions. Rather, we wish to highlight some of the ways in which we believe organizational research has been overly narrow and point to directions for broadening research activities.

Perhaps the most glaring example of the narrowness of organizational research is the overemphasis of the study of mood at the expense of discrete emotions. Research on dispositional affect examines tendencies to experience positive or negative mood states over time. Research on the determinants of affect looks at the way leaders, work environments, or stress influence mood states. Research on the consequences of affect looks at the effects of positive mood states on creativity or helping behavior. Certainly, counterexamples can be found [for example, research on anger (Allred et al. 1997, Fitness 2000, Glomb & Hulin 1997, Pillutla & Murnighan 1996) or the discrete emotional consequences of justice conditions (Weiss et al. 1999b)], but the overwhelming emphasis is on mood states.

A number of reasons can be offered for this imbalance. First, the groundbreaking work of Isen (e.g., 1987) provided a compelling framework for examining the consequences of positive mood states on performance-relevant organizational behaviors. Perhaps no other program of basic research on affect has been as influential for organizational scholars as Isen's. Of equal importance has been the ready availability of measures of mood, particularly measures of positive and negative affect. That is, much of the organizational research on the consequences of affect has used the Positive and Negative Affect Schedule (PANAS) (Watson et al. 1988) or modifications of it (e.g., Burke et al. 1989) as the measurement instrument and Isen's work as the theoretical framework, likely resulting in narrower than desirable methodological and theoretical orientations.

This imbalance in studies of mood and discrete emotions is unfortunate for two reasons. First, an enormous amount of research on emotions has accumulated, and this research highlights processes and outcomes of clear relevance to individual functioning in work settings. Second, it is apparent that discrete emotions are important, frequently occurring elements of everyday experience. Even at work— perhaps especially at work—people feel angry, happy, guilty, jealous, proud, etc. Neither the experiences themselves, nor their consequences, can be subsumed easily under a simple structure of positive or negative states.

The research on discrete emotions is diverse. Evolutionarily influenced psychologists have looked at the universality of basic emotions, including characteristic response patterns as well as the functional value of emotional displays (e.g., Cosmides & Tooby 2000, Fridlund 1994, Izard 1997, Keltner & Ekman 2000). This research can inform studies of emotional contagion and group affective tone and the behavioral and performance consequences of emotional states. Cognitively influenced psychologists examine the appraisal processes that generate emotional states (e.g., Clore & Ortony 2000, Dalgleish & Power 1999, Lazarus 1991). This research can inform the study of emotion generating working conditions and emotional climates. Research programs on particular emotions such as anger, or what have been referred to as "self-conscious emotions" (guilt, shame, pride) (Lewis 2000a), can inform understanding of how these particular emotions play out in organizational contexts. We hope the next few years will see a shift in emphasis to balance the interest in moods with an interest in discrete emotions.

Dispositional affect research in organizational behavior also has been dominated by PA and NA. Measures of PA or NA have been controlled for in stress research and have been correlated with satisfaction and performance and mood states. As we already have noted, in all of this research very little empirical work has been done on the processes by which dispositional affect influences various outcomes. More importantly, there has been little connection between organizational research on dispositional affect and the burgeoning research on the physiology of affect concerning the delineation of multiple affective systems (e.g., Cacioppo et al. 1999, Davidson 1992, Gray 1994) and the development of alternative measures of dispositional affect tied to those systems (Avila 2001, Carver & White 1994). That research points to two systems that control reactivity for positive and negative events. Although these systems are approximately consistent with the PA/NA structure, they are not entirely so. In addition, they suggest more precise ways of examining affective dispositions and may provide for better understanding of how those dispositions operate to produce immediate affective states.

A Process Orientation

Although we asserted that affect-outcome process discussions are more sophisticated than typical satisfaction-outcome process discussions of the past, it is still true that these process analyses can and need to be even more sophisticated. Current research is driven by particular criteria. That is, researchers lay out the important dimensions of performance, look to see what the basic literature says about affect influencing those dimensions, and then demonstrate in the work setting the particular relationship. For example, positive affect enhances helping, so why not show that positive affect at work enhances helping at work? This is a perfectly reasonable activity, both theoretically and practically, and serves as a first step in the study of affect-performance relationships.

What has received less attention, but ultimately may be more useful, is research that is less focused on particular performance dimensions and more focused on broader affect processes. For example, people engage in emotional regulation. These regulatory activities can deplete resources necessary for task performance (Muraven & Baumeister 2000). In a very interesting study, Richards & Gross (1999) showed that attempts to suppress the display of emotional states, a common requirement in many organizations, impaired memory for information encountered during the period of suppression. Similarly, rumination about emotional events can interfere with performance (Mikulincer 1996), and there are measurable individual differences in rumination tendencies (Sarason et al. 1996a). Of course, because people are just as likely to ruminate about positive as negative events, significant emotional events of either valence may negatively impede performance. Such possibilities, derived from a process orientation, have yet to be considered in the organizational literature.

A process orientation requires a better grasp of the state-trait distinction. Few organizational studies have focused on the immediate consequences of momentary affective states, yet many of the outcome processes described in the literature are relatively immediate and time bound. A number of studies have used extended time frames of a week or more (e.g., George 1991, George & Jones 1996, Madjar et al. 2001) to gauge affect at work; even more troublesome, others ask about mood at work but leave the time frame unspecified (e.g., Pelled & Xin 1999). Often, the justification is that moods can be long lasting (hours or days); however, moods also can be rather short lived, fluctuating dramatically over a single day. In addition, although some researchers attempt to use the PANAS structure for state affect, it is not clear that this positive/negative structure is appropriate for describing momentary mood states. Overall, the extent to which these methods adequately operationalize time- and situation-bound processes is unknown.

Some organizational studies have been conducted using experience-sampling methods in which data are collected daily or throughout the day. These designs can have the advantage of better operationalizing affective states, looking at immediate affect processes and better partitioning within subject and between subject effects. However, the studies reported so far in the organizational literature using experience-sampling methods are few in number and generally have not included within-subject outcome or process data commensurate with the level of affect measurement. We think these should and will come, with affect gauged at the moment as well as at other theoretically appropriate levels.

Appreciating Organizational Context

We also see research needs not as directly tied to developments in understanding moods and emotions in other areas of psychology. These needs, in large part, stem from organizational behavior's focus on a particular context, the workplace. First, it is apparent that we know less than we should about features of work environments that are likely to produce particular (positive and negative) moods and emotions among those who spend perhaps the majority of their working hours in them, five or more days a week. We do have narrowly focused theories that tell us, for instance, that if workers are treated unfairly by their employers, they somehow feel bad. What we do not have and need are theories that guide us in identifying specific kinds of work conditions and/or events (physical, social, or economic) associated with specific affective states. For example, it would be helpful to know the kinds of "organizational climates" (e.g., James & Jones 1974) that can be associated with experiencing fear at work. This need for theory likely should be met, in part, by mcthodological approaches more qualitatively rich (e.g., Fineman 1993) than the ones we have reviewed here, for it seems that the theories required must be built from the ground up rather than imported from other areas of psychology.

Second, research stemming from these meta-theories should recognize that a worker's perceptions of his/her work environment are not necessarily equivalent to more objective (e.g., independent) assessments of work events and conditions. Indeed, workers' perceptions of their work environments may be influenced by their affective traits and/or states, and it is those states that supposedly constitute the dependent variables of interest.

Third, returning to the more general literature on moods and emotions, but not leaving behind the problem of worker self-reports, it is important to at least note that workers' reports of how they feel may not adequately tap the constructs of experienced moods and emotions. That is, it appears that affect can be non-consciously processed (e.g., LeDoux 1995, Murphy 2001); affect so processed, although presumably not subject to self-reports, may influence how organizational members think and act. If this may be the case, then organizational researchers are faced with a sizable methodological challenge, incorporating physiological indicators of affect into their research.

Fourth, given that affect at the work group level has been demonstrated to be a meaningful construct, more effort, following the lead of Bartel & Saavedra (2000), ought to be expended to understand the processes by which feelings do and do not come to be shared in the workplace. Moreover, such research should not be limited to work groups. Can, for example, organizations, like work groups, have an affective tone? If so, under what conditions does it come about?

Closing Thoughts

After too many decades, the study of affect in organizational behavior is alive and well. Indeed, Mowday & Sutton's (1993) charge, in an *Annual Review of Psychology* chapter, that organizational behavior's preoccupation with cognitive processes "can lead to theory and research that portrays organization members as cognitive stick figures whose behavior is unaffected by emotions" (p. 197) no longer appears applicable. Considerable change in the field has been initiated in the past few years. Although in their infancy, some recently initiated research programs show considerable promise (for example, those concerned with the effects of leaders on the affective experiences of their followers, with the antecedents and consequences of group affective tone, and with assessing the many hypotheses derived from affective events theory). Much more importantly, we are confident that many, many important questions about the production and consequences of moods and emotions in the workplace have yet to be posed. The opportunity (the challenge) is in front of us. If we are duly enticed by it, then organizational behavior will evolve to and beyond considering workers as people who think and feel; we will more fully appreciate that the groups and organizations to which they belong also exhibit these person-like characteristics.

Visit the Annual Reviews home page at www.AnnualReviews.org

LITERATURE CITED

Agho AO, Price JL, Mueller CW. 1992. Discriminant validity of measures of job satisfaction, positive affectivity and negative affectivity. *J. Occup. Organ. Psychol.* 65(3): 185–96

Allred KG, Mallozzi JS, Matsui F, Raia CP. 1997. The influence of anger and compassion on negotiation performance. *Organ. Behav. Hum. Decis. Process.* 70(3):175–87

Arvey RD, Carter GW, Buerkley DK. 1991. Job satisfaction: dispositional and situational influences. In *International Review of Industrial and Organizational Psychology*, ed. CL Cooper, IT Robertson, 6:359–83. New York: Wiley

Ashforth BE, Humphrey RH. 1995. Emotion in the workplace: a reappraisal. *Hum. Relat.* 48:97–125

Avila C. 2001. Distinguishing BIS-mediated and BAS-mediated disinhibition mechanisms: a comparison of disinhibition models of Gray (1981,1987) and of Patterson and Newman (1993). *J. Pers. Soc. Psychol.* 80:311–24

Bagozzi RP, Burnkrant RE. 1979. Attitude organization and the attitude behavior relationship. *J. Pers. Soc. Psychol.* 37(6):913–29

Baritz L. 1960. *The Servants of Power: A History of the Use of Social Sciences in American Industry.* Middletown, CT: Wesleyan Univ. Press. 273 pp.

Baron RA. 1990. Environmentally induced positive affect—its impact on self-efficacy, task-performance, negotiation, and conflict. *J. Appl. Soc. Psychol.* 20:368–84

Barry B, Oliver RL. 1996. Affect in dyadic negotiation: a model and propositions. *Organ. Behav. Hum. Decis. Process.* 67:127–43

Barsade SG, Gibson DE. 1998. Group emotion: a view from top and bottom. In *Research on Managing Groups and Teams*, ed. DH Gruenfeld, 1:81–102. Stamford, CT: JAI. 272 pp.

Barsade SG, Ward AJ, Turner JD, Sonnenfeld JA. 2000. To your heart's content: a model of affective diversity in top management teams. *Admin. Sci. Q.* 45(4):802–36

Bartel CA, Saavedra R. 2000. The collective construction of work group moods. *Admin. Sci. Q.* 45(2):197–231

Bies RJ. 2001. Interactional (in)justice: the sacred and the profane. In *Advances in Organizational Justice*, ed. J Greenberg, R Cropanzano. Stanford, CA: Stanford Univ. Press

Bies RJ, Tripp TM. 2001. A passion for justice: the rationality and morality of revenge. In *Justice in the Workplace: From Theory to Practice: Series in Applied Psychology*, ed. R Cropanzano, 2:197–208. Mahwah, NJ: Erlbaum

Brief AP. 1998. *Attitudes in and Around Organizations.* Thousand Oaks, CA: Sage

Brief AP, Aldag RJ. 1994. The study of work values: a call for a more balanced perspective. In *Trends and Perspectives in Empirical Social Research*, ed. I Borg, PP Mohler, pp. 99–124. New York: de Gruyter. 375 pp.

Brief AP, Butcher AH, Roberson L. 1995. Cookies, disposition, and job attitudes: the effects of positive mood-inducing events and negative affectivity on job satisfaction in a field experiment. *Organ. Behav. Hum. Decis. Process.* 62(1):55–62

Brief AP, Roberson L. 1989. Job attitude organization: an exploratory study. *J. Appl. Soc. Psychol.* 19:717–27

Burke MJ, Brief AP, George JM. 1993. The role of negative affectivity in understanding relations between self-reports of stressors and strains: a comment on the applied psychology literature. *J. Appl. Psychol.* 78(3):402–12

Burke MJ, Brief AP, George JM, Roberson L, Webster J. 1989. Measuring affect at work: confirmatory analyses of competing mood structures with conceptual linkage to cortical regulatory systems. *J. Pers. Soc. Psychol.* 57:1091–102

Cacioppo JT, Gardner WL, Berntson GG. 1999. The affect system has parallel and integrative processing components: form follows function. *J. Pers. Soc. Psychol.* 76:839–55

Carver CS, White TL. 1994. Behavioral-inhibition, behavioral activation, and affective responses to impending reward and punishment—the BIS/BAS scales. *J. Pers. Soc. Psychol.* 67:319–33

Clark MS, Isen AM. 1982. Toward understanding the relationship between feeling states and social behavior. In *Cognitive Social Psychology*, ed. A Hastorf, AM Isen, pp. 73–108. New York: Elsevier

Clore GL, Ortony A. 2000. Cognition in emotion: always, sometimes, never. In *Cognitive Neuroscience of Emotion*, ed. RD Lane, L Nadel, pp. 24–61. New York: Oxford Univ. Press

Conger JA, Kanungo RN. 1998. *Charismatic Leadership in Organizations*. Thousand Oaks, CA: Sage. 288 pp.

Cooper CL. 1998. *Theories of Organizational Stress*. New York: Oxford Univ. Press. 275 pp.

Cosmides L, Tooby J. 2000. Evolutionary psychology and the emotions. See Lewis & Haviland 2000, pp. 91–115

Cropanzano R, James K, Konovsky MA. 1993. Dispositional affectivity as a predictor of work attitudes and job performance. *J. Organ. Behav.* 14:595–606

Dalgleish T, Power M. 1999. *Handbook of Cognition and Emotion*. Chichester, UK: Wiley

Davidson RJ. 1992. Emotion and affective style: hemispheric substrates. *Psychol. Sci.* 3:39–43

Davis-Blake A, Pfeffer J. 1996. Two steps forward, one step back. *Acad. Manage. Rev.* 21(2):340–43

Eagly AH, Chaiken S. 1993. *The Psychology of Attitudes*. Fort Worth, TX: Harcourt Brace Jovanovich College Publ.

Estrada CA, Isen AM, Young MJ. 1997. Positive affect facilitates integration of information and decreases anchoring in reasoning among physicians. *Organ. Behav. Hum. Decis. Process.* 72:117–35

Fineman S. 1993. *Emotion in Organizations*. Thousand Oaks, CA: Sage. 230 pp.

Fisher CD. 2000. Mood and emotions while working: missing pieces of job satisfaction? *J. Organ. Behav.* 21:185–202

Fisher VE, Hanna JV. 1931. *The Dissatisfied Worker*. New York: Macmillan. 260 pp.

Fitness J. 2000. Anger in the workplace: an emotion script approach to anger episodes between workers and their superiors, co-workers and subordinates. *J. Organ. Behav.* 21:147–62

Folger R, Cropanzano R. 1998. *Organizational Justice and Human Resource Management*. Thousand Oaks, CA: Sage. 278 pp.

Forgas JP. 1998. On feeling good and getting your way: mood effects on negotiator cognition and bargaining strategies. *J. Pers. Soc. Psychol.* 74:565–77

Fortunato VJ, Jex SM, Heinisch DA. 1999. An examination of the discriminant validity of the Strain-Free Negative Affectivity Scale. *J. Occup. Organ. Psychol.* 72(4):503–22

Fridlund AJ. 1994. *Human Facial Expression: An Evolutionary View*. San Diego, CA: Academic

Fried Y, Levi AS, Ben David HA, Tiegs RB. 1999. Inflation of subordinates' performance ratings: main and interactive effects of rater negative affectivity, documentation of work behavior, and appraisal visibility. *J. Organ. Behav.* 20:431–44

Frijda NH. 1993. The place of appraisal in emotion. *Cogn. Emot.* 7(3-4):357–87

Gallupe RB, Bastionatti LM, Cooper WH. 1991. Unblocking brainstorms. *J. Appl. Psychol.* 76(1):137–42

George JM. 1989. Mood and absence. *J. Appl. Psychol.* 74:317–24

George JM. 1990. Personality, affect, and behavior in groups. *J. Appl. Psychol.* 75:107–16

George JM. 1991. State or trait: effects of positive mood on prosocial behaviors at work. *J. Appl. Psychol.* 76:299–307

George JM. 1995. Leader positive mood and group performance: the case of customer service. *J. Appl. Soc. Psychol.* 25(9):778–94

George JM. 1996. Group affective tone. In *Handbook of Work Group Psychology*, ed. M West. Sussex, UK: Wiley. 642 pp.

George JM. 2000. Emotions and leadership: the role of emotional intelligence. *Hum. Relat.* 53(8):1027–55

George JM, Bettenhausen K. 1990. Understanding prosocial behavior, sales performance, and turnover: a group-level analysis in a service context. *J. Appl. Psychol.* 75:698–709

George JM, Brief AP. 1992. Feeling good-doing good: a conceptual analysis of the mood at work-organizational spontaneity relationship. *Psychol. Bull.* 112(2):310–29

George JM, Brief AP. 2001. Personality and work-related distress. In *Personality and Organizations*, ed. B Schneider, B Smith. Mahwah, NJ: Erlbaum. In press

George JM, Jones GR. 1996. The experience of work and turnover intentions: interactive effects of value attainment, job satisfaction, and positive mood. *J. Appl. Psychol.* 81:318–25

George JM, Jones GR, Gonzalez JA. 1998. The role of affect in cross-cultural negotiations. *J. Int. Bus. Stud.* 29:749–72

George JM, Reed TF, Ballard KA, Colin J, Fielding J. 1993. Contact with AIDS patients as a source of work-related distress: effects of organizational and social support. *Acad. Manage. J.* 36(1):157–71

Glomb TM, Hulin CL. 1997. Anger and gender effects in observed supervisor-subordinate dyadic interactions. *Organ. Behav. Hum. Decis. Process.* 72(3):281–307

Gray JA. 1994. Three fundamental emotion systems. In *The Nature of Emotions: Fundamental Questions*, ed. P Ekman, RJ Davidson, pp. 243–47. New York: Oxford Univ. Press

Greenberg J. 1990. Organizational justice: yesterday, today, and tomorrow. *J. Manage.* 16:399–432

Hackman JR. 1992. Group influences on individuals in organizations. In *Handbook of I/O Psychology*, ed. MD Dunnette, LM Hough, 3:199–267. Palo Alto, CA: Consult. Psychol. Press. 1095 pp.

Hart PM, Wearing AJ, Headey B. 1995. Police stress and well-being: integrating personality, coping and daily work experiences. *J. Occup. Organ. Psychol.* 68(2):133–56

Hatfield E, Cacioppo JT, Rapson RL. 1994. *Emotional Contagion*. New York: Cambridge Univ. Press. 240 pp.

Heath C, Jourden FJ. 1997. Illusion, disillusion, and the buffering effect of groups. *Organ. Behav. Hum. Decis. Process.* 69(2):103–16

Heinisch DA, Jex SM. 1997. Negative affectivity and gender as moderators of the relationship between work-related stressors and depressed mood at work. *Work Stress* 11(1):46–57

Hersey RB. 1932. *Workers' Emotions in Shop and Home: A Study of Individual Workers from the Psychological and Physiological Standpoint*. Philadelphia: Univ. Penn. Press

Hochschild A. 1983. Comment on Kemper's "social constructionist and positivist approaches to the sociology of emotions." *Am. J. Soc.* 89(2):432–34

Hoppock R. 1935. *Job Satisfaction*. New York: Harper. 303 pp.

House RJ, Shane SA, Herold DM. 1996. Rumors of the death of dispositional research are vastly exaggerated. *Acad. Manage. Rev.* 21:203–24

Hurrell JJ, Nelson DL, Simmons BL. 1998. Measuring job stressors and strains: Where we have been, where we are, and where we need to go. *J. Occup. Health Psychol.* 3(4):368–89

Isen AM. 1987. Positive affect, cognitive-processes, and social-behavior. *Adv. Exp. Soc. Psychol.* 20:203–53

Isen AM. 1999. Positive affect and creativity. In *Affect, Creative Experience, and Psychological Adjustment*, ed. S Russ, pp. 3–17. Philadelphia: Bruner/Mazel

Isen AM. 2000. Positive affect and decision making. See Lewis & Haviland 2000, pp. 417–35

Isen AM, Baron RA. 1991. Positive affect as a factor in organizational-behavior. In *Research in Organizational Behavior*, ed. BM

Staw, LL Cummings, 13:1–53. Greenwich, CT: JAI Press

Izard CE. 1997. Emotions and facial expressions: a perspective from Differential Emotions Theory. In *The Psychology of Facial Expressions*, ed. JA Russell, JM Fernandez-Dols, pp. 57–77. Paris: Cambridge Univ. Press

James LR, Jones AP. 1974. Organizational climate: a review of theory and research. *Psychol. Bull.* 81:1096–112

Judge TA. 1992. The dispositional perspective in human resource research. In *Research in Personnel and Human Resource Management*, ed. GR Ferris, KM Rowland, 11:31–72. Greenwich, CT: JAI

Judge TA, Ferris GR. 1993. Social-context of performance evaluation decisions. *Acad. Manage. J.* 36:80–105

Kelloway EK, Barling J, Shah A. 1993. Industrial relations stress and job satisfaction: concurrent effects and mediation. *J. Organ. Behav.* 14:447–57

Keltner D, Ekman P. 2000. Facial expression of emotion. See Lewis & Haviland 2000, pp. 236–49

Kornhauser AW, Sharp AA. 1932. Employee attitudes: suggestions from a study in a factory. *Pers. J.* 10:393–404

Kramer RM, Newton E, Pommerenke PL. 1993. Self-enhancement biases and negotiator judgment: effects of self-esteem and mood. *Organ. Behav. Hum. Decis. Process.* 56:110–33

Kumar R. 1997. The role of affect in negotiations. *J. Appl. Behav. Sci.* 33:84–100

Kunin T. 1955. The construction of a new type of attitude measure. *Pers. Psychol.* 8:65–77

Larsen RJ, Ketelaar T. 1989. Extraversion, neuroticism, and susceptibility to positive and negative mood induction procedures. *Pers. Individ. Differ.* 10:1221–28

Lazarus RS. 1991. *Emotion and Adaptation.* New York: Oxford Univ. Press

Lazarus RS, Cohon-Charash Y. 2001. Discrete emotions in organizational life. In *Emotions in Organizations*, ed. R Payne, CL Cooper. Chichester, UK: Wiley. In press

LeDoux JE. 1995. Emotion: clues from the brain. *Annu. Rev. Psychol.* 46:209–35

Lewis KM. 2000a. Self-conscious emotions: embarrassment, pride, shame and guilt. See Lewis & Haviland 2000, pp. 623–36

Lewis KM. 2000b. When leaders display emotion: How followers respond to negative emotional expression of male and female leaders. *J. Organ. Behav.* 21:221–34

Lewis KM, Haviland JM, eds. 2000. *Handbook of Emotions.* New York: Guilford. 2nd ed.

Locke EA. 1976. The nature and causes of job satisfaction. In *Handbook of I/O Psychology*, ed. MD Dunnette, pp. 1297–349. Chicago: Rand-McNally. 1st ed.

Locke K. 1996. A funny thing happened! The management of consumer emotions in service encounters. *Organ. Sci.* 7(1):40–59

Madjar N, Oldham GR, Pratt MG. 2001. There's no place like home: the contributions of work and non-work creativity support to employees' creative performance. *Acad. Manage. J.* In press

McCrae RR, Costa PT. 1991. Adding Liebe und Arbeit: the full five-factor model and well-being. *Pers. Soc. Psychol. Bull.* 17(2): 227–32

Mikulincer M. 1996. Mental rumination and learned helplessness: cognitive shifts during helplessness training and their behavioral consequences. See Sarason et al. 1996b, pp. 191–210

Millar MG, Tesser A. 1986. Effects of affective and cognitive focus on the attitude-behavior relation. *J. Pers. Soc. Psychol.* 51:270–76

Miller DT. 2001. Disrespect and the experience of injustice. *Annu. Rev. Psychol.* 52:527–55

Moorman RH. 1993. The influence of cognitive and affective based job satisfaction measures on the relationship between satisfaction and organizational citizenship behavior. *Hum. Relat.* 46(6):759–76

Motowidlo SJ. 1996. Orientation toward the job and organization. In *Individual Differences and Behavior in Organizations*, ed. KR Murphy, pp. 175–208. San Francisco: Jossey-Bass

Mowday RT, Sutton RI. 1993. Organizational behavior: linking individuals and groups to organizational context. *Annu. Rev. Psychol.* 44:195–229

Muraven M, Baumeister RF. 2000. Self-regulation and depletion of limited resources: Does self-control resemble a muscle? *Psychol. Bull.* 126:247–59

Murphy ST. 2001. Feeling without thinking: affective primacy and the nonconscious processing of emotion. In *Unraveling the Complexities of Social Life: A Festschrift in Honor of Robert B. Zajonc*, ed. JA Bargh, DK Apsley, pp. 39–53. Washington, DC: Am. Psychol. Assoc. 209 pp.

Necowitz LB, Roznowski M. 1994. Negative affectivity and job satisfaction: cognitive processes underlying the relationship and effects on employee behaviors. *J. Vocat. Behav.* 45(3):270–94

Oldham GR, Cummings A, Mischel LJ, Schmidtke JM, Zhou J. 1995. Listen while you work? Quasi-experimental relations between personal-stereo headset use and employee work responses. *J. Appl. Psychol.* 80(5):547–64

Organ DW. 1988. A restatement of the satisfaction-performance hypothesis. *J. Manage.* 14(4):547–57

Organ DW, Near JP. 1985. Cognitive vs. affect measures of job satisfaction. *Int. J. Psychol.* 20:241–54

Parkes J. 1990. Coping, negative affectivity, and the work environment: additive and interactive predictors of mental health. *J. Appl. Psychol.* 75:399–409

Pekrun R, Frese M. 1992. Emotions in work and achievement. In *International Review of I/O Psychology*, Vol. 7, Chap. 5, pp. 153–200. New York: Wiley

Pelled LH, Xin KR. 1999. Down and out: an investigation of the relationship between mood and employee withdrawal behavior. *J. Manage.* 25:875–95

Pillutla MM, Murnighan JK. 1996. Unfairness, anger, and spite: emotional rejections of ultimatum offers. *Organ. Behav. Hum. Decis. Process.* 68:208–24

Plutchik R. 1994. *The Psychology and Biology of Emotion*. New York: Harper Collins Coll. Publ. 396 pp,

Porac JF. 1987. The job satisfaction questionnaire as a cognitive event: first- and second-order processes in affective commentary. In *Research in Personnel and Human Resources Management*, ed. KM Rowland, GR Ferris, 5:51–102. Greenwich, CT: JAI

Pratkanis AR, Turner ME. 1994. Of what value is a job attitude? A socio-cognitive analysis. *Hum. Relat.* 47(12):1545–76

Pruitt DG, Carnevale PJ. 1993. *Negotiation in Social Conflict*. Pacific Grove, CA: Brooks-Cole

Pugh SD. 2001. Service with a smile: emotional contagion in the service encounter. *Acad. Manage. J.* In press

Rafaeli A, Sutton RI. 1990. Busy stores and demanding customers: How do they affect the display of positive emotion? *Acad. Manage. J.* 33(3):623–37

Richards JM, Gross JJ. 1999. Composure at any cost? The cognitive consequences of emotion suppression. *Pers. Soc. Psychol. Bull.* 25:1033–44

Robbins TL, DeNisi AS. 1994. A closer look at interpersonal affect as a distinct influence on cognitive processing in performance evaluations. *J. Appl. Psychol.* 79:341–53

Robbins TL, DeNisi AS. 1998. Mood vs. interpersonal affect: identifying process and rating distortions in performance appraisal. *J. Bus. Psychol.* 12:313–25

Roethlisberger FJ, Dickson WJ. 1939. *Management and the Worker*. Cambridge, MA: Harvard Univ. Press. 615 pp.

Russell JA, Barrett LF. 1999. Core affect, prototypical emotional episodes, and other things called emotion: dissecting the elephant. *J. Pers. Soc. Psychol.* 76(5):805–19

Saavedra R, Earley PC. 1991. Choice of task and goal under conditions of general and specific affective inducement. *Motiv. Emot.* 15:45–65

Saavedra R, Kwun SK. 2000. Affective states in job characteristic theory. *J. Organ. Behav.* 21:131–46

Sandelands L, St. Clair L. 1993. Toward an empirical concept of group. *J. Theory Soc. Behav.* 23(4):423–58

Sandelands LE. 1988. The concept of work feeling. *J. Theor. Soc. Behav.* 18(4):437–57

Sarason IG, Pierce GR, Sarason BR. 1996a. Domains of cognitive interference. See Sarason et al. 1996b, pp. 139–52

Sarason IG, Pierce GR, Sarason BR, eds. 1996b. *Cognitive Interference: Theories, Methods and Findings.* Mahwah, NJ: Erlbaum

Schaubroeck J, Ganster DC, Fox ML. 1992. Dispositional affect and work-related stress. *J. Appl. Psychol.* 77(3):322–35

Schaubroeck J, Judge TA, Taylor LA III. 1998. Influences of trait negative affect and situational similarity on correlation and convergence of work attitudes and job stress perceptions across two jobs. *J. Manage.* 24(4):553–76

Schmitt N, Bedeian AG. 1982. A comparison of LISREL and two-stage least squares analysis of a hypothesized life-job satisfaction reciprocal relationship. *J. Appl. Psychol.* 67(6):806–17

Schneider B. 1987. The people make the place. *Pers. Psychol.* 40(3):437–53

Shaw JD, Duffy MK, Jenkins GD Jr, Gupta N. 1999. Positive and negative affect, signal sensitivity, and pay satisfaction. *J. Manage.* 25(2):189–206

Simon HA. 1982. Comments. In *Affect and Cognition: The Seventeenth Annual Carnegie Symposium on Cognition,* ed. MS Clark, ST Fiske, pp. 333–42. Hillsdale, NJ: Erlbaum

Spector PE. 1996. *Industrial and Organizational Psychology: Research and Practice.* New York: Wiley. 420 pp.

Spector PE. 1997. *Job Satisfaction: Application, Assessment, Causes, and Consequences.* Thousand Oaks, CA: Sage. 96 pp.

Spector PE, Jex SM. 1991. Relations of job characteristics from multiple data sources with employee affect, absence, turnover intentions, and health. *J. Appl. Psychol.* 76(1):46–53

Spector PE, O'Connell BJ. 1994. The contribution of personality traits, negative affectivity, locus of control and Type A to the subsequent reports of job stressors and job strains. *J. Occup. Organ. Psychol.* 67(1):1–12

Staw BM, Barsade SG. 1993. Affect and managerial performance: a test of the sadder-but-wiser vs. happier-and-smarter hypotheses. *Admin. Sci. Q.* 38:304–31

Staw BM, Bell NE, Clausen JA. 1986. The dispositional approach to job attitudes: a lifetime longitudinal test. *Admin. Sci. Q.* 31:56–77

Staw BM, Sutton RI, Pelled LH. 1994. Employee positive emotion and favorable outcomes at the workplace. *Organ. Sci.* 5:51–71

Strati A. 1992. Aesthetic understanding of organizational life. *Acad. Manage. Rev.* 17(3):568–81

Strati A. 1996. Organizations viewed through the lens of aesthetics. *Organization* 3(2):209–18

Sundstrom E, Bell PA, Busby PL, Asmus C. 1996. Environmental psychology: 1989–1994. *Annu. Rev. Psychol.* 47:485–512

Sutton RI. 1991. Maintaining norms about expressed emotions: the case of bill collectors. *Admin. Sci. Q.* 36(2):245–68

Teuchmann K, Totterdell P, Parker SK. 1999. Rushed, unhappy, and drained: an experience sampling study of relations between time pressure, perceived control, mood, and emotional exhaustion in a group of accountants. *J. Occup. Health Psychol.* 4(1):37–54

Thayer RE. 1989. *The Biopsychology of Mood and Arousal.* New York: Oxford Univ. Press. 234 pp.

Thompson LL, Nadler J, Kim PH. 1999. Some like it hot: the case for the emotional negotiator. In *Shared Cognition in Organizations: The Management of Knowledge,* ed. LL Thompson, JM Levin, DM Messick, pp. 139–61. Mahwah, NJ: Erlbaum

Totterdell P. 2000. Catching moods and hitting runs: mood linkage and subjective performance in professional sport teams. *J. Appl. Psychol.* 85(6):848–59

Totterdell P, Kellett S, Teuchmann K, Briner BB. 1998. Evidence of mood linkage in work groups. *J. Pers. Soc. Psychol.* 74(6):1504–15

Varma A, Denisi AS, Peters LH. 1996, Interpersonal affect and performance appraisal: a field study. *Pers. Psychol.* 49:341–60

Vecchio RP. 1995. The impact of referral sources on employee attitudes: evidence from a national sample. *J. Manage.* 21(5): 953–65

Wasserman V, Rafaeli A, Kluger AN. 2000. Aesthetic symbols as emotional cues. In *Emotion in Organizations*, ed. S Fineman. London: Sage. 2nd ed.

Watson D. 2000. *Mood and Temperament.* New York: Guilford. 340 pp.

Watson D, Clark LA. 1992. On traits and temperament: general and specific factors of emotional experience and their relation to the five-factor model. *J. Pers.* 60(2):441–76

Watson D, Clark LA Tellegen A. 1988. Development and validation of brief measures of positive and negative affect: the PANAS scales. *J. Pers. Soc. Psychol.* 54(6):1063–70

Watson D, Slack AK. 1993. General factors of affective temperament and their relation to job satisfaction over time. *Organ. Behav. Hum. Decis. Process.* 54:181–202

Weiss HM. 2002. Deconstructing job satisfaction: separating evaluations, beliefs and affective experiences. *Hum. Resource Manage. Rev.* In press

Weiss HM, Brief AP. 2002. Affect at work: an historical perspective. In *Emotions at Work: Theory, Research, and Application in Management*, ed. RL Payne, CL Cooper. Chichester, UK: Wiley. In press

Weiss HM, Cropanzano R. 1996. Affective Events Theory: a theoretical discussion of the structure, causes and consequences of affective experiences at work. In *Research in Organization Behavior: An Annual Series of Analytical Essays and Critical Reviews*, ed. BM Staw, LL Cummings, 18:1–74. Greenwich, CT: JAI. 373 pp.

Weiss HM, Nicholas JP, Daus CS. 1999a. An examination of the joint effects of affective experiences and job beliefs on job satisfaction and variations in affective experiences over time. *Organ. Behav. Hum. Decis. Process.* 78(1):1–24

Weiss HM, Suckow K, Cropanzano R. 1999b. Effects of justice conditions on discrete emotions. *J. Appl. Psychol.* 84:786–94

Wharton AS, Erickson RJ. 1993. Managing emotions on the job and at home: understanding the consequences of multiple emotional roles. *Acad. Manage. Rev.* 18(3):457–86

White DA. 1996. "It's working beautifully!" Philosophical reflections on aesthetics and organization theory. *Organization* 3(2):195–208

Williams KJ, Alliger GM. 1994. Role stressors, mood spillover, and perceptions of work-family conflict in employed parents. *Acad. Manage. J.* 37(4):837–68

Williams KJ, Suls J, Alliger GM, Learner SM, Wan CK. 1991. Multiple role juggling and daily mood states in working mothers: an experience sampling study. *J. Appl. Psychol.* 76(5):664–74

Williams LJ, Gavin MB, Williams ML. 1996. Measurement and nonmeasurement processes with negative affectivity and employee attitudes. *J. Appl. Psychol.* 81(1):88–101

Winefield AH, Winefield HR, Tiggemann M, Goldney RD. 1991. A longitudinal study of the psychological effects of unemployment and unsatisfactory employment on young adults. *J. Appl. Psychol.* 76(3):424–31

Wright TA, Staw BM. 1999. Affect and favorable work outcomes: two longitudinal tests of the happy-productive worker thesis. *J. Organ. Behav.* 20:1–23

Zajonc RB. 1998. Emotions. In *Handbook of Social Psychology*, ed. DT Gilbert, ST Fiske, G Lindzey, pp. 591–632. Boston: McGraw-Hill

Zohar D. 1999. When things go wrong: the effect of daily work hassles on effort, exertion and negative mood. *J. Occup. Organ. Psychol.* 72(3):265–83

Annu. Rev. Psychol. 2002. 53:309–39

CHILD CLINICAL/PEDIATRIC NEUROPSYCHOLOGY: Some Recent Advances

B. P. Rourke[1,2], S. A. Ahmad[1], D. W. Collins[1], B. A. Hayman-Abello[1], S. E. Hayman-Abello[1], and E. M. Warriner[1]

[1]*Department of Psychology, University of Windsor, Windsor, Ontario, Canada N9B 3P4; e-mail: ahmad@uwindsor.ca, collinw@uwindsor.ca, abello@uwindsor.ca, hayman2@uwindsor.ca, warrin3@uwindsor.ca*
[2]*Child Study Centre, Yale University, New Haven, Connecticut 06510-8009; e-mail: bprourke@aol.com*

Key Words   pediatric neurology, childhood disorders, nonverbal learning disabilities, developmental disabilities

■ **Abstract**   The neuropsychological assets and deficits of several types of pediatric neurological disease, disorder, and dysfunction are described. These are examined from the perspective of the syndrome of nonverbal learning disabilities (NLD) and the "white matter model" designed to explain its complex manifestations. It is concluded that children with some of these diseases exhibit the NLD phenotype, whereas others do not. For the most part, the diseases in which the NLD phenotype is particularly evident are those wherein it has been demonstrated that perturbations of white matter (long myelinated fibers) are particularly prominent.

CONTENTS

0084-6570/02/0201-0309$14.00

INTRODUCTION

This presentation includes a survey of recent neuropsychological evidence regarding a number of types of pediatric neurological disease, disorder, and dysfunction. To organize the presentation theoretically, a neurodevelopmental model is presented and explained. Thereafter, the diseases themselves are examined with a view to their possible explanation in terms of the model. As expected, some of the disorders fit well with the model, whereas others do not.

SYNDROME OF NONVERBAL LEARNING DISABILITIES: CONTENT (CHARACTERISTICS) AND NEURODEVELOPMENTAL DYNAMICS—THE WHITE MATTER MODEL

Speculation regarding the content of the nonverbal learning disabilities (NLD) syndrome began with the seminal work of Myklebust (e.g., 1975). What we have been able to do is to flesh out this content, mostly as a result of our study of subtypes of LD. We have approached this investigative effort from the perspective of developmental neuropsychology, that is, the study of brain-behavior relationships within a developmental context. A review of these studies is available elsewhere (Rourke 1989, 1999). For our current purposes, the relevant dimensions of the conclusions of these investigations are what we take to be the content and dynamics of NLD.

Two features of this description of the NLD syndrome characteristics should be borne in mind:

1. Because of our focus on children and adolescents, manifestations of NLD in persons within these developmental stages are emphasized.

2. This description is couched in terms of the "developmental" manifestation of the NLD syndrome—that is, in terms of its characteristics in a child who has been afflicted since his or her earliest developmental stages. Some modifications in the manifestations of the syndrome are necessary when we turn to considerations of the onset of the syndrome in an older child, adolescent, or adult who has enjoyed a normal early developmental course.

Definition of Nonverbal Learning Disabilities

The syndrome of NLD is characterized by significant primary deficits in some dimensions of tactile perception, visual perception, complex psychomotor skills, and in dealing with novel circumstances. These primary deficits lead to secondary deficits in tactile and visual attention and to significant limitations in exploratory behavior. In turn, there are tertiary deficits in tactile and visual memory and in concept-formation, problem-solving, and hypothesis-testing skills. Finally, these deficits lead to significant difficulties in the content (meaning) and function (pragmatics) dimensions of language. Neuropsychological assets are evident in most areas of auditory perception, auditory attention, and auditory memory, especially for verbal material. Simple motor skills are most often well developed, as are rote verbal memory, language form, amount of verbal associations, and language output. This mix of neuropsychological assets and deficits eventuates in some formal learning (e.g., academic) assets, such as single-word reading and spelling. It also increases the likelihood of significant difficulties in other aspects of formal learning (e.g., arithmetic, science) and informal learning (e.g., during play and other social situations). Psychosocial deficits, primarily of the externalized variety, often are evident early in development; psychosocial disturbances, primarily of the internalized variety, are usually evident by late childhood and adolescence and into adulthood. Table 1 provides diagnostic criteria for research samples with NLD and includes a general list of criteria applicable across the developmental span. Table 2 contains lists of characteristics particularly evident in children with the syndrome: (*a*) up to approximately 6 years of age and (*b*) approximately 7 years of age and older.

NEURODEVELOPMENTAL DYNAMICS   The assets and deficits of the NLD subtype should be viewed within a specific context of cause-effect relationships: that is, the primary neuropsychological assets and deficits are thought to lead to the secondary neuropsychological assets and deficits, and so on to the tertiary and linguistic neuropsychological dimensions. These are seen as causative vis-à-vis the academic and psychosocial/adaptive aspects of this subtype. In this sense, the latter dimensions are, essentially, dependent variables (i.e., effects rather than causes) in the NLD subtype.

THE "WHITE MATTER" MODEL   This model (Rourke 1987, 1988, 1989, 1995a) constitutes an attempt to capture and explain the syndrome of NLD in those types of neurological disease wherein the NLD neuropsychological phenotype is, to a greater or lesser extent, evident. The principal working hypothesis of this model is that the phenotype of NLD will be manifest to the extent that white matter (long myelinated fibers) in the brain is underdeveloped, damaged, or dysfunctional (Rourke 1995a, Tsatsanis & Rourke 1995).

The syndrome is apparent in many individuals who have significant perturbations of right hemisphere systems; thus, significant dysfunction within the right cerebral hemisphere is seen as a *sufficient* condition for the appearance of the NLD syndrome. The syndrome is also apparent in many individuals with significant perturbations of white matter in many, if not most, regions of the brain; thus, significant perturbations of white matter appear to be *necessary* to "produce" the NLD syndrome (phenotype).

We turn now to a discussion of recent research on a number of types of pediatric neurological disease in which the phenotype of NLD is more or less evident. It is

TABLE 1   Diagnostic criteria for research in nonverbal learning disabilities

1. Bilateral deficits in tactile perception, usually more marked on the left side of the body. Simple tactile perception may reach normal levels as the child ages, but interpreting complex tactile stimulation remains impaired.

2. Bilateral deficits in psychomotor coordination, usually more marked on the left side of the body. Simple, repetitive motor skills may reach normal levels with age, but complex motor skills remain impaired or worsen relative to age norms.

3. Extremely impaired visual-spatial-organizational abilities. Simple visual discrimination can reach normal levels with age, particularly when stimuli are simple. Compared to age norms, complex visual-spatial-organizational abilities worsen with advancing years.

4. Substantial difficulty in dealing with novel or complex information or situations. A strong tendency to rely on rote, memorized reactions, approaches, and responses (often inappropriate for the situation), and failure to learn or adjust responses according to informational feedback. Also, especially frequent use of verbal responses in spite of the requirements of the novel situation. These tendencies remain or worsen with age.

5. Notable impairments in nonverbal problem-solving, concept-formation, and hypothesis-testing.

6. Distorted sense of time. Estimating elapsed time over an interval and estimating time of day are both notably impaired.

7. Well-developed rote verbal abilities (e.g., single-word reading and spelling), frequently superior to age norms, in the context of notably poor reading comprehension abilities (particularly so in older children).

8. High verbosity that is rote and repetitive, with content disorders of language and deficits in functional/pragmatic aspects of language.

9. Substantial deficits in mechanical arithmetic and reading comprehension relative to strengths in single-word reading and spelling.

10. Extreme deficits in social perception, judgment, and interaction, often leading to eventual social isolation/withdrawal. Easily overwhelmed in novel situations, with a marked tendency toward extreme anxiety, even panic, in such situations. High likelihood of developing internalized forms of psychopathology (e.g., depression) in later childhood and adolescence.

hoped that the NLD model will assist in putting this very large body of research in perspective.

ASPERGER SYNDROME

Asperger syndrome (AS) is a pervasive developmental disorder characterized by impairments in social understanding, social interaction, and apathy, in the context of average psychometric intelligence and above average to superior mechanical language skills (i.e., single-word reading, spelling, and verbal output) (Klin et al.

TABLE 2   Nonverbal learning disabilities characteristics at younger and older age levels

Characteristics particularly evident in younger children (up to 6 years)

1. Delays in reaching all developmental milestones, including speech, followed by a late but rapid development of speech and some other verbal abilities, usually to above-average levels.
2. Below-normal amount of exploratory behavior.
3. Impaired development of complex psychomotor skills (e.g., climbing, walking).
4. Avoidance of novelty, and preference for highly familiar objects, stimulation, and information.
5. Preference for receiving information in verbal as opposed to visual format.
6. Strengths in simple, repetitive motor activities and in rote verbal memory.
7. Deficits in perception and attention in both the visual and tactile domains.
8. Notably better auditory-verbal memory than visual or tactile memory.
9. Initial problems in oral-motor praxis, and longstanding, mild difficulties in pronouncing complex, multi-syllabic words.

Characteristics particularly evident in older children (7 years and above)

1. Impaired abilities to analyze, organize, and synthesize information, with associated impairments in problem-solving and concept-formation.
2. Very evident and significant impairments in language prosody, content, and pragmatics, despite high levels of verbosity. This is often manifest in the form of "cocktail-party" speech patterns, with high volume of verbal output but relatively little content (meaning) and exceedingly poor psycholinguistic function/pragmatics.
3. Strengths in single-word reading/recognition and spelling, but substantially worse performance in reading comprehension and mechanical arithmetic.
4. Very poor handwriting in early school years, often improving to normal levels but only with considerable practice.
5. Spelling errors predominantly—even almost exclusively—of the phonetically accurate variety.
6. Deficient social perception, social judgment, and social interaction.
7. Poor perception and comprehension of facial expressions of emotion, as well as in reading, interpreting, and providing nonverbal communication signals.
8. Preschoolers and those in early school years are frequently described as "hyperactive"; however, they tend to become normoactive and then hypoactive with advancing years.

1995). Since the first cases were reported by Asperger in 1944, AS has often been considered to be simply another form of autism, and frequently thought to be equivalent to high-functioning autism (HFA; discussed below) (Baron-Cohen et al. 1999, Schopler 1996, Wing 1986). However, as evidence from neuropsychological research has accumulated, it has become clear that despite several similarities, the two disorders have important differences in their presentation, course, and treatment requirements.

Prevalence rates of AS vary from 0.26% to 0.71% (Gillberg & Gillberg 1989, Ehlers & Gillberg 1993), with a notably greater proportion of males than females receiving the diagnosis (Ehlers & Gillberg 1993, Gillberg 1989), but accurate estimates are difficult, given that diagnostic criteria have only recently become fairly standardized. Currently, the DSM-IV (Am. Psychiatr. Assoc. 1994) and International Classification of Diseases-10th Edition (ICD-10) (World Health Organ. 1993) criteria for AS and autism overlap considerably and, although not perfect, the stricter ICD-10 criteria have proven helpful for researchers and clinicians in more accurately separating the two disorders (Craig & Baron-Cohen 1999, Klin et al. 1995, Volkmar & Klin 2000). Other researchers have created their own questionnaires, sometimes emphasizing different abilities (Ehlers et al. 1999, Gillberg & Gillberg 1989, Szatmari et al. 1989a), but these require further research to determine their accuracy and utility.

There is no known cause of AS, although perhaps half of all cases have some form of cerebral dysfunction arising from pre-, peri-, or postnatal distress (Bonnet & Gao 1996, Rickerby et al. 1991, Wing 1981). A genetic component is strongly suggested, particularly given the high incidence of AS features observed in relatives of children with AS (Folstein & Santangelo 2000, Volkmar et al. 1998, Wing 1981).

Wing (1981) described the most commonly found features of AS as (*a*) lengthy, pedantic, and one-sided conversing styles; (*b*) impaired ability to appreciate humor; (*c*) difficulty using and observing nonverbal communication styles, such as prosody and gestures; (*d*) impaired understanding of social norms and rules, resulting in few friendships; (*e*) uncoordinated motor skills; (*f*) extensive knowledge of some circumscribed area or topic, mainly factual information that has been memorized; (*g*) early speech acquisition with no deficits in grammar; (*h*) high verbal output; (*i*) superior rote memory skills; and (*j*) impairments in visual-spatial functioning relative to linguistic strengths. Children with AS perform within the average range on tests of psychometric intelligence and usually have relatively greater verbal than nonverbal abilities (Ehlers et al. 1996, Gillberg 1989, Klin et al. 1995, Ozonoff & Farnham 1994, Ramberg et al. 1996, Szatmari et al. 1989b). Mechanical language skills (i.e., single-word reading, spelling, articulation, and output) and rote verbal memory are intact or above average, but comprehension of text is impaired, as are abilities in motor skills, visual-spatial perception, visual memory, nonverbal concept formation, and higher-order reasoning abilities (Klin et al. 1995, Ozonoff et al. 1991, Craig & Baron-Cohen 1999, Ellis & Gunter 1999).

Although most recent research has confirmed these findings, some characteristics (e.g., motor clumsiness) have not been seen as a consistent or distinguishing deficit in studies of AS populations (Ghaziuddin & Butler 1998, Ozonoff & Griffith 2000, Smith 2000). Abstract reasoning skills can sometimes appear intact in some children, perhaps because their intact verbal skills allow them to obtain correct answers on tests with high verbal content. However, further questioning of their reasoning processes and their performances on nonverbal tests tend to reveal that this is another area of difficulty (Ozonoff et al. 1991).

In addition to the neuropsychological pattern of assets and deficits in AS, the style of social interaction seen in this disorder is important and constitutes a potential aid to proper classification. As in HFA, children with AS are very verbose, but their verbal communication is one-sided, pedantic, and has impaired prosody.

There is very poor understanding or use of nonverbal communication, and children with AS have great difficulty understanding nonliteral aspects of speech (e.g., humor, metaphor, sarcasm) (Ghaziuddin & Gerstein 1996, Klin et al. 1995, Wing 1981). They also show impairments both in their ability to use and read nonverbal cues when conversing or interacting with others; this can lead to poor ability to form and maintain social relationships. Although this also occurs in HFA, children with AS are usually quite aware of, and bothered by, the social isolation that results from these impairments. Even so, children with AS are often unable to compensate successfully for these deficits (Bonnet & Gao 1996, Nordin & Gillberg 1998).

The neuropsychological profile seen in persons with AS is notably different from that seen in HFA, but not all that unique. Indeed, there is a striking amount of overlap with the pattern of neuropsychological assets and deficits seen in the NLD syndrome described by Rourke (1989). Impairments in motor skills and coordination, visual-perceptual abilities, pragmatics and comprehension of language, social understanding and interaction, and nonverbal communication deficits are hallmark symptoms of NLD, particularly in the context of superior single-word reading and abnormally high, fluent, but relatively content-deficient speech production. Despite advances and clarifications in diagnostic criteria for AS, one of the main criticisms of the majority of research to date is that patient populations across studies are not consistently defined, thus limiting conclusions and generalizations from studies conducted in the past few decades. Therefore, future researchers may have to continue investigating many of the same issues (e.g., characteristic features of AS and similar disorders, differential diagnoses, neuropsychological profiles) to properly understand this disorder. Replications of previous work, using modern, more explicit diagnostic criteria, is an important next step for investigating AS.

Finally, with respect to the white matter model (Rourke 1995a), it should be noted that investigations by Berthier (1994) and Lincoln et al. (1998) demonstrate that some white matter pathways (especially callosal fibers) are notably deficient/dysfunctional in persons with AS. Ellis & Gunter (1999) summarized and expanded upon this support for the model.

WILLIAMS SYNDROME

Williams syndrome (WS) is a rare genetic disorder caused by a microdeletion of chromosome 7, which involves the gene for elastin, as well as perhaps 20 other genes (Morris & Mervis 1999, Nickerson et al. 1995). The key characteristics of WS include distinctive facial features, cardiovascular disease, connective tissue anomalies, and in most cases, mental retardation (Anderson & Rourke 1995). WS occurs with equal frequency in males and females, with an estimated incidence of 1 in 20,000 (Martin et al. 1984).

WS is associated with a number of medical complications. The most frequent of these is one form of cardiovascular disease, supravalvular aortic stenosis. Other prominent medical problems include gastrointestinal difficulties, connective tissue abnormalities, ocular/visual problems, musculoskeletal problems, and poor calcium regulation (Anderson & Rourke 1995, Metcalfe 1999, Morris & Mervis 1999). A majority of individuals with WS also have auditory anomalies, typically manifested as otitis media and hyperacusis (Don et al. 1999, Morris et al. 1988). In addition to medical problems, mental retardation occurs in 75% of patients with WS (Davies et al. 1997). Children with WS are typically delayed in achieving motor milestones and exhibit smaller stature in adulthood (Morris et al. 1988).

Neuroimaging studies have rarely reported neuroanatomical or neurovascular malformations in children with WS (Morris & Mervis 1999). However, some evidence of unique neuroanatomical features associated with WS has emerged. Children with WS have reduced cerebral volume compared with controls, but show relatively preserved volumes in cerebellar and limbic structures (Jernigan & Bellugi 1990, Jernigan et al. 1993). In addition, one study of callosal morphology has reported reduced corpus callosum volume in individuals with WS relative to controls (Wang et al. 1992).

Although mental retardation is usually present, individuals with WS show a distinct pattern of cognitive functioning, characterized by relatively strong language function and impaired visual-spatial processing (Anderson & Rourke 1995, Udwin & Yule 1991). Moreover, the neuropsychological profile of WS appears stable throughout the life span (Howlin et al. 1998, Stiles et al. 2000). Children with WS typically perform poorly on academic achievement tests and show a particular weakness for arithmetic compared with reading and spelling (MacDonald & Roy 1988).

Individuals with WS have consistently been shown to have profound difficulties with tasks of visual-spatial-organizational abilities. In particular, children with WS perform poorly on tasks of visual-spatial construction and visual-motor integration (Bellugi et al. 1988, MacDonald & Roy 1988, Stiles et al. 2000, Udwin & Yule 1991). Moreover, children with WS have been shown to perform significantly worse on such tasks than do children with other etiologies of mental retardation matched for verbal IQ (Udwin & Yule 1991). In addition, children with WS tend to perform poorly on tasks of nonverbal problem solving or concept formation (Anderson & Rourke 1995). On simple motor tasks, children with WS perform at control levels but show significantly poorer performance as the visual-construction demands of motor tasks increase (MacDonald & Roy 1988).

Within the verbal domain, auditory rote memory has been consistently shown to be a strength for children with WS (Anderson & Rourke 1995, Klein & Mervis 1999). Studies of vocabulary development have shown that individuals with WS demonstrate a dissociation between preserved phonological processing and deficient lexical-semantic processing (Morris & Mervis 1999). Performance across language tasks in children with WS appears related to task complexity, with relatively better performance on verbal tasks that are mostly receptive in nature as compared with those that are more expressive (Don et al. 1999). Although verbal function is considered relatively spared in WS, language use is atypical. It is often of the "cocktail party" variety, containing an overuse of idioms and social phrases (Udwin & Yule 1990).

The syndrome of NLD provides an explanatory framework to describe the unusual cognitive profile of children with WS (Rourke 1995a,b). NLD is a developmental outcome that is thought to arise from an interaction between primary assets in auditory perception and simple motor skills on the one hand, and primary deficits in visual perception, tactile perception, psychomotor coordination, and adaptation to novelty on the other. Although the overall level of functioning is typically lower in children with WS, they show a profile remarkably similar to children with NLD (Anderson & Rourke 1995, Don et al. 1999, MacDonald & Roy 1988).

In sum, WS is a rare neurodevelopmental disorder resulting from a hemizygous microdeletion of chromosome 7. Individuals with WS display a distinct cognitive profile, consisting of strengths in auditory rote memory and some other dimensions of language and weaknesses in visual-spatial processing. When level of psychometric intelligence is controlled for, individuals with WS show a neuropsychological profile consistent with the NLD syndrome.

Finally, some studies of WS have presented evidence that would be consistent with the white matter model (e.g., Bellugi et al. 1990, Jernigan & Bellugi 1990). Summaries of these and other studies that address some aspects of the white matter model and its relationship to WS have appeared recently (e.g., Anderson & Rourke 1995, Morris & Mervis 1999).

EARLY HYDROCEPHALUS

Hydrocephalus is a condition of increased cerebrospinal fluid (CSF) volume within the cerebral ventricles, resulting in their enlargement. Hydrocephalus in early childhood develops from a wide variety of etiologies, predominantly arising perinatally. Identification of early hydrocephalus depends largely upon the etiology.

The most frequent prenatal etiologies of hydrocephalus include spina bifida, Dandy-Walker syndrome, and aqueductal stenosis. According to recent estimates, fetal neural tube defects occur in North America approximately every 1–2 per 1000 live births (Fletcher et al. 2000). Spina bifida is a malformation caused by a defective closing of the neural tube during the first month of gestation. The most severe and common form of spina bifida is myelomeningocele, which occurs in about 4.4–4.6 per 10,000 live births (Bruner et al. 1999).

Conservative estimates indicate that a minimum of 80% of children with myelomeningocele also suffer from hydrocephalus, primarily due to the Arnold-Chiari II malformation. This malformation is characterized by a herniation of the cerebellum and lower brain stem through the foramen magnum, resulting in the obstruction of CSF flow in the third and/or fourth cerebral ventricles (Fletcher et al. 2000; Hynd et al. 1997). Approximately 20% of children with early hydrocephalus are born with the Dandy-Walker syndrome, a syndrome involving an enlargement of the posterior fossa, resulting in dilation of the fourth ventricle (Cedzich et al. 1999). Aqueductal stenosis occurs in approximately 5 per 10,000 live births and is accompanied by hydrocephalus (Fletcher et al. 2000). Approximately 20% of congenital hydrocephalus cases are the result of aqueductal stenosis. The main cause of the hydrocephalic condition associated with aqueductal stenosis is a blockage of the flow of CSF due to a congenital narrowing in the size of the aqueduct of Sylvius (Scott et al. 1998).

Myelomeningocele, Dandy-Walker syndrome, and aqueductal stenosis are anomalies of neurological development that arise prenatally. Of the postnatal etiologies of hydrocephalus, intraventricular hemorrhage has had considerable attention. An estimated 20–40% of premature infants with very low birth weight rapidly develop posthemorrhagic hydrocephalus because hemorrhage in the germinal matrix has bled into the ventricles and obstructed the flow of CSF (Cornips et al. 1997, Fletcher et al. 2000). Intraventricular hemorrhage and the aforementioned neurodevelopmental anomalies comprise the bulk of early hydrocephalus cases.

Early hydrocephalus is typically treated by draining excess fluid from the ventricles. The most common drainage method is shunt insertion. Though treatment of early hydrocephalus with shunts is well established, complications from shunt treatment are abundant. The following are contemporary areas of investigation related to complication from shunt treatment: intracranial haematomas (e.g., Aguiar et al. 2000), pneumocephalus resulting from air passing through the shunt creating intracranial tension (e.g., Villarejo et al. 1998), postsurgery CSF infection (e.g., Boleans et al. 2000, Wang et al. 1999), and multiple shunt failures (Lazareff et al. 1998). Recent research investigations in treatment of shunts with antimicrobials, alternate shunt drainage systems, and flow-control and programmable valves provide hope for minimizing complications due to shunt treatment (e.g., Boleans et al. 2000, Cornips et al. 1997, Jain et al. 2000, Lazareff et al. 1998, Reinprecht et al. 1997). Despite these efforts, complications from shunt treatment continue to plague patients.

The physiological consequences of early hydrocephalus can be widespread, ranging from head enlargement (macrocephaly) to intracranial tissue pathology. Obstruction of the ventricles results in posterior-to-anterior ventricular expansion and is associated with the risk of white matter damage (Fletcher et al. 1996). Damage to the optic tract and risk of the corpus callosum becoming hypoplastic are also associated with hydrocephalus (Scott et al. 1998).

Children with hydrocephalus, most prominently those who have received shunt treatment, have been repeatedly shown to perform poorly on a variety of neuropsychological measures in comparison with age-appropriate normative data for development (e.g., Bech et al. 1999).

Using numerous assessment measures, many neuropsychologically based research investigations have been conducted to assess a wide array of cognitive skills in children with early hydrocephalus. In support of previous research findings (e.g., Donders et al. 1991), deficits in visuospatial functioning (most notably for shape recognition), simultaneous perception, perception of movement, color perception, orientation, and face recognition have recently been demonstrated in children with hydrocephalus (Houliston et al. 1999). Exploration of verbal and nonverbal skill discrepancies for children with hydrocephalus support a nonverbal poorer than verbal relationship, most notably for children who have received shunt treatment (Brookshire et al. 1995, Fletcher et al. 2000). Recent research investigations have also uncovered a pattern of encoding and retrieval deficits for verbal and nonverbal tasks for children with shunted hydrocephalus. These deficits appear to pose significant difficulties for success on tasks such as serial learning, recognition memory, prose recall, and visuoconstructive memory (Scott et al. 1998). Attentional and speed of processing difficulties have also been found for children with hydrocephalus, possibly providing evidence for underarousal (Fletcher et al. 1996), most notably for children with shunted hydrocephalus.

Research investigations aimed at examining the behavioral adjustment of children with hydrocephalus have been less consistent. Evidence to date supports the need to examine etiology as a major factor in research designs (e.g., Fletcher et al. 1995a) in order to provide clarification regarding the relationship between psychosocial adjustment and hydrocephalus.

The relevance and clinical significance of findings from the neuropsychological literature are consistent with the proposed phenotypic presentation of the syndrome of NLD and with the white matter model of NLD (Rourke 1989, 1995a). Most of the findings regarding significantly poor outcomes of children with hydrocephalus on pathophysiological and neuropsychological test measures are very similar to those expected for children presenting with NLD. Specifically, problems with visual perception, perceptual-motor, and visual-spatial skills, in addition to the verbal-nonverbal discrepancy, are consistently found for children with hydrocephalus, especially those with shunted hydrocephalus. Further, the white matter damage uncovered in hydrocephalus investigations is consistent with expectations based upon the white matter model.

Pathophysiology related to the hydrocephalic condition, treatment history, extent of white matter damage, stage of physical and intellectual development, etiological factors, and other various demographic variables must be considered in future research investigations of early hydrocephalus. A striking resemblance of the pathophysiological and neuropsychological sequelae of early shunted hydrocephalus to the aforementioned models provides a solid framework upon which to focus further research investigation, clinical assessment, and intervention.

TURNER SYNDROME

Turner syndrome is a genetic disorder limited to females that is diagnosed based on an X chromosomal aberration in either all or some cell lines. The most common cause is the absence of an entire X chromosome, denoted 45,X or 45,XO. Other cases of Turner syndrome result from structural abnormalities, partial deletions, X-autosome translocations, or rearrangements of one or both X chromosomes (Downey et al. 1991, Hall & Gilchrist 1990). The variety of karyotypes comprising Turner syndrome contributes to the considerable heterogeneity in severity and type of physical and neuropsychological presentation (e.g., Prandstraller et al.

1999, Ross & Zinn 1999, Rovet & Ireland 1994, Temple & Carney 1993). Epidemiological studies have estimated that between 1 in 2000 and 1 in 5000 females are born with Turner syndrome (Hook & Warburton 1983, Lippe 1991, Berch & Bender 2000).

Individuals with Turner syndrome manifest diverse physical features and associated medical complications. The most consistent features are short stature and gonadal dysgenesis or agenesis. One or more congenital malformations of cardiovascular, skeleto-muscular, renal, and endocrine systems are also frequently present (Davenport et al. 1999, Davies et al. 1995, Elsheikh et al. 1999, Lippe et al. 1988, Prandstraller et al. 1999).

To date, the underlying neurological correlates of Turner syndrome have not been clearly established. However, some initial patterns can be observed in the existing data. Lateralization tests (Netley & Rovet 1982, Elliot & Watkins 1998) and electrophysiological data (Portellano-Perez et al. 1996) suggest atypical hemispheric organization in individuals with Turner syndrome. Positron emission tomography (Clark et al. 1990, Elliot et al. 1996) and magnetic resonance imaging (Murphy et al. 1994, Reiss et al. 1995) studies reported bilateral reduction in function and size of parietal-occipital regions. Computerized tomography scans (Kimura et al. 1990, Lyon & Rumsey 1996), magnetic resonance imaging (El Abd et al. 1997), and postmortem brain examinations (Brun & Skold 1968, Lyon & Rumsey 1996) revealed some disruption in white matter. Abnormalities in the posterior fossa have been observed in magnetic resonance imaging (Reiss et al. 1993) and postmortem exams (Molland & Purcell 1974).

The variability in neuropathological findings is consistent with the diversity of neuropsychological assets and deficits observed in females with Turner syndrome. Despite the individual differences, a general pattern of cognitive, behavioral, and psychosocial functioning has been associated with the syndrome. This profile is quite similar to that evident in nonverbal learning disabilities (NLD). Studies of motor development in girls with Turner syndrome reported no deficits in simple repetitive motor tasks. However, difficulties are apparent on complex tasks with visual or spatial demands, and in particular when sequencing or coordination is involved (Salbenblatt et al. 1989; Ross et al. 1996, 1998). On measures of psychometric intelligence, girls with Turner syndrome tend to score within the average to above-average range on tests in the verbal domain and below average on tests in the nonverbal domain (e.g., McGlone 1985, Pennington et al. 1985, Rovet 1993). This significant verbal IQ–performance IQ discrepancy is evident at very early ages (Pennington et al. 1982) and appears to persist into adulthood (Downey et al. 1991, Romans et al. 1998).

In addition, many studies have shown marked impairments on a variety of visual-spatial processing indices (e.g., Buchanan et al. 1998a, Rovet & Netley 1982, Temple & Carney 1995). In particular, girls with Turner syndrome tend to have more difficulty with visual-spatial location and orientation than with visual object identification (Ross 1996, Buchanan et al. 1998a). Visual-spatial deficits may become more apparent when the stimuli are perceptually complex, unfamiliar, and abstract, and/or when it is difficult to ascribe verbal labels to the stimuli

(Buchanan et al. 1998b, McGlone 1985). In contrast to the abundant research on the primary deficits of girls with Turner syndrome, few studies have explored their neuropsychological assets. Girls with the syndrome tend to have well-developed auditory perception, phonological processing skills, word knowledge, verbal comprehension, and verbal reasoning (Berch & Bender 2000, Romans et al. 1998, Rovet 1995, Temple & Carney 1993).

The difficulties in concentrating and paying attention frequently reported in girls with Turner syndrome may be directly related to their primary assets and deficits (Rovet 1993, Rovet & Ireland 1994). Girls with the syndrome and children with NLD perform in the average range on tasks designed to assess verbal attention. However, on measures of visual attention both groups of children perform at a level significantly below average (Williams et al. 1991). Impaired performance on tests of visual-spatial processing in girls with Turner syndrome has been associated with a specific deficit in visual-spatial working memory (Buchanan et al. 1998a, b). Experiments involving visual and verbal interference tasks have been used to demonstrate the tendency for girls with Turner syndrome to rely on verbal coding to compensate for their weaker visual-spatial working memory (Buchanan et al. 1998b). Inconsistent findings have been reported for measures of verbal memory skills in girls with Turner syndrome. Although individuals with the syndrome demonstrate good rote verbal memory (McGlone 1985, Williams et al. 1991), their verbal recall has been shown to be impaired on tests that involve complex or novel material, speeded retrieval, and those wherein visualization is an alternative strategy to aid recall (Bender et al. 1989, McGlone 1985, Pennington et al. 1985). In addition, individuals with Turner syndrome tend to have impaired performance on tasks of concept formation and problem-solving (Pennington et al. 1985; Romans et al. 1997, 1998).

The most prevalent academic difficulty observed in girls with Turner syndrome is mathematics. They tend to perform at least 2 years behind their classmates (Rovet 1995). On the other hand, single-word reading and spelling appear comparable to same-age peers (Temple & Carney 1993). Girls with the syndrome are often described as immature, hyperactive, and impulsive. This pattern of behaviors tends to change in adolescence, such that older individuals with Turner syndrome are more likely to be less active, anxious, and withdrawn (Rovet 1993, 1995; Williams et al. 1991). Individuals with Turner syndrome frequently have difficulties understanding social cues and need a structured situation to socialize and complete tasks (Rovet 1993, Rovet & Ireland 1994). Low self-esteem and poor body image likely contribute to the social withdrawal evident in early adolescence (Bender et al. 1999, McCauley et al. 1995, Rickert et al. 1996, Swillen et al. 1993).

The complexity of Turner syndrome is only beginning to become apparent. Both genetic and hormonal alterations may significantly impact the development and functioning of the brain. The majority of studies to date have not divided samples of individuals with Turner syndrome according to differential genotypes and have not factored in the role of hormonal deviations in their results. Other methodological problems limiting research in the area of Turner syndrome include small sample sizes, sampling bias because subjects are typically referred for some form of evaluation, lack of controls, reliance on retrospective data, wide age ranges (such that adults and children are included in the same study), and failure to control for the presence or absence of hormonal supplementations (El Abd et al. 1995, Berch & Bender 2000, Rovet & Ireland 1994). Better classification of individuals with Turner syndrome presents an intriguing opportunity to further investigate the interactions between genes and hormones on the development and functioning of the brain, and ultimately their effect on behavioral and cognitive domains.

TRAUMATIC BRAIN INJURY

Traumatic brain injury (TBI) is the leading cause of death in children and one of the major causes of long-term morbidity among children and adolescents (Fletcher & Taylor 1997). A traumatic brain injury refers to a physical injury to the brain caused by an external mechanical force that results in loss of consciousness, post-traumatic amnesia, neurological deficits, or all three (Ragnarsson 1993). The study of pediatric TBI is complicated by continuous changes in brain anatomy, chemistry, and physiology throughout development, as well as changes in the protective capacity of the skull, all of which underscore the heterogeneity of injury and the diversity of outcome within a pediatric population. Furthermore, differences in the severity, mechanism, and pathophysiology of various injuries contribute to a mixed neurobehavioral presentation postinjury.

Injuries may be classified as mild, moderate, or severe on the basis of physiological severity. These injuries may result from motor vehicle accidents, falls, assault, sports accidents or any other sudden blow to the head or change in direction. Following an initial insult to the brain, primary pathophysiological changes may include skull fracture, mass effects, hemorrhage, and vascular and/or neural tissue compression, stretching, and tearing. Secondary injuries include swelling, bleeding, scarring, pressure changes, and local or remote cell degeneration or death, which may result in further neurological damage (Binder 1986, Castejon et al. 1997, Cooper 1982, Maxwell et al. 1997).

Several general principles have emerged from research to date based on analyses of age at injury and injury severity. First, in contrast to the Kennard principle, it is generally agreed that the earlier a TBI is sustained, the more neuropsychological compromise is to be expected. More specifically, skills in ascendancy (i.e., in a rapid state of development) at the time of injury are more vulnerable to the effects of injury because they have not yet been well developed and over learned (Hartlage & Telzrow 1986, Ewing-Cobbs et al. 1995). Second, across studies of TBI it appears that younger children (i.e., younger than age 6 years) are more vulnerable to the effects of severe brain injury.

Children who sustain diffuse or multi-focal TBI are more likely to display greater impairment in psychometric intelligence (Spreen et al. 1995). Initial reductions in both Wechsler performance IQ and verbal IQ scores following severe TBI in children aged 5–14 have been shown to be followed by relative deficits in performance IQ only at 1 year postinjury (e.g., Ewing-Cobbs et al. 1995). Although measures of psychometric intelligence may improve rapidly as children recover from severe TBI, the ultimate levels may not catch up to those of their less injured peers, and deficits in memory, attention, and problem-solving may persist (Fletcher & Taylor 1997).

Memory problems, including impairments in verbal and nonverbal memory, are reportedly the most common impairment in pediatric TBI (Spreen et al. 1995). Children who sustain severe injuries do not recover visual recognition memory or verbal list-learning ability as well as do their mild-to-moderately injured peers (Fletcher et al. 1995b, Yeates et al. 1995). Recent research has also identified deficits in visual-spatial memory relative to auditory-verbal memory among severely injured children only (Farmer et al. 1999).

Ewing-Cobbs and colleagues (1995) identified specific neuropsychological impairments that did not differ according to injury severity or age at injury (e.g., persistent psychomotor impairment) and others that were differentially represented among groups. Severely injured children performed more poorly on visual attention tasks, speeded perceptual-motor tasks, expressive language tasks, and any higher-level cognitive tasks that demand speeded performance. Compared to controls, younger children, regardless of injury severity, obtained worse scores on tests of immediate auditory attention and speeded perceptual motor tasks (Ewing-Cobbs et al. 1998). Deficits in higher-order planning, concept-formation, organization, and mental flexibility occurred frequently following pediatric TBI (Levin et al. 1995), but this area of research has not yet received as much attention as have other neuropsychological dimensions.

To date, a wide variety of psychosocial problems have been reported in the literature, with more confusion and disagreement than consensus. Recent efforts to identify a typology of psychosocial outcome (Butler et al. 1997) may help to elucidate the controversial findings. Butler et al. (1997) identified seven distinct patterns of psychosocial functioning, ranging from completely normal behavior through mild anxiety to severe psychosocial deficits among children with mild to severe TBI. One of the most striking findings in this study was that more than 50% of the children, including those who had sustained severe injuries, demonstrated no or minimal psychosocial problems.

The neuropsychological deficits identified among children with TBI bear some resemblance to the profile pattern exhibited by children with NLD. Many of the deficits are similar, including impairments in complex motor speed, visual-spatial skills, performance IQ (relative to verbal IQ), mental arithmetic, and visual-spatial memory. Certain of the subtypes of psychosocial functioning in TBI overlap with those evident in children with NLD. Further, the main mechanism of injury (i.e., diffuse axonal injury) is consistent with the tenets of the white matter model.

However, children who experience TBI also display significant impairments in verbal memory and language functioning that are not consistent with the NLD model. These impairments most likely result from some combination of the diffuse cerebral dysfunction with the well-documented focal injuries associated with TBI (i.e., frontal and temporal pole contusions from scraping against the bony protrusions on the inside of the skull surface and coups-contrecoups injuries). Thus, it appears that the NLD model maps well onto children who sustain diffuse damage only. The neuropsychological deficits seen above and beyond that pattern of deficits may represent a set of superimposed, unique deficits that relate to focal cerebral insult(s) (Rourke 1989).

ACUTE LYMPHOCYTIC LEUKEMIA

With advances in medical care for children who are diagnosed with acute lymphocytic leukemia and other forms of cancer affecting the brain, more children are surviving the initial course of cancer and living many years beyond diagnosis. However, recent research demonstrates that toxic effects of the treatment regimen may result in progressive neuropsychological compromise that may not be evident until years after the central nervous system (CNS) prophylaxis.

Leukemias (4.3 per 100,000) and cancer of the brain or other nervous system malignancies (3.4 per 100,000) account for more than half of pediatric cancer cases (Ries et al. 1994). Among patients diagnosed with acute lymphocytic leukemia during the early 1960s, less than 5% survived 5 years (Ries et al. 1994). Following the introduction of chemotherapy in the 1970s, survival rates improved, but a secondary proliferation of leukemic cells within the CNS was observed among children who had achieved initial hematological remission. CNS prophylaxis, in the form of intrathecal chemotherapy and cranial irradiation, was then added to the treatment regimen to prevent leukemic meningitis. Cranial irradiation and intrathecal chemotherapy are also used to treat children with primary brain tumors. Unfortunately, the agents of CNS prophylaxis also have toxic effects on healthy cells, and the treatment regimen is associated with acute and chronic side effects. Delayed treatment effects, including leukoencephalopathy, neuroendocrine dysfunction, intracranial calcifications, and cerebral atrophy, are thought to be more worrisome for the long-term survivor than the transient acute effects (e.g., peripheral neuropathy).

Picard & Rourke (1995) conducted a detailed review and analysis of more than 60 articles written since 1975 that addressed the possible effects of CNS prophylaxis on neuropsychological functioning. The majority of empirically sound studies revealed the following: (a) Younger children were more susceptible to the iatrogenic treatment effects; (b) the adverse effects were often not apparent until several years after therapy; and (c) the effects were dependent upon the particular treatment regimen employed. These differential responses to treatment were discussed in the context of disruptions in white matter functioning at various developmental stages and the interruption of skills in ascendancy (Picard & Rourke 1995).

According to Picard & Rourke (1995), the neuropsychological evaluations of children treated with CNS chemotherapy and/or irradiation revealed a pattern of intact functioning during the early phases of CNS prophylactic treatment followed by a gradual emergence of impairment in a variety of cognitive domains. Although anticancer treatment was observed to have a negative effect on psychometric intelligence in comparison to non-CNS treatment, the deficits appeared to be subtle. Verbal IQ–performance IQ discrepancies were in evidence, wherein children demonstrated relatively weaker visual-spatial-organizational skills. Children also exhibited deficits in both visual and auditory attention as documented in the Wechsler scales presumed to reflect these abilities. Mechanical arithmetic skills were frequently impaired in children who received irradiation, but inadequate comparisons with language achievement skills precluded firm conclusions about scholastic performance. Mixed evidence was presented for concept-formation and problem-solving skills. Although the debate continues, basic language-related skills appear to be intact across multiple studies. Of the limited research that addressed the psychosocial sequelae of CNS prophylaxis, most studies did not adequately account for nontreatment variables (e.g., hospitalization, separation from parents) that are frequently influential in children who experience pediatric illness of any kind.

Research by Copeland and colleagues has suggested that the types of impairment most frequently demonstrated by children who received CNS prophylactic treatment are in the nonverbal cognitive domain. Impairment in complex psychomotor skills, visual-motor integration, general attention, and visual-spatial memory have been well-documented by this and other groups (Buono et al. 1998; Copeland et al. 1985, 1988; Dowell et al. 1991; Fletcher & Copeland 1988). Other researchers have confirmed the presence of these largely nonverbal deficits and have cited problems with attention and concentration, visual-spatial processing, visual-spatial memory, and nonverbal reasoning.

Analysis of the pattern of neurocognitive functioning displayed by children who are treated with CNS prophylaxis reveals significant concordance with the NLD pattern of neuropsychological assets and deficits. Recent research confirms and expands the prevalence of nonverbal skills deficits in children who receive CNS prophylaxis (Buono et al. 1998, Lesnik et al. 1998, Regan & Reeb 1998). Striking similarities between children with NLD and children who receive CNS prophylaxis are evident in the following areas: intact simple tactile-perceptual skills and impairment in complex psychomotor skills, visual attention, visual-spatial and abstract memory, and mechanical arithmetic skills. An auditory attention deficit has been demonstrated among this group of children that would not be predicted by the NLD model. Recently, Buono et al. (1998) demonstrated a significant resemblance between the phenotypic expression of children who were treated for brain tumors and those with NLD.

One of the possible neurophysiological underpinnings of the CNS prophylactic toxicity (i.e., leukoencephalopathy) lends further support to the NLD/white matter model explanation of deficits. Neuroimaging studies have demonstrated significant disruption or displacement of white matter following CNS prophylaxis (e.g., Hopewell 1998). In addition, many studies have revealed stronger and more global impairment in children who received prophylactic therapy at a younger age (see Picard & Rourke 1995 for a review). Given the susceptibility of the young, maturing brain to white matter insult, this finding is not surprising and is in accord with the Rourke model.

More research is needed in the following neuropsychological areas to further our understanding of the deleterious effects of CNS irradiation and chemotherapy: visual, auditory, and tactile attention; simple and complex psycholinguistic skills; adaptation to novelty/complexity; higher order problem-solving skills; and psychosocial functioning, including social perception, judgment, and interaction. In addition, the timing of the CNS prophylaxis and concomitant white matter disruption must be investigated carefully, given its putative influence on the expression of impairments in developing children.

TOURETTE SYNDROME

Tourette syndrome (TS) is a neurological disorder characterized by longstanding (longer than one year) multiple, fluctuating motor tics and involuntary vocalizations (Awad 1999, Hogan & Wilson 1999). There are a range of different tics that may arise in TS, in a variety of ways, including obscene words or phrases (coprolalia), obscene gestures (copropraxia), and socially unacceptable verbalizations and actions (coprophilia) (Kurlan et al. 1996).

Prevalence estimates vary due to self-diagnosis and cultural differences. However, TS is currently considered the most severe manifestation of a spectrum of tic disorders, with an estimated 5% of children experiencing transient tic behaviors between the ages of 7 and 11 years (Leckman et al. 1997b). Male:female ratios are consistently found to be approximately 4:1, and average age of onset for TS is approximately 7 to 8 years (Staley et al. 1997).

Recent research evidence implicates disinhibition of the sensorimotor basal ganglia-thalamocortical circuitry in the expression of TS tics (Leckman et al. 1997a). A relationship between dopamine and TS has also been demonstrated, but the precise mechanics behind the dopamine connection to TS remain unclear (Ernst et al. 1999). Despite the lack of clarity for a dopaminergic relationship, TS is frequently treated with dopamine receptor agonists for the purpose of producing a reduction of tic symptoms; the usual side effects (e.g., dysphoria, depression) with this form of pharmacological treatment often plague patients (Bagheri et al. 1999). Alternate pharmacological treatments yielding fewer side effects for children and adolescents with TS is a contemporary area of intense investigation. Pilot investigations in this area have shown promising results (e.g., Salle et al. 2000).

Research investigations of neuropsychological functioning in children with TS have yielded support for performance that is, in general, within normal limits as compared with age-matched peers (Yeates & Bornstein 1996). Some specific differences have been identified. However, the relation of these differences to common comorbid conditions for children with TS complicates interpretation of findings (e.g., de Groot et al. 1997). Persons with TS frequently experience comorbidity for a number of other disorders, such as attention deficit hyperactivity disorder (ADHD), and also frequently display obsessive compulsive symptoms (Lichter et al. 1999). Psycholinguistic, concept-formation, and problem-solving abilities of children with TS appear to be within normal limits, with most studies suggesting that difficulties in these areas may be related to comorbid disorders (e.g., de Groot et al. 1997).

Recent attention has been directed to children with TS who display learning disabilities, although findings in this area have been inconsistent. The results of some studies suggest that patterns of neuropsychological performances in children with TS are similar to those of children with "arithmetic disabilities." The nature of these "disabilities," however, has been proposed to be related to frontal-subcortical circuitry rather than pure numerical processing deficits (Yeates & Bornstein 1996). A further complicating variable in assessing the neuropsychological performance of children with TS is related to attention and impulsivity. Because ADHD comorbidity with TS is high, clarification in this area has been complex. Recent attempts to determine whether children with TS experience attention and impulsivity difficulties independent of ADHD have provided preliminary evidence for a closer relationship of attention problems with children who have both TS and ADHD as compared with children who only have TS (Sherman et al. 1998).

Investigations related to motor ability in TS have provided clearer results. Evidence for mild ocular-motor control dysfunction and difficulties with lateralization of hand movements have recently been demonstrated (Farber et al. 1999, Georgiou et al. 1997). A narrow range of visual-spatial difficulties has also been found and is suspected to be related to basal ganglia dysfunction (Ozonoff et al. 1998).

Examination of behavior and psychosocial functioning in children with TS has shown a complex range of results, depending upon treatment, comorbidity, and age. Recent investigations have provided evidence that aggressive behaviors displayed by children with TS may be related to comorbid ADHD or obsessive compulsive tendencies independent of age or tic severity (Stephens & Sandor 1999). When compared with children with diabetes mellitus, children with TS have also been found to be at elevated risk for poor peer relationships (Bawden et al. 1998).

A review of the pathophysiological and neuropsychological findings related to TS does not provide evidence for a striking similarity between TS and the syndrome of NLD. Although, at a general level, some deficits are shared between the two syndromes (e.g., arithmetic difficulties, visuospatial difficulties), the influence of sequelae-related comorbid disorders with TS may be involved in these similarities. That is, isolation of TS sequelae independent of comorbid disorders does not produce a profile of assets and deficits similar to NLD. Finally, the aforementioned white matter dysfunction apparently related to TS does not coincide with the characterization of the white matter damage/dysfunction outlined in the NLD white matter model. Further research investigations with more precise focus on the complex array of variables, such as comorbidity, age, and tic severity, will undoubtedly shed light on a possible unique pattern of assets and deficits associated with TS.

HIGH-FUNCTIONING AUTISM

According to the DSM-IV (Am. Psychiatr. Assoc. 1994), a child may be diagnosed with autism when there are impairments or delays in three areas: (*a*) reciprocal social interaction, (*b*) communication and language development and/or use, and (*c*) some restrictive, stereotyped patterns of behavior or interests, which may be repetitive motor activities or some intense but very circumscribed area of interest. Further, at least one of these areas must have been impaired in the child before 3 years of age. The majority of children with autism score below average on tests of psychomotor intelligence, but 20–30% of children achieve full scale intelligence quotient scores greater than 70 (Happe 1994, Klin et al. 2000). These children are classified as having high-functioning autism (HFA), and males with autism are nearly nine times more likely than females to be placed in this category (Volkmar et al. 1993).

Some of the first cases were reported by Kanner in 1943 when he published a report of 11 children with deficits in communication, cognitive, and social abilities. They had notable impairments relating to other people—often ignoring them and seeming to prefer solitude—and strong desires to follow set routines. Their speech was also abnormal, characterized by a mechanical, repetitive, and monotonic presentation (Siegel 1998). Kanner referred to this disorder as "early infantile autism." One year later, Asperger published case reports of a group of children with similar deficits, but whose symptoms had appeared later (Klin et al. 1995). In the decades since those reports, researchers and clinicians have attempted to determine whether these investigators were describing the same disorder or two different conditions. Although the controversy is still not entirely resolved, recent improvements in diagnostic criteria and careful investigation have revealed that HFA and Asperger syndrome (AS) have important distinguishing characteristics.

Although the pattern of abilities in children with autism would be expected to vary depending on the severity and nature of their disorder, general patterns in those with HFA have been reported. Mechanical language skills, including discourse, word knowledge, and grammatical skills, are all intact or above average, but delayed in their development (Gillberg & Ehlers 1998, Klin et al. 1995, Siegel 1998). As in AS, their conversational style is one-sided and high in volume; while meaningful, it is perseverative and unusual in content. Unlike AS, however, children with HFA can have impairments in speech articulation (Klin et al. 1995). Pragmatics of speech, as in AS, are also impaired, in that children with HFA have difficulty using and interpreting nonverbal aspects of communication such as gestures and eye contact, and they have a very literal interpretation of speech with little to no comprehension of humor, sarcasm, or intent communicated through tone (Minshew et al. 1995, Siegel 1998).

Other areas of functioning that are usually intact in children with HFA include basic attention (Minshew et al. 1997), sensory-perceptual abilities (Minshew & Rattan 1992, Sussman & Lewandowski 1990), rote verbal memory (Klin et al. 1995), and visual-spatial skills (Minshew et al. 1997, Prior & Hoffman 1990). Intact visual-spatial skills are often considered characteristic of autism, and several researchers have reported consistently better nonverbal than verbal performance on psychometric intelligence tests, with nonverbal problem-solving (e.g., Block Design subtest on the Wechsler scales) often the greatest strength (Casey et al. 1996, Dennis et al. 1999, Ozonoff et al. 1991, Klin et al. 1995). Academically, at least in childhood, children with HFA do not appear to have any particular problems in reading, spelling, or arithmetic (Minshew et al. 1994).

In general, however, when task demands increase in complexity, children with HFA show impairments. In spite of visual-spatial strengths, mental rotation tasks are often failed (Siegel 1998). Reading itself may be intact, but children with HFA have great difficulty extracting meaning or drawing conclusions from text (Jolliffe & Baron-Cohen 1999, Minshew et al. 1995). Even those areas that are relative strengths appear to break down as tasks become more complex and involve more separate pieces of information, particularly when more self-directing strategies to organize and synthesize information are required (Prior & Hoffman 1990, Minshew et al. 1995, Ozonoff et al. 1991, Ozonoff & McEvoy 1994). Children with HFA have notable difficulty when they (*a*) are not provided with specific rules for specific tasks, (*b*) must adapt to changing circumstances, or (*c*) must determine the parameters of a situation or problem on their own (Ciesielski & Harris 1997).

Researchers continue to disagree about whether AS and HFA should be considered separate disorders, but evidence has been accumulating that favors their distinction. Whereas there are several common features between HFA and both AS and NLD, such as strengths in simple verbal and auditory memory and word reading, weaknesses in social interaction, complex reasoning, and in both the use and comprehension of nonverbal communication, there are also important differences. Some language skills, for instance, are initially delayed in both disorders, but in AS and NLD some of these subsequently develop rapidly to at or above average levels (Klin et al. 1995, Rourke 1989). This is the case for expressive, receptive, and writing skills in children with NLD, but is not common in HFA. Even linguistic styles differ, as children with AS and NLD engage others in conversation often, unlike those with HFA (Siegel 1998). Furthermore, the NLD and AS profiles are characterized by difficulties in tactile and visual perception, visual-spatial organization, and psychomotor coordination, whereas none of these are consistent deficits in HFA. Academically, both children with NLD and those with HFA show normal to superior word reading and spelling, but NLD is particularly associated with notable deficits in mechanical arithmetic and HFA is not (Minshew et al. 1994).

Klin et al. (1995) established a system by which children could be classified as having a neuropsychological profile consistent or inconsistent with that in the NLD syndrome. They found that 18 of 22 children with AS met these criteria, whereas only 1 of the 19 with HFA did. Overall, then, it appears that HFA is a syndrome that is distinct from both AS and NLD. Despite the high verbosity and mechanical language skills of children with HFA, the remainder of their neuropsychological profile seems to suggest that they have greater left than right hemisphere dysfunction (Dawson 1983, Rumsey 1992), which stands in contradistinction to the general notion that the NLD syndrome can result from dysfunction confined to the right cerebral hemisphere (Rourke 1989).

TABLE 3   Nonverbal learning disabilities (NLD): overview of manifestations in neurological disease, disorder, and dysfunction[a]

Level 1 (virtually all of the NLD assets and deficits are manifest)
Callosal agenesis (uncomplicated)
Asperger syndrome
Velocardiofacial syndrome
Williams syndrome
de Lange syndrome, hydrocephalus (early; shunted)
Turner syndrome (45, X)
Significant damage or dysfunction of the right cerebral hemisphere

Level 2 (a considerable majority of the NLD assets and deficits are evident)
Sotos syndrome
Prophylactic treatment for acute lymphocytic leukemia (long-term survivors) and
    treatment of children with some forms of brain cancer (long-term survivors)
Metachromatic leukodystrophy (early in disease progression)
Congenital hypothyroidism
Fetal alcohol syndrome (high functioning)

Level 3 (fairly clear evidence of NLD; many of the NLD assets and deficits are manifested by a significant subset of children with these disorders)
Multiple sclerosis (early to middle stages)
Traumatic brain injury (diffuse white matter perturbations)
Toxicant-induced encephalopathy (affecting white matter) and teratology
Children with HIV and white matter disease
Fragile X (high functioning)
Triple X syndrome
Leukodystrophies other than metachromatic (early in disease)
Haemophilus influenzae meningitis
Early-treated phenylketonuria
Intraventricular hemorrhage (early)
Children with cardiac disease treated with ECMO
Children with very low birth weight
Congenital adrenal hyperplasia
Insulin-dependent diabetes mellitus (very early onset)
Fahr's syndrome

Level 4 (research evidence is ambiguous with respect to the phenotype of NLD in these disorders)
Neurofibromatosis 1
Noonan syndrome

Difficult to classify
Cerebral palsies of perinatal origin

Similar, but basically different
Tourette syndrome
Autism (high functioning)

[a]References/notes referring to each neurological disorder may be viewed at
www.nldontheweb.org/Byron_ Rourke_homepage.htm.

CONCLUSIONS AND FUTURE DIRECTIONS

In this presentation we have focused on the neuropsychological characteristics of a number of forms of pediatric neurological disease, disorder, and dysfunction. Our use of the NLD phenotype as the basis for appreciating similarities and differences among and between these was meant to serve as a kind of "anchoring principle" for such comparisons. It is clear that there is much to be done to investigate more exhaustively these forms of neurological disease from a neuropsychological perspective. It is also the case that there are many other forms of neurological disease in which the NLD phenotype is quite evident (e.g., velocardiofacial syndrome; congenital hypothyroidism) and wherein the evidence is equivocal (e.g., Noonan syndrome) (Rourke 1995b).

More generally, the syndrome of NLD is, in our view, best seen as a "final common pathway" for some types of neurological disease, disorder, and dysfunction (Rourke 1987). A hierarchy containing these is shown in Table 3. The increasing hierarchical level corresponds to a decreasing phenotypic similarity of the disease in question to the NLD pattern of neuropsychological assets and deficits (for an up-to-date summary of such considerations, see www.nldontheweb.org/ Byron_Rourke_homepage.htm).

It is anticipated that future research will most likely result in the categorization of other forms of neurological disease, disorder, and dysfunction within this hierarchy. Alterations to the "placement" of neurological conditions within the hierarchical organization are also expected to arise as a result of advances in the quantitative and functional neuroimaging of white matter and increased knowledge regarding the neuropsychological assets and deficits of these and other pediatric neurological disorders.

ACKNOWLEDGMENT

The authors thank Marilyn F. Chedour for her prodigious efforts in assisting with the development of this manuscript.

Visit the Annual Reviews home page at www.AnnualReviews.org

LITERATURE CITED

Aguiar PH, Shu EBS, Freitas ABR, Leme RJD, Miura FK, Marino R. 2000. Causes and treatment of intracranial hemorrhage complicating shunting for paediatric hydrocephalus. *Childs Nerv. Syst.* 16:218–21

Am. Psychiatr. Assoc. 1994. *Diagnostic and Statistical Manual of Mental Disorders.* Washington, DC: APA. 4th ed.

Anderson PE, Rourke BP. 1995. Williams syndrome. See Rourke 1995b, pp. 138–70

Awad Y. 1999. Tics in Tourette syndrome: new treatment options. *J. Child Neurol.* 14:316–19

Bagheri MM, Kerbeshian J, Burd L. 1999. Recognition and management of Tourette's syndrome and tic disorders. *Am. Fam. Physician* 59:2263–72

Baron-Cohen S, O'Riordan M, Stone V, Jones R, Plaisted K. 1999. Recognition of faux pas by normally developing children and children with Asperger syndrome or high-functioning autism. *J. Autism Dev. Disord.* 29:407–18

Bawden HN, Stokes A, Camfield CS, Camfield PR, Salisbury S. 1998. Peer relationship problems in children with Tourette's disorder or diabetes mellitus. *J. Child Psychol. Psychiatry* 39:663–68

Bech RA, Bogeskov L, Borgesen SE, Juhler M. 1999. Indications for shunt insertion or III ventriculostomy in hydrocephalic children, guided by lumbar and intraventricular infusion tests. *Childs Nerv. Syst.* 15:213–17

Bellugi U, Bihrle A, Jernigan T, Trauner D, Doherty S. 1990. Neuropsychological, neurological, and neuroanatomical profile of Williams syndrome. *Am. J. Med. Gen. Suppl.* 6:115–25

Bellugi U, Sabo H, Vaid J. 1988. Spatial deficits in children with Williams syndrome. In *Spatial Cognition: Brain Bases and Development*, ed. J Stiles-Davis, M Kritchevsky, U Bellugi, pp. 273–98. Hillsdale, NJ: Erlbaum

Bender BG, Harmon RJ, Linden MG, Bucher-Bartelson B, Robinson A. 1999. Psychosocial competence of unselected young adults with sex chromosome abnormalities. *Neuropsychiatr. Genet.* 88:200–6

Bender BG, Linden MG, Robinson A. 1989. Verbal and spatial processing efficiency in 32 children with sex chromosome abnormalities. *Pediatr. Res.* 25:577–79

Berch DB, Bender BG. 2000. Turner syndrome. See Yeates et al. 2000, pp. 252–74

Berthier M. 1994. Corticolossal anomalies in Asperger's syndrome. *Am. J. Radiol.* 8:519–27

Binder LM. 1986. Persisting symptoms after mild head injury: a review of the postconcussive syndrome. *J. Clin. Exp. Neuropsychol.* 8:323–46

Boleans JJ, Tan WF, Dankert J, Zaat SAJ. 2000. Antibacterial activity of antibiotic-soaked polyvinylpyrrolidone-grafted silicon elastomer hydrocephalus shunts. *J. Antimicrob. Chemother.* 45:221–24

Bonnet KA, Gao X. 1996. Asperger syndrome in neurologic perspective. *J. Child Neurol.* 2:483–89

Broman SH, Michel SH, eds. 1995. *Traumatic Head Injury in Children*. New York: Oxford Univ. Press

Brookshire BL, Fletcher JM, Bohan TP, Landry SH, Davidson KC, Francis DJ. 1995. Verbal and nonverbal skill discrepancies in children with hydrocephalus: a five-year longitudinal follow-up. *J. Pediatr. Psychol.* 20:785–800

Brun A, Skold G. 1968. CNS malformations in Turner's syndrome: an integral part of the syndrome? *Acta Neuropathol.* 10:159–61

Bruner JP, Richards WO, Tulipan NB, Arney TL. 1999. Endoscopic coverage of fetal myelomeningocele in utero. *Am. J. Obstet. Gynecol.* 180:153–58

Buchanan L, Pavlovic J, Rovet J. 1998a. A reexamination of the visuospatial deficit in Turner syndrome: contributions of working memory. *Dev. Neuropsychol.* 14:341–67

Buchanan L, Pavlovic J, Rovet J. 1998b. The contribution of visuospatial working memory to impairments in facial processing and arithmetic in Turner syndrome. *Brain Cogn.* 37:72–75

Buono LA, Morris RD, Krawiecki N, Norris FH, Foster MA, Copeland DR. 1998. Evidence for the syndrome of nonverbal learning disabilities in children with brain tumors. *Child Neuropsychol.* 4:144–57

Butler K, Rourke BP, Fuerst DR, Fisk JL. 1997. A typology of psychosocial functioning in pediatric closed-head injury. *Child Neuropsychol.* 3:98–133

Casey JE, Enright CA, Gragg MM. 1996. High-functioning autism and the nonverbal learning disabilities syndrome: a comparison of neuropsychological and academic achievement functioning. *J. Int. Neuropsychol. Soc.* 2:40

Castejon OJ, Valero C, Diaz M. 1997. Light and electron microscope study of nerve cells in traumatic oedematous human cerebral cortex. *Brain Inj.* 11:363–88

Cedzich C, Lunkenheimer A, Baier G, Miller J, Kuhner A. 1999. Ultrasound-guided puncture of a Dandy-Walker cyst via the lateral and III ventricles. *Childs Nerv. Syst.* 15:472–76

Ciesielski KT, Harris RJ. 1997. Factors related to performance failure on executive tasks in autism. *Child Neuropsychol.* 3:1–12

Clark C, Klonoff H, Hayden M. 1990. Regional cerebral glucose metabolism in Turner syndrome. *Can. J. Neurol. Sci.* 17:140–44

Cooper PR. 1982. *Head Injury.* New York: Williams & Wilkins

Copeland DR, Dowell RE, Fletcher JM, Bordeaux JD, Sullivan MP, et al. 1988. Neuropsychological effects of childhood cancer treatment. *J. Child Neurol.* 3:53–62

Copeland DR, Fletcher JM, Pfefferbaum-Levine B, Jaffe M, Ried H, Maor M. 1985. Neuropsychological sequelae of childhood cancer in long-term survivors. *Pediatrics* 75:745–53

Cornips E, Van Calenbergh F, Plets C, Devlieger H, Casaer P. 1997. Use of external drainage for posthemorrhagic hydrocephalus in very low birth weight premature infants. *Childs Nerv. Syst.* 13:369–74

Craig J, Baron-Cohen S. 1999. Creativity and imagination in autism and Asperger syndrome. *J. Autism Dev. Disord.* 29:319–26

Davenport ML, Punyasavatsut N, Gunther D, Savendahl L, Stewart PW. 1999. Turner syndrome: a pattern of early growth failure. *Acta Paediatr. Suppl.* 433:118–21

Davies M, Gulekli B, Jacobs H. 1995. Osteoporosis in Turner's syndrome and other forms of primary amenorrhea. *Clin. Endocrinol.* 43:741–46

Davies M, Howlin P, Udwin O. 1997. Independence and adaptive behavior in adults with Williams syndrome. *Am. J. Med. Genet.* 70:188–95

Dawson G. 1983. Lateralized brain dysfunction in autism: evidence from the Halstead-Reitan neuropsychological battery. *J. Autism Dev. Disord.* 13:269–86

de Groot CM, Yeates KO, Baker GB, Bornstein RA. 1997. Impaired neuropsychological functioning in Tourette's syndrome subjects with co-occurring obsessive-compulsive and attention deficit symptoms. *J. Neuropsychiatry Clin. Neurosci.* 9:267–72

Dennis M, Lockyer L, Lazenby AL, Donnelly RE, Wilkinson M, Schoonheyt W. 1999. Intelligence patterns among children with high-functioning autism, phenylketonuria, and childhood head injury. *J. Autism Dev. Disord.* 29:5–17

Don AJ, Schellenberg EG, Rourke BP. 1999. Music and language skills in children with Williams syndrome. *Child Neuropsychol.* 5:154–70

Donders J, Rourke BP, Canady AI. 1991. Neuropsychological functioning of hydrocephalic children. *J. Clin. Exp. Neuropsychol.* 13:607–13

Dowell RE, Copeland DR, Francis DJ, Fletcher JM, Stovall M. 1991. Absence of synergistic effects of CNS treatments on neuropsychologic test performance among children. *J. Clin. Oncol.* 9:1029–36

Downey J, Elkin E, Ehrhardt A, Meyer-Bahlburg H, Bell J, Morishima A. 1991. Cognitive ability and everyday functioning in women with Turner syndrome. *J. Learn. Disabil.* 24:32–39

Ehlers S, Gillberg C. 1993. The epidemiology of Asperger syndrome: a total population study. *J. Child Psychol. Psychiatry* 34:1327–50

Ehlers S, Gillberg C, Wing L. 1999. A screening questionnaire for Asperger syndrome and other high-functioning autism spectrum disorders in school age children. *J. Autism Dev. Disord.* 29:129–41

Ehlers S, Nyden A, Gillberg C. 1996. Asperger syndrome, autism and attention disorders: a comparative study of cognitive profiles of 120 children. *J. Child Psychol. Psychiatry* 38:207–17

El Abd S, Turk J, Hill P. 1995. Annotation: psychological characteristics of Turner syndrome. *J. Child Psychol. Psychiatry* 36:1109–25

El Abd S, Wilson L, Howlin H, Patton M, Wintgens A, Wilson R. 1997. Agenesis of the corpus callosum in Turner syndrome with ring X. *Dev. Med. Child Neurol.* 39:119–24

Elliot T, Watkins J. 1998. Indices of laterality in Turner syndrome. *Child Neuropsychol.* 4:131–43

Elliot T, Watkins J, Messa C, Lippe B, Chugani H. 1996. Positron emission tomography and neuropsychological correlations in children with Turner's syndrome. *Dev. Neuropsychol.* 12:365–86

Ellis HD, Gunter HL. 1999. Asperger syndrome: a simple matter of white matter? *Trends Cogn. Sci.* 3:192–200

Elsheikh M, Conway G, Wass J. 1999. Medical problems in adult women with Turner's syndrome. *Ann. Med.* 31:99–105

Ernst M, Zametkin AJ, Jons PH, Matochik JA, Pascualvaca D, Cohen RM. 1999. High presynaptic dopaminergic activity in children with Tourette's disorder. *J. Am. Acad. Child Adolesc. Psychiatry* 38:86–94

Ewing-Cobbs L, Fletcher JM, Levin HS. 1995. Traumatic brain injury. See Rourke 1995b, pp. 233–59

Ewing-Cobbs L, Prasad M, Fletcher JM, Levin HS, Miner ME, Eisenberg HM. 1998. Attention after pediatric brain injury: a multidimensional assessment. *Child Neuropsychol.* 4:35–48

Farber RH, Swerdlow NR, Clementz BA. 1999. Saccadic performance characteristics and the behavioral neurology of Tourette's syndrome. *J. Neurol. Neurosurg. Psychiatry* 66:305–12

Farmer JE, Haut JS, Williams J, Kapila C, Jonstone B, Kirk KS. 1999. Comprehensive assessment of memory functioning following traumatic brain injury in children. *Dev. Neuropsychol.* 15:269–89

Fletcher JM, Brookshire BL, Landry SH, Bohan TP. 1996. Attentional skills and executive functions in children with early hydrocephalus. *Dev. Neuropsychol.* 12:53–76

Fletcher JM, Brookshire BL, Landry SH, Bohan TP, Davidson KC, et al. 1995a. Behavioral adjustment of children with hydro-cephalus: relationships with etiology, neurological, and family status. *J. Pediatr. Psychol.* 20:109–25

Fletcher JM, Copeland DR. 1988. Neurobehavioural effects of central nervous system prophylactic treatment of cancer in children. *J. Clin. Exp. Neuropsychol.* 10:495–538

Fletcher JM, Dennis M, Northrup H. 2000. Hydrocephalus. See Yeates et al. 2000, pp. 25–46

Fletcher JM, Ewing-Cobbs L, Francis DJ, Levin H. 1995b. Variability in outcomes after TBI in children: a developmental perspective. See Broman & Michel 1995, pp. 3–21

Fletcher JM, Taylor HG. 1997. Children with brain injury. In *Assessment of Childhood Disorders*, ed. EJ Mash, LG Terdal, pp. 453–80. New York: Guilford. 3rd ed.

Folstein SE, Santangelo SJ. 2000. Does Asperger syndrome aggregate in families? See Klin et al. 2000, pp. 159–71

Georgiou NN, Bradshaw JL, Phillips JG, Cunnington R, Rogers M. 1997. Functional asymmetries in the movement kinematics of patients with Tourette's syndrome. *J. Neurol. Neurosurg. Psychiatry* 63:188–95

Ghaziuddin M, Butler E. 1998. Clumsiness in autism and Asperger syndrome: a further report. *J. Intellect. Disabil. Res.* 42:43–48

Ghaziuddin M, Gerstein L. 1996. Pedantic speaking style differentiates Asperger syndrome from high functioning autism. *J. Autism Dev. Disord.* 26:585–96

Gillberg C. 1989. Asperger syndrome in 23 Swedish children. *Dev. Med. Child Neurol.* 31:520–31

Gillberg C, Ehlers S. 1998. High-functioning people with autism and Asperger syndrome: a literature review. See Schopler et al. 1998, pp. 79–106

Gillberg IC, Gillberg C. 1989. Asperger syndrome: some epidemiological considerations. *J. Child Psychol. Psychiatry* 30:631–38

Hall J, Gilchrist D. 1990. Turner syndrome and its variants. *Pediatr. Clin. North Am.* 37:1421–40

Happe FGE. 1994. Current psychological

theories of autism: the "theory of mind" account and rival theories. *J. Child Psychol. Psychiatry* 35:215–29

Hartlage IC, Tolnrow C. 1986. *Neuropsychological Assessment and Intervention with Children and Adolescents.* Sarasota, FL: Prof. Resour. Exchange

Hogan MB, Wilson NW. 1999. Tourette's syndrome mimicking asthma. *J. Asthma.* 36:253–56

Hook E, Warburton D. 1983. The distribution of chromosomal genotypes associated with Turner's syndrome: live birth prevalence rates and evidence for diminished fetal mortality and severity in genotypes associated with structural X abnormalities or mosaicism. *Hum. Genet.* 64:24–27

Hopewell JN. 1998. Radiation injury to the central nervous system. *Med. Pediatr. Oncol. Suppl.* 1:1–9

Houliston MJ, Taguri AH, Dutton GN, Hajivassiliou C, Young DG. 1999. Evidence of cognitive visual problems in children with hydrocephalus: a structured clinical history-taking strategy. *Dev. Med. Child Neurol.* 41:298–306

Howlin P, Davies M, Udwin O. 1998. Cognitive functioning in adults with Williams syndrome. *J. Child Psychol. Psychiatry* 39:183–89

Hynd GW, Morgan AE, Vaughn M. 1997. Neurodevelopmental anomalies and malformations. In *Handbook of Clinical Child Neuropsychology*, ed. CR Reynolds, E Fletcher-Janzen, pp. 42–62. New York: Plenum. 2nd ed.

Jain A, Sgouros S, Walsh AR, Hockley AD. 2000. The treatment of infantile hydrocephalus: "differential-pressure" or "flow-control" valves—a pilot study. *Childs Nerv. Syst.* 16:242–46

Jernigan TL, Bellugi U. 1990. Anomalous brain morphology on magnetic resonance images in Williams syndrome and Down syndrome. *Arch. Neurol.* 47:529–33

Jernigan TL, Bellugi U, Sowell E, Doherty S, Hesselink JR. 1993. Cerebral morphologic distinction between Williams syndrome and

Down syndromes. *Arch. Neurol.* 50:186–91

Jolliffe T, Baron-Cohen S. 1999. The strange stories test: a replication with high functioning adults with autism or Asperger syndrome. *J. Autism Dev. Disord.* 5:395–406

Kimura M, Nakajima M, Yoshino K. 1990. Ullich-Turner syndrome with agenesis of the corpus callosum. *Am. J. Med. Genet.* 37:227–28

Klein BP, Mervis CB. 1999. Contrasting patterns of cognitive abilities of 9- and 10-year-olds with Williams syndrome. *Dev. Neuropsychol.* 16:177–96

Klin A, Volkmar FR, Sparrow SS. 2000. *Asperger Syndrome.* New York: Guilford

Klin A, Volkmar FR, Sparrow SS, Cicchetti DV, Rourke BP. 1995. Validity and neuropsychological characterization of Asperger syndrome: convergence with nonverbal learning disabilities syndrome. *J. Child Psychol. Psychiatry.* 36:1127–40

Kurlan R, Daragjati C, Como PG, McDermott MP, Trinidad KS, et al. 1996. Non-obscene complex socially inappropriate behaviour in Tourette's syndrome. *J. Neuropsychiatry* 8:311–17

Lazareff JA, Peacock W, Holly L, Ver Halen J, Wong A, Olmstead C. 1998. Multiple shunt failures: an analysis of relevant factors. *Childs Nerv. Syst.* 14:271–75

Leckman JF, Peterson BS, Anderson GM, Arnsten AFT, Pauls DL, Cohen DJ. 1997a. Pathogenesis of Tourette's syndrome. *J. Child Psychol. Psychiatry* 38:119–42

Leckman JF, Peterson BS, Pauls DL, Cohen DJ. 1997b. Tic disorders. *Psychiatr. Clin. North Am.* 20:839–61

Lesnik PG, Ciesielski KT, Hart BL, Benzel EC, Sanders JA. 1998. Evidence for cerebellar-frontal subsystem changes in children treated with intrathecal chemotherapy for leukemia: enhanced data analysis using an effect size model. *Arch. Neurol.* 55:1561–68

Levin HS, Ewing-Cobbs L, Eisenberg HM. 1995. Neurobehavioral outcome of pediatric closed head injury. See Broman & Michel 1995, pp. 70–94

Lichter DG, Dmochowski J, Jackson LA, Trinidad KS. 1999. Influence of family history on clinical expression of Tourette's syndrome. *Neurology* 52:308–16

Lincoln A, Courchesne E, Allen M, Hanson E, Ene M. 1998. Neurobiology of Asperger syndrome: seven case studies and quantitative magnetic resonance imaging findings. See Schopler et al. 1998, pp. 145–60

Lippe B. 1991. Turner syndrome. *Endocrinol. Metab. Clin. North Am.* 20:121–52

Lippe B, Geffner M, Dietrich R, Boechat M, Kangarloo H. 1988. Renal malformations in patients with Turner syndrome: imaging in 141 patients. *Pediatrics* 82:852–56

Lyon GR, Rumsey JM. 1996. *Neuroimaging: A Window to the Neurological Foundations of Learning and Behaviour in Children*. Baltimore: Brookes

MacDonald GW, Roy DL. 1988. Williams syndrome: a neuropsychological profile. *J. Clin. Exp. Neuropsychol.* 10:125–31

Martin NDT, Snodgrass GJAI, Cohen RD. 1984. Idiopathic infantile hypercalcaemia: a continuing enigma. *Arch. Dis. Child.* 59: 605–13

Maxwell WL, Povlishock JT, Graham DL. 1997. A mechanistic analysis of nondisruptive axonal injury: a review. *J. Neurotrauma* 14:419–40

McCauley E, Ross JL, Kushner H, Cutler G. 1995. Self-esteem and behaviour in girls with Turner syndrome. *Dev. Behav. Pediatr.* 16:82–88

McGlone J. 1985. Can spatial deficits in Turner's syndrome be explained by focal CNS dysfunction or atypical speech lateralization? *J. Clin. Exp. Neuropsychol.* 7:375–94

Metcalfe K. 1999. Williams syndrome: an update on clinical and molecular aspects. *Arch. Dis. Child.* 81:198–200

Minshew NJ, Goldstein G, Siegel DJ. 1995. Speech and language in high-functioning autistic individuals. *Neuropsychology* 9: 255–61

Minshew NJ, Goldstein G, Siegel DJ. 1997. Neuropsychologic functioning in autism: profile of a complex information processing disorder. *J. Int. Neuropsychol. Soc.* 3:303–16

Minshew NJ, Goldstein G, Taylor HG, Siegel DJ. 1994. Academic achievement in high functioning autistic individuals. *J. Clin. Exp. Neuropsychol.* 16:261–70

Minshew NJ, Rattan AI. 1992. The clinical syndrome of autism. In *Handbook of Neuropsychology. Vol. 7: Child Neuropsychology*, ed. SJ Segalowitz, I Rapin, pp. 65–89. Amsterdam: Elsevier

Molland E, Purcell M. 1974. Bilateral atresia and the Dandy-Walker anomaly in a neonate with 45, X Turner's syndrome. *J. Pathol.* 115:227–30

Morris CA, Demsey SA, Leonard CO, Dilts C, Blackburn BL. 1988. Natural history of Williams syndrome: physical characteristics. *J. Pediatr.* 113:318–26

Morris CA, Mervis CB. 1999. Williams syndrome. In *Handbook of Neurodevelopmental and Genetic Disorders in Children*, ed. S Goldstein, CR Reynolds, pp. 555–90. New York: Guilford

Murphy D, Allen G, Haxby J, Largay K, Daly E. 1994. The effects of sex steroids and the X chromosome on the female brain function: a study of the neuropsychology of adult Turner syndrome. *Neuropsychologia* 32:1309–23

Myklebust HR. 1975. Nonverbal learning disabilities: assessment and intervention. In *Progress in Learning Disabilities*, ed. HR Myklebust, 3:85–121. New York: Grune & Stratton

Netley C, Rovet J. 1982. Atypical hemispheric lateralization in Turner syndrome subjects. *Cortex* 18:377–84

Nickerson E, Greenberg F, Keating M, McCaskill C, Schaffer L. 1995. Deletions in the elastin gene at 7q.11.23 occur in approximately 90% of patients with Williams syndrome. *Am. J. Hum. Genet.* 56:1156–61

Nordin V, Gillberg C. 1998. The long-term course of autistic disorders: update on follow-up studies. *Acta Psychiatr. Scand.* 97:99–108

Ozonoff S, Farnham JM. 1994. Can standard measures identify subclinical markers of autism? *J. Autism Dev. Disord.* 23:429–41

Ozonoff S, Griffith EM. 2000. Neuropsychological function and the external validity of Asperger syndrome. See Klin et al. 2000, pp. 72–96

Ozonoff S, McEvoy R. 1994. A longitudinal study of executive function and theory of mind development in autism. *Dev. Psychopathol.* 6:415–31

Ozonoff S, Roge SJ, Pennington BF. 1991. Asperger's syndrome: evidence of an empirical distinction from high-functioning autism. *J. Child Psychol. Psychiatry* 32:1107–22

Ozonoff S, Strayer DL, McMahon WM, Filloux F. 1998. Inhibitory deficits in Tourette syndrome: a function of comorbidity and symptom severity. *J. Child Psychiatry* 39:1109–18

Pennington B, Bender B, Salbenblatt J, Puck M, Robinson A. 1982. Learning disabilities in children with sex chromosome anomalies. *Child Dev.* 53:1182–92

Pennington B, Heaton R, Karzmark P, Pendleton M, Lehman R, Shucard D. 1985. The neuropsychological phenotype in Turner syndrome. *Cortex* 21:391–404

Picard EM, Rourke BP. 1995. Neuropsychological consequences of prophylactic treatment for acute lymphocytic leukemia. See Rourke 1995b, pp. 282–330

Portellano-Perez J, Bouthelier R, Asensio-Monge I. 1996. New neurophysiological and neuropsychological contributions to Turner syndrome. See Rovet 1996, pp. 93–96

Prandstraller D, Mazzanti L, Picchio F, Mannani C, Berganmaschi R, et al. 1999. Turner's syndrome: cardiologic profile according to the different chromosomal patterns and long-term clinical follow-up of 136 nonpreselected patients. *Pediatr. Cardiol.* 20:108–12

Prior M, Hoffman W. 1990. Brief report: neuropsychology testing of autistic children through an exploration with frontal lobe tests. *J. Autism Dev. Disord.* 4:581–90

Ragnarsson KT. 1993. Model systems of care for individuals with traumatic brain injury. *J. Head Trauma Rehabil.* 8:1–11

Ramberg C, Ehlers S, Nyden A. 1996. Language and pragmatic functions in school-age children on the autism perspective. *Eur. J. Disord. Commun.* 31:387–414

Regan JM, Reeb RN. 1998. Neuropsychological functioning in survivors of childhood leukemia. *Child Study J.* 28:179–200

Reinprecht A, Dietrich W, Czech BT. 1997. The Medos Hakim programmable valve in the treatment of pediatric hydrocephalus. *Child's Nerv. Syst.* 13:588–89

Reiss A, Freund L, Plotnick L, Baumgardner T, Green K, Sozer A, et al. 1993. The effects of X monosomy on brain development: monozygotic twins discordant for Turner's syndrome. *Ann. Neurol.* 34:95–107

Reiss A, Mazzocco M, Greenlaw R, Freund L, Ross J. 1995. Neurodevelopmental effects of X monosomy: a volumetric imaging study. *Ann. Neurol.* 38:731–38

Rickerby G, Carruthers A, Mitchell M. 1991. Brief report: biological factors associated with Asperger syndrome. *J. Autism Dev. Disord.* 21:341–48

Rickert VI, Hassed SJ, Hendon AE, Cunniff C. 1996. The effects of peer ridicule on depression and self-image among adolescent females with Turner syndrome. *J. Adolesc. Health.* 19:34–38

Ries LAG, Miller BA, Hankey BF. 1994. *SEER Cancer Statistics Review, 1973–1991: Tables and Graphs, National Cancer Institute. NIII Publ. No. 94-2789.* Bethesda, MD. http://rex.nci.nih.gov/NCI_Pub_Interface/raterisk/rates31.html

Romans SM, Roeltgen DP, Kushner H, Ross JL. 1997. Executive function in girls with Turner syndrome. *Dev. Neuropsychol.* 13:23–40

Romans SM, Stefanatos F, Roeltgen DP, Kushner H, Ross JL. 1998. Transition to young adulthood in Ullrich-Turner syndrome: neurodevelopmental changes. *Am. J. Med. Genet.* 79:140–47

Ross J. 1996. Estrogen therapy in the treatment

of Turner syndrome. See Rovet 1996, pp. 93–96

Ross J, Kushner H, Roeltgen D. 1996. Developmental changes in motor function in girls with Turner syndrome. *Pediatr. Neurol.* 15:317–22

Ross JL, Roeltgen D, Feuillan P, Kushner H, Cutler GB. 1998. Effects of estrogen on nonverbal processing speed and motor function in girls with Turner's syndrome. *J. Clin. Endocrinol. Metab.* 83:3198–204

Ross JL, Zinn A. 1999. Turner syndrome: potential hormonal and genetic influences on the neurocognitive profile. In *Neurodevelopmental Disorders*, ed. H Tager-Flusberg, pp. 251–68. Cambridge, MA: MIT Press

Rourke BP. 1987. Syndrome of nonverbal learning disabilities: the final common pathway of white-matter disease/dysfunction? *Clin. Neuropsychol.* 1:209–34

Rourke BP. 1988. The syndrome of nonverbal learning disabilities: developmental manifestations in neurological disease, disorder, and dysfunction. *Clin. Neuropsychol.* 2:293–330

Rourke BP. 1989. *Nonverbal Learning Disabilities: The Syndrome and the Model.* New York: Guilford

Rourke BP. 1995a. The NLD syndrome and the white matter model. See Rourke 1995b, pp. 1–26

Rourke BP, ed. 1995b. *Syndrome of Nonverbal Learning Disabilities: Neurodevelopmental Manifestations.* New York: Guilford

Rourke BP. 1999. Neuropsychological and psychosocial subtyping: a review of investigations within the University of Windsor laboratory. *Can. Psychol.* 41:34–51

Rovet J. 1993. The psychoeducational characteristics of children with Turner syndrome. *J. Learn. Disabil.* 26:333–41

Rovet J. 1995. Turner syndrome. See Rourke 1995b, pp. 351–71

Rovet J, ed. 1996. *Turner Syndrome Across the Lifespan.* Toronto: Klein Graphics

Rovet J, Ireland L. 1994. Behavioural phenotype in children with Turner syndrome. *J. Pediatr. Psychol.* 19:779–90

Rovet J, Netley C. 1982. Processing deficits

in Turner's syndrome. *Dev. Psychol.* 18:77–94

Rumsey JM. 1992. Neuropsychological studies of high-level autism. In *High-Functioning Individuals With Autism*, ed. E Schopler, GB Mesibov, pp. 41–64. New York: Plenum

Salbenblatt J, Meyers J, Bender B, Linden M, Robinson A. 1989. Gross and fine motor development in 45 X and 47 XXX girls. *Pediatrics* 84:678–82

Salle FR, Kurlan R, Goetz CG, Singer H, Scahill L, et al. 2000. Ziprasidone treatment of children and adolescents with Tourette's syndrome: a pilot study. *J. Am. Acad. Child Adoles. Psychiatry* 39:292–99

Schopler E. 1996. Are autism and Asperger syndrome (AS) different labels or different disabilities? *J. Autism Dev. Disord.* 26:109–10

Schopler E, Mesibov GB, Kunce LJ, eds. 1998. *Asperger Syndrome or High Functioning Autism.* New York: Plenum

Scott MA, Fletcher JM, Brookshire BL, Davidson KC, Landry TB, et al. 1998. Memory functions in children with early hydrocephalus. *Neuropsychology* 12:578–89

Sherman EMS, Shepard L, Joschko M, Freeman RD. 1998. Sustained attention and impulsivity in children with Tourette syndrome: comorbidity and confounds. *J. Clin. Exp. Neuropsychol.* 20:644–57

Siegel DJ. 1998. Evaluation of high-functioning autism. In *Neuropsychology*, ed. G Goldstein, PD Nussbaum, SR Beers, pp. 109–34. New York: Plenum

Smith IM. 2000. Motor functioning in Asperger syndrome. See Klin et al. 2000, pp. 97–124

Spreen O, Risser AT, Edgell D. 1995. *Developmental Neuropsychology.* New York: Oxford Univ. Press

Staley D, Wand R, Shady G. 1997. Tourette disorder: a cross-cultural review. *Compr. Psychiatry* 38:6–16

Stephens RJ, Sandor P. 1999. Aggressive behaviour in children with Tourette syndrome and comorbid attention-deficit hyperactivity disorder and obsessive-compulsive disorder. *Can. J. Psychiatry* 44:1036–42

Stiles J, Sabbadini L, Capirci O, Volterra V. 2000. Drawing abilities in Williams syndrome: a case study. *Dev. Neuropsychol.* 18:213–35

Sussman K, Lewandowski L. 1990. Left-hemisphere dysfunction in autism: What are we measuring? *Arch. Clin. Neuropsychol.* 5:137–46

Swillen A, Fryns J, Kleczkowska A, Massa G, Vanderschueren-Lodeweyckx M, Van Den Berghe H. 1993. Intelligence, behaviour and psychosocial development in Turner syndrome. A cross sectional study of 50 pre-adolescent and adolescent girls (4–20 years). *Genet. Couns.* 4:7–18

Szatmari P, Bartolucci G, Bremner R. 1989a. Asperger's syndrome and autism: comparisons on early history and outcome. *Dev. Med. Child Neurol.* 31:709–20

Szatmari P, Bremner R, Nagy J. 1989b. Asperger's syndrome: a review of clinical features. *Can. J. Psychiatry* 34:554–60

Temple C, Carney R. 1993. Intellectual functioning of children with Turner syndrome: a comparison of behavioural phenotypes. *Dev. Med. Child Neurol.* 35:691–98

Temple C, Carney R. 1995. Patterns of spatial functioning in Turner's syndrome. *Cortex* 32:109–18

Tsatsanis KD, Rourke BP. 1995. Conclusions and future directions. See Rourke 1995b, pp. 476–96

Udwin O, Yule W. 1990. Expressive language of children with Williams syndrome. *Am. J. Med. Genet.* 6:108–14

Udwin O, Yule W. 1991. A cognitive and behavioral phenotype in Williams syndrome. *J. Clin. Exp. Neuropsychol.* 13:232–44

Villarejo F, Carceller F, Alvarez C, Bencosme J, Diaz C, et al. 1998. Pneumocephalus after shunting for hydrocephalus. *Childs Nerv. Syst.* 14:333–37

Volkmar FR, Klin A. 2000. Diagnostic issues in Asperger syndrome. See Klin et al. 2000, pp. 25–71

Volkmar FR, Klin A, Pauls D. 1998. Nosological and genetic aspects of Asperger syndrome. *J. Autism Dev. Disord.* 28:457–63

Volkmar FR, Szatmari P, Sparrow SS. 1993. Sex differences in pervasive developmental disorders. *J. Autism Dev. Disord.* 32:579–91

Wang KC, Lee HJ, Sung JN, Cho BK. 1999. Cerebrospinal fluid shunt infection in children: efficiency of management protocol, rate of persistent shunt colonization, and significance of 'off-antibiotics' trial. *Childs Nerv. Syst.* 15:38–43

Wang PP, Doherty S, Hesselink JR, Bellugi U. 1992. Callosal morphology concurs with neurobehavioral and neuropathological findings in two neurodevelopmental disorders. *Arch. Neurol.* 49:407–11

Williams J, Richman L, Yarbrough D. 1991. A comparison of memory and attention in Turner syndrome and learning disability. *J. Pediatr. Psychol.* 16:585–93

Wing L. 1981. Asperger's syndrome: a clinical account. *Psychol. Med.* 11:115–29

Wing L. 1986. Clarification on Asperger's syndrome. *J. Autism Dev. Disord.* 6:513–15

World Health Organ. 1993. *International Classification of Diseases.* Geneva: WHO. 10th ed.

Yeates KO, Blumstein E, Patterson CM, Delis D. 1995. Verbal learning memory following pediatric closed head injury. *J. Int. Neuropsychol. Soc.* 1:78–87

Yeates KO, Bornstein RA. 1996. Psychosocial correlates of learning disability subtypes in children with Tourette's syndrome. *Child Neuropsychol.* 2:193–203

Yeates MD, Ris MD, Taylor HG, eds. 2000. *Pediatric Neuropsychology: Research, Theory, and Practice.* New York: Guildford

Annu. Rev. Psychol. 2002 53:341-69

Effects of Psychological and Social Factors on Organic Disease: A Critical Assessment of Research on Coronary Heart Disease*

David S. Krantz and Melissa K. McCeney

*Department of Medical and Clinical Psychology, Uniformed Services University of the Health Sciences, Bethesda, Maryland 20814-4799;
e-mail: dskrantz@usuhs.mil, mmcceney@usuhs.mil*

Key Words health psychology, cardiovascular disease, stress, depression, hostility

■ **Abstract** An extensive research literature in the behavioral sciences and medicine suggests that psychological and social factors may play a direct role in organic coronary artery disease (CAD) pathology. However, many in the medical and scientific community regard this evidence with skepticism. This chapter critically examines research on the impact of psychological and psychosocial factors on the development and outcome of coronary heart disease, with particular emphasis on studies employing verifiable outcomes of CAD morbidity or mortality. Five key variables identified as possible psychosocial risk factors for CAD are addressed: acute and chronic stress, hostility, depression, social support, and socioeconomic status. Evidence regarding the efficacy of psychosocial interventions is also presented. It is suggested that, taken as a whole, evidence for a psychological and social impact on CAD morbidity and mortality is convincing. However, continued progress in this area requires multidisciplinary research integrating expertise in cardiology and the behavioral sciences, and more effective efforts to communicate research findings to a biomedical audience.

CONTENTS

---

*The US government has the right to retain a nonexclusive, royalty-free license in and to any copyright covering this paper.

INTRODUCTION

"...The evidence for mental state as a cause and cure of today's scourges is not much better than it was for the afflictions of earlier centuries.... In short, the literature contains few scientifically sound studies of the relation, if there is one, between mental state and disease...it is time to acknowledge that our belief in disease as a direct reflection of mental state is largely folklore"[1] (Angell 1985).

These statements from an editorial in the prestigious *New England Journal of Medicine* continue to reflect the skeptical view of some in the medical community regarding the possible effects of stress, emotions, and personality traits on both chronic diseases (e.g., coronary heart disease, cancers, AIDS) and acute disorders (e.g., upper respiratory infections). There is an extensive accumulated behavioral science literature in health psychology and related fields that suggests the opposite conclusions, at least in terms of the influence of psychological factors on disease processes (Baum & Posluszny 1999, Cohen & Herber 1996, Kiecolt-Glaser et al. 2002, Krantz et al. 1985, Schneiderman et al. 2001). Therefore, this editorial assault aroused considerable opposition and displeasure in the behavioral science

---

[1]The editorialist specifically excluded from her discussion and conceded the important health effects of personal habits such as smoking, diet, alcohol consumption, compliance with health regimens, and the effects of psychological processes on these behaviors. Therefore, health habits and their psychological antecedents are not considered in this review.

community and has been the subject of considerable debate that continues today (Am. Psychosom. Soc. 2001).

What conclusions can be drawn from this divergence of views between behavioral scientists and some in the biomedical community? An informed resolution of these opposing views must depend on a careful evaluation of the existing research literature. In this chapter we address these issues with respect to coronary artery disease (CAD)—including atherosclerosis and its clinical manifestations such as myocardial infarction (heart attack) and sudden cardiac death—which is among the most widely researched areas in health psychology. Recent *Annual Review* chapters have considered the relevance of psychological factors to acute infectious disease, cancer, AIDS, and other chronic diseases (Cohen & Herbert 1996, Schneiderman et al. 2001, Kiecolt-Glaser et al. 2002). Given the present emphasis on organic disease, we focus only on studies that assess "hard," or verifiable, clinical events (e.g., myocardial infarction and sudden cardiac death) rather than "soft" events (e.g., chest pain, symptoms) that may have an organic basis but that also have a subjective element.

Behavioral research on cardiovascular disorders began with epidemiologic studies documenting the numerous environmental and behavioral lifestyle factors that are involved in the etiology and pathogenesis of CAD. More recently, the ability to combine behavioral research methodologies with methods and techniques in cardiology and medicine to study mechanisms of coronary heart disease pathophysiology has led to increased progress in this area. In addition, a body of evidence suggests that recognizing and treating psychosocial stress in CAD patients might reduce subsequent morbidity and mortality. In light of the breadth of research in this field, we present a selective, rather than comprehensive, review of five key variables that have been identified as possible psychological and psychosocial risk factors for the onset and progression of CAD: acute and chronic stress, behavioral traits of hostility and depression, social support, and socioeconomic status. Evidence regarding the efficacy of psychosocial interventions in CAD patients is also presented.

PATHOPHYSIOLOGY OF CORONARY ARTERY DISEASE IN RELATION TO BEHAVIOR

The Disease Process

Coronary heart disease (or ischemic heart disease) refers to a set of conditions thought to result from coronary atherosclerosis, the accumulation of plaque in coronary arteries. The atherosclerotic process is insidious and quite complex, occurring over a span of many years. It involves a series of biochemical, immune-inflammatory, and hemodynamic processes in interaction with various risk factors (Ross 1999). The first symptomatic presentations of this process may include anginal chest pain resulting from decreased cardiac blood flow (ischemia), myocardial infarction (heart attack), and/or sudden death as a result of malignant distur-bances of cardiac rhythm (arrhythmias). Recent evidence suggests that these clinical manifestations of CAD may be triggered by various behavioral activi-ties such as exercise, mental stress, sexual activity, and/or during sleep (Verrier & Mittleman 1996, Mittleman et al. 1995). However, it is important to note that be-cause of the complex pathophysiology of coronary disease, various psychosocial and behavioral variables may relate to different aspects of the disease process.

Physiologic Effects of Stress

The concept of stress is central to linking psychosocial factors to coronary disease, because stress is known to produce hemodynamic, endocrine, and/or immunologic changes that might plausibly affect the development or progression of atheroscle-rosis or clinical CAD. To the extent that these biological processes are influenced by psychological factors, they lend credibility to the biologic plausibility of psy-chological variables as potential risk factors. It is important to note, however, that many or all of these physiologic changes can also occur in individuals without coronary disease, and these responses by themselves should not necessarily be considered a sign of disease.

The hemodynamic and neuroendocrine responses to stress are characterized by release of catecholamines and corticosteroids, increases in heart rate, cardiac output, and blood pressure (Krantz & Manuck 1984), and changes in processes relevant to clotting processes (hemostasis and thrombosis), such as coronary vaso-constriction, platelet aggregation, or plaque rupture (Muller et al. 1989, Patterson et al. 1995). In patients with atherosclerosis these physiological changes may in-crease vulnerability to clinical events. In this regard, studies making use of current techniques for assessing cardiac function provide evidence for the effects of stress as an acute trigger of myocardial ischemia (Deanfield et al. 1984, Gottdiener et al. 1994, Rozanski et al. 1988). Stress-induced autonomic nervous system activation might also predispose to clinical cardiovascular events by promoting the devel-opment of atherosclerosis over time and/or dysfunction of cells in the coronary artery lining (endothelium), or by directly triggering lethal arrhythmias through alterations of neural transmission to the heart (Muller et al. 1989, Kamarck & Jennings 1991). More recent models of the stress process provide plausible mech-anisms by which chronic stress might affect endocrine and metabolic risk factors (e.g., insulin resistance) for atherosclerosis (e.g., McEwen 1998).

Acute Versus Chronic Risk Factors

In understanding the possible role of behavioral factors in CAD, it is useful to make the temporal distinction between chronic and acute risk factors (Muller et al. 1994). Chronic risk factors—which can be both biological and behavioral—are longstanding and exert their influences over a period of time. Thus, the extent of atherosclerosis can change over time under the influence of longstanding or chronic risk factors such as elevated LDL cholesterol, smoking, hypertension, etc. An acute risk factor is a transient pathophysiologic change that results from exposure to external physical (exercise) or psychological (e.g., acute stress) factors that can trigger clinical events such as ischemia, infarction, or sudden death. Related to the notion of acute risk factors is the concept of psychophysiologic reactivity, referring to changes in response to stress (e.g., Krantz & Manuck 1984, Matthews et al. 1995). Together, chronic and acute risk factors are hypothesized to combine to increase risk of clinical events (see Figure 1). A third category, episodic risk factors, refers to behavioral characteristics (e.g., depression) that are neither acute nor chronic, but range in duration from several months to years (Kop 1999). This framework helps explain the heretofore unpredictable timing of coronary events by identifying the importance of behavioral triggers of clinical events. Individuals with elevated chronic or episodic risk factors and/or known coronary disease are at the greatest risk of clinical events when acute risk factors become elevated (see Muller et al. 1994).

Animal Model Studies

Appropriate animal models enable the controlled application of stress manipulations not possible in humans, and the careful assessment of causal pathogenetic mechanisms in disease. Their shortcoming, of course, is that they cannot identically reproduce the human condition in terms of either behavior or physiology. With regard to animal behavioral models of CAD, recent progress has been made in two areas (McCabe et al. 2000): behavioral influences on the development of atherosclerosis and behavioral influences on the pathophysiology of the heart.

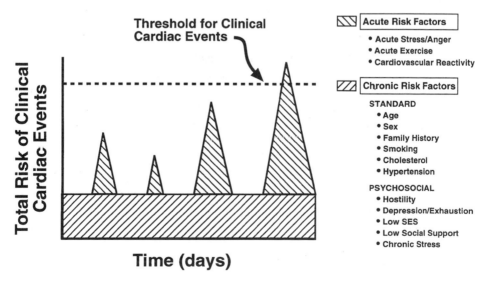

Figure 1   Acute and chronic risk factors combine to reach threshold for clinical cardiac events (myocardial ischemia, myocardial infarction, arrhythmia). Standard risk factors and putative psychosocial risk factors considered in this chapter are listed to the right of the figure. (Adapted with permission from James E. Muller, personal communication.)

With regard to the atherosclerotic process, an important series of studies has been conducted by Kaplan, Manuck and colleagues (see Kaplan & Manuck 1999, McCabe et al. 2000 for reviews). They used cynomolgus monkeys, whose coronary disease pathology closely resembles that of humans. Many of their social behaviors, such as forming a social hierarchy, competition, and aggression, are analogous to those implicated as potential contributors to coronary disease in humans. In addition, premenopausal females of this species are relatively protected from atherosclerosis. For female monkeys, they demonstrated that impaired ovarian function can be induced by the stress of social subordination. This social condition, in turn, eliminates the usual "protection" from atherosclerosis usually demonstrated in females. Furthermore, subordinate premenopausal female animals typically display elevated cortisol levels and exaggerated heart rate responses to stress and display abnormal coronary vasoconstriction (Kaplan & Manuck 1999)—characteristics that have been identified as possible risk factors for CAD in humans.

Other animal models have been utilized to study the effects of stress on hearts with preexisting disease. In this regard, a series of studies (Natelson et al. 1991, McCabe et al. 2000) demonstrated that stress could worsen the effects of heart failure and cardiac death in a hamster model with inherited heart disease. With regard to cardiac arrhythmias and sudden death, studies by Verrier and colleagues (Verrier & Lown 1984) have shown that stress can lower the threshold for malignant arrhythmias in dogs with induced coronary artery blockage. It has also been shown in canines that an acute, socially induced conflict (anger) situation can cause delayed coronary constriction (Verrier et al. 1987) and increase risk markers for arrhythmias (Kovach et al. 2001).

In summary, controlled animal experiments have convincingly demonstrated important effects of social stress and social status on organic disease—the development of atherosclerosis. These studies have investigated mediating mechanisms and have implicated the effects of the sympathetic nervous system in males and disruption of reproductive hormones in females. Research has also convincingly shown that in animals with manifest disease, acute and/or chronic stress may influence cardiac pathology that predisposes to arrhythmias and sudden cardiac death. These data provide strong evidence that social and behavioral factors can affect organic pathology. However, because animal models can only approximate the human condition in terms of either physiology and/or behavior, their relevance to human disease requires additional investigation.

EFFECTS OF CHRONIC AND ACUTE STRESS IN HUMANS

Chronic Stress

The diverse epidemiologic literature on psychosocial stress and coronary heart disease encompasses the effects of chronic stressors including psychological and social conditions at work and in other life domains (e.g., home and family). Some reviewers subsume issues such as social isolation and lack of social support, the effects of emotional distress and depression on prognosis in post-myocardial infarction (MI) patients under the topic of "stress," but these issues are treated in separate sections in this chapter. In this section we briefly consider the effects of occupational stress and of family demands in women.

OCCUPATIONAL STRESS   Research on occupational stress and health has sought to determine which occupations are most stressful and the particular characteristics of occupations that lead to elevated risk of coronary disease (cf. Karasek & Theorell 1990). Working conditions that have been associated with coronary heart disease risk include the psychological demands of the job, autonomy on the job (how much input workers have in making decisions), and satisfaction on the job. Job demands refer to job conditions that tax or interfere with the worker's performance abilities, such as workload and work responsibilities. Level of job autonomy or control refers to the ability of the worker to control the speed, nature, and conditions of work. Job satisfaction includes gratification of the worker's needs and aspirations derived from employment.

Karasek and colleagues (e.g., Karasek & Theorell 1990) proposed that high work demands combined with low decision latitude, resulting in high levels of job strain, are associated with increased risk of coronary disease. Job strain has been shown to predict cardiovascular disease and mortality in several studies of European and American populations (Karasek & Theorell 1990, Karasek et al. 1988, Schnall et al. 1990). However, at least one prospective study of patients who underwent diagnostic testing for coronary disease did not find that occupational stress was related to extent of disease or to subsequent cardiac morbidity or mortality (Hlatky et al. 1995). These negative findings might be attributable to the fact that the study group consisted of a select group of patients, and the effects of job strain may be obscured in such a population. Recent longitudinal studies of male and female civil servants demonstrate that self-reports of low control at work predict CAD in a dose-response gradient (Bosma et al. 1997). Low control is also associated with high concentrations of fibrinogen, a blood clotting factor that predicts cardiovascular disease (Brunner et al. 1996).

FAMILY DEMANDS AND MARITAL STRAIN   It is also of interest that occupational stress interacts with family demands, such that mothers who work outside the home may be at greater risk of developing CAD than mothers who do not work outside the home. An analysis from the Framingham Study reported that this risk increases linearly with the number of children a working mother has (LaCroix & Haynes 1987). Other recent studies helped to confirm that working women, particularly those with children, experience stress owing to work overload and role conflicts both at work and at home. For example, Lundberg & Frankenhaeuser (1999) demonstrated that women in their study experienced more work stress and higher norepinephrine levels than men, owing to greater unpaid workload and greater responsibilities for home and family. Moreover, norepinephrine levels were lower at home than at work for men and women who had no children, but not for working mothers.

Acute Stress and Anger as Cardiac Disease Triggers

Recent research has focused on the role of acute stress and emotions as triggers of the onset of CAD manifestations in individuals with preexisting disease. Epidemiologic evidence suggests that in susceptible patients, clinically important cardiac events (e.g., myocardial infarction, cardiac ischemia) are frequently triggered by activities such as physical or mental stress, rather than occurring spontaneously (Muller et al. 1987; see Krantz et al. 1996 for review). In addition, studies making use of a variety of current techniques for assessing cardiac function in the laboratory and in the field provide evidence for pathophysiological mechanisms and effects of behavioral factors as triggers of myocardial ischemia (Deanfield et al. 1984, Gottdiener et al. 1994, Rozanski et al. 1988).

EPIDEMIOLOGIC STUDIES   Earlier epidemiologic studies observed that there was an increase in cardiovascular mortality among widowers. Other studies have noted that stressful life events, such as death of a spouse and/or other loss events, occurred with increased frequency in the 24 hours preceding sudden cardiac death (e.g., Myers & Dewar 1975, Cottington et al. 1980). However, these and related studies are subject to the criticism of biased recall of stressful events by relatives or friends of sudden death victims, who served as informants in these studies. The occurrence of natural disasters and/or man-made traumas have also been related to increased rates of heart attacks and sudden cardiac deaths. For example, during the Iraqi missile attacks on Israel during the initial days of the 1991 Gulf War, there was a significant increase in fatal and nonfatal cardiac events among the population living close to Tel Aviv (Meisel et al. 1991). Israeli mortality statistics during this period showed that on the day of the first missile strike, excess mortality observed was greater among women than among men (Kark et al. 1995).

Mittleman et al. (1995) used a novel epidemiologic methodology that compares each patient's pre-MI activities to his/her usual levels of activities to assess the immediate physical and mental triggers of onset of heart attack. In a study of patients interviewed a median of 4 days post-MI, there were elevated reports of episodes of anger within the 2 hours prior to myocardial infarction onset. The presence of anger episodes resulted in a doubling of heart attack risk compared with control periods. Other studies by this group established increased infarction rates triggered by acute exercise, an effect that was more pronounced among less fit individuals (Mittleman et al. 1993). However, by its nature, the case-crossover design uses a methodology that relies on retrospective recall of activities. It is important to note that the vast majority of heart attacks occur in individuals with preexisting coronary artery disease, and it is to this population that these studies of acute triggers are most relevant.

STRESS AND CARDIAC ISCHEMIA   Myocardial ischemia is the inadequate supply of blood to the heart that is a clinical manifestation of CAD. The majority of episodes of cardiac ischemia occur during normal daily activities (e.g., Gabbay et al. 1996). Mental stress and emotion also appear to be potent triggers of daily life ischemia in coronary patients (Barry et al. 1988, Gullette et al. 1997, Gabbay et al. 1996). For example, Gabbay et al. observed that the likelihood of ischemia was greatest during intense physical and during stressful mental activities. Strenuous physical activity (e.g., walking) and the experience of intense anger were also triggers of ischemia. Gullette and colleagues (1997) demonstrated that, among cardiac patients during daily life, the relative risk of ischemia was 2.2 during periods when patients reported feeling tension, sadness, and frustration (i.e., about half).

Laboratory mental stressors can provoke ischemia in a substantial subset of CAD patients (e.g., Rozanski et al. 1988, Gottdiener et al. 1994, Goldberg et al. 1996, Blumenthal et al. 1995). Ischemia provides a good model for studying CAD pathophysiology because it is easily provokable and reversible, clinically important, and can be ethically induced in the laboratory in humans. Ironson et al. (1992) further reported that an anger-inducing stressor was a particularly potent psychological stressor in its ability to trigger ischemia.

MENTAL STRESS ISCHEMIA AND PROGNOSIS IN CARDIAC PATIENTS   At least three published studies have shown that the presence of mental stress–induced ischemia has been shown to predict subsequent clinical events in patients with CAD (Jain et al. 1995, Krantz et al. 1999, Jaing et al. 1996). So-called soft events (e.g., referral for revascularization procedures) in these studies that may be influenced by either patient or physician perceptions were included as morbidity endpoints. There is a need for further predictive studies that rely on "hard" outcomes such as myocardial infarction or sudden cardiac death. In this regard, one recent study reported that patients with mental stress ischemia were more likely to die over a 3-year follow-up period (Sheps et al. 2000).

STRESS REACTIVITY   Stress reactivity involves the assessment of physiological changes in response to stress, as opposed to the sole assessment of resting levels of physiologic variables (see Krantz & Manuck 1984, Manuck 1994). Research has examined the possibility that excessive reactivity to stress may itself be a risk factor for coronary disease. In one study of initially healthy men followed for 23 years (Keys et al. 1971), the magnitude of their diastolic blood pressure reactions to a cold pressor test (which involves immersing the hand in cold water) predicted later heart disease. In fact, this physiologic response was a stronger predictor than many of the standard risk factors assessed in the study. However, a later study (Coresh et al. 1992) failed to replicate these findings.

In addition, studies of cynomolgus monkeys fed on a cholesterol-rich diet reveal that high heart rate reactors in response to a standard laboratory stress (threat of capture) had nearly twice the amount of coronary atherosclerosis than did low heart rate reactors (Kaplan & Manuck 1999). Studies of cardiac patients also indicate that high blood pressure reactors to acute stress are also more likely to evidence mental stress-induced ischemia and to show worsened clinical outcomes over time (Blumenthal et al. 1995, Krantz et al. 2000).

COMMENT   Animal studies of acute and chronic stress (e.g., Kaplan & Manuck 1999, Verrier & Lown 1984), and human epidemiological and clinical studies provide significant evidence for the effects of acute and chronic stress on aspects of organic coronary artery disease pathology (e.g., atherogenesis, ischemia, and arrhythmia). However, there remain persistent doubts about the scientific validity and/or clinical relevance of this evidence because of difficulties and inconsistencies in defining and measuring stress in various studies, the multifactorial nature of coronary disease and its onset, and negative results in some studies (e.g., Hlatky et al. 1995). The recent attention to acute triggering events and the effects of stress on infarction, ischemia, and arrhythmia may solidify the connection between acutely stressful events and organic coronary disease endpoints.

SOCIOECONOMIC STATUS: THE GRADIENT WITH CORONARY ARTERY DISEASE

Socioeconomic status (SES), defined as an individual's occupation, economic resources, social standing, and education (Kaplan & Lynch 1997), is a powerful predictor of cardiovascular risk. SES can also refer to the standing of a household, rather than an individual. Evidence is clear that there is a social gradient affecting CAD risk factors and cardiovascular disease (Adler & Ostrove 1999). Much of this research has been done in countries that record social class in some form on death certificates or medical records, such as England (e.g., Smith et al. 1990, Kunst & Mackenbach 1994). However, it has also been demonstrated in the United States that cardiovascular disease is related to SES (e.g., McDonough et al. 1997).

Before the mid-1980s, the study of socioeconomic status and health largely focused on individuals living below the poverty line. Scientists generally held a threshold view of income that held that once household income was above the poverty line, family members no longer suffered ill effects as a result of their SES. However, in the mid-1980s a longitudinal study of British civil servants (the Whitehall study) revealed a "social gradient" in which health improved and mortality decreased at each higher socioeconomic level (Marmot et al. 1984, Adler & Ostrove 1999). This SES-CAD "gradient" has been found in many industrialized countries, although the strength of the association is not necessarily uniform (Adler & Ostrove 1999).

Possible Mechanisms for the Gradient

Numerous pathways have been proposed for the effects of SES on disease, including access to medical care, nutrition, living conditions, and risk-related behaviors, such as low levels of physical activity (e.g., Kuczmarski et al. 1994). In spite of strong relationships, these traditional risk factors explain only about one-quarter of the SES-CAD gradient. More recently, psychological variables have also come under scrutiny as possible mechanisms.

PSYCHOSOCIAL VARIABLES   An analysis of data from more than 2000 Finnish men determined that those in the lower socioeconomic strata (as determined by income) were nearly 2.66 times more likely to die of cardiovascular disease than those in the highest strata (Lynch et al. 1996). The risk ratio was decreased to 1.24 when biologic risk factors (such as blood pressure and serum cholesterol) were controlled, to 1.83 when behavioral factors (such as smoking and physical activity) were controlled, and to 1.71 when psychosocial factors (such as depression and social support) were controlled. However, when all 23 risk factors in the study were controlled, the social gradient was eliminated, suggesting that psychosocial variables do play an important role in the association between SES and CAD.

These psychosocial factors may include lack of social support, job strain, and chronic stress (see below). Because factors such as death and divorce can also result in economic hardship, individuals with fewer economic resources to begin with may not have adequate means for social support. As described later in this chapter, low levels of social support appear to be related to CAD risk. In the Whitehall study, measures of social support in the workplace did not substantially change the SES-CAD gradient (Marmot et al. 1997). However, as discussed in the section on social support, family support may be considerably more predictive of CAD than workplace support.

The interaction of social support with low educational level can also impact on mortality after myocardial infarction. Ruberman et al. (1984) demonstrated that men with low educational levels were more socially isolated and experienced more stress than men with higher educational levels. Men with low educational levels were twice as likely to die from subsequent cardiac events than those with more education and higher levels of social support. Studies like this are important to establish a firm link between social support and SES.

SOCIAL STATUS   An individual's status in society and the way in which he interprets that status may also be linked to cardiovascular disease. In the United States, approaches that place people in hierarchical class strata are generally not well accepted. However, animal models of social structure have provided some insight into this area. Sapolsky & Mott (1987) observed that, in wild baboons, high-density lipoprotein ("good cholesterol") levels were higher in dominant males than in subordinate males. Similarly, it has been observed in civil servants that high-density lipoprotein levels rise incrementally with higher social status (Brunner et al. 1993). It is important to note, however, that low social status is not inherently pathological in monkeys (Kaplan & Manuck 1999), whereas it appears to be a uniform risk factor in humans. Further, social status in humans and dominance status in monkeys are clearly not the same construct (Kaplan & Manuck 1999). However, a measure of social status in humans has been developed and is currently being tested (Bunker et al. 1992, Adler & Ostrove 1999). In addition, other studies are focusing on cardiovascular disease in populations that are believed to struggle with maintaining or improving their social status in this country, such as women and ethnic minorities (e.g., Rogers et al. 1997, Flack et al. 1995).

CHRONIC STRESS AS A MECHANISM   It has been suggested that the aforementioned issues in varying degrees result in greater levels of chronic stress in individuals with lower socioeconomic status (e.g., Baum et al. 1999). There is evidence from the Whitehall study (Marmot et al. 1991) that a stepwise relationship exists between SES and the prevalence of perceived financial strain (Ullah 1990), stressful life events (McLeod & Kessler 1990), low self-esteem (Brown 1986), and fatalism (Eaker et al. 1992). Higher income is associated with more happiness and self-confidence (Link et al. 1993). Individuals in lower socioeconomic strata are likely to live in areas with more crowding, more noise pollution, more crime, and more discrimination. Living in low-SES neighborhoods increases the probability of an individual encountering stressors without having support systems sufficient to meet the demand placed on him (Kessler & Cleary 1980). More definitive prospective studies are necessary to confirm the association between low SES and chronic stress, but it appears stress may account for some of the increased risk of cardiovascular disease morbidity and mortality in lower SES populations. Although there is preliminary evidence that individuals in lower socioeconomic strata experience more stress than those in higher strata, it is too early to conclude that differences in chronic stress account for all SES effects (Baum et al. 1999).

Comment

Of the psychological pathways for the development and progression of cardiovascular disease discussed in this chapter, the theories regarding SES are perhaps the least developed. There is even some controversy regarding what constitutes SES. Some studies have measured SES using only income, whereas others use property ownership. Still other studies have used residential characteristics of the individual's neighborhood, which, in turn, have been shown to predict morbidity and mortality beyond individual SES variables (e.g., Haan et al. 1987). It has further been argued that level of education is a more accurate indicator because it is unlikely to change substantially in adulthood, is unlikely to be influenced by cardiac morbidity, and is available for retired or unemployed persons (Winkleby et al. 1992). Education is more highly associated with cardiovascular disease than with other chronic illnesses. However, education may affect health directly via increased knowledge of health behaviors and promotion of health-promoting psychological attributes such as self-efficacy (Smith et al. 1998). In fact, the validity of this view is uncertain because studies that have examined the effects of income on health while controlling for education's effect on income yield conflicting results (Sorlie et al. 1995, Winkleby et al. 1992).

HOSTILITY AND RELATED TRAITS

Personality characteristics, such as hostility, anger, and mistrust (so-called cynical hostility) (Barefoot et al. 1983) have emerged as correlates of CAD incidence as well as mortality from all causes, although several studies have not found this relationship (see Rozanski et al. 1999, Smith 1992). In support of the notion of hostility as a risk marker, traits of hostility have been related to the development of CAD in high-risk men (Dembroski et al. 1989), to restenosis following coronary angioplasty, and to progression of carotid atherosclerosis (Rozanski et al. 1999). Subsequent research has further suggested that hostility is higher in low SES groups, in men, and in nonwhites in the United States, and also clusters with other risk factors, such as smoking (Siegler 1994).

However, other studies have found no association between hostility and cardiovascular disease. Although several reviews and meta-analyses have reported that hostility is an important risk factor for coronary disease (e.g., Smith 1992), more recent meta-analyses (e.g., Miller et al. 1996, Heminway & Marmot 1999) report that as many as half of the studies of hostility and cardiovascular disease yield null findings. The significant number of negative studies may indicate that the effects of hostility may be difficult to identify and/or do not apply in all populations.

The reasons for these conflicting findings are unclear. One possible issue affecting outcome is that of the possible mediating role of traditional coronary risk factors. Hostility has consistently been associated with age, sex, ethnicity, increased fat and calorie intake, decreased physical activity, and alcohol and tobacco use (Siegler 1994). If these negative behaviors are the mechanism by which hostility impacts cardiovascular disease, then controlling for them in studies may certainly diminish observable associations with hostility.

There are also uncertainties about which populations are at higher CAD risk as a function of hostility. There are few large-scale studies documenting the effects of hostility, chronic anger, and related traits to poorer outcomes in cardiac patients (Rozanski et al. 1999). Demographic characteristics may also affect outcome. For example, evidence also suggests that hostility is more highly associated with cardiovascular outcomes in younger individuals (e.g., Miller et al. 1996). One study of a relatively young sample taken from the general population, with approximately even numbers of men and women, and African-Americans and whites, reported that hostility was significantly associated with extent of coronary calcification, a measure of early subclinical CAD (Iribarren et al. 2000). On the other hand, another recent study reported no association between hostility and calcification (O'Malley et al. 2000). However, the latter study has been criticized for being very selected—i.e., mostly male, mostly white, and consisting entirely of active-duty military personnel.

Comment

The inconsistent data linking hostility and cardiovascular disease precludes drawing firm conclusions that hostility is a risk factor in all populations (e.g., Petticrew et al. 1997). However, meta-analyses do report consistent, if small, associations with measures of organic coronary disease, and there remains a substantial body of literature documenting the effects of hostility, particularly in younger subjects (Siegler 1994). Inconsistencies in this literature derive from the differences among measures and constructs that are used in various studies to measure hostility. Components of hostility and related constructs, such as anger expression and cynicism (e.g., Barefoot et al. 1989, Williams et al. 2000, Angerer et al. 2000), are currently under investigation to determine if their relative importance is stronger than more global hostility scores.

DEPRESSION AND DEPRESSIVE SYMPTOMS

Prevalence

Clinical depression is a syndrome that includes depressed mood and other symptoms such as changes in weight, insomnia, fatigue, and markedly diminished interest or pleasure (Am. Psychiatr. Assoc. 1994). The lifetime prevalence rate is reported to be 13% for major depression, and 5% for dysthymia in the general population (Kessler et al. 1994). Depression rates are higher in cardiac patients, especially postmyocardial infarction patients, with studies reporting prevalence rates of 16–23% (e.g., Schleifer et al. 1989, Frasure-Smith et al. 1993, Carney et al. 1988). As many as 30% of cardiac patients may have depressive symptoms (Frasure-Smith et al. 1995). Depression rates do not appear to increase markedly with severity of cardiovascular disease or increased disability (Carney et al. 1987, Frasure-Smith et al. 1995).

Epidemiological Data

Data are consistent and convincing that depression affects organic disease processes and subsequent morbidity and mortality among individuals who already have cardiovascular disease. For example, Carney et al. (1988) found that patients with cardiovascular disease who met the criteria for major depression were 2.5 times more likely to develop a serious cardiac complication over the next 12 months than nondepressed patients. More than a dozen subsequent studies have controlled for other risk factors and yielded similar results (e.g., Ahern et al. 1990, Ladwig et al. 1991, Kennedy et al. 1987, Barefoot et al. 1996, Schulz et al. 2000). For example, Frasure-Smith and colleagues followed 222 patients after their first MI. These patients received structured psychiatric examinations within 15 days of their first MI and were followed for 18 months. After controlling for other independent risk factors, depression was associated with a 3.5-fold risk of mortality.

This risk is comparable to other major risk factors for mortality, such as congestive heart failure and left ventricular function (Frasure-Smith et al. 1993, 1995).

It appears that the risk of cardiovascular disease associated with depression increases in a linear manner (e.g., Anda et al. 1993, Pratt et al. 1996) and that depressive symptoms are sufficient to increase risk in the absence of major depressive disorder (Anda et al. 1993). In addition, components of depression and/or depression-related characteristics may also increase risk of morbidity or mortality. For example, vital exhaustion refers to fatigue, irritability, and demoralized feelings and has been associated with development of CAD and incidence of cardiac events in healthy and CAD samples (Appels & Mulder 1988, Kop et al. 1994). In one study the presence of exhaustion predicted adverse clinical outcomes in CAD patients undergoing coronary angioplasty, a nonsurgical cardiac procedure (Kop et al. 1994). These results could not be attributed to preexisting disease. Similarly, the absence of hope has also been identified as a possible risk factor. Both observational and prospective studies have linked hopelessness with the development and worsening of coronary artery disease (Brunn et al. 1974; Anda et al. 1993; Everson et al. 1996, 1997).

Mechanisms

Behavioral and physiological mechanisms have been proposed for the association between depression and cardiovascular illness. Depressed individuals certainly are more likely to engage in risk-related behaviors such as smoking or lack of physical activity (Carney et al. 1995). However, after control of traditional risk factors and risk-related behaviors, depression is still associated with poor cardiac outcomes, suggesting that other factors are involved (e.g., Glassman & Shapiro 1998).

We have already described the effects of acute stress and its neurohormonal sequelae on cardiovascular function. Several studies have revealed hyperactive hypothalamic-pituitary-adrenal axis responses to acute mental stress in depressed individuals (e.g., Nemeroff et al. 1984, Arato et al. 1986, Banki et al. 1992). Depression is also associated with high levels of norepinephrine and its metabolites in blood and urine (e.g., Wyatt et al. 1971, Roy et al. 1988), and there is evidence that hyperexcretion of norepinephrine decreases after treatment with tricyclic antidepressants (e.g., Charney et al. 1981, Golden et al. 1988).

Depressed individuals tend to have reduced heart rate variability (beat-to-beat fluctuations in heart rate) (Stein et al. 2000), which has been validated as a measure of autonomic regulation of the heart. Low heart rate variability is associated with poor cardiovascular outcomes (Stein & Kleiger 1999). It has been proposed that loss of cardiac parasympathetic control leaves the heart vulnerable to unopposed stimulation by the sympathetic nervous system and more susceptible to malignant cardiac arrhythmias and sudden death (Gorman & Sloan 2000). Because increased mortality in depressed patients is largely attributable to an increased risk in sudden death, it has been proposed that impaired auto-nomic regulation of the heart predisposes depressed individuals to lethal arrhyth-mias (Frasure-Smith et al. 1993, 1995; Gorman & Sloan 2000). There is also evidence that the association between depression and cardiovascular disease is mediated, at least in part, by changes in blood platelet function (Musselman et al. 1996).

Ongoing Intervention Trials

The possible effect on CAD morbidity and mortality of behavioral and/or phar-macologic interventions to treat depression is currently the subject of active in-vestigation (Shapiro et al. 1999; ENRICHD Investigators 2000). However, as of the writing of this chapter, there has been little published research on the spe-cific effects on hard cardiac endpoints of interventions to reduce depression in cardiac patients, other than to demonstrate the safety of one antidepressant for these individuals (Shapiro et al. 1999). Because depression seems to be clustered with other psychosocial and biological risk factors (Rozanski et al. 1999), other interventions directed at other target behaviors have had the salutary effect of reducing depression. Mendes de Leon et al. (1991) observed that psychosocial interventions, involving stress management and cognitive restructuring, directed at reducing Type A behavior can also reduce depression and other psychosocial risk factors. Behavioral intervention studies are discussed below.

Comment

The evidence linking depression to increased risk of morbidity and mortality in CAD is robust (Hemingway & Marmot 1999, Rozanski et al. 1999, Musselman et al. 1996). These data appear to be more extensive regarding the effects of de-pression and related symptoms in patients with established CAD, although several studies note an increased risk in population studies of individuals initially free of disease. Nevertheless, further studies of initially healthy populations are needed before depression can be firmly established as a coronary risk factor in otherwise healthy populations.

It is also unclear whether depressive symptoms, in the absence of clinical de-pression, are sufficient to increase risk for cardiovascular disease. Individuals with depressive symptoms are more likely to develop coronary disease over time (Anda et al. 1993), but we do not know whether or not their symptoms developed into major depression over the time course of the follow-up period. Depression may also be inherently associated with other behavioral or biological risk factors for coronary disease. For example, depression is associated with feelings of fatigue and lack of interest in activities, which may result in a sedentary lifestyle. The mechanisms by which depression is linked with increased coronary risk in cardiac patients are not entirely clear and may involve biological markers such as reduced heart rate variability and parasympathetic function, impaired platelet reactivity, and/or behavioral factors such as associations with other psychosocial risk factors or reduced compliance with medical regimens. Further studies of these mechanisms might suggest additional useful targets for possible interventions.

SOCIAL SUPPORT

Social support refers to having a variety of social contacts who are available as resources for one's personal benefit (Cohen et al. 2000). Structural support refers to the existence of and interconnections between social ties. Measures of structural support usually include marital status, number of people in one's household, and number of social contacts. These measures are often considered in combination as social integration. Functional support refers to the utility of one's social contacts in providing specific functions, such as emotional support, tangible or instrumental aid, feelings of belonging, and informational support (Cohen et al. 2000, King 1997).

Epidemiological Data

Prospective studies have confirmed the association between low social support and risk of cardiovascular disease. In a 6-year follow-up of residents of South Sweden, Orth-Gomer and colleagues (Orth-Gomer & Johnson 1987) determined that the third of their sample having the lowest number of social contacts were at 50% greater risk of coronary heart disease mortality than those with higher numbers of social ties. At least 4 other studies have yielded similar results (e.g., Kawachi et al. 1996). In a prospective study in the United States, Vogt and colleagues (1992) followed members of a health-maintenance organization for 15 years. Hospital records were then examined to identify incidence of MI. After controlling for standard risk factors, such as hypertension and obesity, they determined that those individuals reporting a wide range of different types of social contacts were less likely to have a heart attack than those who were less socially integrated.

Social support also plays an important role in mortality from preexisting cardiovascular disease. In 1984, Ruberman and colleagues first reported that more socially isolated men were at greater risk of death following an MI. A 4-year follow-up study found that patients who lived alone after a heart attack were at greater risk for recurrent fatal and nonfatal coronary events (Case et al. 1992). Similarly, individuals who were not married and had no confidant have been observed to be more likely to die in the 5 years following an MI (Williams et al. 1992). At least 6 other studies have yielded similar results.

Berkman and colleagues suggest that lack of emotional support may be the reason why social isolation often results in greater post-MI mortality (Berkman et al. 1992). In their longitudinal study, emotional support was measured prospectively, and patients were followed for 6 months. Even after controlling for age, severity of MI, and comorbidity, individuals reporting no sources of emotional support had a threefold higher risk of mortality than those reporting one or more sources.

Mechanisms

Social support is correlated with SES, medication use, medical compliance, and other factors that are directly related to health. It is not clear whether these variables are potential confounders or mechanisms by which social support affects disease (Uchino et al. 1996). However, the association between social support and health remains even after statistically controlling for coronary risk factors and risky behaviors such as medical noncompliance (Bland et al. 1991).

Although social support has been proposed by some to reduce morbidity and mortality through other factors such as reducing depression, most research focuses on the moderating effects of social support on stress. Lepore (1998) suggests at least three possible pathways through which social support could reduce the pathological effects of stress: direct dampening of neuroendocrine activation, which reduces overall arousal due to stress; facilitated coping through cognitive reappraisal processes; and a combination of direct dampening of arousal and facilitated coping.

Comment

Epidemiological data convincingly suggest that social support plays an important role in the development and progression of coronary disease. The specific aspects of social support that are important and the mechanisms by which social support may affect disease are less clear. Many studies are difficult to compare because each used a different instrument to measure social support. Further, many studies fail to report the psychometric properties of the instrument chosen to measure social support (see Uchino et al. 1996). Research in this area would be strengthened by the use of psychometrically sound, standardized measurement tools.

Another important consideration in social support research is the nature of the study samples used. Many studies of social support are conducted on women, based on the popular assumption that females would be more responsive to social support than males. However, the epidemiological data suggests that, in fact, men may be more responsive to social support than women (e.g., Orth-Gomer & Johnsson 1987). The specific needs of the individual may also mediate the beneficial effects of social support. Epidemiological data suggests that a minimum number of social contacts is necessary for cardiovascular health for women in urban areas (e.g., Orth-Gomer & Johnsson 1987, Berkman & Syme 1979). However, women in rural settings have smaller social networks and do not experience negative cardiovascular effects (e.g., Schoenbach et al. 1986). Orth-Gomer & Johnsson (1987) have speculated that women who live in urban areas lead more unstable lives owing to greater changes and contradictory demands from multiple social roles, and therefore require larger social networks.

Not all social contacts provide support. Social relationships may involve demands for attention or assistance, conflict, and criticism. Further, the number of supportive relationships an individual has appears to be only weakly correlated with the number of nonsupportive relationships they have (see Seeman 2000 for a review). It has long been suggested that social integration may actually be harmful if it is accompanied by interpersonal conflict or problems (Medalie & Goldbourt 1976). There is now increasing evidence that positive, supportive relationships are associated with lower levels of cardiovascular and neurohormonal reactivity, whereas nonsupportive relationships are associated with heightened physiological stress responses (e.g., Seeman & McEwen 1996). Therefore, the nature of social relationships may be as important the number, and should be measured as well.

PSYCHOSOCIAL INTERVENTION TRIALS

Behavioral and psychosocial treatment studies have evaluated the efficacy of reducing stress-related characteristics in cardiac patients morbidity and mortality (see Rozanski et al. 1999, Linden et al. 1996). Patients with CAD are often chosen as targets in these secondary and tertiary prevention studies because of their presumed heightened motivation to change their behavior, as well as the ability to readily assess coronary disease endpoints in this population. Intervention studies have employed a variety of behavioral techniques, including relaxation training, cognitive behavioral stress management, meditation, providing home nurse interventions to reduce stress, group emotional support, and cognitive therapy for depression. This literature has recently been reviewed in depth by Rozanski et al. (1999) and in an *Annual Review* chapter by Schneiderman et al. (2001), and will only be considered briefly here.

A meta-analysis was conducted of more than 20 controlled trials utilizing a variety of hard and soft endpoints that evaluated the impact of psychosocial treatments among cardiac patients (Linden et al. 1996). This analysis indicated that patients receiving psychosocial treatments showed greater reductions compared with control conditions in psychological distress, blood pressure, heart rate, and serum cholesterol levels. Morbidity and mortality data, available in only about half of these studies, indicated that patients not receiving psychosocial treatments showed greater mortality and cardiac recurrence rates during the first 2 years of follow-up (Linden et al. 1996).

However, since the publication of this meta-analysis, several important intervention studies have been published, one yielding positive effects on morbidity (Blumenthal et al. 1997) and two yielding no effects or trends in the opposite direction (Jones & West 1996, Frasure-Smith et al. 1997). In their recent comprehensive review, Rozanski et al. (1999) observed that, at the time of their review, 14 psychosocial intervention trials, both large and small, had assessed the impact of psychosocial interventions on cardiac death and myocardial infarction. These trials yielded both positive and negative evidence for the efficacy of psychosocial interventions on morbidity and mortality. However, some or all of the negative findings on morbidity or mortality could be attributed to the fact that the intervention methods used in these studies did not reduce reported psychological distress among participants (e.g., Frasure-Smith et al. 1997).

Comment

Those psychosocial intervention trials that have yielded positive results on cardiac morbidity and mortality (e.g., Friedman et al. 1986, Blumenthal et al. 1997, Ornish et al. 1990) have provided encouraging data for the influence of behavioral factors on cardiac endpoints. However, the existence of negative studies in this area highlights the fact that uncertainties exist in terms of (*a*) the most appropriate and effective types of behavioral and psychosocial interventions and (*b*) how these should be administered in particular groups of patients (Rozanski et al. 1999, Schneiderman et al. 2001). Another important issue is the fact that some of the published interventions yielding positive results have involved small samples of patients (e.g., Ornish 1998, Ornish et al. 1990), and others have either not yet been replicated or yielded negative results when replications were attempted (Frasure-Smith et al. 1997). It has been noted that these negative studies have failed to document a positive impact of interventions on patients' stress levels, so the studies do not refute a possible role for stress in disease progression. These uncertainties support the conclusion that larger controlled clinical trials are needed to establish the demographic and psychological characteristics of appropriate targets for psychosocial interventions, and the physiological and psychological mechanisms by which effective interventions might operate (Schneiderman et al. 2001).

CONCLUDING COMMENTS

Extensive evidence from multiple sources, including animal model studies, epidemiological studies, and human clinical studies (including laboratory studies and intervention trials), suggests that psychological and psychosocial variables can have a significant impact on organic manifestations of coronary artery disease. In our review we noted that this evidence is more consistent for some putative psychological or social risk factors than for others, and that some of these variables appear to be more (or less) important in certain populations (e.g., healthy individuals vs. coronary disease patients). Nevertheless, taken as a whole, these data provide substantial evidence for the effects of psychosocial variables on organic disease.

In light of these data, why the persistent doubts about the scientific validity and/or clinical relevance of this evidence among some in the biomedical community (see Angell 1985, Scheidt 2000)? It is likely that there are those in the biomedical community who will resist acknowledging a role of psychological and social variables regardless of the evidence. With regard to the state of the research literature, in a thoughtful commentary, Scheidt (2000) describes some of the reasons for such doubts among medical practitioners in the case of coronary artery disease, for which some of the strongest evidence exists in the health psychology and behavioral medicine field. These reasons include (*a*) the fact that the literature contains many studies with various design limitations, such as small or selected samples among studies reporting positive (or negative) results, or lack of appropriate control groups; (*b*) inconsistent results among studies; and (*c*) doubts about the actual clinical relevance of behavioral variables and interventions. To these issues, we might add several additional points. There are inconsistencies in defining and measuring various psychosocial measures (e.g., stress, hostility, anger), and gaps in knowledge regarding the applicability of various psychological risk factors in different demographic and health groups. Inconsistencies in psychosocial research findings might result from the use of convenience samples or nonvalidated versions of psychological scales in some studies. Studies may also use different measures of putative psychological risk factors (e.g., anger or hostility), perhaps with differing results.

Another important issue that needs to be addressed is the effective communication of research findings. Most biomedical clinicians and biomedical investigators do not read the psychological research literature, and do not have training needed to understand psychological constructs. To gain the attention and (perhaps) the acceptance of the biomedical community, many behavioral researchers elect to publish their findings in medical journals. In order to accomplish this, however, behavioral researchers need to alter the presentation of their work accordingly (e.g., by eliminating psychological jargon and emphasizing the clinical implications of their work). Further, in order to be accepted by biomedical journals, it is necessary that articles be sophisticated with regard to the medical variables and endpoints in question, and it is here that multidisciplinary research teams that are sophisticated in their knowledge of cardiology variables are important.

Some of these issues may be addressed as more large-scale and carefully controlled clinical trials that measure morbidity and mortality outcomes are conducted (Schneiderman et al. 2001). Moreover, laboratory research on behavioral aspects of coronary artery disease is becoming more and more sophisticated and able to avoid the shortcomings of prior work. This progress has been facilitated as behavioral research begins to incorporate the methodologies and increasing knowledge base in cardiology and related fields (Krantz et al. 2000). Communication and dissemination of research findings to other disciplines will be facilitated by the integration of biomedical methodologies with behavioral expertise. Continued progress in this area is dependent on multidisciplinary research that incorporates the knowledge base in both cardiology and in the behavioral sciences.

ACKNOWLEDGMENTS

Preparation of this chapter was assisted by grants from the NIH (HL47337) and USUHS grant RO7233. The opinions and assertions expressed herein are those of the authors and are not to be construed as reflecting the views of the USUHS or the US Department of Defense.

Visit the Annual Reviews home page at www.AnnualReviews.org

LITERATURE CITED

Adler NE, Ostrove JM. 1999. SES & health: what we know and what we don't. *Ann. NY Acad. Sci.* 896:3–15

Ahern DK, Gorkin L, Anderson JL, Tierney C, Hallstrom A, et al. 1990. Cardiac Arrhythmia Pilot Study (CAPS) investigators: biobehavioral variables and mortality or cardiac arrest in the Cardiac Arrhythmia Pilot Study (CAPS). *Am. J. Cardiol.* 66:59–62

Am. Psychiatr. Assoc. 1994. *Diagnostic and Statistical Manual of Mental Disorders.* Washington, DC: Am. Psychiatr. Assoc. 4th ed.

Anda R, Williamson D, Jones D, Macera C, Eaker E, et al. 1993. Depressed affect, hopelessness, and the risk of ischemic heart disease in a cohort of US adults. *Epidemiology* 4:285–94

Angell M. 1985. Disease as a reflection of the psyche. *N. Engl. J. Med.* 12:1570–72

Angell M, Relman A, Schneiderman N, Williams R, Lumdberg G, Markovitz J, participants. 2001. *Resolved: psychosocial intervention can improve clinical outcomes in organic disease.* Presented at Annu. Meet. Am. Psychosom. Soc., Monterey, CA

Angerer P, Siebert U, Kothny W, Muhlbauer D, Mudra H, von Schacky C. 2000. Impact of social support, cynical hostility and anger expression on progression of coronary artery disease. *J. Am. Coll. Cardiol.* 36:1781–88

Appels A, Mulder P. 1988. Excess fatigue as a precursor of myocardial infarction. *Eur. Heart J.* 9:758–64

Arato M, Banki CM, Nemeroff CB, Bissette G. 1986. Hypothalamic-pituitary-adrenal axis and suicide. *Ann. NY Acad. Sci.* 487:263–70

Banki CM, Karmasci L, Bissette G, Nemeroff CB. 1992. CSF corticotropin-releasing and somatostatin in major depression: response to antidepressant treatment and relapse. *Eur. Neuropsychopharmacol.* 2:107–13

Barefoot JC, Dahlstrom WG, Williams RB. 1983. Hostility, CHD incidence, and total mortality: a 25-year follow-up study of 225 physicians. *Psychosom. Med.* 45:59–63

Barefoot JC, Dodge KA, Peterson BL, Dahlstrom WG, Williams RB. 1989. The Cook-Medley Hostility Scale: item content and ability to predict survival. *Psychosom. Med.* 51:46–57

Barefoot JC, Helms MJ, Mark DB, Blumenthal JA, Califf RM, et al. 1996. Depression and long-term mortality risk in patients with coronary artery disease. *Am. J. Cardiol.* 78:613–17

Barry J, Selwyn AP, Nabel EG, Rocco MB, Mead K, et al. 1988. Frequency of ST-segment depression produced by mental stress in stable angina pectoris from coronary artery disease. *Am. J. Cardiol.* 61:989–93

Baum A, Garofalo JP, Yali AM. 1999. Socioeconomic status and chronic stress: does stress account for SES effects on health? *Ann. NY Acad. Sci.* 896:131–44

Baum A, Posluszny DM. 1999. Mapping biobehavioral contributions to health and illness. *Annu. Rev. Psychol.* 50:137–63

Berkman LF, Leo-Summers L, Horwitz RI. 1992. Emotional support and survival after myocardial infarction. A prospective, population-based study of the elderly. *Ann. Int. Med.* 117:1003–9

Berkman LF, Syme SL. 1979. Social network, host resistance, and mortality. A 9-year follow-up study of Alameda County residents. *Am. J. Epidemiol.* 109:186–204

Bland SH, Krogh V, Winkelstein W, Trevisan M. 1991. Social network and blood pressure: a population study. *Psychosom. Med.* 53:598–607

Blumenthal JA, Jiang W, Reese J, Frid DJ, Waugh R, et al. 1995. Mental stress-induced ischemia in the laboratory and ambulatory ischemia during daily life: association and hemodynamic features. *Circulation* 92: 2102–8

Blumenthal JA, Wei J, Babyak M, Krantz DS, Frid D, et al. 1997. Stress management and exercise training in cardiac patients with myocardial ischemia: effects on prognosis and on markers of myocardial ischemia. *Arch. Int. Med.* 157:2213–23

Bosma H, Marmot MG, Hemingway H, Nicholson A, Brunner EJ, et al. 1997. Low job control and risk of coronary heart disease in the Whitehall II (prospective cohort) study. *Am. J. Public Health* 86:332–40

Brown GW. 1986. Social support, self esteem, and depression. *Psychol. Med.* 16:813–31

Brunn JG, Parades A, Adsett CA, Wolf S. 1974. Psychological predictors of sudden death in myocardial infarction. *J. Psychosom. Res.* 18:187–91

Brunner E, Smith GD, Marmot M, Canner R, Beksinska M, et al. 1996. Childhood social circumstances and psychosocial and behavioral factors as determinants of plasma fibrinogen. *Lancet* 347:1008–13

Brunner EJ, Marmot MG, White IR, O'Brien JR, Etherington MD, et al. 1993. Gender and employment grade differences in blood cholesterol, apolipoproteins, and haemostatic factors in the Whitehall II study. *Atherosclerosis* 102:195–207

Bunker CH, Ukoli FAM, Nwankwo MU, Omene JA, Currier GW, et al. 1992. Factors associated with hypertension in Nigerian civil servants. *Prev. Med.* 21:710–22

Carney RM, Rich MW, Freedland KE, Saini J. 1988. Major depressive disorder predicts cardiac events in patients with coronary artery disease. *Psychosom. Med.* 50:627–33

Carney RM, Rich MW, Tevelde A, Saini J, Clark K, Jaffe AS. 1987. Major depressive disorder in coronary artery disease. *Am. J. Cardiol.* 6:1273–75

Carney RM, Saunders RD, Freedland KE, Stein P, Rich MW, Jaffe AS. 1995. Association of depression with reduced heart rate variability in coronary artery disease. *Am. J. Cardiol.* 76:562–64

Case RB, Moss AJ, Case N, McDermott M,

Eberly S. 1992. Living alone after myocardial infarction: impact on prognosis. *JAMA* 267:515–19

Charney DS, Menkes DB, Henninger GR. 1981. Receptor sensitivity and the mechanism of action of antidepressant treatment. *Arch. Gen. Psychiatry* 38:1160–80

Cohen S, Herbert TB. 1996. Psychological factors and physical disease from the perspective of psychoneuroimmunology. *Annu. Rev. Psychol.* 47:113–42

Cohen S, Underwood LG, Gottlieb BH. 2000. *Social Support Measurement and Intervention: A Guide for Health and Social Scientists.* New York: Oxford Univ. Press

Coresh J, Klag MJ, Mead LA, Liang KY, Whelton PK. 1992. Vascular reactivity in young adults and cardiovascular disease. A prospective study. *Hypertension* 19:218–23

Cottington EM, Matthews KA, Talbott E, Kuller LH. 1980. Environmental agents preceding sudden death in women. *Psychosom. Med.* 42:567–74

Deanfield JE, Kensett M, Wilson RA, Shea M, Horlock P, et al. 1984. Silent myocardial ischemia due to mental stress. *Lancet* 3: 1001–5

Dembroski TM, MacDougall JM, Costa PT, Grandits GA. 1989. Components of hostility as predictors of sudden death and myocardial infarction in the Multiple Risk Factor Intervention Trial. *Psychosom. Med.* 51:514–22

Eaker ED, Pinsky J, Castelli WP. 1992. Myocardial infarction and coronary death among women: psychosocial predictors from a 20-year follow-up of women in the Framingham study. *Am. J. Epidemiol.* 135:854–64

ENRICHD Investigators. 2000. Enhancing recovery in coronary heart disease patients (ENRICHD): study design and methods. *Am. Heart J.* 139:1–9

Everson SA, Goldberg DE, Kaplan GA, Cohen RD, Pukkala E, et al. 1996. Hopelessness and risk of mortality and incidence of myocardial infarction and cancer. *Psychosom. Med.* 58:113–21

Everson SA, Kaplan GA, Goldberg DE, Salonen R, Salonen JT. 1997. Hopelessness and

4-year progession of carotid atherosclerosis: the Kupio ischemic heart disease risk factor study. *Arterioscler. Thromb. Vasc. Biol.* 17:1490–95

Flack JM, Amaro H, Jenkins W, Kunitz S, Levy J, et al. 1995. Panel I: epidemiology of minority health. *Health Psychol.* 14:592–600

Frasure-Smith N, Lesperance F, Prince RH, Verrier P, Garber R, et al. 1997. Randomised trial of home-based psychosocial nursing intervention for patients recovering from myocardial infarction. *Lancet* 350:473–79

Frasure-Smith N, Lesperance F, Talajic M. 1993. Depression following myocardial infarction: impact on 6-month survival. *JAMA* 270:1819–61

Frasure-Smith N, Lesperance F, Talajic M. 1995. Depression and 18-month prognosis after myocardial infarction. *Circulation* 91:999–1005

Friedman M, Thorese C, Gill J, Ulmer D, Powell L, et al. 1986. Alteration of type A behavior and its effects on cardiac recurrences in post-myocardial infarction patients: summary results of the recurrent coronary prevention project. *Am. Heart J.* 112:653–65

Gabbay FH, Krantz DS, Kop WJ, Hedges SM, Klein J, et al. 1996. Triggers of myocardial ischemia during daily life in patients with coronary artery disease: physical and mental activities, anger, and smoking. *J. Am. Coll. Cardiol.* 27:585–92

Glassman AH, Shapiro PA. 1998. Depression and the course of coronary artery disease. *Am. J. Psychiatry* 155:4–11

Goldberg AD, Becker LC, Bonsall R, Cohen J, Ketterer MW, et al. 1996. Ischemic, hemodynamic, and neurohormone responses to mental and exercise stress: experience from the Psychophysiologic Investigations of Myocardial Ischemia. *Circulation* 94:2402–9

Golden RN, Markey SP, Risby ED, Rudorfer MV, Cowdry RW, Potter WZ. 1988. Antidepressants reduce whole-body norepinephrine turnover while enhancing 6-hydroxymelatonin output. *Arch. Gen. Psychiatry* 45:150–54

Gorman JM, Sloan RP. 2000. Heart rate variability in depressive and anxiety disorders. *Am. Heart J.* 140(Suppl. 4):77–83

Gottdiener JS, Krantz DS, Howell RH, Hecht GM, Klein J, et al. 1994. Induction of myocardial ischemia with mental stress testing: relationship to the triggers of ischemia during daily life activities and to ischemic functional severity. *J. Am. Coll. Cardiol.* 24:1645–51

Gullette ECD, Blumenthal JA, Babyak M, Jiang W, Waugh RA, et al. 1997. Effects of mental stress on myocardial ischemia in daily life. *JAMA* 277:1521–26

Haan M, Kaplan GA, Camacho T. 1987. Poverty and health: prospective evidence from the Alameda County Study. *Am. J. Epidemiol.* 125:989–98

Hemingway H, Marmot M. 1999. Psychosocial factors in the aetiology and prognosis of coronary heart disease. Systematic review of prospective cohort studies. *Br. Med. J.* 318:1460–67

Hlatky MA, Lam LC, Lee KL, Clapp-Channing NE, Williams RB, et al. 1995. Job strain and the prevalence and outcome of coronary artery disease. *Circulation* 92:327–33

Iribarren C, Sidney S, Bild DE, Liu K, Markovitz JH, et al. 2000. Association of hostility with coronary artery calcification in young adults: the CARDIA study. *JAMA* 283:2546–51

Ironson G, Taylor CB, Boltwood M, Bartzokis T, Dennis C, et al. 1992. Effects of anger on left ventricular ejection fraction in coronary artery disease. *Am. J. Cardiol.* 70:281–85

Jain D, Burg M, Soufer R, Zaret BL. 1995. Prognostic implication of mental stress-induced silent left ventricular dysfunction in patients with stable angina pectoris. *Am. J. Cardiol.* 76:31–35

Jaing W, Babyak M, Krantz DS, Waugh RA, Coleman RE, et al. 1996. Mental stress induced–myocardial ischemia and cardiac events. *JAMA* 275:1651–56

Jones DA, West RR. 1996. Psychological rehabilitation after myocardial infarction: multicentre randomised controlled trial. *Br. Med. J.* 313:1517–21

Kamarck T, Jennings JR. 1999. Biobehavioral

factors in sudden death. *Psychol. Bull.* 109: 42–75

Kaplan GA, Lynch JW. 1997. Whither studies on the socioeconomic foundations of population health? *Am. J. Public Health* 87:1409–11

Kaplan JR, Manuck SB. 1999. Status, stress, and atherosclerosis: the role of environment and individual behavior. *Ann. NY Acad. Sci.* 896:145–61

Karasek RA, Theorell T. 1990. *Healthy Work, Stress, Productivity, and the Reconstruction of Working Life.* New York: Basic Books

Karasek RA, Theorell T, Schwartz JE, Schnall PL, Pieper CF, Michela JL. 1988. Job characteristics in relation to the prevalence of myocardial infarction in the US Health Examination Study (HES) and the Health and Nutrition Examination Study (HANES). *Am. J. Public Health* 78:910–18

Kark JD, Goldman S, Epstein L. 1995. Iraqi missile attacks on Israel. *JAMA* 273:1208–10

Kawachi I, Colditz GA, Ascherio A, Rimm EB, Biovannucci E, et al. 1996. A prospective study of social networks in relation to total mortality and cardiovascular disease in men in the USA. *J. Epidemiol. Community Health* 50:245–51

Kennedy GJ, Hofer MA, Cohen D, Shindledecker R, Fisher JD. 1987. Significance of depression and cognitive impairment in patients undergoing programmed stimulation of cardiac arrhythmias. *Psychosom. Med.* 270:410–21

Kessler RC, Cleary PD. 1980. Social class and psychological distress. *Am. Sociol. Rev.* 45:463–78

Kessler RC, McGonagle KA, Zhao S, Nelson CB, Hughes M, et al. 1994. Lifetime and 12-month prevalence of DSM-III-R psychiatric disorders in the United States: results from the National Comorbidity Survery. *Arch. Gen. Psychiatry* 51:8–19

Keys A, Taylor HL, Blackburn H, Brozek J, Anderson J, Simonson E. 1971. Mortality and coronary heart disease among men studied for 23 years. *Arch. Int. Med.* 128:201–14

Kiecolt-Glaser JK, McGuire L, Robles TF, Glaser R. 2002. Emotions, morbidity, and mortality: new perspectives from psychoneuroimmunology. *Annu. Rev. Psychol.* 53:83–107

King KB. 1997. Psychologic and social aspects of cardiovascular disease. *Ann. Behav. Med.* 19:264–70

Kop WJ. 1999. Chronic and acute psychological risk factors for clinical manifestations of coronary artery disease. *Psychosom. Med.* 61:476–87

Kop WJ, Appels A, Mendes de Leon CF, De Swart HB, Bar FW. 1994. Vital exhaustion predicts new cardiac events after successful angioplasty. *Psychosom. Med.* 56:281–87

Kovach JA, Nearing BD, Verrier RL. 2001. Angerlike behavioral state potentiates myocardial ischemia-induced T-wave alternans in canines. *J. Am. Coll. Cardiol.* 37:1719–25

Krantz DS, Grunberg NE, Baum A. 1985. Health psychology. *Annu. Rev. Psychol.* 36:349–85

Krantz DS, Kop WJ, Santiago HT, Gottdiener JS. 1996. Mental stress as a trigger of myocardial ischemia and infarction. *Cardiol. Clin.* 14:271–87

Krantz DS, Manuck SB. 1984. Acute psychophysiologic reactivity and risk of cardiovascular disease: a review and methodological critique. *Psychol. Bull.* 96:435–64

Krantz DS, Santiago HT, Kop WJ, Merz CNB, Rozanski A, Gottdiener JS. 1999. Prognostic value of mental stress testing in coronary artery disease. *Am. J. Cardiol.* 84:1292–97

Krantz DS, Sheps DS, Carney RM, Natelson BH. 2000. Effects of mental stress in patients with coronary artery disease: evidence and clinical implications. *JAMA* 283:1800–2

Kuczmarski RJ, Flegal KM, Campbell SM, Johnson CL. 1994. Increasing prevalence of overweight among US adults: the National Health and Nutrition Examination Surveys. *JAMA* 272:205–11

Kunst AE, Mackenbach JP. 1994. The size of mortality differences associated with educational level in nine industrialized countries. *Am. J. Public Health* 84:932–37

LaCroix AZ, Haynes SG. 1987. Gender differences in the health effect of workplace

roles. In *Gender and Stress*, ed. RC Barnett, L
Biener, GK Baruch, pp. 96–121. New York:
Free Press

Ladwig KH, Kieser M, Konig J, Breithardt G,
Borggefe M. 1991. Affective disorders and
survival after acute myocardial infarction: results from the post-infarction late potential
study. *Eur. Heart J.* 12:959–64

Lepore SJ. 1998. Problems and prospects for
the social support-reactivity hypothesis. *Ann.
Behav. Med.* 20:257–69

Linden W, Stossel C, Maurice J. 1996. Psychological interventions for patients with coronary artery disease. *Arch. Int. Med.* 156:745–
52

Link BG, Lennon MC, Dohrenwend BP. 1993.
Socioeconomic status and depression: the
role of occupations involving direction, control, and planning. *Am. J. Sociol.* 98:1351–87

Lundberg U, Frankenhaeuser M. 1999. Stress
and workload of men and women in high-
ranking positions. *J. Occup. Health Psychol.*
4:142–51

Lynch JW, Kaplan GA, Cohen RD, Tuo-
milehto J, Salonen JT. 1996. Do cardiovascular risk factors explain the relation
between socioeconomic status, risk of all-
cause mortality, cardiovascular mortality,
and acute myocardial infarction? *Am. J. Epidemiol.* 144:934–42

Manuck SB. 1994. Cardiovascular reactivity in
cardiovascular disease: "once more unto the
breach." *Behav. Med.* 1:4–31

Marmot MG, Bosma H, Hemingway H, Brunner E, Stansfeld S. 1997. Contribution of job
control and other risk factors to social variations in coronary heart disease incidence.
Lancet 350:235–39

Marmot MG, Shipley MJ, Rose G. 1984. Inequalities in death: specific explanations of a
general pattern? *Lancet* 1:1003–6

Marmot MG, Smith GD, Stansfeld S, Patel
C, North F, et al. 1991. Health inequalities
among British civil servants: the Whitehall II
study. *Lancet* 337:1387–93

Matthews KA, Caggiula AR, McAllister CG,
Berga SL, Owens JF, et al. 1995. Sympathetic reactivity to acute stress and immune
responses in women. *Psychosom. Med.* 57:
564–71

McCabe PM, Sheridan JF, Weiss JM, Kaplan
JP, Natelson BH, Pare WP. 2000. Animal
models of disease. *Physiol. Behav.* 68:501–7

McDonough P, Duncan GJ, William D, House
J. 1997. Income dynamics and adult mortality in the United States. *Am. J. Public Health*
87:1476–83

McEwen BS. 1998. Protective and damaging
effects of stress mediators. *N. Engl. J. Med.*
338:171–79

McLeod JD, Kessler RC. 1990. Socioeconomic
differences in vulnerability to undesirable
life events. *J. Health Soc. Behav.* 31:162–72

Medalie JH, Goldbourt U. 1976. Angina pectoris among 10,000 men. II. Psychosocial and
other risk factors as evidenced by a multivariate analysis of a five-year incidence study.
Am. J. Med. 60:910–21

Meisel SR, Kitz I, Dayan KI, Pauzner H, Chet-
boun I, et al. 1991. Effect of Iraqi missile war
on incidence of acute myocardial infarction
and sudden death in Israeli citizens. *Lancet*
338:660–61

Mendes de Leon CF, Powell LH, Kaplan BH.
1991. Change in coronary-prone behaviors
in the recurrent coronary prevention project.
Psychosom. Med. 53:407–19

Miller TQ, Smith TW, Turner CW, Guijarro
ML, Hallet AJ. 1996. A meta-analytic review of research on hostility and physical
health. *Psychol. Bull.* 119:322–48

Mittleman MA, Maclure M, Sherwood JB,
Mulry RP, Tofler GH, et al. 1995. Triggering of acute myocardial infarction onset by
episodes of anger. *Circulation* 92:1720–25

Mittleman MA, Maclure M, Tofler GH, Sherwood JB, Goldberg RJ, Muller JE. 1993.
Triggering of acute myocardial infarction by
heavy exertion: protection against triggering by regular exertion. *N. Engl. J. Med.*
329:1677–83

Muller JE, Abela GS, Nesto RW, Tofler GH.
1994. Triggers, acute risk factors, and vulnerable plaques: the lexicon of a new frontier. *J.
Am. Coll. Cardiol.* 23:809–13

Muller JE, Ludmer PL, Willich SN, Tofler GH,

Aylmerg I, et al. 1987. Circadian variation in the frequency of cardiac death. *Circulation* 75:131–38

Muller JE, Tofler GH, Stone PH. 1989. Circadian variation and triggers of onset of acute cardiovascular disease. *Circulation* 79:733–43

Musselman DL, Tomer A, Manatunga AK, Knight BT, Porter MR, et al. 1996. Exaggerated platelet reactivity in major depression. *Am. J. Psychiatry* 153:1313–17

Myers R, Dewar HA. 1975. Circumstances surrounding sudden death from coronary artery disease with coroner's necropsies. *Br. Heart J.* 37:1133–43

Natelson BH, Tapp WN, Drastal S, Suarez R, Ottenweller JE. 1991. Hamsters with coronary vasospasm are at increased risk from stress. *Psychosom. Med.* 53:322–31

Nemeroff CB, Widerlov E, Bissette G, Walleus H, Karlsson I, et al. 1984. Elevated concentrations of CSF corticotropin-releasing factor-like immunoreactivity in depressed patients. *Science* 226:1342–44

O'Malley PG, Jones DL, Feuerstein IM, Taylor AJ. 2000. Lack of correlation between psychological factors and subclinical coronary artery disease. *N. Engl. J. Med.* 343:1298–304

Ornish D. 1998. Avoiding revascularization with lifestyle changes: the Multicenter Lifestyle Demonstration Project. *Am. J. Cardiol.* 82:T72–76

Ornish D, Brown SE, Scherwitz LW, Billings JH, Armstrong WT, et al. 1990. Can lifestyle changes reverse coronary heart disease? *Lancet* 336:129–33

Orth-Gomer K, Johnsson JV. 1987. Social network interaction and mortality: a 6-year follow–up study of a random sample of the Swedish population. *J. Chronic Dis.* 40:949–57

Patterson SM, Krantz DS, Gottdiener JS, Hecht G, Vargot S, et al. 1995. Prothrombotic effects of mental and cold pressor stress: changes in platelet function, blood viscosity, and plasma volume. *Psychosom. Med.* 57:592–99

Petticrew M, Gilbody S, Sheldon TA. 1997. Relation between hostility and coronary heart disease. Evidence does not support link. *Br. Med. J.* 319:917–18

Pratt LA, Ford DE, Crum RM, Armenian HK, Gallo JJ, Eaton WW. 1996. Depression, psychotropic medication, and risk of myocardial infarction: prospective data from the Baltimore ECA follow-up. *Circulation* 94:3123–29

Rogers RG, Hummer RA, Nam CB, Peters K. 1997. Demographic, socioeconomic, and behavioral risk factors affecting ethnic mortality by cause. *Soc. Forces* 74:1419–38

Ross R. 1999. Atherosclerosis—an inflammatory disease. *N. Engl. J. Med.* 340:115–26

Roy A, Pickar D, DeJong J, Karoum F, Linnoila M. 1988. Norepinephrine and its metabolites in cerebrospinal fluid, plasma, and urine: relationship to hypothalamic-pituitary-adrenal axis function in depression. *Arch. Gen. Psychiatry* 45:849–57

Rozanski A, Bairey CN, Krantz DS, Friedman J, Resser KJ, et al. 1988. Mental stress and the induction of myocardial ischemia in patients with coronary artery disease. *N. Engl. J. Med.* 318:1005–11

Rozanski A, Blumenthal JA, Kaplan J. 1999. Impact of psychological factors on the pathogenesis of cardiovascular disease and implications for therapy. *Circulation* 99:2192–217

Ruberman W, Weinblatt E, Goldberg JD, Chaudhary BS. 1984. Psychosocial influences on mortality after myocardial infarction. *N. Engl. J. Med.* 311:552–59

Sapolsky RM, Mott GE. 1987. Social subordinance in wild baboons associated with suppressed high density lipoprotein-cholesterol concentrations: the possible role of chronic stress. *Endocrinology* 121:1605–10

Scheidt S. 2000. The current status of heart-mind relationships. *J. Psychosom. Res.* 48:317–20

Schleifer SJ, Macari-Hinson MM, Coyle DA, Slater WR, Kahn M, et al. 1989. The nature and course of depression following myocardial infarction. *Arch. Intern. Med.* 149:1785–89

Schnall PL, Peiper C, Schwartz JE, Karasek RA, Devereux RB, et al. 1990. The relationship between "job strain," workplace diastolic blood pressure, and left ventricular mass index. Results of a case-control study. *JAMA* 263:1929–35

Schneiderman N, Antoni MH, Saab PG, Ironson G. 2001. Health psychology: psychosocial and biobehavioral aspects of chronic disease management. *Annu. Rev. Psychol.* 52:555–80

Schoenbach VJ, Kaplan BH, Fredman L, Kleinbaum DG. 1986. Social ties and mortality in Evans County, Georgia. *Am. J. Epidemiol.* 123:577–97

Schulz R, Beach SR, Ives DG, Martire LM, Ariyo AA, Kop WJ. 2000. Association between depression and mortality in older adults: the Cardiovascular Health Study. *Arch. Intern. Med.* 160:1761–68

Seeman TE. 2000. Health promoting effects of friends and family on health outcomes in older adults. *Am. J. Health Promot.* 14:362–70

Seeman TE, McEwen BS. 1996. Impact of social environment characteristics on neuroendocrine function. *Psychosom. Med.* 58:459–71

Shapiro PA, Lesperance F, Frasure-Smith N, O'Connor CM, Baker B, et al. 1999. An open-label preliminary trial of sertraline for treatment of major depression after acute myocardial infarction (the SADHART Trial). *Am. Heart J.* 137:1100–6

Sheps DS, Pepine CJ, Becker LC, Goldberg AD, Stone PH, Taylor H. 2000. Mental stress ischemia predicts mortality: results from the Psychophysiological Investigations of Myocardial Ischemia (PIMI) Study. *Circulation* 18(Suppl. II)

Siegler IC. 1994. Hostility and risk: demographic and lifestyle variables. In *Anger, Hostility, and the Heart*, ed. AW Siegman, TW Smith, pp. 199–214. Hillsdale, NJ: Erlbaum

Smith GD, Bartley M, Blane D. 1990. The Black report on socioeconomic inequalities in health 10 years on. *Br. Med. J.* 301:373–77

Smith GD, Hart C, Hole D, MacKinnon P, Gillis C, et al. 1998. Education and occupational social class: which is the more important indicator of social risk? *J. Epidemiol. Community Health.* 52:153–60

Smith TW. 1992. Hostility and health: current status of a psychosomatic hypothesis. *Health Psychol.* 11:139–50

Sorlie PD, Backlund E, Keller JB. 1995. Mortality by economic, demographic, and social characteristics: the National Longitudinal Mortality Study. *Am. J. Public Health* 85:949–56

Stein PK, Carnet RM, Freedland KE, Skala JA, Jaffe AS, et al. 2000. Severe depression is associated with markedly reduced heart rate variability in patients with stable coronary heart disease. *J. Psychosom. Res.* 48:493–500

Stein PK, Kleiger RE. 1999. Insights from the study of heart rate variability. *Annu. Rev. Med.* 50:249–61

Uchino BN, Caciopo JT, Kiecolt-Glaser JK. 1996. The relationship between social support and physiological processes: a review with emphasis on underlying mechanisms and implications for health. *Psychol. Bull.* 119:488–531

Ullah P. 1990. The association between income, financial strain, and psychological well-being among unemployed youths. *J. Occup. Psychol.* 63:317–30

Verrier RL, Hagestad EL, Lown B. 1987. Delayed myocardial ischemia induced by anger. *Circulation* 75:249–54

Verrier RL, Lown B. 1984. Behavioral stress and cardiac arrhythmias. *Annu. Rev. Physiol.* 46:155–76

Verrier RL, Mittleman MA. 1996. Life-threatening cardiovascular consequences of anger in patients with coronary heart disease. *Cardiol. Clin.* 14:289–307

Vogt TM, Mullooly JP, Ernst D, Pope CR, Hollis JF. 1992. Social networks as predictors of ischemic heart disease, cancer, stroke, and hypertension: Incidence, survival, and mortality. *J. Clin. Epidemiol.* 45(6):659–66

Williams JW, Paton CC, Siegler IC, Eigenbrodt ML, Nieto FJ, Tyroler HA. 2000. Anger proneness predicts coronary heart disease risk: prospective analyses from the atherosclerosis risk in communities (ARIC) study. *Circulation* 101:2034–39

Williams RB, Barefoot JC, Califf RM. 1992. Prognostic importance of social and economic resources among medically treated patients with angiographically documented coronary artery disease. *JAMA* 267:520–24

Winkleby MA, Jatulis DE, Frank E, Fortmann SP. 1992. Socioeconomic status and health: how education, income, and occupation contribute to risk factors for cardiovascular disease. *Am. J. Public Health* 82:816–20

Wyatt RJ, Portnoy B, Kupfer DJ, Snyder F, Engelman K. 1971. Resting plasma catecholamine concentrations in patients with depression and anxiety. *Arch. Gen. Psychiatry* 24:65–70

Annu. Rev. Psychol. 2002. 53:371–99

Socioeconomic Status and Child Development

Robert H. Bradley and Robert F. Corwyn

Center for Applied Studies in Education, University of Arkansas at Little Rock, 2801 S. University Ave., Little Rock, Arkansas 72204; e-mail: rhbradley@ualr.edu

Key Words   socioeconomic status, poverty, achievement, adjustment, child well-being

■ **Abstract**   Socioeconomic status (SES) is one of the most widely studied constructs in the social sciences. Several ways of measuring SES have been proposed, but most include some quantification of family income, parental education, and occupational status. Research shows that SES is associated with a wide array of health, cognitive, and socioemotional outcomes in children, with effects beginning prior to birth and continuing into adulthood. A variety of mechanisms linking SES to child well-being have been proposed, with most involving differences in access to material and social resources or reactions to stress-inducing conditions by both the children themselves and their parents. For children, SES impacts well-being at multiple levels, including both family and neighborhood. Its effects are moderated by children's own characteristics, family characteristics, and external support systems.

CONTENTS

0084-6570/02/0201-0371$14.00

INTRODUCTION

Socioeconomic status (SES) remains a topic of great interest to those who study children's development. This interest derives from a belief that high SES families afford their children an array of services, goods, parental actions, and social connections that potentially redound to the benefit of children and a concern that many low SES children lack access to those same resources and experiences, thus putting them at risk for developmental problems (Brooks-Gunn & Duncan 1997). The interest in SES as a global construct persists despite evidence that there is wide variability in what children experience within every SES level, despite evidence that the link between SES and child well-being varies as a function of geography, culture, and recency of immigration, and despite evidence that the relation between SES and child well-being can be disrupted by catastrophes and internal strife (Bradley & Corwyn 1999, Wachs 2000).

In this chapter we review the history of SES and provide an overview of the association between SES and children's well-being for three major domains of development (cognitive, socioemotional, health). Attention is given to models that attempt to explicate the connection between SES and these aspects of development. Finally, we offer a rationale for expanding attention to collective SES as a way of more fully instantiating the concepts of developmental systems theory into research on SES.

HISTORY AND DEFINITION

Social scientists have shown continued interest in SES even though there has never been complete consensus on precisely what it represents (Liberatos et al. 1988, McLoyd 1997). There has been something of a tug-of-war between proponents of SES as representing class (or economic position) and proponents of SES as representing social status (or prestige). The idea of capital (Coleman 1988) perhaps best embodies the current meaning psychologists hold of SES (Entwistle & Astone 1994, Guo & Harris 2000). Capital (resources, assets) has become a favored way of thinking about SES because access to financial capital (material resources), human capital (nonmaterial resources such as education), and social capital (resources achieved through social connections) are readily connectible to processes that directly affect well-being. Capital is linked to historic ideas about SES, such as social and material "deprivation," and it brings into focus the important dimension of social relationships (Krieger et al. 1997).

Most widely used measures of SES only partially map onto the concepts of capital described by Coleman. Financial capital is reasonably well assessed by household income, but is more often indexed by occupational status. However, neither fully captures the notion of wealth as described by economists (Smith 1999); wealth may be a better measure of the financial resources available in that it is often a more accurate barometer of access to opportunities (Oliver & Shapiro 1995, Ostrove et al. 1999, Williams & Collins 1995). Income is considered a rather volatile indicator of financial capital (Hauser 1994), and the best way of ordering occupations in terms of their actual contributions to financial well-being has been hotly debated for decades (Davies 1952, Entwisle & Astone 1994, Miller 1991, Grusky & Van Rompaey 1992, Nam & Powers 1983). Most social scientists agree that a combination of income and occupational status provides a better approximation to financial capital than either alone. To more fully capture financial capital, Entwisle & Astone (1994) recommend gathering data on what the family pays for rent or housing. Ostrove and his coworkers (1999) simply asked respondents to estimate the total value of their assets.

Entwisle & Astone (1994) also recommend expanding data collections pertaining to social capital (e.g., number of parents in the home, presence of a grandparent in the home), a suggestion that may garner increasing support given that many children live in households with only one parent. Research showing that occupation often partially determines one's social network suggests that occupational status may also provide some indication of social capital. Likewise, research showing a link between the type of employment parents engage in and parenting practices suggests that occupational status may also capture some of human capital (Kohn & Schooler 1982, Parcel & Menaghan 1990, Rodrigo et al. 2001).

Although there is general consensus that income, education, and occupation together represent SES better than any of these alone (White 1982), there is no consensus on (*a*) how best to composite the set of indicators; (*b*) whether it works best to examine relations between SES and child outcomes using a composite, a statistical procedure that includes each indicator, or each indicator singly; or (*c*) how best to measure each component (Krieger et al. 1997). The predictive value of specific composites have been compared with inconsistent results (Gottfried 1985, Liberatos et al. 1988, White 1982). At times the different indicators seem to be tapping into the same underlying phenomenon, as indicated by their inter-correlations and their similar correlations with outcome measures. At other times, they appear to be tapping into different underlying phenomena and seem to be connected to different paths of influence, as indicated by only modest correlations even among different SES composites and links with different mediating variables (Ostrove et al. 1999). Relatedly, there remains some uncertainty as to whether SES has the same underlying meaning in all ethnic and cultural groups (Williams & Collins 1995).

In overview, the choice of how to measure SES remains open. Part will be determined by the question being examined, part by practical considerations concerning the acquisition of data, and part by the population from whom the data are collected. Regarding this last issue, both theory and empirical findings indicate that SES indicators are likely to perform differently across cultural groups (Bradley 1994, Bronfenbrenner 1995).

SES & WELL-BEING

Health

For years, studies of adults have documented a relation between SES and health (Adler et al. 1994). The data on children is somewhat less complete and less consistent, but evidence points to a substantial relation that begins before birth (US Dep. Health & Human Services 2000b). Children from low-SES families are more likely to experience growth retardation and inadequate neurobehavioral development in utero (DiPietro et al. 1999, Kramer 1987). They are more likely to be born prematurely, at low birth weight, or with asphyxia, a birth defect, a disability, fetal alcohol syndrome, or AIDS (Crooks 1995, Hawley & Disney 1992, US Dep. Health & Human Services 2000b, Cassady et al. 1997, Vrijheid et al. 2000, Wasserman et al. 1998). Early health problems often emanate from poor prenatal care, maternal substance abuse, poor nutrition during pregnancy, maternal lifestyles that increase the likelihood of infections (smoking, drug use), and living in a neighborhood that contains hazards affecting fetal development (toxic waste dumps) (US Dep. Health & Human Services 2000a).

After birth, low-SES infants are more likely to suffer injuries and to die (Overpeck et al. 1998, Scholer et al. 1999). During childhood, SES is implicated in many diseases, including respiratory illnesses (Cohen 1999, Haan et al. 1989, Johnston-Brooks et al. 1998, Klerman 1991, Rosenbaum 1992). Low SES is associated with an increased likelihood of dental caries (US Dep. Health & Human Services 2000b), higher blood lead levels (Brody et al. 1994a, Starfield 1982, Tesman & Hills 1994), iron deficiency (US Dep. Health & Human Services 2000b, Starfield 1989), stunting (Brooks-Gunn & Duncan 1997, Korenman & Miller 1997, Kotch & Shackelford 1989), and sensory impairment (US Dep. Health & Human Services 2000b, Starfield 1989, Wilson 1993). These outcomes likely reflect an array of conditions associated with low SES, including inadequate nutrition, exposure to tobacco smoke, failure to get recommended immunizations, and inadequate access to health care (US Dep. Health & Human Services 2000a,b; Pollitt et al. 1996; Raisler et al. 1999; Sandel & Schrfstein 1999).

On the other hand, SES is not implicated in all illnesses, and the SES/health gradient appears less steep in more egalitarian nations (Adler et al. 1999). Moreover, the relations between particular SES indicators and health factors may be quite complex. For example, the impact of low income appears to depend on how long poverty lasts and the child's age when the family is poor (Bradley & Whiteside-Mansell 1997, Duncan & Brooks-Gunn 1997, Miller & Korenman 1994).

When low-SES children experience health problems, the consequences are often more severe. Low-SES children born preterm are far more likely to suffer health and developmental consequences than their more affluent counterparts (Parker et al. 1988). Children from low-income families are two to three times as likely to suffer complications from appendicitis and bacterial meningitis and to die from injuries and infections at every age (US Dep. Health & Human Services 2000b). The average length of stay for poor children in acute care hospitals is longer than the average for nonpoor children (Bradley & Kelleher 1992). Equally important are findings that early insults to health may have long-term consequences (McLoyd 1998, Bradley et al. 1994). For example, premature children who lived in poverty for the first 3 years of life manifested more problems in growth, health status, intelligence, and behavior (Bradley et al. 1994); children with high lead levels are at increased risk of long-term neurological problems (Needleman et al. 1990);

and low-birthweight children who also had perinatal illnesses experienced more school failure (McGauhey et al. 1991).

Among adolescents, SES is related to health status, but relations are less consistent than for adults (Macintyre & West 1991). Goodman (1999) found that SES was related to depression, obesity, and self-rated overall health (US Dep. Health & Human Services 2000a,b; Call & Nonnemaker 1999). Data from NHANES II indicate that poor teens are more likely to show stunting (Brooks-Gunn & Duncan 1997). However, SES was not associated with asthma and was inconsistently related to suicide attempts and STDs (Goodman 1999).

Biologic impacts during childhood create vulnerabilities that result in adverse health outcomes in adulthood. Power (1991) found that SES measured in middle childhood and adolescence was related to health status at age 23, even controlling for SES at age 23. Hertzman (1999) refers to this as the "biological embedding" of early experience and notes that there is evidence for "latent" effects of early biologic damage (e.g., a higher propensity for adult cardiovascular disease for low-birthweight children). Specifically, he offers the hypothesis that "systemic differences in the quality of early environments, in terms of stimulation and emotional and physical support, will affect the sculpting and neurochemistry of the central nervous system in ways that will adversely affect cognitive, social, and behavioral development" (p. 89). Little research has been completed on this hypothesis, but research shows that anthropometric indicators of undernutrition during infancy predict cognitive performace in middle childhood and adolescence (Pollitt et al. 1996). Also, Treiber and his coworkers (1999) found evidence that low SES was associated with increased systolic blood pressure and increased left ventricular mass among adolescents.

Cognitive and Academic Attainment

For over 70 years findings on the relationship between SES and intellectual/academic competence has accumulated. McCall (1981) presented evidence that the association between SES and cognitive performance begins in infancy. Numerous studies have documented that poverty and low parental education are associated with lower levels of school achievement and IQ later in childhood (Alexander et al. 1993, Bloom 1964, Duncan et al. 1994, Escalona 1982, Hess et al. 1982, Pianta et al. 1990, Walberg & Marjoribanks 1976, Zill et al. 1995). Kennedy and colleagues (1963) reported results from a random sample of first- through sixth-grade African American children selected to represent African Americans living in the southeastern United States. The mean IQ of the highest SES group was 25 points higher than the mean of the lowest SES group.

There has been some debate regarding which aspects of SES most strongly connect to cognitive development. Mercy & Steelman (1982) found that each SES measure used in the Health Examination Survey (family income, maternal education, paternal education) predicted intellectual attainment, with education being the best predictor. Maternal education was a stronger predictor than paternal education. Scarr & Weinberg (1978) found maternal and paternal education to be equally good predictors. This discrepancy may reflect differences in the ages of the children assessed. Mercy & Steelman studied 6- to 11-year-olds, whereas Scarr & Weinberg (1978) studied 15-year-olds. In his meta-analysis White (1982) found that SES accounted for about 5% of the variance in academic achievement. Among the traditional measures of SES, family income accounted for the greatest amount of variance, but SES measures that combined two or more indicators accounted for more variance than single indicators. In a recent study DeGarmo and colleagues (1999) found that each SES indicator (income, education, occupation) was associated with better parenting, which in turn affected school achievement via skill-building activities and school behavior.

Few researchers have concentrated on the relation between parental occupation and cognitive development. However, Parcel & Menaghan (1990) found that mothers who worked in occupations with a variety of tasks and problem solving opportunities provided more warmth and support and a greater number of stimulating materials. Their children manifested more advanced verbal competence. Such findings are consistent with the classic argument of Kohn & Schooler (1982): what parents experience at work, they incorporate into their style of parenting.

There is evidence that the connection between SES and cognitive performance applies to many societies. Mpofu & Van de Vijver (2000) found that among Zimbabwean children social class predicted the frequency with which children used taxonomic rather than functional classification strategies. In their cross-cultural review Bradley and colleagues (1996) found that SES indicators were strongly related to cognitive development from infancy through middle childhood. Evidence suggests a particularly strong relation between SES and verbal skills (Mercy & Steelman 1982). Hart & Risley (1995) found major differences in the language proficiency of children from high-SES and low-SES families. Hoff-Ginsberg (1991) also found substantial SES differences in language performance for children, beginning early in life.

In his meta-analysis White (1982) found some evidence that the relation between SES and intellectual/academic attainment diminishes with age. However, Smith and colleagues (1997) found that the effects of family income on achievement among 7-year-olds were similar to the effects on intelligence for 3-year-olds. Likewise, Walberg & Marjoribanks (1976) suggested that adolescents may benefit as much as younger children from a stimulating family environment. "Uncorrected regression can underestimate environmental effects when there are substantial errors in measuring the environment" (p. 546). Their results suggest that for intellectual and academic attainment there may be a kind of accumulated value to family environment and SES, but thus far there is little evidence to substantiate this.

The relation between SES and cognitive attainment may be quite complex, with different components of SES contributing to the development of particular cognitive skills in different ways and with some components of SES serving to moderate the effects of other components. DeGarmo and colleagues (1999) examined the paths between maternal education, occupation, and income and found evidence of both similarities and differences in their connections to school achievement among 6- to 9-year-olds. Several analyses have indicated that the relations for family income and parental education depend on the number of siblings present in the household (Anastasi 1956, Mercy & Steelman 1982, Walberg & Marjoribanks 1976). Others have discussed the importance of unpacking the effects of socioeconomic status owing to the high level of confounding between socioeconomic and family demographic indicators, but few studies have done so (Brooks-Gunn & Duncan 1997, McLoyd 1998).

SES also appears to affect school attendance and number of years of schooling completed (Haverman & Wolf 1995, Brooks-Gunn & Duncan 1997). The impact on years completed appears to be less than the impact on school achievement. Even so, SES remains one of the most consistent predictors of early high school dropout, with evidence suggesting that it is connected both to low parental expectations and to early initiation of sexual activity (Battin-Pearson et al. 2000).

Socioemotional Development

Although the link between SES and children's social and emotional well-being is not as consistent as the link with cognitive attainment, there is substantial evidence that low-SES children more often manifest symptoms of psychiatric disturbance and maladaptive social functioning than children from more affluent circumstances (Bolger et al. 1995, Brooks-Gunn & Duncan 1997, Lahey et al. 1995, McCoy et al. 1999, McLeod & Shanahan 1993, Moore et al. 1994, Patterson et al. 1989, Sameroff et al. 1987, Starfield 1989, Takeuchi et al. 1991). It is not easy to state the precise relation between SES and socioemotional problems in children. It is often difficult to identify mental illness in young children, owing to the various standards and methods used to assess mental illness. For very young children, there is little evidence of a relation between SES and socioemotional well-being (Earls 1980, Richman et al. 1975). However, the relation emerges in early childhood and becomes reasonably consistent (especially for externalizing problems) in middle childhood (Achenbach et al. 1990, Duncan et al. 1994, McLeod & Shanahan 1993). Among adolescents, low SES is often associated with poor adaptive functioning, an increased likelihood of depression, and delinquent behavior (McLoyd 1997). Conger and colleagues (1997), however, did not find a relation between poverty and adolescent problems. Part of the difference in findings may pertain to who reports on social and emotional well-being. Most often parents and teachers are the reporters, but in the Conger et al. study adolescents reported on their own behavior.

The strength of the relationship between SES and mental disorders varies by type of disorder and race (McLoyd 1997). The relationship is most consistent with schizophrenia and personality disorders, reasonably consistent with mild depression, and inconsistent with neuroses and affective disorders (Ortega & Corzine 1990). Among children 6–17 years old referred to a psychiatric clinic, SES was associated with parent and teacher reports of aggressiveness and delinquency (McCoy et al. 1999).

Higher rates of substance abuse have been reported for low-SES teens, but findings are inconsistent (Wills et al. 1995). The relation is often mediated through friends' use of substances, academic competence, and parental supportiveness. It is also connected with the experience of negative life events (Wills et al. 1992).

Ortega & Corzine (1990) identified a number of factors that complicate our ability to understand relations between SES and socioemotional adjustment. The two leading theories (social causation and social selection/drift) imply opposite causation. The social causation explanation holds that mental disorder results from poverty and its cofactors; the social selection explanation holds that those with mental disorders gradually drift into lower SES strata. For children, there has been little study of the drift hypothesis because it was generated to explain the gradual decline in status for seriously mentally ill adults. A second complication in interpreting research on SES and mental illness derives from the fact that the poor are more likely to be defined as mentally ill even when they manifest the same level of symptomatology as do more affluent individuals.

In overview, there is substantial evidence linking low SES to less optimal outcomes in nearly every area of functioning. Unfortunately, most studies examined only a single outcome and, even when they examined more than one outcome, little attention was given to whether individual children experienced multiple bad outcomes. According to developmental systems theory, it is very difficult to predict developmental pathways with precision in highly complex, self-constructing organisms like humans (Ford & Lerner 1992, Wachs 2000). The same set of circumstances may potentiate any of a number of outcomes (the principle of equipotentiality) depending on individual strengths and vulnerabilities and other conditions present both concurrent and subsequent to the experience of those circumstances.

For low-SES children, it is quite difficult to predict whether a particular health, cognitive, or emotional problem may eventually emerge. However, it is somewhat easier to predict that low-SES children are likely to experience more developmental problems than affluent children. Results from the Infant Health and Development Program showed that 40% of children born prematurely and who lived in chronic poverty had deficiencies in at least two areas of functioning at age three (Bradley et al. 1994). Likewise, Bradley and his colleagues (2000) found that the quality of the home environment was correlated about 0.40 with the number of developmental problems manifested by adolescents from five different sociocultural groups. Correlations with specific problems varied across groups, but the correlation with the number of problems was virtually identical.

Models of Mediating Processes

The SES literature offers a variety of proposed mechanisms linking SES and child well-being. The MacArthur Network on SES and health placed linking mechanisms in two broad categories: environmental resources/constraints and psychological influences (Adler & Ostrove 1999). Most hypothesized mechanisms have not been adequately explored, especially in terms of applicability to different cultural groups; in effect, most have verisimilitude, not established credibility. Many proposed intervening processes are themselves disconnected from broader developmental systems models that not only stipulate moderating and mediating processes but mediated moderating and moderated mediating processes as well (Baron & Kenny 1986). In sum, the literature mostly provides bits and pieces of the larger person-process-context-time tableaux described by Bronfenbrenner (1995).

It is not easy to determine with precision the processes through which SES influences child well-being, partly because low SES frequently co-occurs with other conditions that purportedly affect children (e.g., minority and immigrant status, single parenthood, a family member with a disability or serious mental illness, exposure to teratogens and other potentially hazardous environmental conditions)— the classic "third variable" problem. It is difficult to disentangle SES from such cofactors when there is evidence that they may exacerbate the effects of SES (i.e., they function as moderators). Direct biological damage may also contribute to SES differences. To be more specific, brain disorders, such as those connected with mental illness, can also result from trauma or exposure to pathogens, both of which are more common among individuals who are low SES. Low-SES children are more often the victims of child abuse, peer aggression, and community violence (Garbarino 1999).

In overview, for a given child from a low-SES family, the mechanism leading to a poorer developmental outcome could be one connected to family SES, a particular SES cofactor (such as single parenthood or minority status), a combination of the two, or even a third variable connected to both (e.g., family conflict). During the course of childhood, the meaning and significance of particular cofactors can change (Moen et al. 1995). For preschool children, living in a deteriorated neighborhood may mean less access to stimulating resources and recreational facilities. For an adolescent, the same neighborhood may mean increased likelihood of affiliation with deviant peers.

Resources

NUTRITION   Among the most oft-cited linkages between SES and well-being is access to resources (Klerman 1991). Klerman's model includes seven paths linking low income to health, inability to purchase goods and services essential for health and inability to secure appropriate health services. Mortorell (1980) identified inadequate dietary intake as a key pathway to poor health. According to his model, inadequate dietary intake results in defective nutrient absorption, defective nutrient utilization, and poor defenses against infection. Poor nutritional status, in turn, contributes to an array of morbidities and mortality. Pollitt and colleagues (1996) offer a similar formulation. In addition, they present evidence that poor nutritional status affects brain growth both pre- and postnatally.

Overall evidence supporting the "nutrition pathway" is incomplete, but research showing nutritionally mediated SES impacts on (a) growth (Adler et al. 1999, Brooks-Gunn & Duncan 1997, Miller & Korenman 1994), (b) the increased likelihood of neural tube defects owing to inadequate intake of folic acid during pregnancy (Wasserman et al. 1998), (c) the prevalence of iron deficiency owing to inadequate intake of meats and vegetables rich in iron (US Dep. Health & Human Services 2000a, Oski 1993, Starfield 1989), and (*d*) poor long-term memory following lengthy episodes of poor nutrition (Korenman & Miller 1997) offer support for such a path. Valenzuela (1997) offers evidence that chronic undernutrition can deplete the energy resources of both parent and child, making the child more lethargic and less able to elicit attention from the parent and the parent less sensitive and supportive of the child. The result is not only compromised growth but increased likelihood of insecure attachment, negative affect, and limited mastery motivation.

ACCESS TO HEALTH CARE   It is difficult to determine how much poor nutrition contributes to developmental problems because children who lack access to adequate nutrition also tend to lack access to other resources, such as adequate medical care. It is not easy to determine if a condition connected to poor nutrition actually results from poor nutrition or whether it reflects inadequate prenatal care (Blendon et al. 1989; US Dep. Health & Human Services 2000a,b), inadequate preventive care for the child (e.g., failure to obtain all recommended immunizations) (US Dep. Health & Human Services 2000a, Raisler et al. 1999, Sandel & Schrfstein 1999), failure to obtain necessary medical treatment for acute or chronic medical conditions (US Dep. Health & Human Services 2000b), or increased exposure to infection owing to poor personal hygiene (Rushing & Ortega 1979). For example, prematurity and low birthweight are also associated with delayed or absent prenatal care (Crooks 1995, Frank et al. 1992).

Many poor families cannot purchase needed health care services. Poor children often have no medical insurance and, thus, are more likely to use emergency rooms for medical care and may be in more advanced stages of illness before being treated. The generally inadequate educational backgrounds of many poor adults (and the greater prevalence of ethnic minorities and recent immigrants among the poor) may also reduce the likelihood of their seeking help for symptoms of illness because of beliefs about the causes and cures for symptoms that do not square with modern medical practice. In effect, there may be both a lack of money to purchase service and a lack of fit between the care that is available and the care that is wanted (Bradley & Kelleher 1992).

Research does not make clear how significant a role inadequate medical care plays in the health and developmental problems of low-SES children. Social status differences remain even when there is universal health coverage (Baum et al. 1999). In industrialized countries relative material deprivation, rather than absolute material deprivation, may account for much of the SES differential in well-being. Low social status may limit one's social ties (capital) and lead to feelings of helplessness and lack of control, the first reducing one's protection from potential threats to well-being, the second limiting one's own efforts to deal effectively with those threats (Marmot 1999).

HOUSING   Dilapidated, crowded housing has long been cited as one of the factors responsible for the SES gradient in child health (Marmot 1999). Poor children often live in homes that have cracks in the floor, inadequate heat, pests, open heating appliances, unprotected stairwells, lead paint, and leaky ceilings, and are crowded (Bradley et al. 2001a, Guo & Harris 2000, Mayer 1997). These conditions lead to increased illnesses and injuries (US Dep. Health & Human Services 2000b). Brooks-Gunn and coworkers (1995), Guo & Harris (2000), and Bradley & Caldwell (1980) have also linked the physical quality of the home environment to children's intellectual and social well-being. Evans and colleagues (1999) have, likewise, linked household crowding to cognitive and emotional functioning.

COGNITIVELY STIMULATING MATERIALS AND EXPERIENCES   For over 50 years researchers have argued that low-SES children lack access to cognitively stimulating materials and experiences, which not only limits their cognitive growth but reduces their chances of benefiting from school (Bloom 1964, Hunt 1961). Data from the National Longitudinal Survey of Youth and the National Household Education Survey (Bradley et al. 2001a, Corwyn & Bradley 2000) indicate that children from poor families have less access to a wide variety of different recreational and learning materials from infancy through adolescence. They are less likely to go on trips, visit a library or museum, attend a theatrical performance, or be given lessons directed at enhancing their skills. Access to such material and cultural resources mediates the relation between SES (or family income) and children's intellectual and academic achievement from infancy through adolescence (Bradley 1994, Bradley & Corwyn 2001, Brooks-Gunn et al. 1995, Entwisle et al. 1994, Guo & Harris 2000). The impact becomes greater as the number of negative life events (e.g., family dissolution, loss of employment) and risk conditions (e.g., household crowding, presence of a mentally ill parent) increases (Brooks-Gunn et al. 1995, Sameroff et al. 1993).

Bradley & Corwyn (2001) also found that access to stimulating materials and experiences mediated the relation between SES and children's behavior problems. The connection between SES, stimulating experiences, and children's cognitive functioning is well established (Bradley & Corwyn 1999, Brooks-Gunn & Duncan 1997, McLoyd 1998). Such experiences provide both direct and indirect (i.e., mediated through more capable peers and adults) learning opportunities for children as well as serving as a motivational base for continued learning (Saegert & Winkel 1990). However, the connection between SES, access to stimulating experiences, and behavior problems has been less intensively investigated. Part of the connection would appear to be direct. Human beings are self-constructing organisms that thrive on a diversity of experiences; potentially enriching materials and experiences engage cognitive arousal mechanisms (Ford & Lerner 1992). Learning materials and experiences also afford opportunities for social exchanges and, thereby, engage social arousal mechanisms in a generally productive way. Absent such opportunities, children may become bored and frustrated, leading them to engage in behavior that arouses negative responses from parents and peers. These behaviors may contribute to the kind of coercive styles of parenting that have been hypothesized to increase later behavioral maladjustment (Conger et al. 1997, Dodge et al. 1994, McLoyd 1998).

PARENT EXPECTATIONS AND STYLES   Part of the observed connection between SES, cognitively stimulating experiences, and child well-being probably reflects parental attitudes, expectations, and styles of interacting with children. Adams (1998) identified eight major differences in patterns of socialization for children from different social classes: among them, the emphasis given to verbal skills, independence, achievement, and creativity. High-SES parents engage children in more conversations, read to them more, and provide more teaching experiences (Shonkoff & Phillips 2000). Their conversations are richer, contain more contingent responsiveness, and include more efforts to elicit child speech (Hoff-Ginsberg & Tardif 1995, Hart & Risley 1995). Their teaching style includes more scaffolding and complex verbal strategies (Borduin & Henggeler 1981). Bradley & Corwyn (1999), in their review of research on the home observation for measurement of the environment (HOME) inventory, found that these effects applied to children from infancy through adolescence and generally hold for children from diverse ethnic backgrounds. Such differences in parenting practice are strongly implicated in the relation between SES and children's intellectual and academic performance (Hoff-Ginsberg & Tardif 1995, Walberg & Marjoribanks 1976). Even so, the relation between SES and child cognitive and language competence via the stimulation found in the home appears to be a complex one that is associated with both the degree of crowding in the residence and the number of siblings present (Bradley et al. 1994, Evans et al. 1999, Mercy & Steelman 1982, Walberg & Marjoribanks 1976). The distresses and distractions connected with crowding result in fewer and less-rich exchanges between parent and child. Having more siblings results in less allocation of time and attention to each child.

Low-SES parents are less likely to purchase reading and learning materials for their children, less likely to take their children to educational and cultural events, and less likely to regulate the amount of TV their children watch (Bradley et al. 2001a, Hess et al. 1982). As a result, low-SES children more frequently experience school failure (even in the early grades), which moves them on a trajectory of either conduct problems or withdrawal behaviors (Battin-Pearson et al. 2000).

TEACHER ATTITUDES AND EXPECTATIONS   Teacher attitudes and expectations may also be part of a complex set of mediators linking low SES to school failure and behavior problems via learning materials and experiences. McLoyd (1998) has argued that teachers tend to perceive low-SES pupils less positively (both in terms of their academic and self-regulatory skills). Teachers provide poor children with less positive attention and less reinforcement for good performance. If children, both prior to school entry and during their school years, have less experience with cognitively stimulating materials and experiences at home, they are more likely to fulfill teachers' negative stereotypes. This increases the likelihood of negative interactions with teachers, a problem that may be exacerbated for minority children or recently immigrated children without good skills in English. Over time, the frustrations connected with school failure and negative exchanges with teachers are likely to increase, acting out behaviors (or depression for some children). It also increases the likelihood that children will affiliate with deviant peers.

Stress Reactions

Researchers have consistently argued that stress accounts for much of the difference in outcomes between low-SES and high-SES children (Adler et al. 1999, Bradley & Whiteside-Mansell 1997, McLoyd 1998, Shonkoff & Phillips 2000). Low-SES families experience more threatening and uncontrollable life events, are disproportionately exposed to environmental hazards and violence, and are at increased risk of experiencing destabilizing events such as family dissolution and household moves (Bradley & Whiteside-Mansell 1997, Gad & Johnson 1980). The chronic strain associated with unstable employment and persistent economic hardship can lead to diminished self-esteem, a diminished sense of control over one's life, anger, and depression (Amato & Zuo 1992, Dohrenwend 1990, Pearlin et al. 1981). It also increases the likelihood of partner and child abuse (Garbarino 1992). Coping with these strains also reduces the likelihood that one can engage in health-promoting activities (National Center for Children in Poverty 1990).

ALLOSTATIC LOAD   There are immediate (and more long-term) physiologic responses to stresses associated with low SES and its cofactors (e.g., crowded housing, household and neighborhood violence). Health scientists have proposed the concepts of allostatis and allostatic load to help explain the impact of stress on adaptive functioning (Johnston-Brooks et al. 1998, McEwen & Seeman 1999). Allostatis refers to the body's capacity to adapt and adjust to the demands imposed by environmental stressors via physiological changes. The constant turning on and turning off of stress-related physiologic responses creates allostatic load, including more long-term changes (e.g., persistent elevation in blood pressure). Research done mostly with primates and human adults indicates that allostatic load is connected to a wide array of both biologic and behavioral differences, including growth, the timing of pubertal changes, cognitive functioning, metabolism, and susceptibility to illness.

There has been limited research specifically targeted to children, so the impact of stress mediators during childhood is less clear. There is some evidence for disregulated hypothalamic-pituitary-adrenal axis activity (leading to increased activity level), disregulated serotonergic function (which may lead to increased hostility and suicide), and impaired immune system functioning (which leads to increased illness via changes in cardiovascular activity) (Johnston-Brooks et al. 1998, McEwen & Seeman 1999). What seems clearer is that allostatic load (with its myriad mediating processes) can have numerous lifelong negative consequences, some of which are seriously damaging; however, much remains to be determined about the precise pathways for particular outcomes during each stage of the life course (Francis et al. 1999).

PARENTING   Allostatic load appears to affect parenting (Francis et al. 1999, McEwen & Seeman 1999). The stresses, uncertainties, and low social standing connected to low SES bring about a sense of powerlessness, low self-esteem, learned helplessness, and reduced orientation toward mastery and efficacy (Baum et al. 1999, McLoyd 1998). Longitudinal research on health indicates that living in a low-SES environment over a prolonged period of time tends to deplete energy reserve capacity and leads to negative emotional states such as anxiety, depression, and hostility, which in turn, lead to poorer relationships with family members and friends (Gallo & Matthews 1999, Wilkinson 1999). The MacArthur SES and Health Psychosocial Working Group have termed this set of behaviors "reactive responding" (Taylor & Seeman 1999). Reactive responding includes chronic vigilance, acting on the basis of environmental demands rather than self-generated goals, having simple, short-term goals, developing a narrow range of skills, maintaining a present orientation, reacting emotionally, and using few options to deal with environmental demands.

McLoyd (1990) found that the distress among poor parents can lead to the over use of negative control strategies, low warmth and responsiveness, and failure to adequately monitor children. Animal studies suggest that early caregiving responses help determine the infant's stress reactivity, which then affects risk for disease and, in the longer term, interest in providing care for one's own offspring (Francis et al. 1999). For older children, such parenting behaviors can result in low self-esteem and poor adaptive functioning. McLoyd has also argued that if a parent reacts by becoming too restrictive, it can lead to bonding with peers rather than parents (see also Elder et al. 1985).

Longitudinal studies provide substantial empirical support for the path linking low SES to lower competence and maladaptive behavior via harsh or neglectful parenting and compromised parent-child relationships (Bradley & Corwyn 2001; Conger et al. 1992, 1997; Elder et al. 1985; Felner et al. 1995; Luster et al. 1995; Lempers et al. 1989; McCoy et al. 1999; McLoyd et al. 1994; Morrison & Eccles 1995). Research shows that it is the absence of positive parenting, not just the presence of negative parenting, that links low SES to child well-being (Bolger et al. 1995, Brody et al. 1999, McCoy et al. 1999). For example, Bolger and colleagues (1995) found that maternal involvement mediated 34% of the variance for externalizing behavior problems, 31% of the variance for self-esteem, and 14% of the variance for popularity. Brody and colleagues (1999) reported that economic hardship reduced the likelihood that mothers would set high developmental goals for their children and engage in competency promoting activities. This resulted in poorer self-regulation and less academic and psychosocial competence on the part of African American children ages 6–9. In an earlier study Brody and colleagues (1994b) found that if parents remained optimistic, despite being poor, it served as a protective factor against negative parenting.

Despite general support for the "stress reactions" path, there have been some exceptions (Felner et al. 1995, McLeod & Shanahan 1993), and there is some evidence that age and ethnicity moderate the relation (Bradley & Corwyn 2001). There has also been less support for the hypothesis that parent's emotional responsiveness mediates the relation between low SES and child well-being (McLeod & Shanahan 1993).

Health-Relevant Behaviors/Lifestyle

A third class of processes often mentioned as mediators between SES and child well-being is health-relevant (or lifestyle) behaviors (Adler & Ostrove 1999, Klerman 1991, Williams & Collins 1995). Members of the lower social classes use tobacco and alcohol more but tend to diet and exercise less (Baum et al. 1999, Dohrenwend 1990, Harrell et al. 1998). To some extent these behavioral differences are derivative of the attitudes that distinguish higher and lower social classes (Rank 2000), but they may also reflect stress reactions and social affiliations (Paltiel 1988). These factors are associated with poorer physical and mental health, which may make it harder for low SES parents to provide warm, responsive, stimulating care or to monitor their children (Garbarino 1992, Natl. Res. Counc. 1993). Such parents also provide a less desirable role model for children, albeit the role-modeling hypothesis has not received strong scientific support for all areas of child functioning (McLoyd 1998).

There has been relatively little study of most lifestyle behaviors as mediators of the SES/child well-being relation, although there is evidence of the intergenerational transmission of substance abuse. Wills and coworkers (1995) found that low parental education increased the likelihood of smoking, which was related to adolescent academic and behavioral competence. This, in turn, increased the likelihood that the adolescent would use drugs and would affiliate with friends who also used drugs.

As children move toward adolescence, their own health-relevant behaviors become conduits for adaptive functioning (Harrell et al. 1998, Natl. Res. Counc. 1993). Sedentary lifestyles, poor eating habits, and early engagement in risky behaviors (smoking, substance use, sexual behavior, criminal activities) frequently lead to more serious health and adjustment difficulties. Although the health-relevant behavior path is appealing as a link between SES and child well-being, research findings are inconsistent. These lifestyle behaviors do not appear to account for most of the SES/well-being gradient (Adler et al. 1999, Harrell et al. 1998, O'Malley & Johnston 1999, Wohlfarth & Van den Brink 1998).

In overview, families with more money, higher levels of education, and higher occupational status are likely to purchase an array of goods and services that directly benefit their children. High-SES families may also use their wealth to live in good houses in safe neighborhoods, thereby affording their children protection from harm. The goods and services also become part of more elaborate paths involving chains of mediators (wherein particular goods and services may more indirectly affect child outcomes) (Brody et al. 1999, Conger et al. 1997, Guo & Harris 2000). However, few such models have been tested on multiple populations and few have been tested on children of different ages.

Perhaps most importantly, many of the proposed models reflect developmentally restricted conceptualizations of life-span processes. Some attention has been given to the timing and duration of poverty in its effects on child well-being, with ample evidence to support the hypothesis that persistent poverty has long-term negative consequences (Bradley & Whiteside-Mansell 1997, Duncan & Brooks-Gunn 1997, McEwen & Seeman 1999). There is less evidence for timing effects. Nonetheless, studies on both animals and humans provide some support for the hypothesis that early deprivation has long-term negative consequences (Duncan & Brooks-Gunn 1997, McEwen & Seeman 1999). There is even some tantalizing evidence that changes in family income, somewhat independent of parental education, have consequences for child development (Garrett et al. 1994).

The principles of parallel, convergent, and reciprocal causation are very important to bear in mind when interpreting results of completed studies or when planning future studies on mediation (Anderson 1999). The principle of parallel causation stipulates that several different processes or factors may be sufficient, but not necessary, to produce a particular developmental outcome. The principle of convergent causation stipulates that a particular process may be necessary but not sufficient to produce a particular outcome; its effect depends on the presence of a second factor. The principle of reciprocal causation stipulates that bidirectional influences among several processes and factors interacting across time are required to produce a particular developmental outcome. Bradley et al. (2001b) examined the relation between three aspects of children's home environments (learning stimulation, maternal responsiveness, and spanking) from infancy through adolescence using hierarchical linear modeling. They found that each contributed, independent of the other, to reading achievement and that learning stimulation and spanking contributed to behavior problems, independent of the others.

One of the main limitations of research on SES is the failure to simultaneously consider correlated mediating processes or factors when studying how one particular process operates to influence a specific developmental outcome. Consider again, for example, the nutrition pathway. The same children who experience inadequate nutrition are also more likely to be exposed to environmental hazards pre- and postnatally and to receive inadequate parenting (Pollitt et al. 1996). Low-SES children are more likely to be exposed to drugs (including alcohol and tobacco) prenatally. These exposures are connected to prematurity, low birthweight, interuterine growth retardation, and perinatal complications, not to mention longer-term health, growth, and cognitive difficulties (Hawley & Disney 1992, Korenman & Miller 1997, McLoyd 1998). If one is interested in a possible link between SES and cognitive functioning via poor nutrition, it may be critical to include a consideration of one or more of these other processes. Otherwise, one may attribute cognitive problems to poor nutrition when they actually result from poor parenting or a combination of poor nutrition and prenatal exposure to drugs. The practice of nutrition researchers in controlling for cognitively stimulating materials and experiences when studying the impact of inadequate nutrition on cognitive development is a step in the right direction (Pollitt et al. 1996). A few researchers have used techniques such as structural equation modeling to examine the joint function of multiple mediation processes connecting SES to child functioning (Brody et al. 1999, Dodge et al. 1994). However, model misspecification remains a major impediment to understanding the precise mechanisms that link SES and most child outcomes.

Models of Moderation

Although most research on SES and child outcomes has focused on mediating processes, it is generally acknowledged that these processes are not the same for all children (McLoyd 1998, Wills et al. 1995). For any given mediator model, certain characteristics of children and certain environmental conditions serve as moderators (Wachs 2000). Whereas mediator models are concerned with a process through which SES operates to influence children's development, moderator models are concerned with the conditions in which the process operates. The two models complement one another, with each adding insights into the nature of relations between SES and child outcomes (Baron & Kenny 1986). If researchers obtain weak or inconsistent results when investigating a particular association, it often implicates a moderator effect.

The discovery of a moderator often provides clues regarding a mediating process that underlies the relation between a predictor and outcome variable (Rutter 1990). The connection between mediators and moderators is often tighter (i.e., more fundamental) than may be initially apparent. Although Baron & Kenny (1986) went to great lengths to point out the distinctions between mediators and moderators, they also discussed how each often implicates the other.

The potential value of searching for moderators in regard to SES and child well-being would seem particularly great in light of the two principle classes of mechanisms thought to connect them: access to resources and stress reactions. Taylor & Seeman (1999) compiled a list of possible moderators of the relation between physical and/or psychological health. Belief in personal control, dispositional optimism, social support, self-esteem, coping strategies, and reactive responding were frequently (although not inevitably) observed to be moderators of the SES and health relationship, with social support exhibiting a particularly strong relation to psychological health. Their review emphasized the fact that these same variables may also partially mediate the relation between SES and health. In each case, the characteristic of the individual either increased or decreased resources or increased or decreased harmful stressors. The frequent finding that SES/child development relations differ by race offers another example of a moderator that likely implicates either access to resources or stress exposure as connecting paths. The discrimination and oppression often faced by members of minority groups both reduces the likelihood of accessing resources and increases the likelihood of experiencing stress (Garcia Coll et al. 1996, McLoyd 1990).

Resiliency researchers have identified several factors that may serve as moderators of the relation between SES and child well-being, with emphasis on those that help children cope with the kinds of adversity connected with low SES (Garmezy 1993, Masten & Coatsworth 1998, Rutter 1990). Garmezy (1993) recognizes three broad categories that may function as moderators: (*a*) personality/dispositional features such as self-esteem, locus of control, self-efficacy, optimism, stress reactivity, humor, active coping strategies, communication skills, cognitive competence, affective responses to others, and predictability; (*b*) family characteristics, such as cohesion, shared values, patience, conflict, consistency of rules, orderliness, and the presence of supportive adults; and (*c*) availability of external support systems. Each of these either changes the likelihood of accessing needed goods and services, changes the likelihood of encountering stress, or changes one's reactions to stress-inducing events and conditions. An example from the attachment literature is the finding that infants with difficult temperaments who are in low-resource environments tend to form insecure attachments (Vaughn & Bost 1999). Compas and colleagues (2001) call for research that investigates how social context (e.g., SES) may moderate the relation between individual differences (e.g., temperament) and coping responses to stress.

In contrast to the paucity of research on moderators of the SES child outcome relation, SES is frequently conceptualized as a moderator of relationships effecting children. Examples include the relation between maternal depression and parenting practices (Lovejoy et al. 2000) and the relation between risk factors and adolescent substance abuse (Wills et al. 1995).

COLLECTIVE SES

It is generally acknowledged that SES operates at multiple levels to affect well-being (Adler et al. 1999, Krieger et al. 1997, Leventhal & Brooks-Gunn 2000). Community-level SES measurement can provide information about exposures to violence and hazards as well as access to recreational and institutional resources. For children, it is important to consider community-level SES because there is evidence that neighborhood of residence is associated with health, achievement, and behavioral outcomes even when individual-level income and education are controlled (Baum et al. 1999, Leventhal & Brooks-Gunn 2000, Wasserman et al. 1998). The effects appear to begin prior to birth, with research indicating that living in a lower SES neighborhood increases the likelihood of neural tube defects (Vrijheid et al. 2000, Wasserman et al. 1998). Neighborhood effects on health appear to continue through childhood. Sargent and coworkers (1995) found that living in a densely populated, high poverty community was associated with a ninefold increase in lead burden. Also, adolescent females with a family history of cardiovascular disease showed higher levels of blood pressure and left ventricular mass if they lived in low-SES neighborhoods (Treiber et al. 1999).

Research relating neighborhood SES to health is quite limited and not fully consistent. According to Leventhal & Brooks-Gunn (2000), the most consistent finding is that living in a high-SES neighborhood has positive benefits for school readiness and school achievement, perhaps more so for European Americans than members of minority groups. There is also evidence that living in a low-SES neighborhood may contribute to development of behavior problems and increase the likelihood of nonmarital childbearing (Crane 1991, Loeber & Wikstrom 1993). Osofsky (1999) argued that children growing up in poor urban environments are frequently exposed to guns, knives, drugs, and acts of random violence. As a result, many children manifest posttraumatic stress disorder symptoms. Exposure to such violence also interrupts a child's ability to think clearly and solve problems (Garbarino 1999).

According to the general ecological hypothesis, as the number of stresses in a neigborhood increases and as the number of supports decreases, distress among those living in the neighborhood rises (Zuvarin 1989). Social disorganization theory posits that neighborhoods characterized by a high percentage of low-SES residents, and cofactors of low SES such as single parenthood and ethnic heterogeneity, decrease the likelihood of social order (Sampson 1992). Wilson (1991) stated that neighborhoods with high rates of joblessness and single-parent families tend to produce a feeling of "social isolation" for adults caring for children. This, over time, undermines family management and results in socialization practices and family lifestyles that are not conducive to adaptive functioning (e.g., active problem solving, household organization, warm and stimulating parenting, a focus on schooling, adequate monitoring). It also results in a loss of self- and group identification that sustains customary behavior and prevents deviant behavior (Harrell & Peterson 1992).

Jencks & Mayer (1990) identified four kinds of theories relating neighborhood poverty to maladaptive social behavior: (*a*) contagion theories—the idea that peers influence the spread of problem behaviors; (*b*) collective socialization theories—the idea that role models and monitoring are critical to healthy and adaptive functioning; (*c*) competition theories—the concept that people compete for scarce resources; and (*d*) relative deprivation theories—the theory that individuals evaluate their standing relative to the standing of their neighbors. Duncan & Brooks-Gunn (1997) examined aspects of these theories with both very young children and adolescents. The presence of affluent neighbors had a positive effect on IQ, teenage births, and school dropout, suggesting the influence of adult role models and monitoring as mediating variables. Evidence in favor of the "contagion" effect occurred only for adolescents.

Leventhal & Brooks-Gunn (2000) used a somewhat more concise approach in their review of potential mechanisms linking neighborhood poverty to child well-being. They recognized three classes of mediators: (*a*) institutional resources (e.g., schools, child care facilities, medical facilities, employment opportunities), (*b*) relationships (the characteristics of parents and support networks available to assist parents), and (*c*) norms/collective efficacy. Social and health scientists contend that social capital in the form of social affiliation and social cohesion within neighborhoods and communities may help reduce the risk of morbidity and maladaptive functioning (Kawachi 1999). They argue that informal social control, maintenance of healthy norms, and access to various forms of social support can contribute to both healthier lifestyles and positive well-being. Collective efficacy involves the extent to which there are social connections in the neighborhood and to which residents monitor and supervise the behavior of others in accordance with social standards (Sampson et al. 1997). There is also some support for the collective efficacy hypothesis in the form of the social control of children and affiliation with deviant peers functioning to mediate the relation between neighborhood SES and adolescent behavior, mental health, and achievement (Darling & Steinberg 1997, Elliott et al. 1996, Sampson et al. 1997).

Support for institutional resources as mediators of relations between neighborhood SES and child well-being is quite limited. Few studies have examined the mediating role played by the child care options available, medical resources found in the community, or recreational facilities present. Ennett and coworkers (1997) found that characteristics of schools partially mediated the relation between neighborhood characteristics and rates of cigarette and alcohol use. Entwisle and colleagues (1994) found that mathematics reasoning skills of school-age boys were related to the type of neighborhood the boys lived in. They speculated that this difference may derive from differential opportunities to participate in complex rule-based games with peers.

A companion set of hypotheses relates to how the physical and social quality of neighborhoods affects parenting, Leventhal & Brooks-Gunn's (2000) third class of potential mediators. Parental decisions regarding how far children are allowed to travel from home without supervision depends on the parent's appraisal of potential harm present in the neighborhood (Jacobs & Bennet 1993). Earls and coworkers (1994) reported that parents who live in dangerous neighborhoods admit using more harsh control and verbal aggression with their children. Young & Gately (1988) found that the rates of maltreatment by females was lower when substantial numbers of women with access to material resources were available for support. Garbarino (1999) also demonstrated a relationship between social cohesion and abuse rates. However, few studies have examined the extent to which differences in parenting practices actually mediate the relation between neighborhood SES and child well-being. Klebanov and colleagues (1998) found that the quality of learning experiences in the home mediated the relation between neighborhood and IQ for 3-year-olds. Greenberg and colleagues (1999) also found that the home environment mediated the relation between neighborhood risk and teacher-reported social competence and achievement. Even so, research suggests that most of the variance in parenting is not accounted for by neighborhood of residence (Caspi et al. 2000, Furstenberg et al. 1999).

It is methodologically difficult to establish causal relationships between complex social settings such as neighborhoods and individual behavioral outcomes because results are often consistent with more than one explanation (Duncan & Raudenbush 1999, Natl. Res. Counc. 1993). There are a number of potentially confounding factors that make interpretations about neighborhood effects difficult. Most notably, any differences observed in the incidence of negative behaviors or outcome may be due to the characteristics of those people who selected to live there (a "selection effect" or "omitted variables bias"). Also, major social stressors may have a direct effect on a large proportion of neighborhood residents (an "aggregation effect"). Even so, for certain classes of child outcomes (e.g., congenital anomalies), living in particular low-SES neighborhoods (i.e., near a toxic waste dump) carries a significantly elevated risk of poor development (Vrijheid et al. 2000).

FUTURE DIRECTIONS

The literature reviewed above presents a complex portrait of the relation between SES and child development. Rearchers have specified, and at least partially examined, numerous mechanisms linking SES and child well-being. Not yet fully known is how the various components of SES interact synergistically with each other or with other aspects of family, neighborhood, peer, and institutional contexts to affect the course of development (McLoyd 1998). It is also difficult to attribute causality to SES because children's environments interact with their genetic makeup to impact well-being in many different ways (Huston et al. 1997, Wachs 2000). Children with different genetic attributes will respond differentially to the same environmental circumstances. In the diathesis-stress model of psychopathology, individuals who are genetically predisposed to a particular stress-related problem will be more sensitive to stress-inducing experiences (Paris 1999). On the other side of the equation, environments help determine how genes express themselves (Plomin & Crabbe 2000). Genes could have greater or lesser effects depending on environment. Research in the next decade should help explicate how SES operates through multiple mechanisms simultaneously to affect developmental course, how those paths vary across ethnic and cultural groups, and how different components of SES function conjointly to effect different developmental systems.

Visit the Annual Reviews home page at www.AnnualReviews.org

LITERATURE CITED

Achenbach T, Bird H, Canino G, Phares V, Gould M, Rubio-Stipec M. 1990. Epidemiological comparisons of Puerto Rican and U.S. mainland children: parent, teacher and self reports. *J. Am. Acad. Child Adolesc. Psychiatry* 29:84–93

Adams BN. 1998. *The Family: a Sociological Interpretation*. New York: Harcourt Brace

Adler NE, Boyce T, Chesney MA, Cohen S, Folkman S, et al. 1994. Socioeconomic status and health: the challenge of the gradient. *Am. Psychol.* 49:15–24

Adler NE, Marmot M, McEwen BS, Stewart J, eds. 1999. *Socioeconomic Status and Health in Industrialized Nations*. New York: NY Acad. Sci.

Adler NE, Ostrove JM. 1999. Socioeconomic status and health: what we know and what we don't. See Adler et al. 1999, pp. 3–15

Alexander KL, Entwisle DR, Dauber SL. 1993. First-grade behavior: its short- and long-term consequences for school performance. *Child Dev.* 64:801–14

Amato PR, Zuo J. 1992. Rural poverty, urban

poverty, and psychological well-being. *Sociol. Q.* 33:229–40

Anastasi A. 1956. Intelligence and family size. *Psychol. Bull.* 53:187–209

Anderson NB. 1999. Solving the puzzle of socioeconomic status and health: the need for integrated, multilevel, interdisciplinary research. See Adler et al. 1999, pp. 302–3

Baron R, Kenny D. 1986. The moderator-mediator variable distinction in social psychological research. *J. Pers. Soc. Psychol.* 11: 1173–82

Battin-Pearson S, Newcomb MD, Abbott RD, Hill KG, Catalano RF, Hawkins JD. 2000. Predictors of early high school drop-out: a test of five theories. *J. Educ. Psychol.* 92: 568–82

Baum A, Garofalo JP, Yali AM. 1999. SES and chronic stress: does stress account for SES effects on health? See Adler et al. 1999, pp. 131–44

Blendon R, Aiken L, Freeman H, Corey C. 1989. Access to medical care for black and white Americans. *JAMA* 261:278–81

Bloom B. 1964. *Stability and Change in Human Characteristics.* New York: Wiley

Bolger KE, Patterson CJ, Thompson WW, Kupersmidt JB. 1995. Psychosocial adjustment among children experiencing persistent and intermittent family economic hardship. *Child Dev.* 66:1107–29

Borduin CM, Henggeler N. 1981. Social class, experimental setting and task characteristics as determinants of mother-child interactions. *Dev. Psychol.* 17:209–14

Bradley RH. 1994. The HOME Inventory: review and reflections. In *Advances in Child Development and Behavior*, ed. H Reese, pp. 241–88. San Diego, CA: Academic

Bradley RH, Caldwell BM. 1980. The relation of the home environment, cognitive competence, and IQ among males and females. *Child Dev.* 51:1140–48

Bradley RH, Corwyn RF. 1999. Parenting. In *Child Psychology: A Handbook of Contemporary Issues*, ed. C Tamis-LeMonda, L Balter, pp. 339–62. New York: Psychology Press

Bradley RH, Corwyn RF. 2001. *Age and ethnic variations in family process mediators of SES.* Presented at Conf. Socioeconomic Status, Parenting, Child Dev., Minneapolis, MN

Bradley RH, Corwyn RF, Burchinal M, McAdoo HP, Garcia Coll C. 2001a. The home environments of children in the United States. Part 2: relations with behavioral development through age 13. *Child Dev.* In press

Bradley RH, Corwyn RF, Caldwell BM, Whiteside-Mansell L, Wasserman GA, et al. 2000. Measuring the home environments of children in early adolescence. *J. Res. Adolesc.* 10:247–89

Bradley RH, Corwyn RF, McAdoo HP, Garcia Coll C. 2001b. The home environments of children in the United States. Part 1: variations by age, ethnicity, and poverty status. *Child Dev.* In press

Bradley RH, Corwyn RF, Whiteside-Mansell L. 1996. Life at home: same time, different places. *Early Dev. Parent.* 5:251–69

Bradley RH, Kelleher KJ. 1992. *Childhood morbidity and mortality: the growing impact of social factors.* Presented at Conf. Social Sci. Health Policy: Building Bridges Between Research and Action, Washington, DC

Bradley RH, Whiteside-Mansell L. 1997. Children in poverty. In *Handbook of Prevention and Treatment With Children and Adolescents*, ed. RT Ammerman, M Hersen, pp. 13–58. New York: Wiley

Bradley RH, Whiteside-Mansell L, Mundfrom DJ, Casey PH, Kelleher KJ, Pope SK. 1994. Early indications of resilience and their relation to experiences in the home environments of low birthweight, premature children living in poverty. *Child Dev.* 65:346–60

Brody DJ, Pirkle JL, Kramer RA, Flegal KM, Matte TD, et al. 1994a. Blood lead levels in the U.S. population. *JAMA* 272:277–81

Brody GH, Flor DL, Gibson NM. 1999. Linking maternal efficacy beliefs, developmental goals, parenting practices, and child competence in rural single-parent African American families. *Child Dev.* 70:1197–208

Brody GH, Stoneman Z, Flor D, McCrary C,

Hastings L, Conyers O. 1994b. Financial resources, parent psychological functioning, parent co-caregiving, and early adolescent competence in rural two-parent African-American families. *Child Dev.* 65:590–605

Bronfenbrenner U. 1995. Developmental ecology through space and time: a future perspective. See Moen et al. 1995, pp. 619–48

Brooks-Gunn J, Duncan GJ. 1997. The effects of poverty on children. *Future Child.* 7(2):55–71

Brooks-Gunn J, Klebanov PK, Liaw F. 1995. The learning, physical, and emotional environment of the home in the context of poverty: The Infant Health and Development Program. *Child. Youth Serv. Rev.* 17:251–76

Call KT, Nonnemaker J. 1999. Socioeconomic disparities in adolescent health: contributing factors. See Adler et al. 1999, pp. 352–55

Caspi A, Taylor A, Moffitt TE, Plomin R. 2000. Neighborhood deprivation affects children's mental health: environmental risks, identified in genetic design. *Psychol. Sci.* 11:338–42

Cassady C, Farel A, Guild P, Kennelly J, People-Sheps M, et al. 1997. *Maternal and Child Health Model Indicators.* Washington, DC: Maternal Child Health Bur., US Dep. Health Human Serv.

Cohen S. 1999. Social status and susceptibility to respiratory infections. See Adler et al. 1999, pp. 246–53

Coleman JS. 1988. Social capital in the creation of human capital. *Am. J. Sociol.* 94 (Suppl.):S95–120

Compas BE, Connor-Smith JK, Saltzman H, Thomsen AH, Wadsworth ME. 2001. Coping with stress during childhood and adolescence: problems, progress, and potential in theory and research. *Psychol. Bull.* 127:87–127

Conger RD, Conger KJ, Elder GH. 1997. Family economic hardship and adolescent adjustment: mediating and moderating processes. See Duncan & Brooks-Gunn 1997, pp. 288–310

Conger RD, Conger KJ, Elder GH, Lorenz F,

Simons R, Whitbeck L. 1992. A family process model of economic hardship and adjustment in early adolescent boys. *Child Dev.* 63:526–41

Corwyn RF, Bradley RH. 2000. *Developmental accomplishments and family-child activities of preschoolers in the United States: comparisons across three major ethnic groups and poverty status.* Presented at Meet. Southwest. Soc. Res. Hum. Dev., Eureka Springs, AR, April 13–15

Crane J. 1991. The epidemic theory of ghettos and neighborhood effects on dropping out and teenage childbearing. *Am. J. Sociol.* 96:1126–59

Crooks D. 1995. American children at risk: poverty and its consequences for children's health, growth, and school achievement. *Yearb. Phys. Anthropol.* 38:57–86

Darling N, Steinberg L. 1997. Assessing neighborhood effects using individual-level data. In *Neighborhood Poverty: Policy Implications in Studying Neighborhoods*, ed. J Brooks-Gunn, GJ Duncan, JL Aber, 2:120–31. New York: Russell Sage Found.

Davies AF. 1952. Prestige of occupations. *Br. J. Sociol.* 3:134–47

DeGarmo DS, Forgatch MS, Martinez CR. 1999. Parenting of divorced mothers as a link between social status and boys' academic outcomes: unpacking the effects of socioeconomic status. *Child Dev.* 70:1231–45

DiPietro JA, Costigan KA, Hilton SC, Pressman EK. 1999. Effects of socioeconomic status and psychosocial stress on the development of the fetus. See Adler et al. 1999, pp. 356–58

Dodge KA, Petit FS, Bates JE. 1994. Socialization mediators of the relation between socioeconomic status and child conduct problems. *Child Dev.* 65:649–65

Dohrenwend B. 1990. Socioeconomic status (SES) and psychiatric disorders. *Soc. Psychiatry Psychiatr. Epidemiol.* 25:41–47

Duncan GJ, Brooks-Gunn J. 1997. *Consequences of Growing Up Poor.* New York: Russell Sage Found.

Duncan GJ, Brooks-Gunn J, Klebanov P. 1994.

Economic deprivation and early childhood development. *Child Dev.* 65:296–318

Duncan GJ, Raudenbush SW. 1999. Assessing the effects of context in studies of children and youth development. *Educ. Psychol.* 34:29–41

Earls F. 1980. Prevalence of behavior problems in 3-year-old children: a cross-national replication. *Arch. Gen. Psychiatry* 37:1153–57

Earls F, McGuire J, Shay S. 1994. Evaluating a community intervention to reduce the risk of child abuse: methodological strategies in conducting neighborhood surveys. *Child Abuse Negl.* 18:473–85

Elder G, Caspi A, Van Nguyen T. 1985. Resourceful and vulnerable children: family influences in hard times. In *Development as Action in Context*, ed. R Silbereisen, H Eyferth, pp. 167–86. Berlin: Springer-Verlag

Elliott D, Wilson WJ, Huizinga D, Sampson R, Elliott A, Rankin B. 1996. The effects of neighborhood disadvantage on adolescent development. *J. Res. Crime Delinq.* 33:389–426

Ennett ST, Flewelling RL, Lindroth RC, Norton EC. 1997. School and neighborhood characteristics associated with school rates of alcohol, cigarette, and marijuana use. *J. Health Soc. Behav.* 38:55–71

Entwisle DR, Alexander KL, Olson LS. 1994. The gender gap in math: its possible origins in neighborhood effects. *Am. Sociol. Rev.* 59:822–38

Entwisle DR, Astone NM. 1994. Some practical guidelines for measuring youth's race/ethnicity and socioeconomic status. *Child Dev.* 65:1521–40

Escalona S. 1982. Babies at double hazard: early development of infants at biologic and social risk. *Pediatrics* 70:670–75

Evans GW, Maxwell LE, Hart B. 1999. Parental language and verbal responsiveness to children in crowded homes. *Dev. Psychol.* 35:1020–23

Felner RD, Brand S, DuBois DL, Adan AM, Mulhall PF, Evans EG. 1995. Socioeconomic disadvantage, proximal environmental experiences, and socioemotional and academic adjustment in early adolescence: investigation of a mediated effects model. *Child Dev.* 65:296–318

Ford DH, Lerner RM. 1992. *Developmental Systems Theory: An Integrated Approach.* Newbury Park, CA: Sage

Francis D, Champagne FA, Liu D, Meaney MJ. 1999. Maternal care, gene expression, and the development of individual differences in stress reactivity. See Adler et al. 1999, pp. 66–84

Frank R, Strobino D, Salkever D, Jackson C. 1992. Updated estimates of the impact of prenatal care on birthweight outcomes by race. *J. Hum. Resourc.* 27:629–42

Furstenberg FF, Cook TE, Eccles J, Elder G, Sameroff A. 1999. *Managing To Make It: Urban Families and Adolescent Success.* Chicago: Univ. Chicago Press

Gad M, Johnson J. 1980. Correlates of adolescent life stresses related to race, SES, and levels of perceived support. *J. Clin. Child. Psychol.* 9:13–16

Gallo LC, Matthews KA. 1999. Do negative emotions mediate the association between socioeconomic status and health? See Adler et al. 1999, pp. 226–45

Garbarino J. 1992. The meaning of poverty in the world of children. *Am. Behav. Sci.* 35:220–37

Garbarino J. 1999. The effects of community violence on children. In *Child Psychology, A Handbook of Contemporary Issues*, ed. L Balter, C Tamis–LaMonda, pp. 412–25. New York: Psychology Press

Garcia Coll C, Lamberty G, Jenkins R, McAdoo HP, Crnic K, et al. 1996. An integrative model for the study of developmental competencies in minority children. *Child Dev.* 67:1891–914

Garmezy N. 1993. Children in poverty: resilience despite risk. *Psychiatry* 56:127–36

Garrett P, Ng'andu N, Ferron J. 1994. Poverty experiences of young children and the quality of their home environments. *Child Dev.* 65:331–45

Goodman E. 1999. The role of socioeconomic status gradients in explaining differences in

US adolescents' health. *Am. J. Public Health* 89:1522–28

Gottfried AW. 1985. Measures of socioeconomic status in child development research: data and recommendations. *Merrill-Palmer Q.* 31:85–92

Greenberg MT, Lengua LJ, Coie JD, Pinderhughes EE. 1999. Predicting developmental outcomes at school entry using a multiple-risk model: four American communities. *Dev. Psychol.* 35:403–17

Grusky DB, Van Rompaey SE. 1992. The vertical scaling of occupations: some cautionary comments and reflections. *Am. J. Sociol.* 97:1712–28

Guo G, Harris KM. 2000. The mechanisms mediating the effects of poverty on children's intellectual development. *Demography* 37:431–47

Haan MN, Kaplan GA, Syme SL. 1989. Socioeconomic status and health: old observations and new thoughts. In *Pathways to Health: The Role of Social Factors*, ed. JP Bunker, DS Gomby, BH Kehrer, pp. 176–233. Palo Alto, CA: Henry J. Kaiser Found.

Harrell AV, Peterson GE. 1992. *Drugs, Crime, and Social Isolation: Barriers to Urban Opportunities.* Washington, DC: Urban Inst. Press

Harrell JS, Bangdiwala SI, Deng S, Webb JP, Bradley C. 1998. Smoking initiation in youth: the roles of gender, race, socioeconomics, and developmental status. *J. Adolesc. Health* 23:271–79

Hart B, Risley TR. 1995. *Meaningful Differences in the Everyday Experience of Young American Children.* Baltimore, MD: Brookes

Hauser RM. 1994. Measuring socioeconomic status in studies of child development. *Child Dev.* 65:1541–45

Haverman R, Wolfe R. 1995. The determinants of children's attainments: a review of methods and findings. *J. Econ. Lit.* 33:1829–78

Hawley T, Disney E. 1992. Crack's children: the consequences of maternal cocaine abuse. *Soc. Policy Rep. Soc. Res. Child Dev.* 6(4):1–22

Hertzman C. 1999. The biological embedding of early experience and its effects on health in adulthood. See Adler et al. 1999, pp. 85–95

Hess RD, Holloway S, Price G, Dickson WP. 1982. Family environments and the acquisition of reading skills. In *Families As Learning Environments of Children*, ed. LM Laosa, IE Sigel, pp. 87–113. New York: Plenum

Hoff-Ginsberg E. 1991. Mother-child conversation in different social classes and communicative settings. *Child Dev.* 62:782–96

Hoff-Ginsberg E, Tardif T. 1995. Socioeconomic status and parenting. In *Handbook of Parenting*, ed. MH Bornstein, 4:161–87. Mahweh, NJ: Erlbaum

Hunt JM. 1961. *Intelligence and Experience.* New York: Ronald

Huston AC, McLoyd VC, Garcia Coll C. 1997. Poverty and behavior: the case for multiple methods and levels of analysis. *Dev. Rev.* 17:376–93

Jacobs J, Bennett M. 1993. Decision-making in one parent and two parent families: influence and information selection. *J. Early Adolesc.* 13:245–66

Jencks C, Mayer S. 1990. The social consequences of growing up in a poor neighborhood. In *Inner City Poverty in the United States*, ed. L Lynn, M McGeary, pp. 111–86. Washington, DC: Natl. Acad. Press

Johnston-Brooks CH, Lewis MA, Evans GW, Whalen CK. 1998. Chronic stress and illness in children: the role of allostatic load. *Psychosom. Med.* 60:597–603

Kawachi I. 1999. Social capital and community effects on population and individual health. See Adler et al. 1999, pp. 120–30

Kennedy W, Van de Riet V, White JA. 1963. A normative sample of intelligence and achievement of Negro elementary school children in southeastern United States. *Monogr. Soc. Res. Child Dev.* 28(6) whole issue

Klebanov PK, Brooks-Gunn J, McCarton CM, Mccormick MC. 1998. The contribution of neighborhood and family income upon developmental test scores over the first three years of life. *Child Dev.* 69:1420–36

Klerman LV. 1991. *Alive and Well?* New York: Natl. Cent. Children Poverty, Columbia Univ.

Kohn ML, Schooler C. 1982. Job conditions and personality: a longitudinal assessment of their reciprocal effects. *Am. J. Soc.* 87:1257–83

Korenman S, Miller JE. 1997. Effects of long-term poverty on the physical health of children in the National Longitudinal Survey of Youth. See Duncan & Brooks-Gunn 1997, pp. 70–99

Kotch J, Shackelford J. 1989. *The nutritional status of low-income preschool children in the United States: a review of the literature.* ERIC Doc. ED 308 965 PS 018 152

Kramer MS. 1987. Determinants of low birthweight: methodological assessment and meta-analysis. *Bull. WHO* 65:663–737

Krieger N, Williams DR, Moss HW. 1997. Measuring social class in US public health research: concepts, methodologies, and guidelines. *Annu. Rev. Public Health* 18:341–78

Lahey BB, Loeber R, Hart EL, Frick PJ, Applegate B, et al. 1995. Four-year longitudinal study of conduct disorders in boys: patterns and predictors of persistence. *J. Abnorm. Psychol.* 104:83–93

Lempers JD, Clark-Lempers D, Simons RL. 1989. Economic hardship, parenting, and distress in adolescence. *Child Dev.* 60:25–39

Leventhal T, Brooks-Gunn J. 2000. The neighborhoods they live in: the effect of neighborhood residence on child and adolescent outcomes. *Psychol. Bull.* 126:309–37

Liberatos P, Link BG, Kelsey JI. 1988. The measurement of social class in epidemiology. *Epidemiol. Rev.* 10:87–121

Loeber R, Wikstrom PH. 1993. Individual pathways to crime in different types of neighborhoods. In *Integrating Individual and Ecological Aspects of Crime*, ed. DP Farrington, RJ Sampson, P Wikstrom, pp. 169–204. Stockholm: Natl. Counc. Crime Prev.

Lovejoy MC, Graczyk PA, O'Hare E, Neuman G. 2000. Maternal depression and parenting behavior: a meta-analytic review. *Clin. Psychol. Rev.* 20:561–92

Luster T, Reischl T, Gassaway J, Gomaa H. 1995. *Factors related to early school success among African-American children from low income families.* Presented at Bienn. Meet. Soc. Res. Child Dev, Indianapolis, IN

Macintyre S, West P. 1991. Lack of class variation in health in adolescence: an artifact of an occupational measure of class. *Soc. Sci. Med.* 30:665–73

Marmot M. 1999. Epidemiology of socioeconomic status and health: Are determinants within countries the same as between countries? See Adler et al. 1999, pp. 16–19

Masten AS, Coatsworth JD. 1998. The development of competence in favorable and unfavorable environments. *Am. Psychol.* 53:205–20

Mayer S. 1997. *What Money Can't Buy.* Cambridge, MA: Harvard Univ. Press

McCall RB. 1981. Nature-nurture and the two realms of development: a proposed integration with respect to mental development. *Child Dev.* 52:1–12

McCoy MB, Firck PJ, Loney BR, Ellis ML. 1999. The potential mediating role of parenting practices in the development of conduct problems in a clinic-referred sample. *J. Child. Fam. Stud.* 8:477–94

McEwen BS, Seeman T. 1999. Protective and damaging effects of mediators of stress. See Adler et al. 1999, pp. 30–47

McGauhey P, Starfield B, Alexander C, Ensminger M. 1991. Social environment and vulnerability of low birth weight children: a social-epidemiological perspective. *Pediatrics* 88:943–53

McLeod J, Shanahan M. 1993. Poverty, parenting, and children's mental health. *Am. Sociol. Rev.* 58:351–66

McLoyd VC. 1997. The impact of poverty and low socioeconomic status on the socioemotional functioning of African-American children and adolescents: mediating effects. In *Social and Emotional Adjustment and Family Relations in Ethnic Minority Families*, ed. RD Taylor, M Wang, pp. 7–34. Mahwah, NJ: Erlbaum. 239 pp.

McLoyd VC. 1998. Socioeconomic disadvantage and child development. *Am. Psychol.* 53:185–204

McLoyd VC. 1990. The impact of economic hardship on black families and children: psychological distress, parenting, and socioemotional development. *Child Dev.* 61:311–46

McLoyd VC, Jayaratne TE, Ceballo R, Borquez J. 1994. Unemployment and work interruption among African American single mothers: effects on parenting and adolescent socioemotional functioning. *Child Dev.* 65:562–89

Mercy JA, Steelman LC. 1982. Familial influence on the intellectual attainment of children. *Am. Sociol. Rev.* 47:532–42

Miller DC. 1991. *Handbook of Research Design and Social Measurement.* Newbury Park, CA: Sage. 5th ed.

Miller JE, Korenman S. 1994. Poverty and children's nutritional status in the United States. *Am. J. Epidemiol.* 140:233–42

Moen P, Elder GH, Luscher K, eds. 1995. *Examining Lives in Context.* Washington, DC: Am. Psychol. Assoc.

Moore KA, Morrison DR, Zaslow M, Glei DA. 1994. *Ebbing and flowing, learning and growing: family economic resources and children's development.* Presented at Res. Brief., Board Child. Fam. Washington, DC: Child Trends, Inc.

Morrison LA, Eccles J. 1995. *Poverty, parenting, and adolescents' achievement.* Presented at Bienn. Meet. Soc. Res. Child Dev. Indianapolis, IN

Mortorell R. 1980. Interrelationships between diet, infectious disease, and nutritional status. In *Social and Biological Predictors of Nutritional Status, Physical Growth and Neurological Development*, ed. HS Greene, FE Johnson, pp. 188–213. New York: Academic

Mpofu E, Van de Vijver FJR. 2000. Taxonomic structure in early to middle childhood: a longitudinal study of Simbabwean schoolchildren. *Int. J. Behav. Dev.* 24:204–312

Nam CB, Powers MG. 1983. *The Socioeconomic Approach to Status Measurement.* Houston, TX: Cap & Gown

Natl. Cent. Child Poverty. 1990. *Five Million Children: A Statistical Profile of Our Poorest Young Children.* New York: Columbia Univ. Sch. Public Health

Natl. Res. Counc. 1993. *Losing Generations.* Washington, DC: Natl. Acad. Press

Needleman HL, Schell A, Bellinger D, Leviton A, Allred E. 1990. The long-term effects of low doses of lead in childhood: an 11-year follow-up report. *N. Engl. J. Med.* 322:83–88

Oliver ML, Shapiro TM. 1995. *Black Wealth, White Wealth.* New York: Routledge

O'Malley PM, Johnston LD. 1999. Drinking and driving among US high school seniors, 1984–1997. *Am. J. Public Health* 89:678–84

Ortega ST, Corzine J. 1990. Socioeconomic status and mental disorders. *Res. Commun. Ment. Health* 6:149–82

Oski F. 1993. Iron deficiency in infancy and childhood. *N. Engl. J. Med.* 329(3):190–93

Osofsky JD. 1999. The impact of violence on children. *Future Child.* 9(3):33–49

Ostrove JM, Feldman P, Adler NE. 1999. Relations among socioeconomic indicators and health for African-Americans and whites. *J. Health Psychol.* 4:451–63

Overpeck MD, Brenner RA, Trumble AC, Trifiletti LB, Berendes HW. 1998. Risk factors for infant homicide in the United States. *N. Engl. J. Med.* 339:1211–16

Paltiel FL. 1988. Is being poor a mental health hazard? *Women's Health* 12:189–211

Parcel TL, Menaghan EG. 1990. Maternal working conditions and children's verbal facility: studying the intergenerational transmission of inequality from mothers to young children. *Soc. Psychol. Q.* 53:132–47

Paris J. 1999. *Genetics and Psychopathology: Predisposition-Stress Interactions.* Washington, DC: Am. Psychiatr. Press

Parker S, Greer S, Zuckerman B. 1988. Double jeopardy: the impact of poverty on early child development. *Pediatr. Clin. N. Am.* 35:1127–241

Patterson G, DeBarsyshe B, Ramsey E. 1989.

A developmental perspective on antisocial behavior. *Am. Psychol.* 44:329–35

Pearlin LI, Menaghan EG, Lieberman MA, Mullan JT. 1981. The stress process. *J. Health Soc. Behav.* 22:337–56

Pianta RC, Egeland B, Sroufe LA. 1990. Maternal stress and children's development: prediction of school outcomes and identification of protective factors. See Rolf et al. 1990, pp. 215–35

Plomin R, Crabbe J. 2000. DNA. *Psychol Bull.* 126:806–28

Pollitt E, Golub M, Gorman K, Grantham-McGregor S, Levitsky D, et al. 1996. A reconceptualization of the effects of under-nutrition on children's biological, psychosocial, and behavioral development. *Soc. Policy Rep. Soc. Res. Child Dev.* 10(5):1–24

Power C. 1991. Social and economic background and class inequalities in health among young adults. *Soc. Sci. Med.* 32:411–17

Raisler J, Alexander C, O'Campo P. 1999. Breast-feeding and infant illness: a dose response relationship? *Am. J. Public Health* 89:25–30

Rank MR. 2000. Socialization of socioeconomic status. In *Handbook of Family Development and Intervention*, ed. WC Nichols, pp. 129–42. New York: Wiley

Richman N, Stevenson J, Graham P. 1975. Prevalence of behavior problems in three-year-old children: an epidemiological study in a London borough. *J. Child Psychol. Psychiatry* 16:277–87

Rodrigo MJ, Janssens JM, Ceballos E. 2001. Reasoning and action complexity: sources and consequences on maternal child-rearing behavior. *Int. J. Behav. Dev.* 25:50–59

Rolf J, Masten A, Cicchetti D, Nuechterlein K, Weintraub S, eds. 1990. *Risk and Protective Factors in Development of Psychopathology.* New York: Cambridge Univ. Press

Rosenbaum S. 1992. Child health and poor children. *Am. Behav. Sci.* 35:275–89

Rushing WA, Ortega ST. 1979. Socioeconomic status and mental disorder: new evidence and a sociomedical formulation. *Am. J. Sociol.* 84:1175–200

Rutter M. 1990. Psychosocial resilience and protective mechanisms. See Rolf et al. 1990, pp. 181–214

Saegert S, Winkel GH. 1990. Environmental psychology. *Annu. Rev. Psychol.* 41:441–77

Sameroff AJ, Seifer R, Baldwin A, Baldwin C. 1993. Stability of intelligence from preschool to adolescence: the influence of social and family risk factors. *Child Dev.* 64:80–97

Sameroff AJ, Seifer R, Zax M, Barocas R. 1987. Early indicators of developmental risk: the Rochester longitudinal study. *Schizophr. Bull.* 13:383–94

Sampson RJ. 1992. Family management and child development: insights from social disorganization theory. In *Advances in Criminological Theory*, ed. J McCord, 3:63–93. New Brunswick, NJ: Transaction Books

Sampson RJ, Raudenbush SW, Earls F. 1997. Neighborhoods and violent crime: a multilevel study of collective efficacy. *Science* 277:918–24

Sandel M, Schrfstein J. 1999. *Not Safe at Home: How America's Housing Crisis Threatens the Health of Its Children.* Boston: Boston Med. Cent. Children's Hosp., The Doc4Kids Project

Sargent JD, Brown MJ, Freeman A, Bailey D, Goodman D, Freeman DH. 1995. Childhood lead poisoning in Massachusetts's communities: its association with sociodemographic and housing characteristics. *Am. J. Public Health* 85:528–34

Scarr S, Weinberg RA. 1978. The influence of "family background" on intellectual attainment. *Am. Sociol. Rev.* 43:674–92

Scholer SJ, Hickson GB, Ray WA. 1999. Sociodemographic factors identify US infants at high risk for injury mortality. *Pediatrics* 103:1183–88

Shonkoff JP, Phillips DA, eds. 2000. *From Neurons to Neighborhoods: The Science of Early Childhood Development.* Washington, DC: Natl. Acad. Press

Smith JP. 1999. Healthy bodies and thick wallets: the dual relation between health and economic status. *J. Econ. Perspect.* 13:145–66

Smith JR, Brooks-Gunn J, Klebanov P. 1997.

The consequences of living in poverty for young children's cognitive and verbal ability and early school achievement. See Duncan & Brooks-Gunn 1997, pp. 132–89

Starfield B. 1982. Family income, ill health and medical care of U.S. children. *J. Public Healthy Policy* 3:244–59

Starfield B. 1989. Child health care and social factors: poverty, class, race. *Bull. NY Acad. Med.* 65:299–306

Takeuchi DT, Williams DR, Adair RK. 1991. Economic stress in the family and children's emotional and behavioral problems. *J. Marriage Fam.* 53:1031–41

Taylor SE, Seeman TE. 1999. Psychosocial resources and the SES-health relationship. See Adler et al. 1999, pp. 210–25

Tesman JR, Hills A. 1994. Developmental effects of lead exposure in children. *Soc. Policy Rep. Soc. Res. Child Dev.* 8(3):1–16

Treiber R, Harshfield G, Davis H, Kapuku G, Moore D. 1999. Stress responsivity and body fatness: links between socioeconomic status and cardiovascular risk factors in youth. See Adler et al. 1999, pp. 435–38

US Dep. Health Hum. Serv. 2000a. *Child Health USA 2000.* Washington, DC: US GPO

US Dep. Health Hum. Serv. 2000b. *Healthy People 2010.* Washington, DC: US GPO

Valenzuela M. 1997. Maternal sensitivity in a developing society: the context of urban poverty and infant chronic undernutrition. *Dev. Psychol.* 33:845–55

Vaughn BE, Bost KK. 1999. Attachment and temperament: redundant, independent, or interacting influences on interpersonal adaptation and personality development? In *Handbook of Attachment: Theory, Research, and Clinical Applications*, ed. J Cassidy, PR Shaver, pp. 198–225. New York: Guilford

Vrijheid M, Dolk H, Stone D, Alberman E, Scott JES. 2000. Socioeconomic inequalities in risk of congenital anomaly. *Arch. Dis. Child.* 82:349–52

Wachs TD. 2000. *Necessary but Not Sufficient.* Washington, DC: Am. Psychol. Assoc.

Walberg HJ, Marjoribanks K. 1976. Family environment and cognitive development:

twelve analytic models. *Rev. Educ. Res.* 46: 527–51

Wasserman CR, Shaw GM, Selvin S, Gould JB, Syme SL. 1998. Socioeconomic status, neighborhood social conditions, and neural tube defects. *Am. J. Public Health* 88:1674–80

White KR. 1982. The relation between socioeconomic status and academic achievement. *Psychol. Bull.* 91:461–81

Wilkinson RG. 1999. Health, hierarchy, and social anxiety. See Adler et al. 1999, pp. 48–63

Williams DR, Collins C. 1995. U. S. socioeconomic and racial differentials in health: patterns and explanations. *Annu. Rev. Sociol.* 21:349–86

Wills TA, McNamara G, Vaccaro D. 1995. Parental education related to adolescent stress-coping and substance use: development of a mediational model. *Health Psychol.* 14:464–78

Wills TA, Vaccaro D, McNamara G. 1992. Live events, family support, and competence in adolescent substance use. *Am. J. Commun. Psychol.* 20:349–74

Wilson AL. 1993. Poverty and children's health. *Child Youth Fam. Serv. Q.* 16:14–16

Wilson WJ. 1991. Studying inner-city social dislocation: the challenge of public agenda research. *Am. Sociol. Rev.* 56:1–14

Wohlfarth T, Van den Brink W. 1998. Social class and substance use disorders: the value of social class as distinct from socioeconomic status. *Soc. Sci. Med.* 47:51–68

Young G, Gately T. 1988. Neighborhood impoverishment and child maltreatment. *J. Fam. Issues* 9:240–54

Zill N, Moore K, Smith E, Stief T, Coiro M. 1995. The life circumstances and development of children in welfare families: a profile based on national survey data. In *Escape From Poverty: What Makes a Difference For Children?* ed. PL Chase-Lansdale, J Brooks-Gunn, pp. 38–59. New York: Cambridge Univ. Press

Zuvarin SJ. 1989. The ecology of child abuse and neglect: review of the literature and presentation of data. *Violence Vict.* 4:101–20

Annu. Rev. Psychol. 2002. 53:401–33

ADULT CLINICAL NEUROPSYCHOLOGY:
Lessons from Studies of the Frontal Lobes

Donald T. Stuss[1] and Brian Levine[2]

The Rotman Research Institute, Baycrest Centre for Geriatric Care, Departments of Psychology and Medicine ([1,2]Neurology, [1]Rehabilitation Science), University of Toronto, Toronto, Ontario M6A 2E1; e-mail: dstuss@rotman-baycrest.on.ca, blevine@rotman-baycrest.on.ca

Key Words neuropsychological assessment, brain functions, executive functions

■ **Abstract** Clinical neuropsychologists have adopted numerous (and sometimes conflicting) approaches to the assessment of brain-behavior relationships. We review the historical development of these approaches and we advocate an approach to clinical neuropsychology that is informed by recent findings from cognitive neuroscience. Clinical assessment of executive and emotional processes associated with the frontal lobes of the human brain has yet to incorporate the numerous experimental neuroscience findings on this topic. We review both standard and newer techniques for assessment of frontal lobe functions, including control operations involved in language, memory, attention, emotions, self-regulation, and social functioning. Clinical and experimental research has converged to indicate the fractionation of frontal subprocesses and the initial mapping of these subprocesses to discrete frontal regions. One anatomical distinction consistent in the literature is that between dorsal and ventral functions, which can be considered cognitive and affective, respectively. The frontal lobes, in particular the frontal poles, are involved in uniquely human capacities, including self-awareness and mental time travel.

CONTENTS

0084-6570/02/0201-0401$14.00

INTRODUCTION

The field of adult clinical neuropsychology is not only beyond the scope of a single paper, it also exceeds the limits of most books. We therefore start with a panoramic view to provide a historical and anatomical context to adult clinical neuropsychology, present a framework for adult neuropsychological assessment in general, and proceed to a more narrow focus on one facet of adult clinical neuropsychology, the functions of the frontal lobes. Why have we narrowed our focus thus? The executive functions mediated by the frontal lobes are highly sensitive to brain damage, and executive dysfunction is therefore the most common presenting problem in neuropsychological practice. With the recent explosion in research on frontal lobe functions, it has become increasingly clear that they are involved in nearly every aspect of human neuropsychology. Indeed, as we argue later, they may be what define us as human. In comparison to other cognitive functions such as memory, language, and perception, where many clinical measures have emerged from detailed experimental analysis, few clinical measures reflect recent empirical work on frontal functions. In this sense, the frontal lobes may be considered the final frontier of neuropsychology.

Even with these restrictions, our mandate is not inconsiderable, and further limits have been self-imposed. First, we have limited ourselves to an anatomical/behavior functional relationship to avoid the confusion of multiple terms such as executive functions, the dysexecutive syndrome, the supervisory system, and frontal lobe functions. Second, the focus is on the revelation of fractionation of specific processes and systems within the frontal lobes (Alexander et al. 1986, Cummings 1993, Saint Cyr et al. 2002). Third, our focus is clinical, but the emphasis is on the newest frontal brain-process relationships. The use of clinical frontal lobe tests in various populations is reviewed as much for the information they have provided in relation to frontal localization of function as for their construct validity as individual tests. Indeed, one hoped-for byproduct of this review is that the knowledge of more experimental research in patients with focal lesions might alter the use of such clinical tests. To help us achieve this goal, functional neuroimaging data are presented where possible to support, extend or challenge the more classical clinical neuropsychological lesion research.

A BRIEF HISTORY OF ADULT CLINICAL NEUROPSYCHOLOGY

Neuropsychology, Behavioral Neurology, Neuropsychiatry

Clinical neuropsychology, in its broadest definition, is the understanding of brain-behavior relations and the clinical use of this information. The first noted cortical "localization" of function after brain injury probably was the Edwin Smith Surgical Papyrus, dated sometime around the seventeenth century BC (Walsh 1987). In a real sense, however, the history of neuropsychology started in the nineteenth century, with Carl Wernicke (1874) possibly being the father of neuropsychology. Renewed attention to his work on aphasia and apraxia was a major force that fanned the flames of the burgeoning of interest and activity in neuropsychological issues in the mid- and later twentieth century.

The roots of neuropsychology lie in neurology and psychology, with no real separation existing among these interests in the initial stages. Kurt Goldstein (1934/1995), for example, was an expert in neurology, psychology, psychiatry, and rehabilitation. The psychological basis of neuropsychology began to disengage from medicine in the 1940s, at least in North America (Lezak 1983), the separation occurring to a greater or lesser degree in different regions. Today, three related and relatively new subdisciplines play important interactive and somewhat different roles in brain-behavior studies. Behavioral neurology assumes that at least certain aspects of behavior, even complex behaviors to some degree, are hardwired in the adult central nervous system (Heilman & Valenstein 1985). This assumption provides the framework for behavioral neurology research: In most cases, brain damage in a specific area will result in a certain kind of functional deficit. Neuropsychiatry uses similar assumptions as behavioral neurology, but the emphasis is on the psychiatric manifestations of neurologic disease. Finally, clinical neuropsychology focuses more on psychological testing procedures. Where an individual scientist falls on this spectrum is often an accident of training rather than a result of knowledge, skills, or interest.

Clinical Neuropsychological Assessment Approaches

In the early years of neuropsychological assessment, clinicians would have a sense of "normal" performance, and anything below that indicated a pathological deficit. This dichotomous approach allowed little sense of normal variability. To remedy this, some clinics developed local quantitative procedures, but these usually had no real empirical standardization and no clear generalizable clinical use (Benton 1967). Some clinicians diagnosed "organicity" (meaning brain pathology of some kind) based on "pathognomonic" signs discovered in a patient's response to a test. These early forays in clinical assessment were dramatically altered by Binet and the Stanford-Binet test of psychometric intelligence. Binet developed tests that were objective (procedures were clear and there were precise criteria for satisfactory performance), standardized (the tests were given to samples of different ages, and tests were finally chosen based on specific criteria from these results), and had demonstrable usefulness (Benton 1967).

Binet's transformative method set the stage for the psychometric test battery approach advocated by many neuropsychologists. There was a move from the more dichotomous classification supposedly associated with behavioral neurology to "the measurement of continuously distributed variables within a psychometric tradition that attempts to achieve at least equal interval scaling of the operations in question" (Rourke & Brown 1986. p. 5). Halstead (1947) was a key figure in this shift, with his attempt to use a battery of objective tests to diagnose brain damage and general categories of brain damage. There was a growing desire to create an empirical base to assessment and to make neuropsychology more scientific, with standardized tests for validation, cross-validation, and replication. Within this psychometric approach, a battery of tests was considered superior to individual tests for several reasons (Rourke & Brown 1986). Addition of certain tests improved the rate of accuracy of diagnosis of brain damage. A fixed battery of relatively well-normed standardized tests provided more data on different functions to assist decision making. Individual and global scores could be used. With a fixed battery, issues of generalizability, assessment of different types of validity, and the presence of differential sensitivity of test items all were considered to improve the accuracy of diagnoses. Most importantly, a battery helped avoid the powerful effects of base rates of the condition in the population to which the patient belonged.

Gradually, different procedures were developed to maximize the use of the battery of tests: norms (Reitan & Davidson 1974), keys or decision rules (Russell et al. 1970), and patterns of scores (Golden 1981). The application of multivariate statistics maximized the value of the battery approach by combining information, minimizing variability among groups, and grouping patients by behavioral characteristics (Crockett et al. 1981). For example, factor analysis helped differentiate variables into functional representative groupings and provided a means of examining shared and independent variance to maximize brain-behavior understanding. Discriminant function analysis was an excellent tool for classification of subjects into their proper groups, a major tool of validation of the battery approach (Stuss & Trites 1977).

Not all neuropsychologists followed the psychometric development path for adult clinical neuropsychology. Russian neuropsychology, under the guidance of Luria (1973, 1980), who had training in neurology, psychoanalysis, and psychological testing through his relationship with Vygotsky, was a proponent of a more clinical approach, adapting and improving rather than rejecting neurologists' tools. He emphasized sensitivity to individual differences, including variables such as lesion location, age, sex, handedness, and the individual's history. The approach was more flexible in the assessment of the patient's behavior, with rapid screening, and then focusing on the salient problems. If necessary, new measures would be developed to investigate these deficits; tests would be changed to test limits of abilities, or to provide a more thorough evaluation. Luria developed much of his theory from the investigation of individual patients; that is, he depended to a great degree on what has been a cornerstone of neuropsychology and a major tool of neurologists from the earliest days—case studies. The value of case studies is clear (Crockett et al. 1981). The patient and the deficits can be examined in exquisite detail. Hypotheses about the patient can be developed, tested, and refined, with control over virtually all variables. The case study is rapid and relatively inexpensive, with an ability to deploy and direct resources as required. It is clinically useful, because therapy can be developed based totally on the knowledge of the individual patient.

Luria & Majovski (1977) criticized the battery approach for not having a brain theory on which to base its conclusions. Russell (1986) disagreed, arguing that the battery approach does have many sources for theory: (*a*) a neurological basis, (*b*) its own clinical lore from the use of the battery and (*c*) psychometrics itself. Russell's response clearly demonstrates the key difference between the clinical and psychometric approaches: "In fact, the unique contribution of psychology to neuropsychology, a contribution that cannot be duplicated by neurology or behavioral neurology, can be summarized in one word: psychometrics" (p. 46).

The more clinical approach to neuropsychology can also be seen in a different form in what has been termed the "process" approach, pioneered by neuropsychologists in Australia (Walsh 1987), Denmark (Christensen 1979, who standardized Luria's approach while maintaining the qualitative hypothesis testing nature), and the United States (Kaplan 1988). A major difference of the process approach from the general clinical approach was the push for greater standardization. Qualitative aspects of behavior are identified and quantified and subjected to statistical analyses rather than the method just described. Testing of clinical limits is operationally defined, repeatable, and quantifiable. Whereas diagnosis of brain damage is still a goal in this approach, the questions are different (Milberg et al. 1986). What do the test results mean psychologically and cognitively? How did the patient achieve the final score? The premises underlying the need for this process analysis, at least as presented for the Boston Process Approach (Milberg et al. 1986), are several. Solutions to a test may be achieved by different processes, and each of these may be related to different brain structures. The unfolding of cognitive acts over time provides the opportunity for careful observation of behavior along this temporal continuum, providing a richer source of information than just right or wrong scores. That is, the way a patient responds is as, or more, important than the achievement itself. Because most categories of cognitive function consist of many components, a process approach provides the means to separate and assess these components in a manner not easily achieved by the pure psychometric or battery approach. This is particularly true if you adapt tests to isolate some of the processes. For example, comparing a Digit Symbol copy result to the regular Digit Symbol subtest of the Wechsler Adult Intelligence Scale allows dissociation of the effect of motor speed on Digit Symbol performance.

The strengths of the qualitative and quantitative approaches could be combined. "It is clear that failure to appreciate the appropriate role of qualitative dimensions in the measurement of brain-behavior relationships can lead to a vapid and meaningless generation of irrelevant data" (Rourke & Brown 1986, p. 15).

Modern Clinical Neuropsychology: Integration of Cognitive and Clinical Neurosciences

Our conceptual basis determines how we construct tests (Benton 1967). In the field of intelligence assessment, for example, certain tests were developed based on whether one considered IQ to be a general ability, or to consist of multiple primary abilities. Interestingly, Binet, whose method was a major push for the psychometric approach, avoided the issue—IQ is what the test measures. In this psychometric view the most important criteria are the effectiveness of the test and whether the test meets the critical conditions of objectivity, standardization, and usefulness. Russell (1986) stated that one could not know a function exists unless a test for that function has been developed. Whereas the psychometric approach is truly essential in understanding variability across individuals, the ossification of tests in a fixed battery and the emphasis on the psychometric criteria rather than conceptual bases have limited the ability of neuropsychologists to update the theoretical framework of brain-behavior relations.

The conceptual basis of cognitive and affective faculties derives from modern psychological theory. Clinical neuropsychology therefore should take advantage of current cognitive (and increasingly social) psychological thinking. Furthermore, it must also incorporate the newest neuroanatomical findings in the discovery and dissociation of cognitive processes; in turn, neuropsychology can inform cognitive and affective theory. Moreover, truly understanding the individual cognitive and affective processes of the brain, and their disturbance in brain damage of various types and lesion locations, is a sine qua non for diagnosis and rehabilitation. We also believe that this must be understood in the psychological, psychosocial, and environmental context of the individual, but that is another level of complexity to the clinical story.

The differences in the approaches described above appear to have derived from the background training of the proponents, and by the questions they asked. Take, for example, the following different questions: What is the difference between biological and psychometric intelligence (Halstead 1947); can the presence/absence of brain dysfunction be identified in a particular individual, and with what level of accuracy; what specific cognitive process is impaired in this patient for the purpose of establishing an individualized rehabilitation program; what are the cognitive structure and anatomical underpinnings of, for example, the anterior attentional system? Each of these questions may not only lead to the establishment of different approaches; each may still necessitate the use of a particular approach to answer the question.

In many regards, facets of different approaches are being used in a combined way in modern clinical neuropsychology. For example, case studies (the importance of which is typified in journals such as *Neurocase*) are being directed by sophisticated cognitive theory and assisted by new structural and functional imaging methodologies. Multivariate covariance-based techniques such as structural equation modeling are being used not to differentiate brain damage from non–brain damage but to understand the dynamic interactions of different focal functional brain units (localizationist, brain as a mosaic of separate skills related to distinct areas) in a large neural network (generalist, the hierarchical, sequential, and interactive nature of brain functioning). Methods from case studies and group studies are being combined to enhance the group study approach by providing more in-depth investigations, but also immediate replicability. Our research into the functions of the frontal lobes has benefited from all of these approaches.

The Focus of This Review: The Frontal Lobes

Executive functions are high-level cognitive functions that are involved in the control and direction of lower-level functions. For the purposes of consistency with prior literature, we use the terms "frontal" and "executive" interchangeably when referring to broad classifications of tests, but it will be clear that we adopt a much more specific approach when trying to understand and explain the true functional localization of these processes.

One very general method of separating the different facets of frontal lobe functioning is based on a fundamental neuroanatomical distinction (see Figure 1). The ventral prefrontal cortex (VPFC) is functionally dissociated from the dorsolateral prefrontal cortex (DLPFC), a distinction supported by evolutionary theory of cortical architectonics (Pandya & Yeterian 1996). The DLPFC is part of the archicortical trend originating in the hippocampus. It is involved in spatial and conceptual reasoning processes. Much of what is known about frontal functions in neuropsychological studies is based on patients with DLPFC dysfunction. These cognitive processes form the basis of what is referred to as executive functioning (Goldman-Rakic 1987, Milner 1963).

The VPFC is part of the paleocortical trend emerging from the caudal orbitofrontal (olfactory) cortex. It is intimately connected with limbic nuclei involved in emotional processing (Nauta 1971, Pandya & Barnes 1987), including the acquisition and reversal of stimulus-reward associations (Mishkin 1964, Rolls 2000). The involvement of the ventral medial/orbitofrontal region in inhibition, emotion, and reward processing suggests a role in behavioral self-regulation, as shown in numerous case studies of patients with pathology in this area (Eslinger & Damasio 1985, Harlow 1868). In spite of the obvious importance of these processes to human behavior, they are not adequately assessed by standard neuropsychological assessment.

Further functional/anatomical divisions within the frontal lobes can also be specified. Superior medial lesions can cause an apathetic syndrome, represented in the extreme by akinetic mutism (Cummings 1993, Stuss & Benson 1986). The functional basis of this impairment (i.e., lack of initiation) appears to be separate from more inferior medial frontal effects (Stuss et al. 1998). The superior medial

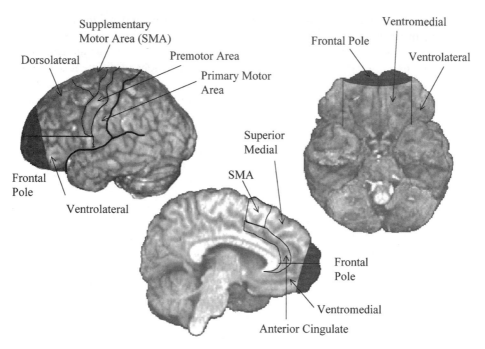

Figure 1   The major functional subdivisions of the human frontal lobes.

frontal region can exhibit dysfunction that at times mimics the lateral regions, and in other instances are unique.

Inferior (ventral) medial frontal regions have been functionally dissociated from ventrolateral and polar regions (Barbas 1995, Bechara et al. 1998, Elliott et al. 2000). Based on connectivity, Carmichael & Price (1995) divided the orbital and medial prefrontal cortex into three regional (and functional) divisions for behavior and emotional responses. The frontal poles, particularly on the right, are involved in more recently evolved aspects of human nature: autonoetic consciousness and self-awareness. The importance of polar regions in specific higher human functions has also been highlighted in studies of humor and theory of mind (Baron-Cohen et al. 1994; Shammi & Stuss 1999; Stuss et al. 2001c,d). We therefore consider the frontal polar region to be distinctly involved in processes that define us as human.

We present data on the effects of frontal lobe lesions, grossly divided into cognitive (DLPFC) and affective (VPFC) functions. As a means of maintaining a coherence of anatomy to function for the purposes of this review, our primary focus is on the DLPFC/VPFC separation, with additional separate consideration of the frontal poles. Whenever possible, these sectors are considered separately according to hemispheric lateralization. Although damage in our patients often crosses medial and lateral sectors, distinctions between these regions are noted where relevant.

COGNITIVE FUNCTIONS ASSOCIATED WITH THE PREFRONTAL CORTEX (DORSOLATERAL)

Our division of executive functions is functional, because this is the approach that would be followed in clinical neuropsychology. Standard tests have come into use through years of clinical practice and form the basis of the "frontal" part of neuropsychological assessment batteries. Some were developed in the context of focal lesion research, but most were classified based upon their face validity as executive measures. Whereas these standard tests have been used clinically with some validation in ancillary focal lesion and functional neuroimaging research, the origin of modern measures is theory-driven research on frontal functions, followed by clinical application.

We review the evidence from both the lesion and functional neuroimaging literature pertinent to the sensitivity and specificity of the standard "frontal" tests as contrasted with novel approaches based on recent cognitive neuroscience research. Our review is organized according to measures of higher-level language, attention, and memory processes. This organization is more pragmatic than theoretical; we acknowledge overlap of control operations across these domains. Owing to space constraints, we limit this review to those in wide usage and those with enough validity data upon which to base a meaningful evaluation. To foreshadow, there is evidence to support the validity of standard frontal tests, but this association depends on careful analysis of task parameters, lesion location, and the exclusion of patients with basic sensory and linguistic deficits from the posterior-lesion control groups. Novel approaches show considerable promise for improving assessment.

Frontal Lobe Language Functions

Excluding motor deficits (e.g., articulation problems), and Broca's aphasia, the language deficits related to the frontal lobes can be grouped globally under activation and formulation (paralinguistic) deficits (Alexander et al. 1989). Activation problems in speech output ("dynamic aphasia") are associated with medial frontal damage (anterior cingulate gyrus and supplementary motor area). Transcortical motor aphasia, with notably truncated spontaneous language as well as other deficits, may occur after damage usually to left DLPFC anterior and superior to Broca's area (Brodmann Areas 44, 46, 6, and 9) (Freedman et al. 1984).

Activation deficits can be tested by requiring the patient to generate a list of words beginning with a specific letter (phonological or letter fluency) or from a specific semantic category (semantic or category fluency). Next to the Wisconsin Card Sorting Test (WCST, see below), letter-based fluency is the most popular frontal test; its face validity derives from its lack of specification by external cues. It is traditionally considered to reflect left frontal function (Milner 1964, Perret 1974), although other areas of damage have been shown to produce impairment on this task (see Stuss et al. 1998 for review).

In our study of 74 focal lesion patients (Stuss et al. 1998), the left DLPFC patients were indeed the most impaired. Right DLPFC and VPFC patients were not impaired. However, patients with left parietal damage were also impaired and in fact could not be distinguished from the left DLPFC patients. Consistent with the role of superior medial regions in activation, superior medial damage on either side was also associated with impaired letter-based fluency. This left DLPFC, parietal, and superior medial frontal regional pattern is activated in functional neuroimaging studies involving word generation (Cabeza & Nyberg 2000). Posterior superolateral temporal regions are also implicated (Wise et al. 1991). We were not able to assess this effect, as our patients' temporal lesions were anterior. Semantic fluency was impaired in all patient groups except for right posterior. Further differentiation of frontal and temporal effects can be derived from process analysis of the size of semantically related clusters of words generated on semantic fluency (related to left temporal lesions) and switching between clusters on either letter-based or semantic fluency, related to left DLPFC or superior medial frontal lesions (Troyer et al. 1998).

The formulation problems, or disorders of discourse, are generative and narrative in nature. They reflect problems in planning and goal attainment. At the level of sentence generation and spontaneous utilization of complex syntax, deficits have only been described with left-sided lesions. At the level of story narrative, lesions in left dorsolateral and prefrontal regions may produce impairments. Left-sided lesions result in simplification and repetition (perseveration) of sentence forms, and omissions of elements. Right-sided lesions cause amplification of details, wandering from the topic and insertion of irrelevant elements, and dysprosody, all leading to loss of narrative coherence (Joanette et al. 1990).

Control of Memory

In considering the role of the frontal lobes in memory, it is useful to distinguish between basic associative processes of cue-engram interaction (mediated by medial temporal lobe/hippocampal structures), and strategic processes involved in the coordination, elaboration, and interpretation of these associations (mediated by the frontal lobes) (Luria 1973, Moscovitch 1992). The role of the frontal lobes on memory tasks is one of control and direction, hence the phrase "working with memory" (Moscovitch & Winocur 1992). Damage to the frontal lobes (other than extension to basal forebrain areas) does not result in clinically diagnosed amnesia.

Given traditional neuropsychology's strength in assessing medial temporal lobe amnesic syndromes, early clinical memory tests were more suited to the measure of associative than strategic processes. This imbalance has persisted. Whereas current clinical neuropsychological memory tests such as the Wechsler Memory Scale (Wechsler 1997b) tap both associative and strategic processes, few attempts have been made to quantify these skills separately, causing the clinical neuropsychologist to resort to qualitative analysis in the interpretation of frontal lesion effects on memory. A major development in this respect is the California Verbal Learning

Test (Delis et al. 1987), an excellent example from the Boston Process Approach of modern clinical neuropsychology, which draws upon cognitive science to improve the specificity of neuropsychological assessment. This test includes measures of serial position learning, semantic organization, interference effects, cued recall, recognition, and response bias. Although similar measures are incorporated into the latest Wechsler Memory Scale revision (Wechsler 1997b), the verbal learning test in this battery contains semantically unrelated words, precluding analysis of semantic clustering.

The effects of frontal brain damage on these and other measures were studied by Stuss and colleagues (1994), who showed that subjective organization (pair-frequency), was specifically affected by frontal damage, although the intrafrontal lesion location was not a factor. Right DLPFC patients had increased intralist repetitions, possibly owing to a monitoring deficit. Category clustering deficits were not found, although these have been reported elsewhere (Gershberg & Shimamura 1995). As expected, frontal damage (especially on the left) affected encoding and retrieval. Contrary to clinical lore, recognition was also affected by frontal damage. Analysis of this effect revealed that it was related to subtle anomia in left DLPFC patients and subtle associative mnemonic deficits in patients with medial frontal damage extending to septal regions. A subsequent meta-analysis confirmed a small but significant role for the frontal lobes in recognition memory (Wheeler et al. 1995), but only on tests that had an organizational component such as categorized lists.

Focal lesion studies have demonstrated the importance of the frontal lobes on retrieval tasks in which monitoring, verification, and placement of information in temporal and spatial contexts are of critical importance (Milner et al. 1985, Stuss et al. 1994). Reduplication, confabulation, and focal retrograde amnesia, all disorders of faulty episodic retrieval, are associated with frontal lesions (Levine et al. 1998a, Moscovitch & Melo 1997, Moscovitch & Winocur 1995, Stuss et al. 1978). In the past decade, the role of the frontal lobes in memory has been greatly elaborated by functional neuroimaging studies (Cabeza & Nyberg 2000), which allow for separation of mnemonic processes not possible in straight behavioral research. Of particular importance is the role of the right frontal lobe in episodic memory retrieval (Tulving et al. 1994), which is consistent with the right lateralization often observed in neuropsychological patients with paramnestic disorders.

More recent imaging work has provided greater intrafrontal specificity in relation to retrieval success, retrieval monitoring, contextual recall, and material specificity (Cabeza & Nyberg 2000). In addition to the right hemispheric bias in retrieval, retrieval operations can also be distinguished according to relative DLPFC/VPFC involvement within the right hemisphere. VPFC is involved in retrieval cue specification, whereas DLPFC is involved in higher-level postretrieval monitoring operations (Fletcher et al. 1998, Petrides et al. 1995). This finding provided greater precision to the earlier patient work (Milner et al. 1991, Stuss et al. 1994) and later case studies (Schacter et al. 1996) on the nature and localization of right frontal executive control in memory retrieval.

Working Memory

Working memory is historically central to research on frontal lobe function (Fuster 1985, Goldman-Rakic 1987), beginning with the observation that monkeys with frontal lobe damage are deficient in making stimulus-guided responses after the stimulus is removed from view (Jacobsen 1936). After 65 years of research, however, the precise role of the frontal lobes in working memory tasks is still a matter of debate. Much of this debate is concerned with separation of working memory processes such as encoding strategies, storage/maintenance, rehearsal, interference control, inhibition, and scanning of working memory buffers (D'Esposito et al. 2000). These processes are addressed in experimental lesion or event-related functional neuroimaging research on working memory and attentional control.

For the purposes of clinical neuropsychological assessment, the important principles follow on those described for long-term memory above. As in long-term memory, the frontal lobes' primary role in working memory is in control and manipulation of information held on-line, hence Baddeley's notion of the "central executive" (Baddeley 1986). Whereas the frontal lobes are certainly involved in simple storage and maintenance, these operations are primarily mediated by posterior regions, such as the inferior parietal lobule ("slave systems") (Baddeley 1986, D'Esposito et al. 1995); frontal involvement increases as information held on-line is threatened by interference or exceeds working memory capacity (D'Esposito et al. 2000). The dorsolateral prefrontal cortex (DLPFC) appears to be preferentially involved in monitoring and manipulation (Owen et al. 1996). The role of the ventral prefrontal cortex (VPFC) is less clear, with hypotheses including maintenance, interference control, and inhibition (D'Esposito et al. 2000).

Working memory is important to many neuropsychological tests, but few widely used tasks seek to directly assess working memory per se. Digit span or spatial span tasks are important for determining working memory storage capacity, but do not provide information relating to rehearsal or executive control. Consistent with the neuroimaging evidence described above, a recent meta-analysis showed no evidence for an effect of frontal lobe lesions on digit or spatial span (D'Esposito & Postle 1999). Reversal of the sequences (e.g., digits backwards) does measure manipulation of information held on-line. Scoring methods that combine forward and backward span confound these capacity and manipulation measures. The latest updates of the Wechsler Instruments have added new tasks stressing manipulation and control (Wechsler 1997a,b) and even allow for a separate "working memory" composite score. This too combines the dissociable processes into a single measure, although the neuropsychologist is still able to examine the more demanding strategic subtests separately. The Brown-Peterson technique taps working memory control processes in the presence of interference (Stuss et al. 1982), and supraspan tests can be used to measure processing when working memory capacity is exceeded (see Lezak 1995 for description).

A modern approach would incorporate additional measures validated in the animal and human experimental literature. Delayed response tasks are among the most-studied tasks in the neuropsychological literature on frontal lobe functioning. Although they have been successfully transferred to clinical research (D'Esposito & Postle 1999, Oscar-Berman et al. 1991), there are many variations on these tasks and no standard administration procedures. The self-ordered pointing and conditional associative learning tests have been validated in both monkey and human focal lesion studies (Owen et al. 1990, Petrides 1989) and in functional neuroimaging studies of healthy adults (Owen et al. 1996; Petrides et al. 1993a,b). Self-ordered pointing requires the monitoring of past responses (such as which objects or spatial locations were selected in a spatial array) and planning of subsequent responses to prevent repetitions. Conditional associative learning requires the acquisition of arbitrary, fixed associations between members of a set of stimuli and a set of responses that are learned through a process of trial and error. Differences in functional localization of these tasks can be revealed through experimental lesion or functional neuroimaging studies, but both are sensitive to DLPFC dysfunction (albeit in different DLPFC regions) (Owen et al. 1990, Petrides 1989). In a sample of patients with focal DLPFC and VPFC lesions, we documented the specificity of conditional associative learning deficits to DLPFC lesions; patients with VPFC lesions were not impaired (Levine et al. 1997).

Anterior Attention Functions

The frontal lobes mediate attentional control in the top-down guidance and direction of other processes. Proper assessment of attentional deficits requires differentiation among distinct attentional processes that can be selectively impaired. Standard assessment is concerned with attentional switching, selective attention, and sustained attention, whereas modern assessment more finely fractionates anterior attentional systems.

ATTENTIONAL SWITCHING: THE WCST AND TRAIL MAKING TEST, PART B   Tests of sorting or grouping have a long history in the psychological assessment of concept formation. Multiple processes contribute to performance on these measures, including generation and identification of concepts, hypothesis testing, maintenance of attention, resistance to interference, utilization of feedback to guide behavior, and when more than one concept is possible, switching categories and inhibiting perseveration of prior categories. In her classic 1963 study, Milner documented a specific effect of frontal cortical lesions on the Wisconsin Card Sorting Test (WCST). In this test the patient must determine the established sorting criterion (color, form, or number) through a process of trial and error, then shift to a new criterion according to a change in examiner feedback. The WCST has since become the most widely used behavioral measure of frontal lobe function (Heaton et al. 1993). However, posterior damage can affect WCST performance (Anderson et al. 1991). In addition, functional neuroimaging studies indicate frontal and posterior activation in association with WCST performance (Berman et al. 1995).

The WCST has been embedded in a larger context of problem-solving by Dias and colleagues (1997). In this framework WCST shifts are regarded as extra-dimensional (across perceptual dimensions, such as from color to form, on the basis of feedback) as opposed intradimensional (shifting within a dimension, such as from red to blue). Extra-dimensional shifting is specifically affected by dorsolateral prefrontal damage in monkeys (Dias et al. 1996) and humans (Owen et al. 1993) and is associated with DLPFC activity in healthy adults (Rogers et al. 2000). This brain-behavior association is consistent with the original development work on the WCST involving patients with DLPFC damage. We directly assessed this DLPFC/VPFC dissociation using the WCST in a large sample of patients with focal lesions (Stuss et al. 2000). Consistent with the monkey data, which indicated that VPFC damage does not affect extra-dimensional shifting, patients with DLPFC lesions were impaired, whereas VPFC patients were not impaired. As noted in earlier work (Stuss et al. 1983), the VPFC patients were prone to loss of set, possibly owing to susceptibility to interference. Set loss was also observed in right DLPFC patients, related to poor sustained attention.

In summary, the classification and use of the WCST as a frontal measure is justified, but with a number of caveats. Within the frontal lobes, the DLPFC is preferentially involved in the set-shifting aspect of the task. Patients with VPFC damage are relatively intact on this key aspect of the WCST, but they are prone to the less frequently reported set loss errors. Finally, the WCST is not completely resistant to the effects of posterior damage. As with any test, similar errors can occur for different reasons, such as comprehension deficits.

Modern neuropsychological approaches to assessing task switching and other functions of sorting tests include the Cambridge Neuropsychological Test Automated Battery (CANTAB) (Robbins et al. 1994), which includes human analogues of the set-shifting paradigms described in the Dias et al. (1996, 1997) studies, and the California Card Sorting Test (CCST) (Delis et al. 1992). The latter presents a wider variety of verbal and visual sorting criteria (see also Levine et al. 1995b). The CCST incorporates standardized manipulations of environmental support, including identification of groupings executed by the examiner and generation of groupings according to cues. Similar cues can be applied in the WCST to investigate the extent to which deficits are due to self-initiated processes as opposed to a more basic deficit affecting perception or detection of the correct sorting criterion (Stuss et al. 2000). This information may be used to generate rehabilitation hypotheses.

The Trail Making Test, Part B (TMT-B), requiring alternating letter-number connecting, has also been used as a frontal test. Although it is interpreted as a measure of attentional switching, its functional and anatomical specificity is affected by several factors, including speed, visual search, and simultaneous maintenance of two sequences. Part A (TMT-A, number connection) is treated as a control for factors other than switching, but it is not well-matched to TMT-B in other respects (Rossini & Karl 1994). Interpretation is further complicated by the standard administration and scoring procedures in which errors and time are confounded. Early focal lesion studies failed to support the widely held claim that TMT-B is sensitive to frontal lesions (Reitan & Wolfson 1995, Stuss et al. 1981). In a direct test of this lesion-behavior relationship, we found that the timing measures were sensitive to frontal pathology, but the differential effect of frontal lesions on time to complete TMT-B was eliminated when this score was corrected for speed on TMT-A (Stuss et al. 2001a). Patients with DLPFC lesions, however, were distinguished from other patients on the basis of errors attributable to difficulties in attentional switching and maintenance of attention. VPFC patients were not impaired (Stuss et al. 2001a). TMT-B errors (but not time), therefore, are a valid measure of DLPFC dysfunction.

SELECTIVE ATTENTION: THE STROOP TEST   Deficient selective attention results in omitted responses to important stimuli or enhanced reactivity to irrelevant information. The Stroop test (Stroop 1935) includes a key demand on selective attention of a given response characteristic (i.e., color naming) to the exclusion of a more dominant one (i.e., word reading). The Stroop interference effect is among the most extensively studied phenomena in experimental psychology (MacLeod 1991), although the experimental work has had no discernable effect on clinical versions of the test. Lesion studies have emphasized right or left DLPFC effects on this measure (Perret 1974, Stuss et al. 1981, Vendrell et al. 1995), whereas functional neuroimaging studies have emphasized the role of medial frontal (in particular anterior cingulate) regions in performance on the Stroop interference condition (Bench et al. 1993, Pardo et al. 1990). In a large sample of focal lesion patients, we recently found that the deficit associated with left DLPFC damage could be accounted for by impaired color naming (rather than interference) (Stuss et al. 2001b). Patients with frontal damage were slowed on all three conditions. Patients with superior medial lesions (especially on the right) committed the most errors, corresponding to this region's role in maintaining the strength of an activated (selected) intention (Devinsky et al. 1995, Goldberg 1985). Inferior medial patients performed normally. The inconsistency with prior lesion research could be explained by the fact that the prior studies did not correct performance in the interference condition for slowing in the color naming condition.

SUSTAINED ATTENTION   There is a surprising lack of widely accepted measures for sustained attention (detection of targets over a prolonged time period) in traditional clinical neuropsychology. Whereas letter cancellation or other "vigilance" tasks are used (Lezak 1995), there are few data relating performance on these paper-and-pencil measures to frontal function. Continuous performance tests are sensitive to right frontal pathology, especially when the target complexity is increased (i.e., respond to "O" following "X"), as opposed to simple vigilance tasks (Reuckert & Grafman 1996, Wilkins et al. 1987) and are associated with right frontal activation in healthy adults (Deutsch et al. 1987, Pardo et al. 1991). Several investigators have highlighted the importance of dull, repetitive tasks in tapping top-down modulation of endogenous arousal (Robertson et al. 1997). Accordingly, slow sustained attention tasks are more sensitive to right frontal pathology than fast-paced ones (Reuckert & Grafman 1998, Wilkins et al. 1987). The Sustained Attention to Response Task (SART; Robertson et al. 1997) and the Elevator Counting Test

(Robertson et al. 1991) are modern neuropsychological tests of these sustained attention abilities stressing maintenance of endogenous arousal.

A COGNITIVE NEUROSCIENCE APPROACH TO ANTERIOR ATTENTION SYSTEMS   The Supervisory Attention System as proposed by Norman & Shallice (1986) distinguished between routine tasks as mediated by contention scheduling and novel, nonroutine tasks in which unmodulated contention scheduling is likely to generate errors, requiring supervisory top-down control (Shallice & Burgess 1993). Although the Supervisory Attention System has been useful for framing problems in frontal lobe research, it is considered to be underspecified in its original form (Shallice & Burgess 1996). Stuss and colleagues (1995) refined an approach to anterior attentional systems by describing five independent supervisory processes: energizing schemata, inhibiting schemata, adjusting contention scheduling, monitoring schema activity level, and control of if-then processes. These control processes are demonstrated in seven attentional tasks: sustaining, concentrating, sharing, suppressing, switching, preparing, and setting.

Context is an important variable in assessing attention. In the WCST we demonstrated that a little information for patients with ventral damage was more destructive than no information (Stuss et al. 2000). We manipulated context by relatively small changes in task difficulty in a "select-what, respond where" attentional task (Stuss et al. 1999). Three different measures of attention were assessed (interference, negative priming, and inhibition of return) across three levels of task difficulty. In certain groups of patients, the brain areas impaired with each attentional measure varied with the task difficulty. For example, when task complexity was manipulated, inhibitory deficits (negative priming) were shown to be related to different regions of the frontal lobe. When the task was simple, deficits were more focally limited to right posterior and right frontal lobe damage. When the task became more complex, impairment was observed after damage in most frontal brain regions (but not all posterior brain regions, in contrast).

Overall Summary

Executive functions, higher-level cognitive functions involved in the control and regulation of lower cognitive operations, are clinically assessed by a small battery of tests that, on the basis of putative sensitivity to frontal damage, are referred to as "frontal." Support for the validity of this claim is variable. There is evidence for the sensitivity of these measures to right or left DLPFC, and in many instances to superior medial area lesions. In some cases this claim is supported by functional neuroimaging data. Because these tests are complex and multifactorial, they do not specifically assess frontal function. Both lesion and functional neuroimaging evidence indicate recruitment of posterior regions involved in the basic linguistic or perceptual operations of the task. Moreover, task complexity could affect which regions of the frontal lobes were involved. As a general rule for some processes, the more complex the function, the more frontal brain regions involved (Stuss et al. 1994, 1999).

In general, modern cognitive neuroscience findings have failed to penetrate clinical assessment of executive functions. The incorporation of measures with greater psychological and anatomical specificity into modern clinical neuropsychology would improve executive functioning assessment. Whether modern or standard, however, a very consistent finding is the relative insensitivity of these measures to VPFC damage.

EMOTIONS, SELF-AWARENESS, AND SOCIAL BEHAVIOR: VENTRAL AND POLAR FRONTAL CORTEX

Functions mediated by VPFC and polar frontal cortex can be considered superordinate for their role in defining human individuality and high level personal decision making and social behavior. Damage to these regions may result in changes so significant that the individual is considered not to be the same person, as in Harlow's classic description of Phineas Gage: "he was no longer Gage." These functions are not properly addressed in standard clinical neuropsychological assessment. Patients with VPFC damage can appear normal on frontal tests of DLPFC functions. Extensive experimental work on this region is important for understanding the basic operations contributing to self-aware behavior. This section suggests that the disorders of self-awareness can be dissociated and that different assessment approaches provide us with different information about the patient.

The critical regions for emotions are located in the subcortical medial wall of the brain: the hippocampal formation including the olfactory apparatus, the gyrus cinguli, mamillary body, hypothalamus, anterior thalamus, amygdala, substantia innominata, midbrain, basal ganglia, and their interconnections (Papez 1937, Watanabe 1998). The area most commonly and strongly related to human emotional and social behavior is the frontal lobes. Connections of the subcortical emotional regions with the prefrontal cortices (the biochemical substrate is admirably described in Arnsten & Robbins 2002) play a critical role in emotional reactions and responsiveness, representing the end point for the interpretation of external percepts (Nauta 1979, Pandya & Barnes 1987), merged with visceral input (Nauta 1973) and integrated with emotional states for the preparation and execution of responses (Mesulam 1985). It is in the frontal lobes, with perhaps a preeminent role of the right frontal lobe, that the complete integration of subjective experience in a fully self-aware person is achieved. We postulate that, at the clinical level, distinction can be made between the effects of ventral medial prefrontal cortex and frontal polar regions.

Emotions, Reinforcement, Self-Regulation, and Decision-Making

LOWER LEVEL OPERATIONS: VENTRAL FRONTAL INVOLVEMENT IN REWARD AND INHIBITION   The ventral prefrontal cortex is intimately connected with more primitive limbic nuclei involved in emotional processing (Nauta 1971, Pandya & Barnes

1987) and processes of information about basic drives and rewards that inform and direct high-level decision-making. Animal work stresses the VPFC's involvement in the acquisition and reversal of stimulus-reward associations (Fuster 1997, Mishkin 1964, Rolls 2000). A double dissociation between VPFC lesion effects on reversal learning (interpreted as affective) and DLPFC lesion effects on attentional (extra-dimensional) set-shifting was reported in the monkey research on set-shifting reported above (Dias et al. 1996, 1997). Similar dissociations have been reported in human research in both focal lesion studies (Freedman et al. 1998) and functional neuroimaging studies of healthy adults (Nagahama et al. 2001).

DECISION-MAKING   More recently, the emphasis has shifted to higher level decision-making tasks involving reward processing in unstructured situations—tasks more in line with distinctly human capacities. One such example is the gambling task developed by Bechara and colleagues (1994) that is both sensitive and specific to VPFC lesions (Bechara et al. 1998). Performance on this task has been dissociated from deficits in working memory and inhibition (Bechara et al. 1998). The gambling results have been interpreted within the Somatic Marker Hypothesis (Damasio et al. 1991), which states that human reasoning is normally constrained by emotional biases acquired through previous conditioning, mediated by the ventromedial prefrontal cortex. Similar findings in patients (Rogers et al. 1999a) and healthy adults using functional neuroimaging (Rogers et al. 1999b) have been found using a different gambling task with parametric manipulation of reward ratios. Separate functional neuroimaging studies have also noted VPFC activation in response to tasks in which choices must be made in under-specified situations (Elliott et al. 2000).

STRATEGIC SELF-REGULATION   The involvement of the VPFC in inhibition, emotion, and reward processing suggests a role in behavioral self-regulation, as shown in numerous case studies of patients with VPFC lesions (Eslinger & Damasio 1985, Harlow 1868). We have used the term "self-regulatory disorder" (SRD) as shorthand for the syndrome exhibited by these patients. SRD is defined as the inability to regulate behavior according to internal goals and constraints. It arises from the inability to hold a mental representation of the self on-line and to use this self-related information to inhibit inappropriate responses (Levine 1999; Levine et al. 1998a, 1999). SRD is most apparent in unstructured situations (e.g., child-rearing, making a major purchase, or occupational decision-making), in which patients fail to inhibit inappropriate responses in favor of those responses that might result in a preferential long-term outcome. This is contrasted with structured situations in which environmental cues or over-learned routines determine the appropriate response (Shallice & Burgess 1993), which is often the case for standard neuropsychological tests. As a result, many patients with SRD appear unimpaired in over-learned, structured situations in spite of significant real-life upheaval (Mesulam 1986, Stuss & Benson 1986).

Shallice & Burgess (1991) attained laboratory concordance of real life SRD in VPFC patients using naturalistic multiple subgoal tasks, setting a quantitative standard for deficits that had heretofore been limited to qualitative description. Subsequent studies in our laboratories and elsewhere have further established the use of such tasks in patients with brain damage (Burgess et al. 1998, 2000; Goel et al. 1997; Levine et al. 2000, 1998b; Schwartz et al. 1999).

Our Strategy Application Test, based on the Six Element Test of the Shallice & Burgess (1991) study, is a paper-and-pencil laboratory task of SRD that requires the selection of targets with high payoff to the exclusion of readily available, but lesser-valued, targets. Every patient with focal VPFC damage (particularly on the right) was impaired (Levine et al. 1998b), despite preserved performance on other tests described above that are sensitive to DLPFC damage (Levine et al. 1995a, 1997). We subsequently revised the test to increase its sensitivity to VPFC damage (Levine et al. 2000). This was accomplished by fostering a response (completion of all items in a sequential manner) applicable early in the task but not as the task progressed, forcing a shift in strategy (selective completion of certain items to the exclusion of other items) to maintain efficiency. In other words, efficient performance depended upon inhibition or reversal of the response pattern reinforced at the beginning of the test (see Figure 2). As in the more basic reversal learning paradigms, this process contrasts with attentional set-shifting (across stimulus dimensions, tapped by the

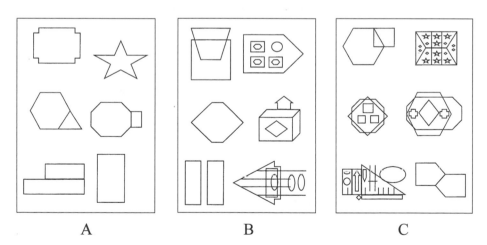

A   B   C

Figure 2   Sample items from the revised Strategy Application Task (R-SAT) (Levine et al. 1999, 2000). On the early pages (*A*), all items can be traced in 5–10 s. As the subject progresses through the task, items increase in duration to completion but not in difficulty of completion (*B* and *C*). Given limited time and an equal amount of points per item, the best strategy is to inhibit the tendency to do all items (established on early pages) in favor of selective completion of brief items on later pages. The test is constructed so that brief items are always available. Subjects are also to complete similarly constructed sentence copying and simple counting items (not shown).

WCST). Initial studies on the revised version of the test (R-SAT) have documented sensitivity and specificity to severe traumatic brain injury (Levine et al. 2000), which causes VPFC damage (Courville 1937). As tasks of this sort are designed to more closely approximate real-life situations than standard neuropsychological tests that are highly structured and examiner-guided, they should be related to real life SRD as measured by outcome questionnaires. In our sample of traumatic brain injury patients, R-SAT performance was significantly related to patients' endorsement of everyday problems in functioning on an outcome questionnaire (Levine et al. 2000; see Burgess et al. 1998 for a similar finding). Replication and extension of these findings in patients with focal lesions and frontotemporal dementia is ongoing.

Episodic Memory, Self-Awareness, and Autonoetic Consciousness

Solid evidence for the role of the frontal lobes in self-awareness derives from memory research. Tulving and colleagues (1994) proposed a hemispheric encoding-retrieval asymmetry model of memory based on functional neuroimaging studies in normal subjects. In simplest terms, left frontal lobe activation is primarily associated with memory encoding, and right frontal lobe activation is primarily associated with retrieval of episodic memories. Episodic memories are those temporally tagged memories that are personally relevant and emotionally salient to the individual. Such memories appear to depend on the autonoetic ("self-knowing") (Tulving 1985) processes—the mental models and self-reflectiveness of the right frontal lobe—that also underlie self-awareness (Wheeler et al. 1997).

Other research supports a preeminent role of the right frontal lobe for personal memory. For example, self-reflective memory is related to right frontal activation (Craik et al. 1999). The right prefrontal and other right hemisphere regions are activated when retrieving emotional memories from the past (Fink et al. 1996). False memories have been shown to be dependent upon subjective feelings that the false information had been previously learned (Loftus & Prickrell 1995). The occurrence of such false memories has been related to right frontal lobe damage (as well as medial temporal lobes) (Melo et al. 1999, Schacter et al. 1996) and right frontal functional imaging activation (Schacter & Curran 1995).

Several dramatic case studies demonstrate the value of the combined anatomical, theoretical, case, and group study approaches in evaluating the effects of right focal frontal lobe damage. Capgras Syndrome (Capgras & Reboul-Lachaux 1923) is defined as a selective and persistent delusion in which a familiar person has been duplicated by a patient (see also Pick 1903). Alexander et al. (1979) described a patient who had suffered a severe traumatic brain injury and, upon eventual recovery, insisted that his wife and four children constituted a new family different from his "first" family, albeit very similar. His neuropsychological test profile revealed no impairment on tests of basic cognitive functioning (memory, basic attention, IQ, etc.) but significant deficits in frontal cognitive tests. He had suffered significant right frontal and right temporal damage. If presented the scenario as if another person had described it, the patient concluded that the situation was "unbeliev able." An in depth review of the recovery course revealed that the reduplicative paramnesia surfaced after the patient had his first visits home about 10 months after the accident. At that time he had recovered sufficiently to be allowed home for a visit, although he still suffered from significant memory and attention deficits. His teenage children had grown notably, the family had a new car, and the wife had altered her hairstyle. It was hypothesized (Stuss 1991, Stuss & Alexander 1999) that the warmth, immediacy, and saliency of that visit home "affectively burnt in" these memories, becoming episodic past memories that define a person. When the patient recovered, he now had two episodic memories of two similar but different families that could not be reconciled owing to his significant and persisting frontal lobe deficits in judgment. The importance of the right frontal lobe in such patients has been repeatedly confirmed (e.g., Hakim et al. 1988, Malloy & Duffy 1994).

We described another patient who had lost all personal past memories after traumatic brain injury (Levine et al. 1998a). That is, he had virtually no episodic memory for pre-injury events, whereas semantic facts about his previous life were retained or relearned. The investigations were driven by theoretical knowledge of the characteristics and anatomical basis of episodic memory. Detailed structural magnetic resonance imaging (MRI) investigations demonstrated a right VPFC lesion that affected frontotemporal connectivity (uncinate fasciculus). New memories about his life after the injury were learned, but these were recalled without any affective valence; that is, they were not episodic in nature. This effect was quantified with the remember/know technique, a self-report measure proposed by Tulving (Tulving 1985; see also Gardiner 1988) to assess episodic reexperiencing. An $H_2^{15}0$ positron emission tomography (PET) study of cued recall revealed that, relative to carefully matched healthy controls and traumatic brain injury patients without retrograde amnesia, anterograde learning and memory were accomplished with reduced right frontal polar activation and increased left hippocampal activation, supporting the hypothesis of impoverished episodic and normal (or enhanced) semantic processes (Levine 1998a).

This case highlighted the need to assess autobiographical memory, including episodic reexperiencing. Lack of standardized assessment in this case led to delayed recognition of his syndrome and even accusations of malingering. The most widely used measure of autobiographical memory is the Autobiographical Memory Interview (Kopelman et al. 1989). This measure includes a thorough assessment of personal semantics (i.e., facts about oneself) as well as elicitation of personal episodes with a qualitative scoring system for separate quantification of autobiographical episodic memory. Moscovitch et al. (1999) described a more detailed protocol analysis.

Another level of self-awareness was revealed by our experience with two patients who had focal right frontal brain damage from two different etiologies (Stuss 1991, Stuss & Alexander 2000). In both there was excellent neurological, functional, and cognitive recovery with intelligence being normal or superior.

Performance on executive tests was normal/superior in one, and only mildly impaired in the other. Both patients could clearly identify their failings, exhibited concern about their problems, and could identify appropriate corrections to the problems. Neither, however, could return to their high-level executive work. The deficits in these patients were not at the level of executive control. Rather, they had a lack of real understanding of the implications of the problems and an inability to act in their own self-interest, despite knowing what to do and at least verbalizing an intent to change. These patients lack a mental model, not of the world, but of their own capacities and role in the world. The discrepancy between their mental model and their experience leaves them without a purpose or ability to organize perceptions and actions for future goals.

Empathy, Sympathy, and Humor

The important role of the right frontal lobe in emotional function suggested by the case studies can be demonstrated experimentally. For example, empathetic psychiatrists showed greater right frontal electrophysiological activation than those less empathetic in therapy (Alpert et al. 1980). During an event arguably associated with potent emotional responsiveness (orgasm), the greatest metabolic activation measured by PET was in the right frontal lobe (Tiihonen et al. 1994).

Two studies have emphasized the potential importance of more polar areas. The appreciation of humor requires the integration of cognition and emotions. When patients with focal lesions throughout the frontal and posterior brain regions were tested on their ability to appreciate jokes and cartoons and to rank how funny humorous sayings were, one group stood out as most impaired: those with right frontal lobe damage, in particular the more medial polar, somewhat more superior, region representing Brodmann Areas 8, 9, and probably parts of 10 (Shammi & Stuss 1999). Moreover, it was the same right frontal group that exhibited the least spontaneous affective responses. The significant correlation of performance with specific cognitive functions (e.g., verbal humor with verbal abstraction ability and mental shifting; cartoon humor with the ability to focus attention to details and to perform visual search effectively) strongly suggested that different systems were necessary for different tasks, but that there was a final common area necessary for humor appreciation. Event-related functional MRI data of normal individuals showed similar results (Goel & Dolan 2001). There were differential systems related to different types of humor tasks, and a "central reward" system with maximum activation in the ventral medial prefrontal region bilaterally and Brodmann Areas 10 and 11 (Goel & Dolan 2001). These imaging data suggest that the functions of the right frontal region may be "preeminent" rather than dominant in relation to self-awareness.

The concept of self-awareness implies a metacognitive representation of one's own mental states, beliefs, attitudes, and experiences. It is this self-reflecting ability that is the basis for understanding the relationship of one's own thoughts and external events, and to understanding the mental states of others. This ability to make inferences about the world, and to empathize with others, allows us to interpret mental states properly and to make social judgments. The neuropsychological basis of this "theory of mind" was tested in focal lesioned patients (Stuss et al. 2001c). On a simple perspective-taking task it was only patients with frontal lobe damage, with some suggestion of a more important role of the right frontal lobe, who were impaired. Detection of deception was impaired after medial frontal lesions, again with a preeminence of the right ventral region. Impairment of abstract awareness of emotions and expectations has been described after right hemisphere damage (Winner et al. 1998). Trauma to the right orbitofrontal region, including orbito-frontal cortex, resulted in significant social aberration in a case study, hypothesized to be based on the ability to generate expectations of others' negative reactions (Blair & Cipolotti 2000).

Functional imaging studies in neurologically intact individuals demonstrated specific right orbitofrontal activation in a task (Baron-Cohen et al. 1994). Whereas ventral and inferior medial damage are frequently observed, the preeminence of the right over the left is not always observed (Fletcher et al. 1995, Goel et al. 1995; see also Stone et al. 1998). Impaired theory of mind was reported in a patient treated with stereotactic anterior capsulotomy (Happe et al. 2001). These data suggest various possible explanations: roles of different brain regions in a functional/anatomical system, differences in processes required to complete the various tasks, variations in the areas of lesions represented among the patients tested, and possible preeminence rather than hemispheric dominance. Regardless, the overlap between the lesion and imaging data is still striking (Shallice 2001) (see Figure 3).

Clinical Implications

Disruption in self-regulation, self-awareness, and social cognition produces a profound alteration in real-life functioning and life quality outcome. These behavioral changes are not limited to the patient; they greatly affect families who must cope with their changed loved one. Although we have illustrated these concepts with dramatic case studies, less dramatic versions of these deficits are likely more common than is currently appreciated but are not revealed for lack of assessment methods (Levine 1999).

So what is today's neuropsychologist to do? Tests of reversal learning and inhibition sensitive to VPFC dysfunction can be readily administered in the laboratory. Tests mimicking real-life unstructured situations with no right or wrong answers (the Gambling test, the R-SAT, or the Six Element Test) are increasingly available. It is also possible to assess real-life functioning with outcome questionnaires, such as the Dysexecutive Questionnaire (Burgess et al. 1996), which includes parallel forms for self- and significant-other ratings. In the realm of memory, the remember/know technique (Tulving 1985) provides a useful self-report of the quality of autonoetic reexperiencing that defines episodic memory and can be easily applied to standard recognition memory tests. Autobiographical memory should be assessed, with emphasis on autobiographical reexperiencing in addition to personal

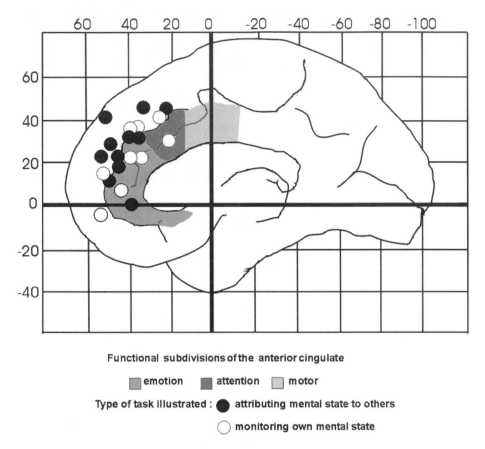

Functional subdivisions of the anterior cingulate

□ emotion   ■ attention   □ motor

Type of task illustrated :   ● attributing mental state to others

○ monitoring own mental state

Figure 3 Location of peak activation in medial prefrontal regions during tasks in which subjects think about their own or others' mental states (C. Frith, personal communication, published in Shallice 2001). This is an updated version of the analysis presented in Frith & Frith (1999). (Reprinted with permission from the author and Oxford University Press.)

semantic knowledge. Finally, it is important to be aware of which patients are most likely to present with these deficits: those with VPFC and polar damage. The highest prevalence of this damage is in traumatic brain injury.

CONCLUSIONS

We have emphasized that adult clinical neuropsychology has evolved through many stages, with different approaches to assessment. Each school has had value, and each is still useful if the question being asked demands that approach. Through the example of recent findings about the frontal lobes, however, we hope we have illustrated that the future of adult clinical neuropsychology lies in an approach that is driven by current cognitive and affective psychological theories, is flexible in the design used (e.g., case study, group comparisons), and takes advantage of the most current methods (e.g., structural imaging for lesion location, various imaging modalities). The most recent findings on the role of the right frontal lobe being key to some of the highest human faculties required all of the above. This brain region has been notoriously nonresponsive to the probing of neuropsychological assessment, a fact considered by many neurosurgeons in their decisions about neurosurgical approaches.

There is an obvious clinical downside—the advocated approach when applied recklessly can lead to the use of tests that do not meet the psychometric criteria. As noted by Russell (1986), however, psychologists are well trained to contribute the psychometrics to the evaluation of brain and behavior. An important goal for future research will be to apply these skills to the analysis of not only the cognitive operations of the brain, but also the emotional and social processes that define us as human. Our contention, however, is not only that the "what" of assessment should not be lost at the expense of the "how," but that it should even precede the "how."

Functional imaging studies, and the lesion research using well-defined patients with damage in different regions, provide different information for use in adult clinical neuropsychology. Lesion research can indicate what brain regions are necessary for a task; imaging research informs us about what areas are involved. Both have clearly demonstrated that neuropsychological assessment must be done in the light of systems and processes (not just brain localization), and context (e.g., variations in task difficulty). In this light, the information provided on localization of processes is for theoretical purposes. The extension to clinical use must be made with caution.

ACKNOWLEDGMENTS

The authors' research reported in this grant was funded primarily by the Canadian Institutes of Health Research and the Ontario Mental Health Foundation. D. Stuss is the Reva James Leeds Chair in neuroscience and research leadership, Baycrest Centre for Geriatric Care, University of Toronto. We are grateful to Drs. M. Moscovitch and William P. Milberg for feedback on early drafts. S. Hevenor, D. Derkzen, and A. Borowiec assisted in manuscript preparation.

Visit the Annual Reviews home page at www.AnnualReviews.org

LITERATURE CITED

Alexander GE, DeLong MR, Strick PL. 1986. Parallel organization of functionally segregated circuits linking basal ganglia and cortex. *Annu. Rev. Neurosci.* 9:357–81

Alexander MP, Stuss DT, Benson DF. 1979.

Capgras syndrome: a reduplicative phenomenon. *Neurology* 29:334–39

Alexander MP, Benson DF, Stuss DT. 1989. Frontal lobes and language. *Brain Lang.* 37:656–91

Alpert M, Cohen NL, Martz M, Robinson C. 1980. Electroencephalographic analysis: a methodology for evaluating psychotherapeutic process. *Psychiatry Res.* 2:323–29

Anderson SW, Damasio H, Jones RD, Tranel D. 1991. Wisconsin Card Sorting Test performance as a measure of frontal lobe damage. *J. Clin. Exp. Neuropsychol.* 13:909–22

Arnsten A, Robbins T. 2002. Neurochemical modulation of prefrontal cortical functions in humans and animals. See Stuss & Knight 2002. In press

Baddeley A. 1986. *Working Memory.* Oxford: Clarendon

Barbas H. 1995. Anatomic basis of cognitive-emotional interactions in the primate prefrontal cortex. *Neurosci. Biobehav. Rev.* 19:499–510

Baron-Cohen S, Ring H, Moriatry J, Schmitz B, Costa D, Ell P. 1994. Recognition of mental state terms. Clinical findings in children with autism and a functional neuroimaging study of normal adults. *Br. J. Psychiatry* 165:640–49

Bechara A, Damasio AR, Damasio H, Anderson SW. 1994. Insensitivity to future consequences following damage to human prefrontal cortex. *Cognition* 50:7–15

Bechara A, Damasio H, Tranel D, Anderson SW. 1998. Dissociation of working memory from decision making within the human prefrontal cortex. *J. Neurosci.* 18:428–37

Bench CJ, Frith CD, Grasby PM, Friston KJ, Paulesu E, et al. 1993. Investigations of the functional anatomy of attention using the Stroop test. *Neuropsychologia* 31:907–22

Benton AL. 1967. Problems of test construction in the field of aphasia. *Cortex* 3:32–58

Berman KF, Ostrem JL, Randolph C, Gold J, Goldberg TE, et al. 1995. Physiological activation of a cortical network during performance of the Wisconsin Card Sorting Test: a positron emission tomography study. *Neuropsychologia* 33:1027–46

Blair RJR, Cipolotti L. 2000. Impaired social response reversal: a case of 'acquired sociopathy.' *Brain* 123:1122–41

Boller F, Grafman J, eds. 1994. *Handbook of Neuropsychology.* Amsterdam: Elsevier

Burgess PW, Alderman N, Evans J, Emslie H, Wilson BA. 1998. The ecological validity of tests of executive function. *J. Int. Neuropsychol. Soc.* 4:547–58

Burgess PW, Alderman N, Evans JJ, Wilson BA, Emslie H. 1996. The Dysexecutive Questionnaire. In *Behavioral Assessment of the Dysexecutive Syndrome,* ed. BA Wilson, N Alderman, PW Burgess, H Emslie, JJ Evans. Bury St. Edmunds, UK: Thames Valley Test Co.

Burgess PW, Veitch E, de Lacy Costello A, Shallice T. 2000. The cognitive and neuroanatomical correlates of multitasking. *Neuropsychologia* 38:848–63

Cabeza R, Nyberg L. 2000. Imaging cognition. II. An empirical review of 275 PET and fMRI studies. *J. Cogn. Neurosci.* 12:1–47

Capgras J, Reboul-Lachaux J. 1923. L'illusion des sosies dans un délire systematisé chronique. *Bull. Soc. Clin. Med. Ment.* 2:6–16

Carmichael S, Price J. 1995. Limbic connections of the orbital and medial prefrontal cortex in macaque monkeys. *J. Comp. Neurol.* 363:615–41

Christensen A-L. 1979. *Luria's Neuropsychological Investigation.* Copenhagen: Munksgaard

Courville CB. 1937. *Pathology of the Central Nervous System.* Mountain View, CA: Pacific Press

Craik FIM, Moroz TM, Moscovitch M, Stuss DT, Winocur G, et al. 1999. In search of the self: a positron emission tomography study. *Psychol. Sci.* 10:27–35

Crockett D, Campbell C, Klonoff H. 1981. Introduction: an overview of neuropsychology. See Filskov & Boll 1981, pp. 1–37

Cummings J. 1993. Frontal-subcortical circuits and human behavior. *Arch. Neurol.* 50:873–80

Damasio AR, Tranel D, Damasio HC. 1991. Somatic markers and the guidance of behavior: theory and preliminary testing. See Levin et al. 1991, pp. 217–29

Delis DC, Kramer JH, Kaplan E, Ober BA.

1987. *California Verbal Learning Test: Adult Version*. San Antonio, TX: Psychol. Corp.

Delis DC, Squire LR, Bihrle A, Massman P. 1992. Componential analysis of problem-solving ability: performance of patients with frontal lobe damage and amnesic patients on a new sorting test. *Neuropsychologia* 30:683–97

D'Esposito M, Detre JA, Alsop DC, Shin RK, Atlas S, Grossman M. 1995. The neural basis of the central executive system of working memory. *Nature* 378:279–81

D'Esposito M, Postle BR. 1999. The dependence of span and delayed-response performance on prefrontal cortex. *Neuropsychologia* 37:1303–15

D'Esposito M, Postle BR, Rypma B. 2000. Prefrontal cortical contributions to working memory: evidence from event-related fMRI studies. *Exp. Brain Res.* 133:3–11

Deutsch G, Papanicolaou AC, Bourbon WT, Eisenberg HM. 1987. Cerebral blood flow evidence of right frontal activation in attention demanding tasks. *Int. J. Neurosci.* 36:23–28

Devinsky O, Morrell MJ, Vogt BA. 1995. Contributions of the anterior cingulate to behaviour. *Brain* 118:279–306

Dias R, Robbins TW, Roberts AC. 1996. Dissociation in prefrontal cortex of affective and attentional shifts. *Nature* 380:69–72

Dias R, Robbins TW, Roberts AC. 1997. Dissociable forms of inhibitory control within prefrontal cortex with an analog of the Wisconsin Card Sort Test: restriction to novel situations and independence from "on–line" processing. *J. Neurosci.* 17:9285–97

Elliott R, Dolan RJ, Frith CD. 2000. Dissociable functions in the medial and lateral orbitofrontal cortex: evidence from human neuroimaging studies. *Cereb. Cortex* 10:308–17

Eslinger PJ, Damasio AR. 1985. Severe disturbance of higher cognition after bilateral frontal lobe ablation: patient EVR. *Neurology* 35:1731–41

Filskov SB, Boll TJ, eds. 1981. *Handbook of Clinical Neuropsychology*. Vol. 1. New York: Wiley

Filskov SB, Boll TJ, eds. 1986. *Handbook of Clinical Neuropsychology*, Vol. 2. New York: Wiley

Fink GR, Markowitsch HJ, Reinkemeier M, Bruckbauer T, Kessler J, Heiss W. 1996. Cerebral representation of one's own past: neural networks involved in autobiographical memory. *J. Neurosci.* 16:4275–82

Fletcher PC, Happe F, Frith U, Baker SC, Dolan RJ, et al. 1995. Other minds in the brain: a functional imaging study of "theory of mind" in story comprehension. *Cognition* 57:109–28

Fletcher PC, Shallice T, Frith CD, Frackowiak RS, Dolan RJ. 1998. The functional roles of prefrontal cortex in episodic memory. II. Retrieval. *Brain* 121:1249–56

Freedman M, Alexander MP, Naeser MA. 1984. The anatomic basis of transcortical motor aphasia. *Neurology* 34:409–17

Freedman M, Black S, Ebert P, Binns M. 1998. Orbitofrontal function, object alternation and perseveration. *Cereb. Cortex* 8:18–27

Frith CD, Frith U. 1999. Interacting minds—a biological basis. *Science* 286:1692–95

Fuster JM. 1985. The prefrontal cortex, mediator of cross-temporal contingencies. *Hum. Neurobiol.* 4:169–79

Fuster JM. 1997. *The Prefrontal Cortex: Anatomy, Physiology, and Neuropsychology of the Frontal Lobe*. New York: Raven

Gardiner JM. 1988. Functional aspects of recollective experience. *Mem. Cogn.* 16:309–13

Gershberg FB, Shimamura AP. 1995. Impaired use of organizational strategies in free recall following frontal lobe damage. *Neuropsychologia* 33:1305–33

Goel V, Dolan RJ. 2001. The functional anatomy of humor: segregating cognitive and affective components. *Nat. Neurosci.* 4:237–38

Goel V, Grafman J, Sadato N, Hallett M. 1995. Modeling other minds. *NeuroReport* 6:1741–46

Goel V, Grafman J, Tajik J, Gana S, Danto D. 1997. A study of the performance of patients with frontal lobe lesions in a financial planning task. *Brain* 120:1805–22

Goldberg G. 1985. Supplementary motor area

structure and function: review and hypothesis. *Behav. Brain Sci.* 8:567–616

Golden CJ. 1981. A standardized version of Luria's neuropsychological tests: a quantitative and qualitative approach to neuropsychological evaluation. See Filskov & Boll 1981, pp. 608–44

Goldman-Rakic PS. 1987. Circuitry of primate prefrontal cortex and regulation of behavior by representational memory. In *Handbook of Physiology: The Nervous System*, ed. F Plum, V Mountcastle, pp. 373–417. Bethesda, MD: Am. Physiol. Soc.

Goldstein K. 1934/1995. *The Organism: A Holistic Approach to Biology Derived from Pathological Data in Man.* Cambridge, MA: MIT Press

Hakim H, Verma NP, Greiffenstein MF. 1988. Pathogenesis of reduplicative paramnesia. *J. Neurol. Neurosurg. Psychiatry* 51:839–41

Halstead WC. 1947. *Brain and Intelligence: A Quantitative Study of the Frontal Lobes.* Chicago: Univ. Chicago Press

Happe F, Malhi GS, Checkley S. 2001. Acquired mind blindness following frontal lobe surgery? A single case study of impaired 'theory of mind' in a patient treated with stereotactic anterior capsulotomy. *Neuropsychologia* 39:83–90

Harlow JM. 1868. Recovery after severe injury to the head. *Publications Mass. Med. Soc.* 2:327–46

Heaton RK, Chelune GJ, Talley JL, Kay GG, Curtiss G. 1993. *Wisconsin Card Sorting Test Manual: Revised and Expanded.* Odessa, FL: Psychol. Assess. Resour. 230 pp.

Heilman KM, Valenstein E. 1985. Introduction. In *Clinical Neuropsychology*, ed. KM Heilman, E Valenstein, pp. 3–21. New York: Oxford Univ. Press

Jacobsen CF. 1936. Studies of cerebral function in primates. *Comp. Psychol. Monogr.* 13:1–68

Joanette Y, Goulet P, Hannequin D. 1990. *Right Hemisphere and Verbal Communication.* New York: Springer-Verlag

Kaplan E. 1988. A process approach to neuropsychological assessment. In *Clinical Neuropsychology and Brain Function: Research, Measurement, and Practice*, ed. T Boll, BK Bryant, pp. 129–67. Washington, DC: Am. Psychol. Assoc.

Kopelman MD, Wilson BA, Baddeley AD. 1989. The autobiographical memory interview: a new assessment of autobiographical and personal semantic memory in amnesic patients. *J. Clin. Exp. Neuropsychol.* 11:724–44

Levin H, Eisenberg H, Benton A, eds. 1991. *Frontal Lobe Function and Dysfunction.* New York: Oxford Univ. Press

Levine B. 1999. Self-regulation and autonoetic consciousness. See Tulving 1999, pp. 200–14

Levine B, Black SE, Cabeza R, Sinden M, McIntosh AR, et al. 1998a. Episodic memory and the self in a case of retrograde amnesia. *Brain* 121:1951–73

Levine B, Dawson D, Boutet I, Schwartz ML, Stuss DT. 2000. Assessment of strategic self-regulation in traumatic brain injury: its relationship to injury severity and psychosocial outcome. *Neuropsychology* 14:491–500

Levine B, Freedman M, Dawson D, Black SE, Stuss DT. 1999. Ventral frontal contribution to self-regulation: convergence of episodic memory and inhibition. *Neurocase* 5:263–75

Levine B, Stuss DT, Milberg WP. 1995a. Concept generation performance in normal aging and frontal dysfunction: preliminary validation of a clinical test. *J. Int. Neuropsychol. Soc.* 1:208

Levine B, Stuss DT, Milberg WP. 1995b. Concept generation: validation of a test of executive functioning in a normal aging population. *J. Clin. Exp. Neuropsychol.* 17:740–58

Levine B, Stuss DT, Milberg WP. 1997. Effects of aging on conditional associative learning: process analyses and comparison with focal frontal lesions. *Neuropsychology* 11:367–81

Levine B, Stuss DT, Milberg WP, Alexander MP, Schwartz M, Macdonald R. 1998b. The effects of focal and diffuse brain damage on strategy application: evidence from focal lesions, traumatic brain injury, and normal aging. *J. Int. Neuropsychol. Soc.* 4:247–64

Lezak MD. 1983. *Neuropsychological Assessment.* New York: Oxford Univ. Press

Lezak MD. 1995. *Neuropsychological Assessment.* New York: Oxford Univ. Press. 2nd ed.

Loftus EF, Prickrell JE. 1995. The formulation of false memories. *Psychol. Ann.* 25:720–25

Luria AR. 1973. *The Working Brain. An Introduction to Neuropsychology.* New York: Basic Books

Luria AR. 1980. *Higher Cortical Functioning in Man.* New York: Basic Books

Luria AR, Majovski LV. 1977. Basic approaches used in American and Soviet clinical neuropsychology. *Am. Psychol.* 32:959–68

MacLeod CM. 1991. Half a century of research on the Stroop effect: an integrative review. *Psychol. Bull.* 109:163–203

Malloy P, Duffy J. 1994. The frontal lobes in neuropsychiatric disorders. See Boller & Grafman 1994, pp. 203–33

Melo B, Winocur G, Moscovitch M. 1999. Memory distortion in people with amnesia and frontal-lobe damage. *Cogn. Neuropsychol.* 16:343–59

Mesulam M-M. 1985. *Principles of Behavioral Neurology.* Philadelphia: Davis

Mesulam M-M. 1986. Frontal cortex and behavior. *Ann. Neurol.* 19:320–25

Milberg WP, Hebben N, Kaplan E. 1986. A Boston Process approach to Neuropsychological Assessment. In *Neuropsychological Assessment of Neuropsychiatric Disorders,* ed. I Grant, KM Adams, pp. 65–86. New York: Oxford Univ. Press

Milner B. 1963. Effects of different brain lesions on card sorting: the role of the frontal lobes. *Arch. Neurol.* 9:100–10

Milner B. 1964. Some effects of frontal lobectomy in man. See Warren & Akert 1964, pp. 313–35

Milner B, Corsi P, Leonard G. 1991. Frontal-lobe contribution to recency judgements. *Neuropsychologia* 29:601–18

Milner B, Petrides M, Smith ML. 1985. Frontal lobes and the temporal organization of memory. *Hum. Neurobiol.* 4:137–42

Mishkin M. 1964. Perseveration of central sets after frontal lesions in monkeys. See Warren & Akert 1964, pp. 219–41

Moscovitch M. 1992. A neuropsychological model of memory and consciousness. In *Neuropsychology of Memory,* ed. L Squire, N Butters, pp. 5–22. New York: Guilford

Moscovitch M, Melo B. 1997. Strategic retrieval and the frontal lobes: evidence from confabulation and amnesia. *Neuropsychologia* 35:1017–34

Moscovitch M, Winocur G. 1992. The neuropsychology of memory and aging. In *The Handbook of Aging and Cognition,* ed. TA Salthouse, FIM Craik, pp. 315–72. Hillsdale, NJ: Erlbaum

Moscovitch M, Winocur G. 1995. Frontal lobes, memory and aging. *Ann. NY Acad. Sci.* 769:119–50

Moscovitch M, Yaschyshyn T, Ziegler M, Nadel L. 1999. Remote episodic memory and retrograde amnesia: Was Endel Tulving right all along? See Tulving 1999, pp. 331–45

Nagahama Y, Okada T, Katsumi Y, Hayashi T, Yamauchi H, et al. 2001. Dissociable mechanisms of attentional control within the human prefrontal cortex. *Cereb. Cortex* 11:85–92

Nauta WJH. 1971. The problem of the frontal lobe: a reinterpretation. *J. Psychiatry Res.* 8:167–87

Nauta WJH. 1973. Connections of the frontal lobe with the limbic system. In *Surgical Approaches in Psychiatry,* ed. LV Laitinen, KE Livingston, pp. 303–14. Baltimore: Univ. Park Press

Nauta WJH. 1979. Expanding borders of the limbic system concept. In *Functional Neurosurgery,* ed. T Rasmussen, pp. 7–23. New York: Raven

Norman DA, Shallice T. 1986. Attention to action: willed and automatic control of behaviour. In *Consciousness and Self-Regulation,* ed. GE Schwartz, D Shapiro, pp. 1–18. New York: Plenum

Oscar-Berman M, McNamara P, Freedman M. 1991. Delayed-response tasks: parallels between experimental ablation studies and findings in patients with frontal lesions. See Levin et al. 1991, pp. 256–72

Owen AM, Downes JJ, Sahakian BJ, Polkey CE, Robbins TW. 1990. Planning and spatial working memory following frontal lobe lesions in man. *Neuropsychologia* 28:1021–34

Owen AM, Evans AC, Petrides M. 1996. Evidence for a two-stage model of spatial working memory processing within the lateral frontal cortex: a positron emission tomography study. *Cereb. Cortex* 6:31–38

Owen AM, Roberts AC, Hodges JR, Summers BA, Polkey CE, Robbins TW. 1993. Contrasting mechanisms of impaired attentional set-shifting in patients with frontal lobe damage or Parkinson's disease. *Brain* 116:1159–79

Pandya DN, Barnes CL. 1987. Architecture and connections of the frontal lobe. In *The Frontal Lobes Revisited*, ed. E Perecman, pp. 41–72. New York: IRBN Press

Pandya DN, Yeterian EH. 1996. Morphological correlations of human and monkey frontal lobes. In *Neurobiology of Decision Making*, ed. AR Damasio, H Damasio, Y Christen, pp. 13–46. New York: Springer-Verlag

Papez J. 1937. A proposed mechanism of emotion. *Arch. Neurol. Psychiatry* 38:725–43

Pardo JV, Fox PT, Raichle ME. 1991. Localization of a human system for sustained attention by positron emission tomography. *Nature* 349:61–64

Pardo JV, Pardo PJ, Janer KW, Raichle ME. 1990. The anterior cingulate cortex mediates processing selection in the Stroop attentional conflict paradigm. *Proc. Natl. Acad. Sci. USA* 87:256–59

Perret E. 1974. The left frontal lobe of man and the suppression of habitual responses in verbal categorical behavior. *Neuropsychologia* 12:323–30

Petrides M. 1989. Frontal lobes and memory. See Boller & Grafman 1989, pp. 75–90

Petrides M, Alivisatos B, Evans AC. 1995. Functional activation of the human ventrolateral frontal cortex during mnemonic retrieval of verbal information. *Proc. Nat. Acad. Sci. USA* 92:5803–7

Petrides M, Alivisatos B, Evans AC, Meyer E. 1993a. Dissociation of human mid-dorsolateral from posterior dorsolateral frontal cortex in memory processing. *Proc. Natl. Acad. Sci. USA* 90:873–77

Petrides M, Alivisatos B, Meyer E, Evans AC. 1993b. Functional activation of the human frontal cortex during the performance of verbal working memory tasks. *Proc. Natl. Acad. Sci. USA* 90:878–82

Pick A. 1903. On reduplicative paramnesia. *Brain* 26:260–67

Reitan RM, Davidson L. 1974. *Clinical Neuropsychology*. New York: Wiley

Reitan RM, Wolfson D. 1995. Category Test and Trail Making Test as measures of frontal lobe functions. *Clin. Neuropsychol.* 9:50–56

Reuckert L, Grafman J. 1996. Sustained attention deficits in patients with right frontal lesions. *Neuropsychologia* 34:953–63

Reuckert L, Grafman J. 1998. Sustained attention deficits in patients with lesions of posterior cortex. *Neuropsychologia* 36:653–60

Robbins TW, James M, Owen AM, Sahakian BJ, McInnes L, Rabbitt P. 1994. Cambridge Neuropsychological Test Automated Battery (CANTAB): a factor analytic study of a large sample of normal elderly volunteers. *Dementia* 5:266–81

Robertson IH, Manly T, Andrade J, Baddeley BT, Yiend J. 1997. 'Oops!': performance correlates of everyday attentional failures in traumatic brain injured and normal subjects. *Neuropsychologia* 35:747–58

Robertson IH, Ward T, Ridgeway V, Nimmo-Smith I. 1991. *The Test of Everyday Attention*. Bury St. Edmunds, UK: Thames Valley Test Co.

Rogers RD, Andrews TC, Grasby PM, Brooks DJ, Robbins TW. 2000. Contrasting cortical and subcortical activations produced by attentional-set shifting and reversal learning in humans. *J. Cogn. Neurosci.* 12:142–62

Rogers RD, Everitt BJ, Baldacchino A, Blackshaw AJ, Swainson R, et al. 1999a. Dissociable deficits in the decision-making cognition of chronic amphetamine abusers, opiate abusers, patients with focal damage to prefrontal cortex, and tryptophan-depleted normal volunteers: evidence for monoaminergic mechanisms. *Neuropsychopharmacology* 20:322–39

Rogers RD, Owen AM, Middleton HC, Williams EJ, Pickard JD, et al. 1999b. Choosing between small, likely rewards and large, unlikely rewards activates inferior and orbital prefrontal cortex. *J. Neurosci.* 19:9029–38

Rolls ET. 2000. The orbitofrontal cortex and reward. *Cereb. Cortex* 10:284–94

Rossini ED, Karl MA. 1994. The Trail Making Test A and B: a technical note on structural nonequivalence. *Percept. Mot. Skills* 78:625–26

Rourke BP, Brown GG. 1986. Clinical neuropsychology and behavioral neurology: similarities and differences. See Filskov & Boll 1986, pp. 3–41

Russell EW. 1986. The psychometric foundation of clinical neuropsychology. See Filskov & Boll 1986, pp. 45–80

Russell EW, Neuringer C, Goldstein G. 1970. *Assessment of Brain Damage: A Neuropsychological Key Approach.* New York: Wiley

Saint Cyr J, Bronstein Y, Cummings J. 2002. Neurobehavioural consequences of neurosurgical treatments and focal lesions of frontal-subcortical circuits. See Stuss & Knight 2002. In press

Schacter DL, Curran T. 1995. The cognitive neuroscience of false memories. *Psychiatr. Ann.* 25:726–30

Schacter DL, Curran T, Galluccio L, Milberg WP, Bates JF. 1996. False recognition and the right frontal lobe: a case study. *Neuropsychologia* 34:793–808

Schwartz MF, Buxbaum LJ, Montgomery MW, Fitzpatrick-DeSalme E, Hart T, et al. 1999. Naturalistic action production following right hemisphere stroke. *Neuropsychologia* 37:51–66

Shallice T. 2001. Editorial: 'theory of mind' and the prefrontal cortex. *Brain* 124:247–48

Shallice T, Burgess P. 1996. The domain of supervisory processes and temporal organization of behaviour. *Philos. Trans. R. Soc. London Ser. B* 351:1405–11

Shallice T, Burgess PW. 1991. Deficits in strategy application following frontal lobe damage in man. *Brain* 114:727–41

Shallice T, Burgess PW. 1993. Supervisory control of action and thought selection. In *Attention: Selection, Awareness, and Control: A Tribute to Donald Broadbent*, ed. A Baddeley, L Weiskrantz, pp. 171–87. Oxford: Clarendon

Shammi P, Stuss DT. 1999. Humour appreciation: a role of the right frontal lobe. *Brain* 122:657–66

Stone VE, Baron-Cohen S, Knight RT. 1998. Frontal lobe contributions to theory of mind. *J. Cogn. Neurosci.* 10:640–56

Stroop JR. 1935. Studies of interference in serial verbal reaction. *J. Exp. Psychol.* 18:643–62

Stuss DT. 1991. Self, awareness, and the frontal lobes: a neuropsychological perspective. In *The Self: Interdisciplinary Approaches*, ed. J Strauss, GR Goethals, pp. 255–77. New York: Springer-Verlag

Stuss DT, Alexander M. 1999. Affectively burnt in: a proposed role of the right frontal lobe. See Tulving 1999, pp. 215–27

Stuss DT, Alexander MP. 2000. The anatomical basis of affective behavior, emotion and self-awareness: a specific role of the right frontal lobe. In *Affective Minds. The 13th Toyota Conference*, ed. G Hantano, N Okada, H Tanabe, pp. 13–25. Amsterdam: Elsevier Sci.

Stuss DT, Alexander MP, Hamer L, Palumbo C, Dempster R, et al. 1998. The effects of focal anterior and posterior brain lesions on verbal fluency. *J. Int. Neuropsychol. Soc.* 4:265–78

Stuss DT, Alexander MP, Lieberman A, Levine H. 1978. An extraordinary form of confabulation. *Neurology* 28:1166–72

Stuss DT, Alexander MP, Palumbo CL, Buckle L, Sayer L, Pogue J. 1994. Organizational strategies of patients with unilateral or bilateral frontal lobe injury in word list learning tasks. *Neuropsychology* 8:355–73

Stuss DT, Benson DF. 1986. *The Frontal Lobes*. New York: Raven

Stuss DT, Benson DF, Kaplan EF, Weir

WS, Della Malva C. 1981. Leucotomized and nonleucotomized schizophrenics: comparison on tests of attention. *Biol. Psychiatry* 16:1085–100

Stuss DT, Benson DF, Kaplan EF, Weir WS, Naeser MA, et al. 1983. The involvement of orbitofrontal cerebrum in cognitive tasks. *Neuropsychologia* 21:235–48

Stuss DT, Bisschop SM, Alexander MP, Levine B, Katz D, Izukawa D. 2001a. The Trail Making Test: a study in focal lesion patients. *Psychol. Assess.* 13:230–39

Stuss DT, Floden D, Alexander MP, Levine B, Katz D. 2001b. Stroop performance in focal lesion patients: dissociation of processes and frontal lobe lesion location. *Neuropsychologia* 39:771–86

Stuss DT, Gallup GG, Alexander MP. 2001c. The frontal lobes are necessary for 'theory of mind'. *Brain* 124:279–86

Stuss DT, Kaplan EF, Benson DF, Weir WS, Chiulli S, Sarazin FF. 1982. Evidence for the involvement of orbitofrontal cortex in memory functions: an interference effect. *J. Comp. Physiol. Psychol.* 96:913–25

Stuss DT, Knight RT, eds. 2002. *Principles of Frontal Lobe Functions*. New York: Oxford Univ. Press. In press

Stuss DT, Levine B, Alexander MP, Hong J, Palumbo C, et al. 2000. Wisconsin Card Sorting Test performance in patients with focal frontal and posterior brain damage: effects of lesion location and test structure on separable cognitive processes. *Neuropsychologia* 38:388–402

Stuss DT, Picton TW, Alexander MP. 2001d. Consciousness, self-awareness, and the frontal lobes. In *The Frontal Lobes and Neuropsychiatric Illness*, ed. S Salloway, P Malloy, J Duffy, pp. 101–12. Washington, DC: Am. Psychiatr. Press

Stuss DT, Shallice T, Alexander MP, Picton T. 1995. A multidisciplinary approach to anterior attentional functions. *Ann. NY Acad. Sci.* 769:191–212

Stuss DT, Toth JP, Franchi D, Alexander MP, Tipper S, Craik FIM. 1999. Dissociation of attentional processes in patients with focal frontal and posterior lesions. *Neuropsychologia* 37:1005–27

Stuss DT, Trites RL. 1977. Classification of neurological status using multiple discriminant function analysis of neuropsychological test scores. *J. Consult. Clin. Psychol.* 45: 145

Tiihonen J, Kuikka J, Kupila J, Partanen K, Vainio P, et al. 1994. Increase in cerebral blood flow of right prefrontal cortex in man during orgasm. *Neurosci. Lett.* 170:241–43

Troyer AK, Moscovitch M, Winocur G, Alexander MP, Stuss D. 1998. Clustering and switching on verbal fluency: the effects of focal frontal- and temporal-lobe lesions. *Neuropsychologia* 36:499–504

Tulving E. 1985. Memory and consciousness. *Can. Psychol.* 26:1–12

Tulving E, ed. 1999. *Memory, Consciousness, and the Brain: The Tallinn Conference*. Philadelphia: Psychology Press

Tulving E, Kapur S, Craik FIM, Moscovitch M, Houle S. 1994. Hemispheric encoding/retrieval asymmetry in episodic memory: positron emission tomography findings. *Proc. Natl. Acad. Sci. USA* 91:2016–20

Vendrell P, Junque C, Pujol J, Jurado MA, Molet J, Grafman J. 1995. The role of prefrontal regions in the Stroop task. *Neuropsychologia* 33:341–52

Walsh KW. 1987. *Neuropsychology: A Clinical Approach*. Edinburgh: Churchill Livingstone. 2nd ed.

Warren JM, Akert K, eds. 1964. *The Frontal Granular Cortex and Behavior*. New York: McGraw-Hill

Watanabe M. 1998. Cognitive and motivational operations in primate prefrontal neurons. *Rev. Neurosci.* 9:225–41

Wechsler D. 1997a. *Wechsler Adult Intelligence Scale—Third Edition*. San Antonio, TX: Psychol. Corp.

Wechsler D. 1997b. *Wechsler Memory Scale—Third Edition*. Boston: Psychol. Corp.

Wernicke C. 1874. *Des Aphasische Symptomenkomplex*. Breslau, Poland: Cohn & Weigart

Wheeler MA, Stuss DT, Tulving E. 1995.

Frontal lobe damage produces episodic memory impairment. *J. Int. Neuropsychol. Soc.* 1:525–36

Wheeler MA, Stuss DT, Tulving E. 1997. Toward a theory of episodic memory: the frontal lobes and autonoetic consciousness. *Psychol. Bull.* 121:331–54

Wilkins AJ, Shallice T, McCarthy R. 1987. Frontal lesions and sustained attention. *Neuropsychologia* 25:359–65

Winner E, Brownell H, Happe F, Blum A, Pincus D. 1998. Distinguishing lies from jokes: theory of mind deficits and discourse interpretation in right hemisphere brain-damaged patients. *Brain Lang.* 62:89–106

Wise R, Chollet F, Hadar U, Friston K, Hoffner E, Frackowiak RS. 1991. Distribution of cortical neural networks involved in word comprehension and word retrieval. *Brain* 15:1803–17

Annu. Rev. Psychol 2002. 53:435–62

GENETIC CONTRIBUTIONS TO ADDICTION*

John C. Crabbe

*Portland Alcohol Research Center, Department of Behavioral Neuroscience,
Oregon Health & Science University, and VA Medical Center, Portland, Oregon;
e-mail: crabbe@ohsu.edu*

Key Words   substance abuse, animal models, QTL, gene-environment interaction,
transgenic

■ **Abstract**   Even the most extreme environmentalists along the nature-nurture continuum in psychology now acknowledge that genes often contribute to individual differences in behavior. Behavioral traits are complex, reflecting the aggregate effects of
many genes. These genetic effects are interactive, *inter se* and with the environments
in which they are expressed. Human studies of addictive behaviors have clearly implicated both environmental and genetic influences. This review selects drug dependence
as a paradigmatic addiction, and further, concentrates on the extensive literature with
genetic animal models. Both traditional studies with inbred strains and selected lines
and studies exploiting the new molecularly based technologies of the genomics era are
discussed. Future directions for further contribution of animal models studies to our
understanding of the brain dysregulations characteristic of addictions are identified.

CONTENTS

DEFINING ADDICTION

Addiction is a lay term, so everyone assumes he or she knows what it means. However, serious discussions of the basis for the motivational dysregulation of behavior that is its core feature must navigate between languages seeking to describe physiological/pharmacological sources of influence and those focused on intrapsychic events whose basis is unspecified. An interesting review of the field that evaluated this distinction forthrightly concluded that both orientations contribute to our understanding of addiction, and that both structural frameworks can offer predictive value (Davies 1998). This review takes up the recent neurobiological evidence. In addition, it focuses on genetic animal models, which have contributed much of our knowledge of addiction biology.

Which behaviors fall into the category of "addiction" is a matter of debate, but genetic studies have helped in some cases to clarify the issues. For example, whereas all would agree that obesity has a behavioral component, the multiple potential sources of dysregulation that lead to obesity (e.g., in appetite, overeating, and physiological processing of foods) can support multiple opinions about the essential pathology. Recent animal studies have identified multiple genes influencing each of these component processes. A review of these individual genes' effects in mice demonstrates that we still cannot explain all forms of obesity simply with these genes, but there are specific behaviors and/or physiological events affected by each (Wahlsten 1999). Armed with this knowledge, we can more readily assess the extent to which certain cases of obesity may represent addiction.

Most would agree that overuse of alcohol and other abused drugs represent clear examples of addictions. Although other addictive behaviors are occasionally discussed, this review concentrates on drug addiction for three principal reasons. First, there is a wealth of data on the genetics of drug dependence. Second, many of the key features of addiction have been modeled successfully in mice and rats. Finally, drugs can be studied from the framework provided by their pharmacology. Drug receptors are localized in the brain, and drug effects are often local to specific brain regions. Specific tools (e.g., antagonist drugs) are often available. Furthermore, the experimenter can arrange access to and delivery of drugs to the subject. These and other specific features of drug dependence, coupled with a population incidence in US adult males diagnosed as alcoholic and/or drug dependent of more than 10%, have led to intense study in this area.

To understand the genetics of individual differences in susceptibility to abuse drugs, we need to consider several aspects of drug response to be comprehensive, including (*a*) susceptibility to an initial challenge with a drug; (*b*) neuroadaptation that occurs with chronic drug administration, represented as reduced (tolerance) or increased (sensitization) sensitivity; (*c*) dependence, as inferred from the presence of withdrawal symptoms when the drug is removed; (*d*) the reinforcing effects of the drug, which may be positive or negative, and in humans are often characterized as craving; and (*e*) the efficiency of metabolism and elimination of the drug. In addition to these issues, drug studies have wrestled with modeling presumptively important, related neurobiological factors such as impulsivity/disinhibition/ loss of control, and various neurobiological and behavioral aspects of stress responses.

The neurobiological bases of drug addiction have stimulated several theoretical approaches. Most evidence historically has centered on explanations that seek to identify dysregulation in the brain circuits underlying reward more generally, primarily in the dopamine systems of the basal forebrain. The various approaches and neurobiological studies testing these hypotheses are reviewed elsewhere (Wise 1996, Self & Nestler 1995, Altman et al. 1996, O'Brien et al. 1998, Robbins & Everitt 1999, Freeman et al. 2001, van Ree et al. 1999, Tzschentke 1998). Genetic strategies have provided much important evidence (Nestler 2000): Before taking up the genetic evidence, a few terms and concepts are introduced. More description can also be found in a recent review of behavior genetics (Wahlsten 1999).

GENETIC APPROACHES TO ADDICTION

Genetics and Genomics

Even the most extreme environmentalists along the nature-nurture continuum in psychology now acknowledge that genes often contribute to individual differences in behavior. No reasonable person would argue that genes determine behavioral outcomes, but understanding their influence is important. Each individual possesses two alleles at each gene, one inherited from each parent. When different alleles at a gene are circulating in a population, the gene is said to be polymorphic, and these different alleles are represented as differences in the base sequence of the DNA coding for the gene product, a protein. So, the first level of genetic variation that can give rise to individual behavioral differences is due to DNA sequence differences.

However, complexity is introduced by several other aspects of gene structure and function. A gene directs production of a protein via the intermediary molecule, RNA. When an RNA is synthesized, or transcribed, many DNA sequences (called introns) are ignored, and the RNA (which will be translated into protein) represents only some of the original genomic DNA, specifically that from the "coding regions" (exons). However, some DNAs lead to multiple splice variants of RNA, hence to multiple proteins. Furthermore, all cells contain identical DNA sequences, but the genes are not expressed all the time. Expression of each gene is regulated differentially among body tissues and organs, at developmental periods throughout life, and even in different regions of the brain. Some genes are not expressed at all in certain tissues.

Finally, behavioral traits are complex. They are rarely affected by only a single gene. Indeed, they have been characterized as multigenic or polygenic in recognition of the fact that any given gene is likely to contribute only a small influence on phenotypic (behavioral) variance. The complexity is also the result of pleiotropy, the term geneticists use for the impact of a single gene on multiple behavioral traits.

As discussed below, the ultimate effects of genes may prove to be very different in different environments.

The recent strides forward in our understanding of genetic influences on behavior have been elegantly reviewed (Wahlsten 1999), and some specific implications of the genomics revolution discussed (McGuffin et al. 2001). The principles of gene action sketched above apply equally to human and nonhuman animal studies. However, the methods for performing experiments and statistically analyzing outcomes are radically different. Because of the much greater experimental control over animal studies, our review concentrates on them. We also follow the lead of other recent reviews (Wahlsten 1999) and concentrate on the complex interactions among genetic and environmental conditions in an attempt to address the problem of addictions from a behavioral genomics perspective, i.e., one that emphasizes the effects of genes on behavioral functions of the whole organism (Plomin & Crabbe 2000). This perspective may be contrasted with the much more prevalent functional genomics and proteomics efforts to identify for each relevant gene the ways in which that gene's protein product affects cellular function.

Human Genetic Studies

TWIN/FAMILY/ADOPTION STUDIES   The classical approaches to complex trait genetics in psychology have been the examination of co-occurrence of or comorbidity for the trait in monozygotic vs dizygotic twins, reared together or apart, and in analogous family studies with other sorts of biological relatives. These studies, particularly when coupled with genetic epidemiological analyses (Merikangas & Swendsen 2001), have provided solid evidence of genetic influence on addictions. Discussions of the older human behavior genetic studies relating to addictions can be found in an earlier review that considers personality, cognitive, and a broad range of psychopathological traits in addition to the addictions (Rose 1995). This review also offers an excellent survey of the complex interpretive issues surrounding family and twin genetic studies, as well as many other helpful insights into such issues as shared versus nonshared environmental effects and the chronic misperception of genetic data by the popular press.

Recent twin studies have explored such issues as the nature of the environmental contributions to alcohol abuse and dependence (Prescott & Kendler 1999; van den Bree et al. 1998a; Johnson et al. 1996b, 1998), caffeine dependence (Kendler & Prescott 1999), and comorbidity of alcohol abuse and depression or other psychiatric disorders (Prescott et al. 2000, Pickens et al. 1995, van den Bree et al. 1998b). An enduring issue in the addiction literature is the potential role of genetic influences in the substantial comorbidity for abuse of alcohol and other drugs. Alcoholism and smoking are highly genetically comorbid (Rose 1995, Madden et al. 1999, Stallings et al. 1999), and alcoholism and drug dependence also share common genetic influences (Rose 1995; Pickens et al. 1991, 1995; Tsuang et al. 1996). However, each disorder also reflects independent genetic influences as well (Enoch & Goldman 2001).

An issue related to comorbidity is whether or not certain personality traits are risk factors for addictions, including substance abuse. This notion has a very long history (Marlatt et al. 1988), but has always faced serious criticism (Nathan 1988). A systematic attempt to identify "addictive" personality traits failed to do so (Rozin & Stoess 1993). Nonetheless, the extensive genetic comorbidity among addictive disorders contributes to the idea's longevity (Patton et al. 1994, Williams 1996). The basic problem in testing the hypothesis of an addictive personality type is that the addictions are diagnosed post hoc, making it difficult to ascribe personality characteristics to the cause or effect column of the ledger. For example, depressive symptoms in many alcoholics resolve after abstinence (Schuckit et al. 1997).

Another example is the potential relationships among pathological gambling, substance abuse disorders, and personality characteristics. A thoughtful review explored these issues and noted the comorbidity of gambling and drug abuse, but did not address potential genetic bases for this relationship (Murray 1993). More recent studies, including a twin study, have also noted this pattern of comorbidity, a notion supported by the *DSM-III-R* and *DSM-IV* criteria for problem gambling (Slutske et al. 2000). A recent review raised the possibility that genetic studies may in fact help to elucidate the nature of excessive gambling behavior and discussed the implications of characterizing problem gambling as an addiction (Shaffer 1999). All investigators agree that it shares with the addictive disorders the feature of diagnostic heterogeneity.

Finally, one set of genetic findings has proven to be especially intriguing. Those individuals with a positive family history for alcoholism have been known to display reduced sensitivity to certain of alcohol's acute effects, such as body sway and subjective intoxication, compared with those who are family-history negative. A cohort of young men was ascertained in the late 1970s and followed prospectively as they entered the age of maximum risk for alcoholism. Family history was expected to predict later risk of alcohol dependence and alcoholism, consistent with a genetic contribution. Family history was indeed found to be predictive of alcoholism in a follow-up 8 years later, but level of initial response to drug challenge was even more highly associated with later alcoholism, and initial responsiveness (which itself is likely to reflect genetic influences) appeared to account for most of the variability in susceptibility to alcoholism (Schuckit & Smith 1996, Schuckit 1999). Other biological correlates of genetic risk for alcoholism have been recently reviewed (Begleiter & Porjesz 1999, Schuckit 2000).

Twin and family studies will continue to contribute to our understanding of the genetic etiology of addictive behavior. However, such studies cannot easily provide evidence of either the number, location, or identity of the responsible genes unless coupled with molecular strategies described in the next section.

MOLECULAR GENE-FINDING METHODS: ASSOCIATION AND LINKAGE STUDIES   One approach to understanding genetic influences on addictions is to relate genetic markers (i.e., specific sequences of DNA in the genome) to the phenotype across individuals. A cogent introduction to these methods for the nonspecialist can be found elsewhere (Gelernter 1999). Studies of this sort have provided a steady stream of reported localizations for candidate genes or for markers at particular genomic loci (see for example Foroud et al. 1998, 2000; Loh et al. 2000). Many alcoholism and substance abuse–related loci have been discussed elsewhere (Reich et al. 1999, Chen et al. 1999). The low sensitivity to alcohol's effects discussed above has recently been mapped to specific markers as well (Schuckit et al. 2001). One interesting recent study suggests that impulsive-aggressive alcoholics were identified by a marker near the serotonin 5-HT$_{1B}$ receptor gene in two populations (Lappalainen et al. 1998). Much neurobiological evidence links serotonin dysfunction, alcoholism, and aggression (Le Marquand et al. 1994a,b). Another study found evidence for quantitative trait loci associations common to both alcohol consumption and smoking (Bergen et al. 1999).

Although association and linkage methods can sometimes provide strong evidence that there must be a gene near the linked marker that affects the trait, the methods are inherently limited by relatively weak effects of specific genes. More importantly, false positive associations are common, largely because populations that appear genetically rather uniform may in fact show a great deal of variation in gene frequencies for genes in the associated region (Gelernter 1999). It is often difficult to avoid situations in which the control and addicted groups are in fact drawn from two genetically distinct populations, a condition called stratification. The transmission disequilibrium test and variants thereof can mitigate this difficulty somewhat. These methods compare marker frequencies among relatives within family groups who share the trait with those who do not. Because all family members are by definition drawn from the same population genetic stratum, differences in some markers but not others are less likely to represent false-positive associations (see Long & Langley 1999, Uhl 1999 for discussion).

In the end, even very strong association and linkage data for markers near the gene for Huntington's disease required many years of additional work before the gene itself was isolated (MacDonald et al. 1993), and this is a single-gene, virtually all-or-none disorder. Final proof that a candidate association has truly captured the relevant gene or genes requires a collection of converging evidence drawn from a wide range of genetic and nongenetic techniques (Belknap et al. 2001).

Genetic Animal Models

Compared to genetic studies of other areas of psychopathology, it is in the area of genetic animal model development and utilization that genetic studies of alcohol and substance addictions are the most advanced. This is due to two factors. First, serious attempts to study voluntary alcohol drinking in rats began in the late 1940s and were followed by studies in mice in the 1960s. These studies had an explicit genetic orientation that has been sustained ever since. The second factor was raised at the beginning of this chapter: Drugs can be administered systematically by the experimenter or the experimental animal, and pharmacology provides a theoretical framework within which attempts to understand their effects can be organized.

INBRED STRAINS   The simplest genetic animal model system is the study of existing genetic variation. In 1959 McClearn & Rodgers studied several inbred strains of mice by offering them a choice between a bottle filled with tap water and one containing alcohol. Same-sex members of an inbred strain are essentially genetic clones owing to many generations of brother-sister matings, which reduces allelic variation at each gene until it eventually disappears entirely. They found that the differences among strains in preference for ethanol far exceeded the within-strain differences (McClearn & Rodgers 1959). This demonstrates a significant genetic contribution to the trait, because differences among strains assessed in as invariant an environment as possible can only arise from the underlying genetic differences. In particular, C57BL/6-strain mice were high preferrers, whereas DBA/2-strain mice were nearly complete abstainers, and other strains showed intermediate preference.

This pioneering study has been followed by dozens of other studies comparing strains for alcohol and drug sensitivity, tolerance, dependence/withdrawal severity, and propensity to self-administer drugs (Crawley et al. 1997, Marks et al. 1989, Stitzel et al. 2000, Seale et al. 1984; for reviews, see Crabbe & Harris 1991, Mogil et al. 1996). A major advantage of the inbred strain work is that the genotypes remain stable over time: Studies of C57BL/6 and DBA/2 mice performed in the 1990s have been compared directly with those from the 1960s, and the result has been a rich accumulation of knowledge about a few strains of mice. A disadvantage, however, is that the specific genes responsible for the strain differences are anonymous. Nonetheless, comparisons among characteristic strain mean responses through correlational analysis have taught us much about codetermination of genetic influence. For example, mouse strains that are high alcohol preferrers tend to be those that show minimal withdrawal severity when the drug is removed. The genetic correlation between these responses has been estimated to be as high as $r = -0.65$ across 15 inbred strains (Metten et al. 1998). A similar analysis of results from 13 inbred strains of mice demonstrated that efficiency of response inhibition assessed in a signaled nosepoke task was highly predictive of low ethanol consumption (Logue et al. 1998). Together, these studies suggest that strains genetically predisposed to experience severe withdrawal and to be able to inhibit responding are those who elect not to self-administer alcohol when it is offered.

There are more than 100 inbred mouse strains available. A new initiative called the Mouse Phenome Project has been undertaken to support systematic collection of behavioral and physiological data in a number (up to 40) of inbred strains and is assembling a relational database for centralizing access to such genetic relationships (Paigen & Eppig 2000). There are also many rat inbred strains, but they are in general less systematically characterized for traits related to addiction.

SELECTED LINES   The oldest technique in behavioral genetics is that of artificial selection. By arranging matings such that extreme responders are mated, lines of mice or rats have been selected to differ genetically in sensitivity, tolerance, dependence, and preference for alcohol and several other drugs of abuse. The principles were derived from agricultural genetics, in which crops and animals are bred for favorable traits. When such selected lines are compared for other traits, they are often found to differ. Ideally, this is because of the pleiotropic effects of the genes underlying the selected trait, but care must be taken to insure that the change in genes caused by the limited population sizes one can actually maintain are not the cause of the differences in correlated responses to selection. Such studies have been of immeasurable value in advancing our understanding of the neurobiological basis for individual differences in drug responses.

The first selected lines relevant to addictions were developed in Chile in the late 1940s, where UChB rats were bred for high and UChA rats for low alcohol preference (Mardones & Segovia-Riquelme 1983). Mardones' studies, and the identification of the propensity of C57BL/6 inbred mice to prefer drinking alcohol solutions mentioned above (McClearn & Rodgers 1959), stimulated the first modern systematic studies of genetic determinants of alcohol and drug responsiveness.

Studies with these selected lines have been reviewed (Crabbe & Li 1995, Eriksson 1972, Crabbe et al. 1994, Li et al. 1994). Most lines have been selected for responses to alcohol, but selection has also been applied for opioid drugs (Mogil et al. 1995, Belknap et al. 1983), nicotine (Schechter et al. 1995), and cocaine (Marley et al. 1998), among other drugs (for reviews, see chapters in Crabbe & Harris 1991, Mogil et al. 1995, Mohammed 2000).

Perhaps the best known of these selected lines are the Preferring and Nonpreferring lines of rats and two additional pairs of lines subsequently derived for the same alcohol preference trait, High Alcohol-Drinking and Low Alcohol-Drinking rats. Many correlated responses have emerged that differentiate these animals, and only a few highlights are summarized here. Under some conditions, Preferring and High Alcohol-Drinking rats self-administer enough alcohol to achieve blood alcohol concentration levels of 200 mg% or greater (Murphy et al. 1986), but more generally, Preferring rats appear to drink for the pharmacological effects and will stop self-administration when blood levels reach 50–70 mg% (Waller et al. 1982a). These levels correspond to 0.05 and 0.07%—most US states now outlaw driving at either the 0.05 or 0.08% level. Preferring rats develop metabolic and neuronal tolerance (Lumeng & Li 1986) and dependence (Waller et al. 1982b) with chronic free-choice ethanol drinking.

Another widely used set of selected lines was bred for the severity of withdrawal symptoms when chronic alcohol exposure was discontinued. Alcohol withdrawal convulsions have been reported to occur in all animal species, including humans. Duplicate lines of mice Withdrawal Seizure-Prone or -Resistant to alcohol withdrawal convulsions following a period of chronic alcohol vapor inhalation were developed (Crabbe et al. 1985). These lines did not differ in sensitivity to several effects of ethanol, or in the magnitude of tolerance development, but Withdrawal Seizure-Prone and -Resistant mice differed in withdrawal severity from diazepam, phenobarbital, and other sedative-hypnotic drugs (Belknap et al. 1987, 1988, 1989). Furthermore, Withdrawal Seizure-Resistant mice were found to drink more alcohol than Withdrawal Seizure-Prone mice in a preference test (Kosobud et al. 1988), consistent with the negative genetic relationship seen in inbred strains, discussed earlier (Metten et al. 1998). They also differed in sensitivity to ethanol place and taste conditioning (Chester et al. 1998). Many other differences between these lines have been reviewed (Crabbe 1996). Although the results of these lines are not obviously consistent with the low response in subjects at risk for alcoholism reported by Schuckit (2000), they suggest that this set of selected lines might offer a model for a genetic propensity to polydrug abuse.

Selection remains a powerful tool in the arsenal of the genetic animal modeler. In the case of drug dependence, many of the contributing factors obvious from a pharmacological perspective have been modeled in selected lines. A particularly useful future strategy might be to breed selectively for and against expression of other traits with presumptive relevance for the intrapsychic effects of drugs, and/or for those personality and behavioral traits found to be comorbid with addiction risk in human populations, such as impulsivity, antisocial behavior, and depression. Highly impulsive mice could then be compared with a low-impulsivity line to see whether they also displayed differences in abusive drug self-administration. Such traits are, of course, intrinsically more difficult to model convincingly in rodents (Altman et al. 1996), but some attempts have been made, particularly for depression (Weiss et al. 1998, Overstreet 1993) and for anxiety, assessed in an elevated plus maze (Liebsch et al. 1998a,b). Rats bred for High-Anxiety-Related Behavior have been found to drink less alcohol than those bred for Low-Anxiety-Related Behavior (Henniger et al., submitted).

QUANTITATIVE TRAIT LOCUS MAPPING   Recent advances in molecular biology have led to an unprecedented explosion in knowledge about the physical aspects of our genes. This has allowed neuroscientists for the first time to begin to translate statistical statements about genetic risk into knowledge of the specific regions on specific chromosomes where genes of importance have been localized. This is a huge first step toward the ultimate identification of those genes and ascertainment of their function. The implications of these technologies for psychology have been discussed in more detail elsewhere (Wahlsten 1999, Plomin & Crabbe 2000).

Studies with genetic animal models in multiple laboratories have established a dense genetic map of distinct DNA sequences scattered throughout mouse and rat chromosomes. Because of our evolutionarily shared ancestor, humans and mice share approximately 80% of these sequence juxtapositions. Practically, this means that when a specific gene's location has been identified in mice, the location of the homologous gene is known in humans 80% or more of the time. During the past 10 years many studies have demonstrated that individual differences in genetic response to drugs of abuse can be reliably associated with particular regions of the genome [termed "quantitative trait loci" (QTLs)]. Whenever the degree of drug sensitivity is reliably associated with a QTL, this implies that a specific allelic form of a specific gene or genes in that region leads to altered drug sensitivity.

There are now more than 30 QTLs mapped for drug response traits in mice, using inbred strains, their F2 and backcross generations, recombinant inbred strains, selected lines, and congenic strains (Crabbe et al. 1999a). The responses mapped range from drug sensitivity (Deitrich et al. 2000, Gehle & Erwin 2000, Jones et al. 1999), tolerance development (Gehle & Erwin 2000, Deitrich et al. 2000), withdrawal severity (Buck et al. 1997, 1999), reinforcement (Risinger & Cunningham 1998), and tendency toward self-administration. QTL studies are beginning to integrate behavioral and neurobiological analyses. For example, QTLs for the severity of withdrawal from alcohol and pentobarbital have been identified in largely the same regions of mouse chromosomes (Buck et al. 1997, 1999), and one region includes genes that code for several of the subunits of the $GABA_A$ receptor. Further studies show significant association between one variant form of the $GABA_A\gamma2$ subunit gene and alcohol withdrawal severity across a panel of inbred strains (Hood & Buck 2000). Although this does not prove that the $\gamma2$ subunit gene is actually responsible for the original QTL association, it is promising that this gene cannot be excluded and supports further efforts to test this candidate gene. It is also encouraging that some human QTL studies with alcohol-dependent subjects have found evidence for an association with this cluster of $GABA_A$ receptor subunit genes (Sander et al. 1999; Loh et al. 1999, 2000; Iwata et al. 2000).

The largest group of studies has mapped genes related to alcohol preference drinking in mice. These studies have been reviewed elsewhere (Crabbe et al. 1999a, Phillips et al. 1998a), but the genetic locations identified have been very similar across laboratories, despite the use of different specific tests of alcohol preference and different mapping populations. Newer studies have also found similar map locations (Vadasz et al. 2000, Whatley et al. 1999). These studies have suggested several candidate genes, some of which have been tested (see next section).

Many studies are now accumulating that do not target addiction-related responses directly but may be of some relevance owing to the comorbidity of anxiety-related disorders and addictions. QTLs for activity in an open field (Gershenfeld et al. 1997; Gershenfeld & Paul 1997, 1998; Turri et al. 1999) and for contextual fear conditioning (Caldarone et al. 1997, Wehner et al. 1997) have been mapped in mice. An interesting, related project in rats has explored the use of factor analyses of data from several behavioral tasks including open field activity to derive factors thought to reflect anxiety. These studies have used multiple rat inbred strains as well as crosses. QTLs for these factors have then been identified. The studies have shown relationships between the serotonin system, stress-related responses, and anxiety-like behavior, reflected as overlapping QTL regions and as co-contributors to specific factors (Castanon et al. 1995; Courvoisier et al. 1996; Kulikov et al. 1995; Moisan et al. 1996; Ramos et al. 1997, 1998, 1999; Ramos & Mormède 1998). Relevance to addictions was addressed in a study that factor analyzed 13 behavioral variables in a number of rat lines selected for high or low alcohol consumption. Although not all variables usually taken to reflect anxiety were correlated across lines, for some variables there was a clear negative association with alcohol preference. That is, high-preferring genotypes loaded lower on factors reflecting anxiety than low-preferring genotypes (Overstreet et al. 1997). And, as noted above, selection for high anxiety was related to high alcohol preference (Henniger et al., submitted).

The current problem is refining these genetic maps to the point that only a few genes are contained in the QTL confidence interval. No group has yet successfully identified a gene through QTL mapping for an addictive drug response, but this has been achieved for some other traits. For example, one QTL for hypertension in rats was subsequently demonstrated to be the gene encoding angiotensin-converting enzyme, known to be important in regulating blood pressure (Jacob et al. 1991). Several groups around the world are using these methods to close in on genes important for addictions. Fehr et al. (submitted) have used specially bred, congenic strains to reduce the confidence interval surrounding a barbiturate withdrawal QTL to a region containing fewer than 20 genes. In parallel, human association and linkage studies are seeking analogous statistical evidence for QTLs related to alcoholism, depression, substance abuse, and other related traits (Foroud et al. 1998), although these studies are intrinsically much more difficult in human populations for a number of technical reasons (see Gelernter 1999).

TARGETED MUTAGENESIS   Sometimes a QTL confidence interval contains a gene whose function appears to be highly relevant to the trait being mapped, as in the example of the $GABA_A$ receptor subunit genes and drug withdrawal given above. Either in pursuit of the genes responsible for QTLs or because a particular gene product is implicated in an addictive behavior based on other neurobiological evidence, investigators have turned to the study of targeted mutants to explore the role of particular proteins. A specific gene can now be inserted into a mouse's germ line, and an over or underexpression transgenic animal studied. Alternatively, the gene can be disrupted or deleted entirely, creating a null mutant or knockout. Many such mutant mice have been shown to display altered drug responses (for review, see Buck et al. 2000). For example, considering only alcohol preference drinking, the genes thus far effectively targeted, or implicated by mapping strategies, include the gene for the serotonin-1B receptor subtype (Crabbe et al. 1996; but see Phillips et al. 1999, Crabbe et al. 1999b), the dopamine D1 and D2 receptor subtypes (El Ghundi et al. 1998, Phillips et al. 1998b), the neuropeptide Y2 receptor gene (Thiele et al. 1998), the protein kinase A gene (Thiele et al. 2000), the protein kinase C epsilon gene (Hodge et al. 1999), the β-endorphin gene (Grisel et al. 1999), and others. In each of these cases, a significant difference was reported in alcohol preference drinking between the null mutant and its control. However, in much the same way that lesioning a brain area and finding a subsequent difference in behavior does not identify that brain area unequivocally as the biological source of the behavior, results from null mutants must be interpreted cautiously. A primary source of caution is the fact that such mutants experience their entire developmental course lacking the deleted gene product, and the highly plastic brain has sought to compensate in unpredictable ways for whatever functions were disrupted (see Wehner & Bowers 1995, Uhl 1999, Gerlai 1996).

RANDOM MUTAGENESIS   Mutations can also be induced at random throughout the genome through X-irradiation of mice (an older technology) or through treatment with a mutagenic chemical such as N-ethyl-N-nitrosourea. A number of large-scale projects have recently begun in which thousands of mice are mutated and their off-spring screened for behavioral and neurobiological abnormalities (Nolan et al. 1997, 2000; de Angelis et al. 2000). If a phenotypically deviant mouse is then bred, and proves fertile, its offspring should also carry the mutated gene, which can then be mapped and identified using the methods alluded to in the QTL mapping section. These methods are too new for it to be known whether they will be efficacious in identifying relevant mutated genes for complex traits, but they are currently highly touted (Nadeau & Frankel 2000). A more balanced assessment of their prognosis suggests that it may be difficult to apply them to the case of complex traits, in which multiple, small gene effects are the rule (Belknap et al. 2001).

Expression Arrays/Gene Chips

Current technology has provided the genetic research community with the power to ask which genes are more or less active in directing synthesis of their protein products (Watson & Akil 1999). With the recent near-completion of the map containing all human genes by the Human Genome Project (Lander et al. 2001, Venter et al. 2001) have come the current generation of gene chips. Using one of several technologies, snippets representing many thousands of individual gene sequences have been bonded to tiny chips (e.g., glass plates). When a sample of DNA is applied, those genes actively expressed in the sample bind to their embedded ligand, and the resulting interaction is visualized. At least 6000 mouse brain DNA probes are available on chips, and the first studies are beginning to identify genes differentially expressed in brain tissue from alcoholics vs controls (Lewohl et al. 2000) and in adrenal tissue from mice acutely withdrawing from ethanol (Thibault et al. 2000). (For review, see Reilly et al. 2001.)

Another study showed a specific pattern of gene-expression changes in nucleus accumbens tissue from primates exposed to cocaine for over a year, including protein kinases and other cell regulatory genes (Freeman et al. 2001). A recent review summarizes the roles that changes in gene expression are likely to play in the addictive process (Nestler 2000). One goal driving a great deal of the interest in gene expression profiling work is the hope that new genes will be identified that will lead to the development of novel drugs useful in therapy (Hefti 2001). Drugs could also be tailored to maximize an individual's response by using specific knowledge of an individual's genotype.

Use of these techniques will increase exponentially for the next several years, and they bring a new challenge—that of making sense of the data. A typical gene-chip expression array analysis identifies dozens of genes whose expression is increased or decreased as a function of the diagnostic or treatment group compared with controls. Occasionally, expression is drastically altered [e.g., exposure of cells to alcohol chronically led to a 20-fold increase in expression of dopamine beta hydroxylase (Thibault et al. 2000)]. Much more common, though, is the finding of numerous genes whose expression is changed about 100–200%. Numerous statistical problems attend the analysis of these studies, including detecting which are true gene expression differences and which are false positive changes, detecting changes in genes with intrinsically low expression levels, and foremost, determining what the pattern of changes in expression of all those diverse genes means to the organism's function (i.e., the behavioral genomics issue).

The current state of the art for such analyses classifies genes according to broadly (and ill-defined) functions such as "cellular metabolism" or "cellular signaling." The categories reveal the intrinsic orientation toward a reductionist and proteomics perspective: They are oriented toward explaining the functions of the protein in the immediate environment in which it is synthesized and acts. A behavioral genomics perspective will be useful here, where the pattern of gene expression is related not only to cellular function per se but also to the behavioral functions in the whole organism that attended the original treatment or diagnostic comparison.

GENES AND THEIR ENVIRONMENTS

The existing genetic animal models have taught us a great deal about the basic pharmacology, physiology, and biochemistry of drugs' effects on the nervous system. They have unequivocally proven that a substantial proportion of individual differences in response to or avidity for drugs of abuse is genetically influenced. Recent studies have begun to isolate the genes responsible for such individual differences. In addition to (and in some cases building on) these gene mapping efforts, candidate gene approaches have also implicated many specific genes as important for drug responses. Three sources of complexity beyond that introduced by pleiotropy need to be considered.

Gene-Environment Interaction

By definition, the behavior of individuals with particular genotypes can only be assessed in an environment, and systematic changes in the environment clearly affect the behavioral outcome. Abundant evidence reveals that different genotypes respond differentially to environmental manipulation. This is termed "gene-environment interaction," and is crucial to the reasonable interpretation of the range and limits of genetic influences on behavior. Ninety-eight recombinant inbred *Drosophila* strains were reared in three environmental conditions, standard medium at two temperatures, and one medium-temperature combination with ethanol added. QTL effects on fitness (reproductive success) could be estimated from the strain means, and the effects of the QTLs depended on the rearing medium (Fry et al. 1998). In another example, inbred strains of mice showed differing degrees of willingness to drink an offered alcohol solution (McClearn & Rodgers 1959). When increasing concentrations of alcohol were offered, some strains (e.g., C57BL/6) continued to self-administer the drug to water, whereas others (e.g., A/HeJ) began to reject it at higher concentrations (Rodgers & McClearn 1962, Belknap et al. 1993). Genotypic differences in alcohol self-administration were also shown to differ in different cage types and according to how food was presented to the rat strains (Adams et al. 2000). Animal-model research in addictions has provided many such examples.

The utility of animal models for exploring gene-environment interaction is especially high because both genotype and environment can be manipulated experimentally. However, even under this very high level of control the specific environmental variables that are potent in differentially affecting genotypes can be hard to identify. A recent study asked whether inbred strain differences in behavior would be the same in three different laboratories when as many environmental and genetic variables as possible were rigorously equated (Crabbe et al. 1999b). Mice from several inbred strains and one null mutant were tested at exactly the same ages on exactly the same days on a battery of six behaviors. The animal husbandry was nearly identical (same laboratory chow, cages changed on the same days, etc.). The apparatus (e.g., elevated plus mazes, water mazes) and test protocols (including how animals were handled) were nearly identical. However, there were some variables that it was impractical to standardize completely, such as the local water and air in the animal facility, and the individual experimenters in the three locations.

As expected, the strains differed a great deal in all behaviors, and for some tests (such as alcohol preference drinking) there were no strong indications of differences in the strain pattern of alcohol preference across sites. However, for some tests (such as the tendency of mice to venture onto the open arms of an elevated plus maze, generally taken as an index of anxiety), there were significant strain X laboratory interactions. In general, the weaker the overall genetic influence on a trait (i.e., the lower the heritability), the more likely there was to be a genotype X–environment interaction.

Do the results of this study imply that behavioral tests in laboratory mice are intrinsically unreliable? Reliability was generally high at each site. The alternative interpretation is that even differences in environmental test situations that are not obvious to the experimenter may have great importance for the animal and may affect animals with different genotypes differently (Crabbe et al. 1999b).

One implication of this finding is that the particular behavioral test employed to assay a given behavioral domain may affect the interpretation of the results. This is potentially a large problem, particularly for experiments characterizing null mutants. For example, an early study with a null mutant lacking one of the multiple variants (5-HT_{1B}) of receptors for the neurotransmitter serotonin found that the knockouts were much less susceptible to the intoxicating effects of an acute alcohol injection than were the wild-type control mice in a test called the grid test (Crabbe et al. 1996). However, a subsequent study tested these animals for alcohol's incoordinating effects using several other tasks, including frequently used tasks such as the rotarod. Null mutants were found to be less sensitive to alcohol on some, but not all, of these tasks. This implies that these different behaviors must not all represent a single, monolithic domain, and a careless investigator might conclude that the 5-HT_{1B} receptor gene was important for "alcohol-induced ataxia," whereas a more careful analysis would reveal that it affects some but not all of the contributing behaviors (e.g., balance, intact proprioceptive feedback, patterned gait, muscle strength, etc.) (Boehm et al. 2000).

Although more difficult to demonstrate in humans, in whom the genotype is much more difficult to control rigorously, gene-environment interaction clearly exists. For example, a classic study of the genetic susceptibility to alcoholism and related behaviors compared Scandinavian men at (or not at) genetic risk (based on diagnosis of close relatives) for one of two broadly defined variants of alcoholism. Type I alcoholism is characterized by relatively mild abuse, minimal criminality, and passive-dependent personality variables, whereas Type II alcoholism is characterized by early onset, violence, and criminality, and is largely limited to males (Cloninger 1987). Multiple variables in the rearing environments were assessed, and individuals were subsequently classified as having been raised in either risk-promoting or protective environments. Individuals at genetic risk for Type I alcoholism were more often diagnosed, demonstrating genetic influence, but this tendency was much more pronounced when they also had higher-risk environments. For Type II alcoholism, genetic loading also increased diagnoses, but there was little further elevation if the rearing environment was also risky (Cloninger et al. 1981). This outcome illustrates the concept that the same environmental risk factors can play a very different role depending on an individual's genotype.

On at least three counts, this is a great oversimplification of a very complex analysis. First, whereas many different diagnostic typologies have been proposed for alcoholism, nearly all support the existence of at least two broadly differentiable variants of the disease (Johnson et al. 1996a, Litt et al. 1992, Babor et al. 1992). Second, multivariate statistical methods were used to categorize variables in the subjects' environmental background as risk-promoting or protective. Finally, a similar analysis of a sample of female alcoholics provided a somewhat different outcome (Bohman et al. 1981). Nonetheless, the interaction seen was substantial.

Gene-Environment Correlation

Genotypes are often not randomly represented in environments. A frequent contributor to relapse to substance abuse is thought to be succumbing to the environmental triggers represented by myriad cues in the patient's environment, e.g., seeing the house where he habitually purchased drugs, hanging around with other drug users. Studies have demonstrated the potency of exposure to previously drug-related cues in eliciting both craving for drugs and increases in physiological responses such as heart rate and pupil diameter (Childress et al. 1999, O'Brien et al. 1998). At least some contribution to substance abuse is likely to be the tendency of genetically susceptible individuals to remain in the risk-promoting environment, thereby potentiating their overall risk. Indeed, many therapies strongly advocate making radical changes in the day-to-day living situation of recovering addicts, a prescription that is unfortunately difficult for many to follow due to limited socioeconomic choices (Budney & Higgins 1998).

It is obviously difficult to conduct controlled studies of gene-environment correlation with humans. However, one underlying principle is that drug responses can often depend upon conditioning to environmental cues. Many animal studies have documented genetic differences in sensitivity to drug-conditioned responses, such as place and taste conditioning (Broadbent et al. 1996, Cunningham 1995, Cunningham et al. 2000, Risinger & Cunningham 1998). The role of conditioning in drug abuse has been reviewed elsewhere (Altman et al. 1996, O'Brien et al. 1998, Robbins & Everitt 1999).

Epistasis

Whenever more than one gene affects a trait, epistatic interactions may be at work. Complex behaviors, including those contributing to addictions, are influenced by many genes, each with relatively small independent effect. Epistasis is the statistical interaction of such individual gene effects. The simplest case is that in which the presence or absence of a particular allele at a second gene significantly modulates the effect of allelic differences at a gene of interest (Browman & Crabbe 1999). A recent example is not strictly about addictive behavior, but rather anxiety, which is extensively comorbid with the addictions. Three groups interested in the stress axis recently independently produced mice in which the corticotropin-releasing hormone (CRH) receptor-2 gene (*Crhr2*) had been deleted. Because of the well-established role of CRH in modulating anxiety-like responses (Weninger et al. 1999, Skutella et al. 1994), all three groups used the elevated plus-maze anxiety test as well as the classic open field test, and each tested both sexes. Many additional variables were also assessed in each study. Although the findings were internally consistent within each group's results, they differed markedly in their conclusions about the role of the CRH-R2 receptor gene in anxiety. One group (Coste et al. 2000) saw no effects on anxiety-related behavior in either sex, whereas the second group (Bale et al. 2000) found greater anxiety in both male and female knockouts. The third group (Kishimoto et al. 2000) saw greater anxiety in male knockouts only, and in only one test.

The source of these differences could simply be that different apparatus, lighting, handling conditions, and other test procedures were used, idiosyncratic to each group. We have already seen that even when such variables are carefully standardized, genetic differences play out differently in different environments. Another possibility is that the CRH-R2 receptor gene has no consistent role in modulating anxiety, but each group used multiple, putative tests of anxiety and each obtained largely consistent results across tests.

It seems more likely that epistasis was at work. The genetically engineered constructs inserted into the embryonic stem cells to produce the gene deletion were different in each laboratory, and each carried a relatively long piece of DNA along with the targeted gene. Thus, other closely linked genes could have been introduced to the recipient mice, and these necessarily differed from laboratory to laboratory. These "passenger genes" could have been interacting epistatically with the CRH-R2 receptor gene to influence behavioral outcomes, such that a given anxiety response was only expressed in the presence of a specific, additional gene in addition to the loss-of-function variant of the CRH-R2 receptor gene. Furthermore, each group introduced its null mutant into a different substrain of 129 inbred mice (these 129 mice served as the source for the embryonic stem cells into which the null mutation was introduced). Different substrains of 129 are very similar genetically, but not identical (Simpson et al. 1997). The mice tested also had varying percentages of the C57BL/6 inbred strain genome, so the effects of the targeted gene could also have been interacting with genes differing in the genetic background, as well as with passenger genes in the construct (Gerlai 1996). There are other possible contributors to these behavioral differences, discussed more fully in the three papers mentioned above and elsewhere (Crabbe 2001).

Researchers are beginning to look for these sorts of interactions in their gene mapping efforts, and it is not surprising that epistasis appears to occur frequently. In a QTL analysis from our group, we were able to demonstrate a significant difference in acute pentobarbital withdrawal severity between mice homozygous for DBA/2J strain alleles in a region of chromosome 11 and those homozygous for C57BL/6J alleles (Buck et al. 1999). This indicated the presence of a gene in this chromosomal region where the DBA/2J-specified gene tended to reduce withdrawal as compared with the C57BL/6J gene. A recent analysis of epistatic interactions, however, showed that this was only true when the animals had DBA/2J alleles in a second region, on the distal end of chromosome 1. If mice had C57BL/6J alleles on distal chromosome 1, there was no difference in withdrawal between mice with C57BL/6J and DBA/2J genomes on chromosome 11 (Hood et al. 2001).

Genes can obviously interact in multiples greater than two. The field is just now beginning to study such interactions, and extension of such analyses to multigenic interactions will require a daunting degree of statistical power. This is because power to detect interactions requires much greater numbers of subjects than are required to detect main effects (Wahlsten 1990). Nonetheless, understanding the complexity of genetic interactions will be crucial. After all, the relevant clinical traits are extensively comorbid (e.g., alcoholism, other substance abuse, impulsivity, attention deficit/hyperactivity disorder, depression, etc.), and their comorbidity is likely to represent a mixture of genetic and nongenetic sources (Crabbe 1999).

TAKE HOME MESSAGES

Interpretation of Genetic Differences

The ubiquitous influence of genes on addiction-related traits must not be over-simplified. "The gene for . . ." syndrome understandably infects the popular press (although scientists have a clear responsibility to lobby strenuously against this kind of reporting). Unfortunately, for many molecularly oriented neuroscientists, a limited result identifying a specific gene with a specific behavioral outcome often also leads to over-naive interpretation. For complex traits, the general rule seems to be that the aggregate contribution of the many genes contributing toward individual differences is no more than 50% of the variance—the rest is explicitly not genetic. Whereas some would argue that teasing apart the relative contributions of genes and environments is a near impossibility (Gottlieb 1998), the general view is that specific domains of genetic influence can, with care, be identified. Nonetheless, it is important to remember that many genes contribute to complex traits, interacting with each other as well as the environments in which they are expressed.

What Specific Contributions Can Animal Genetics Make to the Addictions?

One suggestion raised earlier in this review was that insufficient use has been made of perhaps the most powerful of all behavior genetics techniques, artificial selection. If one wishes to deconstruct the contributions of disinhibition to drug-seeking behavior, it would be a straightforward matter to breed mice for high or low "novelty-seeking" responses and then see whether they differed in drug self-administration. It has been shown that when rats are exposed to an open field, a situation whose novel features cause mild stress, they display different levels of locomotion. High responders can then be shown subsequently to self-administer psychostimulant drugs to a greater degree than low responders. Reviews of these and related studies discuss the neuroendocrine and behavioral profiles characterizing these groups (Piazza & Le Moal 1996, Bardo et al. 1996).

From a genetic perspective, these studies offer no evidence that the behavioral differences are genetic as opposed to environmental. However, simply attempting to select for the novelty response would rapidly answer the question. Of course, the studies reviewed above suggest that it would not necessarily be easy to do this experiment. For example, breeding for high vs low scores on a signaled nosepoke task (Logue et al. 1998) might, or might not, lead to parallel divergence in scores in a delay or probability discounting task (Richards et al. 1997) or in a delayed reinforcement of low rate operant task, even though all three tasks are thought to assay impulsivity. Still, such experiments would be a worthwhile undertaking and could offer much useful insight to the predisposition/comorbidity issues surrounding human genetic studies.

A second area of contribution is the identification of specific genes for risk for or protection from addictive behavior (see "Quantitative Trait Locus Mapping"). The rapid pace of technological development in genetic markers [e.g., the development of many thousands of new genetic markers, much more densely spaced, by ascertaining single nucleotide polymorphisms (Lindblad-Toh et al. 2000, Cargill et al. 1999)] will make the path from QTL to responsible gene much easier in the near future.

Will the proliferation of genetic studies in animals resolve all the most vexing issues facing addiction studies? Almost certainly not. Even this brief review has made it clear that any single addiction diagnosis is etiologically heterogeneous, which probably means that it is both genetically and environmentally heterogeneous as well (not to mention heterogeneous at the intersection of genotype and environment, and so on). Certainly, the history of genetic animal-model research suggests that such studies have great potential for furthering our knowledge of how drugs work in the brain. There is hope among behavioral geneticists that use of genetic information could lead to better diagnostic approaches (Plomin & Crabbe 2000), but the principal, and probably insurmountable, problem is the small effect size of most specific genes of importance. And there is a strong probability that behavioral genomics studies in animals will lead to better therapeutic agents than those currently available. It may not be necessary to identify all the influential genes to devise novel strategies for prevention and treatment of complex disease traits.

Addiction in the Postgenomics World

The rapid proliferation of genetic data–gathering capability has found many a scientist in possession of the DNA from many patients/subjects. Because it is now so comparatively sraightforward to genotype those samples, the potential for misuse of genetic information is great. A fraction of the resources of the Human Genome Project has been devoted to the study of the Ethical, Legal and Social Implications (ELSI) Program and others with similar goals (see http://www.lbl.gov/Education/ELSI/ELSI.html). Privacy and confidentiality issues and their implications for employment and insurance are an extremely complex area. In addition, patients whose DNA leads to patentable discoveries are beginning to sue for a share of the profits.

The need for serious ethical discussions is clear, but the answers will not be simple. As has been the central message of this review, at the heart of the problem is the small effect size of any individual gene contributing to complex traits. The ethical issues surrounding a diagnosis of Huntington's disease are difficult enough, and this is a single-gene disorder for which a yes/no answer to genetic risk can be given. What does it mean to know that an individual has 3 of the 15 (or is it 30?) "bad" genes, e.g., those predisposing to alcoholism, versus having 8 of the 15? Obviously, everyone would prefer the former diagnosis to the latter, but absent knowledge of whether alcoholism is a threshold character or a continuous trait and how the various risk-promoting genes interact with each other in specific combinations, and without environment-related information that is as sophisticated and articulated as the genetic information on risk, it is difficult to see what the appropriate ethical choices are. This does not mean that regulation will not be attempted before the science is clear. Several states have introduced laws regulating genetic privacy.

I am not a bioethicist, but I have been repeatedly exposed to ethical issues during a career devoted to chasing genetic sources of influence on complex traits. In my perusals of the literature relating to ethical decision-making vis à vis genetics, I have been struck by the persistent tendency to raise, rather than answer, questions such as those raised above. The reader is directed to a recent review for other sources of relevance to the ethical questions, where we perpetuated this tendency (Crabbe & Belknap 1998). In addition, the National Institutes of

Health maintains several links to web sites of relevance to ethnicity and genetics, gene patenting, genetic testing/counseling, and gene therapy/gene transfer (http://www.nih.gov/sigs/bioethics/). I suspect that no one with more than a little knowledge in the related scientific areas feels capable of prescribing ethical guidelines. Nearly all scientists I know would agree that it seems unfair, immoral, or a violation of privacy for an insurance company to obtain access to a patient's DNA information without explicit permission and decide that a high risk for a disease justified a higher premium. However, they are much more divided on the issue of whether a patient should retain privacy rights blocking the use of his or her DNA information, freely given with informed consent for a particular genetic linkage study, in a future genetic linkage study for a different trait, in which personal patient-identifying information is doubly blinded. Entire books have been devoted to these complex issues, and it is simply beyond the scope of this review to pursue them in any reasonable depth. The interested reader may also find useful the text of a February 2000 ELSI Research Planning and Evaluation Group Report covering the first 10 years of the ELSI Programs and future plans, and the links cited therein (http://www.nhgri.nih.gov/ELSI/erpg_report.html).

ACKNOWLEDGMENTS

Thanks to Tamara Phillips and Chris Cunningham for their comments, and the VA, NIAAA, and NIDA for support.

Visit the Annual Reviews home page at www.AnnualReviews.org

LITERATURE CITED

Adams N, Hannah JA, Henry W. 2000. Environmental influences on the failure to drink in inbred rats with an ethanol preference. *Physiol. Behav.* 69:563–70

Altman J, Everitt BJ, Glautier S, Markou A, Nutt D, et al. 1996. The biological, social and clinical bases of drug addiction: commentary and debate. *Psychopharmacology* 125:285–345

Babor TF, Hofmann M, DelBoca FK, Hesselbrock V, Meyer RE, et al. 1992. Types of alcoholics. I. Evidence for an empirically derived typology based on indicators of vulnerability and severity. *Arch. Gen. Psychiatry* 49:599–608

Bale TL, Contarino A, Smith GW, Chan R, Gold LH, et al. 2000. Mice deficient for corticotropin-releasing hormone receptor-2 display anxiety-like behaviour and are hypersensitive to stress. *Nat. Genet.* 24:410–14

Bardo MT, Donohew RL, Harrington NG. 1996. Psychobiology of novelty seeking and drug seeking behavior. *Brain Behav. Res.* 77: 23–43

Begleiter H, Porjesz B. 1999. What is inherited in the predisposition toward alcoholism? A proposed model. *Alcohol: Clin. Exp. Res.* 23:1125–35

Belknap JK, Crabbe JC, Laursen SE. 1989. Ethanol and diazepam withdrawal convulsions are extensively codetermined in WSP and WSR mice. *Life Sci.* 44:2075–80

Belknap JK, Crabbe JC, Young ER. 1993. Voluntary consumption of ethanol in 15 inbred mouse strains. *Psychopharmacology* 112:503–10

Belknap JK, Danielson PW, Lamé M, Crabbe JC. 1988. Ethanol and barbiturate withdrawal convulsions are extensively codetermined in mice. *Alcohol* 5:167–71

Belknap JK, Haltli NR, Goebel DM, Lamé M. 1983. Selective breeding for high and low levels of opiate-induced analgesia in mice. *Behav. Genet.* 13:383–96

Belknap JK, Hitzemann R, Crabbe JC, Phillips TJ, Buck KJ, Williams RW. 2001. QTL analysis and genome-wide mutagenesis in mice: complementary genetic approaches to the dissection of complex traits. *Behav. Genet.* 31:5–15

Belknap JK, Laursen SE, Crabbe JC. 1987. Ethanol and nitrous oxide produce withdrawal-induced convulsions by similar mechanisms in mice. *Life Sci.* 41:2033–40

Bergen AW, Korczak JF, Weissbecker KA, Goldstein AM. 1999. A genome-wide search for loci contributing to smoking and alcoholism. *Genet. Epidemiol.* 17(Suppl 1):S55–60

Boehm II SL, Schafer GL, Phillips TJ, Browman KE, Crabbe JC. 2000. Sensitivity to ethanol-induced motor incoordination in 5-HT$_{1B}$ receptor null mutant mice is task-dependent: implications for behavioral assessment of genetically altered mice. *Behav. Neurosci.* 114:401–9

Bohman M, Sigvardsson S, Cloninger CR. 1981. Maternal inheritance of alcohol abuse. Cross-fostering analysis of adopted women. *Arch. Gen. Psychiatry* 38:965–69

Broadbent J, Linder HV, Cunningham CL. 1996. Genetic differences in naloxone enhancement of ethanol-induced conditioned taste aversion. *Psychopharmacology* 126:147–55

Browman KE, Crabbe JC. 1999. Alcohol and genetics: new animal models. *Molec. Med. Today* 5:310–18

Buck K, Metten P, Belknap J, Crabbe J. 1999. Quantitative trait loci affecting risk for pentobarbital withdrawal map near alcohol withdrawal loci on mouse chromosomes 1, 4, and 11. *Mamm. Genome* 10:431–37

Buck KJ, Crabbe JC, Belknap JK. 2000. Alcohol and other abused drugs. In *Genetic Influences on Neural and Behavioral Functions*, ed. DW Pfaff, WH Berrettini, TH Joh, SC Maxson, pp. 159–83. Boca Raton, FL: CRC Press

Buck KJ, Metten P, Belknap JK, Crabbe JC. 1997. Quantitative trait loci involved in genetic predisposition to acute alcohol withdrawal in mice. *J. Neurosci.* 17:3946–55

Budney AJ, Higgins ST. 1998. *A Community Reinforcement Plus Vouchers Approach: Treating Cocaine Addiction.* Rockville, MD: USDHHS-NIH-NIDA

Caldarone B, Saavedra C, Tartaglia K, Wehner JM, Dudek BC, Flaherty L. 1997. Quantitative trait loci analysis affecting contextual conditioning in mice. *Nat. Genet.* 17:335–37

Cargill M, Altshuler D, Ireland J, Sklar P, Ardlie K, et al. 1999. Characterization of single-nucleotide polymorphisms in coding regions of human genes. *Nat. Genet.* 22:231–38

Castanon N, Perez-Diaz F, Mormède P. 1995. Genetic analysis of the relationships between behavioral and neuroendocrine traits in Roman High and Low Avoidance rat lines. *Behav. Genet.* 25:371–84

Charney DS, Nestler EJ, Bunney BS, eds. 1999. *Neurobiology of Mental Illness.* New York: Oxford Univ. Press

Chen CC, Lu RB, Chen YC, Wang MF, Chang YC, et al. 1999. Interaction between the functional polymorphisms of the alcohol-metabolism genes in protection against alcoholism. *Am. J. Hum. Genet.* 65:795–807

Chester JA, Risinger FO, Cunningham CL. 1998. Ethanol reward and aversion in mice bred for sensitivity to ethanol withdrawal. *Alcohol: Clin. Exp. Res.* 22:468–73

Childress AR, Mozley PD, McElgin W, Fitzgerald J, Reivich M, O'Brien CP. 1999. Limbic activation during cue-induced cocaine craving. *Am. J. Psychiatry* 156:11–18

Cloninger CR. 1987. Neurogenetic adaptive mechanisms in alcoholism. *Science* 236:410–16

Cloninger CR, Bohman M, Sigvardsson S. 1981. Inheritance of alcohol abuse.

Cross-fostering analysis of adopted men. *Arch. Gen. Psychiatry* 38:861–68

Coste SC, Kesterson RA, Heldwein KA, Stevens SL, Heard AD, et al. 2000. Abnormal adaptations to stress and impaired cardiovascular function in mice lacking corticotropin-releasing hormone receptor-2. *Nat. Genet.* 24:403–9

Courvoisier H, Moisan MP, Sarrieau A, Hendley ED, Mormède P. 1996. Behavioral and neuroendocrine reactivity to stress in the WKHA/WKY inbred rat strains: a multifactorial and genetic analysis. *Brain Res.* 743:77–85

Crabbe JC. 1996. A genetic animal model of alcohol withdrawal. *Alcohol: Clin. Exp. Res.* 20:96A–100A

Crabbe JC. 1999. Molecular genetics of addiction. See Charney et al. 1999, pp. 591–600

Crabbe JC. 2001. Use of genetic analyses to refine phenotypes related to alcohol tolerance and dependence. *Alcohol: Clin. Exp. Res.* 25:288–92

Crabbe JC, Belknap JK. 1998. Ethical consequences of mapping QTLs for complex human traits. In *Molecular Dissection of Complex Traits*, ed. AH Paterson, pp. 279–85. Boca Raton, FL: CRC Press

Crabbe JC, Belknap JK, Buck KJ. 1994. Genetic animal models of alcohol and drug abuse. *Science* 264:1715–23

Crabbe JC, Harris RA, eds. 1991. *The Genetic Basis of Alcohol and Drug Actions.* New York: Plenum Press

Crabbe JC, Kosobud A, Young ER, Tam BR, McSwigan JD. 1985. Bidirectional selection for susceptibility to ethanol withdrawal seizures in *Mus musculus. Behav. Genet.* 15:521–36

Crabbe JC, Li T–K. 1995. Genetic strategies in preclinical substance abuse research. In *Psychopharmacology: A Fourth Generation of Progress*, ed. FE Bloom, DJ Kupfer, 69:799–811, New York: Raven Press

Crabbe JC, Phillips TJ, Buck KJ, Cunningham CL, Belknap JK. 1999a. Identifying genes for alcohol and drug sensitivity: recent progress and future directions. *Trends Neurosci.* 22:173–79

Crabbe JC, Phillips TJ, Feller DJ, Hen R, Wenger CD, et al. 1996. Elevated alcohol consumption in null mutant mice lacking 5–HT_{1B} serotonin receptors. *Nat. Genet.* 14: 98–101

Crabbe JC, Wahlsten D, Dudek BC. 1999b. Genetics of mouse behavior: interactions with laboratory environment. *Science* 284:1670–22

Crawley JN, Belknap JK, Collins A, Crabbe JC, Frankel W, et al. 1997. Behavioral phenotypes of inbred mouse strains: implications and recommendations for molecular studies. *Psychopharmacology* 132:107–24

Cunningham CL. 1995. Localization of genes influencing ethanol-induced conditioned place preference and locomotor activity in BXD recombinant inbred mice. *Psychopharmacology* 120:28–41

Cunningham CL, Howard MA, Gill SJ, Rubinstein M, Low MJ, Grandy DK. 2000. Ethanol-conditioned place preference is reduced in dopamine D2 receptor-deficient mice. *Pharmacol. Biochem. Behav.* 67:693–99

Davies JB. 1998. Pharmacology versus social process: competing or complementary views on the nature of addiction? *Pharmacol. Ther.* 80:265–75

Deitrich RA, Bludeau P, Erwin VG. 2000. Phenotypic and genotypic relationships between ethanol tolerance and sensitivity in mice selectively bred for initial sensitivity to ethanol (SS and LS) or development of acute tolerance (HAFT and LAFT). *Alcohol: Clin. Exp. Res.* 24:595–604

El Ghundi M, George SR, Drago J, Fletcher PJ, Fan T, et al. 1998. Disruption of dopamine D1 receptor gene expression attenuates alcohol-seeking behavior. *Eur. J. Pharmacol.* 353:149–58

Enoch MA, Goldman D. 2001. The genetics of alcoholism and alcohol abuse. *Curr. Psychiat.* 3:144–51

Eriksson K. 1972. Behavioral and physiological differences among rat strains specially selected for their alcohol consumption. *Ann. NY Acad. Sci.* 197:32–41

Fehr C, Belknap JK, Crabbe JC, Buck KJ. 2001. Congenic mapping of alcohol and pentobarbital withdrawal liability quantitative trait loci to a 0. 9 cM region of mouse chromosome 4: identification of *Mpdz* as a candidate gene. Submitted

Foroud T, Bucholz KK, Edenberg HJ, Goate A, Neuman RJ, et al. 1998. Linkage of an alcoholism-related severity phenotype to chromosome 16. *Alcohol: Clin. Exp. Res.* 22: 2035–42

Foroud T, Edenberg HJ, Goate A, Rice J, Flury L, et al. 2000. Alcoholism susceptibility loci: confirmation studies in a replicate sample and further mapping. *Alcohol: Clin. Exp. Res.* 24:933–45

Freeman WM, Nader MA, Nader SH, Robertson DJ, Gioia L, et al. 2001. Chronic cocaine-mediated changes in non-human primate nucleus accumbens gene expression. *J. Neurochem.* 77:542–9

Fry JD, Nuzhdin SV, Pasyukova EG, Mackay TF. 1998. QTL mapping of genotype-environment interaction for fitness in *Drosophila melanogaster*. *Genet. Res.* 71:133–41

Gehle VM, Erwin VG. 2000. The genetics of acute functional tolerance and initial sensitivity to ethanol for an ataxia test in the LSxSS RI strains. *Alcohol: Clin. Exp. Res.* 24:579–87

Gelernter J. 1999. Clinical molecular genetics. See Charney et al. 1999, pp. 108–20

Gerlai R. 1996. Gene-targeting studies of mammalian behavior: Is it the mutation or the background genotype? *Trends Neurosci.* 19:177–81

Gershenfeld HK, Neumann PE, Mathis C, Crawley JN, Li X, Paul SM. 1997. Mapping quantitative trait loci for open-field behavior in mice. *Behav. Genet.* 27:201–10

Gershenfeld HK, Paul SM. 1997. Mapping quantitative trait loci for fear-like behaviors in mice. *Genomics* 46:1–8

Gershenfeld HK, Paul SM. 1998. Towards a genetics of anxious temperament: from mice to

men. *Acta Psychiatr. Scand.* 393(Suppl.):56–65

Gottlieb G, 1998. Normally occurring environmental and behavioral influences on gene activity: from central dogma to probabilistic epigenesis. *Psychol. Rev.* 105:792–802

Grisel JE, Mogil JS, Grahame NJ, Rubinstein M, Belknap JK, et al. 1999. Ethanol oral self-administration is increased in mutant mice with decreased β-endorphin expression. *Brain Res.* 835:62–67

Hefti F. 2001. From genes to effective drugs for neurological and psychiatric diseases. *Trends Pharmacol. Sci.* 22:159–60

Henniger MSH, Spanagel R, Wigger A, Landgraf R, Hölter SM. 2001. Alcohol self-administration in two rat lines selectively bred for extremes in anxiety-related behavior. Submitted

Hodge CW, Mehmert KK, Kelley SP, McMahon T, Haywood A, et al. 1999. Supersensitivity to allosteric $GABA_A$ receptor modulators and alcohol in mice lacking PKCε. *Nat. Neurosci.* 2:997–1002

Hood H, Crabbe JC, Belknap JK, Buck KJ. 2001. Epistatic interaction between quantitative trait loci affects the genetic predisposition for physical dependence on pentobarbital in mice. *Behav. Genet.* 31:93–100

Hood HM, Buck KJ. 2000. Allelic variation in the $GABA_A$ receptor $\gamma2$ subunit is associated with genetic susceptibility to ethanol-induced motor incoordination and hypothermia, conditioned taste aversion, and withdrawal in BXD/Ty recombinant inbred mice. *Alcohol: Clin. Exp. Res.* 24:1327–34

Hrabe de Angelis MH, Flaswinkel H, Fuchs H, Rathkolb B, Soewarto D, et al. 2000. Genome-wide, large-scale production of mutant mice by ENU mutagenesis. *Nat. Genet.* 25:444–47

Iwata N, Virkkunen M, Goldman D. 2000. Identification of a naturally occurring Pro385-Ser385 substitution in the $GABA_A$ receptor $\alpha6$ subunit gene in alcoholics and healthy volunteers. *Mol. Psychiatry* 5:316–19

Jacob HJ, Lindpaintner K, Lincoln SE,

Kusumi K, Bunker RK, et al. 1991. Genetic mapping of a gene causing hypertension in the stroke-prone spontaneously hypertensive rat. *Cell* 67:213–24

Johnson EO, van den Bree MBM, Gupman AE, Pickens RW. 1998. Extension of a typology of alcohol dependence based on relative genetic and environmental loading. *Alcohol: Clin. Exp. Res.* 22:1421–29

Johnson EO, ˙van den Bree MBM, Pickens RW. 1996a. Subtypes of alcohol-dependent men: a typology based on relative genetic and environmental loading. *Alcohol: Clin. Exp. Res.* 20:1472–80

Johnson EO, van den Bree MBM, Uhl GR, Pickens RW. 1996b. Indicators of genetic and enviromental influences in drug abusing individuals. *Drug Alcohol Depend.* 41:17–23

Jones BC, Tarantino LM, Rodriguez LA, Reed CL, McClearn GE, et al. 1999. Quantitative-trait loci analysis of cocaine-related behaviours and neurochemistry. *Pharmacogenetics* 9:607–17

Kendler KS, Prescott CA. 1999. Caffeine intake, tolerance, and withdrawal in women: a population-based twin study. *Am. J. Psychiatry* 156:223–28

Kishimoto T, Radulovic J, Radulovic M, Lin CR, Schrick C, et al. 2000. Deletion of *crhr2* reveals an anxiolytic role for corticotropin-releasing hormone receptor-2. *Nat. Genet.* 24:415–19

Kosobud A, Bodor AS, Crabbe JC. 1988. Voluntary consumption of ethanol in WSP, WSC and WSR selectively bred mouse lines. *Pharmacol. Biochem. Behav.* 29:601–7

Kulikov A, Castanon N, Mormède P, Chaouloff F. 1995. Cerebral tryptophan hydroxylase activity, and 5-HT$_{1A}$ receptor, 5-HT$_{2A}$ receptor, and 5-HT transporter binding in grouped and isolated Roman RHA and RLA rats: relationships with behaviours in two models of anxiety. *Psychopharmacology* 121:385–95

Lander ES, Linton LM, Birren B, Nusbaum C, Zody MC, et al. 2001. Initial sequencing and analysis of the human genome. *Nature* 409:860–921

Lappalainen J, Long JC, Eggert M, Ozaki N, Robin RW, et al. 1998. Linkage of antisocial alcoholism to the serotonin 5-HT$_{1B}$ receptor gene in 2 populations. *Arch. Gen. Psychiatry* 55:989–94

Le Marquand D, Pihl RO, Benkelfat C. 1994a. Serotonin and alcohol intake, abuse, and dependence: clinical evidence. *Biol. Psychiatry* 36:326–37

Le Marquand D, Pihl RO, Benkelfat C. 1994b. Serotonin and alcohol intake, abuse, and dependence: findings of animal studies. *Biol. Psychiatry* 36:395–421

Lewohl JM, Wang L, Miles MF, Zhang L, Dodd PR, Harris RA. 2000. Gene expression in human alcoholism: microarray analysis of frontal cortex. *Alcohol: Clin. Exp. Res.* 24:1873–82

Li T-K, Lumeng L, McBride WJ, Murphy JM. 1994. Genetic and neurobiological basis of alcohol-seeking behavior. *Alcohol* 29:697–700

Liebsch G, Montkowski A, Holsboer F, Landgraf R. 1998a. Behavioural profiles of two Wistar rat lines selectively bred for high or low anxiety-related behaviour. *Behav. Brain Res.* 94:301–10

Liebsch G, Linthorst ACE, Neumann ID, Reul JMHM, Holsboer F, Landgraf R. 1998b. Behavioral, physiological, and neuroendocrine stress responses and differential sensitivity to diazepam in two Wistar rat lines selectively bred for High- or Low-Anxiety-related Behavior. *Neuropsychopharmacology* 19:381–96

Lindblad-Toh K, Winchester E, Daly MJ, Wang DG, Hirschhorn JN, et al. 2000. Large-scale discovery and genotyping of single-nucleotide polymorphisms in the mouse. *Nat. Genet.* 24:381–86

Litt MK, Babor TF, DelBoca FK, Kadden RM, Cooney NL. 1992. Types of alcoholics. II. Application of an empirically derived typology to treatment matching. *Arch. Gen. Psychiatry* 49:609–14

Logue SF, Swartz RJ, Wehner JM. 1998. Genetic correlation between performance on an appetitive-signaled nosepoke task and voluntary ethanol consumption. *Alcohol: Clin. Exp. Res.* 22:1912–20

Loh EW, Higuchi S, Matsushita S, Murray R, Chen CK, Ball D. 2000. Association analysis of the GABA_A receptor subunit genes cluster on 5q33-34 and alcohol dependence in a Japanese population. *Mol. Psychiatry* 5:301–7

Loh E-W, Smith I, Murray R, McLaughlin M, McNulty S, Ball D. 1999. Association between variants at the GABA_Aβ2, GABA_Aα6 and GABA_Aγ2 gene cluster and alcohol dependence in a Scottish population. *Mol. Psychiatry* 4:539–44

Long AD, Langley CH. 1999. The power of association studies to detect the contribution of candidate genetic loci to variation in complex traits. *Genome Res.* 9:720–31

Lumeng L, Li TK. 1986. The development of metabolic tolerance in the alcohol-preferring P rats: comparison of forced and free-choice drinking of ethanol. *Pharmacol. Biochem. Behav.* 25:1013–20

MacDonald ME, Ambrose CM, Duyao MP, Myers RH, Lin C, et al. 1993. A novel gene containing a trinucleotide repeat that is expanded and unstable on Huntington's disease chromosomes. *Cell* 72:971–83

Madden PA, Heath AC, Pedersen NL, Kaprio J, Koskenvuo MJ, Martin NG. 1999. The genetics of smoking persistence in men and women: a multicultural study. *Behav. Genet.* 29:423–31

Mardones J, Segovia-Riquelme N. 1983. Thirty-two years of selection of rats by ethanol preference: UChA and UChB strains. *Neurobehav. Toxicol. Teratol.* 5:171–78

Marks MJ, Stitzel JA, Collins AC. 1989. Genetic influences on nicotine responses. *Pharmacol. Biochem. Behav.* 33:667–78

Marlatt GA, Baer JS, Donovan DM, Kivlahan DR. 1988. Addictive behaviors: etiology and treatment. *Annu. Rev. Psychol.* 39:223–52

Marley RJ, Arros DM, Henricks KK, Marley ME, Miner LL. 1998. Sensitivity to cocaine and amphetamine among mice selectively bred for differential cocaine sensitivity. *Psychopharmacology* 140:42–51

McClearn GE, Rodgers DA. 1959. Differences in alcohol preference among inbred strains of mice. *Q. J. Stud. Alcohol* 20:691–95

McGuffin P, Riley B, Plomin R. 2001. Genomics and behavior. Toward behavioral genomics. *Science* 291:1232–49

Merikangas KR, Swendsen JD. 2001. Contributions of epidemiology to the neurobiology of mental illness. See Charney et al. 1999, pp. 100–7

Metten P, Phillips TJ, Crabbe JC, Tarantino LM, McClearn GE, et al. 1998. High genetic susceptibility to ethanol withdrawal predicts low ethanol consumption. *Mamm. Genome* 9:983–90

Mogil JS, Flodman P, Spence MA, Sternberg WF, Kest B, et al. 1995. Oligogenic determination of morphine analgesic magnitude: a genetic analysis of selectively bred mouse lines. *Behav. Genet.* 25:397–406

Mogil JS, Sternberg WF, Marek P, Sadowski B, Belknap JK, Liebeskind JC. 1996. The genetics of pain and pain inhibition. *Proc. Natl. Acad. Sci. USA* 93:3048–55

Mohammed AH. 2000. Genetic dissection of nicotine-related behaviour: a review of animal studies. *Behav. Brain Res.* 113:35–41

Moisan MP, Courvoisier H, Bihoreau MT, Gauguier D, Hendley ED, et al. 1996. A major quantitative trait locus influences hyperactivity in the WKHA rat. *Nat. Genet.* 14:471–73

Murphy JM, Gatto GJ, Waller MB, McBride WJ, Lumeng L, Li TK. 1986. Effects of scheduled access on ethanol intake by the alcohol-preferring (P) line of rats. *Alcohol* 3:331–36

Murray JB. 1993. Review of research on pathological gambling. *Psychol. Rep.* 72(3, Pt. 1):791–810

Nadeau JH, Frankel WN. 2000. The roads from phenotypic variation to gene discovery: mutagenesis versus QTLs. *Nat. Genet.* 25:381–84

Nathan PE. 1988. The addictive personality is the behavior of the addict. *J. Consult. Clin. Psychol.* 56:183–88

Nestler EJ. 2000. Genes and addiction. *Nat. Genet.* 26:277–81

Nolan PM, Kapfhamer D, Bucan M. 1997. Random mutagenesis screen for dominant behavioral mutations in mice. *Methods* 13: 379–95

Nolan PM, Peters J, Strivens M, Rogers D, Hagan J, et al. 2000. A systematic, genome-wide, phenotype-driven mutagenesis programme for gene function studies in the mouse. *Nat. Genet.* 25:440–43

O'Brien CP, Childress AR, Ehrman R, Robbins SJ. 1998. Conditioning factors in drug abuse: Can they explain compulsion? *J. Psychopharmacol.* 12:15–22

Overstreet DH. 1993. The Flinders sensitive line rats: a genetic animal model of depression. *Neurosci. Biobehav. Rev.* 17:51–68

Overstreet DH, Halikas JA, Seredenin SB, Kampov-Polevoy AB, Viglinskaya IV, et al. 1997. Behavioral similarities and differences among alcohol-preferring and -nonpreferring rats: confirmation by factor analysis and extension to additional groups. *Alcohol: Clin. Exp. Res.* 21:840–48

Paigen K, Eppig JT. 2000. A mouse phenome project. *Mamm. Genome* 11:715–17

Patton D, Barnes GE, Murray RP. 1994. The reliability and construct validity of two measures of addictive personality. *Int. J. Addict.* 29:999–1014

Phillips TJ, Belknap JK, Buck KJ, Cunningham CL. 1998a. Genes on mouse chromosomes 2 and 9 determine variation in ethanol consumption. *Mamm. Genome* 9:936–41

Phillips TJ, Brown KJ, Burkhart-Kasch S, Wenger CD, Kelly MA, et al. 1998b. Alcohol preference and sensitivity are markedly reduced in mice lacking dopamine D2 receptors. *Nat. Neurosci.* 1:610–15

Phillips TJ, Hen R, Crabbe JC. 1999. Complications associated with genetic background effects in research using knockout mice. *Psychopharmacology* 147:5–7

Piazza PV, Le Moal M. 1996. Pathophysiological basis of vulnerability to drug abuse: role of an interaction between stress, glucocorti-coids, and dopaminergic neurons. *Annu. Rev. Pharmacol. Toxicol.* 36:359–78

Pickens RW, Svikis DS, McGue M, LaBuda MC. 1995. Common genetic mechanisms in alcohol, drug, and mental disorder comorbidity. *Drug Alcohol Depend.* 39:129–38

Pickens RW, Svikis DS, McGue M, Lykken DT, Heston LL, Clayton PJ. 1991. Heterogeneity in the inheritance of alcoholism. *Arch. Gen. Psychiatry* 48:19–28

Plomin R, Crabbe J. 2000. DNA. *Psychol. Bull.* 126:806–28

Prescott CA, Aggen SH, Kendler KS. 2000. Sex-specific genetic influences on the comorbidity of alcoholism and major depression in a population-based sample of US twins. *Arch. Gen. Psychiatry* 57:803–11

Prescott CA, Kendler KS. 1999. Genetic and environmental contributions to alcohol abuse and dependence in a population-based sample of male twins. *Am. J. Psychiatry* 156:34–40

Ramos A, Berton O, Mormède P, Chaouloff F. 1997. A multiple-test study of anxiety-related behaviours in six inbred rat strains. *Behav. Brain Res.* 85:57–69

Ramos A, Mellerin Y, Mormède P, Chaouloff F. 1998. A genetic and multifactorial analysis of anxiety-related behaviours in Lewis and SHR intercrosses. *Brain Behav. Res.* 96:195–205

Ramos A, Moisan MP, Chaouloff F, Mormède C, Mormède P. 1999. Identification of female-specific QTLs affecting an emotionality-related behavior in rats. *Mol. Psychiatry* 4:453–62

Ramos A, Mormède P. 1998. Stress and emotionality: a multidimensional and genetic approach. *Neurosci. Biobehav. Rev.* 22:33–57

Reich T, Hinrichs A, Culverhouse R, Bierut L. 1999. Genetic studies of alcoholism and substance dependence. *Am. J. Hum. Genet.* 65:599–605

Reilly MT, Fehr C, Buck KJ. 2001. Alcohol and gene expression in the central nervous system. In *Nutrient-Gene Interactions in Health and Disease*, ed. N Moussa-Moustaid, CD

Berdanier, 7:131–62. Boca Raton, FL: CRC Press

Richards JB, Mitchell SH, de Wit H, Seiden LS. 1997. Determination of discount functions in rats with an adjusting-amount procedure. *J. Exp. Anal. Behav.* 67:353–66

Risinger FO, Cunningham CL. 1998. Ethanol-induced conditioned taste aversion in BXD recombinant inbred mice. *Alcohol: Clin. Exp. Res.* 22:1234–44

Robbins TW, Everitt BJ. 1999. Drug addiction: bad habits add up [news]. *Nature* 398:567–70

Rodgers DA, McClearn GE. 1962. Mouse strain differences in preference for various concentrations of alcohol. *Q. J. Stud. Alcohol* 23:1:26–33

Rose RJ. 1995. Genes and human behavior. *Annu. Rev. Psychol.* 46:625–54

Rozin P, Stoess C. 1993. Is there a general tendency to become addicted? *Addict. Behav.* 18:81–87

Sander T, Ball D, Murray R, Patel J, Samochowiec J, et al. 1999. Association analysis of sequence variants of GABA$_A\alpha$6, α2, and γ2 gene cluster and alcohol dependence. *Alcohol. Clin. Exp. Res.* 23:427–31

Schechter MD, Meehan SM, Schechter JB. 1995. Genetic selection for nicotine activity in mice correlates with conditioned place preference. *Eur. J. Pharmacol.* 279:59–64

Schuckit MA. 1999. New findings in the genetics of alcoholism. *JAMA* 281:1875–76

Schuckit MA. 2000. Biological phenotypes associated with individuals at high risk for developing alcohol-related disorder. Part 2. *Addict. Biol.* 5:23–36

Schuckit MA, Edenberg HJ, Kalmijn J, Flury L, Smith TL, et al. 2001. A genome-wide search for genes that relate to a low level of response to alcohol. *Alcohol: Clin. Exp. Res.* 25:323–29

Schuckit MA, Smith TL. 1996. An 8-year follow-up of 450 sons of alcoholic and control subjects. *Arch. Gen. Psychiatry* 53:202–10

Schuckit MA, Tipp JE, Bergman M, Reich W, Hesselbrock VM, Smith TL. 1997. Comparison of induced and independent major depressive disorders in 2,945 alcoholics. *Am. J. Psychiatry* 154:948–57

Seale TW, Johnson P, Carney JM, Rennert OM. 1984. Interstrain variation in acute toxic response to caffeine among inbred mice. *Pharmacol. Biochem. Behav.* 20:576–73

Self DW, Nestler EJ. 1995. Molecular mechanisms of drug reinforcement and addiction. *Annu. Rev. Neurosci.* 18:463–95

Shaffer HJ. 1999. Strange bedfellows: a critical view of pathological gambling and addiction. *Addiction* 94:1445–48

Simpson EM, Linder CC, Sargent EE, Davisson MT, Mobraaten LE, Sharp JJ. 1997. Genetic variation among 129 substrains and its importance for targeted mutagenesis in mice. *Nat. Genet.* 16:19–27

Skutella T, Montkowski A, Stohr T, Probst JC, Landgraf R, et al. 1994. Corticotropin-releasing hormone (CRH) antisense oligodeoxynucleotide treatment attenuates social defeat-induced anxiety in rats. *Cell. Mol. Neurobiol.* 14:579–88

Slutske WS, Eisen S, True WR, Lyons MJ, Goldberg J, Tsuang M. 2000. Common genetic vulnerability for pathological gambling and alcohol dependence in men. *Arch. Gen. Psychiatry* 57:666–73

Stallings MC, Hewitt JK, Beresford T, Heath AC, Eaves LJ. 1999. A twin study of drinking and smoking onset and latencies from first use to regular use. *Behav. Genet.* 29:409–21

Stitzel JA, Lu Y, Jimenez M, Tritto T, Collins AC. 2000. Genetic and pharmacological strategies identify a behavioral function of neuronal nicotinic receptors. *Behav. Brain Res.* 113:57–64

Thibault C, Lai C, Wilke N, Duong B, Olive MF, et al. 2000. Expression profiling of neural cells reveals specific patterns of ethanol-responsive gene expression. *Mol. Pharmacol.* 58:1593–600

Thiele TE, Marsh DJ, Ste Marie, Bernstein IL, Palmiter RD. 1998. Ethanol consumption and resistance are inversely related to neuropeptide Y levels. *Nature* 396:366–69

Thiele TE, Willis B, Stadler J, Reynolds JG, Bernstein IL, McKnight GS. 2000. High ethanol consumption and low sensitivity to ethanol-induced sedation in protein kinase A-mutant mice. *J. Neurosci.* 0:RC75(1–6)

Tsuang MT, Lyons MJ, Eisen SA, Goldberg J, True W, et al. 1996. Genetic influences on DSM-III-R drug abuse and dependence: a study of 3,372 twin pairs. *Am. J. Med. Genet.* 67:473–77

Turri MG, Talbot CJ, Radcliffe RA, Wehner JM, Flint J. 1999. High-resolution mapping of quantitative trait loci for emotionality in selected strains of mice. *Mamm. Genome* 10:1098–101

Tzschentke TM. 1998. Measuring reward with the conditioned place preference paradigm: a comprehensive review of drug effects, recent progress and new issues. *Prog. Neurobiol.* 56:613–72

Uhl GR. 1999. Molecular genetics of substance abuse vulnerability: a current approach. *Neuropsychopharmacology* 20:3–9

Vadasz C, Saito M, Balla A, Kiraly I, Gyetvai B, et al. 2000. Mapping of quantitative trait loci for ethanol preference in quasi-congenic strains. *Alcohol* 20:161–71

van den Bree MBM, Johnson EO, Neale MC, Pickens RW. 1998a. Genetic and environmental influences on drug use and abuse/dependence in male and female twins. *Drug Alcohol Depend.* 52:231–41

van den Bree MBM, Svikis DS, Pickens RW. 1998b. Genetic influences in antisocial personality and drug use disorders. *Drug Alcohol Depend.* 49:177–87

van Ree JM, Gerrits MA, Vanderschuren LJ. 1999. Opioids, reward and addiction: an encounter of biology, psychology, and medicine. *Pharmacol. Rev.* 51:341–96

Venter JC, Adams MD, Myers EW, Li PW, Mural RJ, et al. 2001. The sequence of the human genome. *Science* 291:1304–51

Wahlsten D. 1990. Insensitivity of the analysis of variance to heredity-environment interaction. *Behav. Brain Sci.* 13:109–20

Wahlsten D. 1999. Single-gene influences on brain and behavior. *Annu. Rev. Psychol.* 50:599–624

Waller MB, McBride WJ, Lumeng L, Li TK. 1982a. Effects of intravenous ethanol and of 4-methylpyrazole on alcohol drinking in alcohol-preferring rats. *Pharmacol. Biochem. Behav.* 17:763–68

Waller MB, McBride WJ, Lumeng L, Li TK. 1982b. Induction of dependence on ethanol by free-choice drinking in alcohol-preferring rats. *Pharmacol. Biochem. Behav.* 16:501–7

Watson SJ, Akil H. 1999. Gene chips and arrays revealed: a primer on their power and their uses. *Biol. Psychiatry* 45:533–43

Wehner JM, Bowers BJ. 1995. Use of transgenics, null mutants, and antisense approaches to study ethanol's actions. *Alcohol: Clin. Exp. Res.* 19:811–20

Wehner JM, Radcliffe RA, Rosmann ST, Christensen SC, Rasmussen DL, et al. 1997. Quantitative trait locus analysis of contextual fear conditioning in mice. *Nat. Genet.* 17:331–34

Weiss JM, Cierpial MA, West CHK. 1998. Selective breeding of rats for high and low motor activity in a swim test: toward a new animal model of depression. *Pharmacol. Biochem. Behav.* 61:49–66

Weninger SC, Dunn AJ, Muglia LJ, Dikkes P, Miczek KA, et al. 1999. Stress-induced behaviors require the corticotropin-releasing hormone (CRH) receptor, but not CRH. *Proc. Natl. Acad. Sci. USA* 96:8283–88

Whatley VJ, Johnson TE, Erwin VG. 1999. Identification and confirmation of quantitative trait loci regulating alcohol consumption in congenic strains of mice. *Alcohol: Clin. Exp. Res.* 23:1262–71

Williams TG. 1996. Substance abuse and addictive personality disorders. In *Handbook of Relational Diagnosis and Dysfunctional Family Patterns*, ed. FW Kaslow, pp. 448–62. New York: Wiley & Sons

Wise RA. 1996. Neurobiology of addiction. *Curr. Opin. Neurobiol.* 6:243–51

Annu. Rev. Psychol. 2002. 53:463–90

GENE-ENVIRONMENT INTERPLAY IN RELATION TO EMOTIONAL AND BEHAVIORAL DISTURBANCE

Michael Rutter[1] and Judy Silberg[2]

[1]*Social, Genetic and Developmental Psychiatry Research Center, Institute of Psychiatry, London SE5 8AF, UK; e-mail: j.wickham@iop.kcl.ac.uk*
[2]*Virginia Institute for Psychiatric and Behavioral Genetics, Virginia Commonwealth University, Richmond, Virginia 23298-0003; e-mail: jsilberg@hsc.vcu.edu*

Key Words quantitive genetics, molecular genetics, gene-environment correlations, gene-environment interactions, evolution

■ **Abstract** The conceptual and methodological issues involved in the study of gene-environment correlations (rGE) and interactions (GxE) are discussed in historical context. Quantitative genetic findings are considered with respect to rGE and GxE in relation to emotional and behavioral disturbance. Key conceptual and substantive implications are outlined in relation to both genetic and environmental risk mediation, with a brief note on evolutionary considerations.

CONTENTS

INTRODUCTION

Conceptually, gene-environment interactions (GxE) mean that there are genetically influenced individual differences in the sensitivity to specific environmental features (Eaves 1984, Mather & Jinks 1982). That they are likely to be present is evident from the very consistent finding of huge individual differences in people's responses to all manner of stresses and adversities, however severe (see Rutter 2000b, 2001a). That might mean no more than that all behaviors are multifactorially determined, the heterogeneity reflecting the operation of other risk and protective factors, measured or unmeasured. However, that is only part of the explanation because experimental studies in humans and in animals have shown heterogeneity in response to experimentally induced risks even under highly controlled conditions (Petitto & Evans 1999). It may be assumed that organismic factors, which are genetically influenced, play a role in individual differential responsiveness. Gene-environment correlations (rGE) refer to genetic effects on individual differences in liability to exposure to particular environmental circumstances. The likelihood of their occurrence is suggested by the evidence that, through their behavior, people to some extent shape and select their environments (Rutter et al. 1997a). Thus, for example, children showing antisocial behavior are more likely, when adult, to experience seriously stressful life events and to lack social support (Rutter et al. 1995, 1998). A key issue concerns the role of genetic influences in these large individual differences in sensitivity and exposure to environmental influences—the topic of this chapter.

Behavior geneticists have long been aware of the potential importance of rGE and GxE because of their implications for the dynamic mechanisms involved in both genetic and environmental risks (see e.g., Cattell 1965, Eaves et al. 1977, Jinks & Fulker 1970, Plomin et al. 1977, Turkheimer & Gottesman 1996); moreover they play a prominent role in contemporary developmental conceptualizations (see e.g., Bronfenbrenner & Ceci 1994, Rutter et al. 1997a). Nevertheless, all too often, behavior genetic findings have been presented in terms of a partitioning of population variance into separate additive and nonadditive genetic components and shared and nonshared environmental effects, with a disregard for the possible role of rGE and GxE. That is now changing because of a greater realization of the crucial role of gene-environment interplay in risk and protective processes and because of advances in the means to study such interplay. In this chapter we review the methodological considerations, empirical findings, and conceptual implications, with special reference to emotional disturbance (anxiety and depression) and behavioral disorders (oppositional/defiant and antisocial behavior).

Before turning to the evidence on rGE and GxE, it is necessary to put two issues to rest. Although genetic research is far from free of problems, any dispassionate review of the evidence indicates that there are substantial genetic effects on psychopathology, including emotional and behavioral disturbance (Rutter et al. 1999a,b). Additionally, although it is true that much psychosocial research has failed to put environmental mediation hypotheses to the test in rigorous fashion, there are a range of effective strategies that do just that (Rutter et al. 2001), with findings that show the reality of important environmentally mediated risk effects (Rutter 2000a). Accordingly, it is possible to consider G-E interplay in the confidence that there are important gene (G) and environment (E) influences and, therefore, that their interplay is a legitimate topic of study. Moreover, there is substantial epidemiological evidence to suggest that the interplay is likely to be important (Rutter et al. 1997a). Accordingly, an understanding of rGE and GxE should lead to more information on both environmental risk mechanisms and the processes by which genetic factors operate indirectly through effects on exposure to, and sensitivity to, the environment.

GENE-ENVIRONMENT INTERACTION

Conceptual and Statistical Background

Because, in order to analyze gene-environment interaction (GxE) satisfactorily, it is necessary to specify both the environmental influences and the individual genotypes, most of our understanding of the biology, until the advent of molecular genetics, stemmed from experimental work in plants and micro-organisms or from experimental breeding studies of animals (see e.g., Mather & Jinks 1982, McClearn et al. 2001).

The extensive range of studies of GxE in nonhuman species has established several principles (see e.g., Mackay 2001, Mather & Jinks 1982). First, although genetic control of sensitivity to the environment is widespread, the contribution of GxE to the overall population variance is typically smaller than the main effects of G and E even in controlled experiments using extreme environments. However, that does not apply to all biological processes or all genetic effects (see below).

Second, selection and breeding studies show that often different genes affect sensitivity to different features of the environment. There is little indication of a general GxE effect. Rather, there are genetically influenced sensitivities to specific environments, such sensitivities often applying only to minority subsets of the population (Rutter & Pickles 1991). It makes no sense to look for an overall interaction between genes and environments, and hence it is not surprising that "black box" analyses of anonymous G and E have usually failed to show GxE (Plomin et al. 1988).

Third, the genes that influence sensitivity to the environment may be quite different from those that bring about main effects. Moreover, there is both pleiotropy (one gene having diverse phenotypic effects) and polygeny (each phenotype being affected by more than one gene) (McClearn et al. 2001), in addition to genetic interactions, both between alleles within genes (dominance) and across genes (epistasis). The phenotypic expression of even single-gene disorders may be greatly affected by other (background) genes (Weatherall 1999). As a consequence, the detection of GxE is likely to be very difficult unless the individual genotype and the specific environment can be accurately measured. The task of understanding how a gene works in a larger environmental context is likely to prove considerably more difficult than simply finding a susceptibility gene for a multifactorial disorder or even determining what proteins it encodes (Wahlsten 2002).

Fourth, cross-fostering studies of animals genetically at risk (see e.g., Anisman et al. 1998) suggest that risks may be reduced by appropriate rearing—for example, calm, nurturant, nonreactive mothers may provide a buffer against genetically influenced emotional hyper-reactivity (see Suomi 2000). The currently available data are too sparse for firm conclusions, but the experimental approach is clearly a fruitful one.

The seminal theoretical work on the quantitative study of GxE in humans was undertaken by Cattell (1965) some four decades ago when he sought to specify GxE statistically within his multiple abstract variance analysis (MAVA). An early formulation of a model for cultural inheritance also included GxE within the construct of genetic plasticity to the environment provided by parents (Cavalli-Sforza & Feldman 1973). Jinks & Fulker (1970), however, provided a more influential conceptual framework by considering the implications of GxE for second-degree statistics (variances and covariances) and higher-order moments (skewness, kurtosis, and means in relation to the variance) derived from clusters of family members. They showed that, if there were only additive genetic effects on sensitivity to the shared environment, GxE is confounded with main effects of G in the classical design of monozygotic and of dizygotic twins reared together (see also Molenaar et al. 1999). Help can be provided by the study of intrapair variance in separated twin pairs and by higher-order statistics that allow comparison of the effects of environments stratified by genotype (DeFries & Fulker 1985), or the converse if they are independent.

Several other statistical considerations are relevant.

1. There are several different types of gene-environment interaction that give rise to different models and different methods of testing (Kendler & Eaves 1986, Ottman 1996, Rutter & Pickles 1991).

2. It is a serious mistake to equate GxE with the statistical interaction term in a traditional multivariate analysis (see Eaves et al. 1977, Eaves 1984, Rutter 1983, Rutter & Pickles 1991). That is because, in some circumstances, GxE will be entirely absorbed in the main effect (see Rutter & Pickles 1991) and because a statistical interaction will only occur when there is a variation in both G and E (that will not apply, for example, to phenylketonuria when the risk substance is universally present in all ordinary diets or to hay fever, for which the exposure to pollens applies similarly to most people).

3. All forms of interaction (not just GxE) are extremely sensitive to scaling variations (see Brown et al. 1991, for an example with respect to two environmental risk factors). Variance-stabilizing or -normalizing transformations often eradicate apparent GxE (Mather & Jinks 1982). That does not necessarily mean that there was not genetically influenced sensitivity to the environment. There is no one "true" scale. There are parallel dangers of false positives and false negatives.

4. The statistical power for detecting GxE is much less than that for detecting main effects; accordingly, large samples are essential (Eaves et al. 1977; Wahlsten 1990, 1999).

5. Interactions may derive from multi-stage causal chain processes (Pickles 1993). Longitudinal data will be necessary to detect such forms of GxE. However, the interactive nature of a developmental process tends to become invisible after a sufficient time even under the most favorable circumstances (see Molenaar et al. 1999).

6. Although in theory, adoption designs are preferable to twin designs for the detection of GxE because they provide a "cleaner" separation of G and E, they have many disadvantages. That very separation (central to the design) results in there being very few individuals in the key cell that brings together G risk and E risk (see Bohman 1996, Cadoret et al. 1987). That means that the proportion of variance explained by GxE will be a major underestimate of the state of affairs in the general population in which that cell will be very much more common (Rutter 1987). Another problem is that adoptive families severely under-represent high-risk environments (because the choice of parents allowed to adopt excludes them as far as possible) (see Rutter et al. 1999a, 2001) and reflect a narrower range of environments (Stoolmiller 1999). An additional practical problem is that studies of adoptees often involve nonparticipation rates of over 50% (see Cadoret et al. 1995, Ge et al. 1996), raising the possibility of bias.

7. Unless the individual genotype can be specified (through DNA), GxE is difficult to assess satisfactorily in the presence of rGE. Expressed simply, that is because the high psychopathological risk in the G plus E cell could arise either because rGE means that individuals with high G also tend to have high E (with the consequence that the greatest risk, whether due to G or E, will appear to derive from their combination), or because there is a synergistic interaction between G and E (but see Eaves & Erkanli 2001 for a possible solution using Markov chain Monte Carlo methods within a Bayesian framework). Because from an evolutionary perspective both rGE and GxE reflect adaptive effects of G on E (Chadwick & Cardew 1996), it is quite likely in this circumstance that both rGE and GxE are operative, but statistically they cannot readily be differentiated. In multifactorial models it is also necessary to differentiate GxE interactions from ExE interactions (see Eaves & Eysenck 1977).

Molecular Genetic Findings in Internal Medicine

It is clear from all of these considerations that a greatly increased leverage on the study of GxE becomes possible once individual susceptibility genes can be identified, specific environmental risk factors can be accurately identified, and there is some testable hypothesis on a biologically plausible risk process. In the psychopathological arena the only much-studied example concerns the risk of Alzheimer's disease associated with the Apo-E-4 allele (Plassman & Breitner 1996, Rubinzstein 1995). Several GxE effects have been evident. Thus, Mayeux et al. (1995) found that there was no increase in the risk for Alzheimer's disease associated with head injury in the absence of Apo-E-4, a twofold increase with Apo-E-4 alone but a 10-fold increase from the combination of Apo-E-4 and head injury. Similarly, Teasdale et al. (1997), in a 6-month follow-up of patients suffering a severe head injury, found that Apo-E-4 individuals were more than twice as likely to have a bad outcome. Yaffe et al. (2000) found that oestrogen use protected against cognitive decline in older women if they did not have Apo-E-4, but this was much less evident in those who were Apo-E-4 positive, reflecting GxE. More tentatively, there is a possible role for cholesterol in the GxE associated with Alzheimer's disease (Chandra & Pandav 1998).

Ischaemic heart disease provides a good parallel for what may be expected with mental disorders because in both cases causation is multifactorial, with many of the risk and protective factors operating dimensionally with large individual differences in susceptibility to them. Minihane et al. (2000) showed that the Apo-E-4 genotype influences responsiveness to fish oil supplementation effects on lipids. Birley et al. (1997) also used an experimental approach, finding that the lowering of LDL cholesterol associated with diet was greater in those with the NN blood group than in those with MN. Humphries et al. (2001) found that Apo-E-4 was a risk factor for ischaemic heart disease, but this mainly applied to smokers. Talmud et al. (2000) found that individuals with the D9N allele for lipoprotein lipase had a markedly increased risk of ischaemic heart disease when they smoked, the risk associated with smoking being much less in those who did not have this allele.

Other examples of GxE in internal medicine are evident in the marked individual differences in response to infections (Hill 1998, Knight et al. 1999) and to therapeutic medication (Evans & Relling 1999, Wolf et al. 2000). Reed (1985), in reviewing the extensive ethnic differences in alcohol use, abuse, and sensitivity, noted that the most striking difference concerned the lower alcoholism rate in Japanese as a consequence of high alcohol sensitivity of individuals who lack the ACDH-1 isozyme. This GxE effect, of course, concerns alcohol as the E feature. The application of molecular genetic methods to the study of GxE is only just beginning, but it is obvious that it is likely to be highly productive provided that the pathophysiological risk process can be identified in multifactorial disorders, allowing the testing of specific hypotheses on GxE instead of black box analyses of anonymous G and E (see Rutter & Pickles 1991).

Quantitative Genetic Studies of GxE on Psychopathology

Adoption studies have mainly been used to study GxE in antisocial behavior and substance abuse. Cadoret et al. (1983), in a study of 367 adoptees, found a significant GxE such that there was a negligible risk for adolescent antisocial behavior from a genetic factor alone (as crudely indexed by antisocial behavior in the biological parent), no effect from an adverse adoptive family environment alone, but a substantial effect when both were present. An earlier paper (Cadoret & Cain

1980) had shown that the effects of an adverse environment seemed to apply only to males, although biological risks were similar in the two sexes. Cadoret et al. (1995) studied 95 male and 102 female adoptees in Iowa An adverse environment of upbringing was indexed by marital problems, divorce/separation, alcohol/drug problems or anxiety/depression or antisocial behavior in the adopting parents. Genetic risk was indexed by antisocial personality disorder in a biological parent. A significant GxE was found, with no effect of the adverse home environment on aggressivity and conduct disturbance in those without genetic risk but a substantial effect in its presence. Cadoret et al. (1996), in a study of the adult offspring of alcoholic biological parents, found that major depression in females was associated with an alcoholic genetic diathesis only when combined with disturbance in an adoptive parent. The findings in males were negative. Although the numbers in the G plus E cell were too small to show a statistically significant GxE, the pattern of an apparent GxE synergism was evident in studies by Cadoret et al. (1987) and Bohman (1996).

Crowe (1974) found that early institutional care was a risk factor for later antisocial behavior only when a genetic risk factor was present. Legrand et al. (1999) used the Minnesota Twin Family Study to examine the risks for substance use at 14 years associated with parental substance abuse/dependence (as an index of genetic risk) and affiliation with deviant peers (as an index of environmental risk). Both had significant effects, but there was also a significant interaction such that the familial risk effect was greater in the presence of high environmental risk. This implies GxE, but the design did not allow a clear differentiation of G and E.

Riggins-Caspers et al. (1999) used an entirely different putative E risk factor— the moderating effects of adoption agency disclosure of psychopathology in the biological parent. Significant GxE was found for both biological alcoholism and antisocial personality with respect to childhood aggression; the effects on adult antisocial personality in the offspring were much less striking. In other words, the genetic risk for childhood aggression that stemmed from parental psychopathology was increased if the adoptive parents knew about it. Putting the evidence together (but mindful of the limitations of adoptee studies and of the methodological considerations; see above), it may be concluded that the pointers all indicate a likely GxE effect with respect to antisocial behavior and substance use problems.

Twin designs have been employed in the only two studies of GxE with respect to emotional disturbance. Kendler et al. (1995) assessed putative genetic risk for major depression by regarding it as highest when there was an affected monozygotic (MZ) cotwin, lowest when there was an unaffected MZ cotwin, and intermediate with an affected dizygotic (DZ) cotwin (second highest) or an unaffected DZ cotwin (second lowest). The risk of onset of depression following a major life event was greatest in those at greatest genetic risk. This GxE effect implied that genetic factors operate in part by affecting the sensitivity of individuals to the depression-inducing effects of stressful life events. Silberg et al. (2001a), studying adolescent twin girls in the Virginia Twin Study of Adolescent Behavioral Development, used a different strategy. Attention was confined to life events (LE) not showing rGE, with findings indicating a significant increase in heritability in the presence of LE, an increase entirely due to GxE. Phenotypic analyses showed no effect of LE on anxiety/depression in the absence of genetic risk, but a significant effect in its presence. Genetic factors, by contrast, did have a significant effect in the absence of LE, indicating either that there were direct as well as indirect effects on emotional disturbance or that the E risk stemmed from features other than the specific LE assessed.

Koeppen-Schomerus et al. (2000) used the same approach of comparing heritability according to the presence of identified specific environmental risk factors—in their case very premature birth and the associated obstetric and perinatal complications as they affected cognitive scores at age 2 years. The obstetric/perinatal effects were found to be environmentally mediated, but heritability of cognitive level was lowest in the presence of environmental risk, in other words, the opposite form of GxE to that found by anxiety/depression. Similarly, Rowe et al. (1999) in a study of a much older sample, found that the heritabilities for vocabulary IQ were significantly greater among the better educated than the less well educated. However, an earlier study showed only a marginal trend in the same direction (van den Oord & Rowe 1998).

The point of introducing these findings on a quite different phenotype is to underline the fact that GxE effects can be of several different kinds, each having rather different implications for the causal processes. In the case of both antisocial behavior/substance abuse and anxiety/depression, the implication is that an important part of the genetic effect is on sensitivity to key environmental influences (although part seems to operate more directly on the phenotype without the need for environmental mediation). There was little effect, however, from E in the absence of genetic risk. By contrast, in the case of cognitive level, genetic influences were maximal when E risk was low, and vice-versa. The implication is that the effects of G and E on IQ do not involve marked individual differences in sensitivity to the environment, but rather, represent somewhat different routes to the same outcome.

A rather different strategy for examining GxE has been to examine societal moderators either in terms of differences in some broad personal variable or in terms of cohort effects. Heath et al. (1989) noted that the heritability of alcohol consumption was much lower in married than unmarried women—both in younger and older age groups. In another Australian questionnaire study, Heath et al. (1998) showed that a married-like relationship also decreased the genetic effect on depression—again in both younger and older age groups. Boomsma et al. (1999) found that a religious upbringing was associated with a lower heritability for disinhibition; Koopmans et al. (1999) found the same with respect to alcohol use in females (but not in males). Dick and her colleagues (2001, Rose et al. 2001), in a Finnish twin sample, found that genetic influences on adolescent alcohol use were substantially greater in individuals living in areas with many young adults and high migration. They argued that communities characterized by more young adult role models and greater social mobility allowed for an increased expression of genetic propensities that contributed to individual differences in adolescent drinking (although the community differences could reflect differences in genotypes or in genetic variance).

Several studies have examined cohort effects. Heath et al. (1985) found an increase in the heritability of educational attainment in Norway for males, but not females, over a time period in which educational opportunities became more widely available. Conversely, Kendler et al. (2000) found a rise over the twentieth century in the heritability of smoking in women but not men. Heath et al. (1993) found no differences across cohorts in the heritability of smoking initiation. Sellers et al. (1992) found a difference between earlier and later cohorts in the association between smoking and lung cancer (implying a GxE with respect to exposure to smoking). Silventoinen et al. (2000), in a Finnish study, found a marginal increase over time in the heritability of height (76% to 81%). The research strategy is potentially useful, but the results have been rather inconclusive.

On the other hand, large cohort changes in the level of a trait do have implications for the operation of rGE, as pointed out conceptually and mathematically by Dickens & Flynn (2001) in relation to the massive rise in IQ (some 20 points) that has been evident over the past half century (Flynn 2000). That has seemed to provide a paradox in that the cause has to be environmental, but such a large rise would seem to require an enormous environmental difference arising over a short period of time—the equivalent of, for instance, some three standard deviations, which seems implausible (Jensen 1973). Some form of multiplier must operate. Dickens & Flynn (2001) showed that rGE would have such a potentiating effect on E, and given the empirical demonstration of rGE, it seems reasonable to postulate that it may have been responsible. The argument is challenging because some behavior geneticists (e.g., Plomin 1994) have argued that rGE means that E effects have been overestimated in the past because they have included some genetic mediation (but see Eaves et al. 1977). Dickens & Flynn's (2001) model proposed that, although that will be the case to some extent, rGE enhances E and, hence, traditional partitioning of the variance tends to underestimate E. Their argument was directed at the rise in IQ, but it would seem to apply equally to the marked rise in emotional and behavioral disorders in young people that has occurred over the same period of time (Rutter & Smith 1995).

GENE-ENVIRONMENT CORRELATION

Conceptual and Statistical Background

As in the case of GxE, some of the basic insights on rGE stem from work in non-human species in which the environmental impact of parents on offspring may be manipulated through breeding and cross-fostering studies. The genes that influence the rearing environment provided by parents may not be the same as those that influence the offspring's phenotype directly (in which case there is no rGE in relation to the phenotype). For example, human birth weight is almost exclusively determined by the shared environment. However, studies of the children of twins have shown that part of the environmental variation is the result of genetic differences in the mothers (Nance et al. 1983). It was this difference between rGE that did, and did not, contribute to the phenotype of the offspring that led Haley et al. (1981) to refer to "one character" and "two character" models of maternal genetic effects. This basic biometrical understanding of the genetic environment led to Eaves' (1976a,b) treatment of cultural inheritance and sibling interactions in humans.

Cattell (1965) made the important distinction between environments actively shaped by the individual and those brought about because genetically influenced behaviors may provoke particular environmental treatments, thus anticipating one aspect of the future taxonomy of rGE (Plomin et al. 1977). A major inhibition to the widespread acceptance of these early insights [in addition to some mathematical inconsistencies (Loehlin 1965)] was the lack of an explicit and parsimonious formulation of the roles of G and E in human families, a lack partially remedied by Jinks & Fulker's (1970) introduction of model-fitting methods. Among other things, they noted that passive rGE (meaning correlations between the overall family environment and genetic differences among families) may be expected to lead to differences in total variance between children raised by biological parents and those raised by adoptive parents. Subsequently, the rediscovery of Wright's work on path analysis by Morton and his coworkers (Rao et al. 1976) provided the first tractable model for the correlated effects of G and E in kinship data when there was one form of assortative mating (social homogamy). A variety of more general treatments of biological and cultural inheritance followed over the next two decades, allowing for different mechanisms of mate selection and sex differences in the expression of G and E differences (see e.g., Rice et al. 1978, Truett et al. 1994).

In their introduction of a taxonomy for rGE and GxE, Plomin et al. (1977) differentiated between passive, active, and evocative rGE. In the first, the relevant genotypes are those of the parents; their genetically influenced characteristics will help shape the environments they provide for their children. Plomin et al. (1977) pointed out that a direct measure of passive rGE was obtainable from a comparison of the correlations between family environment and child phenotype in adoptive and biological families (see also Plomin 1994). However, this is so only if the range of E, and particularly the proportion of high E risk environments, is similar in the two types of families. Subsequent data have made clear that this is rarely the case, at least with respect to the types of E related to the risk for emotional and behavioral psychopathology (Rutter et al. 1999a, 2001; Stoolmiller 1999).

The understanding of passive rGE involves five rather separate issues. First, there is the question of whether genetically influenced parental characteristics are associated with major differences in the environments of upbringing that they provide for their children. Epidemiological evidence is consistent in showing that there are strong associations between parental psychopathology and the family environments they provide (Murray & Cooper 1997, Rutter 1989).

Second, there is the rather different question of the strength of genetic influences on this association. That is best tackled through studies of adult twins in which the phenotype to be studied is the family environment they provide for their children, as indexed for example by the risk for marital breakdown (Jockin et al. 1996, McGue & Lykken 1992), coercive parenting (O'Connor et al. 1995), marital difficulties (Kendler et al. 1993), or parental overprotection and care (Pérusse et al. 1994)—most of which have been shown to be genetically influenced to some extent. Surprisingly little research on twins has focused on this important question.

Third, there is the question of which parental attribute mediates this genetic effect on the rearing environment. The issue directly parallels that considered in relation to LE (see below), but it has scarcely been addressed so far. Multivariate analyses of twin samples are needed to determine whether, for example, the genetic effects on divorce are primarily mediated through overt antisocial behavior, some temperamental feature (e.g., neuroticism, impulsivity, or sensations-seeking), lack of religiosity, anxiety/depression, or substance abuse. Jockin et al.'s (1996) study is one of the very few to examine some of these possibilities, with the finding that 30–40% of the heritability of divorce risk derived from genetic factors influencing personality.

Fourth, there is the question of the role of passive rGE in the risk mediation from the family environment to the child phenotype. The sampling bias in adoptee studies severely limits their use for this purpose. Offspring of twin designs (see Rutter et al. 2001) would be much more effective, but their use in this connection is only just beginning.

The fifth question concerns the parental mediator of the passive rGE as it applies to the child phenotype. Note that this is not the same as the third question discussed above. The difference is that it concerns the impact on the child behavioral phenotype rather than the family environment phenotype. The Colorado Adoption Project tackled the question with respect to the correlations between the Home Observation and Measurement of the Environment (HOME) and young children's Bayley scores (see Plomin 1994). It might be expected that parental IQ would be the obvious mediator, but surprisingly, that was not found to be the case, leaving open the need to explore other possibilities.

Active rGE differs from passive rGE in that the G concerns the child's genes rather than those of the parents (although obviously the former must come from the latter). It refers to the genetically influenced tendency for individuals to seek, create, or otherwise end up in particular kinds of environments. Longitudinal studies are consistent in showing quite strong associations between children's behavior and their environments in adult life (see e.g., Champion et al. 1995, Quinton et al. 1993, Robins 1966). Active rGE draws attention to the fact that these child behaviors are genetically influenced. Evocative rGE differs from active rGE only with respect to the fact that the E is defined in terms of other people's responses to the individual. In practice, of course, the two frequently overlap, in that people choose which sort of broader social environment they enter (peer group, leisure activity club, etc.) or the person with whom they develop a dyadic relationship (marriage partner, close friend, etc.), but the ways in which they behave towards other people will evoke particular forms of responses from them.

Findings on Gene-Environment Correlations

Twin studies have examined the strength of genetic contributions to quite a wide range of environmental features that have been implicated in the causal mechanisms for emotional and behavioral psychopathology. Thus, Kendler et al. (1993), using the Virginia adult twin registry, found that genetic factors accounted for about 20% of the variance in life events (LE) over the past year; heritability was greater for personal events and negligible for network events (most of which are outside the influence of the individual). Kendler & Karkowski-Shuman (1997) used the MZ cotwin's history of illness as an index of genetic liability to major depression (see Kendler et al. 1995, as described above). This was associated with a significantly elevated risk for LEs; a genetic risk for alcoholism also predisposed to LEs in the personal domain. It was concluded that genes may influence the risk for psychopathology by causing individuals to place themselves in high-risk environments.

Plomin et al. (1990), in the Swedish adoption/twin study of aging (SATSA), found a 40% heritability, which was greatest for controllable LEs and least for uncontrollable ones. Using the same data set, Saudino et al. (1997) found a genetic effect only on controllable life events in women; there was no genetic effect in men. The genetic influence on LE seemed to be mediated by personality characteristics. Thapar & McGuffin (1996), in a Welsh study of children and adolescents, found a high (~0.60) heritability for self-rated LEs but a low one for LEs reported by parents. Genetic factors were also more influential for independent events in girls than boys, although the sample size was too small to test for the statistical significance of the sex difference. A later paper (Thapar et al. 1998) showed that the co-occurrence of LE and depression reflected genetic liability in part (but causal inferences are limited by the fact that the data came from the same informant). Silberg et al. (1999), using the Virginia Twin Study of Adolescent Behavioral Development, also found a significant genetic effect on the liability to life events. Most crucially, not only was the genetic liability to LE and depression shared, but also this was associated with the increasing heritability for depression in girls that is evident during the adolescent age period. Billig et al. (1996) found a heritability of 49% for nonindependent, nonfamily life events in late adolescence (using the Minnesota Twin Family Study), but little genetic component for other life events.

The topic of sex differences in relation to the effects of LEs on emotional disturbance, and the role of rGE, warrants further study. There is some evidence that stressful life events are more likely to lead to major depression in adult women than in men (Maciejewski et al. 2000), but the heritability for major depression seems to be greater in women than in men (Kendler et al. 2001). At first sight, these two findings seem contradictory in that the first appears to suggest that depression in women is largely environmentally determined, whereas the second appears to indicate the reverse. The resolution of this paradox may lie in the effects of rGE and GxE in bringing about, during adolescence, a greater exposure to, and sensitivity to, LEs in females than was present in childhood (when the rates of depression in boys and girls are similar).

Genetic effects on individual differences in other life experiences have been shown for a wide range of features varying in their relevance for psychopathological risk. For example, Deater-Deckard et al. (1999), using the Colorado Adoption Project, found the heritability of parent ratings of negativity, inconsistency, and warmth to be 0.38, 0.04, and 0.26, respectively. Using data from the Non-Shared Environment in Adolescent Development project, Plomin et al. (1994) found an average heritability estimate of 0.27 for 18 composite measures of the family environment, with the genetic influence stronger on child-reported than on parent-reported variables. O'Connor et al. (1995), using the same study, found a nonsignificant heritability for mothers' anger, coercion, and transactional conflict towards adolescents; only fathers' transactional conflict showed significant heritability (27%). They noted, however, a serious problem with the Non-Shared Environment in Adolescent Development project, namely that the differences among sibling groups (full sib, half sib, and unrelated) were inconsistent with genetic theory. Also, the findings with respect to genetic influences on many variables differ according to whether attention is paid to twin comparisons or family comparison findings. Unfortunately, studies of divorced/remarried families inevitably involve troublesome confounds between genetic relatedness and family experiences.

Hur et al. (1996), using the Minnesota Twin Family Study, found heritability estimates for leisure activities that varied from 6% (religious activities) to 57% for intellectual activities. They concluded that interests, and engagement, in aptitude-based leisure time activities were affected by genetically influenced individual talents and abilities. In a study of adult twins using the parental bonding instrument, Pérusse et al. (1994) found heritabilities ranging from 19% (father overprotection) to 39% (mother care). Busjahn et al. (1999) showed that coping styles involved genetic influence. Deater-Deckard & O'Connor (2000), using a study of 125 same-sex preschool twins, found a heritability of 58% for dyadic mutuality. Brussoni et al. (2000) used a Canadian twin sample and found a heritability of 25–45% for a questionnaire measure of adult attachment. Elkins et al. (1997), using the Minnesota Twin Family Study, found significant heritabilities for parent-child conflict; heritabilities were higher at 17 years than at 11 years, possibly reflecting the fact that, as compared with younger children, older adolescents have more choice and impact on the nature of the relationships they have with their parents. Trumbetta & Gottesman (2000), using the Veterans Twin Registry, found that 31% of the variance in pair bonding could be attributed to nonadditive genetic factors, as could 22% of the variance in multiple mates. As already noted, there is a substantial genetic influence on divorce (McGue & Lykken 1992, Jockin et al. 1996). Using the Australian Twin Registry, Dunne et al. (1997) found that the genetic contribution to age at first sexual intercourse was greater in twins age 40 years or less than those aged 41–70 (49–72% vs 0–32%). The authors argued that, in the more laissez-faire social climate that has operated in recent years, there is more opportunity for genetic influences to operate on choices in the initiation of sexual activity.

Although there is considerable diversity in both the quality of the data and of the samples, there can be no doubt that genetic influences play a substantial (albeit not a preponderant) role in influencing individual differences in the likelihood that people will encounter acute and chronic life events and experiences that carry important environmentally mediated risks for psychopathology. That conclusion has been resisted by many commentators on the grounds that it is clearly absurd to suppose that there could be a gene for divorce or for life events (Rose 1995, 1998). That is true, but the criticism completely missed the main point (Rutter 2001b). Most experiences that carry risks for psychopathology involve interpersonal interactions (Rutter 2000a). It must be assumed that people's own behavior will influence those interactions, and there will be genetic influences on that individual behavior. This does not entail genetic determinism because environmental factors have an equally strong (often stronger) impact on the same behaviors that shape or select experiences. Even more crucially, it is not deterministic because the fact that an adverse experience has to come about through genetically influenced individual behaviors does not mean that the effects on psychopathology are genetically mediated (Rutter et al. 1993) (see Environmental Risk Mediation, below).

CONCEPTUAL AND SUBSTANTIVE IMPLICATIONS

Environmental Risk Mediation

All psychologists are trained to appreciate that correlations do not necessarily mean causation. That is both because the statistical association does not indicate the direction of effect and because it could reflect the impact of some third variable. Bell (1968) raised the possibility that many supposed socialization effects reflected children's influence on other people, rather than the effects of rearing on children's behavior. Subsequent research (Bell & Chapman 1986, Rutter et al. 1997a) has confirmed the reality of these child effects. Evocative rGE considers the same point but with the additional consideration of the role of G in the child effect. Thus, both Ge et al. (1996) and O'Connor et al. (1998) found that antisocial behavior in the biological parent was associated with an increased likelihood that the adoptive parent would exert negative control, the main predicting mechanism being the child's own (genetically influenced) disruptive behavior. Without doubt, this evocative effect is important, but it should be noted that O'Connor et al. (1998) found that the association between adoptive parenting style and child behavior was almost as strong in the families in which the adopted child did not have an antisocial parent. The implication is that either there is also a true environmentally mediated socialization effect or the child effects derive from behavior that has been influenced by genetic or environmental risk factors unassociated with antisocial behavior in the biological parent.

There are three main implications of these findings for an understanding of environmental risk mediation. First, it should not be assumed that children's effects on other people necessarily mainly reflect G. Second, it is essential to identify the child behaviors mainly responsible for the evocative effects on other people and the proximal psychological processes by which these effects are mediated, especially in relation to the more extreme parental behaviors carrying high psychopathological risk. Third, with respect to developmental implications, longitudinal studies are needed to determine the ways in which child effects may provoke parental reactions that initiate either risk or protective bidirectional processes. Maccoby & Jacklin (1983) provided a lead, but there is a need for much more to be done. Cross-lagged phenotypic correlations in the context of cross-twin, cross trait analyses, over a developmental period of marked change are needed (see Silberg et al. 2001b for an example in relation to substance use and disruptive behavior).

With respect to third variable effects, behavior geneticists have tended to focus on the implications from evidence of substantial rGE that some effects attributed to environmental influences may, in reality, have been at least in part genetically mediated (Plomin & Bergeman 1991, Plomin 1994). The notion is not new; for example, Jones (1946) suggested that this was likely to be the case because the correlations between parenting features and child behavior were usually much stronger in biological than adoptive families.

However, rGE may reflect three very different mechanisms. First, measures of the environment (E) may be influenced by the characteristics of the person reporting on that environment. Insofar as that is the case, what is supposed to be E may, in reality, reflect the person (P), rather than E, with P being influenced in part by genetic (G) effects. This is the same issue as criterion contamination (i.e., the problem that arises when both the independent and dependent variables derive from reports by the same person). What is new is the recognition that this problem can arise even when the informants are different, if both share the same genes.

Second, the measure of E may be truly valid, but nevertheless, the individual differences in environmental risk exposure may be genetically influenced. Conventional behavior genetic analyses attribute the whole of this rGE to genetics, but this attribution misleadingly assumes that the origins of a risk factor and its mode of risk mediation are necessarily synonymous. The example of smoking clearly indicates that this assumption is false (Rutter et al. 1993). The origins of individual differences in smoking reflect both genetic factors (Silberg et al. 2001b), the availability of cigarettes, and sociocultural influences. However, the risk effects on osteoporosis, lung cancer, coronary artery disease, etc. involve mechanisms that are entirely separate—such as carbon monoxide, nicotine effects on blood vessels, and carcinogenic tars. As part of the broader topic of individual differences in environmental risk exposure (Rutter et al. 1995), it is important to determine the role of genetic influences, but it should not be assumed that this indicates the mechanism of risk mediation. Thus, O'Connor et al. (2000) found that, despite genetic influences on divorce, the effects of divorce on emotional disturbance (at least as measured by teacher report) were environmentally mediated in their study.

Third, the existence of rGE may mean that the associations between E and the psychopathological trait being studied are partially genetically, rather than environmentally, mediated. In other words, because parents pass on genes, as well as influence the circumstances of rearing, any correlation between the family environment and the individual attribute may derive from genetic (G) rather than environmental (E) mediation. Bivariate analyses of twin data, treating E as a phenotype and utilizing cross-trait as well as cross-twin correlations, provide the means of determining the extent of genetic mediation of effects associated with an E variable. Most studies have shown that G accounts for a substantial minority of the risk mediation but far from all of it (see e.g., Kendler et al. 1999, Neiderhiser et al. 1999, Pike et al. 1996, Plomin 1994, Reiss et al. 2000). The mediation that is truly E can be shown through the same approach, but it can also be determined by examining effects within MZ twin pairs (see e.g., Carbonneau et al. 2001, Kendler & Gardner 2001, Kendler et al. 1999, Rutter 2000c, Rutter et al. 2001, Silberg et al. 1999).

Both these methods concern child-specific environmental variables (although their effects can be mainly shared rather than nonshared) (see Pike et al. 1996, Rutter 2000c). Environmentally mediated risks that apply to both twins, but which involve rGE, can be examined by means of the extended twin-family design (see Meyer et al. 2000 for the rationale, the assumptions required, and the limitations). Environmentally mediated effects of early parental loss on the liability to alcoholism (Kendler et al. 1996) and of family maladaptation on antisocial behavior (Meyer et al. 2000) have been shown.

Six main implications for environmental risk mediation follow. First, there needs to be a greater focus on the origins of individual differences in environmental risk exposure, such differences being very large. Selection, shaping and evocative influences (whether or not genetically influenced) play a crucial role in the processes leading to variance in exposure, but societal effects are also important, as reflected in the operation of racial discrimination, availability of guns, local authority housing policies, availability of family planning, and schooling, to mention just a few examples.

Second, genetic designs (as well as other research strategies) have already shown the reality and importance of environmental mediation (see Rutter et al. 2001, Rutter 2000a). In addition, however, they have also shown violations of the equal environments assumption (EEA) that is fundamental to the use of the twin design for genetic purposes. That is to say, the same features (such as stressful life events or parental negativity) that show rGE also show associations within MZ pairs. This means that some of the effects attributed to G are in reality mediated by E. This is not a methodological artifact; rather, it reflects the reality of how G and E operate. Nevertheless, it does mean that twin studies of emotional and behavioral disturbance carry the danger of underestimating specific environmentally mediated risks (see Rutter et al. 2001, 1999a). That may seem surprising in that most reviews have concluded that there is no violation of EEA (see Kendler et al. 1994, Kendler & Gardner 1998).

Two points need to be made in that connection. (*a*) Most tests of EEA have considered features such as the amount of contact between the twins or whether or not they have been dressed alike. It is no surprise that these do not violate EEA because it is exceedingly unlikely that such features carry psychopathological risk. (*b*) EEA can be considered only in relation to specific phenotypes and not as a general phenomenon. Thus, the evidence does suggest violation of EEA with respect to emotional and behavioral disturbance but does not with respect to, for instance, autism or IQ because, so far, environmental risks that operate within MZ pairs have not been identified.

Third, the findings on GxE are challenging in their implication that environmentally mediated risks are slight in the absence of genetic risk. The findings so far are sparse, but they do all point in the same direction. They highlight the great need for further investigation of how environmental risks bring about their adverse effects and what they do to the organism. The findings on the importance of nature-nurture interplay clearly point to the need to study psychosocial risks within the context of biological processes, rather than outside it.

Fourth, several studies have findings that suggest possible differences between males and females in the interplay between nature and nurture (as well as differences between child reports and parent reports). Again, the data are too sparse for anything other than speculation, but it is possible that rGE and GxE may play a role in age-related changes in the sex ratio of some forms of psychopathology. Thus, for example, the data suggest that the rise of depression in adolescence, which is much greater in females than males, may be attributable to genetic effects on both exposure to, and sensitivity to, psychosocial risks, such effects being greater in women than men (Silberg et al. 1999, 2001a), perhaps because of the enhancing role of female sex hormones (see Angold et al. 1999, Petronis 2001).

Fifth, there is the intriguing suggestion from Dickens & Flynn's (2001) modeling of secular changes in IQ that rGE may play a crucial role in enhancing the effects of environmental influences so that they increase over time. There has been remarkably little systematic study of environmental influences on secular changes in rates of psychopathology in young people (Rutter & Smith 1995), and the implication is that twin studies of different cohorts could be informative, provided that they include good measures of the relevant E features.

Finally, rGE and GxE are relevant in relation to the claims that E tends to make siblings different rather than similar—the supposed preponderance of nonshared over shared effects (Plomin & Daniels 1987). These claims have been misleadingly overstated both because they have failed to take measurement error and temporal discontinuity into account (see Rutter et al. 1999a, 2001), because some commentators have misunderstood their meaning (see Turkheimer & Waldron 2000), and because some investigators have misrepresented their own findings (see Pike et al. 2000 in relation to Reiss et al. 2000). The message that it is important to examine child-specific environmental impact (Reiss et al. 1995) remains. However, there is the additional implication that it is necessary to examine how rGE and GxE result in family-wide E-risk features (such as divorce and conflict) impinging differently on different children in the same family. Nonshared influences operate within, as well as outside, the family. Their study will require rather better measurement of environmental risks than has been the case in many behavior genetic studies undertaken so far.

Genetic Risk Mediation

There are four main implications of rGE and GxE for concepts of genetic risk mediation. First, in circumstances in which both are operative (as is the case with emotional and behavioral disturbance), a substantial proportion of the genetic influence will be indirect rather than direct. That is, the genes will be influential, in part, because they affect either exposure, or sensitivity, to the environment rather than because they bring about the psychopathological phenotype directly. Although it is not a necessary consequence, there is the implication that the risk processes may operate through dimensional attributes (such as temperament) rather than on any disorder as such. Thus, the genetic liability to ADHD could come about through effects on sensation-seeking or impulsivity (which predispose to ADHD) rather than through effects on ADHD itself. However, what is clear is that the main research need is not further studies of rGE adding to the list of E features that correlate with G, but rather more systematic investigation of which behaviors mediate the gene-environment connection both with respect to the environment and to the effects of this environment on the child phenotype (see discussion above of passive rGE).

Nevertheless, it is important not to overstate the case for indirect effects. It has proved much easier to identify effects of G in the absence of E risk, than the reverse. Of course, it may be that the measures of E were inadequate in quality or range of coverage. However, it is equally likely that there are important direct G effects that do not implicate the environment. We should not assume just one causal pathway, as highlighted by lessons in the study of comorbidity in internal medicine (Rutter 1997).

Second, up to now, most attention has been paid to active and evocative rGE, and it is apparent that there needs to be much more study of passive rGE. At least during the childhood years, it seems more influential than active or evocative rGE. However, in studying the effects of the environments of rearing that are shaped by genetically influenced parental phenotypes, it will be essential not to assume that effects will impinge equally on all the children in the family. A key research need is studies of the environmentally mediated impact of parental psychopathology with respect to both shared and nonshared effects.

Third, it should not be assumed that genetic risk mediation will operate in the same way with all psychological and psychopathological phenotypes. For example, the GxE found in two studies in relation to cognitive performance operated in the opposite direction to those found for emotional and behavioral disturbance. That is, not only was there no evidence of genetically influenced sensitivity to the environment, but genetic influences seem to be more influential in environmentally low risk homes. Of course, it is quite possible (indeed likely) that active (and evocative) rGE was operative in such a way that genetically advantaged individuals were able to obtain advantaged environments. The study of rGE and GxE must cover the range of different ways in which they might operate, and also pay attention to both risk and protective processes.

Fourth, genetic evangelism and imperialism must temper its claims regarding the pervasive strength of genetic influences through an acceptance that the incorporation of rGE and GxE within the G term misrepresents the situation. Population variance cannot sensibly be partitioned into just G and E because an important minority of the variance has to be attributed to the joint action of G plus E. It should be mentioned, too, that the nongenetic component should not be assumed to be some specific environmental feature; stochastic features related to the probabilistic nature of developmental biological processes may also be operative (see Jensen 1997, Molenaar et al. 1993). However, in chiding some behavior geneticists for hiding the contribution of E within the G term, it is important to go on to accept that the important roles of rGE and GxE in risk and protective processes do indeed mean a centrality for genetic considerations in any study of causal mechanisms in psychopathology.

Evolutionary Considerations

The potential evolutionary importance of gene-environment correlations have been considered in fostering the intergenerational transmission of genes. Thus, Dawkins (1982, 1989) discussed the issue in terms of the concept of "extended phenotypes," reflecting the fact that genetic influences shape environmental selection in the direction of environments that are most adaptive for the individual genotype—a form of "niche-picking" (Scarr & McCartney 1983). There is no doubt that this does occur, but two main cautions need to be made. First, niche construction involves a two-way process that fundamentally changes the co-evolutionary dynamics between genetic evolution and cultural change (Odling-Smee 1996). Thus, nature-nurture interplay will also involve environmental effects on gene frequency. Two examples serve to illustrate the effect. (*a*) Genetic factors determine the ability of adults to synthesize lactose. In areas with long-established dairy farming, the great majority of adults are lactose-tolerant, whereas in other areas the reverse is the case (Bodmer & Cavalli-Sforza 1976, Durham 1991). The reliance on milk in the diet has favored lactose-tolerant genotypes. (*b*) Heterozygote status for thalassaemia constitutes a substantial protection against malaria. Accordingly, in malaria-endemic areas of Africa thalassaemia genotypes have become very common; conversely the frequency appears low in racially comparable individuals living in areas without malaria (although the data are limited and constrained by uncertainties over the ethnic comparability of populations), such as the United States (Davies & Brozovic 1989, Weatherall & Clegg 2001). Environmental features have had an important influence on the frequency of genes according to whether protection against malaria matters.

Second, the term niche-picking implies an active process that is governed by genes, as well as a process that is adaptive. That constitutes a misleading oversimplification because (*a*) the selection of environments need not reflect an active process (Engfer et al. 1994); (*b*) effects on the environment stem from the characteristics of the organism, rather than of the genes (Lehrman 1965, Bateson & Martin 1999); and (*c*) evolutionary advantage applies strictly to reproduction and not to optimal social functioning (Bock et al. 2000). These caveats may be illustrated by considering the effects of antisocial behavior on environment, which are major with respect to a wide range of negative features spanning severely stressful life events, early marriage to a deviant spouse, disrupted close relationships, and lack of social support (Rutter et al. 1997b, 1998). Psychological studies show that environmental effects reflect the ways in which antisocial individuals engage with peers, impulsive actions that lack planning, and coercive interchanges with other people. The fact that they so frequently become parents while teenagers is as likely to reflect lack of planning as deliberate choice. The early childbearing may result in more live offspring, but this is not necessarily a social advantage in an urban industrialized society. Also, genetic influences account for only a moderate proportion of the population variance in the liability to antisocial behavior. In short, niche-picking is not necessarily socially adaptive and is not necessarily primarily driven by genes, although both will be the case in some instances.

CONCLUSION

It is abundantly clear that any adequate understanding of the processes involved in the initiation, remission, recurrence, and persistence of emotional and behavioral psychopathology will require identification of the varied mechanisms involved in rGE and GxE. In this chapter we have sought to summarize in succinct, nontechnical language, some of the conceptual and methodological issues that are involved, as well as the sparse array of empirical research findings. Brief mention was made of a few molecular genetic findings in internal medicine to illustrate the great potential of this field of research with respect to psychopathology (see Plomin & Crabbe 2000, Plomin & Rutter 1998, Rutter 2001b, Rutter & Plomin 1997), but progress will depend not only on the identification of susceptibility genes and their effects on proteins, but also on the use of molecular epidemiological methods of study of nature-nurture interplay (requiring the development of high quality E measures that can be used in very large samples and the development of hypotheses on plausible pathophysiological processes). The challenge can be met, but it will not be easy; the solutions will not come quickly; and success will depend on researchers honestly appreciating the conceptual and methodological hazards that will have to be addressed.

ACKNOWLEDGMENTS

We are deeply indebted to the numerous colleagues who drew our attention to key articles and who generously gave us access to papers not yet published. Special thanks are due to Lindon Eaves, whose thinking has influenced us greatly and whose advice, comments, and suggestions were invaluable in drafting and correcting this chapter. We are also most grateful to Gill Rangel for literature searches and for tracking down elusive references.

Visit the Annual Reviews home page at www.AnnualReviews.org

LITERATURE CITED

Angold A, Costello EJ, Erkanli A, Worthman CH. 1999. Pubertal changes in hormone levels and depression in girls. *Psychol. Med.* 29:1043–53

Anisman H, Zaharia MD, Meaney MJ, Merali Z. 1998. Do early-life events permanently alter behavioral and hormonal responses to stressors? *Int. J. Dev. Neurosci.* 16:149–64

Bateson P, Martin P. 1999. *Design for a Life: How Behaviour Develops.* London: Cape

Bell RQ. 1968. A reinterpretation of the direction of effects in studies of socialization. *Psychol. Rev.* 75:81–95

Bell RQ, Chapman M. 1986. Child effects in studies using experimental or brief longitudinal approaches to socialization. *Dev. Psychol.* 22:595–603

Billig JP, Hershberger SL, Iacono WG, McGue M. 1996. Life events and personality in late adolescence: genetic and environmental relations. *Behav. Genet.* 26:543–54

Birley AJ, MacLennan R, Wahlqvist M, Gerns L, Pangan T, et al. 1997. MN blood group affects response of serum LDL cholesterol level to a low fat diet. *Clin. Genet.* 51:291–95

Bock GR, Goode J, Webb K, eds. 2000. *The Nature of Intelligence.* London: Wiley

Bodmer WF, Cavalli-Sforza LL. 1976. *Genetics, Evolution, and Man.* San Francisco: Freeman

Bohman M. 1996. Predisposition to criminality: Swedish adoption studies in retrospect. In *Genetics of Criminal and Antisocial Behaviour. Ciba Found. Symp. 194*, ed. GR Bock, JA Goode, pp. 99–114. Chichester, UK: Wiley

Boomsma DI, de Geus EJC, van Baal GCM, Koopmans JR. 1999. A religious upbringing reduces the influence of genetic factors on disinhibition: evidence for interaction between genotype and environment on personality. *Twin Res.* 2:115–25

Bronfenbrenner U, Ceci SJ. 1994. Nature-nurture reconceptualization in developmental perspective: a bioecological model. *Psychol. Rev.* 101:568–86

Brown GW, Harris TO, Lemyre L. 1991. Now you see it, now you don't—some considerations on multiple regression. In *Problems and Methods in Longitudinal Research: Stability and Change*, ed. D Magnusson, LR Bergman, G Rudinger, B Törestad, pp. 67–94. Cambridge: Cambridge Univ. Press

Brussoni MJ, Jang KL, Livesley WJ, Macbeth TM. 2000. Genetic and environmental influences on adult attachment styles. *Pers. Relat.* 7:283–89

Busjahn A, Faulhaber H-D, Freier K, Luft FC. 1999. Genetic and environmental influences on coping styles: a twin study. *Psychosom. Med.* 61:469–75

Cadoret RJ, Cain C. 1980. Sex differences in predictors of antisocial behavior in adoptees. *Arch. Gen. Psychiatry* 37:1171–75

Cadoret RJ, Cain CA, Crowe RR. 1983. Evidence for gene-environment interaction in the development of adolescent antisocial behavior. *Behav. Genet.* 13:301–10

Cadoret RJ, Troughton E, O'Gorman TW. 1987. Genetic and environmental factors in alcohol abuse and antisocial personality. *J. Stud. Alcohol* 48:1–8

Cadoret RJ, Winokur G, Langbehn D, Troughton E, Yates WR, et al. 1996. Depression spectrum disease. I. The role of gene-environment interaction. *Am. J. Psychiatry* 153:892–99

Cadoret RJ, Yates WR, Troughton E, Woodworth G, Stewart MAS. 1995. Genetic-environmental interaction in the genesis of aggressivity and conduct disorders. *Arch. Gen. Psychiatry* 52:916–24

Carbonneau R, Eaves LJ, Silberg JL, Hewitt JK, Simonoff E, et al. 2001. *Assessment of the Within Family Environment in Twins: Absolute versus Differential Ratings, and Relationship with Conduct Problems.* Submitted

Cattell RB. 1965. Methodological and conceptual advances in evaluating hereditary and environmental influences and their interaction. In *Methods and Goals in Human Behavior Genetics*, ed. SG Vandenberg, pp. 95–139. New York: Academic

Cavalli-Sforza LL, Feldman MW. 1973. Models for cultural inheritance. I. Group mean and within group variation. *Theor. Popul. Biol.* 4:42–55

Chadwick D, Cardew G, eds. 1996. *Variation in the Human Genome. Ciba Found. Symp. 197.* Chichester, UK/New York: Wiley

Champion LA, Goodall GM, Rutter M. 1995. Behavioural problems in childhood and stressors in early adult life: A 20-year follow-up of London school children. *Psychol. Med.* 25:231–46

Chandra V, Pandav R. 1998. Gene-environment interaction in Alzheimer's disease: a potential role for cholesterol. *Neuroepidemiology* 17:225–32

Crowe RR. 1974. An adoption study of antisocial personality. *Arch. Gen. Psychiatry* 31:785–91

Davies SC, Brozovic M. 1989. The presentation, management and prophylaxis of sickle cell disease. *Blood Rev.* 3:29–44

Dawkins R. 1982. *The Extended Phenotype: The Gene as the Unit of Selection.* Oxford: Oxford Univ. Press

Dawkins R. 1989. *The Selfish Gene.* Oxford: Oxford Univ. Press. 2nd ed.

Deater-Deckard K, Fulker DW, Plomin R. 1999. A genetic study of the family environment in the transition to early adolescence. *J. Child Psychol. Psychiatry* 40:769–75

Deater-Deckard K, O'Connor TG. 2000. Parent-child mutuality in early childhood: two behavioral genetic studies. *Dev. Psychol.* 36:561–70

DeFries JC, Fulker DW. 1985. Multiple regression analysis of twin data. *Behav. Genet.* 5:467–73

Dick DM, Rose RJ, Viken RJ, Kaprio J, Koskenvuo M. 2001. Exploring gene-environment interactions: socio-regional moderation of alcohol use. *J. Abnorm. Psychol.* In press

Dickens WT, Flynn JR. 2001. Heritability estimates vs. large environmental effects: the IQ paradox resolved. *Psychol. Rev.* 108:346–69

Dunne MP, Martin NG, Statham DJ, Slutske WS, Dinwiddie SH, et al. 1997. Genetic and environmental contributions to variance in age at first sexual intercourse. *Psychol. Sci.* 8:211–16

Durham WH. 1991. *Co-Evolution: Genes, Culture and Human Diversity.* Stanford, CA: Stanford Univ. Press

Eaves L, Erkanli A. 2001. *Markov Chain Monte Carlo Approaches to Analysis of Genetic and Environmental Components of Human Developmental Change and GxE Interaction.* Submitted

Eaves LJ. 1976a. The effect of cultural transmission on continuous variation. *Heredity* 37:41–57

Eaves LJ. 1976b. A model for sibling effects in man. *Heredity* 36:205–14

Eaves LJ. 1984. The resolution of genotype x environment interaction in segregation analysis of nuclear families. *Genet. Epidemiol.* 1:215–28

Eaves LJ, Eysenck HJ. 1977. A genotype-environmental model for psychoticism. *Adv. Behav. Res. Ther.* 1:5–26

Eaves LJ, Last KA, Martin NG, Jinks JL. 1977. A progressive approach to non-additivity and genotype-environmental covariance in the analysis of human differences. *Br. J. Math. Stat. Psychol.* 30:1–42

Elkins IJ, McGue M, Iacono WG. 1997. Genetic and environmental influences on parent-son relationships: evidence for increasing genetic influence during adolescence. *Dev. Psychol.* 33:351–63

Engfer A, Walper S, Rutter M. 1994. Individual characteristics as a force in development. In *Development Through Life: A Handbook for Clinicians*, ed. M Rutter, DF Hay, pp. 79–111. Oxford: Blackwell Sci.

Evans WE, Relling MV. 1999. Pharmacogenomics: translating functional genomics into rational therapeutics. *Science* 286:487–91

Flynn JR. 2000. IQ gains, WISC subtests and fluid *g*: *g* theory and the relevance of Spearman's hypothesis to race. In *The Nature of Intelligence. Novartis Found. Symp. 233*, ed. GR Bock, JA Goode, K Webb, pp. 202–16. Chichester, Engl: Wiley

Ge X, Conger RD, Cadoret RJ, Neiderhiser JM, Yates W, et al. 1996. The developmental interface between nature and nurture: a mutual influence model of child antisocial behavior and parenting. *Dev. Psychol.* 32:574–89

Haley CS, Jinks JL, Last KA. 1981. The monozygotic twin half-sib method for analysing maternal effects and sex linkage in humans. *Heredity* 46:227–38

Heath AC, Berg K, Eaves LJ, Solaas MH, Corey LA, et al. 1985. Education and policy and the heritability of educational attainment. *Nature* 314:734–36

Heath AC, Cates R, Martin NG, Meyer J, Hewitt JK, et al. 1993. Genetic contribution to risk of smoking initiation: comparisons across birth cohorts and across cultures. *J. Subst. Abuse* 5:221–46

Heath AC, Eaves LJ, Martin NG. 1998. Interaction of marital status and genetic risk for symptoms of depression. *Twin Res.* 1:119–22

Heath AC, Jardine R, Martin NG. 1989. Interactive effects of genotype and social environment on alcohol consumption in female twins. *J. Stud. Alcohol* 50:38–48

Hill AVS. 1998. The immunogenetics of human infectious diseases. *Annu. Rev. Immunol.* 16:593–617

Humphries SE, Talmud PJ, Bolla M, Cooper J, Day INM, et al. 2001. Apolipoprotein E and coronary heart disease in middle-aged men who smoke: a prospective study. *Lancet* 358:115–19

Hur Y-M, McGue M, Iacono WG. 1996. Genetic and shared environmental influences on leisure-time interests in male adolescents. *Pers. Individ. Differ.* 21:791–801

Jensen AR. 1973. *Educability and Group Differences*. New York: Harper & Row

Jensen AR. 1997. The puzzle of nongenetic variance. In *Intelligence, Heredity, and Environment*, ed. RJ Sternberg, EL Grigorenko, pp. 42–88. Cambridge: Cambridge Univ. Press

Jinks JL, Fulker DW. 1970. Comparison of the biometrical genetical, MAVA and classical approaches to the analysis of human behavior. *Psychol. Bull.* 73:311–49

Jockin V, McGue M, Lykken DT. 1996. Personality and divorce: a genetic analysis. *J. Pers. Soc. Psychol.* 71:288–99

Jones HE. 1946. Environmental influences on mental development. In *Manual of Child Psychology*, ed. L Carmichael, pp. 582–632. New York: Wiley

Kendler KS, Eaves LJ. 1986. Models for the joint effect of genotype and environment on liability to psychiatric illness. *Am. J. Psychiatry* 143:279–89

Kendler KS, Gardener CO. 1998. Twin studies of adult psychiatric and substance dependence disorders: Are they biased by differences in the environmental experience of mono- and dizygotic twins in childhood and adolescence? *Psychol. Med.* 28:625–33

Kendler KS, Gardner CO. 2001. Monozygotic twins discordant for major depression: a preliminary exploration of the role of environmental experiences in the aetiology and course of illness. *Psychol. Med.* 31:411–23

Kendler KS, Gardner CO, Prescott CA. 2001. Genetic risk factors for major depression in men and women: similar or different heritabilities and same or partly distinct genes? *Psychol. Med.* 31:605–16

Kendler KS, Karkowski LM, Prescott CA. 1999. Causal relationship between stressful life events and the onset of major depression. *Am. J. Psychiatry* 156:837–41

Kendler KS, Karkowski-Shuman L. 1997. Stressful life events and genetic liability to major depression: genetic control of exposure to the environment? *Psychol. Med.* 27:539–47

Kendler KS, Kessler RC, Walters EE, MacLean C, Neale MC, et al. 1995. Stressful life events, genetic liability, and onset of an episode of major depression in women. *Am. J. Psychiatry* 152:833–42

Kendler KS, Neale M, Kessler R, Heath A, Eaves L. 1993. A twin study of recent life events and difficulties. *Arch. Gen. Psychiatry* 50:789–96

Kendler KS, Neale MC, Kessler RC, Eaves LJ. 1994. Parental treatment and the equal environment assumption in twin studies of psychiatric illness. *Psychol. Med.* 24:579–90

Kendler KS, Neale MC, Prescott CA, Kessler RC, Heath AC, et al. 1996. Childhood parental loss and alcoholism in women: a causal analysis using a twin-family design. *Psychol. Med.* 26:79–95

Kendler KS, Thornton LM, Pedersen NL. 2000. Tobacco consumption in Swedish twins reared apart and reared together. *Arch. Gen. Psychiatry* 57:886–92

Knight JC, Udalova I, Hill AVS, Greenwood BM, Peshu N, et al. 1999. A polymorphism that affects OCT-1 binding to the TNF promoter region is associated with severe malaria. *Nat. Genet.* 22:145–50

Koeppen-Schomerus G, Eley TC, Wolke D, Gringras P, Plomin R. 2000. The interaction of prematurity with genetic and environmental influences on cognitive development in twins. *J. Pediatr.* 137:527–33

Koopmans JR, Slutske WS, van Baal GCM, Boomsma DI. 1999. The influence of religion on alcohol use initiation: evidence for genotype X environment interaction. *Behav. Genet.* 29:445–53

Legrand LN, McGue M, Iacono WG. 1999. Searching for interactive effects in the etiology of early-onset substance use. *Behav. Genet.* 29:433–44

Lehrman DS. 1965. Interaction between internal and external environments in the regulation of the reproductive cycle of the ring dove. In *Sex and Behavior*, ed. FA Beach, pp. 355–80. New York: Wiley

Loehlin J. 1965. Some methodological problems in Cattell's Multiple Abstract Variance Analysis. *Psychol. Rev.* 72:156–61

Maccoby EE, Jacklin CN. 1983. The "person" characteristics of children and the family as environment. See Magnusson & Allen 1983, pp. 76–91

Maciejewski PK, Prigerson HG, Mazure CM. 2000. Sex differences in event-related risk for major depression. *Psychol. Med.* 31:593–604

Mackay TFC. 2001. Quantitative trait loci in drosophila. *Nat. Rev.* 2:11–20

Magnusson D, Allen VL, eds. 1983. *Human Development: An Interactional Perspective.* New York: Academic

Mather K, Jinks JL. 1982. *Biometrical Genetics: The Study of Continuous Variation.* London: Chapman & Hall

Mayeux R, Ottman R, Maestre G, Ngai C, Tang M-X, et al. 1995. Synergistic effects of traumatic head injury and apolipoprotein-ε4 in patients with Alzheimer's disease. *Neurology* 45:555–57

McClearn GE, Vogler GP, Hofer SM. 2001. Environment-gene and gene-gene interactions. In *Handbook of the Biology of Aging*, ed. EJ Masoro, SN Austad, pp. 423–44. San Diego, CA: Academic. 5th ed.

McGue M, Lykken DT. 1992. Genetic influence on risk of divorce. *Psychol. Sci.* 3:368–73

Meyer JM, Rutter M, Silberg JL, Maes HH, Simonoff E, et al. 2000. Familial aggregation for conduct disorder symptomatology: the role of genes, marital discord and family adaptability. *Psychol. Med.* 30:759–74

Minihane AM, Khan S, Leigh Firbank EC, Talmud P, Wright JW, et al. 2000. ApoE polymorphism and fish oil supplementation in subjects with an atherogenic lipoprotein phenotype. *Arterioscler. Thromb. Vasc. Biol.* 20:1990–97

Molenaar PCM, Boomsma DI, Dolan CV.

1993. A third source of developmental differences. *Behav. Genet.* 23:519–24

Molenaar PCM, Boomsma DI, Dolan CV. 1999. The detection of genotype-environment interaction in longitudinal genetic models. In *On the Way to Individuality: Methodological Issues in Behavioral Genetics*, ed. M LaBuda, E Grigorenko, pp. 53–70. New York: Nova Sci.

Murray L, Cooper PJ, eds. 1997. *Postpartum Depression and Child Development*. New York: Guilford

Nance WE, Kramer AA, Corey LA, Winter P, Eaves LJ. 1983. A causal analysis of birth weight in the offspring of monozygotic twins. *Am. J. Hum. Genet.* 35:1211–23

Neiderhiser JM, Reiss D, Hetherington EM, Plomin R. 1999. Relationships between parenting and adolescent adjustment over time: genetic and environmental contributions. *Dev. Psychol.* 5:680–92

O'Connor TG, Caspi A, DeFries JC, Plomin R. 2000. Are associations between parental divorce and children's adjustment genetically mediated? An adoption study. *Dev. Psychol.* 36:429–37

O'Connor TG, Deater-Deckard K, Fulker D, Rutter M, Plomin R. 1998. Genotype-environment correlations in late childhood and early adolescence: antisocial behavioral problems and coercive parenting. *Dev. Psychol.* 34:970–81

O'Connor TG, Hetherington EM, Reiss D, Plomin R. 1995. A twin-sibling study of observed parent-adolescent interactions. *Child Dev.* 66:812–29

Odling-Smee FJ. 1996. Niche construction, genetic evolution and cultural change. *Behav. Process.* 35:195–205

Ottman R. 1996. Gene-environment interaction: definitions and study designs. *Prev. Med.* 25:764–70

Pérusse D, Neale MC, Heath AC, Eaves LJ. 1994. Human parental behavior: evidence for genetic influence and potential implication for gene-culture transmission. *Behav. Genet.* 24:327–35

Petitto JM, Evans DL. 1999. Clinical neuroimmunology. In *Neurobiology of Mental Illness*, ed. DS Charney, EJ Nestler, BS Bunney, pp. 162–69. New York: Oxford Univ. Press

Petronis A. 2001. Human morbid genetics revisited: relevance of epigenetics. *Trends Genet.* 17:142–46

Pickles A. 1993. Stages, precursors and causes in development. In *Precursors and Causes in Development and Psychopathology*, ed. DF Hay, A Angold, pp. 23–49. Chichester, UK: Wiley

Pike A, Manke B, Reiss D, Plomin R. 2000. A genetic analysis of differential experiences of adolescent siblings across three years. *Soc. Dev.* 9:96–114

Pike A, McGuire S, Hetherington EM, Reiss D, Plomin R. 1996. Family environment and adolescent depressive symptoms and antisocial behavior: a multivariate genetic analysis. *Dev. Psychol.* 32:590–603

Plassman BL, Breitner JCS. 1996. Recent advances in the genetics of Alzheimer's disease and vascular dementia with an emphasis on gene-environment interactions. *J. Am. Geriatr. Soc.* 44:1242–50

Plomin R. 1994. *Genetics and Experience: The Interplay Between Nature and Nurture*. Thousand Oaks, CA: Sage

Plomin R, Bergeman CS. 1991. The nature of nurture: genetic influence on 'environmental' measures. *Behav. Brain Sci.* 10:373–427

Plomin R, Crabbe J. 2000. DNA. *Psychol. Bull.* 126:806–28

Plomin R, Daniels D. 1987. Why are children in the same family so different from each other? *Behav. Brain Sci.* 10:1–16

Plomin R, DeFries JC, Fulker DW. 1988. *Nature and Nurture During Infancy and Early Childhood*. New York: Cambridge Univ. Press

Plomin R, DeFries JC, Loehlin JC. 1977. Genotype-environment interaction and correlation in the analysis of human behavior. *Psychol. Bull.* 84:309–22

Plomin R, Lichtenstein P, Pedersen NL, McClearn GE, Nesselroade JR. 1990. Genetic influence on life events during the last half of the life span. *Psychol. Aging* 5:25–30

Plomin R, Reiss D, Hetherington EM, Howe GW. 1994. Nature and nurture: genetic contributions to measures of the family environment. *Dev. Psychol.* 30:32–43

Plomin R, Rutter M. 1998. Child development, molecular genetics, and what to do with genes once they are found. *Child Dev.* 69: 1223–42

Quinton D, Pickles A, Maughan B, Rutter M. 1993. Partners, peers, and pathways: assortative pairing and continuities in conduct disorder. *Dev. Psychopathol.* 5:763–83

Rao DC, Morton NE, Yee S. 1976. Resolution of cultural and biological inheritance by path analysis. *Am. J. Hum. Genet.* 26:331–59

Reed TE. 1985. Ethnic differences in alcohol use, abuse, and sensitivity: a review with genetic interpretation. *Soc. Biol.* 32:195–209

Reiss D, Hetherington EM, Plomin R, Howe GW, Simmens SJ, et al. 1995. Genetic questions for environmental studies: differential parenting and psychopathology in adolescence. *Arch. Gen. Psychiatry* 52:925–36

Reiss D, Neiderhiser JM, Hetherington EM, Plomin R. 2000. *The Relationship Code: Deciphering Genetic and Social Influences on Adolescent Development.* Cambridge, MA: Harvard Univ. Press

Rice J, Cloninger CR, Reich T. 1978. Multifactorial inheritance with cultural transmission and assortative mating. I. Description and basic properties of the unitary models. *Am. J. Hum. Genet.* 30:618–43

Riggins-Caspers K, Cadoret RJ, Panak W, Lempers JD, Troughton E, et al. 1999. Gene x environment interaction and the moderating effect of adoption agency disclosure on estimating genetic effects. *Pers. Individ. Differ.* 27:357–80

Robins L. 1966. *Deviant Children Grown Up: A Sociological and Psychiatric Study of Sociopathic Personality.* Baltimore: Williams & Wilkins

Rose S. 1995. The rise of neurogenetic determinism. *Nature* 373:380–82

Rose S. 1998. *Lifelines: Biology, Freedom, Determinism.* Harmondsworth, UK: Penguin

Rose RJ, Dick DM, Viken RJ, Kaprio J. 2001.

Gene-environment interaction in patterns of adolescent drinking: regional residency moderates longitudinal influences on alcohol use. *Alcohol. Clin. Exp. Res.* 25:637–43

Rowe DC, Jacobson KC, van den Oord EJCG. 1999. Genetic and environmental influences on vocabulary IQ: parental education level as moderator. *Child Dev.* 70:1151–62

Rubinzstein DC. 1995. Apolipoprotein E: a review of its roles in lipoprotein metabolism, neuronal growth and repair, and as a risk factor for Alzheimer's disease. *Psychol. Med.* 25:223–99

Rutter M. 1983. Statistical and personal interactions: facets and perspectives. See Magnusson & Allen 1983, pp. 295–319

Rutter M. 1987. Continuities and discontinuities from infancy. In *Handbook of Infant Development*, ed. J Osofsky, pp. 1256–96. New York: Wiley. 2nd ed.

Rutter M. 1989. Psychiatric disorder in parents as a risk factor for children. In *Prevention of Mental Disorders, Alcohol and Other Drug Use in Children and Adolescents. OSAP Prevention Monogr. 2*, ed. D Shaffer, I Philips, NB Enzer, pp. 157–89. Rockville, MD: Off. Subst. Abuse Prev., US Dep. Health Hum. Serv.

Rutter M. 1997. Comorbidity: concepts, claims and choices. *Crim. Behav. Mental Health* 7:265–85

Rutter M. 2000a. Psychosocial influences: critiques, findings, and research needs. *Dev. Psychopathol.* 12:375–405

Rutter M. 2000b. Resilience reconsidered: conceptual considerations, empirical findings, and policy implications. In *Handbook of Early Childhood Intervention*, ed. JP Shonkoff, SJ Meisels, pp. 651–82. New York: Cambridge Univ. Press

Rutter M. 2000c. Negative life events and family negativity. In *Where Inner and Outer Worlds Meet: Psychosocial Research in the Tradition of George W Brown*, ed. T Harris, pp. 123–49. London: Routledge

Rutter M. 2001a. Genetic influences and risk reduction: implications for understanding resilience. In *Resilience and Vulnerability:*

Adaptation in the Context of Childhood Adversities, ed. SS Luthar. New York: Cambridge Univ. Press. In press

Rutter M. 2001b. Nature, nurture and development: from evangelism through science towards policy and practice. *Child Dev.* In press

Rutter M, Champion L, Quinton D, Maughan B, Pickles A. 1995. Understanding individual differences in environmental risk exposure. In *Examining Lives in Context: Perspectives on the Ecology of Human Development*, ed. P Moen, GH Elder Jr, K Lüscher, pp. 61–93. Washington, DC: Am. Psychol. Assoc.

Rutter M, Dunn J, Plomin R, Simonoff E, Pickles A, et al. 1997a. Integrating nature and nurture: implications of person-environment correlations and interactions for developmental psychology. *Dev. Psychopathol.* 9:335–64

Rutter M, Giller H, Hagell A. 1998. *Antisocial Behavior by Young People.* New York: Cambridge Univ. Press

Rutter M, Maughan B, Meyer J, Pickles A, Silberg J, et al. 1997b. Heterogeneity of antisocial behavior: causes, continuities, and consequences. In *Nebraska Symposium on Motivation*, Vol. 44. *Motivation and Delinquency*, ed. R Dienstbier, DW Osgood, pp. 45–118. Lincoln: Univ. Neb. Press

Rutter M, Pickles A. 1991. Person-environment interactions: concepts, mechanisms and implications for data analysis. In *Conceptualization and Measurement of Organism-Environment Interaction*, ed. TD Wachs, R Plomin, pp. 105–41. Washington, DC: Am. Psychol. Assoc.

Rutter M, Pickles A, Murray R, Eaves L. 2001. Testing hypotheses on specific environmental causal effects on behavior. *Psychol. Bull.* 127:291–324

Rutter M, Plomin R. 1997. Opportunities for psychiatry from genetic findings. *Br. J. Psychiatry* 171:209–19

Rutter M, Silberg J, O'Connor T, Simonoff E. 1999a. Genetics and child psychiatry. I. Advances in quantitative and molecular genetics. *J. Child Psychol. Psychiatry* 40:3–18

Rutter M, Silberg J, O'Connor T, Simonoff E. 1999b. Genetics and child psychiatry. II. Empirical research findings. *J. Child Psychol. Psychiatry* 40:19–55

Rutter M, Silberg J, Simonoff E. 1993. Whither behavioral genetics? A developmental psychopathological perspective. In *Nature, Nurture, and Psychology*, ed. R Plomin, GE McClearn, pp. 433–56. Washington, DC: Am. Psychol. Assoc.

Rutter M, Smith D, eds. 1995. *Psychosocial Disorders in Young People: Time Trends and Their Causes.* Chichester, UK: Wiley

Saudino KJ, Pedersen NL, Lichtenstein P, McClearn GE, Plomin R. 1997. Can personality explain genetic influences on life events? *J. Pers. Soc. Psychol.* 72:196–206

Scarr S, McCartney K. 1983. How people make their own environment: a theory of genotype → environmental effects. *Child Dev.* 54:424–35

Sellers TA, Potter JD, Bailey-Wilson JE, Rich SS, Rothschild H, et al. 1992. Lung cancer detection and prevention: evidence from an interaction between smoking and genetic predisposition. *Cancer Res.* 52:S2694–97

Silberg J, Pickles A, Rutter M, Hewitt J, Simonoff E, et al. 1999. The influence of genetic factors and life stress on depression among adolescent girls. *Arch. Gen. Psychiatry* 56:225–32

Silberg J, Rutter M, D'Onofrio B, Eaves L. 2001b. *Genetic and Environmental Risk Factors in Adolescent Substance Use.* Submitted

Silberg J, Rutter M, Neale M, Eaves L. 2001a. Genetic moderation of environmental risk for depression and anxiety in adolescent girls. *Br. J. Psychiatry* 179:116–21

Silventoinen K, Kaprio J, Lahelma E, Koskenvuo M. 2000. Relative effect of genetic and environmental factors on body height: differences across birth cohorts among Finnish men and women. *Am. J. Public Health* 90:627–30

Stoolmiller M. 1999. Implications of the restricted range of family environments for estimates of heritability and nonshared environment in behavior-genetic adoption studies. *Psychol. Bull.* 125:392–409

Suomi SJ. 2000. A biobehavioral perspective on developmental psychopathology: excessive aggression and serotonergic dysfunction in monkeys. In *Handbook of Developmental Psychopathology*, ed. AJ Sameroff, M Lewis, S Miller, pp. 237–56. New York: Plenum. 2nd ed.

Talmud PJ, Bujac SR, Hall S, Miller GJ, Humphries SE. 2000. Substitution of asparagine for aspartic acid at residue 9 (D9N) of lipoprotein lipase markedly augments risk of ischaemic heart disease in male smokers. *Atherosclerosis* 149:75–81

Teasdale GM, Nicoll JAR, Murray G, Fiddes M. 1997. Association of apolipoprotein E polymorphism with outcome after head injury. *Lancet* 350:1069–71

Thapar A, Harold G, McGuffin P. 1998. Life events and depressive symptoms in childhood—shared genes or shared adversity? A research note. *J. Child Psychol. Psychiatry* 39:1153–58

Thapar A, McGuffin P. 1996. Genetic influences on life events in childhood. *Psychol. Med.* 26:813–20

Truett KR, Eaves LJ, Walters EE, Heath AC, Hewitt JK, et al. 1994. A model system for the analysis of family resemblance in extended kinships of twins. *Behav. Genet.* 24:35–49

Trumbetta SL, Gottesman II. 2000. Endophenotypes for marital status in the NAS-NRC twin registry. In *Genetic Influences on Human Fertility and Sexuality: Theoretical and Empirical Contributions from the Biological and Behavioral Sciences*, ed. JL Rodgers, DC Rowe, WB Miller, pp. 253–69. Boston: Kluwer Acad.

Turkheimer E, Gottesman II. 1996. Stimulating the dynamics of genes and environment in development. *Dev. Psychopathol.* 8:667–77

Turkheimer E, Waldron M. 2000. Nonshared environment: theoretical, methodological, and quantitative review. *Psychol. Bull.* 126:78–108

van den Oord EJCG, Rowe DC. 1998. An examination of genotype-environment interactions for academic achievement in an U.S. national longitudinal survey. *Intelligence* 25:205–28

Wahlsten D. 1990. Insensitivity of the analysis of variance to heredity-environment interaction. *Behav. Brain Sci.* 13:109–61

Wahlsten D. 1999. Experimental design and statistical inference. In *Handbook of Molecular-Genetic Techniques for Brain and Behavior Research (Techniques in the Behavioral and Neural Sciences)*, ed. WE Crusio, RT Gerlai, 13:40–57. The Netherlands: Elsevier

Wahlsten D. 2002. Genetics and the development of brain and behavior. In *Handbook of Developmental Psychology*, ed. J Valsiner, K Connolly. London: Sage. In press

Weatherall D. 1999. From genotype to phenotype: genetics and medical practice in the new millennium. *Philos. Trans. R. Soc. London Ser. B* 354:1995–2010

Weatherall DJ, Clegg JB. 2001. *The Thalassemia Syndromes*. Oxford: Blackwell. 4th ed.

Wolf CR, Smith G, Smith RL. 2000. Science, medicine, and the future: pharmacogenetics. *Br. Med. J.* 320:987–90

Yaffe K, Haan M, Byers A, Tangen C, Kuller L. 2000. Estrogen use, APOE, and cognitive decline: evidence of gene-environment interaction. *Neurology* 54:1949–53

Annu. Rev. Psychol. 2002. 53:491–517

RATIONALITY

Eldar Shafir and Robyn A. LeBoeuf

Department of Psychology, Princeton University, Princeton, New Jersey 08544;
e-mail: Shafir@princeton.edu, RLeBoeuf@princeton.edu

Key Words   judgment, choice, decision making, normative theories, cognition

■ **Abstract**   This chapter reviews selected findings in research on reasoning, judgment, and choice and considers the systematic ways in which people violate basic requirements of the corresponding normative analyses. Recent objections to the empirical findings are then considered; these objections question the findings' relevance to assumptions about rationality. These objections address the adequacy of the tasks used in the aforementioned research and the appropriateness of the critical interpretation of participants' responses, as well as the justifiability of some of the theoretical assumptions made by experimenters. The objections are each found not to seriously impinge on the general conclusion that people often violate tenets of rationality in inadvisable ways. In the process, relevant psychological constructs, ranging from cognitive ability and need for cognition, to dual process theories and the role of incentives, are discussed. It is proposed that the rationality critique is compelling and rightfully gaining influence in the social sciences in general.

CONTENTS

0084-6570/02/0201-0491$14.00

INTRODUCTION

Assumptions about rationality occupy a central role in practically all fields of inquiry in which human behavior matters. Human rationality has been celebrated as one of the species' greatest achievements and is often considered a trait that distinguishes humans from other animals. Indeed, the rationality assumption has come to constitute perhaps the most common and pivotal assumption underlying theoretical accounts of human behavior in various disciplines. In light of the rationality assumption's dominant role and its comforting view of human competence, it is not surprising that modern critiques of the rationality assumption have met with heated resistance.

The status of the rationality assumption is ultimately an empirical question (but see Cohen 1981, Dennett 1987). Consequently, the field of experimental psychology has been at the forefront of the modern rationality debate. Subtle distinctions of meaning remain outside the purview of this chapter, yet it is worth mentioning that the philosophical literature distinguishes between various senses of rationality (Harman 1995). In this chapter we review recent experimental and conceptual work that critiques the rationality assumption. We then consider recent work that has questioned the relevance or appropriateness of such critiques and conclude that the rationality assumption continues to appear misguided. We propose that its continued replacement with a behaviorally more sophisticated view promises to contribute significantly to the success of social science theories.

It is notable that the predominant theories of rationality are predicated on notions of consistency, not of substance. A person is entitled to a wide range of opinions, beliefs, and preferences; what is important is for these to cohere in a normatively defensible fashion. Thus, the term "rational" conveys a more technical meaning than its general dictionary significance of "agreeable to reason; of sound mind; sane." These latter terms may be applicable to people whose behavior is not well captured by normative accounts of rationality (cf. Simon 1978, Stein 1996). Conversely, one can imagine a person (say, a member of some bizarre cult) who satisfies all the requirements of consistency yet holds beliefs that in common parlance would be considered highly irrational.

Despite its focus on consistency, the rationality assumption remains, at least to some degree, intuitive rather than purely technical in nature. After all, computational (as well as time, attention, memory, and similar) limitations necessitate some failures of ideal rationality. Apart from those theories that are explicitly about idealized rationality rather than about possible human achievement (see, e.g., Stalnaker 1984, Gardenfors 1988), the requirements of rationality typically imposed are those that we expect people, at least to a first approximation, to be able to fulfill. It turns out that a variety of observed failures are not attributable to computational overload but, rather, to the specific ways in which people process information and make decisions. In those instances, whether people are considered to have violated rationality seems largely to depend on whether we had expected them to be able to perform the task in conformity with normative criteria (Bell et al. 1988, Shafir 1993).

For many years the predominant view in the social sciences had been that the rationality assumption is an adequate approximation for modeling and predicting human behavior. Normative theories pertinent to distinct tasks such as logical reasoning (Glymour 1992), probabilistic thinking (Ross 1997), and decision making (Edwards 1961, Luce & Raiffa 1957), served as candidate paradigms of human rationality. But then, motivated by Simon's (1955) notions of bounded rationality and later by Kahneman and Tversky's heuristics and biases program (Kahneman & Tversky 1972, 1973; Tversky & Kahneman 1973, 1974, 1983), the emphasis shifted toward documenting the persistent inadequacy of the rationality assumption. Common to most accounts of rationality is the notion that a person is largely entitled to his or her own views or preferences, but that these should cohere, should adhere to basic rules of logic and probability theory, and should not be formed or changed based on immaterial factors related to, for example, mood, context, or mode of presentation. Many studies from the past three decades, however, have documented numerous ways in which judgments and decisions do not cohere, do not follow basic principles of logic and probability, and depend systematically on just such irrelevant factors. People use intuitive strategies and simple heuristics that are reasonably effective some of the time but that also produce biases and lead to systematic error. In what follows, we briefly review some of the empirical work, mostly in the areas of judgment and choice. We then consider some recent critiques that have arisen concerning these studies' relevance and implications for the rationality assumption. Extensive reviews of the relevant findings can be found in Baron (1994), Camerer (1995), Goldstein & Hogarth (1997), Hastie (2001), Kahneman & Tversky (2000), Mellers et al. (1998), Shafir & Tversky (1995), and Yates (1990).

VIOLATIONS OF NORMATIVE PRINCIPLES

Reasoning

Some of the earliest violations of normative principles documented by experimental psychologists involved systematic deviations from simple principles of logical reasoning (e.g., Wason 1966; see Gilhooly 1988, Oakhill & Garnham 1993 for reviews). Recent contributions to this research have found certain connectives easier to reason about than others; conjunctions (e.g., "and") are easiest, followed by conditionals (e.g., "if ... then"), exclusive disjunctions (e.g., "A or B but not both"), and finally, inclusive disjunctions (e.g., "A or B or both"), which cause participants the most difficulty (Johnson-Laird et al. 1992, 2000). Research has also been motivated by the quest to determine the mechanisms that best account for the observed reasoning competencies and difficulties. Briefly, one view is that people reason by applying abstract reasoning rules to a variety of reasoning tasks (Braine & O'Brien 1998, Rips 1994), whereas the opposing view holds that reasoning is based upon mental models that are constructed to represent the situation at hand (Johnson-Laird 1983, Johnson-Laird & Byrne 1991). All told, research on reasoning has continued to document persistent and systematic shortcomings in reasoning abilities (see Manktelow 1999, Johnson-Laird 1999 for extensive reviews).

Judgment

Early work within the heuristics and biases paradigm concerned people's intuitive probability judgments (Kahneman et al. 1982). The general finding has been that in settings where the relevance of simple probabilistic rules is made transparent, subjects often reveal appropriate statistical intuitions (see, e.g., Tversky & Kahneman 1986). However, in slightly richer contexts, where the applicability of the normative rules is less immediately apparent, people tend to rely on intuitive heuristics that often produce nonnormative judgments.

One such heuristic is the representativeness heuristic, or the tendency to evaluate the likelihood that a target belongs to a certain class based upon the degree to which the target resembles the prototypic class member. Whereas such a strategy may often be reasonably effective, sample sizes, prior odds, and the basic axioms of probability, all of which are highly relevant to likelihood, do not impinge on how representative an observation appears and thus tend to be neglected (Kahneman & Tversky 1972, 1973; Tversky & Kahneman 1983). In a well-known example, respondents are presented with a personality description of a woman, Linda, who is highly similar to a prototypical feminist, and are asked to rate the probability that several statements about Linda are true. The majority of subjects rank the conjunct, "Linda is a bank teller" as less probable than the conjunction, "Linda is a bank teller and is active in the feminist movement" (Tversky & Kahneman 1983), thereby disregarding the fundamental conjunction rule of probability in favor of a judgment based on a highly representative, yet statistically uninformative, description. The notion that people focus on the strength of the evidence with insufficient regard for its weight explains various systematic judgmental biases, including the failure to appreciate regression phenomena and the fact that people are generally overconfident (when evidence is remarkable but reliability is low) and occasionally underconfident (when the evidence is unremarkable but highly reliable) (Griffin & Tversky 1992).

More generally, probability judgments will have gone awry when they are not "well calibrated." Consider a set of propositions, each of which a person judges to be true with a probability of 0.90. If right about 90% of these, the person is said to be well calibrated. If right about fewer or more than 90%, the person is said to be overconfident or underconfident, respectively. People typically tend to be overconfident, whether judging the likelihood that their answers to general-knowledge questions are correct (e.g., Fischhoff et al. 1977, Griffin & Buehler 1999, Lichtenstein & Fischhoff 1977; but see Dawes & Mulford 1996) or estimating the accuracy of predictions about future events or behaviors (Dunning et al. 1990, Pulford & Colman 1996, Vallone et al. 1990). In a typically regressive fashion, overconfidence is most pronounced for difficult tasks, whereas easy tasks occasionally yield underconfidence, in what is known as the "hard-easy effect" (e.g., Lichtenstein & Fischhoff 1977).

Judgments often rely on sets of attributes—for example, a prospective applicant's exam scores, relevant experience, and letters of recommendation—that need to be combined into a single rating, for instance, likelihood of success at the job. Because people have poor insight into how much to weight each attribute, they are typically quite poor at combining these attributes to yield a final judgment. Much research has been devoted to the shortcomings of intuitive ("clinical") judgment, and to the greater predictive success obtained by linear models of the human judge (Dawes 1979, Dawes et al. 1989, Swets et al. 2000). In fact, it has been repeatedly shown that a linear combination of attributes, based, for example, on a judge's past ratings, does better in predicting future (as well as previous) instances than the judge on whom these ratings are based (see, e.g., Swets et al. 2000). Essentially, this "bootstrapping" method takes advantage of the person's insights captured across numerous ratings and improves on any single rating wherein improper weightings of attributes may intrude. Moreover, because attributes are often highly correlated and systematically misperceived, even a unit assignment of weights, not properly devised for the person, can often still outperform the human judge (Dawes 1988). Related methods have extracted from a person's judgments a coherent core that is maximally consistent with those judgments and at the same time comes closer to the observed likelihoods than do the original (incoherent) judgments (Osherson et al. 1994, Pearl 1988).

One recent attempt to model subjective probability judgments, known as support theory (Tversky & Koehler 1994), has focused on the notion that the judged probability that some hypothesis is true will be based on the perceived strength of evidence, or support, for the hypothesis relative to the perceived support for alternate hypotheses. According to support theory, subjective probability is associated not with events but with descriptions of events. Unpacking the description of an event into disjoint components generally increases its support and, hence, its perceived likelihood. As a result, different descriptions of the same event can give rise to different judgments (Brenner & Koehler 1999, Rottenstreich & Tversky 1997, Tversky & Koehler 1994).

As already noted, people's judgments often violate basic normative rules, yet at the same time, people can exhibit sensitivity to and appreciation for the normative principles. This coexistence of fallible intuitions with an underlying appreciation for normative judgment yields a subtle picture of probabilistic reasoning, along with interesting possibilities for a prescriptive approach. In this vein, a large literature on expert systems has attempted to provide analyses and applications (e.g., Hammond et al. 1999, von Winterfeld & Edwards 1986).

Choice

Normative analyses of choice posit consistent preferences that depend on the subjective utilities of anticipated outcomes weighted by their probabilities. To be normative, preferences must satisfy description and procedure invariance, such that logically equivalent representations of a decision problem as well as logically equivalent methods of elicitation yield the same preferences. Recent studies of decision making have captured a number of psychological principles that characterize the decision making process and conflict with these most basic normative requirements. In general, people tend not to have clear and well-ordered preferences: Instead, preferences are actually constructed, not merely revealed, in the elicitation process, and the construction of preference is heavily influenced by the nature and context of the decision.

A number of theories have been proposed to account for the behavioral findings in choice (e.g., Bell 1982, Edwards 1962, Fellner 1965, Luce & Fishburn 1991, Mellers et al. 1997, Shafir et al. 1993a, Tversky 1972), the most influential of which has been prospect theory (Kahneman & Tversky 1979, Tversky & Kahneman 1992). Prospect theory posits that probabilities have nonlinear impacts on decisions (Gonzalez & Wu 1999, Kahneman & Tversky 1979, Prelec 2000, Tversky & Wakker 1995) and proposes an S-shaped value function with three important properties. First, the evaluation of outcomes is defined on gains and losses rather than total wealth. Second, the value function is steeper for losses than for gains: Thus, a loss of $X is more aversive than a gain of $X is attractive. This is commonly referred to as loss aversion (Tversky & Kahneman 1991); one consequence of loss aversion is the "endowment effect," wherein the mere possession of a good can lead to higher valuation of it than if it were not in one's possession (Kahneman et al. 1990). Loss aversion also creates a general reluctance to trade or depart from the status quo, because the disadvantages of departing from it loom larger than the advantages of the alternatives (Samuelson & Zeckhauser 1988). Finally, owing to diminishing sensitivity, prospect theory's value function is concave for gains and convex for losses, yielding risk-averse attitudes in the domain of gains and risk seeking in the domain of losses (except for very low probabilities, in which case these can reverse).

The above attitudes may seem compelling and unobjectionable, yet their combination yields normatively problematic consequences. For example, because prospects can often be framed either as gains or as losses relative to some reference point, and because risk attitudes vary depending upon whether gains or losses are at stake, alternative frames may lead to discrepant preferences with respect to the same final outcome (Tversky & Kahneman 1981, 1986). In one example (Tversky & Kahneman 1986), respondents are asked to assume themselves $300 richer and are then offered a choice between a sure gain of $100 or an equal chance to win $200 or nothing. Alternatively, they are asked to assume themselves $500 richer, and offered a choice between a sure loss of $100 and an equal chance to lose $200 or nothing. Although the two problems are essentially identical with respect to the final outcome, most subjects who choose between gains predictably prefer the $100 for sure, whereas most subjects who choose between losses prefer the probabilistic $200 gamble. This is known as a "framing effect": It occurs when alternative frames of essentially the same decision problem lead to predictably different choices. Framing effects have been replicated across a variety of domains in dozens of studies (for reviews, see Kühberger 1998, Levin et al. 1998; RA LeBoeuf & E Shafir, in preparation).

Influential research has also focused on the relative weighting of options' different dimensions. Because people are often uncertain about the relative importance of various dimensions, the weights assigned to those dimensions are often influenced by relatively immaterial changes in the task, the description, and the nature of the options under consideration. For example, the weight given an attribute tends to be enhanced by its compatibility with a required response. Thus, a gamble's potential payoff is weighted more heavily in a pricing task (in which both the price and the payoff are expressed in the same—monetary—units) than in choice (see Shafir 1993, 1995; Slovic et al. 1990). Consistent with this is the preference reversal phenomenon (Slovic & Lichtenstein 1983, Tversky et al. 1990), wherein subjects choose a lottery offering a greater chance to win over another offering a higher payoff, but then price the latter higher than the former. Preference reversals have been replicated among professional gamblers in a Las Vegas casino (Lichtenstein & Slovic 1973) and in a context offering the equivalent of a month's salary to respondents in the Peoples' Republic of China (Kachelmeier & Shehata 1992). Preference reversals have also been documented in numerous studies involving nonmonetary options, including choice between highway safety programs, job candidates, and interventions intended to address environmental problems (Kahneman & Ritov 1994, Slovic et al. 1990, Tversky et al. 1988).

A related choice pattern, referred to as an evaluability effect, emerges when attributes are difficult to evaluate in isolation (Hsee 1996). In one example, subjects are presented with two second-hand music dictionaries, one with 20,000 entries and a damaged cover, the other with 10,000 entries and a cover that is like new. When evaluating the dictionaries separately, respondents, who have little notion of how many entries to expect, are willing to pay more for the dictionary with the new rather than the torn cover. When these dictionaries are evaluated concurrently, however, most people prefer the dictionary with more entries, despite its inferior cover (Hsee 1996, Hsee et al. 1999).

In further violation of standard value maximization, decisional conflict can lead to a greater tendency to search for alternatives when better options are available but the decision is hard than when relatively inferior options are present and the decision is easy (Tversky & Shafir 1992a). In addition to the conflict or difficulty that characterizes a decision (March 1978), choices have been shown to be influenced, often nonnormatively, by the regret anticipated in cases where another option could have been better (Bell 1982), the reasons used to justify one choice over another (Shafir et al. 1993b, Tetlock 1992), the influence exerted by costs already suffered (Arkes & Blumer 1985, Gourville & Soman 1998), and the effects of temporal ordering on future decisions (Loewenstein & Elster 1992, Loewenstein & Prelec 1993). The methodology used to document the various effects in decision making research is quite rich, including process-tracing methods, such as verbal protocols (Ericsson & Simon 1984), information-acquisition sequences (Payne et al. 1993), and eye-movement data (Russo & Dosher 1983).

Variants of Utility

Whereas discussions generally focus on the descriptive adequacy of utility max-imization, recent research has explored the precise nature of utility. Kahneman (1994) questions whether people maximize the expected experienced utility of a decision, that is, the hedonic experience that the decision will bring, as op-posed to merely the decision utility, that is, the utility perceived at the moment of decision.

It turns out that utility mispredictions are common. The remembered hedonic qualities of past events are subject to biased evaluations that overweigh extreme and final moments, leading to relative "duration neglect" and the occasional preference for events that are remembered more positively owing to an added diminishingly painful final episode, despite the added net amount of pain overall (Kahneman 1994, Kahneman et al. 1993). In addition to misremembering their experiences, decision makers often fail to anticipate increases in liking owing to mere exposure (Kahneman & Snell 1992), neglect the dissipation of satiation (Simonson 1990), misremember options previously encountered (Mather et al. 2000), and fail to fore-see other factors, such as the effects of ownership on the valuation of objects (Van Boven et al. 2000). Finally, when predicting the impact on their lives of specific events, people tend to focus too heavily on those events, consequently overesti-mating the impact these events will have on their lives and their life satisfaction (Schkade & Kahneman 1998, Wilson et al. 2000). In making such forecasts, peo-ple tend to neglect the extent to which they will be able to maintain a level of satisfaction in the face of adversity (Gilbert et al. 1998, Kahneman et al. 1999). In sum, expectations of experienced utility are often inaccurate, whether they stem from biased retrospective evaluations or from misguided theories about the future. Decisions based on expectations that are systematically inaccurate are likely to result in courses of action that fail to maximize well-being, in violation of the standard tenets underlying the rationality assumption.

Emotion

Whereas emotions are typically considered outside the purvue of a rational anal-ysis, recent research has begun to explore the role of emotions in judgments and decisions. It appears that transient moods influence choice and judgment in ways that neither rationality assumptions nor intuition predict. For example, negative moods increase the perceived frequency of risks and of undesirable events (such as homicides) and decrease judged life satisfaction, while positive moods act in the opposite direction (Johnson & Tversky 1983, Schwarz & Clore 1983). Fur-thermore, for those in a positive mood, the pain of a loss is heightened, leading to attempts at "mood maintenance" through greater risk-aversion (Isen & Geva 1987, Isen et al. 1988). Interestingly, moods with the same valence can have differential effects on judgment; thus, anger, a negatively valenced emotion, seems to yield optimism in judgments about future risks, whereas fear, also negatively valenced, generates relative pessimism (Lerner & Keltner 2000).

Furthermore, judgments are often shaped by emotionally evaluative responses in ways not anticipated by accounts of rationality. For example, participants are willing to pay more to insure, and are more likely to seek compensation for, an item that is emotionally meaningful than for an emotionally neutral but equally valuable item (Hsee & Kunreuther 2000). Similarly, the perceived risk of things like nuclear power is related to the amount of dread that they arouse (Fischhoff et al. 1978). The evaluative reaction engendered by stimuli plays a role in the halo effect (Dion et al. 1972), and in the influence of vividness on perceived event frequency (e.g., Lichtenstein et al. 1978).

Such findings have prompted attempts at integrated views of the influences of affect on decision making. Damasio (1994) posited that good decision making requires a somatic marker, or a visceral signal that allows the decision maker to anticipate the pain and pleasure of outcomes. Similar proposals suggest that images, marked by positive and negative affective feelings, often guide decisions; because these images can be consulted more quickly and with less effort then it would take to form a judgment through normative routes, researchers have argued for the existence of an "affect heuristic" (Finucane et al. 2000, Slovic et al. 2001). Findings such as the perceived negative relationship between risk and benefit, strengthened under time pressure and purportedly mediated by affect (Finucane et al. 2000, Fischhoff et al. 1978) and the relative insensitivity to the probability of occurrence of emotionally powerful stimuli (Rottenstreich & Hsee 2001) are seen as further evidence for an affect heuristic. Loewenstein et al. (2001) suggested that anticipatory emotions not only influence cognitive appraisals of uncertain situations but compete with those appraisals in determining a response. In summary, recent decision making research has seen an increased interest in the role of affect: Transient emotions can produce behavioral responses that deviate from what is otherwise seen as the "best" plan, in ways that are not subsumed by the tenets of rationality.

Dual Process Models

People's reasonably sophisticated normative insights, which they are able to formulate upon reflection, alongside the systematic and ubiquitous violations of normative principles in everyday decisions have led to a number of theoretical accounts that have focused on the coexistence of these two apparently discrepant impulses. These accounts have proposed dual-process theories of reasoning and judgment, suggesting that responses can reflect, at different times, the operation of one system or another (Epstein 1994, Evans & Over 1996, Osherson 1995, Sloman 1996, Stanovich 1999). For example, Epstein (1994) suggested that there is a holistic, affective, association-driven experiential system that coexists with an analytic, logical, and reason-oriented rational system. Sloman (1996) proposed an associative system that makes judgments based on similarity and regularities in the environment; this is separate from a rule-based system that operates on symbolic structures and follows explicit rules of computation. Evans & Over (1996) distinguished habitual and tacit "type 1 rationality," which serves to achieve everyday goals, from "type 2 rationality," which enables people to follow explicit normative insights. In his summary of dual-process theories, Stanovich (1999) referred to "system 1" reasoning, which is automatic, largely unconscious, and undemanding of capacity, versus "system 2" reasoning, which is controlled and encompasses analytic intelligence.

Common to these theories is one process of reasoning that makes relatively automatic inferences and judgments through mainly associative means, and another process that makes relatively effortful inferences by following a set of explicitly normative rules. Only when the rule-based, analytic system is engaged, and when it cues a normative response that "overrides" the automatic, associative processing, will people successfully avoid the "irrationalities" that can be generated by the latter. For example, in the context of the Linda problem (Tversky & Kahneman 1983), the associative system might cue the response "Linda resembles a feminist bank teller;" only when the rule-based system recognizes the applicability of the conjunction rule will participants generate the normative response (cf. Epstein 1994, Sloman 1996, Stanovich 1999). It should be noted that these theories share a basic structure with other dual-process theories of information processing, such as Shiffrin & Schneider's (1977) distinction between automatic and controlled processing and Zajonc's (1980) distinction between immediate affective responses and more effortful cognitive responses, as well as theories of attitude change (Petty & Wegener 1999), person perception (Trope & Gaunt 1999), and stereotyping (Fiske et al. 1999; see Chaiken & Trope 1999, for further examples), all of which posit at least two basic modes of processing—one in which heuristic responses predominate and another in which more deliberate strategies take over.

Regardless of the precise account of how reasoning is performed, there seems to be compelling evidence for systematic violations of normative principles alongside the ability to appreciate their normative appeal. Rationality requires that judgments and decisions be far-sighted, contemplated in the aggregate, and made from a global perspective. Instead, research shows that they are often myopic and contemplated from a narrow and local perspective. Nonetheless, some authors have questioned the validity or importance of the empirical findings. It is to these objections that we next turn.

THE OBJECTIONS

A slew of studies and replications have solidified the status of the rationality critique over the past two decades. Perhaps not surprisingly, recent years have witnessed a resurgence in attempts to salvage the rationality assumption. One natural path has been to question the validity or relevance of the accumulated findings. This has been pursued along several lines. The first trivializes the findings by denying their import and applicability to "real" decisions. The second argues that participants are not providing wrong answers but, rather, that the researchers misinterpret the answers as incorrect. The third line holds that researchers' expectations and demands of the participants are inappropriate, unfair, or unrealistic. These arguments and the evidence for or against them are summarized in turn (see Gilovich & Griffin 2001, Stanovich 1999 for related reviews).

Trivializations of the Findings

One way to salvage the rationality assumption is by dismissing the various findings as unsystematic, unreliable, and easily correctable once participants are sufficiently motivated. The simplest version of this argument suggests that irrationalities are nothing more than unsystematic "performance errors," merely the result of a "momentary . . . lapse in ancillary processes" (Stanovich & West 2000, p. 646; see Stein 1996, pp. 9–10). Were this the case, we should expect nothing more than error variance centered around a normative response. This version of the argument can be relatively easily dismissed. The observed deviations from rationality are clearly not random. Errors ranging from the conjunction fallacy (Tversky & Kahneman 1983), to framing effects (Tversky & Kahneman 1981), to preference reversals (Lichtenstein & Slovic 1973) all arise in specific and predictable ways. Furthermore, Stanovich & West (1998c) have found modest correlations between an individual's performance on a host of judgment and reasoning problems; such correlations would not be expected were these nothing but unsystematic errors.

A related argument, however, cannot be quite so easily dismissed. According to this argument, participants who violate basic normative principles may simply lack sufficient motivation; were they motivated, the argument goes, they would think more deeply about the task and obey the otherwise compelling normative principles. This implies that rationality violations ought mostly to emerge on trivial and inconsequential tasks. This prediction has been explored in a variety of ways.

INCENTIVES   Monetary incentives have traditionally been presumed an obvious way to increase motivation. With rare exceptions, however, incentives do not decrease the incidence of nonnormative behaviors. Camerer & Hogarth (1999) reviewed 74 studies that manipulate incentives. An occasional study has been able to, for instance, improve performance on a probability matching task (Castellan 1969), or reduce the influence of an irrelevant anchor (Wright & Anderson 1989). However, most inconsistencies, such as preference reversals (Grether & Plott 1979, Lichtenstein & Slovic 1973, Kachelmeier & Shehata 1992) and framing effects (Levin et al. 1988, Tversky & Kahneman 1981) persist in the face of incentives and can even be exacerbated by them. Arkes et al. (1986) employed a prediction task in which participants had the option of using an actuarial formula; the presence of incentives led to lesser reliance on the formula and to worsened performance. Camerer & Hogarth (1999) concluded that "there is no replicated study in which a theory of rational choice was rejected at low stakes . . . and accepted at high stakes" (p. 33). Note that even when incentives are successful in raising motivation, people still need to apply the correct insights for performance to improve beyond the mere reduction of careless error (cf. Wilson et al. 1996). Without the appropriate insight, increased motivation will lead to more enthusiastic application of an incorrect strategy and will have a small if not a deleterious effect (as in Arkes et al. 1986).

JUSTIFICATION PROVISION   Another method of increasing participants' involvement has been to require them to justify their responses. However, just as incentives do not reduce the occurrence of inconsistency, neither does justification provision. To take framing effects as an example, whereas justification has at times been shown to reduce the incidence of framing effects (Sieck & Yates 1997, Takemura 1994), more often framing effects clearly persist even when justification is provided (Fagley & Miller 1987, Levin & Chapman 1990, Miller & Fagley 1991, Takemura 1993; RA LeBoeuf & E Shafir, in preparation). Again, greater involvement may increase motivation, but without the right insight at the right moment that motivation is unlikely to have a positive effect.

EXPERTISE   An obvious place to look for increased involvement and sophistication is among experts, to whom the task is highly relevant and much more familiar. Numerous studies show that experts can violate the tenets of rationality in much the same fashion as lay people do. For example, Redelmeier & Shafir (1995, Redelmeier et al. 2001) found that physicians, nurses, and legislators who faced choices in their own areas of expertise were prone to violate notions of regularity (Tversky & Simonson 1993) and instrumentality (Bastardi & Shafir 1998) much as nonexperts did. Similarly, McNeil et al. (1982) found that patients, graduate students, and physicians were similarly affected by a framing manipulation of alternative therapies' mortality outcomes. Other studies similarly found expertise and experience to have little impact on the incidence of decision biases (e.g., Benartzi & Thaler 1995, Camerer et al. 1997, Neale & Northcraft 1986, Redelmeier & Tversky 1990).

In a slightly different vein, Dawes et al. (1989) concluded that actuarial decision making is often far superior to expert, or clinical, judgment. Their conclusion stems in part from studies that show that clinicians fall prey to judgmental biases, such as overconfidence (Faust et al. 1988) and the hindsight bias (Arkes et al. 1981). It appears that experts, for whom the tasks are meaningful and relevant, are as likely as nonexperts to violate simple norms of rationality. This strongly suggests that such violations cannot be attributed to lack of interest, involvement, or understanding.

NEED FOR COGNITION   Despite the failure of incentives, justification, or expertise to attenuate the observed inconsistencies and biases, one more variable that has been investigated is participants' inherent need for cognition (NC) (Cacioppo & Petty 1982). NC identifies "differences among individuals in their tendency to engage in and enjoy thinking" (Cacioppo & Petty 1982, p. 116). The NC variable separates those who find fulfillment in intricate thought from those who do not seek out situations that require effortful and elaborate processing (Cacioppo &

Petty 1982). To the extent that a bias is attributable to an insufficiently serious consideration of a problem, NC might moderate the occurrence of such bias

Smith & Levin (1996) reported a lower impact of problem frame on high-NC participants, but both Levin et al. (2001) and RA LeBoeuf & E Shafir (in preparation) found no effect of NC on framing. Stanovich & West (1999) found that those with higher NC scores were more likely, among other things, to recognize the relevance of base rates in likelihood judgments and more likely to recognize the inappropriateness of honoring sunk costs. On the other hand, they found NC scores not to be predictive of insights in hypothesis testing or Prisoner's Dilemma tasks. In fact, higher NC scores did not yield an increase in the tendency to utilize (as opposed to merely recognize the relevance of) base rates. Thus, whereas high-NC participants occasionally give more normative responses than their low-NC counterparts (especially in within-subjects contexts; see RA LeBoeuf & E Shafir, in preparation), increased thought as indexed by NC scores does not appear to rid respondents of observed inconsistencies and bias.

SUMMARY   Deviations from the criteria of rational judgment and choice cannot be seen as mere "performance errors." These deviations are far too systematic, both within and across individuals, to be considered randomly distributed. The systematic biases persist in the face of a variety of attempts to increase incentives as well as other motivational factors. The biases are exhibited by experts as well as novices and cannot be dismissed as random artifacts attributable to trivial, uninteresting, or unrepresentative tasks.

Misinterpretations

Another way to salvage the rationality assumption is to suggest that researchers mistakenly attribute irrationality to what is in fact normative behavior. Such misinterpretation is said to arise owing to experimenters' and participants' purportedly different construals of the tasks (see also Gilovich & Griffin 2001, Stanovich & West 2000). According to this view, participants' responses, which are rational in light of their own construals of the task, are coded as irrational by experimenters who fail to appreciate the participants' construals (Hertwig & Gigerenzer 1999, Hilton 1995, Levinson 1995, Macdonald 1986, Schwarz 1996, Slugoski & Wilson 1998). When studies are redesigned to reduce the likelihood of alternative construals and misinterpretations, purported violations should disappear or at least be markedly reduced (Dulany & Hilton 1991, Fiedler 1988, Krosnick et al. 1990, Politzer & Noveck 1991, Schwarz et al. 1991). We explore this in the following sections.

CONVERSATIONAL IMPLICATIONS   One critique starts with the premise that people must make inferences about a communicator's intent and that, in making such inferences, people typically presume that communicators are following the maxims of relevance and nonredundancy (Grice 1975). Participants in experiments, according to this critique, do not always realize that the experimenter may flout a Gricean maxim, for example, by volunteering irrelevant information. Consequently, they make inferences about the experimenter's presumed intent and base their judgments on inferred as well as available information, whereas the experimenter expects evaluations based solely on available information (Hilton 1995, Levinson 1995, Schwarz 1996).

Prominent targets of this critique have been violations of the conjunction rule as exhibited by performance on the Linda problem described earlier (Tversky & Kahneman 1983). Researchers have investigated the inferences that people draw when presented with the conjunct ("Linda is a bank teller") juxtaposed with the conjunction ("Linda is a bank teller and is active in the feminist movement"). Respondents, it is argued, may expect a cooperative communicator not to pose a trivial question such as "Is A more or less probable than A and B?" and may thus infer that further interpretation is necessary (Politzer & Noveck 1991), leading to the reformulation of the conjunct as meaning "A and not B" (cf. Dulany & Hilton 1991, Levinson 1995).

Anticipating such critique, Tversky & Kahneman (1983) replaced the conjunct with "Linda is a bank teller whether or not she is active in the feminist movement." Whereas the incidence of the conjunction fallacy diminished, the fallacy persisted among the majority of participants. A number of researchers, however, remained unconvinced and further explored potential alternative interpretations of the items.

Dulany & Hilton (1991), for example, found that they could reduce the prevalence of the conjunction fallacy to a minority of subjects (38% or fewer) by rewording the conjunct to include some helpful logical clues. Furthermore, through interviews with participants, they ascertained that the majority who committed the conjunction fallacy did not interpret the conjunct in its extensional, or normative, form. Politzer & Noveck (1991) similarly found that explicit, as opposed to implicit, conjunctions indeed encouraged alternate interpretations of the conjunct. In a related vein, Slugoski & Wilson (1998) found that the tendency to commit the conjunction fallacy was correlated with a person's conversational skill and proposed that the fallacy is due to a process of interpretation, not necessarily an inability to reason.

Despite these observations, it appears unlikely that the conjunction fallacy can be relegated to a flouting of Gricean conventions. First, Tversky & Kahneman (1983) observed the conjunction fallacy across a wide variety of problems, including some for which implicatures are not easily invited (e.g., the "Bjorn Borg" problem). Second, Tversky & Kahneman observed the conjunction effect in a between-subjects design in which the conjunct was rated as less probable than the conjunction even though the two were seen by different participants (but see Hertwig & Gigerenzer 1999, Politzer & Noveck 1991 for questions about the relevance of between-subjects findings). Agnoli & Krantz (1989) found that instruction in set theory could diminish the incidence of the conjunction fallacy, which would not be expected if participants reinterpreted the conjunct to mean that the conjunction was not its subset. Agnoli & Krantz also noted that replacing the conjunct with its purported reinterpretation (A and not B) increased the difference between the likelihood assigned the replacement statement and the original conjunction, a pattern that would not be expected under the spontaneous reinterpretation notion. Finally, Morier & Borgida (1984) included the conjunct, the original conjunction, as well as the purported reinterpretation among the response alternatives. This should have obviated the purported need to reinterpret, yet 77% of participants committed the conjunction fallacy on the Linda problem.

Findings of insufficient reliance on base-rate information in likelihood judgments (Kahneman & Tversky 1973) sparked similar discussions regarding possible conversational inferences (see Schwarz 1996). In a typical experiment, participants are presented with a vignette drawn randomly from some population (consisting, e.g., of 70 lawyers and 30 engineers) and asked the likelihood that the description belongs to a particular member of that population (e.g., a lawyer). Estimates are typically under-influenced by the base rate, and over-influenced by the representativeness of the description (Kahneman & Tversky 1973). It was suggested that perhaps participants are led to infer that the description is important, and that it is this inference, not a general reluctance to rely on base rates, that underlies the apparent error (Schwarz 1996, Schwarz et al. 1991).

In the original studies (Kahneman & Tversky 1973), base rates were given first and then the individuating description was added; this order of presentation, some have proposed, may have suggested that base rates were insufficient for the task. Krosnick et al. (1990) varied the order in which the information was presented and, indeed, found that reliance on base rates increased when base-rate information was presented after the description. Also, in the original studies, in which the personality description was purportedly compiled by psychologists, participants may have inferred that it was carefully constructed and perhaps valid. When the description was said to have been randomly sampled, unreliable, or informative to "statistical" experts, reliance on base rates increased significantly (Ginossar & Trope 1987, Schwarz et al. 1991). Finally, when base rates were made to vary, reliance on base rates increased (Fischhoff et al. 1979, Schwarz et al. 1991). Whereas some instances of base rate neglect may be attributable to conversational factors, as suggested above, the data continue to suggest that an under-reliance on base rates, perhaps less extreme than occasionally observed, nevertheless characterizes people's judgments (Fischhoff et al. 1979, Schwarz et al. 1991).

Conversational considerations have also been invoked with regard to framing effects. In the context of the Asian Disease problem (Tversky & Kahneman 1981), for example, researchers have suggested that the two (purportedly isomorphic) frames presented could be construed as nonisomorphic (Berkeley & Humphreys 1982, Macdonald 1986). However, Stanovich & West (1998b), using a within-subjects design, showed that most participants, especially those of higher cognitive ability, recognize the two frames as extensionally identical. Violations of normative criteria are often overdetermined; many factors can combine to produce such violations, and conversational misinterpretations may be one, but are unlikely to be a major, contributor to the observed effects (cf. Gilovich & Griffin 2001, Schwarz 1996).

ALTERNATIVE INTERPRETATIONS OF TERMS AND TASKS   Some attempts to dismiss the observed findings have focused on the possibility that respondents' interpretations of the terms or tasks are different from those assumed by the experimenters who present them. One such line of criticism hinges on the use of the term "probability." There are at least two distinct philosophical conceptions of probability (Howson & Urbach 1989, Keynes 1921, von Mises 1957). According to one, probabilities refer to the relative frequencies of objective physical events in repeated trials; according to the other, probabilities are epistemic in nature, expressing degrees of belief in specific hypotheses. Note, though, that these different conceptions of probability are arguably constrained by the same mathematical axioms. Adherence to the axioms suffices to insure that probability judgment is coherent. Nonetheless, this distinction is at the core of an ongoing debate concerning the status and interpretation of some experimental findings (see, e.g., Cosmides & Tooby 1996; Fiedler 1988; Gigerenzer 1994, 1996a; Kahneman & Tversky 1996).

For example, Gigerenzer (1994; see also Macdonald 1986) noted that the conjunction fallacy, observed when asking for the probability of single events, violates some theories of probability but does not violate the frequentist conception of probability. Furthermore, Hertwig & Gigerenzer (1999) argued that participants who commit the fallacy generally do not interpret "probability" mathematically. They showed that preceding probability judgments with typicality judgments reduces the incidence of the conjunction fallacy, suggesting that participants can interpret probability mathematically but tend not to do so spontaneously. The conjunction fallacy, however, has also been shown in frequentistic formats (Tversky & Kahneman 1983, Kahneman & Tversky 1996). Furthermore, most respondents do not subscribe to a frequentistic interpretation, because they appear to find the notion of a single event probability natural and clear (Kahneman & Tversky 1996). In fact, it appears that the standard conception of probability endorsed by experimenters is also endorsed by participants with greater cognitive ability (Stanovich & West 1998b).

A similar objection concerns the possible reinterpretation of task instructions. For example, incorrect responses on the Wason selection task (Wason 1966) are typically seen as indicative of errors in deductive reasoning. However, Oaksford & Chater (1996) suggested that participants might see their task as involving optimal data selection for inductive hypothesis testing, which would explain the supposed incorrect responses when the task has abstract or otherwise nondeontic content, as opposed to the improved performance with deontic content. By this account, variations from the modal responses should merely constitute error variance. However, Stanovich & West (1998a) found a larger-than-expected set of participants who gave either the correct or the incorrect response in both the nondeontic and deontic versions, suggesting a frequent construal of the task as one involving deductive reasoning.

A review of the findings suggests that observed violations of the requirements of rationality cannot be explained away by attributing to respondents alternative construals of problems. Of course, understanding participants' construals of situations has been very important, particularly in social psychology (Griffin & Ross 1991). Various considerations that enter into peoples' construals of decision situations have been explored, including fairness (Kahneman et al. 1986), anticipated regret (Bell 1982, Tversky 1975), wishful thinking (Quattrone & Tversky 1984), and impression management (Sen 1993), among others. However, not all construals of every problem can be considered legitimate lest the theory of rational choice be stripped of any normative impact (see Margolis 1987). In fact, some misconstruals may be at the very heart of the counter-normative behaviors they help generate. Stanovich & West (2000, Stanovich 1999) attempted to find an "expert wide reflective equilibrium" such that normative principles, philosophical considerations, intuition, and expert opinion come into balance in regards to whether alternative interpretations are seen as potentially normative; they conclude that the standard normative construals are, for the most part, appropriate.

Inappropriate Tests of Rationality

Other objections to the documented violations of rational choice and judgment focus not on the results as much as on the appropriateness of the tests used to obtain them.

COMPUTATIONAL LIMITATIONS   A fundamental challenge questions whether the observed biases and errors emerge simply because the normative responses are out of reach for people. Clearly, rationality should not be defined in a manner that renders it unattainable by most people (Harman 1995, Stich 1990). If the tasks are unfairly demanding, we learn little from observing participants' inability to solve them.

For many of the findings that form the core of the rationality critique this argument simply does not apply. Simple violations of well-ordering in choice, for example, such as standard framing effects (Tversky & Kahneman 1981), the asymmetric dominance effect (Huber et al. 1982, Simonson & Tversky 1992), the effects of noninstrumental searches (Bastardi & Shafir 1998), and the variety of preference reversals discussed earlier all impose remarkably simple demands; the difficulties appear to reside not in any computational demands, but in the fact that preferences are malleable and thus prone to systematic violations of well-ordering.

Demonstrated, albeit imperfect, improvements in statistical reasoning following instruction also suggest that the difficulties are often not computational but rather conceptual in nature (see, e.g., Agnoli & Krantz 1989, Fong & Nisbett 1991, Frank et al. 1993). Furthermore, various errors and inconsistencies that are systematically exhibited when the applicability of a relevant principle goes undetected are easily avoided once it is transparent (e.g., Fiedler 1988, Tversky & Kahneman 1986, Tversky & Shafir 1992b). As before, the difficulty appears to reside not in the required computation, but in the intuitive heuristic procedures that are used unless their possible inappropriateness is made salient.

INAPPROPRIATE PROBLEM FORMATS   The nature of the particular problems used has also been questioned, particularly in light of findings suggesting that performance can be improved if the problems are altered. Researchers approaching the question of rationality from an evolutionary perspective, for example, have argued that the tasks provided are typically not the tasks that participants' cognitive mechanisms have evolved to be good at. When evolutionarily more appropriate tasks are employed, the argument holds, performance improves (Cosmides & Tooby 1996, Gigerenzer 1996b). For example, it is known that performance can be improved when problems are posed in terms of frequencies rather than likelihood judgments (Cosmides & Tooby 1996, Fiedler 1988, Gigerenzer et al. 1991, Hertwig & Gigerenzer 1999, Tversky & Kahneman 1983), although performance can also be hurt by frequency formats (see Griffin & Buehler 1999). Evolutionary psychologists have proposed that the ability to encode frequencies was useful in the Pleistocene age, and the corresponding cognitive mechanisms were thus selected for, whereas the ability to determine the likelihood of single events was not (Cosmides & Tooby 1996). Similarly, improved performance on the Wason selection task when the content requires participants to check for violations of social contracts is attributed to a "cheater-detection" module that was ostensibly selected for through evolution (Cosmides & Tooby 1992, Gigerenzer & Hug 1992).

Even if these arguments were correct, the fact remains that many problems encountered in everyday life are not presented in evolutionarily advantageous ways and may thus generate incorrect responses. In fact, the successful elicitation of improved performance with certain formats suggests that people do indeed have the required competence and that they tend to agree about the correct norms (Stanovich 1999, Stein 1996). Of course, the fact that some biases are more or less easy to avoid depending on question format is not surprising or inconsistent with nonevolutionary accounts of problem solving and judgment (Gick & Holyoak 1980, Reed 1993). For example, it has been suggested that frequency formats may make extensional considerations easier to bring to mind (Tversky & Kahneman 1983; but see Hertwig & Gigerenzer 1999).

INAPPROPRIATE NORMS   Yet another argument regarding the appropriateness of studies of rationality centers on whether the appropriate normative standards are being used (cf. Gigerenzer 1996a, Gigerenzer et al. 1991, Lopes & Oden 1991, Wetherick 1971). Several economists tried to effect a compromise between normative accounts and descriptive findings by retaining some of the more normatively appealing principles, such as dominance and invariance, while relaxing others, such as independence and transitivity (see Camerer 1990, 1995; Machina 1982). In a similar fashion some researchers have attempted to address the rationality critique by changing some normative criteria so that the normative and descriptive may be more in line (Stein 1996).

Allowing departures from otherwise appealing normative criteria is problematic. For one thing, incoherent judgment entails the possible holding of contradictory beliefs and likelihood judgments that, when translated into bets that the person deems fair, create a set of bets that the person is bound to lose no matter how things turn out (Osherson 1995, Resnik 1987, Stein 1996). Not only do individuals who violate the simple laws of probability or preference leave themselves exposed to situations in which they are bound to lose, but the normative principles are, in fact, typically endorsed by those who occasionally violate them. Stanovich & West (1999) presented participants with normative as well as nonnormative arguments, and found that participants who changed their responses were often more likely to do so in the normative direction (see also Tversky & Kahneman 1983). Furthermore, in many of the tasks that these investigators studied, those who respond normatively score higher on the SAT as well as other cognitive ability measures (Stanovich & West 1998a,b,c). It appears that greater awareness of the normative principles, indexed by cognitive ability, presentation formats, or through explicit explication, is often associated with greater support for their normative appeal (but see Dawes & Mulford 1996, Hoch 1987, Stanovich & West 1998c for instances in which standard normative principles might not be appropriate).

Perhaps the most extreme argument has suggested that rationality is not to be settled empirically, because evolution will have necessarily produced organisms that form true beliefs and that reason rationally (e.g., Dennett 1987, Fodor 1975; see Stanovich 1999, Stein 1996, Stich 1990 for reviews). As others have written, these arguments misconstrue the function of evolution and of natural selection (Lewontin 1990, Stein 1996). There is no basis for assuming that evolution will have produced creatures whose behavior conforms to the rational principles that they have endorsed, and there is, therefore, no reason to question the appropriateness of studies that try to gauge these principles' empirical status.

SUMMARY AND CONCLUSION

Various arguments have been made disputing the accumulation of findings that show people systematically violating fundamental normative principles of reasoning, judgment, and decision. This review suggests that the violations cannot be dismissed as either random or trivial, nor can they be attributed to experimenters' misinterpretation of answers that are actually appropriate to alternative, valid interpretations of the problems. The systematic and well-documented findings cannot be attributed to simple computational limitations, nor does it appear that inappropriate types of questions are being asked or inappropriate norms applied. The compelling nature of the rationality critique is having an ever greater impact on work in neighboring disciplines, most notably in the increasing popularity of behavioral economics (Rabin 1998, Sunstein 2000, Thaler 1992, 1993). It may eventually help alter the social sciences' view of the human agent.

Visit the Annual Reviews home page at www.AnnualReviews.org

LITERATURE CITED

Agnoli F, Krantz DH. 1989. Suppressing natural heuristics by formal instruction: the case of the conjunction fallacy. *Cogn. Psychol.* 21:515–50

Arkes HR, Blumer C. 1985. The psychology of sunk cost. *Org. Behav. Hum. Decis. Process.* 35:124–40

Arkes HR, Dawes RM, Christensen C. 1986. Factors influencing the use of a decision rule in a probabilistic task. *Org. Behav. Hum. Decis. Process.* 37:93–110

Arkes HR, Wortmann RL, Saville PD, Harkness AR. 1981. Hindsight bias among physicians weighing the likelihood of diagnoses. *J. Appl. Psychol.* 66:252–54

Baron J. 1994. *Thinking and Deciding.* New York: Cambridge Univ. Press. 2nd ed.

Bastardi A, Shafir E. 1998. On the pursuit and misuse of useless information. *J. Pers. Soc. Psychol.* 75:19–32

Bell DE. 1982. Regret in decision making under uncertainty. *Oper. Res.* 30:961–81

Bell DE, Raiffa H, Tversky A, eds. 1988. *Decision Making: Descriptive, Normative, and Prescriptive Interactions.* New York: Cambridge Univ. Press

Benartzi S, Thaler R. 1995. Myopic loss aversion and the equity premium puzzle. *Q. J. Econ.* 110:73–92

Berkeley D, Humphreys P. 1982. Structuring decision problems and the "bias heuristic." *Acta Psychol. (Amst.).* 50:201–52

Braine MDS, O'Brien DP, eds. 1998. *Mental Logic.* Mahwah, NJ: Erlbaum

Brenner LA, Koehler DJ. 1999. Subjective probability of disjunctive hypotheses: local–weight models for decomposition of evidential support. *Cogn. Psychol.* 38:16–47

Cacioppo JT, Petty RE. 1982. The need for cognition. *J. Pers. Soc. Psychol.* 42:116–31

Camerer CF. 1990. Behavioral game theory. In *Insights in Decision Making: A Tribute to Hillel J. Einhorn,* ed. RM Hogarth, pp. 311–36. Chicago: Univ. Chicago Press

Camerer CF. 1995. Individual decision making. In *Handbook of Experimental Economics,* ed. JH Kagel, A Roth, pp. 587–703. Princeton, NJ: Princeton Univ. Press

Camerer CF, Babcock L, Loewenstein G, Thaler R. 1997. Labor supply of New York City cab drivers: one day at a time. *Q. J. Econ.* 112:407–441

Camerer CF, Hogarth RM. 1999. The effects of financial incentives in experiments: a review and capital-labor-production framework. *J. Risk Uncertain.* 19:7–42

Castellan NJ. 1969. Effect of change of payoff in probability learning. *J. Exp. Psychol.* 79:178–82

Chaiken S, Trope Y. 1999. *Dual-Process Theories in Social Psychology.* New York: Guilford

Cohen LJ. 1981. Can human irrationality be experimentally demonstrated? *Behav. Brain Sci.* 4:317–70

Cosmides L, Tooby J. 1992. Cognitive adaptations for social exchange. In *The Adapted Mind: Evolutionary Psychology and the Generation of Culture,* ed. J Barkow, L Cosmides, J Tooby, pp. 163–228. New York: Oxford Univ. Press

Cosmides L, Tooby J. 1996. Are humans good intuitive statisticians after all? Rethinking some conclusions from the literature on judgment under uncertainty. *Cognition* 58:1–73

Damasio AR. 1994. *Descartes' Error: Emotion, Reason, and the Human Brain.* New York: Avon

Dawes RM. 1979. The robust beauty of improper linear models in decision making. *Am. Psychol.* 34:571–82

Dawes RM. 1988. *Rational Choice in an Uncertain World.* New York: Harcourt Brace Jovanovich

Dawes RM, Faust D, Meehl PE. 1989. Clinical versus actuarial judgment. *Science* 243:1668–74

Dawes RM, Mulford M. 1996. The false consensus effect and overconfidence: flaws in judgment or flaws in how we study judgment? *Org. Behav. Hum. Decis. Process.* 65:201–11

Dennett DC. 1987. *The Intentional Stance.* Cambridge, MA: MIT Press

Dion K, Berscheid E, Walster E. 1972. What is beautiful is good. *J. Pers. Soc. Psychol.* 24:285–90

Dulany DE, Hilton DJ. 1991. Conversational implicature, conscious representation, and the conjunction fallacy. *Soc. Cogn.* 9:85–110

Dunning D, Griffin DW, Milojkovic JD, Ross L. 1990. The overconfidence effect in social prediction. *J. Pers. Soc. Psychol.* 58:568–81

Edwards W. 1961. Behavioral decision theory. *Annu. Rev. Psychol.* 12:473–98

Edwards W. 1962. Subjective probabilities inferred from decisions. *Psychol. Rev.* 69:109–35

Epstein S. 1994. Integration of the cognitive and the psychodynamic unconscious. *Am. Psychol.* 49:709–24

Ericsson KA, Simon HA. 1984. *Protocol Analysis: Verbal Reports as Data.* Cambridge, MA: MIT Press

Evans JStBT, Over DE. 1996. *Rationality and Reasoning.* Hove, UK: Psychology Press

Fagley NS, Miller PM. 1987. The effects of decision framing on choice of risky vs. certain options. *Org. Behav. Hum. Decis. Process.* 39:264–77

Faust D, Hart KJ, Guilmette TJ. 1988. Pediatric malingering: the capacity of children to fake believable deficits on neuropsychological testing. *J. Consult. Clin. Psychol.* 56:578–82

Fellner W. 1965. *Probability and Profit: A Study of Economic Behavior along Bayesian Lines.* Homewood, IL: Irwin

Fiedler K. 1988. The dependence of the conjunction fallacy on subtle linguistic factors. *Psychol. Res.* 50:123–29

Finucane ML, Alhakami A, Slovic P, Johnson SM. 2000. The affect heuristic in judgments of risks and benefits. *J. Behav. Decis. Mak.* 13:1–17

Fischhoff B, Slovic P, Lichtenstein S. 1977. Knowing with certainty: the appropriateness of extreme confidence. *J. Exp. Psychol. Hum. Percept. Perform.* 3:552–64

Fischhoff B, Slovic P, Lichtenstein S. 1979. Subjective sensitivity analysis. *Org. Behav. Hum. Perform.* 23:339–59

Fischhoff B, Slovic P, Lichtenstein S, Reid S, Combs B. 1978. How safe is safe enough? A psychometric study of attitudes towards technological risks and benefits. *Policy Sci.* 9:127–52

Fiske ST, Lin M, Neuberg SK. 1999. The continuum model: ten years later. See Chaiken & Trope 1999, pp. 231–54

Fodor J. 1975. *The Language of Thought.* New York: Crowell

Fong GT, Nisbett RE. 1991. Immediate and delayed transfer of training effects in statistical reasoning. *J. Exp. Psychol.: Gen.* 120:34–45

Frank RH, Gilovich T, Regan DT. 1993. Does studying economics inhibit cooperation? *J. Econ. Perspect.* 7:159–71

Gardenfors P. 1988. *Knowledge in Flux.* Cambridge, MA: MIT Press

Gick M, Holyoak K. 1980. Analogical problem solving. *Cogn. Psychol.* 12:306–55

Gigerenzer G. 1994. Why the distinction between single-event probabilities and frequencies is important for psychology (and vice versa). In *Subjective Probability,* ed. G Wright, P Ayton, pp. 129–61. New York: Wiley

Gigerenzer G. 1996a. On narrow norms and vague heuristics: a reply to Kahneman and Tversky. *Psychol. Rev.* 103:592–96

Gigerenzer G. 1996b. Rationality: why social context matters. In *Interactive Minds: Life-Span Perspectives on the Social Foundation of Cognition,* ed. PB Baltes, U Staudinger, pp. 319–46. Cambridge: Cambridge Univ. Press

Gigerenzer G, Hoffrage U, Kleinbolting H. 1991. Probabilistic mental models: a Brunswickian theory of confidence. *Psychol. Rev.* 98:506–28

Gigerenzer G, Hug K. 1992. Domain-specific

reasoning: social contracts, cheating and perspective change. *Cognition* 43:127–71

Gilbert DT, Pinel EC, Wilson TD, Blumberg SJ, Wheatley TP. 1998. Immune neglect: a source of durability bias in affective forecasting. *J. Pers. Soc. Psychol.* 75:617–38

Gilhooly K. 1988. *Thinking: Directed, Undirected and Creative*. New York: Academic. 2nd ed.

Gilovich TD, Griffin DW. 2001. Heuristics and biases: then and now. See Gilovich et al. 2001. In press

Gilovich TD, Griffin DW, Kahneman D, eds. 2001. *Heuristics and Biases: The Psychology of Intuitive Judgment*. Cambridge: Cambridge Univ. Press. In press

Ginossar Z, Trope Y. 1987. Problem solving in judgment under uncertainty. *J. Pers. Soc. Psychol.* 52: 464–74

Glymour CN. 1992. *Thinking Things Through: An Introduction to Philosophical Issues and Achievements*. Cambridge, MA: MIT Press

Goldstein WM, Hogarth RM. 1997. *Research on Judgment and Decision Making: Currents, Connections, and Controversies*. Cambridge: Cambridge Univ. Press

Gonzalez R, Wu G. 1999. On the shape of the probability weighting function. *Cogn. Psychol.* 38:129–66

Gourville JT, Soman D. 1998. Payment depreciation: the behavioral effects of temporally separating payments from consumption. *J. Consum. Res.* 25:160–74

Grether D, Plott C. 1979. Economic theory of choice and the preference reversal phenomenon. *Am. Econ. Rev.* 69:623–38

Grice HP. 1975. Logic and conversation. In *The Logic of Grammar*, ed. D Davidson, G Harman, pp. 64–75. Encino, CA: Dickenson

Griffin DW, Buehler R. 1999. Frequency, probability, and prediction: easy solutions to cognitive illusions? *Cogn. Psychol.* 38:48–78

Griffin DW, Ross L. 1991. Subjective construal, social inference, and human misunderstanding. In *Advances in Experimental Social Psychology*, ed. L Berkowitz, 24:319–59. San Diego, CA: Academic

Griffin DW, Tversky A. 1992. The weighing of evidence and the determinants of confidence. *Cogn. Psychol.* 24:411–35

Hammond J, Keeney R, Raiffa H. 1999. *Smart Choices: A Practical Guide to Making Better Decisions*. Boston: Harvard Bus. Sch. Press

Harman G. 1995. Rationality. See Smith & Osherson 1995, pp. 175–211

Hastie R. 2001. Problems for judgment and decision making. *Annu. Rev. Psychol.* 52:653–83

Hertwig R, Gigerenzer G. 1999. The "conjunction fallacy" revisited: how intelligent inferences look like reasoning errors. *J. Behav. Decis. Mak.* 12:275–305

Hilton DJ. 1995. The social context of reasoning: conversational inference and rational judgment. *Psychol. Bull.* 118:248–71

Hoch SJ. 1987. Perceived consensus and predictive accuracy: the pros and cons of projection. *J. Pers. Soc. Psychol.* 53:221–34

Howson C, Urbach P. 1989. *Scientific Reasoning: The Bayesian Approach*. La Salle, IL: Open Court

Hsee CK. 1996. The evaluability hypothesis: an explanation of preference reversals between joint and separate evaluations of alternatives. *Org. Behav. Hum. Decis. Process.* 67:247–57

Hsee CK, Kunreuther H. 2000. The affection effect in insurance decisions. *J. Risk Uncertain.* 20:141–59

Hsee CK, Blount S, Loewenstein G, Bazerman M. 1999. Preference reversals between joint and separate evaluations: a review and theoretical analysis. *Psychol. Bull.* 125:576–90

Huber J, Payne JW, Puto C. 1982. Adding asymmetrically dominated alternatives: violations of regularity and the similarity hypothesis. *J. Consum. Res.* 9:90–98

Isen AM, Geva N. 1987. The influence of positive affect on acceptable level of risk: the person with a large canoe has a large worry. *Org. Behav. Hum. Decis. Process.* 39:145–54

Isen AM, Nygren TE, Ashby FG. 1988. Influence of positive affect on the subjective utility of gains and losses: It is just not worth the risk. *J. Pers. Soc. Psychol.* 55:710–17

Johnson FJ, Tversky A. 1983. Affect, generalization, and the perception of risk. *J. Pers. Soc. Psychol.* 45:20–31

Johnson-Laird PN. 1983. *Mental Models: Towards a Cognitive Science of Language, Inference, and Consciousness.* Cambridge, MA: Harvard Univ. Press

Johnson-Laird PN. 1999. Deductive reasoning. *Annu. Rev. Psychol.* 50:109–35

Johnson-Laird PN, Byrne RMJ. 1991. *Deduction.* Hillsdale, NJ: Erlbaum

Johnson-Laird PN, Byrne RMJ, Schaeken WS. 1992. Propositional reasoning by model. *Psychol. Rev.* 99:418–39

Johnson-Laird PN, Legrenzi P, Girotto V, Legrenzi MS. 2000. Illusions in reasoning about consistency. *Science* 288:531–32

Kachelmeier SJ, Shehata M. 1992. Examining evidence from the People's Republic of China. *Am. Econ. Rev.* 82:1120–41

Kahneman D. 1994. New challenges to the rationality assumption. *J. Inst. Theor. Econ.* 150:18–36

Kahneman D, Diener E, Schwarz N, eds. 1999. *Well-Being: The Foundations of Hedonic Psychology.* New York: Russell Sage Found.

Kahneman D, Fredrickson BL, Schreiber CA, Redelmeier DA. 1993. When more pain is preferred to less: adding a better end. *Psychol. Sci.* 4:401–5

Kahneman D, Knetsch JL, Thaler RH. 1986. Fairness and the assumptions of economics. *J. Bus.* 59(Suppl.):285–300

Kahneman D, Knetsch JL, Thaler R. 1990. Experimental tests of the endowment effect and the Coase theorem. *J. Polit. Econ.* 98:1325–48

Kahneman D, Ritov I. 1994. Determinants of stated willingness to pay for public goods: a study in the headline method. *J. Risk Uncertain.* 9:5–38

Kahneman D, Slovic P, Tversky A, eds. 1982. *Judgment Under Uncertainty: Heuristics and Biases.* Cambridge: Cambridge Univ. Press

Kahneman D, Snell J. 1992. Predicting a changing taste: do people know what they will like? *J. Behav. Decis. Mak.* 5:187–200

Kahneman D, Tversky A. 1972. Subjective probability: a judgment of representativeness. *Cogn. Psychol.* 3:430–54

Kahneman D, Tversky A. 1973. On the psychology of prediction. *Psychol. Rev.* 80:237–51

Kahneman D, Tversky A. 1979. Prospect theory: an analysis of decision under risk. *Econometrica* 47:263–91

Kahneman D, Tversky A. 1996. On the reality of cognitive illusions. *Psychol. Rev.* 103:582–91

Kahneman D, Tversky A, eds. 2000. *Choices, Values, and Frames.* New York: Cambridge Univ. Press/Russell Sage Found.

Keynes JM. 1921. *A Treatise on Probability.* London: Macmillan

Krosnick JA, Li F, Lehman DR. 1990. Conversational conventions, order of information acquisition, and the effect of base rates and individuating information on social judgments. *J. Pers. Soc. Psychol.* 59:1140–52

Kühberger A. 1998. The influence of framing on risky decisions: a meta-analysis. *Org. Behav. Hum. Decis. Process.* 75:23–55

Lerner JS, Keltner D. 2000. Beyond valence: toward a model of emotion-specific influences on judgment and choice. *Cogn. Emot.* 14:473–93

Levin IP, Chapman DP. 1990. Risk taking, frame of reference, and characterization of victim groups in AIDS treatment decisions. *J. Exp. Soc. Psychol.* 26:421–34

Levin IP, Chapman DP, Johnson RD. 1988. Confidence in judgments based on incomplete information: an investigation using both hypothetical and real gambles. *J. Behav. Decis. Mak.* 1:29–41

Levin IP, Gaeth GJ, Schreiber J, Lauriola M. 2001. A new look at framing effects: distribution of effect sizes, individual differences, and independence of types of effects. *Org. Behav. Hum. Decis. Process.* In press

Levin IP, Schneider SL, Gaeth GJ. 1998. All frames are not created equal: a typology and critical analysis of framing effects. *Org. Behav. Hum. Decis. Process.* 76:149–88

Levinson SC. 1995. Interactional biases in human thinking. In *Social Intelligence and Interaction*, ed. E Goody, pp. 221–60. Cambridge: Cambridge Univ. Press

Lewontin R. 1990. The evolution of cognition. In *An Invitation to Cognitive Science*, ed. EE Smith, DN Osherson, 3:229–46. Cambridge, MA: MIT Press. 1st ed.

Lichtenstein S, Fischhoff B. 1977. Do those who know more also know more about how much they know? The calibration of probability judgments. *Org. Behav. Hum. Perform.* 16:1–12

Lichtenstein S, Slovic P. 1973. Response-induced reversals of preferences in gambling: an extended replication in Las Vegas. *J. Exp. Psychol.* 101:16–20

Lichtenstein S, Slovic P, Fischhoff B, Layman M, Combs B. 1978. Judged frequency of lethal events. *J. Exp. Psychol. Hum. Learn. Mem.* 4:551–78

Loewenstein G, Elster J, eds. 1992. *Choice Over Time.* New York: Russell Sage Found.

Loewenstein GF, Prelec D. 1993. Preferences for sequences of outcomes. *Psychol. Rev.* 100:91–108

Loewenstein GF, Weber E, Hsee CK, Welch N. 2001. Risk as feelings. *Psychol. Bull.* 127:267–86

Lopes LL, Oden GC. 1991. The rationality of intelligence. In *Probability and Rationality: Studies on L. Jonathan Cohen's Philosophy of Science*, ed. E Eels, T Maruszewski, pp. 199–223. Amsterdam: Editions Rodopi

Luce RD, Fishburn PC. 1991. Rank- and sign-dependent linear utility models for finite first-order gambles. *J. Risk Uncertain.* 4:29–59

Luce RD, Raiffa H. 1957. *Games and Decisions.* New York: Wiley

Macdonald RR. 1986. Credible conceptions and implausible probabilities. *Br. J. Math. Stat. Psychol.* 39:15–27

Machina M. 1982. "Expected utility" analysis without the independence axiom. *Econometrica* 50:227–324

Manktelow K. 1999. *Reasoning and Thinking.* Hove, UK: Psychology Press

March J. 1978. Bounded rationality, ambiguity and the engineering of choice. *Bell J. Econ.* 9:587–608

Margolis H. 1987. *Patterns, Thinking, and Cognition: A Theory of Judgment.* Chicago: Univ. Chicago Press

Mather M, Shafir E, Johnson MK. 2000. Misremembrance of options past: source monitoring and choice. *Psychol. Sci.* 11:132–38

McNeil BJ, Pauker SG, Sox HC, Tversky A. 1982. On the elicitation of preferences for alternative therapies. *N. Engl. J. Med.* 306:1259–62

Mellers BA, Schwartz A, Cooke ADJ. 1998. Judgment and decision making. *Annu. Rev. Psychol.* 49:447–77

Mellers BA, Schwartz A, Ho K, Ritov I. 1997. Decision affect theory: emotional reactions to the outcomes of risky options. *Psychol. Sci.* 8:423–29

Miller PM, Fagley NS. 1991. The effects of framing, problem variations, and providing rationale on choice. *Pers. Soc. Psychol. Bull.* 17:517–22

Morier DM, Borgida E. 1984. The conjunction fallacy: a task specific phenomenon? *Pers. Soc. Psychol. Bull.* 10:243–52

Neale MA, Northcraft GB. 1986. Experts, amateurs, and refrigerators: comparing expert and amateur negotiators in a novel task. *Org. Behav. Hum. Decis. Process.* 38:305–17

Oakhill J, Garnham A. 1993. On theories of belief bias in syllogistic reasoning. *Cognition* 46:87–92

Oaksford M, Chater N. 1996. Rational explanation of the selection task. *Psychol. Rev.* 103:381–91

Osherson DN. 1995. Probability judgment. See Smith & Osherson 1995, pp. 35–75

Osherson DN, Shafir E, Smith EE. 1994. Extracting the coherent core of human probability judgment. *Cognition* 50:299–313

Payne JW, Bettman JR, Johnson EJ. 1993. *The Adaptive Decision Maker.* Cambridge: Cambridge Univ. Press

Pearl J. 1988. *Probabilistic Reasoning in Intelligent Systems: Networks of Plausible Inference*. San Mateo, CA: Morgan Kaufman

Petty RE, Wegener DT. 1999. The elaboration likelihood model: current status and controversies. See Chaiken & Trope 1999, pp. 37–72

Politzer G, Noveck IA. 1991. Are conjunction rule violations the result of conversational rule violations? *J. Psycholinguist. Res.* 20:83–103

Prelec D. 2000. Compound invariant weighting functions in prospect theory. See Kahneman & Tversky 2000, pp. 67–92

Pulford BD, Colman AM. 1996. Overconfidence, base rates and outcome positivity/negativity of predicted events. *Br. J. Psychol.* 87:431–45

Quattrone G, Tversky A. 1984. Causal versus diagnostic contingencies: On self-deception and on the voter's illusion. *J. Pers. Soc. Psychol.* 46:237–48

Rabin M. 1998. Psychology and economics. *J. Econ. Lit.* 36:11–46

Redelmeier DA, Shafir E. 1995. Medical decision making in situations that offer multiple alternatives. *JAMA* 273:302–5

Redelmeier DA, Shafir E, Aujla P. 2001. The beguiling pursuit of more information. *Med. Decis. Mak.* In press

Redelmeier DA, Tversky A. 1990. Discrepancy between medical decisions for individual patients and for groups. *N. Engl. J. Med.* 322:1162–64

Reed S. 1993. Imagery and discovery. In *Imagery, Creativity, and Discovery: A Cognitive Perspective*, ed. B Roskos-Ewoldson, MJ Intons-Peterson, R Anderson, pp. 287–312. New York: North-Holland

Resnik MD. 1987. *Choices: An Introduction to Decision Theory*. Minneapolis: Univ. Minn. Press

Rips LJ. 1994. *The Psychology of Proof*. Cambridge, MA: MIT Press

Ross SM. 1997. *A First Course in Probability*. Upper Saddle River, NJ: Prentice Hall. 5th ed.

Rottenstreich Y, Hsee CK. 2001. Money, kis-

ses, and electric shocks: on the affective psychology of risk. *Psychol. Sci.* 12:185–90

Rottenstreich Y, Tversky A. 1997. Unpacking, repacking, and anchoring: advances in support theory. *Psychol. Rev.* 104:406–15

Russo JE, Dosher BA. 1983. Strategies for multiattribute binary choice. *J. Exp. Psychol. Learn. Mem. Cogn.* 9:676–96

Samuelson W, Zeckhauser R. 1988. Status quo bias in decision making. *J. Risk Uncertain.* 1:7–59

Schkade DA, Kahneman D. 1998. Does living in California make people happy? A focusing illusion in judgments of life satisfaction. *Psychol. Sci.* 9:340–46

Schwarz N. 1996. *Cognition and Communication: Judgmental Biases, Research Methods, and the Logic of Conversation*. Mahwah, NJ: Erlbaum

Schwarz N, Clore GL. 1983. Mood, misattribution, and judgments of well-being: informative and directive functions of affective states. *J. Pers. Soc. Psychol.* 45:513–23

Schwarz N, Strack F, Hilton D, Naderer G. 1991. Base rates, representativeness, and the logic of conversation: the contextual relevance of "irrelevant" information. *Soc. Cogn.* 9:67–84

Sen A. 1993. Internal consistency of choice. *Econometrica* 61:495–521

Shafir E. 1993. Intuitions about rationality and cognition. In *Rationality: Psychological and Philosophical Perspectives*, ed. KI Manktelow, DE Over, pp. 260–83. Florence, KY: Taylor & Francis

Shafir E. 1995. Compatibility in cognition and decision making. *Psychol. Learn. Motiv.* 32:247–74

Shafir E, Osherson DN, Smith EE. 1993a. The advantage model: a comparative theory of evaluation and choice under risk. *Org. Behav. Hum. Decis. Process.* 55:325–78

Shafir E, Simonson I, Tversky A. 1993b. Reason-based choice. *Cognition* 49:11–36

Shafir E, Tversky A. 1995. Decision making. See Smith & Osherson 1995, pp. 77–100

Shiffrin RM, Schneider W. 1977. Controlled

and automatic human information process-ing: II. Perceptual learning, automatic at-tending and a general theory. *Psychol. Rev.* 84:127–90

Sieck W, Yates JF. 1997. Exposition effects on decision making: choice and confidence in choice. *Org. Behav. Hum. Decis. Process.* 70:207–19

Simon HA. 1955. A behavioral model of ratio-nal choice. *Q. J. Econ.* 69:99–118

Simon HA. 1978. Rationality as process and as product of thought. *J. Am. Econ. Assoc.* 68:1–16

Simonson I. 1990. The effect of purchase quan-tity and timing on variety seeking behavior. *J. Mark. Res.* 27:150–62

Simonson I, Tversky A. 1992. Choice in con-text: tradeoff contrast and extremeness aver-sion. *J. Mark. Res.* 29:281–95

Sloman SA. 1996. The empirical case for two systems of reasoning. *Psychol. Bull.* 119:3–22

Slovic P, Finucane M, Peters E, MacGregor DG. 2001. The affect heuristic. See Gilovich et al. 2001. In press

Slovic P, Griffin D, Tversky A. 1990. Com-patibility effects in judgment and choice. In *Insights in Decision Making: Theory and Ap-plications*, ed. R Hogarth, pp. 5–27. Chicago: Univ. Chicago Press

Slovic P, Lichtenstein S. 1983. Preference re-versals: a broader perspective. *Am. Econ. Rev.* 73:596–605

Slugoski BR, Wilson AE. 1998. Contribution of conversation skills to the production of judg-mental errors. *Eur. J. Soc. Psychol.* 28:575–601

Smith EE, Osherson DN, eds. 1995. *Thinking: An Invitation to Cognitive Science*, Vol. 3. Cambridge, MA: MIT Press. 2nd ed.

Smith SM, Levin IP. 1996. Need for cognition and choice framing effects. *J. Behav. Decis. Mak.* 9:283–90

Stalnaker RC. 1984. *Inquiry.* Cambridge, MA: MIT Press

Stanovich KE. 1999. *Who is Rational? Stud-ies of Individual Differences in Reasoning.* Mahwah, NJ: Erlbaum

Stanovich KE, West RF. 1998a. Cognitive abil-ity and variation in selection task perfor-mance. *Think. Reasoning* 4:193–230

Stanovich KE, West RF. 1998b. Individual dif-ferences in framing and conjunction effects. *Think. Reasoning* 4:289–317

Stanovich KE, West RF. 1998c. Individual dif-ferences in rational thought. *J. Exp. Psychol. Gen.* 127:161–88

Stanovich KE, West RF. 1999. Discrepancies between normative and descriptive models of decision making and the understanding/acceptance principle. *Cogn. Psychol.* 38:349–85

Stanovich KE, West RF. 2000. Individual dif-ferences in reasoning: implications for the rationality debate? *Behav. Brain Sci.* 23:645–726

Stein E. 1996. *Without Good Reason: The Ra-tionality Debate in Philosophy and Cognitive Science.* New York: Oxford Univ. Press

Stich SP. 1990. *The Fragmentation of Reason: Preface to a Pragmatic Theory of Cognitive Evaluation.* Cambridge, MA: MIT Press

Sunstein CR, ed. 2000. *Behavioral Law and Economics.* Cambridge: Cambridge Univ. Press

Swets JA, Dawes RM, Monahan J. 2000. Psy-chological science can improve diagnostic decisions. *Psychol. Sci. Public Interest* 1:1–26

Takemura K. 1993. The effect of decision frame and decision justification on risky choice. *Jpn. Psychol. Res.* 35:36–40

Takemura K. 1994. Influence of elaboration on the framing of decisions. *J. Psychol.* 128:33–39

Tetlock PE. 1992. The impact of accountabil-ity on judgment and choice: toward a social contingency model. In *Advances in Exper-imental Social Psychology*, ed. MP Zanna, 25:331–76. New York: Academic

Thaler RH. 1992. *The Winner's Curse: Para-doxes and Anomalies of Economic Life.* New York: Free Press

Thaler RH. 1993. *Advances in Behavioral Fi-nance.* New York: Russell Sage Found.

Trope Y, Gaunt R. 1999. A dual-process model

of overconfident attributional inferences. See Chaiken & Trope 1999, pp. 161–78

Tversky A. 1972. Elimination by aspects: a theory of choice. *Psychol. Rev.* 79:281–99

Tversky A. 1975. A critique of expected utility theory: descriptive and normative considerations. *Erkenntnis* 9:163–73

Tversky A, Kahneman D. 1973. Availability: a heuristic for judging frequency and probability. *Cogn. Psychol.* 5:207–32

Tversky A, Kahneman D. 1974. Judgment under uncertainty: heuristics and biases. *Science* 185:1124–31

Tversky A, Kahneman D. 1981. The framing of decisions and psychology of choice. *Science* 211:453–58

Tversky A, Kahneman D. 1983. Extensional vs. intuitive reasoning: the conjunction fallacy in probability judgment. *Psychol. Rev.* 90:293–315

Tversky A, Kahneman D. 1986. Rational choice and the framing of decisions. *J. Bus.* 59:251–78

Tversky A, Kahneman D. 1991. Loss aversion in riskless choice: a reference dependent model. *Q. J. Econ.* 106:1039–61

Tversky A, Kahneman D. 1992. Advances in prospect theory: cumulative representation of uncertainty. *J. Risk Uncertain.* 5:297–323

Tversky A, Koehler DJ. 1994. Support theory: a nonextensional representation of subjective probability. *Psychol. Rev.* 101:547–67

Tversky A, Sattath S, Slovic P. 1988. Contingent weighting in judgment and choice. *Psychol. Rev.* 95:371–84

Tversky A, Shafir E. 1992a. Choice under conflict: the dynamics of deferred decision. *Psychol. Sci.* 3:358–61

Tversky A, Shafir E. 1992b. The disjunction effect in choice under uncertainty. *Psychol. Sci.* 3:305–9

Tversky A, Simonson I. 1993. Context dependent preferences: the relative advantage model. *Manage. Sci.* 39:1179–89

Tversky A, Slovic P, Kahneman D. 1990. The causes of preference reversal. *Am. Econ. Rev.* 80:204–17

Tversky A, Wakker P. 1995. Risk attitudes and decision weights. *Econometrica* 63:1255–80

Vallone RP, Griffin DW, Lin S, Ross L. 1990. Overconfident prediction of future actions and outcomes by self and others. *J. Pers. Soc. Psychol.* 58:568–81

Van Boven L, Dunning D, Loewenstein G. 2000. Egocentric empathy gaps between owners and buyers: misperceptions of the endowment effect. *J. Pers. Soc. Psychol.* 79:66–76

von Mises R. 1957. *Probability, Statistics, and Truth.* New York: Dover

von Winterfeld D, Edwards W. 1986. *Decision Analysis and Behavioral Research.* Cambridge: Cambridge Univ. Press

Wason PC. 1966. Reasoning. In *New Horizons in Psychology 1*, ed. B Foss, pp. 135–51. Harmondsworth, UK: Penguin

Wetherick NE. 1971. Representativeness in a reasoning problem: a reply to Shapiro. *Bull. Br. Psychol. Soc.* 24:213–14

Wilson TD, Houston CE, Etling KM, Brekke N. 1996. A new look at anchoring effects: basic anchoring and its antecedents. *J. Exp. Psychol. Gen.* 125:387–402

Wilson TD, Wheatley T, Meyers JM, Gilbert DT, Axsom D. 2000. Focalism: a source of durability bias in affective forecasting. *J. Pers. Soc. Psychol.* 78:821–36

Wright WF, Anderson U. 1989. Effects of situation familiarity and financial incentives on use of the anchoring and adjustment heuristic for probability assessment. *Org. Behav. Hum. Decis. Process.* 44:68–82

Yates JF. 1990. *Judgment and Decision Making.* Englewood Cliffs, NJ: Prentice-Hall

Zajonc RB. 1980. Feeling and thinking: preferences need no inferences. *Am. Psychol.* 35:151–75

Annu. Rev. Psychol. 2002. 53:519–43

CLINICAL ASSESSMENT*

James M. Wood[1], Howard N. Garb[2], Scott O. Lilienfeld[3], and M. Teresa Nezworski[4]

[1]Department of Psychology, University of Texas at El Paso, El Paso, Texas 79968;
e-mail: jawood@utep.edu
[2]Behavioral Health, V.A. Health Care System, Highland Drive, Pittsburgh, Pennsylvania
15206-1297 and Department of Psychology, University of Pittsburgh, Pittsburgh,
Pennsylvania 15213; e-mail: Garb.Howard_N@pittsburgh.va.gov
[3]Department of Psychology, Emory University, Room 206, Atlanta, Georgia 30322;
e-mail: slilien@emory.edu
[4]Callier Center for Communication Disorders, School of Human Development,
University of Texas at Dallas, 1966 Inwood Road, Dallas, Texas 75235-7298;
e-mail: nezworsk@utdallas.edu

Key Words   managed care, multicultural assessment, forensic assessment, clinical
judgment, computerized assessment

■ **Abstract**   Are clinical psychologists' assessment practices cost-effective? Are
they scientifically sound? Are they fair and unbiased? Financial pressures from managed care interests, recent developments in the law, and multicultural issues are forcing
the profession to confront these hard questions regarding accountability. Our review
discusses the important changes that have begun to alter the field of personality assessment and describes recent research on clinical judgment and its implications for the future. We conclude that clinical psychology can adapt to future conditions by developing
assessment strategies that are economical, scientifically sound, and culturally sensitive.

CONTENTS

519

INTRODUCTION

Economic, cultural, legal, and scientific forces are causing profound changes in clinical assessment. The financial pressures of managed care have already altered the assessment practices of many clinicians, and recent developments in the law have encouraged the critical examination of assessment techniques that are used in forensic settings. The rapidly changing ethnic composition of the United States presents new challenges to old practices.

In the first half of this review we discuss the important changes that have begun to alter the field of personality assessment. In the second we discuss progress in research on clinical judgment and its implications for the future. A theme that runs through our review is accountability. Clinical psychologists are being held increasingly accountable for their assessment practices. Forces from both inside and outside the profession are posing hard questions: Are psychologists' assessment practices cost-effective? Are they scientifically sound? Are they fair and unbiased? The answers are already reshaping both the science and the practice of psychological assessment.

THE CHANGING WORLD OF CLINICAL ASSESSMENT

Managed Care

The greatest challenge confronting practicing psychologists over the past decade has been economic. In the era of managed care, clinical practitioners have faced intense and sometimes unreasonable pressure to reduce or defend their services. Psychologists in private practice report a variety of concerns, including loss of income, excessive paperwork requirements, and ethical dilemmas (Phelps et al. 1998).

A survey of 137 psychologists by Piotrowski et al. (1998) gauged the effects of managed care on assessment practices: 55% of respondents reported that in response to managed care they were spending less time giving tests, were using fewer tests, or had discontinued testing altogether (see also Archer & Newsom 2000). Piotrowski (1999) concluded that most psychologists have coped with the pressures of managed care in two ways: (*a*) Some continue to use the same tests as in the past, but less frequently overall, whereas (*b*) others have selectively abandoned tests that are especially time consuming (e.g., the Wechsler Intelligence scales, Rorschach) while continuing to use briefer instruments.

Piotrowski (1999, pp. 792–93) somberly predicted that "economic reality will guide practice in assessment" and "the comprehensive test battery . . . will become a moribund clinical activity." Groth-Marnat (1999), who shared Piotrowski's vision of the future, suggested ways that researchers and clinicians can respond proactively to the financial considerations of managed care. For example, Groth-Marnat suggested that psychologists develop and promote assessment approaches that (*a*) focus on diagnostic issues and client characteristics that are most clearly linked to treatment choice and outcomes, (*b*) reduce the risk of negative outcomes and litigation (e.g., assessment of danger to self or others), (*c*) identify conditions that, when correctly assessed, are likely to result in cost savings, (*d*) are time efficient, and (*e*) integrate treatment planning, progress monitoring, and outcome evaluation. Groth-Marnat urged researchers to demonstrate that their instruments meet such financial criteria as cost-effectiveness, cost-benefit, and cost-containment.

If Piotrowski (1999) and Groth-Marnat (1999) are correct, clinical assessment practices must change if they are to survive the challenge of managed care. Psychologists are already taking a closer look at the cost-effectiveness and utility of traditional assessment techniques, some of which require an excessive amount of professional time and expense for very little tangible benefit (e.g., the Rorschach) (Groth-Marnat 1999, Hunsley & Bailey 1999). Such trends dovetail with the increasing emphasis placed on demonstrating the incremental validity of psychological assessment devices (Butcher et al. 1995, Kuncel et al. 2001).

In addition, there are signs that clinical assessment techniques are being developed or reconceptualized to meet the needs of managed care, as Groth-Marnat (1999) recommended. Several notable examples appear in a recent book by Maruish (1999) that focuses on measurement of treatment planning and outcome. One of the tests described in Maruish's book provides a model of how psychological assessment can adapt to changing trends. The Outcome Questionnaire (OQ-45) (Lambert et al. 1998, 1999), a brief and cost-effective measure, was designed to track treatment progress and outcome for patients with a wide variety of diagnoses. The validity research on the OQ-45 completed thus far is very promising (Lambert et al. 1996, Mueller et al. 1998, Vermeersch et al. 2000). The success of the OQ-45 shows that psychologists can proactively develop new assessment techniques that are both scientifically sound and compatible with the financial constraints of managed care.

Multicultural Clinical Assessment

The ethnic composition of the United States is rapidly changing. The US Bureau of the Census (2000, p. 17) reported that in 1999, 11% of the US population was Hispanic. The projected figure for 2050 is 24%. Other minority groups, especially those from Asia, are also growing. Within 50 years, approximately half of Americans are expected to be people of color (Hall 1997, US Bureau of the Census 2000).

Attention to multicultural clinical assessment has grown in recent years, as evidenced by the publication of several handbooks on the topic (Cuellar & Paniagua 2000, Dana 2000, Fletcher-Janzen et al. 2000, Suzuki et al. 2000). Nevertheless, the quality of research continues to lag far behind what is needed. Studies of American minorities and non-Americans are scarce for many popular assessment techniques, including the Millon Clinical Multiaxial Inventory, third edition (MCMI-III), Personality Assessment Inventory (PAI), Rorschach, Thematic Apperception Test (TAT), projective drawings, and the Hare Psychopathy Checklist-Revised (e.g., see Velasquez 1995). Thus, it is unclear whether these instruments can appropriately be used with American minorities and non-Americans. For example, several recent studies (Boscan 1999, Ephraim 2000, Vinet 2000) indicate that Rorschach scores for relatively normal community samples of Mexicans, Central Americans, and South Americans often differ strikingly from the norms of the Comprehensive System for the Rorschach (Exner 1993, 2001b). In light of these findings, there is substantial reason to doubt whether the norms should be used with Hispanic adults and children in the United States (Dana 1998, Lilienfeld et al. 2000, Wood & Lilienfeld 1999). Studies on "slope bias" (Cleary et al. 1975) are sorely needed to examine possible differences in the validity of Rorschach scores across diverse cultural and linguistic groups.

Although evaluation of multicultural assessment is too often neglected, some recent developments may serve as models for future investigations. First, multicultural research on the MMPI (Minnesota Multiphasic Personality Inventory) and MMPI-2 has been much more common, and often more sophisticated, than research on other assessment techniques (see reviews by Butcher et al. 1998, Handel & Ben-Porath 2000, Zalewski & Greene 1996). This body of research has begun to yield findings of substantial practical importance. For instance, there is now convincing evidence that mean MMPI and MMPI-2 scores of US blacks and Hispanics are usually very similar to the US normative values (Hall et al. 1999, Handel & Ben-Porath 2000, Zalewski & Greene 1996). Similarly, a number of studies now indicate that methodologically careful translations of the MMPI and MMPI-2 tend to yield scale means and standard deviations in international samples that are similar to US normative values (Butcher et al. 1998). Furthermore, in a methodological advance, investigators have used item response theory (Embretson & Reise 2000, Santor & Ramsay 1998) to examine possible race bias on the MMPI-2. By obtaining latent trait estimates for the underlying constructs assessed by MMPI-2 factor scales, Waller et al. (2000) showed that "Whites and Blacks can be meaningfully compared on these scales with little fear that obtained group differences are due to measurement bias" (p. 142) (for other applications of item response theory to the MMPI-2, see Childs et al. 2000, Waller 1998). Similarly, three recent studies (Arbisi et al. 1998, McNulty et al. 1997, Timbrook & Graham 1994) have examined the correlation of MMPI-2 scores with external criteria such as case records and therapists' ratings of patients. Reviewing these studies, Greene (2000, p. 482) concluded that in all three "the most striking finding was the high degree of similarity between the blacks and whites on these external criteria."

The normative studies of neuropsychological tests by Ardila and his colleagues in South America (e.g., Ardila et al. 1994, Ostrosky-Solis et al. 1999) have been a second important development in evaluation of multicultural assessment. Although this review does not cover most developments in neuropsychological testing, the work of Ardila is worth noting because it has systematically identified moderating variables, such as educational level, that should be taken into account in assessments of Spanish-speaking patients (see reviews by Ponton & Ardila 1999, Puente & Ardila 2000).

A third important development has been the publication of several acculturation scales that are suitable for US minorities (Cuellar et al. 1995, Marin & Gamba 1996, Stephenson 2000). Recently developed instruments all conceptualize acculturation as two separate dimensions (i.e., orientation to mainstream US culture and orientation to ethnic culture of origin) rather than as a single bipolar dimension (i.e., acculturated to mainstream US culture versus not acculturated). Acculturation is important in clinical work because, among other reasons, it sometimes moderates the validity of test scores (Cuellar 2000). Perhaps psychologists will eventually be able to routinely assess a client's level of acculturation, linguistic preference, age, and educational attainment and then choose the tests and norms that are most appropriate (Puente & Ardila 2000). Useful advice for researchers in the field of multicultural assessment can be found in Allen & Walsh (2000), Arnold & Matus (2000), Butcher et al. (1998), Handel & Ben-Porath (2000), Okazaki & Sue (1995), and Velasquez (1995, Velasquez et al. 2000).

Forensic Assessment

During the past decade, an increasing number of psychologists have begun to practice in the field of forensic assessment. Custody, competency, and pre-sentencing evaluations probably account for the bulk of forensic assessments. Assessments also play a role in parole decisions, personal injury suits, civil commitments, workers' compensation hearings, Social Security disability evaluations, and even criminal appeals.

At the same time that the field of forensic assessment has been growing, developments in the law have imposed new requirements for accountability. Over the past decade the US Supreme Court has handed down several decisions (Daubert v. Merrell Dow Pharmaceuticals Inc. 1993, General Electric Co. v. Joiner 1997, Kumho Tire Co. Ltd. v. Carmichael 1999) that delineate the legal standards governing the admissibility of scientific and expert evidence in federal courts. The court has described six factors, generally called the "Daubert criteria," that trial judges should consider when deciding whether to admit scientific or expert evidence into court (see discussion by Grove & Barden 1999). Courts in approximately half of the states have also adopted these criteria, which address the following questions: (*a*) Is the theory or technique that forms the basis of the evidence testable? (*b*) Has it in fact been tested? (*c*) Is it generally accepted by the relevant community of scientists? (*d*) Has it been subjected to peer review? (*e*) Does it have a known error rate? (*f*) Are there established standards for its application?

Recent articles have evaluated whether popular assessment techniques meet the Daubert criteria. Serious questions have been raised regarding the legal admissibility of the Rorschach Comprehensive System (Grove & Barden 1999, but see McCann 1998a), projective drawings (Lally 2001), and the MCMI-III (Rogers et al. 1999, 2000b; but see Dyer & McCann 2000, McCann & Dyer 1996). Over the next decade psychologists and lawyers are certain to debate the scientific adequacy of many popular psychological tests.

In the meantime, the expansion of forensic psychology as a practice specialty has stimulated the development of new assessment instruments that address the specific needs and requirements of the legal system. The most extensively researched of these instruments is the Hare Psychopathy Checklist-Revised (PCL-R) (Hare 1991), including the closely related Psychopathy Checklist: Youth Version (PCL:YV) (Forth et al. 1990). The ratings of the PCL-R and PCL:YV are based on structured interviews, observation, and file reviews and have repeatedly been shown to predict violence in prison and psychiatric populations (Hemphill et al. 1998, Salekin et al. 1996). Briefer measures of psychopathy, such as the Psychopathy Checklist: Screening Version (Hart et al. 1994) and the Psychopathic Personality Inventory (Lilienfeld & Andrews 1996), also seem to predict violence in forensic populations, although the supporting research thus far is modest (Douglas et al. 1999b, Edens et al. 1999, Rogers et al. 2000a). A major advantage of these and other brief measures is their potential applicability outside of prison settings (Levenson et al. 1995, Lilienfeld 1998).

Another interesting development has been the revival of interest in mechanical prediction methods (also known as actuarial or statistical methods) (Meehl 1954). Although supported by an extensive research literature extending over half a century (Grove et al. 2000), mechanical prediction is seldom used for clinical decision-making. However, psychologists and other professionals who conduct forensic risk assessments now routinely employ mechanical prediction instruments, which usually consist of linear combinations of demographic and life-history variables (e.g., number of previous crimes, age of onset of crime). Instruments have been developed and validated to predict violence among criminals and psychiatric patients (Douglas et al. 1999a, Hanson 1998, Monahan et al. 2001, Quinsey et al. 1998), recidivism among juvenile offenders (Wiebush et al. 1995), and repeated child abuse and neglect (Baird & Wagner 2000).

Because litigants in civil or criminal cases may sometimes be motivated to exaggerate symptoms of psychopathology, psychologists in forensic settings have a pressing need for measures of malingering. Interest in this area has boomed in recent years (McCann 1998b, Reynolds 1998, Rogers 1997). Malingering subscales have been developed or validated for several conventional personality tests, including the MMPI-2 (Arbisi & Ben-Porath 1995, 1998; Bagby et al. 2000; Nicholson et al. 1997; Rogers et al. 1994), as well as some cognitive and neuropsychological tests, such as Raven's Standard Progressive Matrices (McKinzey et al. 1999) and the Luria-Nebraska Neuropsychological Battery (McKinzey et al. 1997). In addition, promising work has been reported on stand-alone measures of malingering, including the Structured Interview for Reported Symptoms (SIRS) (Rogers 1995, but see Pollock 1996) and the Test of Memory Malingering (TOMM) (Rees et al.

1998, Tombaugh 1997). Effective malingering measures have yet to be developed for the Rorschach and other projective measures, which can be highly susceptible to faking bad (Exner 1991, Schretlen 1997).

Although work on malingering measures is impressive, considerably more research is needed. Replications by independent researchers are often lacking. In addition, research suggests that informed malingerers can sometimes evade detection (Lamb et al. 1994, Storm & Graham 2000, Walters & Clopton 2000; but see Bagby et al. 2000, Iverson et al. 1995).

In closing, it should be noted that there is one area of forensic practice that remains especially problematic: custody evaluations. As O'Donohue & Bradley (1999) pointed out, psychologists who assess parents in custody evaluations commonly rely on techniques that are subjective, unvalidated, or bear no demonstrated relationship to parental fitness. These authors concluded that many custody recommendations are based on little more than "educated guesswork" (p. 321) or the evaluator's own values and prejudices. We hope that future research will provide a better scientific basis for the practice of custody evaluations. In the meantime, we urge custody evaluators to take concrete steps (e.g., arranging for a colleague to supervise or review cases) to ensure that their work is ethical, unbiased, and based on sound evidence.

The Controversy Over the Comprehensive System for the Rorschach

The 1996 chapter on clinical assessment in the *Annual Review of Psychology* (Butcher & Rouse 1996, p. 91) praised Exner's Comprehensive System (CS) for the Rorschach: "Much of the strength of the Rorschach method in contemporary assessment comes from the broad use of the Exner Comprehensive System (Exner 1991, 1993, 1995; Exner & Weiner 1994), which provides a more reliable and objective basis for interpretation than was available prior to its introduction."

At the time that the chapter by Butcher & Rouse (1996) appeared, there were no indications that the CS was about to become the subject of a fierce controversy. Coincidentally, the chapter was published the same year as the first major published critique of the CS (Wood et al. 1996). In ensuing years, heated debates followed in six other journals, including *Psychological Assessment* (Hunsley & Bailey 1999, Viglione 1999), *Assessment* (Acklin 1999, Garb 1999, Weiner 1999, Wood & Lilienfeld 1999), *Journal of Clinical Psychology* (Weiner 2000; Wood et al. 2000a,b), *Clinical Psychology: Science and Practice* (Aronow 2001; Exner 2001a; Hunsley & Di Giulio 2001; Meyer 2001; Widiger 2001; Wood et al. 2001b,c), *Journal of Personality Assessment* (Bornstein 2001, Gacono et al. 2001, Ganellen 2001, Wood et al. 2001a), and *Journal of Forensic Psychology Practice* (Wood et al. 2001d, Hamel et al. 2001). In addition, a full-issue article in *Psychological Science in the Public Interest* critically reviewed the scientific evidence regarding the Rorschach and other widely used projective techniques (Lilienfeld et al. 2000).

We discuss a subset of issues that are central to evaluations of the scientific and clinical merit of the CS. First, it has become apparent that the CS norms for many important variables (Exner 1993, 2001b) tend to make many normal adults and children appear psychologically disturbed (Hamel et al. 2000; Shaffer et al. 1999; Wood et al. 2001b,c; but see Exner 2001a, Meyer 2001). Even Meyer (Meyer & Richardson 2001), a staunch Rorschach proponent, has presented compelling evidence that the CS norms for form quality were inadvertently based on the wrong scoring rules and have been seriously in error since 1983.

Second, critics of the CS and many proponents now agree that most Rorschach scores bear little or no relation to psychiatric diagnoses (Bornstein 2001; Weiner 1999; Wood et al. 2000a,b). Although a few Rorschach scores are moderately valid for detecting conditions marked by thought disorder, such as schizophrenia and bipolar disorder, convincing evidence of incremental validity is often lacking. As Exner's co-author Weiner (1999, pp. 336–37) stated, "The Rorschach Inkblot Method is not a diagnostic test, it was not designed as a diagnostic test, it is not intended to be a diagnostic test, and it does not in fact work very well as a diagnostic test, especially if what is meant by diagnosis is a DSM category."

Third, critics and proponents agree that CS scores are generally unrelated to self-report measures that were once thought to measure the same or similar constructs (e.g., Archer & Krishnamurthy 1993a,b; Greenwald 1990, 1991, 1999; Meyer 1992, 1993, 1996; Nezworski & Wood 1995). CS proponents have recently argued that the negligible relationship between self-report measures and Rorschach scores implies that projective techniques assess different aspects of personality (i.e., implicit characteristics) than do self-report techniques (i.e., explicit characteristics) (Bornstein 2001). If such an argument were correct, the Rorschach should provide substantial incremental validity beyond self-report measures for psychologically relevant external criteria. However, evidence of the Rorschach's incremental validity is limited to a few variables, and the gain in predictive power is often small (Lilienfeld et al. 2000).

Fourth, despite claims that "every variable in the Comprehensive System has demonstrated substantial interrater reliability" (Ritzler 1995, p. 230), there is now considerable evidence that the scoring reliability of many variables is mediocre or poor. Nunnally (1978, pp. 245–46) recommended that test scores used in clinical assessments should have a minimum reliability of 0.90. In contrast, a recent study by Acklin et al. (2000) found that approximately 50% of CS variables had interrater reliabilities below 0.85 and some had reliabilities below 0.30 (see also Gronnerod 1999, Nakata 1999, Shaffer et al. 1999).

Fifth, both critics and proponents agree that at least a few Rorschach scores are valid for certain purposes. Several meta-analyses of published Rorschach studies (e.g., Garb et al. 1998, Hiller et al. 1999, Parker et al. 1988) have yielded a mean weighted validity coefficient of 0.30 ± 0.05. Although this figure may be inflated owing to publication bias and methodological flaws, the findings indicate that "some Rorschach indexes can possess moderate validity" (Hunsley & Bailey 1999, p. 269). Despite the findings of such global meta-analyses, only a handful of individual Rorschach scores possess well-demonstrated and adequate validity (Lilienfeld et al. 2000).

In summary, widely held assumptions regarding the superior psychometric properties of the CS have been abandoned or drastically modified in recent years. Archer (1999, p 309) concluded that "the assumption that the Rorschach Comprehensive System rests solidly and uniformly on an empirical foundation has been forced to undergo a significant re-examination." Ironically, the Board of Professional Affairs (1998, p. 392) of the American Psychological Association recently commended the CS as "perhaps the most powerful psychometric instrument ever envisioned." In response, Wood & Lilienfeld (1999, p. 348) suggested that the Board's commendation is at least as much an overstatement as the old claim that the Rorschach is an X-ray of the mind (Klopfer 1940). It is unclear what will become of practicing psychologists' long, bittersweet romance with the Rorschach. Perhaps the Rorschach will be reconceptualized as an aid to self-exploration in psychotherapy rather than as an assessment device (Aronow 2001, Widiger 2001).

Self-Report Tests

Important developments concerning self-report tests (e.g., their use in multicultural assessment and detection of malingering) were described above. This section focuses on three issues: (*a*) the impact of response options on self-reports, (*b*) the advantages of the MMPI-2 over the Rorschach in clinical practice, and (*c*) the treatment utility of self-report and projective techniques. Each of these topics points to both the strength and continued viability of self-report tests, as well as to potential challenges confronting users of these tests in clinical practice.

IMPACT OF RESPONSE OPTIONS ON SELF-REPORT   Until recently, most personality assessment researchers paid relatively little attention to the selection of response options (e.g., labeling of anchor points on questionnaire items) in the design of self-report measures (see Clark & Watson 1995 for a useful discussion of the pros and cons of differing questionnaire response options). Schwarz and his colleagues have questioned this indifference, arguing persuasively that questionnaire items can be viewed as implicit forms of communication between test developers and test takers (Schwarz 1999). Specifically, they maintain that when participants respond to self-report items, they attempt to discern the pragmatic meaning or intent of the item in addition to its literal meaning. As a consequence, seemingly trivial differences in response options across self-report items can sometimes lead to substantial differences in participants' responses.

For example, in one study (see Schwarz 1999), 39% of patients with psychosomatic disorders reported physical symptom frequencies of more than twice a month when the item anchors ranged from "never" to "more than twice a month." Yet 62% of patients with psychosomatic disorders reported symptom frequencies of more than twice a month when the item anchors ranged from "twice a month or less" to "several times a day." The impact of these different response options was greatest for ambiguous symptoms (e.g., "responsiveness to changes in the weather"). Schwarz and his collaborators contend that these different response options led the two sets of participants to ascribe different interpretations to the same questions. Specifically, participants who were provided with a response scale that implied a higher frequency of symptoms (i.e., "twice a month or less" to "several times a day") interpreted the questions as inquiring about less severe symptoms than did the other participants.

Still other research by Schwarz and his colleagues demonstrates that minor differences in questionnaire format, including the order of items, can sometimes influence substantially not only the mean levels of item endorsement but also the intercorrelations among items (e.g., Schwarz et al. 1991). Although the findings of Schwarz and his collaborators warrant replication by independent investigators, these findings suggest that researchers may no longer be able to treat differing questionnaire response scales as essentially interchangeable. Instead, researchers should remain cognizant of the differing meanings that participants may impute to self-report items and the potential impact of response options on these interpretations.

ADVANTAGES OF THE MMPI-2 OVER THE RORSCHACH   At a time when the scientific status of projective techniques is being vigorously challenged (Lilienfeld et al. 2000), it is worth asking whether self-report instruments could withstand the same level of scrutiny that projective techniques have been exposed to (Archer 1999, Widiger 2001). In this section we compare the MMPI-2 (clinical psychology's most widely used self-report test) and the CS for the Rorschach (the most popular projective technique) and identify five advantages of the MMPI-2 over the CS in clinical practice and managed care settings.

The first advantage of the MMPI-2 is obvious: It can be scored easily and with nearly perfect reliability by a computer. In contrast, scoring of the CS is laborious and complicated, so that Rorschach proponents consider a kappa of 0.61 for interscorer reliability to be "substantial and acceptable" (Acklin et al. 2000, p. 34).

Second, the MMPI-2 is considerably less expensive than the CS, a consideration that is of considerable importance in the era of managed care. If administered and scored by a clerical worker, the MMPI-2 can be interpreted by a psychologist in approximately 30 minutes (Ball et al. 1994). In comparison, the CS must be administered, scored, and interpreted by a psychologist, taking approximately 2.5 hours. In addition, the training required to score and interpret the CS is extremely time-consuming and expensive (Groth-Marnat 1999).

Third, the norms of the MMPI-2 are on much firmer scientific footing than those for the CS. The MMPI-2 norms are based on a stratified probability sample of 2600 American adults that was collected in the late 1980s. In contrast, the CS norms (Exner 2001b) are based on a nonprobability sample of 600 adults that was collected in the late 1970s and early 1980s (Hunsley & Di Giulio 2001). Furthermore, as already discussed, considerable evidence indicates that the CS norms are unrepresentative of normal American adults (Shaffer et al. 1999, Wood et al. 2001b).

Fourth, validity research is stronger for the MMPI-2 than for the CS. Positive findings have been reported for CS scores, but typically they have not been replicated by independent researchers (Lilienfeld et al 2000). Furthermore, research indicates that the clinical judgments of psychologists become more accurate when they use the MMPI but not when they use the Rorschach (Garb 1998, also see Whitehead 1985).

Fifth, the MMPI-2 can be used more confidently with minority groups than can the CS. As discussed earlier, the cross-cultural validity of the MMPI-2 has been examined in many groups and with increasingly sophisticated methods. In comparison, research on ethnic and cross-cultural differences for the CS is extremely limited (Velasquez 1995). In fact, Dana (1993, p. 160) concluded, "The Rorschach and the Exner Comprehensive versions are not recommended for routine cross-cultural applications."

TREATMENT UTILITY   One critical question that has received surprisingly little research attention concerns the treatment utility of self-report tests. The issue of treatment utility applies with equal force to projective techniques. Despite the widespread use of both classes of techniques in clinical practice (Watkins et al. 1995), there is virtually no evidence that they enhance treatment outcome (Hunsley & Bailey 1999, Lilienfeld et al. 2000). One seeming exception to this absence of evidence is the work of Finn and his colleagues (Finn 1996, Finn & Tonsager 1992), who reported that providing clients (college students awaiting psychotherapy) with feedback based on their MMPI-2 scores decreased their psychological distress.

Although Finn's findings (1996, Finn & Tonsager 1992) are a promising first step toward demonstrating treatment utility, they are open to multiple interpretations. Halperin & Snyder (1979), for example, found that snake-phobic clients who received bogus "Barnum" feedback (i.e., highly vague and generalized interpretations of test scores) after completing two psychological tests exhibited enhanced treatment outcome compared with clients who received no test feedback. Moreover, classic research by Sundberg (1955) demonstrates that individuals typically cannot discriminate genuine feedback based on their MMPIs from bogus MMPI feedback at greater than chance levels. Consequently, the work of Finn and his colleagues demonstrates only that assessment feedback to clients can be therapeutic, although it demonstrates neither the treatment utility of the MMPI-2 per se nor even the necessity for accurate MMPI-2 feedback.

A more informative test of treatment utility would involve the use of *manipulated assessment* designs (Hayes et al. 1987). In such designs therapists (who in essence serve as participants) are randomly assigned to receive either information from a given assessment device (e.g., an MMPI-2) or no such assessment information. The extent to which the provision of this information contributes to improved treatment outcome constitutes a direct test of the assessment device's treatment utility (see Harkness & Lilienfeld 1997). To our knowledge, manipulated assessment designs have yet to find their way into the personality assessment literature. Nevertheless, such designs should become a priority among researchers in this area, as the pressures of managed care force practitioners to demonstrate that the psychological tests they administer are therapeutically useful.

CLINICAL JUDGMENT AND DECISION-MAKING

Literature reviews on clinical assessment typically focus on the development and validation of new tests. However, in this section we focus on an equally important component of the assessment process: clinical judgment and decision-making. Steady progress has been made in this area in recent years. Many of the results point out ways that clinical judgments can become more reliable and valid.

Diagnosis

Important insights can be drawn from research on the diagnostic process. First, results from recent studies indicate that agreement between diagnoses made by mental health professionals in the course of their clinical work and research diagnoses based on structured interviews ranges from poor [kappa = 0.24 (Shear et al. 2000), kappa = 0.25 (Strakowski et al. 1997)] to fair [(kappa = 0.45, 0.51, 0.52 (Basco et al. 2000)]. Similar results have been reported in earlier studies (see Garb 1998, pp. 53–54).

When clinicians' diagnoses are compared with diagnoses based on structured interviews, it becomes clear that clinicians underdiagnose a range of mental disorders. This is true for the diagnosis of mental disorders in the mentally retarded, major depressive disorder in terminally ill patients, personality disorders in clients receiving mental health treatment, substance abuse disorders in psychiatric patients, and obsessive-compulsive disorder (and perhaps other anxiety disorders) in substance abuse patients (Garb 1998, pp. 74–77; Hansen et al. 2000; Zimmerman & Mattia 1999a). Underdiagnosis also seems to occur for posttraumatic stress disorder in routine clinical settings (Zimmerman & Mattia 1999b).

Second, and somewhat paradoxically, it also appears that under some circumstances clinicians tend to "overpathologize" patients, perceiving them as more psychopathological than they really are (e.g., Kullgren et al. 1996). In some cases, the tendency to overpathologize clients has been due to the inadequacies of popular psychological tests. For example, as already noted, research indicates that the norms of the CS of the Rorschach are flawed, so that normal individuals tend to appear more psychopathological than they really are (Shaffer et al. 1999, Wood et al. 2001b). Some evidence suggests that CS scores erroneously indicate the presence of depression or a personality disorder in about 75% of normal individuals (see discussions by Exner 1991, pp. 432–33; Wood et al. 2001c).

Third, important results have been obtained regarding the effect of bias on diagnoses. Agreement between clinical diagnoses and research diagnoses has not been significantly different for males and females (Basco et al. 2000, Shear et al. 2000). However, it has sometimes differed for ethnic groups: Agreement between clinical and research diagnoses has been better for whites than non-whites (54%

vs. 35%) (Strakowski et al. 1997), worse for whites than for minority patients (kappa = 0.47 and 0.49 for whites, 0.57 and 0.59 for minority patients) (Basco et al. 2000), and nonsignificantly different for both groups (Shear et al. 2000). It is not clear why results on race bias varied across studies.

Structured interviews really do make a difference, as revealed by the disparity between clinical and structured interview diagnoses. When structured interviews are used, it is more likely that clinicians will adhere to diagnostic criteria and interrater reliability will be at least fair. Also, construct validity is at least fair to good for many structured interviews: For example, structured interviews have routinely been used in studies on psychopathology that have obtained important results (e.g., Keller et al. 2000, McCullough et al. 2000). For these reasons, psychologists should probably increase their use of structured interviews in making diagnoses. Furthermore, clinical graduate programs should place greater emphasis on training students to use such interviews (for further training recommendations, see Grove 2000).

Case Formulation

Perhaps the most difficult judgment task facing mental health professionals involves case formulation. Research reveals that it is surprisingly difficult for clinicians to explain why a client behaves a particular way (Garb 1998, pp. 85–101). Given this body of research, one would hope that psychologists would be cautious when making causal judgments, but this is not always the case. For example, discussing the theory of one psychoanalyst, apparently with approval, Brown et al. (1998) paraphrased her by stressing that "memory for infant trauma is encoded accurately and indelibly" (p. 205) and that implicit memory even for "birth trauma" can have "a profound influence on later development, even when no narrative memory" is available (p. 206). These assertions are not based on convincing empirical evidence, and psychologists who rely on them may be misled into forming false causal conclusions (McNally 1999). A similar situation can be observed for the controversial diagnosis of dissociative identity disorder (formerly known as multiple personality disorder). Here, too, some mental health professionals make questionable causal judgments, tending to attribute their clients' problems to severe childhood trauma and dissociative identity disorder (Spanos 1996), even though " . . . a large proportion—perhaps a majority—of Dissociative Identity Disorder patients . . . exhibit few or no unambiguous signs of this condition prior to therapy" (Lilienfeld et al. 1999, p. 511).

Some things can be done to improve case formulation. Widiger & Clark (2000) recommended that "a means of characterizing a developmental, life span history of a patient's symptomatology should perhaps be provided in DSM-V by recording, for example, age of onset, lifetime history of disorders, and their longitudinal course" (p. 956). Though more descriptive than explanatory in nature, this procedure could help clinicians make more valid causal judgments. Also, collecting this information could lead to a transformation in how psychopathology is viewed. Widiger & Clark gave the following example: "If one comes to understand how an anxiety disorder develops into a depressive disorder with which it shares a common genetic vulnerability, it could be impossible to persist with the notion that they are separate and distinct disorders" (p. 956).

Another promising approach involves using functional analytical clinical case models (Haynes et al. 1997). This approach calls on the clinician to make "low-level" causal inferences (e.g., the clinician may conclude that marital stress led to a client's presleep worry, and that this worry in combination with pregnancy led to a sleep disturbance). An attractive feature of this approach is that causal relations are described pictorially—one can gain an understanding of a client quickly by looking at the "vector-graphic representation of variables and functional relationships" (Haynes et al. 1997, p. 334). In addition, because making causal judgments is in many ways the most difficult task facing mental health professionals (Garb 1998), functional analytical clinical case modeling is promising because it requires judgments that are tied relatively closely to events and observed behavior. One would expect that the interrater agreement among different clinicians would be good given the low level of causal inference typically required, but this needs to be investigated empirically.

Treatment Decisions

Many psychologists, and certainly many mental health professionals, are unfamiliar with the scientific literature on therapeutic interventions. This is one reason why treatment decisions are sometimes inappropriate. The problem of inappropriate interventions is in part an assessment issue, not simply a treatment issue. In a sense, the problem is that some clinicians make inappropriate decisions when assessing clients and formulating treatment plans.

Interestingly, the American Psychological Association (APA) may encourage poor decisions by offering continuing education credits for a range of treatment techniques that have not been empirically supported. APA continuing education credits used to be offered for workshops on thought field therapy, and are still offered for workshops on calligraphy therapy, Jungian sandplay therapy, and neurotherapy (a form of electroencephalographic biofeedback that has sometimes been advertised as a treatment for depression, learning disabilities, attention-deficit hyperactivity disorder, epilepsy, and coma) (Kline et al. 2001, Lilienfeld 1999). APA continuing education credits are even offered for techniques that appear to be harmful. For example, credits are approved for training in crisis debriefing for victims of traumatic events, even though several studies have found this intervention to have negative effects (e.g., Gist & Lubin 1999, Mayou et al. 2000).

One of the most important recent results on decision-making concerns race bias. Race bias has been observed for the prescription of antipsychotic medicine (Segal et al. 1996; also see Garb 1998, pp. 126–29). This finding was replicated in a study on adherence to treatment recommendations conducted by the Schizophrenia Patient Outcome Research Team (Lehman et al. 1998). In this study, 27.4% of minority patients and 15.9% of white patients were placed on excessive dosages of antipsychotic medicine. This finding may be related to data indicating that the risk of violence is overestimated for black psychiatric inpatients and black prison inmates (Garb 1998, pp. 113–14; Hoptman et al. 1999). In a study conducted in Israel (J Rabinowitz, T Shlezinger, M Davidson, manuscript submitted for publication), dosage of psychotropic medicine was found to be related to "the extent to which the patient is believed to constitute a threat to the physician" (p. 2). Thus, minority patients may be more likely than white patients to be perceived as being dangerous, and for this reason a substantial number are put on excessive doses of medicine. Other research has also found a relationship between perception of dangerousness and dosage of medicine (Baldessarini et al. 1995).

Prediction of Violence and Detection of Deception

Researchers have reported encouraging findings about clinicians' ability to predict violence. At one time, some psychologists believed that mental health professionals could not predict violence. For example, in an article in *Science*, Faust & Ziskin (1988, p. 32) concluded that "studies on the prediction of violence are consistent: clinicians are wrong at least twice as often as they are correct." We now know that mental health professionals can make valid short-term and long-term predictions of violence (Garb 1998, pp. 107–9; Mossman 1994). For example, in one study (Hoptman et al. 1999), psychiatrists at a forensic psychiatric hospital were asked to predict assaultive behavior. They made predictions during a 3-month period for a sample of 183 recently admitted male patients. Sixty of the patients became assaultive. The clinicians' overall hit rate was 71%. Fifty-four percent of the predictions of "assaultive behavior" and 79% of the predictions of "no assaultive behavior" were correct.

Positive results were also obtained in a study of deception detection (Ekman et al. 1999). Clinical psychologists and other participants watched silent videotapes of people who were lying or telling the truth about their opinions. Subjects who lied and those who told the truth exhibited differences in facial movements. Clinical psychologists with a special interest in detecting deception were more accurate than other clinical psychologists. This finding is particularly interesting because judgment research indicates that it can be surprisingly difficult to draw inferences from nonverbal behavior (Garb 1998, p. 18). The results of this study, along with those of a prior study in which Secret Service agents performed better than chance in detecting deception (Ekman & O'Sullivan 1991), suggest that experience, training, and/or social intelligence can improve performance in this area. Future studies may clarify the importance of individual differences among judges and examine whether the laboratory findings can be duplicated in more realistic situations.

Clinical Judgment, Computers, and Mechanical Prediction

Clinicians can use algorithms programmed into computers to interpret test results and make judgments and decisions (e.g., diagnoses, descriptions of traits and symptoms, behavioral predictions, and treatment decisions). A recent meta-analysis by

Grove and his colleagues (2000) provides the most thorough and sophisticated review of the research on such "mechanical" algorithms. Grove et al. included studies from both psychology and medicine in which mechanical algorithms and human judges were used to "predict human behavior, make psychological or medical diagnoses or prognoses, or assess states and traits (including abnormal behavior and normal personality)" (p. 20). The analysis included 136 studies, making it the largest review ever conducted on this topic.

The results supported the use of mechanical algorithms to make judgments. This held true across categories: "It holds in general medicine, in mental health, in personality, and in education and training settings" (Grove et al. 2000, p. 25). Mechanical algorithms substantially outperformed predictions made by human judges in 33–47% of the studies. In contrast, judges substantially outperformed algorithms in 6–16% of the studies. In the remaining studies, clinicians and algorithms were about equally accurate. On average, the mechanical algorithms were about 10% more accurate than clinicians. The algorithms were usually superior, regardless of whether clinicians were "inexperienced or seasoned judges" (p. 25).

The Grove et al. (2000) meta-analysis is a landmark study. Its findings strongly suggest that computers can supplement and in some cases improve upon the decisions that clinicians make in their work. However, two important limitations of computerized decision-making should be noted. First, well-validated mechanical decision rules are currently unavailable for most clinical tasks. For example, substantial progress has been made in developing computerized algorithms to predict violence, child abuse and neglect, and recidivism among juvenile offenders (see Forensic Assessment above). However, there are still no well-validated algorithms for making diagnoses, predicting behavior, describing personality traits and psychopathology, or making treatment decisions (Garb 2000). In the future, research is needed to develop and validate computer programs for such tasks.

Second, despite the positive findings of Grove et al. (2000), the highly popular computer programs that clinical psychologists currently use to interpret test results (e.g., the MMPI-2 and the Rorschach) have not generally performed well in validity studies, perhaps because these programs are generally based on the "canned" interpretations of experts, rather than on empirically developed actuarial decision rules. When Butcher et al. (2000) reviewed the literature, they were able to find only four validity studies during the 1990s that had examined these programs. Two of the studies reported negative findings, a third reported mixed results, and the fourth reported only mildly positive results. As Snyder (2000, p. 55) concluded, "studies regarding CBTIs' [computer-based test interpretations'] validity are scarce; for most CBTI systems, they are lacking entirely."

FUTURE DIRECTIONS

As this review has shown, the field of clinical assessment is in the midst of significant change. New pressures are forcing psychologists to demonstrate that their assessment techniques are cost-effective, scientifically sound, and culturally fair.

In concluding, we offer four predictions.

1. The economic constraints on health and psychological services that characterize the era of managed care will not disappear any time soon. Psychologists in the future will be held accountable to show that their assessment techniques yield tangible benefits, are cost-effective, and provide incrementally valid information beyond what can be obtained from less expensive sources. Some traditional assessment techniques will have to be abandoned and new ones developed.

2. As the US population becomes more diverse, valid multicultural assessment will become increasingly important. For many years multicultural issues have been regarded as peripheral to research and practice in clinical assessment. In the future they will become a major focus of attention.

3. Owing to changes in the law, the assessment techniques used by forensic psychologists will face increasingly stringent scrutiny. Current debates concerning the legal admissibility of the MCMI-III and the Rorschach CS are only the first signs of a trend toward greater accountability. Prudent forensic psychologists will pay attention to such debates and base their opinions as much as possible on well-validated assessment approaches. Those who fail to do so will run an ever-higher risk of being embarrassed in court or having their recommendations discounted.

4. Developments in science are likely to introduce radically new and unexpected elements into the assessment process, beyond those we have identified here. For example, Plomin & Crabbe (2000) predicted that advances in behavioral genetics will change clinical psychology: "Here is what the future might look like for clinical psychologists. DNA will be routinely collected. The most powerful potential for DNA is to predict risk so that genes can be used to aid in diagnosis and plan treatment programs" (p. 823). Similarly, neuroimaging techniques for visualizing brain structure and function may become increasingly sophisticated and affordable. It is interesting to imagine a time when psychologists may replace their Rorschach cards with a DNA kit and a pocket scanner.

Visit the Annual Reviews home page at www.AnnualReviews.org

LITERATURE CITED

Acklin MW. 1999. Behavioral science foundations of the Rorschach test: research and clinical applications. *Assessment* 6:319–26

Acklin MW, McDowell CJ, Verschell MS, Chan D. 2000. Interobserver agreement, intraobserver reliability, and the Rorschach Comprehensive System. *J. Pers. Assess.* 74: 15–47

Allen J, Walsh JA. 2000. A construct-based approach to equivalence: methodologies for cross-cultural/multicultural personality assessment research. See Dana 2000, pp. 63–85

Arbisi PA, Ben-Porath YS. 1995. An MMPI-2 infrequent response scale for use with psychopathological populations: the Infrequency-Psychopathology scale, $F(p)$. *Psychol. Assess.* 7:424–31

Arbisi PA, Ben-Porath YS. 1998. The ability of Minnesota Multiphasic Personality Inventory–2 validity scales to detect fake-bad responses in psychiatric inpatients. *Psychol. Assess.* 10:221–28

Arbisi PA, Ben-Porath YS, McNulty JL. 1998. *The impact of ethnicity on the MMPI-2 in inpatient psychiatric settings.* Presented at Annu. Meet. Am. Psychol. Assoc., San Francisco

Archer RP. 1999. Introduction to a special section: perspectives on the Rorschach. *Assessment* 6:307–11

Archer RP, Krishnamurthy R. 1993a. Combining the Rorschach and the MMPI in the assessment of adolescents. *J. Pers. Assess.* 60:132–40

Archer RP, Krishnamurthy R. 1993b. A review of MMPI and Rorschach interrelationships in adult samples. *J. Pers. Assess.* 61:277–93

Archer RP, Newsom CR. 2000. Psychological test usage with adolescent clients: survey update. *Assessment* 7:227–35

Ardila A, Rosselli M, Puente AE. 1994. *Neuropsychological Evaluation of the Spanish Speaker.* New York: Plenum

Arnold BR, Matus YE. 2000. Test translation and cultural equivalence methodologies for use with diverse populations. See Cuellar & Panigua 2000, pp. 121–36

Aronow E. 2001. CS norms, psychometrics, and possibilities for the Rorschach technique. *Clin. Psychol. Sci. Pract.* 8:383–85

Bagby RM, Nicholson RA, Buis T, Bacchiochi JR. 2000. Can the MMPI-2 validity scales detect depression feigned by experts? *Assessment* 7:55–62

Baird C, Wagner D. 2000. The relative validity of actuarial- and consensus-based risk assessment systems. *Child. Youth Serv. Rev.* 22:839–71

Baldessarini RJ, Kando JC, Centorrino F. 1995. Hospital use of antipsychotic agents in 1989 and 1993: stable dosing with decreased length of stay. *Am. J. Psychiatry* 152:1038–44

Ball JD, Archer RP, Imhof EA. 1994. Time requirements of psychological testing: a survey of practitioners. *J. Pers. Assess.* 63:239–49

Basco MR, Bostic JQ, Davies D, Rush AJ, Witte B, et al. 2000. Methods to improve diagnostic accuracy in a community mental health setting. *Am. J. Psychiatry* 157:1599–605

Board Professional Affairs. 1998. Awards for distinguished professional contributions: John Exner. *Am. Psychol.* 53:391–92

Bornstein RF. 2001. The clinical utility of the Rorschach Inkblot Method: reframing the debate. *J. Pers. Assess.* 77:39–47

Boscan DC. 1999. *The Rorschach test: a Mexican sample using the Comprehensive System.* PhD thesis. Fielding Inst., Santa Barbara, CA

Brown D, Scheflin AW, Hammond DC. 1998. *Memory, Trauma Treatment, and the Law.* New York: Norton

Butcher JN, Graham JR, Ben-Porath YS. 1995. Methodological problems and issues in MMPI, MMPI-2, and MMPI-A research. *Psychol. Assess.* 7:320–29

Butcher JN, Lim J, Nezami E. 1998. Objective study of abnormal personality in cross-cultural settings: the Minnesota Multiphasic Personality Inventory (MMPI–2). *J. Cross-Cult. Psychol.* 29:189–211

Butcher JN, Perry JN, Atlis MM. 2000. Validity and utility of computer-based test interpretation. *Psychol. Assess.* 12:6–18

Butcher JN, Rouse SV. 1996. Personality: individual differences and clinical assessment. *Annu. Rev. Psychol.* 47:87–111

Childs RA, Dahlstrom WG, Kemp SM, Panter AT. 2000. Item response theory in personality assessment: a demonstration using the MMPI-2 Depression scale. *Assessment* 7:37–54

Clark LA, Watson D. 1995. Constructing validity: basic issues in objective scale development. *Psychol. Assess.* 7:309–19

Cleary TA, Humphreys LG, Kendrick SA,

Wesman AG. 1975. Educational uses of tests with disadvantaged students. *Am. Psychol.* 30:15–41

Cuellar I. 2000. Acculturation as a moderator of personality and psychological assessment. See Dana 2000, pp. 113–29

Cuellar I, Arnold B, Maldonado R. 1995. Acculturation rating scale for Mexican-Americans-II: a revision of the original ARSMA scale. *Hisp. J. Behav. Sci.* 17:275–304

Cuellar I, Paniagua FA, eds. 2000. *Handbook of Multicultural Mental Health: Assessment and Treatment of Diverse Populations.* San Diego, CA: Academic

Dana RH. 1993. *Multicultural Assessment Perspectives for Professional Psychology.* Boston: Allyn Bacon

Dana RH. 1998. Cultural identity assessment of culturally diverse groups: 1997. *J. Pers. Assess.* 70:1–16

Dana RH, ed. 2000. *Handbook of Cross-Cultural and Multicultural Personality Assessment.* Mahwah, NJ: Erlbaum

Daubert v. Merrell Dow Pharmaceuticals, Inc. 1993. 509 U.S., 113 S. Ct. 2786

Douglas KS, Cox DN, Webster CD. 1999a. Violence risk assessment: science and practice. *Legal Criminol. Psychol.* 4:149–84

Douglas KS, Ogloff JRP, Nicholls TL, Grant I. 1999b. Assessing risk for violence among psychiatric patients: the HCR-20 Violence Risk Assessment Scheme and the Psychopathy Checklist: Screening Version. *J. Consult. Clin. Psychol.* 67:917–30

Dyer FJ, McCann JT. 2000. The Millon clinical inventories, research critical of their forensic application, and Daubert criteria. *Law Hum. Behav.* 24:487–97

Edens JF, Poythress NG, Lilienfeld SO. 1999. Identifying inmates at risk for disciplinary infractions: a comparison of two measures of psychopathy. *Behav. Sci. Law* 17:435–43

Ekman P, O'Sullivan M. 1991. Who can catch a liar? *Am. Psychol.* 46:913–20

Ekman P, O'Sullivan M, Frank MG. 1999. A few can catch a liar. *Psychol. Sci.* 10:263–66

Embretson SE, Reise SP. 2000. *Item Response Theory for Psychologists.* Mahwah, NJ: Erlbaum

Ephraim D. 2000. Culturally relevant research and practice with the Rorschach Comprehensive System. See Dana 2000, pp. 303–27

Exner JE. 1991. *The Rorschach: A Comprehensive System,* Vol. 2. *Interpretation.* New York: Wiley. 2nd ed.

Exner JE. 1993. *The Rorschach: A Comprehensive System,* Vol. 1. *Basic Foundations.* New York: Wiley. 3rd ed.

Exner JE. 1995. *A Rorschach Workbook for the Comprehensive System.* Asheville, NC: Rorschach Workshops. 4th ed.

Exner JE. 2001a. A comment on: The misperception of psychopathology: Problems with the norms of the Comprehensive System for the Rorschach. *Clin. Psychol. Sci. Pract.* 8: 368–88

Exner JE. 2001b. *A Rorschach Workbook for the Comprehensive System.* Asheville, NC: Rorschach Workshops. 5th ed.

Exner JE, Weiner IB. 1994. *The Rorschach: A Comprehensive System,* Vol. 3. *Assessment of Children and Adolescents.* New York: Wiley. 2nd ed.

Faust D, Ziskin J. 1988. The expert witness in psychology and psychiatry. *Science* 241:31–35

Finn SE. 1996. *Manual for Using the MMPI-2 as a Therapeutic Intervention.* Minneapolis: Univ. Minn. Press

Finn SE, Tonsager ME. 1992. Therapeutic effects of providing MMPI-2 test feedback to college students awaiting therapy. *Psychol. Assess.* 4:278–87

Fletcher-Janzen E, Strickland TL, Reynolds CR. 2000. *Handbook of Cross-Cultural Neuropsychology.* New York: Kluwer Acad./ Plenum

Forth AE, Hart SD, Hare RD. 1990. Assessment of psychopathy in male young offenders. *Psychol. Assess.* 2:342–44

Gacono CB, Loving JL, Bodholdt RH. 2001. The Rorschach and psychopathy: toward a more accurate understanding of the research findings. *J. Pers. Assess.* 77:16–38

Ganellen RJ. 2001. Weighing evidence

concerning the Rorschach's psychometric properties: a response to Wood et al. 1999. *J. Pers. Assess.* 77:1–15

Garb HN. 1998. *Studying the Clinician: Judgment Research and Psychological Assessment.* Washington, DC: Am. Psychol. Assoc.

Garb HN. 1999. Call for a moratorium on the use of the Rorschach Inkblot in clinical and forensic settings. *Assessment* 6:313–15

Garb HN. 2000. Computers will become increasingly important for psychological assessment: not that there's anything wrong with that! *Psychol. Assess.* 12:31–39

Garb HN, Florio CM, Grove WM. 1998. The validity of the Rorschach and the Minnesota Multiphasic Personality Inventory: results from meta-analyses. *Psychol. Sci.* 9:402–4

General Electric Co. v. Joiner. 1997. 118 S. Ct. 512

Gist R, Lubin B. 1999. *Response to Disaster: Psychosocial, Community, and Ecological Approaches.* Philadelphia: Brunner/Mazel

Greene RL. 2000. *The MMPI-2: An Interpretive Manual.* Boston: Allyn Bacon. 2nd ed.

Greenwald DF. 1990. An external construct validity study of Rorschach personality variables. *J. Pers. Assess.* 55:768–80

Greenwald DF. 1991. Personality dimensions reflected by the Rorschach and the 16PF. *J. Clin. Psychol.* 47:708–15

Greenwald DF. 1999. Relationships between the Rorschach and the NEO-Five Factor Inventory. *Psychol. Rep.* 85:519–27

Gronnerod C. 1999. Rorschach interrater agreement estimates: an empirical evaluation. *Scand. J. Psychol.* 40:115–20

Groth-Marnat G. 1999. Financial efficacy of clinical assessment: rational guidelines and issues for future research. *J. Clin. Psychol.* 55:813–24

Grove WM. (Chair). 2000. *APA Division 12 (Clinical) Presidential Task Force "Assessment for the Year 2000." Report of the Task Force.* Washington, DC: Am. Psychol. Assoc., Div. 12 (Clin. Psychol.)

Grove WM, Barden RC. 1999. Protecting the integrity of the legal system: the admissibility of testimony from mental health experts under Daubert/Kumho analyses. *Psychol. Public Policy Law* 5:224–42

Grove WM, Zald DH, Lebow BS, Snitz BE, Nelson C. 2000. Clinical versus mechanical prediction: a meta-analysis. *Psychol. Assess.* 12:19–30

Hall CCI. 1997. Cultural malpractice: the growing obsolescence of psychology with the changing U.S. population. *Am. Psychol.* 52:642–51

Hall GCN, Bansal A, Lopez IR. 1999. Ethnicity and psychopathology: a meta-analytic review of 31 years of comparative MMPI/MMPI-2 research. *Psychol. Assess.* 11:642–51

Halperin K, Snyder CR. 1979. Effect of enhanced psychological test feedback on treatment outcome: therapuetic implications of the Barnum effect. *J. Consult. Clin. Psychol.* 47:140–46

Hamel M, Gallagher S, Soares C. 2001. The Rorschach: Here we go again. *J. Forensic Psychol. Pract.* 1:(3):79–87

Hamel M, Shaffer TW, Erdberg P. 2000. A study of nonpatient preadolescent Rorschach protocols. *J. Pers. Assess.* 75:280–94

Handel RW, Ben-Porath YS. 2000. Multicultural assessment with the MMPI-2: issues for research and practice. See Dana 2000, pp. 229–45

Hansen SS, Munk-Jorgensen P, Guldbaek B, Solgard T, Lauszus KS, et al. 2000. Psychoactive substance use diagnoses among psychiatric in-patients. *Acta Psychiatr. Scand.* 102:432–38

Hanson RK. 1998. What do we know about sex offender risk assessment? *Psychol. Public Policy Law* 4:50–72

Hare R. 1991. *Manual for the Revised Psychopathy Checklist.* Toronto: Multihealth Systems

Harkness AR, Lilienfeld SO. 1997. Individual differences science for treatment planning: personality traits. *Psychol. Assess.* 9:349–60

Hart SD, Hare RD, Forth AE. 1994. Psychopathy as a risk marker for violence: development and validation of a screening version of the Revised Psychopathy Checklist. In *Violence and Mental Disorder: Developments in Risk Assessment*, ed. J Monahan, HJ Steadman, pp. 81–97. Chicago: Univ Chicago Press

Hayes SC, Nelson RO, Jarrett RB. 1987. The treatment utility of assessment: a functional approach to evaluating assessment quality. *Am. Psychol.* 42:963–74

Haynes SN, Leisen MB, Blaine DD. 1997. Design of individualized behavioral treatment programs using functional analytic clinical case models. *Psychol. Assess.* 9:334–48

Hemphill JF, Hare RD, Wong S. 1998. Psychopathy and recidivism: a review. *Legal Criminol. Psychol.* 3:139–70

Hiller JB, Rosenthal R, Bornstein RF, Berry DTR, Brunell-Neuleib S. 1999. A comparative meta-analysis of Rorschach and MMPI validity. *Psychol. Assess.* 11:278–96

Hoptman MJ, Yates KF, Patalinjug MB, Wack RC, Convit A. 1999. Clinical prediction of assaultive behavior among male psychiatric patients at a maximum-security forensic facility. *Psychiatr. Serv.* 50:1461–66

Hunsley J, Bailey JM. 1999. The clinical utility of the Rorschach: unfulfilled promises and an uncertain future. *Psychol. Assess.* 11:266–77

Hunsley J, Di Giulio G. 2001. Norms, norming, and clinical assessment. *Clin. Psychol. Sci. Pract.* 8:378–82

Iverson GL, Franzen MD, Hammond JA. 1995. Examination of inmates' ability to malinger on the MMPI-2. *Psychol. Assess.* 7:118–21

Keller J, Nitschke JB, Bhargava T, Deldin PJ, Gergen JA, Miller JA. 2000. Neuropsychological differentiation of depression and anxiety. *J. Abnorm. Psychol.* 109:5–10

Kline JP, Brann CN, Loney BR. 2001. A cacophony in the brainwave: a critical appraisal of neurotherapy for ADHD. *Sci. Rev. Ment. Health Pract.* In press

Klopfer B. 1940. Personality aspects revealed by the Rorschach method. *Rorschach Res. Exch.* 4:26–29

Kullgren G, Jacobsson L, Lynoe N, Kohn R, Levav I. 1996. Practices and attitudes among

Swedish psychiatrists regarding the ethics of compulsory treatment. *Acta Psychiatr Scand.* 93:389–96

Kumho Tire Co., Ltd. v. Carmichael. 1999. 119 S. Ct. 1167

Kuncel NR, Hezlett SA, Ones DS. 2001. A comprehensive meta-analysis of the predictive validity of the Graduate Record Examination: implications for graduate student selection and performance. *Psychol. Bull.* 127:162–81

Lally SJ. 2001. Should human figure drawings be admitted into court? *J. Pers. Assess.* 76:135–49

Lamb DG, Berry DTR, Wetter MW, Baer RA. 1994. Effects of two types of information on malingering of closed head injury on the MMPI-2: an analog investigation. *Psychol. Assess.* 6:8–13

Lambert MJ, Burlingame GM, Umphress V, Hansen NB, Vermeersch DA, et al. 1996. The reliability and validity of the Outcome Questionnaire. *Clin. Psychol. Psychother.* 3:249–58

Lambert MJ, Finch AE. 1999. The Outcome Questionnaire. See Maruish 1999, pp. 831–69

Lambert MJ, Okiishi JC, Finch AE, Johnson LD. 1998. Outcome assessment: from conceptualization to implementation. *Prof. Psychol. Res. Pract.* 29:63–70

Lehman AF, Steinwachs DM, the co-investigators of the PORT project. 1998. Patterns of usual care for schizophrenia: initial results from the Schizophrenia Patient Outcomes Research Team (PORT) client survey. *Schizophr. Bull.* 24:11–20

Levenson MR, Kiehl KA, Fitzpatrick CM. 1995. Assessing psychopathic attributes in a noninstitutionalized population. *J. Pers. Soc. Psychol.* 68:151–58

Lilienfeld SO. 1998. Methodological advances and developments in the assessment of psychopathy. *Behav. Res. Ther.* 36:99–125

Lilienfeld SO. 1999. Pseudoscience in contemporary clinical psychology: what it is and what we can do about it. *Clin. Psychol.* 51:3–9

Lilienfeld SO, Andrews BP. 1996. Development and preliminary validation of a self-report measure of psychopathic personality in noncriminal populations. *J. Pers. Assess.* 66:488–524

Lilienfeld SO, Lynn SJ, Kirsch I, Chaves JF, Sarbin TR, et al. 1999. Dissociative identity disorder and the sociocognitive model: recalling the lessons of the past. *Psychol. Bull.* 125:507–23

Lilienfeld SO, Wood JM, Garb HN. 2000. The scientific status of projective techniques. *Psychol. Sci. Public Interest* 1:27–66

Marin G, Gamba RJ. 1996. A new measurement of acculturation for Hispanics: the bidimensional acculturation scale for Hispanics (BAS). *Hisp. J. Behav. Sci.* 18:297–316

Maruish ME, ed. 1999. *The Use of Psychological Testing for Treatment Planning and Outcomes Assessment.* Mahwah, NJ: Erlbaum. 2nd ed.

Mayou RA, Ehlers A, Hobbs M. 2000. Psychological debriefing for road traffic accident victims: three-year follow-up of a randomised controlled trial. *Br. J. Psychiatry* 176:589–93

McCann JT. 1998a. Defending the Rorschach in court: an analysis of admissibility using legal and professional standards. *J. Pers. Assess.* 70:125–44

McCann JT. 1998b. *Malingering and Deception in Adolescents: Assessing Credibility in Clinical and Forensic Settings.* Washington, DC: Am. Psychol. Assoc.

McCann JT, Dyer FJ. 1996. *Forensic Assessment with the Millon Inventories.* New York: Guilford

McCullough JP, Klein DN, Keller MB, Holzer CE, Davis SM, et al. 2000. Comparison of DSM-III-R chronic major depression and major depression superimposed on dysthymia (double depression): validity of the distinction. *J. Abnorm. Psychol.* 109:419–23

McKinzey RK, Podd MH, Krehbiel MA, Mensch AJ, Trombka CC. 1997. Detection of malingering on the Luria-Nebraska Neuropsychological Battery: an initial and cross-validation. *Arch. Clin. Neuropsychol.* 12:505–12

McKinzey RK, Podd MH, Krehbiel MA, Raven J. 1999. Detection of malingering on Raven's Standard Progressive Matrices: a cross-validation. *Br. J. Clin. Psychol.* 38:435–39

McNally RJ. 1999. Review of the book *Memory, Trauma Treatment, and the Law. Int. J. Clin. Exp. Hypnosis* 47:374–82

McNulty JL, Graham JR, Ben-Porath YS, Stein LAR. 1997. Comparative validity of MMPI-2 scores of African-American and Caucasian mental health center clients. *Psychol. Assess.* 9:464–70

Meehl PE. 1954. *Clinical vs. Statistical Prediction: A Theoretical Analysis and a Review of the Evidence.* Minneapolis: Univ. Minn. Press

Meyer GJ. 1992. The Rorschach's factor structure: a contemporary investigation and historical review. *J. Pers. Assess.* 59:117–36

Meyer GJ. 1993. The impact of response frequency on the Rorschach constellation indices and on their validity with diagnostic and MMPI-2 criteria. *J. Pers. Assess.* 60:153–80

Meyer GJ. 1996. The Rorschach and MMPI: toward a more scientifically differentiated understanding of cross-method assessment. *J. Pers. Assess.* 67:558–78

Meyer GJ. 2001. Evidence to correct misperceptions about Rorschach norms. *Clin. Psychol. Sci. Pract.* 8:389–96

Meyer GJ, Richardson C. 2001. *An examination of changes in Form Quality codes in the Rorschach Comprehensive System from 1974 to 1995.* Presented at Midwinter Meet. Soc. Pers. Assess., Philadelphia

Monahan J, Steadman HJ, Silver E, Appelbaum P, Robbins PC, et al. eds. 2001. *Rethinking Risk Assessment: The MacArthur Study of Mental Disorder and Violence.* New York: Oxford Univ. Press

Mossman D. 1994. Assessing predictions of violence: being accurate about accuracy. *J. Consult. Clin. Psychol.* 62:783–92

Mueller RM, Lambert MJ, Burlingame GM.

1998. Construct validity of the Outcome Questionnaire: a confirmatory factor analysis. *J. Pers. Assess.* 70:248–62

Nakata LM. 1999. *Interrater reliability and the Comprehensive System for the Rorschach: clinical and non-clinical protocols.* PhD thesis. Pacif. Grad. Sch. Psychol., Palo Alto, CA

Nezworski MT, Wood JM. 1995. Narcissism in the Comprehensive System for the Rorschach. *Clin. Psychol. Sci. Pract.* 2:179–99

Nicholson RA, Mouton GJ, Bagby RM, Buis T, Peterson SA, Buigas RA. 1997. Utility of MMPI-2 indicators of response distortion: receiver operating characteristic analysis. *Psychol. Assess.* 9:471–79

Nunnally JC. 1978. *Psychometric Theory.* New York: McGraw-Hill. 2nd ed.

O'Donohue W, Bradley AR. 1999. Conceptual and empirical issues in child custody evaluations. *Clin. Psychol. Sci. Pract.* 6:310–22

Okazaki S, Sue S. 1995. Methodological issues in assessment research with ethnic minorities. *Psychol. Assess.* 7:367–75

Ostrosky-Solis F, Ardila A, Rosselli M. 1999. NEUROPSI: a brief neuropsychological test battery in Spanish with norms by age and educational level. *J. Int. Neuropsychol. Soc.* 5:413–33

Parker KCH, Hanson RK, Hunsley J. 1988. MMPI, Rorschach, and WAIS: a meta-analytic comparison of reliability, stability, and validity. *Psychol. Bull.* 103:367–73

Phelps R, Eisman EJ, Kohout J. 1998. Psychological practice and managed care: results of the CAPP Practitioner Survey. *Prof. Psychol. Res. Pract.* 29:31–36

Piotrowski C. 1999. Assessment practices in the era of managed care: current status and future directions. *J. Clin. Psychol.* 55:787–98

Piotrowski C, Belter RW, Keller JW. 1998. The impact of "managed care" on the practice of psychological testing: preliminary findings. *J. Pers. Assess.* 70:441–47

Plomin R, Crabbe J. 2000. DNA. *Psychol. Bull.* 126:806–28

Pollock PH. 1996. A cautionary note on the de-termination of malingering in offenders. *Psychol. Crime Law.* 3:97–110

Ponton MO, Ardila A. 1999. The future of neuropsychology with Hispanic populations in the United States. *Arch. Clin. Neuropsychol.* 14:565–80

Puente AE, Ardila A. 2000. Neuropsychological assessment of Hispanics. See Fletcher-Janzen et al. 2000, pp. 87–104

Quinsey VL, Harris GT, Rice ME, Cormier CA. 1998. *Violent Offenders: Appraising and Managing Risk.* Washington, DC: Am. Psychol. Assoc.

Rees LM, Tombaugh TN, Gansler DA, Maczynski NP. 1998. Five validation experiments of the Test of Memory Malingering (TOMM). *Psychol. Assess.* 10:10–20

Reynolds CR, ed. 1998. *Detection of Malingering During Head Injury Litigation. Critical Issues in Neuropsychology.* New York: Plenum

Ritzler B. 1995. Putting your eggs in the content analysis basket: a response to Aronow, Reznikov, and Moreland. *J. Pers. Assess.* 64:229–34

Rogers R. 1995. *Diagnostic and Structured Interviewing: A Handbook for Psychologists.* Odessa, FL: Psychol. Assess. Res.

Rogers R, ed. 1997. *Clinical Assessment of Malingering and Deception.* New York: Guilford. 2nd ed.

Rogers R, Salekin RT, Hill C, Sewell KW, Murdock ME, Neumann CS. 2000a. The Psychopathy Checklist—Screening Version: an examination of criteria and subcriteria in three forensic samples. *Assessment* 7:1–15

Rogers R, Salekin RT, Sewell KW. 1999. Validation of the Millon Clinical Multiaxial Inventory for Axis II disorders: Does it meet the Daubert standard? *Law Hum. Behav.* 23:425–43

Rogers R, Salekin RT, Sewell KW. 2000b. The MCMI-III and the Daubert standard: separating rhetoric from reality. *Law Hum. Behav.* 24:501–6

Rogers R, Sewell KW, Salekin RT. 1994. A meta-analysis of malingering on the MMPI-2. *Assessment* 1:227–37

Salekin RT, Rogers R, Sewell KW. 1996. A review and meta-analysis of the Psychopathy Checklist and Psychopathy Checklist-Revised: predictive validity of dangerousness. *Clin. Psychol. Sci. Pract.* 3:203–15

Santor DA, Ramsay JO. 1998. Progress in the technology of measurement: applications of item response models. *Psychol. Assess.* 10:345–59

Schretlen DJ. 1997. Dissimulation on the Rorschach and other projective measures. See Rogers 1997, pp. 208–22

Schwarz N. 1999. Self-reports: how the questions shape the answers. *Am. Psychol.* 54:93–105

Schwarz N, Strack F, Mai HP. 1991. Assimilation and contrast effects in part-whole question sequences: a conversational logic analysis. *Public Opin. Q.* 55:3–23

Segal SP, Bola JR, Watson MA. 1996. Race, quality of care, and antipsychotic prescribing practices in psychiatric emergency services. *Psychiatr. Serv.* 47:282–86

Shaffer TW, Erdberg P, Haroian J. 1999. Current nonpatient data for the Rorschach, WAIS-R, and MMPI-2. *J. Pers. Assess.* 73:305–16

Shear MK, Greeno C, Kang J, Ludewig D, Frank E, et al. 2000. Diagnosis of nonpsychotic patients in community clinics. *Am. J. Psychiatry* 157:581–87

Snyder DK. 2000. Computer-assisted judgment: defining strengths and liabilities. *Psychol. Assess.* 12:52–60

Spanos NP. 1996. *Multiple Identities and False Memories.* Washington, DC: Am. Psychol. Assoc.

Stephenson M. 2000. Development and validation of the Stephenson Multigroup Acculturation Scale (SMAS). *Psychol. Assess.* 12:77–88

Storm J, Graham JR. 2000. Detection of coached general malingering on the MMPI-2. *Psychol. Assess.* 12:158–65

Strakowski SM, Hawkins JM, Keck PE, McElroy SL, West SA, et al. 1997. The effects of race and information variance on disagreement between psychiatric emergency service

and research diagnoses in first-episode psychosis. *J. Clin. Psychiatry* 58:457–63

Sundberg ND. 1955. The acceptability of "fake" versus "bona fide" personality test interpretations. *J. Abnorm. Soc. Psychol.* 50:145–47

Suzuki LA, Ponterotto JG, Meller PJ, eds. 2000. *Handbook of Multicultural Assessment: Clinical, Psychological, and Educational Applications.* San Francisco: Jossey-Bass. 2nd ed.

Timbrook RE, Graham JR. 1994. Ethnic differences on the MMPI-2? *Psychol. Assess.* 6:212–17

Tombaugh TN. 1997. The Test of Memory Malingering (TOMM): normative data from cognitively intact and cognitively impaired individuals. *Psychol. Assess.* 9:260–68

US Bureau Census 2000. *Statistical Abstracts of the U.S.* Washington, DC: US Bur. Census

Velasquez RJ. 1995. Personality assessment of Hispanic clients. In *Clinical Personality Assessment: Practical Approaches*, ed. JN Butcher, pp. 120–39. New York: Oxford Univ. Press

Velasquez RJ, Ayala GX, Pace T, Mendoza S, Choney SK, et al. 2000. Culturally competent use of the Minnesota Multiphasic Personality Inventory-2. See Cuellar & Paniagua 2000, pp. 389–417

Vermeersch DA, Lambert MJ, Burlingame GM. 2000. Outcome questionnaire: item sensitivity to change. *J. Pers. Assess.* 74:242–61

Viglione DJ. 1999. A review of recent research addressing the utility of the Rorschach. *Psychol. Assess.* 11:251–65

Vinet EV. 2000. The Rorschach Comprehensive System in Iberoamerica. See Dana 2000, pp. 345–65

Waller NG. 1998. Searching for structure in the MMPI. In *The New Rules of Measurement*, ed. SE Embretson, SL Hershberger, pp. 185–217. Mahwah, NJ: Erlbaum

Waller NG, Thompson JS, Wenk E. 2000. Using IRT to separate measurement bias from true group differences on homogeneous *and* heterogeneous scales: an illustration with the MMPI. *Psychol. Methods* 5:125–46

Walters GL, Clopton JR. 2000. Effect of symptom information and validity scale information on the malingering of depression on the MMPI-2. *J. Pers. Assess.* 75:183–99

Watkins CE, Campbell VL, Nieberding R, Hallmark R. 1995. Contemporary practice of psychological assessment by clinical psychologists. *Prof. Psychol. Res. Pract.* 26:54–60

Weiner IB. 1999. What the Rorschach can do for you: incremental validity in clinical applications. *Assessment* 6:327–38

Weiner IB. 2000. Using the Rorschach properly in practice and research. *J. Clin. Psychol.* 56:435–38

Whitehead WC. 1985. *Clinical decision-making on the basis of Rorschach, MMPI, and automated MMPI report data.* PhD thesis. Univ. Tex. Health Sci. Center, Dallas

Widiger TA. 2001. The best and the worst of us? *Clin. Psychol. Sci. Pract.* 8:374–77

Widiger TA, Clark LA. 2000. Toward DSM-V and the classification of psychopathology. *Psychol. Bull.* 126:946–63

Wiebush RG, Baird C, Krisberg B, Onek D. 1995. Risk assessment and classification for serious, violent, and chronic juvenile offenders. In *Serious, Violent, and Chronic Juvenile Offenders: A Sourcebook*, ed. JC Howell, B Krisberg, JD Hawkins, JJ Wilson, pp. 171–212. Thousand Oaks, CA: Sage

Wood JM, Lilienfeld SO. 1999. The Rorschach Inkblot Test: a case of overstatement? *Assessment* 6:341–49

Wood JM, Lilienfeld SO, Garb HN, Nezworski MT. 2000a. Limitations of the Rorschach as a diagnostic tool: a reply to Garfield (2000), Lerner (2000), and Weiner (2000). *J. Clin. Psychol.* 56:441–48

Wood JM, Lilienfeld SO, Garb HN, Nezworski MT. 2000b. The Rorschach Test in

clinical diagnosis: a critical review, with a backward look at Garfield (1947). *J. Clin. Psychol.* 56:395–410

Wood JM, Lilienfeld SO, Nezworski MT, Garb HN. 2001a. Coming to grips with negative evidence for the Comprehensive System for the Rorschach: a comment on Gacono, Loving, and Bodholdt (2001), Ganellen (2001), and Bornstein (2001). *J. Pers. Assess.* 77:48–70

Wood JM, Nezworski MT, Garb HN, Lilienfeld SO. 2001b. The misperception of psychopathology: problems with the norms of the Comprehensive System for the Rorschach. *Clin. Psychol. Sci. Pract.* 8:350–73

Wood JM, Nezworski MT, Garb HN, Lilienfeld SO. 2001c. Problems with the norms of the Comprehensive System for the Rorschach: methodological and conceptual considerations. *Clin. Psychol. Sci. Pract.* 8:397–402

Wood JM, Nezworski MT, Stejskal WJ. 1996. The Comprehensive System for the Rorschach: a critical examination. *Psychol. Sci.* 7:3–10

Wood JM, Nezworski MT, Stejskal WJ, McKinzey RK. 2001d. Problems of the Comprehensive System for the Rorschach in forensic settings: recent developments. *J. Forensic Psychol. Pract.* 1:(3):89–103

Zalewski C, Greene RL. 1996. Multicultural usage of the MMPI-2. In *Handbook of Multicultural Assessment: Clinical, Psychological, and Educational Applications*, ed. LA Suzuki, PJ Meller, JG Ponterotto, pp. 77–114. San Francisco: Jossey-Bass

Zimmerman M, Mattia JI. 1999a. Differences between clinical and research practices in diagnosing borderline personality disorder. *Am. J. Psychiatry* 156:1570–74

Zimmerman M, Mattia JI. 1999b. Is posttraumatic stress disorder underdiagnosed in routine clinical settings? *J. Nerv. Ment. Dis.* 187:420–28

Annu. Rev. Psychol. 2002. 53:545–74

DEPRESSION: Perspectives from Affective Neuroscience

Richard J. Davidson, Diego Pizzagalli, Jack B. Nitschke, and Katherine Putnam

Laboratory for Affective Neuroscience and W.M. Keck Laboratory for Functional Brain Imaging and Behavior, University of Wisconsin-Madison, Madison, Wisconsin 53705-2280; e-mail: rjdavids@facstaff.wisc.edu, dpizzag@psyphw.psych.wisc.edu, jnitschke@facstaff.wisc.edu, kputnam@facstaff.wisc.edu

Key Words mood disorders, psychopathology, neurobiology, emotion, emotion regulation

■ **Abstract** Depression is a disorder of the representation and regulation of mood and emotion. The circuitry underlying the representation and regulation of normal emotion and mood is reviewed, including studies at the animal level, human lesion studies, and human brain imaging studies. This corpus of data is used to construct a model of the ways in which affect can become disordered in depression. Research on the prefrontal cortex, anterior cingulate, hippocampus, and amygdala is reviewed and abnormalities in the structure and function of these different regions in depression is considered. The review concludes with proposals for the specific types of processing abnormalities that result from dysfunctions in different parts of this circuitry and offers suggestions for the major themes upon which future research in this area should be focused.

CONTENTS

INTRODUCTION

Affective neuroscience is the subdiscipline of the biobehavioral sciences that examines the underlying neural bases of mood and emotion. The application of this body of theory and data to the understanding of affective disorders is helping to generate a new understanding of the brain circuitry underlying these disorders.

0084-6570/02/0201-0545$14.00

Moreover, parsing the heterogeneity of these disorders on the basis of known circuits in the brain is providing a novel and potentially very fruitful approach to subtyping that does not rely on the descriptive nosology of psychiatric diagnosis but rather is based upon more objective characterization of the specific affective deficits in patients with mood disorders. At a more general level, this approach is helping to bridge the wide chasm between the literatures that have focused on normal emotion and the disorders of emotion. Historically, these research traditions have had little to do with one another and have emerged completely independently. However, affective neuroscience has helped to integrate these approaches into a more unified project that is focused upon the understanding of normal and pathological individual differences in affective style, its constituent components, and their neural bases (see e.g., Davidson et al. 2000a, Davidson 2000).

Affective neuroscience takes as its overall aim a project that is similar to that pursued by its cognate discipline, cognitive neuroscience, but focused instead on affective processes. The decomposition of cognitive processes into more elementary constituents that can then be studied in neural terms has been remarkably successful. We no longer query subjects about the contents of their cognitive processes because many of the processes so central to important aspects of cognitive function are opaque to consciousness. Instead, modern cognitive scientists and neuroscientists have developed laboratory tasks to interrogate and reveal more elementary cognitive function. These more elementary processes can then be studied using imaging methods in humans, lesion methods in animals, and the study of human patients with focal brain damage. Affective neuroscience approaches emotion using the same strategy. Global constructs of emotion are giving way to more specific and elementary constituents that can be examined with objective laboratory measures. For example, the time course of emotional responding and the mechanisms that are brought into play during the regulation of emotion can now be probed using objective laboratory measures. These constructs may be particularly important for understanding mood disorders because patients with depression may suffer from abnormalities in emotion regulation and persistence of negative affect. Patients with such abnormalities may differ from those whose primary deficit may be in reactivity to positive incentives.

Previously constructs such as emotion regulation have mostly been gleaned from self-report measures whose validity has been seriously questioned (e.g., Kahneman 1999). Whereas the phenomenology of emotion provides the subject with critical information that helps guide behavior, it may not be a particularly good source for making inferences about the processes and mechanisms that underlie emotion and its regulation. Though it is still tempting and often important to obtain measures of the subject's conscious experience of the contents of their emotional states and traits, these no longer constitute the sole source of information about emotion.

Because there are recent reviews of the basic literature on the circuitry underlying emotion and emotion regulation (e.g., Davidson & Irwin 1999; Davidson et al. 2000a,d; Rolls 1999), these data are not systematically reviewed in this chapter. We emphasize studies that have been published in the past 3 years because two recent reviews cover much of the earlier literature (Davidson et al. 1999, Drevets 1998). We wish to underscore at the outset that one of the crucial issues that plagues research in this area is the heterogencity of mood disorders. Depression may arise from a multitude of proximal causes and whereas the broad symptoms share a certain similarity, the underlying mechanisms may differ. For example, some depressed patients have pervasive symptoms of negative affect and anxiety as part of their symptom cluster and may suffer from an inability to recover from a stressful event. Other patients may exhibit a pervasive lack of positive affect as their primary dysfunction. For these patients, positive incentives do not possess reinforcing potential. These examples illustrate pathways into depression and are likely mediated by different neural circuits despite the fact that they culminate in a set of symptoms that are partially shared. It is apparent that traditional methods for parsing heterogeneity on the basis of descriptive phenomenology are not yielding clean separation of underlying neural circuitry. For example, the melancholic versus nonmelancholic distinction does not systematically reveal differences in neural correlates (see below). Recommendations for moving beyond phenomenology and toward a more objective, laboratory-based parsing of affective processing abnormalities are provided throughout this chapter.

We have three broad goals for this chapter: (*a*) to review the functional role of the prefrontal cortices, anterior cingulate, hippocampus, and amygdala in affect and emotion regulation [see Figure 1 (color insert) for a depiction of these structures and their locations]; (*b*) to review the functional and structural abnormalities that have been found in these regions in depression; (*c*) based upon the first and second goals above, to advance hypotheses about symptom clusters that may arise as a consequence of dysfunctions in specific regions and to offer suggestions for different ways of parsing the heterogeneity of depression in ways that more directly honor the circuitry of emotion and emotion regulation in the brain.

THE CIRCUITRY OF EMOTION

Prefrontal Cortex

FUNCTIONAL AND ANATOMICAL CONSIDERATIONS FOR UNDERSTANDING ITS ROLE IN AFFECT AND DEPRESSION   Abnormalities in activation of prefrontal regions in depression have been reported more frequently than for any other brain region, mostly in the direction of decreased bilateral or predominantly left-sided activation (Davidson et al. 1999, George et al. 1994). Miller & Cohen (2001) have recently outlined a comprehensive theory of prefrontal function based upon non-human primate anatomical and neurophysiological studies, human neuroimaging findings, and computational modeling. The core feature of their model holds that the prefrontal cortex (PFC) maintains the representation of goals and the means to achieve them. Particularly in situations that are ambiguous, the PFC sends bias signals to other areas of the brain to facilitate the expression of task-appropriate responses in the face of competition with potentially stronger alternatives. In the affective domain we often confront situations in which the arousal of emotion is inconsistent with other goals that have already been instantiated. For example, the availability of an immediate reward may provide a potent response alternative that may not be in the best service of a person's overall goals. In such a case the PFC is required to produce a bias signal to other brain regions that guide behavior toward the acquisition of a more adaptive goal, which in this case would entail delay of gratification.

Affect-guided planning and anticipation that involves the experience of emotion associated with an anticipated choice is the hallmark of adaptive, emotion-based decision making that has repeatedly been found to become impaired in patients with lesions of ventromedial PFC (Damasio 1994). Affect-guided anticipation is most often accomplished in situations that are heavily laden with competition from potentially stronger alternatives. In such cases in particular, we would expect PFC activation to occur. Certain subtypes of depression may be caused by abnormalities of affect-guided anticipation. For example, the failure to anticipate positive incentives and direct behavior toward the acquisition of appetitive goals are symptoms of depression that may arise from abnormalities in the circuitry that implements positive affect-guided anticipation. Our laboratory has contributed extensively to the literature on asymmetries in PFC function associated with approach- and withdrawal-related emotion and mood (e.g., Davidson & Irwin 1999, Davidson et al. 2000a). In this context we suggest that left-sided PFC regions are particularly involved in approach-related, appetitive goals. The instantiation of such goals, particularly in the face of strong alternative responses, requires left-sided PFC activation and hypoactivation in these circuits has been linked to depression. Right-sided PFC regions, alternatively, are hypothesized to be particularly important in the maintenance of goals that require behavioral inhibition and withdrawal in situations that involve strong alternative response options to approach. The prototype of such a process has recently been captured in several neuroimaging studies that involve variants of a go/no go task in which a dominant response set is established to respond quickly, except in those trials on which a cue to inhibit the response is presented. Two recent studies using event-related functional magnetic resonance imaging (fMRI) have found a lateralized focus of activation in the right lateral PFC (inferior frontal sulcus) to cues that signaled response inhibition that were presented in the context of other stimuli toward which a strong approach set was established (Garavan et al. 1999, Konishi et al. 1999).

Depressed individuals with hypoactivation in certain regions of the PFC may be deficient in the instantiation of goal-directed behavior and in the overriding of more automatic responses that may involve the perseveration of negative affect and dysfunctional attitudes. Such deficits would be expected to be unmasked in situations in which decision-making is ambiguous and in which the maintenance of goal-directed behavior is required in the face of potentially strong alternative responses. As we argue below, when the strong alternative responses involve affect, which they often do, the ventromedial PFC is particularly implicated.

Recent neuroimaging and electrophysiological studies suggest that the orbital and ventral frontal cortex may be especially important for the representation of rewards and punishments, and different sectors within this cortex may emphasize reward versus punishment (Kawasaki et al. 2001, O'Doherty et al. 2001). In particular, a left-sided medial region of the orbital frontal cortex (OFC) appears responsive to rewards, whereas a lateral right-sided region appears responsive to punishments (O'Doherty et al. 2001). Kawasaki and colleagues (2001) recorded from single units in the right ventral PFC of patients with implanted depth electrodes for presurgical planning. They found these neurons in healthy tissue to exhibit short-latency responses to aversive visual stimuli. Such studies provide important clues regarding the circuitry that might be most relevant to understanding abnormalities associated with depression. It will be important in the future to evaluate the performance of depressed patients on a task of this kind with neuroimaging. Differential responsivity to rewards versus punishments has been found behaviorally in two studies in our laboratory (Henriques et al. 1994, Henriques & Davidson 2000). In particular, whereas normal individuals exhibited systematic modification of response bias to monetary reward, depressed patients failed to show such changes but did show response bias shifts in response to monetary punishment. On the basis of these findings, we predict that left medial OFC would be hyporesponsive to manipulations of reward in such patients, whereas right lateral OFC activation to punishment would either be normal or perhaps accentuated.

PREFRONTAL CORTEX IN DEPRESSION: THE FINDINGS   Consistent with prior literature, recent reports have documented decreased activation in both dorsolateral and dorsomedial PFC as well as the pregenual region of the anterior cingulate gyrus in patients with major depressive disorder (see Drevets 1998 for comprehensive review). The reduction in activation in this latter region, particularly on the left side, appears to be at least partially a function of a reduction in the volume of gray matter as revealed by magnetic resonance imaging-derived morphometric measures (Drevets et al. 1997). Consistent with the notion that the metabolic reduction found in this region is at least partially a function of the volume reduction, Drevets et al. (1997) have reported that remission of symptoms associated with successful treatment is not accompanied by a normalization of activation in this area.

This general decrease in dorsolateral PFC and in the pregenual region of the anterior cingulate cortex (ACC) tends to be accompanied by an increase in other regions of the PFC, particularly in the ventrolateral and orbital (lateral and medial) zones. Treatment studies have found that activation in dorsolateral PFC, particularly on the left side, increases following successful antidepressant treatment (Kennedy et al. 2001). Less consistent are findings for ventrolateral and orbital PFC regions. Some studies have found increases in these regions (Kennedy et al. 2001), but others have reported decreases (e.g., Brody et al. 1999, Mayberg et al. 1999).

As suggested above, recent reports of anatomical differences in the PFC are of critical import to any claims made about functional differences between depressed patients and normal controls. Consistent with earlier work conducted by Coffey et al. (1993), who found a sample of 48 depressed inpatients to have frontal lobe volumes that were 7% smaller than 76 nonpsychiatric controls, Drevets et al. (1997) reported that unipolar and bipolar depressives with a family history of mood disorders showed a 48% and 39% reduction in subgenual PFC volume, respectively. In a postmortem study by the same group (Öngür et al. 1998b), glial cell number was significantly reduced in subgenual PFC in both unipolar (24%) and bipolar (41%) patients with a family history of major depressive disorder (MDD). No significant effects were observed for nonfamilial MDD or bipolar disorder.

Rajkowska (2000) has further examined alterations in neuronal and glial histopathology in postmortem brains of patients who suffered from mood disorders. She and her colleagues found that left prefrontal cortices (no other brain areas were examined) of MDD subjects had decreases in cortical thickness, neuronal size, and neuronal and glial densities in upper cortical layers (II-IV) of left rostral OFC; decreases in neuronal size and glial densities in lower cortical layers (V-VI); and decreases in neuronal and glial size and density in supra- and infragranular layers. Of note, they found a 12–15% reduction of cortical thickness in the lateral OFC. Furthermore, they argued that the 22–37% reduction in density of large neurons and 6–27% increase of small neurons in the rostral OFC and dorsolateral PFC (DLPFC) may implicate cell atrophy rather than cell loss as the mechanism for the reduced cortical volume seen in depression. Similar results were observed in the left DLPFC of bipolar patients. These brains were characterized by a 16–22% reduction in neuronal density in layer III, a 17–30% reduction in pyramidal cell density in layers III and V, and a 19% reduction in glial density in sublayer IIIc. The fact that these anatomical differences in the brain of patients with mood disorders might account for some of the functional differences noted by Drevets et al. (1997) does not in itself provide any direct measures of causal influence. Longitudinal studies of patients at risk for mood disorders are needed to ascertain whether these structural differences are present prior to the onset of a depressive episode. Heritable factors can be examined by studying monozygotic twins discordant for mood disorders to ascertain whether the anatomical abnormalities are found in the affected twin only.

The common observation in electroencephalographic (EEG) studies of an altered pattern of asymmetric activation in anterior scalp regions in the direction of reduced left relative to right activation in depressed or dysphoric individuals has also been replicated several times in recent years (Bell et al. 1998, Bruder et al. 1997, Debener et al. 2000, Gotlib et al. 1998, Pauli et al. 1999, Reid et al. 1998). However, it should be noted that this asymmetry is not invariably found (e.g., Kentgen et al. 2000, Reid et al. 1998). Reid et al. and Davidson (1998) have discussed various methodological and conceptual issues related to the inconsistencies in the literature. One of the most important of these issues concerns the manner in which statistical tests of the hypothesized group difference in frontal asymmetry are conducted. In the Reid et al. report an analysis of variance (ANOVA) was conducted on the asymmetry scores (log right minus log left alpha power; higher numbers on this index reflect greater relative left-sided activation) (see Davidson et al. 2000b for discussion of EEG recording procedures) with group and site as factors. The site factor was comprised of asymmetry scores from several sites in both anterior and posterior scalp regions. Reid et al. required that the group X site interaction reach significance. The problem with this approach, as noted by Davidson (1998), is that right-sided parietal activation has been reported to be associated with elevations in anxiety (Heller & Nitschke 1998, Davidson et al. 2000c), and of course, many depressed subjects have elevations in anxiety as part of their symptom picture. Thus, a main effect for group rather than a group X site interaction might be expected for depressed subjects with some comorbid anxiety symptoms. Also important is the nature of the control group utilized in these studies. Some studies have used normal control groups that have been screened for lifetime history of psychopathology (e.g., Henriques & Davidson 1991), whereas others have used a more heterogeneous group of controls (e.g., Reid et al. 1998).

Finally, the temporal stability of electrophysiological measures of asymmetric anterior activation may differ in depressed patients relative to controls. Debener et al. (2000) recently confirmed our original observations (Schaffer et al. 1983, Henriques & Davidson 1991) of greater relative right-sided frontal activation in depressed patients compared with controls using data that were averaged across two recording sessions separated by 2–4 weeks. In addition, Debener et al. (2000) confirmed our report of reliable test-retest stability in electrophysiological measures of anterior scalp activation asymmetries (Tomarken et al. 1992). However, Debener et al. also reported that the test-retest stability for depressed patients was poor and suggested that another feature of prefrontal activation asymmetry that marks depression is increased variability. This suggestion, as well as the other procedural and methodological issues noted above, requires careful study in the future.

In an important extension of the work on electrophysiological asymmetries, Bruder and his colleagues (Bruder et al. 2001) examined whether brain electrical asymmetry measures obtained during a pretreatment period predicted response to a selective serotonin reuptake inhibitor (SSRI) treatment. They found that among women in particular, the treatment responders had significantly less relative right-sided activation compared with the nonresponders, though this effect was present in both anterior and posterior scalp regions. Based upon the role of right prefrontal regions in components of negative affect (Davidson 2000) and right posterior regions in arousal and anxiety (Heller & Nitschke 1998), these findings imply that those subjects with global right-activation who would be expected to have symptoms of negative affect and anxious arousal are least likely to show improvements with SSRI treatment.

Anterior Cingulate Cortex

FUNCTIONAL AND ANATOMICAL CONSIDERATIONS FOR UNDERSTANDING ITS ROLE IN AFFECT AND DEPRESSION   Several theories have proposed that the anterior cingulate cortex (ACC) acts as a bridge between attention and emotion (Devinsky et al. 1995, Ebert & Ebmeier 1996, Mayberg 1997, Vogt et al. 1995). In their recent review, Thayer & Lane (2000) described the ACC as "a point of integration for visceral, attentional, and affective information that is critical for self-regulation and adaptability" (p. 211). In light of its anatomical connections (see below), the ACC appears well equipped for assessing and responding to the behavioral significance of external stimuli. Critical roles of the ACC in selective attention (i.e., prioritizing incoming information), affect, and specific characteristic mammalian social behaviors have been described (Devinsky et al. 1995, Vogt et al. 1992). However, in order to fully understand the role of the ACC in psychopathology, affective states, and emotional processing, it is critical to recognize that the ACC is far from being a functionally homogeneous region, and at least two subdivisions can be discerned (Devinsky et al. 1995, Vogt et al. 1992, 1995). The first, referred to as the affect subdivision, encompasses rostral and ventral areas of the ACC (Brodmann's areas 25, 32, 33, and rostral area 24). The second, referred to as the cognitive subdivision, involves dorsal regions of the ACC (caudal area 24' and 32' and cingulate motor area). The affect subdivision possesses extensive connections with limbic and paralimbic regions—such as the amygdala, nucleus accumbens, OFC, periaqueductal grey, anterior insula, and autonomic brainstem motor nuclei—and is assumed to be involved in regulating visceral and autonomic responses to stressful behavioral and emotional events, emotional expression, and social behavior. Owing to its strong connections with the lateral hypothalamus, the subgenual ACC Brodman's area 25 (BA 25) is considered the most important region within the frontal cortex for regulating autonomic function (Öngür et al. 1998a).

Conversely, the cognitive subdivision is intimately connected with the DLPFC (BA 46/9), posterior cingulate, parietal cortex (BA 7), supplementary motor area, and spinal cord and plays an important role in response selection and processing of cognitively demanding information. In functional neuroimaging studies, evidence suggesting a functional differentiation between ventral (affective) and dorsal (cognitive) ACC subdivisions is emerging (Bush et al. 1998, 2000; Whalen et al. 1998) (see Figure 2, color insert).

From a functional perspective, activation of the cognitive subdivision of the ACC has been reported during interference between competing information (Pardo et al. 1990), visual attention (Nobre et al. 1997), monitoring of cognitive (Carter et al. 2000, MacDonald et al. 2000) and reward-related (Rogers et al. 1999) conflicts, task difficulty (Paus et al. 1997), and increased risk-associated outcome uncertainty (Critchley et al. 2001), among other experimental manipulations. A common denominator among these experimental conditions is that they all required modulation of attention or executive functions and monitoring of competition (Bush et al. 2000). Cohen and colleagues (Carter et al. 1999, 2000; Miller & Cohen 2001) have emphasized the role of the ACC in conflict monitoring. These authors proposed that the ACC may serve an evaluative function, reflecting the degree of response conflict elicited by a given task. Conflict occurs when two or more possible task-related decisions compete with or interfere with each other. According to the "competition monitoring hypothesis," the cognitive subdivision of the ACC monitors conflicts or crosstalk between brain regions. If a signal of competition emerges, this output signals the need for controlled processing. The DLPFC (BA 9) is assumed to be critical for this form of controlled processing, in that it represents and maintains task demands necessary for such control and inhibits (see e.g., Garavan et al. 1999) or increases neural activity in brain regions implicated in the competition. Thus, dorsal ACC activation leading to a call for further processing by other brain regions may represent a mechanism for effortful control. Activation of the affective subdivision of the ACC has been reported during various emotional states and manipulations (for reviews, see Reiman 1997, Bush et al. 2000; see also Figure 2). What could be a common denominator underlying activation of the rostral/ventral ACC in such disparate experimental conditions, such as pain, classical conditioning, transient mood, primal affect, Stroop task, and perceiving facial expressions, all of which have been reported in the literature? A possible answer to this question is that the affective subdivision of the ACC may be critical for assessing the presence of possible conflicts between the current functional state of the organism and incoming information with potentially relevant motivational and emotional consequences. This suggestion is based on the observation that the affective subdivision of the ACC is involved in behaviors characterized by monitoring and evaluation of performance, internal states, and presence of reward or punishment, which often require change in behavior.

Evidence suggests that ACC activation may be present when effortful emotional regulation is required in situations in which behavior is failing to achieve a desired outcome or when affect is elicited in contexts that are not normative, which includes most laboratory situations (Bush et al. 2000, Ochsner & Barrett 2001). Similarly it is not surprising that the ACC is one of the most consistently activated regions in patients with different anxiety disorders, such as obsessive compulsive disorder (Breiter et al. 1996, Rauch et al. 1997), simple phobia (Rauch et al. 1995), and posttraumatic stress disorder (Rauch et al. 1996, Shin et al. 1997), in which conflicts between response tendencies and environments are prominent. Interestingly, psychosurgical lesions of the ACC have been used as a treatment for mood and anxiety disorders (e.g., Baer et al. 1995; for review, see Binder & Iskandar 2000), possibly because of a reduction of conflict monitoring and uncertainty that otherwise characterize these psychiatric conditions.

ANTERIOR CINGULATE CORTEX IN DEPRESSION: THE FINDINGS   In major depression, decreased ACC activation relative to controls has been repeatedly reported. In single photon emission computed tomography studies, decreased regional cerebral blood flow in the left (Curran et al. 1993, Mayberg et al. 1994) or right (Ito et al. 1996) ACC has been found in medicated depressed unipolar patients compared with controls. Decreased ACC activation has been replicated with positron emission tomography (PET) (Bench et al. 1992, Drevets et al. 1997, George et al. 1997, Kumar et al. 1993) and fMRI (Beauregard et al. 1998) techniques. Interestingly, as shown in Figure 2, the region of the ACC found to be hypoactive in major depression (dorsal ACC: dorsal region of areas 32, 24′, 32′) appears to be different from the one found to be hyperactive in eventual treatment responders (ventral and rostral ACC, including pregenual areas 24 and 32). Whereas the state of being depressed is associated with reduced dorsal ACC activity (see above), remission has been characterized by increased activity in the same region (Bench et al. 1995, Buchsbaum et al. 1997, Mayberg et al. 1999). Similarly the increased activity in the rostral ACC characteristic of treatment responders (Mayberg et al. 1997; Ebert et al. 1991; Pizzagalli et al. 2001; Wu et al. 1992, 1999) has been shown to normalize (i.e., decrease) in the same subjects after sleep deprivation (Wu et al. 1999, Smith et al. 1999). Based on these findings, recent neurobiological models of depression have highlighted the role of the ACC in the pathogenesis of depression and in the manifestation of its symptomatology (Drevets 2001, Ebert & Ebmeier 1996, Mayberg 1997).

Based on the functional neuroimaging and animal literature reviewed above, it is conceivable to postulate that (*a*) hypoactivation in dorsal regions of the ACC (BA 24', 32') may be associated with impaired modulation of attention or executive functions and impaired monitoring of competition among various response options; and (*b*) hypoactivation in ventral regions of the ACC (BA 24, 32) may be associated with blunted conscious experience of affect, hypoarousal, anhedonia, reduced coping potential in situations characterized by uncertainty, conflict, and expectancy violation between the environment and one's affective state. Whereas future studies will need to specifically test these assumptions, recent findings are in good agreement with some of them. In a recent PET study Brody et al. (2001) found that reduction of anxiety/somatization symptoms was associated with decreased activation in the ventral ACC. Conversely, improvements in psychomotor retardation symptoms were associated with increased activation in the dorsal ACC. In a recent combined EEG-PET study using source localization, we observed that melancholic depressed subjects showed evidence of hypoactivation in BA 25 compared with both nonmelancholic depressed and control subjects (D Pizzagalli, T Oakes, CL Larson, AM Hendrick, KA Horras, RJ Davidson, unpublished data).

The interplay between the affective and cognitive subdivision of the ACC is unknown. From a theoretical perspective, several authors have suggested that the affective subdivision of the ACC may integrate salient affective and cognitive information (such as that derived from environmental stimuli or task demands), and subsequently modulate attentional processes within the cognitive subdivision accordingly (Mega et al. 1997, Mayberg 1997, Mayberg et al. 1999, Pizzagalli et al. 2001). In agreement with this hypothesis, dorsal anterior and posterior cingulate pathways devoted to attentional processes and amygdalar pathways devoted to affective processing converge within area 24 (Mega et al. 1997). These mechanisms may be especially important for understanding the repeatedly demonstrated finding that increased pretreatment activity in the rostral ACC is associated with eventual better treatment response (Mayberg et al. 1997; Ebert et al. 1991; Pizzagalli et al. 2001; Wu et al. 1992, 1999). In an influential paper, Mayberg and colleagues (1997) reported that unipolar depressed patients who responded to treatment after 6 weeks showed higher pretreatment glucose metabolism in a rostral region of the ACC (BA 24a/b) compared with both nonresponders and nonpsychiatric comparison subjects. Recently, we (Pizzagalli et al. 2001) replicated this finding with EEG source localization techniques and demonstrated that even among those patients who respond to treatment, the magnitude of treatment response was predicted by baseline levels of activation in the same region of the ACC as identified by Mayberg et al. (1997). In addition, we suggested that hyperactivation of the rostral ACC in depression might reflect an increased sensitivity to affective conflict such that the disparity between one's current mood and the responses expected in a particular context activates this region of ACC, which then in turn issues a call for further processing to help resolve the conflict. This call for further processing is hypothesized to aid the treatment response.

One of the major outputs from the ACC is a projection to the PFC. This pathway may be the route via which the ACC issues a call to the PFC for further processing to address a conflict that has been detected. Abnormalities in PFC function in depression may thus arise as a consequence of the failure of the normal signals from ACC, or may be intrinsic to the PFC, or both. It is also possible and even likely that there are different subtypes of depression that may involve more primary dysfunction in different parts of the circuitry that we review in this chapter. We address this issue in more detail at the end of the chapter, but for now it is important to underscore the possibility that there may exist a primary ACC-based depression subtype and a primary PFC-based depression subtype. These subtypes might not conform to the phenomenological and descriptive nosologies that are currently prevalent in the psychiatric literature. The ACC-subtype may be reflected phenomenologically in a deficit in the "will-to-change," as such patients would not experience the conflict between their current state and the demands of everyday life. The PFC-subtype may fully experience such conflict and experience pronounced distress because the experience of the conflict between one's current state and the demands of everyday life are not sufficient to activate PFC-based mechanisms to organize and guide behavior toward the resolution of the conflict.

The findings reviewed above on PFC and ACC activation and morphological differences in depressed patients compared with controls underscore the considerable specificity within this region of the brain. There are important differences in connectivity between adjacent regions of cortical tissue, and future studies should examine patterns of functional connectivity in addition to activation differences that may distinguish between depressed patients and controls.

Hippocampus

FUNCTIONAL AND ANATOMICAL CONSIDERATIONS FOR UNDERSTANDING ITS ROLE IN AFFECT AND DEPRESSION   The hippocampus is critically involved in episodic, declarative, contextual, and spatial learning and memory (Squire & Knowlton

2000, Fanselow 2000). It is also involved in the regulation of adrenocorticotropic hormone secretion (Jacobson & Sapolsky 1991). With respect to conditioning, in recent years rodent studies have convincingly shown that the hippocampus plays a key role in the formation, storage, and consolidation of contextual fear conditioning (see Fanselow 2000 for review). In this form of hippocampal-dependent Pavlovian conditioning, fear (e.g., expressed in increased freezing) is acquired to places or contexts (e.g., a specific cage) previously associated with aversive events (e.g., shock). This fact has important implications for our understanding of the abnormalities in affective function that may arise as a consequence of hippocampal dysfunction.

In functional neuroimaging studies, hippocampal/parahippocampal activation has been reported during perception of several negatively valenced stimuli and/or experiencing of negatively valenced affective states, such as trace conditioning (Büchel et al. 1999), perception of aversive complex stimuli (Lane et al. 1997), threat-related words (Isenberg et al. 1999), increasing music dissonance (Blood et al. 1999), tinnitus-like aversive auditory stimulation (Mirz et al. 2000), vocal expressions of fear (Phillips et al. 1998), aversive taste (Zald et al. 1998), anticipatory anxiety (Javanmard et al. 1999), and procaine-induced affect (Ketter et al. 1996, Servan-Schreiber et al. 1998). However, it seems that valence is not the critical variable for evoking hippocampal activation. Indeed, hippocampal activation has been also reported during experimental manipulation of positive affect, such as re-evoking pleasant affective autobiographical memories (Fink et al. 1996), increases in winning in a game-like task (Zalla et al. 2000), and perception of a loved person (Bartels & Zeki 2000). Hippocampal activation was also correlated with long-term recognition memory for pleasant films (Hamann et al. 1999).

To reconcile these findings, we suggest that most of the experimental manipulations leading to hippocampal activation contain contextual cues. That is, we assume that they involve the consolidation of a memory for an integrated representation of a context similar to that associated with the presented stimulus (Fanselow 2000). This is clearly the case during Pavlovian and trace conditioning, for instance, but also during presentation of both positively and negatively valenced visual, olfactory, and auditory cues that may induce re-evocation and consolidation of contextual information associated with a similar situation in the past (see e.g., Nader et al. 2000).

Although in humans the mechanisms underlying contextual conditioning are still unclear, it is possible that plasticity in functional connectivity between the hippocampus and regions crucially involved in decoding the behavioral significance of incoming information, such as the amygdala and the pulvinar, may critically contribute to contextual learning (Morris et al. 1997, 1999), even when the information is presented below the level of conscious awareness (Morris et al. 1999). As recently reviewed by Davis & Whalen (2001), animal studies clearly suggest that the amygdala exerts a modulatory influence on hippocampal-dependent memory systems, possibly through direct projections from the basolateral nucleus of the amygdala. Consistent with this view, stimulation of the amygdala causes long term potentiation (LTP) in the dentate gyrus of the hippocampus (Ikegaya et al. 1995a). Conversely, lesions to (Ikegaya et al. 1994) or local anesthetics within (Ikegaya et al. 1995b) the basolateral nucleus of the amygdala attenuate LTP in the dentate gyrus. Although extending conclusions from these rodent studies to humans is speculative at this stage, it is intriguing that most of the human neuroimaging studies reporting hippocampal activation during aversive affective manipulations also found amygdalar activation (Büchel et al. 1999, Isenberg et al. 1999, Ketter et al. 1996, Mirz et al. 2000, Servan-Schreiber et al. 1998, Zald et al. 1998). Future neuroimaging studies should directly test the interplay between the hippocampus and the amygdala in these processes and in fear-related learning and memory, especially in light of recent animal data suggesting an interaction between these regions for modulating extinction of conditioned fear (Corcoran & Maren 2001).

HIPPOCAMPUS AND DEPRESSION: THE FINDINGS   In their recent review, Davidson, and colleagues (Davidson et al. 2000a) noted that various forms of psychopathology involving disorders of affect could be characterized as disorders in context regulation of affect. That is, patients with mood and anxiety disorders often display normative affective responses but in inappropriate contexts. For example, fear that may be appropriate in response to an actual physical threat but persists following the removal of that threat, or sadness that may be appropriate in the acute period following a loss but persists for a year following that loss, are both examples of context-inappropriate emotional responding. In these examples the intensity and form of the emotion would be perfectly appropriate in response to the acute challenges, but when they occur in the absence of those acute stresses they can be viewed as context-inappropriate.

Given the preclinical and functional neuroimaging literature reviewed above, one may hypothesize that patients showing inappropriate context regulation of affect may be characterized by hippocampal dysfunction. Consistent with this conjecture, recent morphometric studies using MRI indeed reported smaller hippocampal volumes in patients with major depression (Sheline et al. 1996, 1999; Shah et al. 1998; Bremner et al. 2000; von Gunten et al. 2000; Steffens et al. 2000; Mervaala et al. 2000; but see Vakili et al. 2000, Ashtari et al. 1999), bipolar disorder (Noga et al. 2001), posttraumatic stress disorder (Bremner et al. 1995, 1997b, Stein et al. 1997), and borderline personality disorder (Driessen et al. 2000) (for review, see Sapolsky 2000, Sheline 2000). Where hippocampal volume reductions in depression have been found, the magnitude of reduction ranges from 8 to 19%. Recently, functional hippocampal abnormalities in major depression have also been reported at baseline using PET measures of glucose metabolism (Saxena et al. 2001). Whether hippocampal dysfunction precedes or follows onset of depressive symptomatology is still unknown.

In depression, inconsistencies across studies may be explained by several methodological considerations. First, as pointed out by Sheline (2000), studies reporting positive findings generally used MRI with higher spatial resolution

(∼0.5–2 mm) compared with those reporting negative findings (∼3–10 mm). Second, it seems that age, severity of depression, and most significantly, duration of recurrent depression may be important moderator variables. Indeed, studies reporting negative findings either studied younger cohorts [e.g., Vakili et al. (2000): 38 ± 10 years vs. Sheline et al. (1996): 69 ± 10 years; von Gunten et al. (2000): 58 ± 9 years; Steffens et al. (2000): 72 ± 8 years] or less severe and less chronic cohorts (Ashtari et al. 1999 vs. Sheline et al. 1996, Shah et al. 1998, Bremner et al. 2000). In a recent study (Rusch et al. 2002) we also failed to find hippocampal atrophy in a relatively young subject sample (33.2 ± 9.5 years) with moderate depression severity. Notably, in normal early adulthood (18–42 years), decreased bilateral hippocampal volume has been reported with increasing age in male but not female healthy subjects (Pruessner et al. 2001). Finally, in females initial evidence suggests that total lifetime duration of depression, rather than age is associated with hippocampal atrophy (Sheline et al. 1999), inviting the possibility that hippocampal atrophy may be a symptom rather than a cause of depression. Future studies should carefully assess the relative contribution of these possible modulatory variables in the hippocampal pathophysiology and examine hippocampal changes longitudinally in individuals at risk for mood disorders.

Structurally, the hippocampal changes may arise owing to neuronal loss through chronic hypercortisolemia, glial cell loss, stress-induced reduction in neurotrophic factors, or stress-induced reduction in neurogenesis, but the precise mechanisms are not completely known (Sheline 2000). In depression, the hypothesis of an association between sustained, stress-related elevations of cortisol and hippocampal damage has received considerable attention. This hypothesis is based on the observation that the pathophysiology of depression involves dysfunction in negative feedback of the hypothalamic-pituitary-adrenal axis (see Pariante & Miller 2001 for a review), which results in increased levels of cortisol during depressive episodes (e.g., Carroll et al. 1976). Higher levels of cortisol may, in turn, lead to neuronal damage in the hippocampus, because this region possesses high levels of glucocorticoid receptors (Reul & de Kloet 1986) and glucocorticoids are neurotoxic (Sapolsky et al. 1986). Because the hippocampus is involved in negative-feedback control of cortisol (Jacobson & Sapolsky 1991), hippocampal dysfunction may result in reduction of the inhibitory regulation of the hypothalamic-pituitary-adrenal axis, which could then lead to hypercortisolemia. Consistent with this view, chronic exposure to increased glucocorticoid concentrations has been shown to lower the threshold for hippocampal neuronal degeneration in animals (Gold et al. 1988, Sapolsky et al. 1990, McEwen 1998) and humans (Lupien et al. 1998). At least in nonhuman primates, this association is qualified by the observation that chronically elevated cortisol concentrations in the absence of chronic "psychosocial" stress do not produce hippocampal neuronal loss (Leverenz et al. 1999). Conversely, naturalistic, chronic psychosocial stress has been shown to induce structural changes in hippocampal neurons of subordinate animals (Magarinos et al. 1996). In depression, hippocampal volume loss has been shown to be associated with lifetime duration of depression (Sheline et al. 1999), consistent with the assumption that long-term exposure to high cortisol levels may lead to hippocampal atrophy. However, this conjecture has not been empirically verified in humans.

Although intriguing, these findings cannot inform us about the causality between hippocampal dysfunction, elevated levels of cortisol, and most importantly, inappropriate context regulation of affect in depression. Unfortunately, none of the structural neuroimaging studies in depression investigating hippocampal volume were prospective and took into account cortisol data in an effort to unravel the causal link between cortisol output and hippocampal dysfunction.

The possibility of plasticity in the hippocampus deserves particular comment. In rodents, recent studies have shown hippocampal neurogenesis as a consequence of antidepressant pharmacological treatment (Chen et al. 2000, Malberg et al. 2000), electroconvulsive shock (Madhav et al. 2000), and most intriguingly, as a consequence of positive handling, learning, and exposure to an enriched environment (Kempermann et al. 1997; see Gould et al. 2000 for review). Neurogenesis in the adult human hippocampus has also been reported (Eriksson et al. 1998). Further, in patients with Cushing's disease, who are characterized by very high levels of cortisol, increases in hippocampal volume were significantly associated with the magnitude of cortisol decrease produced by microadrenomectomy (Starkman et al. 1999). As a corpus, these animal and human data clearly suggest that plasticity in the human hippocampus is possible (for reviews, see Duman et al. 2000, Jacobs et al. 2000, Gould et al. 2000), a finding that suggests that structural and functional changes in the hippocampus of depressed patients may be reversible.

In summary, preclinical and clinical studies converge in suggesting an association between major depression and hippocampal dysfunction. Future studies should (*a*) assess whether hippocampal atrophy precedes or follows increased onset of depression, (*b*) assess the causal relation between hypercortisolemia and hippocampal volume reduction, (*c*) directly test a putative link between inappropriate context-dependent affective responding and hippocampal atrophy, and (*d*) assess putative treatment-mediated plastic changes in the hippocampus.

Amygdala

FUNCTIONAL AND ANATOMICAL CONSIDERATIONS FOR UNDERSTANDING ITS ROLE IN AFFECT AND DEPRESSION   Although a link between amygdala activity and negative affect has been a prevalent view in the literature, particularly when examined in response to exteroceptive aversive stimuli (e.g., LeDoux 2000), recent findings from invasive animal studies and human lesion and functional neuroimaging studies are converging on a broader view that regards the amygdala's role in negative affect as a special case of its more general role in directing attention to affectively salient stimuli and issuing a call for further processing of stimuli that have major significance for the individual. Evidence is consistent with the argument that the amygdala is critical for recruiting and coordinating cortical arousal and vigilant attention for optimizing sensory and perceptual processing of stimuli associated with underdetermined contingencies, such as novel, surprising, or ambiguous stimuli (see also Davis & Whalen 2001, Holland & Gallagher 1999, Whalen 1998). Most stimuli in this class may be conceptualized as having an aversive valence because we tend to have a negativity bias in the face of uncertainty (Taylor 1991).

AMYGDALA AND DEPRESSION: THE FINDINGS   In major depression, structural and functional abnormalities in the amygdala have been reported. Structurally, several recent studies reported an association between enlargement of amygdala volume and depression. This association has been found in depressed patients with bipolar disorders (Altshuler et al. 1998, Strakowski et al. 1999) as well as temporal lobe epilepsy (Tebartz van Elst et al. 1999, 2000). In a recent study Mervaala et al. (2000) observed significant asymmetry in amygdalar volumes (right smaller than left) in MDD patients but not the controls. In temporal lobe epilepsy patients with dysthymia, left amygdala volume was positively correlated with depression severity (Tebartz van Elst et al. 1999). Although these findings depict a relation between increased amygdalar volume and depression, it is important to stress that (*a*) the causal relations between the two entities are still unknown and (*b*) some inconsistencies among studies are present. Indeed, some studies reported either decreased bilateral volume in the amygdala core nuclei (Sheline et al. 1998) or null findings (Coffey et al. 1993, Pantel et al. 1997, Ashtari et al. 1999). Although the reasons are still unclear, it is interesting to note that two null findings were found in geriatric depression (Pantel et al. 1997, Ashtari et al. 1999).

Functionally, abnormal elevations of resting regional cerebral blood flow or glucose metabolism in the amygdala have been reported in depression during both wakefulness (Drevets et al. 1992) and sleep (Ho et al. 1996, Nofzinger et al. 1999). In a PET study Ho et al. (1996) reported increased absolute cerebral glucose metabolic in several brain regions, particularly the amygdala (+44%), in 10 unmedicated men with unipolar depression during non-rapid eye movement sleep. Further, in his recent review, Drevets (2001) reported data from five consecutive studies, in which increased regional cerebral blood flow or glucose metabolism has been consistently replicated in depressives with familial MDD or melancholic features. In a postmortem study, 5-HT2 receptor density was significantly increased in the amygdala of depressive patients committing suicide (Hrdina et al. 1993). Abnormally increased amygdalar activation has also been recently reported in bipolar depression (Ketter et al. 2001) and anxiety disorders, which often show a high degree of comorbidity with depression (Birbaumer et al. 1998; Liberzon et al. 1999; Rauch et al. 1996, 2000; Schneider et al. 1999; Semple et al. 2000; Shin et al. 1997).

Further establishing a link between depression and amygdalar activation, two studies have reported a positive correlation between amygdalar activation and depression severity or dispositional negative affect in patients with MDD (Drevets et al. 1992, Abercrombie et al. 1998). After pharmacologically induced remission from depression, amygdalar activation has been observed to decrease to normative values (Drevets 2001). In familial pure depressive disease, however, increased (left) amygdalar activation persists during the remitted phases (Drevets et al. 1992),

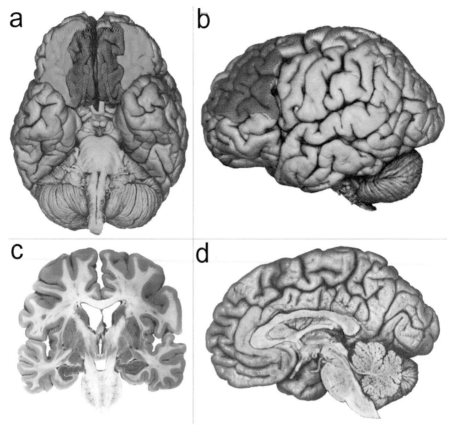

Figure 1 Key brain regions involved in affect and mood disorders. (*a*) Orbital prefrontal cortex (*green*) and the ventromedial prefrontal cortex (*red*). (*b*) Dorsolateral prefrontal cortex (*blue*). (*c*) Hippocampus (*purple*) and amygdala (*orange*). (*d*) Anterior cingulate cortex (*yellow*).

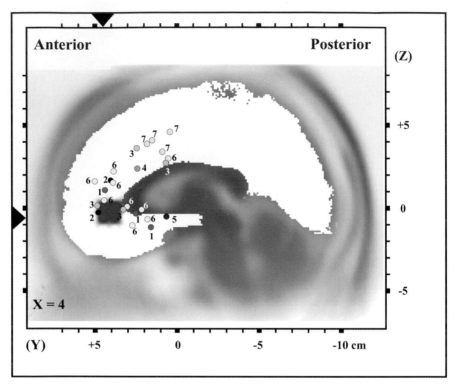

Figure 2 Summary of functional brain imaging studies of anterior cingulate cortex (ACC) involvement in depression as well as during various cognitive and affective task manipulations. Foci of ACC activation or deactivation were registered to a common stereotaxic brain atlas (Talairach & Tournoux 1988) and plotted on a sagittal brain slice (anterior part of the head to the left). The large red area and the black triangles show the location of the ACC cluster found to be associated with degree of treatment response in our previous EEG study (Pizzagalli et al. 2001). The studies of depressed subjects showed pretreatment hyperactivity among patients who responded to treatment (1); posttreatment decreased activity in responders (2); hypoactivity in depressed subjects (3); increased activity with remission of depression (4); and decreased activity with remission of depression (5). Studies involving emotional (6) and cognitive (7) tasks in nonpsychiatric subjects are also reported. Coordinates in mm (Talairach & Tournoux 1988), origin at anterior commissure; (X) = left (-) to right (+); (Y) = posterior (-) to anterior (+); (Z) = inferior (-) to superior (+). Adapted from Pizzagalli et al. (2001).

suggesting that at least in some subtypes of depression amygdalar dysfunction may be trait-like. Interestingly, remitted MDD patients showing symptom relapse as a consequence of serotonin depletion showed increased amygdalar activation prior to the depletion compared with those who do not relapse (Bremner et al. 1997a). Finally, in one of the first fMRI studies using an activation paradigm in depressed patients, Yurgelun-Todd et al. (2000) reported higher left amygdalar activation for bipolar patients than controls in response to fearful faces.

In light of the pivotal role of the amygdala in recruiting and coordinating vigilant behavior toward stimuli with underdetermined contingencies, hyperactivation of the amygdala in major depression may bias initial evaluation of and response to incoming information. Although still speculative, this mechanism may rely on norepinephrine, which (*a*) is oftentimes abnormally elevated in depression (e.g., Veith et al. 1994), (*b*) is involved in amygdala-mediated emotional learning (Ferry et al. 1999), and (*c*) is affected by glucocorticoid secretions, which are often elevated in MDD (e.g., Carroll et al. 1976). Thus, these findings may explain cognitive biases towards aversive or emotionally arousing information observed in depression.

Increased amygdalar activation in depression may also represent a possible bi-ological substrate for anxiety, which is often comorbid with depression. In this respect, elevated levels of glucocortocoid hormones—which characterize at least some subgroups of patients with depression—may be especially relevant, since el-evated glucocorticoid hormones have been shown to be associated with increased corticotropin-releasing hormone (CRH) in the amygdala. Increased CHR avail-ability may increase anxiety, fear and expectation for adversity (Schulkin 1994).

In light of evidence suggesting a link between amygdalar activation, on one hand, and memory consolidation and acquisition of long-term declarative knowl-edge about emotionally salient information, on the other, the observations of dys-functionally increased amygdalar activation in major depression are intriguing. As recently pointed out by Drevets (2001), tonically increased amygdalar activation during depressive episodes may favor the emergence of rumination based on in-creased availability of emotionally negative memories. Although still untested, it is possible that these aberrant processes may rely on dysfunctional interactions between the amygdala, the PFC, and the ACC. Notably, structural abnormalities have been reported in territories of the PFC intimately connected with the ACC (Drevets et al. 1997, Öngür et al. 1998b). ACC dysfunction, in particular, may lead to a decreased capability of monitoring potential conflict between memory-based ruminative processes and sensory information coming from the environment.

SUMMARY AND CONCLUSIONS

This chapter reviewed the circuitry that underlies the representation and regula-tion of emotion. It is this circuitry that exhibits different kinds of abnormalities in depression. Different territories of the PFC and ACC, the hippocampus, and the amygdala were considered. These structures are all interconnected in regionally specific ways and exhibit bi-directional feedback. Abnormalities in the morphometry and functioning of each of these structures have been reported in depression. Because longitudinal studies that involve the measurement of brain structure and function in at-risk individuals have not yet been performed, we cannot specify which of the abnormalities may be primary in the sense of occurring first, and which may be secondary to dysfunctions initially occurring in another brain region. For example, PFC abnormalities may arise as a consequence of ACC abnormalities or may be independent. In addition, a paucity of work has examined functional and/or structural connectivity among these regions. Some of the abnormalities in depression may arise as a consequence of impaired connectivity, either functional, structural, or both. Future research should include measures of both functional (e.g., Cordes et al. 2000) and structural connectivity. The latter can be measured with diffusion tensor imaging (Le Bihan et al. 2001).

We have drawn upon the animal and human literature on basic processes in emotion and emotion regulation to help interpret the abnormalities that have been reported in depression and to highlight the kinds of studies that have not yet been performed but are important to conduct. The findings on the basic processes in animals and normal humans provide the foundation for a model of the major components in affect representation and regulation. The input to affect representation can be either a sensory stimulus or a memory. Most sensory stimuli are relayed through the thalamus and from there they can take a short route to the amygdala (LeDoux 2000) and/or go up to cortex. From both association cortex and from subcortical regions including the amygdala, information is relayed to different zones of the PFC. The PFC plays a crucial role in the representation of goals. In the presence of ambiguous situations, the PFC sends bias signals to other brain regions to facilitate the expression of task-appropriate responses in the face of competition with potentially stronger alternatives. We argued that in the affective domain the PFC implements affect-guided anticipatory processes. Left-sided PFC regions are particularly involved in approach-related appetitive goals, whereas right-sided PFC regions are involved in the maintenance of goals that require behavioral inhibition. Abnormalities in PFC function would be expected to compromise goal-instantiation in patients with depression. Left-sided hypoactivation would result in deficits in pre-goal attainment forms of positive affect, whereas right-sided hyperactivation would result in excessive behavioral inhibition and anticipatory anxiety. Hypoactivation in regions of the PFC with which the amygdala is interconnected may result in a decrease in the regulatory influence on the amygdala and a prolonged time course of amygdala activation in response to challenge. This might be expressed phenomenologically as perseveration of negative affect and rumination.

The ACC is critically involved in conflict monitoring and is activated whenever an individual is confronted with a challenge that involves conflict among two or more response options. According to an influential theory of ACC function (Carter et al. 1999), the ACC monitors the conflicts among brain regions. When such conflict is detected, the ACC issues a call for further processing to the PFC that then adjudicates among the various response options and guides behavior toward a goal. The ACC is very frequently activated in neuroimaging studies of human emotion (see Bush et al. 2000 for review), in part because when emotion is elicited in the laboratory it produces response conflict. There is the general expectation to behave in an unemotional fashion because subjects are participating in a scientific experiment, yet there are the responses that are pulled by the emotional challenge, such as certain patterns of facial expression. This is commonly reported by subjects and is associated with ACC activation.

There is sometimes a conflict between an individual's mood state and the behavior that is expected of the individual in a particular social or role context. For example, among depressed individuals, their dispositional mood state may predispose them to set few goals and engage in little intentional action, yet the demands of their environments may include expectations to behave in specific ways. In an individual with normal levels of ACC activation, the signal from ACC would issue a call to other brain regions, the PFC being the most important, to resolve the conflict and engage in the appropriate goal-directed behavior. However, in an individual with abnormally low levels of ACC activation, the conflict between her dispositional mood state and the expectations of her context would not be effectively monitored and thus, the usual call for further processing would not be issued. The data on ACC function in depression most consistently reveal a pattern of decreased activation in certain regions of the ACC. Interestingly, those depressed patients with greater activation in the ventral ACC before antidepressant treatment are the ones most likely to show the largest treatment responses. In normal individuals, activation of the affective subdivision of the ACC may also be associated phenomonologically with the will to change.

The hippocampus appears to play an important role in encoding context. Lesions to the hippocampus in animals impair context conditioning. In addition, this structure has a high density of glucocorticoid receptors, and elevated levels of cortisol in animal models produce hippocampal cell death. In humans, various stress-related disorders, including depression, are associated with hippocampal volume reductions. Whether such hippocampal volume differences are a cause or a consequence of the depression cannot be answered from extant data. However, to the extent that hippocampal dysfunction is present, we would expect that such individuals would show abnormalities in the context-appropriate modulation of emotional behavior. This type of abnormality would be expressed as the display of normal emotion in inappropriate contexts. Thus, the persistence of sadness in situations that would ordinarily engender happiness could in part arise as a consequence of a hippocampally dependent problem in the context-modulation of emotional responses. We have shown such effects in rhesus monkeys (see Davidson et al. 2000a for review), but they have not yet been studied in depressed patients. The extensive connections between hippocampus and PFC would presumably provide the requisite anatomical substrate for conveying the contextual information to PFC to regulate emotional behavior in a context-appropriate fashion. The connections between hippocampus and PFC are another potential target of dysfunction in depression. It is possible that a certain subtype of individual exists wherein contextual encoding is intact and PFC-implemented goal-directed behavior is intact, but context fails to adequately guide and reprioritize goals. In such cases, the functional and/or anatomical connectivity between hippocampus and PFC might be a prime candidate for dysfunction. The tools are now available to examine both types of connectivity using noninvasive measures.

The amygdala has long been viewed as a key site for both the perception of cues that signal threat and the production of behavioral and autonomic responses associated with aversive responding. As we have noted above, current evidence suggests that the amygdala's role in negative affect may be a special case of its more general role in directing attention and resources to affectively salient stimuli and issuing a call for further processing of stimuli that have potentially major significance for the individual. As with other parts of the circuit we have addressed, there are extensive connections between the amygdala and each of the other structures we have considered. The amygdala receives input from a wide range of cortical zones and has even more extensive projections back to cortex, enabling the biasing of cortical processing as a function of the early evaluation of a stimulus as affectively salient. Also like the other components of the circuit we have described, there are individual differences in amygdala activation both at baseline (Schaefer et al. 2000) and in response to challenge (see Davidson & Irwin 1999 for review). Moreover, it is likely that regions of the PFC play an important role in modulating activation in the amygdala and thus influencing the time course of amygdala-driven negative affective responding. In light of the associations that have been reported between individual differences in amygdala activation and affect measures, it is likely that when it occurs, hyperactivation of the amygdala in depression is associated more with the fear-like and anxiety components of the symptoms than with the sad mood and anhedonia. We have found that amygdala activation predicts dispositional negative affect in depressed patients but is unrelated to variations in positive affect (Abercrombie et al. 1998). Excessive activation of the amygdala in depressed patients may also be associated with hypervigilance, particularly toward threat-related cues, which further exacerbates some of the symptoms of depression.

There are several types of studies that need to be performed in light of the evidence reviewed in this chapter. Studies that relate specific abnormalities in particular brain regions to objective laboratory tasks that are neurally inspired and designed to capture the particular kinds of processing that are hypothesized to be implemented in those brain regions is needed. Relatively few studies of this kind have been conducted. Studies on depressed patients that examine relations between individual differences in neural activity and psychological phenomena almost always relate such neural variation to symptom measures that are either self-report or interview-based indices. In the future it will be important to complement the phenomenological description with laboratory measures that are explicitly designed to highlight the processes implemented in different parts of the circuit that we described.

Such future studies should include measures of both functional and structural connectivity to complement the activation measures. It is clear that interactions among the various components of the circuitry we describe are likely to play a crucial role in determining behavioral output. Moreover, it is possible that connectional abnormalities may exist in the absence of abnormalities in specific structures.

Longitudinal studies of at-risk samples with the types of imaging measures that are featured in this review are crucial. We do not know if any of the abnormalities discussed above, both of a structural and functional variety, precede the onset of the disorder, co-occur with the onset of the disorder, or follow the expression of the disorder. It is likely that the timing of the abnormalities in relation to the clinical course of the disorder varies for different parts of the circuitry. The data reviewed earlier showing a relation between the number of cumulative days depressed over the course of the lifetime and hippocampal volume suggest that this abnormality may follow the expression of the disorder and represent a consequence rather than a primary cause of the disorder. However, before such a conclusion is accepted, it is important to conduct the requisite longitudinal studies to begin to disentangle these complex causal factors.

Finally, we regard the evidence presented in this review as offering very strong support for the view that depression refers to a heterogeneous group of disorders. It is possible that depression-spectrum disorders can be produced by abnormalities in many different parts of the circuitry reviewed. The specific subtype, symptom profile, and affective abnormalities should vary systematically with the location and nature of the abnormality. It is likely that some of the heterogeneity that might be produced by deficits in particular components of the circuitry reviewed will not map precisely onto the diagnostic categories we have inherited from descriptive psychiatry. A major challenge for the future will be to build a more neurobiologically plausible scheme for parsing the heterogeneity of depression based upon the location and nature of the abnormality in the featured circuitry. We believe that this ambitious effort will lead to considerably more consistent findings at the biological level and will also enable us to more rigorously characterize different endophenotypes that could then be exploited for genetic studies.

ACKNOWLEDGMENTS

The authors wish to thank Alexander J. Shackman and William Irwin for invaluable comments, and Andrew M. Hendrick, Kathryn A. Horras, Megan Zuelsdorff, and Jenna Topolovich for skilled and dedicated assistance in the preparation of the manuscript. Additional thanks to William Irwin for preparation of Figure 1. This work was supported by NIMH grants (MH40747, P50-MH52354, MH43454, P50-MH61083) and by an NIMH Research Scientist Award (K05-MH00875) to Richard J. Davidson. Diego Pizzagalli was supported by grants from the Swiss National Research Foundation (81ZH-52864) and "Holderbank"-Stiftung zur Förderung der wissenschaftlichen Fortbildung. Jack B. Nitschke was supported by NIMH Training grant T32-MH18931 and Katherine Putnam was supported by a NARSAD Young Investigator Award.

Visit the Annual Reviews home page at www.AnnualReviews.org

LITERATURE CITED

Abercrombie HC, Schaefer SM, Larson CL, Oakes TR, Holden JE, et al. 1998. Metabolic rate in the right amygdala predicts negative affect in depressed patients. *NeuroReport* 9:3301–7

Altshuler LL, Bartzokis G, Grieder T, Curran J, Mintz J. 1998. Amygdala enlargement in bipolar disorder and hippocampal reduction in schizophrenia: an MRI study demonstrating neuroanatomic specificity. *Arch. Gen. Psychiatry* 55:663–64

Ashtari M, Greenwald BS, Kramer-Ginsberg E, Hu J, Wu H, et al. 1999. Hippocampal/amygdala volumes in geriatric depression. *Psychol. Med.* 29:629–38

Baer L, Rauch SL, Ballantine HTJ, Martuza R, Cosgrove R, et al. 1995. Cingulotomy for intractable obsessive-compulsive disorder. Prospective long-term follow-up of 18 patients. *Arch. Gen. Psychiatry* 52:384–92

Bartels A, Zeki S. 2000. The neural basis of romantic love. *NeuroReport* 11:3829–34

Beauregard M, Leroux JM, Bergman S, Arzoumanian Y, Beaudoin G, et al. 1998. The functional neuroanatomy of major depression: an fMRI study using an emotional activation paradigm. *NeuroReport* 9:3253–58

Bell IR, Schwartz GE, Hardin EE, Baldwin CM, Kline JP. 1998. Differential resting quantitative electroencephalographic alpha patterns in women with environmental chemical intolerance, depressives, and normals. *Biol. Psychiatry* 43:376–88

Bench CJ, Frackowiak RS, Dolan RJ. 1995. Changes in regional cerebral blood flow on recovery from depression. *Psychol. Med.* 25:247–61

Bench CJ, Friston KJ, Brown RG, Scott LC, Frackowiak RS, Dolan RJ. 1992. The anatomy of melancholia—focal abnormalities of cerebral blood flow in major depression. *Psychol. Med.* 22:607–15

Binder DK, Iskandar BJ. 2000. Modern neurosurgery for psychiatric disorders. *Neurosurgery* 47:9–21

Birbaumer N, Grodd W, Diedrich O, Klose U, Erb E, et al. 1998. fMRI reveals amygdala activation to human faces in social phobics. *NeuroReport* 9:1223–26

Blood AJ, Zatorre RJ, Bermudez P, Evans AC. 1999. Emotional responses to pleasant and unpleasant music correlate with activity in paralimbic brain regions. *Nat. Neurosci.* 2:382–87

Breiter HC, Rauch SL, Kwong KK, Baker JR, Weisskoff RM, et al. 1996. Functional magnetic resonance imaging of symptom provocation in obsessive-compulsive disorder. *Arch. Gen. Psychiatry* 53:595–606

Bremner JD, Innis RB, Salomon RM, Staib LH, Ng CK, et al. 1997a. Positron emission tomography measurement of cerebral metabolic correlates of tryptophan depletion– induced depressive relapse. *Arch. Gen. Psychiatry* 54:364–74

Bremner JD, Narayan M, Anderson ER, Staib LH, Miller HL, Charney DS. 2000. Hippocampal volume reduction in major depression. *Am. J. Psychiatry* 157:115–18

Bremner JD, Randall P, Scott TM, Bronen RA, Seibyl JP, et al. 1995. MRI-based measurement of hippocampal volume in patients with combat-related posttraumatic stress disorder. *Am. J. Psychiatry* 152:973–81

Bremner JD, Randall P, Vermetten E, Staib LH, Bronen RA, et al. 1997b. Magnetic resonance imaging-based measurement of hippocampal volume in posttraumatic stress disorder related to childhood physical and sexual abuse—a preliminary report. *Biol. Psychiatry* 41:23–32

Brody AL, Saxena S, Mandelkern MA, Fairbanks LA, Ho ML, Baxter LR Jr. 2001. Brain metabolic changes associated with symptom factor improvement in major depressive disorder. *Biol. Psychiatry* 50:171–78

Brody AL, Saxena S, Silverman DH, Alborzian S, Fairbanks LA, et al. 1999. Brain metabolic changes in major depressive disorder from pre- to post-treatment with paroxetine. *Psychiatry Res.* 91:127–39

Bruder GE, Stewart JW, Mercier MA, Agosti V, Leite P, et al. 1997. Outcome of cognitive-behavioral therapy for depression: relation to hemispheric dominance for verbal processing. *J. Abnorm. Psychol.* 106:138–44

Bruder GE, Stewart JW, Tenke CE, McGrath PJ, Leite P, et al. 2001. Electroencephalographic and perceptual asymmetry differences between responders and nonresponders to an SSRI antidepressant. *Biol. Psychiatry* 49:416–25

Büchel C, Dolan R, Armony JL, Friston KJ. 1999. Amygdala-hippocampal involvement in human aversive trace conditioning revealed through event-related functional magnetic resonance imaging. *J. Neurosci.* 19: 10869–76

Buchsbaum MS, Wu J, Siegel BV, Hackett E, Trenary M, et al. 1997. Effect of sertraline on regional metabolic rate in patients with affective disorder. *Biol. Psychiatry* 41:15–22

Bush G, Luu P, Posner MI. 2000. Cognitive and emotional influences in anterior cingulate cortex. *Trends Cogn. Sci.* 4:215–22

Bush G, Whalen PJ, Rosen BR, Jenike MA, McInerney SC, Rauch SL. 1998. The counting Stroop: an interference task specialized for functional neuroimaging-validation study with functional MRI. *Hum. Brain Mapp.* 6:270–82

Carroll BJ, Curtis GC, Mendels J. 1976. Cerebrospinal fluid and plasma free cortisol concentrations in depression. *Psychol. Med.* 6: 235–44

Carter CS, Botvinick MM, Cohen JD. 1999. The contribution of the anterior cingulate cortex to executive processes in cognition. *Rev. Neurosci.* 10:49–57

Carter CS, Macdonald AM, Botvinick M, Ross LL, Stenger VA, et al. 2000. Parsing executive processes: strategic vs. evaluative functions of the anterior cingulate cortex. *Proc. Natl. Acad. Sci. USA* 97:1944–48

Chen G, Rajkowska G, Du F, Seraji-Bozorgzad N, Manji HK. 2000. Enhancement of hippocampal neurogenesis by lithium. *J. Neurochem.* 75:1729–34

Coffey CE, Wilkinson WE, Weiner RD, Parashos IA, Djang WT, et al. 1993. Quantitative cerebral anatomy in depression. A controlled magnetic resonance imaging study. *Arch. Gen. Psychiatry* 50:7–16

Corcoran KA, Maren S. 2001. Hippocampal inactivation disrupts contextual retrieval of fear memory after extinction. *J. Neurosci.* 21: 1720–26

Cordes D, Haughton VM, Arfanakis K, Wendt G, Turski PA, et al. 2000. Mapping functionally related regions of brain with functional connectivity MR imaging. *Am. J. Neuroradiol.* 21:1636–44

Critchley HD, Mathias CJ, Dolan RJ. 2001. Neural activity in the human brain relating to uncertainty and arousal during anticipation. *Neuron* 29:537–45

Curran SM, Murray CM, Van Beck M, Dougall N, O'Carroll RE, et al. 1993. A single photon emission computerised tomography study of regional brain function in elderly patients with major depression and with Alzheimer-type dementia. *Br. J. Psychiatry* 163:155–65

Damasio AR. 1994. *Descartes Error: Emotion, Reason, and the Human Brain.* New York: Avon

Davidson RJ. 1998. Anterior electrophysiological asymmetries, emotion and depression: conceptual and methological conundrums. *Psychophysiology* 35:607–14

Davidson RJ. 2000. Affective style, psychopathology and resilance: brain mechanisms and plasticity. *Am. Psychol.* 55:1196–214

Davidson RJ, Abercrombie HC, Nitschke JB, Putnam KM. 1999. Regional brain function, emotion and disorders of emotion. *Curr. Opin. Neurobiol.* 9:228–34

Davidson RJ, Irwin W. 1999. The functional neuroanatomy of emotion and affective style. *Trends Cogn. Sci.* 3:11–21

Davidson RJ, Jackson DC, Kalin NH. 2000a. Emotion, plasticity, context and regulation:

Perspectives from affective neuroscience. *Psychol. Bull.* 126:890–906

Davidson RJ, Jackson DC, Larson CL. 2000b. Human electroencephalography. In *Principles of Psychophysiology*, ed. JT Cacioppo, GG Bernston, LG Tassinary, pp. 27–52. New York: Cambridge Univ. Press. 2nd ed.

Davidson RJ, Marshall JR, Tomarken AJ, Henriques JB. 2000c. While a phobic waits: regional brain electrical and autonomic activity in social phobics during anticipation of public speaking. *Biol. Psychiatry* 47:85–95

Davidson RJ, Putnam KM, Larson CL. 2000d. Dysfunction in the neural circuitry of emotion regulation—a possible prelude to violence. *Science* 289:591–94

Davis M, Whalen PJ. 2001. The amygdala: vigilance and emotion. *Mol. Psychiatry* 6:13–34

Debener S, Beauducel A, Nessler D, Brocke B, Heilemann H, Kayser J. 2000. Is resting anterior EEG alpha asymmetry a trait marker for depression? Findings for healthy adults and clinically depressed patients. *Neuropsychobiology* 41:31–37

Devinsky O, Morrell MJ, Vogt BA. 1995. Contributions of anterior cingulate cortex to behaviour. *Brain* 118:279–306

Drevets WC. 1998. Functional neuroimaging studies of depression: the anatomy of melancholia. *Annu. Rev. Med.* 49:341–61

Drevets WC. 2001. Neuroimaging and neuropathological studies of depression: implications for the cognitive-emotional features of mood disorders. *Curr. Opin. Neurobiol.* 11:240–49

Drevets WC, Price JL, Simpson JRJ, Todd RD, Reich T, et al. 1997. Subgenual prefrontal cortex abnormalities in mood disorders. *Nature* 386:824–27

Drevets WC, Videen TO, Price JL, Preskorn SH, Carmichael ST, Raichle ME. 1992. A functional anatomical study of unipolar depression. *J. Neurosci.* 12:3628–41

Driessen M, Herrmann J, Stahl K, Zwaan M, Meier S, et al. 2000. Magnetic resonance imaging volumes of the hippocampus and the amygdala in women with borderline personality disorder and early traumatization. *Arch. Gen. Psychiatry* 57:1115–22

Duman RS, Malberg J, Nakagawa S, D'Sa C. 2000. Neuronal plasticity and survival in mood disorders. *Biol. Psychiatry* 48:732–39

Ebert D, Ebmeier KP. 1996. The role of the cingulate gyrus in depression: from functional anatomy to neurochemistry. *Biol. Psychiatry* 39:1044–50

Ebert D, Feistel H, Barocka A. 1991. Effects of sleep deprivation on the limbic system and the frontal lobes in affective disorders: a study with Tc–99m–HMPAO SPECT. *Psychiatry Res.* 40:247–51

Eriksson PS, Perfilieva E, Bjork-Eriksson T, Alborn A, Nordborg C, et al. 1998. Neurogenesis in the adult human hippocampus. *Nat. Med.* 4:1313–17

Fanselow MS. 2000. Contextual fear, gestalt memories, and the hippocampus. *Behav. Brain Res.* 110:73–81

Ferry B, Roozendaal B, McGaugh JL. 1999. Role of norepinephrine in mediating stress hormone regulation of long-term memory storage: a critical involvement of the amygdala. *Biol. Psychiatry* 46:1140–52

Fink GR, Markowitsch HJ, Reinkemeier M, Bruckbauer T, Kessler J, Heiss W. 1996. Cerebral representation of one's own past: neural networks involved in autobiographical memory. *J. Neurosci.* 16:4275–82

Garavan H, Ross RH, Stein EA. 1999. Right hemispheric dominance of inhibitory control: an event-related functional MRI study. *Proc. Natl. Acad. Sci. USA* 96:8301–6

George MS, Ketter TA, Parekh PI, Rosinsky N, Ring HA, et al. 1997. Blunted left cingulate activation in mood disorder subjects during a response interference task (the Stroop). *J. Neuropsychiatry Clin. Neurosci.* 9:55–63

George MS, Ketter TA, Post RM. 1994. Prefrontal cortex dysfunction in clinical depression. *Depression* 2:59–72

Gold PW, Goodwin FK, Chrousos GP. 1988. Clinical and biochemical manifestations of depression: relation to the neurobiology of stress. *N. Engl. J. Med.* 319:348–53

Gotlib IH, Ranganath C, Rosenfeld P. 1998. Frontal EEG alpha asymmetry, depression and cognitive functioning. *Cogn. Emot.* 12: 149–78

Gould E, Tanapat P, Rydel T, Hastings N. 2000. Regulation of hippocampal neurogenesis in adulthood. *Biol. Psychiatry* 48:715–20

Hamann SB, Ely TD, Grafton ST, Kilts CD. 1999. Amygdala activity related to enhanced memory for pleasant and aversive stimuli. *Nat. Neurosci.* 2:289–93

Heller W, Nitschke JB. 1998. The puzzle of regional brain activity in depression and anxiety: the importance of subtypes and comorbidity. *Cogn. Emot.* 12:421–47

Henriques JB, Davidson RJ. 1991. Left frontal hypoactivation in depression. *J. Abnorm. Psychol.* 100:535–45

Henriques JB, Davidson RJ. 2000. Decreased responsiveness to reward in depression. *Cogn. Emot.* 14:711–24

Henriques JB, Glowacki JM, Davidson RJ. 1994. Reward fails to alter response bias in depression. *J. Abnorm. Psychol.* 103:460–66

Ho AP, Gillin JC, Buchsbaum MS, Wu JC, Abel L, Bunney WE Jr. 1996. Brain glucose metabolism during non-rapid eye movement sleep in major depression. A positron emission tomography study. *Arch. Gen. Psychiatry* 53:645–52

Holland PC, Gallagher M. 1999. Amygdala circuitry in attentional and representational processes. *Trends Cogn. Sci.* 3:65–73

Hrdina PD, Demeter E, Vu TB, Sotonyi P, Palkovits M. 1993. 5-HT uptake sites and 5-HT2 receptors in brain of antidepressant-free suicide victims/depressives: increase in 5-HT2 sites in cortex and amygdala. *Brain Res.* 614:37–44

Ikegaya Y, Abe K, Saito H, Nishiyama N. 1995a. Medial amygdala enhances synaptic transmission and synaptic plasticity in the dentate gyrus of rats in vivo. *J. Neurophysiol.* 74:2201–3

Ikegaya Y, Saito H, Abe K. 1994. Attenuated hippocampal long-term potentiation in basolateral amygdala-lesioned rats. *Brain Res.* 656:157–64

Ikegaya Y, Saito H, Abe K. 1995b. Requirement of basolateral amygdala neuron activity for the induction of long-term potentiation in the dentate gyrus in vivo. *Brain Res.* 671:351–54

Isenberg N, Silbersweig D, Engelien A, Emmerich S, Malavade K, et al. 1999. Linguistic threat activates the human amygdala. *Proc. Natl. Acad. Sci. USA* 96:10456–59

Ito H, Kawashima R, Awata S, Ono S, Sato K, et al. 1996. Hypoperfusion in the limbic system and prefrontal cortex in depression: SPECT with anatomic standardization technique. *J. Nucl. Med.* 37:410–14

Jacobs BL, Praag H, Gage FH. 2000. Adult brain neurogenesis and psychiatry: a novel theory of depression. *Mol. Psychiatry* 5:262–69

Jacobson L, Sapolsky RM. 1991. The role of the hippocampus in feedback regulation of the hypothalamic-pituitary-adrenocortical axis. *Endocrine Rev.* 12:118–34

Javanmard M, Shlik J, Kennedy SH, Vaccarino FJ, Houle S, Bradwejn J. 1999. Neuroanatomic correlates of CCK-4-induced panic attacks in healthy humans: a comparison of two time points. *Biol. Psychiatry* 45:872–82

Kahneman D. 1999. Objective happiness. In *Well-Being: The Foundations of Hedonic Psychology*, ed. E Kahneman, E Diener, N Schwartz, pp. 3–25. New York: Russell Sage Found.

Kawasaki H, Adolphs R, Kaufman O, Damasio H, Damasio AR, et al. 2001. Single-neuron responses to emotional visual stimuli recorded in human ventral prefrontal cortex. *Nat. Neurosci.* 4:15–16

Kempermann G, Kuhn HG, Gage FH. 1997. More hippocampal neurons in adult mice living in an enriched environment. *Nature* 386:493–95

Kennedy SH, Evans KR, Kruger S, Mayberg HS, Meyer JH, et al. 2001. Changes in regional brain glucose metabolism measured with positron emission tomography after paroxetine treatment of major depression. *Am. J. Psychiatry* 158:899–905

Kentgen LM, Tenke CE, Pine DS, Fong R,

Klein RG, Bruder GE. 2000. Electroencephalographic asymmetries in adolescents with major depression: influence of comorbidity with anxiety disorders. *J. Abnorm. Psychol.* 109:797–802

Ketter TA, Andreason PJ, George MS, Lee C, Gill DS, et al. 1996. Anterior paralimbic mediation of procaine-induced emotional and psychosensory experiences. *Arch. Gen. Psychiatry* 53:59–69

Ketter TA, Kimbrell TA, George MS, Dunn RT, Speer AM, et al. 2001. Effects of mood and subtype on cerebral glucose metabolism in treatment-resistant bipolar disorder. *Biol. Psychiatry* 49:97–109

Konishi S, Nakajima K, Uchida I, Kikyo H, Kameyama M, Miyashita Y. 1999. Common inhibitory mechanism in human inferior prefrontal cortex revealed by event-related functional MRI. *Brain* 122:981–91

Kumar A, Newberg A, Alavi A, Berlin J, Smith R, Reivich M. 1993. Regional cerebral glucose metabolism in late-life depression and Alzheimer disease: a preliminary positron emission tomography study. *Proc. Natl. Acad. Sci. USA* 90:7019–23

Lane RD, Fink GR, Chau PM, Dolan RJ. 1997. Neural activation during selective attention to subjective emotional responses. *NeuroReport* 8:3969–72

Le Bihan D, Mangin JF, Poupon C, Clark CA, Pappata S, et al. 2001. Diffusion tensor imaging: concepts and applications. *J. Magn. Reson. Imaging* 13:534–46

LeDoux JE. 2000. Emotion circuits in the brain. *Annu. Rev. Neurosci.* 23:155–84

Leverenz JB, Wilkinson CW, Wamble M, Corbin S, Grabber JE, et al. 1999. Effect of chronic high-dose exogenous cortisol on hippocampal neuronal number in aged nonhuman primates. *J. Neurosci.* 19:2356–61

Liberzon I, Taylor SF, Amdur R, Jung TD, Chamberlain KR, et al. 1999. Brain activation in PTSD in response to trauma-related stimuli. *Biol. Psychiatry* 45:817–26

Lupien SJ, de Leon M, de Santi S, Convit A, Tarshish C, et al. 1998. Cortisol levels during human aging predict hippocampal atrophy and memory deficits. *Nat. Neurosci.* 1:69–73

MacDonald AW 3rd, Cohen JD, Stenger VA, Carter CS. 2000. Dissociating the role of the dorsolateral prefrontal and anterior cingulate cortex in cognitive control. *Science* 288:1835–38

Madhav TR, Pei Q, Grahame-Smith DG, Zetterstrom TS. 2000. Repeated electroconvulsive shock promotes the sprouting of serotonergic axons in the lesioned rat hippocampus. *Neuroscience* 97:677–83

Magarinos AM, McEwen BS, Flugge G, Fuchs E. 1996. Chronic psychosocial stress causes apical dendritic atrophy of hippocampal CA3 pyramidal neurons in subordinate tree shrews. *J. Neurosci.* 16:3534–40

Malberg JE, Eisch AJ, Nestler EJ, Duman RS. 2000. Chronic antidepressant treatment increases neurogenesis in adult rat hippocampus. *J. Neurosci.* 20:9104–10

Mayberg HS. 1997. Limbic-cortical dysregulation: a proposed model of depression. *J. Neuropsychiatry Clin. Neurosci.* 9:471–81

Mayberg HS, Brannan SK, Mahurin RK, Jerabek PA, Brickman JS, et al. 1997. Cingulate function in depression: a potential predictor of treatment response. *NeuroReport* 8:1057–61

Mayberg HS, Lewis PL, Regenold W, Wagner HN Jr. 1994. Paralimbic hypoperfusion in unipolar depression. *J. Nucl. Med.* 35:929–34

Mayberg HS, Liotti M, Brannan SK, McGinnis S, Mahurin RK, et al. 1999. Reciprocal limbic-cortical function and negative mood: converging PET findings in depression and normal sadness. *Am. J. Psychiatry* 156:675–82

McEwen BS. 1998. Protective and damaging effects of stress mediators. *N. Engl. J. Med.* 338:171–79

Mega MS, Cummings JL, Salloway S, Malloy P. 1997. The limbic system: an anatomic, phylogenetic, and clinical perspective. *J. Neuropsychiatry Clin. Neurosci.* 9:315–30

Mervaala E, Fohr J, Kononen M, Valkonen-Korhonen M, Vainio P, et al. 2000.

Quantitative MRI of the hippocampus and amygdala in severe depression. *Psychol. Med.* 30:117–25

Miller EK, Cohen JD. 2001. An integrative theory of prefrontal cortex function. *Annu. Rev. Neurosci.* 24:167–202

Mirz F, Gjedde A, Sodkilde-Jorgensen H, Pedersen CB. 2000. Functional brain imaging of tinnitus-like perception induced by aversive auditory stimuli. *NeuroReport* 11:633–37

Morris JS, Friston KJ, Dolan RJ. 1997. Neural responses to salient visual stimuli. *Proc. R. Soc. London B Biol. Sci.* 264:769–75

Morris JS, Ohman A, Dolan RJ. 1999. A subcortical pathway to the right amygdala mediating "unseen" fear. *Proc. Natl. Acad. Sci. USA* 96:1680–85

Nader K, Schafe GE, LeDoux JE. 2000. Fear memories require protein synthesis in the amygdala for reconsolidation after retrieval. *Nature* 406:722–26

Nobre AC, Sebestyen GN, Gitelman DR, Mesulam MM, Frackowiak RS, Frith CD. 1997. Functional localization of the system for visuospatial attention using positron emission tomography. *Brain* 120:515–33

Nofzinger EA, Nichols TE, Meltzer CC, Price J, Steppe DA, et al. 1999. Changes in forebrain function from waking to REM sleep in depression: preliminary analyses of [18F]FDG PET studies. *Psychiatry Res.* 91:59–78

Noga JT, Vladar K, Torrey EF. 2001. A volumetric magnetic resonance imaging study of monozygotic twins discordant for bipolar disorder. *Psychiatry Res.: Neuroimaging* 106:25–34

Ochsner KN, Barrett LF. 2001. A multiprocess perspective on the neuroscience of emotion. In *Emotions: Current Issues and Future Directions*, ed. TJ Mayne, GA Bonanno, 38–81. New York: Guilford

O'Doherty J, Kringelbach ML, Rolls ET, Hornak J, Andrews C. 2001. Abstract reward and punishment representations in the human orbitofrontal cortex. *Nat. Neurosci.* 4:95–102

Öngür D, An X, Price JL. 1998a. Prefrontal cortical projections to the hypothalamus in macaque monkeys. *J. Comp. Neurol.* 401:480–505

Öngür D, Drevets WC, Price JL. 1998b. Glial reduction in the subgenual prefrontal cortex in mood disorders. *Proc. Natl. Acad. Sci. USA* 95:13290–95

Pantel J, Schroder J, Essig M, Popp D, Dech H, et al. 1997. Quantitative magnetic resonance imaging in geriatric depression and primary degenerative dementia. *J. Affect. Disord.* 42:69–83

Pardo JV, Pardo PJ, Janer KW, Raichle ME. 1990. The anterior cingulate cortex mediates processing selection in the Stroop attentional conflict paradigm. *Proc. Natl. Acad. Sci. USA* 87:256–59

Pariante CM, Miller AH. 2001. Glucocorticoid receptors in major depression: relevance to pathophysiology and treatment. *Biol. Psychiatry* 49:391–404

Pauli P, Wiedemann G, Nickola M. 1999. Pain sensitivity, cerebral laterality, and negative affect. *Pain* 80:359–64

Paus T, Zatorre RJ, Hofle N, Caramanos Z, Gotman J, et al. 1997. Time-related changes in neural systems underlying attention and arousal during the performance of an auditory vigilance task. *J. Cogn. Neurosci.* 9:392–408

Phillips ML, Bullmore ET, Howard R, Woodruff PW, Wright IC, et al. 1998. Investigation of facial recognition memory and happy and sad facial expression perception: an fMRI study. *Psychiatry Res.* 83:127–38

Pizzagalli D, Pascual-Marqui RD, Nitschke JB, Oakes TR, Larson CL, et al. 2001. Anterior cingulate activity as a predictor of degree of treatment response in major depression: evidence from brain electrical tomography analysis. *Am. J. Psychiatry* 158:405–15

Pruessner JC, Collins DL, Pruessner M, Evans AC. 2001. Age and gender predict volume decline in the anterior and posterior hippocampus in early adulthood. *J. Neurosci.* 21:194–200

Rajkowska G. 2000. Postmortem studies in mood disorders indicate altered numbers of neurons and glial cells. *Biol. Psychiatry* 48:766–77

Rauch SL, Savage CR, Alpert NM, Fischman AJ, Jenike MA. 1997. The functional neuroanatomy of anxiety: a study of three disorders using positron emission tomography and symptom provocation. *Biol. Psychiatry* 42:446–52

Rauch SL, Savage CR, Alpert NM, Miguel EC, Baer L, et al. 1995. A positron emission tomographic study of simple phobic symptom provocation. *Arch. Gen. Psychiatry* 52:20–28

Rauch SL, van der Kolk BA, Fisler RE, Alpert NM, Orr SP, et al. 1996. A symptom provocation study of posttraumatic stress disorder using positron emission tomography and script-driven imagery. *Arch. Gen. Psychiatry* 53:380–87

Rauch SL, Whalen PJ, Shin LM, McInerney SC, Macklin ML, et al. 2000. Exaggerated amygdala response to masked facial stimuli in posttraumatic stress disorder: a functional MRI study. *Biol. Psychiatry* 47:769–76

Reid SA, Duke LM, Allen JJB. 1998. Resting frontal electroencephalographic asymmetry in depression: Inconsistencies suggest the need to identify mediating factors? *Psychophysiology* 35:389–404

Reiman EM. 1997. The application of positron emission tomography to the study of normal and pathologic emotions. *J. Clin. Psychiatry* 58:4–12

Reul JM, de Kloet ER. 1986. Anatomical resolution of two types of corticosterone receptor sites in rat brain with in vitro autoradiography and computerized image analysis. *J. Steroid Biochem.* 24(1):269–72

Rogers RD, Owen AM, Middleton HC, Williams EJ, Pickard JD, et al. 1999. Choosing between small, likely rewards and large, unlikely rewards activates inferior and orbital prefrontal cortex. *J. Neurosci.* 20:9029–38

Rolls ET. 1999. The functions of the orbitofrontal cortex. *Neurocase* 5:301–12

Rusch BD, Abercrombie HC, Oakes TR, Schaefer SM, Davidson RJ. 2002. Hippocampal morphometry in depressed patients and controls: Relations to anxiety symptoms. *Biol. Psychiatry.* In press

Sapolsky RM. 2000. Glucocorticoids and hippocampal atrophy in neuropsychiatric disorders. *Arch. Gen. Psychiatry* 57:925–35

Sapolsky RM, Krey LC, McEwen BS. 1986. The neuroendocrinology of stress and aging: the glucocorticoid cascade hypothesis. *Endocr. Rev.* 7:284–301

Sapolsky RM, Uno H, Rebert CS, Finch CE. 1990. Hippocampal damage associated with prolonged glucocorticoid exposure in primates. *J. Neurosci.* 10:2897–902

Saxena S, Brody AL, Ho ML, Alborzian S, Ho MK, et al. 2001. Cerebral metabolism in major depression and obsessive-compulsive disorder occuring separately and concurrently. *Biol. Psychiatry* 50:159–70

Schaefer SM, Abercrombie HC, Lindgren KA, Larson CL, Ward RT, et al. 2000. Six-month test-retest reliability of MRI-defined PET measures of regional cerebral glucose metabolic rate in selected subcortical structures. *Hum. Brain Mapp.* 10:1–9

Schaffer CE, Davidson RJ, Saron C. 1983. Frontal and parietal electroencephalogram asymmetries in depressed and non-depressed subjects. *Biol. Psychiatry* 18:753–62

Schneider F, Weiss U, Kessler C, Muller-Gartner HW, Posse S, et al. 1999. Subcortical correlates of differential classical conditioning of aversive emotional reactions in social phobia. *Biol. Psychiatry* 45:863–71

Schulkin J. 1994. Melancholic depression and the hormones of adversity—a role for the amygdala. *Curr. Dir. Psychol. Sci.* 3:41–44

Semple WE, Goyer PF, McCormick R, Donovan B, Muzic RFJ, et al. 2000. Higher brain blood flow at amygdala and lower frontal cortex blood flow in PTSD patients with comorbid cocaine and alcohol abuse compared with normals. *Psychiatry* 63:65–74

Servan-Schreiber D, Perlstein WM, Cohen JD, Mintun M. 1998. Selective pharmacological activation of limbic structures in human volunteers: a positron emission tomography study. *J. Neuropsychiatry Clin. Neurosci.* 10:148–59

Shah PJ, Ebmeier KP, Glabus MF, Goodwin GM. 1998. Cortical grey matter reductions associated with treatment-resistant chronic unipolar depression. Controlled magnetic resonance imaging study. *Br. J. Psychiatry* 172:527–32

Sheline YI. 2000. 3D MRI studies of neuroanatomic changes in unipolar major depression: the role of stress and medical comorbidity. *Biol. Psychiatry* 48:791–800

Sheline YI, Gado MH, Price JL. 1998. Amygdala core nuclei volumes are decreased in recurrent major depression. *NeuroReport* 9: 2023–28

Sheline YI, Sanghavi M, Mintun MA, Gado MH. 1999. Depression duration but not age predicts hippocampal volume loss in medically healthy women with recurrent major depression. *J. Neurosci.* 19:5034–43

Sheline YI, Wang PW, Gado MH, Csernansky JG, Vannier MW. 1996. Hippocampal atrophy in recurrent major depression. *Proc. Natl. Acad. Sci. USA* 93:3908–13

Shin LM, Kosslyn SM, McNally RJ, Alpert NM, Thompson WL, et al. 1997. Visual imagery and perception in posttraumatic stress disorder. A positron emission tomographic investigation. *Arch. Gen. Psychiatry* 54:233–41

Smith GS, Reynolds CF, Pollock B, Derbyshire S, Nofzinger E, et al. 1999. Cerebral glucose metabolic response to combined total sleep deprivation and antidepressant treatment in geriatric depression. *Am. J. Psychiatry* 156:683–89

Squire LR, Knowlton BJ. 2000. The medial temporal lobe, the hippocampus, and the memory systems of the brain. In *The New Cognitive Neurosciences*, ed. MS Gazzaniga, pp. 765–79. Cambridge, MA: MIT Press

Starkman MN, Giordani B, Gebarski SS, Berent S, Schork MA, Schteingart DE. 1999. Decrease in cortisol reverses human hippocampal atrophy following treatment of Cushing's disease. *Biol. Psychiatry* 46:1595–602

Steffens DC, Byrum CE, McQuoid DR, Greenberg DL, Payne ME, et al. 2000.

Hippocampal volume in geriatric depression. *Biol. Psychiatry* 48:301–9

Stein MB, Koverola C, Hanna C, Torchia MG, McClarty B. 1997. Hippocampal volume in women victimized by childhood sexual abuse. *Psychol. Med.* 27:951–59

Strakowski SM, DelBello MP, Sax KW, Zimmerman ME, Shear PK, et al. 1999. Brain magnetic resonance imaging of structural abnormalities in bipolar disorder. *Arch. Gen. Psychiatry* 56:254–60

Talairach J, Tournoux P. 1988. *Co-Planar Stereotaxic Atlas of the Human Brain.* Stuttgart: Thieme

Taylor SE. 1991. Asymmetrical effects of positive and negative events: the mobilization-minimization hypothesis. *Psychol. Bull.* 110: 67–85

Tebartz van Elst L, Woermann FG, Lemieux L, Trimble MR. 1999. Amygdala enlargement in dysthymia: a volumetric study of patients with temporal lobe epilepsy. *Biol. Psychiatry* 46:1614–23

Tebartz van Elst L, Woermann FG, Lemieux L, Trimble MR. 2000. Increased amygdala volumes in female and depressed humans. A quantitative magnetic resonance imaging study. *Neurosci. Lett.* 281:103–6

Thayer JF, Lane RD. 2000. A model of neurovisceral integration in emotion regulation and dysregulation. *J. Affect. Disord.* 61:201–16

Tomarken AJ, Davidson RJ, Wheeler RE, Kinney L. 1992. Psychometric properties of resting anterior EEG asymmetry: temporal stability and internal consistency. *Psychophysiology* 29:576–92

Vakili K, Pillay SS, Lafer B, Fava M, Renshaw PF, Bonello-Cintron CM. 2000. Hippocampal volume in primary unipolar major depression: a magnetic resonance imaging study. *Biol. Psychiatry* 47:1087–90

Veith RC, Lewis N, Linares OA, Barnes RF, Raskind MA, et al. 1994. Sympathetic nervous system activity in major depression. Basal and desipramine-induced alterations in plasma norepinephrine kinetics. *Arch. Gen. Psychiatry* 51:411–22

Vogt BA, Finch DM, Olson CR. 1992. Functional heterogeneity in cingulate cortex: the anterior executive and posterior evaluative regions. *Cereb. Cortex* 2:435–43

Vogt BA, Nimchinsky EA, Vogt LJ, Hof PR. 1995. Human cingulate cortex: surface features, flat maps, and cytoarchitecture. *J. Comp. Neurol.* 359:490–506

von Gunten A, Fox NC, Cipolotti L, Ron MA. 2000. A volumetric study of hippocampus and amygdala in depressed patients with subjective memory problems. *J. Neuropsychiatry Clin. Neurosci.* 12:493–98

Whalen PJ. 1998. Fear, vigilance, and ambiguity: initial neuroimaging studies of the human amygdala. *Curr. Dir. Psychol. Sci.* 7:177–88

Whalen PJ, Bush G, McNally RJ, Wilhelm S, McInerney SC, et al. 1998. The emotional counting Stroop paradigm: a functional magnetic resonance imaging probe of the anterior cingulate affective division. *Biol. Psychiatry* 44:1219–28

Wu J, Buschbaum MS, Gillin JC, Tang C, Cadwell S, et al. 1999. Prediction of antidepressant effects of sleep deprivation by metabolic rates in the ventral anterior cingulate and medial prefrontal cortex. *Am. J. Psychiatry* 156:1149–58

Wu JC, Gillin JC, Buchsbaum MS, Hershey T, Johnson JC, Bunney WE. 1992. Effect of sleep deprivation on brain metabolism of depressed patients. *Am. J. Psychiatry* 149:538–43

Yurgelun-Todd DA, Gruber SA, Kanayama G, Killgore DS, Baird AA, Young AD. 2000. fMRI during affect discrimination in bipolar affective disorder. *Bipolar Disord.* 2:237–48

Zald DH, Lee JT, Fluegel KW, Pardo JV. 1998. Aversive gustatory stimulation activates limbic circuits in humans. *Brain* 121:1143–54

Zalla T, Koechlin E, Pietrini P, Basso G, Aquino P, et al. 2000. Differential amygdala responses to winning and losing: a functional magnetic resonance imaging study in humans. *Eur. J. Neurosci.* 12:1764–70

Annu. Rev. Psychol. 2002. 53:575–604

INTERGROUP BIAS

Miles Hewstone[1], Mark Rubin[2], Hazel Willis[3]

[1]Department of Experimental Psychology, University of Oxford, South Parks Road, Oxford, OX1 3UD, United Kingdom; e-mail: miles.hewstone@psy.ox.ac.uk
[2]School of Behavioral Sciences, University of Newcastle, Callaghan, NSW 2308, Australia; e-mail: mark.rubin@newcastle.edu.au
[3]School of Psychology, Cardiff University, PO Box 901, Cardiff CF10 3YG, United Kingdom; e-mail: Willishj@cardiff.ac.uk

Key Words conflict, discrimination, prejudice, social categorization, stereotyping

■ **Abstract** This chapter reviews the extensive literature on bias in favor of in-groups at the expense of out-groups. We focus on five issues and identify areas for future research: (*a*) measurement and conceptual issues (especially in-group favoritism vs. out-group derogation, and explicit vs. implicit measures of bias); (*b*) modern theories of bias highlighting motivational explanations (social identity, optimal distinctiveness, uncertainty reduction, social dominance, terror management); (*c*) key moderators of bias, especially those that exacerbate bias (identification, group size, status and power, threat, positive-negative asymmetry, personality and individual differences); (*d*) reduction of bias (individual vs. intergroup approaches, especially models of social categorization); and (*e*) the link between intergroup bias and more corrosive forms of social hostility.

CONTENTS

INTRODUCTION

Intergroup bias refers generally to the systematic tendency to evaluate one's own membership group (the in-group) or its members more favorably than a nonmembership group (the out-group) or its members. Bias can encompass behavior (discrimination), attitude (prejudice), and cognition (stereotyping) (Mackie & Smith 1998, Wilder & Simon 2001). More precisely, this group-serving tendency can take the form of favoring the in-group (in-group favoritism and/or derogating the out-group (out-group derogation). Use of the term "bias" involves an interpretative judgment that the response is unfair, illegitimate, or unjustifiable, in the sense that it goes beyond the objective requirements or evidence of the situation (see Brewer & Brown 1998, Fiske 1998, Turner & Reynolds 2001). Intergroup bias is a general, but not a universal, phenomenon (see Hagendoorn 1995, Hagendoorn et al. 2001), and contemporary social psychology has contributed to a more differentiated and context-dependent view of bias.

In the limited space available we focus on five specific issues. We review first, measurement and conceptual issues; second, the competing claims of currently prominent theories of bias; third, some key moderators of bias, especially those that exacerbate bias; fourth, theory and research on interventions to reduce bias; and, finally, we consider the link between intergroup bias and more corrosive forms of social hostility. We are forced to give a selective overview, and we highlight more recent developments as well as perspectives that we feel offer a unified perspective on why bias occurs, how it is moderated, and what can be done to reduce it.

MEASUREMENT AND CONCEPTUAL ISSUES

Measures of Intergroup Bias

Forms of intergroup bias range from prejudice and stereotyping, via discrimination, injustice, perpetuation of inequality and oppression, to ethnic cleansing and genocide (Hewstone & Cairns 2001). In practice, however, the vast majority of social-psychological studies have investigated weaker forms of bias, as expressed by participants with relatively mild prejudice. A major recent development has been the emergence of implicit measures of bias and analysis of their relationship with explicit measures.

EXPLICIT MEASURES   Researchers often use a large number of well-established explicit measures in the same study. Responses are made consciously and are typically assessed by traditional self-report measures including attribution of group traits (stereotypes), group evaluations (prejudice), and differential behavior toward in-group and out-group targets (discrimination). However, measures of these three cognitive, affective, and behavioral components, respectively, are often empirically dissociated (e.g., Stangor et al. 1991; see Mackie & Smith 1998), with modest-to-weak overall relationships between measures (see meta-analysis by Dovidio et al. 1996).

Studies using multiple measures of bias have tended to show a pattern of inconsistent responses across different measures, which can sometimes be attributed to perceivers making a compromise between the desire to evaluate their own group positively and the wish to maintain a self-image of fair-mindedness (Singh et al. 1998).

IMPLICIT MEASURES   Implicit measures of bias are evaluations and beliefs that are automatically activated by the mere presence of the attitude object (i.e., the target group) (see Dovidio et al. 2001). Implicit measures tap unintentional bias, of which well-intentioned and would-be unprejudiced people are largely unaware; they include (a) the relative concreteness-abstractness of written language in response to expectancy-consistent vs. inconsistent behaviors (for a review, see Maass 1999); (b) indirect self-report measures (e.g., involving attributional biases) (Von Hippel et al. 1997); (c) response-latency procedures following priming (e.g., Dovidio et al. 1997, Fazio et al. 1995, Judd et al. 1995, Wittenbrink et al. 1997); (d) memory tasks (e.g., Crisp & Hewstone 2001, Sherman et al. 1998); and (e) psychophysiological measures (e.g., Phelps et al. 2000, Vanman et al. 1997). Implicit measures have even been developed for use with the minimal groups paradigm (Otten & Moskowitz 2000, Otten & Wentura 1999).

The promise of implicit measures is to assess the true extent of people's bias, given pressures to conform to socially desirable or politically correct norms (see Devine et al. 2001, Judd et al. 1995). The most powerful implicit measures can tap biases despite these norms, because they are beyond both intentional control and awareness. Response latency procedures following priming and the Implicit Association Test (Dasgupta et al. 2000, Greenwald et al. 1998) are especially useful, because they yield individual differences in implicit responding that can be used to predict other responses and behaviors (see Maass et al. 2000).

Priming techniques (with either category labels or faces as primes) (e.g., Fazio & Dunton 1997, Fazio et al. 1995) can be used to assess implicit prejudice by comparing response latencies to differently valenced words (prejudice implies faster responses by white respondents to negative traits after black vs. white primes and to positive traits after white vs. black primes) (e.g., Dovidio et al. 1997, Fazio et al. 1995, Judd et al. 1995, Wittenbrink et al. 1997).

Although popular, questions have been raised about the stability of individual differences for implicit measures of bias and the modest relationships between different measures (see Dovidio et al. 1997, 2001; Fazio et al. 1995; Kawakami & Dovidio 2001). Dovidio et al.'s (2001) meta-analysis yielded a significant, but modest, relationship between different implicit measures of prejudice, but implicit measures appear to have substantial reliability and convergent validity (Blair 2001, Cunningham et al. 2001, Devine et al. 2001).

THE RELATIONSHIP BETWEEN EXPLICIT AND IMPLICIT MEASURES   There are both theoretical and methodological explanations for the generally weak relationship found between explicit and implicit measures (see Blair 2001). If indeed explicit and implicit measures tap different constructs and involve different processes, we should not expect them to be highly correlated (Dovidio et al. 1997, Maass et al. 2000); weak correlations may also reflect the nature of contemporary prejudice, rather than weak measures per se (Dovidio et al. 1998).

The major factor determining the correspondence between explicit and implicit measures appears to be the normative context (Dovidio et al. 2001). Not surprisingly, because implicit measures were designed for use in situations in which explicit measures were unlikely to tap bias, correspondence tends to be weaker for socially sensitive issues, including race (Fazio et al. 1995, Greenwald et al. 1998, Vanman et al. 1997; but see Wittenbrink et al. 1997). Thus, researchers have begun to develop measures of the extent to which people are motivated to inhibit or suppress their biases (Dunton & Fazio 1997, Plant & Devine 1998), which is seen as a precursor to initiating efforts to control prejudice (see Macrae & Bodenhausen 2000).

As Dovidio et al. (1997) argued for racial attitudes, intergroup attitudes may be examined at three levels: public and personal (both explicit) and unconscious (implicit). No one level represents true racial attitudes (any individual having multiple context-dependent attitudes) (see Wittenbrink et al. 2001a,b; cf. Fazio et al. 1995) and different levels predict different types of behavior (public, where social desirability is salient; personal, where responses are private but controlled; unconscious, where behavior is spontaneous).

The development of implicit measures of intergroup bias has facilitated research on important socially sensitive issues, but future research should continue to explore the psychometric properties of both explicit and implicit measures, to uncover the moderators of dissociation between them (Mackie & Smith 1998), and to develop implicit measures for use with children.

In-Group Favoritism vs. Out-Group Derogation

THEORETICAL AND EMPIRICAL PREDOMINANCE OF IN-GROUP FAVORITISM   Self-categorization as an in-group member entails assimilation of the self to the in-group category prototype and enhanced similarity to other in-group members (see Turner & Reynolds 2001); and the in-group is cognitively included in the self (e.g., Smith & Henry 1996). Trust is extended to fellow in-group, but not out-group, members (see Insko et al. 1990, 1998), based on group living as a fundamental survival strategy (Brewer 2001). The extension of trust, positive regard, cooperation, and empathy to in-group, but not out-group, members is an initial form of discrimination, based solely on in-group favoritism, which must be distinguished from bias that entails an active component of aggression and out-group derogation (Brewer 1999, 2000; see also Levin & Sidanius 1999, Singh et al. 1998).

The bias uncovered in social-psychological research predominantly takes the mild form of in-group favoritism, rather than out-group derogation (see Brewer 1999, 2001), as reflected in three distinct lines of research: (*a*) positivity biases associated with in-group identification arise automatically and without awareness, and generalized positive evaluation from in-group pronouns is stronger than generalized negative evaluation from out-group-pronouns (Otten & Wentura 1999, Perdue et al. 1990); (*b*) subtle racism is characterized by the absence of positive sentiments, not the presence of strong, negative attitudes, towards out-groups (e.g., Dovidio & Gaertner 2000, Pettigrew & Meertens 1995, Stangor et al. 1991); (*c*) patriotism (positive national pride and attachment) is distinct from nationalism (belligerence and claimed superiority over other nations) (Feshbach 1994). However, changes to our methodological practices could identify more evidence for out-group derogation (e.g., more frequent inclusion of members of highly racist groups and more potent target groups, and more research in situations of extreme intergroup conflict).

METHODOLOGICAL ISSUES   Various methodological paradigms allow us to separate the two components of in-group favoritism and out-group derogation by including independent assessment of in-group and out-group evaluations (e.g., Bettencourt & Dorr 1998, Brewer et al. 1993, Islam & Hewstone 1993a, Singh et al. 1997). The most accurate conclusions about intergroup bias are likely to be drawn from studies that incorporate two methodological refinements. First, the effect of being categorized should be separated from the effect of judging a target who is categorized as a group member. This can be done, experimentally, by including control conditions in which some participants, as well as some targets, are uncategorized (e.g., Cadinu & Rothbart 1996, Crisp & Hewstone 2000a, Singh et al. 1997). Second, where participants rate individual target group members' performance, products, or outcomes, the valence of these outcomes should be manipulated (e.g., Crisp & Hewstone 2001, Islam & Hewstone 1993a), ideally including positive-, negative- and neutral-outcome conditions.

FROM IN-GROUP FAVORITISM TO OUT-GROUP DEROGATION   Because out-group antagonism is not a necessary extension of in-group positivity and enhancement, when does in-group favoritism give way to derogation, hostility, and antagonism against out-groups (e.g., Brewer 2001, Mummendey & Otten 2001)?

Several recent analyses argue that the constraints normally in place, which limit intergroup bias to in-group favoritism, are lifted when out-groups are associated with stronger emotions (Brewer 2001, Doosje et al. 1998, Mackie & Smith 1998, Mummendey & Otten 2001; M Schaller, submitted). There is ample scope for these emotions in the arousal that often characterizes intergroup encounters, which can be translated into emotions such as fear, hatred, or disgust (Smith 1993, Stephan &

Stephan 2000), and emotions experienced in specific encounters with groups can be important causes of people's overall reactions to groups (e.g., Eagly et al. 1994, Esses et al. 1993, Jackson et al. 1996). Threat (see Key Moderators of Intergroup Bias, below) is one factor that triggers these emotions.

Smith (1993) differentiated milder emotions (e.g., disgust) from stronger emotions (e.g., contempt, anger) most likely to be aroused in an intergroup context, and linked specific emotions, perceptions of the out-group, and action tendencies (see Mackie et al. 2000). Thus, an out-group that violates in-group norms may elicit disgust and avoidance; an out-group seen as benefiting unjustly (e.g., from government programs) may elicit resentment and actions aimed at reducing benefits; and an out-group seen as threatening may elicit fear and hostile actions. Weaker emotions imply only avoidance, but stronger emotions imply movement against the out-group, and these emotions could be used to justify out-group harm that extends beyond in-group benefit (Brewer 2001).

MODERN THEORIES OF INTERGROUP BIAS

In this section we briefly outline and review five relatively recent motivational theories of intergroup bias that have each accrued a substantial literature.

Social Identity Theory

According to social identity theory (Tajfel & Turner 1979), successful intergroup bias creates or protects relatively high in-group status, thereby providing a positive social identity for in-group members and satisfying their need for positive self-esteem. Hogg & Abrams (1990) derived two corollaries from this self-esteem hypothesis: (1) successful intergroup bias enhances self-esteem and (2) depressed or threatened self-esteem motivates intergroup bias. An exhaustive narrative review (Rubin & Hewstone 1998) and meta-analysis (Aberson et al. 2000) of over 50 experiments reveals that the majority of evidence supports corollary 1, but there is little evidence for corollary 2. Before discounting the self-esteem hypothesis, however, it is important to consider some of the controversy surrounding the manner in which it has been tested.

Social identity theory qualifies the self-esteem hypothesis in a number of ways: (a) The need for self-esteem is only thought to motivate intergroup bias that is designed to bring about social change (social competition) (Tajfel & Turner 1979); (b) only specific social state self-esteem is thought to be related to this type of intergroup bias (Rubin & Hewstone 1998, Turner & Reynolds 2001); (c) the need for self-esteem is only thought to motivate intergroup bias among people who identify with their in-group (Branscombe & Wann 1994, Gagnon & Bourhis 1996, Tajfel & Turner 1979); (d) only intergroup bias that is perceived to be successful in bringing about social change is thought to increase self-esteem (Turner & Reynolds 2001). Considering that researchers have tended to ignore these qualifications, it could be argued that the role of positive self-definition and self-esteem in intergroup bias has not yet received a fair test.

Optimal Distinctiveness Theory

Optimal distinctiveness theory (Brewer 1991) proposes that social identity involves a compromise between two opposing needs: the need for assimilation and the need for differentiation. People are motivated to identify with groups that provide an optimal balance between these two needs. Optimal distinctiveness theory puts forward two motivations for intergroup bias. First, bias is motivated by the need to affirm the satisfaction derived from identification with an optimally distinct group (Leonardelli & Brewer 2001). Second, given a certain degree of identification, intergroup bias is motivated by the need for intergroup differentiation (Brewer 1991).

Leonardelli & Brewer (2001) found evidence to support both motives for minimal intergroup bias. Members of optimally distinct minority groups showed greater in-group identification, greater satisfaction with their in-group, and higher self-esteem than members of nonoptimally distinct majority groups. Consistent with the affirmation motive, a positive relationship was found between in-group satisfaction and intergroup bias for minority group members. Consistent with the differentiation motive, a negative relationship was found between in-group satisfaction and intergroup bias for majority group members. Manipulations of distinctiveness have also been conducted independently of group size. Hornsey & Hogg (1999) found a positive association between the perceived inclusiveness of a superordinate category and intergroup bias at the subgroup level. This evidence supports the differentiation motive. Optimal distinctiveness theory is unique in putting forward a dual process model of intergroup bias. However, the specifics of these processes need further elaboration and testing.

Subjective Uncertainty Reduction Theory

Subjective uncertainty reduction theory (Hogg 2000, Hogg & Abrams 1993) proposes that people are motivated to reduce subjective uncertainty. One way to reduce subjective uncertainty is to identify with social groups that provide clear normative prescriptions for behavior. Hogg & Abrams (1993) proposed that the reduction of uncertainty caused by in-group identification imbues people who are associated with this reduction (i.e., in-group members, including the self) with a positive valence. In-group favoritism is explained as a reflection of the resulting perceived differences in intergroup positivity.

Some evidence shows that manipulations of subjective uncertainty influence levels of both in-group identification and intergroup bias. Grieve & Hogg (1999, Experiment 1) showed that participants who completed practice trials prior to taking part in standard minimal group experiments showed lower group identification and intergroup bias than participants with no practice trials. Additional manipulations of pretest task and situational uncertainty produced congruent results (Grieve & Hogg 1999, Experiment 2; Hodson & Sorrentino 2001; Mullin & Hogg 1998; for a review see Hogg 2000). Furthermore, consistent with Hogg and colleagues' research, a positive relationship has been found between the need for closure and both in-group identification and intergroup bias (Shah et al. 1998, Webster et al. 1997).

The evidence suggests that manipulations of uncertainty motivate in-group identification, although some of the operationalizations could surely have affected more than simply uncertainty. Evidence for concomitant increases in self-esteem and reductions in uncertainty is less convincing (Hogg 2000). Given this gap in the evidence, it is possible that subjective uncertainty motivates in-group identification and that identification then moderates the impact of the social identity self-esteem motive.

Terror Management Theory

Terror management theory (see Solomon et al. 1991) proposes that people have a need for self-preservation, and that this need is frustrated by their awareness of the inevitability of their own death. To deal with the potentially paralyzing prospect of their own mortality, people adopt a cultural worldview that imbues subjective reality with stability and permanence (and hence the possibility of symbolic and/or literal immortality) and provides standards of value against which judgments of self-esteem can be made. According to terror management theory, people with high self-esteem feel that they are meeting the values espoused by their cultural worldview, and therefore feel more confident in attaining some form of immortality. Hence, cultural worldviews and, more specifically, self-esteem provide buffers against the anxiety caused by the awareness of death.

Terror management theory proposes that people evaluate in-group members positively because similar others are assumed to support, and therefore validate, their own cultural worldview; but they evaluate out-group members negatively because dissimilar others are assumed to threaten their worldview. Consistent with terror management theory, there is extensive evidence (from studies with minimal and real groups, and with adults and children) that people show greater intergroup bias when they are made aware of their own mortality (Florian & Mikulincer 1998; Greenberg et al. 1990, Experiment 1, 1992; Harmon-Jones et al. 1996; Nelson et al. 1997).

One of the more common criticisms of terror management theory is that the effects of mortality salience can be reinterpreted as the effects of self-relevant threats in general (Greenberg et al. 1994; see also commentaries on Pyszczynski et al. 1997). Consequently the motivational effects of mortality salience on inter-group bias can be reinterpreted as being consistent with corollary 2 of the self-esteem hypothesis (Harmon-Jones et al. 1996). In distinguishing between terror management theory and social identity theory, the crucial question seems to be whether the need for self-esteem stems from a more general need to reduce anxiety about death, or whether the need to reduce anxiety about death stems from a more general need for positive self-esteem.

Social Dominance Theory

Social dominance theory (Sidanius & Pratto 1999) proposes that society contains ideologies that either promote or attenuate intergroup hierarchies. Individual differences in the extent to which these competing ideologies are accepted are represented by social dominance orientation (SDO). Individuals with a high SDO have a strong desire to promote intergroup hierarchies and for their in-groups to dominate their out-groups. According to social dominance theory, men should have a stronger SDO than women. The hypothesized gender difference in SDO is used to explain why men tend to show greater intergroup bias than women (Sidanius et al. 2000; for reviews, see Pratto et al. 1993, Sidanius et al. 1991; cf. Gaertner & Insko 2000).

Jost & Thompson (2000) noted that a problem with the concept of SDO is that it is defined as both a specific desire for one's in-group to dominate out-groups, and a general desire for groups to exist within a hierarchically ordered social system, regardless of whether the in-group dominates out-groups in this system (see Sidanius et al. 1994). Social dominance theory has tended to focus on general, rather than specific, SDO. Hence, there is a large body of evidence showing that SDO (which is only weakly related to authoritarianism) (see Altemeyer 1998) correlates positively with nonegalitarian political and social attitudes, including sexism, racism, chauvinism, patriotism, and nationalism and that men support these attitudes more than women (for reviews, see Sidanius & Pratto 1999, Sidanius et al. 2000). However, there is less evidence showing that people with high SDO engage in specific instances of intergroup bias in order to achieve or maintain in-group dominance (see Pratto & Shih 2000, Pratto et al. 1998 in Pratto 1999). Jost & Thompson (2000) confirmed empirically the distinction between specific and general SDO but found different patterns of correlation with in-group favoritism. There was a positive correlation between specific SDO and ethnic in-group favoritism between African and European Americans. But for European Americans there was a positive correlation between general SDO and favoritism (explained in terms of their trying to maintain their relatively high status), and for African Americans there was a negative correlation (because they are trying to improve their relatively low status). This evidence highlights the need to distinguish between specific and general SDO, especially when considering the relationship between SDO and group status (Federico 1998, Jost & Thompson 2000).

General Issues

Modern theories of intergroup bias tend to explain intergroup bias in terms of various social psychological motivations, and future research should focus on competitive tests between theories, and on how to integrate them (see Turner & Reynolds 2001). We conclude this section by discussing two general issues.

PROXIMAL AND DISTAL MOTIVATIONS   Motivational theories of intergroup bias can be divided into theories that propose proximal motivations and theories that propose distal motivations. Proximal motivations are specifically and directly related to the behavior in question (e.g., social dominance theory); distal motivations are more broad-ranging and less directly related to the behavior in question (e.g., terror management theory and subjective uncertainty reduction theory).

Theories that posit motivations that are too proximal run the risk of providing redescriptions, rather than explanations, of the behavior in question. The problem is not that these redescriptions are incorrect but that they are relatively uninformative. Theories that posit motivations that are too distal also run the risk of losing explanatory power but for a different reason. Distal motivations may be too abstract to relate coherently to specific behaviors and may trivialize and oversimplify the phenomenon to be explained (Hogg & Abrams 1993). Hence, theorists face a difficult balancing act of conceptualizing motivations that are not so proximal as to become redescriptive but not so distal as to become reductionist.

TESTING FOR SATISFACTION   With the exception of social identity theory, researchers have tended to test the effects of motives on intergroup bias without also testing the effects of intergroup bias on motives. Assuming that motives for intergroup bias operate according to the principles of a negative feedback loop, it is important to establish whether bias results in drive reduction. Hence, optimal distinctiveness researchers should investigate whether intergroup bias reduces the need for identity affirmation and differentiation; uncertainty reduction theorists should investigate whether in-group identification reduces subjective uncertainty; terror management researchers should investigate whether intergroup bias bolsters confidence in one's cultural worldview and reduces anxiety about death; and social dominance researchers should investigate whether intergroup bias reduces the need for in-group dominance. The evidence remains incomplete without these confirmatory tests.

KEY MODERATORS OF INTERGROUP BIAS

Whereas Mullen et al's (1992) meta-analysis provided an impressive demonstration of in-group bias, it also pointed to important moderators of the effect. Potential moderators range from culture (more bias in collective than individualist societies) (see Heine & Lehman 1997, Triandis & Trafimow 2001), to education (negatively associated with bias) (see Hagendoorn & Nekuee 1999, Wagner & Zick 1995), to intrapersonal manipulations of affect (positive affect in minimal group settings increases bias) (Forgas & Fiedler 1996; for a review see Wilder & Simon 2001). Future research needs to investigate more thoroughly how these moderators interact with one another. Having mentioned some theory-specific moderators above (e.g., self-esteem, gender, social dominance orientation), here we simply highlight some of the general moderators investigated in recent research.

Identification

There has been a great deal of inconsistency in the way in which identification is conceptualized and measured (see Jackson & Smith 1999). We believe it should be interpreted in the context of intergroup relations, rather than as a stable personality variable (Turner & Reynolds 2001), and when this is done, identification determines whether social categorization results in bias (Oakes 2001). Some scholars argue that in-group identification and bias should be positively related (Hinkle & Brown 1990; cf. Turner & Reynolds 2001), with the theoretical assumption being that identification drives out-group attitudes, rather than vice versa (Jetten et al. 1997; see Duckitt & Mphuthing 1998 for evidence of the reverse causal direction, at least for disadvantaged and subordinate group members). Correlational data point to only a weak and unstable association (Hinkle & Brown 1990, Mullen et al. 1992), but experimental data show that manipulations of identification can increase bias (Branscombe & Wann 1994, Perreault & Bourhis 1999; see also Bourhis et al. 1997).

Group Size, Status, and Power

Although size, status, and power tend to become confounded outside the laboratory (see Simon et al. 2001), there is theoretical and empirical justification for considering their independent effects. Groups in a numerical minority express more bias than those in a numerical majority, whether the groups are real or artificial (Mullen et al. 1992; see also Otten et al. 1996), with the effect of in-group positivity for numerical minorities being mediated by salience (Bettencourt et al. 1999, Study 3). However, when identification is experimentally induced, both majority and minority groups show bias (Leonardelli & Brewer 2001).

Members of high-status groups tend to show more bias than members of low-status groups, especially in laboratory, compared with field, studies, but with several qualifications (for a review, see Brewer & Brown 1998; for meta-analyses, see Bettencourt et al. 2001, Mullen et al. 1992). Members of high-status groups show bias especially on relevant dimensions that favor their own group, and not on status-irrelevant dimensions; they are more likely to show bias when the status gap is perceived to be closing and when the status hierarchy is perceived as legitimate, but they may also show magnanimity when the status gap is very wide (Bettencourt & Bartholomew 1998, Sachdev & Bourhis 1991). Members of low-status groups show more bias when status differentials are perceived as unstable and/or illegitimate and group boundaries are seen as impermeable (Ellemers et al. 1993, Reichl 1997) and on dimensions unrelated to status differences (Brewer et al. 1993, Reichl 1997). However, members of low-status groups may simultaneously show out-group favoritism (see Jost 2001), especially on status-relevant evaluations and when the status difference is large and clear, and they define their inferiority as legitimate and stable (e.g., Boldry & Kashy 1999). To distinguish bias from a consensual description of reality, participants from a third group should also be sampled (see Brauer 2001 on separating asymmetrical intergroup biases from target-group effects).

Finally, intergroup relations between real groups tend to involve groups of unequal power. Members of high- and equal-power groups show more bias than members of low-power groups, and discrimination by members of numerical minorities with high power is especially strong (Bourhis 1994, Sachdev & Bourhis 1991).

Threat

Threat is a central explanatory concept in several of the theories reviewed above and elsewhere in the literature on intergroup bias (see Brewer 1999, Hagendoorn et al. 2001, Stephan & Stephan 2000), although its interpretation varies widely. Threat can be perceived in terms of the in-group's social identity, its goals and values, its position in the hierarchy, even its existence. Threat can be realistic (e.g., intergroup competition over scarce resources) (see Esses et al. 1998) or symbolic (e.g., blocking the in-group's values, customs, and traditions) (Esses et al. 1993).

Threat is frequently conceived, and experimentally manipulated, in terms of heightened intergroup similarity, which poses a potential threat to the in-group's distinctiveness (perceived threat may also moderate the effects of similarity on bias) (Henderson-King et al. 1997). A similar, relevant out-group tends to be perceived as a threat to group identity, leading to attempts to differentiate from it (e.g., Jetten et al. 1996, 1998; Roccas & Schwartz 1993). Jetten et al. (1998) found a curvilinear relation between distinctiveness and differentiation in both laboratory and natural groups, with strongest bias against an out-group that was similar to, but clearly separate from, the in-group. Differentiation was relatively low or nonsignificant when in- and out-groups were too similar or too dissimilar.

Brewer (2001) conceptualized threat in terms of the needs for distinctiveness and assimilation. For example, peripheral group members (who presumably need to assimilate) show more out-group derogation in public than private, whereas context does not affect core members (Noel et al. 1995); core members, however, are more motivated to protect or defend threatened distinctiveness, and show more in-group favoritism (Jetten et al. 1997).

Analyses of xenophobia and hate crimes against social and ethnic minorities provide extra-laboratory evidence of the role of threat. Perceived threat and incidence of violence is greatest when there is a conjunction of faltering economic growth and a high percentage of immigrant minorities (Quillian 1995), with bias fomented by far-right political elites (Green et al. 1998, Pettigrew 1998a).

Positive-Negative Asymmetry

In-group favoritism is generally not found when participants are forced to rate target groups on negative as opposed to positive scales or to make negative rather than positive allocations to in-group and out-group members (e.g., Mummendey et al. 1992, Mummendey & Otten 1998, Otten & Mummendey 2000). Whereas benefiting the in-group is considered normative (Blanz et al. 1997, Platow et al. 1995), normative constraints make it more difficult to justify relative harm towards others, simply because they are out-group members, and participants use strategies to equalize or minimize the amount of aversive stimulation used.

The negative domain tends to be characterized by more elaborate cognitive processing and greater concern with normative inhibitions (Blanz et al. 1997) and may lead groups to recategorize themselves at a superordinate level (Mummendey et al. 2001). Reynolds et al. (2000), however, argued that in-group favoritism is shown on both positive and negative dimensions when both provide a meaningful and relevant basis for self-definition in in-group/out-group terms. A $2 \times 2 \times 2$ taxonomy of social discrimination can be created (see Mummendey & Otten 2001) by crossing valence of resources (positive vs. negative) by type of behavioral mode (direct-inflicting vs. indirect-withdrawing) by target (in- vs. out-group). Gardham & Brown (2001) reported significant in-group favoritism only for instances of beneficiary decisions (i.e., allocating positive, and withdrawing negative, stimuli). Bias in both positive and negative domains can be instigated by aggravating conditions (e.g., when numerical or socially inferior status increases the salience of the intergroup distinction and elicits a threat to social identity and/or the stability of the status hierarchy) (see Mummendey et al. 1992, Mummendey & Otten 1998, Otten et al. 1996).

Personality and Individual Difference Variables

There is a long tradition of attempts to relate personality and individual-difference variables to bias (typically prejudice); recent work points to a positive relationship between prejudice and both right-wing authoritarianism (submitting to established authorities and adhering to social conventions) (e.g., Altemeyer 1998) and strong religious beliefs (e.g., Batson & Burris 1994).

Other individual differences that predict prejudice include general value orientations and more specific social orientations. Endorsement of protestant work ethic values is related to the rejection of out-groups, whereas egalitarian values are associated with more favorable responses to all groups (Biernat et al. 1996; for a discussion of social orientations in the minimal-groups paradigm, see Bourhis & Gagnon 2001). Given the long list of potential individual-difference predictors of bias, and the overlap between some measures, the most useful studies are those that show prediction of bias with a specific measure (e.g., entity vs. incremental lay theories), while controlling for other measures (e.g., need for closure) (see Levy et al. 1998).

Correlations between individual-level predictors and intergroup bias may be generally rather weak for two reasons: (a) Measurement of the predictor is usually taken when an individual's personal identity is salient, whereas intergroup behavior is characterized by the salience of social (in-group) identity (Mackie & Smith 1998, Turner & Reynolds 2001); (b) when people are depersonalized, acting as group members, intragroup homogeneity is enhanced, modifying correlations between intergroup responses and a priori scores on individual-difference measures (see Reynolds et al. 2001, Verkuyten & Hagendoorn 1998).

REDUCTION OF INTERGROUP BIAS

Intergroup bias has both psychological and social components; hence, individual and intergroup approaches can make important contributions to the reduction of intergroup bias (Dovidio et al. 2000a, Eberhardt & Fiske 1996, Oskamp 2000).

Individual Processes

Social-cognitive factors underlying perceiver differences in prejudice can be challenged, especially in young children and adolescents (Aboud & Levy 2000, Levy 1999), to target subtle, unintentional and implicit biases, which may be especially difficult to recognize and, consequently, particularly resistant to change (Gaertner & Dovidio 2000).

DIRECT APPROACHES   Some interventions, often based on motivational processes, attempt explicitly to decrease bias; prejudice must be brought to mind, but in situations that provide solutions to combat it. Monteith's (1993) notion of "prejudice with compunction" makes low-prejudiced individuals aware of "is-ought" discrepancies between their personal values and how they actually respond to minority members. This self-directed guilt should activate control mechanisms aimed at inhibiting and ultimately reducing bias across multiple settings (see Devine et al. 2000). Whereas this approach seems successful (Dovidio et al. 1998), it capitalizes on the good intentions of low-prejudiced individuals (whose bias is surely not the main problem) and demands appropriate levels of awareness, effort, and practice over time.

A controversial idea is that individuals can be made to suppress their biases (see Macrae & Bodenhausen 2000, Monteith et al. 1998). Although this can increase accessibility of negative thoughts, feelings, and behavior when suppression is relaxed, the goal is to help individuals to develop "auto-motive" control of their actions by frequently and consistently pursuing the goal of not being biased. An alternative is more explicit retraining (e.g., Kawakami et al. 2001), but the amount of retraining required is prodigious and, on a large scale, impractical; despite such intensive intervention, change may not be long lasting (Dovidio et al. 2001). Other direct approaches to reducing bias include emphasizing broader, more positive ideologies (e.g., resource allocation) (Pratto et al. 1999); increasing the salience of positive values (e.g., tolerance) (Greenberg et al. 1992); value confrontation (e.g., of right-wing authoritarians) (Altemeyer 1994); and making individuals rationalize or account for their bias (Dobbs & Crano 2001).

INDIRECT APPROACHES   Leippe & Eisenstadt (1994) used dissonance principles to reduce bias indirectly by inducing nonprejudiced behavior from individuals who subsequently showed less biased attitudes, in line with their behavior. Empathy, which has cognitive and emotional aspects, also seems a promising route to generalized positive feelings towards a group as a whole (Batson et al. 1997, Finlay & Stephan 2000, Galinsky & Moskowitz 2000). Empathy can also help decrease threat and reduce anxiety over interacting with members of the out-group (Stephan & Finlay 1999).

Several interventions try to reduce bias by teaching individuals, especially children, to classify others on multiple dimensions (e.g., Bigler 1999, Bigler & Liben 1992). These approaches are indirect because they, for example, teach children about similarities and differences among fictitious children, who are not explicitly related to category memberships but can provide cognitive skills to target prejudice (Aboud & Fenwick 1999).

Intergroup Processes

Many intergroup approaches to bias reduction focus on the need to increase the quantity and quality of intergroup contact. Pettigrew's (1998b) review of recent research on cooperative intergroup contact, supplemented by meta-analytic evidence (Pettigrew & Tropp 2000), pointed to our increased knowledge of the mediating processes by which contact can reduce bias, including empathy and anxiety. Complementing Pettigrew's (1998b) review, we focus here on one major moderator of contact, namely the categorization process underlying intergroup contact (see Brewer & Gaertner 2001, Gaertner & Dovidio 2000, Hewstone 1996, Pettigrew 1998b). We review the three main categorization approaches to contact, considering for each the structural representation of the contact situation that is recommended and the psychological processes that are thought to promote reduced bias in the contact setting (Brewer & Gaertner 2001). Our two primary criteria for evaluating the models are whether contact experiences can be generalized from the target-group member(s) encountered in the contact setting to the out-group in general and whether each model can work in the real world.

REDUCING THE SALIENCE OF CATEGORY DISTINCTIONS

Decategorization   This approach seeks to eliminate categorization via two mutual and reciprocal cognitive processes: "differentiation" (distinctions are made between out-group members) and "personalization" (out-group members are seen in terms of their uniqueness and in relation to the self). Decategorization seeks to reduce bias by moving (former) in-group members (once individuated) away from the self and towards out-group members (thus removing in-group favoritism as the source of bias) (e.g., Brewer 1999). Experimental studies have shown that within contact situations an interpersonal focus is more effective at reducing bias than a task focus (e.g., Bettencourt et al. 1992) and that these effects can generalize to other members of the out-group not involved directly in contact. However, direct individual-to-group generalization is unlikely, because the very conditions that promote personalization will sever the link between the exemplar and the category. More likely long-term positive effects of decategorized contact are that categories are seen as less useful and hence used less often, and the largely atypical out-group members encountered increase the perceived variability of the out-group as a whole (Bettencourt et al. 1992). Decategorization also claims support from survey research showing that having out-group friends reduces bias (e.g., Pettigrew 1997, Phinney et al. 1997).

It is important to note that experimental studies claiming support for decategorization maintained, and did not erase, categorization, and that none of the survey research measured whether categorization was salient for those with out-group friends. Hence, it is not clear that these are pure forms of personalization (as opposed to personal contact moderated by the salience of category distinctions; see below). A further limitation is that the benefits of decategorization may be restricted to majority groups, with members of minority groups showing more bias under interpersonal conditions than when focusing on the task (Bettencourt et al. 1997, 1999).

Recategorization   The common in-group identity (CII) model of recategorization seeks to alter which categorizations are used and to replace subordinate (us and them) with superordinate (we) categorizations (Gaertner & Dovidio 2000). There is extensive experimental support for the CII model (there is also support from survey research, but here the evidence for cognitive mediation is generally weaker) (e.g., Gaertner et al. 1994). Key findings of these experiments are that (*a*) inducing a one-vs. two-group representation of intergroup relations (e.g., via cooperation) reduces bias via its effect on cognitive representations of social categorization (Gaertner et al. 1989, 1990); (*b*) distinctive two-group representations predicted more bias, and stronger superordinate representations predicted less bias (Dovidio et al. 1995). Overall this research finds, as predicted, that bias is reduced primarily by improving attitudes towards former out-group members, owing to their recategorization from out-group to in-group. Intergroup relations are likely to improve over time, rather than immediately, as positivity biases associated with a new superordinate group membership encourage more self-disclosing interactions with former out-group members, which leads later to more differentiated impressions of them (Dovidio et al. 1997, Gaertner & Dovidio 2000).

Most studies of the CII model have not looked at generalization, because the more inclusive superordinate identity is intended to replace the prior in-group/out-group categorization. However, Gaertner et al. (1989) did include a "one group/two groups again" condition in which participants were devolved back into their original groups; bias was intermediate between standard one-group and two-groups conditions. There are, however, two major limitations to the CII solution (Brewer & Gaertner 2001, Hewstone 1996). First, a common in-group identity may only be short-lived, or unrealistic in the face of powerful ethnic and racial categorizations (e.g., former Yugoslavia). Second, for groups with a history of antagonism, and for minorities who are likely to resist assimilation into a superordinate category that is dominated by a majority out-group (Van Oudenhoven et al. 1998), the prospect of a superordinate group identity may constitute a threat, which actually increases bias (Brewer 2000, Hornsey & Hogg 1999).

The fundamental limitation of both decategorization and recategorization models is that they threaten to deprive individuals of valued social identities in smaller, less inclusive groups (Brewer 1999). By eradicating or replacing original categorizations, neither model is likely to meet the needs of assimilation and differentiation, or of cognitive simplicity and uncertainty reduction (Brewer 2000, 2001; Hogg & Abrams 1993). Thus, decategorization and recategorization are temporally unstable solutions to the problem of intergroup discrimination (Brewer & Gaertner 2001).

MAINTAINING THE SALIENCE OF CATEGORY DISTINCTIONS This approach (Hewstone 1996) argues that, to protect against loss of distinctiveness for groups involved in contact, two factors are important: (a) The salience of group boundaries should be maintained during contact to promote generalization across members of the target out-group; (b) each group should be distinct in terms of the expertise and experience it brings to the contact situation, resulting in mutual intergroup differentiation, in which groups recognize and value mutual superiorities and inferiorities.

Positive effects of contact are more likely to generalize to the out-group as a whole when the group membership of a contact partner is made salient (e.g., Van Oudenhoven et al. 1996) or the partner is typical, rather than atypical, of the out-group as a whole (Brown et al. 1999, Study 1). Research has also shown that the intergroup, rather than interpersonal, nature of contact moderates the effect of contact on bias. Positive contact is more likely to be associated with favorable out-group attitudes when contact takes place with a typical out-group member and/or references to nationality are relatively frequent during contact (Brown et al. 1999, Study 2, Brown et al. 2001). Consistent with the mutual intergroup differentiation model, contact more effectively reduces bias when two groups are provided with distinct roles that maintain their positive distinctiveness while cooperating (e.g., Dovidio et al. 1998).

There are two main limitations associated with maintaining category distinctions during contact. First, contact risks reinforcing perceptions of group differences and increasing intergroup anxiety, which increases bias (e.g., Islam & Hewstone 1993b). Second, salient intergroup boundaries are associated with mutual distrust (Brown & Gardham 2001), and this undermines the potential for cooperative independence and mutual liking. To overcome these problems, the intergroup model of contact needs to be integrated with the personalization model. Interpersonal and intergroup contact should be viewed as orthogonal dimensions, which can together create highly effective conditions of out-group contact (i.e., contact should be highly intergroup and highly interpersonal) (Hewstone 1996). Thus, recent approaches have integrated the personalization and intergroup contact models. N. Ensari & N. Miller (submitted) reported that generalization was achieved by the interactive effects of self-disclosure with typicality (Study 1) or salience (Study 2); Hewstone et al. (2000) showed that contact with out-group friends has a stronger effect on reduced bias when participants report being aware of their respective group memberships during contact.

INCREASING THE COMPLEXITY OF SOCIAL CATEGORIZATIONS

Dual Identity The dual identity model (Gaertner et al. 1990, 1994; Gaertner & Dovidio 2000) aims to maximize the benefits of both the CII and the mutual intergroup differentiation models and reduce bias between subgroups who share a common superordinate identity, rather than consider themselves as members of separate groups (Dovidio et al. 1998; Gaertner et al. 1999, 2000; Gaertner & Dovidio 2000). Because the subgroups are both members of the same group at a superordinate level, bringing them together should not arouse motivations to achieve distinctiveness, increase perceived threat to identity, or exacerbate bias; and because the associative link to others beyond the contact situation remains intact, the benefits of a revised common in-group identity should generalize.

Consistent with the dual identity model, equal-status interaction reduced bias when original group identities were salient and not threatened by contact, and reduced bias was mediated by more inclusive group representations (Dovidio et al. 1998, Gaertner et al. 1999). Positive affect added to a dual-identity condition reduced bias further, whereas it led to less inclusive group representations and increased bias in a two-group condition (Dovidio et al. 1998). A dual identity also led to more positive out-group attitudes than a superordinate identity alone (Hornsey & Hogg 2000), especially if the superordinate category was too inclusive and did not afford adequate distinctiveness (Hornsey & Hogg 1999). Gaertner et al's (1994) correlational study in a multi-ethnic high school found less bias the more the student body was perceived in terms of different ethnic subgroups, but "all playing on the same team" (i.e., the school), and when students identified themselves at both subgroup (i.e. ethnic group) and at superordinate (i.e., Americans) levels, rather than at the subgroup level only.

A major problem for the dual-identity approach is that members of majority and minority groups may have different preferences for what model of intergroup relations to adopt. Dominant majority ethnic groups tend to favor assimilation, whereas racial and ethnic minorities favor pluralistic integration (Berry 1997; Dovidio et al. 2000a,b; Van Oudenhoven et al. 1998; Wolsko et al. 2000). Thus, a dual identity may reduce bias for the minority, but not the majority (Zagefka & Brown 2001). A successful superordinate category and identity must be inclusive, and able to represent group differences in a complex way, rather than reflecting too strongly the superior characteristics of a dominant majority group (Mummendey & Wenzel 1999). But even if this is the case, subgroup categorizations and identities are likely to be stronger and more stable than superordinate ones (Brewer 2000).

Crossed Categorization   This approach is based on horizontal, cross-cutting categories, where 'others' can be simultaneously classified as in-group or out-group members on multiple dimensions. Shared or overlapping category memberships reduce bias because they: (1) make social categorization more complex; (2) decrease the importance of any one in-group/out-group distinction; (3) make perceivers aware that the out-group consists of different subgroups; (4) increase classification of others in terms of multiple dimensions; and (5) increase the degree of interpersonal interaction and trust across category boundaries (Brewer 2000, Brewer & Gaertner 2001, Hewstone 1996).

Crossing two categories (i.e., the target is in-group/out-group or partial) does not typically result in less bias than is found in a simple categorization (i.e., the target is only out-group) condition (e.g., Crisp et al. 2001, Singh et al. 1997; see meta-analysis by Mullen et al. 2001), but it reduces the pronounced bias directed against double-out-group targets (i.e., out-group on both available dimensions) (e.g., Crisp et al. 2001, Vanman et al. 1997; see review by Crisp & Hewstone 1999 and meta-analyses by Migdal et al. 1998, Urban & Miller 1998). Cross-cutting social identities or role assignments manipulated as part of cooperative intergroup contact are especially effective, increasing intracategory differentiation and decreasing perceived intercategory differences (Ensari & Miller 2001, Marcus-Newhall et al. 1993). Perceivers may abandon more complex multiple group representations and reduce bias by personalizing new team members from a former out-group (see Urban & Miller 1998), even when groups are asymmetrical in terms of size or status (Bettencourt & Dorr 1998). Positive affect can also augment effects of crossed categorization (Ensari & Miller 1998), generally increasing positive attitudes towards others who share in-group membership on any dimension (see meta-analysis by Urban & Miller 1998).

Several different patterns of bias can be found when categories are crossed (see Crisp & Hewstone 1999, 2000a,b; Hewstone et al. 1993), and bias is not always reduced (for moderators, see Urban & Miller 1998). In particular, the effectiveness of crossed categorization is limited when (*a*) one category dimension is functionally dominant (Crisp & Hewstone 2001, Hewstone et al. 1993, Urada & Miller 2000), (*b*) categories are correlated (Eurich-Fulcer & Schofield 1995), and (*c*) groups are under threat and social identities are defined in more exclusive and less complex terms (Brewer 2000).

INTEGRATION OF INTERGROUP APPROACHES TO BIAS REDUCTION   The three main intergroup approaches (and five models) should be seen as complementary and reciprocal, not competing and exclusive (Brewer 2000, Brewer & Gaertner 2001, Hewstone 1996). This integrative approach responds to the fact that each model can be effective under particular contact conditions, but it also has weaknesses and limitations, particularly with respect to generalization and to finding an intervention that works for both majority and minority groups (Brewer & Gaertner 2001, Gaertner & Dovidio 2000, Hewstone 1996, Pettigrew 1998b). Future research needs to specify how to combine multiple models into high-impact interventions, and to integrate further developmental and social-psychological approaches.

Finally, we need to ascertain which models have the greatest impact on which outcome measures. Many interventions focus on improving out-group attitudes, but because in-group favoritism and out-group derogation are relatively independent components of bias, reduction of extreme negative affect towards an out-group does not necessarily increase positive affect towards out-group members (Brewer & Brown 1998). Given the corrosive nature of many real-world conflicts, out-group liking is often unlikely; achieving other outcomes may be more realistic and as important, including increases in perceived out-group variability, out-group knowledge and perspective taking, and decreased intergroup anxiety. To reduce full-blown intergroup conflict, effective interventions also need to build trust (Kramer & Carnevale 2001), address collective guilt and its related emotions (Doosje et al. 1998), and build intergroup forgiveness (Hewstone & Cairns 2001, Hewstone et al. 2000).

CONCLUSION: BEYOND INTERGROUP BIAS

As we noted earlier, most of the relevant research and theoretical developments on intergroup bias have been directed at its relatively mild forms; they provide a better framework for understanding in-group bias and intergroup discrimination of the positive type than out-group hostility (Brewer 2001). Faced with ethnic cleansing in Bosnia or genocide in Rwanda, there is an evident mismatch between the effect that most research on intergroup bias has studied and most theories have sought to address and the most striking social problems that this research area ought to be able to address.

Social categorization clearly contributes to the most extreme forms of intergroup bias. R.B. Zajonc's (unpublished) analysis of massacres points to several social-psychological processes closely linked to intergroup bias and conflict. These include delegitimizing victims (assigning them to an extreme social category, which enjoys no protection) (Bar-Tal 1990), and morally excluding them (placing them outside the in-group boundary of justice, fairness, and morality) (Opotow 1995, Staub 2001). It would be a mistake, however, to consider ethnic and religious mass murder as a simple extension of intergroup bias. First, the motives of those implicated in ethnic violence may be more complex than simple hatred for an out-group (see Fearon & Laitin 2000) and some perpetrators participate only under duress, and in fear of their own lives. Second, the paradigmatic instances of ethnic and nationalist violence are large-scale events, extended in space and time; hence, they differ from the phenomena that social psychologists normally study, although not necessarily those they (should) seek to explain (see Brubaker & Laitin 1998). Third, social conflict is more complex than intergroup bias and cannot be equated with the outcome of just one psychological process, nor should it be analyzed from just one disciplinary perspective. Real-world intergroup relations owe at least as much of their character to intergroup history, economics, politics, and ideology as they do to social-psychological variables such as self-esteem, in-group identification, group size, and group threat (Tajfel & Turner 1979). Turner & Reynolds' (2001) outline of the general requirements of a social-psychological theory of intergroup conflict includes, but also goes well beyond, theories of intergroup bias (Hewstone & Cairns 2001, Tajfel & Turner 1979).

ACKNOWLEDGMENTS

This chapter was prepared in part while Miles Hewstone was a Fellow at the Center for Advanced Study in the Behavioral Sciences, Stanford. He gratefully acknowledges financial support provided by the William and Flora Hewlett Foundation. All three authors are grateful to the following who provided critical and constructive commentary with commendable celerity: Marilynn Brewer, Richard Crisp, Vicki Esses, Sam Gaertner, Jeff Greenberg, Louk Hagendoorn, Sheri Levy, Sabine Otten, Kate Reynolds, Mark Schaller, Terri Vescio, and Alberto Voci. Finally, we thank Susan Fiske for her own advice, and for her support, encouragement, and patience.

Visit the Annual Reviews home page at www.AnnualReviews.org

LITERATURE CITED

Aberson CL, Healy M, Romero V. 2000. Ingroup bias and self-esteem: a meta-analysis. *Pers. Soc. Psychol. Rev.* 4:157–73

Aboud FE, Fenwick V. 1999. Exploring and evaluating school-based interventions to reduce prejudice. *J. Soc. Issues* 55:767–86

Aboud FE, Levy SR. 2000. Interventions to reduce prejudice and discrimination in children and adolescents. See Oskamp 2000, pp. 269–93

Abrams D, Hogg MA, eds. 1990. *Social Identity Theory: Constructive and Critical Advances.* New York: Harvester Wheatsheaf

Altemeyer B. 1994. Reducing prejudice in right-wing authoritarians. See Zanna & Olsen 1994, pp. 131–48

Altemeyer B. 1998. The other "authoritarian personality." In *Advances in Experimental Social Psychology*, ed. MP Zanna, 30:47–92. San Diego, CA: Academic

Bar-Tal D. 1990. Causes and consequences of delegitimization: models of conflict and ethnocentrism. *J. Soc. Issues* 46:65–81

Batson CD, Burris CT. 1994. Personal religion: depressant or stimulant of prejudice and discrimination? See Zanna & Olsen 1994, pp. 149–70

Batson CD, Polycarpou MP, Harmon-Jones E, Imhoff HJ, Mitchener EC, et al. 1997. Empathy and attitudes: Can feeling for a member of a stigmatized group improve feelings toward the group? *J. Pers. Soc. Psychol.* 72:105–18

Berry JW. 1997. Immigration, acculturation, and adaptation. *Appl. Psychol.: Int. Rev.* 46: 5–68

Bettencourt BA, Bartholomew BD. 1998. The importance of status legitimacy for intergroup attitudes among numerical minorities. *J. Soc. Issues* 54:759–75

Bettencourt BA, Brewer MB, Rogers-Croak M, Miller N. 1992. Cooperation and the reduction of intergroup bias: the role of reward structure and social orientation. *J. Exp. Soc. Psychol.* 28:301–19

Bettencourt BA, Charlton K, Kernahan C. 1997. Numerical representation of groups in co-operative settings: social orientation effects on ingroup bias. *J. Exp. Soc. Psychol.* 33:630–59

Bettencourt BA, Dorr N. 1998. Cooperative interaction and intergroup bias: effects of numerical representation and cross-cut role assignment. *Pers. Soc. Psychol. Bull.* 24: 1276–93

Bettencourt BA, Dorr N, Charlton K, Hume DL. 2001. Status differences and in-group bias: a meta-analytic examination of the effects of status stability, status legitimacy, and group permeability. *Psychol. Bull.* 127:520–42

Bettencourt BA, Miller N, Hume DL. 1999. Effects of numerical representation within cooperative settings: examining the role of salience in in-group favouritism. *Br. J. Soc. Psychol.* 38:265–87

Biernat M, Vescio TK, Theno S. 1996. Violating American values: A "value congruence" approach to understanding outgroup attitudes. *J. Exp. Soc. Psychol.* 32:387–41

Bigler RS. 1999. The use of multicultural curricula and materials to counter racism in children. *J. Soc. Issues* 55:687–706

Bigler RS, Liben LS. 1992. Cognitive mechanisms in children's gender stereotyping: theoretical and educational implications of a cognitive-based intervention. *Child Dev.* 63:1351–63

Blair IV. 2001. Implicit stereotypes and prejudice. See Moskowitz 2001, pp. 359–74

Blanz M, Mummendey A, Otten S. 1997. Normative evaluations and frequency expectations regarding positive versus negative outcome allocations between groups. *Eur. J. Soc. Psychol.* 27:165–76

Boldry JG, Kashy DA. 1999. Intergroup perception in naturally occurring groups of differential status: a social relations perspective. *J. Pers. Soc. Psychol.* 77:1200–12

Bourhis RY. 1994. Power, gender and intergroup discrimination: some minimal group experiments. See Zanna & Olsen 1994, pp. 209–32

Bourhis RY, Gagnon A. 2001. Social orientations in the minimal group paradigm. See Brown & Gaertner 2001, pp. 89–111

Bourhis RY, Turner JC, Gagnon A. 1997. Interdependence, social identity and discrimination: some empirical considerations. In *The Social Psychology of Stereotyping and Group Life*, ed. R Spears, PJ Oakes, N Ellemers, SA Haslam, pp. 273–95. Oxford: Blackwell

Branscombe NR, Wann DL. 1994. Collective self-esteem consequences of out-group derogation when a valued social identity is on trial. *Eur. J. Soc. Psychol.* 24:641–57

Brauer M. 2001. Intergroup perception in the social context: the effects of social status and group membership on perceived outgroup homogeneity and ethnocentrism. *J. Exp. Soc. Psychol.* 37:15–31

Brewer MB. 1991. The social self: on being the same and different at the same time. *Pers. Soc. Psychol. Bull.* 17:475–82

Brewer MB. 1999. The psychology of prejudice: ingroup love or outgroup hate? *J. Soc. Issues* 55:429–44

Brewer MB. 2000. Reducing prejudice through cross-categorization: effects of multiple social identities. See Oskamp 2000, pp. 165–84

Brewer MB. 2001. Ingroup identification and intergroup conflict: When does ingroup love become outgroup hate? In *Social Identity, Intergroup Conflict, and Conflict Reduction*, ed. R Ashmore, L Jussim, D Wilder. New York: Oxford Univ. Press. In press

Brewer MB, Brown RJ. 1998. Intergroup relations. See Gilbert et al. 1998, pp. 554–94

Brewer MB, Gaertner SL. 2001. Toward reduction of prejudice: intergroup contact and social categorization. See Brown & Gaertner 2001, pp. 451–72

Brewer MB, Manzi J, Shaw JS. 1993. In-group identification as a function of depersonalization, distinctiveness, and status. *Psychol. Sci.* 4:88–92

Brown R, Gaertner S, eds. 2001. *Blackwell Handbook of Social Psychology: Intergroup Processes*. Malden, MA: Blackwell

Brown R, Gardham K. 2001. Two forms of intergroup discrimination with positive and negative outcomes: explaining the positive-negative asymmetry effect. *Pers. Soc. Psychol. Bull.* In press

Brown R, Maras P, Masser B, Vivian J, Hewstone M. 2001. Life on the ocean wave: testing some intergroup hypotheses in a naturalistic setting. *Group Proc. Int. Group Rel.* 4:81–98

Brown R, Vivian J, Hewstone M. 1999. Changing attitudes through intergroup contact: the effects of group membership salience. *Eur. J. Soc. Psychol.* 29:741–64

Brubaker R, Laitin DD. 1998. Ethnic and nationalist violence. *Annu. Rev. Sociol.* 24:423–52

Cadinu MR, Rothbart M. 1996. Self-anchoring and differentiation processes in the minimal group setting. *J. Pers. Soc. Psychol.* 70:661–77

Capozza D, Brown RJ, eds. 2000. *Social Identity Processes: Trends in Theory and Research*. Beverly Hills, CA: Sage

Chirot D, Seligman MEP, eds. 2001. *Ethnopolitical Warfare: Causes, Consequences, and Possible Solutions*. Washington, DC: Am. Psychol. Assoc.

Crisp RJ, Hewstone M. 1999. Crossed categorization and intergroup bias: context, process and social consequences. *Group Proc. Int. Relat.* 2:307–34

Crisp RJ, Hewstone M. 2000a. Crossed categorization and intergroup bias: the moderating role of intergroup and affective context. *J. Exp. Soc. Psychol.* 36:357–83

Crisp RJ, Hewstone M. 2000b. Multiple categorization and social identity. See Capozza & Brown 2000, pp. 149–66

Crisp RJ, Hewstone M. 2001. Multiple categorization and implicit intergroup bias: differential category dominance and the positive-negative asymmetry effect. *Eur. J. Soc. Psychol.* 31:45–62

Crisp RJ, Hewstone M, Rubin M. 2001. Does

multiple categorization reduce intergroup bias? *Pers. Soc. Psychol. Bull.* 27:76–89

Cunningham WA, Preacher KJ, Banaji MR. 2001. Implicit attitude measures: consistency, stability, and convergent validity. *Psychol. Sci.* 12:163–70

Dasgupta N, McGhee DE, Greenwald AG, Banaji MR. 2000. Automatic preference for white Americans: eliminating the familiarity explanation. *J. Exp. Soc. Psychol.* 36:316–28

Devine PG, Plant EA, Blair IV. 2001. Classic and contemporary analyses of racial prejudice. See Brown & Gaertner 2001, pp. 198–217

Devine PG, Plant EA, Buswell BN. 2000. Breaking the prejudice habit: progress and obstacles. See Oskamp 2000, pp. 185–210

Dobbs M, Crano WD. 2001. Outgroup accountability in the minimal group paradigm: implications for aversive discrimination and social identity theory. *Pers. Soc. Psychol. Bull.* 27:355–65

Doosje B, Branscombe NR, Spears R, Manstead ASR. 1998. Guilty by association: when one's group has a negative history. *J. Pers. Soc. Psychol.* 75:872–86

Dovidio JF, Brigham JC, Johnson BT, Gaertner SL. 1996. Stereotyping, prejudice, and discrimination: another look. See Macrae et al. 1996, pp. 276–322

Dovidio JF, Gaertner SL, Isen AM, Lowrance R. 1995. Group representations and intergroup bias: positive affect, similarity, and group size. *Pers. Soc. Psychol. Bull.* 21:856–65

Dovidio JF, Gaertner SL, Kafati G. 2000b. Group identity and intergroup relations: the common ingroup identity model. In *Advances in Group Processes*, ed. S Thye, EJ Lawler, M Macy, H Walker, 17:1–35. Stanford, CT: JAI Press

Dovidio JF, Gaertner SL, Validzic A. 1998. Intergroup bias: status, differentiation, and a common in-group identity. *J. Pers. Soc. Psychol.* 75:109–20

Dovidio JF, Kawakami K, Beach KR. 2001. Implicit and explicit attitudes: examination of the relationship between measures of intergroup bias. See Brown & Gaertner 2001, pp. 175–97

Dovidio JF, Kawakami K, Gaertner SL. 2000a. Reducing contemporary prejudice: combating explicit and implicit bias at the individual and intergroup level. See Oskamp 2000, pp. 137–63

Dovidio J, Kawakami K, Johnson C, Johnson B, Howard A. 1997. The nature of prejudice: automatic and controlled processes. *J. Exp. Soc. Psychol.* 33:510–40

Duckitt J, Mphuthing T. 1998. Group identification and intergroup attitudes: a longitudinal analysis in South Africa. *J. Pers. Soc. Psychol.* 74:80–85

Dunton B, Fazio R. 1997. An individual difference measure of motivation to control prejudiced reactions. *Pers. Soc. Psychol. Bull.* 23:316–26

Eagly AH, Mladinic A, Otto S. 1994. Cognitive and affective bases of attitudes toward social groups and social policies. *J. Exp. Soc. Psychol.* 30:113–37

Eberhardt JL, Fiske ST. 1996. Motivating individuals to change: What is the target to do? See Macrae et al. 1996, pp. 369–418

Ellemers N, Wilke H, Van Knippenberg A. 1993. Effects of the legitimacy of low group or individual status on individual and collective identity enhancement strategies. *J. Pers. Soc. Psychol.* 64:766–78

Ensari N, Miller N. 1998. Effect of affective reactions by the out-group on preferences for crossed categorization discussion partners. *J. Pers. Soc. Psychol.* 75:1503–27

Ensari N, Miller N. 2001. Decategorization and the reduction of bias in the crossed categorization paradigm. *Eur. J. Soc. Psychol.* 31:193–216

Esses VM, Haddock G, Zanna MP. 1993. Values, stereotypes, and emotions as determinants of intergroup attitudes. See Mackie & Hamilton 1993, pp. 137–66

Esses VM, Jackson LM, Armstrong TL. 1998. Intergroup competition and attitudes toward immigrants and immigration: an instrumental model of group conflict. *J. Soc. Issues* 54:699–724

Eurich-Fulcer R, Schofield JW. 1995. Correlated versus uncorrelated social categorizations: the effect on intergroup bias. *Pers. Soc. Psychol. Bull.* 21:149–59

Fazio R, Dunton B. 1997. Categorization by race: the impact of automatic and controlled components of racial prejudice. *J. Exp. Soc. Psychol.* 33:451–70

Fazio RH, Jackson JR, Dunton BC, Williams CJ. 1995. Variability in automatic activation as an unobtrusive measure of racial attitudes: a *bona fide* pipeline? *J. Pers. Soc. Psychol.* 69:1013–27

Fearon JD, Laitin DD. 2000. Violence and the construction of ethnic identities. *Int. Org.* 54:845–77

Federico CM. 1998. The interactive effects of social dominance orientation, group status, and perceived stability on favoritism for high-status groups. *Group Proc. Int. Relat.* 2:119–43

Feshbach S. 1994. Nationalism, patriotism, and aggression: a clarification of functional differences. In *Aggressive Behavior: Current Perspectives*, ed. LR Huesmann, pp. 275–91. New York: Plenum

Finlay K, Stephan W. 2000. Improving intergroup relations: the effects of empathy on racial attitudes. *J. Appl. Soc. Psychol.* 30:1720–37

Fiske ST. 1998. Stereotyping, prejudice, and discrimination. See Gilbert et al. 1998, pp. 357–411

Florian V, Mikulincer M. 1998. Terror management in childhood: Does death conceptualization moderate the effects of mortality salience on acceptance of similar and different others? *Pers. Soc. Psychol. Bull.* 24:1104–12

Forgas J, Fiedler K. 1996. Us and them: mood effects on intergroup discrimination. *J. Pers. Soc. Psychol.* 70:28–40

Gaertner L, Insko CA. 2000. Intergroup discrimination in the minimal group paradigm: categorization, reciprocation, or fear? *J. Pers. Soc. Psychol.* 79:77–94

Gaertner SL, Dovidio JF. 2000. *Reducing Intergroup Bias: The Common Ingroup Identity Model.* Philadelphia: Psychology Press

Gaertner SL, Dovidio JF, Nier J, Banker B, Ward C, et al. 2000. The common ingroup identity model for reducing intergroup bias: progress and challenges. See Capozza & Brown 2000, pp. 133–48

Gaertner SL, Dovidio JF, Rust MC, Nier JA, Banker BS, et al. 1999. Reducing intergroup bias: elements of intergroup cooperation. *J. Pers. Soc. Psychol.* 76:388–402

Gaertner SL, Mann JA, Dovidio JF, Murrell AJ, Pomare M. 1990. How does cooperation reduce intergroup bias? *J. Pers. Soc. Psychol.* 59:692–704

Gaertner SL, Mann J, Murrell A, Dovidio JF. 1989. Reducing intergroup bias: the benefits of recategorization. *J. Pers. Soc. Psychol.* 57:239–49

Gaertner SL, Rust MC, Dovidio JF, Bachman BA, Anastasio PA. 1994. The contact hypothesis: the role of a common ingroup identity on reducing intergroup bias. *Small Group Res.* 25:224–49

Gagnon A, Bourhis RY. 1996. Discrimination in the minimal group paradigm: social identity or self-interest? *Pers. Soc. Psychol. Bull.* 22:1289–301

Galinsky AD, Moskowitz GB. 2000. Perspective-taking: decreasing stereotype expression, stereotype accessibility, and ingroup favoritism. *J. Pers. Soc. Psychol.* 73:708–24

Gardham K, Brown RJ. 2001. Two forms of intergroup discrimination with positive and negative outcomes: explaining the positive-negative asymmetry effect. *Br. J. Soc. Psychol.* 40:23–34

Gilbert DT, Fiske ST, Lindzey G, eds. 1998. *The Handbook of Social Psychology*, Vol. 2. Boston: McGraw-Hill. 4th ed.

Green DP, Glaser J, Rich A. 1998. From lynching to gay bashing: the elusive connection between economic conditions and hate crime. *J. Pers. Soc. Psychol.* 75:82–92

Greenberg J, Pyszczynski T, Solomon S, Rosenblatt A, Veeder M, et al. 1990. Evidence for terror management theory II: the effects of mortality salience on reactions to those who threaten or bolster the cultural worldview. *J. Pers. Soc. Psychol.* 58:308–18

Greenberg J, Pyszczynski T, Solomon S, Simon L, Breus M. 1994. Role of consciousness and accessibility of death-related thoughts in mortality salience effects. *J. Pers. Soc. Psychol.* 67:627–37

Greenberg J, Simon L, Pyszczynski T, Solomon S, Chatel D. 1992. Terror management and tolerance: Does mortality salience always intensify negative reactions to others who threaten one's worldview? *J. Pers. Soc. Psychol.* 63:212–20

Greenwald A, McGhee D, Schwartz J. 1998. Measuring individual differences in implicit cognition: the implicit association test. *J. Pers. Soc. Psychol.* 74:1464–80

Grieve PG, Hogg MA. 1999. Subjective uncertainty and intergroup discrimination in the minimal group situation. *Pers. Soc. Psychol. Bull.* 25:926–40

Hagendoorn L. 1995. Intergroup biases in multiple group systems: the perception of ethnic hierarchies. In *European Review of Social Psychology*, ed. W Stroebe, M Hewstone, 6:199–228. Chichester, UK: Wiley

Hagendoorn L, Linssen H, Tumanov S. 2001. *Intergroup Relations in States of the Former Soviet Union: The Perception of Russians. European Monographs in Social Psychology.* Hove, UK: Psychology Press

Hagendoorn L, Nekuee S. 1999. *Education and Racism: A Cross-National Inventory of Positive Effects of Education on Ethnic Tolerance.* Aldershot, UK: Ashgate

Harmon-Jones E, Greenberg J, Solomon S, Simon L. 1996. The effects of mortality salience on intergroup bias between minimal groups. *Eur. J. Soc. Psychol.* 26:677–81

Heine SJ, Lehman DR. 1997. The cultural construction of self-enhancement: an examination of group-serving biases. *J. Pers. Soc. Psychol.* 72:1268–83

Henderson-King E, Henderson-King D, Zhermer N, Posokhova S, Chiker V. 1997. Ingroup favoritism and perceived similarity: a look at Russians' perceptions in the post-

Soviet era. *Pers. Soc. Psychol. Bull.* 23:1013–21

Hewstone M. 1996. Contact and categorization: social psychological interventions to change intergroup relations. See Macrae et al. 1996, pp. 323–68

Hewstone M, Cairns E. 2001. Social psychology and intergroup conflict. See Chirot & Seligman 2001, pp. 319–42

Hewstone M, Cairns E, Judd CM, Voci A, McLernon F. 2000. *Intergroup contact in Northern Ireland: mediational and moderational hypotheses.* Presented at Ann. Meet. Soc. Exp. Soc. Psychol., Atlanta, GA

Hewstone M, Islam MR, Judd CM. 1993. Models of crossed categorization and intergroup relations. *J. Pers. Soc. Psychol.* 64:779–93

Hinkle S, Brown RJ. 1990. Intergroup comparisons and social identity: some links and lacunae. See Abrams & Hogg 1990, pp. 48–70

Hodson G, Sorrentino RM. 2001. Just who favors the ingroup? Personality differences in reactions to uncertainty in the minimal group paradigm. *Group Dynam.: Theory, Res. Practice* 5:92–101

Hogg MA. 2000. Subjective uncertainty reduction through self-categorization: a motivational theory of social identity processes and group phenomena. In *European Review of Social Psychology*, ed. W Stroebe, M Hewstone, 11:223–55. Chichester, UK: Wiley

Hogg MA, Abrams D. 1990. Social motivation, self-esteem and social identity. See Abrams & Hogg 1990, pp. 28–47

Hogg MA, Abrams D. 1993. Towards a single-process uncertainty-reduction model of social motivation in groups. In *Group Motivation: Social Psychological Perspectives*, ed. MA Hogg, D Abrams, pp. 173–90. New York: Harvester Wheatsheaf

Hornsey MJ, Hogg MA. 1999. Subgroup differentiation as a response to an overly-inclusive group: a test of optimal distinctiveness theory. *Eur. J. Soc. Psychol.* 29:543–50

Hornsey MJ, Hogg MA. 2000. Sub-group relations: two experiments comparing subgroup differentiation and common ingroup

identity models of prejudice reduction. *Pers. Soc. Psychol. Bull.* 26:242–56

Insko CA, Schopler J, Hoyle R, Dardis G, Graetz K. 1990. Individual-group discontinuity as a function of fear and greed. *J. Pers. Soc. Psychol.* 58:68–79

Insko CA, Schopler J, Sedikides C. 1998. Personal control, entitativity, and evolution. In *Intergroup Cognition and Intergroup Behavior*, ed. C Sedikides, J Schopler, CA Insko, pp. 109–20. Mahwah, NJ: Erlbaum

Islam MR, Hewstone M. 1993a. Intergroup attributions and affective consequences in majority and minority groups. *J. Pers. Soc. Psychol.* 64:936–50

Islam MR, Hewstone M. 1993b. Dimensions of contact as predictors of intergroup anxiety, perceived out-group variability, and out-group attitude: an integrative model. *Pers. Soc. Psychol. Bull.* 19:700–10

Jackson JW, Smith ER. 1999. Conceptualizing social identity: a new framework and evidence for the impact of different dimensions. *Pers. Soc. Psychol. Bull.* 25:120–35

Jackson LA, Hodge CN, Gerard DA, Ingram JM, Ervin KS, et al. 1996. Cognition, affect, and behavior in the prediction of group attitudes. *Pers. Soc. Psychol. Bull.* 22:306–16

Jetten J, Spears R, Manstead ASR. 1996. Intergroup norms and intergroup discrimination: distinctive self-categorization and social identity effects. *J. Pers. Soc. Psychol.* 71:1222–33

Jetten J, Spears R, Manstead ASR. 1997. Distinctiveness threat and prototypicality: combined effects on intergroup discrimination and collective self-esteem. *Eur. J. Soc. Psychol.* 27:635–57

Jetten J, Spears R, Manstead ASR. 1998. Dimensions of distinctiveness: group variability makes a difference to differentiation. *J. Pers. Soc. Psychol.* 74:1481–92

Jost JT. 2001. Outgroup favoritism and the theory of system justification: an experimental paradigm for investigating the effects of socio-economic success on stereotype content. See Moskowitz 2001, pp. 89–102

Jost JT, Thompson EP. 2000. Group-based

dominance and opposition to equality as independent predictors of self-esteem, ethnocentrism, and social policy attitudes among African Americans and European Americans. *J. Exp. Soc. Psychol.* 36:209–32

Judd CM, Park B, Ryan CS, Brauer M, Kraus S. 1995. Stereotypes and ethnocentrism: diverging interethnic perceptions of African American and White American youth. *J. Pers. Soc. Psychol.* 69:460–81

Kawakami K, Dovidio JF. 2001. Implicit stereotyping: How reliable is it? *Pers. Soc. Psychol. Bull.* 27:212–25

Kawakami K, Dovidio J, Moll J, Hermsen S, Russin A. 2001. Just say no (to stereotyping): effects of training in trait negation on stereotype activation. *J. Pers. Soc. Psychol.* 78:871–88

Kramer RM, Carnevale PJ. 2001. Trust and intergroup negotiation. See Brown & Gaertner 2001, pp. 431–51

Leippe MR, Eisenstadt D. 1994. Generalization of dissonance reduction: decreasing prejudice through induced compliance. *J. Pers. Soc. Psychol.* 67:395–413

Leonardelli GJ, Brewer MB. 2001. Minority and majority discrimination: when and why. *J. Exp. Soc. Psychol.* In press

Levin S, Sidanius J. 1999. Social dominance and social identity in the United States and Israel: ingroup favoritism or outgroup derogation? *Polit. Psychol.* 20:99–126

Levy SR. 1999. Reducing prejudice: lessons from social-cognitive factors underlying perceiver differences in prejudice. *J. Soc. Issues* 55:745–65

Levy SR, Stroessner SJ, Dweck CS. 1998. Stereotype formation and endorsement: the role of implicit theories. *J. Pers. Soc. Psychol.* 74:1421–36

Maass A. 1999. Linguistic intergroup bias: stereotype perpetuation through language. See Zanna 1999, pp. 79–121

Maass A, Castelli L, Arcuri L. 2000. Measuring prejudice: implicit versus explicit techniques. See Capozza & Brown 2000, pp. 96–116

Mackie D, Hamilton D, eds. 1993. *Affect,*

Cognition, and Stereotyping. San Diego, CA: Academic

Mackie DM, Devos T, Smith ER. 2000. Intergroup emotions: explaining offensive action tendencies in an intergroup context. *J. Pers. Soc. Psychol.* 79:602–16

Mackie DM, Smith ER. 1998. Intergroup relations: insights from a theoretically integrative approach. *Psychol. Rev.* 105:499–529

Macrae CN, Bodenhausen GV. 2000. Social cognition: thinking categorically about others. *Annu. Rev. Psychol.* 51:93–120

Macrae CN, Stangor C, Hewstone M, eds. 1996. *Stereotypes and Stereotyping.* New York: Guilford

Marcus-Newhall A, Miller N, Holtz R, Brewer MB. 1993. Cross-cutting category membership with role assignment: a means of reducing intergroup bias. *Br. J. Soc. Psychol.* 32:125–46

Migdal M, Hewstone M, Mullen B. 1998. The effects of crossed categorization on intergroup evaluations: a meta-analysis. *Br. J. Soc. Psychol.* 69:1203–15

Monteith M. 1993. Self-regulation of stereotypical responses: implications for progress in prejudice reduction. *J. Pers. Soc. Psychol.* 65:469–85

Monteith M, Sherman J, Devine P. 1998. Suppression as a stereotype control strategy. *Pers. Soc. Psychol. Rev.* 1:63–82

Moskowitz G, ed. 2001. *Cognitive Social Psychology: The Princeton Symposium on the Legacy and Future of Social Cognition.* Hillsdale, NJ: Erlbaum

Mullen B, Brown R, Smith C. 1992. Ingroup bias as a function of salience, relevance, and status: an integration. *Eur. J. Soc. Psychol.* 22:103–22

Mullen B, Migdal MJ, Hewstone M. 2001. Crossed categorization vs simple categorization and intergroup evaluations: a meta-analysis. *Eur. J. Soc. Psychol.* In press

Mullin B-A, Hogg MA. 1998. Dimensions of subjective uncertainty in social identification and minimal intergroup discrimination. *Br. J. Soc. Psychol.* 37:345–65

Mummendey A, Otten S. 1998. Positive-nega-

tive asymmetry in social discrimination. In *European Review of Social Psychology*, ed. W Stroebe, M Hewstone, 9:107–43. Chichester, UK: Wiley

Mummendey A, Otten S. 2001. Aversive discrimination. See Brown & Gaertner 2001, pp. 112–32

Mummendey A, Otten S, Berger U, Kessler T. 2001. Positive-negative asymmetry in social discrimination: valence of evaluation and salience of categorization. *Pers. Soc. Psychol. Bull.* 26:1258–70

Mummendey A, Simon B, Dietze C, Grünert M, Haeger G, et al. 1992. Categorization is not enough: intergroup discrimination in negative outcome allocations. *J. Exp. Soc. Psychol.* 28:125–44

Mummendey A, Wenzel M. 1999. Social discrimination and tolerance in intergroup relations: reactions to intergroup difference. *Pers. Soc. Psychol. Rev.* 3:158–74

Nelson LJ, Moore DL, Olivetti J, Scott T. 1997. General and personal mortality salience and nationalistic bias. *Pers. Soc. Psychol. Bull.* 23:884–92

Noel JG, Wann DL, Branscombe NR. 1995. Peripheral ingroup membership status and public negativity towards out-groups. *J. Pers. Soc. Psychol.* 68:127–37

Oakes P. 2001. The root of all evil in intergroup relations? Unearthing the categorization process. See Brown & Gaertner 2001, pp. 3–21

Opotow S. 1995. Drawing the line. Social categorization, moral exclusion, and the scope of justice. In *Conflict, Cooperation, and Justice: Essays Inspired by the Work of Morton Deutsch*, ed. BB Bunker, JZ Rubin, pp. 347–69. San Francisco: Jossey-Bass

Oskamp S, ed. 2000. *Reducing Prejudice and Discrimination.* Mahwah, NJ: Erlbaum

Otten S, Moskowitz GB. 2000. Evidence for implicit evaluative in-group bias: affect-biased spontaneous trait inference in a minimal group paradigm. *J. Exp. Soc. Psychol.* 36:77–89

Otten S, Mummendey A. 2000. Valence-dependent probability of in-group favouritism between minimal groups: an integrative view on the positive-negative asymmetry in social discrimination. See Capozza & Brown 2000, pp. 33–48

Otten S, Mummendey A, Blanz M. 1996. Intergroup discrimination in positive and negative outcome allocations: the impact of stimulus valence, relative group status, and relative group size. *Pers. Soc. Psychol. Bull.* 22:568–81

Otten S, Wentura D. 1999. About the impact of automaticity in the minimal group paradigm: evidence from the affective priming tasks. *Eur. J. Soc. Psychol.* 29:1049–71

Perdue CW, Dovidio JF, Gurtman MB, Tyler RB. 1990. Us and them: social categorization and the process of intergroup bias. *J. Pers. Soc. Psychol.* 59:475–86

Perreault S, Bourhis RY. 1999. Ethnocentrism, social identification, and discrimination. *Pers. Soc. Psychol. Bull.* 25:92–103

Pettigrew TF. 1997. Generalized intergroup contact effects on prejudice. *Pers. Soc. Psychol. Bull.* 23:173–85

Pettigrew TF. 1998b. Intergroup contact theory. *Annu. Rev. Psychol.* 49:65–85

Pettigrew TF. 1998a. Reactions toward the new minorities of Western Europe. *Annu. Rev. Sociol.* 24:77–103

Pettigrew TF, Meertens R. 1995. Subtle and blatant prejudice in western Europe. *Eur. J. Soc. Psychol.* 25:57–76

Pettigrew TF, Tropp LR. 2000. Does intergroup contact reduce prejudice? Recent meta-analytic findings. See Oskamp 2000, pp. 93–114

Phelps EA, O'Connor KJ, Cunningham WA, Funuyama S, Gatenby JC, et al. 2000. Performance on indirect measures of race evaluation predicts amygdala activation. *J. Cogn. Neurosci.* 12:729–38

Phinney JS, Ferguson DL, Tate JD. 1997. Intergroup attitudes among ethnic minority adolescents. *Child Dev.* 68:955–68

Plant E, Devine P. 1998. Internal and external motivation to respond without prejudice. *J. Pers. Soc. Psychol.* 75:811–32

Platow M, O'Connell A, Shave R, Hanning P. 1995. Social evaluations of fair and unfair allocations in interpersonal and intergroup situations. *Br. J. Soc. Psychol.* 34:363–81

Pratto F. 1999. The puzzle of continuing group inequality: piecing together psychological, social, and cultural forces in social dominance theory. See Zanna 1999, pp. 191–263

Pratto F, Shih M. 2000. Social dominance orientation and group context in implicit group prejudice. *Psychol. Sci.* 11:515–18

Pratto F, Sidanius J, Stallworth LM. 1993. Sexual selection and the sexual and ethnic basis of social hierarchy. In *Social Stratification and Socioeconomic Inequality: A Comparative Biosocial Analysis*, ed. L Ellis, pp. 111–37. New York: Praeger

Pratto F, Tatar DG, Conway-Lanz S. 1999. Who gets what and why: determinants of social allocations. *Polit. Psychol.* 20:127–50

Pyszczynski T, Greenberg J, Solomon S. 1997. Why do we need what we need? A terror management perspective on the roots of human social motivation. *Psychol. Inq.* 8:1–20

Quillian L. 1995. Prejudice as a response to perceived group threat: population composition and anti-immigrant and racial prejudice in Europe. *Am. Soc. Rev.* 60:586–611

Reichl AJ. 1997. Ingroup favouritism and outgroup favouritism in low status minimal groups: differential responses to status-related and status-unrelated measures. *Eur. J. Soc. Psychol.* 27:617–33

Reynolds KJ, Turner JC, Haslam SA. 2000. When are we better than them and they worse than us? A closer look at social discrimination in positive and negative domains. *J. Pers. Soc. Psychol.* 78:64–80

Reynolds KJ, Turner JC, Haslam SA, Ryan MK. 2001. The role of personality and group factors in explaining prejudice. *J. Exp. Soc. Psychol.* In press

Roccas S, Schwartz SH. 1993. Effects of intergroup similarity on intergroup relations. *Eur. J. Soc. Psychol.* 23:581–95

Rubin M, Hewstone M. 1998. Social identity theory's self-esteem hypothesis: a review and some suggestions for clarification. *Pers. Soc. Psychol. Rev.* 2:40–62

Sachdev I, Bourhis RY. 1991. Power and status differentials in minority and majority intergroup relations, *Eur. J. Soc. Psychol.* 21:1–24

Shah JY, Kruglanski AW, Thompson EP. 1998. Membership has its (epistemic) rewards: need for closure effects on in-group bias. *J. Pers. Soc. Psychol.* 75:383–93

Sherman JW, Klein SB, Laskey A, Wyer NA. 1998. Intergroup bias in group judgment processes: the role of behavioral memories. *J. Exp. Soc. Psychol.* 34:51–65

Sidanius J, Cling BJ, Pratto F. 1991. Ranking and linking as a function of sex and gender role attitudes. *J. Soc. Issues* 47:131–49

Sidanius J, Levin S, Liu J, Pratto F. 2000. Social dominance orientation, anti-egalitarianism and the political psychology of gender: an extension and cross-cultural replication. *Eur. J. Soc. Psychol.* 30:41–67

Sidanius J, Pratto F. 1999. *Social Dominance: An Intergroup Theory of Social Hierarchy and Oppression.* New York: Cambridge Univ. Press

Sidanius J, Pratto F, Bobo L. 1994. Social dominance orientation and the political psychology of gender: a case of invariance? *J. Pers. Soc. Psychol.* 67:998–1011

Simon B, Aufderheide B, Kampmeier C. 2001. The social psychology of minority-majority relations. See Brown & Gaertner 2001, pp. 303–23

Singh R, Choo WM, Poh LL. 1998. In-group bias and fair-mindedness as strategies of self-presentation in intergroup perception. *Pers. Soc. Psychol. Bull.* 24:147–62

Singh R, Yeoh BSE, Lim DI, Lim KK. 1997. Cross categorization effects in intergroup discrimination: adding versus averaging. *Br. J. Soc. Psychol.* 36:121–38

Smith ER. 1993. Social identity and social emotions: towards new conceptualizations of prejudice. See Mackie & Hamilton 1993, pp. 297–315

Smith ER, Henry S. 1996. An in-group becomes part of the self: response evidence. *Pers. Soc. Psychol. Bull.* 25:635–42

Solomon S, Greenberg J, Pyszczynski T. 1991. A terror management theory of social be-havior: the psychological functions of self-esteem and cultural worldviews. In *Advances in Experimental Social Psychology*, ed. MP Zanna, 24:91–159. San Diego: Academic

Stangor C, Sullivan LA, Ford TE. 1991. Affective and cognitive determinants of prejudice. *Soc. Cogn.* 9:359–80

Staub E. 2001. Ethnopolitical and other group violence: origins and prevention. See Chirot & Seligman 2001, pp. 289–304

Stephan WG, Finlay K. 1999. The role of empathy in improving intergroup relations. *J. Soc. Issues* 55:729–44

Stephan WG, Stephan CW. 2000. An integrated threat theory of prejudice. See Oskamp 2000, pp. 23–46

Tajfel H, Turner JC. 1979. An integrative theory of intergroup conflict. In *The Social Psychology of Intergroup Relations*, ed. WG Austin, S Worchel, pp. 33–47. Monterey, CA: Brooks/Cole

Triandis HC, Trafimow D. 2001. Culture and its implications for intergroup behavior. See Brown & Gaertner 2001, pp. 367–85

Turner JC, Reynolds KJ. 2001. The social identity perspective in intergroup relations: theories, themes, and controversies. See Brown & Gaertner 2001, pp. 133–52

Urada DI, Miller N. 2000. The impact of positive mood and category importance on crossed categorization effects. *J. Pers. Soc. Psychol.* 78:417–33

Urban LM, Miller NM. 1998. A meta-analysis of crossed categorization effects. *J. Pers. Soc. Psychol.* 74:894–908

Vanman EJ, Paul BY, Ito TA, Miller N. 1997. The modern face of prejudice and structural features that moderate the effect of cooperation on affect. *J. Pers. Soc. Psychol.* 73:941–59

Van Oudenhoven J-P, Groenewoud JT, Hewstone M. 1996. Cooperation, ethnic salience and generalization of interethnic attitudes. *Eur. J. Soc. Psychol.* 26:649–61

Van Oudenhoven J-P, Prins KS, Buunk B. 1998. Attitudes of minority and majority members towards adaptation of immigrants. *Eur. J. Soc. Psychol.* 28:995–1013

Verkuyten M, Hagendoorn L. 1998. Prejudice and self-categorization: the variable role of authoritarianism and ingroup stereotypes. *Pers. Soc. Psychol. Bull.* 24:99–110

Von Hippel W, Sekaquaptewa D, Vargas P. 1997. The linguistic intergroup bias as an implicit indicator of prejudice. *J. Exp. Soc. Psychol.* 33:490–509

Wagner U, Zick A. 1995. Formal education and ethnic prejudice. *Eur. J. Soc. Psychol.* 25:41–56

Webster DM, Kruglanski AW, Pattison DA. 1997. Motivated language use in intergroup contexts: need for closure effects on the linguistic ingroup bias. *J. Pers. Soc. Psychol.* 72:1122–31

Wilder D, Simon AF. 2001. Affect as a cause of intergroup bias. See Brown & Gaertner 2001, pp. 153–72

Wittenbrink B, Judd C, Park B. 1997. Evidence for racial prejudice at the implicit level and its relationship with questionnaire measures. *J. Pers. Soc. Psychol.* 72:262–74

Wittenbrink B, Judd C, Park B. 2001a. Evaluative versus conceptual judgments in automatic stereotyping and prejudice. *J. Exp. Soc. Psychol.* 37:244–52

Wittenbrink B, Judd C, Park B. 2001b. Spontaneous prejudice in context: Variability in automatically activated attitudes. *J. Pers. Soc. Psychol.* In press

Wolsko C, Park B, Judd CM, Wittenbrink B. 2000. Framing interethnic ideology: effects of multicultural and color-blind perspectives on judgments of groups and individuals. *J. Pers. Soc. Psychol.* 78:635–54

Zagefka H, Brown R. 2001. The relationship between acculturation strategies, relative fit and intergroup relations: immigrant-majority relations in Germany. *Eur. J. Soc. Psychol.* In press

Zanna MP, ed. 1999. *Advances in Experimental Social Psychology*, Vol. 31. San Diego, CA: Academic

Zanna MP, Olsen JM, eds. 1994. *The Psychology of Prejudice: The Ontario Symposium.* Hillsdale, NJ: Erlbaum

Annu. Rev. Psychol. 2002. 53:605–34

LATENT VARIABLES IN PSYCHOLOGY AND THE SOCIAL SCIENCES

Kenneth A. Bollen

Odum Institute for Research in Social Science, CB 3210 Hamilton, Department of Sociology, University of North Carolina at Chapel Hill, Chapel Hill, North Carolina 27599-3210; e-mail: bollen@unc.edu

Key Words unmeasured variables, unobserved variables, residuals, constructs, concepts, true scores

■ **Abstract** The paper discusses the use of latent variables in psychology and social science research. Local independence, expected value true scores, and nondeterministic functions of observed variables are three types of definitions for latent variables. These definitions are reviewed and an alternative "sample realizations" definition is presented. Another section briefly describes identification, latent variable indeterminacy, and other properties common to models with latent variables. The paper then reviews the role of latent variables in multiple regression, probit and logistic regression, factor analysis, latent curve models, item response theory, latent class analysis, and structural equation models. Though these application areas are diverse, the paper highlights the similarities as well as the differences in the manner in which the latent variables are defined and used. It concludes with an evaluation of the different definitions of latent variables and their properties.

CONTENTS

0084-6570/02/0201-0605$14.00

INTRODUCTION

It is impossible to date the first use of latent variables. The idea that observable phenomena are influenced by underlying and unobserved causes is at least as old as religion, where unseen forces affect real world events. In the more secular sphere of everyday living, latent variables find wide application. From the response to "how are you feeling today?" to the description of a worker as "efficient" or a student as "bright," such abstract concepts elude direct measurement. What these examples illustrate is the common practice among humans to explain, to understand, and to sometimes predict events based on the role of concepts that are not directly observable. However, these more metaphysical, and everyday uses of unobserved forces depart from the use of latent variables in psychology and the social sciences. The scientific use of latent variables places a premium on designing research to test hypotheses about latent variables and having the ability to falsify hypotheses about them. In addition, latent variables provide a degree of abstraction that permits us to describe relations among a class of events or variables that share something in common, rather than making highly concrete statements restricted to the relation between more specific, seemingly idiosyncratic variables. In other words, latent variables permit us to generalize relationships.

Psychology has had its critics of latent variables, with Skinner (1976) being a well-known modern one. However, latent variables have been so useful in science that they pervade virtually all fields (see Glymour et al. 1987, pp. 22–26). Psychology and the social sciences are no exceptions. Although latent variables are part of numerous statistical and data analyses models, we do not have a single general definition of a latent variable that would include these diverse applications. Rather we have definitions of latent variables that are closely tied to specific statistical models and few systematic comparisons of these different definitions and the implications of the differences. Furthermore, the common problems that accompany the use of latent variables are obscured by the diverse definitions, each of which is tied to a limited number of applications.

Given the frequent appearance of latent variables in psychology and social science, it is surprising that so little work in these areas has focused on their nature. Borsboom et al. (2001), Edwards & Bagozzi (2000), Hägglund (2001), and Sobel (1994) are exceptions, but overall, my literature search concurs with Borsboom et al.'s conclusion that "... the theoretical status of the latent variable as it appears in models for psychological measurement has not received a thorough and general analysis as yet."

This paper aims to contribute to the discussion of latent variables in psychology and the social sciences. More specifically, the goals of the paper are (*a*) to review the major definitions of latent variables in psychology and the social sciences, (*b*) to formalize an intuitive and general definition of latent variables, (*c*) to examine latent variables in common statistical models in light of these definitions, and (d) to discuss issues that emerge when using latent variables.

I begin by reviewing several common ways of defining latent variables and introduce a "sample realizations" definition that is based on an intuitive notion of latent variables. With these definitions in hand, the next section discusses common properties and issues that arise when employing latent variables. Following this is a discussion of latent variables in a variety of statistical models including multiple regression, limited dependent-variable models (e.g., logistic and probit regressions), factor analysis, latent curve models, item response theory, latent class analysis, and structural equation models. The concluding section reviews the major findings from this review and highlights issues common to the use of latent variables.

DEFINITIONS OF LATENT VARIABLES

Unmeasured variables, factors, unobserved variables, constructs, or true scores are just a few of the terms that researchers use to refer to variables in the model that are not present in the data set. Many definitions of latent variables appear implicitly or explicitly. We can distinguish between nonformal and formal definitions. The next subsection briefly reviews several nonformal definitions. Four subsections that follow will present more formal definitions of latent variables: (a) local independence, (b) expected value, (c) nondeterministic function of observed variables, and (d) sample realization.[1] Next, I apply them to statistical models in psychology and the other social sciences in which latent or unobserved variables appear. This enables us to assess the applicability of these definitions across a range of areas.

Nonformal Definitions

One common set of definitions of latent variables considers them as "hypothetical variables." For instance, Harman (1960, p. 12) refers to factors as "hypothetical constructs." Similarly, Nunnally (1978, p. 96) defines a construct as something that scientists put together out of their imaginations (see also Bartlett 1937, p. 97). From this perspective, a property such as self-esteem is not real, but a hypothetical variable that comes from the mind of the researcher. This perspective contrasts with the Platonic view of latent variables in which the latent variables are seen as real (Sutcliffe 1965). Loevinger (1957, p. 642) makes the distinction between traits and constructs: "Traits exist in people; constructs (here usually about traits) exist in the minds and magazines of psychologists." Similarly, Edwards & Bagozzi (2000,

---

[1]These do not exhaust the formal definitions of latent variables. For example, Shafer (1996, pp. 352–56) uses probability trees and graph theory to briefly discuss latent variables. Similarly Pearl (2000) defines latent variables using graph theory. However, the definitions included here are among the most common formal definitions. Some ideas in the graph theory definitions are closely related to the local independence definitions of latent variables. It is too early to determine the impact of these graph theory–based definitions.

p. 156–57) view constructs as not real but as attempts to measure real phenomena. In their view the construct of self-esteem is not real, but there are real phenomena (or traits) to which researchers apply this term and construct.[2]

Another common definition type treats latent variables as impossible to measure, as unobservable or unmeasurable. Jöreskog & Sörbom (1979, p. 105) state that "latent variables . . . cannot be directly measured." Similarly the *Penguin Dictionary of Economics* (Bannock et al. 1998) defines a latent variable as "a variable in regression analysis which is, in principle, unmeasureable." These definitions presume knowledge that it is impossible to measure a latent variable. In a sense this presupposes that the researcher is able to know the future and that in that future there will be no innovations that will permit direct measurement of the latent variable. Thus, using this definition we would view self-esteem as not now directly measurable or measurable in the future. One difficulty with this definition is the assumption that we know the future and the impossibility of measuring a variable. Unforeseen technological or conceptual developments can occur that might make possible the measurement of variables that previously were treated as unmeasurable. A latent variable as unmeasurable definition does not permit this possibility.

A third type of informal definition defines latent variables as a data reduction device. Harman (1960, p. 5) says that ". . . a principle objective of factor analysis is to attain a parsimonious description of observed data." Thus, the latent variable or factor is a convenient means of summarizing a number of variables in many fewer factors. This definition gives primacy to the descriptive function of latent variables. It does not give much attention to latent variables that researchers define prior to analyzing the data or to the use of statistical procedures that test the implications of latent variable models. With this data reduction definition self-esteem is a term we might assign to a factor to summarize a group of items that "load" on a factor. The term is a shorthand expression for an underlying variable that helps explain the association between two or more variables.

It is possible to combine definitions. For instance, MacCallum & Austin (2000) state that "latent variables are hypothetical constructs that cannot be directly measured." Their definition combines the hypothetical and unmeasurable definitions. Taken individually or combined, these informal definitions do not capture all the ways in which researchers view latent variables. They appear best suited to exploratory analyses in which the nature of the latent variables and their relationships to observed variables is not specified in advance. Furthermore, these definitions are not based on formal definitions about the properties of the latent variables and do not provide technical assumptions about them.

---

[2]Pursuing this distinction between real and hypothetical variables leads to a metaphysical dilemma of deciding when something is real. Defining latent variables as only hypothetical narrows the use of the concept of latent variables and raises metaphysical debates on the meaning of "real variables." It seems preferable to leave the real or hypothetical nature of latent variables as an open question that may well be unanswerable.

Local Independence Definition

The "local independence" definition of a latent variable is one of the most common and popular ways to define a latent variable (Lord 1953, Lazarsfeld 1959, McDonald 1981, Bartholomew 1987, Hambleton et al. 1991). The key idea is that there are one or more latent variables that create the association between observed variables, and when the latent variables are held constant, the observed variables are independent. More formally,

$$P[Y_1, Y_2, \ldots, Y_K] = P[Y_1|\eta]P[Y_2|\eta] \cdots P[Y_K|\eta] \qquad 1.$$

where $Y_1, Y_2, \ldots, Y_K$ are random observed variables, η is a vector of latent variables, $P[Y_1, Y_2, \ldots, Y_K]$ is the joint probability of the observed variables, and $P[Y_1|\eta]P[Y_2|\eta] \cdots P[Y_K|\eta]$ are the conditional probabilities. The joint probability of the observed variables equals the product of the conditional probabilities when the latent variables are responsible for the dependencies among the observed variables. In this definition we permit either continuous or discrete observed or latent variables in recognition of the variety of situations in which this definition of local independence applies. In a factor analysis, for instance, the latent and observed variables would be continuous; in item response theory continuous latent variables would appear in conjunction with discrete observed variables; in latent class analysis both observed and latent variables would be discrete.

McDonald (1981, 1996a) distinguished the above "strong" definition of local independence from a "weaker" form in which the linear association between variables is zero once the latent variables are held constant. An example of this weak form of the definition is

$$\rho_{Y_i Y_j \cdot \eta} = 0 \qquad 2.$$

for all i, j where $i \neq j$. $\rho_{Y_i Y_j \cdot \eta}$ is the partial correlation between two observed variables controlling for the vector of latent variables. If η contains the vector of latent variables underlying these observed variables, then this partial correlation will be zero once they are controlled. If the association remains, then we do not have the complete set of latent variables that underlie the data and we need to add more of them (Bartholomew 1987, p. 5). This is a weaker form of the local independence definition in that it refers to only the linear association between variables, whereas the stronger form of the definition refers to any dependence between the observed variables. Both forms of the local independence definitions define latent variables by their ability to completely explain the association of observed variables. Using this definition we could treat self-esteem as a latent variable if once it is held constant, there is no remaining dependence (or association) among the indicators that measure it. If dependence (association) remains, then we need to introduce additional latent variables or dimensions of self-esteem to capture it.

Several key implications of this definition are that it assumes (*a*) errors of measurement are independent (or uncorrelated), (*b*) observed variables or indicators have no direct or indirect effects on each other, (*c*) we have at least two observed variables, (d) each latent variable must have direct effects on one or more observed variables, and (e) the observed variables (indicators) do not directly affect the latent variable. As I illustrate below, these properties lead to counterintuitive elimination of some variables as latent variables.

Expected Value Definition

The expected value definition of a latent variable is most commonly associated with classical test theory (e.g., Lord & Novick 1968, Lumsden 1976, Jöreskog 1971). Here the term for the underlying variable is the "true score." The true score is equal to the expected value of the observed variable for a particular individual:

$$T_i \equiv E(Y_i), \qquad\qquad 3.$$

where T_i is the value of the true score for the ith individual, $E(.)$ is the expected value, and Y_i is the random observed variable Y for the ith individual. This approach to defining a true score treats it as a value that would be obtained if we could perform a hypothetical experiment in which we could repeatedly observe Y_i for the ith individual without the responses being influenced by previous responses (Lord & Novick 1968, pp. 29–30). The mean of these infinitely replicated experiments would give us the true score value for that individual. Thus, rather than being defined by conditional independence among two or more observed variables, as in the preceding subsection, the expected value definition looks to the mean of the observed variable values for an individual as the true score. If we had an indicator of self-esteem for an individual, the true score on self-esteem would be the expected value of this measure under the hypothetical situation of repeatedly observing the indicator for the same individual where each trial would be independent of the others.

The equation for the observed random variable is

$$Y_i = T_i + E_i, \qquad\qquad 4.$$

where E_i is the error of measurement.

Several properties of the true score latent variable model are (a) its scale is defined by $E(Y_i)$; (b) the error of measurement, E_i, has a mean of zero and is uncorrelated with T_i; (c) the errors of measurement are uncorrelated for two different observed variables; (d) the true scores have direct effects on their corresponding observed variable; (e) the observed variables (indicators) do not directly affect the latent variable; and (f) two different observed variables have no direct or indirect effect on each other. As with the conditional independence definition, I argue that the true score latent variable model can lead to counterintuitive classifications of variables as latent or not.

Nondeterministic Function of Observed Variables Definition

Bentler (1982, p. 106) defines a latent variable as follows: "A variable in a linear structural equation system is a latent variable if the equations cannot be manipulated so as to express the variable as a function of manifest variables only." An interesting aspect of Bentler's definition is that it makes clear that we cannot use observed or manifest variables to exactly determine the latent variable. Although we might be able to manipulate the equations in which a latent variable appears, we cannot manipulate it to the point at which the latent variable is completely determined by the observed variables, that is, the latent variable is a nondeterministic function of the observed variables. In our hypothetical self-esteem example, self-esteem is a latent variable if we cannot manipulate its indicators to exactly express the self-esteem variable. We might be able to estimate or predict a value on the latent variable, but we would not be able to make an exact prediction based on its observed indicators.

This definition does not have the same exclusions as the local independence and expected value true score definitions of latent variables. It permits models with correlated errors of measurement and observed variables that directly or indirectly affect each other. The main restriction for this definition is that it is devised for linear structural equation systems and some latent variable models include nonlinear relations such as models with categorical observed variables. I illustrate below how the definition leads to disturbances being classified as latent variables in one model but not in another, whereas intuitively we would expect a consistent classification.

Sample Realization Definition

The "sample realization" definition that I provide is inspired by the simplest, intuitive understanding of a latent variable. Before giving more details on this definition, I provide a brief orientation of how I view latent variables. I present this orientation here rather than above because I do not assume that this perspective is shared by others who use different definitions of latent variables.

The starting point is the objects of study. The most common objects of study in psychology and the social sciences are individuals or groups. These objects have properties. Properties are characteristics of individuals or groups such as self-esteem, intelligence, cohesion, anxiety, etc. Theories hypothesize relations between these properties. For instance, we might theorize that intelligence promotes self-esteem. To test these ideas we build models. Models formalize the key elements in a theory. The individuals or groups are the objects (cases) in models. The variables in models represent the properties of objects and the model represents the relationships between the variables that are hypothesized in the theory. A model, for instance, could have a variable for self-esteem and another for intelligence, and the model would represent the hypothesized relation between them. The variables in the model are either manifest (observed) or latent (unobserved). Self-esteem and intelligence are both best represented as latent variables. More generally, our interest lies in the latent variables that are in models. The latent variables represent properties in a formal model, but they are not identical to these properties.

The definition of latent variables that I propose is a simple and inclusive definition of latent variables: A latent random (or nonrandom) variable is a random (or nonrandom) variable for which there is no sample realization for at least some observations in a given sample. In some ways this is not a new definition but is a formalization of a common idea that a latent variable is one for which there are no values. The definition permits the situation in which the random variable is latent (or missing) for some cases but not for others. In many situations a variable that is latent for any cases will be latent for all cases in a sample. The term "variable" in the definition refers to something that takes more than one value so that values that are constant across all cases are not included as variables.[3] Note also that the definition for random latent variables relies on the standard definition of a random variable.[4] The latent random variable differs from observed random variables in that for the observed random variable our sample contains realizations. If a random variable has realizations for some cases and not for others, then we can refer to it as latent (or missing) for those missing cases and an observed random variable for the other cases. Similarly, for nonrandom latent variables the variable takes more than one value, but if all or a subset of cases do not have sample realizations, then the variable is latent for those cases.

This definition of latent variables is rather minimalist and as such is more inclusive as to the variables considered as latent compared with the other definitions. For example, latent variables as defined by local independence are a special case of the sample realization definition, as are latent variables that conform to the expected value definition.

From the perspective of the sample realization definition all variables are latent until sample values of them are available. Of course, for many of the variables in the psychological and social sciences we do not have the option of directly observing such variables, so it will be latent for all cases in all samples. Our only option is to indirectly observe it through the sample values of an observed variable.

Another aspect of the definition is that it defines a variable as latent or not with respect to a particular sample. This implies that a variable could be latent in all, none, or just some samples. This permits the possibility that a variable is omitted in one sample but might be observed in another or it allows for the possibility that changes in techniques or advances in knowledge might allow us to measure variables previously treated as latent. For instance, before the invention of accurate thermometers, we could consider temperature a latent variable. But once

---

[3]Regression coefficient parameters, for example, would not be variables if the same parameter holds for all cases in a sample. Alternatively, for random coefficient models in which the regression parameters for the same variable differ across cases, the regression parameters would be a variable by this definition. For an example of the latter case, see the section on latent curve models.

[4]For example, "If S is a sample space with a probability measure and $\mathbf{x}$ is a real-valued function defined over the elements of S, then $\mathbf{x}$ is called a random variable" (Freund & Walpole 1987, p. 75).

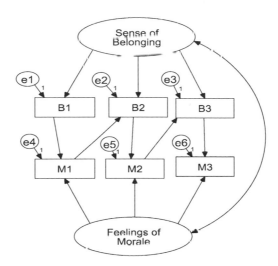

Figure 1 Model of "morale" and "sense of belonging" with response effects indicators (Bollen & Medrano 1998).

such thermometers are in use, their high accuracy permits us to treat their readings as a sample value of the previously latent variable.[5] Similarly to the degree that psychological and social measurement improve, we might reach the point where previously latent variables become observed variables.

The sample realizations definition permits models with correlated errors of measurement, observed variables that directly or indirectly influence each other, and many other nonstandard models. The key criterion is whether a variable has values for cases in a given sample.

Example

An example taken from Bollen & Medrano (1998) provides a means to further explore these definitions of latent variables. Figure 1 is a path diagram of a model with two unmeasured variables, "sense of belonging" and "feelings of morale," enclosed in ovals. Observed random indicators of these variables are in boxes. The unique components of these indicators are also enclosed in ovals and point toward their respective measures. The straight single-headed arrows show the direct effect of the variable at the base of the arrow to the variable at the head of the arrow. The

---

[5]An argument could be made that contemporary thermometers are not perfect, so that the thermometer readings are not synonymous with temperature. However, the degree of measurement error in thermometer readings is miniscule compared with the error in social science measures. Considering thermometer readings as having negligible error is reasonable for the contrasts I wish to make.

curved two-headed arrow between belonging and morale signify the covariance between them. Three indicators of each unmeasured variable are part of the model. In addition, a response set effect is part of the model, where the response to one indicator partially drives the response to the next indicator on the questionnaire. For instance, the first indicator (M1) of feelings of morale follows the first indicator (B1) of sense of belonging. Therefore, the model shows a direct path from B1 to M1. Similarly, additional direct effects correspond to the order in which the indicators are given in the questionnaire.

Are morale and sense of belonging latent variables? The answer depends on the definition of latent variable that we use. In the nonformal definitions these variables would not be latent variables according to the data reduction definition because the primary purpose is not to come up with a descriptive reduction of the data. Rather, these indicators are created based on a theoretical definition of morale and belonging (see Bollen & Medrano 1998).

Whether these variables are inherently unmeasurable or impossible to directly measure is a problematic classification for the reasons described above: The definition presupposes knowledge that it will never be possible to directly measure these variables. Certainly we do not now have the technology or knowledge to do so, but we cannot say that it will never be possible. The last nonformal definition that describes latent variables as hypothetical variables requires a brief explanation before assessing whether morale and belonging are latent according to this definition. If we accept that latent variables are representations of properties of objects as I explained in the sample realization definition section, then the latent variables are not the same as the properties. In that sense they are hypothetical. However, if we push this hypothetical definition to apply to the property the latent variable represents, then the issue is less clear cut. Thus, it is possible that the properties of morale and belonging are real even though the latent variables that stand in for them in a model should not be reified.

Moving to the more formal definitions of latent variables, morale and belonging would not qualify as latent variables according to the local independence definition, because conditional on the values of morale and belonging, we cannot say that the six indicators are uncorrelated. Indeed, the model shows a direct relation between the indicators controlling for the unmeasured variables, thereby ruling out morale and belonging as latent variables. It is interesting to note that if there were no direct paths between the indicators shown in Figure 1, morale and belonging would conform to the local independence definition and thereby be latent variables. It seems counterintuitive to treat the variables as latent or not depending on whether the response set effects are in the model.

Morale and belonging are not latent variables when we apply the expected value definition. There are at least two problems that rule out these variables. One is that the expected value of all of the indicators except B1 would include a term that corresponds to the response set effect from the preceding variable. This would not be captured by morale and belonging. The second problem is that if each indicator has a unique component that is part of the error terms, then this unique component would contribute to the true score but would not be part of morale or belonging.

The nondeterministic function definition would classify morale and belonging as latent because we cannot write each latent variable as a deterministic function of the observed variable. Similarly, the sample realization definition would classify them as latent variables because we do not have sample realizations of these random variables. We can only indirectly observe them through their indicators.

As this example illustrates, the definition makes a difference in whether we would consider a variable as latent or not.

PROPERTIES OF LATENT VARIABLES

In addition to contrasting definitions of latent variables, it is useful to compare some of the issues that often accompany latent variables. In this section I highlight several contrasts that can be gleaned from the literature. The first important distinction is that between *a posteriori* and *a priori* latent variables. These terms are not used in the literature, but they do capture a distinction that is discussed. The *a posteriori* latent variables are latent variables that a researcher derives from the data analysis. In contrast, *a priori* latent variables are hypothesized prior to an examination of the data. The common distinction between exploratory and confirmatory factor analysis (Jöreskog 1969) helps capture this distinction. In exploratory factor analysis, the factors are extracted from the data without specifying the number and pattern of loadings between the observed variables and the latent factor variables. In contrast, confirmatory factor analysis specifies the number, meaning, associations, and pattern of free parameters in the factor loading matrix before a researcher analyzes the data (Bollen 1989, Ch. 7). Historically, the local independence definition of latent variables is closely tied to *a posteriori* latent variables in that latent variables (factors) are extracted from a set of variables until the partial associations between the observed variables goes to zero. The researcher defines the factors as part of a data reduction exercise.

Latent class analysis and other latent variable approaches also are distinguishable in whether they derive the latent variables from the data as part of the analysis or whether they use the data to test prespecified hypotheses about the latent variables. In practice it is probably best to regard the *a posteriori* and *a priori* as two points on a continuum in which most applications fall between these extremes.

A second issue is whether the latent variable is continuous, categorical, or a hybrid that falls between these ideal types. The question of whether the latent variable has gradations of values helps determine its nature. We cannot answer this question from the observed indicators of the latent variable, because it is possible to have a continuous, categorical, or hybrid observed variable with either a continuous, categorical, or hybrid latent variable. For instance, is depression a continuous latent variable with numerous gradations or are people either depressed or not, making it a categorical variable? Or should antisocial behavior be a dichotomy or a continuous variable with a floor of zero? Empirical means cannot always distinguish the nature of the latent variable from the empirical nature of the indicators (e.g., Bartholowmew 1987, Molenaar & von Eye 1994, Borsboom et al. 2001).

The third issue is the identification of the parameters associated with the latent variable in a model. Model identification asks whether it is possible to find unique values for the parameters that are in a model (Wiley 1973; Bollen 1989, Ch. 7; Davis 1993). Failure to achieve identification means that the factor loading or variance of a latent variable might not be unique and that we cannot tell the false from the true parameter values even if we have population data. Identification of latent variables are resolved differently, depending on the latent variable and the type of model, but usually it involves some minimal number of indicators or some constraints on the variance of the latent variables. A necessary condition for identification is that each latent variable must be assigned a scale. Though identification issues are present in simultaneous equations that ignore measurement error, the issues of identification in latent variable models raise additional complications.

Another issue is latent variable indeterminancy. This issue is well studied and debated in the factor analysis literature (e.g., Bartholowmew 1987, 1996; Green 1976; Guttman 1955; Maruan 1996a; McDonald 1996a; McDonald and Mulaik 1979; Mulaik 1996; Schönemann 1996; Steiger 1979, 1996a), but attempting to estimate latent variables from the observed variables is common across applications of latent variable models. Resolution of this indeterminancy is theoretically possible under certain conditions. Three conditions that can affect indeterminancy are (a) when the sample size (N) goes to infinity, (b) when the number of observed variables goes to infinity, and (c) when the squared multiple correlation for the latent variable goes to one and the predictors are observed variables. Of course, it would be highly unusual for one or more of these conditions to hold exactly, but it is possible for a condition to hold approximately, thereby approximately removing the indeterminancy. In the sections on statistical models we illustrate how these conditions can nearly remove the indeterminancy of the latent variable.

A final issue is that of whether the indicators of a latent variable are *causal indicators* or *effect indicators* (Blalock 1964, pp. 162–69; Bollen 1984; Bollen & Lennox 1991; Edwards & Bagozzi 2000). Causal (formative) indicators are observed variables that directly affect their latent variable. Examples include using time spent with friends, time spent with family, and time spent with coworkers as indicators of the latent variable of time spent in social interaction. Time spent watching violent television programs, time spent watching violent movies, and time spent playing violent video games would be causal indicators of exposure to media violence. Effect (reflective) indicators are observed variables that are effects of latent variables. Test scores on several tests of quantitative reasoning would be effect indicators of the latent variable of quantitative reasoning. Degree of agreement with questions about self-worth would be effect indicators of the latent variable of self-esteem. Nearly all measurement in psychology and the other social sciences assumes effect indicators. Factor analysis, reliability tests, and latent class analysis are examples of techniques that assume effect indicators. However, there are situations in which indicators are more realistically thought of as causes of the latent variable rather than the reverse. Tests for causal versus effect indicators have recently become available (Bollen & Ting 2000), but most empirical research implicitly assumes effect indicators. Incorrectly specifying indicators as causal or effect indicators leads to a misspecified model and holds the potential for inconsistent parameter estimates and misleading conclusions (Bollen & Lennox 1991).

In the next sections I illustrate how these varying definitions and properties apply to common statistical models.

LATENT VARIABLES IN STATISTICAL MODELS

Regression Disturbances as Latent Variables

Anyone who teaches courses on factor analysis or structural equation models is likely to have encountered skepticism when the idea of latent or unobserved variables is first mentioned. The reaction might be that such variables are too mystical or are something we should refrain from using. What is not fully appreciated is that it is quite likely that they have already been using unobserved, latent, or underlying variables in the other statistical procedures they have learned. To illustrate this, a convenient starting point is a multiple regression equation:

$$Y_i = \alpha + \beta_1 X_{i1} + \beta_2 X_{i2} + \cdots + \beta_K X_{iK} + \varepsilon_i, \qquad 5.$$

where i indexes cases and runs from $i = 1, 2, \ldots, N$; Y_i is the value of the dependent observed random variable for the ith case; α is the equation intercept; β_k is the regression coefficient that corresponds to the X_{ik} variable where $k = 1, 2, \ldots, K$; and ε_i is the disturbance for the ith case.

It is of interest to examine the definitions of the disturbance term, ε_i. Some authors describe ε_i as a random variable that has three components: (*a*) an inherent, unpredictable random component present in virtually all outcomes, (*b*) a component that consists of a large number of omitted variables that influence Y_i, and (*c*) random measurement error in Y_i (e.g., Johnston 1984, pp. 14–15; Maddala 1988, p. 32). Other authors would add a fourth nonrandom component such as would occur if a researcher assumes a linear relation when a curvilinear one is more appropriate (e.g., Hanushek & Jackson 1977, pp. 12–13; Weisberg 1980, p. 6). Assuming that the nonrandom error is negligible, we can write the regression disturbance as

$$\varepsilon_i = \varepsilon_{ri} + \varepsilon_{oi} + \varepsilon_{mi}, \qquad 6.$$

where ε_{ri} is the inherently random component of the disturbance, ε_{oi} is a collection of the random omitted variables that influence Y_i, and ε_{mi} consists of random measurement error in measuring Y_i. ε_i and each of its components are unobserved variables that explain the discrepancy between Y_i and its predicted values based on the explanatory variables. The regression disturbance indicates a phenomenon in which the unobserved variable is a composite function of two or more latent variables rather than being a single component. In practice, researchers ignore the components of the regression disturbance and treat it as a unitary term, but this is not always the case.

If we consider that the analysis of variance and the analysis of covariance are special cases of multiple regression that also have disturbances, we readily see that much of psychology and the social sciences routinely use such unobserved or latent variables in their statistical modeling. Hence, to purge our models of unobservable or latent variables would require that we eliminate virtually all of the statistical techniques common in the social sciences.

Though the previous paragraphs use the term latent variable to describe the disturbance, not all of the definitions would include ε_i as a latent variable. The local independence definition presupposes at least two observed variables that depend on the latent variable. In multiple regression ε_i influences only Y_i. As such, ε_i would not qualify as a latent variable. The disturbance, ε_i, would also fail to satisfy the expected value definition of a true score (latent variable). By assumption, $E(\varepsilon_i)$ is zero for all cases, unlike the situation in which the expected value of an observed variable would take different values for different cases in the sample. More importantly, the expected value true score definition requires the expected value of an observed variable, whereas ε_i is unobserved.

According to Bentler's (1982, p. 107) definition, the disturbance would not be a latent variable because at the population level we can write $\varepsilon_i = Y_i - (\alpha + \beta_1 X_{i1} + \beta_2 X_{i2} + \cdots + \beta_K X_{iK})$. Thus, the disturbance is a function of observed variables only and hence does not satisfy Bentler's definition of a latent variable.[6] Alternatively, if we consider the components in Equation 6, each component of the disturbance would be a latent variable according to Bentler's definition, even though their sum, ε_i, would not be.

The sample realizations definition would qualify ε_i as a latent variable in that we do not have sample realizations in our sample data. We can estimate it as discussed below, but the estimates are not direct realizations of the random disturbance.

Viewing the disturbance, ε_i, as a latent variable provides the opportunity to introduce two issues common to all latent variables: identification issues and estimating values of the latent variable. Consider identification first. Every latent variable must be assigned a scale and a mean. Neither of these are inherent to a variable but instead are a matter of consensus among those working in an area. In the case of the disturbance in multiple regression, the disturbance is implicitly scaled to have the same units as the dependent variable, Y_i. This follows because the implicit

---

[6]In a sample we have $\hat{\varepsilon}_i$, the sample residual, and do not have the population disturbance, ε_i. From the perspective of the sample, ε_i is a latent variable because we cannot determine its exact value without the population regression coefficients ($\beta_k s$). Bentler (1982) does not make this distinction and considers the disturbance not to be a latent variable.

coefficient for ε_i is 1. Thus, a one-unit shift in ε_i leads to a one-unit shift in Y_i, holding constant the Xs.[7] The disturbance metric matches that of Y_i. The mean of ε_i is set to zero ($E(\varepsilon_i) = 0$). If we failed to make these assumptions, the multiple regression model would be underidentified and we would not be able to find unique values for at least some of the regression parameters. Even with these scaling assumptions, a multiple regression model is not identified. To identify it, we make another assumption about the latent variable, ε_i. We assume that the disturbance is uncorrelated with the Xs. Thus, using the sample realizations definition of a latent variable, the most widely used statistical procedure in the social and behavioral sciences, makes use of a latent variable called a disturbance and makes a number of assumptions about its behavior (coefficient of 1, $E(\varepsilon_i) = 0$, $COV(X_{ik}, \varepsilon_i) = 0$ where $i = 1, 2, 3, \ldots N, k = 1, 2, \ldots, K$).

A second issue that commonly accompanies the use of latent variables is attempts to estimate the values of the latent variable by using weighted combinations of the observed variables. This is linked to the issue of latent variable indeterminancy. In the case of multiple regression, "residuals" is a common name for the estimate of the disturbance, ε_i. The most widely used estimate of the disturbance latent variable is

$$\hat{\varepsilon}_i = Y_i - (\hat{\alpha} + \hat{\beta}_1 X_{i1} + \hat{\beta}_2 X_{i2} + \cdots + \hat{\beta}_K X_{iK}), \qquad 7.$$

where $\hat{\varepsilon}_i$ contains the estimates of ε_i, $\hat{\alpha}$ is the ordinary least squares intercept estimator, and $\hat{\beta}_k$ is the ordinary least squares estimator of the regression coefficients. It is important to remember that the sample residuals, $\hat{\varepsilon}_i$ are not the same as the latent disturbances, ε_i. Unless $\hat{\alpha}$ and $\hat{\beta}_k$ match their corresponding population parameters, the sample residuals will not equal the population disturbances. As I noted above, one condition that sometimes removes latent variable indeterminancy is when the sample size, N, goes to infinity. In the above regression model, as $N \to \infty$, $\hat{\alpha} \to \alpha$ & $\hat{\beta}_k \to \beta_k$ and $\hat{\varepsilon}_i \to \varepsilon_i$, and the indeterminancy is removed. In practice, we have finite sample sizes so that at least some indeterminancy in the values of the disturbances are present. Furthermore, we generally do not have the information that would permit separate estimation of the three components of ε_i described above ($\varepsilon_{ri}, \varepsilon_{oi}, \varepsilon_{mi}$). Their sum is estimated in $\hat{\varepsilon}_i$, but their components remain indeterminant in a regression model even if $N \to \infty$.

Latent Variables in Limited Dependent-Variable Models

Multiple regression assumes that the dependent variable is continuous or nearly so. Categorical dependent variables are common in the social and psychological sciences and thus fall short of this assumption. Logistic and probit regression procedures permit noncontinuous dependent variables. *Limited dependent-variable models* is another term that refers to such models with categorical or censored

---

[7]Below, we introduce the assumption that ε_i is uncorrelated with the Xs. Under this assumption, we need not also assume that the Xs are held constant.

dependent variables (Maddala 1983, Long 1997). These models do not eliminate the need for latent variables, and from one perspective they make further use of latent variables than does the usual multiple regression. A convenient representation for limited dependent-variable models makes use of an equation that appears quite similar to a multiple regression,

$$Y_i^* = \alpha + \beta_1 X_{i1} + \beta_2 X_{i2} + \cdots + \beta_K X_{iK} + \varepsilon_i, \qquad 8.$$

where we can define all variables the same as the preceding multiple regression model except for the new symbol, Y_i^*. Y_i^* is a continuous unobserved variable that has a linear relation to the explanatory variables X_{ik}. The continuous Y_i^* is related to the categorical observed dependent variable. The nature of the relation depends on the nature of the observed categorical variable. For a dichotomous variable $Y_i (= 1$ or $0)$, the relation is

$$Y_i = \left\{ \begin{array}{ll} 1 & \text{if } Y_i^* > 0 \\ 0 & \text{if } Y_i^* \leq 0 \end{array} \right\}. \qquad 9.$$

This equation presents a threshold model where when Y_i^* exceeds 0, the dichotomous variable is one and when Y_i^* is at or below zero, the dichotomous variable is zero. The model assumes that underlying the dichotomous variable is a continuous variable that determines the category of the observed dichotomous variable. To illustrate, suppose the dichotomous variable asks whether a respondent agrees or disagrees with the statement, "I feel that I am as good as others." Though respondents differ widely in their degree of agreement or disagreement, they are left with only two options, agree or disagree. Equation 9 represents this as a threshold model in which once the unobserved degree of agreement passes a threshold of zero, the respondent will give an "agree" response. If they fall short of this threshold, the response will be "disagree." From one perspective, these threshold models are a correction of the crude way in which the original data were collected. From this viewpoint, the variables of interest are conceptualized as continuous, but the response format administered allows respondents to answer only in a restrictive, dichotomous scale.[8] In this formulation we have the disturbance, ε_i, as an unobserved variable as in multiple regression, but we also have Y_i^* as an underlying variable. The ε_i disturbance consists of the same components as in multiple regression ($\varepsilon_i = \varepsilon_{ri} + \varepsilon_{oi} + \varepsilon_{mi}$). Recall that in our discussion of multiple regression the local independence, expected value, and nondeterminant function of observed variables definitions would not classify ε_i as a latent variable, and the sample realization definition would treat it as latent. These same classifications hold for this limited dependent variable model with one exception. The nondeterminant function of observed variables definition would now classify ε_i as a latent variable. The reason is that even knowing the population parameters for

---

[8]It is possible to represent the dichotomous model without using a latent Y_i^* variable (see Long 1997 pp. 50–52).

all coefficients in Equation 8, we still cannot write ε_i as an exact function of observed variables because Y_i^* is unobserved.[9] The different definitions of latent variables would classify Y_i^* the same as ε_i: It is a latent variable according to the sample realization and nondeterminant function of observed variable definitions, but it is not according to the local independence and the expected value definitions.

To take things further we need to make further assumptions. We make the same assumptions about ε_i as we did in multiple regression [coefficient of 1, $E(\varepsilon_i) = 0$, $COV(X_{ik}, \varepsilon_i) = 0$]. These assumptions are sufficient to provide us with the mean of Y_i^* [$E(Y_i^*) = \alpha + \beta_1 X_{i1} + \beta_2 X_{i2} + \cdots + \beta_K X_{iK}$], but the variance of Y_i^* [$VAR(Y_i^*) = VAR(\alpha + \beta_1 X_{i1} + \beta_2 X_{i2} + \cdots + \beta_K X_{iK}) + VAR(\varepsilon_i)$] remains undetermined because we only can estimate the variance of $\alpha + \beta_1 X_{i1} + \beta_2 X_{i2} + \cdots + \beta_K X_{iK}$ and cannot estimate the variance of ε_i [$VAR(\varepsilon_i)$] and we need both to get the $VAR(Y_i^*)$. Strictly speaking, an assumption about the variance of ε_i would be sufficient to identify the variance of Y_i^*. In practice, the most common approach to defining the scale and variance of Y_i^* is to assume that the disturbance variable comes from a specific distribution. If ε_i comes from a standardized normal distribution [$\varepsilon_i \sim N(0,1)$], we have a dichotomous probit regression model. If we assume that ε_i comes from a standardized logistic distribution with a mean of zero and a variance of $\pi^2/3$, we are led to the dichotomous logistic regression model. Either of these assumptions provide the information required to identify the mean and scale for the two latent variables in the model, ε_i and Y_i^*.

This model is readily extended to ordinal outcome variables with more than two categories. Here we would maintain Equation 8, but the equation linking Y_i to Y_i^* becomes

$$Y_i = \begin{cases} 1 & \text{if } -\infty < Y_i^* \le \tau_1 \\ 2 & \text{if } \tau_1 < Y_i^* \le \tau_2 \\ 3 & \text{if } \tau_2 < Y_i^* \le \tau_3 \\ \vdots & \\ C-1 & \text{if } \tau_{C-2} < Y_i^* \le \tau_{C-1} \\ C & \text{if } \tau_{C-1} < Y_i^* \le \infty \end{cases}, \qquad 10.$$

where C refers to the total number of categories for the ordinal variable. The model is similar to the binary outcome model in that we have a nonlinear relation connecting the ordinal variable, Y_i, to Y_i^*, but it differs in that we have introduced "thresholds," τ_j, that are the cutpoints to determine into which category of the ordinal variable a case will fall. This model assumes that the value for the first threshold (τ_1) does not differ across the individuals in a sample. Similarly, the second threshold (τ_2) is constant over individuals, as are all other thresholds. Thus,

---

[9]Bentler's (1982) nondeterministic function of observed variables was proposed for linear structural equation models. The limited dependent variable models are nonlinear in the relation between the categorical dependent variable and the continuous underlying one, so his definition was not devised for such models.

the thresholds are similar to the regression coefficients in that they are population parameters that are the same for all cases in the sample.

As in the dichotomous case, we must ensure that it is possible to identify the mean and variances of the latent variables of ε_i and Y_i^*, but here we have the additional complication of identifying the thresholds. Like the dichotomous outcome model, assuming that ε_i is distributed as a standardized normal or standardized logistic variable will help to identify the means and variances of the latent variables, but now we also need to make assumptions about the thresholds. The two most common are to assume that τ_1 is zero or to assume that the equation intercept α is zero (see Long 1997, pp. 122–23). Either assumption in conjunction with the other distributional assumptions will identify the mean and variances of ε_i and Y_i^* and the thresholds, τ_j, in the model.

Limited dependent variable models such as these have been extended in a number of directions including censored variable models in which the continuous variable is directly observed for only part of its range and remains latent at some minimum or maximum value. Furthermore, multiple regression type models are sometimes combined with limited dependent-variable models such as in sample selectivity correction models (Heckman 1979, 1990; Greene 1997). From the perspective of this article the key aspect of these limited dependent-variable regression models is that they share with the usual multiple regression model the inclusion of unobserved variables. In addition to the unobserved disturbance random variable ε_i, there is a random underlying substantive variable (Y_i^*) that underlies the dichotomous, ordinal, or censored observed variable. The definitions of latent variables do not agree in classifying these variables as latent, and like multiple regression, each unobserved variable must be scaled and given a mean to permit identification of the model. Also similar to multiple regression, the explanatory variables in the model are observed variables.

A difference from multiple regression emerges when one tries to estimate the values of the unobserved variables. In multiple regression we could estimate the latent disturbance, ε_i, as $\hat{\varepsilon}_i = Y_i - (\hat{\alpha} + \hat{\beta}_1 X_{i1} + \hat{\beta}_2 X_{i2} + \cdots + \hat{\beta}_K X_{iK})$. Attempting an analogous procedure for the limited dependent-variable model would lead to $\hat{\varepsilon}_i = Y_i^* - (\hat{\alpha} + \hat{\beta}_1 X_{i1} + \hat{\beta}_2 X_{i2} + \cdots + \hat{\beta}_K X_{iK})$. Unfortunately we cannot calculate this quantity because Y_i^* is latent and we have no value to substitute for it. We can estimate the latent outcome variable, Y_i^*, as $\hat{Y}_i^* = (\hat{\alpha} + \hat{\beta}_1 X_{i1} + \hat{\beta}_2 X_{i2} + \cdots + \hat{\beta}_K X_{iK})$ because we have X_{ik}s and estimates of β_k. The squared multiple correlation (R^2) calculated as described in McKelvey & Zavoina (1975, pp. 111–12) provides a measure of the "closeness" of this predicted latent variable to Y_i^*. The predicted version of the latent variable, $\hat{Y}_i^*$, should not be confused with the actual value of the latent variable. Just as $Y_i \neq \hat{Y}_i$ in a multiple regression with a continuous outcome, we have $Y_i^* \neq \hat{Y}_i^*$ in limited dependent-variable models because we cannot perfectly predict Y_i^*. As the R^2 goes to 1, $\hat{Y}_i^*$ goes to Y_i^* and this is an ideal condition under which the indeterminancy would disappear. Practice falls short of this ideal, so the indeterminancy of Y_i^* remains an issue.

Latent Variables in Factor Analysis

The factor analysis model is one of the first procedures psychologists would think of as a latent variable technique. Because factor analyses treat multiple indicators or observed variables at the same time, the factor analysis model is usually presented in a matrix form. However, I use a scalar form here because it helps point out the similarities and differences of the factor analysis model to the multiple regression and limited dependent-variable models of the prior sections (see section on general structural equation models for matrix expressions for factor analysis as part of the measurement model). Consider the equation for a single indicator from a factor analysis model,

$$Y_i = \lambda_0 + \lambda_1 \xi_{i1} + \lambda_2 \xi_{i2} + \cdots + \lambda_K \xi_{iK} + u_i, \qquad 11.$$

where Y_i is an observed variable or indicator for the ith case, λ_0 is an intercept term, λ_k is the "factor loading" that gives the impact of the kth factor on Y_i, ξ_{ik} is the kth factor for the ith case, and u_i is the "unique" variable or disturbance for the ith case. Factor analysis breaks the unique variable into two components,

$$u_i = s_i + e_i, \qquad 12.$$

where s_i is the specific component and e_i is the random measurement error, each of which is assumed to have a mean of zero and to be uncorrelated with each other and with the underlying factors (Harman 1960, Lawley & Maxwell 1971, Mulaik 1972). The specific component captures the systematic unique aspect of a variable that is uncorrelated with both the factors and with the random measurement error.

The factor analysis model (Equation 11) shares with multiple regression and the limited dependent-variable models the use of unobserved disturbances. The factor model, like multiple regression, has an observed dependent variable, whereas the limited dependent-variable model differs from both of these in its use of an underlying continuous dependent variable. Factor analysis departs from all prior models in its use of unobserved explanatory variables or "factors" as predictors of observed variables. The variables u_i, s_i, e_i, and ξ_{ik} are continuous latent random variables according to the sample realization and nondeterminant function definitions. Only ξ_{ik} are latent variables according to the local independence definition, provided that we have more than one indicator and that the correlation between these indicators goes to zero once the factors are controlled.

The expected value definition is more complicated when applied to this model. According to this definition, the expected value of Y_i would define the latent variable as

$$E(Y_i) = \lambda_0 + \lambda_1 \mu_{\xi1} + \lambda_2 \mu_{\xi2} + \cdots + \lambda_K \mu_{\xi_K}, \qquad 13.$$

where $\mu_{\xi k}$ is the mean of the ξ_{ik} factor. Thus, according to the expected value definition, the linear combination of the means of the factors would define a latent variable, but each separate ξ_k factor would not be a latent variable.

Each latent variable in the factor analysis model must be scaled. One way to scale each factor is to set one of the factor loadings from the factor to an observed variable to one. If for the same variable, we set the intercept to zero we also provide a mean for the factor. In the case in which this observed variable has only one factor influencing it, we get

$$Y_i = \xi_{i1} + u_i. \qquad 14.$$

We can say that ξ_{i1} has the same scale and origin as Y_i in the sense that a one-unit change in ξ_{i1} leads to an expected change of one in Y_i and the latent and observed variable share the same mean (see Bollen 1989, pp. 307–11). An alternative scaling is to standardize each ξ_{ik} to a variance of one and a mean of zero. Other combinations are possible, but each factor must have a scale and an origin assigned. The unique component or disturbance u_i requires the same attention. Factor analysis models handle the scaling of u_i by giving it an implicit coefficient of one and setting its mean to zero.

Factor analysis provides a clear example of the distinction between the *a priori* and *a posteriori* latent variables raised above. In exploratory factor analysis the factors are *a posteriori* latent variables, that is, the factors are derived from the data rather than being defined before the analysis. Confirmatory factor analysis comes closer to the *a priori* latent variables because the factors and their pattern of loadings are determined prior to the data analysis. The *a posteriori* latent variables from exploratory factor analysis are closely associated with the tendency to see latent variables as hypothetical rather than real latent variables. This is easy to understand because the factors extracted in exploratory factor analysis are created by an algorithm and usually are only given "names" after extracted. This does not imply that the *a priori* latent variables in confirmatory factors are uniformly regarded as real.

As I discussed in the section on properties of latent variables, the indeterminancy of latent variables is well known in the factor analysis literature. However, under certain conditions the indeterminancy of a factor can in theory be removed. For instance, the squared correlation, ρ^2 (or "reliability coefficient") between the simple sum of indicators of a single factor and that factor is[10]

$$\rho^2 = \frac{\left(\sum_{j=1}^{J} \lambda_j\right)^2 VAR(\xi_1)}{\left(\sum_{j=1}^{J} \lambda_j\right)^2 VAR(\xi_1) + \sum_{j=1}^{J} VAR(u_j)}. \qquad 15.$$

The j indexes the indicators of the latent ξ_1 factor, $j = 1, 2, \ldots, J$, and each indicator loads only on ξ_1 with a unique component that has a mean of zero and is uncorrelated with all other unique components for the other indicators. With some

---

[10]This formula is derivable from Bollen (1980, p. 378) when there are no correlated errors of measurement.

algebraic manipulations, I rewrite Equation 15 as

$$\rho^2 = \cfrac{1}{1 + \cfrac{\sum\limits_{j=1}^{J} VAR(u_j)}{\left(\sum\limits_{j=1}^{J} \lambda_j\right)^2 VAR(\xi_1)}} \quad . \qquad 16.$$

This equation reveals that ρ^2 goes to one and the factor indeterminancy is removed when the second term in the denominator goes to zero. For instance, suppose that the latent factor and all indicators are standardized to a variance of one and that every indicator has a standardized factor loading of 0.7. Ten such indicators would result in a ρ^2 of 0.94 for their simple sum; 50 indicators would have a squared correlation of 0.99. Of course, the rate of growth in the squared correlation and hence in lessening indeterminancy depends on the magnitude of the factor loadings and errors in addition to the number of indicators, but this example illustrates how increasing the number of indicators ($K \rightarrow \infty$) of a single factor can reduce indeterminancy. See Piaggio (1931, 1933), Mulaik & McDonald (1978), and McDonald & Mulaik (1979) for further discussion of the relation between the number of indicators and indeterminancy of factor scores in exploratory factor analysis.

Latent Curve Models

Latent curve models apply to longitudinal data in which repeated measures are available for the same cases (e.g., Tucker 1958, Meredith & Tisak 1990, McArdle & Hamagami 1991, Willett & Sayer 1994). Though it is possible to formulate these models for categorical outcomes, I limit the discussion to continuous repeated measures. The equations for an unconditional latent curve model are

$$Y_{it} = \alpha_i + \beta_i \lambda_t + \varepsilon_{it}, \qquad 17.$$

$$\alpha_i = \mu_\alpha + \zeta_{\alpha i}, \qquad 18.$$

$$\beta_i = \mu_\beta + \zeta_{\beta i}, \qquad 19.$$

where $i = 1, 2, \ldots, N$ indexes individuals, $t = 0, 1, \ldots, T$ indexes time, α_i is the intercept for the ith case, β_i is the slope of the trajectory for the ith case, $\lambda_t = 0, 1, \ldots, T$ is a time trend variable, ε_{it} is a disturbance for the itth observation, μ_α and μ_β are the means of the intercepts and slopes, and $\zeta_{\alpha i}$ and $\zeta_{\beta i}$ are disturbances. All disturbances are scaled by setting their means to zero and their coefficients to one in the equation in which they appear. By assumption, ε_{it} is uncorrelated with α_i, β_i, $\zeta_{\alpha i}$, and $\zeta_{\beta i}$.

The latent curve model departs from the others we have considered in that the random coefficients, α_i and β_i are unobserved variables. From the perspective of the local independence definition, these are latent variables as long as we have at least two waves of data for the Ys, though we generally require at least three waves of data to identify the model. Similarly, they are latent variables applying the other definitions. This is straightforward for these definitions except for the expected value one. To discuss the expected value definition further, consider the equation for Y_{i1},

$$Y_{i1} = \alpha_i + \varepsilon_{i1}. \qquad 20.$$

Note the similarity of this equation to the true score Equation 4. If we could repeatedly observe Y_{i1} in the sense that I discussed under the expected value definition, then the expected value of Y_{i1} would be α_i, where α_i is a constant intercept for the ith case.[11] An analogous argument holds for β_i if we use the trick of taking difference scores,

$$Y_{i2} - Y_{i1} = (\alpha_i + \beta_i + \varepsilon_{i2}) - (\alpha_i + \varepsilon_{i1}) \qquad 21.$$

$$= \beta_i + (\varepsilon_{i2} - \varepsilon_{i1}). \qquad 22.$$

Using difference scores (Equation 22) appears to be in a form that conforms to the expected value definition of a true score or latent variable. However, one complication is that the errors of measurement for Equations 20 and 21 are correlated, and this violates one of the assumptions for the expected value definition of latent variables. Thus, these only partially satisfy the expected value definition of latent variables, and under the strict definition these would not be latent variables.

The disturbance terms, ε_{it}, $\zeta_{\alpha i}$, and $\zeta_{\beta i}$, are not latent variables according to two definitions. More specifically, only the nondeterministic function and sample realizations definitions would classify these as latent, whereas the local independence and expected value definitions would not. These disturbances and the random coefficients would all be *a priori* in that they are hypothesized prior to the data analysis.

Item Response Theory

Item response theory (IRT) refers to a collection of related techniques that have wide application in psychological measurement (see, e.g., Lord 1980, Hambleton & Swaminathan 1985). They are well suited to handle dichotomous or ordinal observed variables. Though there are many different models for IRT, a simple one-parameter logistic model for dichotomous variables can illustrate the key points with respect to latent variables. We can write this model as

$$P_j(\xi) = \frac{e^{(\xi - \kappa_j)}}{1 + e^{(\xi - \kappa_j)}}, \qquad 23.$$

where ξ is the underlying "ability" variable, e is the mathematical constant, κ_j the item difficulty parameter, j indexes the item (or observed dichotomous variable), and $P_j(\xi)$ is the probability that an item j is correct at ability ξ. κ_j is the item

---

[11]This is different than taking the expected value of the random intercepts over all individuals. In this case the expected value over individuals would be μ_α.

difficulty parameter because the higher its value, the more difficult (i.e., the lower the probability) it is to get a "correct" response to an item. The probability of a correct response for two different items will differ even if the latent variable is at the same value if the item difficulty parameters differ. These models are similar to the limited dependent-variable model in that the observed outcome variable is categorical, but it departs from these models in having an unobserved determinant of the outcome.

Given the nonlinear function connecting the dichotomous item and the underlying variable, ξ would not qualify as a latent true score according to the expected value definition. ξ is not a deterministic function of the observed variables, so this definition of a latent variable would be satisfied with the qualification that the nondeterministic function definition was proposed for linear models. However, the local independence definition of a latent variable is key to IRT, so according to this definition, ξ would be a latent variable provided we have at least two items for the same latent variable. Similarly, the sample realization definition would be satisfied and ξ would be latent by this definition as well. Identifying this model requires that we scale and provide a mean for the latent variable. A common approach is to set the ξ variable's mean to zero and its variance to one (Hambleton et al. 1991, p. 42). Summing items provides a method to estimate the latent variable, but the issue of latent variable indeterminancy remains. Increasing the number of items that tap the unidimensional latent variable can increase the correlation between the sum of the items and the latent variable, but in practice some indeterminancy will persist. More complicated IRT models are available, but the classification of variables as latent or not would follow a similar pattern as that described above.

Latent Class Analysis

In all of the models reviewed the unobserved explanatory variables have been continuous even though the observed variables could be categorical or continuous. In this section I briefly present a model in which both the underlying variable and the observed variables are categorical variables. Lazarsfeld's *latent class model* (Lazarsfeld 1950, 1959; Anderson 1954, 1959; Lazarsfeld & Henry 1968; Goodman 1978; Langeheine & Rost 1988; Heinen 1996) has considerable generality, but to simplify the presentation I only consider a situation in which there are three dichotomous observed variables, X_1, X_2, and X_3, and one dichotomous underlying variable, ξ. The observed and underlying variable each have only two possible values, 0 or 1. The fundamental equation of latent structure analysis is

$$P(X_1 = c_1, X_2 = c_2, X_3 = c_3) = \sum_{c=0}^{1} P(\xi = c)P(X_1 = c_1|\xi = c)$$

$$\times P(X_2 = c_2|\xi = c)P(X_3 = c_3|\xi = c), \qquad 24.$$

where $P(.)$ refers to an unconditional probability, $P(.|.)$ is a conditional probability, c_1, c_2, c_3, and c refer to the value of 0 or 1 for X_1, X_2, X_3, or ξ. This equation says that the unconditional probability of a triplet set of values (c_1, c_2, c_3) for the three observed dichotomous variables (X_1, X_2, X_3) is equal to the sum over c of the unconditional probabilities of the latent variable being in the cth category times the conditional probabilities for each of the observed variables given that the underlying variable is in the cth category. Underlying this probability is the assumption of local independence. That is, any association between X_1, X_2, and X_3 is due to their common dependence on ξ. Within categories of ξ the observed dichotomous variables are independent.

It is not surprising to find that the latent class model conforms to the local independence definition of a latent variable so that using it, we can refer to ξ as a latent variable. The sample realization definition of latent variables would also treat ξ as a latent variable because there are only indicators of it but no direct observations. The nondeterministic function definition was intended for linear structural equation models, but in general we cannot write ξ as an exact function of the dichotomous observed variables so it would be latent. In contrast, the expected value definition would not classify ξ as latent.

Analogous to factor analysis, both *a posteriori* and *a priori* latent variables might appear in latent class analysis. It depends on whether the latent variables are hypothesized before or after the data analysis. Furthermore, indeterminancy of the latent class is an issue, and again, like factor analysis, the number of indicators with properties that conform to the model can lessen the degree of indeterminacy.

Structural Equation Models with Latent Variables

Structural equation models are widely used in psychology and the social sciences. In their most general form they include most of the models from the previous sections (Goldberger & Duncan 1973; Jöreskog 1977; Bentler & Weeks 1980; Muthén 1984; Bollen 1989, 1998; Muthén & Muthén 2001). A slight modification of the LISREL notation presents the model as[12]

$$\eta = \alpha_\eta + \mathbf{B}\eta + \Gamma\xi + \zeta \tag{25.}$$

$$\mathbf{Y} = \alpha_Y + \Lambda_Y \eta + \varepsilon \tag{26.}$$

$$\mathbf{X} = \alpha_X + \Lambda_X \xi + \delta. \tag{27.}$$

Equation 25 is the latent variable model where η is a vector of latent endogenous variables with $\mathbf{B}$ a matrix of regression coefficients for the impact of the latent endogenous variables on each other, ξ is the vector of latent exogenous variables with Γ a matrix of regression coefficients for the latent exogenous variable's impact on the latent endogenous variables, α_η is a vector of equation intercepts, and ζ is the vector of latent disturbances that have a mean of zero and are uncorrelated with ξ. Equations 26 and 27 are the measurement model equations in which the

---

[12]To simplify the discussion, I only present this model for the continuous latent and observed variables. For a discussion of extending this model to categorical variables, see the more recent references cited in the previous sentence.

former relates $\mathbf{Y}$, a vector of observed variables, to η via a coefficient matrix of factor loadings, Λ_Y, α_Y is a vector of equation intercepts, and ε is a vector of unique components that have a mean of zero and are uncorrelated with η, ξ, and ζ. Equation 27 is similarly defined as the indicators for the ξ latent variables. Each equation alone can represent a factor analysis model (Bollen 1989, Ch. 7). As such our previous discussion of the classification of variables as latent or not according to the different definitions of latent variables carries over. Because η and ξ are classified as latent variables via these measurement models (Equations 26 and 27), the only unconsidered unmeasured variable is ζ, but the classification of this variable closely follows the previous discussion of disturbances as latent variables.

DISCUSSION AND CONCLUSIONS

One clear conclusion from this review is that whether we consider a variable latent or not depends on the definition we use. Table 1 summarizes the classifications of the major unmeasured variables that appear in the different statistical models reviewed in this paper. It classifies them as latent according to four definitions of latent variables: local independence, expected value, nondeterminant function, and sample realization definitions. Table 1 reveals that the most inclusive definition is the sample realization definition, closely followed by the nondeterminant function definition. The local independence is perhaps the most common definition of latent variables, yet Table 1 shows it to be fairly restrictive, only exceeded by the restrictiveness of the expected value definition. The other three definitions of latent

TABLE 1   Summary classification of latent variables in statistical models

	Definition			
Model	**Local independence**	**Expected value**	**Nondeterministic function**	**Sample realization**
Multiple regression ε_i	No	No	No	Yes
Limited dep. var. Y_i^*, ε_i	No	No	Yes	Yes
Factor analysis u_i, ξ_{ik}	u_i No, ξ_{ik} Yes[a]	No	Yes	Yes
Latent curve α_i, β_i	Yes[a]	Partially[b]	Yes	Yes
$\varepsilon_{it}, \zeta_{\alpha i}, \zeta_{\beta i}$	No	No	Yes	Yes
Item response theory ξ	Yes[a]	No	Yes	Yes
Latent class ξ	Yes[a]	No	Yes	Yes
Structural equations $\eta, \xi, \zeta, \varepsilon, \delta$	η, ξ sometimes $\zeta, \varepsilon, \delta$ no	No	Yes	Yes

[a]Assumes that error terms are uncorrelated.

[b]Errors for observed variables are correlated contrary to expected value definition, though they otherwise conform. See text.

variables are restrictive forms of the sample realization definition. For instance, if we use the sample realization definition and impose the restriction that the observed variables be independent once the latent variables are controlled, we are led to the local independence definition. The nondeterminant function definition is less restrictive than the local independence and expected value definitions. One of its limitations is that it was devised for linear structural equations, whereas there are other models in which latent variables appear that would not be covered by this definition.

Though the local independence and the expected value definitions are useful in some contexts, they lead to counterintuitive classifications of variables as latent or not. For instance, the local independence and expected value definitions do not classify disturbances as latent variables. In contrast, Arbuckle & Wothke (1999) refer to disturbances as latent variables. Griliches (1974, pp. 976–77) classifies disturbances as one of the three types of latent ("unobservables") variables.

A similar problem occurs in any factor analyses or structural equation models with correlated errors of measurement. The local independence definition would not be satisfied. An example is where we have a single factor with four indicators and correlated errors between the second and third indicators. If the correlated errors were absent, the factor would satisfy the local independence definition for a latent variable. Or I could replace the correlated errors with a single unmeasured variable, uncorrelated with the other factor, with factor loadings fixed to one for the second and third measures. Now both factors would qualify as latent. However, it seems counterintuitive to consider the underlying variable in the model not latent when there are correlated errors, but latent when the correlated errors are replaced with an additional factor.

Higher order factors would be excluded as latent variables with the expected value definition, but these hold an ambiguous status with the local independence definition. If we consider that the indicator variables are uncorrelated once we control for all first order factors, then the higher order factor seems not needed and its status as a latent variable is ambiguous with the local independence definition. This is true even though the first order factors from the same model satisfy the local independence definition when the errors are uncorrelated. Similarly, the unmeasured variable influenced by causal indicators would not be latent according to the local independence definition unless it had at least two effect indicators with uncorrelated errors of measurement. As in the case of disturbances, the sample realization definition would treat the underlying variables as latent in all of these examples.

What explains these different definitions of latent variables? Part of the explanation is that the definitions emerged from different statistical models. For instance, the expected value definition came out of the classical test theory, whereas the local independence definition has roots in latent class and factor analysis. The nondeterministic function of observed variables originates with linear factor analysis and structural equation models. The sample realization definition proposed here was the most inclusive definition because the only requirement is that there is not a sample realization of a variable for a case in a given sample. It is not based on any one of these statistical models but attempts to apply to all of them.

An advantage of the sample realization definition is that it helps make connections between underlying variables in a variety of models and applications. For instance, the distinction between *a posteriori* and *a priori* latent variables holds for all such variables. Issues of identification and scaling are common across these unmeasured variables, as is the problem of latent variable indeterminancy. We also need to decide on the direction of influence between the manifest and latent variables, that is, are there causal indicators or effect indicators? As this review reveals, most attention is directed toward effect indicators, but the sample realization definition holds for unmeasured variables whether there are causal or effect indicators.

In conclusion, there is no right or wrong definition of latent variables. It is more a question of finding the definition that is most useful and that corresponds to a common understanding of what should be considered latent variables. If we stick with the conventional dichotomy of variables being either latent or observed, several interesting questions are posed for the most restrictive definitions. For instance, the factors in a factor analysis model with correlated errors are not latent variables according to the local independence and expected value definitions. They certainly are not observed variables, so what types of variables are they if not latent or observed? Similarly how do we classify disturbances or errors? If we wish to add additional categories of variables beyond latent and observed, what do we gain by creating these new categories? Also, do we miss common properties of variables across these categories by giving them distinct names? These are questions that must be answered if we use the more restrictive definitions of latent variables.

ACKNOWLEDGMENTS

Partial support for this research comes from NIDA grant DA13148. I am grateful for the comments and help from the Carolina Structural Equation Modeling (CSEM) group, the SEMNET Listserv, Denny Borsboom, Susan Fiske, Jennifer Glanville, and Keith Markus. An earlier version of the paper was presented at the International Meeting of the Psychometric Society, July, 2001, Osaka, Japan.

Visit the Annual Reviews home page at www.AnnualReviews.org

LITERATURE CITED

Anderson TW. 1954. On the estimation of parameters in latent structure analysis. *Psychometrika* 19:1–10

Anderson TW. 1959. Some scaling methods and estimation procedures in the latent class model. In *Probability and Statistics*, ed. U Grenander, pp. 9–38. New York: Wiley

Arbuckle J, Wothke W. 1999. *Amos 4.0*. Chicago: Small Waters

Bannock G, Baxter RE, Davis E. 1998. *Penguin Dictionary of Economics*. New York: Penguin

Bartholowmew DJ. 1987. *Latent Variable Models and Factor Analysis*. London: Griffin

Bartholowmew DJ. 1996. Comment on: metaphor taken as math: indetermimacy in the factor model. *Multivariate Behav. Res.* 31:551–54

Bartlett MS. 1937. The statistical conception of mental factors. *J. Psychol.* 28:97–104

Bentler PM. 1982. Linear systems with multiple levels and types of latent variables. In *Systems Under Indirect Observation*, ed. KG Jöreskog, H Wold, pp. 101–30. Amsterdam: North-Holland

Bentler PM, Weeks DG. 1980. Linear structural equations with latent variables. *Psychometrika* 45:289–308

Blalock HM. 1964. *Causal Inferences in Nonexperimental Research*. Chapel Hill: Univ. NC Press

Bollen KA. 1980. Issues in the comparative measurement of political democracy. *Am. Sociol. Rev.* 45:370–90

Bollen KA. 1984. Internal consistency or no necessary relationship? *Qual. Quant.* 18:377–85

Bollen KA. 1989. *Structural Equations with Latent Variables*. New York: Wiley

Bollen KA. 1998. Structural equation models. In *Encyclopedia of Biostatistics*, ed. P Armitage, T Colton, pp. 4363–72. Sussex, UK: Wiley

Bollen KA, Lennox R. 1991. Conventional wisdom on measurement: a structural equation perspective. *Psychol. Bull.* 110:305–14

Bollen KA, Medrano JD. 1998. Who are the Spaniards?: nationalism and identification in Spain. *Soc. Forces* 77:587–621

Bollen KA, Ting K. 2000. A tetrad test for causal indicators. *Psychol. Methods* 5(1):3–22

Boorsboom D, Mellenbergh GJ, Heerden JV. 2001. Philosophy of science and psychometrics: Reflections on the theoretical status of the latent variable. Methodological Rep. 20011. Amsterdam: Univ. Amsterdam Dept. Psychol.

Davis W. 1993. The FC1 rule of identification for confirmatory factor analysis. *Sociol. Methods Res.* 21:403–37

Edwards JR, Bagozzi RP. 2000. On the nature and direction of relationships between constructs and measures. *Psychol. Methods* 5:155–74

Freund JE, Walpole RE. 1987. *Mathematical Statistics*. Englewood Cliffs, NJ: Prentice Hall

Glymour C, Scheines R, Spirtes P, Kelly K. 1987. *Discovering Causal Structure: Artificial Intelligence, Philosophy of Science, and Statistical Modeling*. New York: Academic

Goldberger A, Duncan OD. 1973. *Structural Equation Models in the Social Sciences*. New York: Academic

Goodman LA. 1978. *Analyzing Qualitative/Categorical Data: Log-Linear Models and Latent Structure Analysis*. Cambridge, MA: Abt Books

Green BF. 1976. On the factor scores controversy. *Psychometrika* 41:263–66

Greene WH. 1997. *Econometric Analysis*. Upper Saddle River, NJ: Prentice Hall

Griliches Z. 1974. Errors in variables and other unobservables. *Econometrica* 42:971–98

Guttman L. 1955. The determinacy of factor score matrices with implications for five other basic problems of factor theory. *Br. J. Stat. Psychol.* 8:65–82

Hägglund G. 2001. Milestones in the history of factor analysis. In *Structural Equation Modeling: Present and Future*, ed. R Cudeck, S du Toit, D Sörbom, pp. 11–38. Lincolnwood, IL: Scientific Software Int.

Hambleton RK, Swaminathan H. 1985. *Item Response Theory: Principles and Applications*. Boston: Kluwer

Hambleton RK, Swaminathan H, Rogers HJ. 1991. *Fundamentals of Item Response Theory*. Newbury Park, CA: Sage

Hanushek EA, Jackson JE. 1977. *Statistical Methods for Social Scientists*. New York: Academic

Harman HH. 1960. *Modern Factor Analysis*. Chicago: Univ. Chicago Press

Heckman J. 1979. Sample selection bias as a specification bias. *Econometrica* 47:153–61

Heckman J. 1990. Varieties of selection bias. *Am. Econ. Rev.* 80:313–18

Heinen T. 1996. *Latent Class and Discrete Latent Trait Models*. Thousand Oaks, CA: Sage

Johnston J. 1984. *Econometric Methods*. New York: McGraw-Hill

Jöreskog KG. 1969. A general approach to confirmatory maximum likelihood factor analysis. *Psychometrika* 34:183–202

Jöreskog KG. 1971. Statistical analysis of sets of congeneric tests. *Psychometrics* 36:109–33

Jöreskog KG. 1977. Structural equation models in the social sciences. specification, estimation, and testing. In *Applications of Statistics*, ed. RC Atkinson, DH Krantz, RD Luce, P Suppes, pp. 265–87. Amsterdam: North-Holland

Jöreskog KG, Sörbom D. 1979. *Advances in Factor Analysis and Structural Equation Models*. Cambridge, MA: Abt Books

Langeheine R, Rost J. 1988. *Latent Trait and Latent Class Models*. New York: Plenum

Lawley DN, Maxwell AE. 1971. *Factor analysis as a Statistical Method*. London: Butterworth

Lazarsfeld PF. 1950. The logical and mathematical foundations of latent structure analysis. In *The American Soldier: Studies in Social Psychology in World War II*, Vol. IV. *Measurement and Prediction*, ed. SA Stouffer, pp. 362–412. Princeton, NJ: Princeton Univ. Press

Lazarsfeld PF. 1959. Latent structure analysis. In *Psychology: A Study of Science*, ed. S Koch, pp. 476–543. New York: McGraw-Hill

Lazarsfeld PF, Henry NW. 1968. *Latent Structure Analysis*. Boston: Houghton Mifflin

Loevinger J. 1957. Objective tests as instruments of psychological theory. *Psychol. Rep.* 3:1–18

Long JS. 1997. *Regression Models for Categorical and Limited Dependent Variables*. Thousand Oaks, CA: Sage

Lord FM. 1953. The relation of test score to the trait underlying the test. *Educ. Psychol. Meas.* 13:517–49

Lord FM. 1980. *Applications of Item Response Theory to Practical Testing Problems*. Hillsdale, NJ: Erlbaum

Lord FM, Novick MR. 1968. *Statistical Theories of Mental Test Scores*. Reading, MA: Addison-Wesley

Lumsden J. 1976. Test theory. *Annu. Rev. Psychol.* 27:251–80

MacCallum RC, Austin JT. 2000. Applications of structural equation modeling in psycho-logical research. *Annu. Rev. Psychol.* 51:201–26

Maddala GS. 1983. *Limited-Dependent and Qualitative Variables in Econometrics*. New York: Macmillan

Maddala GS. 1988. *Introduction to Econometrics*. New York: Macmillan

Maraun MD. 1996a. Metaphor taken as math: indeterminancy in the factor analysis model. *Multivariate Behav. Res.* 31:517–38

Maraun MD. 1996b. The claims of factor analysis. *Multivariate Behav. Res.* 31:673–89

McArdle JJ, Hamagami F. 1991. Modeling incomplete longitudinal and cross-sectional data using latent growth structural models. In *Best Methods for the Analysis of Change*, ed. LM Collins, JC Horn, pp. 276–304. Washington, DC: Am. Psychol. Assoc.

McDonald RP. 1981. The dimensionality of tests and items. *Br. J. Math. Stat. Psychol.* 34:100–17

McDonald RP. 1996a. Latent traits and the possibility of motion. *Multivariate Behav. Res.* 31:593–601

McDonald RP. 1996b. Consensus emergens: a matter of interpretation. *Multivariate Behav. Res.* 31:663–72

McDonald RP, Mulaik SA. 1979. Determinacy of common factors: a non-technical review. *Psychol. Bull.* 86:297–306

McKelvey RD, Zavoina W. 1975. A statistical model for the analysis of ordinal level dependent variables. *J. Math. Sociol.* 4:103–20

Meredith W, Tisak J. 1990. Latent curve analysis. *Psychometrika* 55:107–22

Molenaar PCM, von Eye A. 1994. On the arbitrary nature of latent variables. See von Eye & Clogg 1994, pp. 226–42

Mulaik SA. 1972. *The Foundations of Factor Analysis*. New York: McGraw-Hill

Mulaik SA. 1996. On Maraun's deconstructing of factor indeterminancy with constructed factors. *Multivariate Behav. Res.* 31:579–92

Mulaik SA, McDonald RP. 1978. The effect of additional variables on factor indeterminancy in models with a single common factor. *Psychometrika* 43:177–92

Muthén B. 1984. A general structural equation

model with dichotomous, ordered categorical, and continuous latent variable indicators. *Psychometrika* 49:115–32

Muthén LK, Muthén B. 2001. *Mplus: Statistical Analysis with Latent Variables, User's Guide.* Los Angeles: Muthén & Muthén

Nunnally JC. 1978. *Psychometric Theory.* New York: McGraw-Hill

Pearl J. 2000. *Causality: Models, Reasoning, and Inference.* Cambridge, UK: Cambridge Univ. Press

Piaggio HTH. 1931. The general factor in Spearman's theory of intelligence. *Nature* 127:56–57

Piaggio HTH. 1933. Three sets of conditions necessary for the existence of a *g* that is real and unique except in sign. *Br. J. Psychol.* 24: 88–105

Schönemann PH. 1996. The psychopathology of factor indeterminancy. *Multivariate Behav. Res.* 31:571–77

Shafer G. 1996. *The Art of Causal Conjecture.* Cambridge, MA: MIT Press

Skinner BF. 1976. *About Behaviorism.* New York: Vintage Books

Sobel ME. 1994. Causal inference in latent variable models. See von Eye & Clogg 1994, pp. 3–35

Steiger JH. 1979. Factor indeterminancy in the 1930s and the 1970s: some interesting parallels. *Psychometrika* 44:157–68

Steiger JH. 1996a. Dispelling some myths about factor indeterminacy. *Multivariate Behav. Res.* 31:539–50

Steiger JH. 1996b. Coming full circle in the history of factor indeterminacy. *Multivariate Behav. Res.* 31:617–30

Sutcliffe JP. 1965. A probability model for errors of classification. I. General considerations. *Psychometrika* 30:73–96

Tucker LR. 1958. Determination of parameters of a functional relation by factor analysis. *Psychometrika* 23:19–23

von Eye A, Clogg CC, eds. 1994. *Latent Variable Analysis.* Thousand Oaks, CA:Sage

Weisberg H. 1980. *Applied Linear Regression.* New York: Wiley

Wiley DE. 1973. The identification problem for structural equation models with unmeasured variables. In *Structural Equation Models in the Social Sciences,* ed. AS Goldberger, OD Duncan, pp. 69–83. New York: Academic

Willett JB, Sayer AG. 1994. Using covariance structure analysis to detect correlates and predictors of individual change over time. *Psychol. Bull.* 116:363–81

Author Index

Subject Index

CUMULATIVE INDEXES

CONTRIBUTING AUTHORS, VOLUMES 43–53

CHAPTER TITLES, VOLUMES 43–53

Clinical and Counseling Psychology (See also Psychopathology)

Clinical and Counseling Psychology: Specialized Modes of Therapy

Cognitive Processes

Education and Counseling

Educational Psychology

Industrial Psychology
See PERSONNEL-ORGANIZATIONAL
PSYCHOLOGY

Learning and Memory

Marketing and Consumer Behavior

Motivation

Psycholinguistics

See COGNITIVE PROCESSES

Psychopharmacology

Research Methodology

Sensation and Perception

Sensory Processes

Sleep

Social Psychology

ALTRUISM AND AGGRESSION

INTERGROUP RELATIONS, STIGMA, STEREOTYPING, PREJUDICE, DISCRIMINATION

Self and Identity

Social Psychology: Attitude Structure

Social Psychology: Collective Social

Special Topics

Special Topics in Psychopathology: Language and Communication

Timely Topics

Vision